SOCIOLOGY

AQA A-level
Year 2
Student Book

Steve Chapman
Martin Holborn
Stephen Moore
Dave Aiken

CONTENTS

To the student   1

1   Crime and deviance   2

1.1 Functionalist, strain and
     subcultural theories   3
1.2 Labelling theory   12
1.3 Marxist and critical criminologies   20
1.4 Realist theories of crime   30
1.5 Statistics and patterns of crime   39
1.6 Ethnicity and crime   47
1.7 Gender and crime   56
1.8 Social class and crime   66
1.9 Globalisation, human rights,
     state and green crime   73
1.10 Crime and the media   85
1.11 Control, prevention and punishment;
     victims; the criminal justice system   93
     Apply your learning   107

2   Theory and methods   108

2.1 Consensus, conflict, structural,
     social action and interpretivist theories   109
2.2 Feminism   123
2.3 Late-modern and postmodern
     sociological theories   134
2.4 The relationship between sociological
     theories and research methods   143
2.5 Sociology and science   153
2.6 Values and ethics   162
2.7 Sociology and social policy   169
     Apply your learning   178

3   Global development   179

3.1 Defining and measuring development,
     underdevelopment and global
     inequality   180
3.2 Globalisation   199
3.3 The role of TNCs, NGOs and
     international agencies in development   210
3.4 Aid and trade, industrialisation,
     urbanisation, the environment,
     and war and conflict   221
3.5 Aspects of development: employment,
     education, health, population
     and gender   241
     Apply your learning   259

4   The Media   260

4.1 The new media   261
4.2 Ownership and control of the media   272
4.3 The media, globalisation and
     popular culture   283
4.4 The selection and presentation of
     the news   293
4.5 Media representations of gender,
     sexuality and disability   304
4.6 Media representations of ethnicity,
     social class and age   315
4.7 The relationship between the media
     and their content, presentation
     and audiences   328
     Apply your learning   339

5   Stratification and differentiation   340

5.1 Theories of stratification and differentiation 341
5.2 Problems of defining and measuring class   357
5.3 Dimensions of inequality: social class   366
5.4 Dimensions of inequality:
     life-chances and gender   373
5.5 Dimensions of inequality: race and ethnicity   382
5.6 Dimensions of inequality: age   393
5.7 Dimensions of inequality: disability   401
5.8 Changes in inequality and class structure   410
5.9 The nature and significance of
     social mobility   419
     Apply your learning   428

6   Beliefs in society   429

6.1 Ideology, science and religion   430
6.2 Theories of the role and function of religion   445
6.3 Religious organisations   467
6.4 The relationship between religiosity and
     social class, ethnicity, gender and age   481
6.5 Secularisation, globalisation and
     fundamentalism   499
     Apply your learning   516

Looking ahead   517

References   520

Index   532

TO THE STUDENT

The aim of this book is to help make your study of AQA advanced Sociology interesting and successful.

Sociology is an attempt to understand how society works. Fortunately, there are some basic concepts that simplify this ambitious task but some of the sociological theories involved are often abstract and will be unfamiliar at first. Getting to grips with these ideas and applying them to problems can be daunting. There is no need to worry if you do not 'get it' straightaway. Discuss ideas with other students, and of course check with your teacher or tutor. Most important of all, keep asking questions.

There are a number of features in the book to help you learn:

- Each topic starts with an outline of the AQA specification points covered within the topic. This will tell you in which chapter you will find coverage of each point.

- Each chapter starts with a Learning Objectives box to show you what you will learn and the skills you will use throughout the chapter.

- Important words and phrases are given in bold when used for the first time, with their meaning explained in an *Understand the Concept* box. If you are still uncertain, ask your teacher or tutor because it is important that you understand these words.

- Throughout each chapter, you will find evaluation questions. They are written in bold and separated from the main text. You should use them as an opportunity to stop and evaluate what you have learned. These questions often make interesting discussion points.

- Throughout the book, you will find *Focus on Research* features that provide real-life sociological studies and questions to answer about each.

- You will also find *Focus on Skills* features which give you the opportunity to test your ability to pinpoint important information and use key words to inform your response.

- At the end of each chapter, you will find the *Check your Understanding* feature. This is a list of questions which enables you to consolidate your learning and check your knowledge of relevant sociological theories and issues.

- After each *Check your Understanding* feature, there is a *Take It Further* challenge. Here, you will have the chance to put your new-found skills and knowledge into practice.

- Each topic ends with a section called *Apply your Learning*. This is a chance for you to put your knowledge to the test with a mix of short information recall questions as well as longer, more involved ones.

Good luck and enjoy your studies. We hope this book will encourage you to study sociology further after you have completed your course.

1 CRIME AND DEVIANCE

AQA specification	Chapters
Candidates should examine:	
Crime, deviance, social order and social control.	Functionalism, strain and subcultural theories, deviance, social order and social control are covered in Chapter 1 (pages 3–11).
	Labelling theory is covered in Chapter 2 (pages 12–19).
	Marxist and critical criminologies are covered in Chapter 3 (pages 20–29).
	Realist theories of crime are covered in Chapter 4 (pages 30–38).
The social distribution of crime and deviance by ethnicity, gender and social class, including recent patterns and trends in crime.	Statistics and patterns of crime are covered in Chapter 5 (pages 39–46).
	Ethnicity and crime is covered in Chapter 6 (pages 47–55).
	Gender and crime is covered in Chapter 7 (pages 56–65).
	Social class and crime is covered in Chapter 8 (pages 66–72).
Globalisation and crime in contemporary society; green crime; human rights and state crimes.	Globalisation, human rights, state and green crime is covered in Chapter 9 (pages 73–84).
The media and crime.	The media and crime is covered in Chapter 10 (pages 85–92).
Crime control, prevention and surveillance.	Crime control, prevention and punishment, victims and the role of the criminal justice system are covered in Chapter 11 (pages 93–106). Issues relating to social control are discussed throughout the topic.

1.1 FUNCTIONALIST, STRAIN AND SUBCULTURAL THEORIES

LEARNING OBJECTIVES

> Demonstrate knowledge and understanding of functionalist and subcultural theories of crime (AO1).

> Apply the theories to contemporary British society (AO2).

> Analyse the differences between different functionalist and subcultural theories (AO3).

> Evaluate functionalist and subcultural theories of crime (AO3).

INTRODUCING THE DEBATE

Functionalism aims to explain why most modern industrial societies are characterised by social order: that is, why these societies run smoothly and are free from disruption and major conflict. There is a consensus, or general agreement, about basic values which helps to maintain the order. However, such order is potentially under threat from crime – actions that break the laws of society – and deviance – when people fail to abide by social norms or informal rules about how they should behave in particular situations. Social control is the process that aims to prevent, deter or respond to crime and deviance and therefore is essential to social order. It provides the basis for 'policing the boundaries' of what is acceptable and what is not. There are two broad types of social control. Formal control is achieved through the writing of laws and rules. Agencies, such as the police, monitor whether people are obeying the laws and rules, and the criminal justice system punishes those who break them. Informal control is aimed at those who engage in behaviour that is deviant rather than illegal – such as adultery. For example, the use of gossip and public opinion is aimed at discouraging people from behaviour that attracts social disapproval.

Crime and deviance are usually thought of as highly individual acts carried out by people who are ill, evil, misguided, troubled, selfish or simply eccentric. Sociologists, however, are more concerned with the relationship between crime and deviance and the wider social order. Many of the theorists discussed in this chapter see crime and deviance as a product of a society gone wrong rather than as a product of flawed individuals, and sociologists such as Durkheim go as far as suggesting that crime can sometimes be good for society. However, as always in sociology, simple explanations of complex phenomena such as crime can be criticised and are often challenged by new research. This chapter examines how far the explanations originally inspired by functionalism are useful for understanding crime and deviance in Britain today.

GETTING YOU THINKING

Between 6 and 11 August 2011 there was widespread rioting in the UK. It started after the Metropolitan Police shot dead a suspected drug dealer, Mark Duggan. There was rioting and looting in a number of London boroughs and in Salford, Manchester, Birmingham, Bristol and elsewhere. Property was damaged, a number of shops, homes and vehicles were set alight. There were attacks on police officers and others and five people died during the riots. The looting of goods from shops was one of the most widespread features and it was widely reported that social media had been used to coordinate the rioting. Explanations for the rioting varied widely and ranged from those that put the blame squarely on the individuals involved, to those that put more emphasis on institutions or on society as a whole. Greed, consumerism, the media, and gang culture were all suggested as possible causes and an opinion poll found that the public were most likely to cite 'criminal behaviour' as the cause. Research was carried out by the London School of Economics (LSE) in collaboration with *The Guardian* newspaper, in which 270 participants in the riots were interviewed (LSE/*Guardian*, 2012). Those interviewed were most likely to see the riots as anti-police riots expressing resentment at police behaviour, including the shooting of Mark Duggan and the way that the police used 'stop-and-search' powers. Other sources of resentment that helped to motivate the riots were tuition fees and government cuts. Twitter and Facebook were not found to have been significant and nor was gang culture, but BlackBerry Messenger and opportunist theft from shops were. The offenders tended to be from lower-income groups in urban areas.

Of those who took part in the riots, thousands of individuals were prosecuted, but many others were not.

Questions

1. Why might sociologists reject 'greed' and 'criminal behaviour' as plausible and worthwhile explanations of the riots? Why might politicians have a vested interest in such explanations?

2. Would you put greater weight on opinion poll findings or the LSE/*Guardian* research? Explain why.

3. Analyse the reasons why most rioters were from lower-income groups in urban areas.

4. Many sociologists of crime and deviance argue that it is important to study the actions of the police and other law enforcement agencies as well as those of offenders. With reference to the riots, suggest why this could be important.

DURKHEIM, FUNCTIONALISM, CRIME AND DEVIANCE

The idea that deviance is just behaviour that breaks social norms, whilst crime breaks laws that reflect these norms, is based on the belief that society is essentially consensual – that is, the idea that the vast majority of people share similar values. Indeed, it was this approach that was used by Durkheim in his functionalist explanation of deviance and its relationship to crime. Durkheim suggests that every society shares a set of core values, which he called the **collective conscience**. The more behaviour differed from these core values, the more likely

it was to be viewed as deviant. According to Durkheim, a strong collective conscience, backed up by a fair legal system that compensated those harmed by deviant behaviour and punished offenders, formed the basis for social order.

However, Durkheim, perhaps surprisingly, identified two different sides of crime and deviance influencing the functioning of society:

> a positive side, which helped society change and remain dynamic; and

> a negative side, which saw too much crime leading to social disruption.

UNDERSTAND THE CONCEPT

To Durkheim it was not just individuals who had a conscience, society had one too. The **collective conscience** consisted of shared beliefs about what was right and wrong, and it existed over and above individual members of society. Individuals could not change society's values at will. Yet it was also carried within individuals who, in most cases, had taken on or internalised the collective values of society (sometimes referred to as the value consensus by other functionalists).

Positive aspects of crime: social cohesion

According to Durkheim (1895), crime – or at least a certain, limited amount of crime – was necessary for any society. He argued that the basis of society was a set of shared values or collective conscience. The collective conscience provides a framework, with boundaries, which distinguishes between actions that are acceptable and those that are not. The problem for any society is that these boundaries are unclear, and also that they change over time. Crime can play a role in clarifying boundaries between what is seen as acceptable and unacceptable and, where necessary, can initiate change. Specifically, Durkheim discussed three elements of this positive aspect.

1. *Reaffirming the boundaries* – Every time a person breaks a law and is taken to court, the resulting court ceremony, and the publicity in the newspapers, publicly reaffirms the existing values. This is particularly clear in societies in which public punishments take place – for example, where a murderer is taken out to be executed in public or an adulterer is stoned to death.

2. *Changing values* – On occasion some individuals or groups deliberately set out to defy laws that they believe are wrong. Sometimes, these people are ahead of their time and defy laws that will eventually be seen as outdated. Such groups are known as functional rebels because they help to change the collective conscience, and laws based on it, for the better, anticipating and helping to produce changes that will help society to function more effectively and fairly. An example was the former ANC (African National Congress) leader, the late Nelson Mandela, who opposed and helped to overturn the racist apartheid system in South Africa.

3. *Social cohesion* – Durkheim points out that when particularly horrific crimes have been committed, the entire community draws together in shared outrage, and the sense of belonging to a community is thereby strengthened. This was noticeable, for example, in the UK following the July 2005 London Underground bombings.

Other writers have also suggested that crime can have positive effects. The functionalist Kingsley Davis (1937) suggested that crime could be useful as a safety valve which allowed minor criminality or deviance to avoid bigger problems. For example, the institution of marriage could be stabilised by some married men buying the services of prostitutes. Albert Cohen (1993) suggested that crime could boost employment and the economy by creating jobs for police officers and others who work in criminal justice, not to mention criminologists. He also believes that crime can act as a type of early warning mechanism showing that society, or institutions within it are, going wrong. These can then be corrected before too much damage is done and, in the process, crime is brought back under control.

The idea that crime benefits society goes against the common-sense view that crime is harmful. Some contemporary criminologists from different parts of the political and criminological spectrum emphasise the harm done by crime rather than its benefits. Left realists such as Lea and Young (1993) stress that crime can cause real problems for victims, especially those who are already disadvantaged (see pages 31-36). Right realists such as Wilson and Kelling (1982) stress the harm that crime can do to community cohesion and informal social control. If left unchecked, crime can lead to the breakdown of law and order, with disastrous consequences for those living in the affected areas (see pages 95–96).

The negative aspects of crime: anomie and egoism

While a certain limited amount of crime may perform positive functions for society, according to Durkheim, too much crime has negative consequences. Excessive crime could be the result of two problems with the collective conscience – anomie and egoism.

Anomie occurs when there are periods of great social change or stress, and the collective conscience becomes unclear. During a revolution or rapid economic and social change, the old values and norms may come under challenge without new values and norms becoming established. In this situation, there is uncertainty over what behaviour should be seen as acceptable, and people may be partially freed from the social control imposed by the collective conscience.

Egoism occurs when the collective conscience simply becomes too weak to restrain the selfish desires of individuals. It occurs in industrial societies where there are many specialist jobs so that people have very different roles in society. Soldiers and nurses, for example, have to have very different values to carry out their jobs successfully. If individuals are not successfully socialised to accept collective values, for example, through the education system, they can end up putting their own selfish interests before those of society as a whole and committing crime.

Egoism and anomie can be countered, according to Durkheim, by a strengthening of the collective conscience (for example, by teaching moral values in education): but when this is not done effectively, crime rates can become excessive, preventing the healthy functioning of society.

Durkheim's concept of anomie was later developed and adapted by Merton (1938), who suggested that Durkheim's original idea was too vague. Merton, although not himself a subculture theorist, provided the foundation for the development of later subculture theory.

FOCUS ON SKILLS: WHAT IS CRIME?

A protester being stopped and searched in London before a G8 summit

In the last ten years, the government has created 3,000 new criminal offences, adding to a compendium of 8,000 existing offences.

But what sort of misconduct gets classed as a crime, and why?

There are many sorts of crime, and they vary from travelling at 31mph in a 30mph zone, to committing genocide (which is an offence against the Genocide Act 1969). There is, however, no way to be definitive about the core nature of crime because what amounts to a crime changes with every successive historical context.

A crime is simply anything that the state has chosen to criminalise. So, today, offences include activities that for various reasons were not crimes in earlier ages, such as selling glue to children, computer offences and insider trading. Lending money and charging interest used to be the crime of usury, for which perpetrators

were punished. Nowadays bankers and financiers successful in lending money might attract peerages instead. One function of the criminal law is to promote community cohesion. People like to stick together to condemn what they see as very wrong, and this choral rage strengthens the togetherness of the majority. The 19th-century French writer Emile Durkheim noted that crime "draws honest consciousnesses together" and that the punishment of crime helps to "heal the wounds inflicted on the collective sentiments". Whether as citizens we coalesce better by having 11,000 different types of crime we can collectively condemn is another matter.

Source: Slapper (2007)

Questions

1. **Explain** what the article means by saying "there is no way to be definitive about the core nature of crime".

2. **Explain** what Durkheim meant by saying that punishment can "heal the wounds inflicted on the collective sentiments" and give an example from the punishment of a criminal in Britain.

3. **Analyse.** Give an example of your own to show how, over time, in Britain some acts have been criminalised and an example of how some acts have been legalised.

4. **Evaluate** whether 11,000 different types of crime can all reflect the 'collective conscience' of society.

Can you suggest any people who today are seen as criminals and/or deviants but who might be seen as 'functional rebels' in the future? Explain why you think they are ahead of their time in terms of society's values.

Evaluation of Durkheim

Tim Newburn (2013) argues that two aspects of Durkheim's work have been central in the development of sociological thinking on crime.

1. Durkheim was the first to suggest that some level of crime is normal in society.

2. Durkheim had the sociological insight to see that crime was linked to the values of particular societies and these values (and therefore what was seen as crime) could change.

However, Newburn thinks that Durkheim paid too little attention to how the powerful could have undue influence on what acts were seen as criminal. Durkheim exaggerated the extent to which there was a collective conscience (or value consensus) in society. Not everyone agrees with laws and morals, not least many criminals themselves. A further criticism is put forward by Taylor, Walton and Young (1973) who argue that crime itself is not functional for society. It is instead just the publicising of crime and public punishment that help to unite society. A further criticism is that Durkheim was vague in identifying which crimes are beneficial for society; critics have noted that most serious crime such as murder or sex crime / abuse is far from beneficial. Nevertheless Durkheim's work has been very influential, as the section on strain theory demonstrates.

STRAIN THEORY

In the 1930s, Robert Merton tried to develop an explanation of deviance within a functionalist framework. However, Merton did not agree with other functionalists that all aspects of society were always beneficial: aspects of society could become **dysfunctional** and needed to be changed to get society running smoothly again. For Merton, crime and deviance were evidence of a poor fit (or a strain) between the socially accepted goals of society and the socially approved means of obtaining those desired goals. The resulting strain led to deviance. Unlike later theorists, Merton was not a sub-cultural theorist. This is a point of difference between him and Cohen: Merton focused on individual rather than group responses to strain.

UNDERSTAND THE CONCEPT

A part of society that is functional helps society to run more smoothly and harmoniously and/or helps the collective aims of society to be achieved (the aims might include economic growth, the reduction of conflict, inequality or poverty, or improving public health). A part that is **dysfunctional** has the opposite effect, preventing society from running smoothly or making it harder for collective goals to be achieved.

Merton argued that all societies set their members certain goals and, at the same time, provide socially approved ways of achieving these goals. Writing in the USA, Merton saw the main goals as wealth and power, as represented in the 'American dream', which claimed that even the poorest had opportunities to reach the highest levels of society. Americans therefore believed that they could go from a 'log cabin' to the 'White House' if they had the talent and were willing to work hard.

However, Merton was aware that not everyone had the same opportunity to achieve these goals. In an unequal, class-based society, those in the higher classes had more opportunity to succeed than others. They had, for example, access to better schools and more wealth to back them if they wanted to start a business. Merton believed that the system only worked well as long as there was a reasonable chance that a majority of people were able to achieve their goals. However, in a very unequal American society, many among the population were unable to achieve the socially set goals, and they became disenchanted with society and sought out alternative (often deviant) ways of behaving. Merton used Durkheim's term 'anomie' to describe this situation.

Merton identified five different forms of behaviour, or adaptations, that could be understood as a response to the strain between goals and means.

1. *Conformity* – The individual continues to adhere to both goals and means, despite the limited likelihood of success. This was typical of most people.

2. *Innovation* – The person accepts the goals of society but uses different ways to achieve those goals; criminal behaviour is included in this response. This was more common in lower social classes because they had less chance of succeeding than higher classes, partly because they did not

have the same chances of success in education as middle- and upper-class children. To Merton, opportunities were not genuinely equal because the better-off had advantages over those on lower incomes.

3. *Ritualism* – a ritualist is a person who immerses him- or herself in the daily routine and regulations of their job but has lost sight of the goal of material success. An example is the bureaucrat who goes through the motions of doing their job but has given up on trying to get promoted or becoming rich and powerful.

4. *Retreatism* – The individual fails to achieve success and rejects both goals and means. The person 'drops out' and may become dependent upon drugs or alcohol.

5. *Rebellion* – Both socially sanctioned goals and means are rejected, and different ones substituted. This is the political activist or the religious fundamentalist, who has decided society no longer works well and needs to be radically changed.

Merton thought that deviant behaviour was particularly common among those from lower classes who were frustrated by their lack of achievement and turned to crime to get money (innovation) or success or who dropped out of the 'rat race' (retreatists). However, because there was no upper limit on success in society's goals – even the well-off could be greedy for more – there were some middle- and higher-class criminals too, although they were less common than working-class offenders.

Do you think that everyone fits Merton's five adaptations? Can you think of exceptions and, if so, what does this suggest about possible weaknesses of his theory?

Evaluation of Merton

Merton has been criticised by Valier (2001), among others, for his stress on the existence of common goals in society. Valier argues that there are, in fact, a variety of goals that people strive to attain at any one time. For example, people might prioritise altruism or a happy family life or leisure over financial success and power. Some sociologists, such as Taylor, Walton and Young, think that he underestimates the amount of middle- and upper-class crime while overestimating working-class

crime (see the section on white collar and corporate crime in Chapter 3).

Merton has also been criticised for failing to explain crimes that do not produce material reward, and for ignoring the role of subcultures and illegitimate opportunities in crime and deviance (see the ideas of Cohen and of Cloward and Ohlin below). His work has, however, been very influential and to some extent has stood the test of time. The theories discussed below identify weaknesses in Merton's theory, but build on them instead of rejecting them altogether. Some contemporary sociologists, including Robert Reiner (2015) think there is still much mileage in his ideas. Reiner sees them as useful for explaining everything from the 2011 riots in England to the parliamentary expenses scandal, when some MPs were found to be claiming excessive amounts for their personal living expenses.

ILLEGITIMATE OPPORTUNITY STRUCTURE

The idea of strain between goals and means had a very significant impact on the writings of Cloward and Ohlin (1960), who owed much to the ideas of Merton. They agreed with Merton that lack of opportunity in the legitimate opportunity structure was a cause of crime. However, they argued that Merton had failed to appreciate that there was a parallel opportunity structure to the legal one, called the illegitimate opportunity structure. By this they meant that for some **subcultures** in society, a regular illegal career was available, with recognised illegal means of obtaining society's goals (such as getting money, power or status). Where there was organised crime (such as protection rackets, drug dealing or prostitution) young people could look to crime for a successful career.

UNDERSTAND THE CONCEPT

Subcultures are groups within wider social groups (for example, within British society) whose attitudes, lifestyles and values are shared by the subculture members, and are significantly different from those in wider society. This might include, for example, different tastes in music, leisure activities and clothing or different attitudes towards groups in authority. Of course, these groups will also share much in common with others in the wider society/culture but they are sufficiently different to be seen by themselves and/or others to be a separate subculture.

According to Cloward and Ohlin, the illegal opportunity structure had three possible adaptations or subcultures.

1. *Criminal* – There is a thriving local criminal subculture, with successful role models. Young offenders can 'work their way up the ladder' in the criminal hierarchy. Young people were often attracted to a criminal career because they could see examples of people from the same background as them who had become successful career criminals enjoying all the trappings of success. They are often recruited when young by the organisations and if they prove to be dedicated and resourceful are given opportunities to take their criminal careers further.

2. *Conflict* – There is no local criminal subculture to provide a career opportunity but territorial gangs exist which recruit or press-gang young people in the neighbourhood into their service. These gangs often engage in violence against one another because violence is a means of achieving 'respect' or status for young people. This respect may be a substitute for qualifications or a well-paid job, either in mainstream employment or in criminal organisations.

3. *Retreatist* – This tends to occur where individuals have no opportunity or ability to engage in either of the other two subcultures or to achieve success in legitimate ways. They are 'double failures' and the result is a retreat into alcohol or drugs, spending their time with others who have dropped out of society in a similar way.

Evaluation of Cloward and Ohlin

Contemporary sociological research suggests that there is some organised crime in Britain and other western societies. A good example of this is given in Dick Hobbs' book *Bad Business* (1998). Research by Vincenzo Ruggiero and Kazim Khan (2007), based on interviews with 110 imprisoned drug dealers of South Asian origin in the UK, found some evidence of criminal careers being available for those who wanted to make money out of drug dealing. However, all the above researchers stress that large-scale organised crime is limited in the UK and what there is tends to be in loose-knit networks rather than well-structured organisations. Most professional criminals are more like individual entrepreneurs than employees. Cloward and Ohlin's theory also shares some of the weaknesses of Merton's original theory. It is difficult to accept that such a neat distinction into three clear categories occurs in real life. For example, there may be an overlap between criminal subcultures and retreatist

subcultures because heroin addicts are often most responsible for crime in any given neighbourhood. There is no discussion whatsoever about female deviancy or of crimes committed by higher social classes.

STATUS FRUSTRATION AND SUBCULTURE

Writing in the mid-1950s, Albert Cohen (1955) drew upon both Merton's ideas of strain and the ethnographic ideas of the Chicago school of sociology. Cohen was particularly interested in the fact that much offending behaviour was not economically motivated and did not therefore seem to fit Merton's idea of the innovator who tried to achieve financial success by non-legal means. It was therefore non-utilitarian crime (crime committed without any obvious benefit to the offender). Examples of this type of crime include vandalism and violence that is not linked to theft or robbery. Cohen also noted that much delinquent behaviour was a group activity. Merton's theory explained why some individuals might be motivated to commit crime, but not why crimes often took place in groups or gangs.

According to Cohen, 'lower-class' boys strove to emulate middle-class values and aspirations, but lacked the means to attain success. Their upbringing did not equip them to succeed at school, so they found it difficult to get status from exam success. This led to status frustration – that is, a sense of personal failure and inadequacy. The result was that they rejected those very values and patterns of 'acceptable' behaviour within which they could not be successful. He suggests that school is the key area for the playing out of this drama. Lower-class children are much more likely to fail and so feel humiliated. In an attempt to gain status, they 'invert' traditional middle-class values by behaving badly and engaging in a variety of antisocial behaviours. By doing so they gain status from members of their peer group who have adopted similar values. Together they form a subculture with its own distinctive anti-school values opposed to the mainstream values of the school and wider, 'respectable' society. This was why group or gang crime was so attractive. It gave them the chance to have their crimes witnessed by their peer group so they could get more respect from them and increase their status.

Evaluation of Albert Cohen

Cohen's theory has been influential in studies of delinquency, gangs and subcultures generally and offers a plausible explanation for some offending. Steven Box (1981), however, suggests that it may only apply to a minority of offenders who originally accepted mainstream values and then turn against them.

Walter Miller (1962) suggested that opposition to mainstream values was more widespread in the working class because working-class culture does not correspond to the largely middle-class environment of schools. Cohen's theory is limited because it only attempts to explain male delinquency and says nothing about young female offenders whose delinquency may have different causes (see Chapter 7). Cohen also bases his explanation upon success and failure at school and underplays the significance of relationships outside school, which may play a bigger role in the formation of subcultures.

CRITIQUES OF SUBCULTURAL THEORY

Matza and Sykes

Subcultural theory in general and Cohen's work in particular has been criticised by the American sociologist David Matza (Matza and Sykes, 1961). Matza argued that there were no distinctive subcultural values, rather that all groups in society used a shared set of subterranean values. Subterranean values are values at the margins of society, which exist in leisure and mildly deviant activities, particularly leisure activities. They value spontaneity, a degree of rebellion and self-expression which sometimes leads to people straying outside society's norms. The key thing was that, most of the time, most people control these deviant desires. They only rarely emerge (for example, at the annual office party, a political demonstration or a music festival). People suspend observance of mainstream values but they don't reject them altogether. Matza argues that very few individuals are committed to subcultural values. Most 'drift' in and out of subcultures, conforming to mainstream values most of the time.

The seductions of crime

Most of the approaches we have looked at here seek to explain deviant behaviour by looking for some rational reason why the subculture might have developed. Recent postmodern approaches reject this explanation for behaviour. Katz (1988), for example, argues that crime is seductive – young males get drawn into it, not because of any process of rejection but because it is thrilling. In a similar manner, Lyng (1990) argues that young males like taking risks and engaging in 'edgework'. By edgework, he means going right to the edge of acceptable behaviour and flirting with danger.

Neo-tribes

Maffesoli (1996) introduced a postmodernist innovation in understanding subcultures (see Topic 2, Chapter 3 for a discussion of postmodernism), with his argument for the existence of neo-tribes. Maffesoli was unhappy with the idea that subcultures were stable and clearly defined groups whose members all shared very similar values. He suggested that it was much better to think of subcultures in terms of "fluidity, occasional gatherings and dispersal". Neo-tribes then referred more to states of mind and lifestyles that were very flexible, open and changing. Deviant values are less important than a stress on consumption, suitably fashionable behaviour and individual identity that can change rapidly. The shift towards this sort of grouping implies that, rather than subcultures strongly committed to criminal activity, there are only neo-tribes which are more likely to be involved in occasional mildly deviant behaviour.

Deviant values are less important to many neo-tribes than individuality.

Gangs and subcultures

Perhaps the most widely publicised type of subculture is the juvenile gang. But, despite the widespread media coverage of youth gangs, which gives the impression of widespread gang membership, only about 6 to 9 per cent of young people claim to belong or to have ever belonged to a 'gang', and just 2 per cent claim to carry or to have ever carried a knife, according to research by YouGov (2008).

Indeed, researchers suggest that the idea of a gang is defined differently by different young people. This has led Marshall et al. (2005) to suggest that there are three distinct categories of youth groupings, which vary in the degree of seriousness of offending behaviour, but which are often mixed together under the term 'gang'.

1. *Peer groups or 'crews'* – These are unorganised groups of young people who tend to hang around together in a particular place. Any offending behaviour is incidental and does not reflect any great estrangement from society.

2. *Gangs* – Youth gangs in Britain tend to have similar characteristics to peer groups or crews, but instead have a focus on offending and violence. These are the sorts of youth gangs that the majority of the theoretical models of subculture in this topic were intended to explain.

3. *Organised criminal groups* – These are the most serious types of group, who are heavily involved in serious crime. The age of the members vary and there are question marks over the extent to which such groups are integrated.

For details of interactionist approaches, see Chapter 2 and for a neo-Marxist interpretation of subcultures, see Chapter 3.

CONCLUSIONS

The original functionalist theory of Durkheim provided some insights into the relationship between crime, deviance and social order. They have remained influential in persuading sociologists of crime to think about why certain acts are seen as illegal and/or deviant and how this links to changes in society. Durkheim, Merton, Cohen, and Cloward and Ohlin assumed that a widespread and basic consensus about acceptable social values and norms existed. However, this view is hard to sustain in multicultural and unequal societies such as modern Britain. Nevertheless Merton, Cloward and Ohlin, and Cohen have all helped to understand aspects of criminality and its links to wider society. Their ideas seem to provide useful explanations of some types of crime some of the time, but research suggests that their ideas cannot always be applied in contemporary Britain and a greater variety of explanations is required to understand crime and deviance more fully.

CHECK YOUR UNDERSTANDING

1. What is meant by a 'functional rebel'?

2. Explain the meaning of 'collective conscience'.

3. Explain the meaning of 'illegitimate opportunity structure'.

4. Identify three different types of subculture.

5. Which of Merton's five adaptations involved 'dropping out' of society?

6. Briefly explain why Matza's idea of 'drift' challenges subculture theories such as Albert Cohen's.

7. Outline the difference between the concepts of 'neo-tribes' and 'subcultures'.

8. Outline two criticisms of Merton's theory of anomie.

9. Analyse two differences between the theories of Merton and of Cloward and Ohlin.

10. Evaluate the strengths and weaknesses of using the idea of the 'gang' to explain crime in Britain today.

TAKE IT FURTHER

Go to *The Guardian* crime website www.theguardian.com/uk/ukcrime and choose three stories about recent crimes. Choose any one example and analyse the strengths and weaknesses of Durkheim, subculture theorists and Merton in understanding and explaining the crime.

1.2 LABELLING THEORY

LEARNING OBJECTIVES

> Demonstrate knowledge and understanding of labelling theories of crime (AO1).

> Apply the theories to contemporary British society (AO2).

> Analyse the ways in which labelling theories differ from conventional theories of crime (AO3).

> Evaluate labelling theories of crime (AO3).

INTRODUCING THE DEBATE

Most approaches to understanding crime and deviance accept that there is a difference between those who offend and those who do not. On the basis of this assumption, they then search for the key factors that lead the person to offend.

However, since the early 1950s, one group of sociologists known as labelling theorists have questioned this approach, arguing that it is mistaken in its fundamental assumption that lawbreakers are somehow different from the law-abiding since most people break social rules from time to time. Instead they focus on the social reaction to acts seen as criminal or deviant and the effects that the identification of some people as criminals or deviants has on their future behaviour. Labelling theory has been criticised from a number of viewpoints but there is no doubt that it led to a revolution in sociological thinking on crime and deviance.

UNDERSTANDING DEVIANCE: REACTION NOT CAUSE

Labelling theory, which derived from the sociological theory of **symbolic interactionism**, suggests that most people commit deviant and criminal acts, but only some people are caught and stigmatised for it. This is confirmed in self-report studies that suggest that very few people would claim never to break the law or to act in deviant ways. A 2015 survey of 2000 people found that on average British people broke the law 17 times per year, with 63 per cent admitting speeding, 43 per cent having sex in a public place, 33 per cent admitting stealing and 25 per cent taking illegal drugs (Bartlett, 2015). So, if most people commit deviant acts of some kind, it is pointless trying to search for the differences between deviants and non-deviants – instead the emphasis should be upon understanding the reaction to and definition of deviance rather than on the causes of the initial act. As Howard Becker (1963) puts it: "Deviancy is not a quality of the act a person commits but rather a consequence of the application by others of rules and sanctions to an 'offender'. Deviant behaviour is behaviour that people so label."

This is a radically different way of exploring crime; in fact, it extends beyond crime and helps us to understand any deviant or stigmatised behaviour. Labelling theory has gradually been adopted and incorporated into many other sociological approaches. For example, Taylor, Walton and Young (1973) have used it in their updating of Marxist criminology, while left realist and postmodernist approaches also owe much to it. All of these terms will be discussed in later chapters within this topic.

Labelling occurs when particular characteristics are ascribed to individuals on the basis of descriptions, names or labels. These labels are simplified descriptions and often draw upon common stereotypes about certain types of people. These are usually negative ones (for example, scrounger, delinquent, chav). Labels may be expressed publicly or become public knowledge, which leads to other people making assumptions about individuals. For a variety of reasons, the labelled individuals tend to then live up to their label. Their behaviour is often interpreted negatively and their low status makes it more difficult for them to conform.

Symbolic interactionism argues that the social world consists of 'symbols' that have culturally defined meaning to people and suggest appropriate ways of acting. These symbols are not fixed and may change over time. Every time two or more people interact with each other, they amend their behaviour on the basis of how they interpret the behaviour of the other people. A second element of symbolic interactionism is the way that people develop images of themselves and how they should 'present' themselves to other people – what is known as the 'self'. Your self, or self-concept – the sort of person you think of yourself as being – influences the way you interact with others. (See Topic 2, Chapter 1 for a full discussion of symbolic interactionism.)

The best-known exponent of 'labelling theory' is Howard Becker. In *The Outsiders*, Becker gives a very clear and simple illustration of the labelling argument, drawing upon an anthropological study by Malinowski (1948/1982) of a traditional culture on a Pacific Island.

Malinowski describes how a youth killed himself because he had been publicly accused of incest. When Malinowski had first inquired about the case, the islanders expressed their horror and disgust. But, on further investigation, it turned out that incest was not uncommon on the island, nor was it really frowned upon provided those involved were discreet. However, if an incestuous affair became too obvious and public, the islanders reacted with abuse, the offenders were ostracised and often driven to suicide.

Becker therefore argues the following points.

1. Just because someone breaks a rule, it does not necessarily follow that others will define it as deviant.

2. Someone has to enforce the rules or, at least, draw attention to them – these people usually have a vested interest in the issue (in the example of the incestuous islanders, the rule was enforced by the rejected ex-lover of the girl involved in incest).

3. If the person is successfully labelled, then consequences follow (once publicly labelled as deviant, the offender in Malinowski's example was faced with limited choices, one of which was suicide).

Responding to and enforcing rules

Most sociological theories take for granted that once a person has committed a deviant or criminal act, then the response will be uniform. This is not true. People respond differently to deviance or rule-breaking. In the early 1960s, when gay people were more likely to be stigmatised than now, John Kitsuse (1962) interviewed 75 heterosexual students to elicit their responses to (presumed) sexual advances from people of the same sex. What he found was a very wide range of responses from complete tolerance to bizarre and extreme hatred. One told how he had 'known' that a man he was talking to in a bar was homosexual because he had wanted to talk about psychology! The point of Kitsuse's work is that there was no agreed definition of what constituted a homosexual 'advance' – it was open to negotiation.

In Britain today, British Crime Survey statistics show that young Black males are more likely than any other group to be stopped for questioning and searching. From a labelling perspective this can be seen as the result of the police officers' belief that this particular social group is more likely to offend than any other; for this reason, they are the subjects of 'routine suspicion'.

Evaluation

Labelling theory can be criticised for failing to explain the causes of primary deviance. Many people commit crimes knowing their actions are against the law before they have been labelled. Labelling theorists such as Lemert defend themselves from this criticism by saying that crime and deviance are so commonplace that they do not need explaining. However, this fails to distinguish between crimes with different degrees of seriousness and criminals who do different amounts of harm. While most people break minor laws and behave in ways that are mildly deviant from time to time, a smaller minority commit more serious acts such as murder, violent assaults, armed robbery and rape. Labelling theory tends to assume that labelling is either arbitrary, or is based on the biases of those who do the labelling. However, this ignores the possibility that labelling could sometimes be based upon the seriousness of the offence and/or the frequency of the offending and not upon bias in criminal justice. A study conducted by Cambridge researchers in Peterborough (Wilkstrom *et al.*, 2012) found that 4 per cent of young people were responsible for around half of all juvenile crime. Nevertheless, there is strong evidence that some groups are more likely to be labelled than others, which suggests that a full understanding of crime and deviance does require study of both offending and societal reaction through labelling (or non-labelling).

The late Harold Shipman, a GP from Lancashire, was convicted of murdering 15 of his patients, by using lethal injections, but he is suspected of killing more than 250 patients in total, making him Britain's biggest serial killer. How well can labelling theory explain his offending, which went undiscovered for many years?

THE CONSEQUENCES OF RULE ENFORCEMENT

As discussed, being labelled as a deviant and having laws enforced against you is the result of a number of different factors. However, once an individual is labelled as a deviant, various consequences occur.

A clear example of this is provided by Edwin Lemert, who distinguished between 'primary' and 'secondary' deviance (Lemert 1972). Primary deviance is rule-breaking, which is of little importance in itself, while secondary deviance is the consequence of the responses of others, which is significant. To illustrate this, Lemert studied the coastal Inuits of Canada, who had a long-rooted problem of chronic stuttering or stammering. Lemert suggested that the problem was 'caused' by the great importance attached to ceremonial speech-making. Failure to speak well was a great humiliation. Children with the slightest speech difficulty were so conscious of their parents' desire to have well-speaking children that they became overanxious about their own abilities. It was this very anxiety, according to Lemert, that led to chronic stuttering. In this example, chronic stuttering (secondary deviance) is a response to parents' reaction to initial minor speech defects (primary deviance).

The person labelled as 'deviant' will eventually come to see themselves as being bad (or mad). Becker used the term 'master status' to describe this process. He argues that once a label has successfully been applied to a person, then all other qualities become unimportant – they are responded to solely in terms of this master status.

The way in which labelling can make deviance worse is sometimes called a 'deviance amplification spiral'.

Sometimes whole groups can be demonised or seen as dangerous and/or evil. Members of the group are demonised by the media as 'folk devils' – people whom society should fear. This causes what Stanley Cohen (1972) called a 'moral panic', in which labels are applied by the authorities to the group in question with the result that they become more deviant. Cohen applied this idea to the 'mods' and 'rockers', two 1960s youth cultures who sometimes clashed when they met up on bank holidays at seaside resorts. According to Cohen though, the 'problem' was exaggerated and the publicity caused greater deviance over time. Although the example used by Cohen took place several decades ago, there have been many apparent moral panics since. Examples include concerns over so-called 'chavs', knife crime, terrorism, paedophiles, asylum seekers and muggers. (For a full discussion of moral panics see Topic 4, Chapter 4.)

The labelling of individuals and of social groups may produce a self-fulfilling prophecy. A self-fulfilling prophecy takes place when something occurs simply because it has been predicted. Thus, criminal or deviant behaviour could take place because individuals or groups act up to negative labels that have been applied to them and which predict that they will end up in trouble. For example, working-class adolescents labelled as 'chavs' might be more likely to turn to criminal and deviant behaviour if they feel rejected by society, they come to see themselves as 'chavs' and therefore act in deviant ways associated with the 'chav' label.

Another possible effect of labelling is the formation of subcultures based on the label or on the behaviour that has been labelled. Individuals who have all been subjected to labelling may begin to feel a sense of shared identity with others in the same position as themselves. Having been rejected by wider society, they turn to others who are seen as deviant or criminal for status and a sense of identity. There are a number of examples of this in the writings of labelling theorists.

Stanley Cohen (1972) found that labelling of motorbike and scooter riders as dangerous 'rockers' and 'mods' led them to forge stronger links with others who had been given the same label, and to see themselves as members of these two groups. What had previously been informal networks of friends quickly became more integrated subcultures.

In a study of 'hippie' marijuana smokers in Notting Hill, Jock Young (1971) found strong evidence that labelling could lead to deviance amplification and the formation of subcultures. At the start of his study, many people in Notting Hill smoked marijuana but few took harder drugs and there were fewer professional drug users. Most people bought and sold marijuana in small quantities within friendship groups. Smoking marijuana was an occasional leisure pursuit for many people. It was not central to people's lives and people who used the drug and those who did not mixed freely together. However, during his study, public and political pressure mounted for police action against drug users. It was believed by the public and the police that they were a dangerous close-knit subculture with professional pushers, and that they tended to graduate to hard drugs after they had smoked marijuana for a time. This 'fantasy' did not fit the reality, but the police began to clamp down by arresting and charging a number of those who smoked the drug. As a result, a self-fulfilling prophecy occurred – they became more deviant because they had been labelled as such.

This happened for a number of reasons. First, the supply of their drug of choice dried up because of police action, so some did indeed turn to harder drugs. Second, because the risks of selling marijuana increased, it stopped being a casual affair and dealing became concentrated in the hands of a few people prepared to take the risks. Third, whether you were, or were not, a user of the drug became increasingly important. Users no longer trusted non-users to keep their drug use a secret. Increasingly, therefore, drug users mixed with other drug users much more than they did with non-users. Finally, and because of this segregation, a distinctive subculture grew up in which marijuana smoking and other drug use was the basis for the subculture. The drug users became more and more deviant – their deviance was amplified – in response to the police making more arrests and prosecutions.

Evaluation

Labelling theory has been widely criticised for appearing to suggest that labelling will inevitably lead to individuals becoming more deviant. It is therefore sometimes seen as a deterministic theory – a theory in which the behaviour of individuals is controlled by outside forces over which a person has no control. Certainly labelling theorists such as Lemert often sound very deterministic and do not seem to take account of the possibility that labelling and punishment might deter further crime. However, many labelling theorists are very aware that labelling does not always lead to more deviance. As discussed below, some

theorists, such as Becker, see deviance as a 'career' that people may give up rather than getting worse. The idea of moral panics has been criticised as an outdated idea that is no longer useful in the age of digital communications with more sophisticated audiences. However, others argue that moral panics remain a real and significant phenomenon in the UK and elsewhere, and that they continue to lead to labelling and deviance amplification. Labelling theorists suggest that they have sensitised sociologists to the use of official statistics by positivists. Labelling theory demonstrates that statistics are socially constructed: the product of decisions made in the criminal justice system rather than 'facts' about the world. As such, they lack validity.

Finally, labelling theory has raised the important issues of the abuse of police discretion in deciding which individuals to stop and search. The police in the UK have been accused of using this discretion in ways that are discriminatory, particularly against minority ethnic groups.

DEVIANT CAREERS AND THE CREATION OF RULES

Deviant career

These ideas of master status and negotiability led Becker to devise the idea of a 'deviant career'. By this, he meant all the processes that are involved in a label being applied (or not) and then the person taking on (or not) the self-image of the deviant. For example, in a study of marijuana smokers (1963) he noted that people would probably only become persistent users of the drug if they established a regular supply, learned to enjoy the effects of the drug and learned justifications for taking an illegal drug in a subculture of other users. There was always the possibility that they might turn away from their deviant career.

Another example of this is Reiss's (1961) study of young male prostitutes. Although they had sex with other men, they regarded what they did as work and maintained an image of themselves as being 'straight'.

Creating rules

Once labelling theorists began the process of looking at how social life was open to negotiation and that rule enforcement was no different from other social activities, then attention shifted to the creation of rules and laws. Why were they made? Traditionally, sociologists had taken either a Marxist perspective (that they were made in the interests of the ruling class) or a functionalist/pluralist perspective (which argued that laws in a democracy

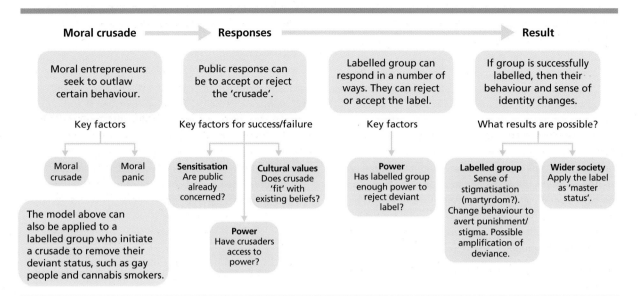

Figure 1.2.1 The process of labelling

reflected the views of the majority of the population). Becker doubted both these accounts and argued instead that "Rules are the products of someone's initiative and we can think of the people who exhibit such enterprises as 'moral entrepreneurs'."

So, labelling theorists argue that laws are a reflection of the activities of people (moral entrepreneurs) who actively seek to create and enforce laws. The reasons for this are either that the new laws benefit the entrepreneurs directly, or these entrepreneurs believe that the laws are truly for the benefit of society. Examples of moral entrepreneurs may be newspaper editors, MPs, religious leaders or individuals who start a campaign. For example, the British MP Tom Watson was important in campaigning about the hacking of mobile phones by journalists.

Becker's most famous example is his study (also 1963) of the outlawing of cannabis use in the USA in 1937. Cannabis had been widely used in the southern states of the USA. Its outlawing was the result of a successful campaign waged by the Federal Bureau of Narcotics which, after the repeal of the prohibition laws (that had banned alcohol), saw cannabis as a growing menace in society. Through a press campaign and lobbying of senior politicians, the Bureau was successful in outlawing the growing and use of the drug. However, Becker points out that the campaign was only successful because it 'plugged in' to values commonly held in the USA:

1. the belief that people ought to be in control of their actions and decisions

2. that pleasure for its own sake was wrong

3. that drugs were seen as addictive and 'enslaved' people.

The term Becker used to describe the campaign was 'moral crusade', and it is this terminology (along with the concept of moral entrepreneurs) that sociologists use to describe movements to pass laws.

Identify some recent examples of moral entrepreneurs: some who have been successful in getting laws changed and others who have not. Suggest reasons why some have achieved their aims and others have not. Can it be linked to power differences?

Evaluation

The idea that there are those who seek to pass laws or to impose rules upon others has been accepted by most sociologists. However, Marxist writers, in particular, have pointed out that there is a wider framework within which this is placed. Are all laws just the product of a particular group of moral entrepreneurs? If so, then what are the conditions under which some groups succeed and others fail? Labelling theory does not really answer this issue very well; in fact, labelling theory does not have a coherent theory of power, as it argues that more powerful groups are able to impose their 'definition of the situation' on others, yet does not explain why some groups have more power than others and are more able to get laws passed and enforced that are beneficial to them. In defence of labelling theory, Becker (1970) does suggest in a famous article ('Whose side are we on?') that there are differences in power and that it is the role of the sociologist to side with the underdog. However, no overall theory of differences in power is given.

PHENOMENOLOGICAL APPROACHES TO DEVIANCE

Phenomenological approaches to studying deviance have many similarities with labelling approaches. Both approaches emphasise the importance of the way that the law is enforced and draw attention to the process of labelling. However, phenomenology does not try to explain why deviance takes place and instead concentrates on the processes by which certain acts are defined as deviant and others are not.

An example of this approach is the research of Aaron V. Cicourel (1976) who studied the way in which delinquency was dealt with in two Californian cities. Cicourel argues that it was not straightforward to define a young person as a delinquent. There was no clear-cut way of distinguishing between delinquents and non-delinquents and instead, he argues, decisions are based upon a process of interaction and negotiation.

The first stage is the decision by the police to stop and interrogate an individual because they feel that they look suspicious, strange, or unusual. This doesn't inevitably lead to them being defined as delinquent, instead a process of negotiation takes place. The young suspect might be able to talk their way out of trouble. However, if they fit the image of the 'typical delinquent' this is more difficult for them. Police and probation officers tend to see the typical delinquent as being from a single-parent family, as having poor attitudes towards authority, a low income and being from a minority ethnic group. These typifications (or ideas about what a typical person from a particular group is like) tend to guide the decision-making.

If the suspect cannot negotiate their way out of trouble with the police officer, they may well be handed over to a juvenile officer (or probation officer) who also tends to act according to these typifications. The meanings held, and mental categories used, by those in authority shape whether individuals are defined as deviant or not rather than any objective assessment of their actions.

Most of those who come to be seen as delinquents are from working-class backgrounds. According to Cicourel, this is partly because they fit the typification of a delinquent, and partly because middle-class parents are better than working-class parents at helping their children to negotiate their way out of trouble. They often convince the police that their child is not a serious or habitual

offender and has simply been temporarily led astray and does not, therefore, pose a serious threat to society.

Evaluation

Cicourel's work illustrates how justice can be negotiated and suggests how important existing mental categories are in the classification of people as deviant or as conforming. However, Taylor, Walton and Young (1973), argue that this approach fails to explain where the meanings come from in the first place. Why is it that the police tend to see the typical delinquent as coming from a working-class background? Taylor, Walton and Young believe that this can be explained in terms of power differences in society. This is something that the phenomenological perspective does not address. With this in mind, phenomenology – while useful for understanding day-to-day interaction – is less useful for understanding the wider reasons for inequality in the criminal justice system.

LABELLING, VALUES AND POLICY IMPLICATIONS

In a famous article, Becker argues that labelling theory has a clear value position – that is, it speaks up for the powerless and the underdog. Labelling theorists claim to provide a voice for those labelled as deviant and 'outsiders'.

However, Liazos (1972) criticises labelling theorists for simply exploring marginally deviant activities as, by doing so, they are reinforcing the idea of pimps, prostitutes and mentally ill people as being deviant. Even by claiming to speak for the underdog, labelling theorists hardly present any challenge to the status quo.

Gouldner (1968) also criticises labelling theorists for their failure to provide any real challenge to the status quo. He argued that all they did in their studies was to criticise doctors, psychiatrists and police officers for their role in labelling – and they failed to look beyond this at more powerful groups who benefit from this focus on marginal groups. More generally, they can be criticised for focusing largely on small-scale interaction and neglecting the wider social structure that might help to shape the interaction.

Labelling theories generally assume that rule-breaking is widespread and generally insignificant unless it leads to labelling. When labelling occurs the offending is likely to become more harmful. The implication of this is that fewer acts should be seen as criminal or deviant and should therefore be decriminalised (made legal after having been illegal). However, in reality society seems to be moving in the opposite direction with more and more laws restricting behaviour in more ways.

An alternative possibility is to develop new types of social reaction to crime and deviance that make further deviance and crime less likely. John Braithwaite (1989) has suggested just such an approach based upon a distinction between two types of shaming.

1. Disintegrative shaming is the type traditionally used in criminal justice. The offender is publicly labelled, for example, at a trial, and the offender is made (or at least encouraged) to feel ashamed by being stigmatised as an offender. This separates the offender from the community.

2. Braithwaite argues that a better approach is to use reintegrative shaming. While the criminal behaviour is acknowledged, the emphasis is more on the criminal acts than the lack of worth of the individual and steps are taken to reintegrate the offender into their community to make it easier for them to return to being law-abiding. For example, the offender may be given the chance to express remorse to their victim and to make some sort of reparation (putting right the wrong they have done) through, for example, community service. If the individual is able to rebuild a sense of self-worth and regain social acceptance, they are less likely to offend again in the future.

FOCUS ON RESEARCH: POLICE INTELLIGENCE AND GANGS IN GLASGOW

Alistair Fraser and Colin Atkinson (2014) conducted research in a predominantly working-class area of Glasgow in which they carried out ethnographic studies both with young people in the area and with police and civilian intelligence workers attached to the police. In both studies they used participant observation supplemented with discussion groups with the young people, as well as 16 semi-structured interviews with police and intelligence workers. The job of the intelligence workers is to analyse information produced by police (for example, from informants and through arrests and investigations), by courts in trials and other sources, such as social media profiles. The intelligence workers then provided police with information on who they thought were gang members in the area, which influenced the individuals the police concentrated on when looking for offenders. However, the research with young people suggested that gang membership was not clear-cut or fixed, with some associations between people being quite loose and individuals having 'multiple affiliations'. Furthermore, much of the information available to the intelligence workers was flawed or wrong. Nevertheless, Fraser and Atkinson argued that being labelled as a gang member could have serious consequences for young people. Their homes might be raided in searches for weapons, and they could be stopped and checked in the streets or banned from community events. Individuals could become stigmatised by association with gangs even if they were never arrested or convicted of offences and this could lead to "corrosive consequences to the life-chances of young people".

Based on Fraser and Atkinson (2014)

Questions

1. Suggest a reason why the researchers carried out group interviews with young people but semi-structured individual interviews with the intelligence workers.

2. Identify an advantage and a disadvantage of the interview type chosen for each group of people.

3. Evaluate the use of social media by intelligence workers as a way of identifying which individuals are gang members.

4. Analyse how useful social media profiles are for studying subcultures. What problems are there in using this data?

5. Evaluate whether 'gang membership' is a real status or just a label imposed on individuals.

6. Explain with examples what you think Fraser and Atkinson mean by the "corrosive consequences to the life-chances of young people" that might result from being labelled as a gang member by intelligence workers.

CONCLUSIONS

As in many other aspects of labelling theory, the idea of reintegrative shaming is probably most applicable to relatively minor acts of deviance or breaches of the law. It might be more appropriate for vandals and noisy neighbours than for murderers and rapists. Labelling theory has problems explaining the most serious deviant acts committed by those who have not been labelled. It also lacks a theory of power to explain why some behaviours are seen as criminal and others are not. However, the approach opened up the sociology of crime and raised basic issues about law and law enforcement that have influenced sociologists ever since. This is particularly true of radical theories, which will be examined next.

CHECK YOUR UNDERSTANDING

1. Explain what is meant by the term 'moral entrepreneur'.

2. Explain what is meant by 'deviant career'.

3. Explain what is meant by 'primary' and 'secondary deviance'.

4. Explain what is meant by 'a deterministic theory'.

5. Identify and briefly outline two recent examples of moral entrepreneurs.

6. Identify and briefly explain two different ways in which a person who been labelled might react to the label.

7. Analyse two differences between 'disintegrative' and 'reintegrative shaming'.

8. Analyse two differences between any one subculture theory and labelling theory.

9. Evaluate the view that labelling theory concentrates too much on the social reaction to crime and deviance.

10. Evaluate the view that labelling theory neglects power differences in society.

TAKE IT FURTHER

Search the *Daily Mail* website for coverage of any group that has been labelled as deviant or criminal (for example, drug users, asylum seekers, benefit 'scroungers', those who have underage sex). Identify one article about a group and analyse it in terms of the following questions.

1. What group is seen as criminal or deviant?

2. What aspects of their behaviour are portrayed as a problem?

3. What kinds of values, beliefs or lifestyles are seen as being threatened by them?

4. To what extent are the dangers exaggerated in your view? (You can search for relevant evidence elsewhere if you wish.)

5. Could the labelling of the group be seen as having any sort of political bias, and if so of what sort?

(Note that when you have read the section on moral panics in Topic 4, Chapter 4, you can refer back to your work on these questions.)

1.3 MARXIST AND CRITICAL CRIMINOLOGIES

LEARNING OBJECTIVES

> Demonstrate knowledge and understanding of Marxist and critical theories of crime (AO1).

> Apply the theories to contemporary British society (AO2).

> Analyse the differences between Marxist and critical theories (AO3).

> Analyse the differences between Marxist and critical theories and non-critical theories (AO3).

> Evaluate Marxist and critical theories of crime (AO3).

INTRODUCING THE DEBATE

Labelling theories of crime introduced the idea that the powerful might impose their own ideas about crime on the less powerful. However, as critics pointed out, labelling theory does not have a well-developed theory of power. Marxism, on the other hand, does. Marxist theories of crime have emphasised the importance of understanding the role of class inequality in understanding crime. Learning from labelling theory, Marxists are well aware that laws and law enforcement are socially constructed and they have consistently argued that power is key to understanding these aspects of crime. But they also look at the causes of law-breaking, and link this to the operation of capitalism and the inequality it produces. Marxists emphasise the role of the economy in understanding and explaining crime, but some neo-Marxists (new Marxists) stress that crime and criminality are not completely controlled by economic factors and they take more account of social action and of other sources of inequality apart from class. This is also true of critical criminologists who broaden the topic beyond illegal acts to actions that also damage the wellbeing of humans and of the planet, whether or not the acts are against the law.

THE TRADITIONAL MARXIST APPROACH

Karl Marx himself wrote very little about crime, but a Marxist theory of crime was first developed by Bonger as early as 1916 and then developed by writers such as Chambliss (1975), Snider (1993) and Reiman (2009). The overall background to this approach was based on the Marxist analysis of society, which argues that society is best understood by examining the process whereby the majority of the population are exploited by the owners and controllers of businesses. Marxists argue that this simple, fundamental fact of exploitation provides the key to unlocking the explanations for the workings of society, since society is largely run in the interests of the rich and powerful. This includes the state which, as part of the superstructure, is dominated by the ruling class, who control the economic base. Although later Marxists have disagreed about exactly how much control the ruling class have over the state, and how direct that control is, they all agree that in the long term it serves ruling-class interests.

The Marxist approach includes analysis of the criminal law and why certain acts are passed but not others. It also looks at law enforcement. Not all laws are enforced with equal vigour and not all offenders are pursued by the authorities. Marxists also discuss the motivations of individual criminals.

The basis of the criminal law

The starting point for Marxist analysis is that all laws are essentially for the benefit of the ruling class, and that criminal law reflects their interests. For example, the laws of property ownership largely benefit those with significant amounts of property. Moreover, it is generally agreed that violent crime is dangerous and needs to be socially controlled but Marxists argue that the ruling class aim to control and monopolise the right to legitimate and use violence through state apparatuses such as the law, the police and the army. Criminal law therefore operates to protect the rich and powerful. Jeffrey Reiman (2009), in *The Rich Get Richer and the Poor Get Prison*, argues that the law of theft appears to be neutral and to protect everyone regardless of their class background. However, it is "a law against stealing what individuals presently own. Such a law has the effect of making the present distribution of property a part of the criminal law". Since Marxists think that wealth is unfairly concentrated in the hands of the rich, this perpetuates injustice.

Laureen Snider (1993) claims that in capitalist societies such as the UK and USA laws that threaten the interests of large corporations by undermining their profits are rarely passed. Indeed the state often spends large sums trying to attract inward investment from corporations. This might take the form of cheap loans, grants and tax concessions. Having done this, governments are reluctant then to enforce laws that regulate pollution, workers' pay, workers' health or minimum wages.

A recent example of this was the official response to the banking crisis of 2008, which was caused by the activities of several big banks; these were sometimes of debatable legality and were certainly harmful. The crisis was so severe that British and American governments had to spend billions of pounds/dollars to bail these banks out. However, very few banks or bankers have been prosecuted and punished for economic crimes (Reiner 2012).

Similarly, Andrew Sayer (2015) believes that the rich largely shape the law so that they are unlikely to end up in prison. For example, they make sure that governments do not close down loopholes that allow the rich and big companies to avoid tax. This includes allowing tax havens – small islands or states where money can be hidden or where tax rates are low. The Tax Justice Network in 2012 estimated that $21–$32 trillion was kept in tax havens, leading to the loss of $250 billion in tax revenues to governments each year (cited in Sayer, 2015). On the other hand, laws against benefits 'scroungers' are strict and punitive. Owen Jones (2014) quotes figures suggesting that tax avoidance may cost the British government more than 20 times as much as benefits fraud, but the government has done relatively little to pass new laws to make deliberate tax avoidance illegal.

Law and ruling class ideology

From a Marxist point of view, in capitalist societies, the ruling class impose their values – that is, values that are beneficial to themselves – upon the mass of the population. This produces a **ruling class ideology** – a dominant pro-capitalist belief system. They do this through a number of ideological agencies, such as the education system, religion and the mass media. Criminal justice is also involved. For example, the constant emphasis on 'benefits scroungers' distracts attention away from law-breaking by the rich and produces a distorted view of social reality. The public are encouraged to believe, for example, that laws about welfare payments are over-generous and poorly enforced so that it is easy to scrounge illegally off the state. For example, a YouGov poll in 2013 found that on average respondents thought that 27 per cent of social security was fraudulently claimed while research suggests the real figure is a mere 0.7 per cent (cited in Jones, 2013).

UNDERSTAND THE CONCEPT

Ruling class ideology is a set of distorted beliefs that benefit the economically dominant class in society by portraying capitalist society as fair and based on equality of opportunity. Problems in society are depicted as being created by individuals or outside forces and not by the capitalist system and the inequality and injustice that Marxists believe it creates.

Not all laws can be seen as pro-capitalist and not all ideas that circulate in Britain today seem to support the capitalist system. Think of some examples and consider how far these examples undermine Marxist views.

Law enforcement and harm

Generally, despite their belief that the law-making process mainly reflects the interests of the ruling class, Marxists also believe that the law has the potential to benefit the majority of the population if it is applied fairly. However, they point out that the interpretation and enforcement of the law is biased in favour of the ruling class, meaning that the police and the judicial system will arrest and punish the working class, but tend not to enforce the law against the ruling class so rigorously. The much stronger enforcement of laws against benefit fraud than those against illegal tax evasion is a case in point. Indeed, tax evaders are much more likely to be given a warning or simply asked to repay the tax than to be prosecuted, whereas benefits fraud is likely to result in prosecution and sometimes imprisonment. There seems to be one law for the rich and powerful and another one, more rigorously enforced, for the poor and the powerless.

Laureen Snider argues that crimes committed by corporations (**corporate crime**) in the USA do far more harm, both economic and physical, than 'street crimes' (crimes such as theft, robbery, assault and murder committed by individuals). One example is the Deepwater Horizon oil spill in the Gulf of Mexico in 2010. An explosion at BP's oil rig killed 11 people and over four million barrels of oil leaked into the sea before it was controlled. This caused health problems for some exposed to the oil, and enormous damage to the environment and to local industries such as fishing and tourism. BP had to pay out more than $40 billion in fines and compensation.

Nevertheless there are generally very few prosecutions for corporate crime. Between 1890 and 1969 under anti-trust legislation (law against monopolies) less than 5 per cent of corporate offenders were given a prison sentence and none of those imprisoned were business leaders. In recent years various financial frauds and scandals have led to few prosecutions of individuals. These include the miss-selling of payment protection and the manipulation of interbank lending rates (the Libor rate) by bankers. Although companies have been fined and have had to repay money to customers (Watt and Treanor, 2012), so far only a handful of offenders have been prosecuted.

UNDERSTAND THE CONCEPT

Corporate crimes are not committed by individuals but by large companies (or corporations) in the pursuit of profit. They might involve false accounting to exaggerate profits, price fixing, failing to pay the minimum wage or taking short-cuts with the health and safety of workers or the public to save costs.

Crimes committed by corporations can also cause death and injury as well as financial loss, but again offenders often get off without punishment. Deaths and injuries at work are sometimes the result of corporate crime but it is particularly difficult to prosecute corporations rather than individuals. The Health and Safety Executive figures recorded that in 2013–14 there were 142 fatal injuries at work, 629,000 non-fatal injuries and 2,538 deaths from previous exposure to asbestos – a cause of death that is common among those who have worked long-term in the construction industry (HSE, 2015). However, the Health and Safety Executive only prosecuted 547 of these cases.

One of the most disturbing examples of corporate crime causing harm was the drug Thalidomide. It was developed by the drug company Chemie Grünenthal but was not adequately tested. It was given to pregnant women in the 1950s to combat morning sickness, but it resulted in about 10,000 infants being born with deformed limbs. There were delays in withdrawing the drug from use yet no individual has ever been prosecuted because of the affair. Another recent example of the effects of corporate crime was the collapse in 2013 of Rana Plaza, a structurally unsound building in Dhaka, Bangladesh. The building housed factories producing goods for many multi-national corporations, including Walmart, Monsoon, Accessorize and Primark. There were 1,129 deaths in the tragedy and over 2,000 people were injured.

Class bias in law enforcement is also evident in the apparently lenient treatment of **white-collar crimes**.

UNDERSTAND THE CONCEPT

White-collar crimes are committed by professionals and managers in the course of their occupations and might include fraud, overcharging customers, bribery and corruption to obtain contracts and stealing from employers. White-collar crimes are primarily designed to benefit the offender rather than the company concerned.

White-collar crimes are often not prosecuted because many are hard to detect. The complexity of some offences involving fraud makes it difficult to mount successful prosecutions. Bribery and corruption benefit both parties involved and so are unlikely to be reported, and the public at large (who are often the victims) may be unaware that they have been victims, or they could lack the resources to bring cases to court (Haralambos and Holborn, 2013). A widely publicised example of white-collar crime was the MPs' expenses scandal of 2009, when MPs were found to be claiming excessive amounts in parliamentary expenses. Most were simply required to repay some money and only four MPs were sent to prison.

Furthermore, many white-collar offenders may not actually be members of the ruling class, but they often work for them or carry out important functions for capitalists, either directly or indirectly. For example, accountants help to minimise the tax bills of corporate clients. As such, Marxists see the treatment of white-collar criminals as further evidence of class bias in criminal justice.

Another type of crime that interests Marxists because it largely benefits the ruling class is state crime, that is, crimes committed by governments – presidents, prime ministers and other ministers – and agencies working on their behalf, that is, the armed forces, the secret police, the intelligence services and so on (see Chapter 9).

The causes of offending

Marxist theory also provides an explanation for actual offending. William Chambliss (1975) argued that capitalism is based upon competition, selfishness and greed, and that this forms people's attitudes to life. Crime is therefore a perfectly normal outcome of these values, which stress looking after oneself at the expense of others. People in all classes, from the working class to the ruling class, use any way they can to get on, if necessary by committing crime. In low-income areas this might involve robbery, burglary or drug dealing, while among higher classes it could involve fraud or corruption. However, the pressure on the poor to commit crime is particularly strong since their income might be insufficient to meet basic needs. These views are further supported by David Gordon (1976) who sees capitalism as criminogenic – inherently likely to produce crime because it produces a competitive dog-eat-dog society. Everybody must fend for themselves and in societies with inadequate welfare provision, such as the USA, crime can be necessary for survival.

This type of explanation appears to account for property crime, in which the offender stands to gain materially and thereby become more successful in a competitive society. But it is less clear how it can explain non-material crimes such as murder, rape and violence, which are not linked to crimes such as robbery. However, Jeffrey Reiman (2009) argues that all crime should be explained in terms of social conditions rather than individual motivation. He believes that social injustice (including poverty, unequal opportunities and racism, as well as other types of discrimination) is the underlying cause of all types of crime.

To Reiman (2009), lack of opportunity is not the result of something going wrong with industrial societies (as Merton, 1938, and Cloward and Ohlin, 1960, believed), but instead it is a 'structural feature' of capitalism itself, which is organised to help keep the rich rich and the poor poor. In a culture dominated by capitalist ideology, in which economic failure is a source of shame, social injustice leading to lack of opportunity inevitably produces crime. Reiman (2015) therefore says, "To the extent that a society makes crime a reasonable alternative for a large number of its members from all classes, that society is itself not very reasonably or humanely organised and bears some degree of responsibility for the crime it encourages."

Crime and control

According to Marxists, crime plays a significant part in supporting the ideology of capitalism, as it diverts attention away from the exploitative nature of capitalism and focuses attention instead on the 'evil' and frightening nature of certain criminal groups in society, from whom we are only protected by the police. These groups tend to be those with little power, such as the working class. This justifies heavy policing of working-class areas, 'stop and searches' of young people, and the arrests of any sections of the population who oppose capitalism.

This theme is taken up by Jeffrey Reiman (2009), who claims that crime is routinely portrayed as being the result of 'individual moral failing' rather than the result of social injustice. It is also portrayed as being carried out largely by the poor and poverty itself is usually seen as the result of moral imperfections such as laziness. This suggests that the poor are poor because they deserve to be poor, or at least because they lack the strength of character to overcome poverty and, since crime is seen as a response to poverty, the problem of crime comes from individual criminals. The population will therefore tend to support ever stronger crackdowns on the poor and on criminals rather than changes in an unjust society. The victims of capitalism, rather than the system itself, are blamed for its problems, making it even easier to control the poor and the working class.

FOCUS ON SKILLS: CORPORATE CRIME AND PUNISHMENT

A protest against corporate crime

A homicide sentence just handed down is novel because it is the first punishment imposed on a company under the Corporate Manslaughter and Corporate Homicide Act 2007.

On 5 September, 2008, Alexander Wright, 27, a geologist, was taking soil samples from a pit which had been excavated as part of a site survey in Gloucestershire. The working practice of the firm was grossly negligent in asking him to be in a deep unsafe pit and the sides of the pit collapsed, crushing him. He was buried alive and died of traumatic asphyxiation.

The company that he worked for, Cotswold Geotechnical Holdings, has just been convicted at Winchester Crown Court of manslaughter and sentenced to a fine of £385,000.

On 2 February 1965, *The Times* reported what was then an important innovation in English law: the first time a company had stood trial for manslaughter. Glanville Evans, a 27-year-old welder, had been killed when the bridge at Boughrood, which he was demolishing, collapsed and he fell into the river Wye. The company had evidently been reckless in instructing him to work in a perilous way but an attempt to convict it for manslaughter at Glamorgan Assizes failed on the evidence.

Even so, the court accepted that a company could be prosecuted for manslaughter. A new crime was recognised. But since then over 44,000 people have been killed at their work or in commercial disasters such as those involving ferries and trains, while prosecutions for corporate manslaughter have totalled at just 38.

The old common law made it very difficult to prosecute companies because the "doctrine of identification" required the prosecution to pin all the blame on at least one director whose will was identified as the "mind" of the company. The new law criminalises corporate killing without the need to find all the blame in one individual.

Globally, more people are killed each year at work or through commercial enterprise than are killed in wars. Work-related deaths number about two million annually whereas war deaths number about 400,000.

The Act will not be working well if there are hundreds more prosecutions following this one – that would mean hundreds more people will have been killed. The Act will be working well if there are few prosecutions because that will mean its deterrent value will have been effective.

Source: Slapper, G. (2011) 'Corporate crime and punishment', *The Times*, 17 February 2011

Questions

1. **Explain** why the writer says that the new Act will not be working well if there are many prosecutions.

2. **Analyse.** Using figures provided here, analyse how serious a problem health and safety at work is.

3. **Analyse.** Compare the treatment of Cotswold Geotechnical Holdings with the way an individual convicted of murder might be treated. Does this provide evidence to support the Marxist view of corporate crime?

4. **Analyse.** From a Marxist perspective, suggest why there have been so few successful convictions of corporations for manslaughter.

5. **Evaluate** whether the evidence here supports or contradicts Marxist theories of punishment. Justify your answer.

Thinking about the urban riots of 2011 in British cities, do you agree with Marxists that crime is used to justify the control of the working class? (The riots involved extensive looting and some violence but strong sentences were imposed on some offenders.)

Evaluation of the traditional Marxist approach

Comparison with functionalism
The traditional Marxist approach avoids a number of weaknesses of the functionalist approach of Durkheim. Marxism does not assume that laws benefit all members of society or reflect a consensus about values, because Marxists recognise that different classes can have different interests and values. Marxism also recognises that the criminal justice system may be manipulated by the powerful and can reflect the economic interests of a dominant ruling class, a group which Durkheim does not even acknowledge as existing. While Durkheim accepts that there can be functional rebels anticipating a better society in the future, he is not clear about what a better society might look like. On the other hand, Marxists have a clear ideal of a more equal, communist society which they would like to see established.

Marxism challenges the view of functionalists such as Merton that something needs to go wrong in capitalist societies before crime occurs, and instead sees it as endemic to capitalism, which is seen as criminogenic.

Comparison with interactionism
Marxism builds upon the work of labelling theorists. It takes account of the ideas of labelling – that both laws and law enforcement are socially constructed and represent the interests of the powerful rather than the unbiased application of laws that reflect a consensus in society. But it goes further than labelling in developing a theory of power that explains where power comes from and examines in some detail how power is distributed. Marxism, in short, has a more developed model of social structure than labelling and interactionism.

Strengths
Marxists are also on strong ground in looking at contemporary societies as capitalist. The UK and USA are indeed based largely upon a capitalist economic system and this system undoubtedly has an important influence on the nature of crime, law enforcement and law-making. Furthermore, Marxism represented an advance on previous approaches to crime precisely because it looked at these three aspects of criminality. It did not just look at the causes of crime, or at criminalisation (the process of making people into criminals) but looked at both. Similarly it looks at both social structure and at social action/agency in examining the actions of criminals and those who enforce the law.

Weaknesses
Nevertheless, Marxism has its critics. The traditional explanation for law creation and enforcement tends to be one-dimensional, in that all laws are seen as the outcome of the interests of the ruling class – no allowance is made for the complexity of influences on law-making, such as the activities of pressure groups or the influence of public opinion, which can sometimes be at odds with the interests of the ruling class.

Similarly, the explanation for crime is one-dimensional – it results from the greed created by the criminogenic capitalist system. Because it implies that the law will always be biased and all groups could become criminal in capitalist societies, Marxism does not really explain changes in criminality over time, or variations in crime rates between different social groups or between countries. Marxism associates high crime rates with capitalism, but Stephen Jones (2009) points out that some capitalist countries (such as Switzerland and Japan) have very low crime rates. Furthermore, Marxists struggle to explain why ruling-class criminals are sometimes prosecuted, convicted and punished. Marxists generally find it difficult to explain the relationship between crime and different ethnic groups (see Chapter 6) or males and females (see Chapter 7). The distribution of power may also be less straightforward than Marxists assume – for example, feminist sociologists draw attention to patriarchal power.

Marxist research on crime often says little about the actual processes of labelling and the interaction between law enforcers and those labelled as offenders. Although some account is taken of the agency of individuals, the emphasis still tends to be more on social structure than social action.

Finally, in common with many other approaches, Marxism has little or nothing to say about the victims of crime. Left-realists, who have been strong critics of aspects of traditional Marxism, suggest that crime cannot be fully understood without looking at the role of victims (see Chapter 11). Furthermore, Marxists tend to ignore the effects of crime on victims and, according to left-realists, most victims are drawn from the working class and the poor.

Despite its limitations, though, Marxism has influenced a range of neo-Marxist and critical criminologies, which have built upon Marxist ideas while trying to take account of some of the weaknesses of traditional Marxism.

NEO-MARXIST AND CRITICAL CRIMINOLOGY

Traditional Marxist approaches to crime and deviance are sometimes seen as a little crude, as lacking in detailed explanations for particular types of crime and as taking little account of the agency and active decision-making of deviants. **Neo-Marxist** approaches to crime and deviance accept the basic ideas behind the Marxist analysis of society but develop those ideas in ways that go beyond conventional Marxism. An example of this is neo-Marxist subcultural theory.

UNDERSTAND THE CONCEPT

Neo-Marxism simply means 'new Marxism' and is used to describe theories that use Marx as their starting point, but disagree with Marx's idea in one or more respects, or that combine Marxism with other theories (for example, in the case of *The New Criminology*, it is combined with interactionism).

Neo-Marxist subcultural theory

This neo-Marxist approach provides a specific explanation for the existence of subcultures amongst the working class. According to The Centre for Contemporary Cultural Studies (a group of writers at Birmingham University), capitalism maintains control over the majority of the population in two ways:

› ideological dominance through the media; and

› economic pressures – people want to keep their jobs and pay their mortgages.

Only those groups on the margins of society are not 'locked in' by ideology and finance, and thus are able to provide some form of resistance to capitalism. The single largest group offering this resistance is working-class youth.

According to Brake (1980), amongst others, this resistance is expressed through working-class youth subcultures. The clothes they wear and the language they use show their disdain of capitalism and their awareness of their position in it. Brake argues that this resistance, however, is best seen as 'magical'. By magical, he means that it is a form of

illusion that appears to solve their problems, but in reality does no such thing. According to him, each generation of working-class youth faces similar problems (dead-end jobs, unemployment, and so on), but in different circumstances – that is, society changes constantly so that every generation experiences a very different world, with the one constant being that the majority will be exploited by the ruling class.

Each generation expresses its resistance through different choice of clothes, argot (slang and patterns of speech), music, and so on. But each will eventually be trapped like their parents before them.

An example of this approach is Phil Cohen's (1972) study of 'Skinheads'. The skinheads were named after their short, cropped hair and they typically wore work shoes or boots, jeans and sometimes braces, reflecting the workwear of male manual workers of previous decades. They were sometimes involved in football violence and could be hostile, and even violent, towards members of ethnic minorities.

Cohen argues that Skinhead subcultures represented a 'magical recreation of working-class culture'. They tried to reassert and relive a lifestyle that was under threat. These young working-class men felt that working-class communities in which they could expect to gain respect were being undermined by a combination of factors. Principally, these were the physical destruction of older working-class housing through urban redevelopments, the loss of jobs in manufacturing and heavy industry and the settlement of members of ethnic minorities in what were previously largely white, working-class areas. Skinhead subcultures were a reaction to these changes, an attempt to resist them and a way in which their members could get a positive sense of identity. Football violence can be seen as an attempt to defend their 'territory' against all the threats from outside.

Criticism of the neo-Marxist subcultural approach

Stan Cohen (1980) pointed out that these writers were biased in their analysis. They wanted to prove that working-class youth cultures were an attack on capitalism, and therefore made sure that they fixed the evidence to find this. He pointed out, for example, that there were many different ways to interpret the subcultural style of the groups, and that the interpretation the Marxist writers had imposed was just one of many possibilities. The researchers used a method called 'semiology', the science of signs. One problem with this method is that it relies on the subjective interpretation of the observer. For example, what one person sees in footwear or hairstyles may be interpreted differently by another observer. The researchers using this method knew what they wanted (signs of subcultural resistance) when they started looking at youth culture, and so they extracted what they needed to prove their theory and ignored what did not fit it.

Blackman (1995) points out that the emphasis on the working-class basis of subcultural resistance ignores the huge variation of subcultures based on variations in sexual identity, locality, age, 'intellectual capacity' and a range of other social factors. Thornton (1995) argues that there is simply no 'real' social-class basis to youth subcultures at all; these are, in fact, creations of the media.

The New Criminology

Another neo-Marxist approach to crime, but one that was more concerned with theory than particular types of crime and deviance, was developed by Taylor, Walton and Young (1973). Partly as a result of the criticisms of what were fairly crude Marxist explanations of crime, and partly as a result of the influence of interactionism/labelling (see Chapter 2), Taylor, Walton and Young attempted to produce what they called a fully social theory of deviance in *The New Criminology* (1973). Their work was very influential.

The new criminologists argued that, in order to understand why a particular crime took place, it was no use just looking at the individual's motivation (for example, alcohol or jealousy) and obvious influences (for example, family background), which is what traditional positivist sociology might do. A neo-Marxist perspective must be taken, looking at the wider capitalist society that is helping generate the circumstances of the crime and the police response to it. It is also important to use interactionist ideas to see how the behaviour of victim, offender, media and criminal justice system all interact to influence how the situation develops. This meant that there were seven aspects of crime that had to be taken into account in any comprehensive study, and these are detailed in Table 1.3.1 (overleaf).

A further element of *The New Criminology* was that, apart from the actual analysis that is suggested, it also argued that any sociology of crime and deviance had to be critical of the established capitalist order. This meant that instead of accepting the capitalist definition of crime and seeking to explain this, its role ought to be to uncover and explain the crimes of the rich. There was no attempt to be unbiased; rather, the approach looked critically at the role of the police, the media and the criminal justice system in general – pointing out how they serve the needs of the ruling class.

Part of this critical approach to crime and criminal justice was to look in a fresh way at the ordinary criminal, who should best be seen as someone who is fighting against injustice in capitalist society, for example, by redistributing wealth to the poor through theft or robbery, or through challenging the established order, for example, through terrorism or protest. The implication was that revolutionary change was needed in society. Taylor, Walton and Young were particularly sympathetic to the decriminalisation of many offences (for example, drug laws and laws against prostitution), since they saw the law as unnecessarily intolerant and restrictive.

Policing the crisis

A good example of the application of *The New Criminology* is the work of Stuart Hall *et al.* (1978) in *Policing the Crisis: The State and Law and Order.* This study adopts a neo-Marxist approach that sees the moral panic about mugging as an ideological attempt to distract attention from the failings of capitalism. By using the idea of moral panics, it draws on interactionism/labelling as well as Marxism.

In the 1970s, London witnessed a growth in 'muggings' – assault and robbery of people in the streets. The media focused on this crime and a wave of publicity forced the problem to the top of the political and policing agenda. Although Hall did not exactly follow the model put forward in *The New Criminology*, the general critical criminological framework was used – see Table 1.3.1.

Evaluation of *The New Criminology*

Paul Rock (1988), argued that *The New Criminology* gave far too romantic a view of criminals, seeing many as politically motivated protestors against injustice. However, Rock argues, this certainly does not apply to most robbers and muggers. In his later writings as a left realist, Young echoed this criticism and suggested it was one of the reasons for his development of left realism.

Feminist criminologists, such as Pat Carlen (1988), pointed out that there was absolutely no specific discussion of the power of patriarchy in the analysis, which simply continued the omission of women from criminological discussion.

Methodologically, it has always been extremely difficult to apply the new criminality perspective, as it is so complicated. The best attempt was made by Hall. Nevertheless, it did point the way towards a more sophisticated and theoretically developed criminology that tried to examine social structure and individual agency simultaneously.

What a fully social theory of deviance must cover, according to Taylor *et al.* (1973)	Application of these ideas in Hall *et al.* (1978)
The wider origins of the deviant act	The 1970s was a period of considerable social crisis in Britain, the result of an international downturn in capitalist economies.
The immediate origins of the deviant act	This turmoil was shown in a number of inner-city riots, conflict in Northern Ireland and a high level of strikes. The government was searching for a group that could be scapegoated, to draw attention onto them and away from the crisis.
The actual act	Mugging – which according to the police was more likely to be carried out by those from African Caribbean backgrounds.
The immediate origins of social reaction	Media outrage at the extent of muggings, linked to racism among the Metropolitan Police.
The wider origins of social reaction	The need to find scapegoats and the ease with which young men from African Caribbean backgrounds could be blamed.
The outcome of social reaction on the deviants' further action	A sense of injustice among ethnic minorities and a loss of confidence by ethnic-minority communities in the criminal justice system.
The nature of deviant process as a whole	The real causes of crime were not addressed and were effectively hidden by the criminal justice system.

Table 1.3.1 *The New Criminology*

CRITICAL CRIMINOLOGY

Traditional Marxism and *The New Criminology* paved the way for a wider approach known as 'critical criminology'. Critical criminologists adopt a wide range of perspectives including feminism (see Chapter 7), anti-racism (see Chapter 6), and environmentalism (see Chapter 9). *The New Criminology* played an important role here because it did not place such exclusive emphasis on class as traditional Marxism, recognising, for example, the importance of the struggle for Black rights in the USA. Despite its diversity, critical criminology has two common unifying features.

1. It sees existing societies and criminal justice systems as unfair and exploitative and in need of change.

2. It does not accept existing laws as being just and as an objective measure of social harm. "Some critical criminologists have responded to these ideas by developing an approach known as 'zemiology' which argues that sociologists of crime should study social harm rather than law-breaking" (Newburn, 2013). For example, the harmful but legal actions of states (see Chapter 9) should be studied alongside harm to the environment, whether legal or illegal (see Chapter 9) and the exploitation of women (see Chapter 7).

While this approach stretches the boundaries of the sociology of crime, and there are likely to be disagreements about what is harmful, it does highlight issues and actions that may be far more damaging to the wellbeing of humans and the planet than the street crimes traditionally studied by criminologists.

Do you think it is justifiable to stretch criminology to include activities that are harmful and not just illegal? Suggest some disadvantages and advantages of this approach.

An overview of Marxist or critical criminological approaches

Marxist and critical criminology have provided a very powerful counterbalance to explanations of crime and deviance that focus on the individual, their family or the community in which they live. Marxist and critical criminology has forced sociologists to explore the wider social, economic and political factors that shape society. Perhaps most of all, they point out that crimes can only happen when people are defined as breaking the law, but that the law itself reflects differences in power between groups. Powerful groups, they claim, can ensure that the law, and the enforcement of the law, reflect their interests, while the harmful activity of the powerful is either not criminalised or is under-policed.

CHECK YOUR UNDERSTANDING

1. Explain what is meant by the term 'corporate crime'.

2. Explain what is meant by the term 'white-collar crime'.

3. Explain what is meant by the term 'zemiology'.

4. Explain what is meant by the term 'ruling-class ideology'.

5. Identify and briefly outline two recent examples that suggest that the law is applied in a way that favours the ruling class.

6. Identify and briefly explain two differences between traditional Marxist theories of crime and *The New Criminology*.

7. Analyse two differences between Marxist criminology and critical criminology more generally.

8. Analyse two differences between Marxist and functionalist theories of crime.

9. Evaluate the view that traditional Marxism gives a one-dimensional view of crime.

10. Evaluate the view that *The New Criminology* is superior to traditional Marxism.

TAKE IT FURTHER

Conduct an online search of *The Guardian* crime section, www.theguardian.com/uk/ukcrime, for one story relating to a recent example of corporate crime and one story relating to an example of white-collar crime. Analyse the differences between the corporate crime and the white-collar crime. Evaluate how well traditional Marxist approaches explain the two examples and, on that basis, identify at least two strengths and two weaknesses of traditional Marxist theories of crime.

1.4 REALIST THEORIES OF CRIME

LEARNING OBJECTIVES

› Demonstrate knowledge and understanding of left and right realist theories of crime (AO1).

› Apply the theories to contemporary British society (AO2).

› Analyse the differences and similarities between left and right realism (AO3).

› Evaluate realist theories of crime (AO3).

INTRODUCING THE DEBATE

Unlike Marxism, critical criminology and labelling theories, realist theories do not see crime as simply being a social construction. They see crime as a very real problem and they have been developed with the intention of providing practical policies to tackle crime. The two realist approaches, **left** and **right** realism, were both developed as a response to the apparent rise in crime in the 1970s and 1980s and consequently both suggest policies to reduce street crime. However, there are important differences between them, and these reflect political differences between the supporters of the two approaches. Left realists tend to see inequality as the main underlying cause of crime but right realists see this as relatively unimportant and instead see the welfare state and a breakdown in informal and formal social controls as the main causes of crime. Although both approaches are controversial and have been criticised, they have had a significant impact on government policy in the UK, USA and elsewhere, and these policies are discussed in relation to issues of policing and crime prevention.

UNDERSTAND THE CONCEPT

Left-wing views emphasise the need for greater equality and believe that free-market capitalism creates too much inequality. They tend to support higher taxation of the rich to pay for welfare spending to help the less well off. **Right-wing** views tend to support less government intervention in the economy and a smaller welfare state, and generally do not see inequality as a major problem. They see private business as the best way to create wealth and to serve consumers.

LEFT REALISM

Comparison with previous theories

Left realism developed out of the Marxist and critical criminology discussed in Chapter 3, but it is also highly critical of aspects of these theories. Left realists criticise Marxists for suggesting that the only way to tackle crime is to abolish capitalism. However, their argument is that the abolition of capitalism is very unlikely to happen and adopting this position meant that those with left-of-centre political views had nothing realistic to say about tackling crime in societies that remain basically capitalist. Left realists believe that crime can only be tackled by reforming capitalism rather than replacing it.

While acknowledging that white-collar crime and corporate crime are important problems, left realists criticise Marxists for their neglect of street crime, that is, crimes such as mugging. Left realism therefore concentrates on filling this gap in left-wing criminology rather than investigating the crimes of the powerful. The founders of left realism, John Lea and Jock Young (1983) pointed out that most victims of street crime were not the rich but the poor, and that burglary, theft and assault made their already difficult lives even harder. They argued that for this reason it was very misleading to portray modern-day criminals as being akin to Robin Hood, stealing from the rich to give to the poor (this position was taken by neo-Marxists in *The New Criminology*).

One of the distinctive characteristics of left realism is its stress on studying victims. Left realists make extensive use of local victim surveys to find out in detail how crime affects the lives of those who live and work in high crime areas. The Islington Crime Survey (Jones, McLean and Young, 1986) is a good example of this left realist approach. It found that inner-city dwellers – who were often working-class, on low incomes and members of minority ethnic groups – had the greatest likelihood of being victims of crimes. These groups also tended to have the greatest fear of crime.

Underpolicing and overpolicing

Left realists argue that some crimes have too much attention and resources devoted to them. These include offences such as soliciting by prostitutes, underage drinking and drug use. However, these crimes do more harm to the offenders than to third parties and can often be dealt with better through medical intervention, education or other types of help rather than through punishment and criminalisation. Other crimes, though, such as sexual assaults and harassment, racially motivated attacks and domestic violence, tended to be underreported and under-investigated. Lea and Young argue that these sorts of crime need more resources devoted to them.

Which types of crime do you think should be taken more seriously by police and other agencies, and which should be targeted less or actually decriminalised? Justify your views and compare them with those of left realists.

The rising crime rate

Some sociologists have been rather dismissive of the view that there has been a rise in street crime since the Second World War. They have questioned this by pointing out that the official crime statistics are invalid because they are socially constructed. However, left realists such as Young (1993) claim that these rises in crime have been so great that they cannot simply be explained away by changes in reporting and recording. Left realists claim that there must have been at least some rise and they take the view that this rise needs explaining.

The explanation of crime

Lea and Young base their attempt to explain crime around three key concepts: relative deprivation, subculture and marginalisation.

> *Relative deprivation* – Left realists point out that in modern societies advertisers stress the importance of economic success and promote middle-class lifestyles and patterns of consumption.

UNDERSTAND THE CONCEPT

A group or individual experiences **relative deprivation** when they feel deprived (lacking in things of importance) in comparison to similar groups or individuals, or when their expectations are not met. In some circumstances, relative deprivation can be experienced despite rising living standards.

Rather like Merton (see Chapter 1), Lea and Young argue that rising crime is partly the result of a rise in people's expectations with regard to what they think they are entitled to consume, combined with the fact that some social groups simply do not have the economic resources to achieve these expectations. Young (1999) argues that increased inequality and increased emphasis on material success have made these problems worse. High levels of cultural inclusion (being involved in the culture of consumer society, for example, through access to glamorous TV shows and the advertising of designer brands) are combined with social and economic exclusion for poorer groups in society (they can't afford to buy most of the desirable goods and services). The feelings of relative deprivation that emerge from this situation are made worse because of the proximity of different social groups. For example, the excluded carry out much routine work for the middle classes, such as working in shops and restaurants.

> *Subculture* – Some groups may develop subcultural strategies and lifestyles in order to cope with the problem of relative deprivation. These may vary. Some,

such as drug-based subcultures, may encourage criminality, while others, such as religious subcultures, may discourage crime. In contrast with functionalists, Young (1999) argues that there is less consensus about moral values than in the past because there is now an increasing variety of subcultures claiming that their values are legitimate, which tends to lead to increased conflict and rising crime, particularly hate crimes committed against marginalised groups (for example, against Black and minority ethnic groups, or against lesbian, gay, bisexual and transgender – LGBT – people).

> *Marginalisation* – Marginal groups generally lack the organisation to represent their interests in political life and consequently their concerns are not generally taken seriously by those in positions of power.

UNDERSTAND THE CONCEPT

Marginalisation involves being pushed to the fringes of society. It tends to mean that people or groups lack power and influence. They may feel that they lack a central role or full involvement in the mainstream life of society.

For example, those in regular employment can join trade unions, but the unemployed and those in casual work are less likely to be unionised. Marginal groups therefore tend to use violence and rioting as forms of political action in order to express their sense of grievance. Lea and Young argue that the key to avoiding marginality is employment because workers feel they have a clear stake in society.

Lee and Young argue that underlying relative deprivation, subculture formation and marginalisation is inequality. Even with reasonable living standards and low rates of poverty, those left behind in an increasingly unequal society could become marginalised, feel deprived and form subcultures that encourage criminality.

The square of crime

As well as developing specific explanations of criminality, left realists have developed a model of the different factors involved in understanding and explaining crime. This is known as 'the square of crime' (see Figure 1.4.1).

According to Roger Matthews (1993) crime can only be understood in terms of the interaction between four elements: the state, the offender, informal social control and the victim. The square of crime acknowledges that

crime is produced through the interaction between what offenders do and the social reaction to their behaviour, both informally from members of the public, and formally from the representatives of the state such as the police and the courts. The idea of the square of crime therefore combines elements from traditional approaches to explaining crime, such as subcultural theory (which focuses on the offender), and from labelling theory (which focuses on the social reaction). However, it goes further than both of these theoretical approaches in seeing victims as also being important.

Many crimes cannot take place without victims and victims are often crucial in determining whether an act is defined as a crime or not. Victims will often be the ones who initially define whether an action is illegal and violent or not and decide whether it should be reported. For example, crimes such as domestic violence and sexual crimes are usually reported by the victims.

The different elements of the square of crime interact with one another. For example, informal attitudes and police policies towards domestic violence and sexual crimes play an important part in influencing whether victims decide to report the crime or not. This is hugely important as the risks of being caught if there is increased reporting may deter potential offenders.

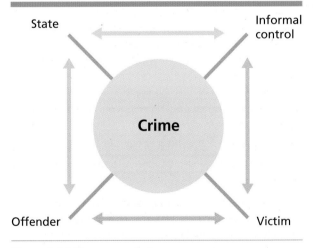

Figure 1.4.1 *The square of crime*

Left realism and policy

Left realists have had some influence upon policies in a number of countries, including Britain. The New Labour government of 1997 to 2010 adopted some policies likely to reduce inequality, including the introduction of tax credits and the minimum wage. These measures can have an impact by reducing relative deprivation. Left realists such as Lea and Young (1984) have also had some influence on policing policy. Young (1997) argued that policing could only be effective with the cooperation of the public and it was therefore important to have democratic control of the police and improve relations between the police and the public, particularly in high-crime areas. They also supported measures such as recruitment of ethnic minority police officers and reduced use of stop and search powers (see Chapter 6), which could help to reduce marginalisation. In line with left realist thinking, attempts were made to consult the public more about policing policy in many inner-city areas and more training has been introduced to counteract racism in the police. More recently, directly elected police commissioners have been introduced to bring some democratic accountability.

Evaluation of left realism

Left realism has been criticised in a number of ways. Hughes (1991) argues that it fails to successfully explain the causes of street crime. Left realists have not gathered empirical data about offenders' motives and the theory therefore lacks direct evidence about the reasons for committing crime. Most left realist research has focused on victim studies, which offer little information about offenders.

Hughes also attacks left realism for its reliance on subcultural theory, which has been heavily criticised (see Chapter 1). Jones (1998) argues that left realism fails to explain why some people who experience relative deprivation turn to crime while others do not. It seems to over-predict the amount of crime that will take place in a consumer society in which everyone potentially wants to consume more. It can also be argued that left realism has not explained why officially recorded crime has fallen in recent years.

Ruggiero (1992) argues that left realists have neglected corporate and organised crime in comparison with Marxist and critical criminologists.

However, Hughes does identify some strengths of left realism. He argues that the concept of relative deprivation is useful in understanding why crime can increase despite rising living standards. He also supports the theory's suggestion that street crime can have harmful effects upon weaker members of society and that it should therefore be taken seriously by left-wing criminologists. Hughes also believes that left realists have provided some useful suggestions for improving policing and, in doing so, have contributed to making the criminal justice system fairer and more effective.

However, perhaps the most important contribution of left realism is to stress the significance of victims and to explore their role in defining what is considered criminal and what is not. No other theory had incorporated the role of victims in the way that left realism has, so it has helped to produce a more rounded way of understanding criminality.

Do you agree that it is important to consider the role of the victim in understanding and explaining crime? Suggest reasons why the victim might be important in some types of crime but not in others.

RIGHT REALIST CRIMINOLOGY

Like left realists, right realists also see crime as a major and increasing problem. They too accept the official crime statistics, which show increases in crime in the 1970s, 1980s and early 1990s in the USA and the UK. Right realists agree with functionalists that it is important to maintain order for society to run smoothly and their theories are aimed at explaining crime in order to find practical ways to combat it.

Right realism first became popular on both sides of the Atlantic in an era when right-of-centre political views, which emphasised individual moral responsibility for crime, were influential. Right realists generally reject the idea that crime can be explained in terms of structural causes, such as increasing inequality, and instead focus more on the individual offender's role and the role of law-enforcement agencies in preventing and deterring crime. However, they do take some account of informal social control as well.

James Q Wilson: crime as rational choice

The American social scientist James Q. Wilson (1975) attacked left-wing solutions to crime. For example, he denied that programmes to eliminate poverty that were tried in the USA in the 1960s had had any success in reducing crime, since the crime rate had continued to rise. Furthermore, Wilson notes, many poor people do not commit crime.

Wilson argues that explaining crime is basically very simple: it is a matter of rational choice. Individuals who contemplate crime weigh up the benefits of criminality, such as financial gain or increased status, and balance these against the risks such as the chances of getting caught and the consequences if they are. According to Wilson, in terms of street crime, the balance of risks and benefits has tipped too much in favour of criminals. In particular, the chance of getting caught has become quite low. Punishment is not effective as a deterrent if there is little chance that you will be caught and prosecuted.

Wilson believed that formal controls were failing to combat crime because the police were solving too few crimes and the law and its punishments were too weak. However, he also believed that informal social controls were breaking down as well. In the past, people may have been deterred from committing crime by the fact that being caught brought public shame and a loss of standing or status in the community. However, Wilson argued that communities were being undermined by the prevalence of crime and, as a result, neighbours had become increasingly distrustful of one another. Moreover, fewer law-abiding citizens were spending time on the increasingly dangerous streets. In these circumstances, reputation and shame had become less important and consequently the prospect of public disgrace was no longer effective at keeping crime down.

Choose four different types of crime and consider whether you can explain the offending in terms of rational choices. Justify your answers.

Wilson and Kelling: broken windows

Wilson and Kelling (1982) further developed the idea that it is crucial to try to maintain informal social controls in neighbourhoods if crime is going to be kept in check. The police can play an important role in doing this by clamping down on the first signs of undesirable behaviour in a neighbourhood. They should try to keep drunks, prostitutes, drug addicts and vandals off the street so that law-abiding citizens feel secure. This means that those who do abide by the law feel safe enough to spend time in public places and consequently they can monitor the behaviour of others and put informal pressure on them to conform.

Wilson and Kelling argue that if just a single broken window is left unrepaired an area can start to deteriorate,

and law-abiding citizens will not feel safe on the streets. Controversially, they therefore argue that the police should concentrate on areas that are just beginning to deteriorate and exercise a policy of **zero tolerance** in those areas. Rather than concentrating solely on the more serious offences, they should deal with all minor offences as well because to leave them unpunished is to risk a rapidly deteriorating situation where offenders feel they can get away with bad behaviour with impunity. However, Wilson and Kelling argue that some areas may be too far gone to save, and that it is better therefore to concentrate resources in areas not yet beyond redemption.

UNDERSTAND THE CONCEPT

Zero-tolerance policies involve removing discretion from police to deal flexibly with minor offences (for example, through informal warnings). When zero-tolerance policies are adopted, the letter of the law is followed rigorously so that potential offenders are left in no doubt about the possible consequences of any offending.

Cohen and Felson: routine activities theory

The rational choice theory of Wilson (see above), was further developed by Lawrence Cohen and Matthew Felson (1979) and their routine activities theory. They argued that in most circumstances social control mechanisms and the risk of getting caught or the simple lack of opportunity prevented crime taking place. Crime therefore needed three conditions to take place.

> Individuals who were motivated to offend.

> The availability of opportunity and targets – for example, with the growth of consumer society more material goods are available to steal, in some cases with little security to prevent their theft.

> The lack of capable guardians (people who were able to prevent offending by controlling the behaviour of potential offenders – for example, police, parents or neighbours).

Most crime was, in their view, opportunist rather than carefully planned in advance. Therefore, if individuals motivated to commit crimes encountered easy opportunities to commit crime in the course of their routine activities in their everyday lives, then crime was likely to occur.

Cohen and Felson believed that changes in the USA had led to the growth of crime. These included an increase in available targets – for example, the growth of car ownership – and reduced control over the behaviour of some social groups, particularly the young, with the growth of single-parent families and single-adult households. More people motivated to offend were spending more time in public places, where there were more targets and fewer capable guardians. Because potential offenders and victims were more often together at the same time and place, there was an increasing likelihood of crime occurring.

Cohen and Felson concluded that in order to reduce crime it had to be made harder to commit crime, for example, with the use of improved locks and alarms on cars (an approach known as 'target hardening'). Furthermore, public spaces had to be better monitored by capable guardians such as by CCTV.

Their approach is one of a number that focus on situational crime prevention. The idea behind this is to cut crime by making it more difficult to commit. It focuses on protecting potential targets of crime rather than on the actions and motivations of offenders (for further details see Chapter 11).

Charles Murray and the underclass

One factor mentioned by Cohen and Felson to explain crime is changes in family structure. A much more central role is given to this by Charles Murray (1990) who largely attributes the growth in crime to the existence of an underclass. According to Murray, a group has developed below the main class system distinguished not so much by its economic position, but by its attitudes and values. The underclass is defined in terms of deviant and criminal behaviour and disregard for the law. Murray believes that this group has grown both in the USA and UK largely because of the increase in single parenthood, which in turn is the result of over-generous welfare systems.

In the past, single parenthood was difficult or impossible. Having children out of marriage was frowned upon by most people. The state did not provide adequate financial support for single mothers either. However, the welfare state now makes it economically viable to be a single parent and, according to Murray, this produces an underclass. Murray argues that young women can get pregnant safe in the knowledge that the state will support them. However, he also argues that young men often do not take responsibility for their children or support them. This encourages welfare dependency, in which people get used to relying on the state for support and have little incentive to earn their own living. Young men,

however, do find they cannot fully fund the lifestyles they would like and consequently turn to crime to supplement their income.

The attitudes and values of the underclass are then passed down to the next generation. Children lack a male role model who goes out to work and earns an honest living. They are influenced more by peer groups who are often themselves involved in delinquent and criminal behaviour. Furthermore, in Murray's view, children in the underclass are inadequately socialised into respect for the law or desire to work by their mothers, and they in turn are likely to end up dependent on benefits.

Some sociologists have seen Murray's underclass theory as 'blaming the victims' of an unjust society for its problems. Explain what you think they mean by this and evaluate their viewpoint.

The influence of right realism

Some aspects of right realist thinking have been very influential. 'Zero-tolerance' policing has been used extensively in the USA and on occasions in the UK as well. This involves clamping down on minor offences in the hope that it will nip criminality in the bud and it is based on Wilson's broken windows theory.

Another policy based on this theory is the use of ASBOs (anti-social behaviour orders), which were first introduced in the UK in 1999. These orders criminalise specific behaviour by named individuals who are deemed to be anti-social. They were replaced by Criminal Behaviour Orders (CRIMBOs) and Crime Prevention Injunctions (CPIs) in 2012.

Right realist ideas have also been influential in encouraging the rise in the prison population, as harsher sentences have been used in an attempt to ensure that 'crime does not pay'. The number of people imprisoned in the USA has risen particularly rapidly but it has also increased in the UK. Generally, both Labour and Conservative governments in Britain were keen to increase the number of police (until recent austerity measures have to led to policy going in the other direction), have stricter sentences and build more prisons in order to catch and punish more criminals more severely.

Evaluation of right realism

The effectiveness of right realist policies is open to dispute, but there are some examples that seem to support the claims. For example, there was a rapid fall in crime in New York when some of its ideas (particularly zero tolerance) were applied by Bill Bratton (New York Police Department Commissioner 1994–96 and later an advisor to David Cameron's government in the UK – see Focus on Skills). The ideas behind situational crime prevention have been extensively used and again there is at least some evidence that they have succeeded. There have been claims that the increased use of imprisonment in the USA has helped to reduce the crime rate by locking up many serious offenders and by deterring other potential offenders. However, no single factor is likely to explain falls in crime that have occurred in much of the western world, regardless of whether right realist policies have been adopted or not.

Some sociologists have directly contradicted the claims of right realists. The broken windows theory has been attacked in various ways. Matthews (1992) examined the research and found little evidence that tolerating broken windows and other minor incidents has led to an increase in crime. Steve Jones (2009) argues that factors such as lack of investment are far more important in determining whether a neighbourhood declines, rather than tolerating broken windows. Furthermore, he argues, concentrating attention on minor offenders might mean that more serious offenders are more likely to get away with their crimes, which is not only unjust but might lead to increased crime. Left realists such as Lea and Young (1984) see the policing policies advocated by right realists as a form of 'militaristic' policing, where the police act almost like an invading army. This just antagonises and marginalises the population further and, if anything, results in even more crime as a result.

The idea that crime is simply a rational calculation has also been questioned. Sociologists such as Katz (1988) and Lyng (1990) suggest that the emotional appeal or thrill of crime is important in explaining crimes, particularly those that give no obvious material benefit to the offender (see Chapter 1). Situational crime prevention has often been criticised for simply displacing crime to areas that have poorer security or less surveillance (see Chapter 11).

Murray's underclass theory as applied to Britain was based on very limited evidence (Haralambos and Holborn, 2013). Tony Fitzpatrick (2011) argues that there is no evidence that most benefits claimants turn to crime and are unwilling to work, and he sees poverty and social exclusion as the key factors leading to criminality in poor areas.

CONCLUSIONS

There are important similarities between left and right realism.

› Both see crime, including street crime, as a real and growing problem and both can be seen as a response to rising recorded crime in the later decades of the 20th century.

› Both concentrate on street crime in poor, inner-city high-crime areas.

› Both have tried to influence actual policies and both have influenced governments in the USA and the UK.

› Both acknowledge that a mix of formal and informal social control is needed to reduce crime.

› Both acknowledge that fear of crime is a significant problem, as well as crime itself.

However the differences between them are greater than the similarities. They come from opposing parts of the political spectrum and, partly because of this, see the causes of crime very differently. While right realists focus on rational choice and deterrence, left realists see the underlying causes as rooted in inequality and lack of opportunity in disadvantaged areas. They also have very different views on solutions. Right realists are much keener on a harsh criminal justice system, with the emphasis on punishment, while left realists are more concerned with tackling underlying processes, for example, reducing inequality, unemployment and poverty. For these reasons, left realists put more emphasis on underlying structural features of society while right realists subscribe to a narrower view that is focused on the motivations of the individual offender.

FOCUS ON SKILLS: ZERO-TOLERANCE POLICING

Theresa May believes the government has a duty to tell the police what the public wants them to do.

The Chief Constable of West Midlands Police has hit out at David Cameron's plans for a US-style zero tolerance of crime by declaring that he will not be "slavishly adopting empty slogans". Chris Sims, commander of Britain's second largest police force, spoke after the Prime Minister caused uproar among senior officers by embracing the approach of Bill Bratton, the American "supercop" he has appointed as an advisor.

His assertion that he answered to the citizens of the West Midlands, not political diktat, will fuel the escalating battle between the government and senior officers. Sims said: "The ethos of local policing has been the bedrock which has allowed collective common sense to prevail."

The government came out with its guns blazing today as police chiefs united to defend their forces and their approach to policing. David Cameron, in a nod to Mr Bratton's crime-fighting philosophy, told *The Sunday Telegraph*: "We haven't talked the language of zero tolerance enough but the message is getting through."

Theresa May insisted that telling senior officers "what the public want them to do" was the Home Secretary's job. She said: "the minister's job is both to ensure that the police know they have support when they get tough and also, it is my job as Home Secretary to ensure that the police know what the public want them to do."

Mrs May also defended the Prime Minister's appointment of Mr Bratton, who made his name crushing New York's gang culture with a zero-tolerance policy and dealt with the aftermath of the Los Angeles riots. Critics of the police budget cuts have, however, noted that Mr Bratton did so partly by vastly increasing rather than decreasing the number of officers.

Sir Hugh [Orde, President of the Association of Chief Police Officers], who has vociferously defended Britain's non-politicised approach to law enforcement, questioned Mr Bratton's appointment. "If you look at the style of policing in the States, and their levels of violence, they are fundamentally different from here," he said.

Iain Duncan Smith, the Work and Pensions Secretary, is meanwhile preparing to lead a hardline crackdown on gangs, involving officially sanctioned campaigns of harassment against members which would bring them before the courts for even the most minor offence. "Gang leaders should receive a knock on the door from the police at least once a day", he told *The Sunday Times*. Those who renounced gang membership, however, would be offered drug treatments and educational help at specially created, heavily 'disciplined' schools. "Instead of going around denying there is a broken society, he has to recognise that in these communities are problem people who are going to destroy the position of London." he said.

Gray, S. (2011) 'Police chief refuses "slavish adoption" of Cameron's zero-tolerance plans', *The Times*, 14 August 2011

Questions

1. **Understand.** What do you think is meant by the sentence, "The ethos of local policing has been the bedrock which has allowed collective common sense to prevail"?

2. **Understand.** What do you think Iain Duncan Smith means by 'problem people'?

3. **Analyse** the ways in which government policy discussed in this article reflects right realist criminology.

4. **Analyse** the ways in which government policy is criticised by the Chief Constable of West Midlands Police in the article.

5. **Identify** two possible strengths and two possible weaknesses of a zero-tolerance approach to crime in Britain.

CHECK YOUR UNDERSTANDING

1. What is meant by 'the square of crime'?

2. Explain what is meant by a 'rational choice' theory of crime.

3. Explain the meaning of 'relative deprivation'.

4. Identify three characteristics of the 'underclass' in Murray's theory.

5. Which of Lea and Young's causes of crime involve the lack of a central role in society?

6. Briefly explain why a 'broken window' can lead to the breakdown of law and order, according to Wilson and Kelling.

7. Outline the ways in which Cohen and Felson believe it is possible to reduce crime through situational crime control.

8. Outline two criticisms of left realist criminology.

9. Analyse two differences between left and right realism.

10. Evaluate the main strengths and weaknesses of right realist criminology.

TAKE IT FURTHER

Go to the website of The Centre for Crime and Justice (http://www.crimeandjustice.org.uk) and find one article about corporate or state crime. (You could try searching for the work of Steve Tombs on the site to help you.) Briefly summarise the material you have found and write a short discussion of how it might support or contradict Marxist theories of crime.

1.5 STATISTICS AND PATTERNS OF CRIME

LEARNING OBJECTIVES

> Demonstrate knowledge and understanding of different types of crime statistics and the statistical patterns shown in them (AO1).

> Apply an awareness of the statistics to current crime trends (AO2).

> Analyse the strengths and weaknesses of different types of crime statistics (AO3).

> Evaluate the reliability and validity of crime statistics (AO3).

INTRODUCING THE DEBATE

Most people think they have a pretty good idea about trends in crime, who commits crime and who is likely to become a victim. However, our common-sense ideas about crime do not always match the picture given in statistics. Many people believe that crime is rising in Britain, but for many years the number of crimes recorded by the police has fallen. Many also think that crime is something committed by the less wealthy against the more wealthy and more vulnerable sections of the community. However, police figures indicate that poorer areas have higher crime rates than wealthy areas, and that young men are more likely to be the victims of crime than old women. But are these figures accurate, and how can we use statistics about crime to help us understand why some people commit crimes and others do not? This chapter examines just these issues.

TYPES OF CRIME STATISTIC

Sociologists use three different ways to build up a picture of crime patterns. Each method provides particular information, but also has a number of weaknesses that need to be identified if the overall picture is to be accurate. The three methods of collecting information are police-recorded statistics, victim surveys and self-report studies.

1. Police-recorded statistics are drawn from the records kept by the police and other official agencies, and are published every six months by the Home Office. These official statistics on crime are particularly useful in that they have been collected since 1857 and so provide an excellent historical overview of changing trends over time. They also give a very accurate view of the way that the criminal justice system processes offenders through arrests, trials, punishments and so on.

2. Victim studies are based on surveys asking a sample of people whether they have been victims of crime and, if so, whether it has been reported to the police. They are useful for estimating unrecorded crime and for looking at trends but they don't cover crimes without victims (such as drug offences). The most important victim study is the Crime Survey for England and Wales (CSEW) conducted annually by the Home Office.

3. Self-report studies involve conducting surveys to ask people if they have committed crimes and they are sometimes conducted by government departments and sometimes by sociological researchers. They rely on the truthfulness of respondents but are useful for revealing the sorts of people who commit different types of crime.

Police-recorded statistics as social constructions

Police-recorded statistics can be seen as a social construction – a product of society rather than objective facts – so they cannot be taken simply at their face value. This is because they only show crimes that are reported to and recorded by the police. Digging a little deeper reveals a lot of hidden issues.

Reporting crime

Police-recorded statistics are based on the information that the criminal justice agencies collect. But crimes cannot be recorded by them if they are not reported in the first place, and the simple fact is that a high proportion of 'crimes' are not reported to the police at all. According to the CSEW (Home Office 2011/2012), individuals are less likely to report a 'crime' to the police if they regard it as:

> too trivial to bother the police with

> a private matter between friends and family – in this case they will seek redress directly (get revenge themselves) – or one where they wish no harm to come to the offender

> too embarrassing (for example, rape).

Other reasons why people might not report crimes to the police are that:

> the victim may not be in a position to give information (for example, a child suffering abuse)

> they may fear reprisals.

On the other hand, people are more likely to report a crime if:

> they see some benefit to themselves (for example, an insurance claim)

> they have faith in the police's ability to achieve a positive result.

Recording of crimes

When people do actively report an offence to the police, you would think that these statistics at least would enter the official reports. Yet a report by Her Majesty's Inspectorate of Constabulary in 2014 concluded that nearly one in five crimes (19 per cent) reported to the police, and that should have been recorded by them, were not included in the statistics. There are large numbers of crimes of which people believe they have been victims but that are not reported and recorded. The total number of unrecorded crimes is known as the 'dark figure'. This dark figure can be estimated but cannot be measured precisely. Because of the dark figure, victim surveys such as the CSEW give different statistics from police-recorded crime. Figure 1.5.1 opposite shows the trends in crime in England and Wales, according to these two sources. These appear to show that in the very long term, crime rates have increased, but since the mid-1990s, according to the CSEW, or the early 2000s, according to police figures, there have been significant falls in numbers of most types of crime. Some researchers have questioned whether this represents an actual fall in crime or whether statistics do not capture the real changes (see Focus on Skills overleaf).

Although the general trends revealed are similar in the police figures and CSEW, numbers of violent crimes recorded by the police have increased in recent years but have declined according to the CSEW. Tim Newburn (2013) suggests this may be the result of changes in police counting rules, which have led to more incidents being counted as separate offences so that there is an apparent increase in offending.

The role of the police

Clearly, the police are filtering the information supplied to them by the public, according to factors that are important to them. These factors have been identified as follows.

> *Seriousness* – They may regard the offence as too trivial or simply not a criminal matter.

> *Classifying* – When a person makes a complaint, police crimes officers must decide what category of offence it is. How they classify the offence will determine its seriousness. So, the police officer's opinion determines the category and seriousness of crime (from assault, to aggravated assault, for example). They must also decide how many offences have taken place, which will also affect the overall figures.

> *Social status* – More worryingly, they may not view the social status of the person reporting the matter as high enough to regard the issue as worth pursuing. This may affect the chances of offenders from different social groups ending up with convictions or being imprisoned. For example, middle-class or white-collar criminals may not be investigated if complaints come from working-class victims. More significantly,

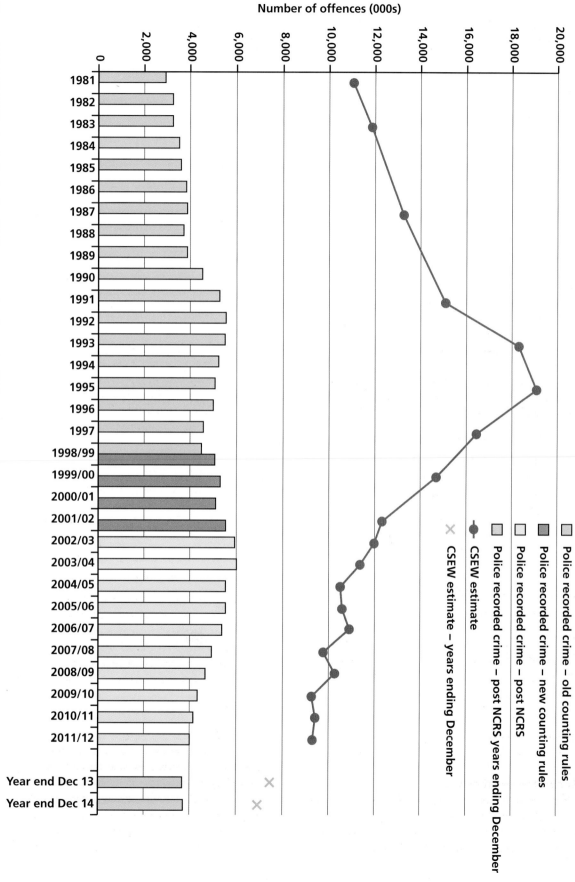

Number of offences (000s)

Figure 1.5.1 ONS (2015) crime in England and Wales, year ending December 2014

Police recorded crime – old counting rules

Police recorded crime – new counting rules

Police recorded crime – post NCRS

Police recorded crime – post NCRS years ending December

CSEW estimate

CSEW estimate – years ending December

the police may exhibit conscious or subconscious bias, which makes them more likely to suspect, investigate, arrest and ultimately label those who fit their stereotypical views on offenders. The next three chapters examine this in detail, looking at evidence of possible class and gender bias and racism in the police.

> *Discretion* – The chances of being arrested for an offence increase markedly depending upon the 'demeanour' of the person being challenged by a police officer (that is, their appearance, attitude and manner). Anderson *et al.* (1994) show that youths who cooperate and are polite to police officers are less likely to be arrested than those regarded as disrespectful. Factors such as class, ethnicity and gender may play a part here.

The dark figure

Because not all crimes are reported, and of those reported not all are recorded, there is a large dark figure of crime that does not appear in the police statistics of recorded crime. It is impossible to be precise about the proportion of crime that does not appear in crimes known to the police.

Some sociologists believe that the exercise of discretion can lead to bias in the criminal justice system against the young, minority ethnic groups, the working class, and (in different circumstances) against males or females. Do you agree that this is likely? Give some examples to support your argument.

FOCUS ON RESEARCH: CRIME SURVEY FOR ENGLAND AND WALES (CSEW)

The Crime Survey for England and Wales (previously called the British Crime Survey or BCS) was first introduced in 1982. The sample size is enormous, with almost 40,000 people being interviewed in recent surveys. The idea behind this victim study is that by asking people directly what crimes have been committed against them, the problems of crime reporting and police recording are avoided. Supporters of the survey suggest that it is more 'valid' than the police statistics because it includes unreported crime.

The sampling technique is based on (a) all households in England and Wales and then (b) anyone over 16 living in these households; since 2009 there has also been a smaller sample of children aged 10–15. The households are randomly selected, using the Postcode Address File, developed by the Post Office to recognise all households in Britain. Interviews last 50 minutes and each person is asked if they have been the victim of a list of selected crimes. There is then a smaller 'sweep'

(a subsample), who are asked to answer questions on selected (sometimes sensitive) issues directly into a laptop computer.

The survey cannot cover all crimes. It is stated: "The CSEW has necessary exclusions from its main count of crime (for example, homicide, crimes against businesses and other organisations, and drug possession). The survey also excludes sexual offences from its main crime count given the sensitivities around reporting this in the context of a face-to-face interview" (ONS, 2014). Is the CSEW more accurate than the police-recorded statistics? It may be that the CSEW is neither better nor worse, but simply provides an alternative, overall picture of crime that helps fill in some gaps in the police-recorded statistics.

Questions

1. How does the CSEW try to maximise the representativeness of the survey?

2. Analyse whether any groups are still left out of, or are under-represented in, the sample for the survey.

3. Analyse reasons why some crimes are excluded from the survey.

4. Explain why respondents in the smaller subsample are asked to input their answers directly into a laptop computer.

5. Evaluate the main strengths and weaknesses of this source of statistics on crime.

The role of the courts

Official statistics of crimes committed and punished also reflect the decisions and sentences of the courts. However, these statistics, too, are a reflection of social processes.

British courts work on the assumption that many people will plead guilty – and about 75 per cent of all those charged actually do so. This is often the result of an informal and largely unspoken agreement whereby the defence will try to get the charges with the lightest possible punishment put forward by the prosecution. (In the USA, this bargaining is far more open than in Britain, and is known as 'plea-bargaining'.) The result is an overwhelming majority of pleas of guilty, yet sometimes these pleas are for less serious crimes than might 'really' have been committed. The statistics will reflect this downgrading of seriousness.

The role of the government and law enforcement agencies

What is considered to be a crime changes over time, as a result of governments changing the law in response to cultural changes and the influence of powerful groups. Any exploration of crime over a period is therefore fraught with difficulty, because any rise or fall in the levels of crime may reflect changes in the law as much as actual changes in crime. The statistics are also influenced by the views of particular police constables. For example, some chief constables pursue users of drugs such as marijuana more vigorously than others. Changing social attitudes can influence the behaviour of the police too. Following the Jimmy Savile case, increased concern about the sexual abuse of children has led to the recording of more and more crimes of this nature, although many of those uncovered took place in the past.

Victim surveys

A second way of estimating the extent and patterns of crime is by using victimisation (or victim) surveys. In these, a sample of the population, either locally or nationally, is asked which offences have been committed against them over a certain period of time.

Strengths of victim surveys

This approach overcomes the fact that a significant proportion of offences are never recorded by the police. It also gives a good picture of the extent and patterns of victimisation – something completely missing from official accounts. The best known victimisation study is the CSEW (see Focus on Research on the previous page).

Weaknesses of victim surveys

There are several disadvantages to victim surveys.

› The problem of basing statistics on victims' memories is that recollections are often faulty or biased.

› The categorisation of the crimes that have been committed against them is left to the person filling in the questionnaire – this leads to considerable inaccuracy in the categories.

› Victim surveys also usually omit a range of crimes, such as fraud and corporate crime, and any crime that the victim is unaware of or unable to report as a crime.

› Despite victim surveys being anonymous, people appear to underreport sexual offences.

Local victim surveys

The CSEW is a typical cross-sectional survey and, as such, may contain some errors – certainly, it does not provide detailed information about particular places. This has led to a number of detailed studies of crime, focusing on particular areas, which provide specific information about local problems.

The most famous of these surveys were the Islington Crime Surveys (Harper *et al.* 1986 and Jones *et al.* 1995). These showed that the BCS underreported the higher levels of victimisation of minority ethnic groups and domestic violence.

Patterns of victimisation

Despite its limitations, victimisation research has produced some interesting findings on the victims of crime. For example, the CSEW has consistently found that young males, in particular the unemployed and low-waged, have a particularly high chance of being victims of violence. Although victim surveys find that there is much more crime than is reported to the police, much (though by no means all) of the unreported crime is of a comparatively trivial nature (for more discussion of patterns of victimisation see Chapter 11).

Self-report studies

The third method for collecting data is by self-report studies. These are surveys in which a selected group or cross-section of the population are asked what offences they have committed. Self-report studies are extremely useful as they reveal much about the kind of offenders who are not caught or processed by the police. In particular, it is possible to find out about the ages, gender, ethnicity, social class and even location of 'hidden offenders'. It is also the most useful way to find out about victimless crimes, such as illegal drug use.

Weaknesses of self-report studies

› *The problem of validity* – the biggest problem is that respondents may lie or exaggerate; even if they do not deliberately seek to mislead, they may simply be mistaken.

> *The problem of representativeness* – because it is easy to study them, most self-report surveys are on young people and students. There are no such surveys on professional criminals or drug traffickers, for example!

> *The problem of relevance* – because of the problem of representativeness, the majority of the crimes uncovered tend to be trivial.

FOCUS ON SKILLS: RICHARD FORD 'CRIME FALL HIDES HUGE RISE IN BANK FRAUD'

Left out of official figures:

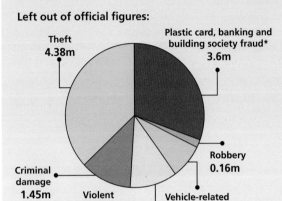

*ONS estimate of fraud

Figure 1.5.2 *True picture of crime*
Source: Crime Survey of England and Wales (2013/2014)

Almost four million crimes are being left out of official figures, disguising the huge scale of fraud across Britain, according to an analysis by the Office for National Statistics.

Inclusion of bank and credit card frauds in the annual Crime Survey for England and Wales would increase the estimated number of annual offences by 50 per cent, taking the overall crime total from 7.3 million to 11 million a year.

The survey has been hailed by ministers as the most authoritative picture of crime because it relies on individuals' experiences rather than incidents reported to police.

However, it does not include bank and plastic card fraud, ostensibly because the victim and location of the crime are difficult to pin down.

The first estimate by the ONS of uncounted crime, published on its website without publicity last month, indicates that every minute about seven people are defrauded.

Marion FitzGerald, visiting professor of criminology at the University of Kent, has said that claims of ever-falling crime were misleading because the crime survey excluded card fraud.

Professor FitzGerald said: "Here we have an admission from its own results that crime is 50 per cent higher than the figure it claims."

The ONS analysis further undermines the reputation of crime statistics after claims this year that police had "fiddled" and "manipulated" figures to meet targets. Statisticians said that the plastic card fraud figures are not included "due to conceptual difficulties with assigning victimisation" — whether the crime is committed against the plastic card holder or the bank or financial institution issuing the card.

The survey only counts crime committed in England and Wales, so fraud involving a card skimmed in the UK but used overseas is not included.

Source: Ford, R. 'Crime fall hides huge rise in bank fraud', The Times, 26 August 2014

Questions

1. **Explain** in your own words why both police and victim survey statistics have underestimated crimes involving bank and credit card fraud.

2. **Analyse** the extent to which this example undermines the statistics suggesting that overall crime has been falling in recent years.

3. **Analyse** why other changes in the nature of crime might affect the validity and reliability of statistics on crime. (You can think about other emerging types of criminality involving internet use and how likely it is that these will be reported and recorded.)

4. **Evaluate** whether in view of this article crime statistics should be see as simply social constructions. (Consult Figure 1.5.2 to answer this question.)

Self-report studies and patterns of offending

Despite these weaknesses, the only information that is available of who offends, other than from the official statistics of people who have been arrested, comes from self-report studies, and they have been very widely used to explore such issues as crime and drug use.

Self-report studies are very useful for trying to determine if there is systematic bias in the criminal justice system that might result in certain types of offender (such as working-class men and people from minority ethnic groups) being more likely to be processed by the criminal justice system and categorised as criminals than other groups, who are more likely to get away with their offending. Evidence on these issues is explored in the next three chapters. Young men from disadvantaged backgrounds who live in inner city areas are much more likely than other types of individual to end up

with convictions or incarcerated (confined in any type of prison or jail), but does this reflect actual patterns of offending?

CONCLUSIONS

Few sociologists of crime and deviance today accept crime statistics at face value, but there are various views on what type of crime statistics are more useful, and how much credence should be given to the picture of crime they provide. These differences reflect the different perspectives on criminal statistics outlined in Figure 1.5.3.

The problems with criminal statistics will be explored further in the next three chapters, which look at patterns of crime in relation to particular social groups.

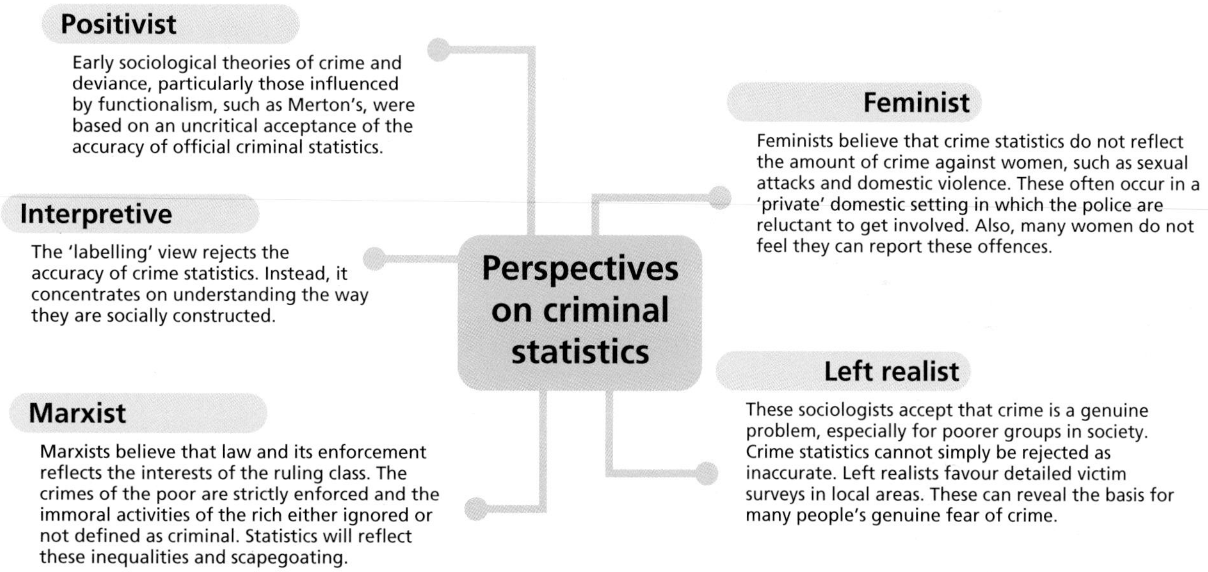

Positivist

Early sociological theories of crime and deviance, particularly those influenced by functionalism, such as Merton's, were based on an uncritical acceptance of the accuracy of official criminal statistics.

Interpretive

The 'labelling' view rejects the accuracy of crime statistics. Instead, it concentrates on understanding the way they are socially constructed.

Marxist

Marxists believe that law and its enforcement reflects the interests of the ruling class. The crimes of the poor are strictly enforced and the immoral activities of the rich either ignored or not defined as criminal. Statistics will reflect these inequalities and scapegoating.

Perspectives on criminal statistics

Feminist

Feminists believe that crime statistics do not reflect the amount of crime against women, such as sexual attacks and domestic violence. These often occur in a 'private' domestic setting in which the police are reluctant to get involved. Also, many women do not feel they can report these offences.

Left realist

These sociologists accept that crime is a genuine problem, especially for poorer groups in society. Crime statistics cannot simply be rejected as inaccurate. Left realists favour detailed victim surveys in local areas. These can reveal the basis for many people's genuine fear of crime.

Figure 1.5.3 Perspectives on criminal statistics

CHECK YOUR UNDERSTANDING

1. Briefly explain what is meant by a 'self-report study'.

2. Briefly explain what is meant by a 'victim study'.

3. Suggest two reasons why a victim might not report a crime to the police.

4. Explain one problem with obtaining a representative sample of victims of crime.

5. Suggest three possible criticisms of victim studies such as the CSEW.

6. Explain how self-report studies can provide evidence about bias in the criminal justice system.

7. Explain three ways in which the police can exercise discretion in deciding how to deal with alleged offenders.

8. Identify and briefly explain three ways in which crime statistics can be seen as socially constructed.

9. Analyse the main differences between the CSEW and police statistics on crime.

10. Evaluate the usefulness of police statistics as a source of data on the extent of crime.

TAKE IT FURTHER

Go to http://www.crime-statistics.co.uk/postcode and enter the postcode for either your home or your school or college. Note down the details of crime in that area for the last month. Now enter the postcode for a very different area – one you are familiar with. Ensure there are some significant sociological differences between the two areas – in terms, for example, of the types of people who live there.

Make sure the second postcode is more than a mile from the first postcode you used. Again, note down crime in the second area. When you have done this:

1. Write a summary of the differences between crime in the two areas (both in terms of the nature of crime and the extent of crime).

2. Suggest sociological explanations for the differences both in terms of factors that might affect the number of criminal acts and the recording of those acts by the police.

1.6 ETHNICITY AND CRIME

LEARNING OUTCOMES

> Demonstrate knowledge and understanding of patterns of offending, sentencing and punishment by ethnic group in the UK (AO1).

> Demonstrate knowledge and understanding of competing explanations of the above patterns (AO1).

> Apply your understanding to contemporary issues about ethnicity and crime (AO2).

> Analyse differences between theories of the relationship between ethnicity, crime and punishment (AO3).

> Evaluate theories of ethnicity, criminality and criminalisation (AO3).

INTRODUCING THE DEBATE

A recurring theme in media reporting of street crime since the mid-1970s has been the alleged disproportionate involvement of minority ethnic groups in crime, particularly young Black males. At certain times, though, and for certain crimes, other minority ethnic groups, including British Asians, have all been seen as a threat to law and order. Does this media concern reflect the evidence? It is difficult to give a definitive answer to this because the evidence is limited and is sometimes contradictory. Furthermore, official statistics on crime could reflect bias and racism in the criminal justice system, as much as real differences in criminality. Therefore, as well as looking at whether there are distinctive causes and patterns of crime across different ethnic groups, this section also considers whether minority ethnic groups are subject to biased treatment from the criminal justice system and are more likely to be victims of crime themselves.

OFFENDING, SENTENCING AND PUNISHMENT

Offending

There are three main ways of gathering statistics on ethnicity and offending and punishment: official police and criminal justice system statistics, self-report studies and victimisation studies provide important information on the chances of different groups being the perpetrators of crime. (The issue of victimisation is covered in detail later in this chapter.)

Official statistics

Official crime statistics based on information provided by the police and courts show that in England and Wales, people from some minority ethnic groups are more likely to be arrested for and convicted of crime than the White ethnic majority. Table 1.6.1 (overleaf) shows that while the Black population makes up just 3.1 per cent of the population, they make up a much higher proportion of those stopped and searched, arrested, convicted or sent to prison. Indeed, proportionately they are more

	White	Black	Asian	Mixed	Chinese or other
Proportion of total population aged 10 or over	87.1 %	3.1 %	6.4 %	1.7 %	1.7 %
Stops and searches	67.1 %	14.2 %	10.3 %	2.9 %	1.3 %
Arrests	79.5 %	8.3 %	5.9 %	3.0 %	1.4 %
Convictions	73.2 %	7.5 %	4.5 %	1.8 %	1.1 %
Sentenced to immediate custody	70.6 %	8.9 %	5.5 %	1.9 %	1.7 %

Table 1.6.1 *Race and the criminal justice system in England and Wales 2011/12*
Source: Ministry of Justice (2013)

than twice as likely as White people to be arrested and convicted of an offence, and almost three times as likely to be sent to prison. Asian ethnic groups are more likely to be stopped and searched than Whites but are otherwise slightly less likely to get into trouble with the law than Whites. Those of 'Mixed' ethnicity have significantly higher arrest rates than Whites.

So do these data show that some minority ethnic groups, particularly Black, are more criminal than other groups? As the previous chapter showed, official crime statistics do not necessarily produce a valid and reliable picture of criminality. The statistics reveal how many people have been suspected of being criminal, or **criminalised** by being defined as criminal, but not how many have committed crimes. They say as much about the actions of the criminal justice system as about offenders. Indeed sociologists of 'race' and crime are divided over whether statistics such as these indicate real differences in offending rates between ethnic groups or simply indicate that the police and courts are biased and are prone to unfairly labelling some ethnic groups more than others, due to conscious or unconscious racism.

UNDERSTAND THE CONCEPT

Criminalisation is the process through which individuals and actions are turned into criminals and criminal actions through the criminal justice system. The term implies that a process of labelling is taking place and that the actions and individuals that are criminalised could be defined as non-criminal if, for example, the law was changed or the courts made different decisions.

What possible explanations could there be for the statistics in the above table? How far should we trust the statistics?

Self-report studies

An alternative way of collecting crime statistics is the use of self-report studies (see Chapter 5). Self-report studies rely upon the honesty and accuracy of respondents, but they do at least give some indication of the extent of offending that has not resulted in arrests and convictions. They can therefore provide an indication of whether offenders from some groups are more likely to be arrested and convicted than those from other ethnic groups. If they are, then this could suggest bias in the criminal justice system.

The last major self-report study of ethnicity and offending in Britain was carried out in 2005, using a sample of more than 10,000 respondents and an extra (booster) sample of minority ethnic groups. It collected data on 20 core offences (broadly street crimes). The highest rates of offending were found among 'Whites', with 42 per cent admitting an offence during their lifetime compared with 39 per cent of those of 'Mixed' ethnicity, 28 per cent of those of 'Black' ethnicity, and 21 per cent of 'Asian' ethnic groups. Whites also had the highest offending rates for more serious offence categories, as shown in Figure 1.6.1. The only category where Black offending rates were higher than White rates was in terms of robbery (2 per cent as opposed to 0.5 per cent), but robbery only accounts for a small proportion of crime and this cannot therefore account for the general overrepresentation of Black offenders and suspects in the criminal justice system. These data therefore suggest that there is some bias in criminal justice because, overall, Whites appear to be more likely to offend than Blacks, but Blacks are much more likely than Whites to be arrested, convicted and imprisoned.

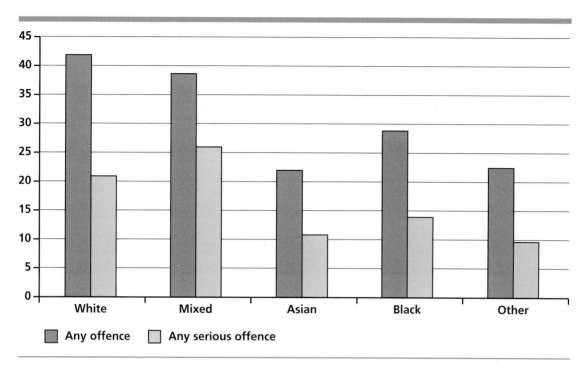

Figure 1.6.1 *Self-reported 'lifetime' offending (%) by ethnic origin, 2003*

ETHNICITY AND VICTIMISATION

Victimisation studies

Victim-based studies (such as the Crime Survey for England and Wales, CSEW) are carried out by asking members of the public whether they have been victims of crime in the preceding 12 months. According to the CSEW in 2012/13, the risk of being a personal victim of crime was higher for non-White groups, at 7.2 per cent, than for White ethnic groups (5.0 per cent). The chances of being a victim of homicide were very much higher in minority ethnic groups than among Whites. Between 2003 and 2012, 11 per cent of homicide victims were from Black ethnic groups and 9 per cent from Asian groups, even though they made up just 3.1 per cent and 6.4 per cent of the population respectively (Ministry of Justice, 2013).

The chances of being a victim of crime are not just, of course, linked to ethnicity. According to Phillips and Bowling (2012), in part, the higher risk of victimisation is the result of the relatively high proportion of minority ethnic groups living in cities, particularly inner cities, where rates of victimisation are generally high.

Some statistics clearly indicate that ethnicity is a factor behind some people becoming victims. The CSEW found that in 2012–13 there were 124,000 racially motivated incidents, and the police actually recorded 30,234 racially or religiously aggravated offences. Those from non-White backgrounds are far more likely than those from White backgrounds to be victims of these hate crimes. Although many of the incidents and offences involve harassment, some are very serious crimes and the police statistics undoubtedly underrecord the number of offences of this type. Interestingly, Phillips and Bowling (2013) report research that suggests that per capita rates of racially motivated offences are higher outside the major cities, particularly in rural areas where there are only relatively small ethnic-minority populations.

Given the high rates of victimisation, and the relatively high proportion of minority ethnic groups who live in inner-city areas, it is not surprising that the CSEW reports greater fear of crime among minority ethnic groups than among the population as a whole. Tim Newburn (2013) comments that fear of crime is greater among minority ethnic groups than among Whites who live in the same types of area. However, minority ethnic groups do not just respond passively by being afraid of crime, there have also been active attempts to combat victimisation through measures ranging from campaigns for greater police protection (such as that following the murder of Stephen Lawrence) to local crime prevention initiatives.

Like all crime statistics, the findings of victimisation studies are not wholly valid and reliable (see Chapter 11). However, they are very consistent in suggesting that ethnic groups are generally more at risk, and this is consistent with police statistics on serious crimes, such as homicide, and evidence on victimisation from racially motivated hate crimes.

FOCUS ON SKILLS: 'ISIS EFFECT' HELPS SPARK 15% RISE IN HATE CRIMES

The 2013 murder of Fusilier Lee Rigby is one factor behind the increase in hate crimes against minority ethnic groups

The number of hate crimes recorded by police in England and Wales has risen by 15% since 2012, with some forces registering increases of up to 67%.

According to figures, 17,605 racially and religiously aggravated harassment crimes were recorded by police in 2014, up from 15,249 in 2012.

Campaigners attribute the rise to a range of factors, including the emergence of Isis, also known as Islamic State, in Iraq and Syria; Israel's military operation against Hamas in the Gaza Strip last year; and the murder of Fusilier Lee Rigby in Woolwich, southeast London, in 2013. The police say better recording of such crimes has, in part, driven the increase.

According to the law, a crime is racially or religiously aggravated if "at the time of committing the offence, or immediately before or after doing so, the offender demonstrates towards the victim... hostility based on the victim's membership, or presumed membership, of a racial or religious group".

Alex Raikes, director of the charity Stand Against Racism and Inequality, said the most common targets were Muslims, and Sikhs mistaken for Muslims, and her organisation had noted growing racism among White women.

"One Sikh taxi driver was verbally abused by a group of young White females as he drove them home. Then they ripped off his turban and set it on fire," she said.

The Community Security Trust, a charity that advises the UK's Jewish population, said the number of anti-Semitic crimes it had recorded in 2014 was more than double that of the previous year.

Stupples, B. (2015) '"Isis effect" helps spark 15% rise in hate crimes', *The Times*, 3 May 2015

Questions

1. **Understand.** What do you understand by the term 'hate crime'?

2. **Analyse.** Why might the emergence of Isis, the murder of Lee Rigby and Israeli bombing of Gaza all be linked to a rise in hate crimes?

3. **Analyse** reasons why there might be better recording and reporting of hate crimes than in the past.

4. **Evaluate** the usefulness of government statistics in estimating the extent of hate crimes.

5. **Evaluate** whether the greater fear of crime in minority ethnic groups than in the White population of Britain is justified.

CRIMINAL JUSTICE, ETHNICITY AND RACISM

This section examines whether there is bias or racism in the operation of the criminal justice system.

Policing

As Tim Newburn comments, there has been a great deal of controversy over relationships between police and minority ethnic groups over recent decades. For example,

the handling of the investigation into the murder of the Black teenager Stephen Lawrence, in London in 1993, drew strong criticism of the police. Despite the availability of good evidence, the police initially failed to successfully prosecute those responsible. The Macpherson Inquiry, which investigated the issue, found that the Metropolitan Police (the London police force) was **institutionally racist** (Macpherson, 1999).

UNDERSTAND THE CONCEPT

The Macpherson Report defined **institutional racism** as "the collective failure of an organisation to provide an appropriate and professional service to people because of their colour, culture, or ethnic origin. It can be seen or detected in processes, attitudes and behaviour that amount to discrimination through unwitting prejudice, ignorance, thoughtlessness and racist stereotyping, and which disadvantage minority ethnic people." Thus there does not have to be deliberate or conscious racism by individuals for institutional racism to take place; it can result simply from inadequate consideration of what is needed for all groups to be treated equally.

In 2009 the Runnymede Trust (Rollock, 2009) reviewed the evidence about whether policing for and of minority ethnic groups had improved since the Macpherson Report. It found that there had been extensive attempts to improve policing, with training to raise awareness of issues relating to 'race', and attempts to recruit more members of minority ethnic groups into the police. However, the report found that despite progress, it was still the case that only 4 per cent of police officers were from minority ethnic backgrounds and there was still evidence of a White-dominated police culture. Police culture has sometimes been seen as the reason for more overt racism in the police. Indeed, the idea of 'canteen culture' argues that police officers have developed distinctive working values and a strong collective identity as a result of the pressure, isolation and hostility they can face in their job. The 'core characteristics' of the culture, according to Reiner (1992), include cynicism, conservatism, suspicion, isolation from the public, macho values and racism. It is undoubtedly much more difficult for police officers now to demonstrate overt racism without being disciplined or dismissed, but hidden or unconscious racism may be more common. BBC documentaries called *The Secret Policeman*, in 2003 and 2008, gave evidence of this (cited in Parmar 2013). Racism in its various forms has sometimes been seen as reflected in statistics on stop and search.

Stop and search

As Table 1.6.1 shows, Black people are nearly five times more likely than White people to be stopped and searched, and those of Asian origin are also more frequently stopped and searched than the population as a whole. Phillips and Bowling (2012) quote evidence that

Black and Asian people are also more likely than White people to be stopped and searched repeatedly and to have more intrusive searches. When serious violence or terrorism is a concern, police can stop and search without reasonable suspicion of a crime, and minority ethnic groups are particularly prone to searches in these circumstances. Phillips and Bowling argue that while there may now be less open targeting of minority ethnic groups by the police than in the past, "stereotypes and prejudices" may still play a role. However, they accept that part of the reason for the disproportionate use of these laws against minority ethnic groups is demographic factors. For example, members of ethnic-minority communities are more likely to be young, unemployed, to live in inner-city areas and to spend leisure time in public places. This probably accounts for some but not all of the statistical differences between ethnic groups. Phillips and Bowling conclude: "disproportionate use of stop and search is clearly a problem: it seems inherently unfair, contributes to the criminalisation of minority ethnic communities, and undermines public support for the police," (2012).

A random stop and search at Notting Hill Carnival

Arrests

Ministry of Justice figures (see Table 1.6.1) show that Black people make up a much higher proportion of arrests (8.3 per cent) than of the population as a whole (3.3 per cent). Phillips and Bowling (2007) quote evidence suggesting that after arrest minority ethnic groups are considerably more likely than the White majority to remain silent, to seek legal advice and to deny the offence. This may suggest that these groups are more suspicious of the police and/or that they are more likely to be arrested for offences they have not committed. People from minority ethnic groups are also less likely than White people to be released after a caution.

Sentencing and imprisonment

Ministry of Justice figures from 2010 show that Whites are slightly more likely than Black and Asian defendants to be convicted of indictable (serious) offences once they have been sent for trial. However, Blacks and Asians are more likely to be given an immediate custodial sentence (that is, sent to prison or a similar institution).

A number of factors can affect whether those convicted are sent to prison, particularly the seriousness of the offence. For this reason the Ministry of Justice (2011) looked at sentencing for specific types of offence. They found that Blacks were slightly more likely than Whites to be sent to prison for the offences of 'actual bodily harm' and considerably more likely than Whites to be sent to prison for possession of class A drugs. Black people were given longer sentences than Whites for burglary, but were slightly less likely to be sent to prison. There is therefore a rather mixed picture in terms of evidence for or against racism in sentencing, but Black minority ethnic groups are certainly overrepresented in prison. In 2012, 11 per cent of the prison population were from Black ethnic groups compared to 3.3 per cent in the population as a whole (Ministry of Justice, 2013). Six per cent of the prison population were from Asian groups, roughly in line with their proportion in the whole population.

Conclusions

Given that self-report studies do not suggest that Black ethnic groups are more likely to offend, the prison statistics do suggest that direct or indirect racism is present in some part or parts of the criminal justice system. Phillips and Bowling (2012) believe that racism plays a part in the British criminal justice system, but they also argue that class factors interact with ethnicity in the experience of different groups. Some sociologists, such as Mayhew *et al.* (1993) emphasise far more than Phillips and Bowling that factors such as age and class differences might explain differences in recorded offending rates between different ethnic groups.

Evaluate whether racism is the main cause of the overrepresentation of some minority ethnic groups in crime statistics.

THEORISING RACE AND CRIMINALITY

A number of sociologists have developed theoretically based approaches to understanding the patterns of offending in different ethnic groups. The first approach to

be discussed – left realism – accepts that there are some real differences in offending between minority ethnic groups and others, though a number of other theoretical approaches reject this view.

Lea and Young: the left realist approach

Lea and Young (1984), leading writers in the left realist tradition, accept that there are racist practices among the police (see Chapter 4 for a discussion of left realism). However, they argue that, despite this, the statistics do bear out a higher crime rate for street robberies and associated 'personal' crimes by Black youths. They explain this by suggesting that British society is racist and minority ethnic groups are disadvantaged in comparison with other groups in society. This is particularly true of young Black males who have much higher than average levels of unemployment. In comparison with their peers from other ethnic groups they tend to be less successful in the labour market, so they suffer from relative deprivation (see Chapter 4). Young ethnic-minority males are also economically and socially marginalised, with little representation, particularly at senior levels, in political parties, trade unions and other organisations with power and influence. This sometimes leads to the formation of subcultures that may react to this situation by turning to crime and/or protest (for example, through rioting).

Lea and Young argue that it would be very surprising if there were not higher levels of crime in groups that are relatively deprived and marginalised. Furthermore, they claim that the statistics on certain types of crime (particularly street robbery) show such a difference in offending rates between ethnic groups that it is unlikely that they could be produced entirely by racist practices. In addition, recorded rates of crime for some minority ethnic groups (for example, British Asians) are relatively low, even though they too could be subject to racism. Recorded rates are also low for Black ethnic groups for some crimes. So, to Lea and Young the patterns of recorded crime do not fit the theory that they are based entirely on police racism and it is likely there are some real and significant differences in crime rates between ethnic groups.

Paul Gilroy: an anti-racist perspective

A second approach draws strongly on critical criminology in developing a radical anti-racist position. Unlike Marxists, who concentrate on class-related inequality and injustice, anti-racists focus much more on the role of racism and ethnic inequality in creating injustice. This approach rejects the approach put forward by Lea and Young. It believes that left realists are wrong to argue that crime rates are higher for minority ethnic groups. Paul Gilroy (1983) describes a 'myth of black criminality'. He attributes statistical differences in recorded criminality between ethnic groups to police stereotyping and racist labelling. Furthermore, he does not see what crime there is among Black British ethnic groups as resulting from relative deprivation, so that people turn to crime to achieve economic success. Instead he sees it as a legacy of the struggle against White dominance in former colonies such as Jamaica. When early migrants came from the Caribbean to Britain they faced discrimination and hostility, and drew upon the tradition of anticolonial struggle to develop cultures of resistance against White-dominated authorities and police forces. Although Lea and Young accept that some criminal acts, such as rioting, could involve protest against marginalisation, Paul Gilroy goes much further, seeing most crime by Black ethnic groups as essentially political and as part of the general resistance to White rule.

Evaluation

Paul Gilroy has been criticised by Lea and Young, who have been particularly scathing, pointing out that the majority of crimes committed by Black people are actually 'intraracial', that is 'Black on Black'. It is hard to see how this can reflect a political struggle against the White majority. Second, they accuse writers such as Gilroy of 'romanticising' crime and criminals, and thereby ignoring the very real harm that crime does to its victims. Certainly Gilroy takes a rather one-sided view of Black criminality and makes little use of empirical evidence. Furthermore, he (like Lea and Young) was writing some time ago and the arguments may have little relevance to today, especially as few migrants today have any experience of taking part in anticolonial struggles.

That is not to say though that Black minority groups may not be politically aware and intent upon resisting racism.

In the case of Lea and Young, their arguments could lack relevance: changes in crime statistics and improved evidence (particularly from self-report studies) suggest that Blacks are not, overall, more criminal than Whites.

Neo-Marxism – capitalism in crisis

A study by Hall et al. (1978) illustrates a particular kind of neo-Marxist approach. This approach takes elements from labelling theories, such as the idea of moral panic, and from Marxism, with its emphasis on the role of the economy in shaping society. It is also influenced by the ideas of The New Criminology (see Chapter 3).

Stuart Hall et al. studied the panic over 'mugging' or street robbery in the 1970s. This was a period of crisis for British capitalism, and Marx emphasised that capitalism would go through periodic crises. The country

was undergoing industrial unrest with widespread strikes. There was a recession in the economy, rising unemployment and political unrest and intense violence in Northern Ireland. When capitalism is in crisis the normal methods of controlling the population may be inadequate: it is sometimes necessary to use force. However, this needed justifying and to do this the media and politicians, basing their arguments on police briefings, highlighted an apparent increase in mugging, particularly by young Black men in London.

According to Hall, the focus on a group who were already viewed negatively served to draw attention away from the crisis and focus blame on a scapegoat – young African Caribbean males. This moral panic (see Topic 4, Chapter 4) then justified increased numbers of police on the streets, acting in a more repressive manner.

According to Hall et al., the problem of mugging was largely manufactured by the police and the media. The crime was nor new and was not increasing any faster than other crimes. The apparent increase in the crime was largely the result of the efforts of a single police officer in the British Transport Police, who was prone, with his colleagues, to arresting groups of young Black men for alleged muggings. Despite the lack of evidence, and even of victims in many cases, the officer was successful in securing many convictions, producing an entirely manufactured crime wave that was then seized on by the media and politicians for their own purposes.

Hall et al. link their case study to the idea of hegemony (political dominance), which means that powerful ruling groups in society were able to justify their position and use force against threats to their dominance by scapegoating young Black men as being the source of political instability. This drew attention away from the failures of the capitalist system and thereby helped to sustain the system itself.

Evaluation

This study is wide-ranging, imaginative and based upon detailed evidence. However, the analysis of Hall et al. has been criticised for not making any actual effort to research the motivations and thinking of young African Caribbean males. Furthermore, the association between criminality and Black youth, made by the police and the media, has continued since the 1970s 'crisis of capitalism', so it may not be necessary to have such a crisis to scapegoat minority ethnic groups. Nevertheless, it was noticeable that, in the wake of the banking crisis and credit crunch of the late 1990s, there was media concern about crime among new groups of immigrants (for example, asylum seekers and immigrants from eastern Europe). The work of Hall *et al.* also has the merit of looking at the big picture and placing ethnicity and crime in the context of social change in a particular place at a particular time. It therefore avoids over-generalising about crime and ethnicity.

Evaluate whether any of the three approaches discussed above offers adequate theories of ethnicity and crime. Are there any important factors that are ignored by all of them?

CULTURAL FACTORS, ETHNICITY AND CRIME

Much of the debate on Black criminality described in this chapter concentrated on whether officially recorded rates of crime were the result of criminalisation by racist police or of higher crime rates resulting from deprivation. Little attention was paid to differences in recorded offending between Black British and British Asian groups. Alpa Parmar points out that at least some Asian groups (particularly those of Bangladeshi and Pakistani origin) have, like Black British ethnic groups, experienced relatively high levels of deprivation but, despite a rise in recorded offending, they are still less likely to be convicted of offences. Furthermore, self-report studies also indicate lower rates of offending among disadvantaged Asian ethnic groups when compared with Black ethnic groups. Parmar notes that this has led a number of researchers to suggest that cultural differences, and particularly differences in family life, may be responsible for the apparent differences in criminality. For example, Webster (2007, cited in Parmar 2013) suggested that high rates of single parenthood in Black ethnic groups meant that boys from these groups were more likely to offend because their behaviour was not 'governed' by fathers and they lacked male role models.

Webster suggested that Asian ethnic groups generally have more stable family structures and larger families, which might "increase the monitoring, social control and household responsibilities thereby acting as a protective factor against offending" (Parmar, 2013).

Parmar is cautious about accepting this argument and raises a number of objections. First, it is dangerous to generalise about family structure in particular ethnic groups. There is great variation within ethnic groups. For example, most Black families are not headed by lone parents and single parenthood is rising in British Asian families. Second, differences in recorded offending are likely to be linked to a variety of social and economic inequalities, including educational achievement (and Black males have relatively low levels of achievement). Third, racism and stereotyping in the criminal justice system are likely to play a major part in differences in recorded offending rates between minority groups. Nevertheless Parmar does suggest that cultural factors may play a part in explaining the differences, alongside other factors.

Other researchers, such as John Pitts (2008), who has carried out extensive research into ethnicity and gang crime in London, argues that both material and cultural factors play a part in explaining ethnic-minority crime. His multi-dimensional approach suggests that both Black and Asian gang culture in the UK develops as a response to poverty, deprivation, unemployment and substandard educational opportunities, particularly on poor council estates. However, global culture also plays a part, particularly in minority ethnic groups with role models offered by American rap groups and Jamaican yardie-gangs.

CONCLUSIONS

The relationship between ethnicity and crime in Britain needs to be understood within the context of difference, inequality and racism, which shapes the experiences of both Whites and minority ethnic groups as victims, offenders and suspects. This relationship changes as the economic situation of particular ethnic groups, ethnic and racial stereotypes and cultures change so the relationships between these different elements are never static. It is clear that ethnicity is a significant factor shaping crime and criminal justice in Britain, but ethnicity also interacts with gender and social class.

CHECK YOUR UNDERSTANDING

1. What is meant by 'criminalisation'?

2. Explain what is meant by 'institutional racism'?

3. Explain the meaning of 'anticolonial struggle'.

4. Identify three ways in which it has been suggested there may be racism in the criminal justice system.

5. Which theory of ethnicity and crime suggests that there are real differences in the offending rates of different ethnic groups?

6. Briefly explain how cultural differences could possibly account for differences in offending rates between minority ethnic groups.

7. Outline the ways in which Hall *et al.* explain the 'moral panic' over mugging.

8. Outline two criticisms of Gilroy's idea that Black criminality is a 'myth'.

9. Analyse two differences between the ideas of Lea and Young and those of Hall *et al.*

10. Evaluate the evidence for racism in the criminal justice system.

TAKE IT FURTHER

Watch the 2008 BBC *Panorama* documentary 'The Secret Policeman Returns'. What evidence is there of racism in this documentary? Discuss how far this could explain the patterns of crime shown in the official statistics.

1.7 GENDER AND CRIME

LEARNING OUTCOMES

> Demonstrate knowledge and understanding of patterns of crime, victimisation and criminalisation by gender in the UK and of theories of gender bias in criminal justice and theories of female criminality and masculinity and crime (AO1).

> Apply your understanding to contemporary issues about gender and crime (AO2).

> Analyse the extent to which male and female patterns of crime really are different (AO3).

> Evaluate theories of gender bias in criminal justice and theories of female criminality and masculinity and crime (AO3).

INTRODUCING THE DEBATE

Perhaps the most predictable and distinctive characteristic of statistics on crime is the disproportionately large number of offences committed by men and the small number committed by women. For as long as records have been kept, and in nearly all countries in the world today, men appear to be much more likely than women to commit crime. But is this a real difference or is it the product of distorted official statistics? Is it more to do with different and biased treatment by the criminal justice system than with what men and women actually do? And, if men really are much more criminal than women, why is this? We consider whether there something in the different construction of femininity and masculinity that can help explain these differences. Furthermore, we ask whether the patterns are changing and, perhaps as a result of changes in male and female roles, women's criminality is increasing towards the level of crime among men.

GENDER DIFFERENCES IN OFFENDING RATES

Table 1.7.1 (opposite) shows that at all stages in criminal justice women are significantly less likely than men to be in trouble with the law. Men are three times more likely than women to be taken to court and to be convicted of offences and more than five times as likely to be arrested. Men are more than 11 times more likely than women to be sent to prison and 19 times more likely to be in prison. There have been fluctuations in the proportion of males and females that are convicted over time, but the statistics have stayed broadly similar. For example, Frances Heidensohn and Marisa Silvestri (2012) found that in 1867 women had been convicted of 23 per cent of crimes.

Government statistics (UK Government, 2013) suggest the proportion of crimes of different types committed by women vary considerably. In 2012 women were less likely than men to be convicted for crimes in every offence group, but the offences with the highest proportion of female offenders were fraud and forgery (29.4 per cent of offenders), and theft and handling stolen goods (24.2 per cent). Women also made up a relatively high proportion of those convicted of violence against the person (15.8 per cent), but very low proportions of those

Data	Female (%)	Male (%)
Population aged 10 and over	51	49
Arrests	15	85
Out of court disposals		
Penalty notices for disorder	23	77
Cautions	23	77
Court proceedings	25	75
Convictions	25	75
Sentenced to immediate custody	8	92
Prison population	5	95
Under supervision in the community	15	85

Table 1.7.1 *Offenders found guilty of, or cautioned for, indictable offences: by sex and type of offence, 2006*

Source: Ministry of Justice (2014)

convicted for burglary (5.2 per cent) and, particularly, sexual offences (1.4 per cent). Shoplifting is one offence where women's conviction rates are particularly high. Indeed, in 2012, 45 per cent of women convicted of indictable offences were found guilty of shoplifting.

Self-report studies

As discussed in earlier sections on this topic, official statistics on crime may be very unreliable, and the people convicted of offences may not be representative of all those committing offences. So have self-report studies supported the official statistics in showing females to be less criminal than males? Newburn (2013) cites a number of self-report studies that have found that males are indeed more likely than females to admit to offences, and are more likely to have committed several offences rather than just one. A study by Stephen Roe and Jane Ashe (2008) for the Home Office on self-reported offending among 10–25-year-olds in England and Wales found that 17 per cent of females and 26 per cent of males admitted that they had committed one of the core offences in the previous 12 months; 12 per cent of males but 8 per cent of females admitted a serious offence and males were also more likely to be frequent offenders (8 per cent as opposed to 3 per cent of females). Data from self-report studies therefore support the picture from official statistics that males are more criminal than women. However, self-report studies also seem to suggest that

the difference in male and female offending rates may not be as recorded in conviction statistics, which imply that men are several times more likely than women to offend. This raises questions about *why* men may be more likely to offend but also about whether males and females are *treated equally* in the criminal justice system.

GENDER AND VICTIMISATION

Women are slightly less likely than men to be victims of personal crime. Figures from the Crime Survey for England and Wales (Ministry of Justice 2014) showed that in 2013, 5 per cent of men but 4.7 per cent of women were victims of personal crime. The gap between men and women was greater in terms of violence, with 2.3 per cent of men but 1.4 per cent of women reporting being the victim of violence. However, women were more likely than men to be the victim of domestic violence (men were particularly likely to be the victims of violence from strangers). Women only account for about 30 per cent of victims of homicide but, on the other hand, women were about twice as likely as men to report being victims of any form of domestic abuse since the age of 16, and about seven times more likely than men to being the victims of sexual abuse, and these are two of the most underreported crimes. Questions have been raised about the fairness of the criminal justice system, not only to female suspects and offenders but also to female victims. Some feminists feel that patriarchal attitudes and structures prevent women from having the same chance as men of receiving justice from the system (see Bias against women, page 58).

Criminologists have sometimes been accused of ignoring women in studying crime. Is there any evidence of this from what you have studied in this topic so far? Can you suggest why this might have happened, if it is true?

GENDER BIAS IN CRIMINAL JUSTICE AND THE CHIVALRY THESIS

Hidden female offenders

One possible explanation for the underrepresentation of women in crime statistics is that women get away with much more unrecorded and undetected crime than men do. This idea was first suggested by Otto Pollak (1950), who claimed that official statistics grossly underestimated female offending because women were naturally more skilled than men at deceiving people. This, he argued, derived from women's ability to hide menstruation because of traditional taboos. Pollack claimed that women often escaped detection for offences such as shoplifting, prostitution and even poisoning relatives and sexually abusing their children.

Unsurprisingly this theory has been attacked as being completely unsupported by evidence by Stephen Jones (2009) and others. Heidensohn (1985) claims that it is nothing more than male bias based on a stereotypical view of women.

The chivalry thesis

A more credible theory does not argue that women are naturally more secretive, but does claim that they are treated more leniently by the criminal justice system. This is sometimes known as the **chivalry thesis.**

UNDERSTAND THE CONCEPT

The **chivalry thesis** suggests that officials in the criminal justice system (from police to judges), who are predominantly men, are more inclined to let women suspects off, or to punish them less severely, than men. The idea of 'chivalry' suggests that men are socialised to be softer and protective towards females while being harder on males.

As noted above, self-report studies do seem to suggest that official statistics may underrepresent female offending while confirming that, overall, females are significantly less criminal than men. In the study by Roe and Ashe, 5 per cent of males and 3 per cent of females were classed as frequent and serious offenders: the group most likely to be convicted of crimes. Yet official statistics suggest that men are four times more likely than women to commit crimes. So it is quite possible that females are more likely to get away with offending than men are.

At several stages in the criminal justice systems is some evidence to support the chivalry thesis. For example, according to a review of research conducted by Haralambos and Holborn (2013):

> women are more likely than men to be given cautions instead of being prosecuted

> women are slightly more likely than men to be given a pre-court sanction (such as a penalty notice) rather than being taken to court

> women are less likely than men to be sent to prison when convicted (in 2009, 14.3 per cent of women but 26.5 per cent of men were given immediate custodial sentences).

In 2009 men were also given longer sentences, on average, than women in every offence group apart from criminal damage. For example, men were given an average sentence of 34 months for robbery whereas women only got 25 months.

However, raw figures like this may not tell the whole story because differences in sentencing are likely to be affected by a number of factors, including the seriousness of the offence. The only study that has fully controlled for these types of factors was carried out by Roger Hood in the West Midlands (Hood, 1992). He still found that women were about a third less likely than men to be given custodial sentences, even when the seriousness of the offence was taken into account.

Evidence against the chivalry thesis

Despite the above evidence, on balance most criminologists are against the chivalry thesis. Some research that tried to take more account of particular circumstances has contradicted the conclusions of Hood and the chivalry thesis. For example, research by Kate Steward (2006) looked at magistrates' decisions on whether to remand men or women in custody. She found the Home Office's own research suggests that whether people are given bail or remanded in custody can almost entirely be explained in terms of the seriousness of the offence. Furthermore, many women are held on remand, despite having committed relatively minor offences such as theft and handling stolen goods.

Home Office research in 2004 (cited in Heidensohn and Silvestri) suggested that courts are actually imposing more severe sentences on women than men for less serious offences. Carol Hedderman (2010) notes that rates of imprisonment for women have been rising in the early years of the 21st century.

Bias against women

Feminists in particular have argued that, far from being chivalrous, the criminal justice system is often biased against women. Sandra Walklate (2004), for example, argues that in rape trials women's complaints are often not taken seriously and a large majority of alleged rapists are found not guilty or never prosecuted. She believes that, in effect, it is the female victim rather than the male suspect who ends up on trial because they are often questioned about their sexual history. Feminists have also long argued that the police do not take domestic violence against women sufficiently seriously. Walklate acknowledges that there have been attempts to improve this situation with changes in both police and court proceedings, which take more account of the interests of victims, but she believes that there are still problems in getting the authorities to treat this as a serious crime in which police should get involved. Louise Westmarland (2010) discusses evidence that suggests that women who are trafficked from one country to another to become sex workers are often treated with hostility by the authorities. If they are discovered, they are often deported back to their countries of origin while traffickers frequently escape unscathed.

Double standards in the criminal justice system

From the above evidence, it appears therefore that the criminal justice system may not be consistently biased, either in favour of men or in favour of women. Instead, the criminal justice system can be seen as **gendered.**

UNDERSTAND THE CONCEPT

If an area of social life is **gendered**, then it is experienced differently by males and females – it differentiates between males and females and gives them different advantages/disadvantages. For example, work is gendered if the expectations of male and female workers are different, or if different jobs are thought suitable for males and females. To say something is gendered does not necessarily imply that one gender is always advantaged at the expense of the other; but it does imply that there is systematic inequality and difference.

Heidensohn (1985) tries to make sense of this by suggesting that there are double standards in the criminal justice system. In particular, women are treated particularly badly when they deviate from the norms of behaviour associated with femininity, for example, by being sexually promiscuous. They are seen as 'double deviants', not just breaking the general noms of society, but also breaking norms suggesting how it is appropriate for women to behave. Double deviance leads to more severe treatment. Sexually promiscuous girls are more likely than promiscuous boys to be taken into care, for example. Yet courts are reluctant to send mothers with young children to prison. Women tend to be divided into virgins or whores, witches or wives and, depending on how they are seen, treated differently.

Some researchers have supported this theory. For example, Kate Steward also found that gender played a part in decisions about on whether to remand women into custody and the final decision was often based upon gender-linked moral judgements about the worth of the individual.

It therefore seems that the British criminal justice system *is* gendered, despite its claims to be based purely upon the principle of equality before the law. However, Carol Hedderman (2015) argues that the differences in sentencing for men and women should not necessarily be seen as bias. Men and women can be affected differently by being sent to prison and offenders have different circumstances. For example, the impact of a prison sentence on a woman with childcare responsibilities can be greater than those on a man without such responsibilities, and there are community-based options that can be effective alternatives to prison for women.

EXPLAINING FEMALE CONFORMITY AND CRIMINALITY

A number of theories have been put forward to explain why a minority of women commit crimes and/or why women appear to be more likely to conform than men.

Biological explanations

This approach has been used by different writers to explain why the vast majority of women do not offend and, conversely, why a small minority do. It starts from the belief that women are innately different from men, with a natural desire to be caring and nurturing – neither of them being values that support crime. 'Normal' women are therefore less likely to commit crime. On the other hand, some women writers, such as Dalton (1964), have claimed that hormonal or menstrual factors can influence a minority of women to commit crime in certain circumstances. However, this fails to explain differences in crime rates for women in different countries or over time. Furthermore, as Tim Newburn (2013) points out, women commit every type of crime so there can be nothing in women's nature that excludes them from becoming criminal. There has not been any convincing research linking criminality to women's hormonal cycles, although attempts have been made to use it as a defence in criminal cases.

Sex-role theory

Sex-role theory argues that women are less likely than men to commit crime because there are core elements of the female role that limit their ability and opportunity to do so. This is often explained in terms of socialisation.

According to this approach, girls are socialised differently from boys. The values that girls are brought up to hold are those that simply do not lead to crime. From a functionalist point of view, Talcott Parsons (1937) argues, for instance, that as most child-rearing is carried out by mothers, girls have a clear role model to follow that emphasises caring and support. Albert Cohen (1955) argued that delinquency was mainly carried out by males because women have the main role in socialisation. Boys therefore may lack a male role model within the household (even in two-parent households) to steer them away from crime and give them a caring, domestic role to aspire to. Instead, boys look to the male gang or subculture, which leads them into crime.

However, some theorists argue that it is the failure of effective socialisation that leads a small proportion of women into crime. Evidence to support this differential socialisation theory was provided by Farrington and Painter (2004) in their longitudinal study of female offenders. They uncovered different patterns of socialisation between offenders and non-offenders. In particular, they found that female offenders were much more likely to have had harsh or erratic parenting, and to have had little support or praise from their parents for their achievements at school and in their community.

While sex roles may play some part in explaining female offending (or lack of offending), they do not seem to provide the whole picture. When asked, women give a wide variety of reasons for their criminality and many reasons are not linked directly to sex-role socialisation. For example, Newburn cites research (Caddle and Crisp 1997, cited in Newburn 2013) that suggests that a variety of reasons for offending were given by women. Caddle and Crisp interviewed over 1000 women in prison and the most common reason for offending, given by 55 per cent of women, was the simple, instrumental one of 'Having no money'; 33 per cent cited 'Having no job' as a reason and 35 per cent 'Drink or drugs'. However, some commonly given reasons did seem to link to sex roles. These included 'Need to support children (38 per cent) and 'Family problems' (33 per cent).

The changing role or 'liberationist' perspective

So far, we have characterised female sex roles as being more passive and less aggressive than those of males. However, a number of writers, including Adler (1975), have suggested that the increasing rates of female crime are linked to their freedom from the traditional forms of social control, discussed earlier, and their acceptance into more 'masculine' roles. More recently, Denscombe (2001) has argued that, because of changing female roles,

increasingly, females are as likely as males to engage in risk-taking behaviour. In his research into self-images of 15–16-year-olds in the East Midlands, in which he undertook in-depth interviews as well as focus groups, he found that females were rapidly adopting what had traditionally been male attitudes. This included such things as 'looking hard', 'being in control' and being able to cope with risk-taking. This provides theoretical support for the fact that female crime levels are rising much more quickly than male ones, not just in terms of numbers but also in terms of seriousness of crimes committed.

Westwood (1999) develops similar ideas when she argues that identities are constantly being reconstructed and reframed. The concept of a fixed female identity has limited our understanding of crime, so we need to understand how women are reconfiguring their identity in a more confident, forceful way, and the possible link to the growth of female crime.

However, Heidensohn (2002) disputes this argument, citing evidence from a number of other studies showing that convicted offenders tend to score highly on psychological tests of 'femininity', indicating, according to her, that they have not taken on male roles. Heidensohn also argues that the women most likely to be involved in crime tend to be poor and/or working-class and not middle-class women, who are more likely to have experienced the benefits of women's' liberation.

Heidensohn and Silvestri suggest that any increase in the numbers of women convicted of violent crime may not reflect real increases in offending but could be the result of increased criminalisation of women, due to the media sensationalising female violence. Heidensohn and Silvestri point out that, in any case, the ratio of male to female offenders has not changed very much in terms of recorded crime over the long term and men still account for the vast majority of recorded offenders.

Does evidence from other areas of social life seem to indicate that liberation has taken place and women now take on very similar roles to men?

FEMINIST PERSPECTIVES ON WOMEN AND CRIME

Some feminists have put forward rather different theories explaining female criminality, or lack of it. Although they might accept some aspects of sex-role theory, they see differences in the roles of men and women in the wider context of power differences in society, and not just in terms of gender roles. Radical feminists tend to see society as male dominated or patriarchal and some socialist feminists also discuss the overlapping role of social class in influencing gender differences in offending.

Heidensohn: radical feminism and social control

According to Heidensohn (1985) females are less likely to commit crime because they are subjected to closer levels of social control than men are. Heidensohn points to the wide range of informal sanctions to discourage women from straying from 'proper' behaviour, including gossip, ill repute and the comments of males.

There are three settings in which there is greater social control exercised over women than men in a patriarchal society.

1. *Control at home* – Women are partly controlled through lack of time because of their primary responsibility for childcare and housework. This keeps them in the home for more hours than men, thus restricting their opportunity to commit crimes outside the home. Women may also be controlled through domestic violence from men or through the financial dominance of male partners, who continue to earn, on average, more than women. Girls also tend to be subject to greater control than boys. For example, as teenagers boys are often allowed to go out more and/or stay out later than girls are.

2. *Control in public* – Women may choose not to go into public places because they fear being ridiculed, raped or attacked, particularly after dark. Heidensohn feels that sexist comments and the risk of being labelled as a 'slag' or something similar limit the freedom of women, for example, by discouraging them from going out alone at night or going into pubs or clubs on their own.

3. *Control at work* – Most managers at work are males and they are therefore in a position to exercise control over females. Trade unions are also largely dominated by men, and various forms of sexual harassment might stop female employees from asserting themselves in the workplace.

Hiedensohn's theory is supported by Hagan (1987), who studied child-raising patterns in Canada and argued that there was significantly greater informal control of daughters' activities in families compared to those of

sons. Similarly, Sunita Toor (2009) has explained the exceptionally low rates of recorded crime among British Asian girls in terms of social control. Toor argues that this can be explained through the strong emphasis upon on the idea of honour (or *izzat*) and shame (*sharam*) in many Asian families. The fear of being ostracised by communities is stronger among Asian girls than boys, according to Toor, and this helps to explain why they largely keep out of trouble with the law.

Nevertheless, Hiedensohn's work is somewhat dated and the social control of women and girls may not be as great as it was in the past. Some liberal feminists argue that significant strides have been made for women in achieving greater freedom from social control; if they are correct, it is difficult to explain why female crime rates remain so low.

Pat Carlen: socialist feminism, women, crime and poverty

Another feminist sociologist who adopts a version of control theory is Pat Carlen (1988), who carried out a study of 39 women, aged between 15 and 46, who had been convicted of a variety of offences. Her research employed in-depth unstructured interviews. She found that the women were overwhelmingly from working-class backgrounds and, unlike many middle-class women, had not enjoyed the benefits of women's liberation. Carlen therefore argued that class and gender interacted in explaining the offending of these women.

Citing control theory, she argues that these women tend to become offenders because they had little reason to conform. They have enjoyed little success in society and they have little to lose by turning to crime. Their criminality was encouraged by a combination of drug addiction (including alcohol), a search for excitement, being raised in care and, above all, the experience of poverty.

According to Carlen many women conform because of what she calls the 'class and gender deals'.

The class deal involves sacrificing personal freedom and working hard in order to earn enough to gain access to consumer goods and enjoyable leisure. But the women in the study had few qualifications and no experience of holding down a reasonably well-paid job. Living in poverty and being unemployed, the women had no incentive to conform in order to keep their jobs and retain their lifestyles.

The gender deal involves accepting marriage, or at least a long-term relationship with a man, for the promise of security, happiness and fulfilment through family life.

Carlen regards this promise as a form of patriarchal ideology; in reality, family life often involves being subject to control (and sometimes abuse) from fathers, brothers, husbands and male partners. The women in the study had little experience of a happy family life, many had been brought up in care; others had been physically or sexually abused by their fathers or male partners. Lacking the experience of the benefits of the gender deal, once again the women had little to lose by rejecting it.

Although Carlen's study was based upon a small sample, there is lots of evidence that most female offenders do come from relatively deprived and insecure backgrounds and have often been brought up in care. For example, the Corston Report (2007) found that 40 per cent of women in prison in the UK have been out of work for five years or more and 61 per cent had no qualifications. Similarly, a study of 25 girls in female gangs by Tara Young (2009) found that all of the girls involved lived in areas of high deprivation and the overwhelming majority had a highly insecure home life.

However, the sort of factors identified by Carlen may well be important in explaining female crime, but they are not unique to women and apply to many male offenders too.

How well can Carlen's theory explain all female offending? What types of crime and what types of criminal does it not seem to apply to?

EXPLAINING MALE CRIME: MALE ROLES AND MASCULINITY

While some criminologists have tried to explain the low offending rate of women, others have tried to explain the high offending rates of men in terms of the concepts of masculinity (or masculinities).

Messerschmidt and normative masculinity

The analysis of masculinity has been strongly influenced by the work of the Australian sociologist, R. Connell (1995). He argued that there were a number of different forms of masculinity, which change over time – although all of them relate to or react against the link between masculinity and control. Although crime was not central to his analysis, the idea of multiple, constructed masculinities was taken up by Messerschmidt (1993).

Messerschmidt argues that a 'normative masculinity' exists in society, and it is highly valued by most men. Normative masculinity relates to the socially approved idea of what a 'real male' is. According to Messerschmidt, it "defines masculinity through difference from and desire for women". Normative masculinity is so prized that men struggle to live up to its expectations. Messerschmidt suggests then that masculinity is not something natural, but rather a state that males only achieve as 'an accomplishment', which involves being constantly worked at.

However, the construction of this masculinity takes place in different contexts and through different methods, depending upon the particular male's access to power and resources. So, more powerful males will accomplish their masculinity in different ways and contexts from less powerful males.

Messerschmidt gives examples of businessmen who can express their power over women through their control in the workplace, while those with no power at work may express their masculinity by using violence in the home or street. However, whichever way is used, both types of men are achieving their normative masculinity and this can result in crime. For example, the businessman might turn to white-collar crime, while less powerful males might turn to domestic violence to control their female partner. Men with low status tend to have more need to use crime to assert their power and express their masculinity.

So it is achieving masculinity that leads some men to commit crime – and, in particular, crime is committed by those less powerful in an attempt to be successful at masculinity (which involves material, social and sexual success). From this point of view, the competitive nature of masculinity and the need for control are central in explaining why men should commit more crimes than women.

Messerschmidt has been criticised by Tony Jefferson (1997) for failing to explain why particular men commit crimes rather than others. If all men have the potential of turning to crime to gain power and control, why is it that not all men, particularly not all less successful men, turn to crime?

FOCUS ON SKILLS: GENDER AND WHITE-COLLAR CRIME

Joyti De-Laurey, a secretary who stole several millions from her employer, the investment bank Goldman Sachs

Janice Goldstraw-White (2012) conducted research comparing male and female white-collar criminals, an area that has been neglected in terms of female offenders. She carried out semi-structured interviews with 32 men and 9 women who were in prison having been convicted of this type of offence. They had all defrauded their employers.

She found some differences between male and female offenders.

› Men tended to be better qualified than the women (34 per cent of men but 22 per cent of women had tertiary qualifications).

› Men were more likely to have offended in cooperation with others, while more women offended alone.

› The average sum involved in the male frauds was £111,250 whereas in the frauds committed by women it was £75,167.

› The average prison sentence given to the men was 40 months while for the women it was 23 months.

› Both men and women were equally likely to attribute their crime to family pressures but men were more likely to offend to 'preserve and maintain a lifestyle', whereas women were more likely to say the reason was to protect their family from problems linked to financial instability. Some of the women could be seen as 'obsessive protectors'.

› Both men and women were likely to give individualistic explanations for their offending (for example, being greedy) but it was only among the men that some people said they had offended to fund addictions (such as gambling or drug use).

When discussing the effects of prison, both men and women missed their families and friends and were disturbed by their loss of freedom, but only men expressed worry about their loss of status after they were released. In general, women were more likely than men to regret their crimes, although two women said they had no choice under the circumstances.

Janice Goldstraw-White concludes that: "What research has shown is that when men and women are placed in similar occupational positions, more women do indeed commit similar frauds to those committed by men – and not always for dissimilar reasons" (Goldstraw-White, 2013). However, she acknowledges that the "complexity of women's position in society" produces a broader range of motives and a greater tendency to be remorseful about their crimes.

Source: Goldstraw-White (2012)

Questions

1. **Identify** and **outline** the main differences between male and female white-collar fraudsters in prison.

2. **Understand**. What do you think Goldstraw-White had in mind when discussing the 'complexity of women's roles in society'?

3. **Analyse**. Identify any evidence here that could be used to support or contradict the following theories:

   A Sex-role theory

   B Female liberation theory

   C Carlen's theory linking poverty to crime

   D Theories of masculinity

4. **Evaluate** the usefulness of this study in understanding the relationship between gender and white-collar crime.

Simon Winlow: social change masculinity and crime

Simon Winlow (2001), in a study of bouncers (doormen) in Sunderland, takes up the issue of masculinity and argues that it remains very important for explaining crime, even though the nature of masculinity has changed in post-industrial societies where heavy industry has declined. In the past, working-class men were able to gain status and respectability through work in traditional industries such as shipbuilding. Therefore there was little in the way of organised crime but men did engage in petty crime and sometimes used violence to assert their status.

By the late 1990s there were few full-time manual jobs available in Sunderland and, in the absence of other sources of status, the use of violence became an increasingly important way of gaining status in male hierarchies. Crime also became an increasingly important way of achieving material success in getting the trappings associated with high status, such as fashionable clothes and cars. In this context, organised crime such as drug dealing became an increasingly important way to achieve success in terms of masculinity. Being a doorman bouncer became an increasingly attractive proposition for those seeking masculine status. It provided opportunities to assert physical prowess, through the use of force in controlling customers, and also afforded opportunities to engage in profitable criminal activities such as drug dealings and protection rackets.

Winlow's research provides an interesting case study of the relationship between masculinity, crime and social change, but it is difficult to know how typical these findings are of crime in other areas of the country.

Masculinity and the thrill of crime

In common with Messerschmidt's ideas, Winlow emphasises the instrumental aims of male criminals: they commit crime in order to achieve success. Other writers, particularly Jack Katz (1988), believe that studies of masculinity rightly emphasise the importance of status, success and control over others for men, but they underestimate the importance of the sheer pleasure and excitement that can be gained from criminal activity. Different crimes provide different thrills, that can vary from the 'sneaky thrills' of shoplifting, to the 'righteous slaughter' of murder. Katz gives the example of robbery, which is largely undertaken, he claims, for the chaos, thrill and potential danger inherent in the act. This idea of the thrill of crime has been used to explain the apparent irrational violence of football 'hooligans', and also the use of drugs and alcohol.

Do you think differences in male and female offending are more to do with social control and opportunity or differences between the way masculinity and femininity are socially constructed?

CHECK YOUR UNDERSTANDING

1. What is meant by 'the chivalry thesis'?

2. Explain what is meant by 'the gender deal'.

3. Explain the meaning of 'normative masculinity'.

4. Identify three ways in which it has been suggested there may be gender bias in the criminal justice system.

5. Which theory of gender and crime suggests that women are naturally better at hiding their criminality than men?

6. Briefly explain how sex-role theory could possibly account for differences in offending rates between minority males and females.

7. Outline the ways in which Heidensohn suggests females are subject to stronger social control than males.

8. Outline two criticisms of the female liberationist explanation for apparently rising rates of female crime.

9. Analyse two differences between the liberationist perspective on female crime and the ideas of Pat Carlen.

10. Evaluate the evidence for the view that there are 'double standards' in the criminal justice system in relation to gender.

TAKE IT FURTHER

Access the publication Statistics on Women and the Criminal Justice System 2013 (or a later edition) produced by the Ministry for Justice, which is available online.

1. Choose any chapter from 3 to 9, which cover: Victims, Police activity, Offender characteristics, Offence analysis, Offender management and practitioners.

2. Summarise the differences between attitudes towards males and females in the criminal justice system covered in that chapter and analyse whether it suggests there is gender bias in criminal justice.

1.8 SOCIAL CLASS AND CRIME

LEARNING OUTCOMES

❯ Demonstrate knowledge and understanding of the relationship between social class, crime and criminalisation (AO1).

❯ Apply your understanding to contemporary issues about social class and crime (AO2).

❯ Analyse competing explanations of the relationship between social class, crime and criminalisation (AO3).

❯ Evaluate competing explanations of the relationship between crime, class and criminalisation (AO3).

INTRODUCING THE DEBATE

Many early studies of crime took social class as being central to the explanation of criminality and assumed that the working class were much more criminal than the middle and higher classes. A number of theories have linked working-class crime with being poor, relatively deprived, or lacking in opportunities. The reasons for this could be directly related to material disadvantage or could be more closely connected to cultural factors that are, at least to some extent, independent of the material inequality. However, some sociologists have argued that the apparent differences in criminality have more to do with the process of criminalisation than with the behaviour of different social groups. From this point of view, being working-class simply makes you more likely to be labelled as a criminal rather than necessarily making you more likely to commit crimes. (The 2014 film *Riot Club*, pictured above, tells the tale of violent crime with very little negative outcome for those involved in a fictional dining club at Oxford University.) This viewpoint puts the focus on the criminal justice system rather than the offender and highlights the importance of power.

Of course, factors related to both criminality and to criminalisation might be important in understanding the relationship between class and crime. Furthermore the relationship might have more to do with the types of crime that different classes commit rather than the amount of crime.

STATISTICS ON SOCIAL CLASS AND CRIME

Deprivation, class and statistics

Statistical evidence is not routinely collected on the class background of offenders in the UK. However, a range of data sources suggest that most people convicted of indictable (serious) offences, especially those who are imprisoned, tend to be from lower social-class backgrounds. Sometimes this is indicated by characteristics that tend to be associated with lower-class backgrounds rather than being based on direct measures of class.

For example, Roger Houchin (2005) found that there was a strong relationship between living in the most deprived wards in Scotland and being in prison. The imprisonment rate in the 27 most deprived wards was around quadruple what it was in Scotland as a whole. In Glasgow no fewer than 60 per cent of prisoners came from the most deprived council estates.

A study of 2,171 adult prisoners imprisoned in England and Wales in 2006 and 2007 (Omolade, 2014) found that 43 per cent had no educational qualifications and only 6 per cent had a degree or equivalent; 36 per cent had been unemployed when sentenced, 60 per cent had been claiming benefits. An earlier study, which looked at the entire prison population of England and Wales (Prison Reform Working Group, 2002), found that 67 per cent were unemployed prior to imprisonment (compared to just 5 per cent in the population as a whole), 32 per cent were homeless (0.9 per cent in the population) and 27 per cent had been brought up in care (as opposed to 2 per cent in the whole population).

Such statistics have their limitations because they do not offer direct measures of the relationship between class and crime and they include only those who have been convicted and imprisoned. Some crimes that are more likely to be carried out by the middle class (such as certain types of fraud and other white-collar crime) are less likely to lead to convictions and imprisonment than crimes that are probably more typically working-class (particularly street crimes such as burglary, robbery and assault). Corporate crimes are only likely to involve those in senior positions in corporations and state crime those in senior positions in government; again there may be low recording, conviction and imprisonment rates for these types of crime (see below).

Self-report studies

One way of testing whether there really is more crime committed by the working class than by the higher classes is to use self-report studies, but again the evidence here is rather limited. Only one recent study, The Offending, Crime and Justice Survey, which was carried out annually between 2003 and 2006, has examined this issue. This study was based on a sample of about 5,000 10–25-year-olds in three of the four surveys and a sample of 10–65-year-olds in one survey. It analysed the independent effects of a number of variables on offending and drug use. The survey found that: "The social class of the family, based on the occupation of the chief wage-earner, was not significantly associated with the likelihood of offending and drug use," (Hales *et al.* 2009). It was not social class but individual circumstances that seemed more important. Self-reported offending was found to be statistically associated with single-parent families, having a parent living with a new partner, inconsistent parental discipline, attending a poorly disciplined school or having a friend or sibling who had been in trouble with the law. This might suggest that factors relating to social control influence whether young people are likely to commit offences, whereas social class has a stronger influence on whether you are criminalised (labelled as criminal) by the criminal justice system. However, because of the nature of the sample, this study reveals little about adult crime.

Based on the evidence here, how strong is the relationship between criminality, criminalisation and social class? How does this compare with the relationship between crime and gender, and crime and ethnicity?

SOCIOLOGICAL EXPLANATIONS FOR WORKING-CLASS CRIMINALITY

Material and cultural explanations: opportunity, inequality and subcultures

Whatever the findings of self-report studies, many theorists have assumed that the working class tend to commit more crimes than the middle class. Some of these theories have already been discussed in detail elsewhere in this topic but it is worth briefly recalling the arguments here. Some emphasise material explanations (seeing crime as related to inequality of income and wealth), while others place more emphasis on cultural factors such as values, attitudes and lifestyle. Most approaches take some account of material and cultural factors, but the exact emphasis and causes suggested vary with individual theories.

Karl Marx, although perhaps the best-known sociological theorist of class and material inequality, hardly discussed crime at all, but when he did he saw it as a product of class inequality. Marx (discussed in Newbun, 2007) associated crime with a group he called the 'lumpenproletariat'. The lumpenproletariat were working class, but not in work, and relied upon income for survival (income they might get from begging, prostitution or crime). Marx saw work as essential to human dignity and he believed the lumpenproletariat had been dehumanised by their lack of work, and it was this that made them turn to crime. Alienation is one source of crime but, according to Marxists, the poverty generated by capitalism also pushes the proletariat towards committing crime. In addition, Gordon (1976) argues that capitalism generates a 'dog-eat-dog' mentality which encourages selfishness and greed. Many of these ideas are also discussed in Chapter 3, along with neo-Marxist ideas about resistance and rebellion.

A more sophisticated explanation of crime was developed by Robert Merton, who discussed the interplay of materialistic factors and culture. Merton (1938) saw crime as resulting from anomie, an over-emphasis upon societal goals and too little emphasis on sticking to the legitimate, accepted and legal means of achieving those goals. The working class had restricted opportunities to succeed in American society, according to Merton, and were therefore likely to turn to illegitimate ways of achieving those goals; that is, to crime. While Merton thought that most criminals were working-class, because they had fewer opportunities than others to achieve success, he accepted that there were some middle-class criminals because there was no upper limit on achievement; people could always want more.

Merton's theory was developed by Albert Cohen (1955) who placed more emphasis on cultural factors. In studying delinquent boys Cohen noted that much of their crime was non-utilitarian – it was not about money or success but was often destructive and apparently pointless (for example, vandalism and joy riding). Furthermore, crime often took place in groups or subcultures in which delinquent boys seemed to thrive off the encouragement they got from their friends. Cohen concluded that their behaviour could be explained in terms of 'status deprivation'. Status deprivation means lacking in prestige or respect. The boys were looked down on by teachers' and others and had failed to achieve academic success. In order to get status, they got together with others in a similar situation and they gave each other status not for success and conformity, but, instead, for breaking the norms of society.

Merton's work was developed further by Cloward and Ohlin (1960), who added the idea that there were also illegitimate opportunity structures, that is, opportunities to succeed where there was organised crime but using illegitimate means. This led to the development of criminal subcultures in some working-class areas. However, in other areas there was little organised crime so there was more use of violence to achieve status in conflict subcultures. Double failures, who had not found success legitimately in the conflict or the criminal subcultures, became retreatists.

Left realists such as Lea and Young (1984) argued that it was not lack of material success itself which led to criminality, but that feeling deprived was most important. They used the idea of relative deprivation and suggested that people were more likely to turn to crime when their expectations were not met: they were not being rewarded as highly as they felt they should be. Lea and Young argued that, in addition, a sense of marginalisation, of being outside the mainstream of society, could lead to increased criminality. Some groups created subcultures to deal with their relative deprivation and marginalisation and to develop collective, criminal responses to their situation. However, Lea and Young also believe that, in addition, the statistics partly reflect bias in criminal justice against the working class (see Chapter 4).

A number of more contemporary criminologists have also argued that material deprivation is linked to higher levels of street crime. For example, Chris Glover (2010) sees levels of inequality, poverty and social exclusion (particularly unemployment) as implicated in causing crime among those on low incomes. The Equality Trust (2011, cited in Reiner, 2015) found a strong relationship between inequality and the rate of serious violent crime, including homicide.

Evaluation of sociological explanations

Critics such as Hall, Winlow and Ancrum (2008) have argued that there is no straightforward statistical relationship between factors such as poverty, unemployment, the state of the economy and crime rates. For example, for most of the second half of the 20th century in the UK, crime continued to rise whether the country was in recession or not and whether unemployment was high or low.

CULTURAL EXPLANATIONS FOR WORKING-CLASS CRIMINALITY

Some explanations for working-class crime place much more emphasis on culture than on material factors. For example, Walter Miller (1958) believed that the lower classes in America developed a distinctive culture, or way of life, which was passed down from generation to generation. This culture started as a response to the low pay and tedium of working-class jobs but then developed a life of its own, independent of the sort of work that particular members of the working class did. According to Miller, this culture has a number of focal concerns, such as 'toughness' 'smartness' and 'excitement'. Toughness brings status in working-class culture, as does smartness (the ability to outwit other people). Excitement involves a search for thrills, particularly at weekends, as a response to the lack of excitement in the daily grind of working-class jobs. Some of these **focal concerns** can lead to trouble with the law, for example, through fights or dangerous or antisocial behaviour when drunk.

UNDERSTAND THE CONCEPT

Focal concerns are central issues in a culture that can influence people's day-to-day decision-making. They may be related to people's attempts to achieve or maintain status and to gain satisfaction in their lives.

Another cultural view of lower-class crime is put forward in Charles Murray's underclass theory. As discussed in the section on right realist theorists (see Chapter 4), Murray argues that the underclass have developed a culture of dependency on welfare in which single-parent mothers raise children who have little respect for the law because they lack suitable adult role models, and young men break the law to supplement their benefits. Rather than seeing poverty as the cause of crime, Murray sees over-generous welfare benefits as encouraging a culture that values laziness and irresponsible behaviour, including criminality.

Evaluation of cultural explanations

Neither of the cultural theories discussed here provides particularly convincing explanations for working-class crime. Miller's work is very dated and many theories question whether there is such a clear-cut lower-class culture in Britain today. Hall, Winlow and Ancrum argue that traditional working-class culture has been replaced by a different set of values based largely on **consumerism**, and working-class involvement in crime is associated with the desire to gain status through acquiring consumer goods. Charles Murray's ideas have been undermined by a lack of empirical evidence (see Chapter 4). Some research has found high rates of criminality among children from single-parent families (Hales *et al.*), but this is generally explained better by the fact that these families tend to have a low income rather than loose morals sometimes cited as a characteristic of the lower classes (Fitzpatrick, 2011, Haralambos and Holborn, 2013).

UNDERSTAND THE CONCEPT

Consumerism involves the purchase and use of consumer goods and services and in a consumer society. This assumes increased importance in people's lives, perhaps to the extent that consumption is increasingly linked to status and a sense of self-worth.

Does the evidence suggest that culture or material deprivation is more important in accounting for working-class criminality?

CRIMINALISATION AND CLASS BIAS

There is an alternative approach to explaining the relatively high conviction and imprisonment rates for lower social classes: arguably, it is the process of criminalisation that is responsible for the statistics, rather than higher rates of offending among the lower classes than among the higher classes. In other words, it is not that the lower classes are actually more criminal, just that their behaviour is more likely to be defined as criminal and prosecuted than is the equally (or more) illegal behaviour of higher social classes. As discussed, self-report studies suggest

that there is no significant difference in offending between working-class and middle-class people aged 10 to 25 (see above) even though it appears that working-class youths are far more likely to be prosecuted, convicted and sent to prison for offences.

There may be a number of factors involved in the greater criminalisation of young people for street crimes. They range from those involving day-to-day encounters between the police and suspects to the broader ways in which power influences law-making and policies and the criminal justice system.

Class bias, street crime and criminal justice

This issue has been explored in a number of American studies. For example, in a classic study, the American sociologist William Chambliss (1973) studied two juvenile gangs. The 'Saints' were from a middle-class background, Their parents were 'pillars of the community' while the 'Roughnecks' were working-class. The 'Saints' got away with far more serious offences (for example, drinking and driving, and deliberately causing road accidents) than the 'Roughnecks', who were more likely to be involved in minor assaults on one another and petty theft. Chambliss argues that the working-class 'Roughnecks' were more likely to be labelled because of pre-existing stereotypes about different classes, the greater visibility of the working-class youth (who were on the streets rather than in private cars and homes,) and their lack of ability to negotiate their way out of trouble by being polite and deferential to the police.

British sociologists argue that similar processes occur in contemporary Britain. For example, Tim Newburn and Robert Reiner (2007) argue that police discretion is very important in influencing which law-breakers are likely to be arrested, given that "breaches of the law outstrip police capacity to process them". They choose to concentrate on those who fit the stereotype of the criminal (lower-class males) engaged in street crimes in public places. Newburn and Reiner (2007) argue that, while people from all social classes commit crime, working-class crime tends to consist of "common and visible predatory street offences … almost by definition the 'crimes of the poor' – which occupy a high proportion of police attention, rather than the more hidden types of crime which happen within the private sphere of the commercial world or within the household," (Newburn and Reiner, 2007).

Hazel Croall (2011), in a review of research, argues that areas with high concentrations of working-class homes are subject to more intense policing and when crimes are committed the 'usual suspects' from lower classes are the focus of most attention. If taken to court then the lower classes are seen as being more at risk of reoffending and are therefore more likely to be sent to prison. Croall also argues that parental status, the areas in which convicted people live, and whether they are unemployed, all affect the chances of imprisonment and mean that the lower classes are punished more harshly than the higher classes.

Criminalisation and the crimes of higher classes

In contrast, offences by higher-status offenders may be less easy to detect; the higher classes have more opportunity to commit white-collar offences that have low detection and conviction rates. There is considerable under-policing of crimes committed by the higher social classes, particularly when they are involved in white-collar and corporate crimes (see Chapters 3 and 9) and state and ecological crimes (see Chapter 9).

A number of Marxist and critical criminologists argue that these differences in the way different social classes are dealt with in the criminal justice system reflect broader power structures. From their point of view, it is no accident that the crimes of the powerful are less likely than lower-class crimes to lead to prosecution and conviction.

For example, Steve Tombs and David Whyte (2010) argue that because corporations have "enormous economic, political and social power" they and their senior managers are largely immune from prosecution even when their activities cause very serious harm. These include:

> harm caused by theft and fraud, such as price fixing and the mis-selling of pensions and payment protection insurance

> harm caused by working, such as the 150 or so workers killed in accidents at work each year

> harm caused by air pollution, which in the UK are estimated at a minimum of 24,000 deaths each year

> harm caused by food poisoning, for example, salmonella and campylobacter kill 100–200 people a year in the UK.

However, the offenders in these sorts of crime do not fit the stereotype of the typical criminal, their offences are difficult to detect, and when they are detected they are usually dealt with by enforcement actions (such as requiring companies to improve health and safety) rather than criminal prosecutions. Because of the power of the corporations and their importance to local and national economies and employment, governments are very reluctant to convict and imprison senior executives.

Are all crimes committed by higher social classes unlikely to result in prosecution and conviction? Are there any crimes predominantly carried out by lower classes that rarely lead to convictions?

CONCLUSIONS

The evidence discussed above suggests that while people from different classes may commit different types of crime, which are treated differently by the criminal justice system, it is impossible to say which classes commit more crimes. There is evidence, however, that crimes committed by the higher classes may do more harm with less chance of prosecution. If this is the case, differences in power between classes may be the key reason. However, whatever the reason for class differences in offending and criminalisation, a full understanding of the relationship between class and crime can only be achieved by looking at offending and criminalisation (see, for example, the left realist idea of the square of crime in Chapter 4).

FOCUS ON SKILLS: TAX EVASION IS AS BAD AS BENEFIT FRAUD

Goods are stolen from shops during the 2011 riots

There is little, if any, moral distinction between withholding money by deception and obtaining money by deception.

Cheat the Government out of £20,000 in benefits and there is a very good chance that you will be put behind bars. Cheat the Government out of double that amount through tax evasion and there is a very good chance you will not. This terrible double standard at the heart of British justice cannot be right.

In May this year Susanne Rees, of Bridgend in Wales, was sentenced to 60 days in prison after pleading guilty to defrauding her local council of £19,000 in housing and council tax benefit. Only three months earlier Michael Frost, a businessman from Cheltenham, avoided jail and was given only 60 hours of community service after pleading guilty to evading £65,000 of income tax through self-assessment fraud.

Probably the only reason Mr Frost escaped going to jail — despite cheating the Government out of more than three times as much as Ms Rees — was because he wore a smart suit and employed an even smarter lawyer. That is not justice.

Sources in the accountancy world say that it is common for wealthy businessmen caught up in tax investigations to do deals with HM Revenue & Customs. The taxman simply does not push for criminal prosecutions when someone is prepared to co-operate.

A quick trawl through court records shows that fewer than one in every 1,000 people subject to HM Revenue & Customs investigation for tax evasion is prosecuted to the degree that a criminal sentence even becomes a possibility. Far fewer end up in prison.

Sentencing must be fair and proportionate, irrespective of your class, wealth or the cut of your suit.

Ellson, A. 'Tax evasion is as bad as benefit fraud', *The Times*, 17 July 2010

Sir Fred Goodwin, formerly boss of the Royal Bank of Scotland.

Fred Goodwin, former boss of the failed RBS, bailed out by UK taxpayers at a cost of £45 billion, merely lost his knighthood and had his pension cut from £703,000 to £342,500 per year. As Michael Meacher points out, the standard penalty for a burglar who stole a ten-millionth of this – £4500 – will be jail, normally for four years.

Nicholas Robinson, an electrical engineering student with no criminal record, was jailed for six months for stealing bottles of water worth £3.50 during the riots in London in August 2011. While the UK government has yet to prosecute any bankers, it immediately set up 24-hour courts to try those arrested in the riots.

Source: Sayer (2014)

Questions

1. **Understand.** What does Andrew Ellson mean by the 'double standard' in criminal justice?

2. **Explain** how the difference between offending and criminalisation can throw light on the evidence and arguments presented here.

3. **Analyse.** Suggest reasons why wealthier and high-status offenders are less likely than poorer and lower-status offenders to be prosecuted and convicted.

4. **Evaluate** whether there are a large enough number of crimes committed by the higher classes to make a difference to the overall relationship between class and offending? (For example, do you think only a small minority of the higher classes are offenders?)

CHECK YOUR UNDERSTANDING

1. What is meant by 'focal concerns'?

2. Explain what is meant by 'consumerism'?

3. Explain the meaning of 'inequality'.

4. Identify three examples of the harm that can be caused by large corporations.

5. Identify one theory of class and crime suggesting that material deprivation leads to high rates of working-class crime.

6. Identify one theory of class and crime suggesting that cultural difference leads to high rates of working-class crime.

7. Briefly explain how police discretion could result in higher arrest rates for the working class.

8. Outline the ways in which Hazel Croall sees criminal justice as being biased against the working class.

9. Outline two criticisms of Charles Murray's view of the underclass and crime.

10. Evaluate the following statement: "The working class and the higher classes commit different types of crime but a similar number of crimes."

TAKE IT FURTHER

Carry out a content analysis of a copy of one tabloid newspaper (for example, *The Sun*) and one broadsheet newspaper (for example, *The Times*) on the same day.

1. Count the stories about crime. Analyse the proportion of stories that concern:

   a. street crime

   b. white-collar/corporate/state crime.

2. Try to identify the class background of offenders mentioned.

3. What images of class and crime are given in the two papers? How well, in your view, does this reflect the reality of the relationship between class and crime?

1.9 GLOBALISATION, HUMAN RIGHTS, STATE AND GREEN CRIME

LEARNING OBJECTIVES

> Demonstrate understanding of the nature of green crime, state crime and human rights violations (AO1).

> Apply your understanding to the impact of globalisation and the state on crime in contemporary society (AO2).

> Analyse the relationship between globalisation and crime (AO3).

> Evaluate the relationship between globalisation and crime (AO3).

> Evaluate competing explanations of green crime, state crime and human rights abuses (AO3).

INTRODUCING THE DEBATE

It has been widely recognised that the world is becoming more interconnected; social life cannot be fully understood simply by looking within local or national boundaries. From this point of view, globalisation has taken place, and crime is also now organised, at least in part, on an international or even global scale. Furthermore, it is increasingly understood that crime cannot be confined just to the actions of individuals or even corporations, but can also involve states, even though they are the very institutions that make national laws. Green or environmental crime is particularly likely to cross national boundaries and to have a global impact – nature does not respect the borders between nation states. The crimes of states themselves also often cross national borders and can involve violations of international law and, at their worst, involve gross violations of human rights. Some criminologists push the boundaries of the subject in discussing state and green crime by arguing that legal definitions of crime are not adequate to identify harms done in these contexts. This section looks at these interconnected issues, all of which can be linked back to the process of globalisation.

GLOBALISATION AND CRIME

Globalisation

Anthony Giddens (1990) defines globalisation as "the intensification of worldwide social relations which link distant localities in such a way that local happenings are shaped by events occurring many miles away and vice versa". By this, Giddens means that social changes have made distance and national borders far less important as barriers between social groups. What happens in one society can quickly affect other societies – anywhere in the world.

Similarly, David Held *et al.* (2002) see globalisation in terms of the greater interconnectedness of social life and social relationships throughout the world.

The globalisation of crime

According to the United Nations Development Programme (1999), globalisation has resulted in a massive growth in the following forms of crime:

> dealing in illicit drugs

> illegal trafficking in weapons

> illegal trafficking in human beings

> corruption

> violent crimes, including terrorism

> war crimes.

The importance of this can be seen by the fact that the total value of transnational organised crime is estimated by the United Nations to be approximately £1 trillion per year.

However, globalisation has also had some benefits in terms of tackling crime. With greater international cooperation between police forces and the more widespread use of extradition agreements (in which suspects can be returned to countries where they are suspected of committing offences) it has become easier to track and prosecute offenders. In 1992 Europol was established to coordinate European policing and its mandate has been extended in recent years (Newburn and Reiner, 2012). Newburn and Reiner also point out that, since 9/11, sharing of information between US and European governments has greatly increased. Many western countries are also making greater efforts to prevent money laundering (partly to combat terrorism) which is essential to tackling transnational organised crime. Nevertheless, most theorists and most research does suggest that globalisation has led to increases in crime, as well as new types of crime, and new ways of organising and committing crime.

Castells: criminal networks and the effects of global crime

Manuel Castells (2010) argues that globalisation involves the development of **networks** that cut across national boundaries, meaning that the notion of self-contained societies is outdated. These networks have developed because of the growth of an information age in which knowledge as well as goods and people can move quickly, easily and cheaply across national boundaries. These changes have resulted in the development of a global criminal economy, in which there are complex interconnections between a range of criminal networks, including the American Mafia, Colombian drug cartels, the Russian Mafia, Chinese triads and the Sicilian Cosa Nostra. These criminal networks operate transnationally, because it reduces the risks and increases their profits. Criminal activities tend to be centred upon countries where the state and its law enforcement are relatively weak. Thus Afghanistan is a centre of heroin production and cocaine is produced in Colombia. However, most sales are made in richer and therefore more profitable markets, such as the USA and UK. Although many criminal networks are transnational/global in their scope, they are often organised along national, regional or ethnic lines. For example, there are links between Chinese triads and Chinese minority ethnic groups worldwide.

UNDERSTAND THE CONCEPT

Networks involve complex sets of interconnections, between people and/or things, that are not normally planned or centrally controlled.

The globalisation of crime has been facilitated by the development of Russian criminal networks, which emerged after the collapse of communism. As state assets were privatised, some Russians collaborated with organised criminal networks from other countries to buy up roubles before dumping them on world currency markets, to slash the value of the currency. This enabled them to buy the former assets of the Soviet state (such as gas and oil fields, hotels and land) at bargain prices. Substantial parts of the gold reserves of the state were stolen and taken abroad to help fund the purchase of privatised assets. Castells argues that, as a result, politics, business and organised crime are now closely intertwined both in Russian networks and across the world.

Castells identifies the drugs trade as the biggest global criminal business, but illegal arms trading, the trafficking of nuclear material (much from the former Soviet Union), and the smuggling of illegal immigrants (for example, from Mexico and the Caribbean into the USA) are also significant. There is also trafficking of children and women, the latter often for the purposes of prostitution, which is closely linked to global tourism. Even body parts, which may be bought from donors or obtained through murder, are trafficked. Money-laundering is also vital to the global criminal economy, as without it the criminals would be unable to use the proceeds of their crimes.

Castells believes that, apart from the harm done to victims, global criminal networks also harm the economy, politics and culture of the world. In some countries the capital held by criminals is so great that it can have a major impact upon the economic policies of the state (for example, in Colombia and Peru). In a number of countries, organised crime is closely linked to corruption within the government, thereby distorting political policies and preventing effective law enforcement. Global crime can also have cultural effects, for example, by making criminal careers more attractive than legitimate careers to young people.

Further effects of the globalisation of crime

Tim Newburn (2013) identifies the following consequences of globalisation for crime and criminology.

1. Globalisation can affect and often reduce the power of the nation state, so that it is hard for individual countries to claim complete sovereignty over issues to do with crime. There may be disputes over crimes that are committed in one country but have effects in another country (for example, internet fraud, which leads to losses in a country other than the one in which the fraudsters are located).

2. It provides opportunities for committing crime in new ways. For example, criminals can take advantage of variations in legislation between countries, variations in duties and of regulation and of the opportunity to escape national jurisdiction, by moving between countries to avoid arrest.

3. Globalisation has also been seen as creating a new awareness of risk from foreign countries, for example, from cyber terrorism, global warming and international terrorism. This in line with the idea of a 'risk society', put forward by Ulrich Beck (see Theoretical approaches to green crime, page 77). This new global consciousness can result either in attempts to produce global or at least international

systems of justice (for example, through international courts and treaties) or amplify fear of outsiders and result in greater efforts to impose social control and exclude immigrants.

CAPITALISM, GLOBALISATION AND CRIME

For socialist criminologists such as Ian Taylor (1997), the development of capitalism is the main driver for the globalisation of crime. The privatisation of state assets (see Castells: criminal networks and the effects of global crime, page 74) and the involvement of markets in more and more activities (a process known as marketisation) are features of capitalist development and help to drive globalisation. In turn, this creates conditions conducive to the growth of both transnational and local crime by elites and working-class offenders alike.

1. For elites, the ability to move finance around the world, with minimal control, enables a whole range of financial crimes, from tax evasion and insider trading to defrauding transnational organisations such as the European Union out of grant and subsidy money. Estimates put losses from the EU at around $7 billion per year.

2. Organised crime gains increased opportunities to launder the profits from illegal activities such as drugs production and distribution, because of loose controls over capital movements and the existence of tax havens.

3. Global capitalism and cheap international transport and communication systems have allowed companies to shift production to countries where production costs are lowest. This generally involves moving from high-tax countries, such as those of Western Europe, with decent welfare provision and health and safety laws, to low-tax countries with no welfare provision or employment laws – for example, in South-East Asia. The resulting decline in employment and income levels in Western European countries has led to increased levels of crime and social disorder and, in some cases, to companies breaking laws in the low-income countries.

Ruggiero (1996) points to a further consequence of the shift in production to low-wage economies. He argues that the decline in employment encourages the growth of small firms in Western Europe that avoid labour laws and operate outside the formal economy. Furthermore, these companies will employ the cheapest labour they can find, often focusing their recruitment on illegal immigrants who can be paid less than the minimum wage.

Crime: the local and the global

Although globalisation might lead to the development of international and transnational criminal organisations, local organisation is also important. Larger organisations are linked to small-scale and locally based criminal activities through networks of connections. Dick Hobbs and Colin Dunningham (1998) studied criminal networks in the north-east of England and found that most organised crime involved networks of interconnected criminals, who worked together from time to time, rather than well-integrated, permanent gangs. Some successful criminals had international contacts that helped them take part in drug smuggling, but they also had lots of local contacts to help them sell the drugs. They argued that crime was not just organised globally but also locally: a combination they refer to as a 'glocal' system. For example, one criminal entrepreneur in the study, 'Dave Peters', made so much money that he ended up living on the Costa del Sol, from where he ran a shipping business and a chain of clubs throughout Europe. However, he maintained strong contacts with his home town in England and owned a warehouse from which he distributed stolen goods. His international operations were still partly grounded in the local networks he had used early on in his career.

In what ways does the idea of 'glocal' crime networks challenge conventional criminological theories of subcultures and organised crime?

GREEN, ENVIRONMENTAL AND ECO-CRIME

Globalisation is closely linked to many crimes that come under the category of green or environmental crime. These categories encompass a wide range of different types of offence and harmful activity and include air pollution, graffiti, producing emissions that contribute to global warming, the dumping of waste, illegal trading in wildlife, the hunting of endangered species, illegal fishing and logging, industrial activity that damages the environment, dropping litter and vandalism. This list shows that offences in these categories include serious criminal offences, minor offences that are dealt with by the civil courts and activities that may not be illegal but are nevertheless harmful to the environment.

Defining crimes against the environment

There is no single agreed definition of crimes against the environment. Narrower definitions tend to be framed in terms of illegality, whereas broader ones are more concerned with harm.

1. Some sociologists limit their definition of crime to actions that are actually against the law. Therefore Situ and Emmons (1999) say that "an environmental crime is an unauthorised act or omission that violates the law". This law could be a national law or it could be part of a transnational or international agreement, for example, agreements on fishing or climate change.

2. A second, more radical approach argues that some actions that are currently legal should also be seen as environmental crimes, as well as those that are illegal. Nigel South (2004) develops this type of argument by using a twofold framework for understanding environmental crimes:

   › primary environmental crimes

   › environmental law-breaking.

Primary environmental crimes are currently legal under international law, but South argues that, because of the extent of environmental damage, they should come under the analysis of criminologists. At present, they tend to be examined simply as 'environmental issues'. South's primary crimes cover such issues as air and water pollution, deforestation and species decline.

Discussing South's approach, Walters (2008) gives the example of the commercial growing of genetically modified crops for profit in the UK, despite the "ecological harm and uncertainties that have been widely documented". Another example is given by Thornton and Beckwith (2004), who claim that 24,000 people die prematurely each year because of air pollution, yet much of the pollution is not illegal and even where pollution is illegal, the law is rarely enforced and the maximum fine is low.

The second part of South's framework covers actions that are already illegal under international law, but these laws may not be enforced. These illegal acts include the dumping of hazardous waste and unauthorised pollution through the discharge of waste. According to Walters (2007), the British nuclear industry has illegally disposed of thousands of barrels of radioactive waste in the seas around the Channel Islands.

South's distinction between primary crimes and the flouting of rules does provide a means of linking two distinct traditions, which can help form the basis of a 'green criminology'.

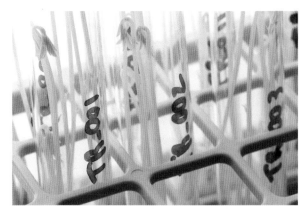

Genetically modified crops: a sign of progress or an environmental crime?

3. Some criminologists go even further than South by disregarding legal definitions of crime altogether and arguing instead that actions should be judged entirely in terms of harm rather than in terms of law. These critical criminologists increasingly argue for the importance of the concept of **zemiology**, which claims there are objective ways of identifying harm, in this case environmental harm, that are quite independent of law.

UNDERSTAND THE CONCEPT

Zemiology is an approach within criminology that argues that national or international laws are inadequate for judging whether actions should be regarded as criminal. This is because laws often reflect the narrow interests of the powerful rather than those of wider groups. Zemiologists argue that whether something is seen as an offence should be based, instead, on whether actions do harm to human beings, to other living creatures, or to the environment.

Reece Walters (2010), for example, argues that it is useful to use the term 'eco-crime' (rather than environmental crime or green crime) to identify actions or omissions that threaten the long-term sustainability of life on Earth or even the "extinction of human and nonhuman life". They are essentially crimes against nature rather than just crimes against individual humans or other species. However, Walters also includes in the category eco-crime, actions that harm the wellbeing of humans or other species, without threatening

long-term sustainability. These types of offence may cause illness, pain and suffering, poverty or shorter life expectancy to humans, or damage other species (including plants as well as animals).

This view is supported by White (2007) who dismisses all anthropocentric (human-centred) definitions of crime as inherently biased. The law assumes that humans have a right to exploit the natural environment for their own ends, but this is a view imposed by humans on nature. White advocates an eco-centric approach that emphasises the interdependence of humans and the environment in which they live. From this viewpoint, damaging the environment is not just harmful in itself but it also damages humans who rely upon the environment for their survival.

Do you agree that humans are anthropocentric in defining crime? Do you agree we should move to an eco-centric approach instead, and if so, why?

THEORETICAL APPROACHES TO GREEN CRIME

Ulrich Beck and risk society

One of the most influential theoretical approaches to understanding green crime is provided by the sociologist Ulrich Beck and his idea of risk society (1992). Beck suggests that economic growth in more affluent countries has meant that the risks resulting from a lack of resources (such as the risk of poverty) have declined and science and technology have allowed humans to overcome many risks from the natural environment. Physical defences, for example, can protect against floods. However, human activity has created new risks such as those of nuclear contamination, toxins in the environment and environmental damage caused by pollution of various types. Many of these risks result from economic growth, for example, the way growth has led to the increased use of motor cars. In the past, the lower social classes tended to be most at risk from misfortunes, but many of the risks created by humans affect all social groups equally. For example, all classes are affected by a nuclear disaster. In *World at Risk* (2009), Beck suggests that there is more global awareness of the risks because of increased publicity.

Beck sees the harm done to the environment as integral to the development of **late modern society**, in which humans attempt to control the world through the use of science and technology. The problem is that in solving one set of problems, humans often create other problems. Nuclear energy, for example, could be used to counteract climate change, but it creates the risk of nuclear disaster (such as those at Chernobyl and Fukushima) as well as the problem of disposing of nuclear waste.

UNDERSTAND THE CONCEPT

A **late modern society** has moved beyond the modern era – based on rational action, secularisation, class divisions and the dominance of nation states – but has not yet changed sufficiently to become postmodern (see Topic 2).

Beck has been criticised for suggesting that all classes are equally vulnerable to man-made risks. For example, Philip Sutton (2015) points out that richer people can afford to live in the parts of the world that are least affected by environmental damage. However, Sutton praises Beck for highlighting some of the environmental harm that comes from the legal use of technology.

Green crime, capitalism and corporate power

Ulrick Beck's ideas have been very influential, but they deal only indirectly with the relationship between crime and the environment. Furthermore, they are rather generalised in terms of explaining why green crime takes place. Some sociologists put much more emphasis on the role of capitalism. For example, Halsey and Whyte (1998) argue that green crime is caused by the dominance of capitalist ideology, which prioritises economic growth over the wellbeing of the environment. More specifically, the blame for environmental harm has often been linked to corporate crime. For example, Nigel South (cited in Walters, 2010) discusses what he calls the "corporate colonisation of nature". By this he means that nature is exploited for corporate profit. Reece Walters (2010) gives some examples of this.

1. Biopiracy occurs when companies take control, sometimes illegally, of plants and animals, preventing them from being used by indigenous people. For example, this might involve stripping rainforests of resources, thus making it difficult or impossible for the local population to thrive and for the rainforest itself to survive.

2. The corporate engineering of nature, such as the use of genetically modified crops, the building of dams and the flooding of valleys, mining and fracking, can all cause great harm to the environment. This can undermine sustainability and diversity, and harm local populations. For example, according to Reece Walters, the introduction of GM crops into Zambia has threatened to contaminate other crops and undermine the local food supply. Corporations have even claimed patents on the genes in local crops contaminated by their GM plantings.

The environment, corporations, states, organised crime and consumers

Capitalist corporations have been responsible for a great deal of green crime and environmental harm. For example, the BP Deepwater Horizon oil spill in the Gulf of Mexico in 2006 caused immense damage to the marine environment. Yet environmental harm is not always the responsibility of corporations. It was the Chinese state that was responsible for building the Three Gorges Dam, completed in 2006, which flooded over 400 square miles of land, damaging the environment, causing soil erosion and drought, and displacing over 1 million people (Watts, 2011).

Some environmental harm is caused by neither corporations nor states, but by organised crime. An example is the disposal of hazardous waste. Nigel South (1998) discusses the role of the Sicilian Mafia in disposing of hazardous waste into the Bay of Naples and he quotes estimates that only 10 per cent of this waste is disposed of legally.

However, if the definition of 'green crime' is extended to include all damage to the environment then, arguably, most people in the world are to some extent responsible. Car drivers, for example, certainly contribute to air pollution and the creation of greenhouse gases which, it is widely agreed, contribute to global warming. It is therefore difficult to lay the blame for green crimes entirely on corporations, states and organised crime. The growth of consumerism and the actions of individual consumers also undermine environmental sustainability.

Which groups do you think are primarily responsible for green crime? What are the most effective ways to tackle it?

FOCUS ON SKILLS: A SCANDAL OF ARROGANCE, GREED AND SKULDUGGERY

In an article published on 21 September 2014 and headlined "Diesel cars built to foil test for toxic fumes", *The Sunday Times* first reported findings by Dutch researchers that onboard car computers were being programmed to fool emissions testers.

Yet it took US officials a full year to wring admission from Volkswagen that its diesels were fitted with "defeat" devices.

These sensed stationary test conditions and reduced emissions that in normal driving proved up to 35 times more noxious.

There were claims yesterday from Norman Baker, the Liberal Democrat former transport minister, that Germany's chancellor, Angela Merkel, had leaned on David Cameron to delay new emission limits in Britain so as to protect the German car industry.

There were also claims that the UK government's failure to act sooner may have contributed to big underestimates of the toll of air pollution.

The government has calculated that thousands of people in Britain may be dying prematurely each year because of exposure to nitrogen dioxide (NO_2).

Dr Anil Namdeo, director of Newcastle University's transport operations research group, said: "We now know that real-world emission factors could be 10 to 35 times higher than lab-based [tests]."

The roots of the diesel scandal stretch back to the early 1990s when European governments were beginning

to worry about greenhouse gases and climate change. In the rush to reduce carbon dioxide (CO_2) emissions, diesel was seen as a potential saviour.

Yet the rush to reduce global warming appears to have blinded regulators to warnings, best expressed in a 1993 Department of the Environment report, that "the impact of diesel vehicles on urban air quality is a serious one... any increase in the proportion of diesel vehicles on our urban streets is to be viewed with considerable concern unless problems of particulate matter and nitrogen oxides emissions are effectively addressed".

Engineers had to find ways of limiting toxic fumes and particles of poisonous soot while retaining the motoring benefits of diesel — long-range fuel efficiency and snappy performance.

Volkswagen's solution was to cheat. It developed a software hack that enabled a vehicle's onboard computer to see government testers coming.

Source: Leake, J. and Allen-Mills, T. 'A scandal of arrogance, greed and skulduggery', *The Sunday Times*, 27 September 2015

Questions

1. **Explain** how and why Volkswagen cheated tests on diesel car emissions.

2. **Analyse.** In what ways would this criminal behaviour harm the environment, owners of VW cars and members of the population, in areas where VWs are common?

3. **Analyse.** Suggest reasons why VW was allowed to get away with this for so long by regulators, when there was already evidence that emissions tests were not reliable.

4. **Evaluate** the view that this was not a victimless crime but a very serious offence on a par with murder.

STATE CRIMES

The nature and extent of state crime

The vast resources of some states make it possible for them to commit crime on a much bigger scale than is possible for individuals. States usually have more ability

than other institutions to use violence and force because of their control over the police and military. States also define what is legal and illegal within their own jurisdiction and run the legal and criminal justice systems. As Penny Green and Tony Ward (2012) point out, they can often maintain secrecy over their actions. For these reasons, it is difficult to define and measure state crime but, despite this, the seriousness and scale of it is beyond question. In some cases states are responsible for actions that are criminal even under their own law.

Green and Ward give the following examples of state crime: genocide (attempts to exterminate whole populations), war crimes, violence by the police, torture and imprisonment of political opponents, and 'grand corruption' when a state elite steals many of the resources of a country for themselves.

Eugene MCLaughlin (2001) divides state crimes into four types.

1. Political crimes, such as rigging elections or appointing officials corruptly.

2. Crimes of the police and security forces, such as torture, illegal detention and using unjustified violence against demonstrators.

3. Economic crimes, such as failing to pay state employees the minimum wage, or breaking health and safety regulations in state-run enterprises.

4. Social and cultural crimes, such as mistreatment of minority ethnic groups, for example, supressing minority languages.

A number of examples cited by Green and Ward can help to illustrate the wide range and sheer scale of state crime.

> Amnesty International research found that a minimum of 111 countries practised torture and ill-treatment in 2009.

> A calculation by Rummel (cited in Green and Ward, 2012) estimated that 262 million people were killed by various forms of state action in the 20th century.

> It is estimated that over 120,000 civilians have been violently killed since the invasion of Iraq in 2003. Many of them have been the victims of actions by the military forces of the states involved.

> An example of grand corruption is the activities of Mubarak, the former leader of Egypt, whose estimated wealth was $70 billion in 2011.

> During the Iraq war the US military tortured prisoners in Abu Ghraib prison.

Defining state crime

State crime can be defined in a number of ways.

1. First it can be defined in terms of breaking the laws of the society in which the crime takes place. States sometimes break their own rules. However, a problem with this definition is that states may legalise actions that would, in most times and places, be seen as criminal. For example, in Saudi Arabia it is legal to imprison, execute or sentence political prisoners to public floggings, simply for criticising the regime (Human Rights Watch, 2015). A further problem is that since offences are not only defined but also prosecuted by the state, it is likely that many offences committed by agents of the state will not come to court.

2. A second approach is to base definitions of state crime on international law. However, international law is open to interpretation and difficult, often impossible, to enforce. Bodies set up to enforce international law, such as the International Criminal Court (based in The Hague) have only been partially successful. Not all countries are signatories to the treaties that recognise this court and it only deals with the most serious offences involving 'crimes against humanity'.

3. The third approach is to use the idea of human rights to provide a basis for determining what is and is not state crime. This approach argues that there are certain general standards against which behaviour can be judged, regardless of the legislation in individual countries or in terms of international law.

State crime and human rights

A number of sociologists define state crime in terms of the violation of human rights. For example, Green and Ward (2004, cited in Green 2010) define state crime as "violations of human rights, perpetrated by agents of the state in the deviant pursuit of organisational goals". This definition is based upon the idea of harm inherent in the idea of human rights rather than legal definitions of unacceptable behaviour (in line with the idea of zemiology, see Chapter 3). This does however raise the question of how harm is defined, and on what basis human rights are established.

The most widely used definition of human rights is given by the UN. Sinšia Malešević (2015) says that the United Nations declaration of human rights "conceptualises human rights as fundamental inalienable rights to which everyone is entitled on the simple account of being a human being. They include the right to life, liberty, security and equality, the preservation of one's dignity, to own property, recognition before the law, freedom of movement and residence, nationality, freedom of thought, conscience and religion".

However, the idea of human rights and the definition that should be used are controversial. Sociologists have objected to the idea of universal human rights on a number of grounds.

> First, it fails to acknowledge that the idea of rights is socially constructed and what is seen as appropriate and 'normal' in terms of rights will vary from society to society. Furthermore, Waters (1996, cited in Malešević, 2015) suggests that the powerful can often impose their own definition of human rights on less powerful groups in society.

> Second, some sociologists have seen the kind of rights identified by the United Nations as having a liberal, Western and individualist bias. For example, Zizek (2005, cited in Malešević) sees the UN rights as "effectively the right of white, male property-owners to exchange freely on the market, and exploit workers and women, and exert political domination".

Zizek believes that women and workers are exploited by UN rights, which he says favour white, male business owners.

Critical social scientists such as Green and Ward (2012) nevertheless insist that universal standards are possible and sociologists can identify behaviours that are harmful to humans, regardless of local customs. They suggest that whether something is a violation of human rights should be judged by a variety of social audiences, including other states, victims, worldwide **civil society** and non-governmental organisations. Violations of human rights are crimes regardless of whether they are against national or international law. Other radical sociologists, such as Herman and Julia Schwendinger (1975), argue that it is the duty of sociology to support human rights and expose abuses by the state, even where this goes against the laws of the countries in which they are citizens.

UNDERSTAND THE CONCEPT

Civil society consists of all non-state organisations apart from businesses, including the family, private life, pressure groups and charities.

As Bryan Turner (2006 cited in Malešević 2015) points out, however, one problem with the idea of universal human rights is that nobody is able to enforce them; states often carry out human rights abuses rather than protect citizens from them.

Stanley Cohen: state crime and the culture of denial

Stanley Cohen (1993) pioneered the study of social reactions to state crime and human rights abuses. He defines state crimes as "gross violations of human rights" against both international law and national law, causing serious harm to humans. Examples include "genocide, mass political killings, state terrorism, torture, disappearances".

Despite the clear and extreme nature of many of these abuses, states often develop a culture of denial to respond to accusations of abuse.

This involves a three-stage spiral of denial.

> In stage 1, it is claimed that the event did not happen, but this can be challenged by non-governmental organisations such as Amnesty International, investigative reporters in the media, and victims who might provide direct evidence that the abuses have indeed taken place.

> In stage 2, the state tries to redefine what has taken place as being something other than a human rights abuse. For example, they might argue that it was an 'accident' or 'collateral damage'.

> In stage 3, the state may argue that, even if the human rights abuse has taken place, it was justified, perhaps because it prevented even greater harm. For example, it could be justified in order to maintain national security or to prevent terrorist outrages. The state therefore uses what Matza and Sykes (1961) called "techniques of neutralisation" to make the abuses seem more acceptable, without challenging the idea that human rights abuses are normally wrong (see Chapter 1).

Cohen gives a number of examples of how states, and individuals acting on behalf of states, can use techniques of neutralisation in response to accusations about violations of human rights.

> *Denial of responsibility* – In this case individuals may say that they are simply following orders or they are just a small cog in a large machine and it was their superiors who were responsible. (This technique was often used by defendants who worked in Nazi concentration camps.)

> *Denial of injury* – This might suggest that the victims didn't really suffer, for example, because they are used to violence.

> *Denial of victim* – An example here is saying that the victims are terrorists and therefore the state is the real victim (for example, when torture is used against suspects).

> *Condemnation of the condemners* – This often involves accusing those making judgements of being hypocrites or of behaving worse themselves. Sometimes it involves accusing the accusers of being racist; for example, Israelis saying they are condemned for abuses because their accusers are anti-Semitic (racist against Jews), or Arab nations claiming the accusations are a result of Islamophobia.

> *Appeal to higher loyalties* – In this case the abuses are seen as justified in pursuit of a greater good such as a "sacred mission ... the revolution ... the purity of Islam, Zionism, the defence of the free world or state security".

Cohen concludes that ordinary people will go along with human rights abuses in certain circumstances, which make it easier to use these techniques of neutralisation. He calls these "crimes of obedience" and suggests they are more likely to occur where the following three conditions are met.

1. There is authorisation by the state, which its citizens are persuaded they have a duty to obey.

2. There is routinisation of the abuse so that it becomes a normal part of a day's work or "no big deal" once the individual has overcome their initial moral repugnance towards action such as killing, torturing, raping and so on.

3. There has been dehumanisation of the people who are regarded as the 'enemy' so that a normal morality does not apply. They become "animals, monsters ... sub-human" and are not therefore part of the person's "shared moral universe".

Cohen's work provides an extra dimension to understanding why human rights abuses continue to occur and remain common despite international agreements, the existence of an international criminal court and legal codes within nation states themselves that often prohibit these abuses. This can apply even in liberal democracies (such as the USA, the UK, and Israel) and not just in undemocratic states. However, more optimistically, Cohen acknowledges that not everyone accepts human rights abuses and state crime and there are usually at least some voices opposing them.

Is there any evidence that the UK ever commits human rights abuses? Do you think you are more aware of abuses by foreign governments than your own, and if so, why do you think this is?

Explanations of state crime and human rights abuses

Stanley Cohen's work helps to explain why state crime involving abuses of human rights is possible even in societies where it is condemned and regarded as immoral. However, it doesn't explain why human rights are abused in the first place. Green and Ward (2012) argue that there are two main approaches to this.

1. The integrated theory of state crime suggests that, in order to occur, crime needs a motive, the opportunity to commit the crime and a failure of any control mechanisms that might prevent it taking place. This theory was developed by Kramer and Michalowski (1990, cited in Green and Ward 2012) and they give the example of the 1986 space shuttle *Challenger* disaster, which was allowed to blast off and subsequently explode despite known faults, because NASA did not want to lose face and put the programme at risk by cancelling the launch.

2. The obedience approach is exemplified by Cohen's ideas on crimes of obedience (see above), which in turn derived from a famous experiment by Milgram in which people were willing to administer what they believed were severe electric shocks to other people.

Green and Ward suggest that both these approaches need to be combined into a **dialectical** approach in order fully to understand state crime, so that both the structural and individual factors are understood. In explaining state crimes committed by supporters of Colonel Gaddafi, the leader of Libya, before he was overthrown in 2011, Green and Ward argue that this was structurally what they call a Sultanistic regime. Power was maintained through a combination of rewards and fear. In this sort of regime individuals will tend to follow orders and commit human rights abuses because they fear for themselves or fear their family might be murdered or tortured.

UNDERSTAND THE CONCEPT

A **dialectic** occurs when opposite views clash but out of this conflict a new viewpoint emerges that combines elements of both.

The Gaddafi regime continued to commit abuses in order to maintain power and so avoid being put on trial and punished for previous crimes.

Of course state crime does not always involve abuse of human rights or the use of violence. Quite often it involves corruption that furthers the interests of both the state and some outside group. This type of crime can be seen as motivated by a desire for power and/or financial reward. Such crime is common in what Weber called "patrimonial states", which Green and Ward define as states based on "personal and economic ties between rulers and subordinates". Examples include Equatorial Guinea, where the state was largely financed by proceeds from smuggling, carried out with the tacit support of the state and Liberia, under its leader Charles Taylor and based on theft of public funds by the leadership. Although such blatant corruption is not so apparent in Western democracies **clientism** is quite common (Green and Ward, 2012)**.**

UNDERSTAND THE CONCEPT

Clientism involves the corrupt granting of favours by politicians in return for financial or political support and is motivated by the desire to retain power. Green and Ward suggest that clientism is well-established in countries such as Italy, Ireland and Greece. In the UK the granting of peerages to people who help fund the governing political party is a form of clientism.

However, as the discussion of human rights abuses shows, state crime cannot just be explained in terms of individual motivation. Structural factors to do with how the state and political parties work are also important.

CONCLUSIONS

Generalised theories of state crime and human rights abuses do not take full account of the varied circumstances in which these types of crime take place. Furthermore, it is sometimes difficult to determine whether actions by the state should be regarded as crimes or not, or whether they could be seen as legitimate self-defence. Nevertheless, given the extraordinary harm that can be done through such crime, they are certainly at least as important a topic for sociological study as street crime. The ideas discussed in this chapter represent at least a beginning in developing an understanding of state offences or 'gross violations of human rights' that have taken place.

CHECK YOUR UNDERSTANDING

1. What is meant by 'globalisation'?

2. Explain what is meant by a 'glocal system'.

3. Explain what is meant by 'gross violations of human rights'.

4. Identify three types of crime that have grown as a result of globalisation and explain why they are linked to this process.

5. Which theory of state crime is based on the idea that people will simply follow orders?

6. Explain the difference between primary environmental crimes and environmental law-breaking.

7. Briefly explain why capitalism might be seen as a cause of green crime.

8. Outline the ways in which Cohen argues that human rights abuses are often denied.

9. Outline two criticisms of the idea that state crimes should only be defined as acts against national laws.

10. Identify two weaknesses of Beck's idea of risk society.

11. Evaluate the view that traditional criminology (such as structural and subcultural theory) is inadequate because it ignores globalisation, state crime and green crime.

TAKE IT FURTHER

Use the search facility of *The Guardian* (http://www.theguardian.com/uk) to identify one story about green crime, and one about the abuse of human rights by a state. Summarise key details about the story. Analyse the two offences by answering the following questions.

1. What were the effects of the two crimes?

2. Which do you consider more serious and why?

3. Analyse what the most plausible explanations are for the two offences.

4. Identify links that can be made between the stories and sociological theories of state and green crime.

1.10 CRIME AND THE MEDIA

INTRODUCING THE DEBATE

It is hard to avoid crime in the media, whether you are reading a newspaper or a book, watching the evening news, or having a night at the cinema, but how accurate is the media portrayal of crime and what effects does it have? It probably won't surprise you that certain types of crime and certain types of criminal get more coverage than others, but why is this? Does this partial, and possibly distorted, reporting and representation actually make crime worse or could it have the opposite effect? There have been many claims that the media cause more crime in general, and violent crime in particular, but sociologists have questioned whether this is really the case and, in the process, have produced more subtle understandings of the ways in which media and audiences interact and the variety of effects that media coverage of crime might have.

MEDIA CONTENT AND CRIME

Research on content

Crime is a mainstay of the media, particularly the mass media such as newspapers, television, radio and cinema. It is extensively covered in both fiction and non-fiction, although most of the sociological research in this area is concentrated on coverage in non-fiction, particularly in the news.

Chris Greer and Robert Reiner (2012) have reviewed studies of newspaper coverage of crime. They found an increase in coverage over recent decades and a tendency for tabloid newspapers to devote a higher proportion of their space to crimes than more serious newspapers do. For example, a study by Williams and Dickinson (1993) found that over 30 per cent of coverage of *The Sun* but just 5 per cent of *the Guardian* was devoted to crime. Research into TV news has found that the proportion of stories about crime is closer to the tabloid figure than that for 'quality' newspapers, and police and crime dramas are very common on TV and in the cinema.

Greer and Reiner's review of a range of studies suggest that violent offences are far more likely to feature in the news than is property crime, and street crimes are given more prominence than white-collar, corporate and state crimes. Homicide is the most widely reported type of crime, making up about a third of all reports. Over time, research suggests that sex crime has taken up an increasing proportion of reporting (Soothill and Walby, 1991) and this is still true, particularly with the recent emphasis on the historical sexual abuse of children.

Offenders in the media

The specific characteristics of crimes and offenders also affect the likelihood of crime being reported. For example, research into the coverage of homicide in three national British newspapers over a four-year period (Peelo *et al.*, 2004) found that only 40 per cent of homicides were reported nationally (though most are mentioned in local papers). Homicides were more likely to get coverage if they involved sexual motives, monetary gain, revenge or jealousy, whereas domestic quarrels that got out of hand and resulted in death got little attention. The nature of the victim was also important. The murder of children, women, and famous or high-status individuals got the most coverage, although the murder of babies generally was not widely reported.

Tim Newburn (2013) suggests that coverage can be somewhat misleading. Compared to the official picture of crime in statistics, news reports are distorted because they:

> disproportionately feature higher-status and older offenders (most offenders are young)

> exaggerate the proportion of crimes that are cleared up by the police (partly because many of the stories are given to the media by the police)

> exaggerate the risk of being a victim of crime, especially for white people and people from high-status backgrounds

> tend to present crime as a series of individual incidents and have little coverage of patterns, trends or underlying causes.

In addition, evidence suggests, media coverage gives the impression that serious violent and sexual crimes are much more common than they are. For example, the homicide rate has declined significantly in Britain over recent decades (Holborn, 2005) but it would be hard to tell this from the reporting of crime in the media.

The selection of content: pluralism

One of the most influential theories of why some stories about crime – but not others – are selected for inclusion in the media is **pluralism**.

UNDERSTAND THE CONCEPT

Pluralists believe that Western democratic societies are run in the interests of the population and are genuinely democratic. However, there are a variety of groups in society with different interests and who want different things. Governments balance these different interests so that each group in society gets some of what it wants, but nobody gets their own way all the time.

From a pluralist point of view, the content of the media reflects the interests of the public. Commercial media rely upon audiences to generate income, so if they run stories or put on entertainment that is not popular, then the audience will go elsewhere and the media organisation will be forced to change, or risk going out of business. However, minority audiences can be catered for in parts of the media that do not require a mass audience to be viable, for example, in magazine publishing and on internet sites. Parts of the media, such as the BBC in the UK, are not commercial organisations. The BBC is funded through the license fee, but it is required by law to give balanced coverage of news events, to avoid political bias and to give alternative viewpoints on controversial issues. For all of these reasons, pluralists believe that the media provide fair, balanced and diverse content in response to demand from the public.

Yvonne Jewkes (2015) notes that pluralists also argue that with the advent of the internet and social media, the media have become even more diverse, so that almost anyone can create media content (for example, through a blog or Twitter). Jewkes suggests that this creates the potential for individuals or groups to challenge government and other establishment views of crime.

However, Jewkes argues, in reality most crime coverage and crime-based entertainment in the popular media continue to "provide homogenised versions of reality that avoid controversy and preserve the status quo. Consequently ignorance among audiences is perpetuated, and the labelling, stereotyping and criminalization of certain groups (often along lines of class, race and gender) persists". There are a number of reasons for this, some of which are dealt with in the next section.

The selection of content: news values

The selection of news content is partly shaped by the idea of news values – journalists' sense of what makes a 'good story'. Yvonne Jewkes (2015) believes there are specific news values applying to crime stories. These include the involvement of sex; celebrity or high-status people and children as offenders or victims; proximity (for example, crime in Britain gets more coverage than crime in distant and culturally dissimilar countries); the involvement of violence; the availability of graphic imagery; and stories that fit a conservative ideology. They also need to reach a high threshold for drama or perceived importance; to be relatively simple (simplicity) and not be too complex to understand; to involve the idea that modern life is filled with risk; and to be explicable in terms of the behaviour of individuals (individualism) and not, for example, organisations. Very unexpected crimes are newsworthy, but predictability can make them worth reporting, too, if they fit a theme that is often covered (for example, violent attacks on the elderly). (For more discussion of news values, including the Marxist perspective, see Topic 4, Chapter 4.)

Crime and the construction of reality

Many sociologists argue that reporting does not just convey 'facts' but instead 'manufactures' or socially constructs a picture of reality. For example, Stan Cohen and Jock Young (1973) argued that there was a manufactured picture of society present in crime news. Robert Reiner (2007) illustrates this view by arguing that three main trends are evident in crime coverage.

1. It accentuates the negative: "Bad news increasingly drives out the good."

2. It highlights victim culture: audiences are positioned to identify with the victims, whose innocence and vulnerability is emphasised. Issues such as the rehabilitation of offenders very rarely feature in coverage, while the need to punish offenders is strongly emphasised.

3. Law and order solutions ("forceful solutions and tough punishments") are portrayed as the only way to tackle a frightening and out-of-control crime wave that requires an ever greater emphasis on security.

Reiner sees these trends as reflecting an increasing emphasis upon individualism in a consumer-oriented capitalist society. In this type of society, everyone is seen as consuming as an individual, and they therefore offend as individuals and are victimised as individuals. More collective aspects of social life get little media coverage. For example, there is little discussion of the role of welfare in preventing crime, or of rehabilitation or poverty reduction in controlling crime, as alternatives to increased security. Media coverage therefore tends to assume that the existing social order is essentially conforming, secure and fair, but that it is constantly under threat from deviant outsiders, and this justifies strict control of these threats. This type of coverage supports a conservative ideology. It is seen as vital to preserve the status quo, to protect it from risk and threats from dangerous forces from outside mainstream society, without reducing inequality or challenging the position of the powerful.

Evaluation of media coverage of crime

Writers such as Cohen and Young, and Reiner, tend to portray media coverage of crime as being very consistent. However, they are aware that not all coverage fits the model they put forward. For example, Reiner accepts that there is increased coverage of police corruption. They nevertheless still underestimate the extent of coverage of crime that reflects badly on those in power. Consider coverage of corporate crime (for example, the BP Deepwater Horizon disaster) and state crime (for example, torture by UK and US military in Iraq). Documentaries on TV and discussion in 'serious newspapers' do comment on police racism, misconduct by bankers or the effects of pollution on climate change. Thus there is some variety in media coverage of crime, even if the dominant coverage does tend to support a consensual view of society.

To what extent do you think crime in TV cop programmes gives a similar picture of crime, criminals and law enforcement to that described by Reiner?

THE EFFECTS OF THE MEDIA ON CRIME

Types of effect

There have been numerous suggestions about the possible effects of the media on crime. Many of these have suggested that the mass media might be criminogenic – that is, new media may make crime worse, and may even produce some new means of committing crime. In particular, the internet "is feared as facilitating all sorts of offences, from fraud, identity theft, child pornography and grooming children for sex, to organising transnational crime and terrorism," (Greer and Reiner, 2012). There is certainly evidence of large numbers of crimes being committed through the internet. In 2015, for the first time, the Home Office published statistics estimating online crime alongside other crime statistics. As a result the total amount of recorded crime doubled, with 5.1 million estimated incidents of online fraud and 2.5 million other cybercrimes (Travis, 2015). Greer and Reiner (2012) identify the following possible criminogenic effects of the media.

› *Opportunity* – The media may have an indirect effect by encouraging consumption, which in turn creates more targets for crime, since more consumer goods are available to steal, including mobile phones, laptops and tablets.

› *Absence of controls* – Some commentators argue that the mass media undermine social control. This includes both external controls (controls outside the individual such as the threat of punishment) and internal controls (controls inside individuals such as a sense of guilt). For example, the media sometimes portray the criminal justice system as corrupt, racist or incompetent, thereby discouraging cooperation with the police and reducing the effectiveness of the system for finding and punishing offenders. More significantly, the media may undermine internal controls by portraying crime and criminals as glamorous. This may lead to disinhibition (where individuals feel less constrained to conform to laws and norms) or desensitisation (where people come to think of criminal behaviour as normal and therefore as not being particularly immoral).

› *Means* – Individuals may learn techniques of crime from the media and commit crimes that they would not otherwise have had the expertise or imagination to carry out. For example, the video game Grand Theft Auto actually asks players to act out the role of a criminal.

› *Motive* – Media coverage can contribute to the motives that may drive criminals to commit crime. The media may stimulate desire for material goods, which can increase the sense of relative deprivation (see the discussion of Lea and Young in Chapter 4) or produce anomie (see the discussion of Merton in Chapter 1), thus leading those who can't afford them to turn to crime. It has often been argued that the media may be a form of **social learning** whereby certain individuals may imitate what they see on the media and commit 'copycat' crime. This effect is often seen as being associated with violent and sexual crime. It is sometimes claimed that this leads to arousal, which motivates crime by encouraging potential offenders to seek excitement and stimulation in risky and sometimes illegal ways.

UNDERSTAND THE CONCEPT

Social learning theory suggests that behaviour is shaped through observing the behaviour of others in the environments in which we spend our time. It could be from other people or from media content that we observe, and there is a tendency to copy or imitate behaviour that we witness.

All the above claims suggest ways in which the media encourage crime. Suggest some ways in which it might discourage it.

Evidence about the media as a direct cause of crime

There has been a great deal of research to consider whether the media do directly cause offending. Much of this research has been based on the hypodermic-syringe model (see Topic 4, Chapter 7) of media effects. This assumes behaviour can be directly caused by viewing media content, whether through a copycat effect, disinhibition or desensitisation. It is assumed that some people, particularly those who might be prone to criminal and deviant behaviour for social or psychological reasons, will act out what they witness in the media in real life. This view was supported in famous experiments conducted as Stamford University (Bandura *et al.*, 1961) in which some children were shown cartoons or films with violent content, while a control group were not shown them. The two groups were then observed playing with bobo dolls (large dolls which could be hit but wouldn't fall over). The former group were found to be twice as aggressive towards the dolls as the latter group were.

This research has been criticised for taking place in an unnatural laboratory setting, for ignoring longer-term effects and for neglecting the possibility that the children were influenced by those conducting the experiment. There have been numerous attempts to repeat this experiment and to conduct other research to measure the extent of imitative violence, but with varied results. Some have shown no effects; some have shown some effects but not always as strong as those in the original experiments.

Some research has shown an association between a tendency to watch violent television media and the likelihood of being convicted of violent offences (for example, Wartella, 1995, cited in Greer and Reiner, 2012). However, Newburn (2013) points out that perhaps greater numbers of violent people choose to watch more violent programmes or films and the content itself has no independent effect on their behaviour.

Furthermore, as Greer and Reiner (2012) note, a number of other factors or variables may influence whether there are effects from witnessing violence or other types of crime. These include "whether violence or deviance was seen as justified, punished, or rewarded, whether the viewers identified with the perpetrator, the variable vulnerability or susceptibility of the viewer, and so on" (Greer and Reiner, 2012).

Another major problem with the idea that exposure to violence in the media has a direct effect on behaviour is the assumption that all members of the audience will interpret the message in the same way. Yvonne Jewkes (2015) stresses that media (such as films, TV programmes or news reports) are open to multiple interpretations. Different audience members will take different messages from the same items. For example, some might see the criminal as a hero and copy their behaviour, while others might see them as evil and be repulsed by their behaviour. Because of this, audience members can act in completely different ways in response to media messages.

As a result, most sociologists of the media argue that any effects of media coverage of violence (and other types of antisocial and criminal behaviour) are likely to interact with a wide range of other factors, rather than simply having a direct effect. The hypodermic-syringe model is therefore very misleading.

OTHER EFFECTS OF MEDIA COVERAGE

The media have been held responsible not only for directly causing crime, but also for causing a range of other effects.

One suggestion is that they may contribute to criminal behaviour, and also affect whether certain acts are criminalised or labelled as deviant. Greer and Reiner (2012) suggest that the media can play an important role in helping to create new types of offence (by highlighting and causing public concern about particular types of behaviour, such as internet bullying or trolling). They can also "change perceptions and sensitivities, leading to fluctuations in apparent crime". For example, a documentary about Thames Valley police in 1982 led to changes in the way allegations of rape were dealt with by the police, helping to increase the willingness of victims to report this type of offence.

There has been considerable research into the effects of the media in causing fear of crime. Generally, it has been assumed that the media cause an irrational and exaggerated fear of crime, by publicising the most serious, atypical and violent offences. For example, Schlesinger and Tumber (1992, cited in Newburn 2013) found that those who were also most likely to read

tabloid newspapers were also most likely to be afraid of becoming a victim of crime, particularly of violent crime. Like other research, though, this raises the question of cause and effect: perhaps those most afraid of crime are most prone to reading about it.

Many Marxist and critical criminologists (for example, Hall *et al.*, see Chapter 3) do believe that the media cause an exaggerated and irrational fear of crime. However left realists (see Chapter 4) argue that the fear is often rational and grounded in real risks.

Jewkes (2015) points out that fear of crime is difficult to measure; fear resulting from high-profile crimes may be short-lived. Other factors, not least direct experience of crime, interact with media coverage and influence the strength of fear. Jewkes suggests therefore that the effects of media coverage tend to be both more long-term and more subtle. The pervasiveness of crime coverage helps to create a climate in which there is widespread support for an emphasis on law and order, along with acceptance of high levels of surveillance and harsh punishment for offenders. Coverage also helps to create a political context in which rehabilitation is seen as being 'soft' on crime and therefore dangerous. Furthermore, crime coverage can act as a diversion from other political issues (such as inequality) and promote a conservative ideology in which anyone who is not 'respectable and middle class' is seen as a potential threat to the consensus in society.

It is, however, very difficult to isolate the effect of crime coverage from other possible causes of prevailing public opinions on crime and law and order.

Suggest why it is so difficult to isolate the effects of media coverage from other possible causes of crime and fear of crime.

Moral panics

The idea of moral panics neatly combines a number of issues relating to media effects, including the possibility that the media are criminogenic, that they can affect the labelling or criminalisation of actions and people, that they can cause fear of crime, and that they can have political effects.

The view that moral panics can be criminogenic is closely connected to the idea of **deviancy amplification**.

UNDERSTAND THE CONCEPT

Deviancy amplification is the process by which deviance (including crime) becomes more frequent and/or more serious as a result of being discovered and labelled as deviant, particularly through the mass media. This process is particularly emphasised by labelling theorists, who believe labelling can lead to the development of a self-concept that makes you more prone to acting up to the label that you have been given, for example, a deviant or criminal label.

The idea of moral panics both overlaps with and complements the concept of deviancy amplification. The term was first used in Britain by Stan Cohen in a classic study (1972) of two youth subcultures of the 1960s – 'mods' and 'rockers'. Cohen showed how the media, for lack of other stories, built up these two groups into folk devils (groups that are widely seen as a threat to society). The effect of the media coverage was to make young people categorise themselves as either mods or rockers. This actually helped to create the violence that took place between them, which also confirmed them as troublemakers in the eyes of the public. It also sensitised the police to look out for trouble at the times and places where clashes were expected (seaside resorts on bank holidays); as a result, even minor incidents led to the arrest of offenders and the possible amplification of their deviance.

Moral panics can die down quickly or continue for some time; they can be linked to deep-seated fears in society about what is believed be an underlying decline in people's willingness to act in legal and moral ways. They can also generate increased fear of crime or be used to justify a clamp-down on groups regarded as folk devils. They can help to create a consensus that certain groups should be seen as a threat and to define moral boundaries about what are acceptable and unacceptable behaviours.

The concept of moral panic and of the role of the media in helping to create them has been widely used in sociology since Cohen's original British work – though perhaps the best adaptation of this is the study by Hall and colleagues of 'mugging' (see Chapter 3).

In recent years there have, arguably, been many bouts of media concern about a wide range of groups including:

> paedophiles

> asylum seekers

> antisocial youths

> Islamic terrorists

> dangerous dogs (and their owners)

> knife crime

> benefits 'scroungers'.

Moral panics: an outdated idea?

The idea of moral panics has been criticised since its original formulation. For example, McRobbie and Thornton (1995) argued that the concept of 'moral panics', as described by Cohen in the 1960s, is outdated and has to be seen in the context of the development of the media and the growing sophistication of the audiences. Whereas moral panics would scapegoat a group and create 'folk devils' in the 1960s, today there is no single, unambiguous response to a panic, as there are many different viewpoints and values in society.

Furthermore, moral panics are much less likely to start in society as a result of media coverage, because it is far less clear today what is unambiguously 'bad'. Society is too fragmented and culturally pluralistic. There is also the danger of rebound for people starting moral panics. For example, politicians who start a campaign about family values, scrounging or drugs have to be very careful about their own backgrounds. (A number of MPs were portrayed as 'scroungers' when MPs' expenses claims were made public in 2009. The claims included one for a duck house and one for cleaning a moat.)

Thornton also argues that the idea of moral panics has entered everyday language and media reporting itself, so that it is now an overused concept lacking a clear meaning. However Cohen himself (Cohen 2002, cited in Newburn 2013) argues that it remains a useful concept because it allows insights into power in society and particularly "the way we are manipulated into taking some things too seriously and other things not seriously enough" (for more detailed discussion of moral panics, see Topic 4, Chapter 4).

Identify a recent issue in relation to crime that has been covered in a way that could be seen as a moral panic. Consider whether the example supports the views of those who support the use of the term 'moral panic' or those who criticise it.

FOCUS ON SKILLS: CRIME AND VIOLENCE IN FILMS

Jewkes believes that crime films have changed dramatically since films such as The Italian Job in the 1960s.

According to Yvonne Jewkes (2015), crime films have changed significantly in the last 35 years. In the 1960s most crime films were about "art burglars, jewel thieves, bank robbers or Cold War spies. Crime was cool and the movies of this period were filled with dashing heroes, dastardly villains and glamorous but merely decorative women". This changed in the 1970s when there was increased fear about violent crime, particularly in the United States, and people were worried about criminals breaking into their homes and committing acts of violence against them. Films about "maverick police officers" whose individual brilliance solved cases and kept citizens safe became common and this type of theme continued in the 1980s. However, by then the maverick cop had "morphed into an all action hero with the excessive physique to make up for his limited dialogue". Typical of this genre was *RoboCop* (1987). The 1990s were characterised by the serial killer movie

(for example, *Silence of the Lambs* (1991) and *American Psycho* (1991). The most recent trends have seen crime films "dominated by technology, terrorists, military combat, environmental disasters and other apocalyptic global threats to the human race".

Jewkes says that "To an extent, this is simply art imitating life and life imitating art. Stories in the cinema run parallel to stories in the news and film-makers are merely picking up on the issues that audiences will recognise and which will provoke the strongest reactions". News values are similar to the values of film producers; for example, violent and sexual crime feature heavily in both. Crime films can also tie into anxieties caused by moral panics, such as children in peril, having been left alone by their parents (*Home Alone*, 1990) or at risk from paedophile neighbours (*The Lovely Bones*, 2009).

Questions

1. **Outline** how the portrayal of crime in movies has changed since the 1960s.

2. **Explain** what Jewkes mean by "art imitating life and life imitating art"? Give an example of how "art imitates life" in crime movies.

3. **Identify** any example, not mentioned here, of a film that seems to tie in with a moral panic about crime.

4. **Analyse** ways in which changes in films might reflect increased fear of crime.

5. **Analyse** the ways in which news values are similar to the characteristics of many films about crime.

6. **Evaluate** the view that the depiction of crime in movies reinforces news coverage of crime.

Positive effects of the media on crime

The discussion of media effects above has very largely concentrated on negative effects of the media in relation to crime. Most sociologists who have considered the issue have also concentrated on the negative effects, but there are also a number of ways in which the effects could be positive.

› Media coverage of crime could help to solve crimes or locate suspects, through programmes such as *Crimewatch,* or through encouraging awareness of risks from serious crimes such as terrorism.

› It can alert the public to the dangers of different types of crime, such as various types of fraud or identity theft, allowing them to take precautions to prevent themselves becoming victims. Social media and local radio channels can be used to alert local populations to particular risks from criminality.

› Media campaigns and public awareness of crime derived from the campaigns could also put pressure on the government or police to take action, for example, over domestic violence and tax evasion by corporations.

> In Durkheim's terms (See Chapter 1), the media can help to define moral boundaries and identify what is acceptable and unacceptable behaviour in a particular society. For example, the media have helped to establish what is and is not acceptable in terms of cyber-bullying.

> In a general sense, the media can deter crime by highlighting the punishment of criminals. Most crime fictions ends with offenders being punished for their crimes.

CONCLUSIONS

Despite the ways in which the media can be seen as having a positive effect in relation to crime, most sociologists emphasise the negative. Whether positive or negative, the effects should not be exaggerated. The research evidence is contradictory about the direct effects of the media on causing crime. The contents of the media are diverse and are not interpreted the same way by all audience members. The media are just one factor amongst many that have an effect on crime.

CHECK YOUR UNDERSTANDING

1. What is meant by 'news values'?

2. Explain what is meant by 'social learning theory'.

3. Explain what is meant by 'deviancy amplification'.

4. Identify three possible effects of media coverage of crime other than actually causing crime itself.

5. Which theory of crime suggests that fear of crime is rational and not just a product of media coverage?

6. Explain two differences between the picture of crime given in media coverage and in official crime statistics.

7. Explain briefly, two effects, relating to crime, of the growth of new media.

8. Outline two criticisms of the idea of moral panics.

9. Identify two weaknesses of the hypodermic-syringe model of media effects.

10. Evaluate the view that the media has more influence on ideas about crime than it has on crime itself.

TAKE IT FURTHER

Watch an episode of *Crimewatch UK* (either a current episode, live or on TV playback, or via an online streaming service). Conduct content analysis of:

i. the type of crimes mentioned

ii. the characteristics of victims

iii. the characteristics of offenders (they might be in photo-fits, CCTV footage, 'wanted' photographs or discussions of previous cases).

1. How representative do you think the cases, victims and offenders are of crime in general?

2. What effects might coverage have in terms of causing crime, preventing crime, helping to clear up crime, contributing to moral panics, shaping public views of the police and affecting fear of crime?

3. Does *Crimewatch* promote conservative ideology? Justify your answer.

Note: For a detailed sociological analysis of *Crimewatch*, read Yvonne Jewkes's book *Media and Crime*, 2010 (London, Sage).

1.11 CONTROL, PREVENTION AND PUNISHMENT; VICTIMS; THE CRIMINAL JUSTICE SYSTEM

LEARNING OBJECTIVES

> Demonstrate knowledge and understanding of theories of crime prevention, theories of punishment, the criminal justice system and patterns of criminal victimisation (AO1).

> Apply sociological theories to the role of punishment in contemporary British society (AO2).

> Analyse and evaluate competing theories of crime prevention, theories of punishment, the criminal justice system and patterns of criminal victimisation (AO3).

INTRODUCING THE DEBATE

This section focuses on responses to criminality rather than criminality itself. The main focus is on social control: the way that society (particularly British society) attempts to limit the extent of crime and deviance by preventing it in the first place, or by using punishment to control offenders or deter future offending. The criminal justice system, which includes prison, plays a crucial role in crime control, so the workings of criminal justice are considered in some detail. However, informal social control is crucial too and this is therefore integrated into the discussion. In the final part of the chapter we look at victims rather than offenders and consider the relationship between victims and offenders, as well as the way that the criminal justice system responds to offenders. These issues are seen rather differently by those with more left-wing and right-wing views and these differences will be explored in this chapter.

SITUATIONAL CRIME PREVENTION AND COMMUNITY SAFETY

Crime prevention can be directed at the specific point at which potential criminals and potential victims or targets come together, at the environment in particular localities (which might encourage or discourage crime) or at the underlying social and community causes that might motivate crime. These three approaches are known as 'situational crime prevention', 'environmental crime prevention' and 'social and community crime prevention' respectively.

Situational crime prevention

Crime prevention, in the formal sense, developed from the writings of a group of criminologists, such as Clarke (1992) who focused on what has become known as 'situational crime prevention'.

Clarke based his ideas on the deceptively simple notion that people will commit offences when the costs of offending (economic or social) are less than the benefits obtained from offending. However, unlike most previous criminologists who argued that the way to make the costs outweigh the benefits was to increase punishment, he argued that it was better to make it more difficult to steal or attack someone. The theory on which this is based, known as 'rational choice theory', assumes that individuals are calculating in pursuit of their own interests. Rather than acting morally or emotionally, individuals simply weigh up whether, on balance, potential offending carries small enough risks and high enough rewards to make it worthwhile. Felson and Clarke (1998) argued that theft was more likely where attractive targets (for example, high-value, easily saleable and portable goods) were accessible (easy to steal without being witnessed) with a good chance of escaping without detection. A contemporary example of an attractive and accessible target is the mobile phone (although counter-measures to make it more difficult to use stolen phones reduce their attractiveness). Counter-measures to make it more difficult to carry out crimes are referred to as 'target hardening'.

To some extent this approach was based upon the ideas of Oscar Newman (1972) who had introduced the idea of 'defensible space', arguing that, by changing the design of streets and housing estates, it was possible to make them safer. The more private space that people had control over, which burglars would have to cross, the less likely burglaries were. Similarly, assaults were less likely in private spaces outside the home than in shared or public space. Low-rise housing with private gardens was seen as safer than high-rise flats with shared entrances and corridors.

Felson (2002) and Cohen and Felson (1999) developed these ideas further by introducing routine activities theory. This stated that crime tended to occur when a likely offender and a likely target came together at a particular time and place where there was no 'capable guardian' to stop or discourage offending. Capable guardians can include anybody who might intervene or report crime, including police officers, community support officers, watchful neighbours, or the parents of local teenagers (so both informal and formal social control were important in this theory). Routine activity theory suggested that opportunity was crucial in explaining most crime. Much crime, particularly low-level crime, such as theft, was not carefully planned but was opportunistic and took place when potential offenders came across easy and relatively risk-free opportunities to profit from crime in the course of their daily routines.

Situational crime prevention was attractive to policy-makers because, potentially, it allowed crime to be reduced, using relatively cheap and simple initiatives that made targets less accessible or attractive, or that increased the monitoring of behaviour. These initiatives could take the form of 'target hardening', which involved ensuring that it was more difficult to steal things. Target hardening could be achieved by, for example, improving locks on houses and windows, the use of car alarms and anti-theft devices, and by marking valuable objects with owners' postcodes in indelible ink so that, should they be stolen, they would be more difficult to sell. At the same time, areas with high levels of crime could have physical changes made in order to limit the opportunities for crime or benefits from it. One of the most widely used preventative measures taken, in line with this approach, is the use of CCTV cameras. There are estimated to be more than 25 million CCTV cameras in the world and more than one million in the UK (Watson, 2008).

Felson gives the Port Authority bus terminal building in New York as an example of the application of these theories. The building, in Manhattan, was notorious as a site of crime before it was redesigned in the 1980s. Some homeless people lived in parts of the building, and they took drugs, had sex, fought with other groups and, in some cases, died there. There were enormous numbers of thefts, assaults, drug trades and incidents of prostitution. According to Felson this was partly because of the design of the building. It provided too much public space for criminals to move into, with poor sight lines so it was difficult to observe criminal activity, and there were quiet corners where it was relatively easy for people to sleep and live. A number of physical changes were made to the facility, to reduce crime. Better lighting was installed so there were no dark corners, graffiti resistant stone walls were introduced, toilet attendants were employed and smaller sinks were fitted in the toilets (making it more difficult for the homeless to wash in them). Similar techniques have become commonplace in cities around the world. For example, obstacles are used to prevent skateboarding, flat surfaces or benches where the homeless might sleep are made uncomfortable and unsuitable for sleeping, and dark corners are lit up. The purpose of such changes is to **design out crime**.

UNDERSTAND THE CONCEPT

The idea of **designing out crime** suggests that urban planning, and the design of buildings and products, can make it so difficult or risky to commit crime that crime can be significantly reduced, regardless of more conventional approaches to tackling crime (such as improved policing or targeting the underlying motives and causes of criminality).

Evaluation of situational crime prevention

Critics of this approach, such as Garland (2001), have argued that it ignores the causes of crime, dealing only with limiting its extent and impact. It takes no account of factors such as inequality and relative deprivation in causing crime. The idea that crime is based on rational calculation is challenged by several other theories. For example, Jack Katz (1988) emphasises the emotional factors behind crime. Lyng (1990) emphasises excitement and risk-taking, and subcultural theory (see Chapter 1) emphasises factors such as the pursuit of status in peer groups.

Furthermore, situational crime prevention is limited to tackling opportunistic street crime. There are many categories of crime that it does not address at all. These include domestic crime (including sexual and violent crime), white-collar crime, state crime, corporate crime and green crime. Crawford and Evans (2013) point out that some critics see it as undesirable because it creates a divided 'fortress society' that reduces civil liberties, increases surveillance and harms some of the most vulnerable (for example, denying even the homeless a relatively comfortable place to sleep).

Furthermore, critics argue, it leads to crime displacement, in which the nature of crime is changed, but the total amount of crime is not reduced. For example, CCTV may limit crime in areas where it is introduced, but crime may rise in neighbouring areas. According to Hakim and

Renert (cited in Crawford and Evans, 2013) displacement can be spatial (the offence is committed in a different place); temporal (it is committed at a different time); tactical (a safer method is used); target-based (a different victim is chosen) or functional (a different and less risky type of crime is substituted). If displacement occurs, then the total amount of crime might stay the same or even increase. While people might commit less serious crimes because of displacement, they might also commit more serious ones. A recent study of Malaga in Spain (Cerezo, 2013) found that the installation of CCTV cameras led to only a very small reduction in crime on the streets where they were installed (a 1.9 per cent reduction according to police figures and 3.6 per cent according to self-report studies). Furthermore, there was clear evidence of displacement as crime rose in some nearby streets that did not have cameras installed.

Despite these criticisms, there is also research that suggests that situational crime prevention can work, at least in certain circumstances, for certain types of crime. For example, better car security has resulted in fewer thefts of cars, although there may have been some displacement to older, less secure cars from newer ones (Newburn, 2013). The redesign of a market in Birmingham, so that stalls were further apart, was linked to a 70 per cent fall in purse thefts over two years (Poyner and Webb, 1997, cited in Newburn). However, these types of measure are likely to be more effective when combined with other types of approach to crime prevention.

Do you think the problem of displacement makes it pointless to introduce situational crime prevention measures?

Environmental crime prevention

Environmental crime prevention focuses on a combination of formal and informal social control measures as a way of preventing crime, or at least preventing areas from deteriorating so that crime becomes endemic. It is based on the influential ideas of the right realist criminologists Wilson and Kelling (1982) and their broken windows theory (right realism is discussed in detail in Chapter 4). This community-based approach argued that high levels of crime occur in neighbourhoods where there has previously been a loss of formal and informal social control over minor acts of antisocial behaviour. They claim that if low-level antisocial behaviour (such as littering, noise, or youths blocking the pavements) can be prevented, then the escalation to more serious criminal acts can be stopped. The analogy that Wilson and Kelling use is of an abandoned building. They point out that once one window gets broken, then all the windows soon get smashed. So if the breaking of the first window is prevented, all the rest are more likely to be saved. In a similar way, stopping the minor crimes makes the major ones much less likely to happen.

The policy implications were that the government should find ways of strengthening local communities to 'fight' crime and antisocial behaviour. The ways chosen have been to introduce policies of zero tolerance and the targeting of relatively minor antisocial behaviour. The idea is to nip offending in the bud, so that an area does not get out of hand, with offenders enjoying free rein in streets where the law-abiding are too fearful to venture out, particularly at night.

In the UK this has involved giving the police and local authorities the powers to issue antisocial behaviour orders (ASBOs), curfews, street drinking bans and dispersal orders (where by you must leave a designated area of a town if a police officer tells you to do so). However, exactly what is to be targeted as 'antisocial behaviour' depends upon local crime and local perceptions. In the USA, Bill Bratton (New York Police Department Commissioner 1994–96) explicitly adopted zero-tolerance policing.

According to Wilson and Kelling, actions by the police to reinforce informal social control can be made more effective by programmes of environmental improvement that make an area less intimidating and more amenable for honest citizens, who can then exercise informal controls.

Another policy adopted in certain US states is the 'three strikes' rule, which allows lengthy imprisonment of offenders who commit three serious offences. The idea behind this is to incapacitate the worst offenders – if they are imprisoned they cannot victimise the public.

Evaluation of environmental crime prevention

There is some overlap between situational crime prevention and environmental crime prevention, but in the latter there is less emphasis on the physical environment and much more emphasis on the role of formal social control through the police. As discussed elsewhere (see Chapter 4), there is limited evidence to support the broken windows theory and some sociologists regard investment in localities, such as providing better leisure facilities or more economic opportunities, as much more effective than zero-tolerance policing in cutting crime. Advocates of situational crime prevention argue that there are simply not enough police to patrol areas that are at risk of deterioration to make a direct impact, and it is unaffordable to employ many more

police to enforce all minor laws (Clarke and Hough, 1984, cited in Reiner, 2015). In the UK, for example, a typical police officer on patrol might have to cover an area with 7,500 houses, making frequent interventions in response to minor offences impractical. Reiner (2015) argues that the police have been more effective in the UK by targeting prolific offenders or 'hot spots', rather than trying to clamp down on antisocial behaviour.

In the UK, ASBOs were widely used under Labour governments until 2010, although their use was beginning to decline by the end of their time in power (Newburn). They were less popular with the Conservative-led Coalition between 2010 and 2015, and were replaced by Criminal Behaviour Orders (CRIMBOs) and Crime Prevention Injunctions (CPIs) in 2012. The Conservative government since 2015 has made more use of PNDs (penalty notices for disorder, which can require on-the-spot fines). However, it also considerably reduced police budgets. The resulting fall in the number of police and community support officers has made it even more difficult to carry out zero-tolerance policing. Despite this, overall crime has continued to fall (Reiner, 2015) suggesting that broader factors may have more influence on crime rates than just policing policies and environmental crime prevention.

Which sociological theories of crime imply that providing more opportunities for disadvantaged young people might be better at reducing crime than zero-tolerance policing?

Social and community crime prevention

Since the mid-1990s a rather broader approach, involving social and community crime reduction (or community safety), has developed. This approach argues that, alongside crime prevention measures, there needs to be a focus on individual offenders and the social context that encourages them to commit crime. This involves:

1. *Intervention* – It is important to identify the groups most at risk of committing crime and to put into action forms of intervention to limit their offending.

2. *Community* – It is also important to involve the local community in combating crime.

Intervention

As described in Situational crime prevention (pages 94–5), policy-makers have taken less interest in the broader causes of crime, and more in what works to stop offending. The concept of '**what works**' has come to dominate thinking on offending in Britain and the USA.

UNDERSTAND THE CONCEPT

The **'what works'** approach suggests that theorising about the causes of crime is less effective than learning lessons from detailed empirical research and from policy initiatives that reveal how crime can be cut. It is pragmatic rather than theoretical.

In Britain, the work of the Cambridge School of Criminology – for example, Farrington (1995) and West and Farrington (1973) – was particularly influential. They took a positivistic research approach, using longitudinal studies in which they compared the backgrounds of young males who offended with those of young males without any police record. They found clear differences between the two groups. Some of the main 'risk factors' linked to early offending were:

> low income and poor housing

> living in run-down neighbourhoods

> a high degree of 'impulsiveness and hyperactivity'

> low school attainment

> poor parental supervision with harsh and erratic discipline

> parental conflict and lone-parent families.

The implications of the research were that intervening to change some or all of these risk factors would lead to lower levels of crime. For example, Farrington (2007) advocated "risk-focused prevention", which included the following components:

> skills training for individuals to counteract impulsiveness

> parental education about the importance of monitoring children and being consistent in disciplining them

> parental training to help parents become more effective

> pre-school programmes to help with attainment

> multiple-component programmes that tackled all of the above.

The importance of pre-school programmes was underlined by the claimed success of the Perry Pre-School Project in Michigan, USA, which can be seen as using an approach in line with left realist thinking. Two groups of African American children aged 3 or 4 from disadvantaged backgrounds were chosen. One group was given pre-school educational support and the family received weekly visits from social workers. The results

were dramatic. By the age of 27, members of the group that received the interventions had half the number of arrests of the group that did not receive interventions.

This risk-based model of offending has been – and still is – extremely influential. Governments in both the USA and Britain decided, where possible, to identify the children at risk of offending and to put various interventions in place. Indeed, it has been argued (Rodgers 2008) that many of the social policy interventions that have been introduced since 1998 – to combat poverty, to redevelop run-down housing estates, to improve schools and to support families – can be seen to be as much anticrime measures as social policies to improve the lives of the poor and marginalised. A recent example is the Troubled Families initiative in the UK, in which the government targeted intervention with the 'most troubled' 120,000 families, in an attempt to increase opportunities for the children and reduce overall crime (See Book 1, Topic 4, Chapter 1).

Community

Running parallel to the risk-based interventions are other policies that emphasise the importance of drawing upon the influence of the community. One example was the Boston Gun Initiative (started in 1996 in Boston USA), aimed at reducing gang gun crime, in which gang outreach workers, community groups and churches offered services to gang members, to entice them away from crime (Newburn). They also reinforced a strong police message, that gun crime would not be tolerated and would be dealt with harshly. Another widely used, community-based intervention has been the use of mentors for young people deemed at risk of becoming criminals.

Evaluation of social and community crime reduction

These approaches have been criticised for doing little to deal with the underlying and deep-seated causes of crime. While they tackle some immediate problems for the disadvantaged, sociologists such as Ian Taylor (1999) argue that structural inequalities in capitalist society are at the root of the problem, rather than dysfunctional families or lack of educational opportunities. Social and community crime reduction programmes can thus be seen as blaming the victims of inequality (or their families and communities) rather than the structure of society itself. These approaches also tend to target working-class crime in inner cities and, like other forms of prevention, do not address white-collar, corporate, and green crime. They have been seen as attempts to increase and spread the power of the state, rather than simply as benign attempts to prevent crime (for example, see the discussions of Garland, Foucault and Cohen in this chapter).

PUNISHMENT, CONTROL AND THE CRIMINAL JUSTICE SYSTEM

If crime cannot be prevented, then the most obvious response is to punish it. But how can punishment be justified? A number of suggestions have been put forward to explain why punishment might be necessary and/or desirable. These have been summarised by Peter Joyce (2006).

Deterrence

The idea behind deterrence is that bringing offenders to justice and publicly punishing them will encourage potential offenders to think twice before committing crime and, hopefully, will result in them deciding that crime is not worth the risks involved. Deterrence can be individual (aimed at particular offenders) or general (aimed at the public at large). For example, individual deterrence might involve having an indeterminate sentence so that the offender has to show that they have reformed before they will be released from prison. General deterrence might entail having very harsh punishment so that people will be scared to offend. Deterrence assumes that the offenders and potential offenders adopt a rational approach towards offending and will be swayed by the severity of punishment as well as the risks of being caught.

Incapacitation

The idea of incapacitation is aimed at protecting potential victims by stopping the offender from repeating their behaviour. Often this involves imprisonment since, unless the offender escapes, this prevents them from committing offences against society at large. Other forms of incapacitation include capital punishment (permanent and complete incapacitation), or restrictions on offenders' freedom outside prison (for example, preventing them from accessing the internet or placing them under house arrest).

Rehabilitation

Like incapacitation and deterrence, rehabilitation is aimed at preventing the offender from committing crimes in the future, but in this case by changing their attitudes, values and behaviour. Examples of techniques used for rehabilitation include psychological and educational programmes in prisons, and some forms of community punishment (such as doing community work) that are designed to encourage a desire to conform to society's predominant norms and values. The rehabilitation approach avoids the use of coercion against offenders but is not always effective.

Retribution

This is not aimed at preventing future crimes, but at society giving a fair and just punishment to offenders who have done harm to others. Joyce says that this is "akin to vengeance" and he says that from this viewpoint "criminals are punished because they deserve it". Retribution may be seen as satisfying the desire of victims, their families and friends, or society at large, for what is seen as 'justice'. Joyce suggests that the idea of retribution is often closely tied to the idea of deterrence.

Not everyone agrees that retribution is morally justified. Some believe that an emphasis on retribution can lead to a spiral of harm, in which the victims of retribution try to inflict punishment on those who have punished them. However, most societies place at least some emphasis upon retribution in their formal and informal systems of social control. An additional function of punishment is restitution. This means that the offender should restore or make amends of the wrong that they have done. In some cases, this may mean giving back the thing that has been lost or making a financial payment to the victim. In some societies, the concept of 'blood money' has been and is a form of restitution. It is worth noting where this takes place given Durkheim's views, which are explained below.

FUNCTIONALIST AND MARXIST PERSPECTIVES ON PUNISHMENT

As well as having perspectives on criminality (see Chapters 1 and 3), functionalists and Marxists also have perspectives on punishment.

Emile Durkheim: the nature and purpose of punishment

Emile Durkheim (1893) developed a functionalist view of the development of the law in society. He argues that the nature of the legal system is related to the division of labour. The division of labour describes the way in which work is divided up between individuals and social groups. In simple societies before industrialisation there was little division of labour, that is, there were few specialist jobs. For this reason, most members of society were very similar to one another and the societies were held together by what he called "mechanical solidarity". Because of their similarity, individuals in the societies have similar moral values and their shared beliefs (or collective conscience) were very strong. People who broke these beliefs were seen as committing seriously deviant acts that offended the whole of society; therefore law was based upon the principle of retribution (retributive justice). Offenders were severely punished and generally all members of society accepted and supported strong punishment.

In modern industrial societies, a more specialist division of labour developed – people took on specialist roles (such as doctor, bricklayer, chef or computer programmer). Because of the differences between roles, people tend to be somewhat different from one another unlike in societies based upon organic solidarity. Everyone relies upon each other to carry out their specialist roles and people are interdependent but, because of the differences between people, the collective conscience is not so strong. According to Durkheim, restitutive justice developed in this type of society. Restitutive justice involves trying to return society to the state it was in before the illegal behaviour took place, for example, by compensating those who have been the victim of dishonesty, by returning the money they have lost. In such societies, Durkheim saw the law as being less vindictive and punishments being less severe, but they still expressed a degree of moral outrage, because wrongdoers still offend the collective conscience, albeit a collective conscience that is weaker than in pre-industrial societies.

Durkheim also saw punishment as having an important role in boundary maintenance. That is, it helped to establish and then reinforce exactly what is acceptable and unacceptable in a particular society at a particular time.

Durkheim has been criticised for assuming that there is a consensus, or collective conscience, in society, whereas in reality there may be different views on what is moral or immoral, just or unjust. Durkheim has nothing to say about the role of power and inequality in shaping the law: issues that are certainly of interest to Marxists.

Marxist perspectives on the law and punishment

Marxists argue that the law is not a product of the shared interest and shared beliefs of all members of society, but rather a product of the interests and beliefs of the ruling class. Although Marx himself wrote little about punishment, the early Marxists Rusche and Kirchheimer (cited in Newburn) outlined a Marxist approach to understanding punishment. They argued that systems of punishment corresponded to the particular economic system in which they developed. They identified three eras in which different systems of punishment were dominant.

> In the early Middle Ages, the main punishments involved religious penance and fines. Workers were in high demand so it did not benefit landowners to imprison potential workers for long periods of time or to execute them.

> In the later Middle Ages, brutal punishment became the norm and capital punishment was used quite widely. The rich now needed to control the poor and

unemployed, who were a potential threat to social order, and the legal system was used to do this.

> By the 17th century there was a shortage of labour and it was in this period that the prison developed, partly because prisoners could be used to produce goods cheaply, thereby helping to plug the gap in the number of workers available to the ruling class.

Marxists such as Melossi and Pavarin (cited in Newburn) have argued that the prison developed in the 17th century in order to impose discipline on workers, a discipline similar to that required in factories. Workers who would not submit to factory discipline could always be sent to prison for a time, so they learned to be a subservient labour force that could be successfully exploited by the ruling class.

Contemporary Marxists such as Reiman (2009) see punishment as a way of enforcing laws that simply protect the private property of the wealthy. While the law and its application might be seen as neutral and fair to all, in reality it is the working class who are far more likely to suffer punishment, even if their behaviour does less harm to society than the behaviour of rich individuals or capitalist corporations (see Chapter 8).

Marxist views on the law and punishment have been subject to considerable criticism (see Chapter 3) and they do seem to provide a rather simplistic explanation of the relationship between punishment and power in society. For example, they take little account of gender or ethnicity, and it is clearly the case that an occasional capitalist finds themselves on the wrong side of the law and ends up being imprisoned or punished in other ways.

How might other sociological theories such as feminism and neo-Marxism see the operation of law and punishment in contemporary societies?

Social control and the criminal justice system

Michel Foucault and *The Birth of the Prison*
A number of writers other than Marxists and functionalists have developed general theoretical approaches to looking at punishment and its relationship to the criminal justice system. One of the most influential theorists is Michel Foucault, whose writings have highlighted the role of prisons in the criminal justice system. In *Discipline and Punish* (1977), Foucault describes the execution of the murderer Damiens in Paris in 1757: "Damiens was placed on a scaffold and had pieces of flesh torn from him using red-hot pincers. Lead, oil, resin and

wax were melted and poured onto his flesh wounds. Next, his four limbs were attached to horses so that he could be torn apart. Still alive, his head and trunk were tied to a stake and set alight."

By the end of the 18th-century this type of extreme public punishment no longer took place and instead punishment was hidden away, with people imprisoned or, if they were beyond redemption, being executed behind closed doors, using swift methods such as the guillotine or hanging. Foucault claims that these changes represented a shift in the way punishment was administered, away from trying to inflict pain on the body, towards trying to change the soul, or more generally change behaviour. This represented a move away from what he calls "sovereign power" (when the King or Queen had control over people's bodies and were entitled to inflict pain on them as a public spectacle) towards disciplinary power, in which power was extended to control behaviour through monitoring or surveillance.

Disciplinary power was first perfected in prisons. A new prison design was developed by Jeremy Bentham and the design was called the 'panopticon'. In a panoptic prison, jailers could watch what prisoners were doing in the different wings of the prison from a central tower that allowed them to see into all the wings. Because of the lighting, however, prisoners could not see whether they were being watched at any particular time so they had to assume that they were being monitored and ensure that their behaviour was appropriate. Prisoners had to self-monitor their behaviour so, in effect, they disciplined themselves.

Foucault argues that disciplinary power became increasingly characteristic of modern society, in which individuals were encouraged to monitor their own behaviour. He saw it as typical of numerous settings, including barracks, schools and factories. Since Foucault was writing, this has been extended further with the widespread use of CCTV, which operates in a similar way to the panopticon prison. Citizens can never be sure whether they are being monitored by CCTV camera but, because of that possibility, they tend to monitor their own behaviour and to conform. Computers also allow the monitoring of many other types of behaviour, and surveillance by the state is widely seen as becoming more extensive and invasive of people's privacy.

Foucault does not see the authorities and the state as monopolising power. Attempts to impose power over populations through surveillance will always meet with a degree of resistance. To Foucault, power is everywhere and is closely tied to knowledge, so it can never be monopolised by a single authority.

Foucault recognises that attempts to control the public by surveillance will always meet with resistance.

Foucault's ideas on surveillance and disciplinary power have been highly influential but they are somewhat contradictory. On the one hand he emphasises the increasing control of centralised state authorities, but on the other hand he insists that people always have the ability to resist this control. Furthermore, some contemporary sociologists argue there has been a shift back towards more direct use of force by the state to control populations.

David Garland and *The Culture of Control*
Another writer who has examined the changing nature of punishment and control in contemporary societies is David Garland (2001). In *The Culture of Control*, he argues that in the USA (and to some extent in the UK) since the 1970s there has been a shift in attitudes towards punishment. He suggests that the traditional method of dealing with crime was penal welfarism, in which the criminal justice system did not just try to catch and punish offenders but also to rehabilitate them, so that they could be reintegrated into society. However, in the later decades of the 20th century, penal welfarism was regarded as failing. In what he calls "late modernity", personal freedom increased but social control was weakened and the economy became more volatile, making life less predictable and more uncertain. Penal welfarism was no longer seen as adequate to contain crime and reassure the public and there was a shift to a new 'culture of control' and a 'punitive state'. The culture of control is as much about reassuring communities as it is about directly dealing with crime and it has three main elements, all of which are aimed at changing society's attitudes to crime and the role of the state in combating offending.

1. *The adaptive response* leads governments to identify certain groups that represent a danger to society and then to intervene in their lives at an early stage, in order to change the way these risk groups think and act.

2. *The expressive strategy* represents a complete change in the way that crime is viewed by society. Increasingly, Garland argues, crime has come to be seen as central to politics and to winning elections. It is more important to politicians to create the perception that crime is declining than to effect any real changes in the levels of crime. Therefore, much government intervention centres on changing perceptions, rather than effective measures to limit crime.

3. *The sovereign state strategy*, which is part of the expressive strategy, emphasises the state taking back direct control through punitive sanctions. A new culture of control is the use of mass imprisonment – that is, imprisoning very large numbers of people. The population is reassured, because it believes that offenders are safely behind bars. The main emphasis is on incapacitation.

Evaluation

Garland's view highlights the importance of 'law and order' politics, in which being tough on crime is seen as important for politicians seeking election or re-election. It certainly seems to be reflected in rising prison populations, both in the UK and USA. It also seems to be reflected in the very high levels of imprisonment of African Americans. Alice Goffman (2014) sees mass imprisonment being used against young Black men as a new form of racial oppression – she points out that 30 per cent of Black men in the USA without college-level education are sentenced to prison by the time they are 30.

Other theorists, however, have provided alternative interpretations of the direction states have taken in producing social control. For example, Stanley Cohen (1985) argues that social control mechanisms have become somewhat diffused and do not just involve the criminal justice system. He argues that the state increasingly uses other professions alongside the criminal justice system. For example, psychiatrists and psychologists are increasingly employed to deal with deviant behaviour. Social workers, teachers, doctors and educational psychologists are all involved in classifying people and identifying 'abnormalities' such as hyperactivity, mental illness or drug use that can justify state intervention.

Cohen's arguments reflect those put forward by Foucault (1977) who argued that the ways of thinking put forward by professional groups (or **discourses**) can contribute to the exercise of power over populations. Certainly, these ideas do draw attention to the much wider exercise of state power beyond the criminal justice system itself.

UNDERSTAND THE CONCEPT

Foucault defined **discourse** as a system of thoughts composed of ideas, attitudes, beliefs and practices that construct, shape and dominate the worlds to which they refer. For example, scientists conduct experiments in particular ways because they have learned from their training, textbooks and peers – the discourse – that there is a 'right' way to do science.

So, if misbehaviour in class is seen in terms of the discourse of hyperactivity, it suggests medical or psychological intervention and gives power to doctors or educational psychologists and turns attention away from any failure by the school to provide stimulating learning for pupils.

In what ways might the dominant discourses about law and order take attention away from underlying social problems that could cause crime?

PRISONS, PUNISHMENT AND COMMUNITY SENTENCES IN CONTEMPORARY BRITAIN

In November 2015 the prison population in England and Wales stood at 87,729, of whom fewer than 4,000 were female (Ministry of Justice, 2015). In comparison, the prison population was just 45,000 in 1990–93 and 62,000 in 1997 (Morgan and Leibling, 2007). Writing in 2012, Liebling and Crewe pointed out that the UK had the highest rate of imprisonment in Western Europe, at 154 per 100,000, although well behind the USA (743 per 100,000).

Part of the justification for the expansion of prisons is the idea that 'prison works' – that it is effective in reducing crime. American right realist social scientists such as Charles Murray (see Chapter 4) believe that prison is effective simply because of incapacitation (taking frequent offenders off the streets), though it also has an important deterrent effect on those who have never experienced prison but fear being sent there, and therefore refrain from criminality. As Liebling and Crewe point out, prisons are also potentially effective at preventing reoffending (or recidivism) by deterring those released from prison (assuming that they have found the experience of prison unpleasant) from future offending. Recidivism is also deterred by reforming offenders through treatment programmes (for example, for alcoholism or impulsive violence) and by resocialising them into less deviant and criminal behaviour.

Liebling and Crewe (2012) however suggest some flaws in these arguments:

> First, far from discouraging crime, the experience of prison might make recidivism more likely when prisoners are released. A period in prison tends to disrupt the prisoner's family life and employment, and stable family life and regular work might discourage criminality.

> Second, in line with labelling theory, the stigmatisation associated with having served a prison sentence could make reoffending more likely, as inmates develop a self-concept in which they see themselves as criminals.

> Third, prisons are environments in which prisoners may be socialised into the values of other criminals, rather than into those of the law-abiding. They can be schools for crime, where people learn both justifications for criminality and criminal techniques.

These reasons may well help to account for high rates of reoffending by ex-prisoners: about 50 per cent are reconvicted of an offence within two years and 35 per cent end up back in prison over the same period (Liebling and Crewe).

These figures can be compared with the number of those who reoffend following community penalties rather than prison sentences. Community penalties can include being required to do unpaid work (community service), undergoing therapy or treatment programmes of various kinds (for example, drug treatment) or being subject to curfews or exclusion from certain places (Raynor, 2012). Probation service staff are responsible for monitoring most of these community penalties. Although reconviction rates vary for different community penalty schemes, overall they are not dissimilar to those for ex-prisoners: a little over 50 per cent. A large number of variables affect reconviction rates, and it is hard to isolate the effects of punishment itself; some criminologists suggest that 'current environment' is much more important than previous punishment (Liebling and Crewe). Nevertheless, it seems that the very expensive policy of large-scale imprisonment is not good value for money, at least for less serious offenders.

Liebling and Crewe therefore suggest that the idea that prison works in purely instrumental terms (it reduces crime) is to miss the point and that the true function of imprisonment may be to "express public sentiment, articulate moral boundaries, and shore up the power of the state" (Liebling and Crewe).

Explain what you think Liebling and Crewe mean by their description of the 'true function of imprisonment'? How far do you agree with their analysis?

FOCUS ON SKILLS: CRIME AND JUSTICE – THE DOG THAT DIDN'T BARK

David Cameron visits a social enterprise scheme in Manchester, set up to reduce crime in the area.

Why, come the 2015 election campaign, was the issue of crime and justice the dog that didn't bark?

At least part of the answer to this lies in the significant degree of consensus that existed between the major parties – at least if their manifestos are to be believed.

For David Garland, writing in 2001 in his much-quoted book, *The Culture of Control*, convergence around a populist agenda represented a narrowing of the debate. Crime policy was no longer the preserve of experts, but a vehicle for the expression of collective anger and righteous demands for retribution. In an increasingly hot political climate, penal measures had to be seen to be "tough, smart and popular with the public".

Labour promised "safer communities", while the Conservatives committed themselves – no less unexceptionably – to "fighting crime and standing up for victims". With the Liberal Democrats outlining their policies under the headline "secure communities" – it was left to UKIP to prioritise removing the "EU's handcuffs" so that foreign criminals could be kept at bay (or rapidly deported) and the Greens to draw attention to the social causes of crime.

Behind the headlines, a more complex picture emerges. So, for example, the former Coalition partners could agree that crime had fallen over the past five years, but not by how much: 20% according to the Conservatives, half that if the Liberal Democrats were to be believed. Labour, on the other hand, claimed that violent crime had increased. UKIP – perhaps rather predictably – blamed an increase in petty criminality on "gangs of thieves, pickpockets and scammers" from overseas.

Only the Liberal Democrats and the Greens were prepared to contemplate fewer people going to prison, although commitments to rehabilitation through education and productive work were common to all parties.

On prison numbers, on victims of crime, drugs, violence against women and hate crime – there was little for the parties to fall out about. Where policies differed, they did so only in their emphasis and at the margins.

Alternatives to the careful orthodoxies of the main contenders were evident in the bold defence of liberal values mounted by the Liberal Democrats, in the Greens' determination to set the problem of crime in the wider context of unemployment, poor education, mental ill-health and social inequality and in UKIP's insistence that Britain's European Union-inspired inability to control its borders was at the root of the crime problem.

Toughness, popularity and an apparently unshakeable belief in the criminal law and the institutions of criminal justice as instruments of social policy continued to hold sway.

Whether the dog finds its voice in 2020 with Jeremy Corbyn in charge of the Labour kennel remains to be seen.

Dixon (2015), discoversociety.org

Questions

1. **Understand.** What do you think is meant by the phrase "convergence around a populist agenda represented a narrowing of the debate"?

2. **Analyse.** Give examples of how some smaller parties tried to widen the debate in 2015 beyond a culture of control.

3. **Identify**, using what you have learned from your study of the sociology of crime and deviance, some issues that in your view should have been introduced to widen the debate even further.

4. **Evaluate** the view that political debate about crime is so narrow in the UK that penal welfarism is unlikely to return in the foreseeable future.

VICTIMS OF CRIME

Defining victims

In 1985 the United Nations defined victims of crime as "persons who, individually or collectively, have suffered harm, including physical or mental injury, emotional suffering, economic loss or substantial impairment of their fundamental rights through acts or omissions that are in violation of criminal laws" (cited in Newburn).

This common-sense definition has however been criticised by Rob Watts, Judith Bessant and Richard Hill (2008), who argue that the difference between a victim and an offender is not always clear-cut. For example, in assault cases that involve a fight between two people it is not always clear who initiated the violence, or whether either party was justified in using violence in self-defence. Nils Christie (1986, cited in Newburn) argues that there is a stereotype of the victim as somebody who is weak and virtuous, but this is not always the case – indeed offenders are themselves more likely to become victims of crimes than other people.

Positivist victimology

According to Miers (1989 cited in Newburn 2007), positivist victimology is mainly concerned with factors affecting rates of victimisation as measured in statistical studies, a focus on violent crime and a concern with how victims might contribute to making the crime happen (known as 'victim precipitation').

As Carolyn Hoyle (2012) points out, the identification of patterns of victimisation has been made possible through the increasing use of victimisation surveys, which are able to supplement official statistics in understanding victims in a number of ways.

> First they can identify victims who have not had their associated offences reported to the police.

> Second, it is possible to do in-depth and local studies and collect far more details about victims than are recorded by police statistics.

> Third, it is possible to produce data on the experience of crime and the effects that victimisation has had on those involved.

Hoyle notes that the British Crime Survey (now replaced by the Crime Survey for England and Wales) has found that the chances of being a victim of most of the crimes measured in the survey are linked to a number of factors.

> *Age* – Young men aged between 16 and 24 have the highest rates of victimisation, particularly of violence.

> *Sex* – Men are generally at higher risk of victimisation than women, except in cases of domestic and sexual violence (See Chapter 7 for a detailed discussion of gender and victimisation).

> *Routine activities* – People who regularly go out at night and consume alcohol are more likely to become victims of crimes than those who do not.

> *Ethnicity* – There is substantial evidence that minority ethnic groups are more likely than the white majority in the UK to be victims of many types of crimes (see Chapter 6).

> *Location* – Crime rates vary substantially between different towns and cities and specific urban areas, and they are often linked to income and social class: poorer, predominantly working-class areas having higher rates of crimes than richer predominantly middle-class areas.

Some vulnerable groups, such as those with learning difficulties or mental health problems, are particularly likely to be victims of crime, according to a study by the mental health charity MIND (2007 cited in Hoyle, 2012).

Patterns of victimisation vary with specific types of crime. For example, the vast majority of sexual assaults and rapes are committed against women by men, and rapes are usually carried out by people who are known to victims rather than by strangers.

Victim precipitation and victim proneness

More controversial aspects of positivist victimology are the ideas of victim proneness and victim precipitation. Victim proneness states that people become victims because of their own characteristics. Thus the old, the young and the mentally ill are said to be victims of crime because they are easy targets for the offender. As early as 1948, Von Hentig (cited in Newburn, 2007) claimed that homicide could be

victim-precipitated, that is, the person who was killed may have started the violence that resulted in their own death. His study of 588 homicides in Philadelphia found that over a quarter could be seen as victim-precipitated. However, this idea has been widely criticised for blaming the victim. The idea of victim precipitation has been particularly criticised in rape cases where, in some court proceedings, judges have occasionally deemed young women wearing revealing clothes partly to blame for their victimisation.

Although it is widely accepted that victims should not be held responsible for the actions of those who victimise them, it is now acknowledged by many criminologists that victims may play some part in the processes that result in crime occurring, and without victims, many crimes would not exist (a theft or assault has to have a victim). This was recognised by left realists such as Lea and Young (1993) in their idea of the square of crime, which highlights the importance of victims in defining acts as criminal and choosing whether or not to report them (see Chapter 4).

Evaluation of positivist victimology

Positivist victimology has been important in identifying broad patterns of crime and for highlighting the problem of victimisation in certain types of offence. For example, it has been useful in highlighting the frequency of sexual assaults on women and the need to tackle sexual and violent offences against female victims within the home. The study of ethnic-minority victims also exposed problems of institutional racism within the police (see Chapter 6). Positivist victimology has, furthermore, highlighted the tendency for the criminal justice system to ignore victims, and has shown that being the victim of even relatively minor offences can be traumatic and potentially debilitating (for example, it can make people feel unsafe within their own home, or make them too afraid of crime to go out at night).

However, positivist victimisation is not without its flaws.

> First, it relies upon data from victimisation surveys that may not be entirely reliable (see Chapter 5).

> Second, some positivist victimology has tended to blame the victim for the offending (for example, Von Hentig).

> Third, it tends to be limited in the range of crimes considered. Crime surveys do not produce statistics on the victims of white-collar, corporate or state crime. Watts *et al.* therefore argue that positivist victimology, because of its reliance upon victimisation surveys, is limited to victims 'that the state chooses to "see"'.

> Fourth, the idea of victim-precipitation carries the serious risk that the victim will not just be seen as involved in the events leading up to the crime, but will be seen as jointly responsible with the offender for causing the crime.

Alternative approaches to victimology have been developed partly because of these criticisms.

Radical and critical victimology

These approaches are critical of positivist criminology for taking a too narrow and uncritical view of victims.

Radical victimology

Radical victimologists suggest that more account needs to be taken of structural factors in understanding victimisation. Thus positivist victimologists might reveal that women and the working class are more likely to be victims of particular types of crime, but they don't tell you why this is the case, because they don't discuss the structure of society. For example, positivists just concentrate on statistical patterns and do not consider the role of patriarchy in crimes of domestic violence. Similarly, left realists such as Lea and Young suggest that any understanding of victimisation needs to consider the way that socially structured class inequality is made worse by the high rates of victimisation among people living in poor inner cities areas (see Chapter 4). For example, using an in-depth local victim survey in Islington, Jones, Maclean and Young (1986) found that the poor are often subject to repeat victimisation, that being a victim was more problematical for the poor, because they often lacked both insurance and the means to protect themselves by designing out further crime. Furthermore, their relationship with the police was often uneasy, which made it difficult for them to report crime. In some cases the police even stereotyped poor victims as troublemakers who were little better than offenders.

Radical victimologists also argue that this area of criminology needs to take account of the victims of crimes other than street crime, including the victims of white-collar, corporate and state crime. For example, Kuazlarich *et al.* (2001, cited in Walklate, 2007) argue that victims of state crime are often found among the poor and vulnerable in a society and, because the offender is the state, they have little chance of getting compensation or seeing the offender prosecuted

Radical victimology has been criticised by critical criminologists for not going far enough in distancing itself from positivist criminology. For example, Walklate suggests that it is sometimes still reliant upon limited and unreliable crime surveys (as was the case with left realist approaches) and upon legal definitions of crime.

Critical victimology

Critical victimologists, according to Walklate, question the whole category of 'the victim', just as labelling theory questioned the idea that the criminal was a clear-cut category. Walklate suggests that the state has a crucial

role in defining who is, and who is not, defined as a victim of crime, and the state often acts in its own interests. For example, states rarely define those who are killed by states themselves (such as the civilians who are killed in military action by armed forces) or people who die in police custody. This approach argues that victims should not just be seen as the unfortunate and passive recipients of harm done to them by criminals, but should be seen more positively as individuals with rights that should be honoured. Critical victimology tends to concentrate on the harm done to relatively powerless people whose rights are violated by the more powerful. This approach has been popular among feminist writers who see women as the victims of oppressive patriarchal practices. Writers such as Walklate accept that political campaigning by victim groups can make some difference and can lead to rights being acknowledged, better enforced or extended (for example, the right of women to be free of domestic violence or sexual harassment at work), but they believe society still largely operates in the interests of the powerful.

Tombs and Whyte (2010) emphasise that many people are victims of corporate crime, often without even realising it. They quote figures that suggest that more than a third of the US population have been victims of fraud or theft and that more than 20,000 people in the UK are killed annually by air pollution. Yet corporations try to ensure that their actions are not prohibited by law or, if they are, that the laws are not enforced. Furthermore, they use their power to obscure the nature and extent of corporate crime (for example, through lobbying governments) so that members of the public do not see themselves as victims. From this point of view, victim surveys are of little use for counting, understanding or explaining victimhood, since many people are not aware that they have been victims of corporate crime. Furthermore, they believe that corporate crime is more common and more damaging than street crime.

Evaluation of radical and critical victimology

Despite the differences between positivist, radical and critical victimology, these approaches to victims may not be mutually exclusive and they could complement one another. Positivist criminology does help to identify the extent of victimisation in different groups, and left realism, a type of radical victimology, highlights the social construction of offenders and victims through the square of crime. The crucial extra issue highlighted by critical victimology is the role of power in defining victims.

Are victims equally important in understanding all types of crime? If not, what makes a difference?

CHECK YOUR UNDERSTANDING

1. What is meant by a 'community penalty'?

2. Explain what is meant by 'discourse'.

3. Explain what is meant by 'restitutive justice'.

4. Identify four possible purposes of punishment.

5. Which perspective from victimology argues that social structures are crucial in understanding victimisation?

6. Explain two differences between situational and environmental crime prevention.

7. Briefly explain two aspects of the culture of control described by Garland.

8. Outline two criticisms of Durkheim's view of the law.

9. Identify two weaknesses of positivist victimology.

10. Evaluate the effectiveness of situational crime prevention.

TAKE IT FURTHER

Imagine you have been appointed Home Secretary. Draw up a 12-point plan for tackling crime in England and Wales, including policies concerned with preventing crime, sentencing, policing and prisons, and briefly justify each measure. What is your underlying approach? How might some criminologists criticise your policies? Compare your policies with those of other students in your class and debate the merits of the different proposals.

APPLY YOUR LEARNING

1. Outline **two** ways in which the criminal justice system may be institutionally racist.   [4 marks]

2. Outline **three** reasons why the mass media's portrayal of crime could lead to an increase in offending.   [6 marks]

3. Read **Item A** below and answer the question that follows.

ITEM A

Punishment

Punishment is often seen as a useful way of dealing with crime because it deters reoffending and first time offenders who don't want to risk punishment such as imprisonment. Imprisonment is sometimes seen as a particularly effective form of punishment because it incapacitates offenders, stopping them from committing crimes by keeping them behind bars. Both community penalties and imprisonment can provide opportunities to rehabilitate offenders so they become law-abiding, but punishment Is not always the most effective way of reducing crime.

Applying material from **Item A**, analyse **two** reasons why punishment might not be effective in reducing crime.   [10 marks]

4. Read **Item B** below and answer the question that follows.

ITEM B

Capitalism and crime

Some Marxist sociologists argue that crime and deviance are caused by the way in which the capitalist system encourages greed and selfishness amongst all members of society, thereby causing criminality in all social classes. They also argue that the law and criminal justice are biased against those from lower classes, ensuring that the actions of the rich are not defined as criminal, whereas those of the lower classes are often treated as criminal.

Applying material from **Item B** and your knowledge, evaluate the usefulness of Marxist approaches in understanding crime and deviance.   [30 marks]

You can find example answers and accompanying teacher's comments for this topic at www.collins.co.uk/AQAAlevelSociology. Please note that these example answers and teacher's comments have not been approved by AQA.

2 THEORY AND METHODS

AQA specification Candidates should examine:	Chapters
Quantitative and qualitative methods of research; research design.	Book 1, Topic 2, Chapter 3 (pages 109–116) covers qualitative research. Book 1, Topic 2, Chapter 4 (pages 117–127) covers qualitative research. Book 1, Topic 2, Chapters 1 (pages 89–96) and 2 cover research design.
Sources of data, including questionnaires; interviews; participant and non-participant observation; experiments; documents and official statistics.	Book 1, Topic 2, Chapters 4 to 6 (pages 117–151) cover these in detail.
The distinction between primary and secondary data, and between quantitative and qualitative data.	This is introduced in Book 1, Topic 2, Chapter 1 (pages 89–96). More detailed discussions are found in Book 1, Topic 2, Chapters 3 to 6 (pages 109–151).
The relationship between positivism, interpretivism and sociological methods; the nature of 'social facts'.	This is covered in Book 1, Topic 2, Chapter 2 (pages 97–108), but related discussions can also be found in Book 1, Topic 2, Chapter 1 (pages 89–96).
The theoretical, practical and ethical considerations influencing choice of topic, choice of method(s) and the conduct of research.	Book 1, Topic 2, Chapter 2 (pages 97–108) covers this.
Consensus, conflict, structural and social action theories.	These theories are covered in Book 2, Topic 2, Chapters 1 and 2 (pages 109–133).
The concepts of modernity and post-modernity in relation to sociological theory.	Book 2, Topic 2, Chapter 3 (pages 134–142) covers this.
The nature of science and the extent to which Sociology can be regarded as scientific.	This is covered in Book 2, Topic 2, Chapter 5 (pages 153–161).
The relationship between theory and methods.	This is covered in Book 2, Topic 2, Chapter 4 (pages 143–152).
Debates about subjectivity, objectivity and value freedom.	These debates are covered in Book 2, Topic 2, Chapter 6 (pages 162–168).
The relationship between sociology and social policy.	This is covered in Book 2, Topic 2, Chapter 7 (pages 169–177).

2.1 CONSENSUS, CONFLICT, STRUCTURAL, SOCIAL ACTION AND INTERPRETIVIST THEORIES

LEARNING OBJECTIVES

> Demonstrate knowledge and understanding of Marxist, functionalist, social action and interpretivist perspectives in sociology (AO1).

> Apply these perspectives to contemporary British society (AO2).

> Analyse the differences between structural and social action or interpretivist perspectives (AO3).

> Evaluate Marxist, functionalist, social action and interpretivist perspectives in sociology (AO3).

INTRODUCING THE DEBATE

Throughout your sociology course you have encountered a range of sociological perspectives applied to particular topic areas. You will have become accustomed to thinking about the strengths and weaknesses of these theories in the context of individual topics. However, you have not had the opportunity, so far, to look at each perspective as a whole, integrated theory, as you will in this chapter. You can draw on the knowledge and understanding you have already developed in studying individual topics to help you grasp the different theories examined here, all of which were developed prior to the 1990s. Some of these theories focused on a study of society as a whole (structural theories), others looked at smaller groups (social action/interpretivist theories). While these two types of theory have usually been regarded as being in opposition to each other, there have also been attempts to combine or integrate these two approaches. One such attempt, Giddens' theory of structuration, is considered at the end of this chapter.

GETTING YOU THINKING

A theory is a set of ideas that provides an explanation for something. A sociological theory is a set of ideas that provides an explanation for human society. Critics of sociology sometimes object to the emphasis that sociologists place on theory, suggesting it might be better to let 'the facts' speak for themselves – but there are no facts without theory. For example, in Western society, the generally accepted facts that the world is round and that it orbits the Sun are inseparable from theories that explain the nature and movement of heavenly bodies. However, in some non-Western societies, whose members employ different theories, the view that the world is flat and the Solar System revolves around it is accepted as a statement of fact. Clearly, the facts do not speak for themselves and it is important to have carefully constructed theories that are also evaluated meticulously to check how robust they are.

Like all theories, sociological theory is selective. No amount of theory can hope to explain everything, or account for the infinite amount of data that exists, or encompass the endless ways of viewing reality. Theories are therefore selective in terms of their priorities and perspectives, and in the data that they define as significant. As a result, they provide a particular and partial view of reality.

Source: Haralambos and Holborn (2013)

1. Suggest two examples of theories from subjects other than sociology.

2. Think about the following 'facts' that are sometimes stated about social life. Suggest what kind of theory lies behind each fact.

   > Humans are basically selfish – everyone looks after their own interests first.

   > Humans have to work together to survive – this is a key feature of humanity.

   > Humans usually live up to the labels that people attach to them.

   > All humans are brought up to understand and accept the culture in which they are raised.

3. Is the time and place in which you live likely to affect the kind of theory of society you believe in? If so why? (Think, for example, about living in countries with different political regimes, religions, and levels of technology. Use the photographs below as a starting point.)

Does the society you live in affect the theories you have of society?

THEORIES OF SOCIETY

This topic explores theories that were prominent in sociological thinking until the 1990s, most of which are still very influential. It considers Marxism, functionalism, social action and interpretivist theories. These theories are divided into structural approaches and social action or interpretivist approaches.

> Structural approaches (also sometimes known as **macro** approaches) attempt to provide a complete theory of society. They begin their analyses from the 'top', by looking first at society as a whole and they place less emphasis on the choices made by individuals. They tend to see individual behaviour as being partly shaped by the structure of society, and major social changes as coming from structural factors. However, not all structural theories go as far as seeing behaviour as actually determined by the structure of society and some leave room for individual decision-making within structures.

> There are two main types of structural theory. The first, functionalism or consensus theory (and its development, neo-functionalism), sees members of society as having shared interests. Functionalists believe that social order benefits all members of society. The second type of structural theory, conflict theories, see society as divided between social groups with different amounts of power. Structural conflict theories include Marxism (and its development, neo-Marxism). Another type of conflict theory is feminism, which is discussed in the next chapter.

> Social action and interpretivist theories (also known as **micro** approaches) do not seek to provide complete explanations for society; instead they start by looking at how society is 'built up' from people interacting with each other. There are differences between social action and interpretivist theories relating to the extent to which it is possible to explain events in society, rather than just understand how people make sense of the world around them.

UNDERSTAND THE CONCEPTS

Macro and **micro** refer simply to the scale that is used to theorise about society, with macro theory looking at society as a whole and its major institutions and micro theory looking at small–scale groups or smaller institutions.

Functionalism

Durkheim and early functionalism

Functionalism has its origins in the work of 19th–century French sociologists, particularly Auguste Comte (1798–1857) who first coined the terms 'sociology' and 'positivism', and Emile Durkheim (1858–1917). In the 20th century, Functionalism was dominant in sociology from the 1940s until the 1970s in the USA; it was very influential in Europe too. After that it fell somewhat out of fashion, but the ideas of some functionalists, particularly Emile Durkheim, still remain influential today.

Emile Durkheim

Durkheim's starting point, was the organic analogy – that is, he imagined society as similar to a living being that adapts to its environment and is comprised of component parts, each performing some action that helps the living being to continue to exist. In the case of human beings, for example, our organs perform functions to keep us alive (for example, the heart pumps blood). It exists for that purpose and it would not exist if there was no need to pump blood. Similarly, institutions exist, or don't, because of their functions for the maintenance of society. Just as our bodies need to resolve certain basic needs in order to survive (for example, the need for food and water), so do societies.

From the organic analogy, the method of functional analysis has developed. This involves explaining why institutions exist in terms of the function they perform for society. (Details of Durkheim's work on the functions of crime are found in Topic 1, Chapter 1 and on the functions of religion in Topic 6, Chapter 2.)

Durkheim was also well known for advocating positivist research methods, based on looking for correlations in statistical data. In particular, he carried out a pioneering study of suicide rates in different European countries (see Chapter 4).

Talcott Parsons

Parsons' aim was to provide a theoretical framework that combined the ideas of Durkheim with a systematic attempt to understand the structures of societies and how they function. Parsons' work represents a very good example of a structural approach in sociology, which examines the functioning of society as a whole and tends to explain human social behaviour in terms of that structure.

Parsons (1951) suggests that there are four basic needs (or functional prerequisites) that all societies have to satisfy:

1. *Adaptation (the economic function)* – Every society has to provide an adequate standard of life for the survival of its members. Human societies vary from fairly basic hunter-gatherer societies to complex industrial societies.

2. *Goal attainment (the political function)* – Societies must develop ways of making decisions. Human societies vary from dictatorships to democracies.

3. *Integration (social harmony)* – Each institution in society develops in response to particular functions. However, there is no guarantee that the different institutions will not develop elements that may conflict. For example, in capitalism, economic inequalities may lead to possible resentment between groups. Specialist institutions, which seek to limit the potential conflict, therefore develop. These could include religions as well as charities and voluntary organisations.

4. *Latency (individual beliefs and values)* – The previous three functional prerequisites all deal with the structure of society. This final prerequisite deals instead with individuals and how they cope. Parsons divides latency into two areas:

   > *Pattern maintenance:* this refers to the problems faced by people when conflicting demands are made of them, such as being a member of a minority religious group and a member of a largely Christian-based society. In contemporary sociological terms, this would be called the issue of identity.

> *Tension management:* if a society is going to continue to exist, then it needs to motivate people to continue to belong to society and not to leave or oppose it.

The existence of institutions such as education and religion is explained in terms of these functional prerequisites (see Book 1, Topic 1 and Topic 6 in this book). Each institution has certain social roles (positions associated with norms or behaviour). Examples include the roles of husband and wife associated with heterosexual families, and teachers and pupils associated with schools. Because of the existence of roles and shared norms, society generally runs smoothly with relatively few misunderstandings. The whole social system is underpinned by a general agreement on values about what is good and desirable, or bad and undesirable. Parsons calls this general agreement a 'value consensus' and, for this reason, functionalism is seen as a **consensus** perspective.

UNDERSTAND THE CONCEPT

A **consensus** is a general agreement about something. In sociology it usually refers to a general agreement about the basic values of society – about what is considered right or wrong. A consensus in this context does not necessarily imply absolute agreement by everyone, however it does imply that the vast majority accept the central values of society.

Social evolution and differentiation

Although all societies share the same functional prerequisites, they do not stay static. Nevertheless, Parsons believes that as societies change they can retain a degree of balance in order to continue functioning effectively. If one part of the social structure changes the other parts adapt to fit round it. For example, if there is a period of immigration or if a new technology is introduced, the institutions of society will adapt to fit around the new elements in society and quite quickly balance will be restored. Parsons refers to this as a 'moving equilibrium'.

As they develop or evolve, modern societies generally become more effective and efficient at raising living standards and meeting the needs of their members. This involves a change in cultural values or what Parsons calls 'pattern variables'. There are two sets of pattern variables, one of which (Pattern Variables B) is more typical of modern societies, whereas the other (Pattern Variables A) is more characteristic of simpler, pre-modern societies. Pattern Variables A is based more on emotional ties than Pattern Variables B, which is based more on rationality and efficiency. The two sets of pattern variables are listed below. Only in families, which are based on close emotional ties, do Pattern Variables A remain centrally important in society today.

Pattern variables A	Pattern variables B
Ascription Status is ascribed; it is determined by the type of family into which a person is born.	**Achievement** Status is achieved through a person's own efforts: for example, through hard work.
Diffuseness People enter into relationships with others to satisfy a large range of needs: for example, the relationship between mother and child.	**Specificity** People enter into relationships with others to satisfy particular needs: for example, the relationship between a customer and shopkeeper.
Particularism Individuals act differently towards particular people: for example, they are loyal to their family but not to strangers.	**Universalism** Individuals act according to universal principles: for example, everyone is equal before the law, so a female police officer would arrest her husband if necessary.
Affectivity Gratification is immediate. People act to gratify their desires as soon as possible.	**Affective neutrality** Gratification is deferred: for example, saving money to put a deposit on a house in the future.
Collective orientation People put the interests of the social groups to which they belong before their own interests.	**Self-orientation** People pursue their own interests first, rather than those of the social group to which they belong.

Table 2.1.1 *Parson's pattern variables*

Do you agree that modern life is characterised by Pattern variables B, at least outside the family? Can you think of any examples that don't fit this theory?

As well as cultures changing as societies evolve, Parsons also sees them as becoming more structurally complex – a process he calls "structural differentiation". Simple societies rely on two institutions to carry out most functions – religion and families – but modern industrial societies develop new and more efficient specialist institutions. For example, schools, colleges and universities take over the educational functions of families, and the welfare state takes over many of the caring roles previously carried out by families and churches.

Criticisms within the functionalist approach

Robert Merton (1957) ascribed to the same functionalist approach as Parsons. However, Merton criticised some of Parsons' arguments, arguing that his view of society was too uncritical, and he proposed two amendments to functionalist theory:

1. Parsons assumed that if an institution was functional for one part of society, then it was functional for all parts. Merton points out that this ignored the fact that some institutions can be both dysfunctional (or harmful) for society, and functional. In particular, he cites the example of religion, which can both bring people together and drive them apart.

2. Merton suggests that Parsons failed to realise the distinction between manifest (or intended) functions and latent (or unintended) consequences of these functions and that latent functions are not always desirable ones. Merton says that this makes any analysis of society much more complex than Parsons' simple model implies.

Criticisms outside the functionalist approach

Sharrock *et al.* (2003) argue that there are several main criticisms of functionalism:

› Functionalism overemphasises the level of agreement or consensus in society. Apart from in the simplest of societies, people have different values and attitudes within the same society. This criticism is made by advocates of perspectives such as Marxism and Feminism, who emphasise class and gender conflict respectively.

› The positivist approach supported by Durkheim and its application to the study of suicide have both been criticised (see Chapter 4).

› Parsons suggests that society is rather like an organism, yet this is not true. Organisms are biological entities that have a natural form and a natural life cycle. Society, on the other hand, is a concept, consisting of the activities of possibly millions of people. There is no natural cycle or natural form.

› Functionalists have real problems explaining social change. If, as Parsons claims, institutions exist to fulfil social needs, then once these needs are fulfilled there is no reason to change them. Societies should never change in form unless there are some external changes that impact on the four functional prerequisites.

› As a method, functional analysis claims to explain why institutions exist but, in fact, it only explains some effects of institutions. Just because something is needed does not explain how and why it actually developed in the first place.

› Parsons seems to ignore differences in power. Yet differences in power can have strong impacts upon the form that society takes and whose interests it reflects.

› Finally, as interactionists point out, human beings in the Parsonian model of society seem rather like puppets having their strings pulled by all-powerful societies via pattern variables. Interactionists, postmodernists and late-modernists all combine to argue that people are much more 'reflexive', making choices and constructing their lives. Functionalism can therefore be seen as too deterministic. That is, it assumes that people's behaviour is determined by external forces and individuals are not credited with having free will – the ability to make their own conscious choices.

Neo-functionalism

Although functionalism has been widely criticised, there are still some writers that follow broadly in the functionalist tradition, including Mouzelis (1995) and Alexander (1985). Both these writers argue strongly for the overall systemic approach provided by Parsons. They dispute criticisms of Parsons that suggest he is not interested in how people act, and argue that, with some modification, Parsonian theory can allow for people to be 'reflexive', making decisions for themselves. These modifications to the theory also help explain social change. However, far more influential than functionalism today are New Right/neoliberal perspectives that owe more to economics and politics than to sociology. They are discussed in relation to social policy in Chapter 7.

Marxism

The second major sociological perspective that, like functionalism, aims to create a total theory of society by linking individual motivations and wider structural context, is the tradition that has developed from Marxism. Marxism derives from the 19th-century writings of Karl Marx (1818–83) who sought to create a scientific explanation of societies. His starting point was that the economic system of any society largely determined its social structure (Marx, 1867/1873). The owners of the economic structure are able to control society and construct values and social relationships that reflect their own interests. Other groups in society, being less powerful, generally accept these values and social relationships, even though these are not in their interests.

Marx began by suggesting that all history can be divided into five periods or epochs, which are distinguished by ever more complex economic arrangements. The history of all societies begins with what he entitled "primitive communism" – simple societies, such as hunter-gatherers, where there is no concept of private property and everything is shared. It then passes through the ancient societies, such as Asia and Rome, through feudalism, until it reaches the crucial stage of capitalism. According to Marx, capitalism would inevitably give way to the final stage of history: communism.

The Marxist model

Marx developed a theoretical model to describe the development of societies through these epochs. In each of the five epochs there is a particular mode of production. A mode of production is a complete economic and social system (for example, communism, capitalism and feudalism) based on a different way of organising the production of goods. In the first epoch, that of primitive communism, production Is based on hunting and gathering and, because there is no surplus to accumulate, there are no social classes. In all other modes of production (at least until modern communist societies are established), society and production are based around the exploitation of one class by another. For example, in feudalism, the feudal lords exploit serfs who have to surrender some of their produce to their masters, and in capitalism, the capitalists exploit the working class.

Classes develop because some people are able to gain ownership and control over the means of production. The means of production are all those things needed to produce goods and the wealth that comes from them. These include land, raw materials, machinery, labour power (human work) and, in capitalism, capital (money used to finance production). In non-communist society, one class owns or controls the means of production, while the class that does not is forced to work for them, since they don't have the means to create wealth themselves. (For example, they don't have land to grow crops or capital to start a business.)

To Marxists, the foundation of society is the economic system or economic base. This consists of the means of production and the class system or the relations of production. The ruling class owns the means of production. This ruling class then constructs a whole set of social relationships that benefit them and allow them to exploit all others who do not share in the ownership of the means of production.

According to Marxist economic theory, the means of production are always advancing, becoming more complex and capable of producing greater wealth – nothing can stop this onward march of technology. However, the values that the ruling group create to benefit themselves tend to move much more slowly. Within each epoch, at the beginning, the values of the ruling class help technology move forward but, over time, because the values do not move as fast, they begin to get in the way of the progress of technology – in fact, they actually impede it. At this point, a new, challenging group arises with values and ideas that would help the means of production advance and, after a degree of conflict, they gain control of society and begin to construct their own relations of production. A new epoch has started and the process begins again.

Applying the model to capitalism

Marx believed that contemporary society has reached the stage of capitalism. The majority of his work was about the state of capitalist society and the factors that would, in his opinion, lead to a communist society.

Within capitalism, there is a ruling class, or 'bourgeoisie', that owns the industry and commerce. All other people who work for a wage, no matter how prestigious or well paid, are members of the working class or proletariat. In between the bourgeoisie and the proletariat is the petite bourgeoisie. This group consists of the self-employed and those with small businesses (for example, shopkeepers). They have enough capital to have their own businesses but not enough to employ and exploit others, at least on a large scale. However, the petite bourgeoisie find it hard to compete with the big businesses of the bourgeoisie. Consequently, they are often forced out of business and have to become waged workers and therefore members of the proletariat. This process is known as 'proletarianisation'.

In capitalism, the bourgeoisie promote a set of distorted beliefs that support their interests by helping to maintain their wealth and power. Self-interested and distorted beliefs are referred to as an 'ideology'. Capitalist ideology supports the view that the enormous inequalities in capitalist societies between rich and the rest are fair and reasonable. However, to Marxists they are unfair, unreasonable and derive from the exploitation of workers.

The majority of the population accept the inequalities of this system because of the way that dominant institutions, such as religion and education, justify the prevailing economic and social situation. Marx describes this majority as suffering from 'false consciousness' – they do not realise that their interests as a class lie in changing society rather than in allowing continued ruling class dominance.

Over time, Marx argued, capitalism will enter periods of crisis which will get progressively worse. The crises have a range of causes. Capitalists will drive down wages to increase their profits, causing many of the working class to become poor. This process is known as 'immiseration' or 'pauperisation'. At the same time, the rich will continue to accumulate wealth, leading to a polarisation between the poor masses and the tremendously rich bourgeoisie. This will make class divisions stark and obvious. Partly for this reason, some members of the proletariat begin to realise that they are being exploited and believe that it is necessary to overthrow capitalism to end their own exploitation. In Marx's terms, they develop "class consciousness", they see through the distorted ideology of the bourgeoisie. Class consciousness manifests itself in terms of strikes and political protest, both of which are examples of class conflict. Eventually, with a tiny minority of very rich capitalists and a huge majority of relatively poor people, radical or revolutionary social change is inevitable. This change will usher in the final epoch of communism.

Criticisms of Marx

Marx's work has probably been subjected to more critical discussion and straight criticism that any other sociological theory. This is mainly because it is as much a political programme as a sociological theory. However, specific sociological criticisms of Marx's work include the following:

> The description of capitalism and its inevitable move towards a crisis has simply not occurred. Indeed, capitalism has grown stronger and, through globalisation, has spread across the world. In most parts of the world, communist systems have either been replaced by capitalist systems (as in the former Soviet Union) or have adopted many of the characteristics of capitalism (as in China).

> The polarisation of people into a tiny rich minority and an extremely poor majority has also not occurred in the way Marx envisaged. There is huge inequality but, at the same time, there has been a massive growth in the middle classes in society – the very group that Marx predicted would disappear.

> Capitalism changed significantly after Marx's death, with the introduction of a wide range of health, pension, housing and welfare benefits, all of which were missing from Marx's analysis.

> Marx paid little attention to other significant social divisions, including those between men and women (gender divisions), ethnic differences, age differences, differing sexualities and so on.

The various criticisms of Marxism discussed above have, in part, helped to stimulate the development of other perspectives (such as feminism) and also attempts to revise Marxism to take account of some of its weaknesses.

Some sociologists believe that Marxism is becoming more relevant because societies such as the UK and USA are becoming more unequal and more capitalist in nature. Do you agree more with them or with critics of Marxism?

Neo-Marxism

Marx's ideas have been taken up and developed by a wide range of sociologists, keen to show that the model, suitably amended, is still the best basis for understanding society. Some neo-Marxist perspectives will now be discussed.

Antonio Gramsci

One of the most influential neo-Marxists was Antonio Gramsci, an Italian who developed many of his ideas when imprisoned by the fascist regime of Mussolini during the 1930s. Gramsci is often seen as a 'humanist Marxist': a Marxist who placed less emphasis on economics and social structure than many other Marxists, and more on the choices or agency of members of different classes. To Gramsci, ideology, alongside economics, was crucially important.

In his *Prison Notebooks*, which were written between 1929 and 1935, he argued that conventional Marxism underestimated both the room for manoeuvre possessed by the state in capitalism and the ability of the proletariat to resist ruling class power. The state could not simply impose its will as it wished on non-capitalists, it had to win consent from large sections of the population to cement its dominance and maintain control. It could retain political and ideological dominance, which Gramsci referred to as 'hegemony', if it made some concessions to the proletariat, through introducing welfare payments or health and safety rules to protect workers, for example.

This was important because the proletariat were never completely taken in by ruling class ideology. Institutions such as the media and religion could fool the proletariat to some extent into accepting capitalism, but the day-to-day experience of exploitation led the proletariat to be critical of capitalism too. This led to the proletariat developing a dual consciousness in which they were partly influenced by ruling class ideology but they were also aware of the injustice they suffered under capitalism. They were never completely taken in by claims that capitalism was fair and that it worked well for everyone. Therefore, the ruling class could never take the loyalty of the proletariat for granted; they had to work at achieving hegemony and sometimes needed to make short-term concessions to achieve this.

Althusser and the concept of relative autonomy

One of the most sociologically influential neo-Marxist approaches was provided by Althusser (1969), who argued that Marx had overemphasised how much the economic system drove society. Althusser suggested that capitalist society was made up of three interlocking elements:

1. *The economic system* – producing all material goods

2. *The political system* – organising society

3. *The ideological system* – providing all ideas and beliefs.

According to Althusser, the economic system has ultimate control, but the political and ideological have significant degrees of independence or autonomy. In reality, this means that politics and culture develop and change in response to many different forces, not just economic ones. Althusser used the term "relative autonomy" to describe this degree of freedom of politics and values. This may not at first seem very important, but what it suggests is that society is much more complex and apparently contradictory than in traditional Marxist analysis. So, the march towards a communist state is not clear, but confusing and erratic.

Althusser also used this argument in his analysis of politics and the state. For Marx, the role of politics was simply to represent the interests of the ruling class, but for Althusser, the state was composed of two elements:

1. *Repressive state apparatuses* – organisations such as the police and the army

2. *Ideological state apparatuses* – the more subtle organisations including education, media and religious organisations.

Both sets of apparatus ultimately work for the benefit of capitalism, but there is a huge variation in the way they perform this task, with some contradictions between them.

Althusser's work provided a huge leap forward in neo-Marxist thinking, as it moved away from a naive form of Marxism (rather similar to functionalism), which simply said that everything that existed did so to perform a task for capitalism. Instead, while recognising this ultimate purpose, Althusser highlighted the contradictions and differences between the various institutions of society. Nevertheless, social action theorists argue that even neo-Marxists emphasise the role of structures far too much and take too little account of human agency – the ability to make decisions and make a difference to what happens in social worlds.

The Frankfurt School

The Frankfurt School is associated with the works of three major neo-Marxists: Marcuse, Adorno and Horkheimer, all of whom were originally at Frankfurt University. In separate books, Marcuse (1964/1991), Adorno (1991) and Horkheimer (1974) criticised Marx for being an economic determinist – that is, he believed society is mainly determined by the economic system. They argued that people's ideas and motivations are far more important than Marx ever acknowledged. Despite Althusser's development of the idea of relative autonomy, he too concentrated on social structure and had little concern with individuals' ability to choose their own course of action – their 'agency'.

The Frankfurt School developed a critique of structural Marxism in three main areas:

1. *Instrumental reason* – According to Adorno, Marx failed to explore people's motivations for accepting capitalism and the consumer goods it offers. Adorno suggests that it was wrong of Marx to dismiss this as simply 'false consciousness'. People work hard to have a career and earn money, but quite why this is their aim is never explored. Thinking in capitalism is therefore rational, in terms of achieving goals, but the actual reasons for those goals may not be rational.

2. *Mass culture* – Marcuse argued that Marx had ignored the importance of the media in his analysis. Marcuse suggested that the media play a key part in helping to control the population by teaching people to accept their lot and to concentrate on trivial entertainment.

3. *The oppression of personality* – The third element of their critique of Marx focused on an area that was neglected in Marx's work: the way that individuals' personalities and desires are controlled and directed to the benefit of capitalism. Before capitalism, there was no concept of 'the work ethic': people did the work that was required and then stopped. Capitalism, and particularly industrial production, needed people who accepted going to work for the majority of their lives and having little leisure. In the early stages of capitalism, therefore, pleasure and desire as concepts were heavily disapproved of – hence the puritan values of Victorian England. But in later capitalism, when it was possible to make money out of desires (and in particular sex), they were emphasised. Sex is now used, for example, to sell a wide range of products. According to the Frankfurt School, therefore, even people's wants and desires are manipulated by capitalism in its own interests.

Evaluation of neo-Marxism

Given that Marx was writing more than a century ago, It is not surprising that his work has been developed and adapted by a range of neo-Marxists. Neo-Marxists have been able to answer many of the criticisms made of Marx's original theory, by incorporating new elements into their version of Marxism or by suggesting a slightly looser relationship between economics and society. However, in the process, Marxist theory has become more complex and, arguably, less powerful as an explanation of how societies develop. Nevertheless, Marxist approaches continue to be influential in a world where inequalities on a global scale are still evident.

FOCUS ON SKILLS: HERE'S HOW TO CUT RUSSELL BRAND DOWN TO SIZE

The following article was written by Janice Turner, a columnist at The Times, *about the comedian, actor and activist Russell Brand. The article was published several days before the 2015 UK General Election.*

Russell Brand, centre

In 2014 the comedian Russell Brand published the book *Revolution*, calling on young people to abstain from voting in elections because mainstream political parties all supported the capitalist system. Instead, he said, a revolution was necessary to change the system entirely.

Here's how to cut Russell Brand down to size.

The pied piper of disenfranchised youth spouts twaddle to millions but simply denouncing him won't be enough.

David Cameron was wrong. Brand is not a "joke" who should be batted away.

Brand has politicised more young people than anyone in Britain.

Brand's critique chimes with the young. Inequality is not an abstract idea to young people who leave college with £40,000 debts and no clear path to adult security. If you're an unpaid intern at a highly profitable firm you might start spouting about 'transnational corporate interests' too. If you are one of three million young adults aged between 20 and 35 back living with your parents – the horror! – knowing you can never buy your own home, the system might look skewed, if not screwed.

Brand's half-baked ideas are easy to mock. His talk of jailing bankers, media hegemonies and tax-dodging Google are clichés, swirling into one great conspiracy theory. But that doesn't negate the fact that disparity of incomes has given London, in particular, a Victorian air. When 1 per cent of Britain has now acquired as much wealth as the poorest 55 per cent, a promised rise in the minimum wage feels like pennies to be scrabbled for in the gutter.

Turner, J. (2015) 'Here's how to cut Russell Brand down to size.', *The Times*, 2 May 2015

Questions

1. **Explain** what is meant by "jailing bankers, media hegemonies and tax-dodging Google".

2. **Explain** what you think the author means by the following sentence: "When 1 per cent of Britain has now acquired as much wealth as the poorest 55 per cent, a promised rise in the minimum wage feels like pennies to be scrabbled for in the gutter."

3. **Analyse.** In what ways are the arguments put forward here similar to Marxist perspectives on society?

4. **Evaluate.** Do you agree with Russell Brand's argument that voting is a waste of time because all politicians essentially support the same capitalist system?

Social action and interpretivist theories

According to social action theories, the way to understand society is not to start analysis at the top (analysing the structure of society, as Marxism and functionalism do), but to begin from the 'bottom' – analysing the way people interact with each other. Social action theorists do not set out to construct a grand theory along the lines of Marxism or functionalism, but are much more content to sketch out the rules of social interaction. These approaches explore the day-to-day, routine actions that most people perform. These theories are based upon a social constructionist approach. This type of approach argues that through language, communication and interaction, humans produce meanings which form the basis of their understanding of the social world. Humans do not experience the world directly in an objective way, but rather they actively create meanings and they then see the world in terms of those meanings. For example, they see other humans in terms of whether they are male or female and they then

interpret their behaviour in terms of their masculinity of femininity. Aspects of the world which are really just socially constructed meanings are nevertheless seen as real, objective and, in some cases natural. For example, gender differences are not seen as the product of the meanings attached to being male and female, but as coming from natural, biological and unchanging differences between the sexes. One of the most influential social action theories is interactionism, which sets out to explain how individuals actually create society through routine actions. Phenomenology takes social constructionist arguments even further.

Symbolic interactionism – the full name for interactionism – derives from the writings of George Herbert Mead (1863–1931) and then Herbert Blumer (1900–1987) at the University of Chicago. Mead's writing (Mead, 1934, published posthumously) provided the foundation for the perspective, while Blumer (1962) helped apply the ideas to sociological issues. Both Marxism and functionalism seemed to suggest that

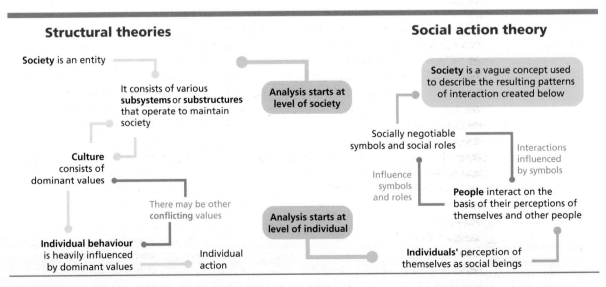

Figure 2.1.1 The difference between structural theories and social action theory

people were like puppets, controlled by the 'relations of production' or the 'pattern variables'. Instead, symbolic interactionism sees people as actively working at relationships and creating and responding to symbols and ideas. It is this dynamic that forms the basis of interactionists' studies.

The theory of symbolic interactionism has four core ideas: the symbol, the self game-playing and role-taking, and the interaction.

1. *The symbol* – The world around us consists of millions of unique objects and people. Life would be impossible if we treated every separate thing as unique. Instead, we group things together into categories, which we then classify. Usually, we then give each group a name (which is a symbol). Examples of symbols include 'trees', 'women', 'gay men', 'terrorists'. You will immediately see that the symbol may evoke some feelings in us; they are not necessarily neutral terms. So, the world is composed of many symbols, all of which have some meaning for us and suggest a possible response or possible course of action. But the choice of course of action that we feel is appropriate may not be shared by everybody.

2. *The self* – In order for people to respond to and act upon the meanings that symbols have for them, they have to know who they are within this world of symbols and meaning. 'I cannot decide how I ought to behave until I know who I am and therefore what is appropriate for me to do in certain circumstances.' Crucially, this involves us being able to see ourselves through the eyes of others. (Another interactionist, Cooley, called this the "looking-glass self" – the responses of others towards us act like a mirror telling us what sort of a person we are.) Labelling theorists developed this idea into that of the self-fulfilling prophecy. If individuals are labelled as a certain sort of person (for example, as a deviant of one kind or another) they come to see themselves in that way and to live up to the label (see Topic 1, Chapter 2 for more discussion of labelling). Mead distinguished two aspects of the self; the 'I' and the 'me'. The 'me' is how you see yourself in a particular role (for example, as a worker or as a consumer). The 'I' is your opinion of yourself as a whole and can also be called your self-concept.

3. *Game-playing and role-taking* – Blumer suggests that we develop the notion of the self in childhood and, in particular, in game-playing. When engaging in a game with others, we learn various social roles

and also learn how these interact with the roles of others. Mead emphasised the importance of role-taking. We imagine ourselves as the other person and try to understand the behaviour we witness from their point of view. This helps us understand the actions of others and helps us decide how we should respond. This brings us to the fourth element of interactionism, the importance of the interaction itself.

4. *The interaction* – For sociology, the most important element of symbolic interactionism is actually the point at which the symbol and the self come together with others in an interaction. Each person in society must learn (again through games) to take the viewpoint of other people into account whenever they set out on any course of action. Only by having an idea of what the other person is thinking about the situation is it possible to interact with them. This is an extremely complex business. It involves reading the meaning of the situation correctly from the viewpoint of the other (What sort of person are they? How do they see me? What do they expect me to do?) and then responding in terms of how you see your own personality (Who am I? How do I want to behave?). There is clearly great scope for confusion, error and misunderstanding, so all people in an interaction must actively engage in constructing the situation, reading the rules and symbols correctly.

Goffman and the dramaturgical approach

Erving Goffman (1968) was heavily influenced by symbolic interactionism in his studies of people's interaction in a number of settings. Goffman's work, which has been called the **dramaturgical** approach, is based on similar ideas to symbolic interactionism in that he explores how people perceive themselves and then set out to present an image of themselves to others. Goffman suggests that people work out strategies in dealing with others and are constantly altering and manipulating these strategies. The basis of his ideas is that social interaction can best be understood as a form of loosely scripted play, in which people ('actors') interpret their roles.

UNDERSTAND THE CONCEPT

Dramaturgy suggests that the social world can be analysed as if it were a giant drama or play in which people act out a variety of roles given to them by society.

Evaluation of symbolic interactionism

Interactionism provides a rich insight into how people interact in small-scale situations. However, as a theory it is rather limited in scope and is as much psychological as sociological. Its main weakness lies in its failure to explore the wider social factors that create the context in which symbol, self, game-playing and role-taking and interaction all exist and the social implications of this. This means that it has no explanation of where the symbolic meanings originate. It also completely fails to explore power differences between groups and individuals, and why these might occur.

Some of these criticisms were answered by Becker (1963) and other writers within the labelling perspective. Labelling theory is an offshoot of symbolic interactionism, that focuses on explaining why some people are 'labelled' as deviant and how this impacts on both their treatment by others and their perception of themselves. Becker specifically introduces the notion of power into his version of symbolic interactionism and demonstrates how more powerful groups are able to brand certain activities or individuals as deviant, with consequences that are likely to benefit themselves and harm those labelled deviant. (For a discussion of symbolic interactionism and methodology see Chapter 4). (For a discussion of symbolic interactionism and methodology see Chapter 4. For a discussion of labelling theory see Topic 1, Chapter 2 on labelling.)

The methodology of interactionist approaches has also been criticised. These approaches (along with others that advocate qualitative research) have been attacked for using methods such as unstructured interviews and participant observation, which rely upon the subjective interpretation of the researcher. They lack reliability because each situation studied is unique and cannot be replicated. This means it is impossible to check the results. Furthermore, they tend to be based on small, unrepresentative samples whose results are difficult to apply more widely. However, interactionists defend their methods as more valid than the quantitative methods supported by many of their critics. (See Chapter 4 for further discussion of perspectives and methods).

Phenomenology: the interpretation of meanings

Although symbolic interactionism takes a very different approach from Marxism and functionalism, by focusing on social structure rather than social action, it still attempts to explain how the social world works in a relatively conventional way. However, some sociological perspectives go further than symbolic interactionism, by arguing that it is not really possible to explain human behaviour as such. One such perspective is

phenomenology: a philosophy that originated in Europe with the work of Edmund Husserl (1859–1938). Phenomenology emphasises that all information about the social world is the product of the human mind. There are therefore no hard facts about the world on which to base explanations. Instead, all you can do is to try to understand the meanings that people give to the world by categorising it in different ways. To make sense of the chaotic world around them, individuals organise the world into phenomena.

Phenomena are things that are held to have characteristics in common – for example, the category 'dog' includes a range of animals with particular characteristics. The emphasis is on the subjective nature of the categorisation. Although a real world exists, how it is categorised is a matter of human choice rather than an objective process. The purpose of phenomenology is to understand the essence of phenomena – the essential characteristics that lead to something being placed in a particular category.

An example of phenomenology is Maxwell Atkinson's work on suicide (1978) in which he studied coroners' courts (see Chapter 4). Atkinson argued that it was impossible to be sure in potential suicide cases whether individuals really intended to take their own lives or whether the deaths were accidents or perhaps murders. Because of this uncertainty, sociologists had no foundation on which to build theories of suicide. All they could do was to look at the factors that influenced the categorisation procedures used by coroners, that is, the reasons influencing their decisions that some deaths were suicides and others were not.

Evaluation of phenomenology

Phenomenologists have been criticised for producing a theory that is too relativistic. According to them, everything is a matter of opinion; all knowledge is just a product of the way in which people classify the world. Logically, though, this also applies to their own theories and research, which are just a product of the viewpoint of phenomenologists themselves. Why should we believe Atkinson's interpretation of coroners' motives rather than someone else's? Most sociologists recognise that there are problems getting reliable and valid data about the social world, but they don't think it is impossible, and they therefore believe that sociology can successfully explain social life as well as describing it. Like interactionism, the sort of qualitative methods used by phenomenologists are criticised by those who prefer quantitative methods and see phenomenological research as being based too much on personal interpretations.

Are there any hard facts that sociologists can rely on? Suggest some possible examples.

UNITING STRUCTURAL AND SOCIAL ACTION APPROACHES

As discussed earlier, there are two main approaches in sociology: structural approaches and social action approaches. Sociologists have increasingly tried to combine these two approaches, arguing that both aspects of society must be considered if a full understanding of society is to be achieved. One of the leading advocates of this view is the British sociologist Anthony Giddens.

Giddens: the theory of structuration

Anthony Giddens advocates what he calls "structuration theory" (Giddens, 1984). The word 'structuration' is a combination of 'structure' and 'action' and, by combining them in one word, he represents his view that structure and action are two sides of the same coin and cannot be truly separated or examined in isolation.

Giddens argues that structures make social action possible. For example, political leaders could not act and have an effect without the civil service, army, police or other institutions of the state. Similarly, students could not study their chosen subjects without an organised and structured education system to facilitate their studies. However, structures are produced, reproduced and maintained by social actions. The state, for example, could not be reproduced without members of the military following orders, nor could the education system be reproduced without students carrying on their studies on

a day-to-day basis. So structures facilitate actions, which in turn reproduce structures; they are part of the same process. Giddens calls this the "duality of structure".

Giddens' view can be illustrated by language. Grammar is the structure of language, but individuals create the structure by talking and writing in ways that follow grammatical rules. If people start to use language in a different way, then grammatical rules will change. However, people can only use language and understand each other because there is some grammatical structure.

In the same way, societal structures and institutions are reproduced through people's actions, but if their actions change, the structures and institutions change. If everybody starts acting differently, existing social structures cannot survive and will change their form or disappear.

Is social life really like language? Suggest some ways in which it might be different.

Evaluation of structuration theory

Critics of Giddens, such as Margaret Archer (1982), argue that he puts too much emphasis on people's ability to change society by acting differently, and that he underestimates the constraints under which people operate. Supporters of more structural approaches believe that it is more difficult than Giddens suggests to change society simply by changing behaviour. However, even structural theorists such as Marx thought that actions could ultimately change society (through a proletarian revolution). Arguably, the best sociological theories try to understand both structures and social actions.

CHECK YOUR UNDERSTANDING

1. What is meant by the 'organic analogy'?

2. Explain what is meant by an 'economic determinist'.

3. Explain what is meant by 'structuration'.

4. Identify four functional prerequisites.

5. Which theory, discussed in this chapter, suggests it is impossible to produce causal explanations of human behaviour?

6. Explain three differences between Marxism and Functionalism.

7. Explain briefly, the difference between a structural and a social action perspective.

8. Outline two criticisms of symbolic interactionism.

9. Identify two weaknesses of conventional functionalism according to Merton.

10. Evaluate the view that Marxist perspectives are still useful for understanding society today.

TAKE IT FURTHER

1. Choose any one significant social event of recent years from the following list, or choose your own example.

   A. The war in Syria

   B. The 2015 terror attacks in Paris

   C. The 2011 British riots

   Carry out research about the circumstances surrounding the event you have chosen.

2. Discuss whether functionalism, Marxism and symbolic interactionism can throw any light on the events.

3. Are the events better explained in terms of individual social action or structural factors?

2.2 FEMINISM

LEARNING OBJECTIVES

> Demonstrate knowledge and understanding of different types of feminist perspective (AO1).

> Demonstrate knowledge and understanding of the influence of feminism on society and on sociology (AO1).

> Apply knowledge of feminist perspectives to British and other societies (AO2).

> Analyse similarities and differences between feminist perspectives (AO3).

> Evaluate the strengths and weaknesses of feminist perspectives and of feminism as a whole (AO3).

INTRODUCING THE DEBATE

Feminism has had a very significant influence, both in society and on sociology. Feminists, of various types, have a long history of campaigning for women's rights and women's liberation across the world and, arguably, have achieved significant success. Within sociology, feminism first became influential in the 1970s, but it has never been a unified perspective and there are therefore several different types of feminism. However, as a minimum, all feminist perspectives agreed that women remain, at least to some extent, disadvantaged and oppressed in society, but they disagree about the extent of that oppression, what should be done about it and what exactly has caused it. There is no doubt that feminism has contributed a great deal to the development of sociology, but it has nevertheless been criticised. Some writers have even challenged whether feminism is still needed today in the West and whether all the important battles for women's rights have now been won. This chapter examines the impact of these important and influential theories and considers the contemporary relevance of feminism.

THE WAVES OF FEMINISM

Feminist sociological ideas grew out of feminism as a movement that has a long history. It is often seen as coming in distinct waves.

The first wave can be traced back to the publication in 1792 of *A Vindication of the Rights of Women* by Mary Wollstonecraft, in which she advocated the provision of education to females so that they could pursue careers, just like men. This was considered a very radical idea at the time, as was the movement to obtain votes for women (the suffrage movement) in the early 20th century.

As a result of the suffrage movement, women aged over 30 were given the vote in 1918 and in 1928 voting rights were extended to women at the same age as men (21).

The second wave of feminism had its origins in the 1960s and grew out of a wider civil rights movement in the USA. This phase of feminism became known as the Women's Liberation Movement. It encompassed some very radical approaches, which aimed at a complete transformation of the relationship between males and females and, in some cases, female dominance. Some more moderate approaches simply looked for more rights for women.

It was during the second wave that feminism first started to influence sociology to any significant degree.

The third wave can be dated to the 1990s and was a response to the claims of some people that the Women's Liberation Movement had achieved its aims and feminism was no longer necessary. A new generation of feminist campaigners asserted that women were still unequal in a number of ways, even in Western societies where legislation has established improved rights for women. While some have argued that we have now entered a post-feminist era, other feminist sociologists strongly assert that feminism is just as essential as it was in the 1960s, even if some inequalities are more subtle now than they were then.

FEMINISM AND SOCIOLOGY

The basic characteristics of feminist theory

Although different types of feminist theories have distinct ideas, they do have some essential characteristics in common.

> First, feminism is a type of conflict theory that sees a conflict of interest between males and females as the most important type of conflict in society. Some feminist theories also see divisions between women as important, while others emphasise the common interests of all women.

> Second, feminists believe that most or all existing and historical societies are – to a greater or lesser extent – patriarchal or male dominated. While they disagree over the nature and extent of patriarchy, they do agree that it exists.

> Third, feminist theories all try to explain inequalities and differences between men and women and suggest what should be done about them.

Sex and gender

In addition to the above points, all feminists are critical of the view that gender differences and inequalities are simply a product of biological differences between men and women. Although some feminists do see biology as having some influence, many see biology as insignificant in itself, though the meanings attached to biology in particular societies are significant.

The foundation on which this view is based is a distinction between 'sex' and 'gender'. This was introduced by Robert Stoller in 1968 and elaborated upon and popularised by Ann Oakley (1972).

The word 'sex' is used to refer to biological differences between men and women such as differences in genitals, body hair, chromosomes and hormones.

'Gender' is used to refer to the beliefs about what it means to be 'masculine' and 'feminine' in different societies and the social roles associated with these beliefs.

The assumption behind this distinction is that there is nothing natural about the differences between men and women in any particular society; the differences are a product of culture not nature.

Oakley backs up this claim with examples of societies where men's and women's roles are very different to those in contemporary Britain.

For example:

> Amongst Tasmanian Aborigines, it was women and not men who did most of the hunting.

> Amongst the Mbuti in the Congo, men are responsible for most childcare.

> In a number of contemporary societies such as Israel, women have long featured as front-line troops.

If the view that gender is cultural not biological is accepted, then it means that there is no reason why the roles of men and women in society cannot be changed to produce greater equality or even to reverse the currently dominant role of men, so that women become dominant instead.

Feminism and the critique of sociology

One of the most important contributions of feminism to sociology has been to highlight the limitations of existing sociological thinking. Many feminists believe that most mainstream sociology (which they call **malestream** sociology) has a masculine bias.

UNDERSTAND THE CONCEPT

Malestream is a corruption of the word 'mainstream' and makes the point that most of the central and most widely accepted sociological theories can be seen as sociology written by men, about men and for men. By implication, then, these theories are seen as inadequate.

Abbott, Wallace and Tyler (2005) identify the following ways in which sociology has been seen as malestream.

> More research has been conducted about men than women and it has been generalised to people as a whole, even when all male samples have been used. This has been particularly true of sociology in the past. For example, very little research was conducted into women and crime until the late 1980s, although the balance has been redressed to some extent in more recent criminology.

> A second criticism of malestream sociology is that issues of particular concern to women have been neglected. These include childbirth, domestic labour, women's health, women's leisure activities, sexism in the workplace and in public places and violence against women. Again, some of these issues have been addressed in more recent sociological writing and research but – arguably – they still take a back seat to research into issues of more concern to men. Even in recent years the same problem sometimes reoccurs; for example, there has been a growth in the study of masculinity that has become, perhaps, more prominent than the study of femininity.

> A third criticism is that women have often been presented in sexist ways in sociological research. For example, in most studies of juvenile gangs, women have been marginalised and seen as the girlfriends of male gang members rather than as rounded human beings in their own right.

> Fourth, feminists have argued that even when females are integrated into research, they are often just added on to existing variables and do not have the central importance feminists believe they should have. From a feminist perspective, gender can be seen as having a more significant impact on people's lives than other variables such as ethnicity, age or social class. People primarily relate to each other as males or females and other social divisions can be seen as secondary (although some, such as Black feminists and difference feminists, do question this).

However, Abbott et al. accept that considerable progress has been made in countering malestream sociology. This is particularly the case in studies of sexuality, the body, identity and culture, that have been reconstructed from a feminist perspective. Feminism has had a less fundamental but still significant impact in areas such as the sociology of education, crime, the family, health and the mass media, but it has had very little impact on studies of class politics and non-feminist sociological theory.

Based on your own knowledge of sociological theory and research, how far would you agree with the feminist critique of malestream sociology?

FEMINIST PERSPECTIVES

Although feminists broadly agree that society is patriarchal and malestream, and that therefore both sociology and society need changing, there are a number of distinctive feminist perspectives that adopt somewhat different positions.

Radical feminism

Radical feminism is particularly associated with certain writers from second-wave feminist thought, who adopted the most extreme position and believed that women are exploited by, and subservient to, men. They are unambiguous in arguing that society is patriarchal, or male-dominated. Indeed, they see patriarchy as the most important organising principle of society. From this perspective, patriarchy is a structural feature of society that is pervasive in all aspects of social life and, for this reason, is very difficult to challenge or change. Because patriarchy is so pervasive, personal life (for example, intimate relationships and domestic life) are political issues to radical feminists, as well as more obviously political issues in wider society.

Radical feminists tend to believe that the apparent improvements in the position of women are relatively superficial and that fundamental inequalities remain largely unchanged. Many radical feminists see patriarchy as a universal feature of society and one that can only be challenged with a fundamental restructuring. Some radical feminists are female supremacists, who believe that women are superior to men and that societies would be better run if women were in charge. Others are female separatists, who argue that women should live independently of men, because it is well-nigh impossible to avoid domination by men in heterosexual relationships. However, the exact proposed solutions to male dominance vary and partly depend upon the explanations for inequality that they put forward. Some radical feminists, for example, explain the inequality in terms of biology, while others see culture or male violence as more important.

Firestone and biology

One early sociological explanation of female oppression was put forward by Shulamith Firestone (1970). She argued that there is a sexual class system resulting from the biological family. Women are at a biological disadvantage in the search for power, because they undergo pregnancy and childbirth, which makes them relatively weak and vulnerable. They are also tied down by the requirements of breastfeeding and hindered by menstruation. Men have taken advantage of these biological facts that make women dependent upon men, particularly in families, and this enables men to monopolise power in society. This in turn leads to power psychology in which both men and women believe the dominance of men over women is inevitable.

According to Firestone, the only way to overcome these problems is by taking what the majority would see as a very dramatic step, to abolish pregnancy through the development of artificial wombs, thus freeing women from the biological constraints that put them at a disadvantage.

Kate Millet: multiple sources of oppression

Kate Millet (1970) denies that biology is the only or main factor causing women's disadvantage, seeing it as one cause among many. According to Millet, several factors work together to keep women disadvantaged and oppressed.

› She admits that biology plays some part, through superior male strength and the use of violence. However, this is more psychological than real as women are perfectly capable of using violence themselves. They are being persuaded by patriarchal ideology that they are weak and vulnerable and lack the physical capability to defend themselves.

› Ideological factors are therefore important in shaping women's views of society, so that, as a result, they are less assertive and ambitious than men.

› Sociological factors relating to women's roles in society are also important. For example, having primary responsibility for childcare restricts opportunities for women to take dominant positions in the workplace.

› Educational and economic inequalities hold women back. According to Millet, women have fewer educational opportunities than men and it is very difficult for women to rise into senior levels in the workplace.

› Myth and religion are used to justify and perpetuate male dominance. For example, most religions either ban women from positions of authority or, even if they do not, are still dominated by male leaders and many religious teachings imply that women are inferior (see Topic 6, Chapter 2).

› Some feminists emphasise the role of violence in the subordination of women. Millet sees this as just one factor among many but, ultimately, if their power is challenged, men can use rape, sexual violence and force to underpin male power.

› Psychology also plays a part, since women interiorise patriarchal ideology. (Patriarchal ideology is the set of distorted beliefs that justify the continuation of male dominance in society.) Women ultimately believe that they are inferior to men and so it is difficult for women to challenge the situation and try to get rid of the structures that lead to patriarchal power.

Overall , Kate Millet believes that women have a caste-like status. In the caste system you cannot change the caste into which you are born; the same is true for women. Because of this, even higher-class women are subordinate to men and gender inequality is more important than class inequality. In class systems, social mobility is at least sometimes possible.

Evaluation of radical feminism

Radical feminism has offered an important challenge to traditional sociological views and has highlighted some very important features of women's oppression. For example, radical feminists were the first to emphasise the role of violence in maintaining male power; this has led to an important recognition of the significance of problems such as domestic violence and rape. They have also been able to emphasise the enduring and apparently intractable problem of male dominance. They have, however, been criticised on a number of grounds, and these criticisms reflect competing feminist perspectives.

Liberal feminists argue that radical feminists tend to underestimate the extent to which women have become less oppressed and more liberated in some societies (particularly Western ones). Radical feminists are also viewed by some feminists as lacking a convincing explanation for what underpins male dominance (for example, by socialist feminists). Various critics suggest that radical feminists exaggerate the degree to which all women are similar and share similar interests. They ignore other social divisions (such as ethnicity) and they underestimate the importance of language in female oppression. Postmodern, difference feminists and Black feminists tend to put forward these types of criticism.

Do you think that radical feminists are correct to see patriarchy as the main source of inequality and oppression in contemporary societies? Justify your answer.

Marxist and socialist feminism

The main features of Marxist and socialist feminism

Marxist and socialist feminists claim that radical feminists attach too much importance to violence, ideology and/or biology and instead argue that economic factors are the key to understanding the position of women in society. Marxist and socialist feminists see the capitalist system as the main source of women's oppression. They claim that it is women's lack of wealth and income that are the underlying factors stopping them from having as much power as men. Generally, they have stressed that women are disadvantaged economically because they tend to do more unpaid labour (as housewives, mothers, and carers for the sick or elderly). They also tend to be less successful, in terms of employment, than men, who continue to have most of the best-paid jobs. Only if women achieve economic equality with men are they likely to free themselves from other forms of inequality. To Marxists this is only likely to come about with a proletarian revolution, which eradicates inequalities in wealth between individuals.

Marxist and socialist feminists have put forward a number of explanations of how the oppression of women started and how it is perpetuated.

Frederick Engels (1872), Karl Marx's friend and collaborator, argued that gender inequality had a materialist base. According to him, in early, primitive communist societies there were no families and people lived in promiscuous hordes (there was no obligation to be faithful to one sexual partner). In these societies there was no inequality between men and women. Goods were shared and there was no opportunity for some people to accumulate wealth at the expense of others. However, when human societies developed the herding of animals, men wanted to pass down the cattle they owned to their offspring. In the promiscuous horde, men could not be sure who their offspring were, so the institution of marriage was started to control women's sexuality and it was from this point that men came to be dominant in society.

Engels' theory, however, is not based on sound empirical evidence. Other writers such as Coontz and Henderson (1966) have also provided a materialist explanation.

They argue that men became dominant due to the practice of patrilocality, whereby wives went to live with their husband's family. This tended to mean that men gained control over women's labour and the wealth they produced, and ultimately this gave men control over society.

In contemporary society, Marxist and socialist feminists (who share very similar views) have suggested a number of ways in which patriarchal domination is maintained.

› Christina Delphy and Diana Leonard (1992) argue that the exploitation of women's labour in the family is important. Not only do women do most of the domestic labour (such as childcare and housework) without payment, they often also help husbands with their careers (e.g. by acting as unpaid secretaries or by entertaining their husband's clients). This helps men to accumulate wealth at the expense of women.

› Fran Ansley (1972) claims that women absorb the frustrations that men experience because of their exploitation and alienation at work. She describes women as the 'takers of shit' because they experience physical and verbal abuse directed at them instead of at employers and capitalism in general.

› A number of Marxist feminists, such as Sharon Smith (2013), emphasise the role of women in reproducing a labour force by bringing up children at no cost to capitalists. If capitalists had to actually pay the full cost of childcare to female carers, it would severely dent their profits.

› Benston (1972) argues that women are used as a **'reserve army of labour'**, who are employed on low wages and thrown out of work when capitalists no longer need so many workers.

UNDERSTAND THE CONCEPT

According to Marxist theory, capitalist economies inevitably go through booms and slumps, with extra workers being needed during the former, and people being thrown out of work during the latter. The workers who are only needed during the booms are known as the **reserve army of labour**.

Evaluation of Marxist and socialist feminism

Marxist and socialist feminists argue that men have retained power because they retain access to the best-paid work and are still, on the whole, much wealthier than women. Engels anticipated that this inequality would diminish and therefore gender inequality in general would decline once women were able to participate fully in the workforce. This seems to fit the idea that there has been some reduction in gender inequality, with women working more and with more women in higher paid jobs than in the past. It also seems to fit the continuing gender inequality in society since women still earn significantly less than men on average.

However, Marxist feminists tend to underplay the significance of non-material causes of inequality stemming from culture and differences between women, for example between women of different ethnicities. By attributing gender inequality entirely to capitalism, they fail to explain continuing inequality in socialist or communist countries. There are also many aspects of gender differences which have no obvious benefits for capitalists.

It can be argued that it is somewhat misleading to argue that all women are in low-paid work, since they are distributed across the workforce and because there are many women in professional jobs. Nevertheless, there are still relatively few women in the best-paid jobs and the average wages of female workers are still substantially lower than those of men (see Book 1, Topic 6, Chapter 2 for a discussion of women and work). Contemporary socialist feminists such as Lizzie Ward (2002) believe that globalisation has undermined the income of women working in the UK, due to competition from low-wage economies, and welfare cuts have disproportionately affected women too.

Certainly economic inequality is an important feature of gender inequality more generally, but it can be argued that it is not the only factor helping to maintain patriarchy. Non-material factors (such as culture, psychology and the use of violence) may also be important. Wealthy women are still women and can face just the same discrimination and sexism as poorer women in everyday life. They are still more likely than men to be victims of domestic violence or sexual harassment, less likely to get into elite positions in society and so on. Therefore, an exclusive emphasis on the economic issues might be misleading.

Liberal feminism

The key ideas of liberal feminists
This perspective is not a distinctive sociological perspective as such, but rather it is a term applied to a range of approaches, which emerged out of the women's rights campaigns, that developed during the second wave of feminism. It seeks reforms rather than revolution and argues that piecemeal improvements in the position of women in society can ultimately lead to equality between the sexes. The ideas behind

it date back to the first wave of feminism, but they were given extra impetus in the 1960s and 1970s by a range of writers. One of them, Betty Friedan (1963), attributed a lack of equal opportunities between males and females to the way in which the mother and housewife roles dominated most women's lives. Like other liberal feminists, Friedan argued that socialisation into distinct gender roles, and dominant cultural ideas about masculinity and femininity, which were perpetuated in the education system, work and the mass media, all contributed to the subordination of women. These issues could be addressed by challenging sex discrimination in all these settings, encouraging non-sexist socialisation and ensuring that men and women had equal rights in the workplace and elsewhere.

Liberal feminism tends to see cultural factors as particularly important in creating inequality between men and women. Compared with Marxist, socialist and some versions of radical feminism, liberal feminists do not place so much emphasis on social structure. Indeed, liberal feminists tend to believe that it is perfectly possible to have a patriarchal society even in the absence of major structural inequalities between men and women. This provides some theoretical justification for the idea that gradual change, including changes in attitudes as well as institutions, can solve the problems identified by feminists.

The influence of liberal feminism
Liberal feminism has perhaps been the most influential of all feminist perspectives and many of the reforms that they have advocated have been implemented over the decades since second-wave feminism emerged. For example, school curricula in the UK have changed to remove certain sexist assumptions about the sort of subjects the boys and girls should study (see Book 1, Topic 1, Chapter 1): females now outperform males in just about every aspect of the UK education system (see Book 1, Topic 1, Chapter 1). Equal rights and equal opportunities legislation have, at least in theory, given women every opportunity for progress at work and the UK government has outlawed discrimination against women in a range of settings. The 1970 Equal Pay Act, the 1975 Sex Discrimination Act and the 2010 Equality Act offer women legal protection against discrimination. Furthermore the 'mother and housewife' role is no longer the norm for mothers, who are now much more likely to continue working after having children than they were in the 1970s.

Liberal feminists, much more than other feminists, accept that women have made considerable progress in gaining rights and improving their position in society.

They still, however, believe there is some way to go before equality is achieved. For example, the liberal feminist Natasha Walter (1998, 2010) believes there remains much that feminists need to change. She thinks that continuing problems of inequality affect all women. Women still tend to suffer from problems such as low pay, lack of affordable childcare, the dual burden of paid employment and domestic labour, poverty and domestic and sexual violence. Furthermore, she argues that sexism is making a return to culture in the UK and elsewhere, creating new problems for women. Popular culture increasingly portrays women in stereotypical ways and has made sexism both respectable and acceptable. She believes there has been a growth of a hypersexual culture in which sexualised clothing is becoming the norm, even for young girls, and cosmetic surgery is becoming commonplace. In these circumstances it is very difficult for women and girls not to aspire to patriarchal ideas of feminine beauty. Furthermore, pornography increasingly shapes men's expectations of women as sexual partners, particularly with it becoming more easily accessible via the internet.

Evaluation of liberal feminism

A major strength of liberal feminism is that its relatively moderate stance has allowed it to take action to improve the position of women in society, without holding out for revolutionary change. The significant reductions in gender inequality since the 1970s do seem to support its theoretical stance that the law, social attitudes and culture are significant in maintaining patriarchal power. Furthermore, adopting this approach has led to worthwhile changes. While it could be argued that economic factors underlie many of these improvements (particularly the growth of female employment and therefore of female income), it seems plausible that a range of factors, including attitudinal change and legal changes, have been significant too.

On the other hand, changes in line with liberal feminism do not seem to have eradicated inequality between men and women. Radical feminists such as Germaine Greer (2000) argue that women have not been truly liberated, and liberation will only occur when women do not have to be like men, or to dress and act in ways that men want them to, in order to succeed. From Greer's point of view, more radical changes in society are necessary.

Some third-wave feminists, such as Catherine Redfern and Kristin Aune, also argue that radical changes are still needed to liberate women fully, as many problems remain (see Focus on Skills). They advocate more contemporary methods to promote this, including the use of blogging and social media, and they point out that whatever the limited success in Western societies in reducing inequality, women in the poorer countries of the Global South generally continue to live in very patriarchal countries.

However, Redfern and Aune could be criticised for underestimating the extent to which greater equality has been achieved in countries such as Sweden and Norway.

FOCUS ON SKILLS: *RECLAIMING THE F WORD* (2010)

A protest demanding equal rights for women

In their book *Reclaiming the F Word*, Catharine Redfern and Kristin Aune (2010) argue that while there has been some progress on the demands of second-wave feminists from the 1970s, there is still much for third-wave feminists to achieve before women are fully liberated. They suggest seven areas in which contemporary feminists need to campaign for improvements.

1. Liberated bodies

In the poorer global South, over 500,000 women die each year in pregnancy and childbirth. The lack of healthcare provision in some places means that women are suffering from rising rates of HIV. Furthermore, there is very strong pressure on women to conform to beauty ideals promoted in the media.

2. Sexual freedom and choice

Cultural practices and inequalities in power continue to limit women's sexual freedom. Furthermore, sexual double standards in which female promiscuity is condemned much more than male promiscuity continue. They also believe that there continues to be significant discrimination against lesbian, gay, bisexual and transgender people.

3. An end to violence against women

Redfern and Aune provide ample evidence that violence against women continues to be commonplace. In the UK, Home Office estimates suggest that 21% of girls experienced some form of sexual abuse as children, while 23% of adult women are sexually assaulted during their lifetime. About one in 20 women, according to Home Office figures, are likely to be raped in the UK during their lives.

4. Equality at work and home

While there have been gains for women in work, women are still significantly disadvantaged both in the UK and elsewhere. They argue that women still experience a glass ceiling, finding it very hard to be promoted to the top positions in any sphere. As evidence, they quote an example showing that only about one in 11 of the directors of the UK's top companies are women. There are also still significant differences in the amounts of unpaid housework and caring done by men and women..

5. Politics and religion transformed

Women are underrepresented in parliaments and in senior political positions in nearly all countries. In 2009, only 19.5% of MPs in the UK were women and there were only 24 countries out of 187 in which women made up 30% or more of political representatives in parliament. Redfern and Aune also highlight the lack of power that women have in many religions.

6. Popular culture free from sexism

Redfern and Aune identify many ways in which popular culture can be seen as sexist: They report that, in 2008, of 64 band members in the indie chart top 30, only four were women. They discuss "the highly sexist content of song lyrics and music videos", saying: "Rap and hip-hop music are often singled out as an extreme example of misogyny and sexualisation."

7. Feminism reclaimed (Redfern and Aune, 2010)

Redfern and Aune finally demand that feminism is reclaimed. They argue that using the 'F Word' (feminism) should no longer be taboo and any negative connotations it has taken on for young women should be challenged and rejected.

Source: Haralambos & Holborn (2013)

Questions

1. **Understand.** What is meant by the term 'glass ceiling'?

2. **Apply.** Suggest one way, other than those mentioned here, in which popular culture can be seen as sexist.

3. **Analyse.** What do the demands of Redfern and Aune have in common with radical, Marxist/socialist and liberal feminism? What type of feminists would you categorise them as?

4. **Analyse.** Suggest one reason, with reference to the source, why many young women are reluctant to define themselves as feminists.

5. **Evaluate.** Identify one way in which the analysis of Redfern and Aune might be criticised by feminists adopting one of the feminist perspectives discussed in this chapter.

Black feminism

The main features of Black feminism

Dissatisfaction with radical, Marxist/socialist and liberal feminism has led to the development of Black feminism. Black feminists regard other types of feminism as **ethnocentric**, meaning that, while claiming to address issues about women in general, they actually concentrate on White women's experience in Western societies.

UNDERSTAND THE CONCEPT

Ethnocentrism means having a built-in bias towards your own culture, nation or ethnic group, so that you see the world its point of view

They argue that other feminists have tended to adopt a 'victim ideology' with regards to Black women, portraying them as the helpless victims of both racism and sexism. Black feminists argue that White feminists cannot claim to speak for the experience of all women and Black women can provide a unique and essential contribution to feminism in general.

The pioneering American Black feminist, Gloria Jean Watkins, better known by her pen name bell hooks (1981), argues that the legacy of slavery has given Black women a unique insight into the nature of oppression, an insight that White feminists do not have.

Black feminist bell hooks

The British Black feminist, Heidi Safia Mirza (1997), argues that a distinctive Black British feminism is essential, in order to challenge distorted assumptions that Black British women are passive victims of racism, patriarchy and class inequality, by representing how they have struggled against domestic violence, and fought to overcome sexism and racism in education and elsewhere. Black feminism has also been important in developing postcolonial feminism, which is particularly concerned with gender inequalities that are partly the result of colonialism in the developing countries of Africa, Asia and Latin America. They have, for example, analysed how the legacy of colonialism has affected women caught up in the AIDS/HIV epidemic in Africa.

Evaluation of Black feminism

Black feminism has succeeded in extending other feminist analysis and highlighting neglected areas of research. It has helped to highlight the value of drawing on the experiences of oppressed women, to understand the social world. It can, however, be accused of emphasising one difference between women (race or ethnicity) at the expense of others (such as class, age and sexuality). Nevertheless, Black feminism opened up the issue of differences between women and questioned the idea that all women shared the same interests. This view has been particularly influential in postmodern feminism.

Can you think of any other groups of women who might develop a distinct feminist perspective? Would all groups of women give distinctive and valuable insights based on their experiences of patriarchy?

Postmodern feminism

The main features of postmodern feminism

Postmodern feminism can be seen as part of third-wave feminism, which reflects on some of the perceived weaknesses of the second wave. It generally rejects the idea that all women share the same interests and that the position of women in society can be explained in terms of a single theory. It emphasises differences between groups of women, based not just upon a single characteristic, but on the whole range of characteristics. Thus, postmodern feminists show an interest in the divisions between groups such as lesbian and heterosexual women, women from different classes and ethnic groups, and women of different ages.

Postmodern feminists follow some of the general views of postmodernists such as Baudrillard and Lyotard (see Chapter 3) in a number of ways:

1. They tend to celebrate difference rather than believing that all women share the same interests.

2. They reject the idea of progress inherent in claims about how women can be liberated in liberal, Marxist and radical feminist accounts. They see such claims as a product of male rationality, which stated that the world can be planned to become a better place.

Postmodern feminists tend therefore to reject the idea of a single path to female liberation. Liberation may mean quite different things to different sets of women and therefore it is impossible to draw up a single set of goals for the feminist movement. Attempts to achieve 'equality' and 'justice', for example, can be seen as adopting male rationality and ignoring what may be more female goals, such as joy and living in harmony with nature.

Post-modern feminism has been very much influenced by a set of ideas known as 'post-structuralism', which emphasises the importance of language in the production of society. Poststructuralism tends towards seeing all aspects of society as being socially created and arguing that significant changes can come about simply as a result of changing the way in which language is used.

From this point of view, women's position can be improved by deconstructing (taking apart and criticising) masculine language and thinking.

Helene Cixous (1993) describes language as phallocentric – male-dominated and reflecting a male view of the world. Sex, for example, from a phallocentric perspective, is often seen in terms of male objectives such as penetration and orgasm. This neglects the female perspective on sex, which is more subtle and has much less focus on a single part of the body. She refers to 'jouissance' – the joyous female sensuality that incorporates the whole body.

Evaluation of postmodern feminism

Rosemary Tong (1998) sees some merit in post-modern feminism and, in particular, its awareness of an acceptance of differences between men and women. Others, however, argue that it rather loses sight of the key importance of inequality between men and women.

For example, Sylvia Walby (1992) criticises postmodern feminism for neglecting the degree to which the experience of oppression and inequality gives women shared interests. Walby accepts that there are differences between groups of women, but believes many still suffer from the effects of patriarchy. This particularly applies to older women, poorly qualified young women and single parents, who all suffer considerable disadvantages. Furthermore, Walby points out, most elite positions continue to be male-dominated.

Postmodern feminists have also been criticised for neglecting important areas such as male use of violence to maintain power and gender inequalities in the home.

One of the most influential feminists today is Judith Butler (1999, first published 1990) whose ideas highlight both the strengths and weaknesses of postmodern feminism. Butler has adopted many of the arguments of postmodern feminism, for example, attaching considerable importance to language in the creation of gender. However, Butler puts much more emphasis upon the acting out or performance of gender, rather than merely the use of language. (She calls this "performativity".) Butler claims that everyday bodily gestures and movements help to create the impression that there are essential differences between men and women. It is not therefore just a matter of how people talk about gender that is important, but also the constant repetition of actions, that helps to

ingrain different practices in male and female bodies. They become a matter of habit and are difficult to change. Examples include differences in the way men and women walk or throw a ball.

Butler's work suggests that gender inequality and female oppression are more complex than any single feminist perspective has grasped.

THE CONTRIBUTION OF FEMINISM TO SOCIOLOGY

There is no doubt that feminism has made a substantial contribution to sociology and to the understanding of society in general. The following are just some of the ways in which it has been important.

> It has highlighted the problems of malestream sociology, such as the use of all-male samples and the tendency to generalise about people without taking into account the distinctive experiences of women in society.

> It has introduced new topics that were previously neglected, including the study of housework, childbirth, gender inequality in the curriculum and female gangs.

> Feminism has also ensured that we know almost as much about women in society as we do about men.

> Perhaps most importantly, it has highlighted the oppression of women and contributed to reducing that oppression. Feminists, particularly liberal feminists, have succeeded in running campaigns that have had at least some impact in tackling problems such as domestic violence, sexual violence against women, sexual discrimination at work and sexist socialisation. It has helped to increase opportunities for women, has raised consciousness of gender inequality and has led to changes in the law in many Western societies.

> Feminists have introduced new methods into sociology, and have effectively criticised a number of male-dominated approaches to studying society. They have argued for distinctive methods that can, in their view, achieve a deeper understanding of the experience of women and, by extension, other oppressed groups. Their methodological views have been challenged, but at the very least they have raised important questions and identified possible sources of distortion in some supposedly 'scientific' approaches to methodology (see Chapter 4 for a more in-depth discussion of feminist methodology).

Feminism has not, however, always succeeded in integrating other inequalities into the understanding of gender and can sometimes be accused of focusing on gender too much. As a social movement, feminism has certainly not eradicated all inequality between men and women; in many countries and at various times there have been backlashes against feminism. In Britain some of the progress that has been made has been undermined by austerity measures, which have led to the closure of rape and domestic violence centres and have cut welfare support for poor and vulnerable women. Furthermore, most women on the planet live in places where liberation has certainly not been achieved for them.

From a sociological point of view, Anna Pollert (1996) attacks the key concept used by feminists: that of 'patriarchy'. According to Pollert, the idea of patriarchy usually involves a circular argument: it is used both as a description and as an explanation of inequality between the sexes. Pollert argues that capitalism is a system with an internal dynamic, but that patriarchy is not such a system. She prefers empirical studies of how class, gender and ethnicity relate to one another, rather than theorising about patriarchy as such. (For a discussion of feminist methodology, see Chapter 4.)

CHECK YOUR UNDERSTANDING

1. What is meant by 'patriarchy'?

2. Explain what is meant by 'jouissance'.

3. Explain what is meant by 'second-wave feminism'.

4. Identify and briefly explain the three main characteristics of liberal feminism.

5. Which theory discussed in this chapter suggests that a complete transformation of society is needed to liberate women?

6. Explain two differences between Marxist/socialist feminism and postmodern feminism.

7. Briefly explain Butler's idea that performance creates gender.

8. Outline two criticisms of Black feminism.

9. Identify two ways in which feminism has made a positive contribution to sociology.

10. Evaluate the view that feminism is still needed in contemporary Britain.

TAKE IT FURTHER

Search *The Guardian* archive for references to feminism. Choose any three articles that you think might be relevant and interesting.

Summarise your three chosen articles.

Analyse what they tell you about gender inequality today.

Analyse what they tell you about the state of feminism in society today.

Discuss whether they seem to offer evidence for, or against any particular feminist perspectives. Explain and justify your reasoning.

2.3 LATE-MODERN AND POSTMODERN SOCIOLOGICAL THEORIES

INTRODUCING THE DEBATE

This chapter examines the relationship between sociological theories and broad changes in social life, particularly in Western societies. Sociology was born in what is sometimes seen as the era of modernity and was a product of the sort of thinking associated with this era. However, some sociologists have argued that the era of modernity has passed. Some even argue that, with that passing, sociological thinking should change radically and that old theories of society are no longer of any use. These different theories can roughly be divided into theories of modernity, theories of late modernity and theories of postmodernity. We shall leave you to decide which approach is most convincing.

THE ENLIGHTENMENT AND MODERNITY

Although the word 'modern' is often used simply to refer to what is new or recent, in sociology it is used more specifically to refer to a particular way of thinking and to the sorts of society associated with this type of thinking. 'Modernity' refers to the era in which modern ways of thinking are (or were) dominant. Modern ways of thinking are usually seen as originating in the 18th century, with a European political and philosophical movement known as the 'Enlightenment'. Enlightenment thinking suggested that human societies did not have to be run simply according to tradition (the way they had always been run) or according to religious belief. It was argued instead that humans could turn to science for knowledge of the world and how the world worked. People could plan societies to make them better or, in other words, to achieve progress. Enlightenment thinkers believed that rational planning, rather than superstition, faith or tradition, could be used to work out how to make societies better and to improve the quality of life for their members.

Enlightenment thinking went hand-in-hand with the transformation of Western societies through urbanisation. This had superseded rural life for much of the population. In addition, industrialisation had demonstrated the productive power that could be unleashed when science was applied to manufacturing.

Perhaps the most influential sociological analyst of modernity was Max Weber (his books were originally published in 1905 and 1920). Weber believed that modernity involved:

> a move towards scientific rationality, in which people decided on their aims and then tried to follow the most efficient means of achieving those aims, based upon scientific knowledge of how the world worked

> gradual secularisation, in which religion continued as a set of personal beliefs

> bureaucratisation, in which large, hierarchical organisations (bureaucracies) were increasingly used to organise society.

Above all though, modernity is based on the idea that humans can ensure progress by planning and shaping their own future and do not need to rely on tradition and trust in fate or divine intervention to make things better.

Most sociological theory up to the 1980s, especially structural or macro theory, can be seen as a product of modernity.

SOCIOLOGY, MODERNITY, LATE MODERNITY AND POSTMODERNITY

Following in the footsteps of natural sciences such as biology and physics, sociology searched for a theoretical perspective that could explain how society was structured, how it functioned and how it changed over time. The theoretical approaches of Marxism and functionalism both claimed to do this. They also claimed to provide the knowledge necessary to ensure that societies worked effectively to meet the needs of their members, whether through evolutionary change and value consensus in the view of functionalists, or through revolutionary change in the view of Marxists. They couldn't agree about how to perfect society, but they did agree that it was possible to perfect it.

By the 1980s (and earlier for feminists), sociologists were aware, through their studies of culture, gender, social class and the economy, that enormous changes were taking place within modern societies. The traditional 'modern' social characteristics of strong social classes, clear gender roles and party-based politics, all linked

to an economic system based on industrial production, were no longer an accurate reflection of British (and most other Western) societies. Because of this, a new breed of theorising emerged.

One group of writers believed that there had been significant changes within modernity, so societies had moved towards what they called 'late modernity' or 'high modernity'. A separate, much more radical group of theorists argued that society really had totally changed and had moved into a period after modernity, or postmodernity – hence the term 'postmodernists'.

The idea of late modernity or high modernity sees society as having changed and having developed new aspects. The task of the late-modernist theory is to adapt more traditional theories of sociology.

Postmodern theorists argue that the whole 'sociological project' was part of a period of history – modernity – in which a particular way of viewing society developed that was closely related to a set of economic and social circumstances. According to these theorists, we have now moved into a new set of economic and social circumstances, based largely on communication and image, and therefore traditional sociological models have little or no value.

Do you think that society has changed so much, in the last 50 years or so, that we now live in a completely different type of society to the society of the past? Why, or why not?

Late or high modernity

Ulrich Beck and the sociology of risk

One of the most influential writers to put forward a theory of 'late modernity' is the German sociologist Ulrich Beck (1992), who argues that a central concern for all societies today is that of risk. This concept has permeated the everyday life of all of us. There are three elements to Beck's thesis: risk society, reflexive modernisation and individualisation.

Risk society

According to Beck, modernity introduced a range of 'risks' that no other historical period has ever had to face. Note that Beck uses the term 'risk' in a very specific way. Throughout history, societies have had to face a wide range of 'hazards', including famine, plague and natural disasters. These were, however, always seen as beyond the control of people, being caused by such things as God or nature, yet the risks faced by modern societies were considered to be solvable by human beings. The belief was that industrialisation, public services, private insurance and a range of other supports would minimise the possibility of risk. Indeed, the very project of sociology began with a desire to control society and minimise social problems.

In late modernity, however, the risks are seen as spiralling away from human control. No longer can risks be adequately addressed to the same standards as they were in modernity. Problems such as global warming and nuclear disaster are potentially too complex for societies to deal with. This is despite the fact that the risks are themselves the product of human actions – humans create risks that get too big or complex for them to control. Furthermore, because of globalisation, risks are not confined to any one country. National boundaries are of little importance with so much movement of people, money, ideas and other things around the world. For example, diseases, pollution, radiation and terrorism cannot be limited to any one country. Within countries, members of the population, even if they are rich, cannot isolate themselves from risks,. The rich cannot eliminate the harm that may result from any of the above risks, whereas in the past they could isolate themselves from risks such as those from poor hygiene or poverty, that were mainly experienced by those on low incomes. For this reason, Beck believes that class differences are no longer important in shaping people's chances in life. He adopts this position so strongly that he calls class a "zombie category" – it still appears in sociology but there is no life left in the concept.

How do we cope with global warming?

Reflexive modernisation
Late modernity, Beck believes, involves people becoming more **reflexive**.

UNDERSTAND THE CONCEPT

Reflexivity refers to the ability of people to reflect upon their lives and to consider different ways to act or live. In modernity this was done by leaders planning society, but in late modernity everyone becomes reflexive and they no longer place such trust in leaders and 'experts'.

The growth of reflexivity leads to people questioning the political and technological assumptions of modernity, for example, the assumption that the growth of scientific knowledge always represents progress. People begin to be aware of risk and how they as individuals are in danger. They also seek ways of minimising risk in all spheres of their lives. Risk and risk avoidance become central to the culture of society. This helps explain the growth in control of young children by parents trying to minimise any possible risk to them from cars, paedophiles and the material they watch on television. It also explains the growth of risk assessment and opposition to new technology such as genetically modified crops or fracking.

Beck argues that although it is the global, political and technological 'system' itself that is the cause of the risk, there has been little attempt to confront the problems at this level; rather, risk avoidance operates at the personal and lower political levels.

Individualisation
Beck links the move towards individualisation with the move away from 'tradition' as an organising principle of society. In modern societies, most aspects of people's lives were taken for granted. Social position, family membership and gender roles, for example, were all regarded as 'given'. In late modernity, however, there has been the move towards individualisation, whereby all of these are now more open to decision-making. So, the background is of risk and risk awareness, and the foreground is of people making individual choices regarding identity and lifestyle as they plan their lives.

Criticisms of Beck
Beck has been criticised by a number of writers. Turner (1994) argues that Beck's distinction between hazard and risk is dubious. People have always faced risk and have always sought to minimise it in whatever ways were available at the time, such as religion or some other means that we might now consider of little value. Nevertheless, there was an awareness that something could be done to combat the hazard.

A second criticism derives from Beck's argument that the response to risk was largely individual. A range of political movements have been formed to combat global warming, eradicate poverty in Africa and stop the spread of HIV/AIDS. These are all political movements that are international in scope and which indicate that people do believe that it is possible to control the risks that Beck identifies.

Beck has been strongly criticised for arguing that social class is no longer important. Skeggs (2015), and many other sociologists, argue that rising inequality has meant that class has an increasing – not decreasing – impact on the opportunities people from different backgrounds have. Similarly, Elliot (2002) argues that Beck's work fails to recognise differences in power. Beck has suggested that the risk is spread across all groups in society and that differences in power are relatively unimportant. Elliot disputes this, suggesting instead that rich and powerful groups are able to limit risk and to have greater influence on the context in which the risk occurs. For example, they can live in areas with little pollution, far away from nuclear power stations.

Postmodernism

Postmodernist approaches to sociology emerged in the 1980s, challenging traditional modernist theories that sought to create an all-encompassing theory to explain society. There are a number of factors that have led to the development of postmodernist approaches but, in part, they have developed as a response to changes produced through globalisation.

At their simplest, postmodern theories argue that there cannot be any overarching theoretical explanation of society. This is because the idea of society exists only as a reassuring 'narrative'. Instead, in order to understand society as it is today, we need to have a deep awareness of the role of the media in creating an image of society that we seek to live out. One role of the media has been to make the process of globalisation possible, which has had, according to many postmodernists, important consequences for the development of postmodern societies.

Globalisation and hybridity

Postmodern approaches developed in the context of globalisation (see Topic 1, Chapter 9 for discussions of globalisation in the context of beliefs and crime and deviance). Globalisation involves a decline in the significance of time and space. David Harvey (1990) calls this "time–space compression", which involves the speeding up of communications so that where you are in the world becomes less significant. With digital media, people in different parts of the world can communicate with one another very easily and information, images, ideas and money can all move around the world almost instantaneously. This leads to what Dominic Strinati (1995) calls "confusions over space and time". Through digital communications, you can witness events that are taking place elsewhere, instantaneously. Digital media can also provide images from the past alongside images from the present. As a result, the sense of being grounded in a particular place and time can be lost for individuals. This makes it difficult for individuals to develop and sustain a single, grounded sense of identity or for places to retain a distinctive culture. With all the information available, individuals can change their identity more easily – for example, choosing to adopt tastes, styles of dress and ways of behaving from different places and times. These can be mixed together with greater **hybridity**.

UNDERSTAND THE CONCEPT

Hybridity is the mixing of different cultures to create something new that combines elements from those different cultures. For example, different musical styles can be combined to form something new and distinctive: contemporary R&B (rhythm and blues) can be seen as a hybrid of soul, funk, pop, hip hop and other types of music, which is nevertheless distinctive in its own right.

To postmodernists, these changes mean that it becomes very difficult to believe in a single theory to explain social life, or to believe that it is possible to have a single plan to improve society. They see the world as too complicated, inter-connected and rapidly changing because of globalisation and hybridity, to reduce the understanding of it to a single theory. From this point of view, it is also impossible to believe in the idea of progress – with so many different perspectives of the world available and none of them being dominant, no one theory of theory of social life is likely to be accepted.

Two key postmodernist writers are Baudrillard (1980, 1994) and Lyotard (1984). Lyotard attacked 'grand theories' of society such as Marxism and Functionalism as being merely big, elaborate stories, that effectively gave comfort to people, by helping them believe there was some rational, existing basis to society. He called these 'stories' **metanarratives**. According to the postmodernists, sociological theory, like science and most other academic subjects, was simply a set of stories or narratives belonging to a specific period in history – the period of modernity.

UNDERSTAND THE CONCEPT

A **metanarrative** is a big story about how the world works and how it can be improved. It provides the foundation for lots of smaller stories about the world, for example, sociological studies based on a perspective. Metanarratives can be sociological (for example, Marxism), religious (for example, Christianity) or scientific (for example, biomedical science), and they include implications about how people should live, as well as what is true (for example, they should abolish social classes, worship Christ, or maintain a healthy body mass).

Lyotard

Lyotard (1984) argues that economic expansion and growth, and the scientific knowledge upon which they are based, have no aim but to continue expanding. This expansion is outside the control of human beings as it is too complex and simply beyond our scope. In order to make sense of this, to give ourselves a sense of control over it and to justify the ever-expanding economic system, metanarratives, such as Marxism are developed.

Incredulity towards metanarratives and technical language-games

In the postmodern society, Lyotard argued, two things change:

> First, people develop "incredulity towards metanarratives" – they no longer believe that a single theory can be used to understand the world and form the basis of perfecting it. Attempts to impose metanarratives on society, for example, Communism under Stalin in the USSR or Fascism under Hitler in Germany, proved disastrous and were rejected. Similarly, according to Lyotard, the metanarratives of sociology (such as Marxism, feminism and functionalism), are, and should be, rejected.

> Second, as a consequence, the search for some sort of ultimate truth is abandoned and metanarratives are replaced by "technical language games". Technical language games are not about searching for the truth, but more about looking for 'what works' on a small scale. People search for useful knowledge, for example, developing new technology, or new ways to reduce the crime rate, rather than for an all-embracing theory of how to perfect the world.

Postmodern society therefore is not organised on the basis of a grand plan. Instead, it is based upon the production and exchange of knowledge that can be sold because it serves some useful purpose. This is a situation that Lyotard welcomes. With people no longer trying to terrorise others by imposing a theory on them, society becomes characterised by tolerance, diversity and creativity. Everyone can get on with living their lives as they choose, solving short-term problems and playing around with their identities, without worrying about some ideal of progress or of a perfect society.

Do you agree that people have generally abandoned grand plans to improve or perfect society? Are there any exceptions to this?

Baudrillard

Like Lyotard, Baudrillard sees society as having entered a new and distinctive phase of postmodernity. However, Baudrillard places more emphasis on the role of the mass media in this process.

The media and the 'death of the social'

Baudrillard notes that, in contemporary societies, the mass of the population expresses a lack of interest in social solidarity and in politics. The hallmark of this postmodern society is the consumption of superficial culture, driven by marketing and advertising. People live isolated lives, sharing common consumption of the media, through which they experience the world. According to Baudrillard this can best be described as the "death of the social".

The media play a central role in the death of the social. Baudrillard argues that people now have limited direct experience of the world and so rely on the media for the vast majority of their knowledge. As well as gaining their ideas of the world from the media, the bulk of the population are also influenced in how they behave by the same media. Baudrillard argues that, rather than the media reflecting how people behave, people increasingly reflect the media images of how they behave. This creates confusion and uncertainty over what is 'real' and what is not. At one time, media content reflected reality, but this is no longer necessarily the case and instead they tend to create what passes as reality.

Sign-objects and the consumer society

In the 21st century, a significant proportion of Western societies are affluent. Members of those societies are able to consume a large number of commodities and enjoy a range of leisure activities. However, Baudrillard argues, this consumption moves people ever further away from social relationships and ever closer to relationships with their consumer lifestyles. Yet the importance of objects in our lives has little to do with their use to us, and much more to do with what meaning they have for us. We purchase items not just because they are functionally useful, but because they signify that we are successful or fashionable. Consumer goods and leisure activities are, in Baudrillard's terms, "sign-objects", as we are consuming the image they provide rather than the article or service itself.

Hyperreality and the simulacrum

Baudrillard argues that, in modern society, it is generally believed that real things or concepts exist and then are given names or 'signs'. Signs, therefore, reflect reality. In postmodern society, however, signs exist that have no reality but themselves. The media have constructed a world that exists simply because it exists. For example, take the term 'celebrity'. A celebrity is someone who is defined as one, they do not have to have done anything or have any particular talent. It is not clear how one becomes a celebrity, nor how one stays a celebrity. Being a celebrity occurs as long as one is regarded as a celebrity. Similarly theme parks such as Disneyland and even cities such as Los Angeles are make-believe worlds based on storytelling. Baudrillard sees them as based on signs rather than an underlying reality.

Where a sign exists without any underlying reality, Baudrillard terms it a **simulacrum**.

UNDERSTAND THE CONCEPT

A **simulacrum** is a sign, such as a word, phrase or image, that represents something that does not exist. For example, 'Harry Potter World' is used to refer to the mythical world of a non-existent child wizard, which is recreated in fantasy theme parks.

Baudrillard believes that the society in which we live is now increasingly based upon simulacra. The fact that so much of our lives is based upon signs that have no basis or reality has led Baudrillard to suggest that we now live in a world of 'hyperreality' – a world of image.

He further believes that, in this process, power has disappeared. Nobody any longer has the power to influence anything. Even American presidents are just puppets caught up in the endless exchange of signs,

with no connection to reality and therefore without any real power to change the world. In Baudrillard's view, it makes no difference who is elected to the US presidency because their power is an illusion.

The implications of postmodernism for social life and for sociology

Writers such as Crook, Pakulski and Waters (1992) have identified a number of consequences for society, resulting from the development of postmodernity.

1. According to Pakulski and Waters (1996), the death of class has taken place. People no longer feel they belong to classes and people who supposedly belong to the same class have little in common. Similarly 'race' ethnicity, gender and age are all much less important than they used to be. In a **consumer society**, it is much more important what people consume, what brands they prefer and what lifestyle they adopt, than what type of job they have or the social groups into which they happen to be born.

UNDERSTAND THE CONCEPT

A **consumer society** is a society in which people's identities are primarily based upon the products they buy and use, rather than other characteristics.

2. Crook, Pakulski and Walters (1992) believe that social changes under postmodernism lead to hyperdifferentiation, in which a fantastic variety of different cultures and cultural products are created. For example, popular music is no longer split into a small number of genres (such as rock music, easy listening, pop, reggae, soul), but instead there is an almost infinite variety of styles and hybrid forms of music. Furthermore, high culture (such as classical music) and popular culture are no longer clearly separate as they influence and borrow from one another (see Book 1, pages 158–9 for a discussion of these terms). This gives people the chance to develop their own individual style, rather than feeling they have to follow the tastes of the social groups in which they are born.

According to postmodernists, as a result of both of the above changes, traditional sociological categories for defining different social groups are no longer of much use for understanding society.

3. Some versions of postmodernism, including those of Lyotard and Baudrillard, deny that it is possible to produce valid information about society. Since they reject 'metanarratives', they argue that there is no solid theory on which to base claims about the social world. Therefore any account of the social world is as good as any other and simply represents how the world looks from a different angle. Each viewpoint is equally valid. (See Chapter 4 for a discussion of postmodern methodology.)

FOCUS ON SKILLS: IT'S NOT A WASTE OF TIME TO MAKE A LIVING FROM THE THROWAWAY SOCIETY

Jenny Dawson, founder of Rubies in the Rubble

Supermarkets are just one of many culprits in an ever-present culture of food waste.

If aliens are up there, our approach to food must be particularly puzzling. In the UK, food banks were required to feed more than 1 million people in the past year. Meanwhile, between a quarter and a third of the country's food is going to waste.

To make matters worse, about 10 per cent of the food thrown away in Britain is fit for consumption – that's enough food for 800 million meals.

Ms Dawson is one of a wave of entrepreneurs building businesses to tackle this problem, particularly the huge amount of food thrown away by the industry because it doesn't conform to standards. This includes apples that are too big, bananas that are too straight and tomatoes that fail the 'prick test', which shows they have 21 days' shelf life. Rubies in the Rubble takes a different approach and sources 'waste' direct from farmers, before processing it into long-life products. Its mission: to create demand for 'ugly' fruit and vegetables, to encourage farmers to harvest their entire yield.

"Food waste is fascinating," says Jenny Dawson, who founded Rubies in the Rubble, a chutney business, in 2011. "You can't blame one culprit: weather is unpredictable, human appetite is unpredictable and supermarket shelves have to look presentable and abundant – so there will always be waste."

Ms Dawson's business sells 3,000 jars of chutney a month through Waitrose, Fortnum & Mason, Ocado and Whole Foods.

A high-end brand with a laudable social purpose can count on high customer loyalty from ethically-minded shoppers.

Source: MacGregor, L. (2015) 'It's not a waste of time to make a living from the throwaway society', *The Times*, 7 December 2015

Questions

1. **Apply.** How could the waste of non-standard food be seen as a product of a rational, modern society? (Think about how rational choices made by profit-seeking companies and busy individuals could cause this.)

2. **Apply.** How could the demand for designer chutneys in luxury food shops be seen as a typical feature of a postmodern society? (Think about how postmodernists emphasise lifestyle choice and its role in identity formation.)

3. **Apply.** In what ways could the waste of food be seen as a feature of postmodern consumer culture? (Think about how a 'throwaway society' might result from consumer culture.)

4. **Evaluate.** Could the existence of food banks be used to criticise some claims made by theorists of late modernity and postmodernity, such as those about the decline or death of class?

Evaluation of theories of postmodernity

There is no doubt that theories of postmodernity have identified some significant trends in contemporary societies. These include an apparent decline in class consciousness (or at least a blurring of the distinctions between classes), the reduction in the significance of some cultural differences, the growing importance of consumer society, the increasing interest in constructing and changing identity and the increasingly pervasive role of the media.

However, theories such as those of Lyotard, Baudrillard and Crook, Pakulski and Waters have also been extensively criticised:

› Lyotard's ideas have been criticised for making the most sweeping generalisations about social change, while backing them up with very little evidence. In effect he produces his own metanarrative about social changes, while at the same time claiming that metanarratives should be rejected. From this perspective he contradicts himself; there is no good reason why his metanarrative should be accepted above all others (including other sociological theories).

› Like Lyotard, Baudrillard uses little research to back up his claims and instead relies upon examples. However, there is no reason to suppose that the customers who visit Disneyland are not aware that it is just a fantasy world with no basis in reality, or that people who watch TV cannot distinguish fact from fiction. Baudrillard went so far as to claim that the first Gulf War (when Iraq invaded Kuwait and was itself invaded by Coalition forces in 1990) did not take place and was just a series of media images. Yet there are millions of witnesses who can contradict this – not to mention the graves of people who were killed in the war.

› Greg Philo and David Miller (2000) argue that the emphasis on language and the media in many theories of postmodernity is dangerous because it can lead to the denial of very real suffering, inequality and injustice. It is a distraction from political and social issues such as rising inequality, war and conflict. Furthermore, their research suggests that audiences are perfectly capable of thinking about the reality behind TV images and, at least to some extent, they can distinguish 'media hype' from 'more authentic accounts'.

› Postmodernists tend to portray the world as one in which people are free to consume what they want. However as Haralambos and Holborn (2013) say: "Postmodernists, with their obsessive interest in culture and style, miss the point that culture is partly shaped by the capitalist economy and differences in what rich and poor can afford to consume." From this viewpoint, class and other social divisions remain much more important than postmodernists assume.

Harvey: a Marxist interpretation of postmodernity

Some of the most recent and interesting sociological theorising within neo-Marxism comes from the work of Harvey (1990). Harvey is unusual for a neo-Marxist in that he develops Marxism within a framework that argues we have entered a postmodern era. As we have seen, postmodernity is seen as involving a fragmentation of society and a move towards image and superficiality in culture. Harvey agrees that this has taken place, not because of the rejection of metanarratives but because of economic changes in the 1970s and the response of capitalists. Due to rising oil prices, capitalist profits fell, which led to a move away from manufacturing to commerce, media and retail as the main employers. Coupled with the development of globalisation, these changes have produced massive changes in capitalism. They have also led to what he calls 'space–time compression'. Space or distance have become less important in social life because of digital communications and faster travel. It is much less important where you are in the world. For example, money, images and ideas can be moved very quickly.

Responding to these changes, capitalists have sought new sources of profit through the creation of whole new areas of commerce – what he calls "flexible accumulation". In particular, they have sought to make money through rapid changes in products (rather than through longterm mass production) and through the manipulation of identity, with developments in fashion, travel and new forms of music. If people can be persuaded that they must constantly reinvent themselves and change their identity by buying new fashionable products and services, then capitalism has an unlimited demand for its products. Globalisation, too, has been utilised to produce cheap goods, which are given added value by being marketed in the more affluent nations.

At the same time, Harvey points out, there have been many real changes that have affected capitalism quite drastically. For example:

› National governments are less powerful than ever before in modernity, and so change now resides at the global, rather than national, level.

› Real political discourse within the traditional frameworks of government and political parties has been replaced by image politics, where what appears to happen is more important than what actually happens.

> Social class as the dominant form of division between members of societies has been joined by a range of divisions linked to gender, ethnicity, sexuality and religion.

Nevertheless, Harvey remains convinced that the capitalist economic system and the social divisions it produces remain the driving force behind social change in the contemporary world. As such, he is highly critical of postmodernists such as Lyotard and Baudrillard who believe that modernist ways of analysing the social world, such as Marxism, are outdated. From Harvey's perspective, real changes can be studied and understood, and their consequences analysed. On this basis, ways of making social life less oppressive can be considered and evaluated. Unlike some other postmodernists, Harvey does not dismiss the idea that progress is possible and he does not believe that modern approaches to understanding social life should be abandoned.

CHECK YOUR UNDERSTANDING

1. What is meant by the term 'modernity'?
2. What is meant by a 'simulacrum'?
3. What is meant by a 'metanarrative'?
4. Identify and briefly explain the three main components of Beck's theory.
5. Which theory discussed in this chapter suggests that postmodernity can be understood through a neo-Marxist perspective?
6. Explain two differences between the idea of late modernity and of postmodernity.
7. Briefly explain Weber's view of modernity.
8. Outline two criticisms of Lyotard.
9. Identify two weaknesses of the idea of 'risk society'.
10. Evaluate the view that modern sociological approaches are of little or no use now we have entered a postmodern era.

TAKE IT FURTHER

Are you modern or postmodern?

1. Do you agree or disagree with each of the following statements?

> You should plan carefully to achieve your objectives.
> Science solves more problems than it creates.
> Oasis is just pop while Mozart is serious music.
> Advertising is not art but Leonardo Da Vinci's work certainly is.
> In the future, things will get better and better.
> Your background largely shapes the sort of person you become.
> Work is more important than shopping.
> Social class is still important in Britain today.
> It is possible to produce the perfect society.
> It is dangerous to follow any political or religious ideology too seriously.

2. Now score your answers. If you have more 'agrees' than 'disagrees', you have chosen answers more in keeping with attitudes supposedly typical of modernity; if the opposite, you have chosen answers more in keeping with attitudes supposedly typical of postmodernity.

3. Now consider each question in turn and explain why agreeing with it is more indicative of attitudes thought to be typical of modernity, and disagreeing is more typical of postmodernity.

4. Taking into account any three of the above questions, use information from other sociological topics you have studied to evaluate whether modern or postmodern views of contemporary society are more plausible.

2.4 THE RELATIONSHIP BETWEEN SOCIOLOGICAL THEORIES AND RESEARCH METHODS

LEARNING OBJECTIVES

> Demonstrate knowledge and understanding of the relationship between sociological theories and research methods (AO1).

> Apply this understanding to examples of sociological research (AO2).

> Analyse the range of methods used by sociologists from different perspectives (AO3).

> Evaluate the strength of the relationship between theory and methods (AO3).

INTRODUCING THE DEBATE

As you have seen in Book 1 (pages 100–104), a mixture of practical, ethical and theoretical factors influences the choice of research methods. This chapter explores the relationship between theories of society and research methods in more depth. It introduces some more advanced arguments about research methods put forward by those who support particular theories. The relationship between perspectives and research methods is not straightforward; there isn't always a perfect match between a particular theory and a particular type of research method: supporters of the same broad perspective can use different types of method. Some theories are more closely linked to particular methods than others and there may be a trend away from rigid support for a particular type of method by sociologists today.

THEORY AND CHOICES IN RESEARCH

Before conducting research, sociologists have to make some basic choices about what they are going to research and how they are going to research it. As discussed in Book 1 (see pages 98–99), one factor that can influence the choice of topic is the theoretical position of the researcher. This is because theories suggest to researchers what sort of topics and issues are of most importance and which are of less significance. Functionalists tend to be interested in topics that relate to social cohesion and social order; Marxists are drawn to topics that relate to class differences and economic inequalities; feminists tend to focus on topics that are relevant to gender inequalities; and interactionists lean towards topics that concern small-scale interaction in groups. The influence of theory on topics is not particularly prescriptive though, since most theories can be applied to a wide range of issues and topics: a theory pushes sociologists in certain directions rather than determining what they will research. Furthermore, as discussed in Book 1, other factors are also important, particularly practical constraints and to a lesser extent ethical issues.

Theory can also affect choices about methodology; perhaps the influence of theory is stronger in this respect than it is on choice of topic. This is also explored briefly in Book 1 (see pages 100–104), where it was pointed out that theory is not the only factor influencing choice of method; practical and ethical issues are also very important in this respect. However, this chapter examines the relationship between theory and method in significantly more detail and draws upon the more sophisticated understanding of theory you will have developed by this stage in the course.

FUNCTIONALISM AND METHODOLOGY

Functionalist theories of society concentrate on analysis of the role and function of institutions in society. Thinking about the functions of the education system, religion or the family does not necessarily require any empirical research; it tends to use thought experiments based upon what would happen if these institutions stopped working. As such, there is not any clear and close relationship between the basic ideas of functionalist theory and particular research methods. Functionalists have therefore used different approaches to try to understand the role of institutions in society. For example, George Peter Murdock (1949) used a variety of secondary sources to look at the nature and role of the family in 224 different societies (see Book 1, Topic 4, Chapter 1) while Talcott Parsons (1951, 1965) relied mainly on abstract theorising.

Many functionalists, and particularly Comte and Durkheim, explicitly support the use of positivist methods. They believe that society should be studied in an objective, scientific way, using quantitative data to look for correlations and causal relationships and to discover laws of human behaviour. Positivist methodology is based upon the idea that it is possible to classify the social world objectively and count incidences of different social facts. It therefore tends to use research methods that are well suited to producing statistical data. Durkheim (1897) used secondary statistical sources, particularly official statistics, to study suicide (see below) and other functionalists have followed suit. Alternatively, when appropriate statistical data is not easily available, they may use the comparative method in order to make systematic comparisons to try to isolate the variables that are causing the phenomenon they are trying to explain (see Book 1, pages 114–15). This process is known as 'variable analysis'.

Functionalists certainly tend to be opposed to the use of in-depth qualitative methods, which they see as being of little use for understanding the overall structure of society. They see such methods as providing only a rather personal and subjective view of the social world and, to

functionalist positivists, this sort of data is not appropriate for studying society in an objective way. (See Chapter 5 for more discussion and evaluation of positivist views of sociology as a science.)

The application of positivist methods: Durkheim and suicide

Durkheim was the first of the functionalists to illustrate in detail how positivist methods could be used to study society. Durkheim (1897) tried to show that suicide was not just a product of individual psychology, and that positivist methods could be used to study and explain the sociological causes of suicide rates. He relied upon existing secondary sources – official suicide statistics from countries across Europe – and he showed that suicide rates varied consistently between countries and within them. Examining the statistics, he found that high rates of suicide were correlated with:

> Protestants rather than Catholics or Jews

> married people rather than single people

> parents rather than the childless

> periods of political stability and peace rather than political upheaval and war

> economic booms and slumps rather than periods of economic stability.

From the statistical patterns, Durkheim claimed to have identified four types of suicide that were linked to how strongly **integrated** people were into society and how strongly **regulated** they were by society. Both excessive integration and regulation, and too little integration and regulation could lead to high suicide rates. Generally, modern industrial societies had low levels of integration and regulation. They have a complex division of labour (where there are many specialised jobs) so people had to be differently skilled to fulfil their different roles in society, and they are more pluralistic in terms of the cultures of the people who lived in them.

UNDERSTAND THE CONCEPTS

Integration is concerned with the extent to which individuals interact with other members of social groups, feel a part of those groups and are accepted by others as members of those groups.

Regulation is concerned with the extent to which society is able to get its members to conform to the formal and informal laws and norms of society.

It was therefore difficult to have a single set of norms governing society. On the other hand, preindustrial societies were close-knit and highly-regulated, so individuals had little freedom to make their own decisions and shared norms were very strong.

Durkheim identified four types of suicide:

> *Egoistic suicide* was caused by insufficient integration into social groups (for example, Protestants had less connection to their Church than Catholics did).

> *Anomic suicide* resulted from too little regulation in industrial societies, especially during times when rapid social change was undermining traditional norms (for example, during economic booms and economic depressions; both of which were linked to high suicide rates).

> *Altruistic suicide* resulted from too much integration in pre-industrial societies (for example, the practice of *suttee* – Hindu widows were expected and required to throw themselves on their husband's funeral pyre to die with them).

> *Fatalistic suicide* resulted from too much regulation in pre-industrial societies (for example, the suicide of slaves).

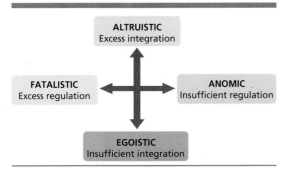

Figure 2.4.1 *Durkheim's four types of suicide*

Evaluation of Durkheim

Although Durkheim's theory of suicide has been highly influential, it has also been widely criticised by interpretive sociologists. They tend to argue that Durkheim could only infer from the statistics what the causes of suicide were. They argue that a far better way to understand suicide is to look at the actual meanings and motives of those who took their own lives. In his general writings about methodology, Max Weber (Weber in Gerth and Mills, 1948) used the idea of verstehen or 'understanding', arguing that you had to understand the meanings and motives of social actions before you could explain them. This view can be applied to suicide. It can't be assumed, for example, that just because suicide rates are higher

amongst Protestants that this has anything to do with their religious beliefs and ways of worshipping; they could be caused by other factors entirely.

Other critics of positivism argue that Durkheim based his research upon statistics, the validity of which cannot be assumed. Ultimately, suicide statistics are just based upon the opinions of coroners about whether someone intended to take their own life. They are not therefore 'social facts', as positivists such as Durkheim assume, but are simply numbers counting the relevance people have attributed to particular acts. These critics therefore advocate different types of methodology that produce more qualitative data.

Did Durkheim really confine himself to looking at the facts in this study? Did he speculate about people's feelings and motives?

INTERPRETIVISM, SOCIAL ACTION AND METHODOLOGY

There are a variety of different types of social action and interpretivist theories of society.

Symbolic interactionism, as developed by George Herbert Mead (1934) and Herbert Blumer (1969), is closely associated with the use of qualitative methods. Herbert Blumer, for example, used in-depth interviews in his studies of the social world. Later writers influenced by symbolic interactionism, such as Erving Goffman (1968) and the labelling theorist Howard Becker (1963, 1970) also used qualitative methods and developed ethnographic research methods, such as participant observation. For example, Becker (1963) used in-depth interviews with marijuana smokers and also used participant observation in studying jazz musicians. Erving Goffman (1968) also used a mixture of in-depth interviews and participant observation, for example, when studying mental hospitals.

Symbolic interactionism, labelling and Goffman's dramaturgy have a strong affinity with qualitative, interpretivist theories because they emphasise the importance of the meanings that individuals attach to social life. Understanding these meanings is difficult – if not impossible – using purely statistical research. Positivists tend to assume that people will react in predictable ways to external stimuli (things in the environment that influence their behaviour) but interpretivists emphasise that people interpret the meaning of these stimuli before reacting to them. This necessitates the understanding of what is going on in people's heads: the subjective ways in which they interpret the events around them before deciding on how to react to them. For these reasons it is rare for interactionist and other interpretivist theorists to make much use of quantitative methods.

The application of interpretivist methods to the study of suicide

A good example of the application of these types of methods to the study of suicide is the work of Jack Douglas (1967). Douglas argued that it was misleading to treat all suicides as the same type of **social fact**, because the meaning of suicide varies greatly in different societies. For example, in Inuit (Eskimo) society, the elderly were expected to kill themselves in times of food shortage for the good of the social group as a whole. In other societies, suicides might mean 'transformation of the soul' (a way of getting to heaven) or be a reaction to social failure (such as a manager responding to their business going bankrupt). From this point of view, statistical data cannot reveal the different meanings of suicide in different societies; therefore, seeking qualitative data from case studies and cultural studies is essential.

UNDERSTAND THE CONCEPT

To Durkheim a **social fact** is any objective feature of society which exists independently of the observer. Statements about social facts are valid because what they are describing is real and the statement is not a matter of opinion. However, some social constructionists argue that many of the things that Durkheim took to be facts, such as suicide statistics, were social constructions – ideas produced by society rather than being real and objective.

Interpretivist theorists such as Douglas are not against explaining the causes of suicide, but they think this is only possible once suicides had been categorised in terms of the different reasons and purposes behind them.

Interpretivist methods face the problem that they rely upon the interpretation of meaning and motives, and these cannot be directly measured, observed or known. It is impossible for a researcher to see inside another person's head and a researcher can only infer what a person's meanings and motives are through observation, interviews, reading qualitative secondary sources or by using similar methods. Other interpretations are often

possible which means that such methods are not reliable. That is, you cannot be sure that two sociologists using the same methods and studying the same thing would produce the same data or reach the same conclusions (see Book 1 page 93 for an explanation of reliability). Statistics on suicide are, in contrast, seen as reliable by most people who prefer quantitative methods. They are based on rigorous and objective court procedures from a positivist point of view (although as we will see shortly, this is disputed by phenomenologists).

Another problem with interpretivist methods is that they tend to be based on small samples. It tends to be time-consuming to gather in-depth data about the meanings and motives of people, so it is unlikely that data can be produced about thousands of respondents in the same way that it can in some questionnaire research. Furthermore, it may be impossible to choose a representative sample, since in-depth qualitative information might only be available about, or from, an untypical group of people. (Many people may be unwilling to take part in in-depth qualitative research, or relevant documents may not be available). It is therefore more likely that interpretive research is unrepresentative than quantitative research. In addition, it can be misleading to generalise from the findings of unrepresentative research (see Book 1, page 95 for an explanation of representativeness and generalisability).

Phenomenology and methodology

Phenomenology goes further than interpretivist theories, in seeing all data as the product of human meanings and categorisation procedures, and therefore as being socially constructed. It adopts methods that allow a greater understanding of the ways in which objects, people and events are classified. This tends towards the use of qualitative methods, such as unstructured interviews and observation/participant observation, because these enable researchers to explore the meanings through which social life is classified. It is difficult to use statistics to express meanings.

Nevertheless, phenomenological researchers may well take an interest in statistics. Rather than seeing statistics as objective facts, as positivists do, phenomenologists observe them as social constructs. Statistics are therefore seen as something to be studied, rather than something to be treated as objective data about the world. From their point of view, statistics help to reveal the mental categories and biases of those who produce the statistics, rather than telling you about the people or things the statistics describe. For example, statistics on ethnicity and crime might reveal police racism rather than actual differences in patterns of offending between ethnic groups.

Phenomenology and the study of suicide

Maxwell Atkinson's research on suicide illustrates these points (Atkinson, 1971). He argued that whether somebody had committed suicide or not was a matter of opinion. The evidence was rarely clear-cut and it was impossible to be certain about the intentions of people who had died. For these reasons, Atkinson believed that Durkheim was wrong to try to explain the causes of suicide by using statistical data, since that data was socially created and not objective.

Atkinson set out to discover the reasons why coroners reached suicide verdicts, rather than trying to find the causes of suicide itself. To do this he used in-depth interviews with coroners' officers (police officers who help coroners to investigate sudden deaths), and he also observed coroners' courts.

Atkinson concluded that coroners took four main factors into account in reaching their decisions:

> Whether the deceased person left a suicide note or had threatened to kill themselves.

> The mode of dying (with road deaths rarely believed to be suicides, but drownings, hangings and drug overdoses more likely to be seen as suicides).

> The location and circumstances of the death. For example, people who were killed on a railway track were more likely to be seen as suicidal if they had no reason for being in that location.

> Consideration of the biography of the deceased, with a history of mental illness, a disturbed childhood or evidence of depression all seen as important indicators of suicidal intent.

According to Atkinson, the statistical patterns in suicide simply reflected the assumptions that influenced the decisions of coroners, rather than any underlying causes of suicide.

Atkinson can be criticised for assuming that it is impossible to determine whether or not a death is a suicide. In some cases, there may be overwhelming evidence, leaving no real doubt. His approach has also been attacked for being too relativistic – seeing all knowledge as a matter of opinion. If all data is simply a matter of interpretation, then why should we accept his account of the factors shaping suicide statistics, any more than an alternative account?

Do you find the arguments of interpretivists/social action theorists more convincing than those of phenomenologists or vice versa? Explain why.

CRITICAL SOCIOLOGY

Critical sociology (or critical social science) refers to sociological or social scientific approaches that regard society as being oppressive and exploitative. This incorporates a wide range of theories including Marxism, neo-Marxism, feminism, anti-racism and theories of sexual oppression, such as homophobia. What all these theories have in common is a determination to be critical of society in order to produce social change. They are also often critical of official statistics, seeing them as being manipulated to serve the interests of the powerful (for example, by disguising the extent of poverty, unemployment, racism or domestic violence). However, given the range of theories involved, it is not surprising that no single research method is used by these theorists, and feminists in particular have devised distinctive methods of their own (see Chapter 5).

Lee Harvey (1990) believes, however, that critical social research does have certain common features.

> First, a concern with abstract concepts and ideology. Critical social scientists claim that beliefs about the social world may be distorted by the powerful (for example, by producing racist, patriarchal or homophobic beliefs). These beliefs can mask the true interests of the group.

> Second, critical sociologists are interested in structures that help to produce or maintain inequality, oppression and exploitation and therefore tend to use methods that can reveal these structures.

This approach to sociology involves reconceptualisation: finding unfamiliar ways to think about familiar aspects of social life. An example is the feminist argument that housework should be analysed as a form of unpaid labour, rather than as part of a family role. This helps to reveal the exploitation involved.

Critical social research is seen as a form of praxis – action designed to change the social world. In this type of research, part of the objective might be to persuade oppressed groups to realise that they are being oppressed and potentially therefore, encourage them to do something to change their situation.

Critical social research is very different to the supposedly objective, neutral and detached approach adopted by positivists, and it is not tied to any single research method. Critical social scientists have used a whole range of research methods, including questionnaires, interviews, case studies and ethnography (the qualitative study of a culture or way of life). When looking at wider social structures, they are more likely to use methods that produce quantitative data. When trying to understand the way that exploited groups experience oppression, they are more likely to use qualitative methods. So, for example, Marxists often use official statistics on the distribution of income and wealth to examine class structures and to study the way capitalism is working. An example is the work of the French Marxist Thomas Piketty (2014) whose study, *Capital in the Twenty-First Century*, has become very influential.

Marxists don't always focus exclusively on the structure of society as a whole: they sometimes examine the day-to-day experience of exploitation and oppression of those from disadvantaged groups such as the proletariat. The neo-Marxist Paul Willis (1977) used ethnography to study the anti-school culture of male working-class schoolchildren. Critical sociologists who look at a range of different inequalities may also use ethnographic approaches. For example, Beverley Skeggs, studying class and gender, used participant observation and in-depth interviews to study working-class women at a further education college in Lancaster (1997).

Because of the range of different theoretical approaches used by critical sociologists, their choice of research method is likely to be influenced as much – if not more – by practical and ethical factors as by theoretical factors. However, the precise theoretical stance does make some difference. For example, neo-Marxists who believe that the economic structure of society does not completely determine how class consciousness develops are more likely to conduct qualitative research into exploited social groups.

This type of research is sometimes called 'critical ethnography'. The American sociologist of education, Phil Carspecken (1996), has described how critical ethnographers should build up a picture of the social world from the viewpoint of those who are in disadvantaged positions in society. Carspecken believes that this should involve the subjects of the research taking an active part in the research process, by checking the data produced by sociologists to see how convincing it is in describing their situation and their lives.

However, to Carspecken, critical research should go further and be used to "discover system relations". That is, it should be used to investigate the overall patterns of inequality, exploitation and oppression, which stem from broader social structures. So, for example, the relationships found in a school might be linked to the content of the mass media, the local labour market or the effects that globalisation is having upon educational policy.

Critical sociology and suicide

Critical sociology has not been extensively used to study suicide, but it was used by Michel Dorais (2004), who studied the high suicide rate among young men in Canada. The study focused on 32 Canadian men aged between 14 and 25, who had attempted suicide at least once. The interview-based research found that most of these attempts could be related to the individuals being regarded as gay or effeminate by other people. As well as interviews, he used statistical data to look at the wider structural patterns and found that suicide and attempted suicide rates were 6 to 16 times higher among young gay men than among young heterosexual men. On this basis, Dorais broadens his arguments not just to cover suicide, but also to develop an argument that dominant ideas about masculinity remain oppressive features of Western societies and that they can lead to effeminophobia (dislike of effeminate men).

FEMINISM AND RESEARCH METHODS

Feminism is a form of critical social science that has developed its own methodologies. Feminists are highly critical of 'malestream' research (male-dominated research, see Chapter 2) and, as a result, have claimed that new research methods need to be developed that reject patriarchal assumptions about social life and the way it should be studied.

One of the pioneers of both feminist sociology and feminist methodology was Ann Oakley.

Feminist interviewing

Oakley (1981) argued that there was a dominant masculine, patriarchal model of interviewing that was typically used by social scientists. It was based upon masculine values of objectivity, control and detachment. Oakley believed that this approach tended to produce invalid data because there was no rapport or true understanding between interviewer and interviewee. According to the dominant approach to interviewing, which Oakley saw as patriarchal, any attempt to establish a relationship between the interviewer and interviewee was seen as likely to distort the validity of the data, because it risked the interviewer influencing the sort of answers given by the interviewee (see the discussion of interviewer bias in Book 1, pages 134–5).

Furthermore, Oakley argues, the patriarchal approach is based on a hierarchical relationship in which the interviewer controls and directs their subject. The interviewee is regarded simply as a passive source of data who is mined for information and then plays no further part in the research.

Oakley argues that feminist interviewing should represent a genuine dialogue in which the people being studied are equally entitled to ask questions as the interviewer. This type of interviewing facilitates the development of a greater rapport and understanding between interviewer and interviewee and is likely to produce more honest, open and full answers. Oakley further regards it as unethical simply to treat the interviewees as subjects to be exploited for information.

As a critical social scientist, she believes in intervention in the social world in order to try to improve it rather than just to describe it. One way to intervene positively is for the interviewer to give something back to her subjects by, for example, offering useful advice. Some of Oakley's early interviews were about the experience of being a housewife; Oakley thought it was appropriate, indeed desirable, for her to help the women being studied with their housework.

Another aspect of feminist interviewing, in this approach, is encouragement of the women to discuss the findings of the research to see whether they ring true with them. Oakley thought that this interactive approach allowed her to check whether she was really understanding and describing a situation accurately. Oakley therefore argues that, in interviews: "personal involvement is more than dangerous bias – it is the condition under which people come to know each other and to admit others into their lives." (1981). It is, indeed, the only way truly to understand the viewpoint of someone else.

Oakley's approach to interviewing has been widely influential, although some sociologists (for example, Pawson, 1992) question whether it is really original or just the development of interviewing techniques used by many interpretivist sociologists. It nevertheless represents a radical departure from the supposed objectivity of positivist methods and – arguably – can produce more valid data about the social world.

Standpoint epistemology

An alternative strand of feminist methodology is known as feminist standpoint **epistemology**.

UNDERSTAND THE CONCEPT

Epistemology is the theory of knowledge, and covers issues to do with what knowledge is and how it can be acquired. For example, positivist epistemologists believe knowledge can be gained through direct observation of facts, while feminist standpoint epistemologists believe it can be gained through experience of oppression.

This approach does not deny that it is possible to discover the truth about society but, unlike positivism, it argues that the truth cannot be discovered through simple observation of the 'facts' and the use of statistical relationships. Instead, it argues, the truth can only be discovered by understanding the experiences of members of society who are oppressed. Advocates of this approach, such as Liz Stanley and Sue Wise (1993), believe that understanding comes from experience and therefore whatever research methods are adopted, the aim of them must be to describe and explain the standpoint of different groups of women accurately, particularly women who are oppressed, rather than White, middle-class or upper-class heterosexual women, who are not oppressed in the same way. This methodological approach tends to favour a variety of qualitative methods, with the aim of producing many different accounts of the world from the viewpoint of different women.

Feminist standpoint epistemology is totally rejected by positivists, who see it as merely producing a variety of personal opinions. It becomes impossible to determine which view of social reality among many is the more accurate, which is why positivists prefer a more detached and, to them, more objective, approach to gathering data.

Evaluation of critical social science methodology

Critical social science methodology is often criticised by positivists for lacking objectivity. They tend to see critical social science as based on little more than the ideologies of those who support them. Whatever they research, Marxists will tend to find class differences and exploitation, feminists will find patriarchy and anti-racists will find racism. In addition, like other research, it is only as credible as the research methods used and all research methods can be criticised. Critical social scientists such as Carspecken argue that this type of research can be perfectly open to changing theories in response to evidence, like any other approach to methodology. In addition, all research is based to some extent on theoretical assumptions about how society works, so the possibility that researchers are influenced by their own values cannot be avoided (see Chapter 6 for a discussion of values).

Do you think critical social scientists can be rigorous researchers, despite their ideological commitment? Is their approach inevitably more biased than that of positivism?

POSTMODERN METHODOLOGY

There is no general agreement among all postmodernists about what sort of methodology should be used to study the social world. However, most postmodernists are quite critical of conventional research methods and, like feminists, they reject positivism. Positivism is an example of modernist methodology from a postmodern point of view, because it is a scientific method that claims that the truth can be discovered through the use of the correct techniques. For example, positivists believe that carefully developed and tested questionnaires can discover facts about society. However, postmodernist sociologists such as Lyotard (1984) argue that there is no way of distinguishing between true knowledge and untrue knowledge. Lyotard sees all knowledge as a form of storytelling and, while some stories might be more convincing, that does not necessarily mean that the convincing stories are true. However persuasive, they are still just stories.

Postmodernists who follow this approach, such as Stephen Tyler (1997), support a type of postmodern ethnography in which the researcher and those being studied work together to produce an account of the social world, as experienced by the subjects of the research. To Tyler, there should be no assumption that this description of the social world is superior or more true than other descriptions of the social world, but it is nevertheless important that different descriptions are produced. According to Tyler, this captures the mood of a postmodern world in which social life is fragmented, and it is impossible to find a single way of understanding complex and ever-changing societies.

Postmodern methodology tends to support qualitative above quantitative methods and is generally sympathetic to the use of techniques such as in-depth interviews and participant observation. These methods are more appropriate than more statistical techniques for producing different stories.

Evaluation

A problem with the types of postmodern method described above is that they abandon any attempt at providing explanations for social phenomena and instead just offer multiple description with no suggestion as to which are more credible. Without explanations, it is impossible to suggest solutions. In these circumstances, postmodern methodology means there is no basis for intervening in the social world and trying to solve social problems. Many critical sociologists therefore see postmodern methods as being very conservative and by implication supporting the status quo. For many sociologists, valid descriptions of the social world should be the starting point for sociological research, but they should not be the end point.

THEORY, TRIANGULATION AND MULTIPLE METHODS

As the above discussion has demonstrated, there is no clear, simple and direct relationship between perspectives on society and the methods used to study society. Some theories, such as interpretivist ones, are quite closely tied to particular research methods but, in reality, researchers following the same broad perspective often use quite different methods. As you saw in Book 1 (see Topic 2, Chapter 1), this is partly because the link between theory and methods is often quite a loose one due to practical and ethical factors intervening. Sometimes, the most ideal method for a researcher to use is not practically or ethically possible. For example, in the study of suicide, it is not possible to interview people who have actually committed suicide because they are no longer alive; also, there may be ethical concerns about interviewing vulnerable people at risk of suicide. Furthermore, differences within perspectives may point towards different types of method (for example, differences between Marxists who might use methods intended to produce more quantitative date and neo-Marxists who might be more likely to use methods intended to produce qualitative data). A further complication is that many sociologists do not adhere to one particular perspective.

There is a trend in contemporary sociological research and writing towards using a mixture of different theories or perspectives. William Outhwaite (2015) claims that sociologists now often draw upon a number of celebrity sociologists in thinking about society. These include Zygmunt Bauman, Anthony Giddens, Pierre Bourdieu and Ulrich Beck. Partly for this reason, and also for practical and ethical reasons, many sociologists now use several research methods in tandem when studying the social world.

Would you agree that using multiple methods is usually preferable to using just one method in sociological research? Explain your answer.

FOCUS ON SKILLS: CONNECTING THEORY AND RESEARCH METHODS

A field experiment to study the impact of labelling students may involve classroom observation.

You will be familiar with the ideas in the following paragraph, which are quite typical of what many students write when asked about the relationship between sociological theory and methods.

"Functionalists like to use quantitative methods. This is because they are positivists and like to treat sociology as a science. Statistics allow them to access large, representative samples, provide clear evidence of social trends and give reasonable chance of achieving value-freedom. In contrast, interactionists like observations; they allow the researcher to gain a genuine empathy with those studied and to gain a truly deep, valid understanding of the small group they are studying."

This kind of response offers a basic account of the traditional relationship between theory and method. However, it is rather simplistic.

Rosenthal and Jacobsen (1968) are interactionists who used field experiments in their research to test the impact of labelling students. The choice of a positivistic method – complete with dependent and independent variables – may be necessary to prove that a teacher-given label actually affects achievement. So it is clearly not as simple as "structuralists prefer positivist methods" and "those who use interviews and observations ignore social structure". The issue of social mobility is one that is stubbornly structuralist in terms of how mobility is measured, but it also lends itself to investigation using interpretivist and interactionist methodologies. Paul Willis, in *Learning to Labour* (1977), for example, famously undertook participant observation in his study of working-class boys and then combined structure and action to argue that these 'lads' chose to fail.

"Researching social life is a complicated business which does not respond well to simple either/or distinctions."

Source: Rogers (2012)

Questions

1. **Explain** what the author means by suggesting that the description in the second paragraph is 'simplistic'.

2. **Explain** why Rosenthal and Jacobsen's method is described as 'positivistic'.

3. **Suggest two reasons** why sociologists might sometimes use methods that do not obviously fit their theoretical approach.

4. **Evaluate.** Discuss the weaknesses of the description of the relationship between theory and methods found in the second paragraph.

SUICIDE AND METHODOLOGICAL PLURALISM

In the study of suicide, a good example of methodological pluralism is the work of Jonathan Scourfield, Ben Fincham, Susanne Langer and Michel Shiner (2012). Their study was based upon a mixture of quantitative evidence (as advocated by positivists) and qualitative data (as supported by interpretivists and phenomenologists). Scourfield *et al.* accept Atkinson's point that suicide verdicts may not be entirely reliable. However, they argue that it is possible to produce reliable statistics on suicide, as long as sociologists critically examine the evidence about deaths and evaluate it so they can determine which deaths really were caused by suicide. They believe that, once the statistics have been refined in this way, it is reasonable to use them to help to understand the structural causes of suicide. However, it is also useful to look at qualitative data to try to understand the circumstances and likely motives behind suicide.

In their research they examined coroners' case files of 100 deaths that had been classified as suicide. Having refined the statistics, they then produced theories about the possible causes of suicide, which were tested further by looking at the qualitative evidence about the likely motives of those who were thought to have taken their own lives.

CONCLUSIONS

The work of Scourfield *et al.* suggests that sociologists do not always need to choose between quantitative and qualitative data, structural and social action approaches or positivist and interpretivist methodologies. A fuller and more in-depth understanding of the social world might be achieved by combining these different elements. While particular theories do therefore tend towards using certain types of method, there are many exceptions; an increasing trend towards theoretical and methodological pluralism suggests that the relationship between theory and methods is likely to become progressively looser as time passes.

CHECK YOUR UNDERSTANDING

1. What is meant by 'praxis'?

2. Explain what is meant by 'standpoint epistemology'.

3. Explain what is meant by 'integration'.

4. Identify and briefly explain three reasons why sociologists might use methods that are not usually associated with their theoretical approach.

5. Identify one methodological approach, discussed in this chapter, that suggests that all knowledge about society is relative, so no facts can be discovered about society.

6. Explain two differences between positivist and feminist methodology.

7. Explain briefly why Atkinson decided to study coroners' courts in order to understand suicide.

8. Outline two criticisms of positivist methodology.

9. Identify two examples of research by critical social scientists.

10. Evaluate the view that no one method on its own is sufficient to produce an adequate sociological understanding of suicide.

TAKE IT FURTHER

1. Choose any one example of sociological research and investigate the theory or theories used by the author(s) and the method(s) used to conduct the research.
   › How closely does the methodology reflect the theory?
   › Suggest reasons why the sociologist(s) chose the methods used.
   › What does the example suggest about the relationship between theory and methods?

2.5 SOCIOLOGY AND SCIENCE

LEARNING OBJECTIVES

› Demonstrate knowledge and understanding of different views on the relationship between sociology and science (AO1).

› Apply this understanding to sociological theories and research (AO2).

› Analyse the similarities and differences between competing views on the relationship between sociology and science (AO3).

› Evaluate the strengths and weaknesses of competing views on the relationship between sociology and science (AO3).

INTRODUCING THE DEBATE

For more than 100 years, sociologists have argued among themselves as to whether or not sociology is a science.

Many early sociologists went out of their way to claim scientific status for sociology. This is partly because both funding and academic prestige are more likely to be gained when subjects are regarded as 'scientific', because it is widely perceived that scientific knowledge is superior to other forms of knowledge.

However, opinions differ over what exactly constitutes a scientific subject and over the theoretical and methodological approach that sociology should adopt. Furthermore, the integrity and objectivity of science have been questioned by some sociologists. For these reasons, a variety of answers have been given to questions about whether or not sociology is a science and, if not, whether it is possible and desirable for it to become a scientific subject.

WHAT IS A SCIENCE?

The positivist approach

There is more than one version of positivist methodology that has influenced sociology, but Durkheim's approach, as illustrated by his study, *Suicide* (1897), is perhaps the most influential and can be used to illustrate a positivist view of science. Durkheim's approach is based upon the following principles.

› There are objective social facts about the social world. These facts can be discovered directly through the senses and, in particular, they can be observed or seen. Facts can be expressed in statistics.

› Such facts are not influenced by the researcher's personal opinion (or subjective viewpoint) or their beliefs about right and wrong (values). If sociologists use appropriate research methods that avoid their becoming subjectively involved (for example, by using questionnaires rather than participant observation), they can remain objective. In his study of suicide, Durkheim himself used official statistics that he assumed were objective Durkheim was therefore an **empiricist**.

UNDERSTAND THE CONCEPT

Empiricism is the view that knowledge comes from sensory experience (for example, seeing, hearing, touching). It tends to downplay the importance of theory.

› Having collected sets of statistics (which Durkheim saw as facts) about the social world, you can look for correlations (patterns in which two or more things tend to occur together).

› Correlations may represent causal relationships, that is, one type of fact causing another (for example, hypothetically it may be proposed that religion causes suicide or prevents it).

› Careful analysis of the effects of different factors (or independent variables) is then needed to check that correlations represent genuine causal relationships. (Today this is usually done through computer programs such as SPSS – The Statistics Package for Social Scientists.)

› Durkheim believed that, by following this approach, it is possible to discover laws of human behaviour – causes of behaviour that are generally true for all societies.

› Durkheim believed that, human behaviour can be explained in terms of external stimuli (things that happen to us) rather than internal stimuli (what goes on in the human mind).

› To be scientific, you should only study what you can observe. It is therefore unscientific to study people's emotions, meanings or motives, which are internal to the unobservable mind of the individual and therefore cannot be studied objectively.

Durkheim's approach has two key features that distinguish it from some other attempts to explain how sociology can be scientific.

› First, it is **inductive** in its approach. That is, in trying to explain how society works, you start by looking at the evidence and from that you induce theories. These are then tested against the evidence.

› Second, it is based upon verification (Giddens, 1978). From this point of view, theories can be confirmed or verified through the collection of evidence.

UNDERSTAND THE CONCEPTS

Induction involves starting with the evidence and examining it to derive a theory to explain it. Deduction involves starting with a theory and testing it by working out what evidence will verify or falsify it and then collecting that evidence (for example, in an experiment).

Positivism and sociology

Not all sociologists who adopt essentially positivist methods accept all features of Durkheim's ideas. For example, many stop short of claiming that universal laws of human behaviour can be discovered; they would claim, more modestly, that they have simply found the correct explanations for particular aspects of social life, in a particular place at a particular time. Furthermore, the idea of induction has been strongly criticised and alternative scientific approaches have been developed, such as that of Karl Popper, which is discussed later in the chapter. However, Durkheim's view is still influential and it gives simple answers to the question of whether sociology can and should be scientific. From Durkheim's point of view, any sociology that uses objective statistical methods, based on data produced by direct observation, is scientific.

Of course, not all sociology fits this description but, in principle, according to Durkheim, any aspect of social life could be studied in this way and therefore it was always possible for sociology to be scientific. Furthermore, Durkheim believed that natural and social sciences can produce knowledge that is equally objective and scientific.

Think of some examples of research based upon positivist methodology. Would you regard the research as scientific? Is the research convincing?

Karl Popper: science as falsification

An alternative approach claiming that sociology can be scientific is put forward by Karl Popper (1959). Popper agrees with Durkheim that sociology can, in principle, be scientific and that it is a good thing for it to be considered as a scientific subject. However, compared to positivists, he has a rather different view of what science is and he rejects some of Durkheim's ideas.

First, he rejects an inductive approach. Popper suggests that whatever you are studying will have to be informed by some sort of initial theory, however undeveloped that theory is. It doesn't particularly matter where this theory comes from – it could be just a hunch, or it could come from data you have collected – but it is nevertheless essential to have a clear theory to test. This is because he supports a deductive approach. When using deduction you deduce, from a theory, what you will find when you collect evidence if that theory is true. If the theory is sufficiently specific and detailed, you can then make precise predictions about what the data will show if it is consistent with the theory.

Second, and following from the above, it is possible to check the theory, not in order to verify it (to confirm it is true) but rather to see if you can falsify it (or prove it wrong). Popper does not believe it is ever possible definitively to verify a theory and therefore to claim that you have discovered a law of human behaviour. It is always possible that, at some point in the future, some evidence, or examples, will not fit the theory and will therefore prove the theory to be untrue. For example, the theory that all swans are white might apparently be confirmed by numerous observations of swans. However, this would be misleading if the observer had not been to Australia, where black swans do exist and a simple observation would falsify the theory.

Popper's highly influential ideas have had important implications for both natural and social sciences. They suggest that scientific knowledge can never be taken to be the final and incontrovertible truth, since it may always be disproved in the future. However, according to Popper, the logic of science still gives us the best knowledge that we can possibly have. If people have repeatedly tried to disprove a theory but have failed, it is far more likely to be true than any theory that has not been rigorously tested.

The problems of social science

The same situation applies to social scientific theories. To Popper though, the problem with much social science is that its theories are not sufficiently precise to be falsified or proved wrong. For example, he was particularly critical of Marxism for predicting a proletarian revolution and the overthrow of capitalism, but not saying when it would happen. It is therefore impossible to say definitively that

Marxism has been falsified (the revolution might happen in the future) and, for this reason, Marxism cannot in Popper's view be considered to be a scientific theory. However, to Popper, sociology can be scientific so long as it makes precise predictions.

The logic of Popper's approach is applied in experimental research in a variety of natural and social scientists' work (see Book 1, pages 113–14). In experiments, hypotheses are deduced from theories, which are then rigorously tested under controlled conditions. Repetition of experiments can be used to try to falsify particular theories. For a number of reasons though, experiments are not widely used in sociology, but sociologists do often use what is called the 'hypothetico-deductive model'. This approach follows the logic of experiments but, where necessary, outside a laboratory setting. It involves developing theories, identifying hypotheses derived from those theories, collecting evidence to test them and, where the evidence does not fit, refining or changing the theories before using revised hypotheses to test the new theories. This process of testing theories with evidence continues until the evidence fits the theory; it can then be tested further to see if it can be falsified. In principle, this logic is certainly used quite widely in sociology and other social sciences although, as we shall see, there are problems in social sciences in finding a perfect fit between theories and evidence.

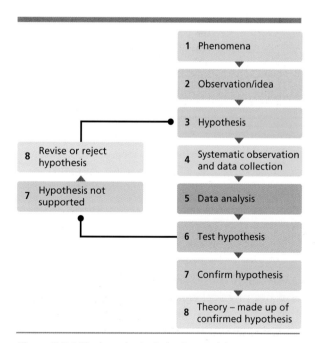

Figure 2.5.1 The hypothetic-deductive model

Sociology and Popper's approach

Most early sociologists, including Parsons, Karl Marx, Durkheim and Comte, did believe they were scientific in approach; many current sociologists also believe that they are being scientific by adopting scientific methods. However, Popper's exacting demands suggest that he would not consider most sociological research to be scientific. Nevertheless, Popper still regarded it as desirable and possible for social scientists to be scientific. It just required precision, rigorous testing and a willingness to admit when you were wrong if your theory was falsified.

Popper's approach, although very supportive of scientific method, does raise some tentative questions about how far scientific knowledge, even in the natural sciences, should be believed. From his point of view, even the most rigorously tested knowledge is ultimately open to question, since it might be proved wrong in the future. This scepticism about the truth of natural and social scientific knowledge has been taken much further by some sociologists, whose views will be examined shortly.

Can you think of any examples of sociological theories that have been proved wrong, rather than just being criticised? Why might it be difficult to prove sociological theories wrong?

QUESTIONING SOCIOLOGY AS SCIENTIFIC: INTERPRETIVIST SOCIOLOGY

Sociological criticisms of sociology as a science

So far, the dominant voices in this topic have been those supporting the notion that sociology can and should be considered scientific. However, since the 1960s, especially with the growth of interactionist and, later, postmodern writings, there has been a range of criticisms from within sociology as to whether it can, or even should, claim to be a science.

Differences between the nature of society and the physical world

The first criticism comes from those who argue that society is not comparable to the natural world and to attempt to transfer the methods and ideas of the natural sciences is a mistake. This argument is less about methods and more about the reality of the world

around us. Is there an objective world outside that exists independently of us, or is the world somehow 'constructed' through the meanings attributed to it by human beings? Interpretivist, interactionist and phenomenological sociologists all believe that the world is socially constructed and that meanings are crucial to understanding it.

To interpretivists and interactionists, for example, meanings such as people's self-concepts shape and influence their behaviour. People attach meaning to the world around them and have motives for acting in particular ways. You can't understand and explain crime, for example, without some reference to why people choose to break the law.

Furthermore, according to phenomenologists and some postmodernists (for example, Lyotard), the external world can only be known, understood and categorised through language; there is no way of observing it directly to record facts about it. To phenomenologists, knowledge is produced through the classification of the world through mental categories, and these mental categories are products of society. For example, whether a death is a suicide or not, and whether a person is a criminal or not, are matters of interpretation, judgement and definition rather than facts. Because of this, there is no solid foundation on which to base a scientific sociology. With no facts, it is impossible to test theories and either verify them or falsify them. It is also impossible to exclude unobservable subjective states from study. What is going on in people's heads matters and can't simply be ignored just because you can't observe it directly. If thought processes are fundamental aspects of social life, excluding them from sociological study would render sociology worthless.

Problems of prediction

Secondly, another problem arises from Popper's claim that scientific subjects should be based upon the testing of precise predictions. This is because it can be argued that the natural and social worlds consist of different types of phenomenon. Most things studied in the natural world (apart from plants and animals) are inanimate and, with the exception of animals, do not possess consciousness. They don't attach meanings to the external stimuli that might influence them. For example, plants don't think about whether it is raining or not and decide whether they are going to grow, nor do rocks interpret the meaning of forces that act on them. The natural world is therefore quite predictable; the human social world is not. Different individuals placed in identical circumstances will often react differently because they have different biographies. They will give different meanings to events around them and they have different motives for acting. Because of this, if sociology were limited to putting forward theories that made precise predictions, these would be constantly proved wrong. The subject would consist entirely of discredited theories and it would not survive long.

From this point of view the unpredictability of humans means that Popper's view of science could not be applied to sociology; it would be inappropriate and counter-productive.

MODERNITY, POSTMODERNITY AND SCIENCE

Quite similar views to those of phenomenologists are put forward by some postmodernists:

› Science and modernity have gone hand-in-hand, according to Rorty (1980), with the belief that rationality, truth and science are all bound together, and that other ways of knowing the world are inferior.

› Postmodernists challenge this view and question how far scientists produce the 'truth' about the natural world. For Rorty, scientists have simply replaced priests as the sources of truth. We want someone to be the expert and to make sense of the world for us. Science has taken on this role. Yet we now know that, despite the advances in science, there may well be concepts and questions that it can never answer – questions about the origins of the universe, the concept of infinity, and so on.

› Lyotard (1984) has also shown that the nature of language limits and channels science, because it provides a framework to approach an understanding of the world. Language both opens up some possibilities and closes down others, since we think within language and are unable to conceive of something that is outside our linguistic framework. For both Rorty and Lyotard then, scientists are deluded in thinking that science can stand apart from the social world in which it is produced and offer an objective and 'true' account of the natural world.

That is not to say that all sociologists reject the idea of sociology being, or becoming, a scientific subject. As we shall see, there are other views of the nature of science apart from those put forward by positivists and by Popper. Some of these do suggest that it is possible for sociology to be scientific (see the realist view below).

Is science objective?

Increasingly, natural science itself has come under fire for not matching the criteria of science discussed above. From the 1960s onwards, a number of sociologists began to put science itself 'under the microscope'. They found the traditional model of viewing science as provider of superior and totally objective knowledge was, to say the least, questionable. An approach known as Science and Technology Studies (S&TS) began to be developed.

An early S&TS sociologist, David Bloor (1976) introduced the idea of **symmetry**.

UNDERSTAND THE CONCEPT

This principle of **symmetry** simply states that all social phenomena, including science, should be explained in the same way. According to Bloor it made no sense to see science as existing outside society, as the one place in which social influences had no effect at all. Instead, he believed that science, like any other part of the social world, is shaped by a variety of social factors that would influence what was accepted as true or false.

A symmetrical approach was developed by Bruno Latour and Steve Woolgar (1979), who studied the way that 'scientific facts' were constructed in a laboratory where they carried out an observational study. The scientists in the study spent a great deal of time trying to get research grants; there was little incentive to try to disprove ideas once they had spent so much time and money making particular claims. Instead they took part in "a fierce fight to construct reality". Constructing reality was a complex process in which the scientists would use other scientists and machines, sometimes specially designed for the purpose of proving that certain entities exist or that particular theories were true. Together scientists, other people and things were 'enrolled' in a network to produce a version of reality. If these people or things were hindering rather than helping they could be 'disenrolled' from the network so that they didn't disrupt efforts to construct reality.

Latour and Woolgar don't address whether or not scientific knowledge is 'true' because this is not relevant to the argument. (Just as sociologists of religion don't usually discuss whether religion is true.) The point is that scientific knowledge, like any other knowledge, is produced through social processes that sociologists can research, analyse and try to understand.

Are there any claims, made by scientists, of which you are sceptical? Why don't you entirely trust them? What does this tell you about science in society today?

THOMAS KUHN: PARADIGMS AND SCIENTIFIC REVOLUTIONS

S&TS approaches to studying science suggest that scientific knowledge is inevitably socially constructed rather than objective and, to some extent, these views are similar to those of Thomas Kuhn (1962/1970).

Kuhn noted that science was usually seen as progressing through the use of the hypothetico-deductive model, which allowed ideas to be constantly refined as theories are found wanting and new theories that fit the evidence better are developed. From this point of view, scientific understanding is constantly improving. However, Kuhn argues, science really develops in a rather different way.

Rather than science being characterised by gradual and continual changes, as scientists evaluated and refined each other's ideas, most of the time scientists accepted, supported and applied existing theories rather than challenging them. Kuhn describes this as 'normal science', which operates within a **paradigm**.

UNDERSTAND THE CONCEPT

A **paradigm** is an accepted framework of theory, concepts and methodologies related to a particular area of knowledge. This framework includes assumptions regarding what is important, the correct procedures and the right sort of questions to be asking.

A paradigm dominates scientific thinking, and traps thought and investigation within it. Any attempt to step outside the accepted conventions is usually ignored or rejected.

For example, in climatology, the idea that human activity was changing the climate was initially treated with scepticism by many scientists and only gradually came to be widely accepted (Sutton, 2015). Similarly, the belief that continents moved or drifted over the Earth's surface was regarded as ridiculous for many decades. When theories such as these are rejected, it is very difficult to conduct research to investigate them because those who propose

them are likely to be marginalised. Most scientists develop their careers while operating within a particular paradigm and they see the world in terms of that approach. They don't consider alternative explanations or research the possibility that the paradigms might be seriously flawed.

It took a long time for the adverse human effect on global warming to be accepted as scientific fact.

However, from time to time, science changes in a scientific revolution that creates a new paradigm. So science changes through occasional, sudden leaps rather than through the gradual refining of theory and accumulation of knowledge. Kuhn suggests that, over time, within normal science there may be a gradual build-up of evidence that does not fit into the accepted paradigm and, at some point, out of this mismatch between theory and evidence, a new paradigm emerges which appears to explain the previous inconsistencies. However, there is likely to be strong resistance to new paradigms and they may not become fully accepted until long after there is strong evidence to back them up.

When a scientific revolution occurs, what was previously taken to be untrue is accepted and a new version of the truth becomes the norm for scientists. For example, in the 20th century, Einstein's theory of relativity superseded previous theories in physics. Another example is Alfred Wegener's theory of continental drift, being finally accepted in the 1950s, when evidence about magnetic fields on the ocean floor in the Atlantic convinced the scientific community that the theory was correct after all.

After a scientific revolution occurs and there is a paradigm-shift, the new paradigm becomes accepted without much question until it too is replaced by a new approach that seems to fit the evidence better.

Kuhn's ideas suggest that there is no reason to believe that the current paradigms will be accepted forever and therefore be taken to be true. Even if a large number of scientists agree, and they have evidence to support their theory, it may be that they are simply interpreting the evidence to fit their theory.

Evaluation and implications for sociology

Kuhn's approach suggests that scientists are influenced as much by their scientific peers and their desire for a successful career as they are by the impartial analysis of the evidence.

Kuhn is himself not free from critics, however. Lakatos (1970) has argued that Kuhn's idea of paradigms is too simplistic and only applies to the past. Lakatos believes that modern science is largely open and much more sophisticated in its thinking. Rarely in the recent history of modern science have central ideas been abandoned. Modern science has not been shaken by paradigm shifts which characterised its earlier history, its central ideas have remained intact and broadly unchanged

Nevertheless, Kuhn's theory provides an interesting way of thinking about sociology. Arguably, in sociology, a single paradigm has rarely been dominant. Perhaps structural functionalism came closest in the 1950s and early 1960s; it was certainly very influential in the USA and, to a lesser extent, in the UK. However, even then alternative paradigms, such as symbolic interactionism in the USA and Marxism and Weberian sociology in Europe, were available to sociologists. Because sociology today seems more characterised by a plurality of paradigms rather than one, it can be argued that it is not a particularly scientific subject. But this could be seen as a strength more than a weakness. It is debatable whether it is desirable for sociology to be scientific in the sense that it accepts a single paradigm. The subject may benefit from using a variety of paradigms (or, in sociological terms, perspectives) rather than trying to rely upon one. Indeed, it seems unlikely that a single theory could explain every aspect of the social world.

Do you think sociology could ever have just one paradigm? Explain your answer.

REALIST VIEWS OF SCIENCE AND OPEN AND CLOSED SYSTEMS

Earlier in this chapter, a number of arguments were considered that suggest that it is impossible and/or undesirable for sociology to be a science. Some sociologists have emphasised that the subject matter of sociology is unsuited to scientific methods; some sociologists and philosophers of science have suggested that scientific knowledge is itself imperfect and, for various reasons, socially constructed. However, some sociologists adopt a different model of science – the realist view – and claim that social sciences such as sociology and natural sciences are not too dissimilar. Andrew Sayer (1992) is one such sociologist who supports the realist view.

According to Sayer, the models of the physical sciences based on positivism and/or Popper are misleading. This is because the models fail to distinguish between the open and closed systems in which scientists operate. The stereotypical image of science is based on sciences such as chemistry or physics, which operate in closed systems. Closed systems only have a limited number of variables interacting and all these variables can be controlled. This makes it possible to carry out laboratory experiments (or similar types of research) and to make precise predictions about what will happen in those experiments. However, other physical sciences, such as meteorology (the study of weather) and seismology (the study of earthquakes), operate in open systems in which there are many variables that cannot be controlled. For example, the Earth's weather system is too complex to allow very precise weather forecasts, and seismology cannot predict when earthquakes will occur. These sciences recognise unpredictability so they cannot conform to Popper's view of science and base their research on making precise predictions.

This does not mean, though, that these are not scientific subjects. Meteorologists can explain the forces producing weather and seismologists can understand how earthquakes occur and identify the areas where they are most likely to happen. They can refine their models and develop their understanding, but they are unlikely ever to be able to make accurate and precise predictions. What they are doing, in producing scientific knowledge, is understanding the underlying structures and processes that are causing the phenomena that require explaining. You can't always see these structures and processes directly – for example, in seismology, seismic waves tend to take place below the Earth's surface – but that doesn't mean you can't work out that they are happening by observing their effects. From this viewpoint, positivists are wrong to believe that you can only study observable phenomena, because many accepted scientific phenomena (including magnetic fields, evolution and sub-atomic particles) cannot be directly seen.

Realism and sociology

According to Sayer's realist viewpoint, the social sciences are no different from many physical sciences. They share with science the aim of uncovering the underlying structures and processes that make things happen, whether these are seismic waves or class conflict.

Realists, for example, might argue that we can only understand conflict between workers and owners by understanding the class structure, or women's experience of work by understanding patriarchy. The realist philosophy of science is often adopted by critical social scientists, such as Marxists and feminists looking for the underlying structures and processes that cause inequality and exploitation.

Realist philosophy of science restores the possibility that sociology can be seen as scientific. However, critics question whether realist approaches actually reveal the structures and processes that shape social life. If they are not observable, other explanations of what is being explained are possible and direct tests of the theory may not be possible. However, its defenders claim that the approach is based on a sound understanding of the nature of the social world and the structures it contains, and it should not therefore be rejected just because it poses some methodological challenges.

FOCUS ON SKILLS: *LANCET* JOURNAL RETRACTS ANDREW WAKEFIELD MMR SCARE PAPER

A leading medical journal has officially retracted the discredited study which sparked a health scare over the MMR (measles mumps and rubella) vaccine.

The Lancet said it now accepted claims made by the researchers, which linked MMR to bowel disorders and autism, were 'false'.

It comes after Andrew Wakefield, the lead researcher in the 1998 paper, was ruled last week to have been irresponsible and dishonest in carrying out the original study on 12 children.

MMR is the combined measles, mumps and rubella vaccine which was introduced in 1988. The fall-out from the research, first published in February 1998, caused vaccination rates to plummet and has been blamed for a resurgence of measles in Britain.

Invasive procedures were carried out on the 12 children without proper ethics committee approval and without due regard to their clinical needs, the GMC found.

Wakefield was also found to have received £50,000 from the Legal Aid Board to carry out the research

on behalf of parents who believed their children had already been harmed by MMR.

Wakefield and two former colleagues, John Walker-Smith and Simon Murch, now face being struck off the medical register if they are found guilty of a further charge of serious professional misconduct later this year.

The three doctors deny any wrongdoing. The *Lancet* had already issued a partial retraction of the paper in 2004, rejecting the interpretation that the vaccine could be linked to health problems.

Rose, D. (2010), '*Lancet* journal retracts Andrew Wakefield MMR scare paper', *The Times*, 3 February 2010

Questions

1. **Understand**. What social factors might have encouraged these researchers to look for a link between the vaccine and bowel disease, and autism?

2. **Apply**. Applying the S&TS approach to this example, explain why it could be seen as evidence that science is socially constructed.

3. **Apply**. Applying Popper's philosophy of science to this example, suggest how it could be seen as an example of science doing its job.

4. **Apply**. Applying the realist view of science, explain how this could just be seen as an example of the problems of scientific research in an open system.

5. **Evaluate** whether it was ethically acceptable for the researchers to be paid by the Legal Aid Board.

SO IS SOCIOLOGY A SCIENCE?

There is no simple answer to this question. According to writers such as Sayer (1992), sociology can be as scientific as the natural sciences by adopting certain procedures. At the other extreme, postmodernists such as Rorty (1980) argue that being scientific is not something sociology should aspire to.

Somewhere in the middle lie the bulk of sociologists who accept that there is a debate over the scientific nature of sociological study, but who get on with their research, attempting to make sense of society in the best and most honest way they can, acknowledging that their arguments are open to criticism, but believing that imperfect knowledge is preferable to simple ignorance about social worlds.

CHECK YOUR UNDERSTANDING

1. What is meant by an 'open system'?

2. Explain what is meant by a 'paradigm'.

3. Explain what is meant by 'falsification'.

4. Identify and briefly explain three reasons why science could be regarded as socially constructed.

5. Identify one theory of science discussed in this chapter that suggests that only observable phenomena should be studied by scientists.

6. Explain two differences between realism and Popper's philosophy of science.

7. Briefly explain how S&TS challenges conventional views of science.

8. Outline two criticisms of positivist theories of science.

9. Identify two examples of scientific revolutions in natural sciences.

10. Evaluate the view that it is desirable for sociology to be scientific.

TAKE IT FURTHER

Go to the Bad Science website at www.badscience.net

The website features articles by Ben Goldacre, a writer for *The Guardian*, who discusses examples of science going wrong. Choose one or more examples from the site and summarise them. Analyse what problems they identify and discuss how they could be used in an essay on sociology and science.

2.6 VALUES AND ETHICS

LEARNING OBJECTIVES

› Demonstrate knowledge and understanding of the competing views on value-freedom and objectivity (AO1).

› Apply understanding to how sociologists work in practice (AO2).

› Analyse the similarities and differences between competing views on value-freedom and objectivity (AO3).

› Evaluate the strengths and weaknesses of competing views on value-freedom and objectivity (AO3).

INTRODUCING THE DEBATE

One of the most bitterly contested concepts in sociology is the question of the place of personal and political values in theory and research. Three distinct positions can be identified on this issue.

1. At one end of the debate are the sociologists who argue that if sociology wants to make any claim to scientific status, then it has to be free of personal and political biases. This is known as 'value-freedom' or 'objectivity'.

2. Some sociologists argue that, in an ideal situation, our personal values should not intrude into our sociological studies, but that in practice it is simply impossible to keep them out – sociology is 'value-laden'.

3. At the other extreme from 'value-freedom', some sociologists argue that sociologists must surely use their studies to improve the condition of those most oppressed in society. Sociology is, therefore, more a tool that helps bring about social change – committed sociology – than an academic subject studying society.

VALUE-FREE SOCIOLOGY

As you have seen in a previous chapter, there is a significant current of opinion in sociology (deriving from Comte and Durkheim) that argues that we should seek to copy the methodology of the physical sciences such as biology or chemistry. One of the key ideas that these sociologists, or positivists, have taken from the physical sciences is the importance of **objectivity** in research. However, it is not just positivists who have argued that an objective sociology is possible.

UNDERSTAND THE CONCEPT

A statement is **objective** if it accurately describes something that exists externally to the person describing it and it is true regardless of the personal (or subjective) viewpoint of the individual making the statement. The idea of objectivity is based upon the assumption that an external reality exists and that it can be described in a way that is not distorted by language or personal beliefs.

Karl Marx believed that his analysis of society was objective and scientific too, even though he also believed that social science (he saw himself as a political economist) should be committed to changing the world for the better (see the discussion of critical sociology below).

As discussed earlier, positivists argue that the nature of sociological research is no different from that of the physical sciences – both branches of science (the physical and the social) study a series of phenomena that exist totally independently of the scientists, and which can be measured and classified. On the basis of this, theories can be constructed and tested.

The 'social facts' positivists refer to are the statistics obtained by direct observation or, where this is impossible, through quantitative methods such as questionnaires, structured interviews and the use of official statistics. Such methods are objective to positivists because they are untainted by personal opinion and preference and simply count what exists, prior to the research, in the social world. According to O'Connell, Davidson and Layder (1994), personal biases and political opinions of researchers are irrelevant, provided that the research is well designed and there is no attempt to distort or alter the findings. Finally, and in line with Popper's ideas on falsification (see pages 154–56), to ensure that no biases have inadvertently intruded, there is the check that comes from publication of the research findings, which will include a discussion of methods used. The publication will be read, replicated and possibly criticised by other researchers.

Would you agree that positivists keep their values out of their theories and research?

VALUE-LADEN SOCIOLOGY

Advocates of this second school of thought believe that, whether it is desirable or not, sociology cannot be value-free and it is a mistake to see it as such. They further claim that sociologists who argue that sociology is value-free are actually doing a disservice to the subject, and they identify a number of ways in which values inevitably enter research.

Historical context
Gouldner (1968) pointed out that the argument for a value-free sociology is partially based in a particular historical context.

Weber has traditionally been associated with the idea that personal and political values should be largely excluded from research. According to Weber, sociologists could be objective in developing research methods, whether qualitative or quantitative. He thought that sociologists could and should ensure that they did not devise methods that would distort the results to suit their own preferences or values. They should then interpret those findings impartially and, if the evidence did not fit their original theories, they should change the theories. To Weber, sociologists should not be involved in using research to argue for particular values or policies. Evidence about how society works, he argued, should be seen as quite separate from beliefs about how social life should be organised, and researchers should not infer the latter from the former. However, Weber did believe that personal values would inevitably influence the selection of a research topic. With an infinite range of possible topics to research, sociologists could only research what they thought was important and this was bound to reflect their personal values.

Yet Gouldner claims that Weber was writing at a time when the Prussian (now German) government was making a strong attack on intellectual freedom. According to Gouldner, Weber was merely trying to prevent the government from interfering in sociology by claiming it was value-free. Furthermore, Weber's own research reflected his own moderately left-wing, reformist view of society and his concern for individual freedom. For example, he expressed concern about the effects that bureaucracy might have on human freedom (Haralambos and Holborn, 2013).

Paying for research
Sociological research has to be financed, and those who pay for the research usually have a reason for wanting it done. Sociologists working for British government departments, for instance, usually have to sign an agreement that if the department does not like the ideas or findings, then it has the right to prevent publication.

In *Market Killing*, Philo and Miller (2000) have argued that, increasingly, all sciences are having their critical researchers silenced. This is through a combination of targeted funding by those who want research undertaken only into topics that benefit them, and by the intrusion of commercial consultancies into research. This means that scientists benefit financially from certain outcomes and lose out if other outcomes are uncovered. They also point out that scientists allow their findings to be manipulated by public-relations companies, operating for the benefit of the funders – even when the findings do not necessarily support the funders' claims.

Career trajectories

As Gouldner (1968) pointed out, all sociologists have personal ambitions and career goals. They want to publish, be promoted and become renowned in their field. These desires can intrude, either knowingly or subconsciously, into their research activities. According to Kuhn (1962/1970), this involves accepting the dominant paradigms at any particular time within all academic subjects (see Chapter 5). This is also likely to encourage sociologists to study subjects that are fashionable in their discipline. For example, there have been fashions about whether or not social class should be seen as important and the subject of research (Holborn, 2015). Similarly, Mark J. Smith (2008) pointed to the great difficulty that environmental or 'green' sociology has had in getting its concerns about the environment accepted by the sociological 'establishment' – as green concerns are seen as peripheral. The struggles of feminists to get their interests and approaches accepted by sociology are also well documented (Abbot and Wallace, 1997).

Personal beliefs and interests

Sociologists are no different from other people, in that they hold a set of values and moral beliefs. They might set out to eliminate these as best they can but, ultimately, all our thoughts and actions are based on a particular set of values and it is impossible to escape from these. According to Gouldner (1970), all researchers have to make basic assumptions – which he calls "domain assumptions" – about social life. These include beliefs about whether people are rational or irrational, assumptions about whether humans are predictable and about whether society requires planned intervention by governments. Without some assumptions you can't start a study and yet assumptions reflect different values about what might be good for individuals and society. (Again, an example is belief about government intervention.)

Similarly, sociologists find certain areas of study 'interesting'. Why are they drawn to these areas in the first place? Often they reflect personal issues and a desire to explore something important to them. This makes it more difficult to extricate personal values from the research process itself. An example of this is the work of Ken Plummer (2000), who has published widely on sexual issues and is a sociologist associated with 'queer theory'. He makes it plain that his own sexual preference encouraged him to become interested in gay issues: "So, in a sense, I was actually exploring my own life side-by-side with exploring sociological theory. And I suppose that has shaped the way I think about these things today."

Similarly, feminist writers are often drawn to subjects of particular interest to women. Often these are topics that men have not researched because, as Harding (1986) argues, male sociologists may be biased in their choice of subject matter and they often neglect subjects that affect women's lives more than men's.

The postmodern critique

Postmodernists such as Lyotard (1984) and Baudrillard (1998) argue that the whole process of sociological and scientific thinking is itself based on a series of values about the nature of society. They dispute the assertion that rational thinking, based upon verifiable evidence, is superior to any other approach to understanding the world. They argue that, in fact, scientific thinking is just one of many possible ways of approaching an understanding of the world and that it is not inherently better – nor does it provide any superior 'truths'. Quite simply, the process of science is based upon a set of values; all that a sociologist does is derived from a set of values that are no 'truer' than any other set of values. In writing about their research, postmodernists have adopted two tactics:

1. *Reflexivity* – This involves sociologists including information about themselves and their roles when actually constructing the research, and seeking to show how they may have influenced it.

2. **Narratives** – This is the name given to the different viewpoints and voices that the researcher allows to be heard in the research. Here, the postmodern sociologist is not trying to dominate the account of the research, but to put forward different views of the various subjects of the research. Plummer (2000) has used this in his accounts of gay men's life histories.

A **narrative** is a story about the social world told by a particular person. In a sociological context, it doesn't have to have a clear structure to be seen as a narrative and can simply consist of a person describing their life.

Postmodernists are sometimes seen as having a conservative bias because they don't question or criticise structural features of society. Would you agree with this? Why?

Foucault

A similar argument is put forward by Foucault (1977) in his analysis of knowledge. He argues that what is considered to be knowledge reflects the ability of more powerful groups to impose their ideas on the rest of society. The way people talk and think about particular issues is called "discourse" by Foucault. If the discourse favoured by a particular group becomes dominant, they also gain control over what is considered knowledge. In an argument similar to that of postmodernists, Foucault therefore argues that the value-free process itself is actually based on a set of values.

Conclusions

This section has suggested that it is impossible to keep values completely out of sociological research and theorising. Sociologists who believe this differ over the extent and nature of the role that values should play in sociology. On the one hand, Max Weber thought it was inevitable that values would influence the topic(s) you choose to study. You couldn't study everything and it made sense to study areas of social life that you thought were important. But Weber thought that, in other ways, values should be kept out of sociological work. At the other extreme, Gouldner argued that it was unavoidable that values would influence all aspects of sociological work. In these circumstances, the best that can be done is to attempt to make these values clear to the readers of the research, so they can make up their own minds about whether the research is distorted by the researcher's values. But many sociologists (including Gouldner himself) go beyond admitting that sociology is bound to be 'tainted' by values, arguing instead that it is a positively good thing to make use of values. Their views will now be examined.

COMMITTED SOCIOLOGY

The third approach comes from those who argue that sociology should not be value-free but should have some explicit values guiding its approach to study – it should be 'committed'. The most ardent advocates of this approach are critical/radical sociologists, including feminists, Marxists, and sociologists who are committed to opposing the oppression of a range of disadvantaged minorities. Thus, critical sociology has challenged racism, homophobia and discrimination against people with disabilities. However, it was two sociologists from rather different traditions who were most influential in developing this approach.

Liberal and radical perspectives

Critical sociologists do not always agree about the line that critical sociology should take. Some, who adopt a liberal view, agree that sociology should be sympathetic to the disadvantaged and oppressed. However, they tend to focus on the disadvantaged and are less concerned with studying those in positions of power directly. Others take a more radical approach and focus specifically on those with power. The former tend to be more inclined towards interpretive and social action research, while the latter place more emphasis on social structure.

These differences are reflected in disagreements between Howard Becker (a liberal) and Alvin Gouldner (a radical), centred on sociological approaches to the study of deviance. Becker is one of the originators of labelling theory – a theory that, he argues, takes the side of the 'underdogs' in society as it focuses on the ways these groups are labelled as deviant and targeted by the forces of social control. Gouldner disagrees. He believes that labelling theory ends up blaming what he calls the "middle dogs" – groups such as the police who actually have very little real power. The study of deviance should instead focus on the really powerful groups who actually make the law and give groups such as the police their orders.

In the 1970s, a famous debate took place between Howard Becker and Alvin Gouldner. Both sociologists agreed that sociology should not be value-free, but the debate that followed went on to ask: 'Well, if we are going to be committed, then what side shall we be on?'

Becker (1970) started the debate by arguing that sociology (or at least the study of deviance, his speciality) had traditionally been on the side of the more powerful,

165

and so had considered issues from the viewpoint of the police officer, the social worker or the doctor, rather than from those of the criminal, the client or the 'mental patient'. Becker called for sociology to look instead from the viewpoint of the 'underdog'. By examining issues from their perspective, new questions and ways of looking at the issues at stake could emerge. This sort of approach is the one that was taken by labelling theorists such as Becker (see Chapter 4).

Gouldner (1968) attacked Becker for this argument, claiming that it did not go far enough – and, indeed, merely strengthened the status quo. Gouldner was therefore more radical than Becker. Gouldner argued that Becker's work still failed to focus on those with most of the power. After all, what real power do police officers, social workers and doctors actually have? According to Gouldner, sociology needs to study the really powerful, those who create the structures of oppression of which police officers are merely unimportant agents.

Gouldner believed that police officers, social workers and doctors do not have any real power.

Marxist perspectives

Exactly this sort of argument was taken up by critical sociologists such as the Marxist Althusser (1969), who argued that the role of sociology (which he viewed as a science) is to uncover the ways in which the ruling class control the mass of the population. In doing so, sociologists hope to achieve the breakdown of capitalism by exposing the truth of how it operates for the benefit of a few. Because Marxists such as Althusser saw their work as scientific, they simultaneously believed that they were being objective and that they should try to promote radical change. Thus their attitude to values in sociology is arguably contradictory.

A good example of this form of argument comes from the critical (Marxist) criminologists Taylor, Walton and Young, who argued in *The New Criminology* (1973) that "radical criminological strategy… is to show up the law, in its true colours, as the instrument of the ruling class… and that the rule-makers are also the greatest rule-breakers."

Feminist perspectives

Feminist writers, such as Spender (1985), would agree with the idea of exposing the workings of an oppressive society, but also argue that the key is to explore how males dominate and control society, not how the ruling class dominate. Again, the aim is exposing the truth, but the result is to free women from patriarchy.

According to Hammersley (1992), there are four elements to feminist research – all of which demonstrate a rejection of searching for objectivity:

1. Feminist research starts with the belief that the subordination of women runs through all areas of social life.

2. Rather than seeking to exclude women's feelings and personal experience, these should form the basis of all analysis.

3. The hierarchical division between the researcher and the researched should be broken down so that the subjects of research should be drawn in to help interpret the data obtained. This would help the research belong to the women under study.

4. As the overall aim of feminist research is the emancipation of women, the success of research should only be measured in line with this, not solely in terms of academic credibility.

Feminist writers accuse sociology of traditionally being malestream, that is, interested in male views and concerns, rather than trying to include views of both males and females.

Does the example of feminism suggest to you that committed sociology is a good idea or a bad idea? Justify your answer.

FOCUS ON SKILLS: *ON THE RUN – RACISM AND CRIMINAL 'JUSTICE' IN THE USA*

In 2014, Alice Goffman published a participant observation study of life in a poor, predominantly Black neighbourhood of Philadelphia. Alice Goffman was a young female, White student at The University of Pennsylvania, who did some tutoring to support her studies. One of her students was Aisha, a secondary-school student from a poor, predominantly Black neighbourhood of Philadelphia. Visiting Aisha's house to tutor her, Goffman gradually got to know her relatives, friends and neighbours. She quickly became aware of the large number of young Black men in the area who were on the run from the police, generally for trivial violations of their conditions of parole. Goffman was very sympathetic to their plight and decided to carry out a participant observation study of the area, as part of a PhD at Princeton University. The study lasted six years, during which time she lived in the area she was studying.

Goffman did not try to keep her distance from those she was studying. On the contrary, she "got to know family members and girlfriends as we cleaned up after police raids, attended court dates and made long drives upstate for prison visiting hours" (Goffman, 2014). Goffman's research was a response to her sense of injustice at the way the 'justice' system in the USA criminalised so many young Black men, and seemed to be institutionally racist. Her research took place in the wider context of unprecedented rates of imprisonment for young Black men in the USA. At the time of her study, 11% of young Black men were imprisoned, compared to about 2% of young White men. Appalled at the allegedly biased treatment she witnessed, Goffman not only tried to help some of the young men caught up the system but she also used her research to argue for something to be done to tackle racism in American criminal justice. She actively joined in the debate about the issues, gave lectures and made media appearances to argue for progressive change.

Questions

1. **Outline.** What evidence is there in this passage that the personal values and subjective experiences of Goffman influenced her choice of research topic?

2. **Analyse** ways in which positivists might criticise this research for not being objective.

3. **Analyse** whether Goffman's research can be seen as adopting a liberal or radical/critical approach to committed sociology.

4. **Evaluate** whether her research should be seen as biased personal opinion or as a very valuable and evidence-based contribution to committed sociology.

Discussion and conclusions

Committed sociologists, whether from the liberal or radical/critical schools of thought, run the risk of being accused of producing sociology that is little more than personal opinion. According to this viewpoint, committed sociology has two serious problems.

> First, sociological interpretations of the social world can become so distorted by the ideology of the researcher that they lack any validity. For example, it could be argued that, whatever they study and whatever their research shows, Marxists will find class exploitation and

feminists will find patriarchy. However, defenders of committed, critical sociology deny that this is the case. For example, Phil Carspecken (1996) argues that critical ethnography can be rigorous and systematic and, just like any other sociologists, critical researchers can and should be open to changing their theories if the evidence does not fit.

> Second, it can be argued that it is inappropriate to base sociology on opinions relating to what is right and wrong, because these are truly personal and cannot be tested by any evidence. One sociologist's

view of a good society is no more credible than that of another and basing sociology on something so subjective discredits it. However, Andrew Sayer (2011) questions this. He argues that it is perfectly possible to do research that examines what kind of societies and social arrangements tend to support the well-being of most of the humans who live in them. (For example, data on murder rates, suicide, life expectancy, and qualitative research on sense of well-being, can all be used to evaluate which societies work well and which don't.) From Sayer's point of view, as long as you can agree some very basic values (such as the desirability of well-being), then sociology can play a role in distinguishing 'good' societies from those that are less good. An example of this approach to values in sociology is Richard Wilkinson and Kate Picket's book *The Spirit Level: Why Equality is Better for Everyone* (2010), which uses a wide range of data to support the claim that very unequal societies have many more social problems than more equal societies.

Has your study of sociology affected your views on what you think a 'good' society might be like? If so, do you think this is based on evidence or personal opinion?

CHECK YOUR UNDERSTANDING

1. What is meant by being 'value-laden'?

2. Explain what is meant by 'critical/radical sociology'?

3. Explain what is meant by 'reflexivity'.

4. Identify and briefly explain three reasons why it could be seen as inevitable that personal values will be involved in any sociological research.

5. Identify the theoretical approach that suggests that sociological research should consist of a range of different narratives.

6. Explain two differences between liberal and critical/radical views on values in sociology.

7. Briefly explain why Andrew Sayer thinks values are not just a matter of opinion.

8. Outline two criticisms of positivist views on value-freedom.

9. Identify two examples of sociological perspectives that could be seen as being committed to particular values and explain why they could be seen in this way.

10. Evaluate the view that it is possible for sociology to be objective.

TAKE IT FURTHER

Choose any sociological study and familiarise yourself with its research methods, main argument and findings. Then answer the following questions.

1. In what ways is this study influenced by the values of the researcher?

2. In what ways (if any) is it able to be objective?

3. Is the study produced by a sociologist committed to trying to change society?

4. If so, do you agree with them on the sort of changes suggested or implied by their research? If not, would it have been better if they had tried to draw some lessons for society from their work?

2.7 SOCIOLOGY AND SOCIAL POLICY

2.7

LEARNING OBJECTIVES

› Demonstrate knowledge and understanding of the relationship between sociology and social policy (AO1).

› Apply this understanding to contemporary Britain (AO2).

› Analyse similarities and differences between different sociological perspectives on the relationship between sociology and social policy (AO3).

› Evaluate the arguments surrounding the extent to which sociology influences social policy and vice versa (AO3).

INTRODUCING THE DEBATE

Sociology is first and foremost an academic subject that sets out to explore the way in which society operates and how it influences our lives, rather than an applied subject designed to help formulate **social policies**. Some sociologists believe that the subject should avoid advocating particular social policies. As Martyn Hammersley (2015) discusses, this was essentially the position adopted by Max Weber. Weber thought the job of the professional sociologist was to work out how the social world worked, but not to intervene in it or to suggest how it should be changed. These roles were best left to politicians. However, as you have seen in the last chapter, it is very hard to keep personal values out of sociology entirely – and, to the extent that values impinge on sociology, this inevitably has implications for social policies. This chapter therefore examines the nature of the relationship between sociology and social policy, with reference to a range of sociological perspectives about what the role of sociology should be and what effects, if any, it has on policy.

UNDERSTAND THE CONCEPT

The Social Policy Association sees **social policy** as involving the way in which governments distribute and redistribute resources to provide 'services, facilities and opportunities' to meet 'human need' and 'promote well-being' (see www.social-policy.org.uk/). Actions taken by non-governmental organisations such as charities can also be seen as social policies if they are designed to have effects on society or sections of it.

SOCIOLOGICAL PROBLEMS AND SOCIAL PROBLEMS

Peter Worsley (1977) was the first to introduce a useful distinction between sociological problems and social problems.

To Worsley, a sociological problem is a feature of social life that requires an explanation, whether or not that aspect of social life is seen as a problem. Sometimes sociologists study aspects of social life that are not regarded as problems. For example, Norbert Elias studied the development of 'good manners' (1978) and Bennett *et al.* (2009) studied the culture of different social classes, neither of which is seen as a social problem.

However, sociological research often does focus on issues that are regarded as social problems, which Worsley defines as "some piece of social behaviour that causes public friction and/or private misery and calls for collective action to solve it" (1977). Examples of social problems that have been studied by sociologists include anti-social behaviour, gang culture, poverty, crime, excessive inequality, educational underachievement and family breakdown.

Of course not all sociologists agree on what social problems are. For example, some see a high rate of imprisonment as a problem, while others view it as a positive feature of criminal justice. There may also be disagreement about how to solve social problems but, nevertheless, many sociologists do believe that the information produced by sociologists should be used to help solve such problems.

John Brewer (2014), a recent president of the British Sociological Association, has argued that sociology can and should address social problems. For example, his own work suggests that the sociology of peace-making can be useful in understanding the way that communities that have been in conflict (such as Protestant and Catholic communities in Northern Ireland) can begin to resolve their differences and live together, in the wake of a political settlement.

While some positivists may deny that sociologists should intervene in social problems, critical social scientists, including feminists and Marxists, do believe that sociology should be used to try to change and improve the social world by exposing injustice, inequality and oppression. They may be reluctant though to work within existing power structures (such as the state) if they believe it is impossible to prevent them from supporting capitalist or patriarchal interests. So, for example, moderate

Marxists and liberal feminists are more likely to work with existing institutions, but radical feminists and Marxists would be more likely to seek change through protest movements.

THE INFLUENCE OF SOCIAL POLICY ON SOCIOLOGY

Before considering the extent to which sociology does influence social policy, it should first be acknowledged that the relationship can work the other way as well, with social policies influencing sociology.

New interventions in the social world – by governments and others – can lead to new sociological research. For example, sociologists have devoted considerable attention to studying the effects of government policies in areas such as education, welfare, health and crime. Sociologists have investigated the effectiveness of CCTV in crime prevention, the effect of academies on educational attainment and the effect of health service reforms on class differences in mortality.

Furthermore, the type of sociological research that gets done is often directly shaped by government priorities. Most government funding for sociology is distributed through the Economic and Social Research Council (ESRC). It is particularly likely to provide funding for research directly concerned with the impact of government policies, maximising value for money and achieving government aims. The effectiveness of research is then measured through the Research Excellence Framework (REF) which tries to measure the impact of research on the world outside academia. Thus, sociologists who wish to be successful in their careers are likely to have to take into account the uses that might be made of their work, and they might bend their research towards issues of government concern. Although some sociologists try to distance themselves from these influences, they are difficult to resist, meaning that government and its social policies are likely to influence sociological research a great deal. Most research is expensive, so such funding is crucial to what gets done. With increased pressure on academics to bring in financial support for research and to get their work published, funding is becoming increasingly important.

Since sociology studies the changing social world, it is bound to be influenced by changes in the social world it studies, which in turn are influenced by the social policies that help to change that world. But, of course, sociology does sometimes try actively to shape the social world as well.

Factors limiting the influence of sociology on social policy

A wide variety of factors affect what influence, if any, sociologists are likely to have on social policy.

Governments are motivated by the desire to attract votes and they are therefore likely to be influenced by opinion polls and focus groups that are used to research public attitudes. For example, David Cameron's 2015 election campaign promise to give voters a referendum on whether Britain should remain a member of the EU was influenced by focus groups and polling, and the public are in turn influenced by the media. The polls and focus groups suggested the Conservatives were in danger of losing support to the UK Independence Party (UKIP), which supports withdrawal from the EU (Ross, 2014).

Even if governments are sympathetic to the policies advocated by particular sociologists, they are not always able to implement them. The effects of globalisation can mean that the power of a particular state can be limited. For example, attempts to introduce new laws that add extra cost to business could result in companies taking work elsewhere. Transnational organisations such as the European Community can also restrict the power of individual governments.

Governments are limited by financial constraints. Eliminating poverty by greatly increasing benefits or even introducing a citizen's wage for everyone would, for example, be relatively simple – yet the problem of raising sufficient funding to do this may prevent it.

Some policies will meet too much opposition from entrenched groups. The 'roads lobby', pharmaceutical and cigarette companies have all been very effective in protecting their interests, despite evidence to show that many of their practices are harmful.

Sociologists are not the only social scientists by whom governments might be influenced: the influence of economists is generally greater than that of sociologists, because economic success is often seen as the key to electoral success.

Political parties often have close links to particular independent research organisations or 'think tanks' (Jones, 2015), which may have more importance than academic sociologists in universities. For example, the Centre for Social Justice, a think tank established by the former Conservative leader, Iain Duncan Smith, proposed the Universal Credit, which Duncan Smith then introduced as Secretary of State for Work and Pensions in David Cameron's government.

Governments are also likely to be influenced by their own broad ideological beliefs. In Britain, different governments have different degrees of sympathy towards the most common strands of sociological thought, with Conservative governments generally less likely than Labour governments to give much credence to sociologists. This is because most sociologists have an ideological position that is left of centre and therefore more similar to that of Labour politicians than that of Conservative politicians. Sociology therefore tends to have different degrees of influence at different times, depending on who is in power.

Politicians can be selective about the sociologists, other social scientists and research organisations, of whom they take note. They are likely to pay particular attention to arguments and research that fit with their own preconceived ideas and which suggest policies that they believe will give them electoral advantage. Sociological research may be used as much to justify policies as to formulate them.

What do you think are the most important factors shaping the social policies adopted by governments? Justify your answer.

THE INFLUENCE OF SOCIOLOGY BEYOND GOVERNMENT

Although the direct influence of sociology on governments may be limited, sociology may have more influence on social policies outside central government. For example, local councils, individual institutions such as schools and local education authorities, and charities may take account of sociological research, even if central government does not. Furthermore, transnational organisations such as the United Nations and the European Community may also be influenced by sociological research. Sociology can also have an indirect impact by changing public attitudes that in turn might influence politicians. Sociological research into domestic violence (for example, by Stanko (2000), see Book 1, page 232) has led to greater public acknowledgement of the issue – and greater efforts by the police to tackle the problem. At an international level, sociology has also raised awareness of issues such as modern-day slavery and people-trafficking. So while the influence of sociology should not be exaggerated, neither should it be underestimated, since it can be indirect and can affect organisations other than central government and help to inform their policies.

FOCUS ON SKILLS: FUNDING, RESEARCH AND CENSORSHIP

Walters findings about youth courts contradicted the positive claims of those funding his research.

In *Critical Thinking about the Uses of Research* (Hope and Walters 2008), Reece Walters claims: "We live in a society where Government manipulates and cherry-picks criminological knowledge and produces distorted pictures of the 'crime problem'."

The book launches a strong attack on the way that government departments, in particular the Home Office (for England and Wales) and the Scottish Executive, fail to fund – or sometimes use confidentiality agreements to restrict – research that contradicts some of the favoured policies that they wish to put in place on crime. Walters and Hope provide some examples of this claimed censorship of research.

Between 2003 and 2006, Professor Walters researched youth court procedures in Scotland with funding from the Scottish Executive. His findings, however, contradicted the positive claims for the youth courts made by the Scottish Executive. The draft report was presented to the Scottish Executive in 2005 and, following several months of the Executive questioning content, a final report was submitted in April 2006. Yet it was not until November 2006 that the Executive published the report on its website.

Walters then wrote a critical article in the academic journal *Youth Justice* (Piacentini and Walters 2006). At this point, Walters states, the Executive complained to his employer, Stirling University, and also refused to pay the final £15,000 of the research contract.

Walters concludes that, despite mounting evidence of censorship, academics are prepared to accept the controls on them in order to obtain funding for their work. He argues that this is detrimental to sociology and has called for a boycott of government-funded work. Walters concludes: "Like field mice scurrying around a python, to appease university obsession with income generation and with the misguided belief that they will change or influence policy, academic criminologists continue to line the corridors of the Home Office and the Scottish Executive with cap in hand hoping to receive a slice of the government's growing financial pie for criminal justice research."

Questions

1. **Understand.** What do you think the author means by describing sociologists as being "like mice scurrying around a python"?

2. **Analyse.** different ways in which the government can use its power to manipulate the production and dissemination of research to get the findings it wants.

3. **Analyse.** Suggest reasons why sociologists might be willing to seek government funding, despite the controls that are placed on their work.

4. **Evaluate.** Would you agree that most sociological research is strongly influenced by government? Are there any exceptions?

SOCIOLOGICAL PERSPECTIVES AND SOCIAL POLICY

Different sociological perspectives have different views on what should be the relationship between sociology and social policy. This section reviews these competing views and considers the extent to which they have actually influenced policies.

Functionalism and positivism

Functionalism

Functionalists such as Comte and Durkheim advocated a largely positivist method of studying society, in which the job of sociology was to produce objective descriptions and analysis of the social world. In theory, such information should carry no implications about what policies should be followed, but should merely analyse what the effects of different policies would be.

However, both early and later functionalists have argued, in different ways, that some things are functional for society and others are not, and have therefore implied what sort of policies should be promoted. Comte went further and claimed that the application of scientific knowledge is preferable to the application of religious beliefs in making decisions about society. Indeed, Comte believed that scientific sociology could be used to promote progress and that sociologists could act like a 'priesthood' guiding government on how to make society better. Durkheim believed that the maintenance of some degree of solidarity was desirable. Durkheim therefore advocated policies to increase the amount of social solidarity in contemporary societies and thereby reduce the rates of suicide and crime. Later functionalists, such as Parsons, supported policies to promote nuclear families and to encourage competition and the desire for individual achievement in education.

Functionalist views have had some impact on social policy, although the quite general theorising that is typical of functionalist sociology has been hard to apply to particular social problems.

Functionalism is often accused of having a conservative bias, in that it tends to support the status quo, since institutions are generally seen as being vital for the efficient functioning of society (Gouldner, 1973). While this is a fair representation of the work of Talcott Parsons, it is less true of some functionalists such as Durkheim. (Durkheim actually advocated the abolition of the inheritance of wealth, for example, to make society more meritocratic.)

Functionalism has generally lost its influence in recent decades and therefore has very little impact on social policies today.

Positivism

Positivist statistical analysis, which is advocated by some functionalists, is – however – extremely important in the development of social policies, as statistical analysis is widely used by government departments and other organisations when deciding between different policies. Most government-funded research produces a range of statistical information, for example, on the effectiveness of different policing strategies and community penalties, and the cost effectiveness of different policies in the health service. However, positivist research does not in itself suggest what kind of aim should be pursued by those making social policies; positivist approaches can be used by sociologists with very different ideological standpoints.

Based on your study of sociology, suggests reasons why it might be dangerous for governments to be over-reliant on positivist research in formulating social policies.

Neoliberalism and the New Right

The foundations of neoliberalism and the New Right perspectives

Neoliberalism and the New Right have been far more influential than functionalism in directing social policies, over recent decades.

The terms 'neoliberalism' and the 'New Right' are both used to refer to right-of-centre political viewpoints, which see the free-market capitalist economy as the solution to most social problems. The term 'New Right' was particularly associated with the advocates of free-market economics and minimal state intervention in the economy in the 1980s and 1990s. It became very influential on policies in the UK and the USA after the election of Margaret Thatcher (as UK Prime Minister from 1979 to1990) and Ronald Reagan (as US President from 1981 to1989). The New Right were associated with traditional, conservative social values as well as free-market economics. For example, they generally disapproved of single-parent families and were supportive of 'family values'. In more recent times, those advocating a right-of-centre political approach are more likely to be referred to as neoliberals, although the term 'neoliberalism' is not as strongly associated with supporting traditional values and is much more focused on free-market economics.

Sociology is not at the heart of New Right/neoliberal thinking, which is more based on ideas from economists. The most influential New Right/neoliberal thinker was the Austrian economist Frederick Hayek, who advocated minimal state intervention in the economy. Hayek believed that the more the state intervened in the economy, the more the state was run in the interests of state employees and the more inefficient the economy became. According to Hayek (1944), free markets produce greater efficiency because competition ensures that only the most successful companies, making products that people want, will survive and inefficiency will be driven out. He also argued that state control led to the centralisation of power and ultimately could lead to a lack of democracy, whereas free markets guarantee the decentralisation of power, particularly into the hands of consumers.

New Right thinkers had no hesitation in arguing that their approach should be used to influence government policy and they have formed a number of think tanks (for example, The Centre for Policy Studies and The Social Market Foundation, Jones, 2015) with the express purpose of helping to direct such policies.

The influence of neoliberalism and New Right sociology

Arguably these perspectives have had far more effect on the policies of UK governments than any other perspectives since the 1980s, influencing not just Conservative governments but also the New Labour governments of 1997–2010.

Although economics has been central to neoliberal/New Right thinking, some sociologists taking the approach have had a considerable influence on social policy.

Charles Murray (1984), theorising that an underclass had developed because welfare benefits created a dependency culture, has been very influential in the development of Conservative Party policies on welfare in the UK, and Republican Party policies in the USA. In both countries it has resulted in a trend towards making receipt of benefits dependent upon looking for work and it has encouraged cuts in benefit levels (see Book 1, pages 415–17).

Policies relating to crime have also been strongly influenced on both sides of the Atlantic by the work of Right Realist criminologists such as Wilson and Kelling (see Topic 1, Chapter 4), who have advocated policies of zero tolerance.

Despite the considerable influence of right realism, most sociologists tend to support left-of-centre political views and they are highly critical of New Right/

neoliberal thinking and policies. (For some examples of these criticisms see Book 1, pages 73–74, 415–417 and 243–245.)

Social democratic perspectives

The characteristics of social democratic perspectives

These views are primarily associated with left-of-centre political parties in Europe, for example, the British Labour Party. They are partly based upon economic ideas, which criticise the views of The New Right/neoliberals, by arguing that a **mixed economy** is necessary.

UNDERSTAND THE CONCEPT

A **mixed economy** is one in which some goods and services are produced by private businesses and others by the state.

The view of social democrats is that capitalist economies, left to their own devices, will tend to produce excessive inequality. Equality of opportunity is undermined because children of the rich gain unfair advantages over other children. This will tend to lead to conflict between social classes. Although the perspective is partly based on economics, sociologists have made a very considerable contribution to the development of social democratic thought. Examples include Peter Townsend's idea of relative poverty, which suggests that income inequality can lead to exclusion from society (see Book 1, pages 396–7) and the social democratic approach to equality of opportunity in education (see Book 1, pages 11, 76–7, 80–82) and the left realist approach to crime (see Topic 1, Chapter 4).

The influence of social democratic perspectives

Social democratic perspectives have had a very strong influence when left-of-centre governments have been in power; this was particularly the case during the Labour governments of the 1960s and 1970s in the UK. They had somewhat less influence during the premierships of Tony Blair and Gordon Brown, between 1997 and 2010. Tony Blair, in particular, supported the approach known as the **Third Way**, which tried to combine left- and right-wing thinking. This approach was developed by the sociologist Anthony Giddens (1999). During Blair's premiership, sociology was able to influence social policies more than at other times, albeit using an approach (the Third Way) that was a hybrid of neoliberalism and social democracy.

The Third Way was heavily criticised by those with more left-wing views, who argued that it was, in effect, a slightly watered-down version of neoliberalism. It has left a lasting legacy for public services – for example, hospital trusts are still struggling to pay for hospital buildings built using private finance under the private finance initiative (PFI).

Radical sociologists have argued that social democrats are unrealistic in claiming that gradual reform of capitalism can lead to a fairer society. Critical sociologists generally argue that reform can only go so far without more fundamental changes in society that would undermine the position of the rich and powerful. Without such change, this group will simply use their power to block reforms that threaten their interests.

How far do you think that social policies today are still influenced by social democratic thinking?

Critical social science

Critical social science includes all forms of social science that argue for a radical transformation of society, involving a fundamental change in its structures. It incorporates Marxist theories and radical feminist theories, both of which argue that it is necessary to develop an overall critique of society, not just of individual social policies, in order to achieve necessary and worthwhile changes. All critical social scientists tend to argue that existing social policies favour the interests of the powerful in society at the expense of others, although they might differ over whom exactly they identify as the powerful.

Marxism

Marxists, like other critical social scientists, have no hesitation in believing that sociological ideas should be used to transform society by producing radically different social policies. Marxists argue that societies are generally run in the interests of a ruling class, who get their power from the ownership of the means of production. Simple Marxist views argue that the state is part of the superstructure of society and it acts in the interests of the ruling class and therefore social policies are designed to favour this group.

Even policies that appear to benefit the mass of the population may be little more than an ideological smokescreen to disguise the continuing exploitation of the proletariat or working classes. For example, Marxists have argued that the welfare state does little to redistribute money from the rich to the poor (see Book 1, pages 418–19), and the education system is biased in favour of those from rich backgrounds (see Book 1, pages 15–16). Policies, they argue, are generally designed to make only token concessions to the lower classes, to prevent the development of class consciousness rather than make any fundamental changes in the distribution of power or wealth in society.

There are, however, different strands of Marxism. Some do accept that the working class may get genuine concessions from the ruling class and so acknowledge that some social policies (such as the development of the welfare state) could, to a limited extent, be progressive.

The influence of Marxism

Marxist perspectives have had relatively little influence upon social policies in the UK. Depending upon your point of view, they could be seen as too extreme to be supported by the electorate or too extreme to be allowed to be put into practice by the ruling class. Nevertheless, they have had some influence on those on the left of Democratic Socialist parties, such as the Labour Party in Britain. (For example, the election of Jeremy Corbyn as Labour leader in 2015, although he is not a Marxist, put the concerns of Marxists on the political agenda.)

Jeremy Corbyn, elected as Labour leader in 2015

Marxist ideas have certainly contributed to debates about issues such as the taxation of companies. For example, pressure groups such as Occupy have succeeded in getting the evasion and avoidance of tax, by corporations, into public debate. Nevertheless, Marxism lost some of its political appeal and influence after the collapse of the Soviet Union and communism in Eastern Europe. Social Democratic critics of Marxism argue that revolutionary change and the establishment of a strong, centralised Marxist state is neither desirable nor likely.

Is Marxism relevant to social policy in Britain today? Justify your answer.

Feminism

Some strands of feminism can be seen as a branch of critical social science. Thus, radical feminism advocates the overthrow of patriarchal societies and their replacement with radically different societies in which women are no longer subservient to men.

A few radical feminists advocate female supremacy, that is, women taking control; some advocate separatism, in which men and women are separated in order to free women from patriarchy. Although radical feminism has generally been too radical to have much direct impact on mainstream political parties, social policy campaigns run by radical feminists have had considerable influence. Radical feminists, for example, have been responsible for highlighting domestic violence and sexual violence against women; their campaigns have led to some improvements in the policing of such crimes against women.

Liberal feminist perspectives, on the other hand, advocate more gradual change in society in order to create more equal opportunities. Thus liberal feminists have tended to advocate the same socialisation for girls and boys, the introduction of new legislation to create more equal opportunities, positive discrimination in favour of women when they are underrepresented in certain spheres of social life (such as all-women shortlists when selecting new candidates to become MPs) and so on. Liberal feminist influence on social policy has been very considerable. It has included the introduction of the 1970 Equal Pay Act, and legislation outlawing discrimination on the basis of sex, as well as changes to school curricula. It is now widely accepted, at least in principle, that equality of opportunity between the sexes should be part of social policy in the UK.

Radical critics argue that liberal feminist approaches have not fundamentally changed the patriarchal nature of society, for example, women still earn less than men and are still responsible for most housework, and women continue to be portrayed as sex objects in the media and popular culture generally. (See Chapter 2 for a detailed discussion of feminism and its influence.)

CONCLUSIONS

There is no doubt that the direct influence of sociological theorising and research on social policy can be exaggerated. Politicians and others responsible for formulating and implementing social policy tend to be selective about the evidence they look at. They are inclined towards using evidence that supports their favoured policies, rather than changing policies on the basis of the evidence. Furthermore, other social scientists are also very influential, particularly economists.

Nevertheless, sociology has some influence on policy. Sociologists have highlighted and raised a whole range of issues that have become issues of public debate. These include violence against women, tax evasion and avoidance by large companies, corporate crime, racism in the criminal justice system and widening inequality. Sociologists are seldom solely responsible for raising these issues. Campaigning organisations and members of political parties also play an important role. However, the role of sociologists can still be very significant and their research is also very useful in evaluating the effectiveness of different policies (whether or not politicians take much notice of the findings). Sociologists can also indirectly affect policies by influencing public opinion and the subject has influenced very large numbers of individuals who have studied sociology at some point in their educational careers and now occupy important positions in a whole range of organisations.

CHECK YOUR UNDERSTANDING

1. What is meant by 'social policy'?

2. Explain what is meant by a 'social problem'.

3. Explain what is meant by a 'sociological problem'.

4. Identify and briefly explain three ways in which social policy can influence sociology.

5. Identify one theory, discussed in this chapter, that suggests that a capitalist economy should be the foundation on which social policies should be developed.

6. Explain two differences between Marxist and social democratic views on social policy.

7. Explain briefly, Giddens' idea of the Third Way.

8. Outline two criticisms of the view that sociology can only influence social policy by changing government policies.

9. Identify two examples of sociology helping to change government policy.

10. Evaluate the view that sociology plays almost no role in influencing social policy.

TAKE IT FURTHER

Choose any one of the following government websites: the Home Office, The Ministry of Justice, The Department for Education, the Department for Business Innovation and Skills, the Department for Work and Pensions, the Department of Health. Briefly review some of the most recent research reports by looking through the summaries. Look up the sorts of research being undertaken.

What is the aim of research? How much research seems to be sociological in nature? Do you think that the criticisms of radical sociologists that sociology is shaped by big business, right-wing politicians and the wealthy are justified?

APPLY YOUR LEARNING

1. Outline and explain **two** advantages of using questionnaires in sociological research. [10 marks]

2. Read **Item A** below and answer the question that follows.

ITEM A

Feminists see society as based upon conflict between men and women. In patriarchal societies, men are able to dominate and exploit women and ensure that society is run in the interests of men. However, different feminists have different views about the causes of male dominance and what should be done about it.

Applying material from **Item A** and your knowledge, evaluate the usefulness of feminist approaches in understanding society. [20 marks]

You can find example answers and accompanying teacher's comments for this topic at www.collins.co.uk/AQAAlevelSociology. Please note that these example answers and teacher's comments have not been approved by AQA.

3 GLOBAL DEVELOPMENT

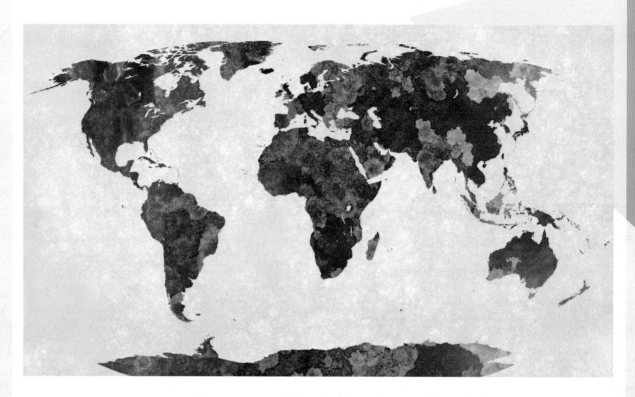

AQA specification	Chapters
Candidates should examine:	
Development, underdevelopment and global inequality.	This is mainly covered by Chapter 1 (pages 180–198) although some aspects may be covered in greater detail and depth in Chapters 3, 4 and 5 (pages 210–258).
Globalisation and its influence on the cultural, political and economic relationships between societies.	This is mainly covered by Chapter 2 (pages 199–209) although economic globalisation is also touched upon by sections on in Chapters 3 and 4 (pages 210–240).
The role of transnational corporations, non-governmental organisations and international agencies in local and global strategies for development.	This is mainly covered by Chapter 3 (pages 210–220) but relevant material can also be found in Chapters 1 and 2 (pages 180–209).
Development in relation to aid and trade, industrialisation, urbanisation, the environment and war and conflict.	This is mainly covered by Chapter 4 (pages 221–240) but relevant material can also be found in Chapters 1, 2 and 3 (pages 210–220).
Employment, education, health, demographic change and gender as aspects of development.	This is mainly covered by Chapter 5 (pages 241–258) but relevant material can also be found in Chapter 1 (pages 180–198).

3.1 DEFINING AND MEASURING DEVELOPMENT, UNDERDEVELOPMENT AND GLOBAL INEQUALITY

LEARNING OBJECTIVES

› Demonstrate knowledge and understanding of the different perspectives on the nature, extent and causes of development, underdevelopment and global inequality, as well as competing definitions of these concepts (AO1).

› Apply the issues of development, underdevelopment and global inequality to contemporary societies (AO2).

› Analyse the differences between development perspectives such as modernisation, dependency, Marxist, neo-liberal, environmentalist and post-development theories (AO3).

› Evaluate sociological explanations in order to make judgements and draw conclusions about definitions, measurements and theories of development (AO3).

INTRODUCING THE DEBATE

The sociology of global development is concerned with explaining why the nations of the world exist in a hierarchy of affluence that ranges from what Harris (1989) describes as "utter destitution to immense wealth". For example, in 2014, the richest 1 per cent of the world's population owned more than 48 per cent of global wealth. Furthermore, the richest 85 people in the world in 2014 shared a combined wealth equal to the poorest 3.5 billion of the world's population. Most of this wealth is concentrated in the so-called developed industrialised world – North America, Western Europe, Japan and Australasia – while most of the destitution is concentrated in the less developed world, which consists mainly of most of Africa, South and Central America, the Indian subcontinent and most of East Asia.

Four competing sociological models of development and underdevelopment have emerged to explain global inequality. Modernisation theory and neo-liberalism argue that developing countries need to closely follow a Western route to development. However, the Marxist-influenced dependency theory argues that countries that follow this path leave themselves exposed to exploitation by the capitalist West, whilst post-development approaches, which mainly represent the views of sociologists living in the developing world, are critical of Western definitions of development because these are often inappropriate to meet the needs of people in developing countries.

GETTING YOU THINKING

1. Look at the two images of children on the right: one forced to work from a very early age and one starving.

   What feelings does each picture provoke in you? Suggest reasons for the predicament of each child. How would you go about improving their lives – even their chances of survival into adulthood?

2. Examine Figure 3.1.1. Place these reasons into three categories: those that blame Africans; those that blame the West; and those that blame geography. Which of these reasons do you think are valid?

criminal leaders · debt · western indifference · western governments · poverty · drought · unfair terms of trade · corrupt governments · civil war · mismanagement · famine · disease

Figure 3.1.1 *Reasons suggested for the extreme poverty in sub-Saharan Africa*

Source: YouGov (2012)

Images of children like those above provoke two distinct sets of feelings among people in the UK:

> Some feel compassion and pity, and perhaps an overwhelming need to help. If you felt this way, you probably constructed a list of solutions that focused on how we in the West might help these children out of poverty. In this case, you are probably the type of person who gives generously to charities that target children in the developing world, such as Make Poverty History.

> Many feel indifference. If this was true for you, the likelihood is that you have seen these types of image so many times now that you may have become immune to their emotional content. If so, you are experiencing what is known as 'compassion fatigue'. Such feelings are likely to be accompanied by nagging questions such as "Why do we always need to put our hands in our pockets?" and "Why don't these people sort themselves out?"

You are likely to find both these sets of feelings present in any group of young people, such as your own sociology class. Neither set is right or wrong.

Our interpretation of the negative images associated with the developing world, such as starving babies or refugee camps, are the product of **value judgements** that we make about how people should live their lives.

UNDERSTAND THE CONCEPT

Value judgements are personal assessments, for example, about what is good or bad, or right or wrong, in terms of one's own standards and priorities.

They are constructed relative to our own experience. Our standard of living in the UK generally ensures that most children in the UK survive healthily into adulthood. We should therefore not be too surprised that our ideas about how societies like these in Africa should change or develop are based on our own Western experiences. Moreover, some of us will quite naturally jump to the conclusion that their problems are created by their failure to adopt our way of life.

It is important to understand that our perceptions, and media representations, of developing countries reflect a wider academic and political debate about how sociologists, politicians and aid agencies should define development. As we shall see, the dominant definitions of development that exist involve the same sorts of value judgement that informed your reaction to the poverty and suffering of children in the developing world.

181

DEFINING DEVELOPMENT AND UNDERDEVELOPMENT

Peet and Hartwick (2015) suggest that development means 'making a better life for everyone'. They note that this is a powerful emotive and ethical ideal because it appeals to people's best instincts, but it is also controversial because it implicitly suggests an egalitarian or fair future for all. They argue therefore that the discourse of development is consequently very contentious.

Most sociologists agree that development should mean, at the very least, improvement or progress for people who desperately need positive change in their lives. Some may argue that development should only meet the needs basic for survival, that is, a diet sufficiently nutritious to maintain good health, shelter, medical care such as vaccination, and so on. However, the main debates about development are underpinned by modernity, meaning that agencies working within the development field aim to replicate within developing societies the material and cultural experience of modern Western societies. Consequently, most sociologists are wedded to the idea that development is about achieving economic growth and its positive social consequences, such as improvements in life expectancy, the lowering of infant and maternal death rates, mass education and literacy, the eradication of diseases of poverty, and so on. Countries that have not yet achieved these modern economic and social goals are often described as either underdeveloped or undeveloped.

The terminology problem

Between 1945 and 1990, it was the norm when discussing development and underdevelopment to use three politically-charged terms.

> The 'First World', which referred to developed industrial-capitalist societies such as the USA, Japan, Australia and those situated in Western Europe.

> The 'Second World', which referred to the communist bloc of the USSR and Eastern Europe, China and Cuba.

> The 'Third World', which referred to the poorest and undeveloped countries that were mainly situated in Africa, Asia and Central and South America.

However, the collapse of communism in Eastern Europe after 1990 and the recent rise of China as an economic power have largely led to the abandonment of those terms. An alternative set of descriptors was used in the Brandt Report (1981), which divided the world into 'North' (the industrialised countries) and 'South' (poor countries) despite the fact that Australia and New Zealand are situated in the southern hemisphere (see Figure 3.1.2). However, many sociologists have been reluctant to use Brandt's terms because they imply that countries within these categories are alike in terms of their development or underdevelopment, which is not the case. As this chapter will illustrate, a diversity of economic and social characteristics exist across both the developed and undeveloped worlds.

Many sociologists and social geographers today prefer the four categories described in Table 3.1.1 when describing and assessing the relative position of societies in the global hierarchy of development.

Although Table 3.1.1 is in general use, its categories are still not entirely satisfactory because they give the impression that underdeveloped countries experience economic and social problems in the same ways. However, it is important to realise that there

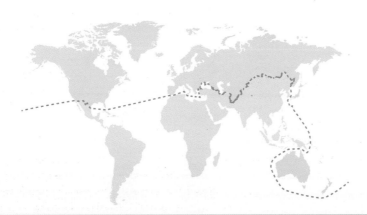

Figure 3.1.2 *The division of the world into developed and undeveloped, as suggested by the Brandt Commission, 1981*

Category	Description of category
More economically developed countries (MEDCs)	These are the wealthy industrial–capitalist countries found in Northern America and Europe, plus Japan, Australia and New Zealand. They generally experience economic growth year-by-year. Their populations generally enjoy a good standard of living, which means that long life expectancy; a happy, disease-free childhood; free primary and secondary education and access to health care, housing and consumer goods are the general norms.
Newly industrialised countries (NICs)	These are the so-called 'Asian Tiger' countries of Singapore, Malaysia, Taiwan, South Korea and China, which have rapidly industrialised in the past 40 years and which today have a large share of the global market in computers, electronics (especially mobile phones), cars, plastics, textiles and so on.
Less economically developed societies (LEDCs)	These are societies such as India, Brazil and Mexico, which have experienced extensive industrialisation and urbanisation, and therefore positive economic growth. However, the economies of these societies are still heavily dependent on agriculture, especially the production of cash crops and the extraction of raw materials. Massive swathes of poverty continue to exist in these countries.
Least economically developed societies (LLEDCs)	These are the poorest countries in the world, such as Bangladesh, Afghanistan and the sub-Saharan countries of Niger, Ethiopia, Sudan, Eritrea and Somalia. Absolute poverty is the daily norm in such societies, as are high rates of child malnutrition and therefore mortality. Other norms include low life expectancy for the adult population because of death from preventable and treatable diseases, and high levels of adult illiteracy. Many of these societies lack basic infrastructure such as roads, electricity, clean water, sanitation and medical services. Collier (2007) estimates that there are about 60 countries, mainly located in sub-Saharan Africa and central Asia, which are home to one billion people who experienced little, if any, economic growth in the 1980s and 1990s.

Table 3.1.1 A global hierarchy of development

are often more differences than similarities between underdeveloped countries, which makes it difficult to place such countries into the same off-the-peg categories. Different societies may have qualitatively different experiences of the same phenomena – for example, poverty – because there are many geographical, religious, ethnic, cultural, political, economic, social and global factors that shape poverty. These are not experienced or shared equally by all underdeveloped societies.

It is also important to understand that the hierarchical ranking of global development described in Table 3.1.1 is not fixed. Development is about progress and change, and therefore some of these countries may rise or fall in these categories. For example, some economists and sociologists today may be tempted to place China in the MEDC category, whereas the economic problems experienced in the European Union during 2014/15 may tempt some to place European societies such as Greece in the Less economically developed societies (LEDCs) category.

Why might First, Second and Third World be considered politically charged terms?

MEASURING DEVELOPMENT AND UNDERDEVELOPMENT

Western governments, international agencies (such as the World Bank and the International Monetary Fund), non-governmental organisations (such as charities like Oxfam) and sociological approaches to development (such as modernisation theory and neo-liberal theory) have tended to measure development in two practical and inter-related ways.

Development as economic wellbeing

First, development is often measured using economic measurements such as Gross National Product (GNP). This is the total economic value of goods and services (expressed in US dollars) produced by a country over the course of a year, that are available for consumption in the marketplace or export to other countries. The total value of GNP is divided by the total population of a country to give a figure per head ('per capita') as per Table 3.1.2. It is argued that GNP signals how economically healthy and successful a society is.

Country	Per capita GNP (US$) 2010	Per capita GNP (US$) 2014
Brazil	9810	11,760
UK	40,470	42,690
Nigeria	1460	2950
USA	48,950	55,200
Japan	41,980	42,000
Bhutan	1990	2390
Dem. Rep Congo	320	410
South Sudan	1080	960
Greece	27,580	22,090
Libya	12,710	7920

Table 3.1.2 *GNP for selected countries, 2010 and 2014*

Source: World Bank (2015)

The use of GNP figures illustrates the very significant gap between the developed and developing worlds in terms of wealth. For example, from Table 3.1.2, we can see that in 2014, GNP per capita in the USA was $55,200, and in the UK it was $42,690, while in the Democratic Republic of Congo it was only $410. Moreover, the figures in Table 3.1.2 show that the USA, the UK and Japan greatly increased their GNP between 2010 and 2014, while the poorest countries, such as South Sudan and Libya (which have both been ravaged by civil war), actually experienced a decline. When economic growth does occur in the developing world, for example, in the case of the Democratic Republic of Congo, the rate of increase is much lower than that of the developed world.

However, GNP as a measure of development is regarded by some sociologists as unsatisfactory for the following reasons:

> There are inconsistencies in the way countries collect such data, so we cannot be sure of its reliability or its value as a comparative tool.

> Black (2002) argues that GNP data collection neglects the invisible and frequently illegal 'economies of subsistence' based on keeping livestock or growing crops for personal use, scavenging through rubbish tips, prostitution, begging, drug-dealing, and so on, that are normal in societies in which poverty is the norm.

> Peet and Hartwick argue that GNP statistics say very little about development. They argue that the social consequences of production are more important. They note that if growth merely produces more 'Walmart junk' than it does schools and hospitals, then it is not really development. Moreover, if growth concentrates wealth in the hands of a few, then that too is not development. For example, the 2014 GNP figure of $55,200 for the USA gives a false impression because it disguises the fact that some social groups in the USA, mainly African Americans and Native Americans, experience disproportionate poverty. Economic growth in terms of GNP therefore does not necessarily result in economic or social development for all members of a population. In fact, GNP has actually grown in modern societies such as the UK, and in developing societies such as Nigeria, while the majority of people in them have experienced greater levels of poverty and inequality.

> GNP may give sociologists some idea of the wealth and prosperity of a developing society, but it fails to document how much of that wealth actually stays in that society. In many developing societies, industry is controlled by transnational companies which transfer profits back to the developed world (see Chapter 3 for more detail). In addition, as we shall see later in Chapter 4, a great deal of the wealth generated by developing societies is lost in aid repayments.

> The focus on GNP as a measure of development implies that materialism and consumerism are somehow central to personal happiness and progress. Two observations can be made in criticism of this. First, a poor person in the developing world may lack personal possessions but this does not necessarily mean that they feel deprived or that they suffer hardship. Other factors such as community, family, religious solidarity and even happiness may be regarded as more important and may positively compensate for the experience of poverty. Second, as Pickett and Wilkinson (2009) argue, the economic prosperity represented by GNP in developed Western societies is often accompanied by profound social problems and unhappiness, as represented by the breakdown of community supports, common feelings of isolation, anomie and alienation, levels of poor physical and mental health, and high suicide and crime rates.

Look at Greece's GNP performance between 2010 and 2014. How might these figures be used to criticise the use of GNP as a measure of development?

Development as social wellbeing

Second, some non-government organisations (NGOs), such as Oxfam and the United Nations (UN) have stressed that measurements of development should also focus on social indicators of development. They argue that development should mean the end of subsistence poverty and the right to experience 'social wellbeing', which means the right for children to survive into adulthood and for adults to live into old age, because they have access to a nutritious diet, safe drinking water, shelter and sanitation, education, and drugs to treat disease.

A good example of this focus on social needs is the Human Development Index (HDI), created by the UN in 1990, which aimed to measure aspects of social wellbeing such as material standard of living as measured by income, years in schooling and adult literacy, the multiple disadvantages experienced by girls, life expectancy at birth, and the number of doctors per 100,000 of the population. The HDI in 2013 showed that underdevelopment as measured by education and life expectancy continues to be a problem. For example, in the USA, 99 per cent of the adult population was literate, while average life expectancy was 78.9 years. However, in contrast, in Sierra Leone, only 43 per cent of the population was literate and average life expectancy was 45.6 years.

SUSTAINABLE DEVELOPMENT: THE ENVIRONMENTALIST PERSPECTIVE

In 1987, the Brundtland Report, published by the UN, proposed the idea of 'sustainable development'. This concept was based on the idea that although social and economic development was important in order to assure human beings of a healthy and productive life, such progress should be eco-friendly and not jeopardise the right of future generations to experience the same living standards as those enjoyed by present generations.

Black (2002) argues that sustainable development not only aims to improve the living standards of people in the developing world, it also proposes to safeguard the environment – the air, soil, water and all forms of life – from the acute pressures of population growth, modern technology and consumer demand. For example, Brundtland noted that poverty in sub-Saharan Africa was often caused by environment degradation, as land was over-farmed, which led to desertification and a reduction in food production. Sustainable development therefore aims to tackle a range of ecological worries – species loss, global warming, deforestation, toxic waste, the depletion of the world's natural resources, and so on – which have come about as a consequence of development. It is

also concerned with ensuring safe water, adequate sanitation and decent affordable housing for the world's poor. Most importantly, it is aimed at making sure that future generations, whether they are in the developed or developing world, live in an environment that is sustainable rather than in terminal decline.

Millennium Development Goals (MDGs)

In 2000, the concepts of economic and social wellbeing, and sustainable development were brought together by the UN in eight Millennium Development Goals that aimed to:

> eradicate extreme poverty and hunger

> achieve universal primary education

> promote gender equality and empower women

> reduce child mortality

> improve maternal health

> combat HIV/AIDS, malaria and other diseases

> ensure environmental sustainability

> develop a global partnership for development.

The eighth MDG was the most contentious goal because it committed underdeveloped nations to addressing the human and social needs of their populations. The developed countries, in turn, agreed to support poorer countries in achieving the previous seven MDGs through the provision and reduction of aid, and more equitable trade relationships.

However, critics of the MDGs argue that they do not go far enough in demanding greater responsibility from those who govern developing nations. Collier (2007) argues that underdevelopment has partly been brought about by poor governance by the elites of these developing nations, who have engaged in corrupt practices and civil wars, and are more concerned with enriching themselves than improving the lives of their peoples. Consequently critics of the MDGs argue that additional development criteria should include the protection of basic human rights; the promotion of religious tolerance; and political freedom, especially the right to vote in democratic and free elections. However, these criteria have been criticised in turn by sociologists actually located in the developing world because such rights and freedoms may reflect Western rather than universal values and any attempt to promote them may be interpreted as Western **imperialism**.

UNDERSTAND THE CONCEPT

Imperialism refers to extending a country's power and influence through colonisation, the use of military force or through the promotion of ideas.

In September 2015, the United Nations announced that the 1990 goals had probably been too ambitious. However, there was good news in that the UN claimed that in Asia, Latin America and Africa a billion people living in extreme poverty – which is defined as living on $1 a day – had been lifted out of poverty (which had therefore fallen by 50 per cent) since 1990. Moreover, global life expectancy had been improved to 70 years. However, 12 per cent of the world's population – one billion people – remained in poverty in 2015 although the UN predicted that extreme poverty would be eradicated by 2030. Later chapters will show some progress in child and maternal mortality rates, although, in 2015, 16,000 children under the age of 5 years were still dying every day of preventable and treatable causes. Over half of these infant deaths were associated with hunger and under-nutrition. Chapters 3 and 4 will deal with the idea that the West could have done more in terms of the provision of aid, the reduction of debt and the establishment of more equitable trade relationships to improve these figures.

FOCUS ON SKILLS: BURGERNOMICS

Sociologists and economists have invented a range of alternative ways in which to measure the development progress of societies. One such example is Pakko and Pollard's (2003) concept of 'burgernomics'. They observed that McDonalds now operate in over 120 countries around the world and that the Big Mac is a valued consumer commodity in most of those countries. However, Pakko and Pollard note that the price of this meal also varies from country to country. Wages differ too across countries. For example, workers in the UK are relatively well paid compared with similar workers in Bangladesh.

These observations led Pakko and Pollard to invent a measurement of development based on how many minutes a worker must work in order to buy a Big Mac. The shorter the period, the more developed they claim the society is. For example, in the USA and UK, a worker only has to work 11 minutes and 15 minutes respectively to earn enough to buy a Big Mac. In contrast, in Mexico, a worker has to work 65 minutes and in the Philippines 112 minutes. In Thailand, the Big Mac costs over three-quarters of the hourly wage of Thai consumers.

Another way of measuring development is through the pursuit of Gross National Happiness (GNH). This aim has been adopted by the government of the Himalayan kingdom of Bhutan, which has rejected Gross National Product (GNP) as a means of measuring development. Bhutan argues that the spiritual and emotional wellbeing of its people should take priority over wealth and income. Bhutan has therefore adopted a holistic approach to development focused on improving the environment in which people should live, regardless of their social backgrounds. It has also promoted the spiritual satisfaction of its citizens by providing them with good governance and an education system that prioritises the teaching of a green philosophy based on conservation and sustainability. Meditation classes too are an important part of the curriculum.

Questions

1. **Explain** why Pakko and Pollard decided to use the concept of burgernomics to measure development.

2. **Analyse** what is meant by a holistic approach to development.

3. **Analyse**. Compare burgernomics with Gross National Happiness. Which of these ways of measuring development do you think is more reliable and why?

4. **Evaluate**. Using information from this source and what you have so far read in this chapter, assess the reliability and validity of the ways in which development is measured.

THEORIES OF DEVELOPMENT AND UNDERDEVELOPMENT

Modernisation theory and defining development

Both McMichael (2008) and Rist (2014) argue that after the Second World War (1939–45), it became clear that many countries in Africa, Asia, Latin America and the Caribbean were remaining poor despite exposure to capitalism. There was concern among the leaders of the West, especially the USA, that widespread poverty, encouraged by the strong mass appeal of communism, could lead to political instability and that this might impede US trade interests. In response to these potential developments, American economists, sociologists and policymakers developed the theory of modernisation.

Modernisation theory believes that societies progress through evolutionary stages. For example, Huntington (1993) describes modernisation as an evolutionary process that brings about revolutionary change. McKay (2004) argues that modernisation theory made a 'beguiling promise' to poorer nations: if they were willing to follow the same growth path pioneered by the richer Western nations they too could achieve development and its economic and social benefits. Modernisation theory therefore set out to identify what economic and cultural conditions might be preventing some countries from developing or modernising. It also aimed to provide an explicitly capitalist solution to global poverty.

Modernisation theory and the ladder of development

The leading modernisation theorist, Walt Rostow (1971), suggested that development should be seen as an evolutionary process in which countries progress up an economic development ladder that has five rungs or stages. Rostow's model of development, described here, follows the pattern of development that he alleged developed countries had experienced between the 18th and 20th centuries.

> Stage 1 – The traditional stage. At the bottom of the evolutionary development ladder are traditional societies whose economies are dominated by subsistence farming: they produce crops in order to survive rather than to make profits. Consequently, such societies have little wealth to invest in science, technology and industry.

> Stage 2 – The preconditions for take-off stage. At this stage Western values, practices and expertise can be introduced into the society to assist the take-off to modernisation. This may take the form

of science and technology to modernise agriculture and to introduce manufacturing industry, and infrastructure such as communications and transport systems. Investment by Western companies and aid from Western governments are therefore essential to this stage. These 'interventions' would act as the fuel for development 'take-off' and produce the beginning of economic growth. As McKay (2004) notes: "the image of take-off is particularly evocative, full of power and hope as the nation is able to launch itself into a bright new future".

> Stage 3 – The 'take-off' stage. This stage involves the society experiencing rapid economic growth as these new modern practices become the norm. Profits from this growth are reinvested in new technology and infrastructure, and a new entrepreneurial and urbanised class emerges from the indigenous (native) population, which evolves into being more individualistic and consequently more willing to take risks and to invest in or start businesses. The country begins exporting manufactured goods to the developed world. Incomes rise, creating a demand for manufactured consumer goods.

> Stage 4 – The drive to maturity stage. This involves continuing economic growth and reinvestment in both new technology and the infrastructure. This stage also sees the introduction of mass education, mass media such as mass circulation newspapers, radio and television, and medical technology, especially birth control. The population takes advantage of the meritocratic educational opportunities available to them to become highly skilled and paid workers and, as a result, it continues to benefit from ever-rising living standards. These economic benefits are reinforced through export earnings as the country strengthens its place in the international trade system. These earnings are invested in health, education and infrastructure.

> Stage 5 – The age of high mass consumption. This is the ultimate stage of development because economic production and growth are at Western levels, and the majority of the population live in urban rather than rural areas, work in offices or in skilled factory jobs and enjoy a comfortable lifestyle organised around consumerism and materialism. Life expectancy is high and most citizens have access to a welfare state that includes health care and free education. Poverty is more or less eradicated.

However, other modernisation theory sociologists argue that development can only occur if cultural barriers in developing societies are overcome. Parsons (1964), in particular, was very critical of traditional

187

undeveloped societies because he believed they were too attached to traditional customs, rituals, practices and institutions and therefore unwilling to entertain social change. Parsons saw modernisation impeded by the following traditional values:

> *Religious values that stress patriarchy* – these particularly prevent intelligent and skilled women from competing equally with men.

> *Ascription* – being born into a particular position, role, family, tribe, caste, gender and so on mean that people lack both the motivation and the innovative ideas to try new roles or ways of doing things.

> *Particularism* – people may be judged and allocated tasks on the basis of affective or family relationships rather than ability and achievement measured by educational qualifications.

> *Fatalism* – people in poverty often subscribe to the view that things will never change. This may mean that people may passively accept their lot rather than actively seeking change.

> *Collectivism* – people may not be motivated to change their material circumstances because they defer to group pressure and put their membership of a social group before self-interest.

Such traditional thinking and practice, from Parsons' perspective, was the enemy of progress. He was particularly critical of the extended kinship and tribal systems found in many traditional societies, which he believed hindered both the geographical and social mobility that are essential if a society is to industrialise quickly and effectively. Parsons believed that people in undeveloped societies need to develop an 'entrepreneurial spirit' if economic growth is to be achieved, and this could only happen if people in these societies became more receptive to Western values such as:

> *meritocracy* – rewarding effort, ability and skill on the basis of examinations and qualifications;

> *universalism* – applying the same standards to all members of society regardless of gender, religion, ethnic group, family of origin and so on;

> *individualism* – putting individual self-interest before the interests of the wider social group to which one belongs. Such self-interest would motivate people to become more ambitious, innovative and increasingly receptive towards change and progress.

Moreover, he argued that traditional societies should be strongly encouraged to replace traditional institutions, such as the extended family and political systems based on tribe, clan, caste or religion, with nuclear families and

democratic political systems respectively. Parsons claimed that traditional institutions stifled the individual initiative, free enterprise and risk-taking necessary for societies to develop and modernise.

Other modernisation sociologists stress the role of education, because literacy means the people of the developing world have access to a wider range of modern ideas. Hoselitz (1960) also encouraged urbanisation because he believed that it was easier and more effective to spread modern ideas among a concentrated city population than among a thinly dispersed rural population.

Modernisation theory therefore thought that all of these motors of development would produce a new capitalist entrepreneurial middle class who would believe in the need for modernity and who would be willing to take risks and therefore drive progress forward. Table 3.1.3 sums how modernisation sociologists see the differences between 'traditional man' and 'modern man'. As Timmons Roberts and Hite (2000) conclude: in a traditional society, the entrepreneur is a social deviant because he is doing something new and different; in a modern society, change is routine, innovation is valued, and the entrepreneur esteemed.

Traditional man	Modern man
Not receptive to ideas	Open to new experiences
Rooted in tradition	Changes orientation
Interested only in immediate things	Interested in the outside world
Denial of different opinions	Open-minded
Uninterested in new information	Inquisitive
Oriented towards the past	Oriented towards the present
Concerned with the short term	Values planning
Only trusts family members	Trusts people to meet obligations
Suspicious of technology	Values technical skills
Highly values religion and the sacred	Highly values education and science
Particularistic	Universalistic
Fatalistic	Optimistic

Table 3.1.3 *Typology of Traditional versus Modern Man*

Based on Table 1, from Peet and Hartwick (2015) which is adapted from Inkeles and Smith (1974) and Scott (1995)

Neo-modernisation theory

The neo-modernisation theorist, Samuel Huntington (1993) has been very influential in recent years. He strongly affirms the importance of culture as the primary variable for development and suggests that Western culture is 'exceptional' compared with that of developing societies. Other neo-modernisation theorists agree that in order to progress developing societies need to develop a 'modern' imagination in both thinking and practice. Landes (1998) suggests Europeans are more rational, ordered, diligent, productive, literate and inventive than non-Europeans. Furthermore he argues that Europeans subscribe to a more advanced value system organised around democracy, freedom of speech, property rights, the rule of law and a work ethic that encourages hard work and the thrifty use of both time and money. Landes argues that these European characteristics need to be adopted by developing societies if they are to escape poverty. Ferguson (2011) agrees with this analysis when he argues that Europe and the USA developed six 'killer apps' – the ability to compete, a scientific approach to problem-solving, a respect for property rights, medicine, consumerism and a work ethic – that produced their economic and material success. The implication of such analysis is that developing societies need to do the same.

Sachs (2005), like Rostow, argues that development is a ladder and that its rungs represent steps towards economic and social wellbeing. However, Sachs argues that a billion people in the developing world are too malnourished, hungry, diseased or young to lift a foot to get on the first rung of the development ladder because they lack certain types of capital that the West takes for granted, such as human capital (good health, nutrition and skills), knowledge capital, infrastructure, business capital (money and technology) and public institutional capital (services).

Sachs argues that it is important to help the developing world because failed economies produce failed states which are a threat to the West because they are hotbeds for terrorism, disease and crime. Huntington also sees undeveloped societies as a threat to the USA and encourages the US administration to invest in 'nation-building', that is, the export of American values, particularly democracy, free trade and women's rights, in order to break the hold of what the Americans see as the tyrannical power of religion and tradition – which they view as the main cause of poverty, inequality and inhumanity in undeveloped societies such as Iraq and Afghanistan. However, this view neglects the Islamic view that poverty and inequality are in fact caused by US economic and cultural imperialism – the very 'modernist' culture that the Americans are attempting to introduce in parts of the Middle East.

> **The theories of Sachs and Huntington have been criticised for being unethical, selfish and cruelly pragmatic. What do you think has led people to voice this criticism?**

Assessing modernisation theory

Strengths

Modernisation theory has had a profound influence on the relationship between the developed and developing worlds. No other sociological theory can claim to match its influence on global affairs. It has influenced Western foreign policy and aid distribution as well as the development policies of the UN, the World Bank and NGOs, such as charities. For example, the 'people first' aid policies of agencies such as Oxfam, Christian Aid and Save the Children aim to help the rural poor in developing societies by helping them take control of agricultural projects through training and education. This aim is based on the quite distinct modernisation principle of 'intervention'. Burkey (1993) argues that "the poor are seldom able to initiate a self-reliant development process without outside stimulation. An external agent must therefore be the catalyst." It is accepted that these agencies have done a lot of good at a localised level.

It may be true that the primary motivation of modernisation theory is the protection of Western trade interests and the ideological desire, prior to 1990, to prevent the spread of communism and, after 9/11, to prevent the spread of religious fundamentalism as part of the 'war on terror'. However, while it has not achieved much for the billion in poverty in the least economically developed societies (LLEDCs), it is partly responsible for the economic growth and improvements in lifestyle for the billions living in the NICs and LEDCs.

Black (2002) also argues that modernisation theory helped raise public consciousness of the poverty problem in the developed world, which led to the emergence of popular movements such as Make Poverty History and the Jubilee Debt Campaign, and the notion of development as a 'moral force' and as an instrument of compassion and social justice. This put pressure on the governments of developed nations, particularly after 2000, to construct aid programmes based on humanitarian motives rather than on strategic and political relationships, although Black acknowledges this was probably short-lived. Moreover, it can be argued that capitalism has brought great benefits to the Western world and that modernisation theory should be praised for wanting to extend these to the developing world, whatever the motive.

Finally, modernisation theory has probably been right (and certainly unpopular) in insisting that in order to reduce poverty, sociologists need to understand culture or at least take it into account when assessing development progress. However, this once deeply unpopular view is again in fashion with some postmodernist accounts of development, suggesting that culture is, and always has been, more important than economics in encouraging social change. However, the difference between modernisation theory and postmodernism with regard to culture is that the former is critical of it because it is seen as an obstacle to development, while postmodernists are more inclined to celebrate it.

The critique of modernisation theory

However, modernisation theory has attracted more criticism than praise for the following reasons:

> Some critics claim that it is ethnocentric because it clearly argues that Western forms of civilisation are technically and morally superior and that the cultures of developing societies are deficient in important respects. Often such societies are defined as 'backward' if they insist on retaining some elements of traditional culture and belief and/or if they apply fundamentalist religious principles to the organisation of their society.

> However Edwards (1992) suggests that the traditional and the modern can in fact be successfully combined. He argues that the economic success of the Asian Tiger economies and China is due to a successful combination of traditional religious values and practices with Western rational thinking and practices. Religions in these societies have encouraged the emergence of a moral and authoritarian political leadership that demands sacrifice, obedience and hard work from its population in return for prosperity. This has paved the way for an acceptance of Western economic and cultural practices, such as widespread respect for meritocratic education for both males and females, commitment to hard work at school and in the workplace, discipline, innovation and ambition.

> Modernisation theory generally ignores the 'crisis of modernism' in the developed world, such as inequalities in the distribution of income and wealth which may be fuelling social problems such as poverty, homelessness, high rates of crime, drug abuse and suicide.

Can you think of two major problems that Europe is experiencing in the mid-2010s because of the failure of modernisation theory and its agents to deal with poverty in sub-Saharan Africa and countries such as Iraq and Afghanistan?

Modernisation theory assumes that all societies will advance in the same way through a fixed set of changes. However, there is no reason to assume that traditional societies share the same features as 18th-century Britain or that capitalism will mould societies in the same fashion. Modernisation theory has been slow to understand that developing societies often have unique features that are not shared by other developing nations. For example, Ethiopia and Somalia are neighbouring LLEDCs but they are quite different from one another in terms of geography, climate, agricultural and industrial output, infrastructure, social structure, culture and so on, and consequently they each require quite different and individually tailored pathways to development.

The modernisation assumption that cultural ideas can initiate economic growth is challenged by empirical evidence collected by Inglehart and Baker (2000), based on a study of 61 traditional societies. They found that all these societies placed a strong emphasis on religion, male dominance in economic and political life, deference to parental authority and traditional gender roles, and the importance of family life. These societies, which were also often authoritarian, found cultural diversity threatening and were generally opposed to social change. In contrast, advanced industrial societies tended to have the opposite characteristics. However, Inglehart and Baker's data suggests that such cultural characteristics were the product of economic insecurity and low levels of material wellbeing rather than being the cause of it. They conclude that culture may be less important than modernisation theory suggests. Instead, they argue that the major reason people in developing societies are slow to welcome social change is unequal access to scarce resources.

Marxists argue that traditional societies cannot develop in the same way as modern Western societies because they exist within a global economy dominated by Western interests. Marxist commentators have pointed out that developing nations cannot follow the same path as the developed world for two inter-related reasons. First, the American economy in the 18th and 19th centuries shared many of the features of the Western European economies. They were able to compete with one another as equals. However, developing countries do not have similar relationship with countries in the developed world.

For example, many developing countries were colonies of Western countries. Furthermore, as Chapters 3 and 4 will show, developing societies are often dependent on the global terms of trade set up by Western powers, and on aid, which often comes with strings attached. In other words, this is no level playing field. In fact, Marxists such as Frank (1971) even go as far as suggesting that developing societies are deliberately kept in a state of economic underdevelopment by the West.

The persistence of global poverty and inequality in 2015, after 70 years of billions of dollars of investment in the developing world, can be seen as the biggest thorn in the side of modernisation theory because most of that spending has been based on their principles. For example, in 2012 the world's richest countries, with only 18 per cent of the world's population, earned 68 per cent per cent of its income. In contrast, nearly half of the world's population only earned 7 per cent. Furthermore, all the evidence suggests that global inequality has actually increased since such investment began. For example, in 1960 the top 20 per cent of the richest people in the world were earning 30 times more than the poorest 20 per cent, but by 1997 this had increased to 74 times. In 2015, the average African household actually consumed 20 per cent less than it did 30 years ago. Furthermore the UN has suggested that there were still a billion people living in extreme poverty in the developing world in 2015. Altogether, these statistics suggest that modernisation theory has failed in its goals, although modernisation thinkers such as Sachs and Landes suggest that the real cause of this failure is the inability of the populations of developing societies to change the way they think and act.

Neo-liberal theories

Neo-liberal theories of development, dominant in the 1990s, were strongly influenced by aspects of modernisation theory. In particular, neo-liberals such as Bauer argued that the only way to achieve development was the whole-hearted adoption of the free-market model of capitalism. Neo-liberals claimed the free market could deliver the benefits of development more effectively than economies that were centrally planned or characterised by government intervention. Consequently neo-liberals argue that government interference in the economy should be kept to a minimum.

Neo-liberal ideas about the free market often shaped the policies of the International Monetary Fund (IMF) and the World Bank, which often lent money to developing countries in the 1990s on the condition that land reform policies – often involving a fairer distribution of land to the poor – were abandoned and/or that government spending on health, education and welfare was reduced. These ideas will be explored further in Chapter 3.

Marxism

Peet and Hartwick observe that Marx never used the term 'development' in the ways in which it is used today, but that he did touch upon global stratification and inequality and why some societies have failed to develop. His theory and history of the class struggle focuses on the class struggles, that characterise early capitalism, between the capitalist class and the feudal nobility and between peasants/workers and the capitalist class. He argues that the capitalist class was able to win these battles because of its 'primitive accumulation' of capital, which originated in earlier periods of history. This capital was accumulated via slavery and colonialism from the wider world and transferred to capitalist economies such as that of the UK. Marx therefore implies that the transition to capitalism from feudalism was facilitated by the exploitation of the developing world and its people.

Traditional Marxists developed the theory of imperialism in which the capitalists of one society exploit the labour power of peasants and workers of other societies. Marxists identify three phases of what they describe as 'Euro-American' imperialism. The first phase of 'mercantile imperialism' lasted from the 15th century to the 19th century and involved conquest of the Americas and much of Asia, particularly the Indian subcontinent. This phase of imperialism involved the plundering of vast wealth from ancient civilisations and the enslavement of the inhabitants of colonies. Mercantilism often involved declaring war on developing nations in order to force them to accept unequal terms of trade that most benefited Western interests. Marxists believed that the profits from these mercantile ventures, and the cheap raw materials that the UK seized from its colonies or produced cheaply on plantations using slave labour, constituted the 'primitive accumulation' of capital that kick-started capitalism in Britain.

The second imperialist phase occurred in the second half of the 19th century as the large industrial countries competed with one another for global domination. This resulted in the carve-up of Africa by Britain, France, Germany, Italy and even Belgium. Japan and the USA were also active in the take-over of traditional societies. For example, Japan took over Manchuria and Korea while the USA expanded its territories in both the Caribbean and the Pacific. These territories and their people were a source of cheap labour, crops and raw materials, as well as new markets in which manufactured goods could be sold.

Some traditional Marxists believe there is a third phase of neo-imperialism led by the USA. However, this neo-imperialism is not motivated by territorial conquest, unlike the first two phases. Rather, neo-imperialism is about control of people defined by the USA as problematic and as a potential threat to the security of the USA. This type of imperialism takes the form of controlling the way people think, or, as Peet and Hartwick put it, "to control global space by conquering the political and economic imaginations of the world's peoples" by having them share in "the expansion of American ideals such as freedom, democracy, equality of opportunity and consumption. American neo-imperialism means spreading certain consumption habits, lifestyle patterns, media orientations, celebrity worship, electoral ambitions, and all the 'good' things that people everywhere have already shown that they urgently and deeply want."

Dependency theory

The economist-sociologist, Andre Gunder Frank (1971), takes traditional Marxism further by arguing that developing countries have found it difficult to sustain development along modernisation lines not because of their own deficiencies, but because the developed West has deliberately and systematically underdeveloped them in a variety of ways, leaving them today in a state of dependency. Hence, Frank's theory is known as dependency theory.

What does this image symbolise about the relationship between the developed and the developing world?

The world capitalist system

Frank argued that since the 16th century, there has existed a world capitalist system organised in a similar fashion to the unequal and exploitative economic or class relationships that make up capitalist societies. This world capitalist system is organised as an interlocking chain. At one end of the chain is the powerful and wealthy 'metropolis' made up of the developed core nations. At the other end of the chain are the undeveloped 'satellite' or peripheral countries. The relationship between the core and the periphery is based on exploitation. The metropolis

is able to exploit the labour, cheap materials and crops of the satellite countries with the cooperation of their ruling elites because it has greater military power and wealth and because it controls the terms of world trade. This exploitation results in the accumulation of wealth in the developed world, and in stagnation and destitution in the developing world. Frank therefore argues that the West has a vested interest in making sure that undeveloped societies remain economically weak and reliant on the West because it fears that the development of these countries would threaten its economic dominance.

Slavery and colonialism

Frank argued that dependency and underdevelopment were established through slavery and colonialism, both of which helped kick-start Britain's industrial revolution. Over a 200-year period (1650 to 1850), the triangular slave trade (see Figure. 3.1.3) shipped approximately nine million Africans aged between 15 and 35 across the Atlantic to work as an exceptionally cheap form of labour on cotton, sugar and tobacco plantations in America and the West Indies, owned mainly by British settlers. This generated tremendous profits for both the British slave-traders and the plantation owners. Britain also enjoyed a virtual monopoly over raw materials such as cotton, tobacco and sugar, which benefited industrial expansion such as that found in the Lancashire/Yorkshire textile industry.

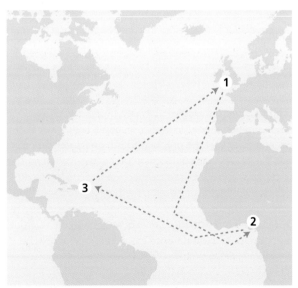

Figure 3.1.3 *The 'Triangular Trade': the slave route*

Colonialism locked much of Africa, Asia, and Central and South America even further into an exploitative relationship with the capitalist West. During the period 1650 to 1900, using their superior naval and military technology, European powers, with Britain to the fore, were able to conquer and colonise many parts of the world. As Harrison (1990) argues, this imperial expansion was to work the greatest transformation the human world has ever seen. The principal result of this European rule was the creation of a global economy in which the colonies were primarily exploited for their cheap food, raw materials and labour. Local industries were either destroyed or undermined by cheap imported manufactured goods from the West.

Neo-colonialism

Many colonies have achieved political independence today, but dependency theory argues that their exploitation continues via neo-colonialism. Frank argued that these new forms of colonialism are more subtle but are just as destructive as slavery and colonialism. Frank identifies three main types of neo-colonialism. First, the terms of world trade are dominated by Western markets and needs. This is explored further in Chapter 4. Second, Frank highlights the increasing transnational exploitation of the economies of developing countries. The forms such exploitation takes in practice are explored in detail in Chapter 3. Third, Frank argues that aid is another means by which Western countries can exploit the developing world because it inevitably leads to such countries being in debt to Western governments and banks. The forms this exploitation takes are explored further in Chapter 4.

A case study of Jamaica carried out by Elliott and Harvey (2000) supports the work of Frank. They conclude that Jamaica's development problems will never be solved by policies that ignore the vast inequalities in power arising from Jamaica's slave and colonial history. They suggest that the root of Jamaica's contemporary problems lie in the creation of the plantation economy by the British, which resulted in vast inequalities in ownership of land that persist to this day. Elliott and Harvey conclude that the Jamaican economy continues to serve the needs of Western markets for cash crops such as bananas, and the Jamaican ruling class, rather than the Jamaican people.

Assessing dependency theory

Strengths of dependency theory

Hoogvelt (2001) argues that dependency theory was a major influence on the political ideologies of many developing countries in the 1960s and 1970s. She notes that political leaders, particularly in Africa, used the principles of dependency theory to argue for 'development as liberation' from Western exploitation. Political and social movements in Africa in this period consequently stressed nationalism, self-reliance and

de-linking from their former colonial masters as a means of countering neo-colonialism. Similar movements can be seen in South and Central America, particularly in Venezuela under Hugo Chavez from 1999 until his death in 2013, in the Sandanista governments of Nicaragua in the 1980s and in present-day Ecuador.

The experience of Cuba, where there was a Marxist revolution in 1959, suggests that a socialist model of development can resist dependency and produce positive benefits. Despite decades of enforced isolationism (until 2015, the USA imposed a trade embargo on Cuba which made it extremely difficult for Cuba to export its goods), Cuba ranks among the top 5 per cent of 125 developing countries in terms of adult literacy rates, infant and maternal mortality rates and life expectancy.

The critique of dependency theory

However, Frank has been criticised for several reasons:

> He failed to be precise in his use of terms. 'Dependency' is an extremely difficult concept to operationalise and therefore test or measure empirically. Some sociologists, such as Myrdal (1968), have attempted to measure the amount of investment put into the developing world by the West and to compare it with the amount of profit taken out. However, it is generally agreed that this is a crude and imprecise method that does not necessarily measure dependency, exploitation and subordination. Similarly, it is unclear how and why Frank categorised particular societies as part of the 'metropolis' or as 'satellites'.

> Frank paints the relationship between the metropolis and satellite as always negative, but some commentators have suggested this is over-simplistic. For example, it could be argued that Canada and Taiwan are satellites of the USA because both are very dependent upon US trade. However, it is doubtful whether these relationships are exploitative. The health of the US economy depends on maintaining positive trade relationships with both countries. In other words, the interconnectedness of the global economy means that capitalist economies are often interdependent. In other words, the USA needs Canada and Taiwan as much as they need the USA.

Born et al. (2003) argue that if the developed world wanted the undeveloped world to be in a constant state of dependency, then the development of the NICs and LEDCs would have been blocked. However, their progress contradicts the dependency argument. Peet (2007), though, argues that dependency now exists in a new financial form.

The fact that the economies of 120 nation states and the livelihoods of 2.5 billion people are under the supervision of US banks and agencies such as the World Bank suggests that financial dependency has actually intensified.

Goldthorpe (1975) argues that it is incorrect to assume that colonialism, transnationals and aid are simply exploitative and that they have brought no benefits to the developing world. The British brought much-needed infrastructure to their colonies in the form of railways, roads, telecommunications, port facilities and urbanisation. Moreover, they provided people with wage-labour and organised land use to make it more efficient. Moreover, countries such as Afghanistan and Ethiopia, which were never colonised, face severe problems of development because they lack the infrastructure provided by the colonial powers.

Frank generally neglects the fact that Western exploitation of developing nations has often occurred with the connivance of the elites of the developing world. Such elites played a crucial role in slavery and colonialism, while today, many of them sit on the boards of the transnational companies that have invested in their countries and they have taken financial advantage of the huge sums of money being injected into their countries via aid. As the Commission for Africa (2005) notes, poor governance and corruption by this **kleptocracy** is partly responsible for the poor condition of many African countries today.

UNDERSTAND THE CONCEPT

The **kleptocracy** are members of the ruling elite in developing societies, who engage in corruption and robbery of the country's economic earnings, money from aid programmes and so on.

Timmons Roberts and Hite note that Frank's version of dependency theory fails to explain why there appear to be greater levels of exploitation over time or why some countries seem to be exploited more than others. Later dependency theorists, such as Evans (1979) and Gereffi (1994), have attempted to address these issues by arguing that the influence of the core is not always homogeneous and that differences among elites in the periphery can explain the different political regimes, economies and class relationships within the peripheral countries.

However, the fundamental weakness of dependency theory is that it offers no realistic economic alternative to capitalism or solutions to global poverty. It is also hamstrung by the fact that capitalism as an economic

system has brought tangible benefits to the world. The credibility of neo-Marxist dependency theory was further undermined by the collapse of the European Communist bloc in the 1990s and the apparent conversion of China to entrepreneurial capitalism in the last decade. Also, North Korea – the country that adheres most strictly to communist principles – is probably not a great advertisement for an attractive alternative to capitalism. However, to be fair to Marxism, the global dominance of capitalism means that disproportionate pressure can be imposed on those societies that experiment with socialist or Marxist development strategies (such as extending land ownership rights to the poor) to make sure they return to the free-market system.

Other neo-Marxists such as Wallerstein (1979) offer an alternative global analysis of the role of capitalism in creating global stratification of developed and undeveloped societies. These ideas are explored in more detail in Chapter 2.

The post-development perspective

Critics of Western models of development, such as Sachs (1992) and Esteva (1992), known as the 'post-development school', argue that development was always unjust, that it never worked and that it has now clearly failed. Black concludes that five decades of development and the expenditure of billions of dollars have produced a form of socio-economic apartheid rather than a more equal world.

There are a number of strands to the criticism of development levelled by post-development writers.

The post-development school criticises the assumption that the developing world is homogeneous and undifferentiated. They argue that the development path of a society and its choices in terms of development goals are mainly historically conditioned and, in the contemporary world, are often shaped by a web of power relations with Western powers and economic interests such as transnational corporations. Development is therefore characterised by disparities in power between the developed world and the developing world. This inequality produces 'development as paternalism' – the developed world is treated 'as a child in great need of guidance'.

Escobar (2008) argues that the discourse of development, particularly that associated with modernisation theory, is ethnocentric. It is a language of power that is only interested in achieving the conditions that are characteristic of already rich Western societies. Consequently it is dismissive of ancient philosophies and concerned with removing the social institutions that have shaped the lives of two-thirds of the world's population for thousands of years. According to Escobar, this is both arrogant and disrespectful and creates the potential for opposition and conflict.

Escobar argues that the Western model of development justifies itself by claiming to be rational, scientific and therefore neutral and objective. However, he claims that in reality it is a top-down approach that treats people and cultures as abstract concepts and statistical figures to be moved up and down in the name of progress. It fails to acknowledge that it is dealing with real people in real situations, and consequently it denies the people of developing societies the opportunity and capacity to make their own choices and decisions.

Other post-development thinkers argue that modernist explanations of underdevelopment rarely seek contributions from sociologists and economists who actually live in the developing world. McKay argues that development strategies are too often in the hands of Western experts who fail to consult local people or take account of their local knowledge and skills. This not only downgrades the role of local initiatives and self-help but also fails to consider that Western values may have little cultural meaning in developing societies.

For example, Sahlins (1997) argues that Western aid agencies often incorrectly assume that people who lack material possessions are in poverty and are unhappy. However, he argues that people in the developing world may have few possessions but this does not mean they see themselves as poor. They may actually be happy because they belong to a supportive community and they have the love of their family. This idea has been practically applied in Bhutan, where development is measured using a Gross National Happiness index (see Focus on Skills). Sahlins argues that the view that poverty inevitably leads to unhappiness is a Western social construction.

Rahnema (1997) argues that development often has little to do with the desires of its target population. Instead it often means a high-octane consumerist society that deprives people of meaning and mental comfort. The idea that materialism is superior to the simple spiritual life, human happiness and ecological awareness is often alien to people living in the developing world.

Korten (1995) argues that Western approaches to development therefore need to be more 'people-centred' and focused on empowering local people in order to encourage them to take more responsibility for their communities. Similarly, Amartya Sen (1987) argues that development needs to be about restoring or enhancing basic human capabilities and freedoms as well as giving

people real choices and power in creating their own livelihoods and in governing their own affairs.

Carmen (1996) argues that Western approaches to development often imply that underdevelopment is the fault of the victim. He argues that this is demeaning, dehumanising and results in dangerous delusions because the people of the developing world often end up internalising the myth that they are incapable and incompetent, and that they themselves are the problem. Sankara (1988) argues that consequently their minds end up being colonised by the idea that they should be dependent and that they should look to the West for direction. Galeano (1992) succinctly summarises this self-fulfilling prophecy consequence as "they train you to be paralysed, then, they sell you crutches".

Post-development sociologists argue that Western models of development have created a diverse set of problems for the populations of developing societies. Indigenous peoples have been forcibly removed from their homelands, grave environmental damage is being done to the rainforests, children's labour is being exploited, and there has been aggressive advertising and marketing of unhealthy products such as baby milk powder, cigarettes and carbonated drinks – all in the name of progress towards the industrial–capitalist model of development.

Some post-development sociologists conclude that development is a 'hoax' in that it was never designed to deal with humanitarian and environmental problems. Carmen, for example, argues that the primary motive of modernist development has always been about allowing the industrialised world, particularly the USA, to continue its economic and cultural dominance of the rest of the world. Consequently, alternative definitions of development grounded in the experience of developing societies are often dismissed as threatening, inferior or backward by Western development experts. For example:

> Socialist models of development, such as that found in Cuba, are often dismissed as extremist, dangerous and threatening to Western economic interests. These types of society often end up isolating themselves – as in North Korea, for example – or the nations of the West side against them and deny them entry to the world's trading system, as was the case with Cuba between 1960 and 2015.

> The Islamic mode of development adopted by Iran has been dismissed by the West as a product of irrational extremism and as the opposite of progress. Islamic societies often regard development as the need to apply Muslim principles to all aspects of their societies – government, law, education, art and so

on, because such societies regard becoming closer to Allah as development and progress. Western secular values are rejected because they are seen as decadent and dangerous. Said (2003) argues that Western commentators tend to regard the Islamic model of development as backward and as a threat to modernity and consequently relationships between Islamic countries such as Iran and Western countries are, at best, tense.

› Some developing societies regard liberation from totalitarian oppression and corruption as more important than industrialisation and economic growth. This was often the goal of the liberation theology resistance movement found in many Central American countries in the 1970s and 1980s. Many of the most repressive, corrupt and totalitarian right-wing regimes in Central and South America were financially sponsored and militarily supported by the USA because the Americans feared that development as liberation would inevitably lead to a communist threat in their 'back yard'.

Ironically, liberation from neo-colonialism and economic dependency on the West is now seen by some post-development sociologists as their ultimate development goal. There are different motives for this. Some, for example, regard industrial development as a problem if it means increasing social and economic divisions within a country (which it inevitably does). Some nationalists and theists (religious people who believe in one god) may resist development because they fear that their local cultures are being undermined by the aggressive marketing of a Western-dominated hedonistic culture that weakens young people's commitment to local traditions, religious practices and nationalism. Some societies may even over-react to this threat, hence, Iran's actions in imprisoning teenagers for posting a video of themselves dancing along to Pharrell Williams's 'Happy', which was reported widely in the media and can be researched online. Even in the West itself, the last decade has seen the rise of a new transnational social movement, Occupy, based on a radical critique of the global capitalist economy and the Western institutions that underpin it.

However, post-development theory has been criticised for three reasons. First, it tends to condemn most Western

attempts to help the developing world as perverse. In particular, it questions the motives of the West and tends to suggest that all development is ultimately carried out for the benefit of the West. This obviously devalues the efforts of those who believe they have a moral imperative to help those worse off than themselves.

Second, it over-romanticises local and indigenous knowledge systems and development programmes, which are seen as automatically superior to rational scientific approaches. Post-development theory therefore engages in what Peet and Hartwick call "a kind of reverse snobbery" but this fails to take into account the global scale of economic forces that threaten local spaces.

Third, post-development theory fails to come up with practical ways in which local initiatives can engage with the global forces that now characterise the world. Martinez-Alier (2013), for example, suggests that economic production and consumption needs to be downscaled so that the world's resource use and waste stays within safe ecological bounds. This is a praiseworthy goal but one that has not been received with much enthusiasm by countries such as the USA, Australia and China, or by many transnational corporations.

CONCLUSIONS

The concept of development is focused on social change. However, defining what form that social change should take is not an easy, straightforward process. There are a number of models of development impacting on global inequality today. All have something to contribute to a sociological understanding of global stratification. Moreover, what is now increasingly being recognised by development agencies is that models of development may have to be individually and locally tailored in order to reflect each country's individual circumstances while also realistically engaging with the consequences of globalisation. You should revisit this chapter throughout your study of the topic to inform the debate between different theories of development.

FOCUS ON SKILLS: MICROCREDIT – BOOM OR BUST?

Microcredit allows the set-up of small businesses across the developing world.

A good example of poorer societies developing different ways of achieving development from those proposed by Western experts is 'microcredit'. This is the invention of Mohamed Yunus, a professor of economics at Dhaka University in Bangladesh. Yunus set up the Grameen Bank, which lends money in tiny amounts at very low rates of interest, particularly to landless women, to establish income-generating activities. These extremely poor women have no collateral and so have been unable to borrow money from conventional banks.

Yunus' Bangladesh enterprise has enjoyed considerable success: it has over 2.3 million borrowers and lends $35 million every month to fund over 500 types of economic activity. Some 98 per cent of loans are repaid. This success has led to Yunus claiming that he has discovered the answer to global poverty. He suggested that it would eradicate poverty within a generation. He also claimed that microcredit has resulted in self-sufficiency, that is, dependence on people's own resourcefulness and skill rather than dependency on Western aid agencies. In this sense, Yunus has claimed that microcredit is people-centred. Interestingly, however, Yunus' scheme is not rejecting the capitalism inherent in most mainstream approaches towards development, but he does claim it is a different way of managing capitalism. He argues that too much of the money involved in development tends to find its way into the pockets of the elite. Little of it trickles down to the poor. Moreover, the big global banks which finance most big development projects believe it is too risky to lend to the poor.

Yunus has argued that in his scheme the poor are able to obtain microcredit and become mini-capitalists.

The success of the Grameen Bank has led to similar microcredit schemes being set up in over 50 developing countries. However, most economists have concluded that microcredit has not reduced poverty or encouraged sustainable bottom-up development. Instead it has turned into a 'poverty trap' for many individuals. This has particularly been the case in South Africa. Bateman (2012) argues that microcredit was aggressively over-sold in South Africa as big banks decided there was profit to be made and it was often aimed at those poor individuals who were most likely to get into personal difficulties. Few checks were carried out on how borrowers intended to use the money. He notes that many of South Africa's poor have voluntarily taken on debt without having any clear idea of what money-making activities they were going to invest it in or how they were going to repay it. Consequently, nearly half of 19 million users of microcredit in South Africa have 'impaired' credit records, meaning they are three or more months in arrears, with a further 15 per cent described as 'debt stressed', that is, one or two months in arrears. This adds up to 11 million people – more than 60 per cent of those who have used microcredit schemes. Such debt is fuelling anti-social problems such as crime in South Africa's cities.

Questions

1. **Explain** what microcredit is.

2. **Analyse** why microcredit was seen as a people-centred alternative to the conventional approaches to development.

3. **Analyse** the reasons for the performance of microcredit in Bangladesh and South Africa.

4. **Evaluate** the view that people-centred schemes such as microcredit are more attractive to people living in developing societies than development schemes promoted by Western governments and agencies.

CHECK YOUR UNDERSTANDING

1. Explain what is meant by the term 'development'.

2. Explain what is meant by 'the crisis of modernism'.

3. Explain what is meant by 'dependency'.

4. Explain what is meant by 'neo-colonialism'.

5. Identify and briefly outline two examples of two cultural values that supposedly prevent traditional societies from modernising.

6. Identify and briefly explain the usefulness of three non-economic measures of development.

7. Analyse two reasons why economic indices of development are seen as unsatisfactory as measures of development.

8. Analyse two differences between traditional societies and societies characterised by high mass consumption.

9. Evaluate the view that the less developed countries have been systematically underdeveloped by Western capitalism.

10. Evaluate the modernisation view that development is an evolutionary process.

TAKE IT FURTHER

1. Conduct a survey that investigates the general public's understanding of the developing world. You should ask questions about:

   > the origin of their ideas about the developing world

   > what they think are the causes of problems in the developing world

   > how they see the developing world solving its problems

   > whether they consider that the West, and especially the UK, makes a contribution in terms of causes and solutions.

   What do your results tell you about which model of development the general public might subscribe to?

2. The United Nations website, www.un.org/millenniumgoals, contains detailed reviews of the Millennium Development Goals. In addition, the United Nations Development Programme website, www.undp.org, is particularly good and contains an impressive range of information about sustainable development projects being carried out by United Nations agencies across hundreds of countries; reports on the Human Development Index (HDI) can be found at http://hdr.undp.org

3. Use the site www.theglobaleconomy.com/compare-countries to update GDP for the countries listed in Table 3.1.2. Add Cuba to this list. This site also includes the performance of countries in terms of human development. Compare and contrast GDP with HI - can you see any similarities or differences?

3.2 GLOBALISATION

LEARNING OBJECTIVES

> Demonstrate knowledge and understanding of globalisation and its influence on the cultural, political and economic relationships between societies (AO1).

> Demonstrate knowledge and understanding of sociological debates about the nature, extent, causes and significance of globalisation (AO1).

> Apply this knowledge to contemporary societies (AO2).

> Evaluate sociological explanations of globalisation in order to make judgements and draw conclusions about its nature, extent, causes and significance (AO3).

INTRODUCING THE DEBATE

Globalisation can be an emotive issue because it does not just affect the lives of people living thousands of miles away. It affects the lives of all citizens both positively and negatively, whether they live in the developed world or the developing world. There are a number of sociological ways in which globalisation is viewed. Modernisation theory implies that globalisation will be achieved once all developing societies reach the age of high mass consumption. However, this analysis suggests globalisation is a long way off. On the other hand, neo-liberals such as Friedman argue that the world should welcome globalisation because it has brought about a golden age of prosperity. He predicts globalisation will eventually see the end of problems such as world poverty. Marxists, who belong to the dependency and world systems approaches, agree that there has been a globalisation of economic activity but argue that this is a merely an expansion of the logic of capitalism into all societies. Marx and Engels predicted this in the Communist Manifesto:

"The bourgeoisie has through its exploitation of the world market given a cosmopolitan character to production and consumption in every country… All old-established national industries have been destroyed or are daily being destroyed. They are destroyed by new industries whose introduction becomes a life and death question for all civilised countries, by industries

that work up raw materials drawn from the remotest zones, industries whose products are consumed in every quarter of the globe… The bourgeoisie, by the rapid improvement of all instruments of production, by the immensely facilitated means of communication, draws all, even the most barbarous, nations into civilisation."

In other words, from a Marxist perspective, globalisation is neither new nor is it novel and unique. Other sociologists have expressed anxiety about the globalisation of culture and the appearance of a global homogeneous mono-culture dominated by American transnational corporations, which is allegedly threatening the existence of traditional local cultures and may even be fuelling resentment of the West. This concern is summed up by Arundhati Roy who claimed in Barsamian and Roy (2004) that "globalization means standardization. The very rich and the very poor must want the same things, but only the rich can have them." However, others such as Martell (2010) suggest that the notion of a global mono-culture imposing the same everywhere is too simplistic. Postmodernists such as Pieterse (2004) argue that it is more likely that when cultures meet they intermingle and create new hybrid forms of culture. However, it may be as Marxists suggest that cultural globalisation is also merely an aspect of the capitalist global drive to enhance profit.

DEFINING GLOBALISATION

Modelski (2003) defines globalisation as a historical process that is characterised by a growing engagement between peoples in all corners of the globe, while Cohen and Kennedy (2000) suggest that it refers to the increasing interconnectedness and interdependency of the world's nations and their people into a single global economic, political and cultural system. As Cochrane and Pain (2000) note, "the lives of ordinary people everywhere in the world seem increasingly to be shaped by events, decisions and actions that take place far away from where they live and work."

THE CAUSES OF GLOBALISATION

Cohen and Kennedy argue that globalisation needs to be understood as "a set of mutually reinforcing transformations" of the world. These transformations take four broad forms:

› Advances in mass communications and computer technology such as the internet, satellite television, mobile phones and social media have transformed the concepts of time and space. Information in all its varied forms – news, ideas, financial transactions and cultural products – can now be transmitted instantaneously to most global destinations.

› The nature of economic and financial markets has changed. They are no longer localised. Countries have become economically interdependent upon one another because of the expansion of international trade, the development of 24-hour global financial trading markets and the global dominance of the so-called 'three sisters of trade': the World Trade Organisation (WTO), the World Bank and the International Monetary Fund (IMF). Moreover, transnational corporations (that have the ability to operate across national borders) have created an international division of labour by situating their manufacturing plants in different locations across the globe, by transferring money, technology and raw materials across national borders and by creating global markets and consumers for their products.

› Culture has become globalised as ownership and control of the world's media, internet providers and websites have become increasingly concentrated in the hands of fewer transnational corporations. Cultural products such as films, television, music, designer fashion, news, social networking sites, food,

drink, brands and sport are primarily developed and manufactured for global consumption. This means that the populations of diverse societies now encounter and consume the same sorts of cultural products. Steven (2004), notes that "despite huge differences in distance, upbringing and social context, many of us now listen to the same music, read the same books and watch the same films and television." (See the Focus on Skills activity in Book 1, Topic 3, Chapter 7 for more on globalisation and branding.)

› **Reflexive modernisation** sociologists such as Beck (1999) and Giddens (2002) argue that risk has also evolved in the sense that the world increasingly shares the same problems, such as terrorism, people-trafficking, climate change and environmental degradation, which emanate from much the same sources.

UNDERSTAND THE CONCEPT

Reflexive modernisation theory is an approach that rejects the idea that modern societies have become postmodern societies. Rather, it believes that modernity has now become reflexive: problems such as harnessing nature to manufacture goods have become secondary to the problems resulting from advanced technology and production processes – the risks to both humanity and the environment of 'manufactured uncertainty', for example, the possibility of nuclear or ecological disaster, global warming and so on. Advanced modern societies are therefore risk societies.

Cohen and Kennedy conclude that these four transformations have led to 'globalism', a new consciousness and understanding that the world is a single place.

THE NATURE AND EXTENT OF GLOBALISATION

Cultural globalisation

Cultural globalisation refers to the rapid movement of ideas, attitudes, meanings, values and cultural products across national borders. It refers specifically to the idea that there is now a global and common mono-culture – transmitted and reinforced by the internet, popular entertainment media, transnational marketing of particular brands and international travel and tourism – that transcends local cultural traditions and lifestyles, and that shapes the perceptions, aspirations, tastes and everyday activities of people, especially young people, wherever in the world they may live. This cultural phenomenon has allegedly increased interconnectedness among different populations and cultures. For example, food is an important part of cultural experience. Most societies around the world have diets that are unique to them. However, the cultural globalisation of food and diet has been promoted by American fast-food and beverage transnationals such as McDonalds, Burger King, Starbucks and KFC. It can be argued that the 35,000 McDonalds restaurants that were operating in 118 countries in 2015 have had a global effect on local diets and eating habits.

However, it is important to understand that cultural globalisation is not new. It actually began centuries ago when languages, religious ideas and cultural values were spread globally via military conquest, trade and missionary work. Consequently, from the 7th century on, Muslim ideas were disseminated globally across Africa, Asia and the Middle East; the Spanish language and Catholicism became global phenomena when Spain conquered much of South America in the 16th century; and the English language, Protestantism and the rule of English law spread globally across much of the Caribbean, Africa and the Indian subcontinent as the British empire expanded in the 18th and 19th centuries. Moreover, the 19th and 20th centuries saw further globalisation because of mass migration to the USA, Canada and Australia. Since the 1950s, large numbers of people have immigrated to the UK from ex-British colonies in the Caribbean and Indian subcontinent. However, despite this historical globalisation of culture, it can be argued that the process of cultural globalisation has dramatically speeded up and intensified because of the fantastic technological advances that have been achieved in the last 30 years.

The global spread of cultural products has been assisted by the spread of new media technology across areas of the world in which it was not previously available. McKay (2000) observes a dramatic and rapid rise in the total number of radio and television sets in Africa, while the Commission for Africa (2005) observes that mobile phone use has spread more rapidly in Africa than in any other part of the world. Research by the Pew Research Center (2014) found that the majority of adults in Uganda, Tanzania, Kenya, Ghana, Senegal, Nigeria and South Africa owned cell phones in 2014, and that 70 per cent of people in Africa use mobiles for online activities such as browsing the web, that many others

might normally perform on laptops or desktop computers, as the technology overcomes weak or non-existent landline infrastructure.

Political globalisation

It is claimed that political globalisation is increasingly transcending local politics. Until the end of the Second World War, national governments were traditionally responsible for maintaining the human rights, security and economic welfare of their citizens. However, using the UK as an example, it can be seen that the UK's membership of and active involvement in global political institutions such as the United Nations, NATO, the European community and the G8, as well as the so-called 'special relationship' with the USA, often shapes or influences domestic political policies. The decision by the Labour government in 2001 to support the USA's invasion of Afghanistan and in 2003 to join the invasion of Iraq has had a huge impact on domestic political decisions to increase spending on home security.

Politics is also intertwined with economic globalisation. In 1976, for example, the IMF lent £2.3 to the UK on condition that cuts were made in public spending. The health of the UK economy may also depend on political decisions made in other countries about interest rates. The austerity measures which have been in place in the UK since 2010 are an indirect result of the lack of any political regulation and controls of banks in the USA, which culminated in the collapse of the Lehman Brothers bank and which led to several banks in the UK having to be bailed out by the Labour government. UK politicians may have to make unpopular political decisions about spending on welfare, education or health because of the size of Britain's overseas debt or because the global economy is experiencing recession.

Both economic and political globalisation have led to the rise of global social protest movements such as Amnesty International and Greenpeace, which aim to protect human rights and the environment. In addition, an anti-capitalist global movement has developed, symbolised by protests outside G8 conferences, as well as the Occupy and Anonymous campaigns. These have used global communication systems to forge alliances with similar dissidents in other countries to protest against the poverty, inequality, greed and corporate tax evasion they associate with global capitalism.

FOCUS ON SKILLS: THE GLOBALISATION OF MOBILE PHONES

The use of mobile phones in Africa is increasing much faster than anywhere else in the world, according to research by the Pew Research Center in 2014. 75 per cent of all telephones in Africa are mobile and Pew forecasts that by late 2019, there will be more than 635m mobile subscriptions in sub-Saharan Africa, and voice call traffic in the region will double. By then, three in four subscriptions should be internet inclusive.

There have been a number of driving forces responsible for the popularity of this form of communication. First, the new range of smartphones are relatively cheap, costing less than £30. Second, people are attracted by the easy access to social media, content-rich apps and video. Third, mobile phones have had a unique impact on Africa because of its relative lack of physical connectivity and access to reliable electricity. Mobile servers on motorbikes are now providing telephone connections in many parts of Africa, while telephone charging points in villages and towns have proved to be very popular and successful. Fourth, mobile phones are popular because of the need for people to keep in touch with family news. They are also used to help poor people in remote areas find employment without travelling long distances.

There is evidence that mobile phone technology is bringing about many indirect spin-offs. Data collection via cellphones has the potential to dramatically increase efficiency within health budgets; pilot schemes in Uganda are already showing savings of as much as 40 per cent. Prepaid phone cards are also beneficial as a form of electronic currency. Africans in the developed world are buying prepaid cards and sending them to their relatives back home, who can then sell the cards to others. Thus the cards have become a form of currency by which money can be sent from the rich world to Africa without incurring the commission charged on more conventional ways of remitting money. The mobile phone is also creating virtual infrastructures.

The spread of mobile phones has been welcomed by some commentators because they are vehicles for commerce, education, development and innovation. Mobile money programmes enable citizens to trade money for goods or services, using their phones in place of banks. Increased connectivity allows entrepreneurs to build support networks and expand their own services. Finally, they may be transforming African culture, infrastructure and politics: studies show that when 20 per cent of a population has the ability to exchange uncensored news and ideas through access to cellphones and text messaging, dictatorial or totalitarian regimes find it hard to retain power. However, despite the dramatic increase in the use of mobile phones in Africa, some commentators point out that the use of phones is not evenly spread across the continent. For example, countries such as Nigeria and South Africa are phone-rich, while societies such as Ethiopia and Eritrea are phone-poor. Also, there is still a huge digital divide in Africa: only a few countries can take internet connectivity for granted. In 2014, only 9.8 per cent of Africa's population had internet access.

Furthermore, some commentators are concerned that the use of mobile phones may create problems by increasing violent conflicts across the continent. Research by Pierskalla and Hollenbach (2013) claims that mobile phones can increase the ability of rebel groups to communicate more easily and to coordinate attacks across geographically distant locations.

Questions

1. **Outline**. What do the statistics tell sociologists about the relationship between Africans and technology?

2. **Explain** why mobile technology is increasing so rapidly in Africa.

3. **Analyse** why mobile phone technology is more common than computer technology in Africa.

4. **Analyse** the positive effects of mobile phone technology for the development of African societies.

5. **Evaluate**. Using information from this source and elsewhere, assess the impact of technologies such as mobile phones on the globalisation process.

Economic globalisation

Neo-liberals such as Friedman argue that there has been a rapid intensification of international trade and investment in the past 30 years and that, as a result, distinct national economies have dissolved into a global free-trade and market economy. This perspective sees global economics as dominated by international agencies such the WTO, the World Bank and the IMF, and a Western transnational corporate and banking culture that is only interested in increasing profit margins, regardless of the often negative effects of the activities of the major corporations on the domestic economies of the countries they operate in. Neo-liberals see such global processes as positive because they argue free trade extends economic and social benefits to all parts of the world.

It is claimed by neo-Marxists such as Frobel *et al.* (1980) that transnational corporations and banks are actually more economically powerful than individual countries and, as a result, have been able to construct an international division of labour through which they systematically exploit the labour of all countries, whether they are developed or not. (The global activities of international agencies such as the WTO and transnational corporations are examined in greater detail in Chapter 3.) However, Frobel argues that globalisation is merely another aspect of capitalism's search for greater profits.

There is no doubt that the development of an increasingly unified global economy is having effects on domestic economies. Decisions made in one society about lifestyle preferences and leisure pursuits can cause problems such as unemployment, debt and the loss of livelihoods for workers and peasants thousands of miles away. For example, if Western demand for a product such as tea, coffee or sugar falls, it can severely undermine the economies of undeveloped societies that may be highly dependent on the export of one of these cash crops. In 1998–1999 the Asian Tiger economies ran into difficulties and were forced to cut back on industrial investment in the UK, which led to a rise in the UK unemployment rate.

Some economists and sociologists suggest that economic globalisation may now be in decline. Stewart (2015) argues that the 2008 global banking crisis has resulted in transnational banks being reluctant to engage in cross-border lending and transnational corporations retreating from foreign investment because of the risks posed by being exposed to what Stewart calls "the ebbs and flows of the international system" symbolised by the 2015 Chinese stock market crash. Geo-political tensions, for example, between the West and Russia, and the rise of right-wing nationalism in several European countries, symbolised by popular fears about migrants and refugees and which are likely to result in tougher immigration policies, are also undermining economic globalisation. Transnational interests are also anxious about the rise of social and political movements that are critical of capitalism, such as the radical Syriza government elected twice in Greece in 2015. Finally, there are signs that globalisation is becoming a scapegoat for mass layoffs and stagnating wages among workers in some developed countries.

GLOBAL RISKS

There is evidence of a spread of crime across international borders, especially the trafficking of heroin and cocaine into the USA and Europe from the developing world, the smuggling of refugees into Europe, internet fraud and illegal arms smuggling. This global crime is estimated to be worth up to $500 billion a year.

Drug-trafficking is particularly profitable. The world turnover in heroin went up 20 times between 1970 and 1990, while cocaine turnover went up 50 times. Drug-trafficking is truly a global phenomenon as it is linked to the poverty of certain countries, which is a result of their weak position within the global economy. The international trading system means that poor farmers in countries such as Bolivia and Afghanistan cannot survive on the income provided by legitimate cash crops and turn instead to the production of coca or poppies (from which heroin can be manufactured) respectively.

Globalisation also increases the possibility of white-collar crime because drug money is often 'laundered' through legitimate global banking operations. This has been made easier by the existence of off-shore banking and 24-hour global financial markets, in which sums of money can be transferred across the world in seconds.

Violence is taking on a global dimension as international drug gangs compete with each other for global dominance. Terrorism, too, has also moved beyond national boundaries. The ISIS and al-Qaeda group have recruited from a range of Arab, Asian and European nations. Moreover, the actions of ISIS and al-Qaeda have become global actions in their choice of targets (for example, US and UK embassies around the world, French cartoonists, and the coastal resorts, hotels, nightclubs and restaurants used by Western tourists), and in their use of media technology (for example, passing on videos of atrocities to the Al-Jazeera television network or posting them on global social network sites, knowing that such images will be transmitted globally, within hours, on television and on the internet).

The Chernobyl nuclear disaster of 1986 demonstrated quite vividly that ecological disasters do not respect national boundaries – today, acres of land in the Lake District and Wales still experience high levels of radiation because of the fall-out from this accident thousands of miles away. Global environment degradation is not only caused by the acid rain and carbon emissions of Western and Chinese industry but also by the unwitting damage caused by the poor in the developing world who engage in over-cultivation and deforestation. The resulting global climate change has implications for everyone in the world.

THEORIES OF GLOBALISATION

Cochrane and Pain note that three theoretical positions can be seen with regard to globalisation.

Globalist theories of globalisation

Globalists argue that globalisation is a fact that is having real consequences for the way that people and organisations operate across the world. They believe that nation states and local cultures are being eroded by a homogeneous global culture and economy. However, globalists are not united on the consequences of such a process.

Hyper-globalism

Hyper-globalists (sometimes called optimists or positive globalists) welcome such developments and suggest globalisation will eventually produce tolerant and responsible world citizens. This is the position of Sen (2002) who suggests globalisation represents hope for all humanity because it will produce a universal techno-scientific culture that will liberate people from poverty. Llosa (2000) suggests that much war and conflict is caused by local cultural differences, therefore the faster local cultures merge into a single global culture the better.

Neo-liberals such as Thomas Friedman (2000) have argued that globalisation has occurred as a result of the global adoption of neo-liberal economic policies. He identifies a neo-liberal economic set of principles that he calls the 'golden straitjacket', which, he argues, all countries need to fit into if they are to achieve success in the global economy. These principles include the privatisation of state-owned enterprises and pensions, the maintenance of low inflation, a reduction in the size of government bureaucracy, the liberalisation of trade and investment, and the reduction of corruption. He argues that this golden straitjacket is "pretty much 'one-size fits all'…it is not always pretty or gentle or comfortable. But it's here and it's the only model on the rack this historical season" (quoted in Ha-Joon Chang, 2008).

Friedman claims that the globalised world economy is the result of most developing countries abandoning state interventionism in the economy, from the 1980s on, and adopting the laissez-faire free-trade policies of deregulation, privatisation and the opening up of free trade and investment. These countries were often shepherded onto the 'right' economic path by the 'good Samaritans' of Western governments, especially the USA and the 'three sisters of free trade': the IMF, the World Bank and the WTO. However, Friedman believes that the global straitjacket will produce prosperity for all in the long run.

Pessimistic globalism

In contrast, pessimistic globalists, such as Chang (2008) and Seabrook (2005), argue that globalisation is a negative phenomenon because it is essentially a form of Western (and especially American) imperialism, peddling a superficial and homogeneous mass form of monoculture and consumption.

Chang takes issue with the neo-liberalist perspective on the joys of economic globalisation. He argues that neo-liberals paint a false picture of the global economy as benefiting all. He claims that much of what happens in the global economy is deliberately meant to benefit the rich countries of the developed world. Neo-liberals preach free market and free trade to struggling poor countries in order to ensure that Western companies can sell their products without interference in developing countries and to prevent companies in the developing world from competing with transnational corporations. The adoption of the free market often means that Western companies can invest in the developing world and take over local businesses because there are no regulations or laws preventing them from doing so.

Chang refers to the World Bank, the IMF and the WTO as the "Unholy Alliance" and claims they exist to "force" developing countries down the free-trade road. For example, the IMF and World Bank will often only lend money to developing countries on the condition that they adopt free-trade policies. Chang points out that, as a result, the neo-liberal world economy is dominated by the developed world – rich countries are responsible for 80 per cent of the output of manufactured goods, they conduct 70 per cent of world trade and are responsible for at least 70 per cent of investment. Chang concludes that Western governments and their agents in the "Unholy Alliance" are actually "Bad Samaritans" rather than good ones in their dealings with developing countries. Chang would probably agree with the observation of Giddens (1999) that this "is less of a global village and more like global pillage".

Seabrook argues that, by definition, globalisation makes all other cultures local and, by implication, inferior. He suggests that globalisation implies a superior, civilised mode of living – it implicitly promises that it is the sole pathway to universal prosperity and security – consequently diminishing and marginalising local cultures. Seabrook suggests that globalisation sweeps aside the multiple meanings human societies and cultures have derived from or imposed upon their environment. He argues that integration into a single global economy is a "declaration of cultural war" upon other cultures and societies and that it often results in profound and painful social and religious disruption.

Many pessimistic globalists are concerned about the concentration of the world's media in the hands of a few powerful media corporations. Media conglomerates, mainly American (such as Disney, Microsoft, Time Warner and AOL) and Japanese (such as Sony) have achieved near monopolistic control of newspapers, film archives, news programmes, advertising, satellites and the production of films as well as television and radio programmes. It is suggested that the media moguls who own and control global media corporations are able to influence business, international agencies and governments and, consequently, to threaten democracy and freedom of expression.

It is also argued that such media corporations are likely to disseminate primarily Western, especially American, forms of culture. There have been concerns that these cultural products reflect a cultural imperialism that results in the marginalisation of local culture. Steven argues that "for the past century, US political and economic influence has been aided immensely by US film and music. Where the marines, missionaries and bureaucrats failed, Charlie Chaplin, Mickey Mouse and The Beach Boys have succeeded effortlessly in attracting the world to the American way." Mass advertising of Western cultural icons such as McDonalds and Coca-Cola has resulted in their logos becoming powerful symbols to people, especially young people, in the developing world because they imply that they need to adopt Western consumer lifestyles in order to modernise.

Cultural globalisation may therefore eventually undermine and even destroy rich local cultures and identities. Barber and Schulz (1995) fear that the globalised world is turning into a monoculture or 'McWorld' in which cultures and consumption will be standardised, while other commentators have expressed anxieties about the 'coca-colonisation' or 'Disneyfication' of the developing world. In his critique of cultural globalisation Seabrook suggests that "it is not only the economies of countries that are reshaped, but also the minds and sensibility of the people. Their value systems are re-formed in the image of the global market."

This cultural change is interpreted by some sections of developing nations as a form of imperialism – an attempt by the West to spread its supremacy – as a colonialism of the mind.

Media corporations are thought to aid the ever-increasing influence of Western culture in the developing world.

Seabrook argues that there are three principal responses to globalisation:

> A fatalistic response which states that the world is simply powerless to resist globalisation. Seabrook argues that most leaders of the developed world take the position that globalisation is inevitable and irreversible. He suggests that these leaders are experiencing an "impotence of convenience" – their confessed powerlessness disguises the fact that the forces of globalisation economically advantage their countries and their economic elites.

> Some cultures may attempt to resist globalisation by reasserting local identity. (See Book 1, Topic 3, Chapter 5 for more on national identity.) This may involve deliberately highlighting and celebrating local folklore and languages. For example, the French government have banned English words such as 'email', 'take-away' and now 'hashtag' and have imposed a 'culture tax' on cinemas showing non-French films. Seabrook identifies another increasing trend called 'commodification'. This involves making local cultures 'sellable' abroad by packaging them up for tourism. For example, Jacobs (2008) has documented how members of the Masai tribe in Kenya perform for tourists 'after carefully taking off their trainers and watches to make the whole thing more authentic'.

However, he notes that globalisation has also seen the emergence of 'vehement' and sometimes violent resistance in the developing world as people interpret it as a 'violation of their identity'. He notes that the rise of old nationalisms and the many fundamentalisms of the age – in the Middle East and elsewhere – are not arbitrary responses, but the reactions of people under overwhelming pressure from global influences. Seabrook concludes that "this is how global terrorism is bred: not by poverty, according to the common wisdom, but as a consequence of the supposed miracle-working, wealth-creating propensities of globalism". Therefore, some religious and ethnic groups may resist globalisation because they interpret the West as having declared an ideological war on local cultures.

Do you think Britain should 'protect' British culture from Americanisation by imposing a culture tax or by banning American words and phrases?

Marxist or radical theories of globalisation

Marxists are traditionalists in that they do not believe that globalisation is a new phenomenon. These sociologists point out that capitalism has been an international phenomenon for hundreds of years. All we are experiencing at the moment is a continuation, or evolution, of capitalist production and trade as the logic of capitalism propels manufacturing and marketing to seek greater profits in the global arena.

World systems theory

Marxists who are unhappy with the explanatory power of dependency theory (see Chapter 1) have subscribed instead to an alternative Marxist theory called 'world systems theory', founded by Wallerstein (1979), which argues that globalisation has always been an important part of the way capitalism organises itself. His theory has four underlying principles:

> Individual countries or nation states are not an adequate unit of sociological analysis. Rather, we must look at the overall social system that transcends (and has done for centuries) national boundaries. Wallerstein argues that capitalism is responsible for creating a 'world order' or Modern World System (MWS) because capital from its beginning has always ignored national borders in its search for profit. At the economic level, then, the MWS forms one unified system dominated by the logic of profit and the market.

> Wallerstein builds upon dependency theory by suggesting that the MWS is characterised by an international division of labour consisting of a structured set of relations between three types of capitalist zone: core, semi-periphery and periphery (see Figure 3.2.1). The 'core', or developed countries, control world trade and monopolise the production of manufactured goods. The 'semi-peripheral' zone

includes countries such as Brazil, India and South Africa, which resemble the core countries in terms of their urban centres but also have extremes of rural poverty. Countries in the semi-periphery are often connected to the core because the latter contract work out to them, such as the call centre or IT work done by Indians on behalf of British companies. Finally, Wallerstein identifies the 'peripheral' countries (such as much of Africa), which are at the bottom of this world hierarchy. These countries mainly supply minerals and cash crops to the core and semi-periphery, and are the emerging markets in which the core countries market their manufactured goods such as cigarettes.

> Wallerstein argues that countries can be upwardly or downwardly mobile in the hierarchy of the MWS, although most countries have not been able to move up. This obviously partially solves one of the weaknesses of dependency theory – the tremendous economic variation in the developing world. It could be argued that the Asian Tiger economies have moved up into the semi-periphery. Some have argued that some European countries, such as Greece and Portugal, are now semi-peripheral economic powers rather than core ones. Wallerstein's model therefore is more flexible

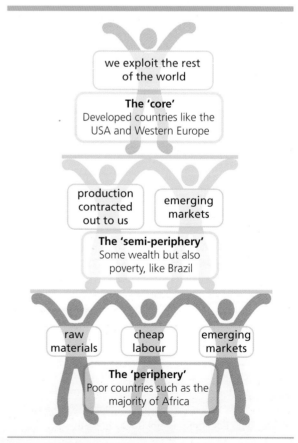

Figure 3.2.1 World systems theory

than Frank's because it allows sociologists to look at the world system as a whole and to explain changes in the fortune of individual countries.

› The processes by which surplus wealth is extracted from the periphery are those already described by dependency theory (historically through slavery and colonialism, and contemporaneously through forms of neo-colonialism).

Wallerstein goes on to suggest that the MWS is constantly evolving in its search for profit. The signs of this are constant commodification (attaching a price to everything), de-skilling (the breaking down of complex skills into simple repetitive skills in order to pay people less) and mechanisation, such as robot computerised technology. Wallerstein shows his Marxist roots by insisting this will supposedly generate so many dispossessed, excluded, marginal and poor people that, in the long term, they will constitute a revolutionary movement that will transform the MWS into a more just, socialist world economy.

In summary, then, Wallerstein's world systems theory can be seen as a global version of the relationship between bourgeoisie and proletariat that Marxists see as the major characteristic of capitalism. Wallerstein notes that the core capitalist nations are the global bourgeoisie, who are engaged in the exploitation of peripheral nations (or the global proletariat) in a modern world capitalist system. Marxists argue that capitalist exploitation has always had a global character in that the labour power of factory and service workers in the West and factory/sweatshop workers and peasants in the developing world are equally exploited.

Assessing world systems theory

The main problem with world systems theory, as with Marxism generally, is that it is guilty of economic reductionism. It assumes that the economy is driving all other aspects of the system (politics, culture, and so on). Bergesen (1990) argues that it was military conquest and the political manipulation of local peoples that imposed economic dependency on developing nations, rather than the logic of capitalism. Wallerstein is also criticised by modernisation theory, which is discussed in detail in Chapter 1, which accuses him of neglecting the importance of internal factors, especially cultural factors, in the failure of some nations to develop. Other critics point out that he ignores the corruption of local elites and their wasteful spending.

The most important criticism, however, is of Wallerstein's methodology. The theory, like Frank's, is highly abstract. It is also rather vague in its definitions of concepts such as 'core', 'peripheral', and so on, and many of its propositions cannot be measured or tested. Wallerstein has also been accused of being vague about how

challenges to the established capitalist order can be mounted and how the socialist world economy will come about.

However, despite these criticisms, Wallerstein's work was one of the first to acknowledge the 'globalisation' of the world (although he himself never uses the concept). He draws attention to the international division of labour which some see as the basis of global inequality. Lately, however, sociologists working from a globalisation perspective have noted that relationships within the world system are far from one-way. Economic interdependence can also mean that problems in the developing world (such as financial crises caused by debt) may have profound ripple effects on the economies of core countries, thereby causing unemployment and the destabilisation of Western currencies.

Transformationalist and postmodernist theories of globalisation

Transformationalists and postmodernists occupy a middle ground between globalists and traditionalists (such as Marxists). They agree that the impact of globalisation has been exaggerated by globalists but argue that it is foolish to reject the concept out of hand. This theoretical position argues that globalisation should be understood as a complex set of interconnecting relationships through which power, for the most part, is exercised indirectly. They suggest that the globalisation process can be reversed, especially where it is negative or, at the very least, that it can be controlled.

Transformationalists are particularly critical of the cultural-imperialist (Marxist) globalisation argument for three reasons:

› These arguments make the mistake of suggesting that the flow of culture is one-way only – from the West to the developed world. This focus fails to acknowledge how Western culture is enriched by inputs from other world cultures and religions.

› It underestimates the strength of local culture. As Cohen and Kennedy observe, "On occasions, some inhabitants of Lagos or Kuala Lumpur may drink Coke, wear Levi 501 jeans and listen to Madonna records. But that does not mean they are about to abandon their customs, family and religious obligations or national identities wholesale even if they could afford to do so, which most cannot."

› Robertson (1992) argues that local cultures are not swallowed up by global or Western culture. Rather the global and the local can actually work well together. He argues that local people tend to select only that which pleases them from the global, which they modify and adapt to local culture and needs. He calls this "glocalisation". Cohen and Kennedy also argue that the local 'captures' the global influence and turns it into an acceptable form compatible with local tastes. They refer to this process as 'indigenisation'. A good example of this is the Indian film industry – 'Bollywood' combines contemporary Western ideas about entertainment with traditional Hindu myth, history and culture. There is evidence that this glocalisation or indigenisation eventually leads to hybridisation – for example, some world music fuses and mixes Western dance beats with traditional styles from North Africa and Asia.

Transformationalists and postmodernists also see the global media as beneficial because it is primarily responsible for diffusing different cultural styles around the world and creating new global hybrid styles in fashion, food, music, consumption and lifestyle. It is argued that in the postmodern world, such cultural diversity and pluralism will become the global norm. Postmodernists therefore see globalisation as a positive phenomenon because it has created a new class of global consumers, in both the developed and the developing world, with a greater range of choices from which they can construct a hybridised global identity.

There is also evidence that global communication systems and social networks can actually assist local cultures to rid themselves of repressive political systems such as dictatorships. It is claimed by Kassim (2012) that the so-called 'Arab Spring' movement that occurred between 2010 and 2013 succeeded in removing totalitarian dictators in Tunisia and Egypt, partly because of the uncensored and accurate information supplied to the Arab public by global social networking websites. They provided activists with an opportunity to disseminate information about government brutality quickly, while bypassing the government censorship found in mainstream media. For example, Facebook was used in Egypt to schedule public protests, Twitter to coordinate, and YouTube to show the world how the authorities had reacted. Kassim points out that these global networks broke down a psychological barrier of fear by helping the Arab people to connect, to share information and to understand that others were experiencing similar inequality and repression. This was the catalyst that gave them the courage to go out onto the streets, which eventually led to some leaders stepping down.

Think about the way the Arab Spring turned out and the rise in influence of groups such as al-Qaeda and ISIS in the region. Have global networking sites always been a good thing?

Some sociologists, such as Giddens (1990) and Beck (2002), have suggested that global communication means that it is now difficult for people to avoid reflecting on world events or acknowledging that we live in a world characterised by 'risks', such as those posed by global warming, war and terrorism. Giddens (1999) suggests that globalisation is often characterised by many as a 'runaway' world which features a greater degree of change, uncertainty, and particularly risk to personal safety, lifestyle and life-chances posed by global terrorism, crime, environmental degradation and climate change.

However, Giddens argues that this may also result in a broadening of identity and political involvement as people choose to champion particular global causes related to issues such as the environment or debt relief. Such of these choices may be partly responsible for the growing popularity of new social movements and, in particular, the anti-globalisation movement among young people.

CONCLUSIONS

Recently, the argument that globalisation has intensified in its cultural, political and economic forms in the past few years because of advancements in technology, such as mobile phones, computers and the internet, has suffered a setback because in 2015 the UN announced that 4 billion people – 57 per cent of the world's population and 90 per cent of those who live in the 48 poorest countries – have no access to the internet. This fact undermines the arguments in favour of cultural globalisation.

However, globalists argue that the economic and political forms of globalisation are still facts of life. Optimistic globalists believe this to be a good thing because it will eventually break down barriers between societies and promote tolerance and understanding. In contrast, pessimistic globalists believe that these forms of globalisation quite simply promote economic and cultural types of imperialism; this in turn perpetuates poverty, inequality and, since some developing societies interpret these as threatening to their existing way of life, potential conflict. Pessimists therefore see globalisation as inevitably leading to dystopia, that is, a world full of risks and conflict, rather than the utopia of human rights, universal access to education and communications, and multicultural understanding envisaged by Cohen and Kennedy.

CHECK YOUR UNDERSTANDING

1. Explain what is meant by the term 'globalisation'.

2. Explain what is meant by 'neo-liberalism.'

3. Explain what is meant by 'cultural globalisation'.

4. Explain what Wallerstein means by the 'core' and the 'periphery'.

5. Identify and briefly outline two examples of political globalisation.

6. Identify and briefly explain three reasons why a global free-trade and market economy has become the norm since the 1980s.

7. Analyse the four transformations of the world that have led to globalisation, according to Cohen and Kennedy.

8. Analyse two differences between local societies and the globalised world in terms of risk.

9. Evaluate the Marxist view that globalisation has always been an important part of the way capitalism organises itself.

10. Evaluate the arguments for and against the idea that globalisation is a positive phenomenon.

TAKE IT FURTHER

1. In order to assess the influence of globalisation in your own life, construct a questionnaire that operationalises the concept of cultural globalisation in terms of your subjects' use of:
   > global brands and logos

   > transnational services such as McDonalds, Burger King and Starbucks

   > clothing and trainers

   > tastes in film, music and television programmes.

   Contact schools abroad via email and ask students to fill in your questionnaire so you can compare your responses with people of a similar age in other countries. Ask your languages teachers whether they can help.

2. The following websites monitor the degree of globalisation in various fields and are well worth a visit.
   - www.resist.org.uk – a site that coordinates the antiglobalisation movement

   - www.globalpolicy.org/globalization/links-and-resources-on-globalization.html – a site that monitors the effects of globalisation

   - http://hociology.emory.edu/faculty/globalisation – a US university site that examines all aspects of globalisation

3. Create a storyboard or picture collage that summarises the different theoretical approaches to globalisation.

3.3 THE ROLE OF TNCs, NGOs AND INTERNATIONAL AGENCIES IN DEVELOPMENT

LEARNING OBJECTIVES

> Demonstrate knowledge and understanding of the role of transnational corporations, international agencies and non-government organisations in the development process (AO1).

> Demonstrate knowledge and understanding of sociological debates about the effectiveness of these three types of organisations (AO1).

> Apply knowledge of the strategies adopted by these of organisations to contemporary issues in the developing world (AO2).

> Analyse and evaluate sociological explanations of the role these three types of organisations have played in global strategies for development (AO3).

INTRODUCING THE DEBATE

This chapter examines the activities of three groups of organisations and agencies which are crucial to both development and globalisation. The first group are the transnational corporations (TNCs). TNCs are global businesses that produce and market goods and brands across both the developed and undeveloped worlds.

The second group are the international political organisations and agencies, membership of which, as Chapter 2 pointed out, may be leading to political globalisation as nation states such as the UK increasingly defer to the global policies, goals and laws laid down by the United Nations, NATO, the G8 and the European Community. Others found in this category are the international trade and banking agencies – the

World Trade Organisation (WTO), which has a huge influence over global trade, the International Monetary Fund (IMF), which deals in short-term loans to nation states, and the World Bank, which was set up after the Second World War by Western governments to make loans to member states at interest rates below those of the commercial banks in order to finance development projects.

The third broad group dealt with in this chapter are non-government organisations (NGOs). These are mainly charities – UK examples include Oxfam, Save the Children Fund and CAFOD – which largely depend on public donations and which usually work at a localised level on small-scale development projects such as providing clean water and education independently of governments in the developing world. McMichael (2008) argues that the category of NGOs should also include organisations such as Greenpeace and Amnesty International, as well as the groups that make up the anti-globalisation movement who are critical of the dominant strategies for development pushed by international agencies such as the WTO.

TRANSNATIONAL CORPORATIONS

Transnationals are businesses that have outgrown their domestic origins and operate across international borders (although the majority of them are still headquartered in the USA, UK, France, Germany and Japan). There were about 7,000 TNCs operating in 1970, but the charity Christian Aid argues that this figure has now increased to about 63,000 operating with about 690,000 subsidiaries in almost all sectors, countries, industries and economic activities in the world.

They have a number of common characteristics:

> They seek competitive advantage and maximisation of profits by constantly searching for the cheapest and most efficient production locations across the world.

> They have geographical flexibility: they can shift resources and operations to any location in the world.

> A substantial part of their workforce is scattered across the world, especially the developing world.

> TNC assets tend to be distributed worldwide rather than focused in one or two countries; for example, 17 of the top 100 TNCs have 90 per cent of their assets in a different country from their head office.

The marketing and sales of TNC products is carried out on a global scale – brands such as GE, Nike, Sony and Coca-Cola are familiar worldwide.

TNCs are economically very wealthy and therefore potentially more powerful than many of the world's countries, especially than some individual developing countries in which they operate. According to Forbes magazine, in 2013, 37 of the 100 largest economies in the world were run by TNCs rather than countries. For example, BP is bigger than Finland, while Chevron is bigger than Ireland. McMichael claimed that TNCs have massive economic global power, in the sense that the combined annual revenue of the 200 largest TNCs exceeded those of the GDP of the 182 nation states containing 80 per cent of the world's population. However, critics point out that statistics relating to TNC revenues and the GDP of countries are measuring different things and are therefore not comparable. Regardless of this methodological difficulty, though, it is generally accepted that TNCs are more powerful in 2015 than they ever have been and are therefore powerful forces in many national economies and key players in the globalised economy.

Frobel *et al.* (1980) note that from the 1970s TNCs set about investing significantly in the developing world because of high labour costs and high levels of industrial conflict in the West, which reduced profits. This investment was greatly helped by developing countries, which actively sought TNC investment by setting up special areas within their borders called export processing zones (EPZs) or free-trade zones (FTZs), in which TNCs were encouraged to build factories producing goods for export to the West (see Figure 3.3.1). There are now some 5000 free or export processing zones in the world today, employing over 43 million workers, the majority of whom are employed in China's Special Economic Zones.

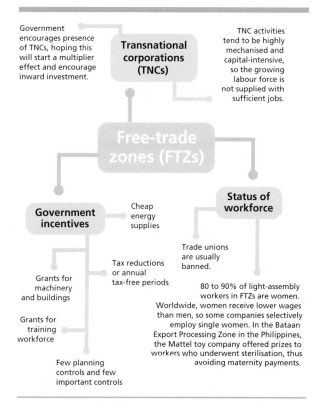

Figure 3.3.1 The elements for free-trade zones

Evaluating TNC activity by theoretical perspectives

Modernisation theory clearly sees TNCs as playing a major positive role in helping societies to develop. Rostow (1971), in particular, saw the injection of capital that is required in his 'pre-conditions for take-off' stage as partly originating in TNC investment. Such companies also bring in technology and knowledge that the host country does not possess. Rostow therefore saw TNCs as essential in kick-starting the economy Similarly, neo-Liberals such as Friedman argue that TNCs benefit societies because they create jobs and provide local people with a regular wage (especially compared with subsistence farming). TNC investment often leads to greater earnings for the developing country from export revenue and taxes. TNCs also invest in education and skills as well as transport and communication infrastructures in the developing world.

In contrast, Marxists are generally critical of the activities of TNCs. They argue that TNC investment in development is part of the modern type of capitalist exploitation known as neo-colonialism. Ellwood (2010) argues, for example, that economically powerful TNCs are bullying smaller, less economically powerful countries to open up their economies to private investment.

Another Marxist concern about transnational behaviour has focused on the deregulation of banks and global finance which, together with the revolution in communication (computers, the internet and email), has led to massive movements of money across the globe. In particular, this globalisation of money has resulted in transnational finance corporations engaging in currency speculation for profit. Some critics argue that the deregulation of banks encourages bankers to act like gamblers and take unnecessary risks with their clients' money. The huge sums of money involved in these deals can in turn have a negative impact on national economies and destabilise them. The collapse of the US bankers Lehman Brothers in 2008 led to the worst global economic crisis since the 1930s: global financial funds and share markets plummeted in value as bank lending dried up. In the UK, banks such as HBOS, Northern Rock and the Bradford & Bingley had to be bailed out by the state. Other countries, such as the USA, Ireland, Iceland and Belgium, had to take similar actions to protect their economies. The total cost to taxpayers worldwide of the 'worst financial crisis in financial history' was estimated by the IMF to be $1.4 trillion.

Bakan (2004) argues that TNCs too often exercise power without responsibility. He refers to TNCs as 'institutional psychopaths', and claims that they are programmed to exploit and dehumanise people for profit. (Bakan's film about transnationals, *The Corporation*, is well worth viewing.) Several examples suggest that TNCs may be guilty of illegal and immoral activities in their pursuit of profit. For example:

> Shell in Nigeria and RTZ in Angola have exploited natural resources with ruthlessness and indifference. Indigenous people have had their land forcibly seized and, despite international protests, have been removed at gunpoint from their homelands by local elites working on behalf of these TNCs.

> The sweatshop conditions of transnational factories in developing countries have been criticised, especially for their use of child labour and exploitative rates of pay. In Britain, chain stores such as Primark and Matalan have been accused of encouraging these exploitative practices.

> TNCs have been accused of causing grave ecological damage in developing countries. For example, in 2003, Coca-Cola was accused of putting thousands of farmers out of work in the Indian state of Kerala by draining up to one million litres of water, which normally fed the farmers' wells, in order to produce Coke for the Indian market. The chemical TNC Trafigura was found to have dumped tonnes of toxic waste in one of Africa's poorest countries, the Côte d'Ivoire, in 2006, which led to 100,000 Ivoirians seeking medical help because of the effects of exposure to these chemicals.

> TNCs have refused to take responsibility for the welfare of local people killed or injured by their factories and plants. The explosion at the US-owned Union Carbide chemical plant in Bhopal, in India, killed 2,800 people and injured 28,000 people in 1984. The company has paid very little compensation. Many victims claim to suffer long-term health problems as a result, the majority of whom have received no financial help with medical bills.

A rally to mark the anniversary of the Bhopal gas disaster in India. Some think that corporate negligence may have caused the tragedy.

> TNCs have influenced tastes and consumption patterns in the developing world in negative ways. For example, Nestlé has been criticised for its aggressive marketing of baby-milk powder in areas without easy access to clean water. Other TNCs have been criticised for their marketing of high-tar cigarettes, drugs and pesticides; many of the latter have been banned in the West for being dangerous to health.

> There is evidence that TNCs have interfered in the internal politics of developing countries and have even financed military coups in developing countries against political leaders they don't like. The military coup against the democratically elected socialist president of Chile, Salvador Allende, in the early 1970s was sponsored by American multinational companies unhappy at his nationalisation of the US-owned copper industry. In 2003, an international boycott of Coca-Cola products was launched by the trade union movement in protest at the company's alleged use of illegal paramilitary groups to intimidate, threaten and kill those of its workers who wished to set up a trade union at its bottling plant in Colombia.

Do you agree with Bakan that the evidence suggests TNCs are institutional psychopaths?

The activities of TNCs illustrate a lack of global control by national governments and agencies such as the United Nations. Quite simply, there is no international law in place to regulate the activities of such organisations, despite their blatant and consistent infringement of human rights.

However, it has to be noted that it is not the function or moral responsibility of TNCs to assist countries to develop. They are private enterprises whose main loyalty is to their shareholders. The primary function of TNCs is to make profit, although most TNCs accept that they should do this in a morally acceptable way. It would also be a mistake to dismiss all transnational investment in the developing world as exploitative. Although concerns about transnational abuse of power and unethical behaviour are legitimate, TNCs can bring about positive change too. As Ellwood notes: "They are at the cutting edge of technological innovation and they can introduce new management and marketing strategies. It's also true that wages and working conditions are usually better in foreign subsidiaries of multinational firms than in local companies."

Do you believe TNCs have a duty to behave in a moral and responsible way in developing societies?

THE ROLE OF INTERNATIONAL ORGANISATIONS

The UK belongs to a number of international organisations that exercise an influence on UK international and domestic policies, and consequently the UK's relationship with the developing world. These include:

The United Nations
The UK was involved in the setting up of the United Nations in 1945 and is a member of the Security Council, which can veto decisions made by the UN Assembly. The UK contributed 6.68 per cent of the United Nation's peacekeeping budget between 2013 and 2015. Much of this peacekeeping involves UN forces policing conflict in the developing world, particularly in Africa. In 2015, the UK contributed about $140 billion to the overall UN budget. The United Nations has a number of agencies working within the developing world that are committed to achieving the UN Millennium Development Goals (discussed in Chapter 1) including the World Health Organisation (WHO), the UN Economic, Scientific and Cultural Organisation (UNESCO) and the UN International Children's Emergency Fund (UNICEF). The UK is committed to the principles and goals of these organisations.

The European Union (EU)
The UK joined the European Community in 1973. This became the EU in 1993. Membership of the EU cost the UK 17 billion euros in 2013. The EU and its member states are the world's largest aid donors. For example, in 2013 they spent 56.5 billion euros on development assistance. This aid is regularly audited and assessed to prevent corruption. According to the EU, developing countries have a strong say in how EU aid is spent, as do NGOs such as trade unions, human rights groups and environmental organisations. The EU also works closely with the UK's overseas aid programme to ensure that aid is not replicated and that money is used effectively.

The G8
The Group of Eight (G8) refers to the group of eight highly industrialised nations – France, Germany, Italy, the United Kingdom, Japan, the United States, Canada and

Russia – that hold an annual summit to discuss and to come to an agreement on global issues such as economic growth, trade, aid and debt, global security, climate change and terrorism. Recent summits have been marred by protests organised by the anti-globalisation movement (AGM) which sees the G8 as primarily motivated by the need to protect their neo-liberal dominance of trade and consequently their share of the world's wealth. The AGM points out that the G8 is not democratic or accountable for the decisions it makes, which often ignore the interests of developing countries. In 1998 protests against the G8 demanded that the developing world's debt be cancelled. In 2005, the Make Poverty History movement pleaded with the G8 for debt concessions for Africa.

The World Trade Organisation (WTO)

In 1947, the General Agreement on Tariffs and Trade (GATT) was signed by the Western powers to govern global trade and to reduce trade barriers and competition between nations. In 1994, the WTO was set up to replace GATT. It currently has 161 member states. The WTO has taken over and extended the GATT agreements on trade in goods, as well as negotiating a new GATT, which covers services such as telecommunications, banking and investment, transport, education, health and the environment.

McKay (2004), Narlikar (2005) and Chang (2009) have criticised the free-trade agenda of the WTO. They claim that global trade rules are unfair and biased against developing countries as the WTO pressures developing countries to open up their economies immediately to Western banks and transnationals, and to abandon tariffs (for example taxes) on imports from the West. However, under the GATTs, the developed countries are allowed to impose quotas restricting the import of manufactured goods from the developing world. It is argued by McKay that the WTO has rigged the rules in favour of the West and consequently the WTO is a rich man's club dominated by the neo-liberal philosophy of the developed industrial nations.

Phillippe Legrain (2002), former special adviser to the Director-General of the WTO, has acknowledged four main criticisms of the WTO:

> It does the bidding of the TNCs.

> It undermines workers' rights and environmental protection by encouraging a 'race to the bottom' between the governments of developing countries competing for jobs and foreign investment.

> It harms the poor.

> It is destroying democracy by imposing its approach on the world secretly and without accountability.

Ellwood argues that the WTO and the TNCs have too much political power and that they often undermine the democratic process and the rule of law in the developing world. He argues that the WTO's free-trade rules have given TNC investment precedence over the democratic and human rights of the population of the developing world.

However, Legrain defends the WTO by suggesting that critics of the WTO have:

> Exaggerated the power of TNCs because he claims that it is consumer choice that shapes the global marketplace.

> Ignored the socially responsible actions of the majority of TNCs.

> Ignored the fact that TNCs have to abide by a battery of government laws and regulations on workers' rights, product liability, health and safety, environmental protection and much else, especially in the West.

> Ignored the power of ordinary people to sue the TNCs which in the USA costs these corporations $150 billion annually.

The World Bank and the International Monetary Fund (IMF)

The IMF specialises in short-term loans to countries, while the World Bank hands out long-term loans. Increasingly, both the IMF and World Bank have become involved in lending money to developing countries whose economies are weak or in trouble because of debt or because of a decline in the value of their commodity exports to the West.

Neo-liberals are very keen on the World Bank and IMF because they believe these agencies can assist developing societies to develop by putting on the 'golden straitjacket' advocated by Friedman (see Chapter 2). They claim that developing countries have a choice between neo-liberal or 'neo-idiotic' economic and political policies. Interventionist or state-led economic policies are derided by neo-liberals as idiotic. They argue that developing countries will only benefit from the global economic system if they adopt the neo-liberal economic approach of free trade, free markets and privatisation of state-owned agencies and services. Since the 1980s, the WTO has pushed for this liberalisation of trade and the removal of domestic rules which regulate foreign investment in developing countries, while both the IMF and World Bank have contributed to the dominance of neo-liberalism and free trade by offering loans only if developing countries adopt neo-liberal policies.

FOCUS ON SKILLS: THE WORLD TRADE ORGANISATION

An anti-WTO demonstration in Cancún, 2003

Narlikar (2005) observes that, for such a small organisation, the WTO arouses a surprising degree of popular interest, emotions and drama. In 2003 NGOs staged massive anti-WTO demonstrations. It is now rare that high-level meetings of the WTO do not attract angry mobs. The WTO might be adored by neo-liberal thinkers but it is detested by many.

Chang (2010) notes that the WTO is committed to the concept of free trade. The WTO believes that unlimited competition in the free market is the best way to organise an economy because it allegedly forces everyone to perform with maximum efficiency. Government intervention is viewed as harmful because it reduces competition via import controls and tariffs and because it confers advantages on others via subsidies. The WTO is committed to removing these obstacles to free trade wherever they may exist.

However, Chang and others argue that WTO policy is biased in favour of Western governments and TNCs because the WTO generally ignores the fact that Western governments do not play by the WTO's own rules of free trade. Chang argues that Western

governments are using the WTO to say to the rest of the world "do as we say, not as we do". He suggests that the West developed and became wealthy as a result of the sorts of interventionist policies rejected by the WTO. Narlikar argues too that the rich countries have historically been reluctant to reduce trade barriers and quick to raise them. WTO policy is therefore based on a historical double standard.

These observations have led to some development sociologists to conclude that the WTO has hidden goals, which are more to do with facilitating the economic success of Western economies and TNCs. Critics claim that WTO decision-making is dominated by a small group of Western members. NGOs have long complained too that the WTO sees trade as more important than values such as human rights, the environment, workers' rights, gender and the eradication of poverty.

Questions

1. **Explain**. Give two reasons why the WTO was established.

2. **Explain** why the WTO is "adored by neo-liberal thinkers".

3. **Analyse** why critics of the WTO claim that WTO policy is based on a "historical double standard".

4. **Analyse** the implications of seeing free trade as a more important goal to be achieved than the protection of human rights and the environment.

5. **Evaluate**. Using information from this source and elsewhere, assess the Marxist view that the WTO is another neo-colonial way of exploiting the developing world.

However, the World Bank and IMF have been criticised by Stiglitz (2001), Ellwood (2004) and Chang (2007) as agents of the neo-liberal WTO. Chang refers to the WTO, the IMF and the World Bank as the 'Unholy Trinity' and suggests that they exist to strong-arm developing countries into accepting neo-liberal political policies in return for economic help. Ní Chasaide (2014) observes that the IMF has engaged in a series of "debt work-outs"-loans with longer repayment timeframes. In return, the developing country has to submit to a set of conditions known as 'structural adjustment programmes' (SAPs). (See Chapter 4 for discussion of debt.)

Chang argues that the World Bank and IMF present themselves as "good Samaritans" whose only motive is to assist the developing world. However, he argues that they are actually "bad Samaritans" because their motives are essentially selfish. As Chang argues, the real point of the WTO, IMF and World Bank is to create an environment in the developing world that is friendly to TNC goods, investment and exploitation of cheap labour. He argues that the SAP conditions for granting loans are often politically biased in the sense that they will only lend the money if the country agrees to abandon any economic interventionist policies and adopts free-trade conditions such as opening up the country's domestic markets to TNCs. Other neo-liberal conditions for loans have included the IMF demanding that taxation be increased, that government spending on public services such as health, education and pensions be cut, that wages for public sector workers should be frozen, that trade union rights should be rescinded, that the minimum wage should be reduced and that elected ministers who support public spending or interventionist economic policies should be sacked and replaced with politicians with neo-liberal sympathies. Hoogvelt (2001) observes that those developing countries that comply with these neo-liberalist demands are rewarded with IMF and World Bank support while those that do not are refused help.

The economist Joseph Stiglitz, who is the former Chief Economist of the World Bank, has also criticised the neo-liberal approach of the IMF and the World Bank. He argues that they are failing to improve the welfare of developing countries because their policies reflect the interests and ideology of the Western financial community. For example, Stiglitz observes that the World Bank claims to tailor assistance strategies for specific poor nations which take on board their unique internal conditions. However, Stiglitz claims this is not true. He claims that World Bank officials are more interested in inspecting the country's five-star hotels and usually arrive with an off-the-peg set of proposals based on a four-step programme which they expect the developing country to sign if the loan is to be agreed.

> Step 1 is the privatisation or selling-off of public utilities such as electricity and water to TNCs. For example, in 2002 Ghana was granted an IMF loan on condition that French and British TNCs were allowed to 'cherry-pick' and privatise the services of the previously state-administered water company.

> Step 2 is 'capital market liberalisation' – the developing country is expected to lift controls on currency and real estate speculation and allow foreign investors in. However, Stiglitz points out that this tends to result in massive amounts of money flowing out of the country in the form of profit for the foreign speculators.

> Step 3 is 'market-based pricing' which means raising prices on food, water and cooking gas, which often leads to what Stiglitz calls 'the IMF riot' – people take to the streets to protest and governments use repressive and violent methods to disperse them. This leads to foreign investment leaving the country in response to the violence and the failure of government services. However, once the violence stops, the TNCs return and buy up the state's assets at fire-sale (extremely discounted) prices.

> Step 4 is free trade – which means wholeheartedly adopting the rules of the WTO and the World Bank in regard to opening the markets of the developing country to TNCs.

Stiglitz concludes that the IMF and the World Bank undermine democracy because:

> They are unelected bureaucrats.

> Their plans for the developing world are devised in secret.

> They are driven by neo-liberal ideology so there is never any discussion or debate about the merits of such thinking and practice. Dissent is simply not allowed.

> They deny citizens of the developing world any participation in the making or evaluation of IMF/World Bank policy.

Stiglitz concludes that these IMF/World Bank policies simply do not work. Despite decades of IMF and World Bank 'help', Africa, for example, is worse off in terms of income and wealth than it was 40 years ago.

On the balance of the evidence presented, are Marxists justified in seeing the WTO, the World Bank and the IMF as agents of neo-colonialism?

THE ROLE OF LOCAL AND NATIONAL NON-GOVERNMENT ORGANISATIONS

Fisher (1997) notes that the globalisation of capitalism has led to a decline in the power of the state, especially in the developing world, and this has produced a growing number of groups that can be termed non-government organisations (NGOs) that have taken on an enormously diverse range of activities including "implementing grass-roots or sustainable development, promoting human rights and social justice, protesting environmental degradation, and pursuing many other objectives formerly ignored or left to governmental agencies". In the view of some observers, the rise in influence of these NGOs constitutes a 'quiet revolution' - they constitute a **civil society** that has the potential to wield power and influence comparable to the nation state.

UNDERSTAND THE CONCEPT

Civil society refers to the notion that the citizens of a society act together in a common cause. For example, Sarnaik (2001) observes that anti-World Trade Organisation demonstrators, volunteer rescue-workers from developed nations helping to save victims of earthquakes, eco-warriors fighting to protect whales and dolphins; people boycotting goods because they have been produced by exploitative or repressive regimes and millions of TV viewers across the world watching rock stars perform in Live Aid in 1985 to raise funds for famine-relief are all aspects of civil society.

It is difficult to generalise about NGOs because of the enormous variety of their activities but there are probably two very broad types of NGO:

> Charities that operate globally, such as Oxfam, Save the Children, the Red Cross and CAFOD, respond to a range of needs in the developing world. These NGOs are funded in two main ways; through public donation (made possible through campaigning, lobbying and advertising) and official aid funds from governments, the EU and the UN. This official funding is based on the fact that NGOs are often the experts on the ground and in the field. They are more in tune with the needs of local people in the developing world because they often work closely with local community associations to identify and respond to local needs.

> There is a loose affiliation of organisations that some have termed the anti-globalisation movement (AGM), which share common concerns about the way the world economy favours Western interests and how trade and neo-liberal economic interests are allowed to ride roughshod over the human rights of people in developing societies. Some members of this alliance, such as Greenpeace, are concerned about the environmental degradation that has resulted from the global pursuit of profit.

According to Escobar (2008), the AGM has enthused ordinary people, especially young people, who have ethical concerns with the way global capitalism operates (and particularly the ways in which it encourages and sustains debt, subsistence wages and child labour in the developing world) and wish to voice these concerns. Many young people who actively protested on the streets at WTO or G8 conferences did so because they had become convinced that governments are in collusion with global

corporations. Klein (2001) argues that what unites all these people is their desire for a citizen-centred alternative – civil society – to the power that neo-liberal capitalism has over their everyday lives.

The AGM has empowered ordinary people by providing a network in which they can engage in levels of protest that suit their situation. This may include, for example:

> attending charity concerts

> boycotting goods because they are produced by environmentally unfriendly methods or by regimes with poor human rights records

> signing petitions for the Making Poverty History movement

> committing to full-blown street protests and anti-corporate behaviour that verges on the criminal, for example, vandalising the stores of global corporate 'villains'.

Escobar concludes that the main achievement of the AGM has been to raise public awareness of the consequences of unfettered global capitalism and the fact that alternative ways of seeing and practising development do exist.

Arguments in favour of NGO activities in the developing world

Sociologists such as Stromquist (1998) view NGOs as positive agencies for change because they are unencumbered and untainted by politics or greed. In this sense, NGOs are idealised as organisations populated by those who simply want to help others. McMichael (2008) argues that NGOs have greater "diversity, credibility and creativity" than official agencies such as the World Bank because they aim to implement "just development" based on "equity, democracy and social justice". Also, the fact that many NGOs are not burdened with large bureaucracies means that they are relatively flexible, innovative in their thinking and practice and fairly efficient at identifying local needs. The main goals of NGOs are therefore seen to have a number of positive effects on the developing world:

1. *The funding and provision of services related to poverty alleviation and welfare* – Lewis and Kanji (2009) sees NGOs as implementers that aim to improve local situations – they mobilise resources to provide goods and services to people who need them in fields as diverse as health care, microfinance, agriculture, emergency relief and human rights. When NGOs such as Christian Aid first got involved in the developing world, their

focus was very much on providing 'basic needs', that is, lifting the poor, especially children, out of poverty and helping to improve diet, access to clean water, shelter, vaccination and so on. However, most NGOs today aim to help local people attain 'social wellbeing' too, that is, the right to be healthy and to live into old age, the right for both sexes to be educated and so on.

2. *Responding to emergencies and disasters* – The larger NGOs often have the infrastructure, contacts and so on to be able to respond quickly when disasters such as earthquakes, or the 2004 tsunami, hit the developing world. They are usually on the front line when responding to human-made disasters – for example, working in refugee camps providing shelter to those fleeing war-zones.

3. *Education and consciousness raising* – Stromquist and Lewis and Kanji stress the role of NGOs in providing education for local people in the developing world that raises their awareness of both local and global issues. In this way, Lewis and Kanji argue, NGOs can be bottom-up catalysts of social change. Desai (2005) argues that NGOs are particularly good for women in terms of challenging customs, ideas and beliefs that perpetuate unequal gender relations. For example, Kilbey (2011) documents how NGOs have set up self-help groups for poor women in India, which have made a massive contribution to women's empowerment, which in turn has led to the alleviation of poverty, a reduction in both maternal and infant mortality rates, an increase in the number of girls in schools and an improvement of women's rights in rural areas.

4. *To hold powerful global organisations to account* – Edwards (1996) argues that NGOs should monitor the activities of the WTO, the World Bank, the G8 and the IMF, as well as those of Western governments and TNCs, so that they become accountable for their decisions and actions in the developing world, especially if these undermine local social wellbeing, human rights or the environment.

5. *Campaigning for sustainable development* – NGOs have played a major role in pushing for sustainable development by campaigning for governments and corporations to take action on a diversity of social and environmental issues, such as the regulation of hazardous waste, the destruction of the rainforests, land mines, child labour, and slavery.

6. *The mobilisation of public opinion and, if necessary, protest* – Edwards argues it is important for NGOs to mobilise support from all sections of society, both in the developed and developing worlds. However, research by Darnton and Kirk (2011) into public perceptions of development suggests that this is the least successful of their goals because their research found widespread public ignorance of the causes of underdevelopment and global poverty. They argue that NGOS need to focus more on educating the Western public about the causes of underdevelopment so there is more public engagement with the issues and the wider systems that create and reinforce poverty.

The critique of NGO activities in the developing world

However, not all sociologists are convinced that NGOs are doing a good job. A number of critiques of NGO activity in the developing world can be seen:

The idealistic view that NGOs are disinterested and politically neutral has probably led people unrealistically to view them as a 'magic bullet' that will somehow make up for the failings of government-sponsored development programmes. However, this is often not possible because NGOs have to work closely with the governments of developing societies and have to operate within what Korten (1990) calls the "sympathetic public space" provided by those in power in the developing world. This space may not be provided willingly. The relationship between NGOs and powerful groups in the developing world is often undermined by political instability and the frequent changes of government that might result, the corruption of elites and the fact that NGO workers on the ground and these elites may not necessarily see eye-to-eye. Some governments and local elites may also see NGOs as a threat to their dominance, and their presence as implicitly critical of their power.

It is often assumed that NGOs are self-funding and that their ability to operate in the developing world is financed by public donations. However, Hulme and Edwards (1996) point out that many NGOs are actually financed by Western governments and international agencies such as the EU and the UN. In other words, many NGOs are contractors who are working on behalf of their clients or funders. Moreover, the degree of NGO funding by Western governments and agencies increased significantly after 9/11 because it was believed that NGOs, by spending money on local projects, could prevent disaffection with the West and therefore terrorism.

Edwards notes that these NGO funders often take a neo-liberal approach to development and consequently their funding is often motivated by a desire to encourage developing societies to adopt free market economies by building societies with the 'right' entrepreneurial attitudes. This close relationship between NGOs and neo-liberal funding has had a number of negative consequences:

1. McCloskey (2015) argues that NGOs are often reluctant to criticise the neo-liberal policies of organisations such as the World Bank or UN who fund them. This obviously undermines the ability of NGOs to hold powerful global organisations to account or to challenge global systems such as world trade that may be keeping poorer societies in a state of underdevelopment.

2. Hilary (2013) argues that the influence of neo-liberalism on NGO funding means that NGOs are likely to distance themselves from radical groups such as the AGM that aim to challenge the existing neo-liberal-dominated power structure by mobilising public opinion and protest.

3. Fisher (1997) argues that neo-liberal influence means that NGOs often abandon 'bottom-up' projects, which generally seek the guidance of local people and experts on what is required, to 'top down' projects which impose Western ideas of development on local communities. This has resulted in NGOs, especially those working within disaster zones, being accused of 'ethnocentric arrogance' because they assume that the decisions they make are the right ones for the people they have failed to consult. Consequently NGOs are increasingly being accused of failing to be accountable to local people, and of failing to raise the consciousness of local people as to the 'true' causes of their poverty.

4. Karat (1988) argues that NGO failure to consult local people and the suspicion that NGOs are agents of free trade capitalism or American political interests can create greater problems. For example, Karat (1988) observed that in India, NGOs with foreign connections were sometimes seen as primarily motivated to disseminate Western political and cultural values rather than alleviate poverty. There is evidence too that suspicion of NGO activities can lead to religious fundamentalism being seen by local people as a viable alternative in meeting local needs. In Pakistan, Afghanistan and Iraq a significant number of NGO workers have been killed in terrorist attacks because they are now often seen by

fundamentalists as the pawns of foreign interests, especially the Americans. For example, NGO workers engaged in vaccinating children against polio have been targeted for assassination by the Taliban who claim that they are actually engaged in a plot to sterilise Muslims.

5. Edwards argues that NGOs are generally toothless and illustrates this by pointing out that, despite over 70 years of NGO activity in the developing world, they have failed to bring about any real change in the systems and structures that perpetuate poverty. Edwards is very critical of those who lead NGOs because logically they should be working themselves out of a job. Yet the number of NGOs has increased. Funds have increasingly been channelled into administrative costs as NGOs have become overly bureaucratic. Moreover, NGOs are not democratic organisations and consequently are rarely accountable for their actions. Farrington and Bebbington (1993) conclude that NGO leaders and bureaucrats actually have a vested interest in the poverty and underdevelopment of the countries in which they work because it is this poverty that ensures their high salaries and job security.

CONCLUSIONS

It is difficult to come to any firm conclusions about NGOs because, as Fisher notes, there is such tremendous variation found within the NGO sector and this makes it very difficult for sociologists to work out their impact at the local, national and global level. They differ from one another considerably in terms of their functions, goals, organisational structures and memberships. This makes it difficult to generalise about their success or failure.

Edwards argues that NGOs have to engage more with aspects of the AGM. This may be uncomfortable for them, considering the source of their funding; however, it would give those without a voice in the developing world membership of a civil society that can powerfully highlight the downside of the globalisation process for poorer countries. He also argues that lobbying by the AGM and NGOs now means that commitment to human rights is regarded by the general public as a basic principle of development. The AGM too has kept the spotlight on the need for reform of international agencies such as the World Bank and the WTO, as well as issues such as unfair terms of trade, global warming and Africa. On a negative note, though, Edwards points out that, despite 70 years of NGO activity in the developing world, the main causes of poverty and inequality in this part of the world remain unchallenged.

CHECK YOUR UNDERSTANDING

1. Explain with examples what is meant by the term 'non-governmental organisation'.

2. Explain what is meant by 'export processing' and 'free-trade' zones.

3. Explain what is meant by the criticism that non-government organisations have a vested interest in the underdevelopment of the countries in which they work.

4. Identify four international organisations involved in the developing world.

5. Identify and briefly outline the functions of non-government organisations such as Oxfam in the developing world.

6. Identify and briefly explain what is meant by the 'unholy trinity of free trade'.

7. Analyse two reasons why critics of transnational corporations believe that they should be subject to international laws.

8. Analyse the role of the anti-globalisation movement in promoting debate about the relationship between the West and the developing world.

9. Evaluate the view that the World Trade Organisation is working in the interests of the developing world.

10. Evaluate the costs and benefits of transnational corporations to the development process.

TAKE IT FURTHER

1. The following websites aim to keep an eye on TNC activities in the developing world. Visit them in order to gather contemporary examples of TNC behaviour.
   www.corpwatch.org – the website of Corporate Watch which monitors TNC behaviour across the world
   www.mcspotlight.org – this site aims to track the activities of McDonalds and other transnationals
   www.sweatfree.org/organizations – identifies those TNCs allegedly running sweatshops in the developing world.

2. Visit the websites of the World Bank, the IMF and the WTO and, using their search facilities, look for policy statements or documents that support the view that these agencies are promoting neo-liberal economic policies.

3. Between 2013 and 2015, 63 NGO health workers were killed by the Taliban while inoculating children against polio in Pakistan. Use newspaper websites to work out why NGO workers are being attacked in this way.

3.4 AID AND TRADE, INDUSTRIALISATION, URBANISATION, THE ENVIRONMENT, AND WAR AND CONFLICT

LEARNING OBJECTIVES

> Demonstrate knowledge and understanding of the role of aid and trade, industrialisation, urbanisation, the environment, and war and conflict on the development process (AO1).

> Demonstrate knowledge and understanding of the sociological debates about the effects of these social phenomena (AO1).

> Apply this knowledge to contemporary society (AO2).

> Analyse and evaluate sociological explanations and debates about the role of aid, trade, industrialisation, urbanisation, the environment and the nature and causes of wars in the developing world (AO3).

INTRODUCING THE DEBATE

This chapter deals with a wide range of topics. Some of these – for example, aid, urbanisation, the environment, war and conflict – will be dealt with in some detail. However, reference to topics such as trade will need to be read in conjunction with sections of Chapter 3, especially the sections on the role of international agencies such as the WTO, the IMF and the World Bank.

AID AND TRADE

'Aid' refers to any flow of resources from developed countries to the developing world, which may take the form of:

> a financial grant or material gift that does not have to be paid back

> a loan with interest, which has to be repaid.

Aid mainly involves the transfer of capital but it may also comprise more concrete forms of assistance. It may take the form of types of expertise; for example, experts may be sent to the donor country to train scientists, technicians, engineers, teachers, health professionals, the armed forces or the police. Aid may also take the form of products such as machines, medicines, contraceptives and weapons.

Types of aid

Bilateral and multilateral aid

Marren (2015) observes that aid from public or official sources accounts for about 80 per cent of all aid flowing from the West into the developing world. Approximately 70 per cent of all official aid is bilateral aid – this means that governments in the developed world give aid directly to governments in the developing world. In the UK this "official development assistance" (ODA) is administered by a branch of the Foreign Office, that is, the Department for International Development (DfID).

The other 30 per cent of official aid is multilateral aid. This means it is delivered by over 200 agencies, including international organisations such as the World Bank, the UN, the EU and NGOs.

Marren observes that in 2012 that the USA provided $30.67 billion in official aid (24 per cent of the total) while the top five donors combined – the USA, the UK, France, Germany and Japan provided over $80 billion or 63 per cent of ODA.

Other sources of aid

The other 20 per cent of foreign aid, according to Marren, comes from NGOs who raise donations from the general public by raising awareness of problems in the developing world. This funding is separate and distinct from multilateral aid. In 2011, NGOs were estimated to have pumped $26.3 billion worth of this type of aid into the developing world. Much of this tends to be humanitarian relief that is raised in response to specific circumstances, such as natural disasters. For example, the worldwide appeal in reaction to the tsunami that devastated South East Asia in 2004 raised $7.5 billion in charitable donations.

Other sources of this type of aid include international foundations ($7.1 billion in 2011) and business corporations such as commercial banks that lend money to developing countries at commercial rates of interest.

The UK government's record on aid

In 1969, a UN commission recommended that 0.7 per cent of rich countries' Gross National Income (GNI) should be given in aid. This excludes both loans and military aid. The UK met this target for the first time in 2014 when it spent £11.4bn – or 0.72 per cent of its GNI – on overseas aid. Moreover, in 2015, the International Development (Official Development Assistance Target) Act legally committed every future UK government to the 0.7 per cent GNI target. Most British aid (approximately 60 per cent) goes to ex-British colonies in Africa, while Asian countries such as India, Pakistan and Bangladesh receive about 30 per cent.

Madden also notes that a recent development trend is aid originating from newly industrialised countries such as China, India and Brazil. China, in particular, has aid relationships with several African countries that came to a total of $2.84 billion in 2011, while India ($790 million) and Brazil ($500 million) are assisting developing countries such as Bangladesh and Bolivia respectively. Cuba too has long been active in terms of offering aid to developing countries such as Angola, particularly in the field of health. The late Socialist leader of Venezuela, Hugo Chavez, was very critical of international agencies such as the IMF, which he saw as an agent of US imperialism. Chavez used Venezuela's oil wealth to offer aid deals to Central and South American countries that were not keen on IMF or World Bank conditions. Marren notes that this alternative type of aid is viewed more favourably by recipients because of their shared history with the donor.

Why give aid?

The most basic reason is probably compassion for others, especially in the face of disaster, and a sense of injustice about global inequalities. According to Haslam *et al.* (2012) this altruism is probably the main reason why ordinary people respond so quickly and generously to emergency aid programmes and involve themselves in movements such as Make Poverty History.

However, this ethical concern with the welfare of others is not shared by officials working for the government or agencies such as the World Bank and IMF. Studies suggest that that foreign aid is shaped by the self-interests of the donor countries. This can be illustrated in a number of ways according to Marren:

> Aid may be "a 'sweetener' used to gain access to markets and resources, to foster trade links". The USA has used aid to guarantee access to scarce resources such as oil, while the increased donor activity of China may be linked to its need for raw materials.

> Aid may be a way of stimulating the donor economy. Some countries attach conditions to aid in that they state a proportion of the funds must be spent on goods manufactured in the donor country. This is known as 'tied aid'. The UK banned this type of aid in 2001, although research by the *Guardian* newspaper found that only 9 out of a total of 117 major DfID contracts and procurement agreements (together worth nearly £750m) since January 2011 had gone to non-British companies. One of the UK's biggest accountants actually offers workshops to British companies eager to win lucrative aid and development contracts.

> Aid may be a way of strengthening political links and securing strategic interests. The UK gives most of its aid to ex-colonies because it believes it has an ethical obligation to these countries but it expects those countries to support British interests in, for example, UN debates. Countries which are viewed by the Americans as positive allies in the 'war against terror' are generously rewarded with aid. Bandyopadhyay and Vermann (2013) looked at the destination of US aid over the 2000s and found that a majority of it was directed towards Afghanistan, Iraq and Egypt. Similarly, Russia may reward allies such as Syria with aid in return for strategic naval bases in the Mediterranean.

> Aid may be used to encourage the adoption of Western and particularly American values in the developing world. Modernisation theory argued strongly in the 1950s that this should be adopted as an aid strategy (See Chapter 1). Radelet (2004) argued aid was an opportunity to promote the American values of openness, prosperity, freedom and democracy. American aid therefore is aimed at ensuring the security of the USA and its citizens because the American government is well-aware that both anti-US sentiments and poverty are forces which may drive anti-US terrorism.

Marren argues that in the end the provision of aid is often based on a complex mix of altruistic, commercial and strategic reasons depending on donor and recipient characteristics.

Is aid a good or a bad thing?

The case for aid

Supporters of aid suggest that targeted aid has had some significant positive effects, especially if systems of accountability are firmly in place. They argue that the problem with most aid is that it is not targeted. It is generally just handed over to the government of the recipient country and often goes astray. Aid from this perspective, therefore, is not a bad thing but it does need to be reformed.

The neo-modernisation thinker Sachs (2005) takes this reformist position when he insists that "aid works, when it is practical, targeted, science-based and measurable". In particular, he argues that aid aimed at improving health, and especially child mortality, has been successful because it has resulted in mass immunisation for millions of children against diseases such as polio, diphtheria and measles. Similarly, Barder (2011) points out that every year foreign aid pays for the vaccinations of 80 per cent of the world's children, which saves 3 million lives a year. The Commission for Africa notes that smallpox in Africa was wiped out by targeted aid worth little more than $100 million, while Burnley (2010) has documented the success of aid in Zambia in the treatment of HIV/AIDS – 82 per cent of those infected are receiving regular anti-retroviral drugs for free, paid for by targeted aid. Moreover, British aid pays for 11 million children in Africa to go to school. Deaton (2013) too concludes that there are roads, dams and clinics in the developing world that would not exist without aid.

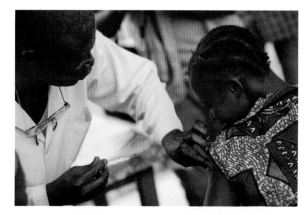

Aid is particularly effective in combating infant mortality.

Sachs notes that aid has also been relatively successful in terms of the 'green revolution' in Asia. Aid from the Rockefeller Foundation and USAID targeted the improvement of agricultural technology in India, China and other South East Asian countries and this resulted in a dramatic rise in rice yields.

These countries were then able to use the capital generated by this to diversify into other cash crops and industry.

The evidence regarding economic growth is also mixed. Addison *et al.* (2013) argue that the overall evidence suggests that aid has had a "respectable" impact on economic growth. There is solid historical evidence, according to Riddell (2014), that the economies of South Korea, Botswana, Malaysia and Indonesia have all extensively benefited from aid.

Paul Collier

Collier's (2008) analysis of aid suggests that aid is merely a "holding operation preventing things from falling apart". However, he does argue that without aid, the countries of the bottom billion of the world's population would have become even poorer than they are today. However, Collier's evidence also indicates that the more aid is increased, the less is the return in economic growth. Collier argues that aid is often rendered ineffective by two obstacles or traps that exist in the recipient countries:

> The conflict trap: too many countries receiving foreign aid are engaged in expensive civil wars or military conflicts with their neighbours.

> The bad governance trap: Collier highlights the problem of the kleptocracies – the corrupt elites – which run many developing societies. The Commission for Africa estimated that the amount of money, often originating in aid, stolen by corrupt elites and held in foreign bank accounts is equivalent to more than half of Africa's external debts.

Collier argues that these traps may mean that the developing countries do not share the priorities of the donor countries. The donor country may want to improve health and education services, but they cannot control how the aid is finally spent. Often the developing country will spend it on military purposes instead.

Peter Riddell

Riddell (2007) argues that aid could be effective but often it is not because of poor governance and corruption in recipient countries. He also suggests that donor countries such as the UK have to shoulder the blame for the failure of aid because:

> They often fail to distribute the aid to the countries that really need it. Riddell argues that less than half of all official aid is channelled to the 65 poorest countries.

> Too much aid is tied. This forces poor countries to buy resources that are not a high priority for challenging poverty.

> There are simply too many donors, aid programmes and projects. Riddell notes that donors often compete with each other to give aid, which results in a lack of cooperation and coordination between agencies and undermines the effectiveness of aid.

> Western aid agencies often do not learn from their past mistakes, because they have insufficient local knowledge and often do not consult with local people about their needs and the particular difficulties they face.

> Aid agencies do little to promote a sense of ownership among the ordinary people of developing nations. Consequently, local people may not be committed to aid projects because they don't really understand their purpose or they misinterpret the intentions of the agency.

The case against aid

The neo-liberal view

Neo-liberals such as Erixon (2005) argue that, although billions of dollars have been given in aid, most African countries, and Asian countries such as Bangladesh and Afghanistan, are poorer today than they were at the time of their political independence. Both absolute poverty and relative poverty (that is, the gap between rich and poor) in the developing world have actually increased in the past 40 years. Erixon also observes that aid to Africa generally seems to have lowered rather than increased economic growth.

Bauer (1981) argues that aid creates a dependency culture and discourages the entrepreneurial spirit vital to economic growth and development. He suggests that people in the developing world are actually demotivated by aid. They are unlikely to produce food if it is being distributed for free.

Moyo (2009) argues that the world lives in a culture of aid in that the majority of people in the West believe that it is "right" that those who are better off should "help" those who are worse off than themselves. In global terms, this is known as aid. Since 1985, this "pop culture of aid" has encouraged the view that the West needs to help more by giving more aid – for example, celebrity figures such as Bono have said "upbraid us for not giving enough," and "scold governments for not doing enough". However, Moyo argues that the idea that aid can alleviate and even eradicate poverty is a myth.

Moyo argues that the $1 trillion in aid that has been transferred from the Western countries to Africa over the past 50 years has been "an unmitigated political, economic and humanitarian disaster". She argues that sub-Saharan Africa remains the poorest region in the world, and the average African is poorer today than two decades ago. Life expectancy in Africa has stagnated, and one in seven children across the continent die before the age of five. Adult literacy across most African countries has plummeted to below 1980s levels, and 50 per cent of the African continent is subject to non-democratic rule.

Moyo argues that the main reason why aid has been unsuccessful is that it has often been distributed with little follow-up to check how it is being used, even when conditions such as structural adjustment programmes (SAP) are attached. This lack of accountability regarding its use has encouraged government corruption – leaders divert aid into their own bank accounts – and created political instability and civil war as groups compete for these funds. Bad governance also means that much aid is wasted. Moyo argues that up to 85 per cent of aid is not used for the purpose it was given.

Aid also undermines the attitudes of local people, and particularly the notion of self-help. Moyo observes that "in an aid environment, governments are less interested in fostering entrepreneurs and the development of their middle class than in furthering their own financial interests". Consequently, the African middle class does not develop the economic skills and attitudes required for economic success. Moyo therefore concludes that aid has actively kept the African continent in a state of underdevelopment that she describes as "childlike".

Give six reasons why Moyo believes foreign aid is a failure.

The Marxist view

Neo-Marxists, particularly Theresa Hayter (1981), reject the view that the primary function of aid is to assist development. Rather, they suggest that it deliberately functions to bring about and sustain underdevelopment, and to reinforce Western monopoly of wealth, consumption and political power. Hayter argues that aid is not meant to benefit the developing world because its primary purpose is to sustain the unequal and exploitative global relationship between the rich capitalist centres of the West and the deliberately underdeveloped and peripheral poor world. Hayter argues that aid is an aspect of neo-colonialism (see Chapter 1) in that aid and particularly the loans distributed by the IMF and the World Bank are ultimately aimed at strengthening unequal trading relations that benefit Western economies.

The imperial nature of aid is revealed by the fact that most aid, whether bilateral or multilateral, is actually tied to Western economies – it is generally spent on Western goods and expertise, and therefore stimulates Western economies. Furthermore, the SAP conditions laid down for IMF or World Bank loans primarily serve the interests of the transnational companies (TNCs) that dominate global capitalism (see Chapter 3). In summary, then, Hayter argues that aid has failed the developing world because it was never really intended to help their economies – rather the true but hidden purpose of aid is to reproduce, maintain and legitimate the interests of the capitalist West.

Dependency theory has also raised concerns about the "aid business", which now employs hundreds of thousands of people worldwide. Hancock (1989) refers to the largely White and Western administrators of the World Bank, the IMF and large charities as the "lords of poverty", because of the large proportion of aid that is spent on bloated salaries, administrative expenses, first-class hotels and attendance at international conferences.

The post-development view

Rist (2010) argues that foreign aid is merely another tool of the US neo-liberalism that has attempted to dominate economic and political thinking worldwide since the end of the Second World War. He argues that aid sends out an ideological message to the developing world that the poor are guilty of not being rich and implies that this can be changed by adopting Western forms of economic thinking and consumer tastes. Post-development thinkers therefore see aid as a vehicle for accelerating the adoption of Western consumerism as a way of life. Post-development thinkers claim that this ideological process is not only disparaging of traditional cultures and communities but also ethnocentric.

Critics of aid acknowledge that the first 20 years of aid – from the 1950s to the 1970s – were relatively successful in improving life expectancy, reducing mortality rates, increasing literacy rates, and improving economic growth and therefore living standards around the world. However, these critics argue that the last 30 years of aid show that this progress has stalled and that aid is failing in its overall goals.

In your opinion, is aid effective or ineffective? Discuss the positives and negatives of giving aid to see if you can reach a conclusion.

The ambiguous role of debt

The effectiveness of aid is undermined by the debt owed by the developing world to the West. For example, in 2012 the external debt of the developing world was almost $5 trillion, according to the World Bank. There are lots of reasons why the developing world is in such debt. Many poorer countries are over-dependent on selling two or three primary commodities. The prices of these have generally fallen over the past few decades while the price of oil and manufacturing goods needed for development have risen steeply. Developing countries have therefore needed to borrow money to make up the difference. In their search for greater profits, Western banks were happy to oblige in the belief that countries never go bust. However, a lot of this money was poorly invested or stolen. Countries therefore were unable to generate the income required to pay back the loans. Meanwhile, the rise in Western interest rates worsened the problem. For example, since the 1970s, the Jamaican government has borrowed about $19 billion, paid back over $20 billion and still owes nearly $15 million because of high rates of interest.

There is no doubt that debt is counter-productive with regard to aid because more income flows out of the developing world in the form of debt repayments than flows in as aid. As Chasaide (2015) observes, this has resulted in an absurd situation where rich governments are giving badly needed aid to developing countries through one channel and taking the money back through another. Nearly a quarter of the aid African countries receive this year will immediately be given back to the West in the form of debt repayments.

The overall effect on the developing world of the debt crisis has been devastating. Debt has actually increased infant-mortality rates and lowered life expectancy because aid that should have been used for developing health care has been diverted to servicing debt.

The future of aid

There is no doubt that aid is in need of reform. The experts, however, are divided on what that reform should look like. For example, Moyo recommends an end to all aid for five years to force the governments of developing societies to turn to tax, investors and the free market to make their economies more accountable, democratic and pro-business. She argues that China insists on accountability for how its aid is used and withdraws it if it is unsatisfied with the response. In contrast, the West gives something for nothing.

Collier argues that aid should be used as reinforcement: if developing societies are willing to tackle corruption and to be more accountable in their use of aid, they should be rewarded with more aid. However, aid should be cut off from less cooperative regimes. However, Collier concludes that aid is only a partial solution to the problems that the bottom billion face; he argues that international laws are needed to regulate the activities of TNCs and that global terms of trade need to be renegotiated so that they positively discriminate in favour of the poorest countries.

Some conclusions about aid

It is difficult to assess the merits of foreign aid because there are probably too many unrealistic expectations associated with it. Some countries, such as China, Cuba and Vietnam, have managed to grow and develop without it. Moreover, as Marren notes, no country has ever developed through aid alone. What is apparent is that aid is necessary, especially in developing societies in which revenues are too inadequate to pay for basic health care and education. However, it is also apparent that aid is never sufficient.

TRADE

Modernisation theory

Modernisation theory highlights the role of trade when climbing the ladder to economic development. Rostow (1971) argues that as countries start to industrialise in the 'take off' stage of development, they will take their place within the international trade system and to start to trade their manufactured goods with the developed world. The 'drive to maturity' stage of development sees export earnings from such trade being reinvested in industry, infrastructure, education, health and so on. Full development implies that societies which successfully climb the development ladder become equal trading partners in the global marketplace.

Neo-liberalism

Reid-Henry (2012) argues that neo-liberalists see global free-trade markets as both the means and the desired end of development (see Chapter 1). Neo-liberal development policy sets out to do whatever is necessary to make local markets and societies 'fit' with this free-market vision. Reid-Henry notes that this usually involves four key organising principles:

> The governments of developing countries are expected to pull down all barriers to Western investment.

> Workers in the developing world are expected to work hard and cheaply without complaint for transnational corporations.

> Public services need to be privatised.

> Social life should be organised around the profit motive.

Reid-Henry refers to this approach to development as the "trade not aid" approach. He observes that the neo-liberal approach to development is to encourage the developing world to get the state out of the way and to get the market conditions right for free trade and especially investment by transnational corporations. If these goals are achieved, neo-liberals see social justice and human development as automatically following. The WTO (see Chapter 3) which was set up to regulate world trade has become the main enforcer of these neo-liberal ideas.

FOCUS ON SKILLS: AID, DEBT AND AFRICA

Calderisi believes that African leaders prioritise their own interests over helping to lift their people out of poverty.

Calderisi (2006), a former World Bank official, suggests that Africa's poverty and debt has been almost entirely self-inflicted. He argues that Africa has failed to use Western aid effectively and accrued massive debt because its leaders are often corrupt and therefore more interested in enriching themselves than helping their own people. Furthermore, these same leaders have badly mismanaged both their economies and their debts. Calderisi argues that corruption in Africa has spread to every level. He claims that corruption undermines development because it saps the energy of the poor, dulls their enterprise and makes them fatalistic and cynical about the possibility of change. Finally Calderisi argues that Africa is characterised by a lack of unity because of tribal and border disputes and this has undermined the ability of African countries to cooperate with one another in trade and in sharing infrastructure such as transport and telecommunications. However, Calderisi can be criticised for neglecting the fact that many African leaders were sponsored by the West for strategic reasons. The West often turned a blind eye to their corruption and their human rights abuses.

Other critics blame international agencies for the ineffectiveness of aid. A good example of this is Sierra Leone, which experienced civil war between 1991 and 2002. When this ended aid advisors from the UK, the USA, the World Bank and the IMF advised the Sierra Leone government on how to tackle poverty. The World Bank and the IMF came up with a complex aid package with lots of strings. Their solution to the problems of the second poorest country in the world was to privatise virtually the entire country, including, most controversially, the national water utility. In 2002, Britain agreed a bilateral aid agreement for £104 million over three years. However, one of the conditions of this package was that Sierra Leone had to agree to privatise 24 public enterprises including shipping, roads, the airline, telecommunications, housing, the postal service, the national power authority and water. It is no surprise that the cost of living in Sierra Leone, and especially the costs of water and electricity, have risen dramatically in the past ten years.

Questions

1. **Explain.** Give two effects of corruption according to Calderisi.

2. **Explain** two economic changes Sierra Leone had to make in exchange for aid.

3. **Analyse** why aid has failed in Africa, according to Calderisi.

4. **Analyse** the influence of neo-liberal economic policies on foreign aid.

5. **Evaluate.** Using information from this source and elsewhere, assess the view that foreign aid is an essential and positive agent of development.

Dependency theory

However, the Marxist-influenced dependency theory is critical of both the modernisation and the neo-liberal stance on trade. Frank (1971) argues that modernisation theory neglects the fact that developing societies already occupy a place in the world trading system as producers of cash crops and raw materials. Before independence, the colonising power simply took these commodities. After independence, developing societies are often still over-dependent on trading in these primary commodities.

Marxists argue that world trade is just another aspect of neo-colonialism (along with aid and TNC exploitation). They are particularly concerned with the recent increase in bilateral free trade agreements (FTAs). For example, in 2007, the EU signed FTAs with India and South Korea. Such FTAs often favour opening up home markets to foreign competitors. The FTA between the EU and India allows the import of poultry and dairy products (despite the fact that 85 per cent of the demand for these products is met by Indian farmers) and the introduction of big supermarket chains into the Indian marketplace.

Marxists argue that the neo-liberal economic policies of the WTO and FTAs can only work on a level playing field. Unfortunately the terms of world trade encouraged by the WTO mean that poor countries are disadvantaged:

> The economies of developing countries are often over-dependent for their export earnings on a narrow range of commodities made up of cash crops or raw materials. According to Ellwood (2004), three commodities account for 75 per cent of total exports in each of the 48 poorest nations, but because of a massive decline in the value of such commodities, the developing nations need to export more and more every year just to stay in the same place. One developing nation leader described this as "running up the downward escalator". For example, in 1960, the earnings from 25 tons of natural rubber would buy four tractors, but today it is not enough to buy one.

> Ellwood argues that the neo-liberal policies of the WTO encourage farmers in the developing world to grow more for export in order to clear their "black hole of debt". He argues that this has resulted in what Greenfield (2004) calls the "social violence of the market" – the constantly escalating pressure on farmers and workers in the developing world by TNCs to produce more for less. This creates a problem called "immiserating trade" – the more a developing country trades, the poorer it gets.

> Raw materials often do not accumulate value until they have been processed in the West, and consequently it is Western TNCs that reap the benefit. For example, when cocoa is processed into a bar of chocolate that costs £1 in the UK, about 77 pence goes to the TNC, 15 pence goes to the government in the form of tax but only 8 pence goes to the cocoa farmer in the developing world.

> Ellwood notes that the WTO does little to stop Western nations from imposing tariffs (a type of import tax that results in goods from the developing world becoming more expensive than home-produced goods), quotas (limits on how much a developed country will import from developing countries) and giving massive subsidies to their own farmers (which means they can undercut the price of the products of the developing world).

> Often the value and price of a commodity is totally out of the hands of the producer country and is actually set by commodity speculators located in Western organisations, such as the London Metal Exchange. In 2006, it was estimated by the bank Merrill Lynch that commodities were trading at prices 50 per cent higher than they would have been without speculators.

Ellwood criticises the WTO for allowing TNCs too much control and power over the global economy, which allows them to insist that developing nations produce more for less or that they reduce production and import more from the richer nations. This is particularly a problem in the food sector. For example, two TNCs control over half the world market in coffee, while four TNCs control 81 per cent of the global beef market.

Hoogvelt (2001) notes that the combination of free trade and TNCs often leads to the corruption of political elites in the developing world. She notes they often become directors of TNC subsidiaries. In some extreme cases, these elites, often military in origin, have even removed threats to foreign interests by violence, while their repressive powers (their control of police and military) serve to assure the cooperation of the masses.

Marxists therefore conclude that the terms of world trade are far from equal. Developing countries are very much junior partners in global trading relationships and consequently are exploited by richer and more powerful countries and their TNC agents.

Alternatives to the neo-liberal dominance of world trade

In the last 20 years, the neo-liberal character of world trade has been rocked by the appearance of a new powerful player – China. This state-capitalist country has been a phenomenal economic success over the past few decades and in its search for raw materials to feed its burgeoning industry, it has offered not only aid in return for access to oil, minerals and food, but also hard cash, when it trades with other nations. Duncan (2015) notes that as a result the developing world can trade on more equitable terms with China, which can afford to pay higher prices for what it wants. In return, the developing world has benefited from the import of cheap Chinese technology such as mobile phones. Duncan argues that the Chinese approach of let's "just do business" is more appealing to the developing world than the neo-liberal approach of the WTO and FTAs, which more often than not involve the developing world having to accept trade conditions that benefit Western interests at their expense.

According to Duncan, the developing world prefers China's attitude to development and business to that of the WTO and FTAs.

There is some evidence too that neo-liberal terms of trade are not entirely necessary for development. The Asian Tiger countries, according to So and Chiu (1995), did not follow the neo-liberal policies of free trade. Rather, they became successful by adopting an interventionist protectionist approach. They used subsidies to reward companies for meeting national targets. They used tariffs and quotas to protect key sectors of their industries from imports.

Many developing countries are now in the process of resisting the neo-liberal dominance over world trade. In 2006, the presidents of Venezuela, Cuba and Bolivia created the Bolivarian Alternative for the Peoples of our America (ALBA) and a People's Trade Agreement in order to reduce Latin America's dependency on the WTO and US markets. The Bank of ALBA and the Bank of the South were also set up to finance infrastructure projects and to fund educational and health programmes, as an alternative to borrowing money from the IMF and World Bank.

Fair Trade

Finally, some developing countries have tried to establish (with the help of NGOs) a more equitable alternative to free trade. McMichael (2011) describes the Fair Trade movement as "a practice that includes social and

environmental costs in the prices of traded commodities, to adequately compensate producers and their habitats, and to render more transparent the conditions of producers and their relation to consumers". In other words, producers of commodities in the developing world would get a fair price for their goods while consumers in the West would gain satisfaction from the knowledge that the goods had been ethically produced, using sound, environmentally friendly practices.

According to McMichael, fair-trade exchanges are increasing, particularly in the fields of organic products such as coffee, bananas, tea and orange juice, as well as cotton jeans. The Fairtrade Labelling Organisations International (FLO) is an umbrella NGO that organises the fair trade market. Products can carry the label 'Fairtrade' if they are produced by democratically organised associations of workers represented by trade unions. Working conditions must be safe and healthy. There should be no child labour. Use of fertilisers and herbicides should be eliminated. Wages should fairly reflect the work done.

Fair trade is gradually making its mark on world trade. For example, Starbucks has attempted to rebrand itself "green capitalist" by adopting a fair-trade variety of coffee products. However, McMichael suggests there are two future paths for the Fair Trade movement – it may turn out to be merely an alternative minority trade movement which ultimately fails to make any real difference to global trade or it may have the potential to educate consumers, mobilise public opinion and harness consumer purchasing power in the West "to democratise the global market".

INDUSTRIALISATION

Bello (2015) argues that the most reliable measures of development are the speed and depth of industrialisation and the variety of manufacturing industries. The prime example often cited is Great Britain, which was the first economy to industrialise and which by the early 19th century was the most powerful economy in the world. Moreover, by the 20th century, the people of Great Britain had experienced a transformation of social life as life expectancy increased, mortality rates fell and wages and standards of living rose. Consequently, Britain's 18th-century industrial revolution is presented as the exemplar of the ideal path to development.

Modernisation theory and neo-liberal theory

Both modernisation theory and neo-liberalism argue that developing countries need to move through the same stages of industrial and economic development as Britain, although they disagree on how this might be achieved.

Modernisation theorists such as Rostow believed that developing countries needed the help of the West via aid and TNC investment to get them onto their industrial feet. In contrast, neo-liberals argued that only by divesting themselves of the protectionist and interventionist state can developing societies be in a position to rapidly industrialise.

The newly industrialised countries

A good example of 'industrialisation as development' is the group of countries known as the 'newly industrialised countries' (NICs). These are described by McMichael as middle-income developing countries that industrialised rapidly and substantially beginning in the 1960s, leaving other developing countries behind.

McMichael identifies these NICs as Hong Kong, Singapore, Taiwan, South Korea, Brazil and Mexico, with Malaysia, Thailand, Indonesia, Argentina and Chile following close behind. These societies were able to develop 'export-oriented industrialisation' (EOI) because of substantial foreign investment in assembly-line production and computerised technology, which produced textiles and particularly electronics for export.

Some have seen the success of EOI as proof of the efficacy of the modernisation model of development. However, the rapid success of these societies could also have been due to the fact some of the Asian NICs, most notably South Korea and Singapore, were 'bureaucratic-authoritarian industrial regimes' in which deferential workers with no labour rights would work extremely long hours because their leaderships stressed this was a matter of national honour.

Another instance which is often cited as an example of the success of the 'industrialisation as development' model is the 'green revolution' – a type of agricultural industrialisation that was championed in the 1960s by the Rockefeller Foundation, a US-based NGO, and backed by the UN and the World Bank. This strategy, which involved industrial-scale farming techniques supervised by agribusiness TNCs, introduced high-yielding hybrid seed technologies into developing countries in Asia and South America, supplemented by industrial fertilisers, intensive irrigation and pesticides.

This green revolution was reasonably successful in terms of wheat and rice production. However, there were disadvantages: it led to unemployment (as machines replaced farmworkers) and environmental problems as the land and the people working it were over-exposed to toxic chemicals.

Dependency theory

Hoogvelt argues that industrialisation is a positive process, but all too often it has been established, organised and developed for the benefit of Western TNCs rather than for the benefit of developing societies. In this sense, it is part of the exploitative process known as neo-colonialism.

Hoogvelt argues that as colonies became independent in the 1950s, they were encouraged to develop along industrial lines through a process called 'technological rents'. This process encouraged the newly independent state to invite TNCs to invest in factories in the developing country. The idea was that the country got the technology and that some workers were trained in technical skills to become managers and, in return for this 'rent', the developing countries provided cheap, unskilled labour for the factory floor. However, this arrangement was more beneficial to the TNCs than the developing world because the TNCs made huge profits that were transferred back to the West, and TNC investment in skills turned out to be negligible.

Why might TNCs be reluctant to train people from developing countries in all the skills required to manufacture goods or to extract natural resources efficiently?

Industrialisation and export processing zones

Critics such as Klein (2001) have noted that many developing countries industrialise by setting up Export Processing Zones (EPZs, see Chapter 3). However, Klein argues that this type of industrialisation inevitably means exploitation as workers, especially women, experience intensive working conditions and long hours, and are denied rights in a way that would not be tolerated outside the EPZ.

The new international division of labour

Marxists such as Frobel et al. (1979) argue that the development of EPZs and developments in manufacturing technology have meant that TNCs have been able to construct a New International Division of Labour (NIDL), in which labour across both continents and countries has been fragmented into a range of unskilled tasks that can be done with minimal training, while computer-controlled technology enables production to be automatically supervised.

Ellwood argues that developing countries often compete with each other to offer TNCs the best terms, such as tax breaks, interest-free loans, a guarantee that trade unions will be outlawed, and publicly-funded sewers, roads and utilities. McMichael notes, for example, that Mexico offers TNCs 100 per cent tax exemption for the first ten years of their investment and 50 per cent for the next ten years. Klein argues that "entire (developing) countries are being turned into industrial slums and low-wage labour ghettos" as a result of these deals.

Why might TNC investment in the EPZs and FTZs lead to unemployment or lower wages in the UK?

The outcome of this NIDL is that most low-paid, low-skilled labour is concentrated in the developing world while most skilled highly paid work is found in the developed world. Neo-liberals believe that the NIDL benefits world consumers by enhancing competition, and therefore keeping the prices of goods reasonably low. However, Frobel *et al.* argue that the NIDL is merely a new form of neo-colonial exploitation. They argue that, in addition to exploiting peasants who grow cash crops for Western consumption, TNCs are now exploiting wage labourers (especially women and often children) in factories and sweatshops throughout the world.

Import Substitution Industrialisation

In the 1950s, some developing countries adopted an alternative industrial path, which introduced nationalist economic policies called Import Substitution Industrialisation (ISI). It involved developing countries manufacturing consumer goods that would normally be expensively imported from the developed world, such as instant coffee, and protecting these from foreign, especially Western competition by using trade barriers such as tariffs and quotas. By the early 1960s, the signs were positive, for example, as Green illustrates (quoted in Hoogvelt): "domestic industry supplied 95 per cent of Mexico's and 98 per cent of Brazil's consumer goods. From 1950 to 1980 Latin America's industrial output went up six times."

However, ISI eventually failed for the following reasons:

> It neglected to address the issue of class and income distribution – that is, the existing elites controlled ISI and this led to further deepening of income and wealth inequalities. These societies therefore became more repressive in their treatment of protest and, as a consequence, politically unstable.

> It was still over-dependent on the West for some technical expertise, spare parts, oil, and so on.

> These societies often borrowed money from Western banks to finance ISI. However, by the 1980s they were heavily in debt. Loan conditions imposed by the IMF and the World Bank often meant getting rid of the barriers that had protected ISI. The WTO and FTAs insisted that the ISI countries had to abide by the same free-trade rules as everyone else.

There is one success story that has come out of ISI in the field of pharmaceuticals. In the 1960s the government of Brazil decided to manufacture generic drugs rather than pay royalties to Western pharmaceutical companies. This reduced the price of drugs on the domestic market by 80 per cent and saved the government $250 million a year in spending on drug imports. The HIV/AIDS crisis also prompted several countries – including Brazil, India and Egypt – to 'copy' and manufacture antiretroviral drugs. Western drug companies were charging anything between $10,000 and $15,000 per person per year for these drugs but these countries managed to produce a generic copy for $600 dollars. The WTO, under pressure from NGOs such as Oxfam and the WHO, has now agreed, despite TNC objections, that countries can import these generic drugs for national health emergencies. This has resulted in one of the pharmaceutical TNCs – GlaxoSmithKline – becoming the first company to sell AIDs drugs at cost price in the developing world.

THE TOURIST INDUSTRY

According to the WTO (2007), in terms of earnings from international trade, tourism is the sixth largest sector of the global economy. More specifically, the tourist industry is generally thought to be the world's largest service sector industry. Tourism to developing countries is on the rise for a number of reasons:

> The growth of communication systems, especially television and the internet, has increased people's curiosity about other lands and people.

> The cheapness of air travel has made previously remote and exotic locations more accessible.

> The growth of higher education has broadened people's interests and stimulated their desire to travel.

The international tourist tends to be Western (although there has been a dramatic increase in Chinese international tourists because tourism is associated with people who enjoy a comparatively high standard of living and have access to education and a variety of mass media.

The tourist industry has a number of benefits to the developing world:

> It brings much-needed Western currency into the country.

> It provides employment opportunities.

> It stimulates the local economy. For example, local food producers sell to hotels and restaurants, and local traders sell to tourists.

However, sociologists such as Urry (1990), Hall (2007) and Harrison (2008) are concerned that international tourism may have a negative impact on the developing world because:

> The country's indigenous population may experience relative deprivation as they compare their lifestyles with that of the tourists. Their perception of a wealth and income gap between themselves and tourists may fuel resentment.

> Local people may interpret activities introduced for the benefit of tourists – such as alcohol, gambling and nude sunbathing – as challenging and insulting to their traditional cultural and religious beliefs. Tourists may also behave in crass culturally insensitive ways.

> Traditional culture, such as tribal dancing, may become commercialised as tourists demand to see and experience it, thereby devaluing it. This may result in a loss of cultural pride.

> Local people may be employed by tourist outlets such as hotels, but these jobs tend to be disproportionately low-skilled, casual and seasonal, low-paid and low-status.

> Tourist resorts only comprise a fraction of the geography of the developing world, but tourists rarely venture out of them. Areas outside the hotel complexes therefore do not benefit economically from tourism.

> Tourism may attract beggars and criminals.

> Tourism may result in environmental degradation as sites of natural beauty are damaged by frequent footfall, or are built on to accommodate ever increasing numbers of tourists.

> Tourism to particular countries may be popular for criminal or deviant reasons; for example, some Westerners may be sex tourists.

> Tourism may actually take more money out of a developing country than it puts in because hotel complexes tend to be owned by foreign investors.

Assess whether the tourist industry is beneficial to the development process.

URBANISATION

In 1900, the only country in the world that could be described as 'urban' was Great Britain. The 20th century, however, saw massive migration from the countryside to the towns and cities of both the developed and the developing world. Cohen and Kennedy (2000) note that there were approximately 185 million people living in the towns and cities of the poorer world in 1940. By 1975, this figure had increased to 770 million. Until the 1950s, most of the world's most populated cities were to be found in the developed world. This situation was reversed only 40 years later and now the most populated cities in the world are (in no particular order) Mexico City, São Paulo, Tokyo, Shanghai, New York, Kolkata (Calcutta), Mumbai (Bombay), Beijing, Los Angeles and Jakarta. Note that only three of these cities are in the developed world. Today, there are three times as many city dwellers in the developing world as there are in the developed world.

In 1950, there were seven cities with populations of over 5 million. It is estimated that this number will rise to 93 by 2025 and that 80 of these will be in the developing world. Some 37 per cent of Africans live in cities, and this is expected to rise by 50 per cent in the next 25 years. By 2030, Africa will be an urban continent. In contrast, urban growth is actually falling in the developed world as people make the decision to move out of cities.

These trends have partly been caused by rapid population growth in the developing world, but the 20th century also saw that population gravitating towards urban areas, through a combination of push and pull factors (see Table 3.4.1). The fact that urban dwellers in developing societies tend to be younger and consequently more fertile than city populations in the West also contributes to rising urban populations in the poorer countries.

Push (from rural areas)	Pull (to the cities)
Poverty	The availability of jobs, especially in transnational factories and services
Displacement by new agricultural technology	The perception that a greater number of waged jobs are available
Loss of land	Access to services such as education and health
Natural disasters, such as drought, flood, earthquakes	Perception that urban life offers greater opportunities in terms of living standards, and bright lights and glamour
Disasters caused by poor governance, such as war, displaced refugees	Escape from traditional constraints of family, culture and religion
Changes in aspirations among younger people as they access modern media	The perception that urbanisation = Westernisation = sophistication

Table 3.4.1 *Push and pull influences on migration to cities in the developing world*

Urbanisation and modernisation theory

Urbanisation is regarded as a universally positive phenomenon by modernisation theorists, because European societies underwent a period of sustained urbanisation in the 19th century and developing societies are encouraged to follow the same development path. Modernisation theory claims that cities promote economic growth by giving industrialist–capitalists access to a massive concentrated pool of labour for their factories. The wages paid to city factory workers supposedly filter down to help develop other city services, such as housing, shops and infrastructure.

Cities are also seen as playing a central role in promoting cultural change. Cross (1979) suggests that cities are catalysts of modernisation in that they loosen ties to traditional institutions and value systems by reducing dependency on community and extended kin. He claims that city life leads to the development of modernist and individualistic values that are more suitable to progress and development. The result is an entrepreneurial urban population more prepared to take risks, more receptive to the possibility of geographical and social mobility,

and willing to make investments in order to accumulate personal profit.

However, this picture of urbanisation has been criticised because:

1. It is based on a false historical picture – urbanisation in Europe and the USA was gradual in that it took place over a period of 200 years. It was also largely responsive to employment opportunities. However, the urbanisation of developing societies has been much more rapid, and population growth has wildly exceeded the number of jobs available.

2. It is guilty of looking at Western urbanisation through rose-coloured spectacles. It ignores the widely accepted view that city life in the West has killed the concept of community and that this, in turn, has led to serious social problems in urban areas in the developed world, including social isolation, alienation, crime and drug abuse.

3. The rapid urbanisation of the developing world has created severe social problems that inhibit development, including the following:

   › High rates of urban unemployment, underemployment and subsistence poverty have led to the development of a dual-sector economy in many cities in the developing world. As Peace (2005) notes, in this situation, a minority of people are lucky enough to find work on reasonable pay in a tiny formal sector, consisting of legitimate, regulated and unionised employment, often in the public sector. Many other inhabitants, however, are forced to eke out a meagre living in the informal sector, dependent on unregulated employment in sweatshops. These are often exploitative (in terms of the wages paid) and dangerous (in terms of health and safety).

   › An estimated one billion live in slums and shanty towns across the developing world. This figure is expected to double by 2030. Asia has 60 per cent of the world's slum dwellers, while Africa has 20 per cent and Latin America has 14 per cent. The infrastructure of these cities – services such as housing, clean water, sanitation, refuse collection and policing – is generally unable to cope with the sheer weight of numbers, and this leads to a set of classic problems associated with lack of development, such as high child and maternal mortality, child malnutrition and low life expectancy.

   › A new set of modern urban problems have appeared as people in the shanty towns turn to illegal or unconventional means to raise their income: crime, especially gun crime, drug-dealing, prostitution or begging. Suicide and mental health problems, too, are becoming major problems in these new urban environments. The Commission for Africa reports that Africa's cities are becoming a powder keg of potential political instability and discontent, and a breeding ground for anti-Western sentiment.

› Rapid urbanisation is leading to environmental degradation. As Esteva and Austin (1987) note, "in Mexico development stinks…The damage to persons…and the degradation of nature which until recently were only implicit in development can now be seen, touched and smelled".

Generally, then, the simple cause-and-effect model that modernisation theory applies to urbanisation (that is, that people will be attracted to cities because of the pull factor of jobs) does not really apply in the developing world.

Urbanisation and dependency theory

The way in which modernisers have supported the notion of urbanisation as the focus for development planning and policy is something that has been criticised by dependency theory. In contrast, dependency theory suggests that urbanisation in the developing world is not acting as an effective force for development – rather, it is likely to sustain underdevelopment. Marxists point out that European urbanisation was a response to industrialisation, when people migrated to towns and cities to take work in factories. In developing societies, people have migrated to cities, leaving behind land on which they lived and grew food or kept livestock, but factory jobs in the cities are not widely available because TNC factories tend to highly mechanised.

An urban underclass

These urban migrants end up in the slums, and their existence is so poor that some Marxists argue that they constitute a class below that of the proletariat – a lumpen-proletariat or underclass.

Dependency theorists partly blame the rapid growth of cities in the developing world on colonialism. Cities in poorer satellite countries were established by the occupying colonial powers as the administrative centres for transferring capital, raw materials and cash crops to the developed world. They argue that cities in developing societies continue to act as staging-posts for neo-colonial exploitation of the labour, raw materials and cash crops of the developing world because TNCs establish their operational headquarters and factories in urban areas.

Dependency theorists argue that cities play a key role in ensuring that poorer countries remain in a state of underdevelopment because these cities monopolise any surplus capital that might be generated by exports or aid. This capital is often spent on expensive vanity projects, such as airports, hotels and conference centres, that enhance the look of the city, but which only benefit local elites or tourists.

THE RELATIONSHIP BETWEEN DEVELOPMENT AND THE ENVIRONMENT

In the last 25 years, there has been a rise in interest in the relationship between development and the environment. In particular, there is a growing awareness that environmental degradation cannot continue at its present rate without having major implications for the living standards of people in the developed and developing worlds alike.

There are concerns about how long current developmental processes can continue before local and global ecological systems collapse. Kingsbury et al. (2004) point out that environmental degradation does not respect state boundaries and widespread environmental collapse is no longer a case of 'if', but of 'when and where'. Environmental degradation can be illustrated in several ways:

› *Species extinction* – Ellwood (2001) notes that the global extinction crisis is accelerating, with dramatic declines in wildlife. Habitat loss is the major cause of the decline in numbers of many species. Ellwood notes that, in the past 500 years, mankind has forced 816 species into extinction.

› *Deforestation* – Kingsbury and colleagues argue that deforestation is the world's most significant environmental problem. Deforestation has a number of major implications because rainforests absorb carbon dioxide as well as producing the oxygen upon which all life depends. It is estimated that some of the world's major rainforests, in areas such as Indonesia, Borneo, Chile and the Amazon Basin, will be completely deforested within 30 years.

› *Desertification* – This is mainly the result of the over-cultivation and overgrazing of poor-quality land by the poor, who are often forced to keep using unsustainable land in order to survive. The more fertile land in many developing countries is owned by TNCs who use it to grow cash crops for export, such as the cut flowers found in British supermarkets in the winter. Kingsbury and colleagues point out that desertification is getting worse. In 1970, Africa was self-sufficient in food production, but by 1984, a quarter of Africa's population was being kept alive by food aid and imported grain because of desertification, soil erosion and drought.

> *Water pollution* – Kingsbury and colleagues note that the pollution of the world's waterways – rivers, streams and lakes – for industrial and food purposes has reduced the amount of clean drinking water and seriously threatens the continuing existence of some animal and plant life. In particular, he argues that access to clean drinking water is probably the world's most immediate environmental problem, because it has been seriously threatened by the waste products of industrialisation, the increased use of pesticides, insecticides and chemical fertilisers, and population growth. In 2012, 800 million people globally did not have access to piped water or had less than the recommended minimum amount. For example, in Pakistan in 2012, a large majority of the country's 135 million people did not have access to drinkable water.

Environmental pressure points

A number of causes have been identified by environmentalists with regard to environmental degradation.

> *Population growth* – Ehrlich (1968) has argued that the Earth's resources cannot sustain present levels of population growth because some areas of the world have very limited capacity and are more prone to degradation because of overuse. These areas tend to be in the very poorest parts of the world, such as sub-Saharan Africa. Ehrlich's ideas are explored in more depth in Chapter 5.

> *Economic necessity* – Many of the poor in developing countries have no choice but to use and reuse environmental resources. In other words, this type of behaviour is a matter of economic necessity and survival. Ellwood (2001) argues that "the desperately poor do not make good eco-citizens. Tribal peoples plunder the forest on which they depend for survival; animals are poached and slaughtered by impoverished African villagers for their valuable ivory or their body parts."

> *Greed and corruption* – The desire of local elites and international corporations to accumulate wealth, usually at the expense of others, results in the exploitation and selling-off of environmental resources. At the same time, cost-cutting in order to increase profits may lead to unscrupulous behaviour, such as the illegal dumping of toxic waste.

> *Poverty and debt* – Chakravarty et al. (2012) argue that deforestation is partly caused by the poverty and debt that characterises the economies of the developing world. In order to pay off their debts, developing countries have expanded their raw

material and cash-crop exports, often with the strong encouragement of neo-liberal international agencies such as the WTO, the World Bank and the IMF. For example, between 1978 and 1996, Brazil cleared 12.5 per cent of rainforest in the Amazon Basin in an attempt to meet loan repayments to the World Bank and commercial banks in the West. There is a human cost, too, as the indigenous Amazon tribes are forced off their land and, in some cases, murdered by commercial loggers.

> *Western consumption* – However, some environmentalists argue that the real problem is Western over-consumption and waste of the world's resources. For example, Rees (1996) estimates that about 10 to 14 acres of land are used to maintain the lifetime consumption of the average person in the West, but the total available productive land in the world, if shared out equally, would only come to 4.25 acres per person. The rich world is therefore consuming the resources of the poor. Moreover, the 'throwaway economy' created by the consuming class produces vast amounts of waste – much of which is toxic or made of materials and wrapped in packaging that is not eco-friendly, so that it may inflict damage on the environment because it does not naturally break down.

> *Industrial and agribusiness development* – Industrial technology, both in the West and in those countries relatively new to industrialisation, has had – and is still having – profound effects on the global environment and climate. For example, carbon dioxide levels in the atmosphere continue to rise because of the burning of fossil fuels, such as coal and oil, in factories, cars, tankers and jet-planes. It is estimated that if China continues on its present path of economic growth, it will contribute 40 per cent of global carbon dioxide emissions by 2050. The expansion of agribusiness TNCs has led to the increasing poisoning of the world's rivers and lakes through the massive use of fertilisers and pesticides.

Sustainable and appropriate development strategies

In the 1980s, there was a move towards introducing more **sustainable** forms of **development** in order to protect the global environment in the long term. There was an increasing realisation among agencies such as the World Bank that development had a global dimension, and that it should be targeted at what Korten (1995) calls "the global threefold human crisis" of deepening poverty, social disintegration and environmental destruction. Development strategies in the 1980s, therefore, focused on ameliorating problems which might otherwise threaten chaos at a global level.

Sustainable development

In 1987, the World Commission on Environment and Development (WCED), or Bruntland Commission, concluded that economic development in both the West and the developing world should be compatible with greater responsibility for the global environment.

Bruntland advocated the policy of sustainable development. A central component of this idea was the acknowledgement that poverty in the developing countries might be a major cause of global environmental problems such as global warming. Bruntland therefore argued that the construction of a more equitable economic relationship between the developed and developing worlds would reduce the need for the developing world to over-exploit their environments and thus slow down environmental destruction. Moreover, Bruntland argued that rich countries should aim to reduce pollution and put clean air before higher living standards. In the 1990s, 178 UN member states agreed to pursue sustainable development. The United Nations, too, adopted sustainable development as part of its Millennium Development goals.

Foster (2004) argues that the World Bank's projects and practices are creating environmental problems despite its supposed commitment to sustainable development. Foster accuses the World Bank of encouraging logging in tropical rainforests and of entering into partnership with some of the most notorious producers of hazardous pesticides.

Some of the world's biggest polluters – the USA (which accounts for 36 per cent of carbon emissions) and Australia (the biggest polluter per capita in the world) have been very slow to commit to reducing their emission of industrial pollutants such as carbon dioxide (that is, greenhouse emissions). However, in 2014 the United States agreed to cut its emissions to 26–28% below 2005 levels by 2025 whilst in 2015, China, the world's largest carbon emitter, pledged to cut its greenhouse gas emissions per unit of gross domestic product by 60–65% from 2005 levels. However, despite this progress, sustainable development is always going to be undermined by the developed world's level of consumption and the continual rises in living standards and social expectations regarding consumption in the developing world itself. China, for example, has openly stated that it will not adopt environmental goals that prevent its people enjoying the standards of living that people in the Western world take for granted.

Appropriate development

The concept of sustainable development has been supplemented by the concept of appropriate development. This suggests that 'small is beautiful' and ecological outcomes should have precedence over GNP. Moreover, such development should be operated by people in their localities, without the need for Western expertise or capital.

A good example of inappropriate development would be the provision of diesel-powered electric generators, which rely on both oil and spare parts from the developed world. An example of appropriate development is technology that is not only sustainable – wind or solar power, for example – but can also be operated using only local experts. Elkington (1999) notes that there is tension between economic development and environmental concerns "with one side trying to force through new rules and standards, and the other trying to roll them back". The slogan "think global, act local" is fast becoming the mantra of sustainable development. Elkington argues that if the world does not put environmental and social responsibility on a similar level to economic prosperity, it will run the very real risk of extinction.

Wind farms such as this are an example of appropriate development: sustainable and relatively low maintenance.

How important is the environment to your decision-making when you decide to buy or upgrade a mobile phone? What do you think happens to your obsolete phone when you dispose of it?

WARS AND CONFLICT IN THE DEVELOPING WORLD

Duffield (2001) observes that, in the early 1990s, the main concern of the international community regarding conflict in the developing world was essentially humanitarian and focused on supporting civilians in war zones. However, the emphasis shifted during the mid-1990s, and the need to address the issue of war and conflict became a central concern within development theory. Duffield goes on to argue that "development is ultimately impossible without stability, and, at the same time, security is not sustainable without development." In other words, war impedes development.

Duffield argues that this new interest in the relationship between development and conflict has been motivated by globalisation – specifically the realisation that an excluded developing world may encourage international instability through war, criminal activity and terrorism. As Duffield notes, within this new security framework, "underdevelopment has become dangerous" and is often a motivation to engage in conflict and war.

"Old" wars and "new" wars

A useful way to begin an analysis of war and conflict in the developing world is to examine Mary Kaldor's (2006) distinction between "old" wars and "new" wars. According to Kaldor, old wars, which mainly took place in the first half of the 20th century, have five major characteristics:

› They were total wars in that they involved a vast mobilisation of men and arms by nations.

› They were public confrontations because they generally involved battles between opposing armies on battlefields although the Second World War saw the "privatisation of war and conflict" – civilians or non-combatants were targeted for the first time through mass indiscriminate bombing and concentration camps.

› Violence was socially organised and legitimised. Ideologies such as patriotism, antifascism, communism

and democracy became the justifications for the old wars.

› Technology and industry were focused on the mass production of weapons of destruction, such as tanks, ships and aircraft, and atomic and nuclear weapons.

› Democratic countries entered into alliances with one another, for example, in organisations such as NATO.

Kaldor argues that the wars that have broken out in the developing world differ considerably from old wars. She refers to wars in the developing world as "new" wars. Keen (1995) refers to them as "privatised" or "informal" wars because they are not normally focused on attacking other countries but rather they involve internal groups competing for resources and territory. Duffield (1998) calls them "postmodern" wars because they take advantage of new media technologies such as satellite phones, while Shaw (2000) refers to such wars as "degenerate" wars because they often have genocidal aspects.

The characteristics of "new wars"

Kaldor suggests the new wars of the developing world have the following characteristics.

› *Identity politics* – many of the new wars are focused on identity politics – groups develop grievances based on national, clan, tribal, religious and linguistic differences. For example, Collier observes that the Rwandan civil war in the 1990s was caused by tribal differences and resentments. Many rebel groups are financed by members of their communities who have chosen to live or have been exiled abroad (**diaspora** communities). For example, the Tamil Tiger rebels in Sri Lanka were funded by Canadian Tamils.

UNDERSTAND THE CONCEPT

The **diaspora** refers to ethnic or religious communities that have exiled themselves, usually in the West, because of persecution, war or lack of economic opportunities in their own countries.

› *Different modes of warfare* – the new wars involve guerrilla warfare and counter-insurgency rather than mass battles. Territory is captured and controlled by sowing fear and hatred, and the use of forced resettlement and genocidal mass murder, known as 'ethnic cleansing', is common. This type of violence is therefore mainly aimed at civilians rather than soldiers of the opposing army. It has produced a dramatic increase in the number of refugees and displaced persons. Widespread human rights abuse is now a central feature of today's new wars.

> *Globalised financing* – new wars are financed by a globalised war economy. Rebels finance themselves through plunder, hostage-taking and the black market, or through external assistance – funding from their diaspora, the hijacking of aid, and support from neighbouring governments.

> *Shadow economies* – Duffield suggests that war and conflict in the developing world are made worse by the development of informal or 'shadow' economies which involve trade in drugs, blood diamonds, ivory and oil. TNCs may advance massive amounts of funding to rebel movements in return for resource concessions in the event of a rebel victory. Western arms companies, in all likelihood, will provide the weapons required.

> *The effects of globalised culture* – Kaldor notes that rebel leaders or warlords are often influenced by globalised culture. She argues that "the effect of television, radio or videos on what often is a non-reading public cannot be overestimated." Rebel leaders and their followers often display the symbols of a global mass culture – Mercedes cars, Rolex watches, Ray-Ban sunglasses – combined with the labels that signify their own unique brand of cultural identity.

War and underdevelopment

In 1998, a study of 34 of the world's poorest countries found that two-thirds of them had either recently been involved in a civil war or were currently in one. It can therefore be concluded that poverty and underdevelopment are high risk factors with regard to civil conflict.

Collier agrees that underdevelopment can lead to civil war. He argues that civil wars, particularly in Africa, often occur in countries in which state revenues have declined because the economy is failing to grow. Collier notes that low income produces poverty and low economic growth produces hopelessness. Young men, who are the recruits for rebel armies, come cheap in an environment of hopeless poverty. Collier argues that life itself in developing societies is cheap, and joining a rebel movement gives young men a chance of riches.

Collier also highlights the "coup trap". Many governments are more at risk from coups by their armed forces than from rebellion. Duffield argues that coups and civil war violence complicate and deepen poverty and underdevelopment. Collier describes civil war as "development in reverse" because it damages both the country and its neighbours. On average, a civil war reduces economic growth by around 2.3 per cent. A seven-year civil war can mean that a country is 15 per cent worse off in terms of economic growth. Economic growth also stagnates because conflict often destroys or undermines agricultural and industrial production, trade and development assets such as power grids and transport systems.

Education, which is central to development, is also massively disrupted by war. For example, Short (1999) notes that the 15-year civil war in Mozambique destroyed 70 per cent of the country's schools. Social capital, too – particularly community stability – is disrupted by war because ethnic groups no longer trust one another.

The experience of having been through a civil war roughly doubles the risk of another conflict. Collier estimates that there is only a 50:50 chance of achieving 10 years of peace in developing societies that have recently experienced civil war. For the majority of young, poor members of rebel groups, killing is the only way they know to earn a living. Moreover, in many countries in the developing world, the surplus of cheap guns does not help improve the prospects for a peaceful future.

The effects of armed conflict on children
During civil war, rebel groups often recruit children as child soldiers. Children are also likely to be the victims of such conflicts. Despite international treaties, thousands of children worldwide fight in armies and paramilitary forces. In 1999, Amnesty International claimed that at least 300,000 children under the age of 18 were actively involved in armed conflict in countries such as Sierra Leone, Liberia, Congo, Sudan, Uganda, Sri Lanka and Burma. Many child soldiers are involved in conflicts and atrocities involuntarily. They are coerced into violence through fear that they themselves will be killed. Children are also disproportionately the victims of war in terms of deaths and, alongside women, are disproportionately likely to be displaced from their home and to be refugees. (See the Focus on Skills activity in Book 1, Topic 3, Chapter 5 for more reasons why young people become involved in violent conflict.)

FOCUS ON SKILLS: CIVIL WAR AND BLOOD DIAMONDS

From 1991 to 2002, the West African nation of Sierra Leone was ravaged by civil war when the Revolutionary United Front (RUF) took up arms against the government. The conflict was particularly brutal. The RUF soldiers destroyed villages and raped women. A high number of children were killed but many were also recruited as soldiers and given hallucinogenic drugs and amphetamines. These child soldiers became notorious for hacking off people's limbs with machetes. Over 100, 000 people were mutilated in this fashion. Much of Sierra Leone's infrastructure, its schools and hospitals, was destroyed by the RUF. 2 million refugees were created by the war which put immense economic pressure on Sierra Leone's neighbours, therefore creating more political instability in the region.

The RUF were initially motivated by a desire to rid the country of the vast inequalities that existed between the urban elites and the rural poor but their leaders were eventually corrupted by the riches offered by Sierra Leone's diamond reserves. The civil war therefore became a war for the control of the diamond mines. Thousands of people were enslaved by the RUF to work in them. Diamonds therefore made the RUF leaders very wealthy and also funded the weaponry and the army of young men required to sustain the civil war.

The rebel leader, Laurent Kabila, said that as little as $10,000 could buy an army of young men. These men were desperate for some sort of income and security, and therefore often had little alternative but to fight. Also, those who did try to leave were often executed for disloyalty.

Diamonds from Sierra Leone and other war-torn regions are known as 'blood' or 'conflict' diamonds because thousands of people have died either in the attempt to control the local trade or in the illegal mining operations. These diamonds were being traded on the open market, despite their origins, by diamond transnationals in the 1990s. However, after a global protest movement which put pressure on global transnational corporations dealing in diamonds, all diamond-producing countries and diamond-trading TNCs agreed to sign up to the Kimberley Process in 2003 which means that all diamonds have to be certified 'conflict free' before they can be bought and sold in the global diamond market.

Questions

1. **Explain.** Give two examples of ways in which the RUF terrorised the local population.

2. **Explain** why Laurent Kabila argues that all that is needed to start a civil war is $10,000.

3. **Analyse** why Kaldor might describe the civil war in Sierra Leone as a 'new war'.

4. **Analyse** the impact of the Kimberley Process on war in the developing world.

5. **Evaluate.** Using information from this source and elsewhere, assess the relationship between poverty and war in the developing world.

CONCLUSIONS

Most sociologists working in this field conclude that war in the developing world should not be dismissed as a 'little local difficulty'. Rather, they argue that such wars are linked to the way that the global system of trade is organised, in that it creates the conditions for poverty in the developing world. Most importantly, these wars have implications for the West. Duffield (2007) notes that globalisation has also brought into existence a "shrinking and radically interconnected world", in which war and conflict in distant lands, which 20 years ago would have had little relevance to our everyday lives, now directly affect the security of our society and the standard of living we take for granted. Consequently it is now quite normal for the leaders of Western societies to conclude that poverty, civil war, failed states and terrorism are inter-linked, and that therefore we ignore war and conflict in developing societies at our peril.

CHECK YOUR UNDERSTANDING

1. Explain what is meant by the term 'bilateral aid'.

2. Explain what is meant by 'the bad governance trap'.

3. Explain what is meant by 'the green revolution'.

4. Explain what is meant by 'tied aid'.

5. Identify and briefly outline two differences between 'old wars' and 'new wars'.

6. Identify and briefly explain how export-oriented industrialisation was responsible for the success of the Asian Tiger economies.

7. Analyse two differences between cities in the developed world and cities in the developing world.

8. Assess the impact of foreign aid on developing societies.

9. Evaluate the view that development is undermined by war and conflict.

10. Evaluate the view that trade, industrialisation and urbanisation are essential components of the development process.

TAKE IT FURTHER

1. Bananas provide a really interesting topic to research if you want to understand the way that world trade is loaded in favour of the developed world. In 2003, a 'trade war' broke out between Europe (which supports bananas produced by a confederation of Caribbean countries) and the USA (which supports bananas produced by American transnationals in Latin America). Find out as much as you can about this. Your school or college Geography department may have copies of the following useful books: *Global Challenges* (Digby, 2001) or *Population, Resources and Development* (Chrispin and Jegede, 2000). You could also visit the website of the Caribbean Banana Exporters Association – www.cbea.org – in order to investigate how they view their relationship with the developed world.

   Your research should focus on the following:
   > the role of past colonial relations

   > the role of TNCs

   > tariffs

   > trade blocs

   > the role of the World Trade Organisation

   > the impact on both Caribbean and South American farmers.

2. Update yourself on recent crises caused by debt by visiting the following sites: www.debtchannel.org and www.makepovertyhistory.org

3. If you are interested in researching the effect of blood diamonds on conflict in developing societies, visit www.stopblooddiamonds.org. or www.globalwitness.org/campaigns/conflict-diamonds
   You could also watch the film *Blood Diamond* from 2006.

3.5 ASPECTS OF DEVELOPMENT: EMPLOYMENT, EDUCATION, HEALTH, POPULATION AND GENDER

LEARNING OBJECTIVES

> Demonstrate knowledge and understanding of the employment, education, health, population and gender aspects of development (AO1).

> Demonstrate knowledge and understanding of the different sociological perspectives on the patterns and causes of these aspects of development (AO1).

> Apply this knowledge to contemporary societies (AO2).

> Evaluate sociological explanations in order to make judgements and draw conclusions about the significance of these aspects of development (AO3).

INTRODUCING THE DEBATE

Modernisation and neo-liberal theories of development stress that if countries are to progress up the development ladder and to achieve the economic success that is taken for granted by the developed West, they need to slow down their population growth and invest in education and health care. It is particularly argued that if girls and women are educated, then fertility, birth and infant mortality rates will naturally fall especially if jobs for women are available. However, critics of these theories argue that this process is not as simple and straightforward as modernisation theory and neo-liberals claim.

THE CHANGING NATURE OF EMPLOYMENT AS A RESULT OF DEVELOPMENT

Peet and Hartwick (2015) observe that economic activity – work, labour and trade – has become globalised. There now exists a global division of labour (see Chapters 2, 3 and 4), as transnational corporations increasingly outsource work that was once exclusively done in Western workplaces to factories, call centres and packing plants in the export processing zones (EPZs) or free trade zones (FTZs) of developing countries. For example, India has benefited enormously from foreign corporations creating jobs in IT, financial services, pharmaceuticals and automotive components, which exist to service the West. McMichael observes that, in one Delhi call centre servicing British bank customers, Indian recruits receive a 20-hour crash course in British culture – "they watch videos of British soap operas to accustom them to regional accents. They learn about Yorkshire pudding. And they are taught about Britain's unfailingly miserable climate."

Explain why Indian call centre workers are taught about British culture.

The development of the world economy and the globalisation of labour have transformed employment across the world in a number of ways. According to the World Development Report (2015), more than 3 billion people in the world have jobs, but the nature of those jobs varies greatly.

> Some 1.65 billion workers have regular wages or salaries. Most of these workers are in the developed world. Most of this labour is formal in that the worker leaves their home, goes to a place of business, works a number of set hours and is paid a wage or salary on which they pay tax.

> However, the nature of this work has changed dramatically over the past 50 years in Western countries such as the UK. The economy and therefore work in the UK used to be dominated by manufacturing industry. The workforce was found mainly in factory environments. However, UK industry went into decline from the 1960s as demand for British goods was undermined by cheaper exports from China

and the developing world. Many British corporations also chose to outsource work to the EPZs and FTZs of the developing world because costs were lower and profits higher. The UK economy shifted so that it became more service-oriented. Formal wage labour in the UK is now mainly provided by service industries such as the government and financial sectors as well as the retail and personal service industries, for example, hotels, restaurants, coffee shops, fast food outlets.

> Formal waged work is increasingly found in the cities, EPZs and FTZs of the developing world in which transnational corporations have built factories, although such work often lacks the legal protection that Western workers take for granted. It is often insecure, casual, low-paid, demeaning, poorly unionised and involves long unsociable hours.

> The majority of workers in the developing world (1.5 billion) work in the informal sector. This type of work often involves maintaining crops or livestock on family plots of land. This does not pay a wage. Its economic value lies in the fact that it is a means of ensuring the family's survival. Other types of informal work found in the developing world include the recycling of waste products (which 'employs' 250,000 people in Mumbai, India), casual agricultural labour (such as picking vegetables, fruit and cotton), selling fruit, vegetable and cooked foods on the streets, working from home preparing raw materials for processing in TNC factories and so on. This type of work and the money that it generates cannot be considered as a regular income. It is often casual and precarious. Fields (2014) argues that all of these types of informal work involve people 'working hard but working poor'.

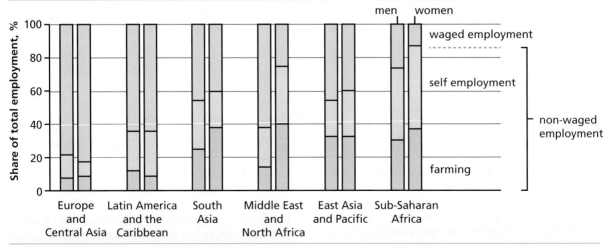

Figure 3.5.1 A job does not always come with a wage

Source: World Development Report, World Bank (2013)

> Global migration, especially from the developing world to the developed world, as well as from rural regions to the cities of the developing world, has led to a massive increase in the global number of domestic workers. According to the International Labour Organisation (ILO) there were at least 52 million domestic workers worldwide in 2014. Domestic workers work in the homes of others for pay and provide a range of services such as cleaning, washing, cooking, caring for children, gardening and driving. In the Middle East, one out of three women waged employees is a domestic worker, and in Latin America and the Caribbean, the figure is one in four. There is some evidence that some domestic labourers are kept in a state of near-slavery (especially in the Middle East) and/or subjected to moral, sexual and physical abuse.

Employment and women

Martell (2010) observes that women are increasingly a resource for global capitalism because millions of women have been incorporated into the production process, particularly in developing societies as low-wage labour. Peet and Hartwick suggest that "women arguably are becoming the majority of the new global working-class, pitted against global financial and industrial capital that is male-dominated." 1.2 billion (40 per cent) of the world's 3 billion workers are female. Peet and Hartwick argue that global development has pushed women in the developing world into jobs that have changed their social and economic status. A number of observations can be made about women's employment:

> Women are more likely to have paid jobs and careers in middle-income developing societies and the developed West.

> Women continue to earn significantly less than men, whether they are in the developed or developing world.

> 90 per cent of workers in factories in the developing world are female. Martell argues that this is positive because it means such women have incomes that are independent of men and consequently they can gain some independence from patriarchal structures. However, Martell also points out that such work is often exploitative, both in conditions and pay, and is often unprotected by law. Female workers are often dismissed if they fall ill or pregnant. Membership of trade unions is often illegal.

> The poorer and more undeveloped a country is, the less likely it is that women will have paid jobs. For example, in Pakistan, only 28 per cent of women work, compared with 82 per cent of men.

> The World Bank notes that there are 79 countries in the developing world that have laws that restrict the types of jobs that women can do.

> Martell argues that unemployment has become feminised because women's unemployment has risen faster than men's. The World Development Report (2015) shows that almost 2 billion working-age adults in the developing world are neither working in waged work nor looking for it; the majority of these are women.

> Despite the increase in numbers of jobs in factories in the developing world, the majority of women are in informal employment. For example, the UN observes that in many rural areas, women depend on small-scale subsistence farming for their survival. The UN also estimated in 2014 that in South Asia, over 80 per cent of women in non-agricultural jobs were in informal employment compared with 74 per cent in sub-Saharan Africa.

> Martell notes that women from developing societies are more likely to be involved in 'sex work' in developed societies because of human trafficking, which often involves deception or force. Global tourism means that women may be involved in sex work in their home country too.

> Women workers in both the developed and undeveloped worlds often have to cope with the dual burden of work outside the home and domestic responsibilities within the home. Time use studies around the world clearly show that women spend considerably more time than men in non-market unpaid family work. However, it should be noted that 'housework' in the developing world is very different from that done by Western women because it includes tasks such as fetching water, gathering firewood as well as nursing children. Women in the developing world often lack the domestic technology that women in the developed world probably take for granted. This means that women in the developing world probably have less leisure time than women in the developed world.

What social and cultural factors might be responsible for the majority of women in a society failing to seek work?

Child labour

The World Development Report observes that although global child labour is in decline, it still affects 1 in 8 children. The International Labour Organization (ILO) defines child labour as any work by a child under age 12 or, for a child above age 12, any work that impedes education or is damaging to health and personal development. Worldwide, 306 million children were at work in 2008. Of these, 215 million were engaged in activities that constituted child labour, and 115 million were involved in hazardous work. Most of these children are unpaid family workers. More than half live in Asia and the Pacific region; but the highest numbers are found in sub-Saharan Africa, where child labour affects 1 in 4 children (or 65 million of them).

Recent research shows that children work for diverse and complex reasons. These include:

> The need for all members of a family to work in order to overcome household poverty. In this sense, children are economic assets.

> There may be no schools available or schooling may not be affordable without the income from a job. The majority of children who attend school in many parts of the developing world are also working, according to the World Development Report.

In family farming and small household enterprises, children's work leads to the acquisition of skills important to subsistence.

The impact of urbanisation on employment

Before 2020, more than half of the total population in developing countries is expected to be living in cities and towns. The growth of the non-agricultural labour force in the developing world now exceeds the growth of the agricultural labour force. Observers have noted that the transformation from rural to urban is so quick that families may have a foot in both agricultural and industrial-urban employment. For example, one member of a family may have a job in an EPZ factory, another may have a service industry job as a taxi-driver, while some women and children may work on a smallholding tending animals and crops, or in a cottage industry in the home preparing textiles for the local factory.

Women in particular have benefited from urbanisation, especially in Asia. There are many more job opportunities in cities for women, especially in the factories of the EPZs and FTZs. Women often have to work because the wages of their husbands' jobs often do not generate enough income to support the family.

Migration to the cities is likely to increase urban unemployment, particularly among young people. The World Development Report identifies 200 million people in the developing world as unemployed and actively looking for work. A disproportionate number of these are young people. The ILO reports that most urban unemployment in developing countries is actually underemployment, in which people are obliged to undertake any available informal economic activity, however poorly paid and unproductive, because there is no welfare state. In Ghana, for example, one survey put the unemployment rate at 1.6 per cent of the workforce, but the rate of underemployment was nearly 25 per cent.

In sub-Saharan Africa, the urban informal sector (which can include such activities as small-scale peddling, petty services or work in unregistered factories) is estimated to employ more than 60 per cent of the urban labour force at extremely low incomes. In Latin America, and the Caribbean, 83 per cent of all new jobs created between 1990 and 1993 were in the informal sector; the bulk of these jobs were low-paid, insecure, unsafe and of low productivity.

Employment and poverty

In 2015, the World Bank announced that, for the first time, less than 10 per cent of the world's population will be living in extreme poverty by the end of that year. This decline has occurred because of increased employment opportunities, especially the creation of millions of new, more productive jobs, mostly in Asia. More people in the developing world have jobs now than ever before, and those jobs, despite being low-paid (compared with wages in the developed world) provide a better standard of living than subsistence agricultural work.

However, jobs in the developing world are vulnerable to global economic downturns. Economic crises, which may start in a single country, often become global and can have a devastating effect on labour markets in both the developed and developing worlds. For example, in 1997, a speculative attack on Thailand's currency severely affected the economies of Indonesia, Malaysia and South Korea. In 2007, an alarming rise in food prices across the world resulted in problems with food supply and inflation, increased poverty and reduced real wages in parts of the developing world. The 2008 banking crisis initiated a global crisis that resulted in 22 million new unemployed in a single year. It is estimated that the 2008 crisis cost China between 20 million and 36 million jobs, particularly among migrant workers in export-oriented sectors. In Mexico, it caused a decline of half a million jobs between 2008 and the second quarter of 2009, particularly among women, young and older workers, as well as a 10 per cent drop in real wages.

Migration of skilled labour to the developed world

Dodani and LaPorte (2005) argue that a "brain drain" is taking place as skilled workers from the developing world emigrate, either legally or illegally, to the developed world. They suggest this is not only for 'pull' reasons, such as the availability of jobs, a better quality of life, higher salaries, and access to advanced technology, but also for 'push' reasons, such as unstable political conditions (the civil war in Syria is an example), religious persecution and unemployment in their country of origin. This brain drain has a negative impact on developing societies, as they experience a shortage of doctors, nurses, scientists, teachers, engineers and so on. However, on a positive note, there is evidence that such migrant workers may assist the development of their home countries by sending money home. For example, $530 billion was transferred to developing countries in 2012 by migrants working in the West.

Some politicians argue that the UK benefits greatly from migrant labour while others suggest that it brings about unemployment and lowers wages. Using the NHS as an example, assess the pros and cons of migrant labour.

THE ROLE OF EDUCATION IN DEVELOPMENT

Most sociologists working in the development field see education as an essential component of development. One of the eight Millennium Development Goals (MDGs), for example, focuses on the need to achieve universal primary education. Most people working in the field accept that education is a basic human right and a significant factor in the development of children, communities, and countries. It is seen as essential in breaking inter-generational chains of poverty because education, especially for girls, is fundamentally linked to other development goals, such as economic growth, gender empowerment, improving maternal health, reducing child mortality and fighting the spread of HIV. For example, education and qualifications can empower females both economically and personally, and this enables them to make confident choices that benefit their health and futures, such as delaying marriage, choosing to use contraception and choosing to reject female genital cutting. This is supported in the study by Murthi *et al.* (1995), who found that in quantitative terms the effect of female literacy on lowering child mortality is extraordinarily large.

Modernisation theory and education
Modernisation theory subscribes to human capital theory, the notion that if money is invested in a population, then the return in terms of skill, aspiration and efficiency will greatly benefit the economy. Hoselitz (1960) argued

that the introduction of meritocratic education systems (paid for by official aid and borrowing) would speed up the spread of Western values such as universalism, individualism, competition and achievement, measured by examinations and qualifications. These values are seen as essential to the production of an efficient, motivated, geographically mobile factory workforce in the developing world.

Modernisation theory also suggested that the children of the political and economic elites of traditional countries should be educated in Western schools, universities and military academies so that these future leaders of the developing world could then disseminate Western values down to the mass of the population. See also Chapter 1 for more discussion of the role of education, especially the creation of the 'modern entrepreneurial man' in modernisation theory.

Sen (1999) argues that education is the key that unlocked the economic success of China and the Asian Tiger countries. He notes that when China turned to marketisation in 1979 it already had a highly literate people, and good schooling facilities across the country. South Korea and Taiwan also had educated populations, who grabbed the economic opportunities being offered by a supportive market system.

The state of global education
Despite the focus on education in the MDGs, the evidence regarding global education is not positive. A UNESCO report published in 2014 stated that 175 million – or one in four – young people in developing countries lacked even basic literacy skills, and that poor-quality education had left a "legacy of illiteracy" more widespread than previously believed. An estimated 250 million children were not learning basic reading and maths skills, according to the report, even though half of them had spent at least four years in school. Many developing countries have rapidly increased their teacher numbers by hiring people without training. This may help get more children into school but UNESCO warned that it puts education quality in jeopardy. This "global learning crisis" is costing developing countries billions of dollars a year in wasted education funding.

There is little sign of progress in adult literacy. In 2014, there were 775 million illiterate adults, a decline of 1 per cent since 2000. This figure is projected to fall only slightly, to 743 million, by 2015. Ten countries – India, China, Pakistan, Bangladesh, Nigeria, Ethiopia, Egypt, Brazil, Indonesia and the Democratic Republic of the Congo – account for almost three-quarters of the world's illiterate adults. Globally, almost two-thirds of these illiterate adults are women, a figure that has remained almost static since 1990.

245

UNESCO argues that literacy and adult education have suffered from relative neglect because attention has mainly focused on boosting primary school attendance rates in poor countries. Moreover, this target has obscured differences in wealth and poverty. For example, if current trends continue, the wealthiest boys in sub-Saharan Africa will achieve universal primary completion in 2021, while the poorest girls will have to wait until 2086.

The Brookings Institute (2015) estimates that if education is measured by average levels of attainment – how much children have learned and how long they have spent in school – then the developing world is about 100 years behind developed countries. These poorer countries still have average levels of education in the 21st century that were achieved in many Western countries by the early decades of the 20th century. Furthermore, Brookings found that the education levels of the adult workforce in the developed world, measured by average numbers of years of school, is double that of workers in the developing world.

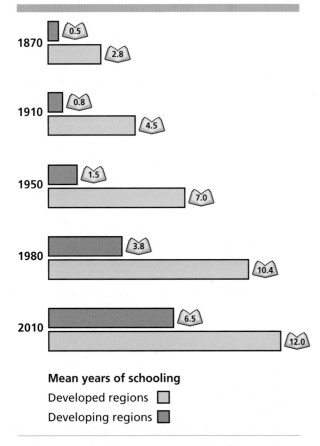

Mean years of schooling

Developed regions ▢
Developing regions ▣

Figure 3.5.2 A graph to show the average number of years of education finished by an adult in the developed world and the developing world

Source: Morrisson and Murtin (2013)

Dependency theory

Marxists identify a number of reasons for inequalities in education between the developed and developing world:

> Governments in developing societies often lack the financial resources to invest in education, because the country does not earn enough in foreign exports, or because money that could be invested in education has been diverted into debt repayments.

> The IMF or the World Bank may have attached conditions to loans that insist on cutting public spending on free education.

> Poverty means that people, especially in sub-Saharan Africa, cannot afford to pay for education, which in many societies is not free.

> Poverty may mean that parents may prefer that their children work to supplement household income, do household chores, or care for sick family members. In African countries afflicted by AIDS, children may stay out of school to care for sick parents or orphaned siblings.

> Poverty may blind parents to the value of education. They may believe that jobs in the local economy do not require academic skills, or they may simply be unaware of the opportunities that exist, especially if they are uneducated themselves.

> A government may lack the political will to meet its citizens' educational needs because of corruption or because it practises discrimination against particular groups.

> Some societies practise patriarchal discrimination against females because of their cultural and religious traditions. If parents live in a community that devalues education or frowns upon educating girls, they may be reluctant to violate social norms.

In addition, the poverty that exists in developing societies may mean that schools are housed in inadequate buildings. They may also lack resources such as textbooks, writing materials and science laboratories. Developing societies may not be able to afford to train or pay teachers. Attendance at school may be affected by the fact that children may not be vaccinated against diseases such as malaria. Civil war also disrupts education.

Freire (1972) argued that imposing Western-style education in developing societies, with its emphasis on competition, individualism and achievement, is inappropriate. He argued that education in the developing world should be organised around the value-systems of the developing world. In this sense, education should be collaborative, teaching should be a process of dialogue and enquiry, and educational knowledge should focus on how people could value their indigenous culture and their environment. He regarded education as an empowering process which could eventually alter the unfair and exploitative social, cultural and economic relationships that the developing world has had with the West by providing transformative local community-based solutions to development problems.

Finally, McCloskey (2015) suggests that "development education" should focus on educating people in the developed world so that they understand the underlying causes of global inequality. Julius Nyerere, the former president of Tanzania, echoed this point when he said, "Take every penny you have set aside in aid for Tanzania, and spend it in the UK explaining to people the facts and causes of poverty" (quoted in McCloskey).

McCloskey argues that if people knew the real causes of poverty in the developing world:

> the unequal nature of world trade

> the ineffectiveness of aid

> how debt undermines spending on education and health

> the exploitation of the economies of poor countries by TNCs

> the neo-liberal conditions attached to loans

they might support the efforts of the anti-globalisation movement as well as putting pressure on their own politicians to bring about change.

In your opinion, is education of young people in the developed world about the causes of underdevelopment essential to tackling global inequality?

HEALTH-CARE SYSTEMS AND HEALTH AND ILLNESS IN DEVELOPING COUNTRIES

The nature of health and illness in developing countries

In the wealthy developed countries, the main causes of death are the so-called 'diseases of affluence' – cancer, strokes and heart disease – mainly caused by 'excessive' lifestyles, for example, too much fatty food, obesity, alcohol and smoking. In contrast, people in the developing world are more likely to die of 'diseases of poverty' – preventable and treatable diseases – caused by lack of access to amenities that Western populations take for granted, such as nutritional diets, clean water, vaccination and maternal care.

Some countries have made impressive gains in achieving health-related targets relating to the MDGs, but there are still major inequalities in health outcomes between the developed and developing world. For example:

> In some parts of sub-Saharan Africa premature adult death rates are nearly four times higher than those experienced in Western European countries. The most shocking fact is that, while life expectancy is generally increasing across the world, in Africa the reverse is true – adults in Africa today die younger than in 1990.

> Half a million women die each year as a consequence of pregnancy and childbirth. Of these deaths, 99 per cent are in the developing world. The maternal death rate in developing countries in 2014 was 479 per 100,000 live births, compared with 27 per 100,000 in developed countries.

> According to the World Health Organisation, the world infant mortality rate for under-fives per 1,000 live births has decreased from an estimated rate of 63 in 1990 to 32 in 2015. However, according to the World Bank, infant mortality rates in developing countries in 2015 are significantly higher than the UK. For example, Angola has an infant mortality rate of 157 per 1,000 live births whilst it is 120 in Sierra Leone and 91 in Afghanistan compared with a rate of only 4 in the UK. Globally 6.3 million children under the age of five died in 2013. More than half of these early child deaths are due to conditions that could be prevented or treated with access to simple, affordable interventions.

> It is estimated that 30,000 children a day die of preventable diseases, especially communicable diseases caused by infected and polluted water supplies, and particularly in sub-Saharan Africa. Thirteen million African children were killed by diarrhoea alone in the 1990s. In 2014, about a quarter of all children in developing societies – 800 million – were suffering from malnutrition, which weakens resistance to infections such as measles, and to other diseases.

> In 2014, about 35 million people were living with HIV/AIDS, the majority of them in low-income African countries.

Modernisation theory and health

Modernisation theory argues that developing societies need to follow the same evolutionary path as developed societies. The latter also experienced diseases of poverty in the early years of industrialisation, but as they experienced economic growth, the standard of living of Western societies improved, which meant that the mass of the population had access to nutritious food, better public health in terms of clean water and sanitation, improved housing, and an increasingly sophisticated system of health care. Life expectancy therefore dramatically increased and mortality rates fell, especially among children and women. It is therefore argued that developing societies will soon make this progress as their economies grow along Western lines. In the meantime, foreign aid programmes can assist by building hospitals, vaccinating children and importing antiretroviral drugs for the care of HIV/AIDS patients.

Dependency theory

Marxists identify a number of neo-colonial reasons why developing societies experience inequalities in health:

1. Poverty, which from a Marxist perspective is caused by the deliberate underdevelopment of poorer countries by the West, is the main cause of health inequalities. Poverty has a number of consequences for health.

   › It often results in malnutrition for children, which makes it difficult for them physically to fight disease.

   › It means societies often lack the cash to invest in public-health systems such as clean water, toilets and sewerage systems. Water-borne diseases caused by sewage are major causes of death in many developing societies.

   › It means that many developing societies do not have the money to invest in national health-care systems or even to immunise their children. This means that, while richer nations have on average one doctor for every 520 people, in the poorest developing countries, the ratio is one doctor for every 17,000 people. Developing societies also often lack the funds to import drugs and vaccines from Western pharmaceutical companies.

2. The fact that many developing countries are in debt to the West is one of the reasons they lack the money to invest in health-care systems. There is evidence that the more a country pays to reduce its debt as a percentage of its earnings, the more likely its infant mortality rate is to increase, because it has less money to invest in essential medicines

or the wages of doctors and nurses. Moreover, the conditions attached by agencies such as the IMF and the World Bank often result in cuts in public spending in areas such as health. Peet and Hardwick (2015) claim that the "structural adjustments" required of developing countries by the World Bank in the 1980s ended up killing millions of children.

3. Another problem faced by the developing world is the high cost of manufactured pharmaceuticals and medical technology, which are mainly produced by Western-based multi-national companies and which developing societies often cannot afford. These big-pharma TNCs have been accused of exploiting the African AIDS epidemic for profit, in that the prices they charge the developing world for these drugs is well in excess of their costs. Some developing countries have responded to this by producing generic copies of essential drugs such as those aimed at treating HIV/AIDS and selling these at cost price to other developing nations (see Chapter 4).

4. Western companies have also been accused of creating further health problems in the developing world through irresponsible and aggressive advertising of unhealthy products such as baby-milk powder, cigarettes and pesticides as well as the dumping of toxic materials in the developing world.

5. Western countries have been accused of 'poaching' health-care professionals from developing countries. This has led to a 'brain drain' from the developing world to the West as health professionals migrate to secure better jobs. The NHS is heavily dependent on health workers from the developing world and would be in dire straits without them. For example, 10 per cent of nurses and 26 per cent of doctors working in the NHS come from developing societies. Sharples (2015) argues that this global brain drain exacerbates global health inequalities for two reasons.

   › It takes much needed health workers from the environment in which they are needed the most. For example, in 2014, during the Ebola crisis, Sierra Leone only had 136 doctors and 1,017 nurses, that is, one doctor for approximately every 45,000 people. In contrast, 27 doctors and 103 nurses trained in Sierra Leone were working in the UK in 2015.

   › The migration of health professionals works out to be cheaper than training indigenous British workers. In 2006 it was estimated that the money saved by the UK through the recruitment of Ghanaian health workers may have exceeded the value of the aid given to Ghana by the UK for health.

Health-care systems

Developing countries are often influenced in their choice of health-care system by the developed world. They tend to adopt systems based on the biomedical model of health intervention, which believes that the treatment of illness and disease should be left to doctors. These medical professionals often promote mass immunisation programmes to prevent the spread of diseases such as malaria, or treat those already infected by using drugs developed by big-pharma TNCs. However, this is an expensive approach and consequently funding may be inconsistent. Mortality statistics too suggest that this type of care faces a slow uphill battle in reducing health inequalities.

A more effective bottom-up approach may be that adopted by health NGOs. These tend to focus on public health initiatives located in particular communities, and involve, for example, promoting health education in areas such as hygiene, contraception, sexual activity and childcare. Such initiatives also spend money on local clean water and sanitation schemes.

However, both these approaches to health care are accused of neglecting or ignoring altogether local cultural approaches towards health care and imposing Western systems and ways of thinking about health on local people. Many traditional cultures tend to have a **holistic approach to health** in that they see the causes of illness as located in a breakdown in the relationship between the body and the mind/spirit of the ill person. Consequently these approaches believe that the mind or spirit needs to be treated in conjunction with the body if the problem is to be cured.

UNDERSTAND THE CONCEPT

A **holistic approach to health** is an approach that addresses all aspects of an individual's wellbeing together – the physical body, the environmental in which the individual is located and the individual's emotional, mental and spiritual levels of satisfaction.

In many developing countries the only health care available until a few decades ago was that based on traditional medicine and spiritual healing. Many developing governments have therefore created health systems that strike a balance between modernity and tradition. For example, India tries to make traditional remedies safely available to as many people as possible, but has modern biomedical techniques available too.

How important is poor health in holding back progress in developing societies?

DEMOGRAPHIC CHANGE: TRENDS, CAUSES AND SIGNIFICANCE FOR DEVELOPMENT

The sociological study of population change is known as 'demography'. Sociologists believe that it is important to study demographic trends, such as those associated with birth, fertility, infant mortality, death and migration, because they can produce insights into why societies experience social change.

World population growth

In 1925, there were only two billion people on the planet. In 2015, the population of the world was 7.3 billion people. The world has therefore experienced a massive rise in population in the past 100 years. Two aspects of this rise stand out:

> The increase in world population has been phenomenally rapid. This can be illustrated with the fact that the fifth billionth human born is about 12 years old, the fourth billionth is about 25 years old, while the third billionth is approximately 40 years old.

> Most of this increase has occurred in the developing world. World population increases by about 83 million people annually. Ninety-nine per cent of this increase occurs in the less developed regions of Africa, Asia, Latin America and the Caribbean. Six countries account for half of the increase in world population: India, China, Pakistan, Nigeria, Bangladesh and Indonesia. In contrast, the population of the developed world has fallen.

The United Nations forecasts that, by 2050, the world's population will hit 9.2 billion. Nine out of every ten people in 2050 will live in a developing country. In contrast, only three of the more developed countries, the United States, Russia and Japan, are expected to remain among the most populous by 2025. In particular, population levels in Europe are projected to decline sharply.

Sociological explanations: neo-Malthusian modernisation theory

In his *Essay on the Principle of Population* in 1798, Thomas Malthus (1766–1834) argued that populations increase in size at a much faster rate than the ability of those same populations to feed themselves. He concluded that these limits on food supply would lead to natural checks on population, such as famine and malnutrition – and perhaps even war – as people fought over scarce resources. Such checks limit population because they increase death rates.

Malthus's ideas have been adopted by the biologist Paul Ehrlich who, in his book *The Population Bomb* (1968), argued "the battle to feed all humanity is over" after studying the figures for birth rates and death rates and comparing them with food production and

FOCUS ON SKILLS: HEALTH CARE IN CUBA

According to the UN's World Health Organization (WHO), Cuba's health care system is an example for all countries of the world. The Cuban health system is recognised worldwide for its excellence and its efficiency. Despite extremely limited resources and the dramatic impact caused by the economic sanctions imposed by the United States for more than half a century, Cuba has managed to guarantee access to care for all segments of the population and obtain results similar to those of the most developed nations.

With an infant mortality rate of 4.2 per thousand births, the Caribbean island is the best performer on the continent and in the Third World generally. This is also demonstrated by the quality of its health care system and the impact it has on the well-being of children and pregnant women. The infant mortality rate in Cuba is lower than it is in the United States and is among the lowest in the world.

With a life expectancy of 78 years, Cuba is one of the best performers on the American continent and in the Third World, achieving results similar to those of most developed nations. On the average, Cubans live 30 years longer than their Haitian neighbors. In 2025, Cuba will have the highest proportion of its population over the age of 60 in all of Latin America.

Cuban expertise in the field of health also benefits the people of the Third World. Indeed, since 1963, Cuba has sent doctors and other health workers throughout the

Third World to treat the poor. Currently, nearly 30,000 Cuban medical staff are working in over 60 countries around the world. In 2014, LABIOFAM, the Cuban chemical and biopharmaceutical research institute, launched a vaccination campaign against malaria in no fewer than 15 West African countries. Similarly, Cuba trains young physicians worldwide in its Latin American School of Medicine (ELAM). Since its inception in 1998, ELAM has graduated more than 20,000 doctors from over 123 countries.

In praising Cuba, the WHO stresses that it is possible for Third-world countries with limited resources to implement an efficient health care system and provide all segments of the population with social protection worthy of the name. Cuba's health care system is based on preventive medicine and the results achieved are outstanding. According to WHO, the world should follow the example of the island in this arena and replace the curative model, inefficient and more expensive, with a prevention-based system.

Source: Cuba's Health Care System: a Model for the World by S. Lamrani, 8th August 2014, The Huffington Post

Questions

1. **Identify** two obstacles that Cuba has overcome to provide its people with an excellent health system.

2. **Explain** how Cuba benefits the health of other developing societies.

3. **Analyse** how Cuba compares with other countries, both developed and developing, with regard to infant mortality and life expectancy.

4. **Analyse** how Cuba has managed to achieve such an outstanding health care system.

5. **Evaluate**. Using information from this source and elsewhere, assess the reasons why many of the Millennium Development goals on health in the developing world have not been achieved.

malnutrition rates. Ehrlich argues that the high birth rates of developing countries have led to a population explosion that has put too much strain on their limited resources of food and energy. This, he alleges, is responsible for problems in the developing world, such as famine, malnutrition, poverty, war, desertification, (because of overuse of land), deforestation (because more land is required for housing) and increasing environmental pollution. He concludes that "the birth rate must be brought into balance with the death rate or mankind will breed itself into oblivion".

Why might high population be bad for the environment?

Modernisation theory cites overpopulation as yet another internal obstacle preventing countries from adopting Western forms of development. It is argued that the economic growth necessary for industrial development is difficult to achieve because any spare capital is unlikely to be reinvested in developing industry. Instead, it is likely to be spent feeding the growing population in order to avoid civil unrest and political instability. In addition, the infrastructure of such societies, especially their health and education systems (which are already basic), are stretched to the limit. Modernisation theory has suggested that traditional cultural beliefs are mainly responsible for this overpopulation. Modernisation highlights two types of cultural tradition as creating these barriers to development:

> Traditional religions such as Islam and Roman Catholicism, which are responsible for the high birth rates in the developing world because they oppose contraception.

> Patriarchal belief systems that deny women access to contraception, education and employment.

Solutions to overpopulation

Modernisation theory has suggested three broad solutions to the problem of overpopulation.

Family planning

Some countries such as Singapore and China have experienced state-enforced compulsory family-planning or anti-natalist schemes aimed at reducing population. Between 1966 and 1987, Singapore encouraged families to have only one child but in the late 1980s the government became concerned at the failure of female university graduates to marry and bear children because they preferred to follow a career. Moreover, there were insufficient workers to fill job vacancies and the population was ageing. In 1987 the Singapore government announced a public relations campaign to promote the joys of marriage and parenthood. It also offered financial incentives for families to have more than two children.

China restricted couples to one child for more than three decades because, in the 1950s, China's population was growing too quickly – by 1.9 per cent per year – which the Chinese government believed was unsustainable. Couples found to have more than one child were stripped of their state benefits and fined. However, this law resulted in mass abortions and dramatically changed the makeup of the population in that China now has a rapidly ageing population, a shallow labour pool and an imbalance between the sexes. The UN estimates that there are 33 million more men than women and that by 2050, China will have nearly 440 million over-60s. In 2015, China changed the law to allow all couples to have two children in an attempt to address potential future labour shortages and to address the imbalance between the sexes.

A poster for China's one child policy, which was in place until 2015

Why is an ageing population a problem in both the developed and developing worlds?

Western aid

Official aid from the West has been used to encourage the governments of developing countries to adopt family-planning and health-education policies. For example, in 2006, USAID spent over $400 million on 'population stabilisation' in developing nations in which birth rates were starting to fall. However, Catley-Carlson (1994) argues that the West's motives for family planning have been questioned in developing societies. For example, there is some evidence that some Islamic societies see birth control as part of a Western plan to reduce their populations to impose control over them more easily.

The education of women

The education of women is seen as the most important strategy required to reduce population in the developing world. It is based on the assumption that, given the choice, women would want to have fewer children. It is argued that if women's employment opportunities were improved, this would provide them with alternative sources of status and satisfaction beyond childbearing. Educated women are also generally better able and more willing to use contraceptives.

The critique of neo-Malthusianism

Ehrlich's predictions have failed to come true. Cohen and Kennedy point out that predictions of population explosions and world collapse are usually based on present trends (that is, from the period in which the author is writing). However, these are often wrong because "people change their conduct in response to earlier plausible warnings." Carnell (2000) argues that Ehrlich expected food production to decrease but it has actually increased faster than population growth because of advances in agricultural technology.

Sociological explanations: dependency theory

Sociologists working from a Marxist or socialist dependency theory perspective are very critical, for several reasons, of the neo-Malthusian idea that developing countries are responsible for the high population they experience.

1. Adamson (1986) claims that neo-Malthusians misunderstand the relationship between poverty and population. He claims that Ehrlich makes the mistake of supposing that population causes poverty. However, Adamson argues that poverty causes high population because in developing societies, children are economic assets in terms of their labour power and the extra income they can generate. They are also vital for providing security and welfare in old age, especially if no welfare state exists. Dependency theorists therefore argue that birth-control programmes will always fail if poverty is not tackled. Adamson argues "look after the population and the population will take care of itself."

2. Dependency theory also identifies a number of crucial differences between the experience of developed countries and developing nations

that undermine the neo-Malthusian argument. For example:

› Population growth in the developing world has been compressed into a much shorter period of time, and population growth rates are therefore steeper and more dramatic.

› Europe was relatively wealthy before industrialisation. It did not face the problems that the developing world faces today in terms of debt and a disadvantaged position in world trade.

› There were more economic opportunities for European populations because population increased just as the industrial revolution was taking off.

3. There is some evidence that the argument that people in the developing world are "having too many babies" is quite simply wrong. Instead, it is argued that high population growth is mainly due to a major decline in the death rate in developing societies. As the demographer Nick Eberstadt (quoted in Carnell, 2000) observed in relation to population growth: "It's not because people started breeding like rabbits. It's that they stopped dying like flies." Western-led public health education and medical advances in the eradication of diseases have significantly contributed to a fall in the death rates of the developing world. The developing world's increasing birth rate also looks problematical because the birth rate of the developed world has fallen steeply.

Why has the birth rate fallen in most developed societies?

4. Adamson argues that the real problem is not overpopulation but instead over-consumption. He argues that the unequal global distribution of resources, such as food and energy, between the developed and the developing world is far more important than population as a cause of underdevelopment, and especially the over-consumption of the world's resources by the West and the wasteful nature of Western standards of living. For example, the average American consumes 300 times more energy than the average Bangladeshi, because although the USA has only 6 per cent of the world's population, it consumes 40 per cent of the World's resources. Adamson points out that the 16 million babies born each year in the rich world will have four times as great an impact

on the world's resources as the 109 million born in the poor world.

Adamson argues that much of the neo-Malthusian concern with population is unconsciously racist because it reflects concerns among Western people with white skin that people with black and brown skins may start to demand a fairer share of the world's resources, and this may impact on White affluence. Family-planning policies, from this perspective therefore end up "substituting condoms for justice".

Compare the population and consumption arguments. Is Adamson justified in saying that family planning introduced by aid agencies in the developing world is racist?

5. Adamson argues that famine is not caused by overpopulation. He argues that famine is caused by inequalities in land ownership, which has resulted in the poor being pushed onto less arable and consequently over-farmed land. More fertile land in developing societies is often owned by local elites or TNCs and is used for to produce cash crops for export to the West.

    Dependency theory does agree with modernisation theory that the education of females is essential if population growth is to be slowed. Studies show that female education and health services reduce birth rates. For example, the 1992 World Bank report pointed out that women without education, on average, have seven children, but education reduces the average to three children. Evidence from Bangladesh showed a 21 per cent decrease in **fertility rates** between 1975 and 1991 because of a national family-planning programme. McMichael argues that there is a clear correlation between improving women's rights and declining fertility rates.

UNDERSTAND THE CONCEPT

The **fertility rate** refers to the number of live births per 1,000 women aged 15 to 44 over one year. The Total Fertility Rate (TFR) is the number of children that are born to an average woman during her childbearing life.

Some conclusions about population

In conclusion, the sociological debate about population can be divided into two broad camps. Some critical sociologists argue that the over-consumption of resources by the West is more important than population growth. Others suggest that population growth in the developing world needs to be stopped or slowed down. Commentators such as Porritt (1985) argue that if societies are to develop women need to be educated. This is the focus of the next section of this chapter.

THE SIGNIFICANCE OF GENDER IN RELATION TO DEVELOPMENT

Women in developing countries

Although women in the developed world lag behind men in terms of pay, they enjoy opportunities with regard to education, health, access to jobs and legal rights that suggest greater equality with men than is experienced by women in the developing world. Patriarchy is not dead and buried in the West, but it is no longer all-powerful. However, patriarchal control in the developing world can be all-consuming and exert control that can often threaten women's lives in different ways.

Leonard (1992) argues that "the conditions of underdevelopment – dependency, powerlessness, vulnerability and inequality of income – are experienced by women to a greater extent than men". Steinem (1995) suggests that women in developing countries make up a "fifth world", in that they are more at risk than men in these countries from subsistence poverty, poor health care and exploitation in factories and sweatshops, as well as the sex trade. The evidence seems to confirm these observations, as can be seen in the following examples:

> Women participate in labour markets in the developing world on an unequal basis with men and earn less. (See earlier discussion of other employment inequalities experienced by women in the developing world.)

> A woman's lifetime risk of dying from pregnancy-related causes in Africa is 1 in 16; in Asia, it is 1 in 65; and in Europe, it is 1 in 1,400. Pregnancy and the complications of childbirth are the leading cause of death for young women aged between 15 and 19 in the developing world.

> AIDS has a disproportionate effect on women; 25 million people have AIDS in Africa and 57 per cent of them are women. For example, in Zambia, women are three times more likely to be infected with the HIV virus than men.

> Ninety million girls receive no education at all in the developing world. Two-thirds of the 867 million illiterate people in the world are women.

> Both the developed and the developing world have experienced a feminisation of poverty – 70 per cent of the 1.5 billion people living on $1 a day or less are women. Many are denied access to credit, land and inheritance in both worlds.

> There is evidence that women are more likely to be subjected to violence than men. In war, rape is often used as a weapon against the female population and women prisoners are often subjected to sexual slavery. 72 per cent of the world's 33 million refugees are women and children.

> In Africa, it is estimated that 6,000 girls every day are subject to genital cutting or female circumcision (removal of the clitoris), often referred to as female genital mutilation (FGM), in order to enhance their future husband's enjoyment of sex. Circumcision is also intended to make wives less likely to commit adultery and to make them more docile and submissive.

> There is evidence that, in rural India, between five and ten women a day die because of bride-burning (or dowry death), where husbands kill wives so that they become free to marry again and attract a dowry.

Explanations for the position of women in developing countries

Modernisation theory

Modernisation theory blames internal cultural factors for women's subordination in the developing world. It is argued that some cultures, and especially the religious ideas that underpin the values, norms, institutions and customs of the developing world, ascribe status on the basis of gender. In practice, this means that males are accorded patriarchal control and dominance over a range of female activities and, consequently, women have little status in many developing societies. Van der Gaag reports that in many countries today, the birth of a boy is still something to be celebrated whereas the birth of a girl is a cause for commiseration.

Modernisation theory would argue that the low status of women in developing societies is another obstacle to development, for two reasons:

> Their potential contribution to the economy is not being fully realised.

> Their status as mothers contributes to overpopulation.

The Commission for Africa (2005) called for greater educational opportunities for adolescent girls in order to break the cycle of early childbearing. The Commission argues: "Getting girls into school, studies show, is crucial for development. Economic productivity is raised by educating girls. Infant and maternal mortality is lowered. Nutrition and health improve. The spread of HIV is reduced. Providing girls with one extra year of education boosts their eventual wages by 10 to 20 per cent."

Modernisation theory also argues that attitudinal change needs to be promoted. In particular, fathers, husbands and brothers need to be encouraged to view their female relatives as equal to themselves. Young men must challenge the ways they have been brought up and the traditional ways in which they see themselves. It is argued that as long as women are considered second-class citizens, young women will never be able to achieve their full potential.

Feminist perspectives

Feminist theories of development focus on how patriarchal structures produce subordination and exploitation in the developing world. These patriarchal structures may be the products of traditional structures but they may also be introduced by the West in the form of development aid. Feminists are particularly critical of modernisation theory. Scott (1995) suggests that modernisation theory is **malestream** because it is underpinned by patriarchal inequality. This is because modernisation theory states that the feminised world of the extended family is an obstacle to modernity since it encourages irrational traditional norms and customs thinking.

UNDERSTAND THE CONCEPT

Malestream is a feminist concept that means particular types of sociological theories are biased because they reflect masculine ways of looking at the world.

Modernisation theory argues that the nuclear family and rational modes of thinking are more conducive to development. She also criticised modernisation theory for assuming that women would become productive once they had access to technology and family-planning because this ignores the larger and more influential social processes – cultural traditions and oppressive patriarchal structures that mainly shape women's lives in the developing world. However Scott was also critical of dependency theory for ignoring women altogether in its Marxist analysis of underdevelopment.

Why might the encouragement of the nuclear family and rational thinking be accused of being patriarchal?

In the early 1970s, feminist thinking on development focused on the marginalisation of women. Boserup (1970) was particularly critical of the way in which Western aid agencies assumed that modernisation meant imposing western ideas of the sexual division of labour on developing societies. Boserup points out that traditionally women are the main food producers in the majority of African societies but the new agricultural technologies introduced by aid agencies focused on training men to use them, thereby marginalising women, making them dependent on men and reducing their status, power and income.

Similar criticisms were made by Leonard, who argued that aid is not gender-neutral because it often comes with Western male-oriented values attached. Aid workers bring with them the patriarchal prejudices about women and technology found in their own societies. Moreover, aid planners tend to neglect other aspects of female work, such as domestic tasks, because they do not consider this 'real work' as it is unwaged, or because they undervalue its role. They also make the mistake of seeing men as the main breadwinners. Moreover, Leonard argues that, in Africa many men are unused to the status of being a wage-earner and they see their wage as their own money rather than as a means of supporting their families.

However, Chowdhry (1995) criticises Boserup and Leonard because they imply that – once women are given technology and aid agencies target women as well as men – women's position in developing societies will improve. This assumption fails to take into account the influence that social factors such as class, ethnicity, religion, family and culture have on women's position in the developed world. Moreover, Marxists suggest that it avoids questioning women's subordination and oppression in the developing world as part of a wider global system of capitalist exploitation.

Pearson (2001) notes that, since the mid-1990s, the major development agencies have responded positively to the critique that women's issues were neglected by development policy. Consequently, gender has been incorporated into the indices of development used by multilateral aid agencies such as the UK's Department for International Development, the World Bank and the United Nations. For example, the MDGs include the promotion of gender equality, the empowerment of women and the improvement of maternal health. The Gender Empowerment Measure (GEM) indicates whether or not women play an active part in economic and political life across both the developed and developing world. All of these agencies now check, as a matter of course, that gender is considered across a range of projects, including civil engineering works and famine relief.

In particular, NGOs have championed a number of projects aimed at alleviating the feminisation of poverty. For example, microcredit schemes in countries such as India and Bangladesh make small amounts of credit available to the poor to cover subsistence needs, so that they can invest in livestock, equipment, fertiliser, and so on. These schemes are seen particularly to empower women (who are often responsible for domestic production). Research by Kilby (2001) into 80 microcredit schemes suggests that women who take part in these self-help schemes experience increased mobility, respect, dignity, assertiveness and support.

What patriarchal prejudices exist in the West with regard to the relationship between women, science and technology?

Marxist-feminists argue that women's poverty and subordinate position in developing societies is caused by the fact that an exploitative global system of capitalism has been imposed on developing societies and that women workers are regarded by TNCs as more pliable and docile compared with male workers and less likely to resist low pay and poor conditions. The exploitation of these women takes several forms:

> Low pay – Women workers in the EPZs are paid lower rates than male workers. Wages are often only about 10 per cent of those in developed societies, and working hours are often 50 per cent higher. Consequently, women in the EPZs are producing more for less pay.

> Western owners do not invest a great deal in training female workforces. The work is generally regarded as unskilled, despite high skill levels being evident. However, because women have often already learned these skills in the home – for example, the sewing skills needed in sweatshops – the skill is downgraded.

> TNCs take advantage of what Elson and Pearson (1981) call "women's material subordination as a gender", that is, the fact that women in these countries are more likely to put up with lower wages and to accept oppressive working conditions. They do this

because either there is no alternative or because the patriarchal conditions of their society mean the job is only temporary until they achieve the more important cultural goal of marriage and childbearing. Foster-Carter (1993) argues that industrial jobs for women in the developing world often bring with them "new forms of exploitation" in which the price of gaining some freedom from men's authority and an income of one's own is often submission to long hours, low wages, a precarious form of job security and chauvinist male bosses.

However, in criticism of the exploitation thesis, it can be argued that:

> The wages earned from such work are superior to the subsistence living eked out in rural existences.

> Such work allows some escape from forms of patriarchy found in the countryside, such as arranged marriages.

> This type of work may be more attractive than others available. For example, women in countries such as Thailand are often trafficked into sex work.

FOCUS ON SKILLS: THE CHALLENGES OF LOW STATUS FOR WOMEN

Nasrin Akther, aged 21, is from Bangladesh and until recently worked from 8am to 10pm every day in a clothing factory. In the Bangladeshi clothing manufacture industry, about 80 per cent of the workforce are female. They produce clothes for many of the big Western brands but work in appalling conditions for very low wages. Nasrin says: "There are no childcare or medical facilities. The women don't receive maternity benefits. We have two days off a month. In my factory, it is very crowded, very hot and badly ventilated. I could not support myself with the wage I was getting. Because we have to work very long hours, seven days a week, we have no family life, no personal life, no social life … Our lives have been stolen. Any workers who attempt to get together a union are fired immediately and may be blacklisted.'

Women in Bangladesh, and some other countries in Asia, who defy traditional gender roles and speak out against the oppression of women are routinely subject to threats, intimidation and assassination. Projects, schools and businesses run by women are often the target of hateful attacks. In Bangladesh, more than 200 girls and young women were mutilated in acid attacks last year, leaving them scarred and blinded. Reported reasons for the acid-throwing attacks include the refusal of an offer of marriage, dowry disputes, domestic fights and arguments over property.

Questions

1. **Explain.** Give two examples of ways in which women in Bangladesh are exploited in sweatshops.

2. **Explain** why TNCs outsource work to sweatshops.

3. **Analyse** why religious fundamentalists such as the Taliban are threatened by women who defy traditional gender roles.

4. **Analyse** the implications for underdevelopment of universal free education for girls.

5. **Evaluate.** Using information from this source and elsewhere, assess the view that undeveloped countries are more patriarchal than developed countries.

Hunt (2004b) notes that postmodernists have drawn attention to how the category of 'woman' has been constructed, and particularly how specific female groups in the developing world have been perceived by Western feminists. Mohanty (1997), for example, is critical of the way Western feminists have presented women in the developing world as "ignorant, poor, uneducated,

tradition-bound, domestic, family-orientated, victimised, etc." and in need of help from Western women. Western women, on the other hand are presented as "educated, modern, as having control over their own bodies and sexualities, and possessing the freedom to make their own decisions." Mohanty argues that Western feminists have not always understood the nature of the developing world. She suggests that their insistence that men are the enemy has failed to understand that women in the developing world have different priorities such as acquiring the reproductive rights, education and human rights that women in the developed world have already obtained. Gender and patriarchy are not the only causes of women's oppression in the developing world – culture, religion, poverty, war, religion and globalisation are just as important. Moreover, women in the developing world are physically at risk from male violence for even daring to campaign for such rights.

The prognosis for women in the developing world is, at best, mixed. On the plus side, the expansion of both education and family-planning does constitute progress. Adamson argues that there is now a generation of women such as Malala Yousafzai in the developing world who see education as the norm and not the exception. Malala Yousafzai has since written a memoir of her plight, *I Am Malala*, and has been depicted on screen in *He Named Me Malala*. These women will demand more input into political and domestic decision-making, and will pass down these attitudes to their daughters. Moghadam (2005) is positive about women's future because she observes that a global women's movement is now emerging to challenge gender inequality. She argues that globalisation has exposed more women to education, information and connections with women from different countries.

However, according to Van der Gaag (2004), the advances women have made over the last 20 years cannot hide the fact that for millions of women life is still very grim. While noting the improvements in women's lives – better education, longer life-span, better prospects of a career in business or politics, legislation against domestic violence and action against genital cutting – some brutal facts remain:

> The vast majority of the world's women still have very little power, at work, in their relationships at home, or in the wider social world. Worldwide, 60 per cent of the world's 550 million poor in 2014 were women, as are two-thirds of illiterate adults. One in four women is beaten by her husband or partner. Every day, 1,300 women still die unnecessarily in childbirth or pregnancy.

> There has been a growth in the numbers of women and girls from the developing world being trafficked for the purpose of sex tourism and prostitution. The UN estimates that four million women a year are trafficked from the developing world for prostitution use in the developed world.

> FGM still continues. In 2014, it was estimated that it affected up to 140 million women and girls. In December 2012, the United Nations general assembly unanimously voted to work for the elimination of FGM throughout the world.

> There is a lack of political will to tackle the exploitation of women and children's labour in sweatshops to meet Western demand for cheap clothing.

> The rise of religious extremism and fundamentalism has resulted in heightened legal and social restrictions for women. Van der Gaag notes that often Islamic fundamentalists see women's rights as the product of Western **decadence**. They often oppose such rights because men believe that women generally should serve men as wives and mothers.

UNDERSTAND THE CONCEPT

Decadence refers to moral decline. Islamists see modern ideas as decadent because modernism encourages the abandonment of historical tradition and the adoption of Western ideas, which are often the reverse of long-held practices and customs.

> The increasingly militarisation of the world is having a disproportionate negative effect on women and children who, for example, make up the majority of refugees fleeing war-zones. Women are often the victims of ethnic cleansing and rape.

> Environmental degradation may be having a disproportionate negative effect on the lives of women in the developing world. Ecofeminists argue that women are naturally closer to the land or the environment because they are more likely than men to work the land. Problems such as deforestation, desertification and exposure to toxic chemicals are allegedly more likely to affect women's livelihoods and health.

> Van der Gaag claims there has been a global male backlash against women's rights because, in some developing countries, men believe that women have too many rights. In South Africa, women are experiencing high levels of violence, which may be partly fuelled by a male backlash against the progress women have made. This 'neo-patriarchy' is another attempt to exert male authority through a culture of violence.

Finally, there has also been a growing realisation in development theory that the concentration on women in recent years has led to neglect in the understanding of men and masculinity. Researchers have now begun to focus on examining how masculinity is constructed in the developing world in order to understand the nature of patriarchal gender-relations.

CHECK YOUR UNDERSTANDING

1. Explain what is meant by the term 'demography'.

2. Explain what is meant by the 'informal economy'.

3 Explain what is meant by 'biomedical health-care systems'.

4. Explain what is meant by 'ecofeminism'.

5. Identify two cultural factors that, according to modernisation theory, lead to overpopulation, and briefly outline one example of each.

6. Identify and briefly explain how education can improve the position of females in the developing world.

7. Analyse two reasons why there are global inequalities in health.

8. Analyse two differences between work in the formal sector and work in the informal sector.

9. Evaluate the relationship between population, urbanisation and the environment.

10. Evaluate the view that women's experience is similar across the world.

TAKE IT FURTHER

1. Conduct a social survey to find out what view of population is held by a representative sample of people. Ask people whether they agree or disagree with the following statements, using a scale of 1 to 5 in which 1 means 'strongly agree' and 5 means 'strongly disagree'.

   › They have too many babies in the developing world.

   › The world's population is out of control.

   › We consume more than our fair share of resources in the West.

   › The developing world needs more contraception.

   › The world just cannot support all these extra mouths.

   › High population results in more poverty.

   › There are simply not enough resources to go around.

   › The cause of high population in the developing world is poverty.

   › The world's food resources are not fairly distributed.

   › Obesity in the developed world is linked to starvation in the developing world.

2. Compare the attitudes to women across the world at Human Rights Watch (www.hrw.org).

APPLY YOUR LEARNING

1 Outline and explain **two** ways in which official aid may assist the development of poorer countries.   [10 marks]

2 Read **Item A** below and answer the question that follows.

ITEM A

Most development sociologists are agreed that countries with high rates of illiteracy and gender gaps in educational attainment tend to be poorer and underdeveloped. The education of females has the effect of reducing fertility rates and slowing population growth. Infant and child mortality rates also fall and family health improves. Moreover, educated women are more likely to go out to work and contribute to family income. Educated women are also more politically active and better informed about their legal rights.

Applying material from **Item A**, analyse **two** reasons why educating females is regarded as crucial to development.   [10 marks]

3 Read **Item B** below and answer the question that follows.

ITEM B

Most countries of the developing world aspire to the economic growth and wealth experienced by Western nations. However, the evidence suggests that if developing societies ever achieved the West's current level of economic and industrial development, it would put an intolerable strain on the world's resources and ecological stability.

Applying material from **Item B** and your knowledge, evaluate the relationship between development and the environment.   [20 marks]

You can find example answers and accompanying teacher's comments for this topic at www.collins.co.uk/AQAAlevelSociology. Please note that these example answers and teacher's comments have not been approved by AQA.

4 THE MEDIA

AQA specification	Chapters
Candidates should examine:	
The new media and their significance for an understanding of the role of the media in contemporary society.	Chapter 1 covers this (pages 261–271), although there are also references to it in Chapters 2, 3 & 4 (pages 272–303).
The relationship between ownership and control of the mass media.	Chapter 2 covers this (pages 272–282), although there are also references in Chapter 4 (pages 293–303).
The mass media, globalisation and popular culture.	Chapter 3 covers this (pages 283–292).
The processes of selection and presentation of the content of the news.	Chapter 4 covers this (pages 293–303).
Media representations of age, social class, ethnicity, gender, sexuality and disability.	Chapters 5 and 6 cover this (pages 304–327).
The relationship between the mass media, media content and presentation, and audiences.	Chapter 7 covers this (pages 328–338).

4.1 THE NEW MEDIA

LEARNING OBJECTIVES

> Demonstrate knowledge and understanding of the competing views on the nature and significance of digital media (AO1).

> Demonstrate knowledge and understanding of the growth, diversity, control and use of new media (AO1).

> Apply this knowledge to contemporary society (AO2).

> Analyse and evaluate sociological explanations in order to make judgements and draw conclusions about the use and significance of new media (AO3).

INTRODUCING THE DEBATE

The term 'mass media' refers to those forms of communication that transmit information, news and entertainment to mass audiences. Traditionally, this was done via newspapers, magazines, advertising campaigns, radio, television, cinema and music. However, mass communication is now increasingly being dominated by 'new' forms of media.

The term 'new media' generally refers to the emergence of new forms of communication that have appeared in the last 25 years. These include cheap laptop computers, tablets, smartphone technology, digital television and texting, which were only developed for the mass market from the mid-1990s on. The most innovative technology that has appeared in the last 20 years is probably the internet – a global multimedia library of information and services in cyberspace made possible by a global system of interconnected super-computers. The development of high-capacity broadband wireless networks means more people than ever can connect at high speed to this information superhighway.

The new media differ enormously from traditional older forms of media such as newspapers and magazines, books, DVDs, CDs, the radio, the cinema and analogue television. For example, at the beginning of the 1990s in the UK, most people received television pictures through aerials and analogue signal television sets, and there were only five terrestrial television channels that could be accessed. Today, however, people are increasingly buying digital, high-definition, flat-screen or curved-screen smart televisions fuelled by dual core processors and subscribing to digitalised satellite and cable television that offer a choice of hundreds of television and radio channels and give access to download streaming services such as Netflix and Amazon Prime. Moreover, these new television sets offer the consumer a greater set of services, including web browsers for online shopping, game-play, Facebook and Twitter integration, and wi-fi for app, video and game sharing direct from a smartphone.

The growing popularity of new media has led to two broad sociological positions. Some sociologists – the neophiliacs – welcome this new technology because, in their view, it offers consumers more choice. Moreover, they argue that new media is good for democracy because people can now monitor and criticise the activities of the powerful, and organise protest via social networking sites. From this perspective, every citizen has the potential to be an active participant in the democratic process.

In contrast, cultural pessimists argue that the democratic potential of new media is exaggerated because such forms of media are increasingly bought up by the same media corporations that own older forms of media such as newspapers and television. The implications of these processes are also discussed in Chapter 2. Moreover, cultural pessimists argue that the new media are problematic because, in their various forms, they are leading to cultural illiteracy, the dumbing-down of popular culture, the decline of community and the emergence of a new set of social problems.

GETTING YOU THINKING

Item A

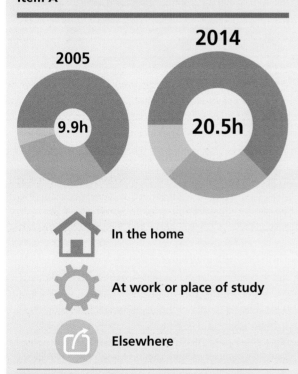

In the home

At work or place of study

Elsewhere

Figure 4.1.1 *Estimated hours spent online per week*
Source: Ofcom (2015)

Item B
Like crying infants, our smartphones are constantly demanding that we pick them up and pay attention to them. When they emit the slightest noise, we rush to attend to them, interrupting work and social occasions. Even when our devices are silent, we obsessively check them multiple times a day, hearing phantom rings and notifications, and becoming anxious if they are not in our possession at all times. FOBO (Fear Of Being Off-line) seems to be growing exponentially. In a survey circulated last year by Iowa State University of Science and Technology to gauge the extent of nomophobia — smartphone separation anxiety — people admitted that they would feel "worried and nervous" if they and their family and friends could not communicate instantly, they would be "annoyed and uncomfortable" without constant access to information through a smartphone and that running out of battery was something to be "scared" about.

Source: McMahon (2015)

Item C
According to the former CIA contractor Edward Snowden, America's National Security Agency and Britain's GCHQ have been spying on people through popular smartphone apps such as Angry Birds. He also claims they are using mobile base stations to gather data from phones on users' ages, location, financial status and even sexual orientation.

Source: Kennedy (2014)

Questions

1. Examine Item A and identify the trends in the use of new media between 2005 and 2014.

2. How, in your opinion, have new media technologies such as the smartphone and digital TV improved the quality of your life?

3. New media have been accused by some critics of undermining the notion of community and creating social anxiety. How does Item B support these ideas?

4. In what way does Item C identify smartphones as a danger to democracy?

THE CHARACTERISTICS OF THE NEW MEDIA

New media share a number of important characteristics which distinguish them from old media.

Digitalisation
The growth of digital technology in the 1990s resulted in changes in the way information is stored and transmitted. All information, regardless of format (for example, images, text and sound) is now converted into binary code.

Technological convergence
Digitalisation resulted in the convergence of different types of information – text, photographs, video, film, voices and music – into a single delivery system, available to media such as smart television, laptop, tablet and smartphone. As Boyle (2005) notes, digitalisation allows information to be delivered across a range of media platforms that were once separate and unconnected technologies. It is now possible to watch television and films, to take photographs, consult maps and use GPS, to download and listen to music, play games, send texts and emails, and upload photographs, videos and comments to social networking and sharing sites on one device.

Economic convergence
This technological convergence has also produced economic convergence. Media and telecommunication industries that once previously produced separate and distinct systems of communication, such as the telephone, television programmes or computers, began to make economic alliances with each other because digitalisation reduced the boundaries between media sectors. It was this cross-fertilisation of ideas and resources, underpinned by digitalisation, that produced these new forms of converged multimedia delivery systems.

Cultural convergence
Jenkins notes that media convergence has also produced cultural convergence because it has changed the way that members of society interact with both the media and each other. For example, the new media have changed the nature of consumerism in the UK. In 2012, the Organisation for Economic Co-operation and Development (OECD) found that six out of ten British adults used the internet to buy products such as food, clothing, music, insurance or holidays, compared with only three out of ten adults in other OECD nations. Moreover, the new media have changed the way that people interact with one another. For example, a report by Ofcom (2014) found that Facebook remains the default social networking site for 96 per cent of UK adults who are online, while over 9 million people in the UK communicate with others via Twitter.

What impact has cultural convergence had on your family?

Interactivity
The new media are interactive media that are responsive in 'real time' to user input through clicking on links or selecting menu items with a mouse. The internet epitomises such interactive media because it lets users select the stories that they want to read or watch, in the order that they want or to read watch them. They can also mix and match the information they want – for instance, people may access news from several different sources.

Choice
Jenkins argues that media audiences today can now interact with a variety of media, often using a single device in their search for entertainment, information, social relationships, services and so on. This means that today's new media audience has a greater degree of choice compared with pre-1990s media audiences. Boyle (2005) notes that society's use of television has evolved from a system of supply-led television to a demand-led television, organised around the idea that the viewers or subscribers should choose what they want to watch and when. Viewers are no longer constrained by television schedules.

Participatory culture
New media audiences are no longer passive receivers of entertainment, knowledge and so on. Instead they often actively collaborate with new media and other users by uploading content to sharing sites such as Facebook, YouTube and Ted Talks, by sharing music files, by writing reviews on consumer sites and by letting others know about their opinions via Twitter and Reddit. Jenkins therefore argues that convergence and interactivity have produced a "participatory culture". In other words, media producers and consumers no longer occupy separate roles – they are now participants who interact with each other according to a new set of rules that are constantly evolving.

Collective intelligence
Jenkins also suggests that this participatory culture is producing a "collective intelligence". He notes "none of us can know everything; each of us knows something; and we can put the pieces together if we pool our resources and combine our skills". He claims that this collective intelligence, which is constructed by new media users,

challenges traditional and official ways of seeing the world provided by media owners, politicians, civil servants and so on. Jenkins claims that new media content is an alternative user-led source of information that is often critical of information produced top-down by traditional forms of media.

Explain why texting and websites that you regularly use can be categorised as 'participatory'.

WHO IS USING THE NEW MEDIA?

Ofcom's report 'Adults' media use and attitudes' (2015) documents the extent of media literacy – defined as the ability to use, understand and create media and communications in a variety of contexts – in 2015 and how the media landscape has changed since 2005.

2006	2007	2008	2009	2010	2011	2012	2013
Twitter Blu-ray BT Vision	iPlayer iPhone Kindle Virgin Media	Android Sky+ HD Spotify Chrome	WhatsApp Angry Birds Windows 7	iPad Instagram 3D TV Kinect	Google+ Raspberry Pi	Netflix UK Smart TV 4G YouView	Xbox One PS4 Chromecast

Figure 4.1.2 *Media launches since 2006*

Ofcom noted in 2015 the following changes in media use since 2005:

› 84 per cent of adults in the UK accessed the internet, using a variety of devices inside and outside the home, compared with 54 per cent in 2005.

› 69 per cent of people accessed the internet via smartphones and tablets as well as PCs and laptops.

› The claimed weekly hours of internet use among all adults had doubled from 9.9 hours to 20.5 hours.

› Texting was the preferred form of social contact for the majority – at least 96 per cent of people did this at least once a week.

› 7 in 10 internet users had a social profile on a social networking site such as Facebook. 81 per cent of those with a profile claimed to visit social media sites at least once a day. This rose to 93 per cent for the 16–24 year age group.

› Watching TV remained hugely popular, but it had increasingly converged with the internet, tablets and smartphones. Viewers were increasingly constructing their own schedules, using catch-up services, subscriptions to streaming sites such as Netflix and technology such as Sky+.

› Consumption of short-form user-generated online platforms such as YouTube, Wikipedia and IMDB as a source of information had increased considerably since 2005.

The generation divide

Boyle (2007) notes that new media are often associated with young people. Some sociologists have consequently suggested that there exists a generational divide in terms of how people use new media. For example, surveys conducted by Ofcom suggest that 12- to 15-year-olds are more likely than adults to be engaged in some form of cross-media multi-tasking – for example, texting friends while browsing across several web windows, or watching television while doing their homework. However, on the whole, the 2015 Ofcom survey suggests that the generation divide may be in decline as older age groups increasingly engage in online activities such as social networking via smartphones and tablets.

Boyle argues that there is no doubt that the media experience of young people growing up in the UK in 2015 is markedly different from that of previous generations because the generation that has grown up in the last 15 years has had a more intensive experience of new media across a shorter period of time. The new media of the internet, social networking sites, the smartphone and texting are 'now' media, significantly different from previous media because of their immediacy and accessibility. Consequently, the ways in which young people access and seek out entertainment and news differ from previous generations. They are more likely to want it all now – and tailored to their specific needs and identities.

Compare what media were available to an 18-year-old in 1990 compared with an 18-year-old in 2016.

Boyle observes that adult anxieties about the use of media by young people have always existed. (See Chapter 7 for concerns about young people's exposure to screen violence.) However, young people's access to a greater range of new media gadgets has amplified traditional concerns and led to new social anxieties about children and young people accessing pornography and terrorist propaganda, as well as the new forms of bullying and grooming that are appearing in mobile phone text messaging or on social networking sites.

The digital class divide

It has been suggested that the poor are excluded from new media usage because they are a digital underclass who cannot afford to keep up with the middle-class use of new media technology. Ofcom surveys indicate that although the digital class divide has narrowed in recent years, it still exists. For example, the 2015 Ofcom survey found that 95 per cent of the AB socio-economic group use a range of new media devices to go online in any location compared with only 75 per cent of the DE socio-economic group and 86 per cent of all socio-economic groups. Three-quarters of ABs own a smartphone, compared to only 54 per cent of DEs.

However, Helpser (2011) claims that despite this narrowing of the class divide, a digital underclass – characterised by unemployment, lower education levels and low digital skills –does exist in the UK. The evidence suggests that this group has increased its use of the internet at a much slower rate than other social groups and those members of this group that do have internet access rate their skills as poorer than other more educated groups.

The digital gender divide

Li and Kirkup (2007) found significant gender differences between men and women in the UK in their use of new media technology. Men were more likely than women to use email or chat rooms, and men played more computer games on consoles such as the Xbox than women did.

However, Ofcom (2015) reported that in 2014:

> Males were more likely than females to access the internet (23.3 hours per week compared with 17.8 hours).

> Women are more likely than men to go online to look at social media sites (67 per cent versus 60 per cent).

The Internet Advertising Bureau (IAB) conducted research in 2014 that suggests that women now account for 52 per cent of those who play digital games, and this is closely related to the popularity of the smartphone, which has extended the availability of computer games beyond those using dedicated consoles such as the Xbox, PlayStation and Nintendo Wii. The IAB survey found that mobile puzzlers such as Candy Crush Saga and Angry Birds were particularly attractive to females because they were free, intuitive, accessible and did not require much learning time.

However, Olson et al. (2008) found that boys were more likely to play violent video games because they wanted to express fantasies of power and glory, to master exciting and realistic environments and to work out their anger and stress. The same study noted that an increasing number of girls were also using violent video games as a means of coping with anger, although Hartmann and Klimmt (2006) found that women gamers generally disliked violent content and preferred the social interaction aspect of games. Royse et al. (2007) studied female gamers who played between 3 and 10 hours a week and found them to be mainly motivated by the technical competition offered by games that allowed them to challenge gender norms.

Compare the gaming habits of males and females in your Sociology class or your friendship groups.

The global digital divide

According to the World Economic Forum (WEF) in 2014, the digital divide between developed nations and developing nations, especially the least developed countries (LLEDCs), is worsening. See Topic 3, Chapter 1 for more on the global hierarchy of development.

Figures 4.1.3 and 4.1.4 clearly show that the developed world has greater access to mobile broadband and the internet than the less developed world.

According to the World Bank, by 2012 about three-quarters of the world's population had access to a mobile phone. There were 6 billion mobile phones in use worldwide, of which nearly 5 billion were in developing countries. Mobile phone use has spread particularly quickly in Africa.

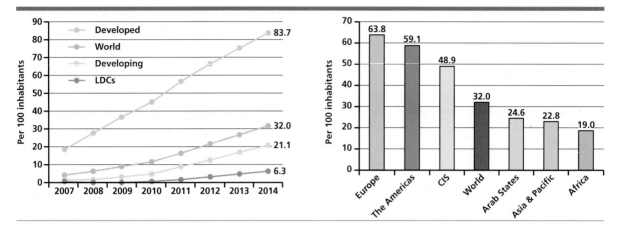

Figure 4.1.3 *Active mobile broadband subscriptions by level of development, 2007–2014 (left) and by region (estimate) (2014)*

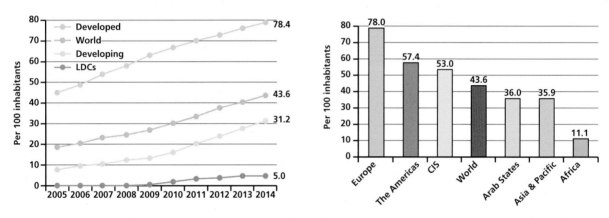

Figure 4.1.4 *Percentage of households with internet access by level of development, 2005–2014 (left) and by region (estimate) (2014)*

Source: ITU World Telecommunication/ICT Indicators database (2014)

In 2014, GSMA estimated that 72 per cent of Africans use mobile phones but this fact creates a false impression of a digital revolution:

> It masks the fact that mobile connectivity is limited.

> Only 18 per cent of these phones are smartphones

> There are regional disparities in access to mobile phones – for example, in Eritrea, only 5 per cent of the population owns a mobile phone.

> Only 7 per cent of Africa's inhabitants are online.

> Difficulties of access are compounded by the fact that most of the language of the internet is English.

> A fairly large proportion of African countries have high levels of illiteracy.

DEBATES ABOUT NEW MEDIA

According to Curran and Seaton (2003), two perspectives dominate the debate about the new media in the UK:

1. 'Neophiliacs' are optimistic about the spread and influence of new media technologies, which they see as offering more choice and the opportunity to participate more interactively and effectively in the democratic process.

2. The 'cultural pessimists' suggest that new media are not really that new, that interactivity is an illusion because ownership of new media is still overwhelmingly concentrated in the hands of powerful corporations, and that consequently the new media contribute to the undermining of the democratic process. Cultural pessimists have also suggested that new media content is a factor in the decline in the quality of popular culture. It is also leading to new social problems such as cyberbullying, addiction to pornography and online sexual grooming.

The neophiliac perspective

Neophiliacs argue that new media are beneficial to society for several reasons, outlined below.

Increased consumer choice

Neophiliacs argue that the convergence and interactivity that characterise media technology and delivery today have increased consumer choice. There are now literally hundreds of entertainment and news channels on television. Moreover, people can choose from a number of media delivery systems. For example, people may choose to buy music in CD form or to download it from iTunes; they may listen to it by playing a CD, or through a television, personal computer, a tablet, an MP3 player or a mobile phone. Pluralist neophiliacs argue that the competition between this diversity of media will improve the quality of media output.

An e-commerce revolution

The internet has also led to a revolution in e-commerce in recent years. E-retailers such as Amazon and eBay have been great economic successes and have undermined high-street sales of books, films and music. Most major commercial companies now have their own websites. It is claimed that this e-commerce trend has resulted in more choice for consumers because it increases competition, leads to lower prices and puts consumers in control as they can compare prices from a huge range of products and services.

Does the evidence regarding the digital divide support the view that the new media offer more choice for consumers?

Revitalising democracy

It is argued that new media technologies offer opportunities for people to acquire the education and information required to play an active role in democratic societies, and to make politicians more accountable to the people. The internet is a means of communicating information that the giant corporations who own and control the world's traditional media are unlikely to want to report. The internet, in particular, has been highlighted in this respect because it is a public sphere that anybody can access, usually at little or no cost. It provides people with the opportunity to access a wide range of information and alternative interpretations and viewpoints, which are unlikely to be found in the conventional mainstream media that traditionally have set the agenda for debate in wider society.

Seaton notes that many believe that the internet is advancing progressive politics: "Internet technology converts the desk into a printing press, broadcasting station and place of assembly. This enables 'many-to-many communication', which allegedly is changing the way we do politics. In this view, the net is rejuvenating civil society, generating political activism and launching exciting experiments of popular participation in government. Established centres of power and monopolies of communication are being bypassed … and a process of progressive mobilisation is under way that will empower the people."

Some media sociologists have therefore suggested that the internet can revitalise democracy because it gives a voice to those who would otherwise go unheard. It allows like-minded people to join together and take action that may lead to social change.

Some neophiliacs who are part of the antiglobal-capitalism movement have used the internet to challenge power elites. As Itzoe (1995) argues, the internet is "a loose and anarchic confederation of millions of users around the world who communicate in perhaps the freest forum of speech in history". The internet has therefore been used in a variety of political ways by these activists:

> to monitor the illegal or immoral activities of big businesses

> to harness mass support for causes such as Make Poverty History

> to coordinate protesters and activists, ranging from hunt saboteurs and anti-vivisectionists to anti-austerity protesters and those disrupting G8 meetings.

Hacktivist networks such as Anonymous have defaced corporate and government websites and engaged in virtual sabotage such as 'web sit-ins' (sending so much information to a site that it crashes), email bombing, and information theft, especially computer code theft.

FOCUS ON SKILLS: THE POWER OF TWITTER

Protesters in Egypt, aided by Twitter, staged a large-scale demonstration against President Mubarak's regime.

Murthy (2013) has empirically investigated the impact of Twitter, which has 140 million users worldwide. He claims that Twitter has proved extremely useful as a news-gathering medium in terms of communicating information about events such as the Tohuku earthquake in Japan in 2011, and social movements such as the Occupy protests in London and New York in 2011 and the Arab Spring anti-government movements that spread across the Middle East and North Africa between 2011 and 2012.

Murthy argues that Twitter was particularly effective in the Egyptian protests, that toppled President Mubarak, in two ways. First, Twitter helped enable a mass movement of people out onto the streets (although Murthy notes that high unemployment, persistent poverty and police brutality were the main causes of the movement). Murthy also notes that both the internet and Twitter were regarded by the Egyptian authorities as so threatening in their dissemination of activist

information that they were shut down for a week by the government in January 2011. Second, Murthy argues that Twitter helped to bring international attention to what was going on by acting as a valuable news source for international journalists.

Murthy concludes that "even if tweets did not bring feet to Egyptian streets, they helped to facilitate a diverse global network of individuals who participated in a wide-ranging set of mobilisation efforts from the retweeters in Starbucks to those sending letters to their Congresspeople/Ministers or participating in activist movements both online and offline."

He notes that although Twitter may not be able to topple governments, as a young communications medium it has the potential to shape many aspects of people's social, political and economic lives. However, not all media sociologists agree – Hader (2011) describes Twitter as symbolic of ineffectual pseudo-laptop/iPad revolutionaries.

Questions

1. **Identify** two examples of events in which Twitter proved to be useful as a news-gathering medium.

2. **Explain** why Twitter has the potential to shape people's social, political and economic lives.

3. **Analyse** the role of Twitter in the toppling of President Mubarek in Egypt.

4. **Evaluate,** using information from this source and elsewhere, the view that new media devices and networks can revitalise democracy.

The cultural pessimist perspective

Cultural pessimists believe that this revolution in new media technology has been exaggerated by neophiliacs. There are a number of strands to their argument.

'Not-so-new' media

Cornford and Robins (1999) argue that the so-called 'new media' are not that new. 'Old' technology – television and telephone landlines – is still integral to the use of new media such as computer game consoles, and broadband and wireless connections to the internet. They suggest, further, that interactivity is not something new, because people have written to newspapers and phoned in to radio and television for many years. The

only thing that is new about new media is its speed – information, news and entertainment can be accessed in 'real time'. The most convincing example of this is still the plane hitting the second World Trade Center tower on 9/11: audiences around the world watched the event as it actually happened. Cornford and Robins suggest that what the new technologies permit is the refinement, extension and embellishment of traditional media. They suggest we might consider the relationship of new media to old as "being like that between an old Hollywood movie and its re-make: the characters are the same, the story is the same, but the special effects are more spectacular, and the marketing budget is much larger."

Domination by media conglomerates

Cultural pessimists criticise the idea that new media are increasing the potential for ordinary people to participate more fully in the democratic process and cultural life. They argue that the role of the transnational media **conglomerates** in the development and control of the new media undermines the potential for media democracy.

UNDERSTAND THE CONCEPT

Conglomeration refers to a business corporation that consists of different companies with diversified interests in a very wide range of products or services.

Jenkins (2008) argues that most new media have developed as a result of investment by the big media corporations. In particular, he argues that the cross-media ownership that began in the 1980s was the first phase of media concentration and technological convergence. Owning different types of media made it more desirable for companies to develop content across a variety of media platforms and delivery systems. As Jenkins notes, "digitalisation set the conditions for convergence; corporate conglomerates created its imperative".

The internet, in particular, is dominated by a small number of media corporations – for example, Microsoft has developed most of the software required for accessing the net. Comcast, which is the largest broadcasting and largest cable company in the world by revenue, is the USA's biggest internet provider. These multinational companies enable people to log on in the first place, direct users to particular commercial services and play a key role in online advertising. Most of the internet's commercially viable content is therefore controlled and/or commissioned by the big entertainment, press, telecommunications, advertising and software companies. For example, in the UK, the top five internet sites in 2015, measured by visitor traffic, were Google, Facebook, YouTube, Amazon and eBay. The BBC, Daily Mail Online and the Telegraph were in the top 20 sites visited.

These media superpowers have many advantages over individuals in setting up websites – they have back catalogues, funds for investment, technical expertise, close links with the advertising industry, brand visibility and cross-ownership, so it is relatively easy for them to cross-promote products – for example, Comcast owns NBC Universal which produces films, television programmes, popular music, computer games, books, newspapers, magazines and comics, as well as owning

cable companies and amusement parks. Chapter 2 examines the implications of these patterns of ownership and control in more depth.

Commercialisation

As a result, the internet is now extremely commercialised. Moreover, millions of people use the internet to manage their bank accounts, pay bills, and buy services such as insurance and consumer goods. In short, over ten years there has been a major shift in internet activities from educational use to commercial use.

Cornford and Robins agree that these new technologies may produce more choice for the consumer, but there are also some dubious side effects. For example, many companies that sell products and services on the internet engage in consumer surveillance. Technologies such as cookies can monitor and process the data generated by interactive media usage, so they can segment and target potential future audiences, and thus enhance profits. Some Marxist sociologists have grown alarmed at this commercialisation of the internet, smartphones and digital television because they claim that it encourages materialism, consumerism and false needs, and thereby furthers capitalist domination and control.

Reinforcing elite power

Cornford and Robins are sceptical of the view that new media will lead to a more democratic communications structure that will bring about a new political and social order. They note that through a series of assertive tactics – alliances, mergers, takeovers, licensing deals, patents and copyright restrictions – media corporations seek to monopolise key strategic links within the new media. Jenkins, too, notes that not all the participants in the new media are created equal. Corporations – and even individuals within corporate media – still exert greater power than any individual consumer or even aggregates of consumers. Political elite power-holders too, such as government departments and agencies, political parties, and the security services, have not been slow to see the power of new media delivery systems and have constructed sophisticated and elaborate websites to make sure their view of the world dominates the internet. The ex-CIA analyst Edward Snowden claimed in 2015 that the British security services have the technology to access private information stored on people's smartphones.

From a cultural pessimist perspective, media technologies are therefore mainly strengthening the power of the existing elites rather than promoting alternative ideas, free speech or democracy. The digital class divide also contributes to this inequality because it is probably those who are unable to access the internet who have the most genuine political grievances.

Seaton (2003) argues that online political involvement probably mirrors the level of ordinary people's political involvement in the real world. Studies conducted by Hill and Hughes (1997) found that only 6 per cent of webpages were devoted to political issues. They also challenged the view that cyberspace is more likely to contain web content that supports alternative minority political issues or views. Seventy-eight per cent of political opinions expressed on the American websites were mainstream. Seaton remarks "when the net was a marginal experimental sphere in which counter-cultural movements were especially active, the net had a different significance, but those halcyon days are over." Even when the net was used to plan and mobilise the anti-globalisation protests, it was only one of a number of strategies used, which included leaflets, posters, graffiti, mainstream news reports and cheap air travel. As the media corporations successfully colonised most of the net with their news, entertainment, business and sport sites, minority political views and civic discourse were shifted to the margins.

Decline in the quality of popular culture

Cultural pessimists argue that increased choice of media delivery systems, and particularly the digitalisation of television, has led to a decline in the quality of popular culture. Harvey (2008), for example, suggests that digital television may have dramatically increased the number of channels for viewers to choose from, but this has led to a dumbing-down of popular culture as television companies fill these channels with cheap imported material, films, repeats, sport, reality television shows and gambling.

Harvey argues that, increasingly, television culture transmits a "candy floss culture" that speaks to everyone in general and no one in particular. It is argued that both ITV and the BBC have experienced a process of "tabloidisation" over the past 10 years because they now have to compete with Sky and other satellite channels. This has allegedly resulted in a decline in documentaries and news coverage and an increase in reality television programmes. Consequently, cultural pessimists argue that more choice is simply more of the same.

Lack of regulation

It is argued by sociologists, politicians and cultural commentators that new media, particularly the internet, is in need of state regulation. All points of view are represented on the internet, but it is argued that easy access to pornography, and to sites that are homophobic or racist, or incite terrorism, is taking free speech too far.

Moreover, the increased use of new media, particularly by the young, has given rise to a new set of problems for society, including global cybercrime, cyberbullying, abusive on-line **trolling** of minority groups and the sexual grooming of children by adults.

UNDERSTAND THE CONCEPT

Trolling refers to the use of online new media, particular sites such as Twitter, by some individuals to anonymously abuse or threaten people whose opinions or activities they dislike.

Some commentators, however, believe that the irresponsible use of the internet is a price worth paying for the free expression and exchange of information that it provides. In any case, the control of information on the web is largely outside the government's control because many ISPs operate outside UK territory.

Alone together

Turkle (2011) refers to new media users as "cyborgs" because they are always connected to each other, regardless of where they are, via their laptops, tablets and smartphones. She argues that people now live full-time on the web and are devoted to their communication devices, particularly their smartphones, which constantly have to be checked for texts, emails and social network updates.

However, Turkle points out that although new media connects its users to more people, it has also resulted in greater anxiety and isolation. She notes "we enjoy continual connection but rarely have each other's full attention … We brag about how many we have 'friended' on Facebook, yet Americans say they have fewer friends than before … The ties we form through the internet are not, in the end, the ties that bind. But they are the ties that preoccupy. We text each other at family dinners, while we jog … when we misplace our mobile devices, we become anxious – impossible really." Livingstone (2009) in a similar analysis argues that children today communicate more with the virtual outside world than with adult members of their own family. Parents often have to text or Facebook their children to gain their attention at meal times.

How true are Turkle's and Livingstone's observations of your own relationship with new media?

New media as chaos

Keen (2008) is very critical of aspects of the new media, especially the internet, which he claims is chaotic. He claims that it has no governing moral code and that it is a place where truth is selective and frequently subject to change. He makes four specific criticisms of new media:

› Social networking sites such as Facebook and blogging do not contribute to the democratic process in any way because they are merely vehicles for narcissistic self-broadcasting. He claims they exist purely for individuals to indulge in shameless self-promotion.

› User-generated sites such as Wikipedia are open to abuse and bias, and consequently they are unreliable as sources of information. Keen also argues that the internet has created a generation of 'cut and paste' plagiarists and intellectual thieves.

› Much of the output of new media outlets such as Twitter and blogs is unchecked, and consequently uninformed opinion, lies and trolling are the norm, rather than considered analysis and expertise.

› The internet is contributing to cultural illiteracy. Keen claims that young people are less actively engaged with researching the world around them because the web gives them easy access to 'facts'. Consequently, he says, young people have shorter attention spans and poor problem-solving skills.

CONCLUSIONS

While neophiliacs are very upbeat about the future role of new media technologies, cultural pessimists remind us that we need to be cautious about how the new media may be employed. Both perspectives probably exaggerate how far the media is being transformed. The last two decades have seen both continuity and, at the extreme, evolutionary rather than revolutionary change. Television is still the most popular medium, and newspapers, despite fears that they were going to be replaced by the internet, still sell extremely well. Books are holding up remarkably well too despite the development of e-books and reading devices such as Kindle and Nook. Moreover, a small number of very powerful media companies are still very much in control of both traditional and new media.

CHECK YOUR UNDERSTANDING

1. Explain what is meant by the term 'interactivity'.

2. Explain what is meant by the 'digital underclass'.

3. Explain what is meant by 'collective intelligence'.

4. Explain what is meant by 'e-commerce'.

5. Identify and briefly outline two examples of how new media might reinforce elite power.

6. Identify and briefly explain how more choice in new media might lead to a 'candy-floss culture'.

7. Suggest and analyse two reasons why new media may play an active role in democratic societies.

8. Analyse two differences in the way that males and females use new media.

9. Evaluate Keen's view that the internet is a chaos of useless information.

10. Evaluate the neophiliac view of the new media.

TAKE IT FURTHER

1. Design a questionnaire and conduct a survey within your school or college to assess the differences in access to and consumption of new media in relation to class, gender, ethnicity and age. Consider both household ownership and personal consumption of the various forms of the new media.

2. What skills are required by users of new media? Visit YouTube and search for the video The *New Media Literacies* by Project New Media Literacies and the TEDxWarwick talk by Doug Belshaw, *The essential elements of digital literacies*.

4.2 OWNERSHIP AND CONTROL OF THE MEDIA

INTRODUCING THE DEBATE

This chapter focuses on sociological concerns over the ownership and control of the mass media in both its traditional and new forms. There are essentially four positions:

> Pluralists argue that the market largely determines the content of the media. If a media product does not sell and make a profit, the media company goes out of business. Pluralists see media personnel as doing their best in an impartial way to give people the media products that they want.

> In contrast, instrumental Marxists argue that media owners manipulate and control media content on behalf of a capitalist ruling class in order to ensure the existing economic system remains unchallenged.

> Hegemonic Marxists, however, argue that this interpretation is too simplistic and that owners exercise little power. Rather, control of media content is in the hands of professionals who produce media designed to appeal to the masses and to offend as few people as possible. The motive of these professionals is to make profit rather than to make political or ideological points although hegemonic Marxists point out that this means that media content is rarely critical of a status quo that benefits the powerful.

> Finally, postmodernists argue that the nature of media has changed so much in recent years that it is individual consumers rather than media owners and professionals who 'own' and 'control' media content.

OWNERSHIP AND CONTROL OF THE MEDIA

Concentration of ownership

Bagdikian (2004) points out that in 1983, 50 corporations controlled the vast majority of all news media in the USA. However, by 1992, 22 companies owned and operated 90 per cent of the mass media – controlling almost all of the USA's newspapers, magazines, TV and radio stations, books, records, movies, videos, wire services and photo agencies. Bagdikian argues that if the USA's media were owned by separate individuals, there would be 25,000 owners; instead, by 2014, media ownership in the USA was concentrated in six corporations: Comcast, Disney, 21st Century Fox/News Corporation, Time Warner, Viacom and CBS Corporation. Chapter 1 documented how a small number of corporations dominate the ownership of the new media. Internet providers, social networking sites and the content of digital media are increasingly being bought up by the companies that dominate the old media.

The British newspaper industry

Curran (2003) suggests that there has been a similar concentration of ownership in the British newspaper industry since the early 20th century. For example, in 1937, four men – Lords Beaverbrook, Rothermere, Camrose and Northcliffe, known as the 'press barons' – owned nearly one in every two national and local daily newspapers sold in the UK. In 2015, little has changed. Seven individuals dominate the ownership and content of UK national daily and Sunday newspapers:

> News Corp (owned and controlled by the Australian-American Rupert Murdoch and his family) produces *The Times*, *The Sun*, *The Sun on Sunday* and *The Sunday Times*.

> DMG, formerly Associated Newspapers (owned by Lord Rothermere) owns the *Daily Mail*, the *Mail On Sunday*, and *Metro* as well as 54 regional papers.

> Northern & Shell is owned by Richard Desmond and produces the *Daily Express* and the *Sunday Express*, the *Daily Star* and *OK!* magazine.

> The *London Evening Standard*, The *Independent*, The *Independent on Sunday* and the *i* newspaper are owned by Alexander Lebedev and his son Evgeny.

> The *Telegraph* group (*Daily and Sunday*) is owned by the Barclay Brothers.

Only two national newspaper groups are controlled by companies rather than individuals. Trinity Mirror owns the *Daily Mirror*, *Sunday Mirror*, *Sunday People* and *Daily*

Record (Scotland's biggest selling paper), as well as over 150 regional daily newspapers. The Guardian Media Group is controlled by a board of trustees – the Scott Trust – which owns both the *Guardian* and the *Observer*.

The British broadcasting media

There is evidence of concentration of ownership in British commercial and satellite television. For example, the content of commercial terrestrial television is mainly controlled by one company, ITV plc, which currently owns 12 of the 15 regional commercial television franchises. Channel 5, on the other hand, is currently owned by Richard Desmond. Access to satellite, cable and digital television in the UK is generally controlled by three companies – Sky plc (39 per cent of Sky's shares are owned by Rupert Murdoch's News Corp), Virgin Media and BT Total Broadband.

Horizontal integration

Concentration of ownership is consolidated by cross-media ownership or horizontal integration. This refers to the fact that the bigger media companies often own a range of different types of media outlets. For example, News Corp, which owns newspapers in Britain and Australia, also owns the publisher HarperCollins as well as interests in the USA, including the *New York Post*, Fox TV and 20th Century Fox film studios. It also owns a big chunk of Sky and the biggest Asian satellite channel, Star TV.

Vertical integration

Concentration of ownership is also strengthened by vertical integration. This refers to the increasing trend of media multinationals to control all levels of media production. For example, Time Warner makes its own films and distributes them to its own cinema complexes while News Corp owns television and film studios as well as the satellite television channels that show them. Vertical integration therefore gives media multinationals greater economic control over their operating environment.

Lateral expansion

Lateral expansion also assists concentration of media ownership. It occurs when media companies diversify into new business areas in order to spread economic risk. Losses made in one area may be compensated for by profits in another. The Virgin group owned by Richard Branson is a good example of a diversified corporation – it has major media interests in music, publishing, film production and cinemas. However, it also sells insurance and banking services as well as running an airline, a train service and health services.

Global conglomeration

Concentration of media ownership has been assisted by the erosion of traditional national boundaries and the globalisation of both economics and culture (see Topic 3). Media companies such as Sony, Samsung and Viacom have invested in or bought up media companies outside their countries of origin. Globalisation has opened up new international markets, particularly in new media such as the internet and smartphones. Concentration of ownership has therefore become global and a small number of media companies have transformed themselves into transnational conglomerates that monopolise ownership of a diversity of media across dozens of countries. For example, News Corp owns hundreds of different types of media companies across Asia, Europe and North America.

Synergy

Concentration of ownership is increasingly strengthened by a marketing strategy known as 'synergy'. This involves media transnationals using their diversity to package the same product in several different ways therefore increasing profit. For example, a film will often be accompanied by a soundtrack album, a computer game, a downloadable ring tone, toys and so on, produced by different arms of the same media company. The film may be marketed by advertisements in newspapers.

Technological convergence

Technological convergence (see Chapter 1) refers to the trend of putting several technologies into one media delivery system such as the smartphone, tablet or laptop. This, too, consolidates concentration of media ownership because in the past these media delivery systems would have been produced by distinct companies that specialised in those products. However, transnational media companies are increasingly investing in and working closely with companies such as Samsung (producers of smartphones), Apple, Orange, Microsoft and Facebook to explore ways to bring about even greater technological convergence, so making their media products – music, films, television, apps and games – more accessible to a global audience.

THEORIES OF MEDIA OWNERSHIP AND CONTROL

Doyle (2002) suggests that we need to study media ownership and control because it is important for societies to have a diverse and pluralistic media provision so that all points of view can be heard. She argues that if concentration of media ownership occurs in a society there is a danger that abuses of power and influence by elites will go unnoticed and that democracy and justice will suffer as a result.

The pluralist theory

From a pluralist perspective, modern capitalist societies are democratic – all interest groups, whether they are right-wing, centrist or left-wing, are given a media platform to express their views to the electorate, and the most persuasive arguments will result in their representatives being voted into power. The mass media are therefore seen by pluralists as essential and impartial facilitators of this democratic ideal, because most people obtain their knowledge about politics from newspapers, television and the internet.

The economics of media ownership

Pluralists subscribe to a market model of media ownership and control in that they argue that the free market and the pursuit of profit (at the expense of other media companies) is always going to trump the idea that media corporations are a means by which owners could impose their political will on audiences and consumers. In free-market economies, media owners compete against each other in order to attract people to their product. Pluralists argue that readers, viewers and listeners are the real power holders because they exercise consumer sovereignty, which is the right to buy or not to buy. In other words, they have freedom of choice. If they did not like the choices that media owners are making available to them, or if they suspected the media product was biased one way rather than another, the media audience would probably respond by not buying the product and the media company would go out of business.

Pluralists point out that this global media marketplace is segmented. Mass media corporations produce an amazing variety of media products aimed at different markets. For example, the mobile phone market is very different to the pop music market or the magazine market. Pluralists therefore argue that such variety and diversity counters any attempt to influence a mass audience. Moreover, media corporations often tailor their products to appeal to particular social groups. This empowers the consumer because they have access to more diverse media products. Their choices can make or break that product. A good example of this is the failure of Blackberry (which dominated the mobile phone market for young people and professionals in the early 2000s) to update the features on phones that most appeal to the young. They lost significant ground (and earnings) as smartphone media produced by Apple and Samsung overtook them. Power, then, according to pluralist thinkers, lies with the consumer or audience rather than with media owners. An individual may own a media corporation but the control of what that media corporation produces is in the hands of those consuming in the media marketplace. From a pluralist point of view, the bottom line is that it is the market that determines media content and product, not the owner.

Pluralists also claim that the rationale for the concentration of media ownership and control is essentially economic. They argue that media products are costly to produce and that, therefore, the concentration of ownership is aimed at the maximisation of audience size in order to reduce costs and to attract advertising revenue. The globalisation of the media and the conglomerates that have resulted from this are merely attempts at finding new audiences or customers in order to increase profits. Pluralists maintain that processes such as vertical and horizontal integration, synergy, lateral expansion and convergence are aimed at reducing the costs involved in contracting services out to other media companies that might be competing with them. Profits are also enhanced because they are no longer subjected to the fluctuating prices charged by other companies.

Pluralists argue that the diversity of media products worldwide means it that it is practically impossible for owners to influence their content. For example, it is doubtful whether Rupert Murdoch has the time or capability to control the content of the dozens of newspapers he owns or to interfere with programmes on the TV channels his conglomerate runs. Whale (1977) suggests that "media owners have global problems of trade and investment to occupy their minds" and so do not have the time to think about the day-to-day detailed running of their media businesses.

The media as a democratic mirror

Pluralists claim that the range of media products available is extremely diverse and that, as a result, all points of view in a democratic society are catered for. If some viewpoints have a greater range of media representing them, this is not necessarily biased. It merely mirrors what the audience wants or sees as important. For example, if the majority of UK newspapers raise concerns about Jeremy Corbyn refusing to push the nuclear button, pluralists would argue that owners, editors and journalists are merely mirroring the concerns of the majority of UK citizens about the external threat to Britain's security.

Public service broadcasting

Pluralists point out that a significant share of the media market in the UK is taken up by public service broadcasters (PSB), that is, media outlets controlled by the state, which have a worldwide reputation for impartiality, and which cater for every conceivable taste and opinion. The British Broadcasting Corporation (BBC) is the most obvious example of this, although Channel 4 is also a public service broadcaster.

The BBC was set up in 1926 by a Royal Charter, which clearly states that the BBC has a legal obligation to provide specific services – to inform, to educate and to entertain the full audience spectrum (that is, all social groups in society must be catered for). Government reviews of BBC output have consistently stressed the importance of impartiality in the reporting of news, of catering for all segments of society and of the education of audiences so that they can make informed decisions about political issues. Pluralists therefore see PSB as the epitome of impartial and objective media and a counterweight to any potential bias that might occur in the private sector.

However, a number of commentators have suggested that the BBC is increasingly abandoning its PSB aims because it is losing its audience to commercial and satellite television. As a result, the BBC has become more commercialised and populist in its programming in an attempt to keep its audience. Some pluralists argue that this is not a problem because PSB and ITV have had to offer more choice to their audiences in order to compete with Sky and Virgin; for example, the setting up of the BBC digital channels and an internet news site are a rational response to this increased competition, which pluralists claim can only be good for audiences.

State controls

Pluralists note that the power of media owners is also restricted by state or government controls. For example, in some societies, governments do not allow owners to own too many media or different types of media, in order to reduce the possibility that one person's or group's views or products might become too dominant. In the USA, the huge film studios have been prevented from owning film production, film distribution and cinemas at the same time. Many countries have cross-ownership rules preventing companies from owning more than one media form in the same area – for example, an owner may only be able to own one television station rather than several.

Another state constraint on media ownership is the fact that both the BBC and ITV have some formal legal requirements imposed upon them by a powerful regulator – the Office for Communications (Ofcom) – which was set up in 2003. Ofcom's function is to monitor the content and quality of television and radio output on both the

BBC and the commercial channels, and to investigate viewer and listener complaints. Pluralists argue that this combination of audience and regulator prevents unscrupulous media owners imposing biased content upon the general public.

Media professionalism

Pluralists stress the professionalism of journalists and editors, arguing that editors would never allow owners to compromise their independence. They argue that journalists have too much integrity to be regularly biased in favour of one particular perspective. Pluralists also point out that the media have a strong tradition of investigative journalism, which has often targeted those in power. The Washington Post's reporting of the Watergate scandal which found that President Nixon had authorised the bugging of his opponent's offices led to his resignation in 1972. Newspapers in the UK have also uncovered corruption in high places and forced politicians to resign from office.

Critique of the pluralist theory

There are a number of criticisms that can be made of the pluralist view of the media:

> Curran argues that there is plenty of evidence that media owners have undermined newspaper independence and balance in subtle ways by choosing the editors that they want and getting rid of editors and journalists that 'fail' to toe their owner's line. Moreover, he observes that journalists deliberately self-censor their reports to omit controversial issues that might draw the owner's attention to them. Conforming to the owner's requirements brings rewards in terms of interesting assignments and promotion, whilst dissident journalists are often sacked.

> Pluralists have been criticised for over-stating the impartiality of journalists. Blumler and Gurevitch (1995) point out that many journalists are over-reliant on official sources – particularly politicians and the police – for information and stories, and this undermines journalistic objectivity. Surveys of the general public demonstrate that significant numbers do not trust journalists.

> Trowler (2004) observes that 500 journalists were embedded with British and American troops during the invasion of Iraq. This resulted in one-sided, rather than balanced, reporting of the conflict as journalists formed personal attachments with the soldiers with whom they were living.

> Feminists are critical of pluralism because they argue that the range of female voices made available in the marketplace is actually very narrow. They argue that media content is very male-oriented and that this can clearly be seen in media representations of females, which on the whole are defined by sexual objectification, domesticity or motherhood. See Chapter 5 for a detailed exploration. Little space is afforded to alternative representations of this critique of women and, as Thornham (2007) notes, all too often feminist perspectives are dismissed by journalists as extreme and threatening.

> It is difficult for ordinary people to decide what they want to see or hear if the media provide their only source of information. Powerless groups do not have the resources to set up media companies to communicate their points of view. Consumers therefore do not have access to a diversity of media reflecting every conceivable opinion because particular views are deemed unacceptable or too extreme by owners and media professionals. Media consumers therefore cannot make genuine choices because the media have constructed a highly censored marketplace.

The Marxist theory

Marxists argue that the capitalist economic system of the UK is deeply unfair because it generally benefits a minority – the capitalist class – at the expense of the majority, and especially the working class. Marxists believe that inequalities in wealth and income and therefore poverty are the direct result of the way capitalism is organised.

The role of ideology

Marxists suggest that the capitalist class uses **ideology** to make sure that the working class accepts capitalism and does not threaten its stability.

UNDERSTAND THE CONCEPT

Ideology refers to a set of ideas that usually originate with a powerful group and which contain elements of untruth. However, these ideas are often presented to the population as facts or common sense. An example of a successful ideology is the notion that the UK is a meritocracy in which talent and hard work are always rewarded. The evidence from social mobility studies does not support this ideological 'truth' (see Topic 6).

In order to disseminate this ideology to the mass of the population, Marxists argue that the capitalist class uses its cultural power to dominate institutions such as the education system, religion and the mass media. The role of these agencies is to transmit ruling-class ideology, which aims to convince people of the benefits of capitalism and to justify inequalities in income and wealth. Those who fail to benefit from capitalism are encouraged to believe it is their fault for not working hard enough. Consequently, Marxists argue that the outcome of ruling-class ideology is that the poor fail to see the real cause of their poverty – the exploitative and deeply unequal organisation of the capitalist system that benefits the few at the expense of the many. Ruling-class ideology therefore produces false class consciousness among the working class – they are unable to see the true cause of their social and economic situation.

The Marxist instrumentalist theory

Marxist theories of the mass media strongly challenge the pluralist theory of ownership and control. Marxists such as Miliband (1973) take a manipulative or instrumentalist approach to the ownership and control of the media. Miliband argued that the mass media represent an ideological instrument which plays a key role in the reproduction and justification of class inequality. Marxists believe that media owners do this by transmitting a conservative and conformist ideology in the form of news and entertainment. The role of the media (along with other ideological agencies, such as education) is to convince the general public that ruling-class ideology is 'truth' and 'fact'. By doing this, Miliband argued, media owners shape and manipulate how people think about the world they live in. For example, the media rarely inform the general public about why people continue to live in poverty or, if they do, they represent the poor as somehow responsible for their situation. The media do not encourage people to be critical of the capitalist system. Media representations of wealth are, on the whole, very positive, as are media representations of the Royal Family.

Marxists also argue that media representations of ethnic minorities tend to portray them as criminals, migrants and extremists in order to divide and rule the working class. Marxists such as Castles and Kosack (1973) argue that it suits the capitalist class for white working-class people to view ethnic minorities as a threat because this distracts them from the real cause of inequality, that is, the organisation of the capitalist system. (A more detailed discussion of these media representations of poverty, wealth and ethnic minorities can be found in Chapter 6.) Marxists argue that the mass media ensure

that members of society only get a narrow range of 'approved' views and knowledge, with the result that 'alternative' and critical points of view are rarely heard or are dismissed as extremist. Marxists, particularly those who belong to the Frankfurt School, such as Marcuse, argue that media owners play a key role in helping to control the working class through a **'bread and circuses'** approach, meaning that they deliberately make sure that media output is mainly entertainment-oriented so that people are kept happy and docile.

UNDERSTAND THE CONCEPT

The phrase **'bread and circuses'** is used to describe superficial entertainments used to satisfy populations so that they are distracted and diverted from real issues such as the causes of poverty therefore keeping them happy, and most importantly, docile and ignorant.

Marxists argue that the media are happy to transmit ruling-class ideology through television and newspapers because media owners are part of the ruling capitalist class and have a vested interest in it not being criticised or dismantled. The last thing they want is equality for all, because this would mean less wealth for them.

Tunstall and Palmer (1991) argue along similar lines with regard to government regulation of media conglomerates. They suggest that governments are no longer interested in controlling the activities of media owners because the class interests of media owners and the political elite often overlap. Rather, 'regulatory favours' are the norm – newspapers owned by a media conglomerate will directly support a government or neglect to criticise government policy or even withhold information from the general public in return for governments failing to enforce media regulation or even abolishing it altogether.

Evidence for the Marxist instrumentalist theory
The problem with this Marxist account is that it implies that media owners, wealth – holders and the political elite are united in some sort of ideological conspiracy to manipulate the opinions of the UK population. There is some evidence for this cooperation in other societies – for example, in Italy, it has been demonstrated that Silvio Berlusconi's control of three television stations (which reached 40 per cent of the Italian audience) was

instrumental in his party winning the general election in 1994 and Berlusconi becoming Prime Minister.

Curran's detailed systematic examination of the British press also suggests that the evidence for owner interference in and manipulation of UK newspaper content is strong. He suggests that four distinct periods can be seen with regard to owner intervention and the consequent undermining of journalistic and editorial integrity.

› From 1920 to 1950, press barons such as Lord Beaverbrook, who owned the Express newspaper group, openly stated their ideological intentions. For example, Beaverbrook famously said: "I run the *Daily Express* merely for the purpose of making propaganda and with no other motive."

› Curran argues that from 1951 to 1974 there was greater delegation by owners to editorial and journalistic authority and autonomy. Consequently this was the great era of investigative reporting by journalists into abuses of power, although owners still insisted their newspapers supported particular political ideologies and political parties.

› From 1974 to 1992, Curran argues, a new more interventionist proprietorship appeared, as symbolised by Rupert Murdoch – "a businessman first and foremost" – who acquired both *The Sun* and *The Times*. Murdoch was oriented towards what sold rather than what furthered a party interest or ideological viewpoint. Curran notes that Murdoch shifted his newspapers to the Right because he believed that right-wing economic policies were the key to making vast profits.

Murdoch introduced a new personalised style of management to the production of newspapers in the UK – he read proofs, wrote leaders, changed content and layout. Most importantly, he handpicked compliant editors and managing directors and sacked those who opposed his ideological position. Between 1979 and 1992, Murdoch was a strong supporter of Margaret Thatcher's Conservative government because it pursued economic policies he agreed with and actively encouraged, to such an extent that he was dubbed the "phantom prime minister".

› Since 1997, Curran argues, media ownership has been based on an ideology of "global conservatism", as British newspaper groups have moved into the global marketplace. The most successful media entrepreneur in this period has been Rupert Murdoch, who Bagdikian dubbed "lord of the global village". Curran notes how, in 1997, Murdoch instructed his newspapers to abandon support for the Conservative Party and to support

Tony Blair's New Labour. However, this was not due to Murdoch's sudden conversion to social democracy. Rather, it was a hard-nosed business decision, because Blair was willing to lift state controls that prevented cross-media ownership. Curran argues that Murdoch was right-wing, but perceived Blair to be "the only credible conservative worth supporting in 1997. In effect, a tacit deal was made between two power-holders – one a market-friendly politician and the other a pragmatic businessman – in a form that sidelined the public". As Curran concludes, "the Murdoch press thus changed its political loyalty but not its politics."

Critique of the Marxist instrumentalist theory

Instrumental Marxists have been criticised because they rarely explain how an owner's media manipulation works in practice. The evidence they present tends to be anecdotal and partial rather than based on empirical research.

Instrumental Marxists are economic reductionists, which means they are only interested in how media ownership and control relates to social class relationships and inequalities. Consequently, feminists would argue that they ignore the role of media owners in transmitting patriarchal ideology.

They also assume that ruling-class ideology has an effect upon its audience in the form of false class consciousness although there is little evidence for this. Neo-Marxists such as Gramsci argue that the working class are likely to experience 'dual consciousness'. They may agree with aspects of ruling – class ideology but their experience of everyday life and work means that they have the ability to see through and reject the ideology transmitted by owners of the media.

Marxists fail to acknowledge that many journalists and media publications still see themselves as the guardians of the public interest and dedicate their careers to exposing members of the establishment who abuse their powers.

It is argued that the growth of the new media, especially social networking sites such as Twitter and Facebook, means that media owners and the ruling-class elite are now subject to more surveillance and criticism from ordinary people. This 'citizen journalism' allegedly means that the actions of those in power, including media owners, are under constant public scrutiny. These ideas will be further explored in Chapter 4.

Curran's analysis of media ownership does partly support the instrumentalist position because his evidence suggests that, until the 1970s, press barons generally subscribed to a right-wing ideology in the management of the content of their newspapers. However, Curran argues that the evidence regarding media owners from the 1970s on does not always support the Marxist instrumentalist argument because today such owners are primarily motivated by profit rather than ideology. Moreover, their actions are not united and collectivised; media owners and conglomerates ruthlessly compete with each other in an attempt to obtain a bigger share of the market. Murdoch's instructions to Fox News to support the Iraq War, and his decision that Sky News should not cover pro-democracy protests in China, seem to have been motivated simply by his desire to increase his audiences and therefore profits in the USA and China respectively. However, Curran suggests that there is sufficient evidence to suggest that the actions of media owners produce media content that, in the long term, benefits capitalism. In this sense, Curran's analysis fits in with the analysis of the Glasgow University Media Group (GUMG), which takes a **hegemonic** approach to media ownership and control.

UNDERSTAND THE CONCEPT

Hegemony means economic, social and cultural domination of one group over another. From a Marxist perspective, a minority – the ruling or capital class – exercises hegemony over the majority of the population.

The hegemonic Marxist theory

The Glasgow University Media Group suggests that media content does support the interests of those who run the capitalist system but this hegemony is probably an accidental by-product of the social backgrounds of journalists and broadcasters. These tend to be overwhelmingly White, middle-class and male. Sutton Trust reports in 2006 and 2012 found that over 50 per cent of the top 100 journalists in the UK were educated in independent private schools (which educate only 7 per cent of all pupils). The Sutton Trust asks the important question: is it healthy that those who are most influential in determining and interpreting the news agenda have educational backgrounds that are so different from the vast majority of the population?

The GUMG claims that these journalists and broadcasters tend to believe in 'middle-of-the-road' (consensus) views and ideas, which are generally unthreatening and which, they believe, appeal to the majority of their viewers, listeners and readers. Such journalists and broadcasters tend to see anyone who believes in ideas outside this media consensus as 'extremist' and, consequently, such people are rarely invited to contribute their opinion in newspapers or on television. When such alternative views are included in newspapers or television broadcasts, they are often ridiculed by journalists.

Economic pressures

However, the GUMG argues that this journalistic desire not to rock the boat is mainly motivated by profit rather than a desire to transmit capitalist ideology. Most media companies aim to make profits by attracting advertising, and advertisers are attracted to a specific type of media by the number of readers and viewers. If, for some reason, those viewers or readers are put off the television programme or newspaper or magazine because its content is interpreted as offensive or upsetting, then profits decline. Those who commission television programmes or decide newspaper or magazine content consequently play safe by excluding anything that might offend or upset viewers, readers and advertisers.

Agenda setting

The result of this journalistic consensus, says the GUMG, is that the media decide what issues should be discussed by society and which ones should be avoided. This is known as 'agenda setting'. The GUMG argues that the media present a fairly narrow agenda for discussion. For example, the media are happy to talk about the size and shape of a female singer's bottom, but don't often discuss the massive inequalities that exist in society. The *Sun* readers are more likely to be outraged by the fact that Jeremy Corbyn did not sing the national anthem at the 2015 Remembrance Sunday ceremony than by the number of people living in poverty. In this way, ordinary members of the public never really question the workings of capitalist society. The GUMG argues that consequently we are not presented with the really important information that would help ordinary members of society make real choices about how society should be run. Agenda setting therefore results in 'cultural hegemony', with the basic principles of capitalism – private enterprise, profit, the 'free market' and the rights of property ownership – being presented by the media as 'normal' and 'natural'.

UNDERSTAND THE CONCEPT

Imperialism refers to a country's ability to impose its power and influence on other countries, usually through military conquest. Cultural imperialism suggests that such power and influence is imposed by mass media and cultural products rather than through force of arms.

GLOBALISATION

Steger (2005) defines globalisation as a "set of social processes that are thought to transform our present social condition into one of globality". Steger sees globality as a "social condition characterised by the existence of global economic, political, cultural and environmental interconnections and flows that make many of the currently existing borders and boundaries irrelevant".

Crothers (2012) observes that a combination of economic, political and cultural factors promotes globalisation in three ways:

> New and increased relationships that have been created between people, social networks and ideas go beyond traditional nation state borders. For example, people in 'traditional' societies are now exposed to modern technologies such as mobile phones and 'modern' ideas such as democracy, equality and tolerance for others. However, this is not one-way traffic – modern societies are exposed to and influenced by the values of the developing world with regard to the environment, alternative medicine, religion and so on.

> People are linked in new ways as both the production of goods as well as the flow of finance capital, and their consumption, take place 24 hours a day around the world. For example, workers in the West and in the developing world may find themselves employed by the same transnational corporations. Economic problems in one part of the world now have a knock-on effect on the rest of the world, as demonstrated by the 2008 meltdown in the subprime mortgage market in the USA. People the world over consume McDonalds burgers, drink Coca-Cola and use Chinese-manufactured Apple computers and iPhones.

> Global events and issues have become local events and issues because of the speed of communication and the expectation of instantaneous contact. For example, Islamist groups such as the so-called Islamic

State have taken particular advantage of satellite television channels such as Al-Jazeera, online social networks and smartphones to disseminate live images of beheadings or the destruction of antiquities quickly to a global audience.

Bell (2015) observes that there has never been a form of global media with the power to report and disseminate events with the speed and geographic reach of Twitter. She argues: "America holds its first television debate for Democratic candidates, Donald Trump live-tweets it. If London Bridge is closing down, Twitter provides the eyewitness reports and pictures ahead of the broadcast news media. Journalists when they wake in the morning don't first switch on the radio they reach for their smartphones and scroll through Twitter. Their subjects and sources, from politicians to pop stars, do the same."

As people are exposed to this increasingly complex world, their ideas and identities are shaped and reshaped. For example, some media sociologists argue that social networks such as Twitter and Facebook can give people who live in repressive societies the confidence to dissent and take to the streets to demand change.

Bell observes that Facebook has 1.2 billion active users worldwide who are constantly engaged in constructing and reconstructing their identities through the posting of textual and visual representations that add up to their personal profile or identity.

THE MEDIA AND GLOBALISATION

The mass media have played a key role in creating this global world. Advances in mass communications, digitalisation and cyber technology such as satellite television, the internet – particularly its user-generated and social network sites – streaming services and mobile phones – particularly recent developments in 4G and 5G smartphones – have transformed the world's concept of time and space. Information in all its varied forms – news, ideas, financial data and cultural products such as film, music and television – can now be transmitted instantaneously 24 hours a day to most global destinations.

The globalisation of media outlets and products has been assisted by the economic growth of transnational media and cybercorporations such as News Corp, Apple and Microsoft. Since the 1990s, the ownership of the world's media companies has become increasingly concentrated in the hands of a small number of transnational corporations. McChesney (2002) observes that the overwhelming majority of the world's film production,

It is argued that the growth of the new media, especially social networking sites such as Twitter and Facebook, means that media owners and the ruling-class elite are now subject to more surveillance and criticism from ordinary people. This 'citizen journalism' allegedly means that the actions of those in power, including media owners, are under constant public scrutiny. These ideas will be further explored in Chapter 4.

Curran's analysis of media ownership does partly support the instrumentalist position because his evidence suggests that, until the 1970s, press barons generally subscribed to a right-wing ideology in the management of the content of their newspapers. However, Curran argues that the evidence regarding media owners from the 1970s on does not always support the Marxist instrumentalist argument because today such owners are primarily motivated by profit rather than ideology. Moreover, their actions are not united and collectivised; media owners and conglomerates ruthlessly compete with each other in an attempt to obtain a bigger share of the market. Murdoch's instructions to Fox News to support the Iraq War, and his decision that Sky News should not cover pro-democracy protests in China, seem to have been motivated simply by his desire to increase his audiences and therefore profits in the USA and China respectively. However, Curran suggests that there is sufficient evidence to suggest that the actions of media owners produce media content that, in the long term, benefits capitalism. In this sense, Curran's analysis fits in with the analysis of the Glasgow University Media Group (GUMG), which takes a **hegemonic** approach to media ownership and control.

UNDERSTAND THE CONCEPT

Hegemony means economic, social and cultural domination of one group over another. From a Marxist perspective, a minority – the ruling or capital class – exercises hegemony over the majority of the population.

The hegemonic Marxist theory

The Glasgow University Media Group suggests that media content does support the interests of those who run the capitalist system but this hegemony is probably an accidental by-product of the social backgrounds of journalists and broadcasters. These tend to be overwhelmingly White, middle-class and male. Sutton Trust reports in 2006 and 2012 found that over 50 per cent of the top 100 journalists in the UK were educated in independent private schools (which educate only 7 per cent of all pupils). The Sutton Trust asks the important

question: is it healthy that those who are most influential in determining and interpreting the news agenda have educational backgrounds that are so different from the vast majority of the population?

The GUMG claims that these journalists and broadcasters tend to believe in 'middle-of-the-road' (consensus) views and ideas, which are generally unthreatening and which, they believe, appeal to the majority of their viewers, listeners and readers. Such journalists and broadcasters tend to see anyone who believes in ideas outside this media consensus as 'extremist' and, consequently, such people are rarely invited to contribute their opinion in newspapers or on television. When such alternative views are included in newspapers or television broadcasts, they are often ridiculed by journalists.

Economic pressures

However, the GUMG argues that this journalistic desire not to rock the boat is mainly motivated by profit rather than a desire to transmit capitalist ideology. Most media companies aim to make profits by attracting advertising, and advertisers are attracted to a specific type of media by the number of readers and viewers. If, for some reason, those viewers or readers are put off the television programme or newspaper or magazine because its content is interpreted as offensive or upsetting, then profits decline. Those who commission television programmes or decide newspaper or magazine content consequently play safe by excluding anything that might offend or upset viewers, readers and advertisers.

Agenda setting

The result of this journalistic consensus, says the GUMG, is that the media decide what issues should be discussed by society and which ones should be avoided. This is known as 'agenda setting'. The GUMG argues that the media present a fairly narrow agenda for discussion. For example, the media are happy to talk about the size and shape of a female singer's bottom, but don't often discuss the massive inequalities that exist in society. The *Sun* readers are more likely to be outraged by the fact that Jeremy Corbyn did not sing the national anthem at the 2015 Remembrance Sunday ceremony than by the number of people living in poverty. In this way, ordinary members of the public never really question the workings of capitalist society. The GUMG argues that consequently we are not presented with the really important information that would help ordinary members of society make real choices about how society should be run. Agenda setting therefore results in 'cultural hegemony', with the basic principles of capitalism – private enterprise, profit, the 'free market' and the rights of property ownership – being presented by the media as 'normal' and 'natural'.

The media and the Establishment

Jones (2015) generally supports the hegemonic Marxist perspectives on the media. He sees media owners, editors and journalists as part of the 'Establishment', which he defines as an alliance of unaccountable powerful groups "bound together by common economic interests and a shared set of mentalities"; these groups aim to protect their dominant position in society by managing democracy to make sure that it does not threaten their interests. Jones argues that it should be the job of the media to scrutinise the activities of the Establishment but he notes that "the British media is an integral part of the British Establishment; its owners share the same underlying assumptions and mantras." Consequently journalists turn a blind eye to the Establishment and instead critically attack and vilify the behaviour of the poor, the unemployed and other benefit claimants, immigrants and public sector workers. This deflects attention and "anger away from those who actually wield power in British society".

Critique of the hegemonic Marxist theory

The criticisms of the hegemonic model are similar to those of the instrumental model in that hegemonic Marxists are also vague about what constitutes ideology and the effects it allegedly has upon powerless groups. The GUMG's exclusive focus on media professionals implies that owners have little or no input into media production, which is probably unrealistic. Some critics have noted that it is difficult to see the difference between the instrumental Marxist focus on manipulation and the hegemonic Marxist focus on agenda-setting or the role of the media as part of the British Establishment.

It also neglects to consider that, because the media is largely owned and controlled by men, agenda-setting is a patriarchal exercise that serves to limit women's roles in media production and content. Finally, some critics see the new media and citizen journalism as having the potential to counter the influence of the establishment-orientated media identified by the GUMG and Jones.

FOCUS ON SKILLS: MEDIA SILENCE ON GEORGE OSBORNE'S NUCLEAR DEAL WITH CHINA

George Osborne meets Chinese Premier Li Keqiang.

George Osborne addressed the Conservative Party conference on 5 October 2015, fresh from a sales trip to Beijing. His efforts to promote more trade between the two nations saw Chinese state-owned companies invited to participate in the development of nuclear generating power plants in Britain. However, Henderson (2015) points out that the British mass media has been strangely quiet about this deal, especially considering that:

> The Chinese have a poor health and safety record with regard to building nuclear power stations.

> China has a deeply corrupt economy and there are fears that companies operating in Britain may attempt to side-step safety measures and regulatory agencies.

> Though technically state-owned, it is the Communist Party of China and the People's Liberation Army, not government agencies, that control the Chinese companies building these power stations. The £2 billion guarantee promised by Osborne to these Chinese companies will result in the British taxpayer subsidising the Chinese Communist Party.

> The question of Chinese state (and thus Communist Party) involvement in Britain's power stations, is a matter of national security.

Henderson concludes that the nuclear deal with China is, in effect, a trade-off for allowing financial services (the only economic sector the British government privileges) to penetrate the Chinese market. This means the government is set to embark on a potentially very dangerous path. Had this deal been negotiated by Jeremy Corbyn as Prime Minister, the media would have been wondering if he were in the pay of the Chinese government. But George Osborne? Surely not.

Based on Henderson (2015), theconversation.com

Questions

1. **Suggest two reasons** why the British government is keen to get the Chinese involved in building British nuclear power stations.

2. **Explain** why Henderson believes the British media should take a more critical position with regard to the deal between the British and Chinese.

3. **Analyse** the reasons why pluralist media sociologists might argue there was nothing wrong with media reporting of this deal.

4. **Evaluate** and **assess**, using information from this source and elsewhere, the view that the media reporting of this deal supports Marxist theories of the media.

Postmodernist theories

Postmodernists such as Strinati (1995) argue that countries such as the UK have been transformed in the past 30 years from industrial modern societies with manufacturing economies to postmodern and post-industrial societies with service economies.

Postmodernists argue postmodernist society has three characteristics that have an impact on the ownership and control debate.

› First, postmodern society is a media-saturated society. As Trowler observes in Haralambos and Holborn (2008), "the media are not just one aspect among many of the postmodern condition, but are its intimate, defining aspect".

› Second, postmodern societies are underpinned by globalisation – media transnationals have used communications technology such as the internet and satellite television to remove the distinction between the global and the local and to increase consumer choice in the range of media available for consumption.

› Third, in the postmodern world, it is claimed that people no longer have any faith in great absolute truths. Postmodernists argue that people have become sceptical, even cynical, about the power of science, politics or media to change the world. Consequently, postmodernists insist that truth is both unattainable and irrelevant in the postmodern world. Instead, postmodernism stresses the relativity of knowledge, ideas and lifestyle today. This means that all ideas contain an element of truth. As Trowler observes "in postmodernity, the norm is complexity: there are many meanings and not one deep, profound meaning."

Postmodernists argue that these characteristics mean that sociologists can no longer claim that owners, editors and journalists influence audiences by disseminating a particular view of the world, for two reasons:

› Baudrillard (1998) argues that the postmodern revolution in communications media means that audiences are immersed in so much information that they find it difficult to distinguish between real life and the media version of reality, which Baudrillard calls "hyper-reality". In a

media-saturated postmodern world there are multiple versions of hyper-reality and this has undermined the power of both 'truth' and 'objectivity'. It has resulted in individuals subjecting media content to multiple interpretations. Trowler argues that media messages in the postmodern world are "**polysemic**" – each media message or text is now interpreted in a variety of ways, which makes it difficult for any one message to be more powerful than another.

UNDERSTAND THE CONCEPT

Polysemic refers to the idea that there are multiple ways in which to interpret media content. For example, a comic may be viewed as pleasurable, as a source of information, as satirical, as ironic, as humorous and so on.

› Postmodernists argue that this has resulted in the distinction between media producers and media consumers becoming less clear-cut. Postmodernists argue that there has been a shift in media production away from global corporations to individuals who are increasingly engaged in the production of new media content, for example, through blogging, vlogging, uploading to social network sites and the construction of user-generated websites. Individual consumers of the media are also involved in re-inventing and subverting the existing media products of global corporations in imaginative and playful ways, for example, the Lego-based parodies of the Star Wars films. From a postmodern perspective, control of media production is no longer exclusively in the hands of global media corporations, owners or advertisers.

› Postmodernists argue that if there are multiple interpretations of media content, then the power to disseminate knowledge circulates in a fluid way rather than being concentrated in the hands of a few media owners. Levene (2007) observes that members of society now have a greater choice in their access to a greater diversity of media, which makes it easier for them to reject or to challenge the meta-narratives proposed by the powerful. He documents how university students in 2007 were able to utilise media products such as Facebook and Twitter to construct a 'viral' campaign to defeat the corporate giant HSBC, which had proposed to introduce overdraft fees.

However, there are a number of criticisms of postmodernist theory of the media. First, the arguments are often vague, impressionistic and frequently based on anecdotes rather than research-based evidence. Second, postmodernists probably exaggerate the impact of the 'information explosion' on ordinary people's capacity to bring about change. The evidence actually suggests that media saturation has produced passive participation in a mass culture in which more choice simply means more of the same. Third, postmodernists simply fail to acknowledge the overwhelming evidence for the existence of structural inequalities in wealth and power relations, which makes it difficult for powerless groups, whatever access they might have to the media, to bring about any meaningful change to their everyday lives.

CONCLUSIONS

The pluralist theory of media ownership and concentration seems increasingly out of touch with the modern global world because it has failed to acknowledge that journalistic or editorial integrity no longer has a great deal of influence in the global marketplace. Instrumental Marxists, however, are probably guilty of over-simplifying the relationship between media owners and the political elite. However, the hegemonic Marxist approach of the GUMG is probably right to stress that the way the media are organised, and the social backgrounds of journalists, have resulted in media content generally reflecting the cultural hegemony of capitalist values and ways of seeing the world. Jones' contribution to this debate – that the media are part of an informal Establishment and, as such, are the guardians of a specific set of economic and ideological interests – is worth further investigation. Finally, if the postmodernist claim that people subscribe to multiple interpretations of media content is true, then the influence of media owners may not be as powerful as Marxists argue it is.

CHECK YOUR UNDERSTANDING

1. Explain what is meant by the term 'concentration of ownership'.

2. Explain what Jones means by the 'Establishment'.

3. Explain what is meant by 'synergy'.

4. Explain what is meant by 'polysemic'.

5. Identify and briefly outline the differences between horizontal and vertical integration.

6. Identify and briefly explain why pluralists believe that media content is shaped by the market.

7. Analyse trends in the ownership of the media in the UK.

8. Analyse the role of public service broadcasting, according to the pluralist theory of the media.

9. Evaluate the relationship between media owners and their editors and journalists, according to Curran.

10. Evaluate the view that the mass media is an ideological apparatus that functions to reproduce and legitimate class inequalities.

TAKE IT FURTHER

1. Watch an episode of 'Keeping up with the Kardashians' or any other similar reality programme, and make a list of how the hyper-real narrative and scenes in the programme may differ from your experiences. Does everybody in your class share your interpretation of what happened during the programme?

2. Design and conduct a small-scale survey to discover to what extent people from different social classes, ages, religious and ethnic backgrounds believe that the content of the media reflects a wide variety of opinions and beliefs.

3. Watch Mr Thirkill's series of videos on YouTube outlining the pluralist and conflict views of the media.

4.3 THE MEDIA, GLOBALISATION AND POPULAR CULTURE

LEARNING OBJECTIVES

› Demonstrate knowledge and understanding of definitions of culture (AO1).

› Demonstrate knowledge and understanding of the causes and significance of global media and popular culture on contemporary society (AO1).

› Apply this knowledge to contemporary society (AO2).

› Analyse the effects of globalisation on popular culture and the role of the media in cultural imperialism (AO3).

› Evaluate sociological explanations in order to make judgements and draw conclusions about the relationship between the media, globalisation and popular culture (AO3).

INTRODUCING THE DEBATE

Cohen and Kennedy (2000) argue that societies that were once distant, disparate and independent from one another are increasingly becoming interconnected and inter-dependent because of a process known as 'globalisation'. It is argued that the world, which in 2015 was made up of 196 separate nation states, has become a single global society or village because of a series of economic, social and cultural transformations that took place in the late 20th century and which are still ongoing.

Cochrane and Pain (2000) summed up the consequences of these transformations when they observed: "Drugs, crime, sex, disease, people, ideas, images, news, information, entertainment, pollution, goods and money now all travel the globe. They are crossing national boundaries and connecting the

world on an unprecedented scale and with previously unimaginable speed. The lives of ordinary people everywhere in the world seem increasingly to be shaped by events, decisions and actions that take place far away from where they live and work."

This chapter will explore the role that the mass media have played in these transformations, and the effect of this global change on popular culture. In particular, it will critically examine the two broad views that dominate the sociology of globalisation: the view that globalisation is generally a positive social force; and the view that globalisation is merely a misnomer for the global dominance of American popular culture, and that this so-called globalisation is actually a form of cultural **imperialism**.

GLOBALISATION

Steger (2005) defines globalisation as a "set of social processes that are thought to transform our present social condition into one of globality". Steger sees globality as a "social condition characterised by the existence of global economic, political, cultural and environmental interconnections and flows that make many of the currently existing borders and boundaries irrelevant".

Crothers (2012) observes that a combination of economic, political and cultural factors promotes globalisation in three ways:

› New and increased relationships that have been created between people, social networks and ideas go beyond traditional nation state borders. For example, people in 'traditional' societies are now exposed to modern technologies such as mobile phones and 'modern' ideas such as democracy, equality and tolerance for others. However, this is not one-way traffic – modern societies are exposed to and influenced by the values of the developing world with regard to the environment, alternative medicine, religion and so on.

› People are linked in new ways as both the production of goods as well as the flow of finance capital, and their consumption, take place 24 hours a day around the world. For example, workers in the West and in the developing world may find themselves employed by the same transnational corporations. Economic problems in one part of the world now have a knock-on effect on the rest of the world, as demonstrated by the 2008 meltdown in the subprime mortgage market in the USA. People the world over consume McDonalds burgers, drink Coca-Cola and use Chinese-manufactured Apple computers and iPhones.

› Global events and issues have become local events and issues because of the speed of communication and the expectation of instantaneous contact. For example, Islamist groups such as the so-called Islamic

State have taken particular advantage of satellite television channels such as Al-Jazeera, online social networks and smartphones to disseminate live images of beheadings or the destruction of antiquities quickly to a global audience.

Bell (2015) observes that there has never been a form of global media with the power to report and disseminate events with the speed and geographic reach of Twitter. She argues: "America holds its first television debate for Democratic candidates, Donald Trump live-tweets it. If London Bridge is closing down, Twitter provides the eyewitness reports and pictures ahead of the broadcast news media. Journalists when they wake in the morning don't first switch on the radio they reach for their smartphones and scroll through Twitter. Their subjects and sources, from politicians to pop stars, do the same."

As people are exposed to this increasingly complex world, their ideas and identities are shaped and reshaped. For example, some media sociologists argue that social networks such as Twitter and Facebook can give people who live in repressive societies the confidence to dissent and take to the streets to demand change.

Bell observes that Facebook has 1.2 billion active users worldwide who are constantly engaged in constructing and reconstructing their identities through the posting of textual and visual representations that add up to their personal profile or identity.

THE MEDIA AND GLOBALISATION

The mass media have played a key role in creating this global world. Advances in mass communications, digitalisation and cyber technology such as satellite television, the internet – particularly its user-generated and social network sites – streaming services and mobile phones – particularly recent developments in 4G and 5G smartphones – have transformed the world's concept of time and space. Information in all its varied forms – news, ideas, financial data and cultural products such as film, music and television – can now be transmitted instantaneously 24 hours a day to most global destinations.

The globalisation of media outlets and products has been assisted by the economic growth of transnational media and cybercorporations such as News Corp, Apple and Microsoft. Since the 1990s, the ownership of the world's media companies has become increasingly concentrated in the hands of a small number of transnational corporations. McChesney (2002) observes that the overwhelming majority of the world's film production,

TV show production, cable and satellite system ownership, book publishing, magazine publishing and music production is dominated, in terms of the revenue generated, by fewer than ten global media corporations.

CULTURE

Scott and Marshall (2009) define culture as all that which, in human society, is socially rather than biologically transmitted. Culture therefore refers to all that is learned from others in society. When people are born, they join a social world with a culture already in existence. Children learn how things are done culturally. They learn what is culturally important – **values**, **norms**, rules and traditions – in order to successfully take their place in society.

UNDERSTAND THE CONCEPT

Values refer to the beliefs and goals that members of societies agree are important, while **norms** refer to how societies expect their members to behave in particular situations.

High culture
Most societies, especially those based on status differences such as social class, differentiate between high culture, folk culture and popular or mass culture. High culture refers to what the elite of a particular society regard as the highest intellectual achievements in areas such as art, music, literature, poetry and theatre. High cultural products such as classical and modern art paintings, sculpture, classical music, opera, ballet, Booker Prize-nominated novels and Royal Shakespeare Company productions are regarded as aesthetically superior to all other cultural products. This is because they are regarded as saying something profound about the human condition. High culture is seen as vital to the social and cultural health and wellbeing of a society, according to those who have the power to define it, because societies globally judge one another on the basis of standards such as creativity, expression and philosophy. For example, English high culture is globally renowned because of Shakespeare. In 2012, the World Shakespeare festival saw his plays performed in over 50 languages.

The importance of high culture can be assessed by examining the British mass media's focus on it in the broadsheet newspapers. These often contain supplements that focus exclusively on art exhibitions, reviews of classical music concerts and CDs, ballets and operas, as well as articles discussing the artistic merits

of novelists, poets, playwrights and painters. Television also devotes considerable time to high culture. BBC2, BBC4, and Sky Arts, are channels on which high culture is regularly featured.

Folk culture refers to the traditions and rituals of societies which have been passed down, usually by word of mouth, through the generations for hundreds of years. For example, in the UK, these might include practices such as Bonfire Night, fairs and festivals, folk-singing, folk-dancing and dressing in national costumes. Folk culture is regarded as authentic because it reflects what goes on in everyday life in local communities.

There is evidence that folk culture is becoming increasingly globalised as tourists demand to see the performance of 'traditional' dance or song in the countries they are visiting.

Popular culture
Mass or popular culture refers to the products of the mass media in modern capitalist societies, such as television programmes, films, popular fiction, magazines and comics, and popular music, which are enjoyed by the majority or mass of the population. These products are mainly focused on entertainment although new forms of media have extended the function of popular culture to include both the exchange of information – for example, Twitter, Snapchat and Reddit – and the construction of identity – for example, Facebook and Instagram.

Some sociologists have argued that this type of culture is manufactured for mass consumption rather than created for its own sake and, consequently, has little aesthetic or artistic merit, compared with the products of high culture. Barnett and Seymour (1999), for example, describe popular culture as a "superficial candyfloss culture" that has resulted in the dumbing down of intelligence, creativity and critical thinking.

The globalisation of popular culture
Entertainment media have become globalised via satellite television, the global marketing and branding of mobile phones, computer technology, films, music, and internet user-generated social networks such as Facebook, YouTube and Twitter. Consequently, a large section of the world's population engages with much the same popular culture: the same films, the same television programmes – *Friends* was a global phenomenon – and the same music – Coldplay, Kanye West and Justin Bieber are global icons. Sport too has been globalised through global events such as the Olympic Games, the World Cup and the African Cup of Nations. Some sociologists have suggested that the globalisation of culture has led to its **homogenisation**,

in that people's consumption habits in the field of popular culture, wherever they are located in the world, is now very similar.

THE EFFECTS OF GLOBALISATION ON POPULAR CULTURE

The postmodernist perspective

Postmodernists argue that the mass media have played a big role in the way societies have changed from being modern societies, based on industrial manufacturing, to being postmodern societies, based on the consumption and dissemination of information and culture. In particular, postmodernist sociologists have argued that the rapid expansion in media technologies between 2005 and 2015 has led to postmodern societies becoming 'media-saturated'. As a result, the media – and the popular culture that they generate – are now more influential in the shaping of personal identity and lifestyle than traditional influences such as family, community, social class, gender, nation or ethnicity.

The mass media and identity

Postmodernists also argue that the media have also changed and shaped consumption patterns by making consumers more aware of the diversity of choices that exist in the postmodern world. Strinati (1995) argues that in the postmodern world the distinction between high culture and popular culture has become blurred and this too has increased consumer choice, because popular culture is increasingly assimilating high culture and vice versa. For example, classical music and opera often accompany television coverage of global sporting events, while classical performers such as Vanessa Mae have adopted marketing strategies similar to those of rock stars.

The global expansion of new media, especially social networking websites and smartphone technology, has attracted a global presence and audience in a short period of time. Postmodernists argue that globalisation is essential because it increases the consumption choices and opportunities that are now available to media audiences and society in general, particularly with regard to personal identity and lifestyle. These types of global media have therefore been essential in the rapid spread of the consumption of global images, logos and brands, which have become central features of global consumption and the way people present their identities to the rest of the world via Facebook, YouTube, and so on.

Media saturation, the rejection of meta-narratives and the relativity of knowledge

An important aspect of the general theory of postmodernism is that people today are disillusioned with grand political, philosophical and scientific theories or meta-narratives about the way society works or should work. Postmodernists argue that a media-saturated society produces a more media-literate audience that, because of the sheer diversity of media output, is aware that there is no such thing as a single and absolute truth, and that knowledge is actually underpinned by diversity, plurality and difference. In other words, knowledge and ways of looking at the world are relative. All points of view therefore have some value. This media-led way of looking at the social world has allegedly produced a more critical and participatory global, culture.

Henry Jenkins and participatory culture

Jenkins (2008), in particular, has developed the concept of global participatory culture, which is a term Fuchs (2014) defines as "the involvement of users, audiences, consumers and fans in the creation of culture and content". This might include contributing to a Wikipedia page, uploading videos to YouTube, writing a blog or the creation of short messages on Twitter. Jenkins and others such as Shirky (2011) have argued that global culture and society have become more democratic because users and audiences are enabled "to produce culture themselves and to not just listen or watch without actively making and creating culture" (Fuchs). For example, Shirky argues that global social media such as Facebook have resulted in the "wiring of humanity" and free time – which is used to interact with social media through the uploading of texts and images – has become a shared global resource. Jenkins also argues that this participatory culture creates new forms of community because those involved feel connected to one another, in that they care about what other people feel about what they have created.

Jenkins et al. (2013) observe that the globalisation of popular and participatory culture has been enhanced by the very rapid spread of social media. If audiences are not encouraged to get involved with actively shaping the flow of content on social media, it is unlikely that the medium will globally expand. As Jenkins *et al.* argue, "if it doesn't spread, it's dead" (quoted in Fuchs). Jenkins argues that audience participation empowers consumers. For example, he argues that global social media allow fans of television shows that have been cancelled to speak back to the networks and to lobby for the return of their favourite programmes. He also celebrates blogs because, he argues, they are a means through which their authors can challenge the meta-narratives associated with the mainstream news media.

The globalisation of media and popular protest

Murthy (2013) has empirically investigated the impact of Twitter, which had 300 million users worldwide in 2015, and concludes that global media sites such as Twitter and Facebook can help increase political awareness of issues such as human rights abuses, repression and protest, and consequently help coordinate a mass political response to these issues. Murthy concludes that, as a young communications medium, Twitter has the potential to shape many aspects of people's social, political and economic lives. (See Chapter 1 for more on the political potential of Twitter.)

A similar point about the global reach of new media is made by Spencer-Thomas (2008) who observed that mass anti-government demonstrations in Burma in 1988 failed to receive much media attention because the military regime banned overseas journalists from the country. In contrast, the mass demonstrations of 2007 received far more global attention because the Burmese people had access to new media technology, such as the mobile phone and the internet, and were able instantaneously to send messages and, in particular, images of the Burmese army's violent reaction to the protests, thereby generating instant global criticism of the Burmese government's actions.

New media technology resulted in widespread awareness of the Burmese people's demonstrations in 2007.

In your opinion, is it possible to protest effectively in 140 characters?

The effect of global media on local cultures

Thompson (1995) argues that the globalisation of communication has become so intensive and extensive that all consumers of the global media are citizens both of the world and of their locality. However, he argues that global media products are often domesticated by local folk cultures and this usually creates a hybridised media culture that makes sense within local communities. Local cultures are not therefore swallowed up by global media culture; rather, local culture adapts to global culture. In India, for example, Bollywood films are produced by a local film industry that is organised around both Hollywood and Indian entertainment values.

Cohen and Kennedy too argue that local people do not generally abandon their cultural traditions, family duties, religious beliefs and national identities because they listen to Adele or watch a Disney film. Rather, they appropriate elements of global culture, and mix and match them with elements of local culture, in much the same way as the citizens of the USA and UK do. British culture has been increasingly hybridised as British people encounter other cultures via migration and the global media.

Can you think of ways in which British culture has been influenced by culture from other parts of the world, apart from the USA?

In conclusion, postmodernists generally agree that the globalisation of media and popular culture is generally beneficial because it is primarily responsible for diffusing different cultural styles around the world. It is argued that, in the postmodern global world, cultural hybridity rather than global homogenisation is now the global norm.

The critique of the postmodernist perspective

Postmodernists have been criticised for exaggerating the degree of the social changes that they associate with global media and popular culture. Evidence from attitude surveys indicates that many people still see social class, ethnicity, family, nation and religion as having more influence over their lives and identities than global media or culture. Media influence is undoubtedly important, but it is not the determining factor in most people's lifestyle choices.

There is also a rather naïve and unrealistic element to postmodernist analyses, in that they tend to ignore the fact that a substantial number of people are unable to make consumption choices because of inequalities brought about by traditional influences such as unemployment, poverty, racial discrimination and patriarchy. Traditional forms of inequality remain a crucial influence, as access to the internet, digital television and so on is denied to many people in the UK and across the world. Research by the Policy Exchange thinktank (2014) reported that four in ten of those aged over 65 in the UK do not have access to the internet at home. Africa as a continent may have more access to mobile phones but large swathes of that continent are unable to access the internet.

The cultural imperialist argument against the globalisation of media and popular culture

The cultural imperialist approach is very influenced by the Marxist Frankfurt School, which argues that popular culture is an ideological product aimed at distracting poorer groups from the exploitation and inequality which is a feature of their everyday lives. Marxists claim that it encourages conformity and a lack of critical thinking, especially about the organisation of capitalism. Marcuse (1964) claimed that this conformity is the product of media audiences being encouraged by media companies to subscribe to three ways of thinking and behaviour:

> *Commodity fetishism* – the idea that the products of popular culture have special powers that somehow enhance the life of the user. For example, Turkle's (2011) research suggests many people see their smartphones as extensions of their self and feel lost and disconnected when they are without the device.

Do you have a smartphone? Consider the relationship you have with your phone or that you see others have – do you (or other people) fetishise it?

> *False needs* – this is the idea generated by the media through marketing, advertising and branding that, in order to conform to a modern lifestyle, consumers need to have a particular product. These products are not essential, hence the description of them as 'false needs', but the consumer is persuaded that they are central to their lifestyle and

identity. Such products are deliberately designed to be obsolete, that is, they have a fairly short life-span before the next range of such products appears. Adorno claimed that these 'false-need' products exist in order to bind consumers to producers.

> *Conspicuous consumption* – particular products of the media and the popular culture it generates are presented as having more status than other items for consumption. Consequently, certain brands are credited with imbuing the consumer with more status than others. People are therefore encouraged by the media to 'conspicuously consume' – to be seen with the 'right' cultural products, such as designer labels, in order to attract praise and status from others.

Marxists such as Adorno and Marcuse argued that the role of the global mass media is to indoctrinate global consumers into capitalist ideology and to produce a homogenised culture that mainly promotes capitalist values such as materialism and consumerism, therefore producing a **false consciousness** that inhibits any criticism of the global capitalist system. The global mass media are from this Marxist perspective agents of a cultural imperialism shaped by capitalist ideology.

UNDERSTAND THE CONCEPT

False consciousness refers to people's failure to look critically at the social world or their circumstances because they have been ideologically indoctrinated by the media and other agencies to see their experience of capitalism as fair and just.

Globalisation as Americanisation

The spread of global media and popular culture has led sociologists such as Flew (2007) to claim that globalisation is a misnomer for Americanisation. Flew argues that this amounts to "cultural imperialism", in a powerful cultural force – the USA that is imposing its media products and therefore its popular culture on less powerful nations.

There is no doubt that American culture is ubiquitous. Crothers observes that American-produced "audio-visual media like movies, music and television provide a significant means by which images of the 'American' way of life, whether political, social, or economic, are transmitted around the world. Likewise, fast-food restaurants like McDonalds, drink companies like Coca-Cola and Pepsi, sports like NBA basketball and major league baseball, and clothing like Levi's jeans are global cultural icons. Facebook and sites like it serve as hubs through which American popular culture reaches ever-widening parts of the world. It is through these artefacts (and many others) that the rest of the world sees American values and lifestyles."

Can you think of any ways in which American culture has been influenced by the culture of other societies?

McChesney and others argue that the domination of this American cultural imperialism is a direct result of the increasing concentration of the world's media companies in the hands of a few powerful American transnational media corporations. Companies such as Disney, Microsoft, Time Warner, Apple, News Corp, Google, Facebook and Comcast have achieved near monopolistic control of newspapers, film archives, news programmes, television and radio, advertising, satellites, streaming and digital services as well as ownership of huge chunks of the internet.

Cultural imperialism as Americanisation is seen as having several interrelated effects on cultures across the world:

› There have been concerns that the globalisation of American culture will result in the marginalisation or destruction of rich and diverse local cultures and identities. Mass advertising of Western cultural icons such as McDonalds and Coca-Cola may result in their logos becoming powerful symbols to people (especially children) in the developing world of the need to adopt American consumer lifestyles in order to modernise. The cultural imperialism thesis therefore sees the globalisation of the media and American popular culture as aimed at replacing the authenticity, vitality and diversity of local cultures with the homogeneous, dumbed-down and standardised sterility of American popular culture. For example, Kellner (1999) suggests that this global media culture is about sameness and that it erases individuality, specificity and difference. As Crothers (2012) observes: "The fear is that in time everyone everywhere will end up eating the same thing, reading the same thing, and wearing the same thing. Under such circumstances, cultural diversity will be lost forever. What would be left is a world of soulless consumers just looking for the next thing to buy that is exactly like what everyone else in the world already has and wants until

the corporations generate the next must-have item. One culture, consumer capitalism, would dominate the world".

There are a number of alternative terms that describe this process. For example, Hannerz (1992) coined the term "coca-colonisation" to describe how American cultural products like Coca Cola were penetrating the cultures and consciousness of people in less-developed countries in order to convince them that their wants, desires and even needs should be defined by American popular culture. Ritzer (1993) uses the term 'McDonaldisation' and Klein uses the term 'McWork' to describe the increasing tendency in the developing world for cultural products, whether they are burgers or television shows, to be delivered as per the American popular culture model in a standardised and predictable way.

› Barber (2003) argues that one extreme response to American cultural imperialism has been the rise of Islamic fundamentalism and the provoking of what he calls 'jihad', which he defines as "bloody holy war on behalf of partisan identity that is metaphysically defined and fanatically defended". In other words, fundamentalists see American popular culture as a threat that undermines their people's commitment to God. This may therefore be a rationale for terrorist attacks on US targets. To put it another way, the ubiquity of American popular culture may be bringing about a world characterised by more risk.

Fuchs argues that the owners of transnational corporations not only dominate world trade in popular culture, thereby denying true choice to consumers, but they are also able disproportionately to influence governments, thus threatening democracy and freedom of expression. Fuchs is very dismissive of the notion of the participatory popular culture championed by Jenkins because, he argues: "an internet that is dominated by corporations that accumulate capital by exploiting and commodifying users can never be participatory." Other critics such as Keen (2008) argue that global media such as Twitter and Facebook are too wrapped up in 'me-culture' to be effective tools for social change.

Putnam (1995) and Turkle have expressed concerns about how the spread of global media, and especially the global use of smartphones and social network sites, may have the side-effect of bringing about civic disengagement in countries across the world. Turkle argues that in the West people are no longer willing to get involved in their communities. They would rather stay at home and watch television, surf the internet or update their social profile on Facebook. Many critics of global popular culture are concerned that people may feel that they no longer belong to real communities. Turkle has argued that the proto-communities of internet chat-rooms, blogging and online fantasy gaming such as Second Life, and the imagined communities of television soap operas, are increasingly replacing real communities composed of family, extended kin and neighbours.

> How much time do you spend texting or updating your profile on social networking sites such as Facebook? Do you agree that the cyber-communities to which you belong are more important than physically being in the company of others?

FOCUS ON SKILLS: SOME COUNTRIES REMAIN RESISTANT TO AMERICAN CULTURAL EXPORTS

Tyler Cowen in the *New York Times* rejects the notion of cultural imperialism when he observes that Hollywood movies and American music have done very well in Europe but not so well in Asian countries such as India. Cowen argues that loyalties to cultural goods and services – be it pop music or ballet – is important when people are involved in networks of status, power and caste. He claims that people use local culture to connect to others like themselves, to construct their identity and to signal their place in local hierarchies. For example, an Indian Muslim might listen to religious Qawwali music to set himself apart from local Hindus. The Indian music market is 96 per cent domestic in origin, in part because India is such a multifaceted society – it literally contains hundreds of ethnic and religious groups and cultures that are proud of their differences and compete with one another for cultural space. Loyalty to local culture makes clear and reinforces those differences.

Cowen notes that local culture is a very powerful influence in Islamic societies because religion often underpins all aspects of those societies, including music, theatre, dance and art. Consequently the populations of these societies are likely to be faithful to their own cultural products. For example, many Arab people use Al-Jazeera as the source for news rather than CNN or the BBC. Similarly Sunni Muslims will use cultural products to differentiate themselves from Shia Muslims.

Cowen points out that smaller countries have been less welcoming of American cultural imports. For example, it is the norm in Central America and in African countries such as Ghana for domestically produced music to command up to 70 per cent of market share. Cowen observes that this makes sense because these countries tend to be poor and the poorer a country is, the more likely it is that it will buy and listen to its own cheaply produced domestic music. However, he observes, such societies are more likely to watch American films and television because these are expensive to produce domestically.

Cowen argues that cultural imperialism is more likely to occur in Europe (although countries such as France have attempted to control the number of American films shown in their cinemas). Cowen suggests Hollywood movies are popular in Europe in part because of the successes of European welfare states and of European economic integration. The adoption of welfare states has resulted in fewer differences between citizens and less need to reinforce these by using cultural products. Western Europe has also moved away from an aristocratic class society, and high culture now has much the same status as popular culture. Europe also has strong global connections. All those factors favour an interest in American and global popular culture, and consequently Hollywood movies often capture 70 per cent or more of a typical European cinematic market. Social democracy, which the Europeans often hold up in opposition to the American model, ironically has resulted in cultural imperialism by making Europe more egalitarian – there are fewer cultural differences between sections of Danish society than in Pakistani society, for example.

Cultural tastes across countries in Western Europe have therefore become very similar.

Finally, Cowen observes: "Western cultural exports are as likely to refresh foreign art forms rather than destroying them. Western technologies have spurred creativity worldwide." He suggests that Nigerian funk was partly influenced by the American funk of James Brown and Funkadelic, while Indian authors have acknowledged the influence of Charles Dickens in their writing. Cowen concludes that American or global popular culture does not therefore necessarily diminish the cultures of other poorer societies.

Questions

1. **Suggest three reasons** why Cowen believes that American popular culture is unlikely to dominate the cultures of societies such as India or Iran.

2. **Explain** why Cowen believes that European cultures may be undermined by the globalisation of American popular culture.

3. **Analyse** the reasons why Europe has been more receptive to American popular culture.

4. **Evaluate**, using information from this source and elsewhere, the view that the export of American popular culture is a type of cultural imperialism.

Criticisms of the cultural imperialist argument

Held *et al.* (2003) argue that the cultural imperialism argument makes the mistake of suggesting that the flow of culture is one-way only – from the West to the developed world. This focus fails to acknowledge 'reverse cultural flows' – how Western culture is enriched by inputs from the popular culture of other societies. These flows are likely to produce hybridisation as people in both the West and the developing world select from the global only that which pleases them and then alter it, so that it is adapted to local culture or needs, or mix it with local media to produce completely new forms of media. For example, many Western musicians such as Damon Albarn and Robert Plant have worked with African and Arab musicians to fuse genres of music into new forms.

The cultural imperialist perspective may underestimate the strength and richness of local cultures. For example, young people in developing countries may enjoy aspects of American culture but this does not mean they are going to abandon their customs, family and religious obligations or national identities wholesale.

CONCLUSIONS

The globalisation of both the mass media and the largely American popular culture it has generated has led some sociologists to argue that the USA is engaged in cultural imperialism. It is predicted that such imperialism will inevitably lead to cultural disaster for the people of the developing world as their own cultures are replaced by the bland uniformity of global popular culture. There may even be a jihadi-type response to these global processes. However, Cohen and Kennedy optimistically conclude that globalisation of media and popular culture will, in fact, eventually lead to improvements in human rights, universal access to education and communications and greater multicultural understanding.

CHECK YOUR UNDERSTANDING

1. Explain what is meant by the term 'globalisation'.

2. Explain what is meant by a 'media-saturated society'.

3. Explain what is meant by 'civic disengagement'.

4. Explain what is meant by 'cultural imperialism".

5. Identify and briefly outline two examples of the globalisation of American popular culture.

6. Identify and briefly explain why Marxists are critical of the globalisation of popular culture.

7. Suggest and analyse four reasons why the globalisation of media and popular culture has spread so quickly in the last 30 years.

8. Analyse two ways in which global media may produce a participatory culture.

9. Evaluate the postmodernist approach to the globalisation of the media and popular culture.

10. Evaluate the view that the globalisation of the media and popular culture has been a positive process.

TAKE IT FURTHER

1. Make a list of all the ways that your cultural life is touched by American popular culture. Compare it with the lists compiled by other students in your class. Compile a second list of all the ways that your cultural life is touched by British culture. Discuss with your classmates whether British culture is in danger of disappearing because of your use of American culture.

2. www.globalization101.org/pop-culture contains some excellent material focused on the effect of the globalisation of popular culture. Look on YouTube too. It contains some excellent videos on this topic.

4.4 THE SELECTION AND PRESENTATION OF THE NEWS

INTRODUCING THE DEBATE

A major source of information for most citizens is the news. This chapter will examine how news is gathered and presented to audiences. There are two broad sociological approaches to the news. The first, which is associated with journalists themselves, argues that news-gathering is a fairly objective process, based on a set of criteria called 'news values', which reporters and editors use to work out the newsworthiness of a particular event. Journalists also point out that news is also influenced by the nature of the news organisation for which they work, for example, news journalists at

The Sun newspaper gather and write news in a different way to those who work for Channel 4 News.

In contrast, critics of the news-gathering process argue that it is far from an objective process. Rather, they argue, news is socially constructed by a collection of social actors – media owners, politicians, spin doctors and public relations companies – that ensure that news content is generally bland and uniform, that alternative sources and versions of news are excluded and that the news acts as an ideology of the powerful.

NEWS AS A WINDOW ON THE WORLD

News is presented in a variety of forms in the 21st century. Up to the 1990s, the main sources of news in the UK were tabloid and broadsheet newspapers, radio and terrestrial television news programmes, particularly on the BBC and ITV. However, the 21st century saw the appearance of new media sources of news such as 24-hour rolling news on satellite channels (for example, Sky News, CNN, BBC, Fox), specialist news sites on the internet (for example, the Huffington Post), social networking sites such as Facebook and Twitter, and blogs (for example, Guido Fawkes at http://order-order.com).

However, despite the growth of new media, the majority of the population still rely on traditional methods of news coverage. In 2014, according to Ofcom, 75 per cent of people indicated that television was their most-used platform for news. Newspapers were used by 40 per cent of the population and radio was used by 36 per cent. However, Freedman (2010) observes that national newspaper circulation is steadily declining in the UK. Between 1995 and 2014, the number of adults reading a national daily paper declined by 28 per cent from 13.2 million to 9.5 million. The 2014 Ofcom survey showed that only 33 per cent of the 16–24 age group read newspapers whereas 60 per cent relied on the internet and apps, particularly via their smartphones, for news. This trend has led some sociologists to speculate that younger audiences are deserting traditional sources of news for the immediacy and **interactivity** of new media.

UNDERSTAND THE CONCEPT

Interactivity refers to the dialogue that occurs between a person and internet websites; for example, uploading photographs to Facebook.

However, Benson (2010) suggests that the use of new media as sources of news may not be that revolutionary, because those using the internet and/or apps to consume news are mainly using the websites of the traditional news-gatherers. In 2014, Ofcom reported that the BBC was the most popular source of news on the web, with about 60 per cent of market share. News websites run by the *Guardian* and the *Telegraph*, and the *Mail online* are also very popular. Social media such as Facebook and Twitter were used by 20 per cent of online news users, while 19 per cent used search engines such as Yahoo. In 2015, Twitter launched 'Moments' – an attempt to edit Twitter streams into a more orderly news format so that users could get an immediate overview of the most tweeted stories.

Ofcom surveys suggest that a majority of the UK population trust television news more than any other news source and that they regard it as a 'window on the world' offering an accurate and trustworthy account of events as they actually happen. In contrast, despite the fact that 9.5 million newspapers are read every day in the UK, most newspaper readers recognise that their newspaper is not impartial but identifies with a particular political and ideological position. For example, *The Times* supports the ideology of the Conservative Party while the *Daily Mirror* does the same for the Labour Party.

THE CONSTRUCTION OF NEWS

McQuail (1992) argues that events happen, but this does not guarantee that they become news – not all events can be reported because of the sheer number of them. The reality is that news is actually a socially manufactured product because it is the end result of a selective process – gatekeepers such as editors and journalists, and sometimes proprietors, make choices and judgements about what events are important enough to cover and how to cover them.

Media sociologists point out that the process of news selection is generally dependent upon three broad influences:

> the news values held by media organisations

> organisational or bureaucratic constraints/routines

> ownership of media news organisations.

News values

Spencer-Thomas (2008) defines news values as general guidelines or criteria that determine the worth of a news story and how much prominence it is given by newspapers or broadcast media. Brighton and Foy (2007) suggest that news values are "often intangible, informal, almost unconscious elements". News values define what journalists, editors and broadcasters consider as **newsworthy**.

UNDERSTAND THE CONCEPT

Newsworthy refers to what is regarded as interesting enough to appeal to and attract a significant readership or audience.

What is regarded as newsworthy will vary from newspaper to newspaper because they may be aimed at different types of readership. What television editors and journalists regard as newsworthy may also differ from newspapers, and between channels – for example, Channel 4 tends to focus on more social policy issues than does the BBC or ITV.

Pluralists believe that values are of crucial importance because news producers are under great commercial pressure to increase their audience or readership in order to generate the advertising revenue that makes up most of a media organisation's profit. Hence, market forces shape news values.

The best known list of news values was supplied by Johan Galtung and Marie Holmboe Ruge (1970). They analysed international news across a group of newspapers in Norway in 1965 and identified a number of values shared by Norwegian journalists and editors as to what constituted a worthwhile news story. These included:

› *Extraordinariness* – rare, unpredictable and surprising events have more newsworthiness than routine events because they are extraordinary. As Charles A. Dana famously put it: "if a dog bites a man, that's not news. But if a man bites a dog, that's news!" Disasters and the deaths of celebrities, especially if young, fit this criteria – for example, the deaths of Michael Jackson and Amy Winehouse as they were unexpected.

› *Threshold* – the 'bigger' the size of the event, the more likely it is that it will be nationally reported. There is a threshold below which an event will fail to be considered worthy of attention, and will not be reported. For example, national newspapers report murder but rarely report street robberies or burglaries.

› *Unambiguity* – events that are easy to grasp are more likely to be reported than those that are open to more than one interpretation, or where understanding of the news depends on first understanding the complex background to an event. A survey of 300 leading media professionals across the USA, conducted by The Columbia Journalism Review (2000), revealed that the most regular reason why stories don't appear is that they are "too complicated for the average person".

› *Reference to elite persons* – the famous and the powerful – those at the top of the socio-economic hierarchy – are often seen as more newsworthy than those who are regarded as 'ordinary'. Media sociologists have noted that, in the past ten years, a 'cult of celebrity' has developed that has extended the definition of who counts as worthy of public interest, so that celebrity gossip is increasingly front-page news, especially in the tabloid newspapers.

› *Reference to elite nations* – this relates to cultural proximity: stories about people who speak the same language, look the same, and share the same cultural preoccupations as the audience receive more news coverage than those involving people who do not. Events in the USA and Australia are more likely to be covered in British newspapers than events that happen in Asia or Africa.

› *Personalisation* – if events can be 'personalised' by referring to a prominent individual or celebrity associated with them, then they are more likely to be reported. Consequently, journalists often try to reduce complex events and policies to a conflict between two personalities. For example, British politics is often presented as a personal showdown between the two party leaders.

› *Frequency* – this refers to what Dutton (1997) calls "the time span taken by the event". Murders, motorway pile-ups and plane crashes happen suddenly and therefore their meaning can be established quickly. However, structural social trends are often outside the 'frequency' of the daily papers because they occur slowly and often invisibly over a long period of time. For example, inflation or unemployment may only be reported when the government releases figures on them.

› *Continuity* – once a story has become 'news' and is 'running', it may continue to be covered for some time. This is partly because news teams are already in place to report the story, and partly because previous reportage may have made the story more accessible to the public.

› *Negativity* – bad news is regarded by journalists as more exciting and dramatic than good news and is seen as attracting a bigger audience. Generally, good news, for example, "there were no murders today", is regarded as less interesting and entertaining than "three people were shot to death today". Stories about death, tragedy, bankruptcy, violence, damage, natural disasters, political upheaval or simply extreme weather conditions are therefore always rated above positive stories.

The threshold for reporting bad news is lower than that for reporting good news because it usually incorporates other news values – it is often unambiguous; it occurs in a short space of time; it is often unexpected; and it may be big – for example, a disaster.

› *Composition* – however, most news outlets will attempt to 'balance' the reporting of events, so that if for example, there has been a great deal of bad or gloomy news, some items of a more positive nature, especially human interest stories, may be added. If there is an excess of foreign news, for instance, the least important foreign story may have to make way for an inconsequential item of domestic news.

Galtung and Ruge argued that events become newsworthy and are more likely to be reported if they conform to some of these news values. However, Galtung and Ruge have been criticised by Brighton and Foy, who point out that their research was limited to Norwegian newspapers. They also point out that broadcast news programmes "were in the first flush of youth, newspapers were still essentially serious publications and the internet did not exist. There was little trans-national broadcasting." In other words, it is not clear whether their list of news values is still relevant today.

Harcup and O'Neill (2001) updated Galtung and Ruge in their study of British newspapers. They concluded that there were ten criteria newspaper reporters use to judge whether a story is newsworthy:

› power elite
› celebrity
› entertainment
› surprise
› bad news
› good news
› magnitude
› relevance
› follow-ups
› media agenda

Harrison (2006) compiles a similar list but adds elements of media or journalistic practice such as the availability of pictures or film, the need for balance and the potential for sensationalism.

Brighton and Foy criticise all of these lists because their compilers assume that there is consensus or general agreement, among both journalists and audiences, as to what is newsworthy. However, this is unlikely, especially in a media industry that features several types of news outlets. For example, putting together television news is very different from putting together a newspaper. Audiences too are made up of a very diverse range of people in terms of education, social class, ethnicity and so on, and may be attracted to news outlets that meet their needs. The news needs of the typical *Sun* reader may be very different to that of someone who regularly

watches Channel 4 or somebody who listens to the *Today* programme on Radio 4.

Second, Brighton and Foy point out that cultural expectations about news vary from country to country – what the typical Mexican regards as newsworthy may be quite different from the typical German or Briton. Finally, Brighton and Foy argue that journalism is undergoing change and that traditional news values may no longer be relevant in the age of spin doctors, churnalism and citizen journalists.

The influence of spin doctors on the news
There is evidence that some powerful groups may attempt to circumvent news values altogether and use their influence either to plant or to shape news stories sympathetic to their cause. For example, since 1884 political reporters (known as the lobby) based at Parliament have been fed news by government ministers on the understanding that they do not identify the specific source of this information. The last three governments have also appointed an unprecedented number of press officers, known as 'spin doctors', whose role is to meet journalists in order to 'manage' news stories so they are favourable to the government. As a consequence, the existence of both lobby journalists and spin doctors challenges the idea that all news stories are the product of news values. Some news stories are clearly constructed to favour particular political points of view.

Churnalism
Many viewers and readers rather naively believe that news stories are generated by journalists pounding the streets looking for a newsworthy story. This once was true but, in order to save costs, news companies have made thousands of journalists redundant in recent years and now uncritically source news from cheaper outlets such as the Press Association (PA) or Reuters – companies that sell brief reports of world or national news 24 hours per day.

Davies argues that journalists should be renamed 'churnalists' because they are largely engaged in uncritically churning out 'facts' or stories given to them by government spin doctors, and particularly by public relations companies working for celebrities and corporate interests. He notes that: "where once journalists were active gatherers of news, now they have generally become mere passive processors of unchecked, second-hand material, much of it contrived by PR people to serve some political or commercial interest." Davies suggests that up to 80 per cent of stories found in tabloid newspapers come from these official sources rather than journalists using their own news-gathering skills.

Phillips (2010) agrees with Davies's analysis and points to the widespread practice of reporters being asked to rewrite stories that have appeared in other newspapers or on the BBC or Sky News websites, and to lift quotes and case histories without any attribution. Messner and DiStaso (2008) found that US journalists often quote bloggers who in turn derive their information from uncorroborated sources, particularly rumours circulating on social networking sites such as Facebook and Twitter. The implication of churnalism is that news stories are characterised by uniformity, which reduces the choice available to the news reader. There is little opportunity to see other sides of the story.

Citizen journalism

The development of the internet, digital and satellite technology, smartphones and social networking sites such as Facebook and Twitter, and the 27.8 million blogs that have been set up since 1999, have led Matt Drudge, a leading blogger (www.drudgereport.com) to observe that a new form of journalism – citizen journalism – is increasing in importance as a source of news. In the UK, the term refers to anyone who posts even one story or photograph on a mainstream news site. For example, BBC viewers are encouraged to text information or send pictures and video clips of news events direct to the BBC newsroom via their mobile phones. Most of the 'live' pictures from the attacks in Paris in 2015 came from the mobile phones of 'citizen journalists'.

FOCUS ON SKILLS: CITIZEN JOURNALISM

Drudge claims that citizen journalism "allows every citizen to be a reporter and have his or her voice equated with that of the rich and powerful". Furthermore, citizen journalists are not constrained by any system of news values that might prevent certain facts coming to light. For example, the BBC was accused of not reporting knowledge of Jimmy Saville's crimes because he occupied a powerful position within the BBC. Drudge argues that citizen journalism circumvents these obstacles and consequently improves the democratic process. It therefore challenges the idea that news is shaped by news values and supports the postmodern notion (see Chapter 2) that mass media content is now characterised by diversity.

In 2006 the TV journalist Jon Snow claimed that input from ordinary people taking pictures at the scene of events was "gold dust flying our way" although he acknowledged that "there's loads of rubbish out there". However, Keen (2008) dismisses citizen journalism as offering up "opinion as fact, rumour as reportage and innuendo as information". Couldry (2010) empirically

investigated the impact of citizen journalism in the USA and concludes that it has had minimal effect on both the news-gathering process and the democratic process.

However, supporters of citizen journalism in the UK argue that it is useful for monitoring those in power and authority because of its whistle-blowing potential. Citizen journalism may also improve knowledge of what is going on in societies that Western journalists may find it difficult to access, or in which they are prevented from freely moving around. For example, during the Arab Spring uprisings in Tunisia and Egypt in 2012, a great deal of information was passed on by citizen journalists to Western news agencies.

However, Gillmor (2006) points out that citizen journalism is often the product of a narrow and privileged part of society because it requires education, technical skills, money and time. It is therefore doubtful that the traditional voiceless sections of society – the poor and powerless – are going to be citizen journalists.

Questions

1. **Suggest three reasons** why Keen is critical of citizen journalism.

2. **Explain** why Gillmor argues that citizen journalism may not represent all sections of society.

3. **Analyse** the arguments in favour of citizen journalism.

4. **Evaluate** and **assess**, using information from this source and elsewhere, the view that news values are the main influence on the news-gathering process.

Organisational or bureaucratic routines

Some observers of news production suggest that it is important to look at the organisational or bureaucratic routines and rules that exist within particular news organisations. They argue that the logistics of collecting news may bias what news is gathered or how it is actually presented and reported. This can be illustrated in a number of ways.

Financial costs

News-gathering is an expensive business and sending personnel overseas and booking satellite connections incurs great costs. The last ten years have seen a decline in expensive forms of news coverage such as investigative reporting and foreign affairs coverage (apart from conflict in which the UK is involved) because television networks have been cutting costs since the 1990s. For example, the BBC has been affected by severe budget cuts brought about by the government freezing the cost of the television licence fee in 2010 for six years and the decision by the Chancellor of the Exchequer in 2015 that the BBC should fund the £650 million cost of free TV licences to people aged 75 and over, which has taken up one fifth of its budget. Newspapers are not immune to these financial pressures. As readerships have fallen over the last 20 years, newspapers have attempted to cut costs by making thousands of journalists redundant.

Cost-cutting has two effects on the quality of the news. First, as Williams (2010) argues, it has severely undermined the quality of investigative journalism in the UK. He argues that newspaper investigative journalism in the 21st century has largely been reduced to "digging up dirt and revealing secrets about the private lives of the Royals, MPs, footballers and rock stars". However, this comment may be a little unfair because there are still journalists who are engaged with attempts to expose the unacceptable face of capitalism, such as those who work for the *Guardian* and *Private Eye* magazine.

Second, Franklin (1997) argues that entertainment has now superseded the provision of information in the construction of the news, both in newspapers and on television. He calls this "infotainment". Davies argues infotainment is attractive to media companies because it attracts large audiences and therefore advertising revenue. Williams concludes that "news is increasingly seen as lost among a tsunami of trivial and sensational copy". He concludes that the change from news to infotainment is a profound threat to culture and democracy because it often blurs the distinction between the fictional and the factual.

There is evidence that television news is also pursuing a more populist and tabloid news agenda. ITV's evening news contains more lifestyle and celebrity stories, while an Ofcom survey criticised BBC news coverage for being more "Madonna than Mugabe".

Time or space available

News has to be tailored to fit either the time available for a news bulletin or the column space in a newspaper. For example, both the BBC's and ITN's evening news programmes contain, on average, 15 items transmitted over a 25–30-minute period. In contrast, Channel 4 News is an hour long, which means items can be treated in more depth and detail. Similarly, a newspaper only has a fixed amount of space for each news category. Sometimes news stories are included or excluded simply according to whether they fit the time or space available.

Deadlines

Television news, especially 24-hour satellite-based news, has an advantage over newspapers because it can report news as it happens, as it did in 2001 when the World Trade Center in New York was hit by two planes. In contrast, newspapers have deadlines (usually about 10pm, if the news is to be included in the morning edition) and consequently they focus more on the previous day's news. This is why broadsheet newspaper coverage of stories generally tends to be more detailed and analytical than most television news coverage.

Immediacy and actuality

Events are much more likely to be reported on television news if they can be accompanied by sound bites and live film footage from the location of the event because these are thought to add dramatic reality. Recent technological advances in news-gathering have also made possible a level of immediacy unimagined a few decades ago. For example, BBC News 24 is now able to inform the UK about news events through live streams, labelled 'breaking news' on all the BBC websites, and by uploading news to apps received by smartphones.

The audience

Pluralists would argue that the content of the news and the style in which it is presented are very much a reaction to the type of audience that is thought to be watching, or the social characteristics of a newspaper's readers. For example, *Five News* is characterised by short, snappy bulletins because it is aimed at a young audience. Tabloid newspapers such as *The Sun* are aimed at a working-class youngish readership and so use simplistic language because this is what they believe their readership wants. It is also suggested that it reflects the educational level of the target audience. Newspapers traditionally referred to as broadsheets, such as the *Guardian*, on the other hand, may be considered to be aimed at the more qualified professional middle classes (as is Channel 4 News).

Who is perceived to be watching a news broadcast at particular times of the day also influences the selection of news. A lunchtime broadcast is more likely to be viewed by a stay-at-home parent, and so an item relating to a supermarket 'price war' might receive more coverage than it would in a late-evening news bulletin.

Journalistic ethics

Keeble and Mair (2012) have highlighted the unethical culture and practices of some sections of the news media. All British newspapers are signed up to the Press Complaints Commission's (PCC) voluntary code of conduct. The first clause of this insists that the "press must take care not to publish inaccurate, misleading or distorted information, including pictures". However, this code of conduct has been criticised as not powerful enough – the PCC has no statutory or legal powers to punish any irresponsible media behaviour. Ofcom, which was set up by the government, is the communications regulator in the UK. It is responsible for protecting people from being exposed to harmful or offensive material, from being treated unfairly and from having their privacy violated by television or radio.

In 2011, the biggest scandal to engulf the tabloid news media since the 1990s unfolded. News International (owned by News Corp) admitted that the hacking of voicemails by journalists employed by the *News of the World* (*NOW*) newspaper was a common practice. There was widespread outrage when it was discovered that the *NOW* had hacked the voicemail of the murdered teenager Milly Dowler after her abduction in 2002, and had even deleted some of her messages on her phone in an attempt to here new messages that might land.

In response to this scandal, the government set up an inquiry, chaired by Lord Justice Leveson, which concluded in 2012 that phone-hacking was common and encouraged by editors, that the culture of the press frequently and unethically demonstrated a blatant disrespect for people's privacy and dignity, and that news stories frequently relied on misrepresentation and embellishment. Leveson recommended the setting up of an independent regulatory body that would hear complaints from the victims of unfair press treatment, and would have the power to impose fines on news organisations. Leveson also recommended that this body be underpinned by

legislation to make sure it was doing its job properly. In 2013, the Coalition government rejected the majority of Leveson's recommendations and instead introduced a new press watchdog. However, all news organisations have so far refused to sign up to it.

Ownership, ideology and bias

Galtung and Ruge's concept of news values implies that the criteria of newsworthiness that they identify are objectively and reflexively used by journalists and editors in their role as gatekeepers of what counts as news. Pluralist sociologists suggest that this gatekeeping process is generally apolitical and impartial because journalists are dispassionate, neutral and objective pursuers of truth and facts (see Chapter 2).

The Marxist critique

Marxists are very critical of the idea that truth-telling is the primary function of journalists and that newsgathering is mainly based on a set of objective news values. McChesney (2002) argues that this is an ideological myth invented by media owners in order to present the corporate media monopoly as a 'neutral' and unbiased contributor to democracy. He argues that, in reality, democracy is undermined by the fact that extremely powerful media owners are able to influence the social manufacture of the news by shaping the editorial approach or policy of their news media, and this affects the choice of stories pursued by their editors and the way in which those stories are presented. In other words, an owner does not have to exercise day-to-day control – compliant editors who value their jobs know what their employer expects. For example, as instrumental or manipulative Marxists (see Chapter 2) have observed, a number of national newspapers carried a story in July 2007 detailing Rupert Murdoch's contacts with the Prime Minister, Tony Blair, in the run-up to the Iraq war. The story was not featured at all in any of Murdoch's newspapers.

Herman and Chomsky (1988) argue that news-gathering is largely shaped by market forces – particularly the power of advertisers – and that, built into the capitalist system, there is a range of filters that work ceaselessly to shape a news output that generally supports and disseminates capitalist ideology. They argue that this is not surprising because most news agencies are part of profit-seeking media corporations partly funded by advertisers who want their advertising to appear in a supportive selling environment. Consequently, news and news values are not objective – instead, they constitute a form of propaganda, because news-gathering and output are shaped by a neo-liberal and politically conservative ideology, which extols the virtues of free-market capitalism and is critical of any alternative point of view.

McChesney (2000) argues that the media see official sources of information – big business, government and wealthy individuals – as legitimate, but he notes that the perspectives of the poor and powerless are often portrayed by journalists as unreliable. Similarly, Bagdikian (2004), writing about the USA, notes how capitalist values often imperceptibly permeate news; for example, most newspapers have sections dedicated to business news, which present corporate leaders as heroes or exciting combatants, and they frequently report corporate and stock-market information uncritically. In contrast, very little attention is paid to ordinary Americans and the economic pressures that they face; for example, the news media seem uninterested in the growing gap between rich and poor in the USA.

Edwards and Cromwell (2006) argue that the media's role as a propaganda machine for capitalism means that subjects such as corporate criminality or the poor human rights record of the UK allies, such as China or Saudi Arabia, are often ignored by the British news media.

The hierarchy of credibility

The neo-Marxist Stuart Hall (1973) suggests that news is supportive of capitalist interests because those in powerful positions have better access to media institutions than the less powerful. Hall argues that most journalists rank the views of politicians, police officers, civil servants and business leaders (**primary definers**) as more important (or credible) than those of pressure groups, trade unionists or ordinary people.

UNDERSTAND THE CONCEPT

Primary definers are powerful groups that have easier and more effective access to the media, such as government ministers, spin doctors, the police and PR companies.

Hall argues that this 'hierarchy of credibility' means that journalists often report what prominent people say about events rather than the events themselves; indeed, what such people say may constitute an event in itself – powerful people 'make news'. The media's focus on primary definers means that minority groups are often ignored by the media or are portrayed negatively, as threats to society. Manning (2001) notes that less powerful groups have to tone down anything extreme or radical in their message in order to get heard by the media.

The social background of media professionals

However, the Glasgow University Media Group (GUMG) (1981), which takes a hegemonic Marxist perspective, argues that the way in which news is gathered and presented is actually the product of the middle-class backgrounds of most journalists and editors. The GUMG claims that journalists unconsciously side with the powerful and rich because they have more in common with them. Journalists often do not welcome the sorts of radical change proposed by the representatives of the poor and powerless. The GUMG therefore argues that news journalists engage in agenda setting – they choose to include certain types of news stories and to exclude others that do not fit their view of the world.

The GUMG studied news broadcasts and found that the language and images used by journalists were more sympathetic to the interests of the powerful and often devalued the points of view of less powerful groups. Fiske (1987) found that trade unions were typically presented by news journalists as 'demanding', which is a word that implies greed and disruption, whereas management made 'offers', which is a word that implies generosity.

Recent GUMG research has focused on news as a 'circuit of communication' in which production, content and reception of news are constantly affecting each other, although in unequal ways. Philo and Miller (2005) identify four groups who take part in this communication process:

1. *Social and political institutions, such as business organisations, government, lobbyists, the PR industry, and research and interest groups* – These have a great influence on the supply of information that becomes news.

2. *The media* – Within news broadcasting, the media tend to prioritise certain types of issue and to cultivate certain types of relationship. Official sources tend to be accorded most weight but, increasingly, commercial forces drive media content. This is reflected in the shift towards lifestyle features, reality TV and live reports, and away from detailed or investigative journalism.

3. *The public, which consists of different social, professional and political groups* – The audience will bring varying degrees of prior knowledge to their understanding of reported events, just as they will bring different cultural values and interests.

4. *The government* – There may be official criticism of news output or official pressure brought to bear

on news reporting. For example, the BBC's 2015 interview with the CIA whistleblower, Edward Snowden, was criticised by government ministers as disloyal.

This 'circuits of communication' approach involves a simultaneous examination of these four elements in order to understand how news content is both produced and received. The GUMG argue that clear agendas drive the news, but some sections of the audience may be critical of the messages conveyed, particularly if they have direct experience of the issues being reported.

Schlesinger (1990) is critical of Marxist theories. He argues that the media do not always act in the interests of the powerful – contemporary politicians are very careful what they say to the news media because they are aware that news can shape public perceptions of their policies and practices, influence voting behaviour and result in pressure on them to resign. Schlesinger argues that the Marxist notion that there is a unified media, engaged in manufacturing news as capitalist propaganda, is severely undermined by the fact that news outlets are engaged in stiff competition to grab larger audiences, to attract a greater percentage of advertising revenue and to make bigger profits than one another. Another criticism of Marxism comes from feminists who argue that Marxists neglect the way that women are represented in the news. This will be explored in depth in Chapter 5.

What sociological approach to the media do you think Schlesinger supports?

Moral panics

Moral panics are covered in terms of their impact on crime and deviance in Topic 1, Chapter 10. This section focuses on the role of the news media in their construction and presentation.

The news media sometimes focus on particular groups and activities and, through the style of their reporting, define these groups and activities as a problem worthy of public anxiety and official control. The term 'moral panic' was popularised by Stanley Cohen (1972), in his classic work *Folk Devils and Moral Panics,* to refer to the consequences of this type of news reporting in terms of the anxiety and sense of threat that it produces among the general population. In turn, this anxiety or panic puts pressure on the authorities to control the problem and to discipline the group responsible. However, the moral concern is usually out of proportion to any real threat to society posed by the group or activity.

Cohen focused on the news media's reaction to youth 'disturbances' on Easter Monday 1964. He demonstrated how reporters blew what were essentially small-scale scuffles and vandalism out of all proportion by using headlines such as 'Day of Terror' and words such as 'battle' and 'riot' in their reporting. Little time or interest was expended by journalists on what actually happened, which was a series of localised scuffles. Cohen argued that the events were reported in a way that far outweighed their importance. Moreover, the media analysed the disturbance as a conflict between two youth cultures – mods and rockers – and presented these groups as a threat to national law and order. The news media attempted to impose a culture of control on these groups by calling for more policing and severe punishment. Cohen outlined a number of stages that news reporting goes through in the construction of a moral panic, which are outlined in Figure 4.4.1 overleaf.

Why do certain types of news reporting result in moral panics?

The types of issues and events that result in moral panics may conform to the news values on Galtung and Ruge's list. In other words, these are newsworthy events.

There have been moral panics in recent years on internet grooming, migrants at Calais trying to enter the UK, and paedophile celebrities – in your opinion, which of Galtung and Ruge's news values make these newsworthy?

Cohen and Young (1981) suggest that moral panics originate in the consensual nature of the news media in the UK today. Journalists see 'problem groups' as newsworthy because they assume that their audiences share their moral concerns about the direction that society is taking. In this sense, journalists believe that they are giving the public what they want.

Moral panics may also simply be the product of the desire of journalists and editors to sell newspapers – they may be a good example of how audiences are manipulated by the media for commercial purposes. In other words, moral panics sell newspapers.

The neo-Marxist Stuart Hall (1978) studied news coverage of Black muggers in the 1970s and concluded that the moral panic that resulted functioned to serve capitalist interests because news stories labelled young African Caribbeans as criminals and as a potential threat to White people. This served ideologically to divide and rule the

Moral panics go through a number of stages, which some sociologists have termed a 'cycle of newsworthiness'.

STAGE 1

The tabloid media report on a particular activity/incident or social group, using sensationalist and exaggerated language and headlines.

STAGE 2

Follow-up articles identify the group as a social problem. They are demonised and stigmatised as 'folk devils': the media give them particular characteristics, focused particularly on dress and behaviour, which helps the general public and police to identify them more easily.

STAGE 3

The media oversimplify the reasons why the group or activity has appeared, e.g. young people out of control, a lack of respect for authority, a decline in morality. The media predict further outbreaks of trouble.

STAGE 4

Moral entrepreneurs, e.g. politicians and religious leaders, react to media reports and make statements condemning the group or activity; they insist that the police, courts and government take action against them.

STAGE 5

There is a rise in the reporting to the police by the general public of incidents associated with the group or activity as the group or activity becomes more visible in the public consciousness.

STAGE 6

The authorities stamp down hard on the group or activity – this may take the form of the police stopping, searching and arresting those associated with the activity, the courts severely punishing those convicted of the activity or the government bringing in new laws to control the activity and group. Other institutions, e.g. shopping centres may ban the group or activity.

STAGE 7

The group may react to the moral panic, overpolicing, etc., by becoming more deviant in protest, or the activity may go underground where it becomes more difficult to police and control. This is known as deviancy amplification.

STAGE 8

More arrests and convictions result from the moral panic and the statistics are reported by the media, thereby fulfilling the initial media prophecy or prediction that the group or activity was a social problem.

Figure 4.4.1 *Stages of a moral panic*

working-class by turning White working people against Black working people. It also diverted attention away from the mismanagement of capitalism by the capitalist class and justified heavier policing of Black communities.

The study of moral panics has drawn attention to the power of the news media in defining what counts as normal or deviant behaviour. However, moral panic theory has been subject to a number of criticisms:

› Jewkes (2015) claims that moral panic theory is too vague in its definition of deviance. For example, she notes that it fails to consider that there are different levels of deviancy and that consequently news stories on cannabis use and the moral panic that results cannot be equated with news stories and moral panics about paedophilia.

› Jewkes argues that not all folk devils can be said to be vulnerable or unfairly maligned by the news media. For example, the social reaction to paedophiles is probably justified.

› Critcher (2009) believes that the concept of moral panic is too abstract to be testable and that the news

characteristics associated with it, such as sensationalism and disproportionality, are too vague and potentially value-laden. For example, what constitutes a disproportionate response to a perceived problem will differ according to the political or moral position taken by the journalist or editor or the general public.

› Jewkes is critical of the idea that the general public naively and passively trust the news reports that underpin moral panics. She argues that audiences are "well qualified to see through the ideological veils put up by journalists and reporters". This idea will be explored further in Chapter 7.

› Postmodernists are critical of moral panics because they are seen to be the product of a dominant discourse but they argue that media content that posits the notion of a moral panic is no longer passively consumed by the audience without question. Instead, it is subjected to a diversity of media interpretations, all of which claim relevance and, consequently, media audiences are less likely to accept that the problem presented by the media is real. For example, new media allow all groups – including those potentially defined as deviant – a say in any media attempt to define a particular group as a social problem. Consequently, moral panics are no longer straightforward – they are hotly contested.

❯ McRobbie and Thornton (1995) argue that new media have radically changed the relationship between the media and their audience and consequently undermined the overall impact of moral panics. Audiences are allegedly now more sophisticated in how they interpret news stories. Competition between different types of news media – newspapers, television, twenty-four-hour rolling satellite news channels, Facebook, Twitter, blogs and other internet gossip websites – means that audiences are exposed to a wider set of news interpretations about potential social problems and are consequently more likely to be sceptical of their moral panic status.

However, critics of new media, such as Keen, suggest that interactive new media may have the opposite impact, in that unsubstantiated rumours about the deviant

behaviour of celebrities or political figures may circulate on social networking sites and trigger moral panic news stories in tabloid newspapers. In other words, interactive new media may actually accelerate the appearance of moral panics.

CONCLUSIONS

The news may not be as impartial as the general public like to think it is. Critics of news-gathering suggest that a range of influences mean that the news is a socially manufactured product that may reflect the interests and ideology of powerful groups rather than its audience. From a Marxist point of view, news is a type of ideology that supports ruling-class interests and censors any challenge to the economic and social inequalities that characterise UK society. Moreover, the evidence suggests that journalists sometimes create moral panics that cause an unnecessary rise in levels of social anxiety about particular groups.

CHECK YOUR UNDERSTANDING

1. Explain what is meant by the term 'churnalism'.

2. Explain what is meant by 'citizen journalists'.

3. Explain what is meant by 'moral panics'.

4. Explain what is meant by 'news values'.

5. Identify and briefly outline two reasons why television news programmes are seen as the most reliable source of news.

6. Identify and briefly explain how the hierarchy of credibility works as part of the news-gathering process.

7. Analyse the implications of the Leveson Report for news-gathering.

8. Analyse the stages of a moral panic.

9. Evaluate the impact of bureaucratic constraints and news values on the social construction of the news.

10. Evaluate sociological explanations as to why some news reporting results in moral panics.

TAKE IT FURTHER

1. List the first ten news items from an edition of the BBC evening news. Do the same for ITN news on the same evening. What are the differences? Can they be explained in terms of 'news values'?

2. Look at the websites of the following newspapers on the same day: *The Sun*, the *Daily Mail*, the *Daily Telegraph*, the *Guardian*. Compare the presentation of their main stories.

4.5 MEDIA REPRESENTATIONS OF GENDER, SEXUALITY AND DISABILITY

LEARNING OBJECTIVES

> Demonstrate knowledge and understanding of media representations of gender, sexuality and disability (AO1).

> Demonstrate knowledge and understanding of the nature, causes, trends and significance of media representations of femininity, masculinity, sexuality and disability (AO1).

> Apply this knowledge to contemporary society (AO2).

> Analyse changes in the media representation of gender, sexuality and disability (AO3).

> Evaluate sociological explanations in order to make judgements and draw conclusions about media representations of gender, sexuality and disability (AO3).

INTRODUCING THE DEBATE

This chapter aims to examine media representations of a range of groups, many of whom have traditionally occupied a subordinate position in society. Women and gay people have experienced significant social progress in the past thirty years. Equality between men and women, and between homosexuals and heterosexuals, has largely been achieved in many areas of social life.

This chapter therefore aims to see whether such change is reflected in the way the media portray these groups. In contrast, the disabled as a minority group have not yet achieved the goal of equality with the able-bodied. Pressure groups for disabled people, such as Disability Rights UK, suggest that negative mass media representation is a social barrier that undermines disabled people's identity and potential independence. This chapter will therefore examine the evidence to assess whether this argument stands up.

MEDIA REPRESENTATIONS OF FEMININITY

Symbolic annihilation

Tuchman *et al.* (1978) used the term 'symbolic annihilation' to describe the way in which women are represented by the media. They argue that women's achievements are often not reported, or are condemned or trivialised by the mass media. Moreover, when women are portrayed, they are generally shown in a narrow and limited range of social roles and their achievements are often presented as less important than their looks and sex appeal.

Limited roles

Tunstall (2000) argues that the presentation of women in the media is biased because it mainly represents women as busy housewives, as contented mothers, as eager consumers and as sex objects in various stages of undress. It generally ignores the fact that well over half of British adult women go out to work. Tunstall observes that, in contrast, men are often portrayed as active and in positions of power. The male body is rarely sexually objectified in the mainstream media and little reference is made to men's marital and domestic status.

The 'Just the Women' report (2012), based on a fortnight's analysis of 11 national newspapers in September 2012, concluded that just over 1300 news reports portrayed women in limited roles. The report found that the tabloid press in particular often focused on women's appearance and reduced them to sexual commodities to be consumed by what Mulvey (1975) calls the **male gaze**. According to Kilbourne (1995), the media often present women as mannequins: tall and thin, often size zero, with very long legs, perfect teeth and hair, and perfect skin. Kilbourne notes that this mannequin image is used to advertise cosmetics, health products and anything that works to improve the appearance of the body for the benefit of the male gaze (rather than for female self-esteem). Wolf (1990) argued that the dominant media message aimed at women is that their bodies are a project in constant need of improvement.

Bates (2014) argues that the music industry is particularly guilty of sexually objectifying women in lyrics and videos. She observes that as consumers of the music industry young girls: "learn that women are, almost without exception, required to bare as much skin as possible when singing … while male artists, remaining fully clothed themselves, will strew writhing bikini-clad women around the sets of their videos like Christmas decorations."

> ### UNDERSTAND THE CONCEPT
>
> The **male gaze** refers to the way the camera looks at a woman in the same way as a man does and consequently portrays women as sexual beings or as decorative. It is assumed by a male-dominated media that this is what the male audience wants.

The 'Just the Women' report also found that 'women's issues' were often covered in a very narrow and stereotyped way and women who had achieved some level of social status as politicians or actors were often denigrated and humiliated by the media. For example, Salinas (2015) observes that journalists often pass negative comment on the way women dress, their weight and looks and their sexual and family lives. In 2015, the leader of the Scottish National Party, Nicola Sturgeon, remarked: "…What annoys me or worries me most…, I'm used to reading pretty derogatory things about me in the newspapers about how I look, and my hair… and it's water off a duck's back, but … younger women, who might be thinking about going into politics, they'll read that about me and think: 'I don't fancy putting myself in the firing line for that.' It worries me that it puts women off going into politics."

Similarly, research by Martinson *et al.* (2012) found that there were few media stories about women's abilities or expertise and that the experts consulted by the media in the fields of business, politics and economics were overwhelmingly men. Cochrane (2011) found similar levels of symbolic annihilation in television's relationship with women. She found that a range of television output – news and current affairs as well as political and comedy panel shows – were dominated by males. Radio was also characterised by an under-representation of females. For example, Cochrane found that 84 per cent of reporters and guests on BBC Radio 4's *Today* programme were male.

In your opinion, do women have 'special' needs that justify women's pages in newspapers or television programmes such as *Loose Women*?

Another good example of the symbolic annihilation of women's activities is the media coverage of women's sport in newspapers and on television. Packer *et al.* (2015) found that at the time of the 2012 Olympics, 4.5 per cent of articles in national newspapers related to women's sports but this fell to 2.9 per cent in 2013. What coverage does exist tends to sexualise, trivialise and devalue women's sporting accomplishments. For example, Duncan and Messner (2005) note that commentators, (97 per cent of whom are men), use different language when they talk about female athletes. Women in sports are often described as 'girls', whereas males are rarely referred to as 'boys'.

Orbach (1991) argues that the media perpetuate the idea that slimness equals success, health, happiness and popularity. She accuses the media, especially women's magazines, of encouraging young girls and women to be unhappy with their bodies. She notes that they create the potential for eating disorders by constantly exhorting females to be concerned with their weight, shape, size and looks, by using pictures of size-zero supermodels to illustrate articles and, through adverts, encouraging dieting and cosmetic surgery. Banyard (2010) cites research that suggest that only five minutes of exposure to thin and beautiful images of women result in female viewers feeling low self-esteem about their own bodies in comparison to viewing neutral objects.

In your opinion, do media representations of models 'cause' girls to be unhappy with their bodies?

Do the modern media empower women?

Gauntlett has drawn attention to 21st-century media aimed at young women, which, he claims, differ in character from the media of 20 years ago. He argues that magazines for young women today emphasise that women must do their own thing and be themselves. This set of media representations suggests that women can be tough and independent while "maintaining perfect make-up and wearing impossible shoes". He claims that surveys of young women and their lifestyles suggest that these media messages are having a positive and significant impact on the way young women construct their identities today.

Green and Singleton (2013) argue that it is in the field of new media, particularly those underpinned by digital technology, that women are most empowered. It has been argued by Plant (1997) that the internet is a feminine technology that has the potential to destabilise patriarchy because its use allows women to explore, subvert and

create new identities. There is some evidence that the internet, in the form of Twitter, Facebook and websites such as everydaysexism.com, have been very useful as tools for challenging negative media representations of women.

In your opinion, how might girls and women use new media such as Twitter and Facebook to challenge sexist stereotypes of women in the mainstream media?

However, research also indicates that women who use new media such as the internet may experience the sorts of everyday sexist representations encountered in older forms of media. For example, women's rights campaigner Caroline Criado-Perez was subjected to 50 rape and murder threats every hour for two days in 2013 from internet and Twitter online trolls, while the academic Mary Beard and the MP Stella Creasy have also received threats and sexist abuse via Twitter. It is a fact that under almost any article on an internet news site that positively focuses on women's issues or rights there will be huge numbers of sexist comments. The internet may help disseminate feminist ideas more widely but it also does the same for its polar opposite – misogyny or woman-hating views. Green and Singleton also acknowledge that women's participation in internet online communities such as Mumsnet and Facebook may merely reinforce the notion that women should perform the 'emotional work' for the family.

MEDIA REPRESENTATIONS OF MASCULINITY

There has been little analysis of how the media construct, inform and reinforce cultural expectations about men and masculinity compared with the dozens of studies of how the media represent women and femininity.

In 1999, the research group Children Now asked boys between the ages of 10 and 17 about their perceptions of the male characters they saw on television, in music videos and in movies (Children Now, 1999). Their results indicate that media representations of men do not reflect the changing work and family experiences of most men today. The study found the following representations of masculinity were dominant:

> males are violent

> men are generally leaders and problem-solvers

> males are funny, confident, successful and athletic

> men and boys rarely cry or show vulnerability

> male characters are mostly shown in the workplace, and only rarely at home.

More than a third of the boys had never seen a man doing domestic chores on TV. These images support the idea that traditional images of masculinity generally continue to dominate mass-media coverage of boys and men.

McNamara (2006) analysed a wide variety of media – newspapers, magazines and television – and claimed that media representations of men and boys generally failed to portray the reality of masculine life. McNamara found that:

> 80 per cent of media representations of men were negative. Men and boys were routinely shown as "violent and aggressive thieves, thugs, murderers, wife and girlfriend bashers, sexual abusers, molesters, perverts, irresponsible deadbeat dads and philanderers, even though, in reality, only a small proportion of men act out these roles and behaviours."

> Men and boys were also shown as irresponsible risk-takers and, in particular, incapable of communicating their feelings or controlling anger.

In contrast, McNamara did find that 20 per cent of media representations of masculinity focused on men and boys who were in touch with their feminine side and expressed this through their appearance – the **metrosexual male** – and, through fatherhood especially, the need to connect emotionally to their children. However, on the whole, McNamara concludes that men are demonised by media representations of masculinity.

UNDERSTAND THE CONCEPT

The **metrosexual male** refers to men who take care of their appearance in terms of consuming toiletries and fashion products and who are unafraid to express emotional vulnerability. The 'hipster' is thought by some to be symbolic of this metrosexual ideal.

Gauntlett suggests that men's media such as *FHM* and *Men's Health* transmit metrosexual values because they portray men as "fundamentally caring, generous and good-humoured". Gauntlett argues that these magazines are often centred on "helping men to be considerate lovers, useful around the home, healthy, fashionable, and funny". However, Gauntlett does acknowledge that images of the "conventionally rugged,

super-independent, extra-strong macho man still circulate in popular culture", although men's magazines that present women for the benefit of the 'male gaze', such as *Nuts* and *Penthouse,* are becoming increasingly obsolete.

There are, then, signs that media representations of masculinity are moving away from the emphasis on traditional masculinity, to embrace new forms of masculinity that celebrate fatherhood and emotional vulnerability. Similarly, it is important not to exaggerate changes in representations of masculinity, as the overall tone of media representations still strongly supports hegemonic versions of what it is to be a man.

THEORETICAL PERSPECTIVES AND MEDIA REPRESENTATIONS

Feminist perspectives

Feminists are the main sociologists working in this field. They have been very critical of the representations of men and women in the media because they believe that the mass media play a major role, alongside the family and education, in the social construction of gender roles: how children learn to be feminine or masculine. The media emphasis on females as domestic goddesses and sex objects is seen as problematic because it is believed to have a limiting effect on young females' behaviour and aspirations, especially in adolescence.

Liberal feminists believe that media representations are slow to change in response to women's achievements in society. This 'cultural lag' is due to the fact that women rarely achieve high positions in media organisations. For example, there have been very few female editors of British national newspapers. Mills (2014) argues that the newsroom is a very male culture that can be off-putting to females. She observes that "the tabloid newsroom is far from being woman-friendly – visitors would be lucky to see a woman anywhere near a news desk. There is a deeply entrenched bloke culture. It's all about the boys' club, promotions are dished out in the pub and women aren't invited."

Lauzen (2015) found that in 2014–15 women accounted for only 27 per cent of creators, directors, writers, producers, executive producers, editors, and directors of photography working in prime-time television. In 2014, females only comprised 12 per cent of protagonists, 29 per cent of major characters, and 30 per cent of all speaking characters in the top 100 grossing films. Women continue to be disproportionately found in costume design, make-up and hair, which have less status and are paid less than male-dominated technical areas such as camera, sound and lighting.

million **homophobic** comments. In 2015, BT were criticised by LGBT organisations such as Stonewall for providing parents with the option of using an internet filter for children that blocks access to gay and lesbian lifestyle content as well as information on abortion, STIs and contraception.

UNDERSTAND THE CONCEPT

Homophobia refers to prejudicial attitudes and actions against LGBTs.

In conclusion, critics of mass-media representations of LGBTs agree that there has been an increase in the number of positive representations of LGBTs in commercials, films, and television shows but there is still a long way to go before such sexualities are portrayed in ways that are neither stereotypical nor judgemental.

REPRESENTATIONS OF DISABILITY

There are two broad sociological views of disability. The first suggests that disabled people are disabled by their physical and/or mental impairments. This view, known as the bio-medical model, suggests that they need constant care from medical practitioners and their families: the disabled are dependent upon the able-bodied.

The second view, held by many sociologists who have experienced disability firsthand, such as Colin Barnes and Tom Shakespeare, suggests that the disabled are actually disabled by society, particularly by prejudicial stereotypes and attitudes. These result in discriminatory practices, known collectively as 'disablism', that reinforce the notion that the disabled should be dependent upon able-bodied others or that they should be segregated from the rest of society (see Book 1, Topic 5, Chapter 1 and Topic 5, Chapter 7 of this book).

Media stereotypes
The mass media are seen by disabled sociologists as partly responsible for the dissemination of these stereotypes and prejudices. Barnes (1992) identified a number of recurring stereotypes of disabled people, which he claimed regularly appear in media representations of the disabled:

1. *Pitiable and pathetic* – Barnes claims that this stereotype is a staple of television documentaries, which often focus too heavily on disabled children and the possibilities of 'miracle' cures.

2. *Sinister and evil* – Disabled people are often portrayed as criminals or monsters. For example, villains in James Bond films often have something physically wrong with them.

3. *Atmospheric or curio* – Disabled people might be included in drama to enhance an atmosphere of menace, unease, mystery or deprivation. Disabled people are therefore used to add visual impact to productions. Television documentaries often see the disabled as curios to be watched in fascination by able-bodied audiences.

4. *Super-cripples* – Barnes notes that the disabled are often portrayed as having special powers: for example, blind people might be viewed as visionaries with a sixth sense or super-hearing. He notes the existence of 'super-cripple films' such as *My Left Foot* and *The Theory of Everything*, in which disabled people (often played by able-bodied actors) overcome their impairments. Channel 4's coverage of the Paralympics also fits this category because it involved Channel 4 celebrating disabled people doing extraordinary things. Ross (1996) notes that for disability issues to be reported, they have to be sensational, unexpected or heroic to be interpreted by journalists as newsworthy.

5. *Sexually abnormal* – It is assumed by media representations that the disabled do not have sexual feelings or that they are sexually degenerate.

6. *Incapable of participating fully in community life* – Barnes calls this the stereotype of omission and notes that disabled people are "rarely shown as integral and productive members of the community; as students, as teachers, as part of the workforce, or as parents".

Roper (2003) suggests that telethons such as *Children In Need*, which aim to raise money for the disabled, rely too heavily on 'cute' children who are not representative of the range of disabled people in the UK. Telethons act to keep the audience in the position of givers and to keep the disabled in their place as grateful and dependent recipients of charity. She notes that telethons are about entertaining the public rather than helping able-bodied society to understand the everyday realities of what it is like to be disabled. Consequently, these media representations merely confirm social prejudices about the disabled; for example, that they are dependent on the help of able-bodied people.

Shakespeare (1999) argues that media stereotypes of the disabled on television and film are "crude, one-dimensional and simplistic". He suggests that "the use of disability as character trait, plot device, or as atmosphere is a lazy short-cut. Such stereotypes reinforce negative attitudes towards disabled people, and ignorance about the nature of disability" (quoted in Wood 2012). Barnes agrees and observes that television and films rarely portray disabled people as normal, ordinary people who just happen to have an **impairment**.

UNDERSTAND THE CONCEPT

Impairment refers to the loss of or damage to a body part such as the loss of a limb or limbs, paralysis, a physically degenerative disease, such as motor neurone disease or MS, or to a characteristic such as blindness or Down's syndrome that means that they are prevented from doing something the able-bodied take for granted. However, the impaired are disabled by society's failure to provide the means by which they could partake in the same activities as the able-bodied. For example, inability to walk is an impairment, whereas an inability to enter a building in a wheelchair because the entrance has a flight of stairs and no ramp is a disability.

Newspaper representations of the disabled

Williams-Findlay (2009) examined the output of two broadsheet newspapers, *The Times* and the *Guardian*, to see whether their coverage of the disabled had changed between 1989 and 2009. Williams-Findlay found there was a steep decline in the use of stereotypical words such as 'brave' but argues that both negative and stereotypical representations of the disabled were still present in both newspapers in 2009 because journalists still assumed that disability was 'tragic' and disabled people were 'afflicted'. Williams-Findlay also suggests that disability is not regarded as newsworthy by either journalists or their audiences. Consequently, stereotypical representations of the disabled persist because disabled people and their organisations are rarely used as sources and, as a result, they have little influence over the language used by journalists, or over how disabled people and disability are represented.

Watson, Philo and Briant (2011) compared and contrasted tabloid media coverage of disability in five British newspapers in 2010–11 with a similar period in 2004–5 and found that there had been a significant increase in the reporting of disability. However, the proportion of articles that described disabled people in sympathetic and deserving terms had fallen and the media portrayal of some groups of disabled people, particularly those with mental health conditions and 'hidden' disabilities, was particularly negative because journalists often described them as welfare 'scroungers' who were undeserving of benefits.

Watson *et al.* found that articles focusing on disability benefit and fraud increased threefold between 2005 and 2011, and that this increased negative media attention was leading members of the general public to believe that many disabled people were fraudulently claiming benefits. In contrast, the research found that there were rarely articles that described the reality of daily life for the disabled or discrimination against them. Moreover, Watson *et al.* reported a significant increase in the use of derogatory language used by journalists and other media contributors to describe disabled people, such as 'cheat' and 'skiver', which reinforced the idea of disabled benefit claimants as undeserving.

Theories of representations of the disabled

Pluralists argue that media representations of the disabled reflect the dominant medical view that disability is dysfunctional for both the individual and society. Media representations realistically mirror social anxieties about impairment, for example, that individuals experience it as a problematic and abnormal state. However, it is argued that media representations of the disabled also reflect society's admiration of the 'courage' shown by some disabled individuals, especially if they are young. Pluralists therefore argue that media representations of the disabled portray the reality of the everyday conditions of the disabled and their carers.

How might the portrayal of disability in the media be a product of the news values discussed in Chapter 4?

However, media representations of the disabled are seen very differently by sociologists who are themselves disabled and belong to the social constructionist school of disability. For example, Oliver (1998) and Barnes and Mercer (2003) argue that it is important to understand that the social reaction to people with impairments produces the social condition and experience of disability. The social constructionist theory argues that impaired individuals are disabled by society and that mass media representations play a significant part in that process. They argue that there are three main reasons why mass media representations of disability take the form they do:

1. Medical professionals set the agenda for media portrayal of disability. They are at the top of the hierarchy of credibility. Their view that disability is

unhealthy, unfortunate and tragic, and that disabled individuals are dependent upon others, dominates journalist's perspectives on disability despite the fact that these are non-disabled assumptions of what it is like to experience impairment.

2. Media representations reflect the prejudice that able-bodied people feel towards the disabled. This prejudice is the result of fear in that the disabled represent everything that the 'normal' world most dread – personal tragedy, loss and the unknown.

3. The disabled are rarely consulted by journalists because they concur with the medical view that disabled people are incapable of leading a 'normal' life. Negative representations therefore reflect the low status, oppression, exclusion and inequality experienced by the disabled in a society dominated by the able-bodied.

Finally, postmodernists argue that the dominant medical discourse, which has shaped the societal and media treatment of the disabled, is fragmenting in the 21st century, as the disabled politically organise themselves, find their voice and independently construct their own identities. Consequently, the medical metanarrative is in decline and the perspective of the disabled that impairment does not mean unhealthy, deficient and dependent is increasingly heard and acted upon. This is reflected in more positive media representations, especially in the coverage of sport.

However, Gauntlett (2008) points out that all sociological theories of media representations need to be cautious in their approach because of the sheer diversity of media that exist in the UK. It is difficult, if not impossible, to generalise these critiques to all types of media. For example, television representations of the disabled may be positive on the BBC and Channel 4 but negative on Channel 5 and in tabloid newspapers.

CHECK YOUR UNDERSTANDING

1. Explain what is meant by the term 'disablism'.

2. Explain what is meant by 'symbolic annihilation'.

3. Explain what is meant by 'the male gaze'.

4. Explain what is meant by 'demonisation'.

5. Identify and briefly describe two stereotypes that are apparent in the media's representation of women.

6. Identify and briefly explain how television and newspapers represent disabled people.

7. Analyse the mass-media representation of masculinity.

8. Analyse why disabled sociologists are critical of telethons.

9. Evaluate mass-media representations of alternative sexualities.

10. Evaluate sociological explanations of mass-media representations of femininity.

TAKE IT FURTHER

1. Compare the views of young men and young women about the representations of men and women in the media. You could do this by conducting in-depth interviews or by using a questionnaire. Try showing respondents examples of men's and women's magazines to get them talking.

2. David Gauntlett is the author of *Media, Gender and Identity: An Introduction*. Go to his book's website at www.theoryhead.com/gender. Select "Bonus discussions and interviews" and read his articles and the discussions about men's and women's magazines. To what extent do you agree with Gauntlett's views? It is well worth exploring some of the 'related features', including links to other websites.

3. Watch the films *Suffragette* (2015) and *Lara Croft: Tomb Raider* (2001) and compare how each film represents women.

4.6 MEDIA REPRESENTATIONS OF ETHNICITY, SOCIAL CLASS AND AGE

LEARNING OBJECTIVES

> Demonstrate knowledge and understanding of media representations of ethnicity, social class and age (AO1).

> Demonstrate knowledge and understanding of the nature, causes, trends and significance of media representations of ethnicity, social class and age (AO1).

> Apply this knowledge to contemporary society (AO2).

> Analyse changes in the media representation of ethnicity, social class and age (AO3).

> Evaluate sociological explanations in order to make judgements and draw conclusions about media representations of ethnicity, social class and age (AO3).

INTRODUCING THE DEBATE

This chapter aims to examine media representations of a disparate set of groups. First, the chapter will focus on media representations of ethnic minorities. An Ofcom survey conducted in 2013 suggests that members of minority ethnic groups are at the forefront in terms of their use of new media, such as mobile phones, the internet and multichannel television take-up. For example, members of minority ethnic groups in the under-45 age group are more likely to own a mobile phone and access digital TV and the internet than the average person under 45.

The take-up of media technology among minority ethnic groups is therefore well developed. However, the evidence suggests that media representations of minority ethnic groups is problematic because they, like women, may be experiencing symbolic annihilation in that they are generally underrepresented across the British media and, when they are visible, they are represented in stereotyped and negative ways across a range of media content. In this sense, media representations of minority ethnic groups may be undermining the concept of a tolerant multicultural society and perpetuating social divisions based on colour, ethnicity and religion.

The second section will focus on representations of social class groups. Sociologists working in this field suggest that high-status groups tend to be positively represented in the media whilst low-status groups, particularly, the poor and people receiving state benefits, tend to be stigmatised and demonised by the media.

The final section of this chapter examines media representations of different age groups. It is suggested by criminologists that the activities of young people, in particular, are often unfairly exaggerated and sensationalised by the media via moral panics (see Chapters 4.4 and 1.10) and consequently young people are often constructed as a social problem by journalists.

Pressure groups working on behalf of the elderly also claim that the elderly are depicted through what Milner *et al.* from the International Council on Active Aging call a "lens of decline and diminishing value, emphasising the 'burdens' of growing old". Milner *et al.* claim that such stereotyping has resulted in a distorted view of the ageing process as well as a culture which has low expectations of the elderly and that often shows them scant respect.

MEDIA REPRESENTATIONS OF MINORITY ETHNIC GROUPS

Van Dijk (1991) conducted a content analysis of tens of thousands of news items across the world over several decades. He noted that news representations of Black people could be categorised into three stereotypically negative types of news: ethnic-minority people as criminals; ethnic-minority people as a threat and ethnic-minority people as unimportant.

Minority ethnic groups as criminals

Van Dijk and Davies *et al.* (2007) argue that journalists have demonised Black young people, particularly African Caribbeans, as a threat to law-abiding White society for decades. Studies by Law (2002), Sveinsson (2008) and Cushion *et al.* (2011) confirm the persistence of this stereotype.

Law conducted a content analysis of news output from press, radio and television sources between November 1996 and May 1997. He found that "the linkage of race, violence, dangerousness and crime remains a high-profile theme." Wayne *et al.* (2007) examined news coverage of a range of UK national news programmes and found that close to 50 per cent of news stories concerning young black people dealt with them committing crime. Sveinsson examined the reporting of violent crime in relation to the ethnicity of both victim and perpetrator and concluded that violent crime is portrayed as endemic within ethnic communities and that notions of race tint the (journalistic) lens through which criminality is viewed and reported by the media.

Cushion *et al.* monitored a range of daily and Sunday newspapers, nightly television news and radio news programmes for a period of 16 weeks over the period 2008–9. The research clearly shows that Black young men and boys are regularly associated with negative news values. Close to 7 in 10 stories of Black young men

and boys were related in some form to crime, especially violent crime involving knives and/or gangs. Cushion *et al.* point out that the news media often represent Black crime as irrational and senseless or as motivated by gang rivalries. There is little attempt to provide context or to discuss the possible structural or social factors that might contribute to motivations for crime.

What structural or social factors do you think might contribute to young Black people's motivations for committing crime?

Watson (2008) argues that moral panics often result from media stereotyping of Black people as potentially criminal. This effect was first highlighted by Hall *et al.* (1978) who examined a 1970s moral panic that was constructed around the folk devil of the 'Black mugger'.

Back (2002) argues that the reporting of inner-city race disturbances involving members of minority ethnic groups in the UK over the last 25 years often stereotypes them as 'riots'. This implies that such disturbances are irrational and criminal, and conjures up images of rampaging mobs that need to be controlled by justifiable use of police force. Journalists very rarely use the word 'uprising', because this suggests that members of minority ethnic groups may have a genuine grievance in terms of being the victims of racial attacks, discrimination by employers and police harassment. The idea that people are angry enough to take to the streets because they want to rebel against injustice very rarely forms part of the media coverage of such events.

Minority ethnic groups as a threat

Van Dijk's content analysis suggested that a common news stereotype was the idea that minority ethnic groups are posing a threat to the majority White culture. In recent years, three groups seem to constitute the greatest threat in the UK, according to newspapers and television. Moral panics have therefore been constructed around:

> *Immigrants* – who are seen as a threat in terms of their 'numbers', and because of the impact they supposedly have on the supply of jobs, housing and other facilities.

> *Refugees and asylum seekers* – who are often portrayed as coming to Britain to abuse the welfare state. The Information Centre about Asylums and Refugees (ICAR) notes that studies of media coverage of asylum seekers have shown that the media have constructed an image of migrants as a problem or threat to British identity and cohesion (Greenslade 2005). The ICAR study found the British media often repetitively used negative and judgemental language to describe asylum seekers and refugees. ICAR argues that there is often a link between media coverage and community tensions. They conducted research in London and discovered that unbalanced and inaccurate media images of asylum seekers made a significant contribution to their harassment by local residents.

> *Muslims* – who are often portrayed as the 'enemy within'. Poole (2000, so written before 9/11), argued that Islam has always been demonised and distorted by the Western media, and presented as a threat to the security of the UK and British values. Media representations of Islam have therefore long been predominantly negative. Consequently Muslims have been homogenised by Western journalists as "backward, irrational, unchanging **fundamentalists** and misogynists who are threatening and manipulative in the use of their faith for political and personal gain".

UNDERSTAND THE CONCEPT

Fundamentalists are people who take their religions literally. They are often traditional and conservative in outlook and reject modern ideas such as equality of the sexes or tolerance of homosexuality.

Other studies confirm Islamophobic media content. For example, Whitaker (2002) found that Muslims are stereotypically presented by the media as "intolerant, misogynistic, violent or cruel, and finally, strange or different". Moore *et al.* (2008) analysed the content of the British media between 2000 and 2008. They avoided 2001 and 2005, in the aftermath of 9/11 and 7/7 respectively,

because they wanted to focus on the everyday coverage of British Muslims.

The research found that, between 2000 and 2008, over a third of stories focused on terrorism, while a third of stories focused on differences between the Muslim community and British society by highlighting forced marriages and the wearing of the hijab and the veil. In contrast, stories about attacks on Muslims and **Islamophobia** were fairly rare.

UNDERSTAND THE CONCEPT

Islamophobia refers to prejudice and discrimination practised against Muslims.

Moore *et al.* conclude that there are four negative ideological messages in British media representations of Islam:

> Islam is dangerous, backward and irrational compared with Western thought and actions.

> Multiculturalism with its stress on diversity and tolerance is allowing Muslim extremists to spread their message across Muslim communities in the UK.

> There is a clash of civilisation between the West, which is presented as democratic, tolerant and focused on equality for all, and a Muslim world that is presented as oppressive, intolerant, misogynistic and all too willing to persecute minorities.

> Islam is a major threat to the British way of life. For example, stories often focused on the idea that Muslims wanted to replace British law with **Sharia law**.

UNDERSTAND THE CONCEPT

Sharia law refers to the basic Islamic legal system derived from the religious precepts of Islam, particularly those found in its holy texts: the Quran and the Hadith.

Ameli *et al.* (2007) note that media discussion around the issue of the wearing of the hijab and the veil is also problematic because journalists often depict such clothing as a patriarchal and oppressive form of control that exemplifies the misogyny of Islam and symbolises the alleged subordinate position of Muslim women. Ameli argues that the negative language used by journalists to describe women who wear hijabs and veils reduce Muslim women to victims. The idea that women choose to wear the hijab, and the actual everyday problems or challenges that Muslim women face, and which are caused by their socio-economic conditions or by racism, are generally ignored because journalists only want to see them in the context of a repressive form of Islam.

Nahdi (2003) also argues that this generally hostile and careless news coverage destroys trust among Muslim readerships and audiences. He argues that the general decline in the standards of Western media and journalism, with the move towards sound bites, snippets and quick and easy stories, has actually legitimised the voice of extremist Islam. Most importantly, it disguises the vast diversity and range of perspectives among Muslims and equates the outlook and actions of a few individuals to over one billion people worldwide.

In what ways might Islamophobic media stories about Muslims affect the Muslim minority's relationship with the White majority?

Minority ethnic groups as unimportant

Van Dijk notes that some sections of the media imply that the lives of White people are somehow more important than the lives of non-White people. The British African pressure group, Ligali (2006), argued that Black victims of crime are not paid the same degree of attention by the news media as White victims of crime. In 2006, Sir Ian Blair, the Metropolitan Police Commissioner, agreed with Ligali when he claimed that institutionalised racism characterised the British media's reporting of violent crime, because journalists paid a lot of attention to White victims of such crime while seriously neglecting Black victims.

Many of the studies of media representations of ethnic minorities described in this chapter have used content analysis to gather their data. What are the strengths and limitations of this method?

Institutional bias

Some sociological studies suggest that when members of minority ethnic groups do appear on television, they experience the following institutional problems:

> They are often portrayed in stereotypical low-status roles.

> They may appear in a programme because of **tokenism**. A former BBC executive, Shah (2008), argues that broadcasters overcompensate for the lack of executives, producers, directors and writers from minority ethnic groups by putting too many Black and Asian faces on screen, regardless of whether they authentically fit the programmes they are in. In this sense, ethnic-minority actors are merely 'props'.

UNDERSTAND THE CONCEPT

Tokenism refers to the practice of making only a perfunctory or symbolic effort to do a particular thing. With regard to television drama, it means recruiting a small number of actors from minority ethnic groups in order to give the appearance of racial equality.

Actors used in this way are rarely shown as ordinary citizens who just happen to be Black or Asian. More often than not they play 'Black' roles, in which their attitudes, behaviour and interaction with other social groups are shaped by their ethnic identity.

Consider ethnic-minority characters in soap operas you are familiar with – is it true that their ethnicity is important to the storylines?

Bennett *et al.* (2006) found that minority ethnic groups rarely identify with much of the nation's TV culture because television culture offers little space for ethnic-minority interests or identities. Audience research suggests that members of minority ethnic groups believe that media institutions produce a media content geared to the interests of White people because, as Shah has noted, it is dominated by a metropolitan, liberal, White, male, public-school and Oxbridge-educated, middle-class cultural elite.

FOCUS ON SKILLS: GANGSTA RAP

Black cultural media products such as music are often criticised by the White mainstream media for encouraging drug use and gang violence. In both 2003 and 2006, moral panics occurred as 'gangsta rap' music came under attack from politicians and newspapers for its alleged contribution to an increase in gun crime and for its misogynistic lyrical content.

Best and Kellner (1999), in defence of rap music, argue that it articulates the experiences and conditions of young Blacks living on the margins in inner-city areas or on deprived council estates who feel that they are being stereotyped and stigmatised. They argue that rap provides the means through which they can communicate their anger and sense of injustice about racism and inequality. It therefore supplies a voice for people excluded from mainstream society. It is also a symbol of Blackness in that it celebrates Black culture, pride, intelligence, strength, style, and creativity. As Best and Kellner note: "rap is thus not only music to dance and party to, but a potent form of cultural identity."

However Best and Kellner do acknowledge that at its worst, it is: "racist, sexist, and glorifies violence, being

little but a money-making vehicle that is part of the problem rather than the solution. Many of its images and models are highly problematic, such as the gangsta rap celebration of the outlaw, pimp, hedonistic pleasure seeker, and drug dealer." Best and Kellner therefore argue that rap music is complex and many-sided, with contradictory effects. It attracts a large White audience who can gain some insight into the Black experience. They argue that: "rap music makes the listener painfully aware of differences between Black and White, rich and poor, male and female. Rap music brings to White audiences the uncomfortable awareness of Black suffering, anger, and violence." However, successful male rap artists undermine this potential awareness by expressing misogyny, violence towards women and homophobia in their lyrics. Ironically, some rappers direct their rage towards other members of their community, such as women and homosexuals, rather than those who are responsible for their oppression and subordination.

Questions

1. **Suggest two reasons** why moral panics focused on gangsta rap occurred in 2003 and 2006.

2. **Explain**, using three examples, why rap music is a potent symbol of cultural identity.

3. **Identify** and **analyse** the negative content and consequences of rap music.

4. **Evaluate**, using information from this source and elsewhere, the view that minority ethnic groups in the UK are subject to symbolic annihilation by the mass media.

Some theoretical perspectives on media representations of ethnicity

The studies included in this chapter clearly show that media representations of ethnic minorities are generally negative. There are a number of explanations as to why some ethnic minority groups such as young Blacks and Muslims are negatively stereotyped and demonised.

The pluralist perspective

Pluralists tend to see the media as a window on the world, which reflects and reports on the social world in an objective fashion. Journalists are seen as watchdogs of the public interest. Moreover, media content is also shaped by

the market. If the media do not give the public what they want, they become unprofitable and go out of business. From this perspective, then, problematic representations of Black people as criminal or Muslims as a threat reflect real fears. They are supposed to be the fears of the predominantly White readers of certain tabloid newspapers such as *The Sun* or the *Daily Mail* about what they perceive as 'outsider' groups with very different cultures from their own. From a pluralist perspective, then, newspapers are simply acting in the interests of their readers by demanding that those in power take action to control ethnic minority groups, for example, by restricting immigration or by recruiting more police officers.

The editors of these newspapers would probably argue that if they did not run these stories, their readers would desert them for other newspapers. Pluralists also argue that people can choose not to buy these newspapers because there is a diversity of media products, some of which portray ethnic minorities in a neutral or positive way.

However, in criticism of this view, many White people may not have come into contact with Black people or Muslims, and may not have formed opinions about them. Their only source of information is the media. If this is the case, the media are not mirroring their anxieties about ethnic minorities: journalists are actually constructing and shaping racist ideologies on behalf of their readers.

The Marxist perspective

Marxist sociologists believe the media to be an ideological apparatus which functions to divide and rule the working class, to distract their attention from inequality and the mismanagement of the capitalist system. Hall, for example, has suggested that ethnic minorities may be subject to media moral panics which aim to criminalise them and to present them as folk devils which threaten the stability of White society. This justifies more official spending on the social control of ethnic minority communities and plays on White working-class fears that processes such as immigration and radicalisation of young Muslims are more problematic than extreme inequalities in income distribution or poverty.

The evidence for this Marxist explanation is rather limited. Hollingsworth (1990) uncovered some anecdotal evidence that some tabloid owners, editors and journalists subscribed to racist views but this is probably only a very small proportion of media professionals. Some newspapers, notably The *Gutrdian,* are assiduously anti-racist, for example, Cottle (2000) notes that between 1993 and 1998, there were 347 news reports in the *Guardian* focused on investigating the death of the Black teenager Stephen Lawrence and the institutional racism that undermined the investigation into his murder. Moreover, the media marketplace is very competitive and very diverse. These facts mean that it is unlikely that the media as a whole, or even particular sectors of the media, are pursuing the same ideological goals.

The hegemonic Marxist perspective

The hegemonic Marxist theory of the media may be more useful. This makes several interrelated points that may explain why mass media representations of ethnic minorities tend to be negative.

› Most owners, editors and journalists are White, and consequently subscribe to a particular consensual view about how society should be. They share this view with their predominantly White audience or readership.

› This is the product of economics rather than ideology or racism. White opinion and interests are reflected in the media because White people constitute the majority audience. Large audiences attract advertising revenue and consequently profit.

› This consensus approach means that media professionals do not want to risk alienating their White audience by focusing on minority cultures or interests. Moreover, this consensus approach probably results in ethnic minority media professionals distancing themselves from acting as advocates for minority groups. Consequently, then, the interests of Black people and Muslims are marginalised or rendered invisible.

› This consensus approach means that White experts and sources are at the top of the hierarchy of credibility. This means that journalists tend to go to the police or government for information on crime, immigration and radicalisation. Cottle observes that this means that media professionals devote little energy or resources to non-institutional or ethnic minority sources.

› Cottle argues that the pursuit of large audiences has led to the tabloidisation or dumbing down of news. This means that complex issues, for example, the impact of multiculturalism or fundamentalist religions, are less likely to be explained to audiences. Rather news is likely to be reduced to simplistic soundbites and dramatic statements that highlight conflict but fail to capture or illuminate the complexity of race relations in the UK.

Some conclusions about media representations of ethnic minorities

It is important to realise that both the media and society are in a constant state of change. There are signs that the media are growing more diverse in terms of positive representations of ethnic minority culture, especially as more ethnic minority professionals take up media careers and develop media institutions and agencies that specifically target the interests and concerns of ethnic-minority audiences. Some have chosen to work within the established system by developing aspects of institutional media, such as the BBC Asian digital network and programmes such as *Ebony* and *Café 21*. There is also a range of home-grown media agencies that are owned, managed and controlled by minority ethnic groups themselves, including newspapers and magazines such as *Eastern Eye* and *The Voice*, radio stations such as *Sunrise Radio* and *Asian FX*, and new media websites such as www.brasian.co.uk.

HOW DO THE MEDIA REPRESENT SOCIAL CLASS?

Mass-media representations of social classes rarely focus on the social tensions or class conflict that some critical sociologists see as underpinning society. In fact, as Chapter 2 has indicated, some neo-Marxist sociologists suggest that the function of the media is to ensure the cultural hegemony of the dominant capitalist class and to ensure that inequality and exploitation are not defined as social problems so that they do not become the focus of social debate and demand for social change.

Representations of the upper class

Neo-Marxists argue that mass-media representations of social class tend to celebrate hierarchy and wealth. Those who benefit – the monarchy, the upper class and the very wealthy – generally receive a positive press as celebrities who are somehow deserving of their position. The UK mass media hardly ever portray the upper classes in a critical light, nor do they often draw any serious attention to inequalities in wealth and pay or to the overrepresentation of public-school products in positions of power.

Sociological observations of media representations of the upper classes suggest that popular films and television costume drama tend to portray members of this class in either an eccentric or a nostalgic way. In films such as *The King's Speech* and television costume dramas such as *Downton Abbey*, a rosy, idealised picture is painted of a ruling elite characterised by honour, culture and good breeding.

Representations of the monarchy

Nairn (1988) notes that the monarchy has successfully converted much of the modern mass media to its cause, so that, until fairly recently, it was rare to see any criticism of this institution or the individuals in it. Nairn argues that this is because after the Second World War the monarchy, with the collusion of the media, reinvented itself as a 'Royal Family' with a cast of characters, not unlike our own families, who stood for national values such as 'niceness', 'decency' and 'ordinariness'. Members of this 'family' were presented as 'like us' but 'not like us'; for example, the Queen was just an 'ordinary' working mother doing an extraordinary job. This successful makeover resulted in a national obsession with the Royal Family, reflected in media coverage that has focused positively on every trivial detail of their lives, turning the Queen and her family into an ongoing narrative or soap story, but with a

glamour and mystique far greater than any other media personality. Mass-media representations of the Queen are also aimed at reinforcing a sense of national identity, in that she is portrayed as the ultimate symbol of the nation. Consequently, the media regard royal events, such as weddings, births and funerals, as national events to be celebrated.

How do you feel about the Royal Family? What is your main source of information about this institution?

Representations of wealth

Newman (2006) argues that the media focus very positively on the lifestyles of the wealthy and the privileged. He observes that the media focus too heavily on consumer items such as luxury cars, costly holiday spots and fashion accessories that only the wealthy can afford. Newman also notes the enormous amount of print and broadcast media dedicated to daily business news and stock market quotations, despite the fact that few people in the UK own stocks and shares. He notes that: "international news and trade agreements are reported in terms of their impact on the business world and wealthy investors, not on ordinary working people." He observes that the media rarely focus on the inequities of capitalism, such as the size of bankers' bonuses, the fact that top business people are rewarded with huge pay-offs for failure, or the growing divide between rich and poor.

However, from a pluralist perspective, it can be argued that representations of the rich, their lifestyles and the business world are justified for three reasons:

1. The media view the UK as a meritocracy and the media portrayals of the wealthy are representative of the idea that talented people are deserving of high rewards.

2. Such stories may motivate people to work hard in the belief that they can attain these rewards, which benefits the economy.

3. The focus on finance, stocks and shares may merely reflect the importance of these sectors for the economy.

How do the British tabloid media view celebrity, materialism and wealth?

Representations of the middle classes

Some sociologists argue that the middle classes (professionals, managers, white-collar workers) and their concerns are overrepresented in the media. There is not a great deal of British sociological research in this area, but four broad sociological observations can be made:

1. In general, the middle class are overrepresented on TV (while the working class are underrepresented). In dramas, apart from soaps and situation comedies, middle-class families are predominant. They are generally portrayed as concerned about manners, decency and decorum, social respectability, and so on.

2. A lot of British newspapers – such as the *Daily Mail* and *Daily Telegraph* – and magazines are aimed at the middle class and their consumption, tastes and interests in material goods such as computers, music, cars, house and garden design that can only be afforded by those with a good standard of living.

3. The content of newspapers such as the *Daily Mail* suggests that journalists believe that the middle classes of middle England are generally anxious about the decline of moral standards in society and that they feel threatened by alien influences such as the euro, asylum seekers and terrorism. Newspapers often crusade on behalf of the middle classes and initiate moral panics on issues such as immigration and asylum seekers coming to Europe.

4. Most of the creative personnel in the media are themselves middle class. In news and current affairs, the middle classes dominate positions of authority – the 'expert' is invariably middle class.

Representations of the working class

Marxists argue that some mass-media representations of the working class are also part and parcel of capitalist ideology. Newman notes that there have been very few situation comedies, television dramas or films in the past 10 years focusing on the everyday lives of the working class, despite the fact that this group constitutes a significant section of society.

Jones (2011) argues that media coverage of working-class people constitutes a middle-class assault on working-class values, institutions and communities. He claims that many middle-class journalists suffer from a "liberal bigotry" – they assume that all working-class people are feckless,

promiscuous, foul-mouthed racists who hate minority ethnic groups, refugees and multiculturalism. The reporting of issues such as poverty, unemployment and single-parent families, however, often suggests personal inadequacy, rather than government policies or poor business practices, is the main cause of these social problems.

Curran and Seaton (2003) note that newspapers aimed at working-class audiences assume that they are uninterested in serious analysis of either the political or social organisation of UK society. Political debate is often reduced to a simplistic conflict between personalities. The content of newspapers such as *The Sun* and the *Daily Star* assume that such audiences want to read about celebrity gossip and lifestyles, trivial human interest stories and sport. Marxists see such media content as an attempt to distract the working-class audience from the inequalities of capitalism. In contrast, pluralists argue that this is what tabloid newspaper readers want: the proof of the pudding lies in the sales of these newspapers. For example, in 2013 just under 13.5 million people read *The Sun* or *The Sun on Sunday*, either in print or online every week, whilst the *Daily Mail* attracts 12m readers across its daily and Sunday print titles and the *Mail Online*.

Moreover, some media representations of working-class people portray them very sympathetically. The 'kitchen-sink' British cinema of the 1960s, represented by films such as *Saturday Night and Sunday Morning* (1960) and *Kes* (1969), television drama such as *Our Friends in the North* (1996) and films such as *The Full Monty* (1997), *Brassed Off* (1996), *Made in Dagenham* (2010) and *Pride* (2014) have portrayed working-class life and problems in a dignified, realistic and supportive way, and even commented upon and challenged social inequality, class exploitation and racial intolerance.

Representations of poverty and the underclass

McKendrick *et al.* (2008) studied a week's output of mainstream media in 2007 and concluded that coverage of poverty is marginal in the UK media, in that the causes and consequences of poverty are very rarely explored through the news, documentaries or drama. Cohen (2009) argues the UK mass media is so concerned about "trumpeting the good fortune" of British capitalism that it pays less attention to its 'casualties'. Cohen argues that journalists, entertainers and artists are hopeless at realistically reporting or dramatising the plight of the poor. He argues that some sections of the media actually revel in the suffering of the poor by commissioning shows that deliberately portray the poor as parasitic scroungers. The media therefore reinforces the popular view that the poor are poor because of their own depravity and weakness. Most importantly, says Cohen, the media fail to see the connection between deprivation and wealth.

Another development, in the 21st century, in media interest in the poor has been the media labelling of some sections of the poor as 'chavs' or 'shirkers', which Shildrick and MacDonald (2007) suggest is another way of suggesting that the poor are undeserving of public sympathy. As Hayward and Yar (2006) argue, the label 'chav' is now used by newspapers and websites as a familiar and amusing term of abuse for young poor people. Lawler (2005) argues that the media use this discriminatory and offensive form of language to vilify and **socially stigmatise** what they depict as a peasant underclass or White trash, symbolised by stereotypical forms of appearance, such as the wearing of tracksuits, idleness, fraudulent benefit claims, anti-social behaviour, drug use and criminality. These media representations neutralise any public concern or sympathy for their social and economic plight.

UNDERSTAND THE CONCEPT

Social stigmatisation refers to extreme disapproval of (or discontent with) a person or group because of their behaviour or characteristics. This often results in a negative label or stigma being attached to them, which serves to **distinguish** them from other members of society.

How do programmes such as the Jeremy Kyle show generally view the underclass?

Some conclusions about media representations of social class

Despite the lack of empirical research in this area, it can be argued that media representations of the powerful – the upper class and the middle class – tend to be more positive than representations of the less powerful working class and the poor.

Marxists would argue that this is because the mass media are an ideological agency that functions to maintain, legitimise and reproduce class inequalities and to bring about a state of false class consciousness in those who occupy the bottom rungs of society. Profit and wealth

need to be justified as deserved (when in reality they are the product of the capitalist class's exploitation of labour) whereas media representations of poverty serve to suggest that this economic status is self-inflicted rather than caused by the social organisation of capitalism.

In contrast, pluralists argue that these representations reflect the reality of capitalist society – that they are reported because they fit news values of what is newsworthy and that if working-class people didn't like them, they would not invest in the types of media in which these representations are mainly found.

REPRESENTATIONS OF AGE

Media representations of different groups of people based on age (children, adolescents and the elderly), also generalise and categorise people on the basis of stereotypes. The media encourage audiences to assume that specific representations in terms of image and behaviour can be applied wholesale to particular age groups. However, functionalist sociologists argue that these representations are an essential part of the socialisation process because, alongside other agencies of socialisation – the family, education and religion – the mass media functions to equip children and young people with the appropriate values and norms required to be good citizens. Once children and young people have been instilled with that shared culture, media representations engage in **boundary maintenance**.

UNDERSTAND THE CONCEPT

Boundary maintenance refers to the social control aspect of the socialisation process. Children need to be socialised into social rules of behaviour but they and adults need to be reminded every now and then of the social boundaries of their behaviour; that certain types of behaviour attract the social disapproval of others, and therefore, possible punishment.

Media stories about children and young people reinforce social expectations as to how those groups should behave and, importantly, what happens to them when they do not. Media representations help to control the behaviour of young people socially and, as such, they are regarded as crucial to safeguarding both conformity and social stability.

Representations of childhood

British children are often depicted in the UK media in fairly positive ways. Content analyses of media products suggest that six stereotypes of children are frequently used by the media:

> *Cute* – This is a common stereotype found in television commercials for baby products or toilet rolls.

> *Little devils* – Another common stereotype especially found in drama and comedy – Bart Simpson, for example.

> *Brilliant* – Perhaps as child prodigies or as heroes for saving the life of an adult.

> *Brave little angels* – Suffering from long-term or terminal disease or disability.

> *Accessories* – Stories about celebrities such as Madonna, Angeline Jolie or the Beckhams may focus on how their children humanise them.

> *Modern* – The media may focus on how children 'these days' know so much more 'at their age' than previous generations of children.

Heintz-Knowles's (2002) study of children on American television found that children are often portrayed as motivated primarily by peer relationships, sports and romance and, least often, by community, school-related, or religious issues. They are rarely shown as coping with societal issues such as racism or with major family issues such as child abuse and domestic violence.

However, Heintz-Knowles also found that most representations of children are positive and show them engaged in pro-social actions such as telling the truth and helping others; about 40 per cent of television drama, nevertheless, depicted children engaged in anti-social actions, such as lying or bullying. However, one very noticeable feature of children's television that has occurred in the last 15 years has been the move to more realistic drama featuring issues from a child's rather than an adult's point of view.

Children are also represented in television commercials in ways that socialise them to become active consumers. They are encouraged by television advertising and film merchandising to have an appetite for toys and games. Evans and Chandler (2006) note that this has led to the emergence of a new family pressure: **pester power**, the power of children to train or manipulate their parents to spend money on consumer goods that will increase the children's status in the eyes of their peers. They suggest that pester power is creating great anxiety among poorer parents, who will often go into debt to provide for their children's desires.

UNDERSTAND THE CONCEPT

Pester power refers to the ability of children to pressurise and persuade their parents into buying them products, especially items such as toys advertised in the media.

Sociological knowledge about media representations of children in the UK is actually quite limited. Most studies have been American and, consequently, there may be cultural differences in the way children are portrayed by the media in the USA and the UK. The limited numbers of studies that are available tend to generalise to all children but, in the UK, children's experience of both childhood and media representations of it may be subject to influences such as social class, gender, ethnicity, religion. For example, media representations of Islamic children may be quite different to those of children from other religious backgrounds. Finally, there is an absence of studies that explore children's interpretations of media representations.

Representations of youth

There are generally two very broad ways in which young people have been targeted and portrayed by the media in the UK. On the one hand, there is a whole media industry aimed at socially constructing youth in terms of lifestyle and identity. Magazines are produced specifically for young people. Record companies, internet music download sites, mobile telephone companies and radio stations all specifically target and attempt to shape the musical tastes of young people. Networking sites on the internet – such as Facebook, Instagram and Snapchat – allow youth to project their identities around the world.

However, youth are often portrayed by news media as a social problem, as immoral or anti-authority, and they are consequently constructed as folk devils and part of a moral panic. The majority of moral panics since the 1950s have been manufactured around concerns about young people's behaviour, such as their membership of specific 'deviant' subcultures (teddy boys, hoodies, for example) or because their behaviour (for example, drug-taking or binge drinking) has attracted the disapproval of those in authority. For further details and explanations of moral panics constructed around youth, see Chapters 1.6 and 4.4.

Research by Wayne et al. confirms this overwhelmingly negative portrayal of youth in the UK. Their analysis looked at 2,130 news items across all the main television channels during May 2006 and found 286 stories that focused specifically on young people. Of these, 28 per cent focused on celebrities, but 82 per cent of the remainder focused on young people as either the victims of or, more commonly, the perpetrators of violent crime. In other words, young people were mainly represented as a threat to society. Wayne and colleagues also found that it was very rare (only 1 per cent) for news items to feature a young person's perspective or opinion. They note that the media only deliver a one-dimensional picture of youth, one that encourages fear and condemnation rather than understanding. Moreover, they argue that it distracts from the real problems young people face in the modern world – such as homelessness, not being able to get onto the housing ladder, unemployment, mental health – that might be caused by society's or the government's failure to take the problems of youth seriously.

Some theoretical perspectives on media representations of young people

Functionalists argue that media representations function to maintain and normalise boundaries of socially expected behaviour. Young people may be subjected to negative peer pressure and be encouraged to indulge in deviant behaviour. Media representations remind adolescents what is socially expected of them and the punishments they can expect if they transgress.

Pluralists argue that such media representations simply reflect social reality – young people commit more crime and deviance than any other social group. Moreover, criminal behaviour is newsworthy: people want to read about it and so it sells newspapers.

Interactionists argue that young people are frequently labelled by older generations as a threat to social stability because they often challenge their authority. Media representations and the moral panics that often result from these are attempts at social control.

As the Glasgow University Media group have observed, most journalists subscribe to a consensus view of society that places older people at the top of the hierarchy of credibility with regard to their sources. Consequently, the agenda as far as the reporting of youth is concerned is set by older people and consequently is negative.

Finally, postmodernists argue that in media–saturated, postmodern societies, negative portrayals are only a small aspect of media representations, which are actually diverse and pluralistic. In particular, postmodernists highlight the role of the new media and the fact that young people are accomplished creators and users of such media. For example, young people, in their desire to construct unique identities, use a plethora of new media – especially social networking sites such as Facebook, Twitter, Instagram, YouTube, Snapchat – to construct positive (and sometimes very profitable) media representations of themselves.

As a teenager, do you believe that the media portrays your age group fairly?

Representations of old age

Research focusing on media representations of the elderly suggests that age is not the only factor that impacts on the way the media portrays people aged 65 and over. For example, Newman notes that upper-class and middle-class elderly people, usually men, are often portrayed in television and film dramas as occupying high-status roles as world leaders, judges, politicians, experts and business executives and are portrayed as both healthy and fit, as well as socially involved.

Gender seems to interact with age in a positive way for men in some sections of the media. For example, female film and television stars are often relegated to character parts once their looks and bodies are perceived to be on the wane, which seems to be after the age of 40, while male actors continue to play leading roles, regardless of their age. Stoller and Gibson (1999) observe that: "although men also face negative stereotypes and loss of status as they get older, these experiences occur at a more advanced age.......Negative consequences of ageing for men focus more on occupational success than physical attractiveness." They argue that elderly women are mainly shown in social, family and recreational settings and represented as passive, socially isolated, unpleasant and poor. Finally, sociologists have observed that news programmes seem to work on the assumption that an older male with grey in his hair and lines on his face somehow exudes the necessary authority to impart the news. They are often paired with attractive young females, while older women newsreaders are often exiled to radio.

Media stereotyping of ageing and the elderly

It can also be argued that old age is generally devalued by some parts of the media industry. The emphasis on youth and beauty in television, film and advertising imply that ageing should be avoided at all costs, which in itself strongly implies that to be old is a stigmatised identity.

The charity Age Concern (2000) argus that the elderly are underrepresented in general across a variety of mass media and that media portrayals are generally **ageist** in that the old tend to be portrayed in stereotypically negative ways:

> *Grumpy* – This stereotype paints elderly women as shrews or busybodies and males as curmudgeons who spend their time waxing lyrical about the past, bemoaning the behaviour of young people and complaining about the modern world. These characters tend to be portrayed as conservative, stubborn and resistant to social change.

> *Mentally challenged* – This stereotype ranges from those elderly who are forgetful or befuddled to those who are suffering from senility, so that they are feeble-minded or severely confused. This stereotype suggests that growing old involves the loss, or at least the decline, of people's mental functions.

> *A burden* – The elderly are portrayed as an economic burden on society (in terms of the costs to the younger generation of pensions and health care) and/or as a physical and social burden on younger members of their families (who have to worry about or care for them).

UNDERSTAND THE CONCEPT

Ageism refers to prejudice and discrimination practised against age groups.

However, recent research suggests that media producers may be gradually reinventing how they deal with the elderly, especially as they realise that this group may have more disposable income – the **grey pound –** to spend on consumer goods. Lee *et al.* (2007) note that representation of the elderly in advertisements is still fairly low – 15 per cent – but the majority of these advertisements (91 per cent) portray the elderly as 'golden agers', who are active, alert, healthy, successful and content. On the other hand, some research suggests that this positive stereotype may be unrealistic because it does not reflect the wide range of experiences that people have as they age, including loss of status, poverty, loneliness and the loss of their partner.

UNDERSTAND THE CONCEPT

The **grey pound** refers to the economic power of elderly people.

Robinson *et al.* (2008) compared how older adults and college students perceived the stereotypes of the elderly found in magazine adverts. They found that their elderly sample liked those adverts that showed them as clever, vibrant and having a sense of humour. Interestingly, neither the elderly nor the student respondents liked those adverts that poked fun at the elderly or presented them as out of touch or unattractive. Media representations of age, alongside other agencies of socialisation such as family experience and education, are important in shaping public attitudes towards other age groups. However, research in this field, especially with regard to the very young and the elderly, is fairly limited. Perhaps this fact, too, is illustrative of the low status that society generally attributes to these age groups.

In your opinion, how are the elderly mainly portrayed by the British mass media?

Some conclusions about media representations of age

Sociological research on representations of age in the UK media is both mixed and partial. Despite the fact that most research in this field is American, media representations of children in the UK are also probably positive because childhood is regarded as a time of innocence and dependency in which children are viewed as vulnerable and special. However, some critics have recently suggested that media representations of childhood are becoming more problematic because the media are increasingly guilty of over-sexualising childhood, especially girls' childhood. Feminist commentators have observed that some media representations of childhood result in girls worrying about their appearance and weight and that both boys and girls are put under pressure to take an interest in sex at too young an age.

In contrast, representations of youth in traditional media such as newspapers are generally negative. Teenagers are generally presented as a problem and the notion that there is a generation gap between adolescents and parents has become something of a media cliché despite surveys of young people clearly demonstrating that teenagers and their parents share many values and beliefs. However, there is evidence that representations of youth in new media are positive and celebratory because most new media content today is actually constructed by the young for consumption by other young people.

Finally, representations of the elderly are mixed. Ageist media stereotypes are common but the evidence suggests that whether the elderly are subjected to soft or hard forms of negative labelling by the media is dependent on social class and gender. The evidence suggests that media representations of older people are both patriarchal, that is, ageing women are more likely to be stigmatised than ageing men, and dependent on social class, that is, older people with spending power are more likely to be portrayed positively compared with elderly people who live in poverty.

CHECK YOUR UNDERSTANDING

1. Explain what is meant by the term 'Islamophobia'.

2. Explain what is meant by 'folk devils'.

3. Explain what is meant by 'ageism'.

4. Explain what is meant by 'tokenism'.

5. Identify and briefly outline two examples of how the media portray youth.

6. Identify and briefly explain why critics of the media view many news representations of Muslims as Islamophobic.

7. Analyse the mass media representation of the working class and the poor.

8. Analyse why the mass media have been accused of being ageist.

9. Evaluate mass media representations of the monarchy and wealth.

10. Evaluate the view that the mass media generally portray minority ethnic groups in negative and stereotypical ways.

TAKE IT FURTHER

1. Interview a sample of over-60s about how they view representations of the elderly in the media. Focus the discussion by showing participants some well-known personalities. To what extent are they concerned about stereotyping in the media?

2. Visit the European Network Against Racism website at www.enargywebzine.eu, which monitors the content of social media and provides in-depth analysis of how such sites are being used to disseminate racism and hate. There is a particularly useful article called 'Hate on the internet' at www.enargywebzine.eu

4.7 THE RELATIONSHIP BETWEEN THE MEDIA AND THEIR CONTENT, PRESENTATION AND AUDIENCES

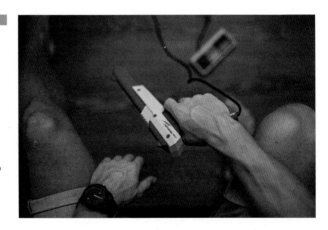

LEARNING OBJECTIVES

› Demonstrate knowledge and understanding of the different theories concerning and methodological issues of researching the effects of media on their audience, especially violent content (AO1).

› Apply this knowledge to contemporary society (AO2).

› Analyse the findings of sociological studies that aim to explore the relationship between media content, and the actions and attitudes of diverse audiences (AO3).

› Evaluate sociological explanations in order to make judgements and draw conclusions about the relationship between the media, their content and presentation, and audiences (AO3).

INTRODUCING THE DEBATE

Many people believe that the media influence behaviour and what we think or believe. Influential psychologists, pressure groups such as Mediawatch-UK, religious leaders and politicians suggest that there is a fairly direct causal link between violence in films, television programmes and computer games, and violent real-life crime. Moreover, some feminist and Marxist sociologists argue that media content may have some effects on audiences too. What all these groups have in common is that they believe media content exerts an overwhelmingly negative effect on mass audiences, and particularly the impressionable young. These beliefs have led to official attempts to control Britain's television and film media output, particularly their violent, sexual and anti-social behaviour content, although easy access to the relatively uncensored world of the internet has seriously undermined attempts to control media content. This chapter therefore aims to analyse and assess whether media content has any effect on behaviour or attitudes.

THE HYPODERMIC SYRINGE MODEL OF MEDIA EFFECTS

The hypodermic syringe model of media effects believes that a direct correlation exists between the violence and antisocial behaviour portrayed in films, on television, in computer games, in rap lyrics, and so on, and real-life violence and antisocial behaviour, such as drug use and teenage gun/knife crime. The model suggests that children and teenagers are vulnerable to media content because they are still in the early stages of socialisation and therefore very impressionable. Some sociologists, such as Gerbner *et al.* (1986), have focused on representations of violence in certain types of media, especially Hollywood films, and suggest that these contribute to violent crime and antisocial forms of behaviour in real life, especially that committed by the young.

However, some sociologists have also taken a hypodermic syringe approach to how the mass media may shape non-violent forms of behaviour. Feminist sociologists such as Orbach (1991) and Wolf (1990) have argued that media representations of femininity may be producing a generation of females who suffer from eating disorders, whilst others such as Dines (2011) have argued that men's consumption of pornography may be harmful in terms of encouraging negative attitudes towards women. Some early Marxist commentators, particularly those belonging to the Frankfurt School, such as Marcuse (1964), believed that the media transmitted a 'mass culture' which was directly injected into the hearts and minds of the population, making them more vulnerable to ruling-class propaganda. Norris (1999) claims that media coverage of political issues can influence voting behaviour.

On a more positive note, functionalists believe that the mass media have a hypodermic effect in that, alongside the family, education and religion, they are responsible for boundary maintenance – mass media representations of crime reinforce social expectations about normal and abnormal behaviour.

The media effects debate is therefore both complex and crowded. This chapter intends to focus on two important aspects of this debate:

1. The effect of media on violent behaviour

2. The effect of media on social attitudes.

Imitation or copycat violence
Early hypodermic model studies of the relationship between the media and violence focused on conducting experiments in laboratories. For example, Bandura *et al.*

(1963) looked for a direct cause-and-effect relationship between media content and violence. They showed three groups of children real, film and cartoon examples of a self-righting doll ('bobo doll') being attacked with mallets, while a fourth group saw no violent activity. After being introduced to a room full of exciting toys, the children in each group were made to feel frustrated by being told that the toys were not for them. They were then led to another room containing a bobo doll, where they were observed through a one-way mirror. The three groups who had been shown the violent activity – whether real, film or cartoon – all behaved more aggressively than the fourth group. On the basis of this experiment, Bandura and colleagues concluded that violent media content could lead to imitation or 'copycat' violence.

Bandura's research on children was carried out in a laboratory context – what practical, ethical and theoretical limitations can you identify with this type of method?

In a similar vein, McCabe and Martin (2005) argue that screen violence has a **'disinhibition'** effect – it convinces children that, in some social situations, the 'normal' rules that govern conflict and difference can be suspended: that discussion and negotiation can be replaced with violence.

UNDERSTAND THE CONCEPT

Disinhibition refers to lack of restraint caused by the lifting or suspension of the normal rules that govern everyday behaviour. A good example of disinhibition is road rage.

Desensitisation
Newson (1994) argued that violent images in films are too easily available and that exposure to screen violence encouraged young viewers to identify with violent perpetrators rather than victims. Moreover, she noted that children and teenagers are subjected to thousands of images of killings (for example, it is estimated that the average 18-year-old in the USA has viewed 16,000 television murders) and acts of violence as they grow up, through viewing television and films. She suggested that such prolonged exposure to media violence may have a 'drip-drip' effect on young people over the course of their childhood and result in their becoming desensitised to violence – they become socialised into

accepting violent behaviour as normal, especially as a problem-solving device.

Newsom's conclusions are supported by four pieces of research. Huesmann *et al.* (2003) carried out a study of 300 young people who were monitored from the age of eight into their 20s. They found that those respondents who watched violent shows at an early age were more likely to be aggressive in their 20s. Johnson *et al.* (2002) also found a significant relationship between the amount of time spent watching TV during their respondents' teenage years and aggressive behaviour as young adults. Peter and Valkenburg (2008) found that exposure to pornographic internet sites increased adolescents' likelihood to engage in casual sex. Research conducted by Anderson and Bushman (2009) on 257 college students who played violent computer games found sustained exposure to these games increased the students' levels of aggression and made them more accepting of real-life violence. Anderson and Bushman concede that prolonged exposure to media violence does not result in copycat behaviour but they claim that it does change the way people think about violence.

Censorship

Newson's conclusions had a great impact on society and politicians. Her report led directly to increased censorship of the film industry. The British Board of Film Classification (BBFC) was given the power to apply age certificates, (for example, U, PG, 12A, 15 and 18) for films, DVDs and music videos. The BBFC can also insist that film-makers make cuts relating to bad language, scenes of drug use and violence.

The television companies agreed on voluntary censorship by adopting the nine o'clock watershed, which means that television programmes that feature bad language or scenes of a sexual or violent nature should not be shown before this time. Television channels also issue warnings before films and programmes with regard to sexual or violent content.

Critique of the hypodermic syringe model

A number of critiques have developed of the hypodermic syringe model of media effects:

Preventing real-life violence

Some media sociologists claim that media violence can actually prevent real-life violence, in the following ways:

> *Catharsis* – Fesbach and Sanger (1971) found that screen violence can actually provide a safe outlet for people's aggressive tendencies. This is known as **catharsis**. They looked at the effects of violent

TV on teenagers. A large sample of boys from both private schools and residential homes were fed a diet of TV for six weeks. Some groups could only watch aggressive programmes, while others were made to watch non-aggressive programmes. The observers noted at the end of the study that the groups who had seen only aggressive programmes were actually less aggressive in their behaviour than the others. Fesbach and Sanger therefore claim that media violence has a cathartic effect – watching an exciting film releases aggressive energy into safe outlets as the viewers immerse themselves in the action.

UNDERSTAND THE CONCEPT

Catharsis refers to the safe release of violent or aggressive impulses by taking part in sport, playing computer games or watching screen violence. However, the value of the concept has been questioned in recent years.

> *Sensitisation* – Similarly some sociologists argue that seeing the effects of violence – and especially the pain and suffering that it causes to the victim and their families – may make viewers more sensitive of its consequences and so less inclined to commit violent acts. This is supported by research by Ramos et al. (2013) who found that participants in their research were significantly more **empathetic** towards victims' suffering when they knew they were watching real violence rather than fictional violence.

UNDERSTAND THE CONCEPT

Empathy refers to a person's ability to identify with and understand another person's situation from their perspective.

Methodological problems

The methods used by the hypodermic syringe studies have also been questioned.

Gauntlett (2008) is critical of studies, such as that carried out by Bandura, that have been conducted in the artificial context of the laboratory. He argues that this makes their findings questionable because people, especially children, do not behave as naturally under laboratory conditions as they would do in their everyday environment. For example, a laboratory context rarely takes into consideration the fact that children's media habits are generally controlled by parents, especially when they are very young. Moreover, there may be a laboratory effect, as research subjects work out what is expected of them. In other words, the data may not be valid because it merely reflects the desire of the research subjects to please the experimenters. This may especially be the case with children.

The hypodermic syringe studies are not clear about how 'violence' should be defined. There are a number of different types: cartoon violence; authentic violence as seen in images of war and death on news bulletins; sporting violence, such as boxing; and fictional violence. Moreover, it is often unclear in media effects studies whether these different types of violence have the same or different effects upon their audiences or whether different audiences react differently to different types and levels of violence. The effects model has therefore been criticised: because it only focuses on particular types of fictional violence, it tends to be selective in its approach to media violence.

The effects model often fails to put violence into context – for example, it views all violence as wrong, however trivial, and fails to see that audiences interpret it according to narrative context. This point is supported by Morrison (1999), who showed excerpts from violent films – to groups of women, young men and war veterans. All of the interviewees felt that the most violent and disturbing clip was a man beating his wife in the film *Ladybird, Ladybird*. It caused distress because of the realism of the setting, the strong language, the perceived unfairness, and also because viewers were concerned about the effect on the child actors in the scene. In contrast, a clip from *Pulp Fiction* – in which a man is killed out of the blue during an innocent conversation, spraying blood and chunks of brain around a car – was seen as 'humorous' and 'not violent', even by women over the age of 60, because there was light-hearted dialogue. Morrison's research therefore suggests that the context in which screen violence occurs affects its impact on the audience.

The scene from Ladybird, Ladybird (above) was considered more violent and disturbing than the one from Pulp Fiction (below).

Another critique suggests that any studies of the hypodermic syringe model tackle social problems such as violence backwards. For example, Belson (1978) showed violent teenagers violent videos and claimed that, because they reacted positively to them, this type of viewing had obviously caused the violence in the first place. Gauntlett points out that these studies merely tell us about the viewing preferences of violent teenage boys rather than the effects of such habits on their behaviour. Aggressive boys may merely like aggressive films.

Children as sophisticated media users

Some sociologists believe that people, and particularly children, are not as vulnerable as the hypodermic syringe model implies. For example, some research indicates that children can distinguish between fictional/cartoon violence and real violence from a very early age, and generally know that it should not be imitated. Research by Millwood Hargrave (2003) found no evidence of confusion in children's minds between fictional and real-life violence.

However, research summarised in the Ofcom report *Children and Parents: Media and Attitudes* (2015) suggests that children may lack online understanding – nearly one in ten children do not question what they see online and, consequently, they are likely to believe that what they see on social media sites, particularly on YouTube or apps, is true and accurate. Only 52 per cent of children aged 12–15 who watch YouTube are aware that advertising is the main source of funding on the site, and less than half (47%) are aware that 'vloggers' (video bloggers) are often paid to endorse products or services.

Furthermore, the Institute of Public Policy Research (IPPR) found in 2014 that sending sexually explicit pictures by mobile phone is now part of everyday life for almost half of British teenagers, while almost half of the survey's sample said there was "nothing wrong" with looking at pornography. The research also found that teenagers ranked pornography sites on the internet higher than parents as a source of information about sex and relationships and that easy access to online pornography was putting pressure on both girls and boys to look and act in certain sexual ways.

Do you have a tendency to believe uncritically that information you have read on the internet is true?

Scapegoating the media

In April 1999, two students took guns and bombs into their school – Columbine in Colorado – and killed 13 people. A number of media influences were cited by supporters of the hypodermic syringe model as being primarily responsible for the boys' actions, such as playing the computer game *Doom*, listening to the 'violent' music and lyrics of Marilyn Manson and watching violent videos, most notably *The Basketball Diaries*. This incident is an excellent example of how the media are scapegoated for violence by the supporters of the hypodermic syringe model.

However, the hypodermic syringe model often fails to consider other social and psychological factors that may motivate violent or antisocial behaviour, such as poor parenting, childhood trauma, the peer group, drug abuse or mental illness. It is therefore highly likely that violence is caused by a range of factors interacting with one another. As Michael Moore points out in his documentary film *Bowling for Columbine*, blaming one cause – the media – for the Columbine massacre makes as much sense as blaming ten-pin bowling, which both killers were very keen on. Media content therefore may possibly be an influence on real-life violence but it is very unlikely to be the sole influence.

An interesting observation made by Ferguson (2015) is that youth violence in the USA has fallen by 83 per cent in the past two decades despite an explosion in the number of violent computer games. He argues that violent games may have a beneficial effect on society because they give individuals prone to aggression an opportunity to play out that aggression and, most importantly, these individuals are no longer on the streets potentially commiting violent crime because they are too busy playing these games.

Conclusions about the hypodermic syringe model

Overall, the evidence claimed in support of the hypodermic syringe model is weak. Studies of societies in which the availability of television is fairly recent have found minimal change in young people's behaviour. For example, Charlton *et al.* (2000) carried out research on the island of St Helena in the South Atlantic Ocean, which received television transmissions for the first time in 1995, but found no evidence that programmes were producing imitation, disinhibition or desensitisation.

Guy Cumberbatch (2004) looked at over 3,500 research studies into the effects of screen violence, encompassing film, TV, video and, more recently, computer and video games. He concluded: "If one conclusion is possible, it is that the jury is still not out. It's never been in. Media violence has been subjected to a lynch mob mentality with almost any evidence used to prove guilt." In other words, there is still no conclusive evidence either way that violence shown in the media influences or changes people's behaviour.

ACTIVE AUDIENCE APPROACHES

Active audience approaches argue that media content does not lead to imitation or desensitisation. They are critical of the hypodermic syringe model because of the assumption that audiences are homogeneous, that is, that they share similar characteristics. However, in reality, audiences have very different social features in terms of age, maturity, social class, education, family background and so on. These characteristics will influence how people respond to and use media content.

Active audience approaches believe that people who constitute audiences have considerable choice in the way they actively use and interpret the media. Audiences are not merely passive recipients of media content. They interpret it and make active choices in how they respond to it. There are a number of active audience models.

The two-step flow model

Katz and Lazarsfeld (1965) suggest that personal relationships and social networks are dominated by 'opinion leaders'. These are people with influence because other members of social networks to which they belong look up to and listen to them. These people usually have strong ideas or opinions about a range of matters, which they have formed by exposing themselves to different types of media and content. Katz and Lazarsfeld suggest that media content goes through two steps or stages before it has an 'effect':

> The opinion leader is exposed to the media content.

> The opinion leader disseminates their interpretation of that content and those who respect the opinion leader are influenced by that interpretation.

Consequently, media audiences are not directly influenced by the media. The audience, in the form of the opinion leader, is not passive, but active. However, critics have pointed out two problems with this model:

> There is no guarantee that the opinion leader has not been subjected to an imitative or desensitising effect; for example, a leader of a peer group such as a street gang might convince other members that violence is acceptable because he or she has been exposed to screen violence that strongly transmits the message that violence is an appropriate problem-solving strategy.

> People who are most at risk of being influenced by the media may be socially isolated individuals who are not members of any social network. Such individuals do not have access to an opinion leader who might help interpret media content in a healthy way.

The selective filter model

Klapper (1960) suggests that, for a media message to have any effect, it must pass through the following three filters:

> *Selective exposure* – The audience must choose to view, read or listen to the content of specific media. Media messages can have no effect if no one sees or hears them! However, what the audience chooses depends upon their interests, education, age, gender, social class and so on. Hollywood makes specific types of genre film with this in mind; for example, most horror movies are aimed at a teenage audience. Moreover, the film certificate system denies some audiences entry to particular films.

> *Selective perception* – The audience may view media content but may decide to reject it because it does not fit their perception of the social world. For example, a heavy smoker may choose to ignore the content of a television programme that stresses the link between smoking and lung cancer. Festinger (1957) argues that people usually seek out media that confirm their existing attitudes and view of the world.

> *Selective retention* – Media content has to 'stick' in the mind if it is to have an effect but research indicates that most people have a tendency to remember only the things they broadly agree with. Berry's (1986) research into knowledgeable, well-motivated, grammar-school sixth-formers found that they only retained 60 per cent of the news information that they were tested on, just minutes after viewing. Postman (1986) argued that we now live in a 'three-minute culture': the attention span of the average member of society is only three minutes or less.

Klapper therefore suggests that these three filters involve a degree of active choice on the part of the audience. Most importantly, they challenge the implicit hypodermic syringe notion that audiences are homogeneous and that they react to media content in similar ways.

The uses and gratifications model

Blumler and McQuail (1968) and Lull (1995) see media audiences as active users of media content. Their 'uses and gratifications' model suggests that people use the media in order to satisfy particular needs that they have. Blumler and McQuail argue that these needs may be biological, psychological or social. Moreover, these needs are relative – the way the audience uses the media to gratify its needs will depend upon influences such as social class, age, gender and ethnicity.

Blumler and McQuail identify four basic needs that people use television to satisfy:

> *Diversion* – Watson (2008) argues that "we may use the media to escape from routines, to get out from under problems, to ease worries or tensions." People may immerse themselves in particular types of media to make up for the lack of satisfaction at work or in their daily lives. For example, some people may compensate for the lack of romance and excitement in their marriages by reading books such as *Fifty Shades of Grey* or watching sexually explicit television programmes. There is some evidence that disabled people may use online virtual reality sites such as Second Life, Smeet and WeeWorld because, via their avatars they can walk, run and even dance.

> *Personal relationships* – Watson notes that we often know more about characters in soap operas than we do our own neighbours. The media may therefore provide the means to compensate for the decline of community in our lives. For example, socially isolated elderly people may see soap opera characters as companions that they can identify with and worry about in the absence of interaction with family members.

> *Personal identity* – People may use the media to 'make over' or to modify their identity. For example, a teenager who suspects he or she is gay may use the experience of a gay character in a teenage soap opera such as *Hollyoaks* or *Skins* to help them make decisions about how they might deal with their own sexuality. Sites such as Facebook, Instagram and Pandora allow people to use the media to present their particular identities to the wider world in a way that they can control.

> *Surveillance* – People use the media to obtain information and news about the social world in order to help them make up their minds on particular issues. In recent years, the **gratification** of this need is increasingly taking on an interactive quality, with the growing popularity of online blogging, Twitter and websites to which people can add their own knowledge such as Reddit, Ted Talks and Wikipedia.

UNDERSTAND THE CONCEPT

Gratification refers to gaining pleasure or satisfaction from a particular activity, for example, achieving a particular level in a computer game.

However, the uses and gratifications approach has been criticised for several reasons:

> It is argued that the methodology of the approach has not done enough research on how media audiences interpret and gratify themselves by using media content. It is too dependent on the interpretations of the researchers of the audience's motivations.

> It fails to appreciate that different age-groups, social classes or ethnic groups may interpret and use the same media content differently and that therefore the media may gratify them in very different ways.

> Marxists argue that it exaggerates the audience's freedom to interpret media content in the way that they choose. The GUMG, for example, suggest that the agenda is already set by the media and consequently it is difficult for audiences to interpret media content outside ideological constraints. For example, if media content on the Royal Family is always positive and never negative, this restricts gratification to one particular ideological interpretation.

> Postmodernists argue that each individual has specific needs and that the function of a media-rich or saturated, postmodern society is to provide a plurality of media choices in order to meet individual tastes in different types of gratification.

FOCUS ON SKILLS: USING THE MEDIA

Lull (1990) carried out a participant observation study of families' use of television and found that families actively used media in five 'relational ways' ways:

1. Families used the television to communicate with one another. The content of television programmes was often the main topic of conversation between family members. The TV show *Gogglebox* demonstrates this.

2. Television reinforced family 'affiliation'. Some television shows such as *Britain's Got Talent* transcend age differences and consequently whole families sit down to watch them.

3. People may use television, computer games, music and the internet as a means of avoiding others. Since, other sociologists have argued that this trend may lead to the decline of face-to-face social interaction and community because the use of new media, particularly the smartphone, computer games and notebooks and tablets probably means less communication and interaction between family members.

4. Some people may use the media, especially the internet, to solve problems, to seek guidance, to access information and learning, and to find role models.

5. People may use the media to gain intellectual validation and/or status. For example, answering the questions posed by TV quiz shows or

contributing to user-generated internet sites may increase self-esteem.

Recent research has focused on new media and especially social networking sites (SNS) such as Facebook. Park *et al.* (2009) found the major uses and gratification factors of SNS users are: socialising, entertainment, the seeking of self-esteem and information. Ellison *et al.* (2007) found that SNS users wished to gratify such needs as meeting new people and saw Facebook as a means of sustaining offline relationships with friends and family they did not have time to see on a regular basis. Raake *et al.* (2008) found this led to a sense of wellbeing among SNS users. Haridakis and Hanson (2009) found that socially active, young males used YouTube to fulfil entertainment needs such as thrill-seeking and information-seeking. Park *et al.* found that young people used sites such as Facebook, Istagram and SnapChat in order to present themselves as cool or to develop their career.

However, Marxists are critical of the uses and gratifications model because they suggest that social needs may be socially manufactured by the media. Marxists argue that the mass media in capitalist societies, especially the advertising industry, promote the ideology that consumption and materialism are positive goals to pursue. This may mean that people mistake 'false needs' for personal or social needs.

Questions

1. **Outline** two consequences of the increased use of new media by teenagers, according to Watson.

2. **Outline** and **explain** the five ways people use the media to gratify their needs, according to Lull.

3. **Analyse** the relationship between people's social needs and social networking sites.

4. **Evaluate**, using information from this source and elsewhere, the view that media audiences actively engage with the variety of media available to them rather than being merely 'injected' with media content.

The reception analysis model

The reception analysis model of media effects suggests that people interpret the same media content in a variety of different ways because of their different social

backgrounds. Morley (1980) researched how 29 different groups, made up of people from a range of educational and professional backgrounds, interpreted the content of a news programme. He concluded that people actively choose to make one of three readings or interpretations of media content:

> *Preferred (or dominant) reading* – This interpretation of media content is dominant because it reflects the consensus. People go along with it because it is widely accepted as legitimate. For example, the British people generally approve of the Royal Family, so very few people are likely to interpret stories about them in a critical fashion.

> *Oppositional reading* – A minority may oppose the views expressed in media content. For example, people who are anti-monarchy or Republicans may be critical of stories about Royal celebrities.

> *Negotiated reading* – The media audience may reinterpret media content to fit in with their own opinions and values. For example, they may not have any strong views on the Royal Family but enjoy reading about celebrity lives.

Imagine a breaking news story that focuses on drug arrests at Glastonbury and identify possible preferred, oppositional and negotiated readings.

Morley suggests all three interpretations or readings of media content can be generated within the same social group. However, Morley argues that the average person belongs to several subcultural groups and this may complicate a person's reading of media content in the sense that they may not be consistent in their interpretation of it. For example, a young British Jewish person may respond to the Israeli–Palestinian problem in a number of ways:

> As a socially aware, educated person, they may feel that the Palestinians have not been given a fair deal by the Israelis.

> As a British person, they may feel that this conflict has very little impact on them.

> As a Jewish person, they may feel a strong sense of identification with Israel.

> As a young person, they may feel that politics is fairly boring and consequently not show much interest.

These subcultural characteristics are not predictable in the way they influence responses to media content – for example, belonging to a Jewish subculture does not bring about automatic identification with media stories sympathetic to Israel.

Reception analysis theory suggests that audiences are not passive, impressionable and homogeneous. They act in a variety of subcultural ways and, for this reason, media content is 'polysemic': it attracts more than one type of reading or interpretation. However, Morley did concede that his research might have been compromised by the fact that his sample did not see the news programme used in the research in their natural environment. The responses of the sample to the news content therefore may have been influenced by the research context. For example, demand characteristics (see Topic 2, Chapter 4) may have undermined the quality of the interviews conducted by the researchers.

The cultural effects model

The Marxist 'cultural effects' model sees the media as having a very powerful ideological influence that is mainly concerned with transmitting capitalist values and norms. There is disagreement among Marxists about why this process occurs. As highlighted in Chapter 2, some suggest it is because of the influence of media owners, others suggest that it is due to capitalist market conditions in which the imperative is to make profit, while the Glasgow University Media Group (1981) suggest that it is an accidental by-product of the social and educational backgrounds of most journalists, who are happy to subscribe to a consensus view of the world.

In its focus on audiences, the cultural effects model, like the reception analysis model, recognises that the media audience is made up of very different types of people from a variety of social backgrounds who have had very different experiences. This means that they interpret what they see, read and hear in many different ways. For example, a programme about life in an inner-London borough may be interpreted as evidence of racial conflict and deprivation, or as evidence of interesting cultural diversity, depending on who is doing the watching.

However, Marxist cultural effects theory argues that media content contains strong ideological messages that reflect the values of those who own, control and produce the media, whether in the form of newspapers, magazines, television, pop music or film. Consequently, media producers expect audiences (who often lack direct experience of an issue) to interpret media content in a particular way, that is, to agree with their own preferred reading.

The cultural effects model argues that media coverage of particular issues results in most people coming to believe that media perspectives on particular issues are correct – and that these perspectives reflect a consensus perspective that generally fails to challenge ruling-class ideology and, in many cases, actually reinforces it. For example, media coverage of unemployment and single-parent families gives the general impression that these situations are often the result of choice and so the claiming of benefits by these groups is probably unjustified. This leads to many people seeing claiming benefits as a form of scrounging.

What other examples of media coverage of particular issues could be criticised in this way?

Marxists believe that audiences have been exposed over a long period of time to a 'drip-drip' effect, through which media content has become imbued with ideological values. Cultural effects theory believes that television content, in particular, has been deliberately dumbed down and consequently audiences no longer think critically about the state of the world. It is argued that the long-term effect of this preferred reading of media content is that the values of the rich and powerful come to be unconsciously shared by most people – people come to believe in values such as 'happiness is about possessions and money', 'the Royal Family deserve their wealth and social position', 'most asylum seekers are just illegal immigrants' and 'Black people are potential criminals'.

The cultural effects model is supported by research conducted by Iyengar and Simon (1993), who found a framing effect in their study of news coverage of the Gulf War. Respondents who relied the most on television news, which emphasised the view of journalists embedded with US troops, expressed greater support for a military rather than a diplomatic solution to the crisis. Andsager (2000) analysed the attempts by interest groups to frame the abortion debate of the late 1990s. She found that the pro-life group in the USA was more successful in getting their interpretation into press coverage because this fitted the consensus view held by male journalists. Reese and Lewis (2009) found that news reports after 9/11 in the USA shared and uncritically transmitted the political administration's response to the attack as a 'war on terror', therefore helping to justify the US invasions of Afghanistan (2001) and Iraq (2003). (See Topic 4, Chapter 4 on news and Chapter 5 on representations of gender for other examples of such cultural effects.)

How does the Marxist view of journalists explain why the pro-life lobby was more successful than the pro-abortion lobby in terms of press coverage?

The cultural effects model suggests that media content helps those who manage (and benefit from) capitalist society to obtain the active consent of the majority (who do not particularly benefit from the organisation of capitalist society). It recognises that audiences interpret media messages in different ways but within certain confined limits. As Curran (2003) argues, the frequent reading of particular newspapers means the immersion of the reader into a particular ideological way of seeing and interpreting the world. Consequently, it is argued, this view of the world may affect some readers in that they may interpret such ideology as common sense or as a product of their own choices. Cultural effects theory argues that most types of media probably have these ideological effects in the long term.

Criticism of the cultural effects model

However, in criticism of this Marxist model, it has to be said that these cultural effects are very difficult to operationalise and measure. Pluralists too question the Marxist view that these cultural effects benefit the capitalist elite because pluralists believe that the professionalism and objectivity of modern journalists ensure that media output is constructed for the benefit of the audience. If the media do project a particular point of view at the expense of another, pluralists say, this is because the audience already believe in it and therefore demand it. Moreover Pluralists argue that the sheer diversity of media content means that the Marxist concern that the media is creating an homogeneous worldview underpinned by capitalist ideology is simply untrue.

The postmodernist model

According to theories of postmodernity, the media are central to the creation of the postmodern world because the choices they offer mean that members of society create their own unique set of values and understandings from the global information around them. In particular, postmodernists believe that individuals in postmodern societies are involved in a search for their 'true' or authentic self and that this often gives way to a 'playfulness' in which personal identity is experimental and is expressed and invented by choosing from the diversity of lifestyles on offer through the media.

Postmodern perspectives on the effects of media content are essentially an extension of reception analysis. Whereas the reception analysis model focuses on explaining the influence of subcultural differences in the ways audiences might respond to media messages, the postmodern model focuses on how individual members of audiences create their own meanings from a media text. As Philo (2002) argues, postmodernists see media content as producing multiple definitions of reality, each of which has the same degree of importance as the others. Moreover, these interpretations of media reality are constantly changing and being modified. They are not fixed. Philo notes that postmodernists argue that "All definitions of reality are just that – mere definitions which are constantly changing with each new interpretation of what is real or what has occurred. There is, therefore, no 'fixed' way of describing anything – it all depends on what is seen and who is describing it. There is no way of saying that reality is distorted by media images since there is no fixed reality or truth to distort. It is all relative to who is looking; 'truth' and 'reality' are in the eye of the beholder." In other words, rather than seeing the audience as an undifferentiated mass (as does the hypodermic syringe model) or as divided into cultural or other groupings (as do the active audience approaches) postmodernists argue that generalisations about media effects and audiences are impossible, since readers and viewers may react to the same media message in a variety of different ways. However, because postmodernists believe that there is no such thing as absolute truth, all these reactions and interpretations have relative value. Consequently, it is impossible to judge whether media content is having a positive or negative effect.

Conclusions about active audience approaches

All these 'active audience' approaches see the audience as interpreting media messages for themselves, so it is difficult to generalise about the effects of the media. What is apparent is that the media does have the potential power to influence public belief, but the role of audiences in interpreting and modifying media messages cannot be overestimated.

CHECK YOUR UNDERSTANDING

1. Explain what is meant by the term 'desensitisation'.

2. Explain what is meant by 'selective exposure'.

3. Explain what is meant by 'catharsis'.

4. Explain what is meant by 'opinion leaders'.

5. Identify and briefly outline two examples of how audiences may positively use media content to bring about gratification.

6. Identify and briefly explain the stages of the selective filter model of the media.

7. Analyse the postmodern approach to media effects.

8. Analyse how the reception analysis model works.

9. Evaluate the Marxist view that the media shape the attitudes and opinions of their audiences so that these are generally supportive of capitalist values.

10. Evaluate the view that mass-media representations of violence and antisocial behaviour are responsible for the real-life violent and antisocial behaviour of young people.

TAKE IT FURTHER

1. Conduct a content analysis of part of one evening's TV programmes on any one major terrestrial channel. Add up the number of times acts of violence are depicted. After noting down each act of violence, explain the type of programme (for example, news, cartoon, drama) and the type of violence (for example, real, humorous). What do your results tell you about the amount and type of violence on television?

2. Watch Gerbner talk about violence in the media in *The Killing Screens: Media & the Culture of Violence* on YouTube. To what extent do you agree with the views expressed? Read David's Gauntlett's assessment of the 'effects model' at www.theory.org.uk/effects.htm

APPLY YOUR LEARNING

1. Outline and explain **two** ways in which screen violence may affect audiences.   [10 marks]

   Read **Item A** below and answer the question that follows.

ITEM A

Curran argues that owners of media curtail editors' freedom of action by an implicit understanding of how owners expect the newspaper to develop. Journalists tend to be selected on the grounds that they will fit in. Conformity to the owner's vision brings rewards in terms of good assignments, promotion and peer group esteem. Resistance, on the other hand, invites punishment. Dissident reporters who do not deliver what the owner expects suffer professional death.

2. Applying material from **Item A**, analyse **two** ways in which owners influence the content of the media.   [10 marks]

3. Read **Item B** below and answer the question that follows.

ITEM B

Research suggests that ethnic-minority audiences want to see more realistic representations of ethnic-minority people on television and less stereotyping in the news media. Asian viewers are particularly fed up with being represented as extremists and as victims of religious discrimination, while African Caribbeans are disgruntled with news media because it disproportionately focuses on Black boys as violent or as gang members. Ethnic minority groups want to see realistic media portrayals of their everyday real world and the problems they face, which are often completely unrelated to race.

3. Applying material from **Item B** and your knowledge, evaluate the view that the media portray ethnic minority groups in a stereotypical way.   [20 marks]

You can find example answers and accompanying teacher's comments for this topic at www.collins.co.uk/AQAAlevelSociology. Please note that these example answers and teacher's comments have not been approved by AQA.

5 STRATIFICATION AND DIFFERENTIATION

AQA specification	Chapters
Candidates should examine:	
Stratification and differentiation by social class, gender, ethnicity and age.	Theories of stratification and differentiation are examined in Chapter 1 (pages 341–356) and Chapters 3, 4, 5, 6 and 7 (pages 366–409).
Dimensions of inequality: class, status and power, differences in life-chances by social class, gender, ethnicity, age and disability.	Differences in life-chances by social class are examined in Chapter 3 (pages 366–372), by gender in Chapter 4 (pages 373–381), by ethnicity in Chapter 5 (pages 382–392), by age in Chapter 6 (pages 393–400) and by disability in Chapter 7 (pages 401–409).
The problems of defining and measuring social class; occupation, gender and social class.	This is covered in Chapter 2 (pages 357–365).
Changes in structures of inequality, including globalisation and the transnational capitalist class, and the implications of these changes.	This is the main focus of Chapter 8 (pages 410–418).
The nature, extent and significance of patterns of social mobility.	This is covered in Chapter 9 (pages 419–427).

5.1 THEORIES OF STRATIFICATION AND DIFFERENTIATION

LEARNING OBJECTIVES

> Understand the concepts of social differentiation and social stratification (AO1).

> Demonstrate knowledge and understanding of different types of stratification systems (AO1).

> Demonstrate knowledge and understanding of different sociological theories of stratification (AO1).

> Apply knowledge of theories of stratification (AO2).

> Evaluate the strengths and weaknesses of the theories of stratification covered (AO3).

INTRODUCING THE DEBATE

Human beings are both similar to and different from one another. The concept of 'social differentiation' refers to the differences between people that are socially recognised and acted upon. For example, many cultures, historically, have treated left-handedness as deviant and it wasn't so long ago in Britain that left-handed primary school children were forced to write right-handed. Even a characteristic as seemingly innocuous as hair colour can attract social approval or censure, or indeed both at the same time, as in 'blonde bombshell' and 'blonde bimbo'!

Social inequality exists when resources, opportunities or rewards in a society are distributed unequally, for example, if some groups have more money or higher status than others.

When socially recognised differences are associated with structures of inequality, sociologists talk about

social stratification. This term borrows from geology the concept of strata – or layers of rock laid one on top of another – to describe the ordering of societies into layers with unequal amounts of wealth, status and/ or power.

Social stratification always has the potential to generate opposition from those disadvantaged by it. The appearance in the 2010s of organisations such as UK Uncut, Occupy and The People's Assembly against Austerity illustrate this in a British context.

Stratification is not just about material inequalities; it is also concerned with some of our most intimate emotions: feelings of social worth or worthlessness, respect and contempt, as well as social inclusion and exclusion. It is no wonder therefore that social stratification has been at the heart of sociology since its inception.

GETTING YOU THINKING

The extract below is taken from an opinion piece written by Will Hutton, a regular columnist for a left-of-centre national Sunday newspaper, *The Observer*.

Of course class still matters – it influences everything that we do.

The only way to create a fairer society is to start talking about it. The discussion starts here.

Nobody wants to believe that British society is as class-bound as it is. Tens of millions watch the X Factor in the belief that talent and effort will rule in the end. We like to think that, while schools like Eton exist, in essence, Britain is a 21st-century democracy where merit, rather than privilege, is the route to the top.

Humans are keenly aware of a sense of fairness. We formulate intentions, exert ourselves to deliver them and the outcomes are there for all to see. We expect to be proportionally rewarded for our efforts in producing good results and duly punished for bad ones. Of course there is good luck – of family, talent and natural advantages – and bad. By and large, we consider good outcomes delivered by good luck to be less valuable than those delivered by effort and the sweat of our brow. You can't stop people thinking these things; it is as natural as love and fear. It is not envy that inspires discussion of private schools – it is a sense of fairness.

For the distribution of reward and positions in today's Britain does not mainly correspond to proportional talent, effort and virtue. It has been largely predetermined by the good luck of to whom and where you were born. There are 10 million men and women in work earning less than £15,000 a year; nearly all their parents were in the same position, as will be their children. There are nearly 3 million people of working age who do not even make themselves

available for work, again reproducing itself through the generations.

Meanwhile, the middle and upper classes are becoming increasingly effective at ensuring that their children have the capabilities and qualifications to populate the upper echelons of the economy and society, what the great sociologist Charles Tilly called opportunity hoarding.

David Cameron can claim to have made the most of his luck, a luck he acknowledges. However, the fact remains that he had the luck for which Britain does too little to compensate. Those who weren't so lucky know how unfair it is; they feel it instinctively. Certainly, Labour and the prime minister should stop harping on about Eton and toffs; it cheapens the whole debate. But they should talk their heads off about fairness, including private education. The media effort to close the conversation down as irrelevant should be resisted. Only those without the advantage have the right to say that private education no longer matters. And they never will.

Hutton, W. 'Of course class still matters – it influences everything that we do', *The Observer*, 10th January 2010

Questions

1. Explain the concept of 'opportunity hoarding' in your own words.

2. Do you think that the fact that the PM, David Cameron, attended Eton matters?

3. What do you think is more important: that people have an equal opportunity to reach the top of society or that the gap between the top and the bottom isn't too wide?

4. Do you agree with Hutton that British society is still 'class-bound'?

FORMS OF STRATIFICATION

Historically, systems of social stratification have varied along two main dimensions: the degree of inequality they embody and the extent to which people could change the position they were born into – how 'open' or 'closed' they were to movement up or down the social strata (what sociologists call social mobility). In terms of the latter, two polar extremes can be identified: systems based on ascribed status and systems based on achieved status:

› *Ascribed status* – given at birth either through family (e.g. the Queen) or through physical, religious or cultural factors (e.g. in some societies, women and girls are regarded as second-class citizens simply because they are female)

› *Achieved status* – the result of factors such as hard work, educational success, marriage, special talent or sheer good fortune (for example, winning the lottery).

In reality, few societies are totally open or closed and each could be placed somewhere along a continuum.

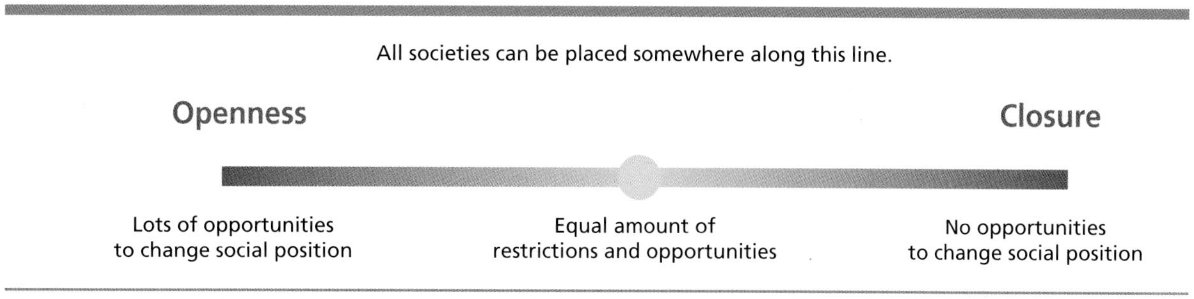

All societies can be placed somewhere along this line.

Openness   Closure

| Lots of opportunities to change social position | Equal amount of restrictions and opportunities | No opportunities to change social position |

Figure 5.1.1 *Open or closed: the continuum of social status*

Traditional societies tend to be more closed, as shown in Table 5.1.1, because of the greater influence of religion and tradition, which means that people can only play a limited range of roles and these tend to be fixed at birth. Modern societies, which seem more fluid and open, may actually experience significant levels of closure, in that some groups, for example, racial minorities and disabled people, face social barriers and obstacles when attempting to improve themselves.

	The caste system	The feudal estate system
Place and time	Although officially banned in India today, the Hindu caste system of stratification is still enormously influential.	The feudal estate system was found in medieval Europe.
Structure	There are four basic castes or layers, ranging from the Brahmins (religious leaders and nobles) at the top, to the Sudras (servants and unskilled manual workers) at the bottom. 'Untouchables' exist below the caste system (hence, 'outcastes') and are responsible for the least desirable jobs, such as sewage collection.	The king owned all the land and, in return for an oath of loyalty and military support, he would allocate the land to barons who, in turn, would apportion parts of it to knights. The majority (95 per cent) were peasants or serfs who had to work the knight's land and, in return, were offered protection and allowed to rent land for their own use.
Restrictions	People are born into castes and cannot move out of them during the course of their lives. There are strong religious controls over the behaviour of caste members – for example, you cannot marry a member of another caste, nor can you do certain jobs because these are assigned exclusively to certain castes.	Feudal societies were mainly closed societies – people's positions were largely ascribed and it was rare for people to move up. Marriage between groups was rarely allowed and feudal barons even restricted the geographical movement of the peasants.
Possibility of social mobility	The system is based upon religious purity – the only way people can be promoted to a higher caste is by living a pure life and hoping that they will be reincarnated (reborn) as a member of a higher caste.	On rare occasions, exceptional acts of bravery could result in someone being given a gift of land, or being granted their freedom.

Table 5.1.1 *Examples of traditional societies based on ascribed status*

SOCIAL CLASS

Social class is the stratification system associated with industrial capitalism. However, whether post-industrial societies like contemporary Britain can still be usefully labelled as 'class societies' is a matter of debate – a debate that will be explored in this and the following chapters.

Social classes are groups of people who share a similar economic position in terms of occupation, income and ownership of wealth. Class systems are different from previous systems in the following ways:

343

> They are not based on religion, law or race, but on economic factors.

> There is no clear distinction between classes – it is difficult to say where the working class finishes and the middle class begins, for example.

> All members of society have equal rights irrespective of their social position.

> There are no legal restrictions on marriage between the classes.

> Social-class societies are reputedly open societies – you can move up or down the class structure through, for example, jobs, the acquisition of wealth or marriage.

> Such systems are also reputedly **meritocratic** – that is, people are not born into ascribed roles. Individuals are encouraged to better themselves through achievement at school and in their jobs, by working hard and gaining promotion.

UNDERSTAND THE CONCEPT

A **meritocracy** is a society or system in which success or failure is based on merit. Merit is seen as resulting from a combination of ability and effort or hard work. In principle, this could be seen as a fair system but it is difficult to define and measure merit, and the prior existence of inequality makes it very difficult to have a system that genuinely rewards merit.

Just how meritocratic social-class societies really are, and the extent to which factors such as race, gender and age can affect access to opportunity, will be a key focus of subsequent chapters.

Do you think it is possible to have real equality of opportunity in a stratified society?

Explaining social stratification

Virtually all societies since the earliest hunter-gatherer communities have been socially stratified, although there have been conscious attempts to eradicate stratification, most notably perhaps among the Israeli *kibbutzim* – small-scale communities in which property is owned communally and which seek to be both democratic and egalitarian.

Sociologists disagree about how best to account for stratification, and a number of competing theories have been developed. The main ones can be divided into consensus theories (functionalism), conflict theories (Marxism, Weberianism and feminism) and postmodernism. The rest of this chapter will be devoted to outlining and evaluating these theories.

CONSENSUS THEORIES

Consensus theories in sociology are so-called because they assume that what holds societies together is a consensus – a general agreement – on fundamental values. Indeed, without such a widespread agreement it would be difficult to even talk about a collection of people as a 'society', in their view. The principal example of a consensus theory is functionalism.

Functionalism

Durkheim

Among sociology's founding fathers, it was Emile Durkheim (1858–1917) who developed functionalism as a key sociological perspective. Durkheim did not directly confront the issue of why social stratification existed, but he lived at a time when issues of class inequality and class conflict were prominent both in society and in political and social commentary and so was obliged to address them.

For Durkheim, societies – like human bodies – could exist and thrive only if their various constituent elements worked in harmony. This did not mean that he naïvely dismissed the existence of conflict in society. Indeed, in 1893, he stated "It is neither necessary or even possible for social life to be without conflicts". But it did mean that class conflict was for him an 'abnormal' state of affairs associated with the early stages of industrialisation and the difficult transition that had to be negotiated from traditional to modern society.

This transition was understood by Durkheim as a movement from one type of **social solidarity** – 'mechanical solidarity' – to another, which he called 'organic solidarity'. Traditional societies, he argued, were held together by a strong, religiously based conscience collective (or value consensus) but, as societies grew in both size and complexity, the power of religion waned. Solidarity in modern society – organic solidarity – would instead be produced through people's recognition of their mutual dependence on each other as the division of labour grew ever more specialised.

UNDERSTAND THE CONCEPT

Social solidarity is a concept often used by functionalists to describe the unification of diverse groups so that they feel a common sense of mutual interests, shared values and norms and of belonging to a particular community or society.

Durkheim took it for granted that different occupations would be differentially rewarded (some would pay better than others), but considered that this would not undermine social solidarity so long as "social inequalities exactly express natural inequalities", by which he meant individual differences in ability and application.

This would require the development of what we would now call 'equality of opportunity' (or meritocracy), which is widely seen today as justifying the existence of inequality on the basis that it offers everyone the chance to compete for higher pay and status.

The risk of class conflict would also be lessened, Durkheim believed, by the development of occupational associations which, alongside the state, would help to regulate conflicts of interest between employers and workers (for example, through collective bargaining and laws of contract).

Parsons

It was the American sociologist, Talcott Parsons (1902–1979), who – along with Davis and Moore (see below) – drew on Durkheim's earlier work to develop a functionalist theory of stratification as such.

As we have seen, Durkheim thought that class conflict would disappear as industrialisation became established but, writing in 1949, Parsons argued that "class conflict is endemic in our modern industrial type of society" and identified half-a-dozen reasons for this, among them:

› Competition for occupational prestige produces winners and losers – winners tend to be arrogant; losers display a 'sour-grapes' attitude.

› The organisation of the division of labour requires discipline and authority. These do not exist on a grand scale without generating some resistance (in other words, people don't generally like being told what to do!).

› A "general tendency for the powerful to exploit the weak".

However, Parsons goes on to say, pointedly, "I do not ... believe that the case has been made for believing that it [class conflict] is the dominant feature of every such society and of its dynamic development". Indeed, for Parsons, class conflict was no more than an unfortunate and relatively insignificant by-product of social stratification, rather than an inevitable and central feature of capitalism, as we shall see it was for Marx and Engels

Parsons saw stratification as a ranking system based on moral evaluation – that is, based on respect, prestige, social honour, social approval and disapproval. Inequalities in possessions and power were seen as secondary to this status ranking and as deriving from it.

Stratification was both inevitable and functional in Parsons' view. It was inevitable because people would be differentially evaluated in terms of the degree to which they exemplified society's value system, whatever that was (occupational success in **advanced industrial societies**). And stratification was functional, because it helped "in the stabilisation of social systems".

UNDERSTAND THE CONCEPT

Functionalists tend to talk about **advanced industrial societies**, Marxists advanced capitalist societies. They are talking about the same societies, so why the difference in names? The answer has to do with their different views about the crucial distinguishing features of such societies. For functionalists it is the level of technology and the associated occupational division of labour; for Marxists it is the pattern of ownership of the forces of production and the associated relations of production (that is, class relationships).

Davis and Moore

Davis and Moore (1945) argue that all societies have to ensure that their functionally most important positions are filled with the most talented people. They therefore need to offer such people high rewards in the form of income and status in order to motivate them to make the necessary sacrifices in terms of earnings foregone during education and training.

Furthermore, they argue that class societies are meritocracies. Educational qualifications (and hence the stratification system) function to allocate all individuals to an occupational role that suits their abilities. Hence, people's class position is a fair reflection of their talents.

Davis and Moore also claim that most people agree that stratification is necessary because they accept the meritocratic principles on which society is based.

Stratification, moreover, encourages all members of society to work to the best of their ability. For example, those at the top will wish to retain their advantages while those placed elsewhere will wish to improve on their position. Stratification thus ensures that the 'functional prerequisite' (a precondition of an efficiently functioning society) of effective role allocation and performance is satisfied. In sum, for Davis and Moore – like Parsons – stratification is both necessary and functional.

Saunders
A similar view to that of Davis and Moore has been proposed by the New Right thinker, Peter Saunders (1996). He points out that economic growth has raised the standard of living for all members of society, and social inequality is thus a small price to pay for society as a whole becoming more prosperous. Saunders is influenced by Hayek (1944) – one of the architects of **neoliberalism** – who argued that capitalism is a dynamic system that continually raises everybody's standards of living, so the poor in society today are much better off than they were in the past. Moreover, capitalist societies offer incentives to those with talent and enterprise in the form of material wealth. Saunders argues that if these incentives did not exist, then many of the consumer goods that we take for granted today, such as cars, ballpoint pens, computers and iPods, would not exist, because talented people would not have been motivated to produce them. Saunders acknowledges that stratification is not the only way to ensure effective role allocation, but the only alternative, he claims, would be the threat or use of physical force. Stratification systems, therefore, are not inevitable, but they are desirable because the alternative would be far worse.

UNDERSTAND THE CONCEPT

The key idea informing **neoliberalism** is that individual freedom is best guaranteed by the 'free market' and that the role of the state is to promote private enterprise (for example, through privatisation) and remove barriers to the free operation of markets (for example, by removing government regulation). Beyond this, the state should do as little as possible consistent with maintaining social order and providing a minimal safety net for those genuinely unable to support themselves (for example, because of illness or disability).

Evaluation of the functionalism
Functionalists assume that status ranking is the key feature of stratification. Not all theorists agree.

Others point out that some functionally important jobs – nurses, refuse collectors, care workers, say – are not generally highly rewarded; nor are the people who occupy high-status positions necessarily the most talented. Also, opportunity hoarding by the higher strata militates against the downward mobility of their children. Consequently, functionalists ignore the fact that class societies are not necessarily meritocratic.

Some groups may be able to use economic and political power to increase their rewards, against the will of the majority. High rewards sometimes go to people who play no functionally important roles but who simply live off the income generated by their wealth.

The 'dysfunctions' of stratification are neglected by Davis and Moore. For example, poverty is a major problem for people and has a negative impact on mortality, morbidity, education and family life.

The theory sheds no light on why the *degree* of stratification varies from one society and one time to another. Is *any* degree of stratification functional, never mind how extreme?

Do you think that Davis and Moore's neglect of the possible dysfunctions of stratification invalidates their theory?

CONFLICT THEORIES

Conflict theorists reject the organic analogy favoured by functionalists and claim that societies are best understood as made up of groups with conflicting interests engaged in a struggle for dominance. Social order is seen as the product of an uneasy truce rather than of a value consensus and social stratification is ultimately a reflection of the unequal power of these different groups.

Marxism
According to Marx (1818–83), the driving force of virtually all societies is the conflict between the rich and powerful minority who control the society, and the powerless and poor majority who survive only by working for the rich and powerful. These two classes are always in conflict as it is in the interests of the rich to spend as little as possible in paying their workers.

Causes of conflict

The heart of this class conflict is the system of producing goods and services – what Marx called the 'mode of production'. This is made up of two things:

> *the forces of production* – the resources needed to produce goods, such as capital (money for investment), land, factories, machinery and raw materials

> *the social relations of production* – the ways in which people are organised to make things; in other words, the way in which roles and responsibilities are allocated among those involved in production.

Together, these represent the economic base, or 'infrastructure', of society and all the other social institutions – the family, education, religion, the state, and so on – make up what Marx called the 'superstructure'.

Also included in the superstructure are 'ideologies' – belief systems that served to justify the existing social arrangements in the interests of the dominant class. For example, the belief that people are naturally competitive and always wish to outdo others, rather than cooperative, suggests that attempts to promote greater equality are bound to fail because they "go against nature". Similarly, religious teachings which insist that the "meek will inherit the earth" militate against doing anything to change it in the here and now. For Marx, religion was "the opium of the masses". Ruling-class ideology produced false consciousness among the subordinate class, which meant that they failed to see that they were being exploited.

Marx described Western societies as capitalist societies and suggested that they consist of two main classes:

> *the bourgeoisie* – the capitalist or ruling class, who own the means of production; they are the owners or, today, the large shareholders in businesses, and control decisions about employment, new investment, new products, and so on.

> *the proletariat* – the working or subordinate class, who sell their ability to work (labour power) to the bourgeoisie; most people make a living by working for a profit-making business, but they have no say in business decisions or how they are put to work, and rely on the success of the company for which they work.

Marx argued that the social relations of production between the bourgeoisie and proletariat are unequal, exploitative and create class conflict. Capitalism's relentless pursuit of profit means that wages are kept as low as possible and the bourgeoisie pockets the difference between what they pay their workers and the value of the goods produced by workers, once other production costs are covered. This 'surplus value', forms the basis of their great wealth. Moreover, workers lose control over their jobs as new technology is introduced in order to increase output and therefore profits. Workers become alienated by this process and are united by a shared exploitative class experience. This common class experience means that the working class is objectively a 'class-in-itself'.

Marx believed that the conflict inherent in the capitalist system would come to a head, because the increasing concentration of wealth would cause the gap between rich and poor to grow and grow; the classes would become polarised, so that even the most short-sighted members of the proletariat would see that the time for change had come. Marx predicted that, eventually, the proletariat would unite, overthrow the bourgeoisie, seize the means of production for themselves and establish a fairer, more equal society – initially a socialist society, but ultimately a communist one. For Marx, then, radical social change was inevitable as the working class was transformed from a class-in-itself into a revolutionary 'class-for-itself', with false consciousness replaced by class consciousness.

Evaluation of Marxism

Marx's ideas have probably been more influential than those of any other political thinker, and had a huge impact in the 20th century. They inspired communist revolutions in many countries, such as China and Russia. However, his ideas have also come in for a great deal of criticism, especially since the communist regimes of Eastern Europe crumbled in the 1990s.

> Marx is accused of being an economic 'determinist' or 'reductionist', in that he thought that the nature of all the social institutions in capitalist society was determined by the economic base. Critics, including some neo-Marxists, have challenged this claim, arguing that the superstructure is relatively autonomous (that is, has some degree of independence from the economic base). For example, they would deny that the state in advanced capitalist societies is bound to represent capitalist interests.

> For Marx, all inequalities were ultimately reducible to class. For example, the conflict in Northern Ireland between Catholics and Protestants, although apparently religious in nature, would be seen by Marxists as driven by underlying class differences. Critics would argue that many contemporary conflicts, such as those rooted in nationalism, ethnicity and gender, cannot be explained adequately in economic terms.

> Marx is criticised for underestimating the importance of the middle classes. He did recognise a third class made up of professional workers, shopkeepers and clerks, which he called the 'petite bourgeoisie'. However, given their relative numerical insignificance in Marx's day, they were deemed unimportant to the class struggle. In his view, as the two major camps polarised, members of this class would realign their interests accordingly with either one.

> Marx's prediction that the working class would become 'class conscious' because they would experience extreme misery and poverty, and therefore seek to transform the capitalist system, has not occurred. Neoliberal sociologists would claim that this is because people appreciate the freedoms associated with capitalism. Neo-Marxists would argue that people have been bought off by the false promises of consumerism.

> Interpretivist sociologists are critical of both functionalism and Marxism for being over-deterministic, reducing all human behaviour to a reaction to the social and/or economic structure. This is a valid criticism of functionalism, but fails to acknowledge that Marx recognised the role of human agency. He famously wrote: "Men [sic] make their own history", going on to say "but they do not make it as they please; they do not make it under self-selected circumstances, but under circumstances existing already, given and transmitted from the past" (1852). In this way, Marx saw a two-way ('dialectical') relationship between people and society.

Do you think the Marxist notion of 'false consciousness' has any validity in Britain today?

Neo-Marxist approaches

Marxist writers who have attempted to adapt and extend Marx's own writings since his death to cope with these and other criticisms are known as 'neo-Marxists'. Their work on stratification has gone in various directions, two of which will be examined below. One strand has sought to deal with the problem posed for Marx's prediction of class polarisation by the growth of the middle classes. The other has sought to account for the non-occurrence of revolution in advanced capitalist societies.

Erik Olin Wright

Wright, an American sociologist, has devoted a great deal of effort to developing a theoretical framework within the Marxist tradition that can deal adequately with the complexity of the class structure that has developed within the advanced capitalist societies.

Some people who operate with a simplistic view of Marxism dismiss this as a problem by arguing that there are still just two basic classes: owners and workers. If you have to work for a living then, by definition, you are a member of the proletariat. There are two major problems with this view:

1. Does it really make much sense to suggest that the CEO of a FTSE 100 company and his/her lowest-paid employee are in the same class?

2. This view offers no way in which to understand divisions in class consciousness and class action that clearly exist among those who 'work for a living'. For example, those CEOs who insist that they must be paid many hundreds of times their lowest employee's rate of pay as they operate in a global market for talent.

Wright's key conceptual innovation is the concept of contradictory class locations, which he uses to describe the position of those who are neither clearly capitalists nor workers. The allegiances of such employees are, in a sense, torn between the owners of their employing organisation and their work colleagues, hence *contradictory* class locations.

Wright (2000) argues that the two key dimensions along which one can usefully distinguish between employees in the class structure are, first, their relationship to authority within production and, second, their possession of skills or expertise. Each of these dimensions is divided into three categories: the authority dimension into managers, supervisors and non-management; the skills/expertise dimension into graduates, non-graduates and the unskilled. This generates nine class locations for employees. Wright also distinguishes between three levels of 'owners': capitalists, small employers and the self-employed. The resulting class schema is illustrated in Table 5.1.2 on the next page.

As we shall see shortly, Wright's class typology appears at first sight to be not dissimilar to those that have been developed drawing on the work of Max Weber. However, Wright insists that there are two key differences between the latter and his own typology, namely that for Marxists these classes are involved in antagonistic relations with each other and that these relations are exploitative – each class benefiting from the surplus value produced by the class/classes below it.

	Owners of means of production	Non-owners (wage labourers)			
Owns sufficient capital to hire workers and not work	1 Bourgeoisie	4 Expert managers	7 Semi-credentialled managers	10 Uncredentialled managers	+
Owns sufficient capital to hire workers but must work	2 Small employers	5 Expert supervisors	8 Semi-credentialled supervisors	11 Uncredentialled supervisors	>0
Owns sufficient capital to work for self but not to hire workers	3 Petty bourgeoisie	6 Expert non-managers	9 Semi-credentialled workers	12 Proletarians	−
		+	>0	−	

Skill/credential assets

Organisation assets

Table 5.1.2 *Assets in the means of production: Wright's typology of class locations in capitalist society*

Source: Erik Olin Wright (1985)

The Frankfurt School

The Frankfurt School of Marxists, writing since the 1930s, have focused on the role of the media in creating a popular culture for the masses that has diverted working-class attention away from the unequal nature of capitalism towards consumerism, celebrity culture and trivia. Marcuse (1964), for example, noted that capitalism has been very successful in bedazzling the working class with what he saw as 'false needs' to buy the latest consumer goods. Neo-Marxists argue that the latest soap storylines, and the lifestyles of the rich and famous, are now given more priority by the media, especially the tabloid newspapers and commercial television, than political and economic life. As Lawrence Friedman (1999) argues, the lifestyle of the rich and famous is now the modern opium of the masses.

Consequently, the mass of society is now less knowledgeable about how society is politically and economically organised. The result of this ideological barrage is that the working class is less united than ever, as people compete with each other for the latest material goods. As a result, stratification and class inequality are rarely challenged. This has led to Reiner (2007) arguing that the 'class war' has been won to devastating effect by the capitalist class, echoing the view of one of the USA's richest businessmen – Warren Buffet – that "There's class warfare, all right, but it's my class, the rich class, that's making war, and we're winning" (Stein, 2006).

Evaluation of neo-Marxist approaches

One problem for Wright's analysis is how to deal with those working in the public sector (employed by the state) and third sector (employed by non-profit organisations) rather than the private sector. Critics such as Callinicos (2006) are sceptical about Wright's attempt to locate them in the class structure in terms of the 'class interests' which they are supposed to serve.

Marcuse's concept of 'false needs' begs the question of how/whether these can be objectively distinguished from 'true' needs. The concept of 'false consciousness' is similarly problematic in that it presupposes that a Marxist interpretation of society is *the* (only) true one and if people don't share this interpretation, they've got it wrong. Saunders (1990) points out rather sarcastically "Marxists know the true situation because Marxist theory is true".

FOCUS ON SKILLS: IN PRAISE OF KARL MARX

Karl Marx

There is a sense in which the whole of Marx's writing boils down to several embarrassing questions: Why is it that the capitalist West has accumulated more resources than human history has ever witnessed, yet appears powerless to overcome poverty, starvation, exploitation, and inequality? What are the mechanisms by which affluence for a minority seems to breed hardship and indignity for the many? Why does private wealth seem to go hand in hand with public squalor? Is it, as the good-hearted liberal reformist suggests, that we have simply not got around to mopping up these pockets of human misery, but shall do so in the fullness of time? Or is it more plausible to maintain that there is something in the nature of capitalism itself which generates deprivation and inequality, as surely as Charlie Sheen generates gossip?

Marx was the first thinker to talk in those terms. This down-at-heel émigré Jew, a man who once remarked that nobody else had written so much about money and had so little, bequeathed us the language in which the system under which we live could be grasped as a whole. Its contradictions were analysed, its inner dynamics laid bare, its historical origins examined, and its potential demise foreshadowed. This is not to suggest for a moment that Marx considered capitalism as simply a Bad Thing, like admiring Sarah Palin or blowing tobacco smoke in your children's faces. On

the contrary, he was extravagant in his praise for the class that created it, a fact that both his critics and his disciples have conveniently suppressed. No other social system in history, he wrote, had proved so revolutionary. In a mere handful of centuries, the capitalist middle classes had erased almost every trace of their feudal foes from the face of the earth. They had piled up cultural and material treasures, invented human rights, emancipated slaves, toppled autocrats, dismantled empires, fought and died for human freedom, and laid the basis for a truly global civilization. No document lavishes such florid compliments on this mighty historical achievement as *The Communist Manifesto*, not even *The Wall Street Journal*.

That, however, was only part of the story. There are those who see modern history as an enthralling tale of progress, and those who view it as one long nightmare. Marx, with his usual perversity, thought it was both. Every advance in civilization had brought with it new possibilities of barbarism. The great slogans of the middle-class revolution—"Liberty, Equality, Fraternity"—were his watchwords, too. He simply inquired why those ideas could never be put into practice without violence, poverty, and exploitation. Capitalism had developed human powers and capacities beyond all previous measure. Yet it had not used those capacities to set men and women free of fruitless toil. On the contrary, it had forced them to labour harder than ever. The richest civilizations on earth sweat every bit as hard as their Neolithic ancestors.

Source: Eagleton (2011)

Questions

1. **Explain,** using the material on Marxist perspectives on stratification above, Eagleton's view that there is something in the nature of capitalism itself that generates deprivation and inequality.

2. **Explain** why, according to Eagleton, it is misguided to suggest that Marx thought that capitalism was "simply a bad thing".

3. **Explain.** The phrase "Liberty, Equality, Fraternity" is associated with the French Revolution of 1789. Explain each term in your own words.

4. **Evaluate** Eagleton's view that Marx is still relevant today.

Max Weber

Another classical theorist, Max Weber (1864–1920), disagreed with Marx's view on the inevitability of class conflict: class conflict in his view was a possible, but by no means inevitable, feature of capitalist societies. Weber also rejected the Marxist emphasis on the economic dimension as the fundamental determinant of inequality. Weber saw 'class' (economic relationships) and 'status' (perceived social standing) as two separate but related sources of power that have overlapping effects on people's life-chances. For example, status differences connected with ethnicity or religion or gender can cut across class divisions. He also recognised what he called *'party'* as a further dimension. By this, he meant the political influence or power an individual might exercise through membership of pressure groups, trade unions or other organised interest groups. However, he did see class as the most important of these three interlinking factors.

Like Marx, Weber saw classes as economic categories organised around property ownership, but argued that the concept should be extended to include 'occupational skill' because this created differences in life-chances (income, opportunities, lifestyles and general prospects) among those groups that did not own the means of production, namely the middle class and the working class. In other words, if we examine these two social classes, we will find status differences within them. For example, professionals are regarded more highly than white-collar workers, while skilled manual workers are regarded more highly than unskilled workers. These differences in status are associated with differences in pay which lead directly to differences in life-chances and therefore inequality.

Weber defined social classes as clusters of occupations with similar life-chances and patterns of mobility (people's opportunities to move up or down the occupational ladder). On this basis, he identified four distinct social classes:

1. Those privileged through property or education

2. The petite bourgeoisie (the self-employed, managers)

3. White-collar workers and technicians (the lower middle class)

4. Manual workers (the working class).

Weber was sceptical about the possibility of the working class banding together for revolutionary purposes – becoming class conscious – because differences in status would always undermine any common cause.

Social classes were too internally differentiated, and this undermined any potential for group identity and common action.

Class and status

Weber recognised that income and wealth confer status, but suggested that a person can have wealth but little status – like a lottery winner, perhaps – or, conversely, high status but little wealth – such as a church minister. He suggested that it is very rare that high-status groups allow wealth alone to be sufficient grounds for entry into their status group. He noted that such groups may exclude wealthy individuals because they lack the 'right' breeding, schooling, manners, culture, and so on. This practice of **social closure** will be explored in more depth in later topics. Conversely, someone may be accepted as having high status by the wealthy, despite being relatively poor in comparison, such as the aristocrat who has fallen on hard times. Weber rightly points out that high status and political power can sometimes be achieved without great economic resources.

UNDERSTAND THE CONCEPT

Social closure is a key concept within Weberian theories of stratification. It refers to the practices used by dominant groups to hold onto their privileges by excluding others on the basis of some kind of arbitrary criteria, such as skin colour, gender, sexuality, accent and so on. Weber called the strategies adopted by excluded groups to challenge their exclusion usurpationary strategies; for example, those adopted by gay rights activists in their struggles against heterosexist laws.

Evaluation of Weber

For functionalists, class and power are subsidiary to status. For Marxists, status and power are subsidiary to class – money buys both! For Weberians, class, status and party are all aspects of the unequal distribution of power. This dispute is not easily resolved.

For Weber, classes are distinguished by their unequal life-chances. They may be involved in antagonistic relationships, for example, in terms of negotiations over pay and working conditions, but class conflict is far from inevitable. For Marxists, on the other hand, class relationships are exploitative and so class conflict is highly likely.

If classes are distinguished by life-chances, there is inevitably a boundary problem: exactly how unequal do life-chances have to be before one can talk about different classes existing? In other words, where is the boundary drawn between one class and another?

Which do you think is the most crucial feature of social stratification: status inequalities, economic inequalities or power inequalities? Why?

FEMINISM

"The feminist agenda is not about equal rights for women. It is about a socialist, anti-family, political movement that encourages women to leave their husbands, kill their children, practice witchcraft, destroy capitalism and become lesbians." Pat(rick) Robertson (US tele-evangelist), 1992

Feminism, like most social movements that seek to challenge entrenched privileges, is routinely misrepresented by its opponents. Pat Robertson's claims are extreme, to say the least, but negative views of feminism and of feminists are not uncommon in the media, so students need to be aware of this.

Moreover, this negative representation helps to explain the paradoxical finding that there is widespread support today for equal treatment of men and women, but this exists alongside a reluctance to self-identify as feminist. In 2013, a YouGov survey of adults in Great Britain found that a large majority of both men (80 per cent) and women (81 per cent) were in favour of gender equality, but only a minority of men (10 per cent) and women (27 per cent) identified themselves as feminist.

In general, feminist theories – prior to postmodern feminism – are posited on the distinction between sex and 'gender': that 'sex' is biologically determined, while gender is a social construct and ideas about masculinity and femininity are historically and culturally variable – a conceptual distinction introduced by Ann Oakley.

Feminism, loosely defined, refers to a body of ideas and a social movement dedicated to achieving gender equality. It dates back a long way and encompasses a wide variety of tendencies and strategies. Its history is conventionally divided into three phases or 'waves' (Rampton, 2014). The first wave, which began at the end of the 18th century and culminated with the granting of the vote to women at the same age as men in the UK in 1928, was narrowly focused on female suffrage (meaning the right to vote, hence 'suffragettes'). The second wave, associated with the Women's Liberation Movement, ran from the 1960s to the 1980s and embraced a wide range of demands, including equal pay and the outlawing of sexual discrimination. The third wave runs from the 1990s to the present day and has been associated with what Walby (2011) has called the 'mainstreaming' of gender issues.

Women protest against sexism and inequality during the second wave of feminism.

Feminist theories of stratification

During the second wave of feminism, a range of competing theories of female subordination emerged and continue to inform debates about gender stratification. Different theories take different views about the exact form gender stratification takes, but they share the view that class theories had previously ignored women's position in society. They can be examined under five main headings.

Liberal feminism

Liberal feminism is so-called because its focus is on women's rights as individuals to be treated equally. Liberal feminists are in favour of reform rather than revolution, believing that equal rights can be achieved within the existing structure of society. An influential text was *The Feminine Mystique* (1963) in which Betty Friedan talked about what she called 'the problem without a name' – the widespread unhappiness of American housewives in the 1950s and 1960s. The cause she identified was the set of ideas embodied in dominant notions of femininity, in particular that women were by nature fulfilled by devoting their lives more or less exclusively to being mothers and housewives. Equal rights could be achieved by challenging this mystique, changing the ways in which girls (and boys) were socialised within the family and the school and by the mass media, and tackling sex discrimination in schools and workplaces.

Thus, liberal feminists challenged children's books that depicted boys and girls in stereotypical gender roles, school curricula that offered different subjects to boys (woodwork and metalwork) and girls (home economics and needlework) and gendered toys (Barbie Dolls for girls and Action Men for boys).

In the 1990s, some liberal feminists suggested that these processes were coming to an end. Sue Sharpe's work on the attitudes of teenage girls (1994) suggests that education and careers are now a priority for young women. Females have also enjoyed greater educational success than males in recent years. Liberal feminists, therefore, have an optimistic view of the future for women. In the family, they see evidence of both partners accepting equal responsibility for domestic work and childrearing. They also argue that dual-career families in which both partners enjoy equal economic status are becoming the norm. Legislators too are beginning to recognise male responsibility for childcare with the recent increases in paternity rights.

Radical feminism

For radical feminists, sexist attitudes and institutions needed to be understood as surface manifestations of a much more deep-seated structural phenomenon which they called 'patriarchy'. Patriarchy literally means rule by the father, but can be understood as referring to a system dominated by men in general.

In 1969, Kate Millet argued that patriarchy was a system that preceded other systems of stratification and was both trans-historical and cross-cultural. Patriarchy was a belief system that, on the basis of women's reproductive function, had built a collection of ideas about women's 'natural' role, status and temperament – expressed as 'masculinity' and 'femininity' – which served to keep women subordinated. Male domination was not only present in the wider society, but in the most intimate area of men's and women's lives – sex – where women were expected to be passive and docile or risk being seen as 'unfeminine'. Hence, for Millet, "the personal is political".

Similarly, in a book published the following year, Shulamith Firestone argued that men and women occupied separate classes and that there was a "sex class system" that predated the social-class system, imposed on women because of their biological role. She advocated the abolition of the nuclear family in favour of communal living arrangements and looked forward to the time when reproductive technologies would free women from their reproductive role.

More recently, Sylvia Walby (1990), while critical of the view that patriarchy is universal and unchanging, nevertheless argued that the concept is crucial for an understanding of gender inequality.

She identified six "patriarchal structures" which operated to maintain male dominance in British society at that time:

1 *The area of paid work* – Women experience discrimination from employers and restricted entry into careers because of the ideology that 'a woman's place is in the home'; when they enter work they experience low pay, low status and so on.

2 *The household* – Female labour is exploited in the family.

3 *The state* – This acts in the interests of men rather than women in terms of taxation, welfare rules and the weakness of laws protecting women at work.

4 *Cultural institutions such as the mass media* – These represent women in a narrow set of social roles, such as sex objects and as mother–housewives or wives and girlfriends, rather than people in their own right.

5 *Sexuality* – A double standard persists in modern society that values multiple sexual partners for men but condemns the same behaviour in women.

6 *Violence against women* – Sexual assault, domestic violence and the threat of violence are used by men to control the behaviour of women.

Socialist feminism

Socialist feminists are critical of various features of radical feminism. In particular, they reject the claim made by some radical feminists that patriarchy is monolithic and unchanging, and disagree with the strategy of separatism – that women should organise separately from men to tackle male domination. They are also critical of liberal feminism's claim that gender equality can be achieved under capitalism since, in their view, capitalism and patriarchy are interdependent systems.

An influential text within socialist feminism is *Beyond the Fragments: Feminism and the making of socialism* (1979, reissued 2013) by Sheila Rowbotham, Lynne Segal and Hilary Wainwright. The 'fragments' referred to were the various parties, tendencies and groups on the left politically who, the authors claimed, needed to stop fighting amongst themselves and join together to promote a new kind of socialism that was informed by feminism.

Drawing on Marxism, they argue that as capitalism developed, so a division between the 'public' sphere of work and political life and the 'private' sphere of the home was established and women were increasingly confined to the private sphere. Moreover, during Victorian times a patriarchal ideology developed which justified the idea that 'a woman's place is in the home' by reference to men's and women's supposed different natures. Women's unpaid labour in the home played a vital role in terms of the reproduction of labour (by bearing and raising children) and commodity production, since it freed their husbands to concentrate on paid employment. It also meant that women could act as a 'reserve army of labour' that could be drafted into commodity production if circumstances demanded – for example, during times of war.

Black feminism
Black feminism can be seen as a response to the recognition by women of colour that the perspectives already outlined did not adequately relate to either their experience or their concerns.

Black feminists argued that the intersection of racism with sexism complicated the situation facing minority women, many of whom occupied lower class positions. Hazel Corby (1982), for example, pointed out that black men could be victims of racism by white women as well as agents of male dominance, leaving black women with divided loyalties. Similarly, while white feminists had identified the family as a source of male oppression, for black women it was a site of resistance against racism. Black feminism has therefore concerned itself with mapping the intersections between oppressions connected with race, class and gender rather than seeking to develop a distinctive position on the origins of gender inequality (Mirza, 1997).

Postmodern feminism
Lorber (2010) suggests that liberal and socialist feminism, despite their differences, can be categorised as what she calls 'gender reform feminisms'. Politically, their goal is a 'reformed gender social order' in which men and women are positioned equally in society and have equal power, prestige and economic resources – although for liberal feminists this would be under a capitalist system, while for socialist feminists it would require the replacement of capitalism by socialism.

By contrast, radical feminists are unpersuaded that gender equality can be achieved without a frontal attack on patriarchy. Lorber categorises radical feminism as a type of 'gender resistance feminism', which argues that progress for women requires resistance to patriarchy.

Indeed, not merely resistance, but subversion: confronting the existing gender order by turning it upside down and valuing women and womanly attributes over men and manly attributes – emotional sensitivity over objectivity, nurturance over aggression, parenting over the marketplace and so on.

Postmodern feminism is classified by Lorber as a type of 'gender rebellion feminism' because, for postmodern feminists, the problem is the very notion of gender itself and progress for women (and men) requires a rebellion against (what they see as) the tyranny of gender categories.

Postmodernists are critical of what they call 'gender essentialism' – the idea that men and women are inherently different. Indeed, they reject the binary dualisms (pairs of opposites) – male/female, masculine/feminine, heterosexual/homosexual – with which other feminist perspectives operate.

For postmodernist feminists like Judith Butler (1990), earlier – 'modern' – feminists had made a mistake by trying to assert that 'women' (and 'men') were a group with common characteristics and interests. Gender, for Butler, is not an expression of something we are, but something we do. It is not a manifestation of our biological natures, but a performance we put on: "There is no gender identity behind the expressions of gender, ...identity is performatively constituted by the very 'expressions' that are said to be its results." In other words, we've been so good at performing masculinity and femininity that we've persuaded ourselves of the reality of there being just two types of human beings.

For postmodern feminists, then, the way forward is not to push for the interests of women against men, but for people to stop 'doing' gender according to the existing social scripts. Butler wanted people to refuse to conform to existing gender norms and to lead their lives however they wanted, thereby producing a proliferation of genders.

Evaluation of feminist theories
The theories developed during the second wave of feminism played a crucial role in transforming both sociology and society. Sociology's side-lining of women's lives – its 'male-stream' bias – was identified and effectively challenged, and feminist activism from the 1960s onwards set about addressing the entrenched patriarchal features of so many societies.

It is now clear that both liberal and radical feminism equated the concerns and interests of relatively affluent white women with those of all women. While some of their concerns could indeed be seen as universal – for example, the problem of male violence – others could not. If the degree of gender inequality in society varies cross-culturally and historically, as arguably it does, radical feminist theories of patriarchy struggle to account for this.

Socialist feminism has been criticised, for example by Cynthia Cockburn (2013), for underestimating the problems women face outside the economic sphere: "Largely absent are issues women have in their lives as mothers, daughters, sisters, and domestic and sexual-service providers to men" – particularly those issues related to male violence.

Gender oppression, as Black feminists have pointed out, intersects with other oppressions (for example, racism, heterosexism, ageism, disablism). This can produce cross-cutting allegiances that render the prioritisation of gender oppression problematic.

The distinction between sex and gender, which underlies many feminist theories, implies that biology plays no part at all in influencing men's and women's temperament and behaviour, a claim that remains far from settled among scientists. Postmodern feminism sees gender as entirely fluid – as a matter of individual choice. If, in fact, there are inherent differences between men and women that cannot be simply wished away, the very foundations of postmodern feminism are built on shaky ground.

Postmodernism and second modernity

Postmodernist sociologists believe that towards the end of the 20th century a raft of social and economic changes marked the transition from modernity to postmodernity in the advanced industrial societies. Among these changes were: the decline of manufacturing and the growth of service occupations, globalisation, the growth of the mass media and increasing individualisation.

For these writers, classes no longer exist in the way they did in modern societies, that is, as social groups with a shared sense of collective identity, shared ways of life ('class subcultures') and the capacity for acting politically in their own interests (even if they did not always do so). It is important to recognise that this does not mean that they think social inequalities have disappeared, but it does mean that they believe that class is no longer a valid way of talking about these inequalities.

Bauman

One writer who exemplifies these views is Zygmunt Bauman. In 1988 and 2007, he argued that countries such as the UK are more accurately referred to today as 'consumer societies' than as industrial societies because people's identity is based more on what

they buy than on their job. The relevance of class has therefore declined and class subcultures have, allegedly, been replaced by a multiplicity of 'lifestyles' based around consumption.

Consumer societies are still unequal societies, but for Bauman the main social cleavage in these societies is between the majority who are able to participate in consumption, whom Bauman calls the 'seduced', and the minority who are not, whom he calls the 'repressed' – the unemployed, the low paid, those in insecure or casual employment, recently arrived migrants and so on.

Pakulski and Waters

A similar argument is presented by the Australian sociologists Jan Pakulski and Malcolm Waters in 1996. Like Bauman, they argue that consumerism has become the dominant feature of post-industrial societies and that classes have been replaced by status groups linked to consumption, a system which they call 'status conventionalism'.

In a later essay, Pakulski (2001) argued that social inequalities in contemporary advanced societies increasingly approximate to what he calls 'complex (classless) inequality'. Because such societies are increasingly fragmented, there are numerous strata that form around shared market, status or political interests and these may or may not survive in the long term. In order to label such strata, Pakulski argues, one would need multiple descriptors, such as 'unskilled migrant women', or 'white-collar urban Blacks' or 'Catholic intelligentsia'.

Beck

Ulrich Beck, a German sociologist, was critical of postmodernists because he felt they should not be content with describing what was happening by simply looking backwards, but should seek to understand where society was going. However, he shared the view of postmodernists that class was now redundant. Indeed, he called class a 'zombie category' – a concept that was past its sell-by date but which refused to lie down and die! Beck (1986) argues that we have moved into a new period in human history, which he calls 'risk society', or more recently, 'second modernity', characterised by global ecological and economic crises, widening transnational inequalities (for example, between the rich countries of the north and the poor countries of the south), precarious forms of paid work and threats from international terrorism. Nation states are unable to control these global threats and individuals are increasingly left to cope with the uncertainty of this globalised world by themselves. What was needed, he argued, was a new kind of international politics, which he called 'cosmopolitanism'.

Evaluation of postmodernism

Undoubtedly, other sources of inequality besides class have forced themselves on the attention of society, and of sociologists, through social movements in the second half of the 20th century connected with race, gender, sexuality and disability in particular. As a result, 'class politics' appears to have declined and 'identity politics' increased.

Recognition of these types of social diversity – alongside others, such as ethnicity and age, together with greater geographical mobility – has produced an increasingly pluralised society in which class differences no longer stand out.

However, research indicates that most people, if prompted, will still identify themselves with a class. An Ipsos/MORI poll conducted in 2012 found that 93 per

cent of British adults were prepared to label themselves working or middle class, with only 7 per cent opting for 'Don't know'.

Will Atkinson (2010) argues that rather than individualisation having obliterated class, people now interpret the influence of class in more individualistic ways, rather than in terms of deprivation and inequality. Indeed, Roberts (1995) argues that our experiences are still broadly predictable on the basis of our class background and suggests the term 'structured individualisation' to describe this.

The irony of such findings is that the decline in the social significance of class has coincided with an almost unprecedented increase in economic inequality in the UK in recent decades. Atkinson suggests that neoliberalism – the set of political ideas that have been dominant in Britain since the 1980s – has served both to conceal and legitimate these 'class' inequalities.

CHECK YOUR UNDERSTANDING

1. Distinguish between 'ascribed' and 'achieved' status.

2. Why is stratification inevitable, according to Parsons?

3. Identify two criticisms of functionalist theories of stratification.

4. What do Marxists mean by 'exploitation'?

5. Explain the Marxist distinction between a 'class-in-itself' and a 'class-for-itself'.

6. What are the three dimensions of stratification according to Weber?

7. What is the 'boundary problem' in Weberian analyses of class?

8. What do feminists mean by 'patriarchy'?

9. What criticism does Black feminism make of other feminist perspectives?

10. Give two reasons why postmodernists see class as a redundant concept today.

TAKE IT FURTHER

Interview a sample of people under 20 and over 50 about whether they think social classes still exist today. Do they see themselves as belonging to a particular social class? If so, what effect do they think it has/ had on their life? Also, do they think that social classes have shared or opposed interests? Then analyse your results. Do there appear to be any generational differences in the views expressed? What limitations might there be in the representativeness of your sample? What do the answers suggest about whether class still matters?

5.2 PROBLEMS OF DEFINING AND MEASURING CLASS

LEARNING OBJECTIVES

> Demonstrate knowledge and understanding of social class and the difficulties of defining and measuring it (AO1).

> Demonstrate knowledge and understanding of the distinction between subjective and objective ways of measuring class and of different class schemas (AO1).

> Apply knowledge and understanding of problems of measuring class (AO2).

> Evaluate the strengths and weaknesses of different class schemas (AO3).

INTRODUCING THE DEBATE

Social classes were defined in the previous chapter as "groups of people who share a similar economic position in terms of occupation, income and ownership of wealth". As we saw, sociologists disagree about whether social classes still exist in societies such as present-day Britain. This is partly because different sociologists focus on different facts and/or interpret the same facts differently, but it's also because they define class differently. This chapter will therefore seek to clarify the different meanings that the term can have and the associated problems of measuring class.

WHAT ARE (SOCIAL) CLASSES?

'Class' derives from the Latin *classis* referring to any of the six orders or ranks into which the Roman people were divided on the basis of their wealth for tax purposes. The origin of the term points to the two key features that characterise it and on which all sociologists agree:

> Class is concerned with economic differences between groups of people.

> These groups are arranged in some kind of hierarchy.

Beyond this, however, things get more complicated. This is because classes are multi-faceted. Four aspects of class are typically distinguished:

> a shared economic situation

> shared attitudes, beliefs, values and behaviour ('class subcultures')

> awareness of membership ('class consciousness')

> action to promote their shared interests ('class action').

Do you think that all four aspects need to be present before one can validly talk about a collection of people as a 'social class'?

It follows that people could, objectively, be in the same or a similar economic situation, yet, subjectively, be unaware of this. This was what Marx was referring to in his distinction between a 'class-in-itself' and a 'class-for-itself'. (In sociological terms, this is the distinction between a 'social category' and a 'social group'.) It also follows that people could think and behave in similar ways because of their shared class position yet not recognise this influence. Similarly, people could belong to a class and, on the one hand, feel that this was an important aspect of their identity, or, on the other hand, see it as insignificant. Hence, class consciousness is not inevitably associated with

FOCUS ON SKILLS: SUBJECTIVE CLASS IDENTITIES

Semi-structured interviews were used by Savage et al. to study class identity.

Mike Savage and his colleagues carried out semi-structured interviews between 1997 and 1999 with 178 people living in four areas in and around Manchester. They identified three groups of people in terms of subjective class identity:

> First, there was a small minority of their sample who strongly identified themselves as belonging to a specific class. These were often graduates who had the cultural confidence to express their class position in an articulate fashion.

> The second group was also well educated, but did not like to identify with a particular class position. Rather, this group tended either to reject the notion of social class, because they saw themselves as individuals rather than a product of their social-class background, or they preferred to debate the nature of social class rather than acknowledge their belonging to any particular group. Some felt happier differentiating themselves from other social classes rather than focusing on their own membership of a particular social class.

> The third group, which made up the majority of the respondents, actually identified with a social class, but did so in an ambivalent, defensive and uncommitted way. Some of this group prefaced their 'belonging' with remarks such as "I suppose I'm ..." or "Probably, I'm ..." Savage and colleagues suggest that identification with the concepts of 'working class' and 'middle class' for this part of their sample was based on a simple desire to be seen as normal and ordinary, rather than any burning desire to be flag-wavers for their class.

They conclude as follows: "We have argued that class identities are generally weak. However, this should not be taken as evidence that class does not matter. For, in sustaining and articulating the kinds of individualised identities that do matter to people, reference is made to external benchmarks of class as a means of 'telling their story' ... We see then, in people's accounts of class, a highly charged, but complex ambivalence in which classes and individuals are held to be different yet also inherently related." (Savage, Bagnall and Longhurst, 2001).

Questions

1. **Explain** what is meant by 'subjective class identity'.

2. **Identify** how the majority of interviewees responded to the question of what class they saw themselves as belonging to.

3. **Analyse.** The authors report that the interviewees saw the concept of class as 'highly charged'. What do you think they mean by this?

4. **Evaluate** what the findings of this research suggest about whether class still matters.

class action. Consequently, when sociologists argue about whether class still matters, part of the difficulty in arriving at an answer lies in the fact that the term 'class' carries a number of distinct yet interrelated associations.

The other main problem with the meaning of class has to do with how the classes that are identified are seen as relating to each other. For some sociologists they are seen simply as occupying different *levels* in terms of income and wealth (the 'gradational' approach), but for others they are seen as involved in an antagonistic relationship or relationships, meaning that they have opposing interests. This distinction is sociologically important. If classes are simply categories of people enjoying or suffering different standards of living, then that is one thing; but if the higher standards of living of some classes are the result of an exploitative relationship with lower classes, then that is something else.

COMPETING VIEWS OF THE CLASS STRUCTURE

Given the complexity of the concept of class, it is perhaps unsurprising that sociologists have produced a range of competing views about the class structure of the advanced industrial societies. Four influential assessments are briefly described below.

Giddens

Anthony Giddens (1973) endorsed the widespread conventional view that society can be divided into an upper class, middle class and lower (or working) class. Drawing on Weber, he argued that class position is determined by 'market capacity' (in simple terms, the way people make a living) and distinguished three different types of market capacity, detailed below:

Class	Market capacity
Upper class	Capital ownership
Middle class	Educational credentials
Working class	Labour power

Table 5.2.1 *Giddens's view of the British class structure*

Giddens acknowledged that one can identify subdivisions within each of these classes, for example, between graduates and non-graduates among the middle class, but nevertheless saw these three divisions as fundamental.

Wright

As we saw in Chapter 1, Erik-Olin Wright's main concern was to 'rescue' the Marxist framework in light of the growth of 'middle' classes between the **bourgeoisie** and the proletariat. To do this he added to the concept of ownership of economic resources the additional concepts of organisational assets and skills/credential assets. The resulting matrix generated ten 'contradictory class locations' between the bourgeoisie (owners of large enterprises) at the top and the proletariat (unskilled manual workers) at the bottom. (See Table 5.1.2 in Chapter 1 for a full description of Wright's (1985) 12-class schema.)

UNDERSTAND THE CONCEPT

Bourgeoisie is a French word that translates as 'middle class', yet the section above on Wright talks about his concern to explain the growth of 'middle classes' between the bourgeoisie and the proletariat! The explanation of this conundrum is that the bourgeoisie were indeed 'in the middle' between the aristocracy and the peasants when feudalism was giving way to capitalism, but as capitalism developed they became the new ruling class – merging with the aristocracy in Britain, sending the aristocracy to the guillotine in France! So, although bourgeoisie does translate as 'middle class', it is used by Marxists to refer to the dominant class in capitalist societies.

Runciman

Another influential attempt to map the contours of the class structure, in this case relating specifically to British society, is provided by Gary Runciman (1990). For Runciman, classes are "sets of roles whose common location in social space is a function of the nature and degree of 'economic power' [quotes added] attaching to them". He identifies three sources of economic power: that deriving from ownership of the means of production, that deriving from control of labour or capital and that deriving from 'marketability' – the possession of an attribute or capacity that is of value in the labour market.

On this basis, Runciman claims to identify seven classes occupying qualitatively different locations in terms of economic power. These are shown in Table 5.2.2, with his estimate of the approximate size of each at the time he was writing.

Class	Estimated size in 1990
Upper class	0.1–0.2%
Upper middle class	<10%
Middle middle class	15%
Lower middle class	20%
Skilled working class	20%
Unskilled working class	30%
Underclass	5%

Table 5.2.2 *Runciman's view of the British class structure*

Those at the top – the upper class – are distinguished by their considerable wealth, their positions as senior executives, or their possession of scarce and highly valued knowledge and skills. Those at the bottom – the underclass – are seen as lacking in any economic power and as "more or less permanently at the economic level where benefits are paid by the state".

Bourdieu

Giddens, Wright and Runciman were all concerned with mapping the contours of the class structure of modern societies. Pierre Bourdieu (1984), a French conflict theorist who drew heavily on the work of both Marx and Weber, had a different concern. He wished to explain how the class structure was reproduced across space and time and how the privileges of those at the top came to be seen as just and fair – in Marxist terms, how they were 'legitimated'.

Bourdieu's crucial innovation was to suggest that capital was not just a matter of money, but also of the possession of valued cultural attributes and social connections. He identified three different types of capital that people could possess:

> *economic capital*: income, wealth, inheritance and other money assets

> *cultural capital*: attitudes of mind, tastes, educational qualifications and so on

> *social capital*: the range and depth of people's contacts based on their social networks.

Once any of these are perceived and recognised as legitimate they provide their possessors with what Bourdieu calls 'symbolic capital', that is they come to represent high status in the eyes of others (wearing an Armani suit, say, or visiting the Royal Opera House in Covent Garden). Hence, for Bourdieu, it is not just wealth that those at the top of the class structure possess, but specific kinds of tastes and cultural preferences

as well as useful contacts which enable them to resist downward mobility.

Post-modernists argue that the former distinction between high ('highbrow') culture and low (popular) culture no longer exists. Do you agree?

Dale Southerton (2009) draws on a Bourdieuian perspective to analyse how different groups use consumption practices to mark themselves off from each other in a new town – Yate, near Bristol. Against the post-modern view that consumption increasingly reflects individualisation and personal choice, he argues that class continues to structure consumption practices and displays. For example, for working-class groups the kitchen is seen in functional terms (as a place to prepare and consume food), but for middle-class groups it was a place to display one's identity and 'taste' through its design, layout, decoration and choice of kitchen equipment.

PROBLEMS OF MEASURING CLASS

It might appear that, if sociologists wished to establish the class structure of a society, there is a straightforward way to do this: simply ask a representative sample of people what class they belong to and map the results! However, there are a number of reasons why, in practice, things are more complicated.

First, in asking people about their class position there is the danger of unwittingly prompting a positive response when the respondent does not in fact identify with a class, but feels that it might reflect badly on them or that they would be seen as uncooperative if they were to admit this. In other words, how do you ask people about their 'class identity' without using the word 'class' and thereby leading their response?

Second, even if people genuinely identify with a class, the class they feel they belong to may not coincide with the class that they objectively belong to. If the sociologist's goal is to establish how people's objective class location relates to, say, their life-chances, classifying people on the basis of their self-ascribed class would not be helpful. (Subjective measurements of social class are considered in more detail below.)

Third, if an objective approach is followed, there is the problem of how to operationalise class. That is, how to turn what is an abstract concept into something that can actually be measured. This requires the identification of variables that can act as indicators of class, such as wealth or income. Yet people are notoriously cagey about telling strangers what they earn, let alone how much money they have in the bank! Consequently, sociologists have tended to use occupation as their principal indicator of class, as this can be readily and – usually unproblematically – established.

Scales of social class

The Registrar General's scale
This occupational scale was used by government from 1911 until 2000 and involved the ranking of thousands of jobs into six classes, based on the occupational skill of the head of household:

› Class I: Professional – for example, accountants, doctors

› Class II: Lower managerial, professional and technical – for example, teachers

› Class IIINM: Skilled non-manual – for example, office workers

› Class IIIM: Skilled manual – for example, electricians, plumbers

› Class IV: Semi-skilled manual – for example, agricultural workers

› Class V: Unskilled manual – for example, labourers, refuse collectors.

This scheme differentiated between middle-class occupations (non-manual jobs were allocated to classes I to IIINM) and working-class occupations (manual jobs were allocated to classes IIIM to V). The Registrar General's scheme has underpinned many important social surveys and sociological studies, particularly those focusing on class differences in educational achievement and life expectancy.

Criticisms of the Registrar General's scale
The Registrar General's scale was the main way in which class was measured in official statistics. Most sociological research conducted between 1960 and 2000 uses this classification system when differentiating between different classes. However, it does have disadvantages:

› Assessments of jobs were made by the Registrar General's own staff – hence, there was a bias towards seeing non-manual occupations as having a higher status than manual occupations.

› Reliance on occupation meant that those whose economic position was based on wealth and unearned income disappeared from view.

› Feminists criticised the scale as sexist – the class of everyone in a household was defined by the job of the male head of household. Women were assigned to the class of their husbands (or their fathers, if unmarried).

› It glossed over the fact that workers allocated to the same class often had widely varying access to resources such as pay and promotion.

› It failed to distinguish between the employed and self-employed – this distinction is important because evidence shows that these groups do not share similar experiences. For example, the shadow economy is much more accessible to the self-employed: they can avoid paying tax and VAT by working at a cheaper rate 'for cash', which cannot be traced through their accounts, or by not fully declaring all the work they do.

The Hope-Goldthorpe scale
Sociologists were often reluctant to use government-inspired scales as they lacked sufficient sociological emphasis. In order to study social mobility (see Chapter 9), in the early 1970s John Goldthorpe – working with Keith Hope – created a more sociologically relevant scale that has proved very popular with social researchers. Goldthorpe recognised the growth of middle-class occupations – and especially the self-employed – and based his classification on the concept of market position: income and economic life-chances, such as promotion prospects, sick pay and control of hours worked. He also took account of work or employment relations: whether people are employed or self-employed, and whether they are able to exercise authority over others. The Hope-Goldthorpe scale also acknowledged that both manual and non-manual groups may share similar experiences of work and, for this reason, Goldthorpe grouped some of these together in an intermediate class. Instead of the basic non-manual/ manual divide used by the Registrar General's scale, Goldthorpe introduced the idea of three main social divisions into which groups sharing similar market position and work relations could be placed: he referred to these as the **service class**, the intermediate class and the working class (see Table 5.2.3).

UNDERSTAND THE CONCEPT

The term **service class** refers to those employees whose employment relationship is based on a code of service and so involves trust as a key element. It is also associated with relatively high levels of autonomy (people are trusted to get on with the job without close supervision). The term can be misleading since it is easily confused with work in the 'service sector' or service industries (such as hairdressing or care work). Consequently, the term 'salariat' is sometimes used instead.

Class	Occupation
Service class	
1	Higher professionals
	High-grade administrators; managers of large companies and large proprietors
2	Lower professionals
	Higher-grade technicians; supervisors of non-manual workers; administrators; small-business managers
Intermediate class	
3	Routine non-manual (clerical and sales)
4	Small proprietors and self-employed artisans (craftspersons)
5	Lower-grade technicians and supervisors of manual workers
Working class	
6	Skilled manual workers
7	Semi-skilled and unskilled manual workers

Table 5.2.3 *The Hope–Goldthorpe Scale*

Source: Goldthorpe (1980)

Goldthorpe's scale was first used in studies conducted in 1972, published in 1980. The scale more accurately reflected the nature of the British class system, but it was still based on the male head of household. He defended this position by claiming that, in most cases, the male worker still determined the market situation and lifestyle of a couple, because the male was still the main breadwinner. However, many feminists remained unconvinced by this argument. They argued that scales based on the idea of a male 'head of household':

> overlook the significance of dual-career families, where the joint income of both partners can give the family an income and lifestyle of a higher class

> ignore situations where women are in a higher-grade occupation than their husbands

> overlook the significance of the increasing number of single working women and single working mothers, who were classified by Goldthorpe according to the occupation of their ex-partners or fathers.

A feminist alternative: the Surrey Occupational Class Schema

This scale was developed by the feminist sociologists Dale, Gilbert and Arber (1985) in an attempt to overcome what they saw as the patriarchal bias inherent in the Hope–Goldthorpe scale. In this scheme, women are classified on the basis of their own occupations, whether they are married or not. The gendered nature of work in contemporary society, especially the growing service sector of the economy, is also taken into account. This is most evident in class 6 which is divided into 6a (sales and personal services – female dominated) and 6b (skilled manual – overwhelmingly male) (see Table 5.2.4).

Class	Occupation
1	Higher professional
2	Employers and managers
3	Lower professional
4	Secretarial and clerical
5	Supervisors, self-employed manual
6a	Sales and personal services
6b	Skilled manual
7	Semi-skilled
8	Unskilled

Table 5.2.4 *The Surrey Occupational Class Schema*

Source: Dale, Gilbert, & Arber (1985)

However, the inclusion of women in such occupational classifications does present some difficulties because women's relationship to employment is generally more varied than that of men. More women work part time or occupy jobs for short periods because of pregnancy and childcare. It is therefore difficult to know whether the class assigned provides a meaningful insight into their life experience as a whole or whether it merely reflects a short-term or temporary experience that has little impact on lifestyle and life-chances.

A new scale for the 21st century: the National Statistics Socio-Economic Classification (NS-SEC)

The NS-SEC scale, which essentially is a variation on the Hope–Goldthorpe scale, fully replaced the Registrar General's scale for government research and statistics, and was used for the first time to classify data from the 2001 census (see Table 5.2.5).

Like the Hope–Goldthorpe scale, the NS-SEC is based on:

> employment relations – whether people are employers, self-employed or employed, and whether they exercise authority over others

> market conditions – salary scales, promotion prospects, sick pay, how much control people have over the hours they work, and so on.

Occupational classification	% of working population	Examples
1 Higher managerial and professional	11.0	Company directors, senior civil servants, doctors, barristers, clergy, architects
2 Lower managerial and professional	23.5	Nurses, journalists, teachers, police officers, musicians
3 Intermediate	14.0	Secretaries, clerks, computer operators, driving instructors
4 Small employers and self-accountable workers	9.9	Taxi drivers, window cleaners, publicans, decorators
5 Lower supervisory, craft and related	9.8	Train drivers, plumbers, printers, TV engineers
6 Semi-routine	18.6	Traffic wardens, shop assistants, hairdressers, call-centre workers
7 Routine	12.7	Cleaners, couriers, road sweepers, labourers
8 Long-term unemployed or the never-worked		

Table 5.2.5 *The National Statistics Socio-Economic Classification (NS-SEC)*

Source: Rose and Pevalin (with K. O'Reilly) (2001)

Strengths of the NS-SEC

> It no longer divides workers exclusively along manual and non-manual lines. Some categories contain both manual and non-manual workers.

> The most significant difference between the Hope–Goldthorpe scale and the NS-SEC is the creation of Class 8, the long-term unemployed and never-employed unemployed. Some sociologists, most notably from New Right positions, have described this group of unemployed as an 'underclass'.

> Feminist arguments have been acknowledged and women are now recognised as a distinct group of wage earners. They are no longer categorised according to the occupation of their husbands or fathers.

Weaknesses of the NS-SEC

> The scale is still based primarily on the objective criterion of occupation. This may differ from what people understand by the term 'social class' and their subjective interpretation of their own class position.

> Those who do not have to work because of access to great wealth are still not included.

> Some argue that the scale still obscures important differences in status and earning power, for example, headteachers are in the same category as classroom teachers.

The Great British Class Survey (GBCS)

The most recent attempt to map Britain's class structure (Savage *et al.*, 2013), draws on Bourdieu's view that class is not just a matter of economic inequalities, but also of two other forms of 'capital': social and cultural.

Working with the BBC, Savage and his colleagues devised an on-line questionnaire that people were invited to fill in. It asked questions designed to establish the amounts and types of economic, cultural and social capital participants possessed. Economic capital was assessed by questions about household income, household savings, whether people lived in rented property or were owner-occupiers and, if the latter, the value of their house. Cultural capital was measured by questions about people's leisure interests, musical tastes, use of the media and food preferences. Finally, social capital was measured by asking people whether they knew anyone in 37 different occupations, ranging in status from cleaner to chief executive.

The web survey was launched in January 2011 and, by July that year, 161,400 completed responses had been submitted. However, analysis of these responses revealed a strong selection bias, with the sample significantly skewed towards more affluent and well–educated social groups. In order to compensate for this problem, a further nationally representative face-to-face survey of 1,026 adults was carried out by a market research company called GfK, using the same questions. Results were analysed by applying a statistical technique that searched for patterns in the data in order to determine classes. The resulting class map is detailed in Table 5.2.6.

Class	%GfK	%GBCS	Description
Elite	6%	22%	Very high economic capital (especially savings), high social capital, very high highbrow cultural capital.
Established middle class	25%	43%	High economic capital, high status of mean (average) contacts, high highbrow and emerging cultural capital.
Technical middle class	6%	10%	High economic capital, very high mean status of social contacts, but relatively few contacts reported, moderate cultural capital.
New affluent workers	15%	6%	Moderately good economic capital, moderately poor mean score of social contacts though high range, moderate highbrow but good emerging cultural capital.
Traditional working class	14%	2%	Moderately poor economic capital, though with reasonable house price, few social contacts, low highbrow and emerging cultural capital.
Emergent service workers	19%	17%	Moderately poor economic capital, though with reasonable household income, moderate social contacts, high emerging (but low highbrow) cultural capital.
Precariat	15%	<1%	Poor economic capital and the lowest scores on every other criterion.

Table 5.2.6 *Summary of GBCS social classes*
Source: Savage *et al.* (2013)

Does the type of concert you attend reflect your social class?

Evaluation of the GBCS

One strength of the GBCS is that, because it does not use occupation as an indicator of economic status, it takes account of both income and wealth. This allows it to identify a distinct 'elite' class at the top of the class structure, which would simply be subsumed into the highest paid category when using occupation-based scales. It also avoids accusations of being sexist.

Another strength is that, by measuring cultural and social factors, it acknowledges that class is not just a matter of economic position. However, it is doubtful whether the people who are allocated to these 'classes' are likely to identify with them, let alone engage in collective action to promote their 'class' interests.

Rose and Harrison (2013) are critical of the inductive methodology used to identify the seven classes, arguing that if the authors had chosen different key criteria "then very likely different classes would have emerged". They are also critical of the fact that Savage *et al.* assign an average age to each class grouping, arguing that age should be irrelevant to class.

Finally, sociologists who see classes as existing in antagonistic relationships with one another – because the advantages enjoyed by higher classes are dependent on the exploitation suffered by lower classes – are critical of the gradational basis of the GBCS model. Standing (2013), for example, argues that Savage *et al.* confuse socio-economic groups with social classes, adding that "classes exist in tension with one another".

SUBJECTIVE MEASUREMENTS OF SOCIAL CLASS

Social surveys suggest there is often a discrepancy between how objective measurements of social class classify jobs and how people who actually occupy those jobs interpret their social status or class position. For example, many teachers like to describe themselves as working class despite the fact that both the Registrar General's classification of occupations and the NS-SEC objectively class them as middle class. This is because many teachers have experienced upward mobility through educational qualifications from working-class origins and feel that their perspective on the world is still shaped by working-class values and experience. This subjective awareness of class position often conflicts with official objective interpretations.

More importantly, it is the subjective interpretation of class position that is responsible when it comes to social interaction, for the sharp boundary lines that exist between the social classes in the UK. In other words, there is some evidence that those people who interpret themselves as, say, 'working class' or 'middle class' have very clear ideas about what characteristics people who 'belong' to their class should have. Moreover, they tend to have very strong views about the characteristics of other social classes. These subjective interpretations may have little or nothing in common with official and objective attempts to construct broad socio-economic classifications based on employment.

The 'Focus on Skills' exercise provides an example of research exploring subjective social class identities.

CHECK YOUR UNDERSTANDING

1. Explain what is meant by saying that 'class' is multi-faceted.

2. Distinguish between a gradational and a relational view of classes.

3. What are the four kinds of capital distinguished by Bourdieu?

4. Identify three difficulties in measuring class.

5. Why has occupation been the most widely used indicator for measuring social class?

6. Analyse the strengths and weaknesses of the Registrar General's scale.

7. How does the NS-SEC scale address the weaknesses of the RG scale?

8. How might the NS-SEC scale still be said to be lacking?

9. Identify one difference between the NS-SEC and GBCS scales.

10. Identify one strength and one weakness of the GBCS.

TAKE IT FURTHER

We have seen above that, in order to measure a concept, sociologists usually have to identify something that will act as a valid and reliable indicator of it. For example, many sociologists have used occupation as an indicator of class position.

Assess the validity, reliability and practicality of each of the following possible alternative indicators of people's economic position. You'll need to think about such considerations as: is the information visible or will you have to ask people about it? If the latter, are they likely to be happy to provide the information? Are they likely to be honest?

> Type of housing lived in

> How someone dresses

> Visible tattoos

> The neighbourhood they live in

> Which supermarket they shop in

> Whether they own a car and, if so, the make and model

5.3 DIMENSIONS OF INEQUALITY: SOCIAL CLASS

LEARNING OBJECTIVES

> Understand how the political focus on inequality in the UK has moved from class to social exclusion to 'troubled families' in recent decades (AO1).

> Demonstrate knowledge of growing income and wealth inequality in the UK and how this can be explained (AO1).

> Apply knowledge and understanding of the links between class and life-chances (AO2).

> Analyse the links between class and life-chances in relation to education and health (AO3).

> Evaluate the continuing relevance of class inequalities to life-chances (AO3).

INTRODUCING THE DEBATE

As we saw in Chapter 1, some sociologists have seen the growing importance of consumption, social fragmentation and individualisation as evidence that the UK is no longer a class society, and that the occupational status and the market rewards attached to social class are no longer the main source of identity and inequality today. Rather, these sociologists argue that social divisions – such as those between neighbourhoods, regions and status groups – are now far more important. However, other sociologists do not accept the validity of this picture of the United Kingdom. They argue instead that, although the nature of social class in the UK is changing, it is still the most important influence on all aspects of our lives.

In Chapter 2, we saw that class is a multi-faceted concept and that it would be perfectly possible for class to have become less significant in subjective terms while continuing to play an important role in terms of its impact on people's life experiences and life-chances. This chapter will seek to establish how far class does still impact on people's life experiences and life-chances by looking at changes in the distribution of income and wealth and the impact of class on education and health. But first we will look at the changing political discourse around social disadvantage in recent decades.

THE POLITICS OF DISADVANTAGE

From class inequality to social exclusion

Under the combined influences of structural changes to society and neoliberalism, 'social class' has largely disappeared from the discourse of politicians over the last few decades. David Cameron, in 2008, expressed the view that "I don't believe this is a class-ridden society. I think that's a load of rubbish." Coming from a **right-wing** politician, this was perhaps predictable. But **left-wing** politicians are no more willing to talk about class, even when it is clear that this is what they have in mind. Thus, for example, one of the key themes of Ed Miliband's campaign in the run-up to the 2015 election was the (alleged) growing plight of the middle classes, but the phrase used to refer to this was always the 'squeezed middle', never squeezed middle classes.

UNDERSTAND THE CONCEPT

The terms **left-wing** and **right-wing** are used to refer to sets of political beliefs, ideologies and parties. They originated with the National Assembly following the 1789 French Revolution, where supporters of the king sat on the right of the president and supporters of the revolution to the left. The left is associated with a belief in equality, state regulation, a mixed economy and republicanism. The right is associated with a belief in individual freedom, a small state, a free-market economy and monarchy. The terms are associated particularly, though not exclusively, with class politics, so those who believe class no longer matters tend to see the terms as outmoded.

Why do you think most politicians in the UK are reluctant to use the word 'class' today?

Under the 'New Labour' governments of 1997 to 2010, the 'Old Labour' concern with class inequality as a source of disadvantage was largely replaced by a concern with 'social exclusion'. One of Tony Blair's first initiatives on becoming PM was the establishment of a Social Exclusion Unit as part of the Office of the Deputy Prime Minister. In 2006, the SEU was merged with the PM's Strategy Unit to form the Social Exclusion Task Force. One of the reasons for this was that Tony Blair (PM between 1997 and 2007)

was heavily influenced in his political thinking by the British sociologist Tony Giddens.

Giddens and Diamond (2005) argue that social class is no longer an important source of inequality or identity in the 21st century. They suggest that the UK is a meritocratic society in that equality of opportunity is now the norm: all members of society are objectively and equally judged on their talent and ability. Social background, and therefore social class, is now less important than ever before. Giddens and Diamond's argument appeared as a chapter in a book they edited, which they called *The New Egalitarianism*. 'Egalitarians' are people who believe in equality, a principal generally associated with the Left in politics. The view of these "new egalitarians" was that disadvantage today is no longer associated with class, but with a number of distinctive cleavages or disparities between the social experiences of particular social groups, such as:

> between different types of families – for example, single-parent families do not experience the same opportunities as dual-career families

> between homeowners and those who live in council housing

> between those living in neighbourhoods with high levels of crime and antisocial behaviour, and little community spirit, and those living in ordered and integrated communities

> between those with secure well-paid jobs and those in insecure casual or temporary low-paid work and those who are long-term unemployed

> between the disabled and the able-bodied

> between ethnic groups

> between the elderly and younger members of society

> between male pupils and female pupils.

In short, the new egalitarians rejected the notion of an overarching class-based structure of inequality and argued instead that social exclusion was a more accurate term for 'the range of deprivations' (for example, low wages, child poverty, lack of educational and training opportunities, low levels of community belonging, and the lack of integration into a unified national identity) that prevent a diverse range of groups from taking their "full part in society". In response, social policy under New Labour concentrated on the fields of education, training and welfare with the concept of *social inclusion* in mind – that is, it aimed to target these groups so that they could become part of mainstream society again.

From social exclusion to troubled families

If New Labour had refined the focus of concerns around social disadvantage, from the broad problems associated with class inequality to the narrower ones associated with social exclusion, the Coalition Government narrowed them still further to that of 'troubled families' and individuals, often associated in Conservative discourse with a disaffected and self-reproducing 'underclass'. The Social Exclusion Task Force was abolished in 2010 by the new Coalition Government and the language of social exclusion was replaced by that of 'social justice'. In 2011, the Department for Communities and Local Government announced the Troubled Families programme, designed "to meet the national ambition of turning around the lives of 120,000 families".

In 2012, the Coalition Government published *Social Justice: transforming lives* which explained the government's plans for giving individuals and families with multiple disadvantages "the support and tools they need to turn their lives around". This programme continues under the new Conservative government elected in 2015. Indeed, in 2015, David Cameron praised the Troubled Families programme for its "unprecedented success" and announced it would be working with up to 400,000 new families.

SO DOES CLASS NO LONGER MATTER?

The views associated with the new egalitarians and those subsequently expressed by the Coalition Government have not been embraced by all sociologists and social commentators. As Steve Chapman (2008) has put it, these sociologists and commentators – known as the 'new traditionalists' – argue that "equality of opportunity is generally undermined by the main cause of social problems in the UK today: the economic and social inequalities brought about by the free-market capitalist economy. In other words, they believe that social class is still the central problem of the UK in the 21st century."

Thus, Mike Savage (2000), for example, rejects the new egalitarian view that we now live in a society "where most social groups have been incorporated into a common social body, with shared values and interests", describing the concepts of social exclusion and inclusion as "bland and inoffensive" and arguing for the continued importance of social class divisions.

Similarly, Owen Jones (2011) argues that the last few decades have seen a growing 'demonisation' of the working class as 'chavs', members of an 'underclass' who are both permanently unemployed and unemployable, happy to live off benefits, and given to petty crime, racism and unwanted pregnancies. In reality, Jones argues, what has happened has been the systematic destruction of working-class communities, jobs and workplaces, which has created council housing estates and areas of low-quality, privately rented accommodation where few jobs are available and where those that are available are low-paid and insecure.

That there are individuals and families that are both troubled and, indeed, troublesome is not in dispute. Nor indeed that targeted help may well be worthwhile. What is at issue is whether these problems are restricted to a small minority of the population who have largely been the authors of their own fate, or whether it is that the problems associated with growing class inequalities have simply hit this group the hardest and that they have then been vilified as the cause of wider problems in society. As David Cameron put it in 2011, "Whatever you call it, we've known for years that a relatively small number of families are the source of a large proportion of the problems in society."

The new traditionalists would probably agree, but the families they would point the finger at would be those at the top, with the power to influence who gets what in society. The dispute between the new egalitarians and new traditionalists cannot be easily settled, because it is as much about conflicting political beliefs and ideologies as it is about facts. However, facts are important and the rest of this chapter will explore at least some of the relevant data.

TRENDS IN INCOME AND WEALTH

A number of observations can be made about the distribution of income and wealth over the last few decades.

Income

Between 1979 and 1997 (during an unbroken period of Conservative government), income inequality between the rich and poor in Britain widened until it was at its most unequal since records began at the end of the 19th century. No other Western industrialised country, apart from the USA, had experienced this level of inequality. Average income rose by 36 per cent during this period, but the top 10 per cent of earners experienced a 62 per cent rise, while the poorest 10 per cent of earners experienced a 17 per cent decline. According to the Organisation for Economic Cooperation and Development (OECD) (2015) – an organisation of the world's 27 leading economies – the UK today is the fifth most unequal in terms of income distribution. The average income of the richest 10 per cent is almost ten times as large as that of the poorest 10 per cent. The OECD average is 9.5 (for comparison, in France and Germany it is around 7, in the USA, 16).The share of the top 1 per cent of income earners increased from 6.7 per cent in 1981 to 12.9 per cent in 2011. Recent data up to the 2012/13 fiscal year suggests income inequality overall has been constant since 2010. However, this is not the case at the top of the income range. A report by the High Pay Commission in 2015 revealed that FTSE 100 CEOs earned, on average, 183 times the median pay for a full-time employee in 2014 – just under £5m compared to just over £27,000. The figure for 2010 was lower at 160 times more.

On the release of the figures on CEO pay in 2015, the deputy director of the Adam Smith Institute commented that "Good decision-making from the top might not be invaluable, but CEO pay reflects that it is as close to invaluable as one can get." Do you agree?

It is widely believed that these large inequalities in income are mitigated by a 'progressive' tax system in the UK (that is, a system in which the more you earn, the higher the proportion you pay in tax). According to Power and Stacey (2014), nearly seven out of ten people in the UK hold this belief. In fact, however, the UK tax system overall is regressive: a household in the bottom 10 per cent pays 43 per cent of its income in tax, while the average household and a household in the top 10 per cent both pay 35 per cent – eight percentage points less. The misconception arises because many people imagine that income tax, which is progressive, is responsible for most of the tax burden. But actually income tax accounts for only just over a quarter of the tax take and many of the other taxes – such as VAT, excise duty and fuel duty – are regressive.

Wealth

The 20th century did see a gradual redistribution of wealth in the UK. In 1911, the most wealthy 1 per cent of the population held 69 per cent of all wealth yet, by 1993, this had dropped to 17 per cent. However, this redistribution did not extend down into the mass of society. Rather it was very narrow – the very wealthy top 1 per cent distributed some of its wealth to the wealthy top 10 per cent via trust funds in order to avoid paying taxes in the form of death duties. The result of this redistribution within the economic elite is that in 2003, the top 1 per cent and top 10 per cent owned 18 per cent and 50 per

cent of the nation's wealth respectively. This polarisation of wealth in the UK has also been encouraged by a soaring stock market (investments in stocks and shares) and property values, which, as Savage notes, "have allowed those who were already wealthy to accumulate their wealth massively". In contrast, half the population shared only 10 per cent of total wealth in 1986, and this had been reduced to 6 per cent by 2003.

Rising house prices are increasing the wealth of those with housing assets.

According to a report by the Centre for the Analysis of Social Exclusion (2013), the most authoritative current estimates were produced by the ONS's Wealth and Assets Survey between 2008 and 2010. These include personal possessions, net financial assets, housing assets (net of mortgages), and the value of people's non-state pension rights. The survey found that median household wealth in Great Britain stood at about £230,000, with the top 10 per cent having wealth of at least £967,000 and the bottom 10 per cent no more than £12,600 at most. The poorest 1 per cent of households had negative wealth (debts) of £3,600 or more.

Wealth is distributed much more unequally than income. The total wealth of the top tenth of households in 2008–2010 amounted to 850 times as much as the total owned by the bottom 10 per cent! Nevertheless, on an international basis, the unequal distribution of wealth in Britain is not particularly pronounced: compared to other OECD countries, the distribution is more equal than the OECD average.

EXPLAINING BRITAIN'S GROWING LEVEL OF ECONOMIC INEQUALITY

Kersley and Shaheen (2014) identify six main drivers of growing economic inequality in the UK:

> globalisation

> technology

> financialisation

> declining trades union membership and labour market liberalisation

> government redistribution policies

> political capture.

(For an extended treatment of these drivers, see Book 1, Topic 6, Chapter 1.)

We now turn to an examination of the issue of how far class continues to impact on life-chances by examining two crucial areas: health and education.

Class and health

> Life expectancy for all social classes has increased over the last 50 years. However, there is evidence, explored in some detail in Book 1, Topic 5, that there is a significant health gap between social classes in terms of mortality rates, life expectancy and the chance of developing chronic illness. It also suggests that, despite attempts by successive governments to challenge and narrow this gap, little progress has been made. The Acheson Report (1998) found that the health gap had actually widened since the Black Report in 1980 and the 2010 Marmot Report found the gap "had not narrowed" since 1998. Marmot found that people living in the poorest neighbourhoods in the UK die 7 years earlier, on average, than those living in the richest neighbourhoods and that the average difference in disability-free life expectancy between the two was 17 years.

> It is therefore still the case, as Bottero (2005) concluded, that "there is a strong socio-economic gradient to almost all patterns of disease and ill-health. The lower your socio-economic position, the greater your risk of low birth-weight, infections, cancer, coronary heart disease, respiratory disease, strokes, accidents, nervous and mental illnesses."

Class and education

Kynaston (2008) argues that most studies of meritocracy recognise that education is the prime engine of social mobility. However, he points out that meritocracy in the UK is undermined by the existence of private schools, which generally reproduce the privileges of the economic elite, generation by generation. Only about 7 per cent of all children are educated at private schools, but these pupils take up 45 per cent of Oxbridge places and a disproportionate number at other top UK universities. As ex-Labour leader Neil Kinnock once observed, private schools are the "very cement in the walls that divide British society".

Empirical evidence supports this view. For example, The Sutton Trust (2007) ranked the success of schools, over a five-year period, at getting their pupils into Oxbridge. Top was Westminster public school, which got 50 per cent of its students into Oxbridge and which charges annual boarding fees of £25,956 for the privilege. This means that the wealthy parents of Westminster pupils have a 50/50 chance of their child making it into Oxbridge. Altogether, there were 27 private schools among the top 30 schools with the best Oxbridge record; 43 in the top 50; and 78 in the top 100. The Sutton Trust concluded that the 70th brightest sixth-former at Westminster or Eton is as likely to get a place at Oxbridge as the very brightest sixth-formers at a large comprehensive school. Kynaston concludes that these figures suggest that private education is a "roadblock on the route to meritocracy". Other Sutton Trust studies show that those in high-status jobs are disproportionately recruited from private schools: 35 per cent of MPs, 35 per cent of High Court judges, 51 per cent of bank CEOs, 51 per cent of medics. Moreover, the 'old school tie' network ensures important and valuable social contacts for years to come, particularly in the finance sector of the economy. This is, almost certainly, still the most influential pathway to the 'glittering prizes' of top jobs and 'super-salaries'. This educational apartheid means that only the talents of the children of the wealthy elite are genuinely being unlocked.

Leaving aside the independent sector of education, middle-class parents can afford to buy into areas that have state schools with good league-table standings. Also, middle-class parents are able to use their knowledge, expertise, contacts and greater confidence in expressing themselves and in dealing with fellow professionals – their cultural capital – to ensure that their children are well served by the educational system. All of these factors undermine the view that the UK is a meritocracy. (See Book 1, Topic 1, Chapter 2 for an extended treatment of class and educational achievement.)

FOCUS ON SKILLS: SOCIAL CLASS IN AN 'INDIVIDUALISED' SOCIETY

Furlong et al. concluded that class still affects young people's social experiences.

Furlong *et al.* (2006) carried out research to test the claim that young people's experiences have become increasingly individualised in recent years and are no longer predictable on the basis of social class. The research aimed to identify the main routes that describe the transitions of young people from school into work. Using data from a longitudinal study carried out in the west of Scotland, the research studied the experiences of over 1,000 young people born in 1987, who were between the ages of 15 and 23. The research identified eight transitional routes:

1. *Long higher education* – university

2. *Short higher education* – shorter courses such as HND

3. *Enhanced education* – Highers (equivalent to A-levels), then employment

4. *Direct job* – leave school at 16 to go to work

5. *Assisted* – on government training schemes

6. *Extended periods of unemployment*

7. *Domestic* – time out of the labour market to have and/or care for children or family

8. *Other* – mainly made up of young people who were sick or disabled.

The researchers found that these transitional routes can largely be predicted on the basis of educational achievement, which, in turn, is predicted by social class. Some 58 per cent of those following the long higher education route had parents in the professional and managerial classes (Classes I and II), while only 17 per cent of children who had taken the assisted route did. 16 per cent of those who had taken the unemployed route and 14 per cent of those who had taken the domestic route were from these classes. In contrast, only 9 per cent of those who had taken the long higher education route were from semi-skilled and unskilled backgrounds (Classes V and VI), while 27 per cent of those who had taken the assisted route, 27 per cent of those who had taken the unemployed route and 24 per cent of those who had taken the domestic route were from these classes. Furlong *et al.* conclude that although the social experiences of young people may appear to be more fluid today, concepts such as social class still help sociologists to understand the distribution and persistence of socio-economic inequalities.

Questions

1. **Explain** why the word 'individualised' is in inverted commas in the title of the report of this research.

2. **Identify** the proportion of the sample who had taken the long route who were from Classes I and II, compared to the proportion who were from Classes V and VI.

3. **Evaluate** the degree to which the transitional routes followed by young people in Scotland still reflect the influence of class background.

CONCLUSIONS

The new egalitarians are undoubtedly correct in drawing our attention to the fact that a diversity of social groups, such as the long-term unemployed, single mothers and asylum-seekers, are socially excluded from mainstream society and so experience a range of social and economic deprivations. However, their reluctance to acknowledge the role of social class and its indicators (such as inequalities in income, wealth, housing, health and education) is problematic, given the weight of the evidence available. As Savage (2000) concludes: "In recent years, whatever people's perceptions of their class might be, there is no doubting that class inequality has hardened. People's destinies are as strongly affected and perhaps more strongly affected, by their class background than they were in the mid-20th century."

CHECK YOUR UNDERSTANDING

1. Identify two reasons why Giddens and Diamond believe class divisions have declined.

2. What groups are typically socially excluded, according to the new egalitarians?

3. What is the main difference between new egalitarians and new traditionalists?

4. What has happened to income inequality in the UK since 1980?

5. Why have income inequalities widened in the UK over the last 30 years?

6. What have been the main trends with regard to wealth redistribution in the UK since 1980?

7. Explain what is meant by the 'health gap'.

8. What has happened to the health gap between classes since 1980?

9. What percentage of children in England and Wales attend independent, fee-paying schools?

10. Identify two ways in which class inequalities undermine equal educational opportunities.

TAKE IT FURTHER

Residents of council housing estates are often on the receiving end of negative portrayals in the media. It is important that sociology students avoid adopting the negative stereotypes such portrayals promote and seek instead to gain an impartial and balanced picture of such communities.

One way of doing this is through conducting case studies of specific communities. A fascinating case study would be provided by the Easterhouse estate on the outskirts of Glasgow, typical of large peripheral council estates in Britain. It is of particular note for social scientists because a professor of social policy – Bob Holman – chose to give up his job in academia and go and live there. He helped set up a community organisation – Family Action in Rogerfield and Easterhouse (Fare) – which is still active. Use the internet to see what you can find out about life on this estate today. How far does it correspond with the claim made by Lynsey Hanley in her book *Estates* (2007) that estates such as Easterhouse represent 'class ghettos'?

5.4 DIMENSIONS OF INEQUALITY: LIFE-CHANCES AND GENDER

LEARNING OBJECTIVES

› Demonstrate knowledge and understanding of how gender inequalities have changed over the last 50 years (AO1).

› Demonstrate knowledge and understanding of gender difference in life-chances in relation to work, education and health (AO1).

› Demonstrate knowledge and understanding of sociological explanations of these differences (AO1).

› Apply knowledge and understanding of links between gender and life-chances (AO2).

› Evaluate the different sociological explanations of (changing) gender differences in life-chances (AO3).

INTRODUCING THE DEBATE

Ending female subordination has been high on the political agenda for a number of decades, not only in the UK but globally. In 1995 the United Nations reaffirmed its commitment to gender equality in what became known as the 'Beijing Declaration' and, surveying the progress made since then, declared in 2015 that "Over the last 20 years, the lives of women around the world have improved in many areas", while cautioning that "in many domains, women remain disadvantaged".

What of the UK? Does it make a difference to your life-chances any longer whether you are born male or female? An Ipsos/MORI survey across 15 developed countries in 2014 found over two-thirds (69 per cent) of adult female respondents in Great Britain agreeing with the statement "I have full equality with men and the freedom to reach my full dreams and aspirations" (14 per cent agreeing 'very much', 55 per cent agreeing 'somewhat') with 31 per cent disagreeing. But when both men and women were asked in the same survey whether they agreed that "there is currently an inequality between men and women in terms of social, political and/or economic rights in my country", a very similar response was obtained, with 70 per cent agreeing (20 per cent 'very much', 50 per cent 'somewhat') and 30 per cent disagreeing!

This chapter will try to help resolve this conundrum by examining what light sociology can shed on gender and life-chances in contemporary Britain in three important areas: work, health and education. We will begin with work.

GENDER AND WORK

The idea that women were not involved in paid employment before the 20th century is mistaken. Many single women were. However, most ceased paid employment on marriage. According to Grint and Nixon (2015), the biggest change in occupational activity in the 20th century was the increased rate of employment for married women and mothers. From a figure of fewer than 1 in 10 married women in employment at the start of the 20th century, the proportion had increased to 74 per cent by 2009. Moreover, by 2011, the employment rate of mothers had grown to a point where it matched the overall female employment rate of 67 per cent.

Consequently, today the UK labour force is very nearly equally split between men and women in numerical terms, with men making up 53 per cent of the labour force in 2013 and women 47 per cent. However, these figures mask significant differences in rates of full and part-time work, with a much smaller percentage of men than women in part-time employment. In 2012 there were 5.85 million women working part-time, but only 2.11 million men (Women's Business Council, 2012).

Only since 1970 has the law supported the idea that men and women doing the same work should be paid the same. The 1970 Equal Pay Act (EPA) was enacted by a Labour Government following a successful campaign in which women machinists working for Ford Motors in Dagenham protested about being paid at the same rate as unskilled male manual workers (celebrated in the 2010 film *Made in Dagenham* and the recent West End musical of the same name). The EPA was followed in 1975 by the Sex Discrimination Act and, a few years later, once it had become clear that some employers were attempting to circumvent the EPA by ensuring that men and women didn't work alongside each other, by the 1983 Equal Pay (Amendment) Regulations, requiring equal pay for work of equal value.

Do you think the state should place any limits on the kind of work men and women are allowed to do?

Commentators disagree about how much real difference this legislation made, but it had at least three important consequences. First, it largely put an end to the most blatant cases of unequal pay. Second, it began the process of breaking down occupational segregation (based on the ingrained idea that there were 'women's jobs' and 'men's jobs'). And finally, it had an important symbolic effect in providing state backing to the idea that gender discrimination was morally wrong.

Since the 1980s there has been a slow but steady narrowing of the gender pay gap. According to the ONS, the gap in median hourly earnings in the UK for those working full-time had narrowed to 9.4 per cent in 2014, compared to a gap of 17.4 per cent in 1997. However, because a much higher proportion of women than men work part-time – mainly due to childcare responsibilities – and part-time work is more often lower skilled and therefore lower paid, so the gender gap in median hourly earnings for all employees (both full-time and part-time) is higher at 19.1 per cent – though here too the gap has narrowed, from 27.5 per cent in 1997. In international terms, the gap of 19.1 per cent compares with an EU average of 16.4 per cent, placing the UK among the lower-performing EU countries.

In terms of unpaid work, while men have become significantly more involved in childcare in recent decades, primary responsibility usually remains with women. This is evidenced by the fact that 38 per cent of women with dependent children work part-time, compared to 7 per cent of men with dependent children (Resolution Foundation, 2012). Moreover, women – with or without children – who work spend 15 hours a week on average doing household chores, while men spend only five (Durrant, 2009) – the so-called 'dual burden' of paid work and housework shouldered by employed women.

Explaining the gender pay gap

Part of the explanation for the gender pay gap has to do with the continued existence of differences in both the kinds and level of work done by men and women. Catherine Hakim (1979) refers to these differences as "occupational segregation" and suggests that there are two types of occupational segregation:

> Horizontal segregation – men and women are concentrated in different types of jobs in different sectors of the economy.

> Vertical segregation – women occupy the lower levels of pay and status in particular jobs.

Horizontal segregation

Table 5.4.1 gives an insight into how occupations are gender segregated. In the public sector, women are mainly employed in health and social work, and in education, where they made up 79 per cent and 73 per cent of the workforce respectively in 2006. In the private sector, women are over-concentrated in clerical, administrative, retail and personal services, such as catering, whereas men are mainly found in the skilled manual and upper professional sectors (EOC 2006).

Occupation	Women (%)	Men (%)
Caring, leisure and other services	82	18
Administrative and secretarial	77	23
Sales and customer service	63	37
Professional	50	50
Elementary	46	54
Associate professional and technical	43	57
Managers and senior officials	33	67
Process, plant and machine operatives	11	89
Skilled trades	10	90

Table 5.4.1 *The percentage of workers in each occupation group that are women, April to June 2013, UK*

Source: Labour Force Survey, ONS (2013)

There is some evidence that horizontal segregation may be in decline because there has been a decline in work traditionally done by men, such as that found in the primary sectors (for example, engineering, coal-mining) and secondary sectors (for example, car manufacturing) of the economy. Also, increasing female educational success, especially in higher education, has resulted in more women entering areas of work previously dominated by men, such as the medical, legal and financial sectors of the economy. For example, in 2005, according to the Women and Work Commission, 75 per cent of pharmacists, nearly 40 per cent of accountants and about 50 per cent of solicitors were women. Similarly, more men have been entering areas of work previously dominated by women, such as primary teaching, nursing, airline stewarding and even midwifery.

Vertical segregation
The evidence suggests that, within occupational groups, women tend to be concentrated at the lower levels. When women do gain access to the upper professional or management sector, the evidence suggests that they encounter a **glass ceiling** – a situation in which promotion appears to be possible, but restrictions or discrimination create barriers that prevent it.

UNDERSTAND THE CONCEPT

The **glass ceiling** refers to an alleged invisible barrier that prevents women from reaching the top positions in both the public and private sectors, or at least makes it much harder for them to do so.

In 2012, research by the BBC found that fewer than a third of the most senior positions across 11 key sectors of the economy were held by women. For example, women made up only 16 per cent of directors of the top 100 British companies, 13 per cent of high–court judges, 12 per cent of university vice-chancellors and 17 per cent of the top ranks in the police.

SOCIOLOGICAL EXPLANATIONS OF GENDER STRATIFICATION IN EMPLOYMENT

Functionalism and human capital theory
The functionalist position is particularly associated with the work of Talcott Parsons in the mid-20th century (see Chapter 5.1). Parsons felt that separate gender roles for men and women were helpful to societies. He claimed that women were more suited by nature to what he called "expressive roles" – those emphasising caring and emotions – while men were the ideal candidates for "instrumental roles" – those that required qualities of competition, aggression and achievement. The implications of Parsons's view are that women will be more suited to domesticity and less suited to the labour market, than men. Therefore, he argued, it is not surprising that they are, on average, paid less.

Some economists have gone on to suggest that the pay gap between men and women is justified because it reflects the fact that men have more **human capital** than women because of their greater orientation to paid work. It is suggested that women are less committed to paid work and are more likely to take career breaks or to opt for part-time work in order to continue to care for

UNDERSTAND THE CONCEPT

Human capital is the stock of knowledge, skills and personal attributes, possessed by individuals or groups, that can be used to create economic value. It reflects such things as education, training, experience, judgement and creativity.

their families. Men, however, will be able to build up their skills, qualifications and experience because they are in receipt of more education and on-the-job training and their employment is not interrupted by family commitments.

Evaluation of functionalism and human capital theory

Parsons's theory was based on the idea that men and women were suited to different roles by nature. This view is now seen as questionable, at the very least, although the nature/nurture debate as it applies to gender roles is far from resolved. Nevertheless, the fact that there has been a turn-around in the educational performance of boys and girls over the last 50 years points strongly towards the role of nurture.

Human capital theory has been criticised by Olsen and Walby (2004). They used data from the longitudinal British Household Panel Survey to investigate the causes of pay differences between men and women. They accept that pay differentials partly reflect the fact that women tend to experience less full-time employment than men and take more career breaks, but they argue that the main cause of women's low pay is "systematic disadvantage in acquiring human capital". For example, pay is lower in occupations where there are high concentrations of women. This could well be because these jobs provide fewer training and promotion prospects than those jobs in which men are in the majority. Furthermore, human capital theory assumes that experience of employment increases wages, yet experience of part-time work (which is mainly taken up by women) is actually associated with a slight reduction in wages.

Dual labour-market theory

Many sociologists have looked for explanations for gender stratification within the structure of the labour market as a whole. Barron and Norris (1976), writing from a Weberian perspective, argue that there is a dual labour-market: the labour market is divided into two sectors:

1. a primary sector consisting of secure, well-paid jobs with good prospects

2. a secondary sector characterised by poor pay, insecurity and no ladder of promotion.

It is very difficult to move from the secondary to the primary sector. Barron and Norris argue that women are more likely to be found in the disadvantaged secondary sector for three reasons.

Women's 'unsuitability'

There is some evidence that employers may hold stereotypical beliefs about the 'unsuitability' of women for primary-sector roles. Studies by West and Zimmerman (1991) and Hartnett (1990) both noted that employers in the 1980s subscribed to myths and negative stereotypes about women workers such as:

> Male workers do not like working for a female manager – employers are therefore reluctant to promote females to management positions.

> Women are less dependable because they often take time off work to deal with family commitments.

> Women will stop work when they marry and have children, so there is little point investing in their long-term training.

> Children are psychologically damaged by their mothers spending long periods of time at work rather than spending quality time with them. In order to protect children, women should not be given management jobs because these involve long and unsociable hours.

Disrupted career development

Jobs with good promotion prospects often recruit people at a young age and require several years of continuous service. It is difficult in most jobs to take long periods of time out of work and return to a similar position. However, social pressure to have a family often leads to women taking extensive time out of employment. Consequently, they lack experience, compared with men, and often miss out on promotion when they do return to the workplace. Abbott and Wallace (1997) argue that women's continuous employment is also undermined by the fact that the husband's career and pay is often regarded as more important. Therefore, if his job requires a move to another part of the country, the wife is often forced to interrupt her career and give up her job.

Weak legal and political framework supporting women

Barron and Norris claimed that both the Equal Pay and Sex Discrimination Acts were ineffective because they failed to protect women's employment rights. Coussins (1976) described the Sex Discrimination Act as "feeble", because it did not apply to many areas of employment. Furthermore, she doubted the commitment of governments to eliminating gender inequality. She noted that the government had done little to promote free or cheap nursery care and encourage employers to provide crèche facilities for their workers who are mothers. However, recent changes in the legal position of part-time workers have benefited women considerably and some attempt has been made to recognise that men, too, have some responsibility for child-rearing, with the introduction of recent legislation to allow paid leave for either partner. Since 2015, couples living in Great Britain have been able to take Shared Parental Leave of up to 50 weeks, with up to 37 weeks statutory maternity/paternity pay between them.

Evaluation of dual labour-market theory

The theory was put forward nearly 40 years ago so it would be surprising if social change hadn't affected its plausibility. For example, one would expect that stereotypical assumptions about women's 'unsuitability' for paid work would have largely disappeared. Yet the Fawcett Society (2015) claims that "stereotypes around men and women's roles and value in the workplace still exist". Moreover, some of the changes that have taken place have actually increased the plausibility of the concept of a dual labour-market. Lansley (2011) argues that, over the last 30 years, there has been an increasing polarisation of the jobs market with "a rise in the number of well-paid professional and managerial jobs, a decline in the number of middle-paid and skilled jobs, and a rise in the number of routine low-paid service jobs … offer[ing] poor conditions of work, minimal rights and little security"– jobs in which women are over-represented. Moreover, Walby (2011) argues that the effects of the 2007/8 financial crisis have affected women more severely than men. For example, women's jobs were hit particularly hard by reductions in public expenditure, since women make up the majority of public-sector employees.

However, the theory has been weakened by the gradual but nevertheless significant decline in gender segregation in the UK labour market. According to the European Commission (2009), while the UK is in the middle range of EU countries for its degree of occupational segregation by gender, it was one of six countries experiencing relatively fast desegregation between 1997 and 2007 – although it is unclear whether this trend has continued since the financial crash. In addition, Bradley (1996) points out that the theory fails to explain vertical segregation (gender inequalities in the same sector). For example, teaching is not a secondary labour-market occupation, yet women are less likely than men to gain head-teacher posts.

Gender segregation in the UK labour market is falling, meaning you are now more likely to see a female scientist or a male primary school teacher.

Feminist theories

Chapter 1 described feminist theories of gender stratification in general. Here, we will simply highlight two concepts from these theories that are potentially relevant to explaining the gender pay gap.

Gender-role socialisation

Liberal feminists argue that traditional forms of gender-role socialisation found in the family, but also in education and the mass media, are responsible for reproducing a sexual division of labour in which masculinity is largely seen as dominant and femininity as subordinate and which therefore reinforces both horizontal and vertical segregation in employment.

However, in the 1990s, some liberal feminists suggested that these processes were coming to an end. Sue Sharpe's work on the attitudes of teenage girls (1994) suggests that education and careers are now a priority for young women. Females have also enjoyed greater educational success than males in recent years.

The reserve army of labour

For Marxists, capitalism, because of its internal contradictions, is doomed to alternate between booms and slumps (the so-called business cycle). It therefore needs a pool of workers – in Marxist terms, a reserve army of labour – that can be drawn upon in booms and cast off during slumps. Marxist feminists see women as part of this reserve army of labour, which is hired by firms in times of economic expansion and fired when recession sets in.

Marxist feminists argue that women are more vulnerable to trends such as economic recession, downsizing and mergers, and therefore constitute a more disposable part of the workforce for a number of reasons:

> They change jobs more frequently than men because of pregnancy and childcare, or because their job is secondary to that of their partner – they may be forced to change jobs if their partner is relocated to another part of the country.

> They are generally less skilled (though in the 21st century, this is not necessarily the case.), more likely to work part-time, and less likely to be members of trade unions. As a result, it is easier for employers to sack them.

> Patriarchal ideologies mainly locate women in the home, as 'natural' carers and home-makers.

However, the reserve army of labour theory fails to explain why women ended up with responsibility for domestic labour, especially considering that historical evidence suggests that in the pre-industrial period, this was the responsibility of children and older adults of both sexes rather than exclusively female.

Moreover, the ideological underpinning of the theory appears to have been fatally undermined. An international survey by Reuters/Ipsos in 2010 found that over three-quarters (78 per cent) of respondents in Great Britain disagreed with the statement 'a woman's place is in the home'. Indeed, it's hard to imagine a politician standing up in the House of Commons today and suggesting that the unemployment problem could be solved if only women would revert to their traditional role of housewives. In the 21st century, women would appear to be too well integrated into the labour market at nearly all levels to act as a reserve army of labour. This is not to say, however, that public attitudes towards women working make no distinction between the situation of women with and women without young children, or between full-time and part-time working in the case of the former [see findings of Scott (2008) below].

Preference theory

Catherine Hakim (2000) has examined data about gender and work from across the world. She argues that reliable contraception, equal-opportunities legislation, the expansion of white-collar and part-time jobs, and the increase in lifestyle choices give women in modern societies more choices than ever before. However, women do not respond to these choices in the same ways. She identifies three main types of work–lifestyle preferences that women may adopt:

> *Home-centred* – 20 per cent of women prefer not to be in employment because family life and children are their main priorities.

> *Adaptive* – The majority of women (about 60 per cent) want to combine family and paid work in some way.

> *Work-centred* – 20 per cent of women see careers or other involvement in public life as their priority. Women without children are concentrated in this category.

It follows from Hakim's theory that at least part of the explanation for gender differences in pay is the rational choices that women make in relation to paid employment, particularly in terms of whether to pursue part-time or full-time work.

Hakim's ideas seem to be supported by Scott, who found that support for gender equality appears to be declining across Britain because of concerns that women who play a full role in the workforce do so at the expense of family life (Scott *et al.* 2008). She found

that both women and men are becoming more likely to believe that both the mother and the family will suffer if a woman works full-time. In 1994, 51 per cent of women in Britain and 52 per cent of men said they believed family life would not suffer if a woman went to work. By 2002, those proportions had fallen to 46 per cent of women and 42 per cent of men. As Scott notes, "It is conceivable that opinions are shifting as the shine of the 'super-mum' syndrome wears off, and the idea of women juggling high-powered careers while also baking cookies and reading bedtime stories is increasingly seen to be unrealisable by ordinary mortals." However, Scott also found that there was a continuing decline in the proportion of women and men who think "it is the husband's job to earn income and the wife's to look after the children". In 1987, 72 per cent of British men and 63 per cent of British women agreed with this proposition but, by 2002, the proportion had fallen to 41 per cent of men and 31 per cent of women.

Evaluation of preference theory

Hakim's theory has provoked considerable opposition from feminists, perhaps because it has placed women's own agency (the ability to exercise choice) at the centre of its explanation for gender inequalities rather than seeing women as the victims of men's actions or of patriarchal structures. Feminists have argued, for instance, that part-time women workers are no less committed to their jobs than full-time women workers, that there are many factors besides 'personal preference' that shape women's attitude to paid employment and that the 'choices' women make are heavily constrained by the structure of employment opportunities (the availability of flexible working, for example, and women's earning power relative to men's), the availability and affordability of childcare, men's willingness to take on childcare responsibilities, and so on.

Feminist critics are certainly correct in pointing out that choices are never entirely 'free', being shaped and constrained by a wide range of cultural and structural influences. Nevertheless, to imply by this that women have no real choice about their employment is to err too far on the side of **social determinism**.

UNDERSTAND THE CONCEPT

Social determinism is the claim that social influences are so powerful that the behaviour of members of society is completely shaped by them and that people are left with no choice about how to behave. The opposite of determinism is *voluntarism*.

FOCUS ON SKILLS: WOMEN AND MANUAL TRADES

I started training as a painter and decorator with an east London council's large direct labour organisation (DLO) on 7 October 1985, alongside 41 other women. The DLO carried out all of the repairs and maintenance on the council's large domestic stock portfolio, including all cyclical and planned works as well as some new building.

During my years 'on the tools', I took down my share of inappropriate calendars and challenged the use of unacceptable language pointed at women. I recollect working on a large refurbishment site when all the female operatives were told that we could no longer use the site canteen because several male subcontractors were coming on site for second fixing and they took priority over women operatives.

I remember returning to a Portakabin on an external painting site to be met on the steps by Cecil, a kind, elderly, West Indian painter who told me not to go into the cabin as he feared that I would be as upset as he was about what was being said about me and the other women. We sat on the steps of the cabin and had our lunch together that day, and many other days after that.

So, like most women who work in the trades, I experienced some negatives. These were, however, far outweighed by the positives. I made many good friends among the men on the tools and, later, among operational managers, and some of these friendships have stood the test of time, some 30 years on. I was paid exactly the same sum and worked the same number of hours as my male counterparts, both during my training and afterwards as a fully qualified operative.

[Today] my perception is that basic equalities around pay and hours are routinely implemented. Dodgy calendars are pretty much consigned to the dustbins of the past.

However, in terms of the number of new female recruits into the manual trades, it seems that things are getting worse: fewer women are training and working in the manual trades in the 21st century than was the case when I joined the industry in the mid-1980s. Data from the Office for National Statistics confirms this. In 2012/13, there were 14,209 women identified as working in construction-related manual trades, out of a total workforce in the sector of nearly 1.2 million (so women accounted for 1.18 per cent).

Source: Nelson (2014)

Questions

1. **Identify** examples of sexual discrimination experienced by the author when working 'on the tools'.

2. **Suggest reasons** for the very low level of female employment in manual trades.

3. **Suggest reasons** for the decline in female representation in manual trades since the 1980s.

4. **Evaluate**. Does the very low number of women in manual trades mean that the notion of 'women's jobs' and 'men's jobs' is still a valid one?

GENDER AND EDUCATION

Education is widely recognised as playing a crucial role in terms of life-chances. For at least two decades, girls have been outperforming boys at every level of the education system in England and Wales. In 2013, for example, girls did better than boys at GCSE level in every subject other than Maths. For the same year at A-level, girls were more likely to get A* to C grades in every subject other than French. And in 2012 women were a third more likely to start a degree than their male counterparts and also more likely to gain a first or upper-second degree classification. At the same time there is, however, still a significant degree of gender segregation in subject choice, with more girls studying Humanities and more boys Science and Maths.

While the significance of these differences can be exaggerated – they are outweighed by class and ethnic differences, for example – they are nevertheless likely to affect future employment possibilities. (See Book 1, Topic 1, Chapter 4 for an extended consideration of gender and education.)

GENDER AND HEALTH

Life-chances in the literal sense of the term are directly related to health.

There is a significant gender gap in life expectancy. In the UK, a female born in 2014 can expect to live until she is 82.5 years old, while a male born in the same year can expect to reach the age of 79.5. About two-thirds of deaths that occur before the retirement age of 65 years are male. Consequently, 58 per cent of people who survive beyond the age of 65 are female.

The situation in relation to morbidity is less clear-cut. Indeed it is difficult to establish whether males or females experience more ill health once allowance is made for women's greater willingness to seek medical help when they are unwell and their greater life expectancy. Nevertheless, there are clear gender differences in the prevalence of particular illnesses or health-damaging behaviours. For example, women are more likely to experience depression and anxiety, eating disorders and dementia; men are more likely to engage in hazardous drinking, be diagnosed with antisocial personality disorder and commit suicide. (See Book 1, Topic 5, Chapter 3 for an extended consideration of gender and health.)

CONCLUSIONS

In many respects, the life-chances of women in the UK have been transformed over the last 50 years. The second wave of feminist activism achieved tangible changes in women's lives. Sexism, while far from extinct, is widely condemned, females outperform males at every level of the education system and the gender balance in many professions is rapidly approaching parity.

Yet gender inequalities clearly remain. Neither horizontal nor vertical gender segregation in the labour market has disappeared. Women are still under-represented in positions of power – following the 2015 general election, for example, just 29 per cent of MPs were female. The problem of male violence against women still blights many women's lives (this was highlighted at the premiere of the movie *Suffragette* in 2015, where Sisters Uncut demonstrated against government cuts to services supporting the victims of domestic violence). Moreover, evidence suggests that unconscious sexist bias in recruitment practices still disadvantages women. When orchestras in the USA began using 'blind' auditions, where the recruiters didn't know the gender of the musicians, the likelihood of female musicians being selected increased by 50 per cent. How gender relations progress in the future will be largely down to those of you reading these words now.

CHECK YOUR UNDERSTANDING

1. According to Grint and Nixon, what was the biggest change in female employment patterns in the 20th century?

2. What is the main reason for women's higher part-time employment rate?

3. Using your own words, explain the difference between 'horizontal segregation' and 'vertical segregation'.

4. How can dual labour-market theory be used to explain the gender pay gap?

5. How does human capital theory justify the gender pay gap? How can it be criticised?

6. Identify two criticisms of the theory that women form a reserve army of labour.

7. Identify the three different sets of work/lifestyle 'preferences' that Hakim claims women display today.

8. Identify two criticisms made by feminists of Hakim's theory.

9. Do males or females obtain more first and upper-second degrees?

10. Why is it difficult to establish whether men or women experience more ill health?

TAKE IT FURTHER

First, conduct a detailed study of the gender breakdown of the authority structure of the school/college where you are studying (the number of men and women at each level of the organisational hierarchy).

Then, conduct informal interviews with your teachers. In the first part of the interview, ask them whether they think that men and women compete on an equal footing when pursuing careers in teaching/lecturing. In the second part, present them with your findings and ask them whether they think the authority structure in your/their school/college supports or undermines their views. (Bear in mind that this is potentially a sensitive topic and that it may well raise questions of confidentiality which will need to be addressed.) Write up your findings, making sure you anonymise interviewees.

5.5 DIMENSIONS OF INEQUALITY: RACE AND ETHNICITY

LEARNING OBJECTIVES

> Demonstrate knowledge and understanding of race and ethnicity as social constructs (AO1).

> Demonstrate knowledge and understanding of how Britain has become increasingly ethnically diverse in recent decades (AO1).

> Apply knowledge and understanding of the links between ethnicity and life-chances (AO2).

> Analyse the position of BAME groups in the UK and the impact of this on their life-chances (AO3).

> Understand and evaluate sociological explanations of ethnic stratification (AO1 and AO3).

INTRODUCING THE DEBATE

At the start of Chapter 4 we asked the question "Does it make any difference to your life-chances in the UK if you are born male or female?" This chapter will explore the same question in relation to race and ethnicity.

If racial and ethnic equality were merely a matter of legal protection against discrimination, equality should by now be firmly established. The first Race Relations Act was passed 50 years ago in 1965. The Act outlawed discrimination on the "grounds of colour, race, or ethnic or national origins" in public places. The scope of the Act was extended by further legislation in 1968 and 1976, extended again in 2000 and 2003 and consolidated in the Equality Act of 2010. Moreover,

according to the British Academy (2015), "Britain is arguably the EU member state [that has made] the greatest strides towards racial equality in many professions – from the police to politics."

On the other hand, as the British Academy goes on to point out, Black men are 28 times more likely to be stopped and searched as White men, unemployment rates are much higher for Black Britons than for their White peers, and it took 19 years for two suspects to be found guilty in 2012 of the murder of the young Black Londoner Stephen Lawrence in 1993.

However, before we can explore this topic in more detail, we need to clarify what we are talking about.

THE MEANING OF RACE AND ETHNICITY

Both race and ethnicity are social constructs. Normally, to refer to something as a social construct is not to imply that it is 'imaginary' or 'doesn't really exist', only that the thing being talked about could be understood or perceived differently at a different time or in a different society. However, in respect of race, it turns out that races don't really exist!

In the 19th century Europeans believed that human beings could be divided into three racial categories (negroid, caucasoid and mongoloid) and that Black people belonged to the least evolved category. This provided a convenient but pseudo-scientific rationale for both slavery and colonialism. However, most scientists and sociologists accept that in the 20th century the science of genetics has clearly shown that all human beings have evolved from a single set of African ancestors and **race** as a scientific concept is "well past its sell-by date" (Steven and Hilary Rose, 2005) although stereotypical beliefs about racial differences continue to underpin political debate as well as the prejudice and discrimination practised against ethnic minorities in the UK.

UNDERSTAND THE CONCEPT

Race can be defined as a social category of people who are mistakenly regarded as biologically distinct because they are believed to share certain visible physical characteristics.

Today, the term 'ethnicity' has largely replaced that of race. Ethnic groups are groups defined by 'race', religion and/or national origin who share a common cultural heritage, so the focus is more on culture than biology. Yet ethnicity is still a social construct in that the categorisations involved can and do vary over time and cross-culturally. The preferred term to refer to ethnic-minority groups in Britain is Black and Minority Ethnic (BME) groups, or more recently Black, Asian and Minority Ethnic (BAME) groups.

Misunderstandings and misconceptions

In everyday life, the topics of race and ethnicity are replete with misunderstandings. For example:

1. It is important to understand that everybody has an ethnic identity, so talking about 'ethnic' fashions, say, is meaningless. The ethnic majority in the UK is officially identified as 'White'.

2. Most ethnic-minority people living in the UK are not immigrants – they were born here.

3. The term 'ethnic minority' suggests a homogeneity and shared sense of identity that may not actually exist. For example, there is no such thing as an all-encompassing Asian culture. People of Asian origin have come to the UK from different countries (among them India, Pakistan, Bangladesh, Hong Kong and Japan) so they have different religious beliefs (Hinduism, Sikhism, Islam, Buddhism, Christianity) and cultural practices and speak a variety of languages.

4. Political debate about race and ethnicity often uses language which is far from neutral. Think about the implications of words and phrases such as 'hordes' and 'swarms' to refer to refugees seeking asylum in Britain, for example.

'Migrants' are people who have left one country (emigrants) and gone to live in another (immigrants). Why do you think that British people who have emigrated to Spain to live there in retirement are almost always referred to in the British media, not as migrants, but as 'ex-pats'?

Britain as a multi-ethnic society

Britain has been an ethnically diverse society for a very long time. Many centuries ago, invasions by Romans, Saxons, Vikings and Normans brought increasing diversity. People have been immigrating to – and emigrating from – Britain ever since, so it is important to have some historical perspective when politicians today express concerns about the impact of migration on Britain's way of life.

Nevertheless, it is the case that Britain has become significantly more ethnically diverse since the 1950s and, in the last couple of decades, the historical pattern of net outward migration (more people emigrating than immigrating) has been reversed. Indeed, since the 1990s, immigration has become the main engine of population growth. Of the 3.7 million increase in Britain's population between 2001 and 2011, 2.1 million is attributable to immigration (Jivraj, 2012, cited in Pilkington, 2015).

As Pilkington explains, there have been two main phases of immigration since World War II. The first phase, from the late 1940s to the early 1970s, involved the primary migration of people from Britain's former colonies in the Caribbean and the Indian subcontinent particularly, to meet Britain's post-war labour shortage. Many came planning to return to their native countries once they had accumulated some assets, and some did, but many settled permanently. The second phase dates from the 1980s and involved three main categories of immigrants: the secondary migration of dependants of those who had come in the first phase, asylum seekers and – with the expansion of the European Union – significant numbers from other European countries. Together, these two phases have produced a situation where the

proportion of the population categorised as 'White' in England and Wales has declined from 94 per cent at the time of the 1991 census to 86 per cent in 2011, the date of the most recent census.

The ethnic composition of England and Wales in percentage terms, according to the 2011 census, is shown in Figure 5.5.1. The fact that ethnicity is not simply a given is evidenced by the fact that in 1991, when the census first included a question about ethnicity, respondents were offered a choice of nine categories to choose from, but by 2011 the choice had expanded to eighteen (the four White categories offered have been collapsed into one in Figure 5.5.1).

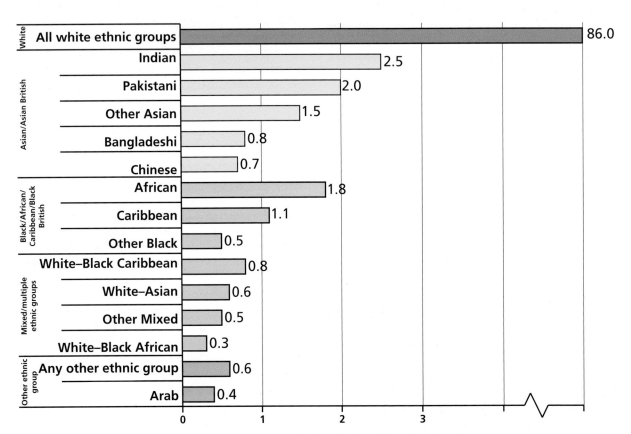

Figure 5.5.1 *Ethnic group of usually resident population England and Wales, 2011; all usual residents*

Source: 2011 Census, Office for National Statistics (2012)

ETHNICITY AND LIFE-CHANCES: THE EVIDENCE

We are now in a position to return to the question at the start of the chapter and examine the evidence concerning the impact of ethnicity on life-chances. Does it make any difference today what your ethnic identity is?

Employment and unemployment

Although the pattern is mixed, the overall picture is one of ethnic-minority disadvantage in the labour market, with ethnic-minority employees concentrated in low-paying occupations (for example, sales, catering, elementary personal services, hairdressing, textiles and clothing) and more likely than White employees to receive less than the living wage. On the other hand, more than a quarter of Indian and Chinese men are employed in professional occupations, a significantly higher proportion than White men, and the wage gap between White and ethnic-minority employees within occupations was limited (Brynin and Longhi, 2015). Nevertheless, research by The Joseph Rowntree Foundation (Clark and Drinkwater 2007) found that men from ethnic minorities in managerial and professional jobs earn up to 25 per cent less than their White colleagues. Black African and Bangladeshi men were most likely to face the greatest pay discrimination. Indian men were the least likely to be discriminated against, but they were still earning less than White men doing the same job. Pay differentials were smaller for women than for men.

In relation to unemployment, the picture is one of consistent ethnic-minority disadvantage. For instance, the unemployment rate for all people aged 16+ in the UK between October, 2013 and September 2014 was 6 per cent, but for Black groups it was 15 per cent, Asian 10 per cent and other ethnic-minority backgrounds 11 per cent. The picture in relation to youth unemployment (16–24 years) is even more pronounced, with an unemployment rate for White youngsters of 16 per cent compared to 32 per cent for Black youths, 25 per cent for Asians and 28 per cent for all other ethnic-minority backgrounds (Dar and Mirza-Davies, 2015).

Poverty and deprivation

According to the Joseph Rowntree Foundation (JRF, in Platt, 2007), there are stark differences in poverty rates according to ethnicity. Risks of poverty are highest for Bangladeshis, Pakistanis and Black Africans, but are also above average for Caribbean, Indian and Chinese groups. Over half of Pakistani, Bangladeshi and Black African children were growing up in poverty. Overall, 40 per cent of ethnic-minority communities live in poverty – double the poverty rate of the White British communities – and are most likely to live in London, parts of the north and the Midlands than elsewhere in the UK. Half of all ethnic-minority children in the UK live in poverty.

More recent research by the JRF also found that all ethnic-minority groups were more likely than the White majority to live in deprived neighbourhoods in England and that this was true in both 2001 and 2011. Based on the Index of Multiple Deprivation (which combines scores on seven aspects of deprivation – income, employment, health, education, barriers to housing and services, crime and living environments –

to produce a single score for an area of about 1500 people), more than 1 in 3 Pakistani and Bangladeshi households lived in deprived neighbourhoods in both 2001 and 2011.

Education

Research by the Runnymede Trust (2012) found that levels of academic attainment have improved significantly for some ethnic minorities, relative to the ethnic majority, over the last couple of decades in England and Wales. For example, in 2011, Chinese (79 per cent), Indian (74 per cent) and Bangladeshi (60 per cent) pupils outperformed their White British (58 per cent) peers in obtaining five or more GCSEs at grades A* to C, with Black African pupils matching the White British percentage. However, Pakistani (53 per cent) and African Caribbean (49 per cent) children were still performing below White pupils at GCSE (though these figures conceal a significant difference in performance between male and female African Caribbean pupils, with girls scoring 12.5 per cent higher than boys). (See Book 1, Topic 1, Chapter 3 for an extended examination of ethnicity and educational achievement.)

Health

According to the Parliamentary Office of Science and Technology (2007), BAME groups generally have worse health than the ethnic majority although the picture is far from uniform and patterns vary from one health condition to another. For example, surveys commonly show that Pakistani, Bangladeshi and African Caribbean people report the poorest health, with Indian, East African Asian and Black African people reporting the same health as White British, and Chinese people reporting better health. (See Book 1, Topic 5, Chapter 2 for further information on ethnicity and health.)

HATE CRIME

In 1998, the Crime and Disorder Act (CDA) criminalised race-based **hate crimes** by creating new laws focused on 'racially aggravated offences'. In 2011–12, over 80 per cent of hate crimes recorded by the police were racially motivated. The overwhelming majority of victims were members of BAME groups. Moreover, criminologists using victim surveys estimate that this type of crime is significantly under-reported. For more on race-based hate crime, see Topic 1, Chapter 6.

Hate crime is defined by the Home Office as "any criminal offence that is perceived by the victim or any other person to be motivated by hostility or prejudice based on a personal characteristic". In England and Wales there are five categories of hate crime where enhanced sentences can be imposed by the courts: race, religion, sexual orientation, disability and gender identity.

EXPLAINING ETHNIC–MINORITY DISADVANTAGE

The evidence presented above indicates that, while the picture is far from uniformly negative and there are areas of society where ethnic-minority groups enjoy considerable success, overall the life-chances of BAME groups in Britain are worse than those of the ethnic majority. How can we explain this?

Sociologists have developed a number of competing theories to account for ethnic stratification. However, before examining these it will be helpful to outline some of the key concepts that sociologists employ in their theories.

Racism
Racism refers to a set of beliefs – an ideology – based on the flawed notion of race examined earlier, that serves to justify discriminatory treatment of people on the basis of their supposed membership of a 'racial' group. The term is usually employed to refer to both such beliefs and the social practices that derive from them.

Modood (1992) has sought to extend the meaning of racism by introducing the concept of 'cultural racism'. He argues that "colour, class and culture are the three distinct dimensions of race" and that "the more distant an individual or group is from a White, upper-middle class, British, Christian/agnostic norm, the greater the marginality or exclusion". Modood has focused particularly in his writing on the demonisation of Asian minorities who are Muslims (principally from Pakistan and Bangladesh) and the cultural racism they have experienced in Britain. He urges that the state should promote **multiculturalism** and that a more inclusive concept of 'Britishness' should be developed which would embrace cultural and religious diversity as part of an expanded idea of what it means to be British.

Multiculturalism is the belief that the best way to promote social integration in an ethnically diverse society is for the state to provide some level of public recognition and support for ethnic minorities to maintain and express their distinct identities and practices, rather than expect them to abandon these and assimilate into the culture of the ethnic majority.

Racial prejudice
Racial prejudice refers to attitudes, usually of a negative kind, held about people seen as racially different. Prejudice involves pre-judging someone, usually on the basis of stereotyped ideas about the social group to which they are assumed to belong.

The British Social Attitudes Survey has asked a representative sample of British people a question about prejudice annually since 1983. The question is: "Would you describe yourself as very prejudiced/a little prejudiced against people of other races?" The percentage describing themselves as either 'very' or 'a little' prejudiced declined from a high point of 38 per cent in 1987 to a low of 25 per cent in 2001, but since then the trend has been upwards, hitting 38 per cent again in 2011, dropping to 26 per cent in 2012 and then rising again to 30 per cent in 2013.

Racist stereotyping probably originates in a number of diverse cultural sources:

Britain's colonial past
Britain's imperial power, exercised during the 19th and 20th centuries, clearly saw Black and Asian people as subordinate to and heavily dependent upon White people. The teaching of Britain's imperial history in schools may reinforce stereotypes of ethnic minorities picked up during family socialisation and in the media.

Language
Language often contains implicit cultural messages. For example, some socio-linguists have noted that words associated with Black people – e.g. 'things are looking black', 'accident black spot', 'black sheep of the family' – are negative. Black is also symbolic of evil and wrong-doing. Whiteness, on the other hand, is associated with innocence, purity, goodness, and so on. The use of this type of language may therefore reinforce racist stereotypes passed down through socialisation.

The mass media

Rothon and Heath (2003) argue that the rise in prejudice since 2001 has been fuelled by hostile newspaper coverage of immigration and asylum seekers. They argue that mass media representations of ethnic minorities are symbolic of a new type of prejudice that is the product of New Right politicians and journalists. This type of prejudice highlights 'cultural difference' and suggests that traditional White British/English culture is under threat from ethnic-minority culture because ethnic minorities are allegedly not committed to integration with their White neighbours.

In what ways are ethnic minorities presented as a problem or threat by sections of the media?'

Ethnocentrism

Much of what is called 'racism' in the media would more correctly be labelled as 'ethnocentrism'. Ethnocentrism refers to the tendency, present in all cultures, to view the world from the standpoint of one's own culture and to take for granted its superiority to others. Cultural differences are then interpreted as moral deficits. So, for example, the French don't drive on the other side of the road, but the wrong side of the road!

Racial discrimination

If prejudice is to do with attitudes, discrimination is to do with behaviour. Racial discrimination involves treating someone less favourably because of their assumed racial identity and, as we saw at the start of the chapter, is illegal in the UK. The law covers both direct and indirect racial discrimination. Direct discrimination involves treating someone less favourably because of who they are (or are assumed to be). Indirect discrimination occurs when an organisation's practices, policies or procedures have the effect of disadvantaging people who share certain protected characteristics, such as race or ethnicity, whether or not the effect is intended.

In 2004, a BBC survey showed ethnic-minority applicants still face major discrimination in the job market. CVs from six fictitious candidates – who were given traditionally White, Black African or Muslim names – were sent to 50 well-known firms covering a representative sample of jobs. All the applicants were given the same standard of qualifications and experience, but their CVs were presented differently. White 'candidates' were far more likely to be offered an interview than similarly qualified Black or Asian 'names'. Almost a quarter of applications by two candidates given traditionally 'White' names – Jenny Hughes and John Andrews – resulted in interview offers. But only 9 per cent of the 'Muslim' applications, by the fictitious Fatima Khan and Nasser Hanif, prompted a similar response. Letters from the 'Black' candidates, Abu Olasemi and Yinka Olatunde, had a 13 per cent success rate.

Four years later, the National Centre for Social Research was commissioned by the DWP to replicate this research. The researchers found that it took an average of nine applications for a positive response if the applicant appeared to be White, but 16 if they appeared to be African or Asian.

Institutional racism

Lord Macpherson's 1998 report into the murder of the Black teenager Stephen Lawrence by White youths in 1993 concluded that the London Metropolitan Police were guilty of 'institutional racism', which was defined as "unwitting prejudice, ignorance, thoughtlessness and racial stereotyping which disadvantaged minority-ethnic groups". For example, when the police arrived at the scene, they initially failed to understand that Stephen had been murdered because he was Black and they also assumed that all Black people near the site of the killing (including Stephen's best friend, who had witnessed the attack) were suspects rather than witnesses. The Macpherson report denounced the Metropolitan Police as fundamentally racist for its handling of the investigation into Stephen's death.

It is important to understand that institutional racism is neither conscious nor intentional. Not all members of key institutions are necessarily racist – they may or may not be. However, it is the manner in which some institutions operate that has racist outcomes. Teachers, for example, may be committed to antiracist education, but schools still expel four times as many Black pupils as White.

FOCUS ON SKILLS: SOCIAL INTEGRATION

The article below appeared in The Telegraph newspaper. It is based on a report by the Social Integration Commission (2014) entitled 'Social Integration: A Wake-up Call'. The research it refers to involved an on-line survey carried out by Ipsos/MORI of a nationally representative sample in January, 2014.

Decades of efforts to promote multiculturalism have gone into reverse, major new research showing teenagers are no more likely to mix with people from other racial backgrounds than those 40 years older suggests.

The study, which analyses the social lives of almost 4,300 people from 13 to 80, shows that a clear trend towards each successive generation becoming more integrated than the one before breaks down when it comes to under-18s.

Despite growing up in a more diverse society than ever before at a time when mass migration has transformed the make-up of Britain, today's teenagers have almost 30 per cent fewer friends from other ethnic backgrounds than people in their 20s and early 30s.

Overall the analysis found that the current generation of teenagers show similar levels of social segregation as middle aged people.

The surprise finding emerges from the first phase of research by the Social Integration Commission, a study backed by charities and business to examine the impact of increasing diversity in Britain.

Source: Bingham, J. 'Multiculturalism in reverse as teenagers buck the trend towards integration', *The Telegraph*, 29 June 2014

Questions

1. **Explain** what is meant by multiculturalism.

2. **Suggest reasons** why one might expect successive generations to be more ethnically integrated.

3. **Suggest reasons** why this trend appears to have been reversed among 13 to 17 year olds.

4. **Evaluate** the implications of this finding for racial and ethnic integration.

SOCIOLOGICAL THEORIES OF ETHNIC–MINORITY DISADVANTAGE

The host–immigrant model or assimilation theory

A sociological approach, stressing the importance of culture, was Patterson's (1965) theory – the host–immigrant model – which shares many of the assumptions of functionalist sociology. Patterson depicted Britain as a basically stable, homogeneous and orderly society with a high degree of consensus over values and norms. However, she claims that this equilibrium was disturbed by the arrival of immigrant "strangers" in the 1950s who subscribed to different cultural values. Patterson argues that this resulted in a culture clash between West Indians (who were regarded as boisterous and noisy) and their English "hosts" (who valued privacy, quiet and "keeping oneself to oneself"). Patterson argued that these clashes reflected understandable fears and anxieties on the part of the host community. She claimed that the English were not actually racist – rather they were unsure about how to act towards the newcomers.

She therefore suggested that there were three main causes of racial prejudice, discrimination and racial inequality:

> xenophobia and ethnocentrism: fear on the part of the host culture (White people) of strangers, cultural difference and social change

> resentment in the host culture, particularly the working class, at having to compete with ethnic minorities for scarce resources such as jobs and housing

> the failure of ethnic minorities to assimilate, that is, to become totally British and integrate –tending instead to live in segregated communities rather than mixing socially.

Patterson's theory is implicitly critical of the insistence of ethnic minorities that they should retain their own cultural values and practices because these allegedly make White people anxious. However, she was reasonably optimistic about the future of race relations in the UK and argued that ethnic minorities would eventually move towards full cultural assimilation by shedding their 'old' ethnic values and taking on English or British values.

Evaluation of the host–immigrant model

Patterson's view of culture sees it as static and fixed. British culture has in fact changed significantly since the 1950s, not least because it has absorbed elements of BAME cultures – chicken tikka masala is now apparently Britain's favourite dish, for example.

The assumption that progress towards racial harmony requires assimilation not only ignores other possible forms of co-existence but is also unrealistic. Racial integration can take different forms, including a pluralistic form in which ethnic groups live in harmony while respecting each other's cultural differences. 'Multiculturalism' has in fact been the preferred model in Britain over recent decades, even if it has recently come under sustained criticism (Pilkington, 2015). Also, expecting ethnic minorities to abandon their cultural heritage in the short to medium term is unrealistic: few of the British who retire to Spain learn Spanish, convert to Catholicism or embrace bull-fighting!

Patterson's focus on cultural differences as the barrier to integration underplays the significance of racism as an independent variable. African Caribbeans are arguably the most assimilated of all ethnic-minority groups – most speak English as a first language at home, they intermarry into the White population, their children mix freely and

easily with White children and they are usually Christian. However, they continue to be economically, socially and educationally disadvantaged.

Neo-Weberian theories

The work of Max Weber (1864–1920) has had a significant influence on explanations for racial discrimination and inequality. He noted that modern societies are characterised by class divisions in terms of income and wealth – but also by status inequality. Status and power are in the hands of the majority ethnic group, thereby making it difficult for ethnic-minority groups to compete equally for jobs, housing, and so on. Ethnic-minority individuals who do manual jobs are technically part of the working class, but they do not share the same status as the White working class. This is because they are likely to face prejudice and discrimination from the White working class, who see them as in competition for the same scarce resources, in this case, jobs. Ethnic-minority groups therefore suffer from status inequality as well as class inequality. Even middle-class Asians doing professional jobs may experience status inequality in the form of prejudicial attitudes held by members of both the White middle and White working classes.

Organisation of the job market

Such prejudice and discrimination can be seen in the distribution of ethnic-minority workers in the labour force. The "'dual labour-market theory'" of Barron and Norris (1976) focuses on ethnic inequalities as well as gender inequalities in employment. They suggest that there are two labour markets:

> the primary labour sector – characterised by secure, well-paid jobs, with long-term promotion prospects and dominated by White men

> the secondary labour sector – consisting of low-paid, unskilled and insecure jobs.

Barron and Norris point out that women and Black people are more likely to be found in this secondary sector. They argue that Black people are less likely to gain primary-sector employment because employers may subscribe to racist beliefs about their unsuitability and practise discrimination, either by not employing them or by denying them responsibility and promotion.

Women and Black people are more likely to have jobs in the secondary labour sector.

Underclass

Another Neo-Weberian approach is that of Rex and Tomlinson (1979), who argue that ethnic-minority experience of both class and status inequality can lead to poverty, which is made more severe by racism. They believe that a Black underclass has been created, of people who feel marginalised, alienated and frustrated. (Note: when both Barron and Norris and Rex and Tomlinson were writing in the late seventies, the term 'Black' was used to refer to what would now be called BME or BAME groups.)

However, there is considerable overlap between the White and BAME population in terms of poverty and unemployment, although the constant threat of racism does suggest that some members of the White working class do not recognise the common economic situation they share with BAME workers. The concept of status inequality may therefore help to explain the apparent divisions between the White and ethnic-minority working class and the outbreaks of 'racial' conflict between White and Asian people in some northern towns in 2001.

Evaluation of neo-Weberian theories

As we saw in relation to gender, the concept of a dual labour market remains plausible as a description of contemporary Britain. However, the spread of BAME groups throughout the occupational hierarchy – albeit in different proportions to White groups – undermines the plausibility of this theory.

The same developments have undermined the idea of a BAME underclass. Indeed, while the concept itself remains controversial, its proponents either no longer emphasise the ethnic dimension or, if they do, they focus today on White ethnicity ('chavs').

Nevertheless, the evidence above of continuing racial discrimination in the labour market points to the utility of the Weberian concept of social closure – the use by the ethnic majority of racial or ethnic markers to exclude members of ethnic minorities and thereby preserve their privileged position.

Marxist theories

Marxists such as Castles and Kosack (1973) argue that ethnic minorities are generally part of the exploited working class and it is this that determines their fate in capitalist society. Marxists see racial conflict, discrimination and inequality as symptoms of some deeper underlying class problem. They see these symptoms as deliberately encouraged by the capitalist class for three ideological reasons.

Legitimisation

Racism helps to justify low pay and poor working conditions because ethnic-minority workers are generally seen as second-class citizens undeserving of the same rights as White workers. Capitalist employers benefit from the cheap labour of people from ethnic minorities in terms of profits made. Some Marxists argue that ethnic-minority individuals, like women, are a reserve army of labour that is only taken on in large numbers during periods of economic boom but whose jobs are often the first to be lost in times of recession. However, the existence of racism means that the plight of ethnic-minority people in the job market is rarely highlighted.

Divide and rule

If ethnic-minority and White workers unite in pursuit of a common economic interest, they are in a stronger position to campaign for better wages and conditions. Castles and Kosack argue that racism benefits employers because it divides the workforce. The White workforce will fear losing their jobs to the cheaper labour of ethnic-minority workers. Employers play on these fears during pay negotiations to prevent White workers from demanding higher wages or going on strike.

Scapegoating

When a society is troubled by severe social and economic problems, widespread frustration, aggression and demands for radical change can result. Instead of directing this anger at the capitalist class or economic system, White people are encouraged by racist ideology and agents such as the mass media to blame relatively vulnerable groups such as ethnic minorities for unemployment, housing shortages and inner-city decline: "they have come over here and stolen our jobs", for example. Ethnic minorities become the scapegoats for the social and economic mismanagement of capitalism. This process works in the interest of the wealthy and powerful capitalist class because it protects them from direct criticism and reduces pressure for radical change.

However, some Marxists, such as Miles (1989), have been influenced by the Weberian argument that the concept of 'status' should be used alongside the concept of 'class' to explain racism and racial inequality. Miles argues that the class position of ethnic minorities is complicated by the fact that they are treated by White society as socially and culturally different, and consequently they have become the victims of racist ideologies that prevent their full inclusion into UK society. At the same time, ethnic minorities also "set themselves apart" from the White majority by stressing and celebrating their unique cultural identity. Miles suggests that, as a result, ethnic minorities are members of "racialised class fractions". He argues that the White working class stress the importance of their ethnicity and nationality through prejudice and discrimination, while ethnic minorities react to such racism by stressing their ethnicity in terms of their observance of particular religious and cultural traditions.

Evaluation of Marxist theories

Significantly higher levels of BAME unemployment during times of recession support the idea that ethnic minorities form a reserve army of labour. Similarly, the growing support for UKIP between 2010 and 2015 supports the idea that ethnic-minority groups – widely (if inaccurately) perceived as 'immigrants' – are scapegoated for macro-economic problems not of their making.

For Marxists, racial and ethnic stratification are derivatives of class stratification and would therefore disappear with the demise of capitalism. Grint and Nixon (2015) argue that: "The experience of non-capitalist societies, ancient and modern, [suggests] that nothing of the sort is likely".

Marxist theories often assume that racism represents a form of 'false consciousness', a failure by those involved to recognise their shared class interests in the face of racial or ethnic divisions. The problem with 'false consciousness' is that its usefulness as an explanatory concept relies on the validity of the underlying Marxist theoretical framework it rests on. If that is rejected, its explanatory power is forfeited.

Postmodernist approaches

Postmodernists reject the sociological theories we have looked at so far that seek to generalise and offer blanket explanations for the position of ethnic or racial groups as a whole. This is because they reject both the idea of 'essentialism' – that there is some core, fixed feature that determines the nature of racial or ethnic groups ('Blackness', say or 'cultural uniqueness') – and the idea that any single identity overrides any others.

They suggest that both White and ethnic-minority identities are being eroded by globalisation and consumption, and so members of such groups are less likely to have their identity shaped by membership of their ethnic group. Postmodernists suggest that in the 21st century, the young, in particular, have begun to 'pick and mix' their identity from a new globalised culture that interacts with both White British culture and the ethnic-minority subcultures that exist in the UK.

This process has produced new **hybrid identities**. Gill (2009), for example, writes about the adoption by some young British Asians of a 'Blasian' identity that fuses elements of Black and Asian culture.

UNDERSTAND THE CONCEPT

Hybrid identities involve the fusion of elements from two or more cultural sources to produce a new identity. The concept is linked particularly with globalisation and migration. It can be illustrated by the rapper Eminem whose identity draws on elements not only from his White, American, working-class roots but also from Black hip-hop.

As a result, racial or ethnic differences are not fixed and imposed by membership of an ethnic group. Instead, identity has become a matter of choice. The implication of these trends is that as ethnicity and race are reduced in importance and influence, so racism and racial disadvantage will decline.

Evaluation

Postmodernism has played a useful role in reminding us that both race and ethnicity are social constructs and challenging essentialist conceptions. It has also usefully emphasised that ethnicity is not fixed and that people have the ability to choose how they self-identify and, to some extent, construct a narrative of their lives that makes sense to them.

However, identities are not only chosen; they are also imposed. The fact that a young person of Indian or Caribbean ancestry sees themselves primarily as, say, a footballer or a dancer is unlikely to make any difference to the racist thug who wishes to humiliate them! Moreover, identities are shaped by people's material lives: experiences of unemployment, poverty, poor housing and inner-city deprivation are likely to leave their mark.

To say that cultures are fluid is true, but at any particular point in time they have a massive influence on people's identity through the processes of socialisation and internalisation. As a result they shape who we are in fundamental ways, some of which we may not even be aware of. Postmodernism's picture of 'pick and mix' identities overlooks this. As Gill points out, young Asians may well construct new stylistic – Blasian – identities, but they are still one of the least likely groups to marry outside of their ethnic group. As he pithily concludes: "Style is one thing, but making a life commitment across ethnic boundaries is something quite different."

CHECK YOUR UNDERSTANDING

1. Explain what is meant by saying that both race and ethnicity are 'social constructs'.

2. Why might it be factually incorrect to refer to someone from a BAME group as an 'immigrant'?

3. What proportion of the population of England and Wales belonged to BAME groups in 2011?

4. Identify two sources of racial prejudice in British society.

5. Explain why members of organisations deemed 'institutionally racist' may not necessarily be racist individuals.

6. Distinguish between direct and indirect discrimination.

7. Identify two weaknesses of the immigrant–host theory of ethnic inequality.

8. Explain the relevance of the Weberian concept of 'social closure' to accounts of ethnic inequality in the workplace.

9. How do Marxists argue that racism benefits capitalism?

10. Identify one criticism of the postmodern idea that ethnicity no longer matters because people can now choose their identity.

TAKE IT FURTHER

The concept of multiculturalism is often in the news. Carry out some research on the internet to try to find out more about the different ways in which the concept is used and understood and the arguments of both its supporters and opponents. Write up your findings in summary form. The writings of the sociologist Tariq Modood would be a good place to start your research – you will find some of his articles on 'openDemocracy' (www.opendemocracy.net).

5.6 DIMENSIONS OF INEQUALITY: AGE

LEARNING OBJECTIVES

> Demonstrate knowledge and understanding of age stages as social constructs the ways in which some young people and old people may be disadvantaged (AO1).

> Apply knowledge and understanding of links between age and life-chances to contemporary society (AO2).

> Analyse the role of ageism in society (AO3).

> Evaluate sociological explanations of the position of older people in society (AO3).

INTRODUCING THE DEBATE

Are age stages a natural or social creation? Ageing is a physical process that all human beings experience, and all societies recognise distinct stages in life. In the UK today, the stages that are typically distinguished are childhood, youth or adolescence (being a teenager), early adulthood, middle age and old age. But the stages that are distinguished vary from society to society and from time to time. In many preindustrial and tribal societies, for example, the period of youth is notably absent, because at puberty children go through 'rites of passage' – often involving physical ordeal – that transform them into adults with much the same responsibilities as other adult members of the society.

These age categories therefore, are not 'natural' but created by society. That is, they are social constructions. Society also constructs sets of social expectations about 'appropriate' behaviour and lifestyle, responsibilities to others, independence and dependence, and so on in terms of the age stages it distinguishes. These are not, of course, entirely independent of chronological age, but the limits that the latter provides are highly flexible. When state education was first introduced in Britain, for example, the school-leaving age was set at ten.

Do you think that society still operates with social norms regarding age-appropriate behaviour, or are people free to do as they like without risking censure? Think about Mick Jagger and Dame Helen Mirren, for example, who are pictured above.

Age categories also tend to differ in terms of their status. When this happens we can talk about 'age strata'. Again, in preindustrial and tribal societies, the elderly are generally treated with great respect and consequently have high status because their longevity is seen as conferring wisdom. In modern societies however, the rapidity of social change, connected particularly with new technology, means that the old risk being seen as 'out of touch' and – given the institutionalisation of retirement – even as a 'burden'. Indeed, because of the status attaching to employment in modern societies, both the old and the young risk being assigned a lower status.

THE ELDERLY: THE DEMOGRAPHIC PICTURE

The decline in the death rate and the birth rate, and increased life expectancy over the last 50 years have led to an ageing of the UK population – a pattern reproduced throughout the developed world (See Fig 5.6.1). Life expectancy at birth has increased significantly over this period by roughly two years for every decade, standing at 79 for men and 83 for women in 2013. There are increasing numbers of people aged 65 and over and declining numbers of children under 16. Since 1971, the proportion of the population aged 65 and over has grown by 47 per cent, and represented 18 per cent of the total in 2014. While the gap in life expectancy between males and females has been narrowing – it was 8 years in 1980/82 – a marked gender gap remains apparent within the elderly population, with 127 women for every 100 men aged over 65 in the UK (ONS, 2011).This increase in life expectancy has led to the recognition of new age stages among the elderly, with gerontologists increasingly talking about the 'young old' (65–74), the 'middle old' (75–84) and the 'old old' (85+).

AGE AND INEQUALITY

Bradley (1996) refers to old age as the most neglected and hidden dimension of social stratification and hence inequality – for example, pensioners are one of the most significant groups that make up the poor. Age UK reported in 2011 that 1 in 6 pensioners (1.8m) live in poverty (defined as below 60 per cent of median household income after housing costs). Age interacts with social class and gender to bring about inequality. People who are poor in old age are most likely to be those who have earned least in their working lives – women and those employed in manual jobs. This can be seen especially with regard to pension rights. Many of those working in professions, such as teaching and finance, can supplement their state pension with a company or private pension. However, many manual occupations fail to provide this extra.

Davidson (2006) notes that the majority of those people who are not eligible for – or who cannot afford the contributions required for – participation in private occupational pension schemes are female. This is because they are more likely to have their careers interrupted by pregnancy and childcare, and are more likely to be employed in low-paid, part-time work for a significant period of their lives. Oppenheim and Harker (1996) found that 73 per cent of male employees receive company pensions, compared with only 68 per cent of female full-time employees and only 31 per cent of female part-time workers. Consequently, women are more likely

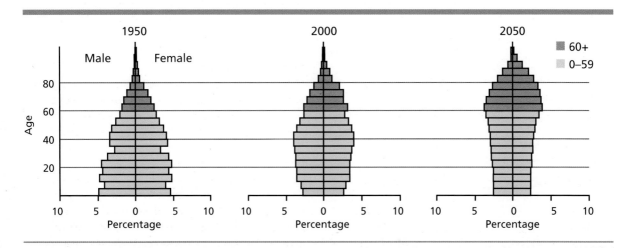

Figure 5.6.1 *Population pyramids, 1950 to 2050*

Source: Europe, Population Pyramids, UN Ageing Report 2003

in later life to be dependent on a husband's occupational pension or on a state pension supplemented by benefits. Mordaunt *et al.* (2003) report that, as a result, twice as many elderly women compared with men rely on benefits and one in four single (never-married, widowed or divorced) women pensioners in the UK live in poverty.

Davidson also notes that the proportion of ethnic-minority elders reaching retirement is higher now than ever before. She argues that interrupted work patterns, low pay and racial discrimination mean that ethnic-minority workers also have less opportunity to pay into private occupational pension schemes. They also have less economic potential to save and invest for old age. Ethnic-minority women are further disadvantaged.

However, in recent years some government policies have benefited the elderly. In 2010, the newly elected coalition government introduced what it called a 'triple lock' on the state pension, which guaranteed that it would rise every year by whichever was the highest: price inflation, earnings or 2.5 per cent. (The Conservative government elected in 2015 has pledged to continue with the triple lock.) In 2011, compulsory retirement was outlawed, allowing people to continue working after 65 should they so wish. The employment rate for people aged 65 and over increased from 5 per cent in 2001 to nearly 10 per cent in 2013. As a result, the proportion of the elderly living in poverty in the UK has been falling in recent years, from 2.2m in 2005/6 to 1.8m in 2011.

The effects of ageism

Robert Butler (1969) has defined ageism as a process of negative stereotyping and discrimination against people purely on the grounds of their chronological age.

Butler suggested that ageism was composed of three connected elements:

› prejudicial attitudes towards older persons, old age and the ageing process

› discriminatory practices against older people

› institutional practices and policies that perpetuate stereotypes about older people.

The elderly have mainly been the victims of this discrimination, but Best (2005) notes that the young, especially youth, can be victims of ageism too. Moral panics that focus negatively on the activities and cultural habits of young people are cited as evidence of such ageism. However, it can be argued that ageism practised against the elderly has greater negative consequences than that practised against the young, in terms of self-esteem and social wellbeing, because the young

will get older but the only escape for old people is through dying.

Ageist attitudes

There is evidence that negative stereotypes underpin social attitudes about the elderly in the modern UK and dehumanise members of this group. Recent surveys suggest that the negative stereotyping of the elderly is still a mass problem. The 2008 European Social Survey (ESS) showed that ageism is rife across Europe. In particular, the elderly faced the problem of subtle forms of prejudice, such as the idea that older people are passive, needy and frail. However, older people in the UK were more likely than their European counterparts to report that they had been treated disrespectfully or had been ignored and patronised. The report found that these subtle types of prejudice are just as harmful as overt discrimination, because they make it difficult for older people to feel empowered and to be able to assert their preferences and choices. Research from the English Longitudinal Study of Ageing (ELSA) in 2013 also found that one in three men and women aged 52 and older report that they have been discriminated against because of their age in a number of settings, including the workplace, shops, restaurants and the health services.

The sorts of ageist stereotypes outlined above result in the elderly being associated, particularly by the young, with dependence, vulnerability and disability. They are generally seen as making little or no contribution to society, and even as a burden on society, despite the fact that a significant proportion are involved in providing informal care for family members and/or voluntary work as well as paid work. The ascribed characteristics of age therefore serve to exclude many elderly people from full involvement in society.

Institutional ageism

Until quite recently, there was no legal protection against age discrimination in the UK. It wasn't until 2006 that the first steps to combat it were taken, with legislation that banned age discrimination in further and higher education. Four years later, in 2010, the Equality Act extended protection against age discrimination to employment and the provision of all goods and services. However, Greengross (2004) argues that the National Health Service (NHS) is guilty of institutional ageism because older patients in the NHS are often omitted from clinical trials or are denied particular treatment or operations on the basis of their chronological age. (See Book 1, Topic 5, Chapter 4 for more detailed coverage of ageism in access to health services.)

At this institutional level, Ray and colleagues claim that ageism can mean exclusion from the workplace and positions of power or decision-making because employers assume lower competence. Finally, it might be assumed that it is natural for older people to have lower expectations and reduced choice and control. Consequently, less account is taken of their views.

Ageism and the mass media

Another type of institutional ageism is found in the mass media. Representations of men and women in the UK media tend to focus on the 'body beautiful'. Ageing – and its outward signs, such as wrinkles, grey hair, and so on – is often presented as a threat to our wellbeing that needs to be resisted at all costs. Carrigan and Szmigin (2000) argue that the advertising industry either ignores older people or stereotypically presents them as physically unattractive, mentally deficient, senile, cranky, grumpy, cantankerous or difficult. Age Concern UK (2005) commissioned a social survey of a representative sample of adults in Great Britain, which was conducted in 2004. It found that 58 per cent of people they surveyed believed that the UK media portrayed the elderly in a negative way. Older people portrayed on television are often marginalised, comical or based on offensive stereotypes. Older women in particular are underrepresented on television. For example, while TV presenters are broadly reflective of the general population in age terms, a large majority (82 per cent) of those over 50 are men (The Commission on Older Women, 2013).

Why do you think older women are underrepresented in the visual media compared to men?

The 'demographic time-bomb'?

Another aspect of ageism is the debate about the so-called 'demographic time-bomb'. In 2014, people aged over 65 years outnumbered people aged under 16 for the first time, and the gap is predicted to widen in the future. The number of people over retirement age in 2021 is projected to be 12.2 million. New Right thinkers have assumed, almost without question, that these elderly people are going to be dependent on younger people, that they are going to put intolerable strain on services such as healthcare, and that they will be a drain on the economy because of the disproportionate costs of the healthcare, social services and housing assistance they will supposedly need. Generally, then, this demographic time-bomb is seen as potentially leading to a crisis for the welfare state, family and economy.

However, the concept of a demographic time-bomb is based on a number of ageist assumptions that do not stand up to scrutiny:

> One such assumption is that elderly people are likely to be dependent because of poor physical and mental health. While ageing is associated with some biological decline in physical and mental abilities, there is little evidence that this has a significant effect on the lifestyle of the elderly. For example, only one in 20 people over 65 and one in five people over 80 experience dementia.

> In terms of physical health, some authors suggest that there is a 'medical myth' that misleadingly suggests ageing is synonymous with disease. Walker (2014) argues that prolonged exposure to an unhealthy environment and lifestyle is three times more significant than the ageing process itself in terms of producing age-related illness.

> There is also an assumption that the elderly are incapable of doing paid work because the ageing process makes them incompetent. However, Ray and colleagues note that experiments indicate that there is no significant difference between the abilities of younger and older workers, with each group performing particularly well or poorly in different areas.

> Taylor-Gooby (1996) points out that the number of pensioners increased from 6.5 million in 1951 to 10 million in 1991 without causing any major economic or social problems.

THE YOUNG

Like the elderly, the young also make up a large subgroup of the poor. A quarter of children live in households receiving less than 60 per cent of the average median income. In addition, many young people of working age face social deprivation caused by low pay, student loans and, in some cases, ineligibility for benefits and unemployment. In 2012, the UK unemployment rate for those under 25 was 22 per cent, compared to the rate for all over 16 of 8 per cent. However, the increase in those on training schemes masks the true figure. Again, this is affected by other factors, such as ethnicity – for example, twice as many young African Caribbean males are unemployed compared with young White males.

Furthermore, the extended transitions into adulthood that characterise the experience of young people in advanced industrial societies often bring with them extended periods of relative deprivation and reduced social standing. It is now more likely that there will be intermediate stages between leaving school and entry into the labour market, between living in the parental home and having a home of one's own, and (perhaps) between being a child in a family and being a parent or partner in one. Declining opportunities for those in vulnerable groups has led to increases in homelessness and financial hardship among the young, especially in run-down urban areas. Beatrice Campbell in *Wigan Pier Revisited* (1985) and *Goliath* (1993) referred to adaptations some young people make in the absence of access to the mainstream routes to adult status. She suggests that some young women use having a baby as a means of acquiring adult status in a society which has increasingly closed down other options for them, while young men with little prospect of work turn to drug addiction and crime.

Young people at work

Most young workers earn relatively little, and they are given less responsibility and status in almost every occupational sector. Many young people are on the minimum wage. The hourly rate for those aged 21 and over in 2015/16 is £6.70, but for 18–20-year-olds it is £5.30 and for under-18s it is £3.87. For apprentices it is even less: £3.30. From April 2016, employers must pay the 'National Living Wage' to workers aged 25 and over. Those under 25 are exempt from this law. Young people are also overrepresented on zero-hour contracts.

Young people have been particularly hard hit by the 2007/8 crash and the ensuing policy of austerity. CLASS (The Centre for Labour and Social Studies) estimates that real wages overall fell by 8 per cent between 2007/8 and 2013, but the fall for young workers has been significantly higher. Writing in 2013, Danny Dorling argued that "if you are young in Britain today, you are being taken for a ride". Among the disadvantages he mentions are the removal of the Educational Maintenance Allowance (EMA), increases in higher education (HE) fees and the resulting debt, rising housing costs, reductions in benefit entitlements and the rise in long-term unemployment among the young. The Conservative government in 2015 announced that it would cut housing benefit for those under 21 and replace JSA for 18–21 year olds with a new 'youth allowance'.

Do you think that young people are victims of ageism in the UK today?

THEORETICAL EXPLANATIONS OF AGE INEQUALITY

Functionalism

Functionalists, such as Cummings and Henry (1961), suggest that the way society treats the old has positive benefits for both society and the elderly. The ageing process and the social reaction to it is part of a mutual process in which the elderly are encouraged to abandon their occupational roles within the specialised division of labour and withdraw from wider engagement with society. The individual is thereby relieved of the stresses and strains associated with employment and allowed time to come to terms with their eventual demise. In their view, the withdrawal of older people from work roles and social relationships was both an 'inevitable' and a 'natural process'. This process of 'social disengagement' functions to allow younger members of society to take the place of the old in the specialised division of labour with minimum disruption to both social order and economic efficiency. It was also functional in terms of helping both the individual and society prepare for the ultimate disengagement: death.

Critics of disengagement theory have questioned how far the process of disengagement could be 'mutual' under regimes of compulsory retirement. Second, they claim that it promotes an uncritically negative view of old age as a time of stagnation and withdrawal. Third, they claim that the theory is ageist in that it – unintentionally – serves to justify the neglect of the experience, skills and talents of older members of society that could still be of great benefit to society. Finally, disengagement theory ignores the fact that many old people continue to be active participants in society.

Do you agree that disengagement theory is based on ageist assumptions, or is it just being realistic?

Conflict theories

Marxists, such as Phillipson (1998), suggest that the logic of capitalism, which is about exploiting workers and consumers for profit, is incompatible with the needs of the elderly. Retirement from paid work often means that the elderly lose a major source of status, respect, identity and economic security. This has resulted in the elderly, despite their greater needs, being neglected by the capitalist system because they no longer have the disposable income or spending power which is so attractive to capitalists. Moreover, because their labour-power is no longer of any use to capitalism, the elderly are seen as a drain on its resources through their use of welfare and health provision: "Older people came to be viewed as a burden on western economies, with demographic change … creating intolerable pressures on public expenditure." Consequently, then, in capitalist societies such as the UK, early retirement and increasing life expectancy mean that the elderly have little or no status because they are likely to possess little economic power. Cultural and ideological stereotypes of the elderly help justify this state of affairs. As a result, the elderly are more likely to be in poverty and to experience ill-health as an aspect of that poverty.

On the other hand, Alan Walker (2006), drawing more on Weber, points out that the elderly are divided along lines of class, ethnicity and gender and that their position in old age is mainly a product of their circumstances in middle age. Some old people, particularly those from an upper-middle-class background, have more power and status because their earning power during their working lives was greater and they were able to accumulate savings and wealth. Indeed, social commentators have coined the term the 'grey pound' to refer to the relatively high levels of disposable income enjoyed by such people. This privileged sector of the elderly has the economic power to consume services, such as private health schemes, and they therefore enjoy greater life expectancy and better health.

Labelling theory

Ray *et al.* (2006) generally take a social action or interactionist approach to the treatment of the elderly. They note that there is evidence that the mental capability and wellbeing of the elderly can be negatively affected by exposure to stereotypical labels and experiences of ageism. Their labelling theory suggests that a self-fulfilling prophecy may be the result of exposure to ageism, which can cause a person to behave in a way that confirms these beliefs. They note that research has shown that the use of 'baby talk' or infantilised language causes older people to accept the implication that they are no longer independent adults, thus causing them to behave in a passive and dependent manner. In addition, research has shown that the linguistic expression of pity, particularly from medical professionals, conveys the idea that older people are helpless. Some older people may internalise this message and, as a result, increase their dependence on others – a process known as 'learned helplessness'.

Postmodernist theory

Postmodernists such as Blaikie (1999) argue that chronological age, ageism and age-determined inequality are less likely to shape people's life experience in the 21st century. He suggests that UK society has undergone a social transformation from social experiences, based on collective identities originating in social class and generation, to an increasingly individualised and consumerist culture in which old age can be extended by investing in a diverse choice of youth-preserving techniques and lifestyles.

Featherstone and Hepworth (1991) talk about the "mask of ageing" in describing how the outward physical signs of ageing conceal the essentially still-youthful self beneath: "Inside, I don't feel any different." The conditions of postmodernity will allow older people to experiment with roles and identities made available by the erosion of cultural constraints defining what is – and what is not – 'age-appropriate'. For example, people will be able to use emerging technologies, such as cosmetic surgery, to modify the appearance of ageing.

However, Featherstone and Hepworth, and also Blaikie, acknowledge that class, gender and ethnicity continue to structure to some degree the experience of old age, and that choices are inevitably reduced as people move towards the final years of their lives. Gilleard and Higgs (2000), on the other hand, argue that the 'baby boomers' of the post-WWII years are the first 'young old' generation to have appeared when consumerism was becoming established and that this has created a wide variety of 'cultures of ageing' that cut across class divisions. Class can no longer, in their view, compete with the multiplicity of influences connected to growing individualism, globalisation and choice around lifestyles.

Critics of postmodernist views of ageing argue that class, ethnicity and gender continue to structure the opportunities old people have to 'experiment' with new identities and lifestyles, particularly the opportunities – or, rather, lack of opportunities – of those who find themselves living in poverty. Postmodernists also overlook the possibility that consumerism may be a means to achieving class-determined ends through, say, **conspicuous consumption**. Moreover, while some feminists view cosmetic surgery as 'empowering', others stress the extraordinary – and, in their view, malign – pressure that is exerted by a patriarchal and ageist society on women, much more than on men, to look younger.

UNDERSTAND THE CONCEPT

The term **conspicuous consumption** was coined by an American sociologist called Thorstein Veblen and refers to consumption that involves the ostentatious display of consumer products intended to demonstrate the status and taste of those who have purchased the item(s).

Is the use of cosmetic surgery to reverse physical signs of ageing empowering for women or evidence that they are victims of both patriarchy and ageism?

FOCUS ON SKILLS: 'BABY BOOMER' MYTH CHALLENGED

There is a widely touted belief that there is a uniform group of older people in the UK – so-called 'baby boomers' – who have benefited at the expense of younger age groups.

The report by the Ready for Ageing Alliance, which defines baby boomers as people between the ages of 55 and 70, argues that the term has become an overused and potentially dangerous shorthand to inaccurately describe everybody in a single age group. It provides compelling evidence that baby boomers are in fact a diverse group of people in virtually every aspect of their lives.

While many boomers have benefited from house price inflation, just under half of those aged 55 to 64 in England fully own their property and 24 per cent are still renting. Although some boomers can expect to live a long time in good health, men in the most deprived parts of England can expect to live to 52.2 years in good health compared with 70.5 years in the least deprived areas. Furthermore, 6.7 million people aged 55 to 64 have a long-standing illness or disability. While some boomers benefited from free further education, under 1 in 5 of those aged 55 to 64 in the UK have a degree. Evidence in the report also shows that while some boomers will retire with good pension provision, almost 3 in 10 of

55 to 64 year olds in Great Britain do not have any pension provision.

David Sinclair, spokesperson for the Ready for Ageing Alliance, said: "The term 'baby boomer' seems to be increasingly used to inflame divisions and resentment between younger and older generations.

"The report highlights that while some boomers are ageing successfully, there is huge diversity in income, wealth and experiences of those aged 55 to 70.

"If we are to ensure that our increasingly ageing society is prosperous for all future generations, we must find ways of bringing older and younger together rather than pitch them against each other."

Source: Age UK (2015)

Questions

1. **Identify**. To whom does the label 'baby boomers' apply?

2. **Explain** why it is incorrect to see baby boomers as a homogeneous group.

3. **Analyse** why some people see them as particularly fortunate.

4. **Evaluate** the claim that they "have benefited at the expense of younger age groups".

CHECK YOUR UNDERSTANDING

1. Explain what is meant by describing age strata as social constructs.

2. What proportion of the UK population were over 65 in 2014?

3. Give two examples of ageism.

4. Identify two recent government policies that have benefited the elderly.

5. Why do some commentators suggest that the increasing numbers of elderly people constitute a 'demographic time-bomb'?

6. Analyse how the view in question 5 can be criticised.

7. What is disengagement theory?

8. Why, according to Marxists, are old people marginalised in capitalist society?

9. How does ageism exacerbate patriarchy in the view of feminists?

10. How has the growth of consumerism affected old age in the view of postmodernists?

TAKE IT FURTHER

As a class exercise, come up with as many phrases as you can think of that are used to describe old people (for example, 'old dear', 'codger'). Then categorise each of them according to whether they carry negative, positive or neutral connotations. Discuss what your results suggest about the existence of ageism.

5.7 DIMENSIONS OF INEQUALITY: DISABILITY

LEARNING OBJECTIVES

› Demonstrate knowledge and understanding of the distinction between impairment and disability (AO1).

› Demonstrate knowledge and understanding of the heterogeneity of the population classified as disabled (AO1).

› Apply knowledge and understanding of links between disability and life-chances (AO2).

› Analyse the ways in which disabled people are both enabled and disabled by society (AO3).

› Evaluate the changing role of government policy (AO3).

› Understand and evaluate competing models of disability (AO1 and AO3).

INTRODUCING THE DEBATE

Until fairly recently, sociology had little to say about disability. It was seen essentially as a medical issue, a problem located firmly within the individual, and therefore one that fell outside the domain of sociology.

This is no longer the case. The change came about because of the success of disabled rights activists in the late 20th century in promoting a social model of disability in opposition to the previously dominant medical model.

The social model drew an important distinction between 'impairment' and 'disability'. An impairment, according to the World Health Organisation, is "any loss or abnormality of psychological, physiological or anatomical structure or function", such as suffering from clinical depression, being blind or lacking a limb. Disability, the social model insisted, was not an attribute of an individual, but "the loss or limitation of opportunities to take part in the normal life of the community on an equal level with others due to physical and social barriers" (Barnes, 1992). Impairment was seen as a feature of individuals and disability as a product of society and thus an issue for sociology.

The idea that impairment and disability – like sex and gender – are completely separate is open to question and will be examined later, but it is certainly true that society can either enable or disable people with impairments. For example, the present writer has a visual impairment which would prevent him from producing this text were it not for the fact that society has enabled him by the provision of spectacles. This chapter will be exploring how far UK society enables or disables people with significant impairments. (See Book 1, Topic 5, Chapter 1 for further discussion of a number of the sociological issues surrounding disability.)

THE DEMOGRAPHICS OF DISABILITY

According to the government's Office for Disability Issues, there were 11.6 million disabled people in Great Britain in 2011/12, or roughly 19 per cent of the population. The figures relate to people with a longstanding illness, disability or infirmity that causes them to have significant difficulties with day-to-day activities.

The prevalence of disability rises with age. Around 6 per cent of children, 16 per cent of working-age adults and 45 per cent of adults over State Pension age are disabled. Mainly as a consequence of the fact that women generally live longer than men, females make up a larger proportion (54 per cent) of disabled people than males (46 per cent). The most commonly reported impairments are those connected with mobility or with lifting and carrying.

Disability: myths and misunderstandings

There are many myths and misunderstandings surrounding disability, among them the idea that all disabled people are sick and in constant pain, need to use a wheelchair and are unable to speak for themselves. Such myths relate to stereotypical views of disability that treat disabled people as a homogeneous category who all share the same – generally negative – characteristics. In reality, the only thing they share is the fact that they have one or more impairments that make daily living 'significantly' more difficult for them than for others.

Moreover, the location of the dividing line between disabled and non-disabled people is inevitably somewhat subjective. 'Longstanding' in the statistics above, for example, is defined as lasting for 12 months or more. A shorter or longer period would produce higher or lower estimates, respectively, of the size of the disabled population.

Perhaps the most problematic misunderstanding is the idea that disabled people are not 'normal'. The Work and Pensions Secretary, Iain Duncan Smith, said in the House of Commons in 2015, while defending the government's record on getting disabled people back into employment, that "we are looking to get [the employment rates of disabled people] up to the level of *normal*, non-disabled people who are back in work".

Statistically speaking, of course, disabled people aren't normal: they constitute a numerical minority of the population. But the word 'normal' inevitably carries evaluative connotations. As George Walkden, lecturer in Linguistics at the University of Manchester, pointed out on the BBC's *Ouch!* website on 10 September 2015, "The use of the word implicitly divides people into two groups – with abnormal, the currently used antonym, carrying negative connotations." Disabled people, then, are not abnormal, or – at least – they are no more or less abnormal than the rest of the population.

Composition of the disabled population

In contrast to stereotypical views, it is important to recognise the diversity of the disabled population. There are three main sources of diversity (Prime Minister's Strategy Unit, 2005):

> type of impairment (see below) and its variation by severity, duration, age of onset and evolution over time

> socio-demographic characteristics – including variation by social class, region, ethnicity, age and gender

> impact of different barriers – attitudinal, physical and socio-economic.

The main types of impairment that can be distinguished are (with examples): learning disabilities (Down's syndrome); developmental disabilities (autism); mental health problems (schizophrenia); physical impairments (paraplegia); sensory impairments (blindness); and long-term medical conditions (multiple sclerosis).

DISABILITY AND LIFE-CHANCES

The role of government

Until relatively recently, government policy in relation to disability was mainly concerned with either the care or the control of disabled people, rather than with issues relating to equality. The 1970 Chronically Sick and Disabled Persons Act marks a watershed in that it was the first in the world to recognise and give rights to disabled people (Rescare, 2012).

However, it was not until the 1995 Disability Discrimination Act (DDA) that a frontal attack on the barriers facing disabled people was launched by a (Conservative) government persuaded to act by decades of campaigning by the disability rights movement. The Act made it unlawful to discriminate against disabled people in connection with employment, the provision of goods, services or facilities or the disposal or management of premises. The scope of the Act was extended by subsequent amendments and the 2005 DDA introduced a Disability Equality Duty, which obliged public authorities to take a more proactive role in promoting the equality and inclusion of disabled people.

Also in 2005, the Prime Minister's Strategy Unit published its final report of a series entitled *Improving the life-chances of disabled people*. The response of the (Labour) government was to set a target that "By 2025, disabled people in Britain should have full opportunities and choices to improve their quality of life and will be respected and included as equal members of society." The strategy to achieve that target was to be driven forward by a new Office for Disability Issues (ODI) reporting to the Minister for Disabled People. Four years later, in 2009, the government signed up to the United Nations Convention on the Rights of Disabled People (UNCRDP), introduced in 2006, and to the Convention's optional Protocol, which allows individuals or groups who consider themselves to be victims of any violation of the Convention to submit a complaint to the UN's Committee on the Rights of Persons with Disabilities.

In 2010, the provisions of the preceding DDAs were incorporated into a new Equality Act which combined all previous anti-discrimination legislation into a single Act to be overseen by a new commission – the Equality and Human Rights Commission (EHRC). Also in 2010, the Labour government was replaced by a coalition government of the Conservatives and Liberal Democrats. The Coalition government was ostensibly equally committed to disability equality, retaining the ODI, the Equality Act, the EHRC and the Public Sector Equality Duty. In July, 2013 the Coalition government published its own disability equality strategy: *Fulfilling Potential – Making it Happen*, and in September 2014, it launched The Accessible Britain Challenge, designed to encourage communities to be more inclusive and accessible.

The evidence on disabled people's life-chances

It would appear then, that in the last couple of decades, UK governments have done a great deal to promote disabled people's life-chances. How successful have they been?

One useful piece of evidence is provided by the findings of a longitudinal survey launched in March, 2009 by the ODI and carried out by the ONS – the Life Opportunities Survey. The survey compares the activities of disabled and non-disabled people across a wide range of situations. Among the key findings of the first wave of interviews conducted in 2009/10 were:

> 17 per cent of adults with impairments, compared with 9 per cent without, said they faced barriers to using learning and training services.

> 56 per cent of adults with impairments, compared with 26 per cent without, said there were barriers to the kind of work they did or the hours they could work.

> 45 per cent of adults with impairments, compared with 29 per cent without, said they would find it hard to pay an unexpected bill, pay off a loan or have a holiday.

> 29 per cent of adults with impairments, compared with 7 per cent without, said they found it difficult to get into and move about in buildings outside their home.

Data relating to education, employment and living standards also point to continuing disadvantages:

> Disabled adults are nearly three times as likely to have no formal qualifications as non-disabled adults (30 per cent v 11 per cent) and are about half as likely to hold a degree-level qualification (ODI, 2012).

> Disabled people capable of working are four times more likely to be out of work than non-disabled people (JRF, 2014). Almost half (48 per cent) of unemployed disabled people said that flexible working would have helped them stay at work, but that they were not given this option (Scope, 2013).

> A "substantially higher proportion" of individuals who live in families with a disabled member or members are in poverty compared to individuals who live in families where no one is disabled (ODI, 2014) and disabled people's day-to-day living costs are 25 per cent higher than those of non-disabled people (Leonard Cheshire Disability, 2014).

HATE CRIME

The evidence above suggests that disabled people continue to be disadvantaged in many areas of life. But perhaps the most significant area, in terms of life-chances, is their experience of harassment, including hate crime. The EHRC published a report in 2011 (*Hidden in plain sight*) which examined ten cases in which disabled people had died or been seriously injured in recent years because of abuse, including the case of Fiona Pilkington who, in 2007, set fire to her car when she and her learning-disabled daughter were in it, following years of harassment. The report states that:

> Cases of disability-related harassment that come to court and receive media attention are only the tip of the iceberg.

> Disabled people often don't report harassment because they are unclear about who they should report it to, are fearful of the consequences of reporting it or are afraid they won't be believed.

> There is a systematic failure by public authorities to recognise the extent and impact of harassment and abuse of disabled people, to take action to prevent it happening in the first place, or to intervene effectively when it does.

In March 2012 the Home office estimated that 65,000 disability hate crimes occur each year in England and Wales, while disability charities claim it could be as high as 100,000. Moreover, the trend appears to be upwards: in 2013/14 there were nearly 2,000 recorded disability hate crimes in England and Wales, double the number recorded in 2008 (though one must be cautious in interpreting these figures since they could reflect an increase in disabled people's willingness to report hate crime). Disability charities insist not only that the increase is genuine, but that it has been fuelled by the Coalition government's 'benefit scrounger' rhetoric. In 2012, the DWP suggested that three in four people claiming incapacity benefit were faking disabilities. After this figure was challenged, it admitted that in fact only an estimated 0.3 per cent of the incapacity benefit budget was overspent due to fraud!

DISABILITY AND GOVERNMENT ANTI-AUSTERITY POLICY

In 2015, it was confirmed by the campaigning organisation Disabled People Against Cuts (DPAC) that the UN's Committee on the Rights of Persons with Disabilities (CRPD) was carrying out an inquiry into "systematic and grave violations of disabled people's human rights by the UK government".

The inquiry was triggered by DPAC, which submitted evidence to the Committee that disabled people had been disproportionately harmed by the Coalition government's austerity policies. DPAC's concerns were focused initially on the government's decision to end the Independent Living Fund and transfer responsibility for supporting disabled people to live independently to local authorities.

But its case against the government subsequently grew to include concerns about the reliability of work capability assessments for Employment and Support Allowance, the impact of the 'spare bedroom tax', cuts to social care, the impact of benefit sanctions on disabled people, and the government's unwillingness to assess the cumulative impact of its cuts and reforms as a whole on disabled people.

At the time of writing, the outcome of the inquiry is not known, but it would be the first of its kind in relation to the UNCRPD Protocol, and the CRPD would not have begun an investigation unless the evidence submitted by DPAC was viewed as "reliable". (See Book 1, Topic 5, Chapter 1 for further information on disability and life-chances.)

UNDERSTANDING DISABILITY AS A SOCIAL PHENOMENON

Historically and cross-culturally, disability has been understood in a number of different ways. Before examining the two main models that offer an explanation for the disadvantaged position of disabled people in society today – the medical model and the social model – it is worth looking at two additional models since their influence in society is still apparent.

The eugenics model

Eugenics is the 'science' of improving humankind through selective breeding. It originated in the late 19th century in Britain following the publication in 1859 of Darwin's *Origin of Species* and was enthusiastically embraced in the early years of the 20th century by many prominent people on both the Right and Left of politics, such as Winston Churchill, Theodore Roosevelt, H.G.Wells and George Bernard Shaw. Indeed, at this time, eugenics was seen as an aspect of medical sociology.

Eugenic ideas fed into the world view of the Nazis in Germany in the 1930s. It is widely recognised that their belief in the existence of 'inferior' and 'superior' races led to the genocide of six million Jews in the Holocaust.

What is less widely known is that the same ideas led to the killing of an estimated 275,000 disabled people (BBC – *Ouch!*, 2014). Nazi propaganda portrayed disabled people as "useless eaters" who had "lives unworthy of living" and stressed that the high cost of supporting disabled people represented an "unfair burden" on society. A widespread compulsory sterilisation programme was introduced by the Nazis when they came to power in 1933, and the killing of disabled people started in 1939.

After World War II, eugenic ideas fell into disrepute but it would be naïve to think that they have entirely disappeared. Tom Shakespeare (1998) has written about the use of prenatal tests to screen for Down's syndrome (aka Trisomy 21), which are now offered to all pregnant women on the NHS. He does not oppose a woman's right to choose to have an abortion should such a test prove positive, but argues that parents are rarely provided with full information about living with disability or the support available to families. As a result, more than 90 per cent of Down's syndrome pregnancies detected antenatally are terminated. As Shakespeare argues, the provision of a test suggests the advisability of that test, and taking a test implies acting on the results. The inescapable corollary is that the life of someone with Down's syndrome is not worth living. Today, there is a growing 'Down's pride' movement (Gordon, 2015) and on-line campaigns challenging negative views of Down's syndrome, such as downsideup.com, forceofnature21.com and thefuturesrosie.com.

The eugenics model inevitably raises some profound and uncomfortable questions about society's view of disability. Sociology cannot provide answers by itself because medical, political and ethical issues as well as sociological ones are involved, but it can usefully draw attention to the way disabled people have been, and sometimes still are, treated as 'other'.

Should the NHS provide all pregnant women with the option of a test for Down's syndrome?

The charity model

If the eugenics model embodies a potentially malign attitude towards disability, the charity model could be seen as representing a benevolent stance. This model sees disabled people as victims of heredity or circumstance, deserving of pity and in need of practical and financial support from those who have been more fortunate in life's lottery. Indeed, historically, many disabled people have been represented and cared for by charitable organisations funded and run by non-disabled people, such as Scope, Mencap, RNIB and RNID. Charitable giving to help disabled people is still encouraged by advertising and events such as Red Nose Day.

It might seem that such philanthropy is entirely laudable, yet it has been roundly criticised by disabled rights organisations. Swain *et al.* (2003) for example, argue that "Charity advertising provokes emotions of fear, pity and guilt, ostensibly to raise resources on behalf of disabled people. The images and language have built upon and promoted stereotypes of disabled people as dependent and tragic ... Charity advertising sells fear ... and fails to find a solution because it itself is the problem."

Organisations such as Disabled People's International and the UK Disabled People's Council (both founded in 1981 by disabled people themselves) call for "Rights, not Charity" and are highly critical of the fact that disabled people have often not had a voice in the voluntary organisations that are supposed to represent them (Davies, 1994).

However, the growing influence of the social model of disability has affected the charity sector and many of the traditional organisations have not only rebranded themselves (for example, The Spastics Society became Scope in 1994, and in 2002 the RNIB changed its name from The Royal National Institute for the Blind to The Royal National Institute of the Blind), but have become increasingly focused on the rights of disabled people to be fully integrated into society. Moreover, organisations of disabled people are increasingly influential politically.

A campaign against public sector cuts affecting disabled people

Do you think that donations to charities supporting disabled people should be encouraged or discouraged?

EXPLAINING DISABLED PEOPLE'S DISADVANTAGED POSITION

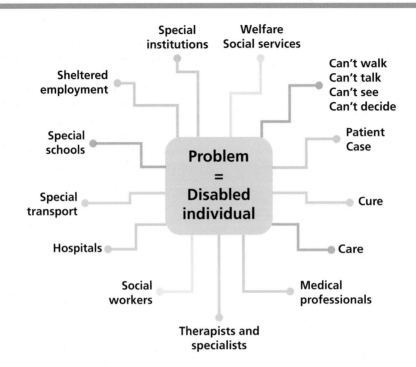

Figure 5.7.1 *The medical model*

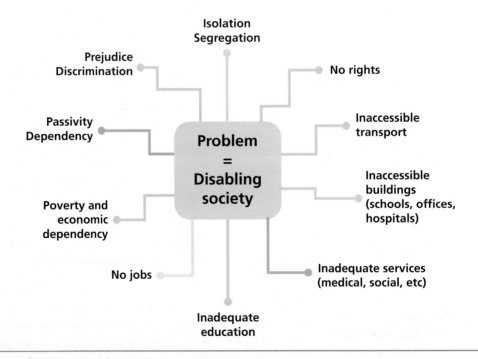

Figure 5.7.2 *The social model*

Source: World Bank/IMF Poverty Reduction Paper Strategy, 1999

The medical model

The idea that disability is determined by impairment is the product of the medical model – an approach that sees disabled people as needing constant care from medical personnel. This model takes an individualistic approach in that it treats disability as a property of individuals who, because of their impairment, are unable to take advantage of the opportunities enjoyed or taken for granted by able-bodied people. The medical model explains the disadvantaged position of disabled people (and therefore their position at the bottom of the stratification system) as an inevitable consequence of their individual impairment, with the degree of severity of their impairment determining the degree of their disadvantage.

Evaluation of the medical model

Strengths

Many, though by no means all, disabled people rely on medical intervention to function or, in extreme cases, to stay alive.

Medicine can offer palliative care (for example, the provision of prosthetic limbs) and, in some cases, the prospect of finding a cure for painful and debilitating conditions.

By offering both diagnoses and prognoses it can provide disabled people with information that allows them to understand the nature of their impairment.

Weaknesses

A narrow focus on the individual fails to recognise the significant role of society in disabling people who have an impairment.

The medical model has led to a person's impairment becoming their 'master status': the impaired person is seen purely in terms of what is wrong with them, so that impaired people become identified with their impairment : 'the blind', 'the deaf', 'the crippled' and so on. Care and dependency take precedence over rights, autonomy and independence (Thompson, 1993).

Writing from an interpretivist position, Shakespeare and Watson (2002) offer a more radical critique of the medical model, arguing that "there is no qualitative difference between disabled people and non-disabled people, because we are all impaired. Impairment is not the core component of disability (as the medical model might suggest), it is the inherent nature of humanity."

The social model

For the social model, the disadvantaged position of disabled people is a product of society rather than impairment.

At least two strands can be discerned in sociologists' writing about the social model. One strand, deriving from interpretivism, emphasises that disability can be seen as a social construct: what counts as a disability is culturally and historically variable. (The social constructionist approach is covered in Book 1, Topic 5, Chapter 1.) The other strand derives from conflict theory and the power imbalance between disabled and non-disabled people and examines how social factors such as the built environment, social attitudes and organisational practices, cause people with impairments to be disabled.

The social model emerged in the last decades of the 20th century as an explicit critique of the medical model. Shearer (1981), for example, argued that 'disability' is something imposed on people with impairments by the patterns and social expectations of a society organised by and for the non-disabled. These act as barriers preventing disabled people from participating fully in society. The term 'disablism' was coined to describe these barriers, defined by Thompson (1993) as "the combination of social forces, cultural values and personal prejudices which marginalises disabled people, portrays them in a negative light and thus oppresses them".

Oliver (1990), writing from a neo-Marxist perspective, suggests that the marginalisation and oppression of disabled people takes a unique form in Western capitalist societies. He argues that in preindustrial, agricultural society, most people worked either on the land or in the textile trade as spinners, weavers, and so on. Moreover, they lived in small, tight-knit communities. He suggests that attitudes and practices in regard to disabled people were very different then – they often played a key role in the economic life of such communities.

Oliver argues that industrialisation and the factory system transformed economic life by introducing a more intensive labour process, such as assembly-line production and, as a result, the worth of individuals came to be assessed according to their economic value – efficient, quick work was seen as immensely profitable. Paid employment, especially in factories, became the main source of identity and status. As Hyde (2001) notes, the dominant ideology of capitalism was 'competitive individualism' and those among the working-class who were not employed – the chronically sick and disabled – were therefore seen to have an inferior social status compared with waged workers.

Oliver argues that the social exclusion of disabled people from economic life was reinforced by state policy in the 19th century. This had two main social consequences for them:

1. The state transferred their responsibility for the assessment, treatment and care of disabled people to medical professionals. This resulted in the ideological dominance of the medical model of disability.

2. Disabled people were increasingly committed to long-stay hospitals and asylums – in other words, treatment of disabled people often resulted in institutionalisation in what Goffman (1961) called **total institutions**. Such institutions treated disabled people by stripping them of their identity.

UNDERSTAND THE CONCEPT

The term **total institutions** refers to places of communal residence, cut off from the wider society, where a group of people lead an enclosed, formally administered round of life under close and continuous supervision. Examples given by Goffman included prisons, mental hospitals, military training camps and boarding schools. The phrase 'total' refers to the fact that the totality of inmates' lives takes place within the boundaries of the institution.

FOCUS ON SKILLS: DISABLED BY SOCIETY

Tell Them The Truth

There goes the mongol up the street

Getting on the loonybus

The schoolbairns call

Making funny faces at us

Calling us names

Headcase, spassy, wally

Nutter, Dylan, Twit!

There goes the dumb-bell in the nuthoose!

The schoolbairns are all daft themselves

They should see a psychiatrist

About their brains

It makes you mad, it boils up your blood

Their wooden heads are full of nonsense

They've got nothing else to do

Except make fun of us

We are human beings

And should be treated as equals

Treated as adults

Tell them the truth

Group poem written by Donald Lack, Robert Drysdale, Margaret Williamson, Derek Mustard, J.R. Grubb, Joan Cargil, Robert McMahon (St Clair Centre, Kirkcaldy), quoted in Davies (1994)

Questions

1. **Explain**. The opening line of the poem refers to 'mongols'. What word is more normally used to describe this group of people today?

2. **Analyse**. How does the poem illustrate the way in which disabled people are sometimes identified with their impairments?

3. **Explain**. Why do you think the authors – who are adults – write that they should be treated as adults (line 18)?

4. **Evaluate**. How does this poem link to the social model of disability?

Evaluation of the social model of disability

Strengths

By drawing attention to the physical, attitudinal and organisational barriers faced by people with impairments, the social model paved the way for a major shift in society's understanding of disability.

It has also provided the rationale for significant institutional and organisational changes, including legislation outlawing discrimination against disabled people in many countries.

The social model has drawn attention to the objectifying and dehumanising consequences of identifying people with their impairments. As Shakespeare and Watson (2002) put it, "the social model was and remains very liberating for disabled individuals."

Weaknesses

Critics have argued that the social model denies the reality of impairment. Morris (1992) argues that "there is a tendency within the social model of disability to deny the experiences of our bodies, insisting that our physical differences and restrictions are entirely socially created. While environmental barriers and social attitudes are a crucial part of our experience of disability – and do indeed disable us – to suggest that this is all there is to it is to deny the personal experience."

By implying that disability has nothing to do with impairment, the social model fails to confront the complexity of disability. As the WHO (2002) put it, disability is a complex phenomenon that is both a problem at the level of a person's body and a social phenomenon. The fact that there are different types and degrees of impairment and that severe impairments will inevitably have an impact on people's social existence cannot be simply wished away.

CHECK YOUR UNDERSTANDING

1. Roughly how many people in contemporary Britain are officially classified as disabled?

2. Distinguish between 'impairment' and 'disability'.

3. Identify two sources of diversity among disabled people.

4. Explain the eugenics model of disability.

5. Why are disabled rights activists opposed to charitable support for disabled people?

6. Identify three ways in which disabled people are disadvantaged in society.

7. What is meant by saying that impairment can act as a 'master status'?

8. Explain the concept of 'disablism'.

9. Identify one strength and one weakness of the medical model of disability.

10. Identify one strength and one weakness of the social model of disability.

TAKE IT FURTHER

Shakespeare and Watson argue that we are all impaired to a greater or lesser degree. Hold a class discussion on whether this represents a useful way of undermining what is inevitably a somewhat arbitrary distinction between disabled and non-disabled people or a denial of the fact that some people have impairments of such severity that they will be disabled however society is organised.

5.8 CHANGES IN INEQUALITY AND CLASS STRUCTURE

LEARNING OBJECTIVES

› Demonstrate knowledge and understanding of the link between globalisation and developments in capitalism since the eighties (AO1).

› Demonstrate knowledge and understanding of the link between the transnational capitalist class and the growth of secrecy jurisdictions (AO1).

› Demonstrate knowledge and understanding of different views of the contemporary UK class structure (AO1).

› Apply knowledge and understanding of changes in inequality and class structure (AO2).

› Analyse and evaluate continuities and changes in the UK class structure (AO3).

INTRODUCING THE DEBATE

We have seen in the preceding chapters that a number of social and economic changes over recent decades have had an enormous impact on occupations and on inequality in the UK.

One change is the significant decline in the proportion of the workforce engaged in manual occupations, from about 55 per cent in the mid-1950s to about 25 per cent today. This decline has been matched by an increase in professional and routine white-collar jobs as Britain has become a post-industrial society.

Another change in occupations is the virtual disappearance of 'jobs for life' and the growth of people involved in various forms of 'precarious employment': short-term contracts; zero-hours contracts; agency employment, casual employment and the like.

These changes are linked to increasing economic inequality. Between 2009 and 2015, the number of billionaires in the UK more than doubled and pay for top company directors increased by more than 40 per cent, while the average UK worker experienced a 9 per cent decline in their real income – that is, allowing for inflation (Inequality Briefing, 2015).

Alongside these changes, as we saw in Chapters 1 and 2, has been an ongoing debate about the continuing salience of class. Rather than retracing these arguments, this chapter will focus on how the UK class structure has changed since the 1980s and on sociologists' attempts to describe how it looks today. But first we need to explore in more detail how we got here.

GLOBALISATION AND ITS IMPACT

Globalisation, as defined earlier, involves all parts of the world becoming increasingly interconnected, so that national boundaries – in some respects, at least – become less important. It is associated with increasing global flows of information, ideas, goods and people.

Sociologists differ in their understanding of globalisation and its impact on society. Some have focused on its cultural implications, reflected particularly in the work of postmodernists. Some, such as Beck (1992), have focused more on its societal implications and the possibilities it offers for a more cosmopolitan and cooperative global society – essential, in Beck's view, to deal with the growing ecological and economic crises that are beyond the scope of nation states to deal with. Yet others, influenced particularly by Marxism, have focused more on the economic and political consequences of globalisation and it is these that are particularly relevant to an understanding of how the class structure has changed.

William I. Robinson (2004) argues that globalisation represents the latest stage in the historical transformation of capitalism. For most of the 20th century, capitalism was organised on a nation state basis, but in the 1970s this system was faced with a crisis of stagnant growth and rising prices ('stagflation') and falling profits. Over the next two decades, Robinson argues, capitalism was reorganised on a global scale with the growth of multi-national or transnational corporations (TNCs), under the influence of neoliberal ideas. Welfare capitalism in the developed world was rolled back, the socialist project in the Second World ended with the so-called 'collapse of communism' and the countries of the developing world faced a debt crisis resulting from the failure of their developmentalist projects.

Robinson identifies four mechanisms by means of which capitalism reorganised itself trans-nationally. One was by promoting a new set of capital-labour relations based on the notion of labour flexibility and by weakening trades unions through legislation. Another was through both the intensification of capitalism itself – via policies of privatisation and commodification (that is, widening the range of things that could be bought and sold, such as health, happiness and security) – and the incorporation into the capitalist system of regions and areas that had previously operated outside its scope (China, the former USSR, Angola, Mozambique, and others). The third was the creation of a global legal and regulatory structure to facilitate profit accumulation: the creation of the World Trade Organisation; the setting up of hundreds of multilateral, bilateral and global free trade agreements;

and the conversion of the IMF and World Bank into promoters of neoliberalism. The final mechanism, according to Robinson, was the imposition of **neoliberal structural adjustment programmes** on any nations who were unable to repay international loans and therefore needed to seek help from the IMF or World Bank. (The reforms demanded of Greece in return for a further bailout by the EU in 2015 could, arguably, be seen as an illustration of this.)

UNDERSTAND THE CONCEPT

Neoliberal structural adjustment programmes emphasise the market allocation of resources, decreased public sector spending, liberalisation (reduction of barriers that inhibit free trade), deregulation (reduction of state control over flow of goods and services), and privatisation (sale of state-owned enterprises, shifting provision of many social services to the private sector).

In summary, Robinson claims that the present phase of global capitalism displays four novel features:

> Transnational capitalism, based on an integrated, global production and financial system

> The development of a transnational capitalist class

> The creation of a transnational 'state' apparatus into which nation-states are increasingly incorporated

> New global relations of power and inequality that cut across the old north-south, east-west divisions.

THE TRANSNATIONAL CAPITALIST CLASS

Robinson's reference to a transnational capitalist class (TCC) draws on the earlier work of Leslie Sklair (2000), who argued that globalisation had produced a new global power elite, dominant class or inner circle. Sklair wrote: "The transnational capitalist class can be analytically divided into four main factions: (1) owners and controllers of TNCs and their local affiliates (2) globalising bureaucrats and politicians (3) globalising professionals (4) consumerist elites (merchants and media)."

According to both Sklair and Robinson, the TCC share similar lifestyles, patterns of higher education and ideas and, while not always entirely united on every issue, are willing to form strategic alliances. Moreover, they seek to protect their interests through global organisations such as the World Bank, the IMF, the G20, the World Economic Forum (held annually in Davos, Switzerland), the Bilderberg Group, the Bank for International Settlements and other transnational associations.

Inextricably linked to the TCC is a social practice known as 'offshoring'. In a recent article based on his book of that name, John Urry (2014) writes: "Offshoring involves moving resources, practices, peoples and monies from one national territory to another but hiding them within secrecy jurisdictions as they move through routes wholly or partly hidden from view. Offshoring involves evading rules, laws, taxes, regulations or norms. It is all about rule-breaking, getting around rules in ways that are illegal, or go against the spirit of the law, or which use laws in one jurisdiction to undermine laws in another. Offshore worlds are full of secrets and lies."

'Secrecy jurisdictions' are also known as tax havens (or Treasure Islands, as Nicholas Shaxson called them in an influential book published in 2011). Urry states that since the 1980s there has been an "astonishing growth" in the movement of finance and wealth to and through the 60 to 70 tax havens that can be identified. They include Switzerland, Jersey, Manhattan, the Cayman Islands, Monaco, Luxemburg, Panama, Dubai, Liechtenstein, Singapore, Hong Kong, Gibraltar, the City of London and the state of Delaware in the USA.

The scale of offshored money, according to Urry, has grown from US$11 billion in 1968 to US$6 trillion in 1998 and to US$21 trillion in 2010 (equivalent to about one-third of annual world income). And it is the TCCs who are the main beneficiaries, he argues. Almost all major TNCs (83 per cent) have offshore accounts/subsidiaries, more than half of world trade passes through secrecy jurisdictions and almost all 'high net worth' individuals possess offshore accounts, enabling them to avoid or evade tax in the countries where they are domiciled.

THE UK CLASS STRUCTURE TODAY

The economic changes associated with globalisation examined above have inevitably had an impact on Britain's class structure. Moreover, since the election of Margaret Thatcher as Prime Minister in 1979, UK governments have, with varying degrees of enthusiasm, embraced neoliberal ideas and, since 2007/8, austerity programmes. These ideas and their associated policies have also affected Britain's class structure, not least because, as indicated in the introduction, they have been associated with growing economic inequality.

The main impacts on the UK class structure can be summarised as:

> Growth in the numbers of the very rich (members of the TCC) residing in the UK and benefiting from 'non-dom' status (i.e. not paying UK tax on their foreign earnings)

> Growth of insecure employment as firms seek to cut their costs and increase the flexibility of their workforce

> Growth of work in the ICT sector associated with the global scale of operations of TNCs

> Decline of work in manufacturing and heavy industry as TNCs have offshored production to the newly developing economies with cheaper labour and laxer employment regulations – which has impacted on the size of the traditional working class particularly.

It should also be noted that globalisation has led to significant changes in the demographic composition of the different classes because of increasing migration. The 2014 Labour Force Survey found that there were approximately 2.9 million people who were not British citizens working in the UK, with roughly 1.7m from other EU countries and 1.2m from non-EU countries.

There have been three main attempts to identify the UK class structure in the 21st century. Two of these have already been examined in Chapter 2: the Office for National Statistics Socio-Economic Classification (NS-SEC), introduced in 2000, and the Great British Class Survey (GBCS), introduced in 2013. The third has been offered by Guy Standing in two recent books, *Work after Globalisation* (2009) and *The Precariat: The New Dangerous Class* (2011) which, as the title suggests, was focused on the emergence of what Standing sees as an important new social class – the 'precariat' – produced by the changes in global capitalism examined earlier.

Table 5.8.1 provides a simplified comparison of these three competing views of the UK class structure today.

The three classifications differ from each other in terms of their underlying rationales, their perceptions of the nature of social classes and, to some extent, in terms of the picture of the class structure they present, although sometimes the choice of terminology means that differences are more apparent than real, as is the case for 'established middle class' and 'salariat'. They also point to both continuity and change in Britain's class structure, with both of the more recent class scales including categories absent from the NS-SEC.

The rest of this chapter will seek to explore this issue of continuity and change by examining some of the classes identified in more detail.

NS–SEC (% of working population)	GBCS (% of population)	Standing (relative sizes not estimated)
1 Higher managerial and professional (11%)	1 Elite (6%)	(Plutocracy)
2 Lower managerial and professional (23%)	2 Established middle class (25%)	1 Elite
3 Intermediate (14%)	3 Technical middle class (6%)	2 Salariat
4 Small employers and self-employed workers (10%)	4 New affluent workers (15%)	3 Proficians
5 Lower supervisory, craft and related (10%)	5 Emergent service workers (19%)	4 Proletariat
6 Semi-routine (19%)	6 Traditional working class (14%)	5 Precariat
7 Routine (13%)	7 Precariat (15%)	6 Long-term unemployed
8 Long-term unemployed or the never-worked (not estimated)		7 Lumpen precariat (or underclass)

Table 5.8.1 *Three views of the UK class structure in the early 21st century*

The Rich

The Rich are Always with us was the title of a famous 1932 Hollywood movie starring Bette Davis. The title may be a truism, but it is one sociology, as a whole, in recent decades has largely ignored. (See Focus on skills.) This is no longer the case.

Social class classifications based on occupation – such as the NS-SEC – will inevitably mask the existence of the rich because their economic position generally owes more to wealth and the income generated by certain forms of wealth (such as stocks and shares, savings accounts and property for rent) than to earnings. However, the extraordinary increase in both the wealth and income of those at the top of the class structure in recent years has forced itself on the attention of sociologists.

Both the GBCS and Standing identify the rich in their class classifications, though they choose to use the term 'elite'. (The term in brackets at the top of Standing's class scale – 'plutocracy' – refers to the super-rich who have homes in many different countries and who typically reside in one country while being 'citizens' of another to minimise their tax bills.) The issue of nomenclature – what to name this group at the top of the class structure – is not a trivial one because different terms carry different associations and link to different theoretical perspectives. 'Upper class', for example, fits with a gradational view of class, while 'ruling class' is associated particularly with a Marxist perspective and carries the implication of political power

as well as wealth. The term 'elite', for social scientists, also links with power, as in C. Wright Mills's (1956) 'power elite'; for laypeople, however, Sayer believes that it somewhat misleadingly implies special qualities and merit. Another term used in the past, for example, by John Scott (1982), and recently revived by Owen Jones (2014), is 'the establishment'.

Despite their differences, what all these terms seek to convey is that it is not simply wealth that defines this group, but shared ideas, interests and political influence. They are united today by their embrace of neoliberalism: a belief in so-called 'free markets', in privatisation, and in low taxes and opposition to state 'interference' in the economy and to any collective organisations that are critical of the *status quo*, such as trades unions. Their political interests are centred on the Conservative Party, although the Labour Party under Tony Blair and Gordon Brown (New Labour) was constructed to be acceptable to the rich with its 'pro-business' stance and embrace of the City. Influence is gained through donations to political parties, the funding of sympathetic think-tanks (such as the Institute of Economic Affairs, the Adam Smith Institute and the Centre for Policy Studies) and the fact that the majority of the press in Britain is owned by wealthy proprietors sympathetic to neoliberalism (Rupert Murdoch, the Barclay Brothers, Viscount Rothermere and Richard Desmond).

FOCUS ON SKILLS: THE RICH – THE ELEPHANT IN THE SOCIOLOGY ROOM

We simply cannot afford to ignore the rich, given their extraordinary rise over the last 30 years and their increasing domination of politics, but sociology has taken surprisingly little interest in them. The most striking feature of the growth in income and wealth inequalities in the UK, the US and many other countries is the pulling away of the 1% from the rest.

Yet the vast majority of sociological writing about class and economic inequality has been about the working class, and to a lesser extent the middle class, while the upper class or the rich class is hardly recognised. This is now beginning to be remedied …

The astonishing success of Thomas Piketty's book on the rich (*Capital in the Twenty First Century*, 2014) has caught sociology looking the other way. As Piketty and associates have shown, the rich have made a remarkable comeback; the post-war boom was an exceptional period when the share of national income in the UK going to the rich fell from its early 20th century figure of nearly 20% to less than 6%. Now it's climbing back to over 15%.

Few people realise just how fast wealth is concentrating at the top:

Collective wealth of UK's 1,000 richest people
1997 = £98 billion
2008 = £413 billion
2010 = £336 billion
2012 = £414 billion
2013 = £450 billion
2014 = £519 billion

Source: *The Sunday Times* Rich List

In these times of austerity, the wealth of these people increased by 15% just between 2013–2014. That £519 billion would fund the UK education system for 5.9 years, or the state pension bill for 3.7 years, or the NHS for 4.2 years.

Source: Sayer, A. 'Viewpoint: The rich - the elephant in the sociology room', *discoverysociety.org*, 1 December 2014

Questions

1. **Explain** the title: *The rich – the elephant in the sociology room.*

2. **Identify** how the share of national income going to the top 1 per cent has fluctuated over the last 100 years.

3. **Suggest** reasons why the share of national income going to the top 1 per cent has increased over the last few decades.

4. **Evaluate** the relative merits of the following terms for the rich: the upper class, the ruling class, the elite, the establishment.

The Middle Classes

Non-manual workers (traditionally seen as middle-class) comprise roughly three-quarters of the UK workforce today (Nomis, 2015). The tertiary or service sector of the economy that is organised around education, welfare, retail and finance has expanded hugely in the past 30 years.

The term 'middle classes' is now widely used in place of 'middle class' because it is a far from uniform category. As early as the late 1970s, Roberts et al. (1977) argued that the middle class was becoming fragmented into a number of different groups, each with a distinctive view of its place in the stratification system. Savage *et al.* (1992) agree that it is important to see that the middle class is now divided into strata, or 'class fractions', such as higher and lower professionals, higher and middle managers, the petite bourgeoisie and routine white-collar workers.

The established middle class

Traditionally, the middle class was seen as composed of people in professional and managerial occupations.

Savage and colleagues argue that higher and lower professionals mainly recruit internally – in other words, the sons and daughters of professionals are likely to end up as professionals themselves. The position of professional workers is based on the possession of educational qualifications. Professionals usually have to go through a long period of training – university plus professional examinations – before they qualify. Savage argues that professionals possess both economic capital (a very good standard of living, savings, financial security) and cultural capital (seeing the worth of education and other cultural assets such as taste in high culture), which they pass on to their children. Moreover, they increasingly have social capital (belonging to networks that can influence decision-making by other professionals such as head teachers). Professionals also have strong occupational associations, such as the Law Society and the British Medical Association, that protect and actively pursue their interests (although the lower down the professional ladder, the weaker these associations/unions become). The result of such groups actively pursuing the interests of professionals, especially those in the state sector in areas such as the NHS, includes high rewards, status and job security.

Given the impact of government austerity policies since 2007/8, how far do you think that it still remains true that professionals in the state sector are protected from insecurity in employment?

By contrast, managers have assets based upon a particular skill within specific organisations. Such skills (unlike those of professionals) are not easily transferable to other companies or industries. Savage *et al.* note that many managers have been upwardly mobile from the routine white-collar sector or the skilled working class. Many have worked their way up through an organisation that they joined at an early age. They consequently often lack university degrees. Their social position is therefore likely to be the result of experience and reputation rather than qualifications. They note too that most managers do not belong to professional associations or trade unions. Consequently, they tend to be more individualistic in character and are less likely to identify a common

collective interest with their fellow managers – whom they are much more likely to see as competitors. However, managers, despite being well paid, are less likely to have the cultural or social capital possessed by professionals.

Savage argues that job security differentiates professionals from managers – managers, particularly middle managers such as bank managers, are constantly under threat of losing their jobs because of recession, mergers and downsizing. They are consequently more likely to be potentially downwardly mobile.

The salariat

Standing (2009) argues that over the previous 20 years or so, a group of higher executives – the salariat – has appeared. These individuals run companies on a day-to-day basis, are on spectacular salaries and often have share options worth millions. The Income Data Services showed that nearly half of all senior executives of Britain's 350 largest public companies made more than £1 million a year, with eight directors on packages of £5+ million (Cohen 2005).

Adonis and Pollard (1998) claim that the salariat make up approximately 15 per cent of middle-class occupations. According to Adonis and Pollard, the lifestyle of this class revolves around nannies and servants, second homes, private education for their children, private health schemes, exotic foreign holidays and investment in modern art. The salariat tend to live in 'gated communities' patrolled by private security companies. Some sociologists have suggested that this group is no longer middle-class because it has more in common with the unified wealth elite at the top of the class structure.

The technical middle class

Clark and Hoffman-Martinot (1998) highlight the growth of a technological elite of 'wired workers' – new professionals who are as productive as entire offices of routine non-manual workers because of their use of technology, and who spend most of their days behind computers, working in non-hierarchical settings. The GBCS calls this group the technical middle class, while Standing refers to them as "proficians". They enjoy considerable autonomy, are paid extremely well, often working flexibly, sometimes from home, and are engaged in dynamic problem-solving activities. Such workers can be found in a wide range of new occupations regarded as part of the 'infotech sector' – areas such as web design, systems analysis, e-commerce, software development, graphic design and financial consultancy.

THE WORKING CLASS

One of the main motives for the development of the NS-SEC was the conviction that the manual/non-manual distinction, on which the earlier Registrar-General's scale was based, was no longer either a valid or a useful way of identifying class differences. On the one hand, the earnings of many skilled manual workers far exceed those of routine white-collar workers; on the other, the working conditions of many white-collar employees (such as those working in call centres) increasingly resemble those of factory workers – a process that Marxists labelled 'proletarianisation'.

Nevertheless, a significant minority of the population are still involved in skilled/semi-skilled/unskilled manual work (for example, electricians, lorry drivers, cleaners, respectively) and are identified by the GBCS as the traditional working class and by Standing as the proletariat.

Fulcher and Scott (1999) point out that, until the late 20th century, the working class had a strong sense of their social-class position. Virtually all aspects of their lives, including gender roles, family life, political affiliation and leisure, were a product of their keen sense of working-class identity. Lockwood's (1966) research found that many workers, especially in industrial areas, subscribed to a value system he called 'proletarian traditionalist'. Such workers felt a strong sense of loyalty to each other because of shared community and work experience, and so were mutually supportive of each other. They had a keen sense that capitalist society was characterised by inequality and unfairness. Consequently, they tended to see society in terms of conflict – a case of 'them' (their employers who were seen as exploiting them) versus 'us' (the workers united in a common cause and consciousness).

Later research has claimed that this type of class identity is in decline because the service sector of the economy has grown more important as the traditional industrial and manufacturing sectors have gone into decline. Moreover, recession and unemployment linked to globalisation have undermined traditional working-class communities and organisations such as trade unions.

A recent study of the views of people who identify as working class carried out by a 'strategic research agency', BritainThinks (2011), found that 24 per cent of people identified themselves as working class, compared to 67 per cent in the late 1980s. Using focus groups in Rotherham and Basildon, they found that their sample felt "disenfranchised, isolated and threatened on all sides". Most felt unrepresented by any of the leading political parties (Conservative, Labour, Lib-Dems), were scathing about politicians and regretted what they saw as the decline of trades unions. They also reflected anti-immigrant views – seeing immigration, especially from Eastern Europe, as having depressed wages – and claimed that the term 'working class' had been devalued through its association with 'chavs' – a group from which the participants were anxious to disassociate themselves.

THE PRECARIAT

Two of the class scales summarised in Table 5.8.1 identify a new class, which they call the 'precariat'. The term is a neologism – a new word – formed from an adjective 'precarious' (meaning unstable) and a noun 'proletariat' (meaning worker). This class is not only new but growing, as more and more workers are 'precariatised', that is, habituated to expecting a life of unstable employment.

In the GBCS, the precariat are the bottom group and are described as "the most deprived group of all". Standing disagrees with this description, arguing that the precariat are not at the bottom of the class structure, a position occupied in his view by what he calls a "lumpen precariat" or underclass – (see below). Nevertheless, for both the GBCS and Standing, the precariat is characterised by insecure and unstable labour associated with casualisation, informalisation, agency labour, part-time labour, phoney self-employment and **crowd-labour**.

Many believe that trade unions no longer have the power they once had.

> ## UNDERSTAND THE CONCEPT
>
> **Crowd-labour** refers to work outsourced to a large, geographically dispersed group of people via the internet. It represents a specific type of crowdsourcing using people who work from home, when needed, on specific projects.

How do you think crowdsourced labour should be viewed: as an enterprising way of spreading work around or as the creation of digital sweatshops?

Besides the distinctive employment situation of its members, Standing identifies a number of additional features that characterise the precariat:

> It depends almost entirely on money wages, with limited rights to access the forms of social security developed under welfare capitalism (which, in any case, are increasingly restricted under austerity policies).

> Its members lack the sense of a secure occupational identity and the notion of a career traditionally associated with occupations.

> Members must engage in a lot of work outside of paid labour in order to make and keep themselves employable and the division between work and leisure becomes blurred as members need to be available more or less on call.

> Members are often over-qualified for the work they do.

Members have distinctive relations to the state. They are 'denizens' rather than citizens "pushed to rely on discretionary and conditional hand-outs from the state and by privatised agencies and charities operating on its behalf" (Standing, 2014).

Standing argues that the precariat is comprised of three groups in tension with one another, each characterised by a different form of relative deprivation. The first consists of those with few educational qualifications, dropping out of old working-class communities, who feel deprived relative to a lost past, real or imaginary. The second consists of migrants and ethnic minorities who feel deprived of a sense of belonging, of feeling at home in the present. And the third consists of those who feel deprived of a future, despite the fact that they have acquired educational qualifications.

Collectively, for Standing, they represent a 'class-in-the-making' and one that has the potential to become a class-for-itself and therefore a driver of social change. As such, they pose a threat to the *status quo* – hence the subtitle of Standing's 2011 book: *The Precariat: The New Dangerous Class*. They are "dangerous" in his view because:

> They share a "powerful sense of status frustration and relative deprivation".

> They reject the "old mainstream political traditions".

> They feel unrepresented by the established political parties.

But, Standing argues, they are also dangerous in that they could easily fall victim to extreme right-wing political parties exploiting their frustrations and sense of alienation from mainstream political parties.

Standing's thesis has been subjected to fierce criticism from Marxists who have argued either that those experiencing precarious employment are simply a segment of the working class (Bailey, 2012) or that precariousness is increasingly experienced by nearly all classes below the 'ruling bloc' and that therefore this is not a new class-in-the-making (Breman, 2013). It has also been criticised by the GBCS team, who argue that people higher up the class structure, who face precarious employment, possess cultural resources and have social networks that ensure the experience will be temporary. Standing has responded to such criticisms by emphasising the various ways in which, in his view, the precariat is distinctive in terms of its relationship to the processes of capitalist production and distribution and to the state, and therefore does have the potential to become a class-for-itself.

THE UNDERCLASS?

The claim advanced by neoliberal social scientists such as Charles Murray, David Marsland and Peter Saunders, that an 'underclass' exists below the class structure of societies such as Britain and the USA, was examined in detail in Book 1, Topic 6, Chapter 4 and 5. The conclusion reached there was that "there is little evidence to support the (alleged) existence of a large, permanently excluded underclass in Britain".

The only one of the three class scales summarised in Table 5.8.1 that refers explicitly to an underclass is Standing's, but it is clear from his description of this group that he is not using the term in the same way as neoliberals. In particular, Standing's underclass – or 'lumpen precariat' – is not a large group but consists of "sad people lingering in the streets, dying miserably" (Standing, 2014). Moreover, Savage – the lead researcher on the GBCS – has stated (*Guardian*, 10 April 2013) that the GBCS team consciously avoided using the term 'underclass' as they felt it had been used to denigrate the poor and disadvantaged.

CONCLUSIONS

The evidence presented in this chapter suggests that globalisation has been associated with both global and local changes in class structure. Globally, a new transnational capitalist class has emerged. Locally, Britain's class structure has become increasingly polarised, with a very wealthy class increasingly detached from the rest and increasing numbers lower down experiencing a precarious existence. Whether, as Standing argues, the latter represent a full-blown class-in-the-making, only time will tell. But what is clear, as Savage (2013) has argued, is that the concept of class is still needed if we are to understand how widening economic inequalities connect to social and cultural changes in society.

CHECK YOUR UNDERSTANDING

1. Identify three features of the global organisation of capitalism today.

2. Identify the four groups that make up the transnational capitalist class, according to Sklair.

3. Explain what is meant by 'secrecy jurisdictions'.

4. Why has there been a renewed interest within sociology in studying the wealthy in recent years?

5. Identify two ways in which the elite promote their shared (class) interests.

6. Identify three distinct groupings within the middle classes.

7. Why has there been a decline in working-class solidarity in recent decades?

8. Identify four forms of precarious employment today.

9. Why does Standing refer to the precariat as "the new dangerous class"?

10. How does Standing's view of the underclass differ from that of neoliberal social scientists?

TAKE IT FURTHER

If you are interested in exploring further the issues of class in Britain today, look at the following books written for the 'interested layperson'. A left-wing perspective is provided by Owen Jones in *Chavs* (2011) and *The Establishment* (2014), and a more right-wing view by Ferdinand Mount in *Mind the Gap: The New Class Divide* in Britain (2005).

5.9 THE NATURE AND SIGNIFICANCE OF SOCIAL MOBILITY

LEARNING OBJECTIVES

> Demonstrate knowledge and understanding of the different types and sources of social mobility (AO1).

> Demonstrate knowledge and understanding of social mobility studies and what they reveal about patterns of absolute and relative mobility (AO1).

> Apply knowledge and understanding of social mobility (AO2).

> Analyse the uses and limitations of these studies (AO3).

> Evaluate the debate surrounding the degree to which Britain is a meritocracy (AO3).

INTRODUCING THE DEBATE

Social mobility refers to the movement of individuals or groups up or down a system of social stratification. Social mobility is important sociologically because it represents the major way in which economic inequalities are legitimised in modern societies and because social mobility influences the formation of social class subcultures: high rates of mobility are likely to hinder the formation of distinctive social class subcultures, whilst low rates are likely to promote them.

The idea that all should have an equal opportunity to be upwardly mobile – a view more or less taken for granted today in the UK – is historically, relatively recent. Until well into the 20th century, people were expected to 'know their place' and make the best of whatever cards life's lottery had dealt them. However, as the century progressed so demands began to grow for a more open or fluid society. The passing of the 1944 Education Act, with its provision of free secondary education for all and with access to different types of state schooling being dependent on performance in a competitive exam (the '11-Plus'), marked the transition to widespread acceptance of the idea that society should be meritocratic – based on ability and effort rather than birth.

Today, the idea of equal opportunity is embraced by all political parties, and governments are, on paper at least, committed to promoting it through their social and educational policies. This chapter will examine how sociologists have conceptualised and measured social mobility and how successful governments have been in promoting equal opportunities. But first we need to look a little more closely at the key concept of meritocracy.

MERITOCRACY

Literally, a meritocracy would be a society ruled by those with the most merit (defined as effort plus ability). Today, the term is widely used as simply another word for equal opportunity. The term was coined by the British sociologist Michael Young who, in a novel entitled *The Rise of the Meritocracy 1870–2033,* first published in 1958, envisioned a future society based on meritocracy, which he painted as a 'dystopia' (an undesirable society). It would be undesirable, he felt, because those who reached the top would legitimately feel that they had 'earned' their position and so would have no qualms about their resulting privileges. For Young, a socialist as well as a sociologist, a good society would be one based not on equality of opportunity (associated with meritocracy), but on equality of condition (or equality of outcome, as it is also known).

The term no longer carries the negative connotations with which Young invested it, much to his dismay ('Down with meritocracy', *The Guardian,* 29 June 2001), but students need to recognise that a meritocracy essentially embodies the idea that everyone should have an equal chance to end up better off than others. Whether such a society is more desirable than one based on greater equality of condition is a matter of debate, since it involves making value judgements. Nevertheless, few would deny that a society in which status was based on achievement rather than ascription is fairer, so sociology can play a useful role in examining how open society actually is.

Another way of describing meritocracy – and the one used in the British Social Attitudes Survey in 2009 – is a society in which everyone has 'an equal opportunity to get ahead'. This is equivalent to 'an equal chance to end up better off than others' and yet the two phrases evoke different emotional responses. Why do you think this is?

SOCIOLOGICAL PERSPECTIVES ON MERITOCRACY

Functionalist

As we saw in Chapter 1, functionalists take it for granted that industrial societies need to be meritocratic if they are to function efficiently, for two main reasons. First, social solidarity would be undermined if people did not have an equal opportunity to compete for high-status positions because they would see the system as unfair. Second, without equal opportunities, the functionally most important positions would not be filled by those most capable of performing the roles associated with them and society would therefore not function efficiently. From this perspective, any barriers to meritocracy, such as racial discrimination, would be dysfunctional.

Marxist

For Marxists, the idea that capitalist societies are meritocratic is essentially a myth that helps to legitimate social class inequalities. Moreover, in their view, education, far from being an engine of meritocracy, is one of the crucial means by which social classes are reproduced from one generation to another. They do not, of course, deny that there is some social mobility within capitalist societies, but argue that it is impossible for children lower down the class system to have the same opportunities to be upwardly mobile as those higher up. In any case, for Marxists, the 'good society' is not one based on equal opportunities for people to end up unequal, but one based on equality of condition.

THE NATURE OF SOCIAL MOBILITY

There are two main ways of looking at social mobility:

> *Intergenerational mobility* – movement between generations; for example, a daughter moving higher up the social scale than her mother.

> *Intragenerational mobility* – movement of an individual within their working life; for example, an individual may start off as an office junior and work their way up to office manager, win the lottery or marry someone wealthy.

Sources of mobility

It is important to recognise that there are two quite different sources of social mobility in a society. If, over time, the shape of the stratification system changes – if, say, the number of higher-status jobs increases – this will lead to an increase in upward mobility even if there is no change in the openness of the society (other things, such as fertility rates, remaining the same). Such mobility is known as 'absolute' or 'structural' mobility.

If, on the other hand, the shape of the stratification system stays the same over time, mobility is only possible if some move down in order for others to move up. In other words, the link between the status of parents and their offspring has to weaken. Such mobility is known as 'relative' mobility and its extent depends on how 'open' or 'fluid' the society is.

Problems of measuring social mobility

A number of problems attend the measurement of social mobility. Normally, mobility is measured in terms of movement between social classes but, as we saw in Chapter 2, there is much debate about how best to measure class. For example, class scales based on occupation offer a relatively straightforward way of locating people, but such scales focus on the working population and say little about the very rich and the very poor – important groups in society, but ones for whom occupation is unlikely to provide their main source of income and wealth. Also, over time, some occupations disappear and new ones emerge; or the relative position of occupations may change – for example, clerical work is no longer paid more than skilled manual work. Another difficulty is that 'intragenerational' mobility poses problems for the measurement of 'intergenerational' mobility: for example, if people are socially mobile during their working life, at what point do you compare one generation with another? Finally, and again relating to intergenerational mobility, if both parents worked, which one do you compare their offspring with?

Partly because of such problems, some sociologists – alongside economists – have in recent years started using income rather than occupation to measure mobility. They do this by dividing the population into income groups and measuring whether a younger generation ends up in a higher, lower or equivalent income group to its parents (allowing for changes in the level of earnings over time). This method is not without its problems either, for example, it still leaves wealth out of the picture and people may be reluctant to reveal their income.

These and other problems mean that measuring mobility is difficult and that one must treat the findings of mobility studies with caution. Nevertheless, these problems are far from insuperable and there is no reason to think that mobility studies should not be able to reveal broad patterns and trends. So what have mobility studies found?

Social mobility studies

The Oxford Mobility Study (OMS)

The OMS (Goldthorpe, 1980) used a large sample survey to examine the position of sons in 1972 relative to their fathers. Fathers and sons were classified using the 7-point Hope-Goldthorpe class scale (see Chapter 2). The study found relatively high rates of both 'long-range mobility' (movement across several classes) and 'absolute mobility', with much greater numbers of people from working-class origins (classes 6 and 7) being upwardly mobile into the service class (classes 1 and 2) compared with the 1950s and 1960s. For example, 7.1 per cent of sons of class 7

fathers were in class 1 in 1972, over a quarter of the men in class 1 in 1972 had working-class origins and in none of the seven classes did more than 50 per cent of the sample originate from the same class.

Explaining the findings

Goldthorpe suggested three main reasons for the increase in upward mobility he found:

1. Changes in the economy and therefore the class structure. The size of the service class had increased, while the intermediate class (classes 3, 4 and 5) and working class had decreased. Consequently, there was more 'room at the top'.

2. There had been differences in the fertility rate of social classes and consequently in the number of children being born. The fertility rate of the service class had been too low to cope with the growth of service-sector jobs. This sector therefore had no choice but to recruit from other social classes.

3. Education had dramatically expanded since the Second World War. In particular, the introduction of free secondary education in 1944 and the expansion of higher education had facilitated upward mobility because, for the first time, people from working-class backgrounds had access to higher educational qualifications.

However, this increase in absolute mobility had occurred without any change in 'relative mobility'. The chances of upward mobility had increased for all social classes because there was more room at the top of the class structure, but there was no evidence of any narrowing of the gap between classes in their relative chances of being upwardly mobile. The relative chances of those born between 1938 and 1947 of making it into the service class were roughly the same as those born between 1908 and 1917: boys from the service class were roughly four times more likely to obtain a service-class job than boys from the working class and twice as likely as boys from the intermediate class for both birth cohorts. The *Sunday Times* dubbed this "the 1–2–4 rule of relative hope" and argued that, while absolute mobility had increased, there was little to suggest that this had been accompanied by greater equality in opportunities for all social classes.

The OMS was in many ways a path-breaking piece of research, but it was not without its limitations. In particular, it was focused exclusively on males and was unable to shed any light on entry into the very top of the class structure – the elite – because class 1 in the Hope-Goldthorpe scale covers quite a broad range of occupations and, as indicated in Chapter 2, excludes wealth.

Recent studies of social mobility

Numerous further studies of social mobility have been carried out since the OMS and, up to the end of the 20th century, they largely concurred with the findings of the OMS. This later research also covered female mobility.

However, a study published in 2005 suggested that rates of relative social mobility were actually declining.

The study, carried out by Blanden, Greg and Machin at the Centre for Economic Performance (CEP), looked at intergenerational mobility based upon income rather than class. The CEP research analysed data from two British birth-cohort studies: the National Child Development Study (following children born in 1958) and the British Cohort Study (following children born in 1970). Their key finding was that the earnings of men and women in the 1970 cohort (when they were in their early thirties) was more closely associated with their family incomes at the age of 16 than those of the 1958 cohort were. For the 1958 cohort there was a 30% chance that income differences in childhood would be reflected in their early adult earnings, but for the 1970 cohort there was a 40% chance.

The CEP research has been very influential. Indeed, according to John Goldthorpe, writing in 2012, the idea that social mobility in Britain has stalled has become so widely taken for granted that he dubs it the 'consensus view'. However, the reliability of the CEP research has been challenged by a number of writers. Gorard (2008), for example, points out that whilst both cohorts had around 17,000 children at the outset, the results of the research are based on only around 2,000 in each, for whom the necessary data was available. Moreover, he states that while the researchers time-averaged the income of parents across two different points of time for one cohort – thereby increasing the reliability of the measurement of parental income – they didn't do this for the other cohort. Additionally, Goldthorpe criticises the CEP researchers for not making explicit that their research was focused on relative mobility and that their conclusions said nothing about what was happening to absolute mobility.

The majority of other research since 2000 – for example, Paterson and Ianelli (2007) and Goldthorpe and Mills (2008) – either claims that there has been no significant change in relative rates of mobility since the middle of the last century, or suggests that there is some evidence of slightly greater fluidity in class terms (Li and Devine, 2011). There has, however, been a slowdown in rates of absolute mobility for men, but not for women.

Gender and social mobility

For much of the twentieth century, female social mobility lagged a long way behind that of males. This is no longer the case. Roberts (2001) argues that "Recent school-leaving cohorts have been the first waves of young women in modern times whose mothers worked for the greater part of their adult lives and during their daughters' (and sons') childhoods. These mothers (and fathers) have encouraged their daughters to aim for decent jobs – not to be left in the typing pools or at the supermarket check-outs."

Wilkinson (1994) argues that towards the end of the century there was what she calls a "genderquake" in female attitudes. Females were increasingly prioritising employment and careers over having children. At the same time, there was a remarkable improvement in female educational performance, with females outperforming males at all levels of the British educational system.

Research by Li and Devine (2011), using the 1991 British Household Panel Survey and the 2005 General Household Survey, found that absolute upward mobility had increased significantly for women and downward mobility had declined slightly over the 14-year period between the two surveys. Nevertheless, while upward mobility clearly outweighs downward mobility for men (40.6 per cent compared with 31.3 per cent in 2005), the reverse is true for women (35.9 per cent compared with 36.8 per cent in 2005). Moreover, as these figures indicate, women are still less likely to be upwardly mobile and more likely to be downwardly mobile than men. Additionally, as Chapter 4 indicated, the evidence suggests that women continue to encounter a 'glass ceiling', barring them from entry to elite positions in society – or, at least, making it more difficult.

Ethnic minorities and social mobility

According to the Centre on Dynamics of Ethnicity (2013), ethnic minorities in Britain are experiencing increasing absolute upward mobility, with growth in clerical, professional and managerial employment, but still face significant barriers to enjoying the levels of social mobility of their White British peers (relative mobility).

First-generation members of ethnic minorities (immigrants) have lower rates of social mobility than do the rest of British society. Indeed, Platt (2005) notes that many immigrants to the UK in the 1950s and early 1960s experienced downward mobility due to racial discrimination. But the second and third generations (their children and grandchildren) have experienced rates of upward mobility that are similar to their White

British peers. Platt conducted a study of second- and third-generation Asians and African Caribbeans and compared job destinations with parents. She found that 35 per cent of her Indian sample and 22 per cent of her African Caribbean sample had service-class jobs, compared with 38 per cent of her White control sample. This has been facilitated by significant improvements in educational attainment among many ethnic minority groups. Chinese, Indian, Irish, Bangladeshi and Black African students now outperform their White British peers in obtaining five or more GCSEs at grade A* to C, and all BAME groups have significantly improved their access to higher education. Indeed, by 2011, Chinese, Indian and Black African groups had a higher proportion of people with degree-level qualifications than White groups.

Nevertheless, despite this mobility, the second and third generations still face significant ethnic penalties in the labour market. Improved levels of educational attainment have not translated into improved outcomes in employment. For example, Black male unemployment has remained persistently double that of Whites, and while self-employment has provided an important avenue of upward mobility for many Asian minorities, it is marked by, for example, disproportionate clustering in the transport sector (taxi-cabs) for Pakistani men.

SO HOW MERITOCRATIC IS BRITAIN?

In recent years, as Britain has become a more unequal society economically, the issue of meritocracy has become increasingly prominent politically. As Gaffney and Baumberg (2014) argue, "Growing inequality means that the consequences of social mobility are much more significant than they were in the past – the rewards and penalties of social mobility or immobility are that much greater."

Having looked at a range of evidence relating to social mobility, we should now be in a position to answer the question posed above. However, it turns out that the answer is far from straightforward. This is partly, as we have seen, because social scientists sometimes disagree about how the evidence should be interpreted, but it is also because they disagree about which facts matter most – for example, whether absolute or relative mobility is more important. Consequently, the issue of how meritocratic Britain is has become the focus of intense debate.

Peter Saunders

The leading sociological proponent of the view that Britain is essentially meritocratic is the New Right sociologist, Peter Saunders (*Social Mobility Myths*, 2010).

In his view, "people in Britain are getting allocated to occupational class positions mainly according to meritocratic principles."

While accepting that entry to elite positions – 'the top 1 per cent', as he describes it – is not based on meritocratic principles, entry to the remaining 99 per cent of positions is, he claims. Yet most sociologists, he argues, disagree because their perceptions are biased by their left-wing commitments: nine out of ten sociology professors in Britain describe themselves as 'hard left' or 'moderate left' (Halsey, 2004). This ideological commitment has allegedly produced a left-wing orthodoxy he calls "the SAD thesis" – the theory that 'social advantages and disadvantages' are conferred at birth and that children born in modest circumstances have the odds massively stacked against them.

This 'biased' view has generated four 'social mobility myths', Saunders claims. These are:

> the myth that Britain is 'a closed-shop society' in which life-chances are heavily shaped by the class into which you are born

> the myth that social mobility, already limited, is now getting even more so

> the myth that differences of ability between individuals either do not exist or are irrelevant in explaining differential rates of success

> the myth that governments can increase social mobility via top-down social re-engineering within the education system and forcing more income redistribution.

Joan Garrod (2011) has usefully summarised the evidence Saunders presents in seeking to rebut these alleged myths:

> Based on a 3-class scale (professional/managerial, intermediate and working), more than half the population are in a different class from that into which they were born.

> Claims that social mobility is lower in Britain than elsewhere are based on shaky statistics.

> Almost all research shows that social mobility is not falling and some research shows that it is increasing, especially for women.

> Children born to middle-class parents tend to succeed because bright people tend to become middle-class and these people have bright children.

> Most bright working-class children do succeed and are upwardly mobile (though less bright middle-class children do not necessarily move down).

> In terms of adult occupational status, based on cognitive ability at 11, ability is almost twice as important as class origin, three times more important than the level of parental interest in education and five times more significant than parents' level of education or their aspirations for their children.

'Social Mobility Myths': an assessment

Clearly, the contemporary UK is not a caste society, but neither is it a perfect meritocracy, as Saunders concedes. So the issue is not whether Britain is a meritocracy, but the degree to which it is meritocratic.

Some of Saunders' claims about so-called left-wing sociologists are unjustified. Most sociologists would not describe Britain today as a 'closed-shop society' and few claim that social mobility overall is declining. Most sociologists acknowledge that absolute social mobility for women has been increasing. However, Saunders's other claims are disputed.

First, most sociologists argue that relative mobility – fluidity – is more important than absolute mobility in assessing the degree of meritocracy. Saunders disagrees, arguing that absolute mobility is more important than relative mobility because it has had a profound effect on how people think about their social status and class position, and how they judge what is fair in modern society. In particular, Saunders argues that absolute mobility has had a crucial effect upon people's attitudes towards the future – it has resulted in the working class becoming more aspirational and seeing upward mobility as a very real possibility for their children. This may well be true but, whether Saunders likes it or not, it is relative mobility that is the crucial test of meritocracy.

Second, most sociologists do claim that people's life-chances in Britain are heavily shaped by the class into which they are born. For example, recent research by Blanden, Gregg and Macmillan (2013) compared the educational performance of children in the top fifth and the bottom fifth of the population in England, based on family income at 14. They found that children from the top fifth were 40 per cent more likely to get five GCSEs at A* to C grades, twice as likely to get one or more A Levels and three times as likely to participate in higher education.

Saunders's response to such findings is to claim that they are misleading because they ignore the role of intelligence and effort. Saunders argues that there is a genetic basis to social mobility. He suggests that people with middle-class jobs are generally brighter than those with working-class jobs and, because intelligence is heritable, middle-class parents tend to have bright children. He also suggests that middle-class parents are better at motivating their children. Consequently, it is inevitable that middle-class children will outperform working-class children in the competition for high-status positions.

The glass floor and the class ceiling

The issue of the heritability of intelligence is a highly contentious one, which is still far from resolved. Against Saunders, Roberts, for example, argues that it is impossible to measure innate ability. He notes that "performance in intelligence tests, the construction of these tests, and what we mean by ability, are all socially contaminated." Moreover, since Saunders also claims that "most bright working-class children do succeed", it would appear that their alleged lack of motivation is not a crippling disadvantage.

However, Saunders's position on the role of intelligence is undermined by research which indicates that, even when measured intelligence is held constant, middle-class children still tend to be more successful. For example, research by Abigail McKnight (2015), based on the British birth cohort survey, looked at earnings at the age of 42 years. She found that children from more advantaged social backgrounds who are assessed at age 5 as having low ability are nonetheless 35 per cent more likely to be high earners as adults than children from poorer families who show early signs of high ability. The research concludes that middle-class parents are successful in creating a 'glass floor' that prevents their children from downward mobility. (Compare the concept of 'opportunity hoarding', introduced in Chapter 1, Getting you Thinking.)

Another recent piece of research has identified a 'class ceiling' (similar to the 'glass ceiling' affecting women). It limits any prospects that people from working-class backgrounds who actually are successful in being upwardly mobile might have of enjoying earnings equivalent to people from upper middle-class backgrounds. An analysis of the 2014 Labour Force Survey, by Friedman and Laurison (2015), found that those in NS-SEC class 1 occupations whose parents were in classes 6 or 7 earn on average £6,200 less a year than their colleagues from class 1 backgrounds, even after controlling for a host of factors known to affect earnings, such as educational qualifications, job tenure, training, gender, age, hours worked and firm size. Similarly, research by Ashley et al. (2015), based on interviews with staff from 13 elite law, accountancy and financial services firms, found that as many as 70 per cent of job offers in 2014 were to graduates who had been educated either at a selective state school or a fee-paying school, even though such schools educate only 4 per cent and 7 per cent of children respectively.

FOCUS ON SKILLS: WHAT THE HELL AM I DOING HERE?

My first experience of moving significantly outside of my class came at Cambridge University. It was the first dinner there. I had no family or friends to tell me how to wear the stupid over-sized gown, so I improvised, searching Google to find images of people wearing them, so I could work out how it was supposed to be worn.

That first dinner was a fascinating experience. It was black tie with silver service. What would now be termed 'imposter syndrome' oozed through me as I sat at the top table, watching waiters and waitresses bring out the three course dinner (with wine and port). Staring at the cutlery in front of me, I pulled out memories of how to best use it, using the only experience I had: years of waiting on tables and performing silver service at Cheltenham race-course. I wasn't comfortable enough in my surroundings to ask for help – I already felt like I didn't fit in, and felt a stronger bond to those waiting tables than those sat around me.

How and where you grow up affects how you think – about the world, about others and about yourself. Coming from a working-class, or lower socio-economic background, and trying to culturally fit into middle-class lifestyles and jobs can be incredibly difficult.

Middle class is a scary place, full of unwritten rules that are alien to someone coming from a background where survival is paramount. Growing up poor, your brain is constantly working out how to get through today; and planning to work out tomorrow when it comes to it. It's hard to plan a future, a route through career structures, pensions and life – when you have grown up focusing on the next pay packet, and are thinking about how to make sure you have enough food and electricity to last.

When you come from a poor background you are unlikely to have cultural experiences that can form the basis of many conversations. You don't have the same shared experiences of locations visited, shows, plays and museums seen. I was nearly 20 before I saw my first play that wasn't on a school trip. Food is different (hummus is awesome – I didn't know of its existence until the first time I had to make it working as a chef), clothing is different (you mean you don't just buy the cheapest things that look ok?) attitudes towards people are different (there's a lot more subtext, nuance and casualness among friendships), relationships are different, and your cultural reference points are different.

Coming from lower income backgrounds, we start off feeling inferior – because life and our experiences have told us that we are. We then risk continuing to feel inferior because we are stuck in circles surrounded by people who constantly have access to knowledge and cultural experiences we haven't.

Source: Brook (2014), quantumplations.org.

Questions

1. **Explain**. What do you think the author means by 'imposter syndrome' (line 10)?

2. **Identify** some of the ways in which the author felt ill-prepared to cope as a Cambridge undergraduate.

3. **Analyse** how the content of this blog links to the concept of a 'class ceiling'.

EDUCATION, ECONOMIC INEQUALITY AND SOCIAL MOBILITY

Saunders claims that the idea that governments can increase social mobility "via top-down social re-engineering of education" is also a myth. But the truth of this claim is highly dependent upon just how radical governments are prepared to be. Governments can do nothing to stop affluent parents investing in private tuition, but they could do something about the widespread social practice of middle-class parents buying houses in the catchment area of more successful state schools by, for instance, insisting that children are allocated to schools by lottery rather than area of residence. They could also do more to address the advantages enjoyed by children who attend independent schools – in terms , for example, of facilities, small class sizes and social networking – by addressing the charitable status enjoyed by such schools, or – more radically – abolishing them. Less controversially, they could simply increase investment in state schools, although this is unlikely to happen under the present austerity regime.

Finally, Saunders claims that the idea that governments can increase social mobility by "forcing more income redistribution" is also a myth. The evidence is not on his side. The claim cautiously put forward first in 2005 by Blanden, Gregg and Machin – on the basis of a comparison of eight developed societies – that mobility is lower where inequality is higher has been supported by further research since then. For example, Corak (2013) provides powerful evidence, based on a comparison of 13 advanced economies, that there is a significant positive correlation between higher levels of income inequality and higher levels of intergenerational earnings inelasticity – in other words, higher income inequality is associated with a tighter link between the earnings of parents and children – see Figure 5.9.1. The 'Gini coefficient' represents the income distribution of a nation.

What the chart shows is that, as you move from left to right on the horizontal axis, you move from more equal to less equal countries in terms of income distribution, and as you move from bottom to top on the vertical axis, you move from countries where there is a looser association between the income of parents and their children to one where there is a closer association. On this measure, the USA, Italy and the UK all have higher levels of inequality and higher intergenerational income inelasticity, while Finland, Norway and Denmark have lower levels of both.

The curve was dubbed 'The Great Gatsby Curve' by Alan Kreuger in 2012, then Chairman of the US Council of Economic Advisers, after the eponymous character of the famous American novel by F. Scott Fitzgerald.

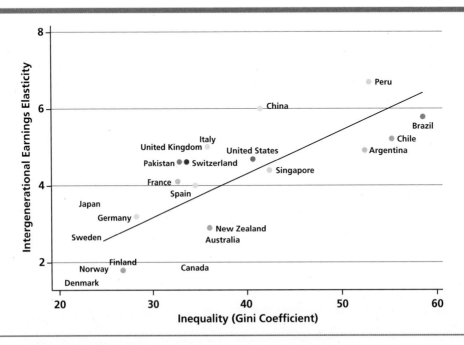

Figure 5.9.1 *The Great Gatsby Curve*
Source: Corak (2012)

CONCLUSIONS

The possibility of social mobility is often used to justify the existence of inequalities of condition: so long as all have the chance to acquire the 'glittering prizes' associated with occupational success, inequalities of outcome can be presented as fair. However, it turns out that, in practice, large inequalities of condition militate against the achievement of equal opportunities. Rather than equal opportunity offsetting inequality of condition, the latter makes the achievement of the former much more difficult. As the gaps between the rungs of the ladder grow ever wider in Britain (see Chapters 3 and 8), the achievement of a more meritocratic society is likely to become ever harder.

CHECK YOUR UNDERSTANDING

1. Distinguish between 'intergenerational' and 'intragenerational' mobility.

2. What is the difference between 'absolute' and 'relative' mobility?

3. Why did absolute upward social mobility increase significantly in the second half of the 20th century?

4. What is the 1–2–4 rule of relative hope?

5. What has happened to female social mobility in the last couple of decades?

6. What has happened to ethnic minority social mobility in the last couple of decades?

7. Identify Saunders's four 'social mobility myths'.

8. Why does Saunders not see higher rates of middle-class upward mobility as evidence of a lack of meritocracy?

9. How does evidence of the existence of a 'class ceiling' and 'glass floor' challenge Saunders' claims?

10. Explain what the 'Great Gatsby Curve' shows.

TAKE IT FURTHER

The Sutton Trust was set up by Sir Peter Lampl in 1997 to promote greater social mobility through education. As well as being a think tank, having commissioned over 140 research studies, it describes itself as a 'do tank', having funded over 200 programmes designed to address educational inequality. It also operates as a pressure group, lobbying government on policies to promote greater meritocracy.

Have a look at some of its research at www.suttontrust.com.

APPLY YOUR LEARNING

1 Outline and explain two ways in which women continue to be disadvantaged in the contemporary UK.   [10 marks]

2 Read **Item A** below and answer the question that follows.

ITEM A

Recent analyses of changes in the UK class structure have drawn attention to the emergence of a new class – the precariat – composed of people in insecure and generally poorly paid employment.

Applying material from **Item A**, analyse **two** reasons for the emergence of the precariat in recent decades.   [10 marks]

3 Read **Item B** below and answer the question that follows.

ITEM B

Sociologists disagree about how meritocratic British society is. Some argue that those who are bright and work hard will be successful whatever their starting point, while others argue that the dice are loaded in favour of those born into more affluent backgrounds.

Applying material from **Item B**, and your knowledge, evaluate the debate around meritocracy in the UK.   [20 marks]

You can find example answers and accompanying teacher's comments for this topic at www.collins.co.uk/AQAAlevelSociology. Please note that these example answers and teacher's comments have not been approved by AQA.

6 BELIEFS IN SOCIETY

AQA specification	Chapters
Candidates should examine:	
Ideology, science and religion, including Christian and non-Christian religious traditions.	Chapter 1 (pages 430–444) covers ideology and science. Sociological theories of religion are covered in Chapter 2 (pages 445–466).
The relationship between social change and social stability, and between religious beliefs, practices and organisations.	These relationships are discussed in Chapter 2 (pages 445–466).
Religious organisations, including cults, sects, denominations, churches and new-age movements, and their relationship to religious and spiritual belief and practice.	Chapter 3 (pages 467–480) covers this.
The relationship between different social groups and religious/spiritual organisations and movements, beliefs and practices.	These relationships are discussed in Chapter 4 (pages 481–498).
The significance of religion and religiosity in the contemporary world, including the nature and extent of secularisation in a global context, and globalisation and the spread of religions.	A discussion of this can be found in Chapter 5 (pages 499–515).

6.1 IDEOLOGY, SCIENCE AND RELIGION

LEARNING OBJECTIVES

> Demonstrate knowledge and understanding of science as a social construct and sociological definitions of religion (AO1).

> Apply this understanding to contemporary society (AO2).

> Analyse the differences between science and religion as belief systems and ideologies (AO3).

> Evaluate sociological explanations of the relationship between science and religion (AO3).

INTRODUCING THE DEBATE

It is not easy to work out what counts as a religious belief system or the characteristics a system must have to qualify as 'religious'. Moreover, there are thousands of different religions, many of which claim to be more 'truthful' than the others and superior to non-religious belief systems such as science.

Hamilton (2001) observes that everyone at some point asks 'big' questions about things that are beyond their understanding: "sleep and dreams, death, catastrophes, war, social upheaval, the taking of life, suffering and evil". Berger (1971) points out that every culture throughout history has developed religious belief systems that address these questions and which aim to give meaning and purpose to the world.

In the 21st century, religious belief systems continue to have a very great influence on the way many people view their moral obligations and responsibilities and organise their daily lives. This includes their appearance, dress, diet, family life and children's education. Religion is an important aspect of identity which marks its followers out as both similar to other followers and different from members of other groups. Religion is also rarely just a personal or local experience: increasingly, world events are triggered and swept along by global religious belief systems, as people with particular religious beliefs identify with their peers worldwide.

GETTING YOU THINKING

Transcendental Meditation

The belief system of Transcendental Meditation (TM) is composed of a set of ancient traditions originating in Hindu India. It does not require faith or belief in any god or gods. It teaches that our spiritual fulfilment lies inside ourselves and can only be achieved through the practice of meditation and the use of a mantra or repetitive chant that promotes deep relaxation and the simplest form of human awareness. According to its founder, Maharishi Mahesh Yogi, the practice of TM by its present 5,000,000 practitioners has a spill-over effect on the rest of the world's population, because it reduces societal stress, crime, violence, and conflict, and increases positivity and peace.

Roman Catholicism

The Roman Catholic belief system states that God created the world and sent his only son, Jesus, via a virgin birth to preach his word 2,000 years ago. During his time on Earth, Jesus turned water into wine, healed the sick, raised the dead, and walked on water. Jesus was crucified by the local authorities, but after three days he rose from the dead and ascended to heaven. Catholics also believe that praying to saints will cause them to intercede with God on their behalf. Lourdes in France is a major pilgrimage site because the Virgin Mary appeared to a local teenager – Bernadette Soubirous – and asked for a church to be built on the site of the visions.

Nazism

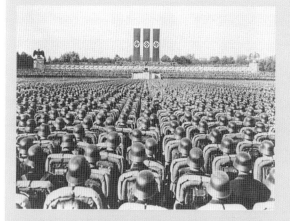

In Germany between 1933 and 1945, the belief system of Nazism stated that the German people were genetically and physically superior to people of other races and cultures. It also suggested that some races were sub-human. This belief became more important than belief in God. Nazism presented its leader, Adolf Hitler, as a messiah-like figure. Nazi rallies involved thousands of people enthusiastically engaged in the quasi-worship of Hitler. Millions of Germans were happy to pledge their allegiance to him and many sacrificed their lives in the name of the Nazi cause during the Second World War.

Scientology

The belief system of Scientology states that people are actually immortal spiritual entities called thetans who originally took on human form many millions of years ago in a far distant galaxy. Humans have forgotten their thetan past and the powers that they once possessed. For example, when a human, or thetan, dies, the thetan side merely occupies the body of a newly born baby. Scientology claims that it can help people get in touch with their thetan selves through a process called auditing. This involves moving through a number of stages (costing money) which will rid the body of engrams (stress) and eventually enable the follower to 'go clear'. A 'clear' can tap into their higher thetan intelligence and abilities.

The Exclusive Brethren

The belief system of the Exclusive Brethren states that they should keep themselves separate from other people (including other Christians) as far as possible. This is based on the idea that the outside world is a place of wickedness. The Exclusive Brethren are opposed to the products of the modern world. Reading novels, watching television and using computers are forbidden because these are considered to be the tools of the devil. Until recently, any Brethren who left the group would be shunned by other members. They would lose their job because most members work for Brethren companies. Their families would never be allowed to see them or talk to them again.

Denominations of religions

I was walking along the Golden Gate Bridge and I saw a man about to jump. I said, "Don't!"
He said, "Nobody loves me."
I said, "God loves you."
He said, "Really?"
I said, "Of course! Are you a Christian or a Jew?"
He said, "A Christian."
I said, "Me too! Protestant or Catholic?"
He said, "Protestant."
I said, "Me too! What denomination?"
He said, "Baptist."
I said, "Me too! Northern Baptist or Southern?"
He said, "Northern."
I said, "Me too! Northern Fundamentalist Baptist or Northern Reformed?"
He said, "Northern Fundamentalist."

I said, "Me too! Northern Fundamentalist Great Lakes Conference or Northern Fundamentalist Eastern Seaboard?"

He said, "Northern Fundamentalist Great Lakes Conference."

I said, "Me too! Northern Fundamentalist Great Lakes Conference Council of 1879, or Northern Fundamentalist Great Lakes Conference Council of 1912?"

He said, "Northern Fundamentalist Great Lakes Conference Council of 1912."

I said, "Die, heretic!" And I pushed him over.

Source: A joke told by the comedian Emo Philips

Questions

1. Examine the passages. In your opinion, which of these belief systems qualify as religions? Justify your decision in each case.

2. Using the passages and your own knowledge about religion, make a list of six characteristics that you think religious belief systems are likely to share.

3. In your opinion, what are the main differences between religious belief systems and scientific belief systems such as physics, chemistry and biology?

4. What sociological observations about religious belief systems can you make using the final passage?

ISSUES IN DEFINING RELIGION

There is such a great diversity of religious belief systems and organisations that sociologists have struggled to produce a single definition of religion that is accepted by all. This is partly because Western sociologists have tended to use Christianity as their starting point; they are said to be **Christocentric**. However, Christianity is only one of several world religions. Definitions of religion have to include all world religions (see Table 6.1.1).

UNDERSTAND THE CONCEPT

Christocentric refers to the fact that Western sociologists of religion tend to over-focus on Christianity and neglect the influence and impact of non-Christian religions.

Sociologists have attempted to define religious belief systems in three main ways.

Inclusive or functional definitions of religion

This approach defines a set of beliefs as religious if such beliefs have a positive social and psychological use or function for individuals and societies. From this perspective, any belief system can be defined as religious if it functions to inspire individuals and to unite communities in terms of faith, devotion and commitment.

It may do this by claiming that it can explain to social groups, the purpose or meaning of existence. As Chapter 6.2 will later show, the theory of functionalism and especially the work of Durkheim takes this approach to defining religion.

However, inclusive definitions of religion can be criticised for the following reasons.

> They may be too broad. Aldridge (2013) argues that they include too much. Many non-religious belief systems such as science and philosophy are also concerned with explaining the problem of the human condition. For example, Aldridge observes that "on some inclusive definitions, all human beings are religious, even if they are professed atheists and utterly reject religion", because atheism is a distinct belief system that offers an explanation for the human condition.

> Scharf (1970) argues that inclusive definitions of religion "allow any kind of enthusiastic purpose or strong loyalty, provided it is shared by a group, to count as a 'religion'". Similarly, Aldridge observes that inclusive definitions would class devotion to a nationalistic cause such as Nazism or to a mass movement such as communism or fervent commitment to a football team or Justin Bieber as 'religious'. Some sociologists therefore argue that it is too easy for something to qualify as a religion, based on this approach. To get around this problem, the term 'civil religion' is used to describe belief systems that are not religious in a conventional sense but have a **quasi-religious** effect (see Chapter 2 for more about civil religion).

Buddhism	Buddhism is a non-theistic religion or philosophy, meaning that it does not teach the existence of a god or gods. It includes a variety of traditions, beliefs and spiritual practices that are largely based on teachings attributed to Gautama Buddha, commonly known as the Buddha. It is practised by 535 million people, which is about 8 per cent of the world's population.
Chinese traditional religion	The Chinese traditional religion is a polytheistic religion that venerates nature deities or gods and the power of the spirits of ancestors. It has about 394 million followers, which is about 5.5 per cent of the world's population.
Christianity	Christianity is a monotheistic religion based on the person and teachings of Jesus Christ. There are two broad Christian traditions: the Roman Catholic Church and non-Catholic denominations known as Protestant. The latter group is made up of thousands of competing churches and theologies. Christianity is the world's biggest religion – about one third of the world's population self-identifies as Christian.
Hinduism	Hinduism is a religion that believes that there is one true god – a supreme spirit called Brahman – who takes various god-like forms such as Vishnu and Krishna. For this reason, it cannot really be described as monotheistic or polytheistic. It is the world's oldest religion and has 1 billion adherents, which is about 14 per cent of the world's population.
Islam	Islam is a monotheistic religion that believes that there is one true God, Allah, whose teachings were revealed to the world by his prophet Muhammad. It is the second biggest religion in the world with about 1.6 billion followers, which is about 23 per cent of the world's population. Most Muslims are either Sunni (about 85–90 per cent) or Shia (about 10 per cent). Sunnis regard themselves as the orthodox branch of Islam and exclusively follow the sayings and actions of the Prophet Muhammed. In contrast, followers of the Shia sect also believe in following the teachings of the Prophet but, in addition, they also believe that their actions should be guided by the wisdom of the Prophet's descendants, particularly his son-in-law Ali. However, the Sunni believe that this Shia belief is heretical and consequently tension and conflict has existed for centuries between these two branches of Islam. Sunnis make up about 90 per cent of the population of countries such as Saudi Arabia and Egypt, whilst Shia Muslims are in the majority in Iraq and Iran.
Judaism	Judaism is a monotheistic religion that believes God appointed the Jews to be his chosen people, in order to set an example of holiness and ethical behaviour to the world. There are about 16 million Jews worldwide.

Table 6.1.1 *The main world religions*

UNDERSTAND THE CONCEPT

Quasi-religious means that an event or activity resembles religion with respect to its followers' devotion, but lacks a superhuman or spiritual dimension. For example, fervent fans of Doctor Who may faithfully watch every episode, follow every word of the scripts, dress up in costumes and loyally attend every convention, but they generally would not consider themselves to belong to a religion.

Aldridge argues that inclusive definitions of religion prevent sociologists from assessing whether religion is growing, stable or in decline. If virtually everything is considered religious, it is almost impossible to operationalise and measure the influence of religion empirically.

Inclusive definitions also assume that all groups share the same interpretation of the purpose of religion. However, the major world religions – Christianity, Islam, Hinduism, Judaism and Buddhism – do not agree on the purpose of religion. Moreover, Christianity as a belief system is generally divided into Catholicism and Protestantism.

There are about 30,000 Protestant religious belief systems and therefore at least as many different interpretations of the purpose of Christian teaching worldwide. Similarly, although there is disagreement about precise numbers, it is estimated that there are at least 70 schools or sects within Islam. Each has its own unique interpretation of the Qur'an.

Exclusive or substantive definitions of religion

These definitions attempt to explain what religion is by referring to characteristics unique to religious belief systems, such as belief in a god or gods. They highlight actions and practices that assume the existence of superhuman, supernatural, mystical or magical beings and powers. These beings and powers are viewed as transcending humanity and society, and as shaping the past, present and future. Political, philosophical and scientific belief systems have a completely different set of defining features.

All religions distinguish between the sacred and the profane. The sacred includes anything – beliefs, rites, objects, daily activities, buildings, places, times, events or people – that is seen as symbolic of divine or supernatural power and venerated as holy. As Marsh and Keating (2006) observe, the sacred is "superior in dignity and power, protected and isolated through a sense of awe and thus treated with special respect". In contrast, the profane refers to ordinary things that must remain at a distance from the sacred. For example, a piece of wood or iron is a profane thing but once it is fashioned into the shape of the Christian cross or Islamic crescent, it becomes sacred. This is especially true if it is situated in a sacred place, such as a church or mosque respectively. Giddens (2013), observes that lighting a candle to light a room is profane, but becomes sacred when it is done for the soul of a loved one, as in Catholic churches.

Why in January 2015 were some Muslims offended by the content of the French magazine Charlie Hebdo?

Substantive definitions, however, are regarded as problematic for the following reasons.

It is unclear what can be or cannot be defined as 'supernatural' and, therefore, religious. For example, belief in magic, energy lines, UFOs, aliens, crystals and even ghosts could be considered religious according to this definition.

Many people in modern societies are superstitious. This suggests that they believe in a force beyond their control – luck or fate – which can have a positive or negative effect upon their life. This has led some sociologists to classify beliefs in superstition, magic and fate as 'subterranean' religions, in order to differentiate them from the more mainstream world religions.

Giddens suggests that many definitions of religion do not focus exclusively on the relationship between the supernatural and humanity. This is because many religious belief systems do not reference the supernatural or divine, or suggest that gods created humanity, or suggest that gods insist people behave in particular ways. Religions such as Buddhism, TM and Confucianism do not include the idea of a divine power that exists in some metaphysical place invisible to human perception. For example, Buddhism teaches that all life is interconnected and that humanity needs to learn compassion, morality and wisdom through the practice of meditation. Many of the 'new religious movements' that have appeared over the past 70 years stress the 'spiritual' or psychological rather than the divine. In other words, they suggest that humanity should be looking within for fulfilment, rather than outwards towards some powerful, supernatural being or force. Consequently, some sociologists dismiss substantive definitions as too exclusive.

Religion as a social construction

Some sociologists such as Beckford (2003) argue that it is important to understand that religious belief systems are **social constructions**. There are two ways of interpreting this.

UNDERSTAND THE CONCEPT

A **social construct** refers to a phenomenon, category or perception that is manufactured or constructed by society and/or powerful groups.

First, some sociologists such, as Durkheim and Marx, believe that there is no such thing as a divine or supernatural power, and that gods and therefore religions are the product of humans. They argue that religions have been socially invented by societies to explain the unexplainable and either to bring communities together in a common cause or to justify power inequalities. Similarly, some feminist sociologists believe religions have deliberately been created by men to justify patriarchy.

The second position is relatively neutral as far as belief in God or divine power is concerned. However, it acknowledges that recognising particular belief systems as religious may benefit the interests of particular groups, especially those with more power and influence than the majority. This position observes that the mass acceptance and legitimacy of a belief system as a religion depends on where it lies on this power continuum. The following examples illustrate this.

> Before the conversion of the Roman emperor Constantine, Christianity was a minority religion which was in danger of dying out. After its acceptance by the Romans, it grew in power and, over the course of 1,000 years, it persecuted believers in non-Christian religions if they refused to convert. Consequently, religions that worshiped the ancient gods, and had dominated societies such as Greece, Rome and Scandinavia, eventually disappeared altogether. Few people worship these gods today.

> The Protestant religion of Anglicanism dominates religious thought and practice in the UK because the ruling elite broke away from Catholicism and set up the Church of England over 500 years ago. In the first 200 years of Anglicanism, other religions were unable to claim legitimacy in the UK because Anglicanism persecuted them, with the support of the monarchy and the political establishment. Some people who practised other religions were forced to flee Britain for America, while some, such as Lollards, were wiped out altogether. The Catholic religion was severely affected by Protestant power and this is the main reason that only about 8 per cent of the British population is Catholic today.

> The power of a religion to dominate a society and to suppress other religious belief systems can result from the sheer number of followers it has. For example, Sunni Islam is the largest Islamic belief system with 1.2 billion followers, or approximately 87–90 per cent of Muslims. It dominates countries such as Saudi Arabia, Egypt, Turkey and Syria. Shia Muslims, who comprise about 200 million people or 10–13 per cent of Muslims, dominate societies such as Iran, Iraq and Pakistan.

From a social constructionist point of view, it is important to note that the prevalence of Sunni and Shia Islam may make it impossible to follow other religious belief systems, including minority Islamic beliefs such as the Bahai and Sufi traditions. In some Islamic countries, apostasy – conversion to another religion or the renunciation of Islam – is a crime punishable by death. In November 2015, a poet in Saudi Arabia was sentenced to death for allegedly renouncing Islam, whilst in 2016

Sunni-dominated Saudi Arabia's execution of a Shia cleric resulted in Shia-dominated Iran cutting off diplomatic relations.

Powerful groups can deny religious status to belief systems or insist that they make major changes to their beliefs. This can dilute the influence of those belief systems on society. This is particularly true for those belief systems that have a minority following and which governments view as threatening or dangerous to their followers and to society. For example, Aldridge (2013) documents how several countries, including Germany, Belgium, Finland and others, refuse to recognise Scientology as a religion. Aldridge also observes how the American occupying power in Japan, immediately after the Second World War, was able to insist that the Japanese changed a central tenet of the dominant religion in Japan, Shintoism. The religion taught that the Japanese emperor was a god. The USA forced the emperor to renounce his divinity and imposed secularisation on Japan.

Find out why some countries see Scientology as threatening or dangerous.

With regard to defining religion, Aldridge points out that many participants in a religion may not necessarily be actively religious. He observes that "the experience of being a Jew, or a Hindu, or a Mormon is often more about doing things than believing things: about abstaining from pork, or beef, or tea, coffee and cola drinks. Often too, it is the doing and the not-doing that provoke hostile social reactions to particular religions: Jehovah's Witnesses rejecting blood transfusions, Quakers refusing to enlist in the armed services, 19th-century Mormons practising polygamy". Aldridge argues that religion should be defined as a "cultural resource" that shapes and influences people's everyday behaviour, rather than a set of beliefs that result in slavish devotion and worship.

TYPES OF RELIGION

A bewildering variety of religions has existed in the past and exists in societies today. Sociologists use the following categories to classify them.

Animism
Animism refers to beliefs, often held in pre-industrial and non-industrial societies, that a spiritual or supernatural force organises and shapes the physical or material world. Consequently, animals, plants, rocks, mountains,

volcanoes, rivers and other natural things are believed to contain a spirit that can positively or negatively affect the human world. For example, angry spirits may cause natural disasters, illness, accident and death. In 2015, local people blamed a group of Western tourists who had posed for a series of nude photographs at the top of Mount Kinabalu in the Malaysian state of Sabah for a major earthquake. They believed that the mountain spirits had been angered by the tourists' lack of respect for the mountain.

Animistic beliefs tend to be associated with religions that are no longer followed, such as Greek, Roman, Aztec and Inca religions, or with smaller tribal cultures. For example, the Navajo, a North American tribe, believe that owls are spies for evil spirits. However, world religions such as Hinduism are also underpinned by elements of animism. For example, the Hindu god Ganesha has the head of an elephant, while the cow is regarded as a symbol of the divine power of giving life and is therefore protected and venerated.

According to the 2011 census, paganism has about 53,000 followers in the UK. Pagans subscribe to animistic beliefs in that they believe spirits reside in mountains, lakes, springs and rivers. They also believe that powerful spirits are associated with different seasons and that the Earth itself is a goddess named Gaia.

Totemism

Animism may be expressed through totemism. This is when tribes or clans adopt a totem as their divine protector and provider. A totem is some aspect of nature, such as an animal or plant, which may be believed to contain spirits, souls, demons or magic. Followers of these religions draw images of the totem onto stones or carve their images in wood to create a totem pole. The totem stone or pole symbolises the divine and consequently becomes the centre of worship and veneration.

Durkheim carried out an analysis of Australian aboriginal totemism and observed that these stones or wooden objects were regarded by the aboriginal clans as sacred and taboo. That is, customs had developed that prohibited and restricted disrespectful behaviour around them. Durkheim observed that these totemic symbols were not only representative of the supernatural power that a clan revered, but they were also emblematic of the clan itself, in much the same way that the Union Flag is symbolic of the UK. Durkheim argued that all forms of religion have their origins in totemism.

Theistic religions

Theistic religions focus on belief in a sacred, higher and controlling power: that is, a god or gods. This power is viewed as the source of moral codes of behaviour and is seen as worthy of great reverence. There are two types of theistic religions.

> *Monotheistic religions* believe in one divine power. These include the major world religions Christianity, Judaism and Islam. However, there are variations on monotheism. For example, Roman Catholics believe in one God but they also pray to the Virgin Mary and often ask saints to intercede on their behalf.

> *Polytheistic religions* believe in a plurality of gods. Examples include the religions of ancient Greece and Rome, Hinduism and paganism. Some religions may be monotheistic in belief but polytheistic in practice. Sikhs, for example, believe in one God but also celebrate the major polytheistic festivals of their parent religion, Hinduism.

Not all religions are theistic – many religions make no reference to the supernatural, divine powers or gods. For example, Buddhism, Confucianism and many 'new-age religions' (see Chapter 4) generally reject the idea of an external authority such as a god. They hold the view that people can discover 'truth' for themselves through experience, by following a personal spiritual path and by exploring their inner self. The main goals of these types of religions are spirituality and inner peace rather than worshipping a god.

THE RELATIONSHIP BETWEEN RELIGION AND SCIENCE

Religion and science are both belief systems that attempt to explain how the world works. However, until about 200 years ago, science and religion did not exist as separate and distinct types of knowledge. Science was dominated by religious thinkers who believed that the primary purpose of science was to document the glory of God. This science bore little relationship to the systematic, rational and positivist approach to research that is associated with science today.

Dixon (2008) observes that scientific belief systems became separate and distinct from religious belief systems during the 18th century. During this time, societies such as the UK progressed from a pre-scientific era, dominated by religious explanations of how the natural world works, to a modern era in which religious explanations were largely superseded by scientific belief systems, particularly in the fields of biology, physics and chemistry. These belief systems were characterised by rational and logical thinking and underpinned by evidence and facts. This period became known as the Enlightenment.

It would be wrong to assume that the Enlightenment resulted in a major rift between religion and science, although there were conflicts of interest, most notably when Darwin published his theory of evolution. Weber (1905) argues that the rapid scientific progress which transformed everyday life in the 18th and 19th centuries – transport, communications, work and leisure – could never have occurred without religion. He observes that the emergence of Protestant religions such as Calvinism in the 18th century was crucial to this social change (see Chapter 2).

However, the success of science in raising people's standard of living led to a widespread public faith in science that only started to diminish in the late 20th century. For example, as medicinal science eradicated many diseases and increased life expectancy, it was widely believed that scientific knowledge could explain, predict and control the natural world. In some religious belief systems, particularly Christian ones in the West, the number of people who profess faith in God appears to have declined over the past century. However, not all sociologists agree either that this decline is happening (see Chapter 5), or that science is responsible for it. It is possible to be both scientific and religious, as many scientists are.

The differences between religious and scientific belief systems

Dixon compared the belief systems of science and religion and identified the following differences between them.

Science is an 'open belief system' because the data collected by scientists are always open to rational scrutiny, criticism and testing by others. According to Karl Popper, the more a hypothesis or theory stands up to attempts to disprove it, the more likely it is to be a scientific truth. In science, the claim to factual truth or validity lives or dies by the evidence. Scientific knowledge is therefore cumulative: it builds on the achievements of previous scientists to develop a greater understanding of the world.

In contrast, religion is generally considered to be a 'closed belief system' because religious knowledge is sacred and cannot be challenged. It cannot grow or change because it is regarded as the absolute truth, which is to say the word of God. Those who challenge it may be punished for their **heresy**.

UNDERSTAND THE CONCEPT

Heresy refers to beliefs or opinions that are viewed as provocative because they are at odds with religious belief systems. In the Middle Ages, Christianity usually punished heretics by execution (the last execution for heresy in Europe, by the Catholic Church, was in 1826 in Spain) or excommunication (being deprived of particular religious rights such as communion). The author Salman Rushdie was subjected to a fatwa (In his case, a religious decree proclaiming he should be killed) issued by the Iranian spiritual leader Ayatollah Khomeini in 1989, because his novel *The Satanic Verses* was viewed as heretical by Islamic scholars.

The most famous illustration of this closed religious thinking is the case of the Italian mathematician and astronomer Galileo. Galileo was prosecuted by the Catholic Church in 1632 for hypothesising that the Earth and other planets revolve around the Sun, after conducting mathematical calculations on the basis of rigorous observations using a telescope. His hypothesis contradicted Catholic theology, which favoured the view that the Earth was the centre of the universe. Galileo was found guilty of heresy, forced to recant (that is, to deny that the Sun is the centre of the universe) and placed under house arrest for the rest of his life.

Scientists gather scientific knowledge by observing the natural world and formulating logical hypotheses or conjectures, which are ideas or informed guesses usually based on existing scientific knowledge.

In contrast, religion is concerned with the metaphysical or spiritual world, which is presumed to exist by religious people but which cannot be observed in a scientific sense.

Scientists collect their data in standardised and rational ways through systematic observation and experimentation. These methods are considered reliable because they can be used by other scientists to re-test and validate findings.

In contrast, the existence of God and other religious phenomena cannot be proven, because it cannot be subjected to normal scientific procedures. Religions therefore make claims about knowledge that cannot be successfully overturned. This is because religious truths are believed ultimately to come from God or God's agents. This may involve supernatural means such as revelation in the form of visions or voices in the head, faith, prayer, healing and conversion.

Scientists regard science as an objective and value-free discipline that is only interested in the disinterested pursuit of evidence. They aim to ignore their personal feelings and remain objective, meaning free from the influence of social, political or religious bias at all times, particularly when conducting scientific research. The truth or falsity of scientific knowledge is judged by universal, objective criteria such as testing, and not by the personal views or prejudices held by the scientist.

In contrast, religious knowledge depends on faith, which is deeply subjective and often irrational in character. Religious experiences are personal, exclusive and unique to the individual. They cannot be replicated or even generalised. Religious faith is often seen by critics of religion as at the heart of a 'circularity of false reasoning or logic' in which religious beliefs use 'this' to prove 'that' whilst also claiming that 'that' is caused by 'this'. For example, 'I know God exists because I have faith' and 'My faith is sustained by God's existence'. It is also argued that religious beliefs are generally circular, because they claim that if followers do not believe in them, they will be subjected to an eternal damnation of pain and suffering. Religious documents such as the Bible, the Qu'ran and the Torah are used to justify these claims. Believers argue that these documents are 'true' and the fact that some people do not believe in them does not distract from their truthfulness. Moreover, it is often argued by religious leaders that their religious claims must be true because so many people believe in them. Another circular argument suggests science has not found evidence of God's existence because He does not wish this to happen.

Can you think of any examples of circular logic in religion?

Scientific enquiry continues to work in fields in which religious ideas were once dominant. For example, the Big Bang theory and the search for the 'God Particle' using the Large Hadron Collider in Geneva implicitly question the notion that God created the universe. Similarly, geologists have questioned biblical assertions about the age of the Earth. Scientists involved in cloning and stem cell research are thought to challenge the notion that only God can create life. However, it is important to understand that scientists have not set out deliberately to undermine religion – these findings are simply the outcome of rational scientific enquiry.

There is some evidence that such research may not be having a significant impact on the nature or extent of religious belief, even in the technologically advanced West. For example, American scientists are leaders in many areas of scientific research, yet the USA is the most religious of the advanced industrial democracies. Forty-two per cent of Americans consistently reject the idea of natural evolution because it conflicts with the biblical account of creation. Of those Americans who do support the idea of evolution, a further 21 per cent believe such evolution is guided by a supreme being.

Creationism continues to exert an influence on American education. In Alabama, biology textbooks have to carry a sticker warning children that the theory of evolution is only one theory that explains the origin of the human species. In Kansas, all references to evolution were actually removed from the science curriculum between 1999 and 2006.

UNDERSTAND THE CONCEPT

Creationism is the belief that God created the world, as stated by the Bible. Creationists believe that the Earth is about 6,000 years old. They tend to oppose the theory of evolution.

A new battlefront opened up in the 1990s with the emergence of 'intelligent design' (ID) theory, which asserts that there is scientific evidence that life was created by an 'intelligent designer'. This theory claims the physical properties of an object are so complex that they could only have been 'designed' by a greater power and could not possibly have evolved over thousands or millions of years. This theory, which claims to be a science, does not challenge the idea of evolution. However, it disputes Darwin's idea that the cause of biological change is wholly blind and undirected. It argues that life on Earth, and more generally in the universe, shows so much order and purpose that there must have been a designer. Most intelligent design arguments avoid any reference to scripture and try to eliminate anything that might look as if it was derived from religious belief.

However, opponents of ID claim that it is religion dressed up as pseudo-science. They argue that its claims cannot be tested and verified by observation or experiment and that the notion of an intelligent designer or engineer is essentially the same thing as God. Critics such as Richard Dawkins have consequently compared teaching ID theory to teaching flat Earth theory and said that it is akin to mentally abusing children. In June 2007, the Council of Europe concluded that "creationism in any of its forms, such as 'intelligent design', is not based on facts, does not use any scientific reasoning and its contents are pathetically inadequate for science classes".

Assessing the claims of science

The notion that science is an open belief system has, however, been challenged by Feyerabend (1975), who argues that science is not as open as it claims. This can be illustrated in a number of ways.

Feyerabend suggests that what scientists say they do is often different from what they actually do. He claims that there is no such thing as a scientific logic model that all scientists faithfully follow. He argues that individual scientists follow their own rules and often deviate from rational thinking and practices.

Kaplan (1964) points out that many scientific discoveries are not the product of logic at all. Instead, many are the product of accident, inspired guesses, imagination and luck. Many scientists make false starts or collect data that mislead them temporarily before they get back on track. Kaplan argues that when scientists write up their accounts of the research process in scientific journals, they 're-construct logic'. This means that their account is partly fictionalised. They add in the logic and rationality that their fellow scientists expect to see.

According to Kaplan, cheating is fairly commonplace in science because scientists are heavily biased towards proving their own theories right. There is little chance of being caught because there is no prestige in re-doing someone else's work, meaning that little attempt is made to replicate and verify the work of other scientists. Reliability in this sense may therefore be overrated.

Kuhn (1962) challenges the openness of science by observing that scientists often refuse to consider any challenges to their existing knowledge. He argues this is because they work within 'paradigms' – sets of shared assumptions into which all scientists are socialised during their education and training, and which shape dominant scientific thought and actions for hundreds of years. This is similar in some ways to how religious faiths influence people's actions. Scientists who follow the rules of the paradigm are rewarded with research grants, awards and professorships.

Kuhn points out that the research findings of any scientist who works outside the paradigm, or who attempts to challenge it, is unlikely to be accepted by the scientific community in the short term because the paradigm makes it difficult for the majority of scientists to think outside the box. The anti-paradigm scientists may find that their work is mocked and they may consequently find it difficult to find a research or teaching post (see Topic 2, Chapter 5 for more on Kuhn's work). Scientists may accumulate enough evidence to contradict the dominant paradigm, and this may eventually result in a period of scientific revolution in which old ideas are replaced by new ways of thinking about and doing science. However, this process may take decades.

FOCUS ON SKILLS: EVOLUTION AND RELIGION – SEPARATE OR COMPLEMENTARY?

From September 2014, evolution will be taught in primary schools. It's an important development, which raises some interesting cultural questions and implications. Some of these wider issues are religious. Many conservative Muslims see any idea of evolution – especially human evolution – as contrary to the traditions of Islam, and oppose its teaching in schools. My own conversations with Muslim school students in London over the past five years suggest that some of them see the compulsory teaching of evolution in schools as part of a western anti-Islamic agenda, and thus react against evolution for non-scientific reasons. The same issue arises, although to a lesser extent, within British Christianity, where forms of "creationism" (generally holding that the world was created in six days about 6,000 years ago) are becoming increasingly influential, particularly within fundamentalist Christian religions such as Pentecostalism.

There are really two issues here: the theoretical question of how evolution relates to religious faith, and the more pragmatic question of what can be done to lessen religious anxieties about evolution. Because these questions are complex, raising different issues for different faith traditions, I will focus on Christianity, and allow readers to make any necessary adaptations. There are three broad positions to consider.

First, there is the view that science and faith are completely separate worlds of thought and action, and ought to be kept apart. Science gets taught in the classroom, and faith gets taught in the home or at church. It's a neat solution in some ways, and keeps science and religion out of each other's way. But it's problematic. What, for example, if religion teaches something that is scientifically questionable? Or if some scientists resist a new theory because it seems "religious"? The astronomer Fred Hoyle famously resisted the Big Bang theory because it sounded too much like religious ideas of creation.

Second, there's the view — often referred to as the "warfare model" or "conflict thesis" — which holds that science and faith are locked in mortal combat. This approach began to emerge in the late 19th century, and has been popularised in recent decades by the biologist Richard Dawkins, particularly in his *God Delusion* (2006). Dawkins believes in a permanent conflict between science and religion, and regards Darwin's theory of evolution as the atheist's weapon of choice against faith. For Dawkins, any talk about an "alleged convergence" between religion and science can only be "a shallow, empty, hollow, spin-doctored sham".

The third position is a mediating approach which holds that science and religious faith exist in a complex relationship. This is characterised by moments of tension and synergy, yet opens the way to an enriched vision of reality which is both existentially and rationally satisfying. I belong to this school of thought, and see it as a way of holding together and affirming the strengths of science and faith, while recognising the limits of both.

What can be done to lessen religious anxieties about evolution? In a recent article in *The New York Times*, Brendan Nyhen considers what happens when science and faith are in tension. His argument deserves to be heard: "We need to try to break the association between identity and factual beliefs on high profile issues." If religious believers of whatever type are made to feel that they must choose between their faith or evolution, they are likely to choose their faith. Religious fundamentalists are the chief beneficiaries of the ridiculously simplistic slogan 'you can't believe in evolution and God'."

Based on McGrath, A. 'Evolution and religion: separate or complementary?', *The Times*, 29 August 2014

Questions

1. **Understand.** Give two reasons that McGrath identifies that cause Muslims to object to the teaching of evolution to primary school children.

2. **Explain** the warfare model of science and faith.

3. **Analyse** why Christian critics object to evolutionary theory being taught to primary school children.

4. **Evaluate.** Using information from this source and elsewhere, assess the view that science and religious faith can never be reconciled on subjects such as evolution.

The overlap between science and religion

It can be argued that science actually resembles religion in many ways and that there are more similarities than differences. For example:

> Science is not necessarily anti-religious. Many classical scientists such as Newton set out to document the glory of God, whilst many religions are quite accepting of scientific ideas such as evolution.

> They are both anthropocentric approaches in that they both see human beings as the centre of the universe.

> They are both dominated by dogma or accepted ways of doing things (Kuhn calls these paradigms) that result in alternative ways of thinking or practice being dismissed as heretical or wrong.

> They both include 'stories' that are dependent on faith. For example, although many scientific theories have been proven by evidence, many have not, but scientists have faith that they are probably 'true'.

> They both contain saints and priests – a collection of people, usually men, who are revered and whose teachings or views are regarded as sacred and rarely questioned. The writings of these scientific saints and priests have a 'holy' status in the scientific community.

> Lay-people who prefer science over religion often do so without any understanding or comprehension of how the science works in practice. In other words, they have blind faith that the scientist is right.

> There has been intolerance on both sides of the religion–science divide. Dixon notes that "the story is not always one of a heroic and open-minded scientist clashing with a reactionary and bigoted church". He says that in reality, "the bigotry, like the open-mindedness, is shared around on all sides".

> Postmodernists argue that both religion and science are metanarratives.

> Marxists and feminists argue that both religion and science are ideologies.

Postmodernism, religion and science

Lyotard (1984) argues that science and religion are metanarratives or 'big stories' that falsely claim to possess the truth. In the postmodern world, Lyotard argues that people have become sceptical of all metanarratives that tell them what is right or wrong and tell them how to live their lives. Consequently, many people have grown disillusioned with both science and religion. For example, many people believe science creates as many problems as it solves, such as global warming, the risks associated with nuclear power and bombs, pollution and environmental destruction.

Postmodernism argues that, in the postmodern age, people no longer seek truth from a single belief system or metanarrative. Instead they can pick and choose from a variety of alternative belief systems that have emerged as critiques of conventional metanarratives. For example, people may use alternative or complementary medicines, as well as conventional medical science. In the field of religion, they may turn away from conventional religions, churches and denominations to **new-age** spiritual movements, sects and cults.

UNDERSTAND THE CONCEPT

New age refers to a broad spiritual movement characterised by alternative approaches to traditional Western culture, with an interest in inner peace, human potential, mysticism, holism and environmentalism.

The postmodernist view of the relative ideological merits of religion and science has been criticised in two ways.

> First, it is argued that scientific beliefs are tested against evidence and are therefore still seen by members of society as more objective and valid forms of 'truth' than religious or political beliefs. Bruce (2002) observes that people can see that science always has superior outcomes to religion. For example, people will always see that astronomy is more believable than astrology or that medical science works better than prayer.

> Second, it is important not to exaggerate the extent to which science has lost influence. Scientific technology underpins the smooth running of modern societies, as well as most people's identity and lifestyle. However, it is probably true that people today are more aware of the negative effects of science than in the past.

IDEOLOGY, RELIGION AND SOCIETY

Sociologists use the term 'ideology' to illustrate how belief systems relate to the distribution of power in society. An ideology is a set of beliefs that aim to legitimate or justify the position of powerful groups in society, and divisive and unfair social structures. Marxists and feminists, in particular, suggest that religion is an ideology that works for the benefit of the capitalist ruling class and for men respectively (see Chapter 2). Religion can be seen to be ideological in non-capitalist and non-patriarchal contexts, as the following examples illustrate.

> It was believed in medieval Europe that monarchies were divinely ordained via the Pope. Consequently, they had absolute power and did not have to explain their actions to their people. They were answerable only to God. This was known as the 'divine right of kings'. This prevented any challenge to their power, because challenging the power of kings meant challenging the power of God. This merited the worst possible punishment: excommunication from the Catholic Church, which made entry to heaven impossible.

> The system of stratification that dominates India – caste – is underpinned by the Hindu religious beliefs of reincarnation, karma and dharma. The caste system is a rigid, hierarchical and closed system of stratification based upon birth and fate. People are born into high status or low status groups known as castes, in which they remain all of their life. Membership of a particular caste determines a person's job, status, who they marry and where they live. People generally accept their social situation and position without question because they believe in the Hindu principles of karma

and dharma. Karma, or fate, means their position is a result of their actions in a previous life. Dharma tells them that, if they are good in this life, they will be reincarnated as a member of a higher caste.

Critics of science argue that its progress and priorities reflect the ideology and interests of powerful groups. Many advances in supposedly 'pure' science have been driven by the need of powerful groups to justify inequalities in power and wealth. Gomm (1982) argues that Darwin's theory of evolution was used in an ideological way by supporters of the British Empire to justify British colonialism. The Darwinian idea that evolution was about the 'survival of the fittest' encouraged Victorian Britons to see themselves as superior to the people of conquered territories. In other words, science was used to justify racism and imperialism (empire-building). However, this is also true of the Christian religion: according to Leach (1982), Christian thought was used to describe slaves and indigenous people in British colonies as sub-human, degenerate, damned souls and the product of the devil rather than God. The science of eugenics (a set of beliefs and practices that aimed to improve the genetic quality of the human population) was used by the Nazis to justify their extermination of people 'unfit' to reproduce, such as those with mental and physical disabilities and members of minority groups. Feminists such as Terry (2014) argue that male scientists and doctors either perceive post-natal depression as an individual mental illness or they ignore its existence altogether; for example, it was until fairly recently excluded from the American Psychiatric Association's Diagnostic and Statistical Manual (DSM). This is because they subscribe to a dominant patriarchal ideology that disseminates the myth of motherhood – that being a mother should be the central defining feature of a woman's life, achievement and identity. Acknowledging the existence or importance of post-natal depression undermines this patriarchy ideology and myth.

MARXISM AND SCIENCE

Marxists also view science as an ideology that works in favour of powerful groups. Many advances in supposedly 'pure' science have been driven by the need of the capitalist class for more profit and power. This can be illustrated in a number of ways.

Marxists point out that science and technology are the foundation stones of capitalist production, such as assembly line production. This revolutionised the labour process and, from a Marxist perspective, made it easier to exploit the working class for their surplus value.

Scientific advancements in technology, such as the magnetic compass, the sextant, the marine chronometer, shipbuilding, mapping techniques, aerospace, the telegraph, radio, satellites, computers, the world-wide web and digitalisation, have resulted in the spread of global capitalism and the economic dominance of Western states and transnational companies. Science was also responsible for developing the weapon technology that imperial powers such as the UK used to suppress and colonise countries in the developing world, in order to exploit their raw materials and labour.

The 20th century also saw a green revolution in many developing countries, as scientists developed high-yield seed crops as well as fertilisers and pesticides that dramatically increased agricultural production. In recent years, scientists have also developed genetically-modified seeds that resist insects and herbicides. These scientific developments in agriculture have tended to benefit agribusiness and food transnationals, and consequently global capitalism, rather than the people of the developing world, because these Western companies control the cost and distribution of seeds, fertilisers and pesticides.

How might scientists justify spending billions on the Large Hadron Collider rather than spending it on poverty relief or a cure for cancer?

From a Marxist perspective, explain why the British government might be happy to spend millions of pounds on the science involved in sending Major Tim Peake to the International Space Station in a period of austerity welfare cuts.

Marxists believe that science is ideological because it is presented as a positive force for good, in that it has increased life expectancy and substantially improved living standards. This ideological image of science distracts members of society, especially the poor, from the fact that the wealthy have used science and technology to acquire wealth and power at their expense. The emphasis scientific ideology places on individual benefits, such as the smartphone, may blind people to manufactured future risks such as environmental destruction, global warming and pollution.

However, there is some evidence that science and technology may be used to construct platforms that are critical of global capitalism. For example, groups such as Anonymous (a hacker action group), the anti-globalisation movement, the Make Poverty History campaign and

WikiLeaks have used the internet and social networking sites such as Twitter and Facebook to organise and coordinate actions and protests against Western governments and global economic powers, such as the World Trade Organisation. A cyber-democracy movement can also be seen in the coordination of the Arab Spring protests, which saw the removal of totalitarian dictators in Tunisia and Egypt in 2011.

FEMINISM AND SCIENCE

Crasnow *et al.* (2015) argue that the institutions of science have a long tradition of excluding women as practitioners. For example, Marks (1979) describes how patriarchal ideology based on science was used to justify the exclusion of women from education until the 1930s. Male doctors, scientists and educationalists in this period often expressed the view that the education of females would lead to the creation of "a new race of puny and unfeminine" females and "disqualify women from their true vocation", namely the nurturing of the next generation. Similarly, Oakley describes the psychological theory of maternal deprivation, which appeared in the 1950s, as a scientific ideology that justified men dominating paid work while women stayed at home to raise children.

Crasnow *et al.* also argue that the ideology of science is routinely used to marginalise women as subjects of scientific enquiry and to suggest that the sciences are an inherently masculine domain to which women are unsuited. When women do enter science, this ideology adjusts to suggest that the institutions of science are a model of gender-neutral meritocracy. This means that when women fail to climb the scientific hierarchy, it is suggested that there are innate sex-linked differences in talent. For example, men may be thought to have superior mathematical skills and women may be considered less driven than men. However, research suggests that patriarchal prejudice and discrimination are mainly responsible for gender inequalities in science employment.

Religion has also been criticised as ideological by Marxists and feminists. These ideas are explored in depth in Chapter 2.

Using Topic 2, Chapter 4, give examples of how ideology might influence a sociologist's choice of research subject.

CONCLUSIONS

The debate about what forms or approaches religion and science take are important because they influence what evidence will be accepted or rejected when discussing these belief systems. For example, this chapter has shown that characteristics normally associated with science, such as reliability or evidence, may be exaggerated or may not always exist. It can also be concluded that science may not be a superior belief system to religion. It does not appear to possess a special form of knowledge, because faith and other quasi-religious characteristics can clearly be seen in the way that it operates. Similarly, it is important to be precise when identifying the characteristics of religion because this has implications for other sociological debates, such as whether secularisation (the decline in religious beliefs and practices) is actually occurring.

Science and religion continue to exist side by side, but not without tensions. Where scientific evidence and long-held religious belief come into direct conflict, many religious people continue to reject science in favour of the teachings of their faith tradition. The next chapter will examine the role of religion in societies. Regardless of our own religious beliefs, an objective and scientific approach to sociological research shows that religion has many benefits for society – although some sociologists argue that religions can be problematic too.

CHECK YOUR UNDERSTANDING

1. Explain the term 'theism'.

2. Explain what is meant by 'the Enlightenment'.

3 Define the concept of 'totemism'.

4. Explain what is meant by a 'paradigm'.

5. Identify and briefly illustrate two reasons why postmodernists are critical of science.

6. Identify and briefly explain some similarities between the belief systems of religion and science.

7. Analyse two ways of defining religion.

8. Analyse two ways in which science is not as open as it claims.

9. Evaluate the view that science and religion are very different types of belief systems.

10. Assess the usefulness of the idea that scientific knowledge is gathered to benefit all, rather than used to justify the power of a few.

TAKE IT FURTHER

1. Ask your friends some 'big questions' covering topics such as the meaning of life, life after death, belief in God, superstitious beliefs. Make sure you get informed consent from them before the interview, as this sort of questioning sometimes upsets people. What sort of belief systems do their answers reveal? To what extent can their beliefs be described as 'religious'?

2. Visit the websites of the National Secular Society at www.secularism.org.uk and the British Humanist Association at www.humanism.org.uk. What problems does each organisation believe religion causes for societies?

3. Look up the Scopes Monkey Trial on the internet or watch the film *Inherit the Wind*. What does this tell you about the relationship between science and religion in the USA?

6.2 THEORIES OF THE ROLE AND FUNCTION OF RELIGION

LEARNING OBJECTIVES

> Demonstrate knowledge and understanding of the sociological theories of the role and function of religion (AO1).

> Demonstrate knowledge and understanding of the impact of social change on religious belief, practices and organisations (AO1).

> Apply this understanding to contemporary society (AO2).

> Analyse evidence that suggests religion is either a conservative force that provides stability or a force for social change, and that it is a cause of conflict.(AO3).

> Evaluate sociological explanations of religion in order to make judgements and draw conclusions about its functions (AO3).

INTRODUCING THE DEBATE

This chapter examines the role of religion in wider society and asks whether it is beneficial or detrimental to society. Some sociological theories, notably functionalism, are very positive about religion. They suggest that religious belief systems are generally very beneficial for society because they promote social stability, harmony and consensus in the form of agreed moral codes of behaviour which regulate personal and social life. Functionalists see religion as essentially conservative, as most do not like social change. However, this is generally regarded as a good thing because social change often brings social instability and conflict.

Marxists and feminists also view religion as a **conservative force** but believe that this is generally detrimental to society, particularly the working class and women. These theories see the role of religion as ideological and argue that its function is to prevent subordinate social groups from recognising the true cause of their social condition and acting to change their social world. Not all critical theories see religion in such black-and-white terms. For example, some neo-Marxists believe religion is an occasional catalyst of change for oppressed groups. Similarly, Max Weber sees a particular Protestant religion – Calvinism – as partly responsible for spurring profound economic and social change during the emergence of the capitalist economic system in the 17th century.

UNDERSTAND THE CONCEPT

In the context of the Sociology of Religion, the concept of **conservative force** means fear of or opposition to social change, because that change is thought to disrupt the status quo and undermine traditional ways of doing things that have been in place for hundreds of years and which are seen to work, especially by the powerful who have benefitted from them. Conservatism often also means a rejection of liberal ideas such as equal rights for minorities.

FUNCTIONALISM

Functionalists regard society as a social system – a set of parts which work together to form a whole. These parts are the social institutions of society, such as the family, religion and education. Functionalists assume that society has certain basic needs or prerequisites that must be met in order to survive. First and foremost is the need for social order. It is assumed that social order requires a certain degree of cooperation and social solidarity. This is made possible by a consensus or agreement about society's values and norms. Without this value consensus, people would constantly act in opposition to one another, and conflict and chaos would result. Second, there is a need for 'social integration' – a sense of belonging to society. This acts like a social glue, binding people together as one nation or community. When analysing any part of society, such as religion, functionalists often aim to uncover its function, meaning its contribution to the maintenance and wellbeing of the social system.

Emile Durkheim

The most influential interpretation of religion from a functionalist perspective is that of Emile Durkheim. Durkheim believed that religion was a set of myths and imaginary forces, constructed by human beings, that functioned to bring about social order in societies. He believed that the divine and supernatural had no foundation in reality. However, this did not prevent him from seeing religion as a power for social good in society. In fact, he went as far as suggesting that religion and its rituals are as necessary for everyday life as food is for physical life.

Durkheim's study of aboriginal totemism convinced him that for members of any society the totem, or any other sacred or religious representation, is both the symbol of a god and the symbol of society. The totem stands for the sacred, in that it symbolises the power of the divine and supernatural, but it also represents the collective conscience, meaning the cultural beliefs, values, traditions and norms that members of society share. Sacred things symbolise the fact that society is more powerful and important than the individual. In other words, from Durkheim's perspective, god and society are one and the same thing. Durkheim argues that in worshipping a god and venerating the sacred and divine, what people are really doing is worshipping society.

Durkheim argues that religion in all its forms is an important agent of secondary socialisation. The major function of religion is to socialise society's members into a collective conscience, meaning common agreement about values and ways of behaving. This can work by investing particular values with a sacred quality, or by encouraging a sense of belonging to society.

Investing particular values with a sacred quality

Most religions infuse particular values with religious symbolism and special significance. These values become 'moral codes' – beliefs that society agrees to revere and set above all other principles. Examples might include respect for human life, honesty, compassion and charity. Religions may differ in their choice of moral codes; for example, Islam morally disapproves of gambling, in contrast to some other religions. However, the function of all moral codes is essentially the same. They provide codes of behaviour that people and societies can use to regulate both personal and social life. Socialisation into such codes is seen as integral to a child's upbringing, if he or she is to become a 'decent' upstanding citizen.

In your opinion, what other examples of modern values, morals and ethics in your society have been influenced by religion?

Encouraging a sense of belonging to society

Durkheim believes that the act of group worship and celebration of the divine serves to integrate individuals socially into the larger moral community and therefore to forge social identity and solidarity. Religion and its associated rituals help people to understand the reality of social relations, to communicate with one other, to establish obligations between kin, neighbours and strangers and to maintain stable boundaries, to avoid conflict with other belief systems that exist alongside them.

Durkheim believes that it does not matter what form worship takes or what its expressed purpose is. All that matters is that people come together as a group to worship. The worship of god or the coming together of individuals as Christians, Buddhists, Muslims, Jews, Sikhs and so on is actually recognition that society is more important than the individual.

Talcott Parsons

The American functionalist Talcott Parsons agrees with Durkheim that religion is an important component of society and suggests that religion performs three major functions.

1. It provides moral guidelines (taken from religious teachings and texts) into which people can be socialised by priests, imans and so on when attending religious institutions, in education via assemblies, RE and citizenship classes and in families through grandparents and parents passing down religious and moral knowledge. People's actions are compared with these guidelines and they are consequently judged either as good citizens or as deviant. These guidelines often underpin the legal systems of societies because they are a primary source of the laws that govern everyday behaviour.

   This is sometimes referred to as 'generalisation'. People may not recognise their condemnation of adultery in relationships as religiously-inspired but it stems from bibical teachings. Similarly, the act of taxation is based upon the idea that individuals should help others, even those they do not know and may never meet. This resonates with the idea of the Good Samaritan.

2. Religion provides a means of adjusting to events that cannot be predicted or controlled and that may disrupt social order. For example, religious ceremonies unite a nation following the death of its leader, a disaster, or an event with a national resonance. Beckford (in Fenn 2008) observes that religion played a significant role in drawing the nation together after the death of Diana, Princess of Wales, in 1997, regardless of social class or ethnicity.

3. Religion may function by applying a higher meaning and purpose to events that have the potential to disrupt society. Most importantly, religious ceremonies provide people with reasons for potentially stressful events, such as the death of a close relative.

In Parsons' view, most funerals are suffused with religious sentiment and particularly the notion that death is the result of God's will. The death of a loved one can cause the bereaved to feel helpless, alone and unable to cope with life. Bereaved people often withdraw for a period from their social roles; for example, they may take time off work. However, the funeral ceremony brings people together to celebrate the contribution that the deceased has made to the community. It also assures the bereaved that the deceased has moved on to a better place and that the community exists to support the bereaved through this stressful period. This helps to re-integrate bereaved people into their social roles and society.

Bronislaw Malinowski

Malinowski believes religion functions to appease the stress and anxieties created by life crises such as birth, puberty, marriage and death. These events have the potential to undermine people's commitment to their role in wider society and therefore to social order.

Malinowski argues that most societies have evolved religious rite of passage ceremonies in order to minimise any potential social disruption. In addition to the funeral service, rites of passage underpinned by religious sentiments and rituals aim to reduce anxieties about other potentially stressful social events such as the birth of a child, the movement from childhood to adulthood and marriage.

Malinowski also argues that religion functions to relieve the tensions and fears that arise from unpredictable situations. His **anthropological** study of the Trobriand Islanders found that they carried out religious ceremonies before dangerous activities over which they felt they had little control. Before fishing activities in the relatively safe harbour of the lagoon, no religious ceremonies took place. However, before going out to fish in the less predictable Pacific Ocean, the islanders performed religious ceremonies in which they committed themselves to the protection of their gods. As a result, deaths at sea were interpreted by the rest of the islanders as the will of the gods, minimising grief and therefore the potential for disorder.

UNDERSTAND THE CONCEPT

Anthropology is the study of the development of human societies and cultures. Many anthropologists have focused on pre-industrial and non-industrial cultures such as Samoa (Margaret Mead) or African tribal cultures (Evans-Pritchard).

Functionalist thinkers are likely to agree with Aldridge (2013) that religion is not necessarily about religious belief. Aldridge argues that it is a cultural resource, a means of cultural identification that functions to bring people with similar cultural traditions together. This is nicely summed up by Freedland (2015) who observes: "for many, it is about belonging and community, a matter of ethnic or familial solidarity rather than theological creed. For Anglicans, it works that way too. Singing hymns in church is a comfort, reminding them of their childhood and leaving them with a glow of warmth towards neighbours they might otherwise never meet" (*The Guardian*, 26 September 2015).

Functionalism, social control, stability and social change

In conclusion, functionalists generally see religions as forms of benevolent social control that set the parameters of acceptable and unacceptable behaviour and bring people together into integrated communities. From this perspective, religions and religious organisations are generally conservative in that they help to preserve the status quo. However, functionalists believe that this status quo is based on consensus. Religions therefore benefit all members of society, because they help bring about social stability and order. Social change, on the other hand, disrupts that stability and order and brings with it the possibility of social conflict. Functionalists therefore regard religion as a means of helping to manage such change by making sure that is of a gradual nature, rather than sudden and potentially disruptive to the smooth running of society.

The critique of the functionalist theory of religion

Some sociologists, notably Bruce (2002), have pointed to the decline of religious practices in Western societies and have argued that it is difficult to see how religion can socialise the majority of society's members into morality and social integration, if only a minority of people regularly attend church, for example (see Chapter 5 for further investigation of the topic of religious decline, or secularisation). In defence of functionalism, one should note that religious practice and belief are not the same thing and that the 2011 census results suggest that most of the UK population subscribes to some sort of religious belief. Moreover, it may be that religious beliefs are now generally viewed by society as social values. These still underpin many aspects of social life in the UK, such as the law, beliefs regarding how education and family life should be organised, holidays and festivals. Finally,

this functionalist analysis of the function of religion may still be regarded as relevant because religion is extremely powerful globally, particularly outside of Western Europe.

Religion may not be functional or beneficial for a society. There is evidence that religion can be **dysfunctional,** but Durkheim chooses to ignore this. As Hamilton (2012) observes, Durkheim is happy to stress that religion can inspire morality and heroism, but fails to acknowledge that it also can inspire mob mentality, lack of logical reasoning and atrocity. As well as bringing people together as communities, it can create conflict and huge suffering.

UNDERSTAND THE CONCEPT

Dysfunctional means causing social harm or damage.

Many of the world's current conflicts are underpinned by fundamental differences in religious beliefs. For example:

> Christians have conducted anti-Semitic ethnic cleansing and pogroms for hundreds of years.

> The period between 1969 and 1999 saw conflict between Catholics and Protestants in Northern Ireland that caused approximately 3,600 deaths.

> During 2006 and 2007, tens of thousands died in the Sunni–Shia civil war in Iraq.

> In India, over 10,000 people have been killed in Hindu–Muslim communal violence since 1950.

> The current conflict between Islamist movements such as al-Qaeda and ISIS/Daesh and Western governments, which Islamists see as underpinned by a conspiracy against the Muslim world by Christian crusaders and Zionists, has resulted in thousands of deaths across the world since 2001.

Religion can therefore produce conflict rather than consensus and integration.

How do the attacks on Paris in 2015 fit into this analysis?

Hamilton argues that Durkheim's theory is more suited to societies in which one religion dominates. He argues that it fails to account for the emergence of religious pluralism and diversity in modern societies, which often lead to tensions, divisions and conflicts between social groups. This undermines social integration and solidarity.

Some have argued that Durkheim's analysis is based on flawed evidence and that he misunderstood both totemism and the behaviour of the aboriginal clans themselves. This is because he never directly observed them. He depended entirely on secondary sources, such as missionary reports of the aborigines' behaviour and practices. Critics have also suggested that totemism is not very representative of the diversity of religions worldwide. Some have even suggested that totemism was not even typical of aborigines across Australia.

The idea that religion can be seen as the worship of society depends on an assumption that worship is a collective act of people joining together to celebrate their god or gods. However, religious belief may be expressed individually. For example, many 'new-age' religions are not collectivistic. Adherents of these religions tend to follow the belief systems individualistically. It is rare that these individuals come together as a group.

Marxists and feminists are critical of the idea that religion functions for the good of all society. They argue that religious belief systems are ideologies that aim to justify and reproduce inequality and particularly the status and wealth of powerful groups such as the capitalist elite and men.

Neo-functionalism

The neo-functionalist Robert Bellah introduced the concept of civil religion, which he believed had become the most influential type of belief system in the USA. He defined a civil religion as a belief system that induces a mass response, with similar levels of passion, dedication and commitment to those found in mainstream religions. For example, Nazism and communism are viewed as civil religions because their belief systems substituted belief in God, for beliefs in nationalism and Marxism respectively. They provided their millions of followers with charismatic leadership, secular saints and objects, and codes of behaviour in much the way a conventional religion does.

Bellah argues that the USA is dominated by a civil religion he calls 'Americanism', which unites the American people, regardless of class, race or creed. He argues this has given the American nation state an identity which emphasises equally, commitment to God and to American nationalism. What is particularly interesting about this American civil religion is that God is not Catholic, Protestant, Jewish or Muslim – he is an American first and foremost, who welcomes all religious creeds as long as they put American values first. American values such as the **American Dream** – the principle of making the most

of opportunity and belief in the free market – are regarded as 'sacred' and virtuous values that deserve veneration.

UNDERSTAND THE CONCEPT

The **American Dream** is an influential idea in the USA. It that states that people who have talent and are willing to work hard will be rewarded with economic success, regardless of social background and race.

Bellah claims that Americanism can be seen in most aspects of American life. For example, in some parts of the USA schoolchildren pledge allegiance to the USA and God. The phrase 'In God we trust' is found in most courtrooms and on dollar bills. The phrase 'God bless America' ends speeches given by the president of the USA and ends national events such as the Super Bowl. Bellah observes that particular objects such as the American flag, people such as George Washington and Abraham Lincoln, holidays such as Thanksgiving, and places such as Mount Rushmore or the site of the 11 September attacks have taken on sacred qualities.

Bellah, like other functionalists, argues that the worship of God in the USA is inevitably the worship of American society and values. This has probably come about because the USA is a relatively new society, dependent on immigration. Americanism as a civil religion has an integrating effect: it brings together people from very different backgrounds and creeds and unifies them relatively quickly into one nation under God.

In your opinion, does 'Britishness' have the potential to become a civil religion?

Critics such as Beckford reject the concept of civil religion because there is little empirical evidence for its existence or for the effects it is supposed to have. It is a very generalised concept, and is probably subject to the same criticisms aimed at the substantive definition of religion (see page 434 in Chapter 6.1). In other words, all nationalistic activity could be interpreted as civil religious behaviour. For example, Moosa (2010) observes that all countries have a national activity, such as a sport, that creates common values that could qualify, using Bellah's definition, as a civil religion.

Moosa is also critical of civil religion because, he argues, it does not benefit all Americans equally. There has recently been a spate of police killings of young Black men (which has resulted in the campaign Black Lives Matter). Furthermore, Muslim-Americans who, Moosa argues, were committed to the American Dream have been subjected to increased surveillance and arrests, because all Muslims became suspects post 9/11. Moosa observes that consequently "you had to be Christian and White to be counted among those people who automatically have a God; others must prove to the rest that they have a God and, moreover, make sure that their God resembles the Christian God". He concludes that American civil religion is a misnomer for a toxic nationalistic ideology that excludes poorer American citizens on the basis of their race and creed.

Finally, other critics of civil religion argue that is is doubtful whether it commands the same sort of loyalty, passion and commitment that characterises the daily lives of people with strong, conventionally religious beliefs.

MARXISM

Aldridge observes that Marx was strongly influenced by Ludwig Feuerbach. Feuerbach (1854) argued that God is merely a projection of humanity, while Christianity is a form of wish fulfilment. He believed that God is a fictive being who is socially constructed by societies as the perfection of human knowledge, love, benevolence and power, but makes people unhappy by compelling them to behave in particular ways if they wish to avoid being punished after death. Feuerbach argued that God is a representation of human fears, anxieties and aspirations. People fear death, for example, so they idealise it with the concept of heaven and hell. He concluded that the concept of God impoverishes humanity because, as Aldridge notes, "religion is a delusion not just of the human intellect, but of the human will and the human heart, and is therefore something far deeper than an intellectual error or a priestly fraud" (2013). Feuerbach claimed that religions are dangerous because they encourage dogmatism, intolerance, arrogance and conservatism, which justify the persecution of unbelievers and heretics.

How do images of God or Jesus suggest that the Christian version of God is a projection of humanity?

Marx, an atheist, was convinced by Feuerbach's analysis of religion, but he adds two important elements to this

view. First, Marx took what he believed to be a scientific approach to the study of society and objected to the fact that the Christian Church had resisted and attacked both science and socialism. Second, Marx was mainly concerned with what he saw as the oppressive nature of capitalism, and claimed that religious ideas and practices are ideological.

Marx believed capitalism to be organised into two interrelated structures. The infrastructure, which embodies the economy and workplace, is the site in which one class – the bourgeoisie – exploits the labour of another class – the proletariat or working class. Class inequalities in wealth and power therefore originate in the infrastructure. The second structure is the superstructure, which is composed of all of society's important institutions, including the family, education, government, mass media and religion. The superstructure is concerned with the production and dissemination of ideology. Ideology refers to a set of powerful ideas which are essentially false but which are widely accepted as true and even as commonsense. The ideological role of the superstructure is threefold: it hides or disguises inequality; if this is impossible it propagates ideas that justify or legitimate inequality; and most importantly, it maintains and reproduces inequality generation by generation.

Religion as ideology

Marx saw religion as ideological in two broad ways. First, it promotes the idea that the existing socio-economic hierarchy – the class system – is natural and God-given and therefore unchangeable. Marx argued that the ideology of the Protestant religion in the 18th century attracted the newly emerging capitalist class because it emphasised individualism, reward through hard work and thrift. Material success was viewed as a sign of God's favour, while poverty was viewed as an outcome of sin. In other words, socio-economic positions or social classes were pre-ordained by God. This ideology is reflected in the popular hymn *All things bright and beautiful*, which clearly states (in what is today a rarely sung verse): The rich man in his castle, the poor man at his gate, God made them high and lowly, and ordered their estate.

Secondly, Marx argued that the ideological power of religion is mainly aimed at convincing the poor and the powerless – the proletariat – that their socio-economic position is God's will and that they will be compensated for their suffering by God in an afterlife. Religious arguments for this view include the following.

Some religious denominations and sects attract the poor, by explaining poverty and inequality in supernatural terms. Some religious belief systems convince the poor that poverty is a symbol of their sin and therefore deserved. Other religions state that poverty is a virtue because it is a test of commitment to God. Those who suffer poverty without complaint are thus the 'chosen ones' in a world of sinners. A verse from the New Testament stating that it is easier for a camel to pass through the eye of a needle than for a rich man to enter the kingdom of Heaven is often selectively quoted to support this idea.

Religious belief systems often offer compensation for poverty by promising rewards in an afterlife or a return to a 'promised land'. Rastafarians, for example, believe that they will return to the promised land of Judah, thought to be in Ethiopia, when Ras Tafari, their messiah, is resurrected. Some religions even promise that the human cause of their misery will be destroyed by God. For example, the Black Muslim and Rastafarian religions both promise that White society will be destroyed by Allah or Jah respectively, in the future.

Marx described religion as the "sigh of the oppressed creature, the heart of a heartless world, just as it is the spirit of a spiritless situation. It is the opium of the people" (1844). Likewise, Lenin described religion as a "spiritual gin". As Hamilton observes, Marx compared religion with opium because the consolation or 'high' that a person gets from drugs is only temporary. It also often comes at the cost of blunting the senses and blinding people to reality, and has undesirable side effects. In the case of religion, these take the form of **false class consciousness**: unawareness of the true extent of the exploitation and oppression of the poor by the capitalist class.

UNDERSTAND THE CONCEPT

False class consciousness refers to the idea that working-class people are indoctrinated by ruling-class ideology into believing that their problems are caused by factors other than their exploitative relationship with their employers.

In this sense, Marx believed that religion provides no real solution to the problems of the poor and powerless and that it actually inhibits any real solution or social change to their situation by claiming to make suffering and repression bearable. Religion therefore plays a major role in perpetuating capitalism and the class inequalities that are its inevitable product. It convinces the poor that this has been ordained by a higher authority that they should

never question. They consequently become fatalistic and apathetic about whatever social or economic context they are in.

Marx believed that, following the advent of communism, religion would no longer be necessary. The means of production would be communally owned by all members of society, so no individuals would dominate wealth and power, and there would be one class. Without oppressing classes, there would be no need for religion, as its sole purpose was to legitimate ruling-class power. Religion would therefore disappear under communism.

China is apparently a communist society. Has religion in China disappeared?

Marxism, social control, stability and social change

Marx generally agreed with the functionalist theory that religious belief systems acted as mechanisms of social control and that religion was a conservative social force that aimed to preserve the status quo and inhibit social change. However, whereas functionalists claim this works for the benefit of all, Marx argued that religion is an ideology that benefits the bourgeois few. Moreover, Marx claimed that it contributes to the oppression of the working class because it blinds them to the cause of their poverty, or excuses it on divine grounds. In this way, Marx argued, religions are dangerous conservative forces because they help to prevent crucial, revolutionary, social change in capitalist society.

Evaluating Marx's theory of religion as a conservative ideology

Marx's critique of religion does have some support. First, Leach (1988) argues that there is a strong connection between the ruling class or Establishment, state and religion in the UK. The Queen is Head of State as well as Defender of the Faith and Supreme Governor of the Church of England. Church of England bishops sit in the House of Lords and can consequently influence legislation. There is evidence that those who control the Anglican Church tend to share a similar background with the economic, social and political elites. In 2014, 48 of the 96 serving bishops whose schooling could be determined were educated in the independent sector. The current Archbishop of Canterbury, Justin Welby, was educated at Eton College. Only 13 per cent of bishops attended comprehensive schools. Forty-two per cent of bishops took a first degree at Oxford or Cambridge. Most members of the clergy come from middle-class backgrounds. This has prompted Leach to suggest that most have little idea about how the poor live or how they feel.

Some sections of the political elite believe that the Church is too left-wing because the Church has been very critical of the government's austerity policies, bankers' pay and the failure of corporations to pay their fair share of tax. However, critics of the Church of England suggest that these calls for the government to address inequality are particularly hypocritical in the light of the Church's own great wealth and landholdings, and particularly its dealings in share markets.

In your opinion, is the Church of England a left-wing organisation?

Another example that supports the Marxist case is the role of the American Religious Right (a group of religiously motivated conservative voters, politicians and lobbyists), which Martin (2005) observes have been influential in US politics since the 1980s. Lugg (2000) describes the Christian-Right as a collection of evangelical Christian interest groups (although Catholics and Mormons are also involved) that generally collaborate in terms of supporting the Republican Party (for example, it is estimated that evangelicals make up 40 per cent of Republican supporters). The Christian Right has also been credited with playing a significant role in the election of Republican Presidents (who subscribe to ideas and policies that resonate with them), for example, Ronald Reagan who won in 1980 and 1984 elections appealed to the Religious Right because of his views on 'Godless communism'. The Christian Right was also seen to have made a significant contribution to the Presidential election victories of George W Bush in 2000 and 2004. He was open about his evangelical beliefs and his faith in the power of prayer.

The Christian Right also sponsored Sarah Palin's attempt to become Vice President in 2008. She openly subscribes to the theological view that the world has entered the End Times and that there will be a future apocalypse in which Christianity will triumph over other religions. She suggested that the American invasion of Iraq was part of God's plan. Palin's attempt failed but she remains an influential figure in US politics in 2016. Moreover, Ted Cruz and Donald Trump, Republican candidates for the Presidential election In 2016, have both made attempts to be seen as the evangelical candidate. Cruz has come out against abortion and Planned Parenthood, whilst Trump has responded to surveys showing that evangelicals are particularly worried about immigration and Muslims, by promising stricter controls on who can enter the USA.

Other Religious Right conservative initiatives have focused on preventing, slowing down or repealing liberal policies such as gay and lesbian rights (and especially same-sex marriage) and abortion rights. Education has been a very significant target for the Christian-Right, who have attempted to remove sex education and the teaching of evolution in schools across many states, whilst lobbying in favour of school-sponsored prayer and abstinence-only sex education. Finally, the Christian Right has announced its opposition to environmentalism and its scepticism about global warming, on the basis that environmentalists held 'anti-human' beliefs which only benefit Satan and that they deal in exaggeration, myths and outright lies.

There is also support for the Marxist assertion that religious belief is at its strongest among the poor and powerless. For example, Norris and Inglehart (2011) argue that poorer societies are more religious than affluent societies (see Chapter 5 for further examination of these ideas). Chesnut (2014) also supports the Marxist case by observing that US missionaries in Latin and Central America have been extremely successful in converting the poor to Pentecostalism, a type of fundamentalist Protestant Christianity. Chesnut notes: "In the case of the poor, they are especially attracted to prosperity theology, also known as the health and wealth gospel. It gives people hope that they can move up regardless of their station. People are told that, with sufficient faith and active petition of God, eventually the things that you want in life will be yours. That's a very powerful message to someone who has very little."

Eli Halevy claims that non-conformist religions such as Methodism were the reason that Britain was one of the few countries unaffected by working-class revolution in the 18th and 19th centuries. According to Halevy, the preaching of the founder of Methodism, John Wesley (1703–1791), persuaded large numbers of working-class people that the Anglican Church was decadent and corrupt and had little interest in the working class. Wesley set up the Methodist Church, a Protestant religion which prided itself on its plainness. For example, Methodist chapels rarely had altars or stained glass windows because Methodists emphasised the worship of God without the distraction of wealth. Methodism also stressed non-conformity with Anglicanism and, by implication, with the values of the ruling class. Halevy argues that working people consequently regarded their membership of this religion as a form of protest against their employers and the political elite. Methodism thus had mass appeal and was often the most popular religion in working-class urban areas. However, according to Halevy, this meant that working people were less likely to take to the streets in any attempt to bring about social changes in their working conditions. In this sense, Halevy claimed that Methodism had a conservative effect on the politics of the British labouring classes and immunised them against revolution.

Critique of Marxism

The Marxist theory of religion has also been subjected to criticism.

› Functionalists argue that Marx ignored the positive benefits of religion to society, including the way in which religion creates social stability and the shared values necessary for social order. For example, UK society is not generally characterised by religious conflicts or tensions, despite the fact that Britain is a multicultural society. Functionalists would argue that this is because religions in the UK generally promote tolerance rather than hatred.

› Those who favour the secularisation thesis argue that religion can no longer be a powerful ideological force working in favour of the capitalist ruling class, if religious beliefs and practices are in decline. However, the degree to which UK society is experiencing secularisation is highly contested (Chapter 5 covers this issue in more detail). Marxists also argue that it does not matter if religion is getting weaker, because it is only one part of the superstructure. The other parts of the superstructure, including the family, mass media and the education system, focus on the same ideological goals.

› Marx has been criticised for being very narrow in focus. He almost exclusively focuses on religion as an ideology and consequently neglects the much broader range of effects that religion might have. For example, faith offers comfort and religion addresses questions about key problems such as why we exist and what happens after death. These effects have helped it survive, despite the rise of science. Marx therefore

fails to consider the full meaning that religion has for individuals.

› Feminists argue that religion acts to preserve male or patriarchal power as well as class inequality and that Marxists tend to neglect how religion helps maintain gender-based forms of inequality.

› Marxism tends to focus on Christian traditions and neglect world religions. It has also failed to keep pace with the emergence of more individualised, new-age religions, whose followers often do not defer to an external divine authority and which are often totally uninterested in the economic world.

› Marx predicted that religion would not be necessary in the communist world, and that it would therefore disappear. However, attempts to suppress religion in communist countries have not been successful. It was predicted in 2015 that China would be the world's most Christian nation by 2030.

› Halevy's view of religion and history was challenged by the historian Chris Hill, who argues that Methodism was never as powerful or as influential as Halevy suggests. Hill counterclaims that the real antidote to revolution in Britain was a ruling class who knew when to make concessions to the middle and working classes. They consequently never came close to losing control. There is also evidence that Methodism was not as conservative as Halevy claimed. Methodism was instrumental in the abolition of slavery in the UK, as well as in setting up trade unions and the Labour Party.

› Marx believed that everything within the superstructure, including religious beliefs and practices, was determined by the economic base or infrastructure of capitalist society. However, some neo-Marxists suggested that parts of the superstructure might be capable of producing ideas independent of the infrastructure.

Neo-Marxism

Marx (1845) stated that, at any point in history, "the ideas of the ruling class are … the ruling ideas" and consequently the consciousness of the ruling class becomes a dominant ideology. This is because the dominant class is not only dominant in economic terms of wealth, property and income, but also politically and culturally. Gramsci (1971) refers to this combined economic, political and cultural authority as "hegemony".

Gramsci believed that hegemony was extremely influential because the subordinate class were subjected to ideological influences in the family, education system, mass media and religion. However, he did not believe this meant that the poor and powerless were totally hypnotised by dominant ideology. This is because their daily experience of work, poverty and other aspects of oppression made them conscious that there was another way of looking at the world, which was opposed to the dominant ideology. In other words, the poor and powerless did not necessarily experience false class consciousness. Instead, Gramsci argued, many experienced a **dual consciousness**. This meant, for example, that they might support the ruling class in the face of an external threat to the country, by enlisting in the army, but that they generally retained their self-respect by subscribing to political outlooks and practices based on everyday experience. This allowed them to contest ruling-class hegemony.

UNDERSTAND THE CONCEPT

Dual consciousness refers to the idea that ordinary people may subscribe to some aspects of ruling ideology, while their daily experience may make them critical of others. For example, people may believe that the royal family is essential, even while their experience of low-paid work or unemployment makes them aware that the capitalist system is unfair.

Gramsci also rejected the traditional Marxist view that the superstructure was dependent on the economic infrastructure and therefore functioned solely to transmit ruling class ideology. In his view, the superstructure was more autonomous and independent than Marx acknowledged. It could produce 'ideas' that were not always in tune with ruling class ideology. With regard to religion, Gramsci acknowledged that state-sanctioned religions such as the Church of England or the Catholic Church often served the interests of the state and ruling class. However, Gramsci also argued that non-hegemonic religious ideas and practices could independently emerge from the superstructure. These ideas are most likely to develop out of everyday observation and experience of poverty and exploitation. They are adopted by working-class leaders as a means of raising working-class consciousness and challenging the ideology and hegemony of the ruling capitalist class.

Religion and social change

Maduro (1982) developed Gramsci's ideas further. He suggests that, in particular circumstances, religious ideas might actually promote social change and override ruling-class ideology. He observes that in societies with totalitarian dictatorships, all political protest is usually banned. For example, opposition parties and trade unions are often made illegal and street protests and demonstrations are often brutally put down by the police and army. People are often arbitrarily arrested, tortured, imprisoned and executed. Conventional means of protest are therefore blocked and unavailable.

Maduro observes that the only places in which people can gather together safely in large numbers are religious places – churches, temples and mosques in which they worship and pray. Maduro also notes that some local religious leaders are charismatic leaders, led by conscience. They may speak out against inequality and repression in their sermons, although this will often be couched in religious terms. Political leaders are often reluctant to arrest or kill such religious leaders because they are 'sacred'. Their assassination would turn them into martyrs. This might inspire mass uprising. Maduro argues that these religious leaders eventually raise the consciousness of their followers. He argues that this may lead to political activism, despite its dangers, and to attempts to overthrow the ruling elite through civil war.

There is evidence that some religious ideas and movements have been instrumental in bringing about radical and revolutionary religious change during the course of the last century. Examples include the following.

> The Reverend Martin Luther King and the Southern Baptist Church were at the forefront of the civil rights movement in the USA in the 1960s. King's non-violent demonstrations played an important role in dismantling segregation and acquiring political, social and economic rights for Black people in the USA.

> The Catholic Church in Poland and the Protestant Church in East Germany played an important peaceful role in the collapse of communism in those countries in the early 1990s.

> The liberation theology movement in South America in the 1980s made a fundamental contribution to raising revolutionary consciousness in the peasant class in countries such as Nicaragua and El Salvador. Catholic priests in Central and South America developed liberation theology in response to the failure of the Vatican to respond critically to the oppression of the poor by right-wing dictators. This theology essentially combines the teachings of Jesus and Marx. It encourages people actively to change their societies, through violence if necessary. Such priests played a leading role in the Sandinista Revolution in Nicaragua, throughout the 1970s, in which the repressive dictator Somoza was eventually overthrown. Many priests encouraged civil war or actually took up weapons and

became guerrilla fighters in the conflict. The Vatican responded to the involvement of liberation theology priests by excommunicating (expelling) them from the Catholic Church. Somoza eventually lost the war in 1979 and Nicaragua has been a democracy ever since.

› The Arab Spring was a revolutionary wave of demonstrations and protests that swept across the Middle East and North Africa (i.e. the Arab world) between 2010 and 2014. Islamic groups, many of them composed of moderate Muslim activists, made use of social media. They raised awareness of corruption, nepotism, one-party state systems and police brutality, and organised and publicised acts of civil resistance, such as peaceful demonstrations, marches and rallies. Initially, the Arab Spring was very successful. Totalitarian dictators were forced from power in Tunisia, Egypt, Libya and Yemen. In Egypt, the Muslim Brotherhood won the 2012 election and formed a government. However, the success of this Arab Spring has since been questioned. Control of Libya has fragmented into violent conflict between tribal and religious groups, while attempts at an Arab Spring in Syria degenerated into a bitter civil war that has claimed the lives of thousands and resulted in Islamism taking a hold in the region. The Muslim Brotherhood government of Egypt was deposed by a military coup in 2013 and its leaders were imprisoned.

These examples demonstrate that religion can bring about radical social change, although it cannot guarantee that such change will have a lasting effect. Neo-Marxists therefore argue that, in some unique cases, religions can develop into political movements that seek and achieve real social change in the here and now.

Religion and conflict

Casanova (1994) claims that the irrational nature of religious belief has caused much more war, persecution and human suffering than any other belief system. A number of examples can be used to illustrate this viewpoint.

› Conflicts within the Muslim world between Sunni Muslims represented by Saudi Arabia and Shia Muslims represented by Iran have fuelled a proxy war in Yemen. Saudi Arabia and Iran support different factions in the Syrian civil war. It is estimated that 100,000 Sunni Muslims have been killed by Shia militias in Iraq since 2003 and 150,000 Shia civilians have been killed by Sunni insurgents, through car bombs and assassination.

› Fundamentalist Islamists, who see Western countries as 'crusaders' intent on wiping out Islam, have launched terrorist attacks on Christians. Examples include the al-Qaeda attacks on New York in 2001, Madrid in 2004, London in 2005 and Burkina Faso in 2016, and ISIS acts

of terror such as the beheading of Western hostages, attacks on Paris and Tunisian beach resorts, and the downing of a Russian airliner over Egypt in 2015. Other Islamist groups that use terror tactics in their respective regions include Boko Haram (Nigeria), Al-Shabaab (Kenya), Hezbollah (Lebanon), Hamas (Palestine and Israel) and the Taliban (Afghanistan and Pakistan).

› When Yugoslavia broke up in 1991, ethnic and religious tensions led to the outbreak of civil war in the Balkans in 1992, as Islamic Bosnia and Catholic Croatia declared independence. The largest region in the Yugoslav federation – Orthodox Christian Serbia – invaded both Bosnia and Croatia. It engaged in ethnic cleansing, which resulted in a number of massacres of the Muslim population, most notably at Srebrenica. It is estimated that over 100,000 people died and two million were displaced by this conflict.

› In India, violent conflict between Hindus and Muslims is commonplace. For example, over 1,000 Hindus and Muslims were killed and 200,000 people displaced as a result of religious clashes in Gujarat in 2002.

Evaluation of religion as a cause of social conflict

Critics argue that conflicts apparently based on religion are really about other issues. For example, in Northern Ireland, the conflict could be interpreted as political rather than religious, as one faction wanted to remain part of the UK whilst the other wished to be part of a United Ireland. Moreover, it can be argued that much of the conflict between Hindus and Muslims in India was caused by the decision of the UK government to partition its Indian empire along sectarian lines, before granting independence in 1947 to India and Pakistan. Similarly, it could be argued that the Balkan war between the Catholic Croats, the Orthodox Serbs and the Muslim Bosnians as well as the Palestinian conflict between Jews and Arabs, is about territory, rather than a clash of religious beliefs.

Others argue that much of the conflict between Christianity and Islam in 2016 is caused by American foreign policy and its interest in obtaining cheap oil rather than by differences in theology. Some critics argue that Islamist acts of terror are a reaction to globalisation, especially the spread of Western consumerism and materialism, which are interpreted as decadent and lacking in spiritual fulfilment. These secular ideas are seen as a form of imperialism that are 'infecting' and corrupting the religious faith of young people via fashion, pop music, films and ideas such as equal rights for all. Islamists therefore oppose secular or non-religious ideas, rather than Christianity.

Finally, it needs to be stated that some of the biggest conflicts that have occurred in the past century, and which have involved millions of deaths, have had nothing to do with religion. The First and Second World Wars, the Holocaust, the Korean and Vietnam wars, the Falklands War and the 1994 Rwandan genocide were not inspired by religious differences.

MAX WEBER

Weber (1905) began his analysis of religion by looking at connections between different types of religion and specific social groups. He rejected the **economic reductionist** model of Marx, which argued that religions were ideologies that reflected, justified and reproduced the wealth or poverty of particular social groups. He also rejected theories of religion that see such belief systems as mere responses to deprivation and resentment. Instead, Weber believed that religious ideas exist independently of other influences.

UNDERSTAND THE CONCEPT

Economic reductionism refers to the idea that everything can be reduced to economic relationships, particularly social class relationships.

Weber believed the role of religion was to meet social and psychological needs. He observed that many religious belief systems share the view that those who have experienced misfortune are being punished by divine powers for doing something wicked. Conversely, religions often justify good fortune as the result of divine reward and favour, rather than hard work or mere luck. Hamilton (2002) argues that Weber sees religion as "fundamentally a response to the difficulties and injustices of life which attempts to make sense of them and thereby enables people to cope with and feel more confident when faced by them. Religious conceptions arise as a result of the fact that human beings desire certain things but find that their desires are not always fulfilled." In this sense, Weber argued that religion can make people feel more secure and hopeful because it makes the world look and feel more meaningful, predictable and ordered.

Weber observed that people's social and economic position in society is mainly a product of the way society is organised. Inequality is not random, nor is it the product of divine intervention. However, different social groups will adopt different religious outlooks or answers called

theodicies to explain and justify their social experiences to themselves and others. Weber saw theodicies as people's attempts to understand their relationship with divine powers. For example, theodicies often focus on why bad things such as illness, poverty and persecution seem to happen to good people.

UNDERSTAND THE CONCEPT

A **theodicy** is a religious explanation or justification for something, such as 'God made the volcano erupt because he is angry with us'.

Weber observed that different social groups adopt different types of theodicies. For example, the affluent adopt 'theodicies of good fortune', which emphasise that prosperity is a sign of God's blessing and therefore deserved. In contrast, poorer people adopt 'theodicies of misfortune', which stress that affluence is evil or unfairly come by and that the suffering that results from inequality and poverty will be rewarded by God in the afterlife. Some of these theodicies justify keeping things as they are, while others encourage change.

Examples of religious theodicies include the following.

> Many Western religions teach that suffering in this life will bring rewards in the next.

> Hinduism suggests that living in the 'right way' in this life will lead to a better future life on Earth through reincarnation.

> Some theodicies include a belief in fate: people believe their lives are predestined and they can do nothing to change them. Some people may devise ways to convince themselves that this predestination works in their favour. For example, by working hard and becoming an economic success, they can demonstrate that they are favoured, and therefore reassure themselves of their ultimate place in heaven.

Theodicy and social change
All these theodicies have social consequences. For example, Islamic fundamentalists may gain strength from trade sanctions imposed on their countries by Western powers that disapprove of their fundamentalism. One Islamic theodicy is the belief that suffering plays a role in gaining entry to heaven. Western sanctions and the deprivation that results from them are therefore seen as a means to divine salvation and so provide greater religious resolve.

The influence of religious leadership on social change

According to Weber, religious authority usually takes one of three forms.

1. *Charismatic* – people obey a religious leader because of their personal qualities. Well-known charismatic figures might include Jesus Christ and Hitler. Charisma has been a common feature of leadership in some religions. If the charismatic leader attracts enough followers, these religions can bring about significant changes to a society.

2. *Traditional* – those who exercise authority do so because they continue a tradition and support the preservation and continuation of existing values and social ties. Those in authority give orders and expect to be obeyed because the office they fill gives them the right to. Though generally conservative, this kind of authority can be responsible for change in the face of modernising regimes. The authority of Islamic leaders in Afghanistan and Iran are recent examples.

3. *Legal–rational* – this type of authority is not based on the personal qualities of the individual, but on laws and regulations. Orders are only to be obeyed if they are relevant to the situation in which they are given. Individuals within the Anglican Church exercise this form of authority.

Social change may be brought about because influential religious leaders challenge legal–rational authority – the form exercised by the state or government. Charismatic leaders have been responsible for the establishment of many alternative social arrangements, which have often brought them into conflict with mainstream society or legal–rational authority. For example, Joseph Smith was the charismatic leader of the Church of Jesus Christ of Latter-day Saints, known as Mormons. He was imprisoned and eventually killed at the hands of a mob because he encouraged male Mormons to practise **polygyny**. His charismatic successor, Brigham Young, led Mormons into the American West to escape persecution from the legal–rational authorities and founded Salt Lake City and the state of Utah. The Mormons agreed to outlaw polygyny but their relationship with the federal government of the USA has not always been straightforward.

UNDERSTAND THE CONCEPT

Polygyny means marrying more than one woman.

Religious organisations and social change

According to Christiano and Swatos (2015), American religious organisations tend to reflect theodicies. They argue that mainline Churches in the USA with their middle-class congregations tend to promote order, stability and conservative social values. They generally approve of existing social arrangements and consequently see little need for social change. These religious organisations reflect a theodicy of fortune. Implicitly, they approve of capitalism, and the inequality it generates, because their main source of income is dependent on the fact that their members are relatively affluent, compared with the rest of the population.

In contrast, poorer Americans are attracted to evangelical forms of Christianity such as the Baptist and Pentecostal Churches. These reflect a theodicy of misfortune, albeit one that encourages justice and fairness. Such religions often encourage their congregations to change modes of behaviour that are seen as contributing to their poverty. Alcoholics Anonymous, for example, originated in an evangelical Christian group in the 1930s, known as the Oxford Group. The Oxford Group believed that all people are sinners, that all sinners can be changed and that confession is a prerequisite to change. Evangelical religions therefore encourage their followers to change aspects of their personal behaviour, that are viewed by God as sinful or wicked and to adopt virtues such as industry, respectability, marriage and prayer. They claim these will bring about positive material changes in their followers' lives.

Weber, the Protestant ethic and social change

Weber (1905) identified one particular theodicy – the Protestant religion of Calvinism – which he claimed had facilitated dramatic economic and social change during the course of the 16th and 17th centuries. After carrying out a historical comparison of Europe, India and China, he noted that the biggest economic and social change of the last 300 years – the movement from agricultural production to the industrial–capitalist mode of production – had only occurred in Western Europe. This puzzled Weber because all three regions had access to raw materials, science and technology, a labour force and capital.

Weber came to the conclusion that religious ideas were the main catalyst for the emergence of industrial capitalism in Europe. In contrast, the religious ideas that were popular in India and China acted conservatively to inhibit any change towards capitalism. For example, Hinduism in India had produced the caste system, which made it virtually impossible for individuals to achieve on the basis of merit. The Hindu theodicy also viewed economic activity as less important than spiritual fulfilment. Similarly, the dominant religion in China, Confucianism, saw the creation of wealth as an inappropriate goal.

Weber argued that some European religions, particularly Roman Catholicism, were also not suited to capitalism. Catholicism taught that poverty was an expression of godliness and that private wealth should be used to do good deeds and for acts of public charity. The Catholic Church also taught that money-lending and charging interest were morally wrong.

Weber claimed that the emergence of the Protestant religions in the 16th century provided the religious ideas that ultimately sparked capitalist activity in Western Europe. According to Weber, the most influential Protestant religion in Europe was Calvinism. This religion believed in 'pre-destination', the idea that God had already chosen those who would ascend to heaven – the 'elect' or 'saved'. People's damnation or salvation was fixed in advance, and the fact that people had no way of knowing their fate created anxiety. Calvinists developed a theodicy to help them cope with the fear that they might not be amongst the chosen. This worked on the assumption that any form of social activity has religious significance. By being industrious and achieving economic success, Calvinists set out to 'prove' to themselves and to others that they were predestined or chosen by God. They saw work as a way of glorifying God, as a sacred calling. In this sense, economic success and spirituality were intimately intertwined. Prosperity was seen as evidence of God's favour.

Weber argued that this Calvinist theology led to the development of an ethos he termed the 'spirit of capitalism'. This involved the adoption of a set of attitudes and rational working practices known as the Protestant work ethic. These attitudes regarded industry, hard work, good time management, diligence, thrift and asceticism as sacred godly virtues. Meanwhile, idleness, time-wasting, spending money on luxuries and pleasurable activities such as drinking, gambling, dancing and sex were condemned as wicked and sinful – mainly because they distracted people from economic activity. The Calvinists, inspired by a desire to serve God, possessed an obsessive work ethic and self-discipline. This prompted them to reinvest their profits in technology and the expansion of their manufacturing empires, rather than spending their money on luxuries.

Hunt (2008) claims that Calvinism led to the following massive social and economic changes.

> He argues that Calvinist ideas played a major role in accelerating the start of the capitalist system in Europe, although Weber did not claim it was the sole influence. Other non-Calvinists who could see the economic benefits of this Protestant ethic quickly adopted these ideas, so that they eventually came to be seen as normal business practice. In this sense, the Protestant work ethic underpinned and shaped a 'spirit of capitalism' that became attractive to other entrepreneurs.

> He argues that Calvinist business success led to massive investment in science and technology and the eventual introduction of mass production techniques such as the assembly line, in order to improve profits.

> He argues that the Protestant work ethic was exported to the USA where it became the basis of the American Dream.

> He argues that the Protestant work ethic led to the globalisation of capitalism, in the search for new markets.

Criticisms of Weber

Some countries with large Calvinist populations, such as Scotland, Norway and Sweden, did not industrialise. However, as Marshall (1982) points out, Weber did not claim that Calvinism caused capitalism or that it was the only influence on its emergence. He only suggested that it was a major contributor to the climate of change. Calvinist beliefs had to be supplemented by a certain level of technology, a skilled and mobile workforce, and rational modes of law and bureaucracy. These may have been missing from some of the societies in which Calvinism was popular.

Marxists such as Frank (1967) have suggested that slavery, colonialism and piracy were more important than Calvinist beliefs in accelerating the development of capitalism. This was because these activities meant that countries such as the UK had already accumulated the capital required for fast and effective industrialisation. Moreover, having an empire and colonies allowed Britain to obtain raw materials extremely cheaply compared with other countries. This gave the British economy an advantage over the rest of Europe.

MacKinnon (1993) claims that Weber misinterpreted Calvinist theology and that the religion was actually opposed to greed and the pursuit of money. He accuses Weber of selectively choosing only those parts of Calvinist teaching that suit his hypothesis. However, Weber never argued that Calvinists set out to make money or wealth. Work itself was a spiritual activity. Profit and wealth were accidental by-products of the adoption of the Protestant work ethic. Calvinists used these outcomes as evidence of godly approval.

The Marxist Kautsky (1953) took issue with Weber's idea that Calvinism pre-dated capitalism. Kautsky argued that capitalism pre-dated Calvinism and that Calvinist ideas were adopted by early capitalists as an ideology to justify their pursuit of profit and the inequalities associated with capitalist exploitation of workers.

Despite these criticisms, Weber's ideas have proved influential because he suggested that religious ideas could change history. This challenges Marx's idea that tackling the class inequality caused by the economic infrastructure is the only way of changing history.

Weber influenced modern-day sociologists such as Berger (2003) and Redding (1990), who also argue that religious ideas can fuel economic and social change. Redding argues that modern Confucianism has encouraged a 'spirit of capitalism' among the people of Asian Tiger economies such as Singapore. He argues that the values of Confucianism inspire hard work, self-discipline, frugality, deference to authority and a commitment to self-improvement. The effect of this value system is very similar to that of the Protestant ethic in that it leads to sustained economic productivity and success.

Aldridge (2013) argues that the economic success associated with the US state of Utah and its capital, Salt Lake City, is closely linked with the Mormon adoption of the Protestant work ethic. Mormon theology encourages hard work, thrift and deferred gratification. It also promotes conservative values, such as upholding family life, traditional roles for husbands and wives, children's obedience, opposition to homosexuality, pre-marital sex, gambling and the prohibition of alcohol, tobacco and all drinks containing caffeine.

Attanasi and Yong (2012) argue that Pentecostalism is encouraging the development of capitalism in Brazil today, in the same way as Calvinism did in Europe in the 16th and 17th centuries. Latin American Pentecostalists embrace a work ethic and lifestyle that demand an ascetic way of life, emphasising personal discipline, hard work and abstinence from alcohol. Moreover, Pentecostalists encourage converts to start their own businesses and pull themselves out of poverty. In this way, Pentecostalism encourages its members to prosper and become upwardly mobile. Chesnut argues that Pentecostalism has a strong affinity with modern capitalism. He claims the religion has resulted in an active Pentecostal middle class, who are responsible for Brazil's recent economic success. However, critics such as Meyer (1999) and Freston (2008) are sceptical that Pentecostalism can economically modernise Brazil.

FOCUS ON SKILLS: PENTECOSTALISM – PROTESTANT ETHIC OR CARGO CULT?

Until recently Brazil was quite correctly perceived as a Catholic country. It is still the largest such country in the world, if one counts all those who are nominally Catholic. However, evangelical Pentecostalism has been challenging this Catholic hegemony. Pentecostalism in Brazil is characterised by a strong belief in Biblical authority, the importance of a personal ('born again') conversion experience, the efficacy of prayer and the duty to engage in missionary activity, and, last not least, conservative morals. Pentecostals share all these beliefs, but they add their own defining ones— glossolalia ('speaking in tongues'), spiritual healing, exorcisms and other alleged miracles.

The new faith was introduced into Brazil in the early years of the 20th century, by missionaries from the United States, via Europe. It began very modestly indeed. The big explosion began in the 1950s. Out of a total population of about 175 million, it is estimated that there are now some 20 million Brazilian Pentecostals and other 'charismatic' Christians (the dividing lines between these groupings are somewhat vague, and certainly flexible).

There are two distinct views on how Pentecostals relate to society. David Martin (1990) has suggested that Pentecostals are a new embodiment of what Max Weber called the "Protestant ethic" – a morality of self-discipline, hard work and saving – which, he argued, was an important factor in the birth of modern capitalism. If Martin is right, Pentecostalism is a modernising force, certainly in terms of economic behaviour, possibly also as a "school for democracy". Not least of its revolutionary qualities is the transformation it seeks in family life and the role of women – broadly speaking, toward gender equality.

The other approach associated with Meyer and Freston sees Pentecostalism very differently – as a kind of "cargo cult". This was a curious movement in Melanesia in the first half of the 20th century. Its core belief was that ships (and, later, airplanes) would come and shower the inhabitants of those Pacific islands with all the material goods of modernity – and that magic and ritual practices could make this happen. No special effort was required by the recipients of the "cargo", other than the faith that the magic would work – certainly not sweaty Protestant entrepreneurship. If that interpretation is correct, Pentecostalism is not modernising at all – in fact, it is a carry-over from a pre-modern worldview that actually inhibits modernisation.

Both interpretations have data to back them up. My view of the matter is quite simple: Given the enormous number of people involved in the Pentecostal phenomenon worldwide, it is very plausible that both types can be found – the busy Protestants working to produce the "cargo", and those who sit back and wait for the magic to bring the goodies to them (though this outcome can be positively influenced by giving money to the preacher-magician).

Source: Berger, P. 'Pentecostalism – protestant ethic or cargo cult?', *The American Interest*, 29 July 2010

Questions

1. **Identify** five characteristics of Pentecostalism.

2. **Understand.** What proportion of Brazil's population is Pentecostal?

3. **Analyse** why Martin and other sociologists believe that Pentecostalism resembles Calvinism.

4. **Analyse** why Meyer and Freston are critical of the idea that Pentecostalism encourages modernisation.

5. **Evaluate.** Using information from this source and elsewhere, assess the view that religious ideas can independently bring about profound economic and social change.

FEMINISM

Aldridge (2013) observes that the debate about the role of women in all world religions is between traditionalists and modernisers. Traditionalists argue that since religion and faith are divinely ordained, fixed and sacred, they are distinct from culture, which is a human creation. Aldridge observes that traditionalists regard feminism and any other opposition to the religious control of women as a 'secular contagion'. Modernisers, on the other hand, argue that there is no such thing as a culture-free religion. They point out that, in all the major world religions, religious practices differ enormously between societies and across history. They observe that a lot of so-called 'traditions' were invented recently and that traditionalists are often selective in what they include and what they leave out.

Feminism, ideology and social change

The main group of modernisers are feminist sociologists, who see the organisations of most societies as patriarchal – that is, based on male domination and female subordination. Many feminist sociologists therefore regard religion as a patriarchal institution that reflects and perpetuates this inequality between men and women. They believe religious beliefs function as a patriarchal ideology that preserves, justifies and helps to reproduce male power in patriarchal societies, generation by generation. In other words, religion is a conservative social force in that it usually legitimates and reproduces the dominant male view of the social world and is actively engaged in repressing female attempts to increase their autonomy. It therefore discourages social change aimed at improving the rights of women.

Feminism is usually divided into a number of schools of thought. Liberal feminists argue that many societies, including modern ones such as the UK, and their religious institutions are patriarchal. Liberal feminists argue that society and its institutions need to be reformed so that equal rights and opportunities, as well as justice for all, are the norm. For example, they believe that many religions have a 'stained-glass ceiling'. If women are allowed to become religious leaders (and in many religions they are not) they can only progress so far. They can see the top jobs but the religion has placed obstacles – theological rules – in their way that prevent them from achieving high-status religious positions.

Socialist or Marxist feminists see patriarchy as an aspect of capitalist exploitation and inequality. For example, Marxist-feminists see religion as an ideology working on behalf of the capitalist class, to legitimise the idea that women's primary function is to be mothers and take responsibility for religious socialisation in the home. However, this also functions for the benefit of capitalism, in that capitalism profits from women's disadvantaged position as low-paid and part-time workers and their unpaid domestic labour, which maintains the fitness of the current male workforce and reproduces and raises the future one.

Radical feminists consider all women as oppressed by a patriarchal system that is both all-powerful and inescapable because it is presented by cultural organisations such as religions, as the natural order of things which has been pre-ordained by God. Radical feminists argue that all men directly and profoundly benefit from women's low status, exploitation and oppression, whether they want to or not. Many radical feminists argue that religions are patriarchal because what counts as culture (and religion is a cultural institution) is constructed by men and consequently men are able to dominate how religious texts are interpreted with regard to the roles and activities of men and women.

Simone de Beauvoir, in her pioneering feminist book, *The Second Sex* (1953), argued that men use religion to control and oppress women. Religion is also a way of compensating women for their second-class status. Religion deceives women into thinking they are equal to men, while in reality they are disadvantaged as the 'second sex'. It also gives women the false belief that they will be compensated for their suffering on Earth by equality in heaven. She concludes: "[Religion] gives her the guide, father, lover, divine guardian she longs for nostalgically; it feeds her daydreams; it fills her empty hours. But, above all, it confirms the social order, it justifies her resignation by giving hope of a better future in a sexless heaven." This is very similar to the Marxist theory of religion discussed earlier in this chapter.

De Beauvoir's ideas are supported by a variety of examples of women's subordination across a range of world religions. In some religions, there are taboos that regard menstruation, pregnancy and childbirth as a problem. These biological states are seen as 'polluting' religious rituals. Consequently, women experiencing these conditions may not be allowed into sacred spaces. For example, in Islam, menstruating women are not allowed

to touch the Qur'an and in Hinduism women cannot approach family shrines when pregnant or menstruating. Furthermore, places of worship often segregate the sexes and marginalise women; for example, they may be seated behind screens while men occupy the central spaces. Women's participation may be restricted, in that they often cannot preach, lead prayers or read from sacred texts.

De Beauvoir observes that religious laws and customs may give women fewer rights than men, such as access to divorce. Religious influences on cultural norms may lead to unequal treatment, such as genital mutilation or more severe punishments for women than men if they commit sexual transgressions. For example, in some Islamic countries, women may be stoned to death for adultery, while men are subjected to a public whipping. Many religions also stress that the only roles for women are as mothers and homemakers. These religions may police women's behaviour, to make sure they do not act in ways that are not approved by religious thinkers or texts.

In your opinion, to which feminist school of thought does De Beauvoir belong?

Many Christian feminists argue that there will never be gender equality in the Church as long as God is interpreted as male. Mary Daly (1973, 1978) argues that Christianity itself is a set of patriarchal myths. Although originally a Catholic herself, she argues that the early Christian Catholic Church deliberately eliminated religions in which female gods were either dominant or equal in power to male gods. It also purposely reduced the role of female figures such as Mary Magdalene, who, she argues, played a key role in the growth of Christianity. She argues, that the beliefs and practices of Catholicism actually embody misogyny. For example, she observes that women are not allowed to be priests because the Catholic Church blames them for 'original sin' and associates them with sexual temptation. She claims that women are excluded from the priesthood because their presence is thought to make celibacy more difficult for priests.

In what ways does the Catholic Church attempt to control women's reproduction and sexuality?

Daly argues that Christianity is also inherently patriarchal, with men made in 'the image and glory of God' and women made 'for the glory of man'. The following passage from the New Testament illustrates this: "Wives be subject to your husbands, as to the Lord. For the husband is the head of the wife as Christ is the head of the church" (Ephesians 5:22–24). Furthermore, Daly observes that the primary roles in the Bible are reserved for males. For example, all the most significant Old Testament prophets, such as Isaiah and Moses, are male. In the New Testament, all the apostles are men. In contrast, Daly claims that the most prominent females in the Bible, Eve and Mary, can be interpreted as figures that reinforce patriarchal ideas. Eve, who was made from one of Adam's ribs, represents the dangers of female sexuality, while Mary symbolises the virtues of motherhood. Finally, Daly highlights attempts by the Catholic Church to control women's reproduction and sexuality by banning abortion and artificial contraception.

In contrast, the Muslim–feminist Nawal El Saadawi (1980) argues that religious belief systems such as Islam and Christianity are not in themselves patriarchal or responsible for the oppression of women. For example, El Saadawi argues that the cultures of early Arab societies were patriarchal – men were viewed as superior to women – and consequently men were able to use their power to occupy positions of influence within Islam. This meant that men dominated the writing and interpretation of the scriptures. Men became scholars, sharia lawyers and preachers or imams. This cultural power enabled male religious thinkers to impose patriarchal ideas on their interpretation of religious texts. For example, the Qur'an stipulated that both men and women could be stoned to death for adultery, but this fate was very unlikely to befall men. This was because Arab culture permitted men to have several wives and allowed men to divorce their wives. There was therefore little need for men to commit adultery. El Saadawi also argues that female circumcision is not a product of Islam itself because the Qur'an gives no justification for the practice. The fact that it is not practised in all Islamic societies, and that it is practised in some non-Islamic African countries, suggests that it is the product of culture rather than Islam.

In your opinion, is El-Sadaawi a liberal, Marxist or radical feminist or none of these things?

Kurtz (2016) points out that in some Islamic societies today women tend to have a 'separate but equal' status. This generally means that women exercise power and command great respect from men in their role as mothers and homemakers but are excluded from or denied equality in public spheres, such as at work or in public

places. Kurtz agrees with El Saadawi when he concludes that this is partly due to patriarchal Arab culture. This "is often carried with the religion as it diffuses" and encourages men to exercise cultural control over the scriptures and the organisational practices of Islam.

The debate about the role of Islam in women's lives can be illustrated by examining arguments about the function of the veil and headscarf for Muslim women. In public, some Muslim girls and women wear the hijab (a headscarf that covers their head and hair), some wear the niqab (a full face veil) and others wear the burqa (a body-length garment with a mesh covering the face). In some Islamic societies, such as Saudi Arabia, Iran and Taliban-controlled areas of Afghanistan, these garments are compulsory.

Some feminists see these garments as a powerful tool of patriarchy that nullifies the individuality of the women who wear them. Burchill (2001), for example, describes the burqa as a "mobile prison". Feminists often believe that girls and women are not given a choice to dress in this way but are pressured by their parents, husbands, the local Muslim community and radical clerics and activists to do so. They believe any sudden change from Western forms of dress to these Islamic modes of clothing may be a sign of the adoption of extreme fundamentalist beliefs and practices.

However, there are signs that Western Muslim girls and women, especially those who are middle-class and educated, are increasingly choosing to wear the hijab in particular. Research data collected by Watson (1994) and Gilliat-Ray (2010) suggests three interrelated reasons why Muslim women in the UK choose to adopt the hijab.

› It may enable Muslim women to express their identity as devout British Muslims and to affirm their commitment to Islam. For example, the Qur'an instructs that women should maintain their modesty and that boundaries should be maintained between the sexes.

› It may be the result of a trade-off between Muslim girls and their parents. Muslim girls increasingly enter further and higher education, and embark on careers. Parental approval for these choices may be more readily given if they dress modestly outside the home.

› Some Muslim women see the hijab as liberating because it frees them from the voyeuristic gaze of males which often devalues women as sexual objects.

It is easy to assume that these religious practices are intended as tools of patriarchy and oppression. However, as Watson and Gilliat-Ray demonstrate, it is important to examine how Muslim women themselves interpret their use of the hijab, niqab and burqa.

In your opinion, are the hijab, niqab and burqa repressive forms of dress?

The critique of feminism

We should not automatically assume that all religions are equally oppressive to women. There have been some successful challenges to the patriarchal structure of organised religion, such as the following examples.

> Many religions, including Quakerism, Methodism, Unitarianism, Christian Science and the Salvation Army, are gender blind, meaning that men and women are generally treated as equals. Kaur-Singh (1994) observes that Sikh gurus have consistently supported equal rights for women in Indian society.

> Some religions have changed their stance on men's and women's roles and have become more liberal and progressive. For example, the Church of England appointed its first female UK bishop in 2015. Non-Orthodox Judaism appointed its first female rabbi in 1972.

Aldridge suggests that although religions may be patriarchal, this does not mean that they exploit and oppress women or that women do not possess power over their lives. A number of studies support Aldridge's assertion that some patriarchal religions may "provide a haven for women who yearn for the comfort and security of traditional gender roles" (2013). For example:

> Davidman (1991) studied two Jewish communities in the USA and found that women occupied an exalted status in these communities, despite the patriarchal organisation of the religion. Jewish men were taught to be closely involved in home and family life, and to be deeply respectful of their wives and mothers.

> Brasher (1998) studied Christian fundamentalists and found that, although men were in charge of the daily running of the church, women were not passively

dependent on men. Fundamentalist women organised themselves to participate in a wide range of religious activities. Consequently, women played a major role in organising Bible study, providing counselling services and spreading the gospel in the local community.

> Woodhead (2002) refers to charismatic Christianity or Pentecostalism as an "indigenous feminist movement" because it emphasises both the Word of God and the Spirit of God. The former is patriarchal in that it confirms that God is male, that church leaders should be male and that women should occupy domestic roles. However, the Spirit of God is essentially feminine, in that it is loving and gentle. Consequently, female qualities are exalted by the Pentecostal movement. In Latin America, such an approach has been instrumental in challenging 'machismo' and teaching male converts the feminine virtues of love, kindness, gentleness and faithfulness, to respect women, and to take more responsibility for their families.

There is some evidence that some of the new religious movements (NRMs) that have appeared since the 1960s, especially new-age religions, may be more female-friendly. There is a strong feminist element in contemporary Paganism in which the most important God is Gaia, the Earth Goddess. The appeal of other NRMs to females will be discussed further in Chapter 3.

POSTMODERNISM

Postmodernist theorists believe that the UK and other Western societies have experienced major economic and cultural change in the past 20 years. They claim that this transformation from modern society to postmodern society has profound implications for religious organisations and the way religion is practised. However, as Hunt (2003) observes, postmodernism does not provide a coherent theory of society. Rather, it offers a "series of interpretations of contemporary social life".

Postmodernists argue that over the past 40 years the UK has experienced fundamental change. They argue that the UK was once characterised by certainty. It was a manufacturing nation in which people were born into particular statuses based on traditional hierarchies such as social class, patriarchy, age, ethnicity and religious affiliation. These hierarchies shaped the identity and lifestyle of communities. Individuals had little or no control over these social processes. They were born into these statuses and rarely escaped them over the course of their lifetime. Big 'truths' or metanarratives such as science, political ideologies and world religions were used by those in power, to explain to the less powerful why the world was organised in the way that it was.

In contrast, the postmodern UK is characterised by uncertainty and fluidity. Traditional sources of influence and power have receded. For example, the UK economy is no longer dependent on manufacturing, and consequently relationships and authority based on social class are allegedly no longer important. The UK economy today is a service economy – this means that it is organised around the consumption of goods and information. The UK today is more media-saturated. It is also more receptive to other cultural and economic global influences.

Postmodernists argue that, in postmodern societies, there are no longer absolute truths. Lyotard (1984) argues that ideologies no longer exist and that people have become disillusioned with metanarratives. Postmodern societies accept that there are many ways of looking at the social world and that there are multiple ideas and wisdoms, all of which have relative value for helping people to understand the world. There is also a greater degree of choice in postmodern societies for constructing personal identity and lifestyle: people are no longer forced down particular social paths. They have become more individualistic. Postmodern societies are **pluralist** societies in which people freely choose to construct their identities from a diverse range of sources.

UNDERSTAND THE CONCEPT

Pluralist societies are diverse societies in which people are free to pursue their own beliefs, but tolerate other beliefs, even if these do not match their own.

Postmodernism and religion

› Hervieu-Léger (2000) argues that if religious communities are to remain healthy and vibrant then it is important that societies hand down a religious chain of memory, comprising traditions, beliefs and practices, to the next generation, via the Churches, family life, formal education and everyday routine. However, she argues that conventional mainstream religions have lost their status and authority today, because they do not suit postmodern societies that are in a constant state of dynamic change. She argues that, in postmodern societies, people have become less and less capable of handing down traditional religious ideas and practices to younger people, because these have to compete with other religious and social interpretations of how the world works. This de-traditionalism has come about because in postmodern societies, people are

more likely to subscribe to rationalism, Individualism and moral relativism. They reject belief systems that claim a monopoly over truth and instead see 'truth' and 'morality' as relative: that is, they see a variety of viewpoints as containing 'grains of truths'. They also demand the right to be individualistic in their religious beliefs, to think for themselves. Moreover, Hervieu-Leger observes that there now exists a marketplace of competing religious and philosophical beliefs, in which people can shop around for religious or spiritual beliefs that can be tailored to their individual identity. Consequently, as a result of this postmodern set of social changes, societies are now experiencing 'cultural amnesia'. Young people, are now less likely to inherit a fixed and compulsory religious identity. They are now free to choose their own spiritual paths or to ignore religion and spirituality altogether.

› Lyon (2000) argues that, in postmodern societies, traditional religions have become dis-embedded or de-institutionalised, because of the globalisation of the mass media. The global media via satellite channels and live internet streaming has lifted religious beliefs out of traditional institutions – Churches – in which they have been embedded for hundreds of years and made them available in the privacy of people's homes. Consequently, religion is no longer characterised by collective acts of worship. It has become individualised. Moreover, globalisation has expanded religious consciousness by introducing people to a greater range of religious and spiritual ideas, especially those taken from non-Christian traditions. Consequently, rather than being embedded in one religion over the course of their lifetime, people are now spiritual shoppers, sampling religious and spiritual wares from a global supermarket of beliefs and practices. This 'pick and mix' by postmodern spiritual 'shoppers' helps them to express their spirituality or to find meaning in their lives.

› Religion in postmodern society is now treated like any other commodity. Religions have to compete for consumer attention in a globalised religious marketplace characterised by greater diversity and choice. If a religion cannot keep up with the constant change found in postmodern societies, it may fail altogether or have to re-invent itself. However, Lyon (2000) argues that the new forms of global spirituality, which have become more visible and available because of globalisation, mean that postmodern society is actually characterised by religious resurgence and revival in the form of both new unconventional forms of spirituality and a rise in **fundamentalist** religious ideas and practices. These are explored in more detail In Chapters 4 and 5.

Fundamentalism refers to extreme forms of religion that tend to believe in a literal interpretation of holy texts and whose followers are often opposed to modernity and liberal practices.

In your opinion, is it true that young people today take their religious or spiritual outlooks from a variety of religious belief systems?

Evaluation of postmodernism

There is no doubt that the religious marketplace has expanded and that there is a staggering variety of religions for consumers to choose from. However, Bruce (2002) argues that this is not a specifically postmodern characteristic. There has always been a plurality of religions. Furthermore, the evidence suggests that globally the world religions Christianity, Islam, Hinduism, Judaism and Buddhism are probably more popular than ever. There is little sign that they (or science) have declined as metanarratives.

Bruce also argues that many of the new religions are fairly weak religions. He suggests that they, unlike the world religions, fail to exert a profound effect on people's lives, moralities and identities. He claims that many new religions go through a phase of being fashionable but they often fade into obscurity once their interest or charm has declined. This compares very poorly with the lifelong commitment that billions of people still make to the world religions. Bruce is also sceptical that the spread of global media has disembedded traditional religion. He argues that those religions that use television or the internet are mainly preaching to the converted. Most viewers are already regular church attenders who supplement their weekly attendance with media extras. Finally, Bruce rejects the postmodern notion that group identities are no longer important. He concludes that postmodernism has greatly exaggerated the rise of individualism and the decline of traditional sources of authority such as social class.

CONCLUSIONS

This chapter has focused on three main themes: the role and function of religion, the relationship between religion and social change, and the idea that religion has brought about global conflict.

McGuire (2000) makes a number of points about the relationship between religion and social change. First, if religion is deeply embedded in the culture of a particular society, or a central religious authority exercises strong social controls, then religion is likely, as functionalists argue, to contribute to the stability of that society. This might be, for example, by socialising and integrating individuals into a common identity and sense of unity or by policing, by consensus, moral and religious behaviour. It is therefore unlikely that in such societies people would feel a need for social change because they benefit from the social order that results. This 'feeling' might be false consciousness, as Marxists and feminists argue, but the effect is the same, in that social change is generally unwelcome and seen as a potential source of conflict.

Second, in societies in which religion plays a relatively minor role, it is unlikely to play a major role in bringing about social change. For example, a major social change in recent years in the UK has been the improvement in rights for gays and lesbians, despite the objections of religious leaders.

Third, McGuire notes that if religious leaders are close to an oppressed, exploited or disenfranchised group of people they may use their influence to bring about social change especially if other avenues of change are blocked. This, of course, reflects the neo-Marxist ideas of Maduro as well as those of Max Weber. Another way of looking at the relationship between religion and social change is the postmodern idea that it is not religion that promotes or inhibits change. Rather religion itself has undergone change because it has had to adapt to the novel demands of a postmodern society fixated on consumption and identity.

Finally, the idea that religion is solely responsible for much of the conflict that exists in the world may be over-stated. Religious differences are probably unfairly scapegoated as the cause of global conflict. A range of non-religious factors such as territorial claims, poor political and imperial decision-making and globalisation may actually be the true causes of many of the wars that have blighted the world over the course of the last century. Moreover, there is a case for arguing that religion has functioned to minimise conflict, by providing a moral consensus and therefore a sense of order. On the other hand, there are signs that the decline of religion – secularisation – and the social changes that result from it, may have increased the potential for social conflict, as people become less sure about what social rules they should be following.

CHECK YOUR UNDERSTANDING

1. Explain what is meant by the term 'the spirit of capitalism'.

2. Explain what is meant by 'civil religion'.

3. Explain what Marx meant when he described religion as 'the opium of the people'.

4. Explain what postmodernists mean by the privatisation of religion.

5. Identify and briefly illustrate three features of American civil religion.

6. Identify and briefly explain how the neo-Marxist theory of religion differs from the Marxist theory of religion.

7. Analyse the relationship between religion and conflict.

8. Analyse the idea that a major function of religion is to provide people with a code of behaviour that regulates their personal and social life.

9. Evaluate the view that religion acts as a conservative force in modern society.

10. Assess the usefulness of the idea that religious belief systems are merely patriarchal ideologies that benefit men at the expense of women.

TAKE IT FURTHER

1. Watch the BBC series *The Protestant Revolution*. Focus especially on episode 4, 'No rest for the wicked', which discusses Max Weber's ideas about the spirit of capitalism.

2. Interview or conduct a focus group with a small number of other students who attend religious events on a regular basis. Try to cover a range of religions. Ask the participants about their beliefs and their views about society. Include the following points.

   › Do they argue for social change or are they content with the way things are?

   › If they want change, what sort of changes are they looking for?

   › How do they think these might come about?

3. Visit the Faith in Feminism website at www.faithinfeminism.com for news on the latest debates about the relationship between women and religion.

4. Research the Indian Bharatiya Janata political party to ascertain the influence of the Hindu religion on its policies. Which theory of religion do your findings support?

6.3 RELIGIOUS ORGANISATIONS

LEARNING OBJECTIVES

> Demonstrate knowledge and understanding of the characteristics of different types of religious organisations (AO1).

> Demonstrate knowledge and understanding of the explanations for the growth or decline of different forms of religious organisations (AO1).

> Apply this knowledge to contemporary society (AO2).

> Evaluate sociological explanations for the existence of a plurality of religious organisations and their relationship to religious and spiritual beliefs and practices (AO3).

INTRODUCING THE DEBATE

Many members of society express their religious beliefs through religious organisations, and often those organisations are responsible for shaping the religious and spiritual beliefs and practices of their members. Sociologists generally agree that there are five broad types of religious organisation in the UK: Churches, denominations, sects, cults and new-age movements. This chapter will identify the characteristics of these types and will examine sociological reasons for their relative growth or decline.

Be aware that the terminology in this section can be confusing. Denominations and sects often refer to themselves as 'churches'. For example, the Unification Church is actually a sect, while the Methodist Church is a denomination. Furthermore, the mass media, and even some sociologists, use the terms 'sect' and 'cult' interchangeably. These terms tend to be used in a very negative way; for example, Beckford (2010) notes that cults are 'reviled' as a 'deadly threat' by journalists, television documentary makers and politicians. As this chapter will show, sects and cults are actually quite different from one another. In many cases, they engage in 'normal' religious beliefs and practices, and their threat to individuals and societies has been grossly exaggerated.

CATEGORISING RELIGIONS

Sociologists have identified five major forms of religious organisation:

> The Church

> The denomination – Wallis (1984) refers to recent denominations such as Pentecostalism as world accommodating new religious movements (NRMs).

> The sect – Wallis refers to these as world rejecting NRMs.

> The cult – Wallis refers to these as world affirming NRMs.

> The new-age spiritual movement – Heelas refers to this as the "holistic milieu":

These five organisational types are models or ideal types that indicate typical features; however, not all examples will have all these features. Some religious groups may even have features that overlap between types, such as characteristics associated with both sects and cults. For example, Scientology is difficult to categorise because it contains elements of the denomination, the sect and the cult. Christian Science has both sect-like and cult-like characteristics.

The Church

Weber (1920) and Troeltsch (1931) identified the following five characteristics which are specific to Churches.

> They normally have a large universal membership. 8.5 million people identified with the Church of England in 2014, about 17 per cent of the British population. Meanwhile, 9 per cent of British people identified themselves as Catholic. The majority of Christians in the UK, therefore, identify with these two religious organisations.

> Churches have inclusive memberships. This means that members are born into the Church and are recruited as children, long before they can understand its teachings.

> Churches have large, complex bureaucratic structures and hierarchies, and consequently tend to resemble large business organisations. Power in the form of policy making and decision making is concentrated at the top. For example, the Church of England is led by the Archbishop of Canterbury. Like any other business, it employs thousands of bureaucrats to fulfil its religious and non-religious functions, including education, welfare, charity fundraising, investment banking and land management. It is extremely wealthy and invests in stocks, shares and pension funds as well as owning extensive landholdings.

> Churches have professional salaried clergy who undertake training, follow a professional ethos, compete for promotion and receive pensions when they retire.

> Churches are often formally tied to the state and ruling establishment. For example, the Queen is both the symbolic head of the Church of England and the symbolic Head of State. Bishops sit in the House of Lords. In European societies such as the Republic of Ireland, Spain and Poland, there are strong ties between the state and the Roman Catholic Church. In contrast, France is secular, which means the state and religion are entirely separate entities.

Examine these characteristics and explain why Churches tend to be ideologically conservative and show little support for radical social change.

The denomination

Niebuhr (1957) suggests that denominations are likely to share the following ideal characteristics.

> Denominations have relatively large followings. For example, there are thought to be just under one million Pentecostals in the UK, while the Methodists reported 208,000 members in 2014 and the Baptist Union of Great Britain reported 140,000 members.

> Denominations often have many members from working-class and lower middle-class backgrounds.

> Some of the older denominations, such as Methodism, Congregationalism and Unitarianism, have inclusive membership. People are born into them and members consequently tend to identify with the religion for life. Newer denominations, particularly Pentecostalism, have mainly exclusive memberships, meaning that members have probably been converted via evangelism.

> Denominations are usually national organisations: denominational places of worship can be found in most towns and cities across the UK. They consequently tend to have formal bureaucracies and hierarchies to administer the everyday affairs of the religion. However, these tend to be looser than those employed by Churches; for example, they rarely have bishops.

> Denominations usually employ part-time or full-time professional clergy. However, they often use unpaid volunteers or lay preachers as well.

> Some denominations require a level of commitment from their memberships beyond attendance. For example, Methodists expect their members to refrain from drinking alcohol and gambling. Pentecostals may expect members to go out into the community and evangelise.

> Most denominations are happy to live tolerantly alongside other religions and to accept religious diversity. However, Pentecostals see themselves as the one 'true' religion because when the 'day of judgement' (also known as the 'end times' or the 'rapture') occurs only they will be saved by God, while the rest of the world will be destroyed.

Evaluating the concept of Church

Bruce (1996) argues that the definition of 'church' is more appropriate to religion in pre-industrial Britain. At this time, the Church of England controlled and dominated most aspects of religious, political, educational and social life in Britain, and the Catholic Church exercised much the same powers over many European societies. The definition of 'church' may also be more appropriate to religion in some contemporary non-Christian societies. For example, Iran describes itself as an Islamic state, and Islam consequently exerts church-like domination over all aspects of Iranian society.

In the past 200 years, Christianity in the UK has fragmented into a variety of denominations and sects. There are now literally hundreds of competing **Protestant** interpretations of Christianity in the UK, in addition to Anglicanism. This means that the Church of England no longer commands universal loyalty. Bruce argues that identification with the Church of England is largely symbolic, because in 2014 only 800,000 people attended Anglican services on a regular basis. Consequently, Bruce argues that it has lost its church status and is merely another denomination. Religiously, therefore, the UK is now a pluralistic society. As such, it is not dominated by any one religious outlook or church.

UNDERSTAND THE CONCEPT

Protestantism is one of the three main types of Christianity in addition to Roman Catholicism and Eastern Orthodoxy. There are over 30,000 Protestant denominations and sects worldwide. Protestants differ from Catholics in a number of ways. For example, Protestants believe that the Bible is the only source of God's teachings, whereas some Catholic beliefs and practices, such as praying to saints, the veneration of Mary and so on, have no basis in scripture. Protestants also reject the idea that the Pope in Rome speaks for God.

This religious pluralism was confirmed in 2015 by the Commission on Religion and Belief in British Public Life (CRBBPL) led by high-court judge Dame Elizabeth Butler-Sloss. The CRBBPL consulted 20 religious and academic thinkers from every major religious tradition, as well as the British Humanist Association. It concluded that the concept of a dominant 'church' in the UK exhibiting the characteristics described by Weber and Troeltsch was now redundant. Butler-Sloss observes that Britain's religious landscape has changed beyond recognition in

the last 30 years. Consequently, she argues that concepts such as the 'church' may no longer be relevant for the following reasons.

> Almost half the population of the UK identifies as having no religious affiliation or identity (NatCen, 2015).

> There has been a substantial decline in the number of members of the Anglican Church and the Catholic Church.

> Denominational forms of evangelical Christianity have increased in popularity.

> There has been a rapid demographic growth in the numbers of those following Islamic, Sikh and Hindu faiths in the UK.

The CRBBPL recommended that schools should no longer face a legal requirement to provide daily acts of worship of a Christian nature, that the next coronation ceremony should reflect a more religiously pluralist society, and that the number of Church of England bishops in the House of Lords should be reduced. Nick Clegg, former leader of the Liberal Democrats, went even further by recommending in 2014 the **disestablishment** of the Church of England because the UK is increasingly becoming an atheistic and multi-faith society.

UNDERSTAND THE CONCEPT

Disestablishment refers to the severing of the formal bonds between the government, the monarchy and the Church of England.

It may therefore be time to abandon the ideal type categories of 'church' and 'denomination' and to adopt the more neutral concept of 'faiths'. This would encourage sociologists to examine non-Christian religions in the UK more closely.

NEW RELIGIOUS MOVEMENTS

Wallis (1984) developed the conceptual category of the 'new religious movement' (NRM). This describes religious organisations and movements that have evolved from the early 1950s, mainly in the West, and which claim to offer some sort of spiritual or possibly philosophical guidance that significantly differs from the guidance offered by traditional mainstream religions.

Many sociologists, such as Arweck (2002), use the term 'new religious movement' in an extremely generalised way to describe religious groups perceived by the general public and mass media as 'cults'. These include groups that the media and the state accuse of using 'brainwashing' and 'mind control' techniques to recruit, manipulate and exploit members, to break up families, to deceive the public and to promote totalitarian and autocratic forms of leadership and thought.

Wallis argued that this use of the term NRM was too narrow and too value-laden. He specifically objected to the fact that the media and many sociologists use the terms 'sect' and 'cult' interchangeably, arguing that there are important differences between these types of religious organisation. He championed the use of more neutral categories, to avoid the prejudicial and derogatory assumptions associated with sects and cults. He particularly wished to avoid the idea that all sects and cults are deviant and dangerous rather than respectable. With these points in mind, Wallis argued that all Western religious organisations that have appeared in the last 70 years can be categorised into three types: world accommodating, world rejecting and world affirming.

World accommodating NRMs

These NRMs are the Pentecostal and Baptist denominations, which have experienced fantastic global success, especially in the developing world. There are 279 million Pentecostals and 100 million Baptists worldwide. Wallis suggests that these religions should be classed as 'world accommodating' NRMs because their members lead conventional lives and conform to mainstream social rules.

However, these religions are usually dismayed at the state of the world and the state of organised mainstream religions. They seek to re-establish older certainties, while giving them a new vitality. They therefore believe that their role is to restore spiritual purity to secular societies, especially now that the world has entered the 'end of days', an era prophesied in the Bible, which precedes the end of the world. They believe that it is their spiritual duty to save as many souls as possible through evangelism. They place a high value on inner religious life. Pentecostals believe that the Holy Spirit inhabits them and gives them the sacred gift of speaking with the tongues of angels.

These NRMs tend to subscribe to very conservative beliefs. For example, they are more likely than average to be in favour of traditional roles for women, to be anti-abortion and anti-gay rights, and to believe that society is in moral decline because of the easy availability of contraception and divorce. They are therefore not supportive of social change, especially the movement towards a more liberal society.

Evaluating denominations or world accommodating NRMs

Some critics suggest that the concept of world accommodating NRMs implies similarity of belief and practice within denominations. However, within particular denominations, there are actually profound differences in belief and practice. For example, there is tremendous diversity within the denomination of Pentecostalism, as illustrated by the fact that there are approximately 170 different types of Pentecostalism in the UK and about 400 globally.

Second, the concept of denomination is made complicated by globalisation. For example, in the state of Utah in the USA, the Church of Jesus Christ of Latter Day Saints, otherwise known as the Mormons, has Church status but, in the rest of the USA, this religion has denominational status. However, Mormon missionaries have successfully exported Mormonism to other parts of the world such as the UK in which there are 190,000 Mormons. This begs the question as to whether Mormonism is a denomination or sect in the UK.

Third, the category of denominations is also undermined by the fact that older Christian denominations in the UK, such as Methodism, Unitarianism and Congregationalism are very different in character, membership and objectives to the newer denominations such as Pentecostalism. For example, the congregations of the older denominations are overwhelmingly White and are quite sober and conventional in terms of their beliefs and practices. In contrast, the Pentecostal and Charismatic churches have large Black congregations, often have charismatic leaders, engage in very energetic worship and are evangelical in the sense that they set out to convert others to their faith. In other words, there are more differences than similarities between them, which suggests they should not occupy the same category.

Fourth, secularisation – the decline in religious attendance – is also undermining the denominational status of some religions. For example, the Methodist denomination has a rapidly ageing congregation which is not being replaced by younger worshippers. This has led some observers to believe that Methodism could shrink in the next 30 years to sect status.

World rejecting NRMs or sects

Wallis argues that the terms 'sect' and 'cult' should always be used distinctly. He uses them to describe two very different types of religious organisation with very particular characteristics, although there are some religious organisation that have both sect-like and cult-like features. Barrett (2008) observes that a useful distinguishing factor is that sects (like Churches) see themselves as legitimised by God and therefore as the only true path to salvation, while members of cults (like most denominations) believe they are following one path among many towards spiritual awareness or satisfaction.

Wallis described sects as world rejecting NRMs because they tend to be highly critical of the outside secular world. Given this world rejecting stance, Wilson (1961) suggests that sects may belong to the following categories.

> *Introversionist* – sects such as the Plymouth Brethren and the Amish cut themselves off from what they perceive to be a sinful, secular world. Introversionist sects often reject modernity and live a communal life away from conventional society.

> *Conversionist* – sects such as the Jehovah's Witnesses and the Jesus Army use evangelical methods to convert people to their faith in order to save them from damnation.

> *Reformist* – sects such as the Quakers are philanthropic. They aim to make society a better place by carrying out good deeds to demonstrate God's love.

> *Manipulationist* – sects such as the Salvation Army and the Mormons believe that people need to remain spiritually pure by abstaining from harmful behaviour and substances.

> *Thaumaturgical* – sects such as Christian Science believe that God shows his presence through miracles and faith healing.

> *Revolutionist or millenarian* – sects such as the Nation of Islam and Rastafarianism believe that God will one day transform the world by destroying the cause of their problems.

All of these categories of sects tend to share common features.

> Many of them, although not all, will have been initiated and directed by a charismatic or inspirational founder and leader who claims to have been chosen by God or by some other unworldly power to lead the world out of its spiritual wilderness. For example, Sun Myung Moon led the Christian Unification Church – which is actually classified as a sect – until his death in 2012. He claimed revelations from God, Jesus, Confucius and the Buddha. He declared that Jesus had told him to unite all the world's religions and that Jesus' second coming would take place in Korea.

> Sects are relatively small compared with Churches and denominations. They are normally composed of hundreds of individuals, although some of the older sects that exist in the UK have thousands of members. For example, the Mormons and Jehovah's Witnesses, which are probably the biggest sects in the UK, claim 186,000 and 134,000 active members respectively. In contrast, it is estimated that only 1,200 followers of the Unification Church and at most a couple of hundred followers of the International Society for Krishna Consciousness are currently active in the UK.

> Sect membership tends to be exclusive. This means that members have generally been converted to the belief system or have been inspired to join by the preaching of the charismatic leader.

> Most sects in the UK do not have professional clergy or formal bureaucracy and hierarchy. Larger sects in the UK that originated in the USA tend to be exceptions to this rule.

> Sects tend to be 'total institutions'. This means they demand a great deal of commitment from their members. This aspect of sect life has attracted a great deal of media hostility, based on the fear that sects brainwash their members. Some American sects have come into conflict with law enforcement. This led, for example, to the suicide of over 900 members of Jim Jones' People's Temple in 1978. Seventy-six members of David Koresh's Branch Davidians died following an FBI siege of their Waco compound in 1993. Thirty-nine members of the California-based Heaven's Gate sect committed suicide in 1997. Members of the Japanese Aum Supreme Truth sect killed 12 people and injured 5,000 by releasing poisonous gas on the Tokyo subway in 1995. These incidents reinforced the negative perception of sects (or 'cults' as the media mistakenly call them) in the popular imagination.

Some commentators believe that the Islamic group known as ISIS, IS, ISIL or Daesh is a fundamentalist religious sect because its members' lifestyle and activities are based on a literal interpretation of the Qur'an. Those who do not share their specific belief system are seen as apostates and as such deserve death. Recent ISIS attacks in Tunisia and Paris on Western civilians have been accompanied by the attackers chanting religious slogans.

Examine the characteristics of sects listed earlier in this chapter. In your opinion, is ISIS a sect?

Most sects are not destructive organisations but do demand that their followers demonstrate their devotion to their religious beliefs. Different sects demand different levels of commitment. For example, this might mean changing one's name to a spiritual alternative. The US sect Nation of Islam, for example, suggests members give up their 'slave' name and adopt an Islamic name. The boxer Cassius Clay changed his name to Muhammad Ali after joining this sect.

Other sects might insist that their members live and work together on a commune, giving up contact with friends and kin. Sects such as the Plymouth Brethren believe that this is a necessary part of a highly disciplined and spiritually pure or ascetic way of life. However, when the Unification Church insisted in the 1970s that new converts do this, the media accused them of brainwashing. Families and friends of converts found it too difficult to understand the radical change that had taken place in the life of their loved one. Members of some sects may subordinate their identity and individuality to that of the greater whole. For example, members of the International Society for Krishna Consciousness adopt a communal look by shaving their heads, leaving just a pigtail. They also wear flowing gowns of a particular colour depending on the day of the week. Krishna Consciousness devotees repeat the same mantra 16 times a day.

Some other sects use 'tithing' to indicate commitment. This means giving up one-tenth of one's income or wage to the sect. Others will merely demand that their members follow particular moral codes, such as abstaining from sex before marriage, drinking alcohol or gambling. Some sects, such as the Quakers, encourage their members to do good deeds in their local communities.

The People's Temple

Set up in 1955 by the Reverend Jim Jones, this group recruited affluent White followers and Black people from San Francisco ghettos. It had a radical theology based on a combination of religion and Marxism. The sect was strictly controlled by the charismatic Jones, who claimed to perform medical miracle cures. Under investigation by the US authorities, Jones moved the sect to Jonestown in a rainforest of Guyana in South America. Here, members withdrew from the outside world. In 1978, the sect was again investigated and a visiting USA congressman and several journalists were killed by Jones' bodyguards. Fearing the consequences, sect members agreed to commit mass suicide. The entire sect of over 900 people died: most committed suicide by drinking soft drinks laced with cyanide, although some appeared to have been injected or shot.

Another possible reason why sects attract suspicion and hostility is that many claim a monopoly over religious truth (although some denominations do this too). Members of sects often claim that they are the elect. This means they are special, because they have been chosen by God and people who do not heed their teaching will suffer eternal damnation. This may lead them to go out into the wider community to evangelise aggressively; that is, to share their 'special' knowledge with non-believers in order to convert and save them. For example, Jehovah's Witnesses evangelise by knocking on people's doors or by giving away free literature in city centres.

Evaluating the concept of a sect

It is important to understand that there are thousands of sects across the world. Very few share the same beliefs or theologies. Even those with origins in the same world religions are unique in their particular worldview and practices. Consequently, both Wilson and Wallis have been criticised for attempting to fit sects into categories. However, they both argued their categories were ideal models or types, aimed at helping sociologists to identify similarities and differences between religious groups, rather than a definitive list of characteristics all sects must have.

It is also probably unfair of the media to dismiss sects as dangerous and evil 'cults'. This is not only misleading terminology, but is also based on the behaviour of only a handful of sects and is therefore unrepresentative. As Barrett (2008) observes, the result is that any small or unusual religious movement is likely to be stigmatised as deviant, deluded, fanatical and abusive. However, Beckford (2010) observes that the stereotypical negative characteristics applied to sects by the media such as financial exploitation, sexual abuse, racism and cruelty towards children are also often found in mainstream religions.

Barrett argues it is important to remember that many conventional religions started off as sects. For example, Christianity began as a sect that was labelled deviant and dangerous, and consequently members were mercilessly persecuted by the Romans.

World affirming NRMs or cults

Wallis defines world affirming religions as those that accept the world as it is and aim to teach people techniques for participating with others more effectively and releasing their spiritual and creative potential.

Beckford observes that sociologists are reluctant to use the term 'cult' because of its negative connotations. They prefer the more neutral term 'world affirming NRM' because it conveys less prejudice and stigma. Wallis suggests that cults may share some of the following features.

> Their belief systems do not generally involve believing in or worshipping God. However, their beliefs may sometimes include a supernatural element. Pagans, for example, believe that the planet is a living creature, whilst clairvoyants believe in a spirit world.

> Most are concerned with the spiritual development of the individual. Their main goal is to affirm or improve the individual's place in the social world.

> They generally offer a service in return for a fee to show individuals how they might enhance their lifestyle or improve their social or creative skills. People who are interested in the spiritual beliefs or therapeutic activities of cults are therefore viewed as clients or customers, rather than converts or worshippers. For example, cults such as Insight Seminars and Landmark Worldwide provide training courses at great expense. These allow individuals to discover a 'centre' within them that supposedly contains the solutions to all their problems. Transcendental Meditation, founded by the Hindu guru Maharishi Mahesh Yogi in the early 1950s, places an emphasis on 'finding oneself' through positive thinking.

> There is rarely a physical sacred place in which followers congregate as a community. Involvement in cults is therefore usually loose and informal. For example, clients rarely come into contact with one another.

> Cults, unlike sects, rarely offer radical alternative lifestyles. They do not demand a radical break with conventional society and do not seek to restrict or control people's behaviour. Cults rarely demand any commitment, compared with other religious organisations.

> Cults will usually tolerate other beliefs, mainly because their own beliefs or theologies tend to be very vague. Most believe that people are responsible for their own actions and for discovering their own truths.

> Cults often come and go depending on fashion or market demand. Consequently, they normally have a fairly small number of clients compared with the members of Churches, denominations and sects. They are not mass movements.

Cultish activity

In addition to considering cults as organisations, Stark and Bainbridge (1985) have observed that ordinary people often engage in cultish activity for a number of reasons. Some may adopt physical exercise such as yoga, Pilates and tai chi because they believe these can bring about a healthy balance between their body and mind. Others might engage in cultish activity because it is fashionable. In the 1990s, people used Feng Shui to reorganise their homes, believing this would create strong and vibrant energy and bring health, happiness and good fortune. Others may participate in cultish activity for fun or because they are uncertain about their futures; for example, they may read horoscopes, pay for a Tarot card reading, have their palm read or visit a clairvoyant.

Evaluation of the concept of NRMs

The term 'new religious movement' is not value-laden, but it is still problematic in some ways.

> Most significantly, many NRMs are not actually new, and some are not even new to a particular culture. For example, some sects that are popular in the UK, such as Jehovah's Witnesses, Mormons, Christian Science and Seventh-day Adventists, originated in the USA in the 19th century.

> Measuring affiliation with NRMs in the UK presents a number of difficulties because smaller NRMs do not keep formal records of membership. Sociologists often have to resort to estimating membership statistics, which is invalid. Data may also be unreliable because many people may continue to practice cult techniques such as meditation, individually and in private, long after ending their contact with an organisation.

> The NRM categories tell sociologists very little about levels of commitment to religious beliefs and practices. While those who devote themselves to their movement full time are generally quite visible, part-time commitment is more difficult to identify.

> Wallis' categories do not take sufficient account of the diversity of views that often exist within a single

category of NRM. For example, there are hundreds of varieties of Pentecostalist beliefs within the world accommodating category. These beliefs may be more important than organisational features in shaping the behaviour of those who lead and follow the religion.

> Some religious organisations are still difficult to categorise. For example, it can be argued that Scientology is world accommodating, world rejecting and world affirming, because it exhibits some features of denominations, sects and cults. Aldridge (2013) argues that religious groups such as the Mormons have an ambiguous position, because they constitute a denomination in the USA, but in the UK they are a sect.

NEW-AGE MOVEMENTS

In the last 30 years, a large number of new and unconventional religions and therapies have appeared which have been labelled and grouped together by sociologists such as Heelas (1996) and Davie (1996) as 'new age movements' (NAMs). This term includes an esoteric mix of beliefs and practices, based on environmentalism, alternative medicine, Eastern and Western philosophy, psychology and psychoanalysis, and criticisms of science. The general aim shared by NAMs seems to be the achievement of self-discovery, personal growth, self-perfection, the harnessing of inner potential and spiritual awareness. NAMs are seen as 'me-religions' or 'self-religions' because they often claim to be the only means by which people can find spiritual satisfaction or life-affirming skills. The following belief systems are characteristically 'new age'.

> *A belief in natural energy* – this includes 'good' and 'bad' energy, both of which have impacts on human actions, and the belief that negative energy can be controlled in various ways, such as using crystals, aromas and feng shui, or wearing glass or metal bangles.

> *The Pagan belief in the power of nature or the environment* – this has encouraged some to establish ecological new age communities such as Findhorn in Scotland and to use natural or traditional herbal remedies.

> *A belief in the notion of inner human potential* – followers of new age religions often believe this can be unlocked by new age psychotherapy techniques aimed at improving confidence and enhancing communication skills.

> *A belief in reincarnation* – this has encouraged new – age practices such as past-life regression therapy and re-birthing.

> *A belief in clairvoyance or psychic reading* – this depends on the notion that there is another dimension or spirit world that can be contacted for advice or healing.

> *A belief in fate* – this is symbolised by occult practices such as Wicca witchcraft, shamanism, Tarot, palmistry and astrology.

> *A belief in extra-terrestrials* – an example is Maitreya, the 'World Teacher', who will supposedly appear to show humanity the 'divine path'.

NAMs are difficult for sociologists to research because they compose a loose and informal network of beliefs that tend to be vague, extremely flexible, experimental and subject to constant change. However, Bruce (2002) suggests that NAMs contain a number of common themes which differentiate them from mainstream religion.

> *The self is divine* – NAMs aim to strip away the negative residue caused by the environment and circumstances, to free the real or true self.

> *Everything is connected* – NAMs are holistic because they see the self, the environment and the supernatural world as part of a greater whole.

> *The self is the final authority* – NAMs do not attempt to impose absolute truths on communities. Rather, they give status to each person and value whatever works for that person. Bruce observes that 'personal experience is the only test that matters' (2002).

> *They constitute a 'global cafeteria' of relative truths* – the new-age stresses the right of the individual as a consumer or 'spiritual shopper' to choose and buy what they want to believe. As a result, Bruce observes that many apparently incompatible things can all be true at the same time.

> *Self-improvement and self-gratification are the main goals of NAMs* – the rituals and ideas of NAMs are deliberately therapeutic and are intended to make people more successful, healthier and happier.

NAMs are probably best represented by their marketplace and this is probably the best basis for researching them. The marketplace is mainly found on the internet, although annual new-age conventions and festivals take place in London and at new-age sites such as Stonehenge and Glastonbury.

Evaluation of NAMs

It is difficult to ascertain the national importance and impact of new age beliefs and practices in statistical terms. In the 2011 census only about two per cent of the population identified with religions that might be defined as new age. Bruce (2002) argues that new age spiritually is only superficially popular. He claims that most interest in it is slight and consequently most involvement is shallow. He also questions whether such religions are radical or alternative. He claims NAMs are merely "an extension of the doctor's surgery, the beauty parlour and the gym. Furthermore, as new age practices such as yoga become mainstream, they become distanced from their spiritual origins and lose their religious significance. They simply become another lifestyle choice".

However, after observing the growth of new age beliefs and practices in the Lake District town of Kendal, Heelas *et al.* (2004) predicted that Christianity will be eclipsed by new age spirituality in the UK, within the next 20 to 30 years.

Some sociologists have contested the homogeneity of NAMs. In particular, White (2015) argues that contemporary Paganism is not a new age belief system because its beliefs in nature gods, magic and witchcraft render it closer in substance to mainstream religions than to NAMs. Pike (2004) also notes that Paganism involves reinventing religions from the past, while the new age is concerned with transforming the future of individuals. Moreover, Pagans claim that many new age religions are patriarchal. They also criticise the fact that many new age teachers charge fees.

A Pagan ritual

A final criticism is that it is difficult to see the difference between cults or world affirming NRMs and new age movements. However, Heelas (1996) is adamant that the new age movement is not a NRM or a collection of NRMs. He argues that the way new age beliefs and practices appear across cultural channels – the internet, films, music,

exhibitions, fitness and health centres, clinics and shops – is what distinguishes them from the beliefs and practices of NRMs, which have not had the same cultural impact.

In what ways have new age beliefs and practices had a cultural impact in the town or city in which you live?

EXPLANATIONS FOR THE GROWTH OF DENOMINATIONS, SECTS, CULTS AND NEW AGE MOVEMENTS

Disillusion with an established church or faith

Until the 16th century, there was one dominant Church in Europe – the Catholic Church – and therefore only one conception of God. In 1517, Martin Luther published his 95 Theses, which rejected many of the teachings and practices of the Catholic Church. Luther believed that the Church was corrupt and rejected in particular the dominant idea that people could buy God's forgiveness by giving money to the Church. His critique of Catholicism resulted in his **excommunication** by the Pope. However, his ideas led to the Reformation in the 16th and 17th centuries. This saw the growth of greater religious freedom and the emergence of different types of Protestant religion, with competing conceptions of God. King Henry VIII of England took advantage of the emergence of the Protestant religions to break with Rome and set up the Church of England. By the 17th century, this had become the dominant religion in Britain.

UNDERSTAND THE CONCEPT

Excommunication refers to a rare church practice in which the religious authorities deprive an individual of religious rights such as being allowed to worship formally or enter heaven. This is believed to consign them to a spiritual future of damnation and hell.

Barrett *et al.* (2001) estimate that there are now approximately 31,000 Protestant denominations and sects across 238 countries in the world. Protestantism broke away from Catholicism because some people believed that the Catholic Church had compromised its beliefs and practices, but many of the 31,000 competing

Protestant denominations and sects have similarly broken away from other Protestant belief systems. Many Christians separated from the Church of England in the 16th, 17th and 18th centuries. Many of these Christians, such as the Lollards, were persecuted to extinction by the Anglican Church and the political elite. Other groups, such as the Puritans, fled to America in order to pursue their beliefs freely. In the 19th century, John Wesley's critique of Anglicanism led to the establishment of the Methodist denomination.

Nelson (1987) suggests that this disillusion with mainstream Protestantism was responsible for the increase in the popularity of Christian world accommodating NRMs and world rejecting NRMs or sects in the 1980s, particularly those associated with the evangelical Pentecostal movement. He argues that evangelical Christians interpreted Anglican services as too formal, too lacking in religious creativity and not spiritual enough. Nelson argues that the growing popularity of Pentecostalism indicates that some Christians believed there were more genuine and exciting ways of satisfying spiritual needs and being in contact with God than those provided by the Anglican Church and chose to leave. There is also some evidence that converts to Pentecostalism in Latin America are deserting the Catholic Church in large numbers for similar reasons.

The impact of social change

Wallis argues that many NRMs, especially sects, took off in the 19th century in the USA because Americans were anxious about the scale and consequences of the social changes that were occurring around them: industrialisation, urbanisation, immigration and secularisation. The charismatic leaders of sects such as the Jehovah's Witnesses (Charles Taze Russell), the Church of Jesus Christ of the Latter Day Saints, also known as Mormons (Joseph Smith and Brigham Young), Christian Science (Mary Baker Eddy) and the Seventh-day Adventists (Joseph Bates) were able to offer hope and certainty in an uncertain and increasingly secularised world. These sects equipped converts with a community, purpose and moral codes which compensated for the destruction of the traditional world that social change was threatening.

Wallis also argues that social change was probably responsible for the hundreds of NRMs that appeared in the 1960s and 1970s, which were mainly world rejecting sects and world affirming new age cults. The belief systems of this second wave of NRMs had their roots in a range of world religions and non-religious disciplines such as philosophy and psychology. These religions were very successful in recruiting mainly middle-class, university-educated young people who had become disillusioned with various aspects of mainstream US society, such as involvement in the Vietnam War and racial segregation. Examples of these NRMs include the Unification Church, the Children of God (subsequently called The Family of Love and Family International), Scientology, Rajneesh and Transcendental Meditation.

Wallis argues that young people experienced alienation in response to USA foreign and domestic policy, the increase in access to higher education and experimentation with drugs. This may have brought about a counterculture which expanded the consciousness of young people and caused them to reject the individualism, selfishness, consumerism and materialism that they associated with their parents' generation. Many of these young people were probably attracted by the communal living offered by NRMs in which property, work and even relationships were shared among members. Barker suggests NRMs such as the Unification Church acted as a 'surrogate family' for their converts. Many NRMs based on Eastern mysticism and led by gurus from the Indian subcontinent were attractive because of their emphasis on inner experience, which was seen as uncontaminated by the dominant parent culture.

However, Wallis has been criticised for placing too much emphasis on the idea that NRMs are the product of a counterculture rebellion. Moreover, Wallis fails to explain the sheer diversity among the NRMs that arose in this period and why they adopted qualitatively different strategies to oppose mainstream values. For example, Wallis does not make clear why some groups cut themselves off from society while others went into society seeking converts.

Hamilton (2001) observes that the modern, impersonal world is dominated by bureaucratic social structures that have undermined or threatened community. He suggests this may explain the continuing attraction of world accommodating and world affirming NRMs. He argues that these NRMs help people adapt to social change, by providing them with identity, community, self-respect and purpose.

There is some evidence that a third wave of NRMs appeared in the late 1990s, motivated by the approach of the millennium in 2000. Many sects saw this as the year in which the world would end or the year in which Jesus or aliens would reveal themselves. A number of sects promised salvation from these potential disasters. The best-known is Heaven's Gate, whose members killed themselves, in order to release their souls from their human shells, to join an intergalactic spacecraft concealed in the tail of the Hale–Bopp comet, which was passing close to Earth.

The impact of deprivation

Some sociologists, notably Glock (1964), have suggested that social change is linked to **relative deprivation**. He argues that involvement in an NRM may be a rational response to a particular type of deprivation that may be partly brought about by social change.

UNDERSTAND THE CONCEPT

Relative deprivation refers to the idea that some people may be attracted to religion because they feel economically or socially deprived in some way, compared with others. Involvement with a religion may compensate in some way.

Economic deprivation

There is evidence that NRMs, especially world rejecting NRMs and world accommodating NRMs, may appeal to people experiencing economic deprivation or poverty. They offer a supernatural explanation for these people's social and economic suffering and promise a way to improve the individual's place in the social world. Weber (1905) called this explanation a "theodicy of misfortune" because religions, especially sects, promise compensation for poverty in the form of salvation. (See Chapter 2 for a fuller discussion of 'theodicy' and especially its links to the global success of Pentecostalism.) This theodicy could also explain why world rejecting sects, such as Rastafarianism or the Nation of Islam, appeal to some members of ethnic minority groups.

Similarly, Norris and Inglehart (2011) suggest that poorer people, especially in the developing world, may turn to NRMs because they provide security, comfort and compensation for the life-threatening risks posed by poverty. (These ideas, which are known as 'existential security theory', will be discussed more fully in Chapter 5.)

Social or status deprivation

NRMs may attract skilled manual workers and members of the lower-middle classes who are experiencing 'social' or 'status' deprivation at work. This type of worker may feel socially deprived because they lack job satisfaction or are denied creative power at work. Glock and Stark (1969) suggest that evangelism may be an alternative and compensatory means of obtaining status. They suggest

this may be why some types of worker are particularly attracted to the evangelical goals of world rejecting NRMs such as the Jehovah's Witnesses and the Mormons and world accommodating NRMs such as Pentecostalism. Involvement in an NRM may provide an opportunity to achieve positions of responsibility, authority and status denied to them in work and wider society.

Organismic deprivation

'Organismic deprivation' refers to physical, mental and addiction problems. People affected by this type of deprivation may turn to NRMs in the hope of being healed. NRMs may claim to have faith-healing powers or provide social support to help people develop self-discipline and reject deviant forms of behaviour such as drug addiction or alcohol abuse.

Ethical deprivation

The theology and ethos of NRMs may attract some people because they experience ethical deprivation, meaning that they feel the world is wicked and in moral decline. They may choose to retreat into world accommodating denominations such as Pentecostalism, or even into world rejecting NRMs because they provide moral certainty in societies undergoing secularisation. For example, Griffith (1997) argues that women with traditional ideas about gender may be attracted by some Pentecostal denominations and sects, because they encourage a traditional domestic division of labour and generally reject the notion of equality between the sexes.

Psychic deprivation

Some people may reject the socially dominant values of individualism, materialism and consumerism and wish to explore spiritual alternatives. They may wish to discover their spiritual selves, or 'find themselves', because they may experience the world as too materialistic, lonely and impersonal. This rationale for involvement with NRMs, especially cults or new age movements, is most often associated with the middle classes. These people may not lack material wealth, but feel spiritually or psychically deprived. Research suggests that middle-aged, middle-class groups may take up cultish or new age services, because they are more likely to be disillusioned with material values and in search of more positive meaning in their lives.

Glock's ideas linking social change to relative deprivation were criticised by Beckford (1975), who argues it has never been proven that those involved in NRMs experience this alleged sense of deprivation. There is too often an assumption that deprivation is felt.

FOCUS ON SKILLS: SPIRITED AWAY – WHY THE END IS NIGH FOR RELIGION

In the beginning there was the Church. And people liked to dress up in their best clothes and go there on Sundays and they praised the Lord and it was good. But it came to pass that people grew tired of the Church and they stopped going, and began to be uplifted by new things such as yoga and t'ai chi instead. And, lo, a spiritual revolution was born.

Study after study appears to prove that people are increasingly losing faith in the Church and the Bible and turning instead to mysticism in guises ranging from astrology to reiki and holistic healing. The Government, significantly, said this week that older people should be offered t'ai chi classes on the NHS to promote their physical and mental wellbeing. More and more people describe themselves as 'spiritual', fewer as 'religious' and, as they do so, they are turning away from the Christian Church, with its rules and 'self last' philosophy, and looking inwards for the meaning of life. Twice as many people believe in a 'spirit force' within than they do an Almighty God without, while a recent survey hailed a revival of the Age of Aquarius after finding that two thirds of 18 to 24-year-olds had more belief in their horoscopes than in the Bible.

If you don't believe it, take a walk around Kendal, Cumbria, population 28,000. Since the millennium dawned, this town has been the subject of a spiritual experiment. Linda Woodhead and Professor Paul Heelas, both specialists in religion at Lancaster University, chose the town to measure the growth of the 'holistic milieu' and the decline of Christian congregational worship. The conclusion of their new book, *The Spiritual Revolution*, is dramatic: Christianity will be eclipsed by spirituality in this country within the next 20 to 30 years.

Kendal mirrors the national statistics with eerie precision: 2,207 people in the town — 7.9 per cent of the population — attend church on Sunday while 600 — 1.6 per cent of the population of the town and environs — take part in some kind of holistic activity. During the 1990s, when the town's population grew by 11.4 per cent, participation in the 'new spirituality' grew by 300 per cent. Woodhead and Heelas point out that, in Kendal, the holistic milieu now outnumbers every single major denomination apart from Anglican. (There are 531 Roman Catholics, 285 Methodists and 160 Jehovah's Witnesses.)

Critics will say that this is merely the end product of a prosperous me-me-me society that has encouraged navel-gazing and pampering of the self via routes ranging from personal therapy to facial massage. This is too simplistic, insist Heelas and Woodhead. "It is standard to lash this kind of thing and cite it as evidence of the narcissistic self," says Woodhead. "Trying to become yourself but better through your relationships with others is a very noble activity." Heelas adds: "It's a shift away from (the idea of) a hierarchical, all-knowing institution and a move towards (having) the freedom to grow and develop as a unique person rather than going to church and being led. A lot of the comfort of religion is in postponement — a better life after death. But belief in Heaven is collapsing, so people believe it is more important to know themselves and make themselves better people now."

But must the rise of new forms of spirituality necessarily mean the decline of Christianity? There are life-long Christians who think not. Among them is Victor de Waal, 75, the former Dean of Canterbury Cathedral. He meditates daily. "I don't see it as an alternative; I see it as deepening one's faith," he says. "Because it's not committed to a particular tradition, it is open to all". But isn't it self-indulgent to look inwards? "It is not about discovering your ego, but the divine within yourself," he says. It is about finding one's deepest humanity. People who have been on the fringes or have given up the Church enter into their own spiritual selves and discover it again."

Source: Midgley, C. 'Spirited away: why the end is nigh for religion', *The Times*, 4 November 2004

Questions

1. **Understand**. What do Heelas and Woodhead mean by the 'holistic milieu'?

2. **Understand**. What evidence from Kendal does the article cite in support of the idea that the spiritual is replacing the religious?

3. **Analyse**. What are the arguments for and against the view that new age religions are the 'end product of a prosperous me-me-me society that has encouraged navel-gazing and pampering of the self'?

4. **Assess**. Using information from this source and elsewhere, assess the view that most new religious movements are fringe organisations that are inevitably short-lived and have little influence in contemporary society.

POSTMODERN EXPLANATIONS OF NEW RELIGIOUS MOVEMENTS AND NEW AGE MOVEMENTS

Postmodernists argue that society has undergone profound social change as it has evolved from a modern society to a post-modern society focused on consumption, choice and individualism. However, this social change has brought about 'a crisis of meaning' for some individuals. This means that they are concerned about the lack of satisfaction and fulfilment in their lives and confused about their role in postmodern society.

The traditional sources of certainty and explanation – mainstream religion and science – which used to dominate people's thinking about the state of the world have gone into decline. Postmodernists argue that people are no longer interested in the metanarratives, or big truths, provided by mainstream religions and science, which claim other points of view are worthless. In postmodern society, people are more individualistic and consequently believe in the relativity of knowledge: all points of view have relevance and validity. Consequently people are happy to seek personal rationales for their unhappiness or lack of spiritual satisfaction through the process of 'spiritual shopping' in a global religious and spiritual marketplace. This gives them the freedom to try out without judgement, and even mix and match various religious and spiritual alternatives in their own time and at their leisure, rather than having it Imposed on them by organised religion. Hervieu-Leger refers to people who embark on such spiritual journeys as "pilgrims".

Postmodernists are particularly interested in why people are attracted to new age cultish activities. They suggest that new age and world-affirming movements fit with the tendency within postmodern society towards greater individualism, self-improvement and personal indulgence.

People today feel more empowered to change what they are not personally happy about, by spending money on themselves in ways that would relatively recently have seemed selfish. Gym memberships, health spas, counselling, alternative therapies and the rapidly growing number of tourism centres, such as yoga retreats that focus on wellbeing and personal growth, are evidence of this trend. Some world affirming NRMs sell techniques and knowledge that they claim can transform a person's life by maximising their inner spiritual energy and psychic potential.

Some postmodernists argue that the decision to get involved in some cultish activity stems from the rejection of metanarratives in postmodern society. For example, people have become disillusioned with science – new agers tend to be very critical of scientists who they see as closed-minded and as responsible for the spiritual decline of society, with their emphasis on rationality and logic. They also see science as responsible for environmental damage and for making the world a riskier place. In contrast, new age religions tend to stress beliefs and practices that are alternatives to the scientific approach, such as ancient and traditional ways of thinking focused on ecology and environmentalism. Many new age religions claim that the planet is a living organism and that all living things are sacred. Those who follow new age religions are usually very sympathetic to the green movement, are more likely to practise alternative medicine and to be vegetarians or vegans.

However, postmodernists have been criticised for overstating the extent of individual choice. Critics such as Bruce (2002) point to the continuing influence of group membership on identities. This is shown by the ways in which factors such as class, gender and ethnicity continue to influence the spiritual life course. This is explored further in Chapter 4.

CONCLUSIONS

The number and variety of religious organisations that exist across the world is enormous. This makes it particularly difficult for sociologists to categorise them. There are consequently a number of definitions and typologies that can ultimately prove to be confusing. This is demonstrated by the lack of sociological agreement as to what constitutes a sect or cult. The debate about how to categorise religious organisations is also Christocentric and it is not clear whether the existing categories – Church, denomination, sect, cult and new age movement – are suitable for documenting non-Christian religions.

CHECK YOUR UNDERSTANDING

1. Explain what is meant by the term 'new religious movement'.

2. Explain what is meant by the term 'crisis of meaning'.

4. Explain what is meant by 'theodicy of misfortune'.

5. Explain what is meant by 'inclusive' and 'exclusive' membership of religious organisations.

6. Identify and briefly outline three differences between a 'Church' and a 'denomination'.

7. Identify and briefly explain what has happened to religious metanarratives, according to postmodernists.

8. Analyse the reasons why young, middle-class, university-educated people were attracted to sects in the 1970s.

9. Analyse the relationship between different types of deprivation and involvement in new religious movements.

10. Examine the view that most sects are 'destructive total institutions'.

11. Evaluate the difficulties sociologists face in measuring involvement in new religious movements.

TAKE IT FURTHER

1. a) Conduct a survey or interview a sample of other students to discover the extent of new age beliefs among your peers. Try to assess their knowledge and experience of new age practices such as Tarot cards, crystal healing and astrology. If any students say they have used these practices, ask whether they believe they are effective or have used them for entertainment value.

   b) Identify a small sample of students who participate in organised religious activity. Conduct semi-structured interviews, aiming to discover what appeals to them about their particular religious group. Do you find any differences between those who are involved in different kinds of religious organisations?

2. a) Visit the website of the Cult Information Centre at www.cultinformation.org.uk and explore some of the organisations and incidents mentioned. Note that this site often uses the word 'cult' to refer to what you have learned are 'sects'.

   b) Visit the website of Inform at www.inform.ac and examine the latest information on new religious movements.

   c) Many websites represent and discuss Churches, sects and cults. Many belong to the groups themselves. Access the websites of Churches, sects and cults to explore whether they have the social characteristics described in this chapter.

3. Search online for the Kendal Project website, which outlines the project's methods and results.

6.4 THE RELATIONSHIP BETWEEN RELIGIOSITY AND SOCIAL CLASS, ETHNICITY, GENDER AND AGE

INTRODUCING THE DEBATE

This chapter will demonstrate four key relationships between religious belief, practice and particular social groups. First, it will explore the relationship between social class and religiosity, including reasons why churchgoing in the UK is largely a middle-class activity and why working-class people, especially those living in deprived inner city areas, are largely indifferent to most religions. Second, it will examine the relationship between ethnicity and religion, especially the idea that religion is a central component of the ethnic identity of minorities who have been in the UK for over 60 years as well as recent immigrant groups. Third, it will examine the argument that females are more religious than males. Fourth, it will assess the relationship between age and religion, especially the idea that the young are largely apathetic about religion. However, it is important to note that all these social factors – class, gender, ethnicity and age – often intersect with each other. They can therefore create variations in belief and practice even within particular social groups.

RELIGIOSITY AND SOCIAL CLASS

Research into the relationship between social class, religiosity and church attendance is generally sparse, but the limited evidence that does exist suggests the following.

Church attendance

Ashworth and Farthing (2007) found that churchgoing is mainly associated with the middle classes rather than the working classes. For both sexes, their research found that those in middle-class jobs had an above-average frequency of church attendance, while those in skilled, semi-skilled and unskilled working-class jobs were less likely to attend regularly. Ashworth and Farthing also found that those entirely dependent on state benefits because of sickness, unemployment or old age were the least likely group to regularly attend church.

A YouGov survey of 7000 adults conducted in 2015 found that 62 per cent of regular churchgoers were middle-class. The 2012 British Social Attitudes (BSA) survey found that 73 per cent of skilled manual workers claimed they had never attended a religious service, compared with 63 per cent of professional and managerial workers. However, the BSA research did not focus exclusively on services of religious worship – it also included weddings, christenings and funerals.

Research conducted by Voas and Watt (2014), on behalf of the Church of England," does not make any direct reference to social class, but makes three observations about churchgoing that may be relevant to social class distinctions. First, they point out that attendance in rural churches is twice as high as attendance in urban parishes. Second, they found some evidence that church attendance is higher in the South of England than in the North and the Midlands. Third, they noted some growth in church attendance, especially in those suburban areas which had academically high-performing church primary and secondary schools. Like the findings of the other researchers mentioned above, this research suggests that church attendance is higher among the middle classes than the working classes.

How might the three observations made by Voas and Watt contribute to the notion that churchgoing is mainly a middle-class activity?

Religious belief

> Lawes (2009) found that with regard to religious beliefs, **lifelong theists** disproportionately come from semi-skilled and unskilled manual backgrounds and are less likely to have academic qualifications. This contradicts the findings relating to church attendance. As such, it seems to support Grace Davie's hypothesis that "believing [in God] without belonging" (1994) is very common in contemporary UK society. In contrast, **lifelong atheists**, disproportionately, come from higher professional and managerial backgrounds. This group is also more likely to have experienced higher education. Atheism has historically been a minority movement even among better-educated people, but it is becoming much more prominent in the UK and worldwide.

UNDERSTAND THE CONCEPT

Lifelong theism refers to people who have always believed in a god, as opposed to people who have recently been converted. **Lifelong atheists** are those who have never believed in a god.

Sociologists need to be cautious when generalising about religiosity, church attendance and social class because other factors may distort the statistics, most notably ethnicity, immigration, gender and age. For example, there is evidence that church attendance in deprived inner city areas of large cities is higher than in other urban areas. This is particularly so in the churches of the Methodist, Pentecostal and Baptist denominations and the chapels of Christian sects such as Christ Embassy and the Living Faith Church. Africans and other recent immigrants to the UK who tend to have a deeper religious faith than the majority White population, are disproportionately likely to live in these areas. These immigrant groups are relatively poor and are therefore objectively working-class. Immigration may also explain why the decline in attendance at Catholic churches has been less steep than at Anglican churches: Catholic churches are more likely to attract Irish, Polish and African working-class immigrants in inner city parishes.

Religious and social class organisations

The Church of England

The Church of England has always had a close relationship with the monarchy, the state and the establishment. The Queen is the 'Defender of the Faith and Supreme Governor of the Church of England', while the prime minister is partly responsible for choosing bishops. Because of its elite connections, the middle classes often regard churchgoing as the 'decent', 'respectable' and 'deferential' thing to do.

In contrast, Ahern and Davie (1987) argue that working-class people are generally distrustful of institutions such as the Anglican Church, which they see as hierarchical and too closely tied to the ruling establishment. Ahern's survey of inner city residents in London demonstrated that they viewed the relationship between the working class and Churches as one of 'them versus us'. Inner city residents saw the Anglican Church and its ministers as incomprehensible, patronising, gloomy and boring. They also claimed that ministers were culturally embarrassed by the presence of working-class people in church. Ahern and Davie also argue that working people are attracted to religious non-conformity because they perceive mainstream religion as too formal, middle-class and authoritarian. Working people may resent and reject instructions from their social and religious 'betters' on how they should behave.

Halevy (1972) argued that these working-class concerns with the Anglican Church would have resonated with workers who left the Church of England and converted to Methodism in the 18th and 19th centuries. He also claimed that the Anglican Church and clergy generally sided with employers, at the expense of the workers. Wesley preached in favour of equality of worship and urged working people to become lay preachers. Many of these preachers went on to become trade union leaders and to help found the Labour Party in 1900.

The attendance of middle-class people in mainstream churches, especially in rural and suburban areas, may be a reflection of their social and geographical mobility. Brierley (1999) argues that churches may ease the transition of middle-class newcomers into rural and suburban communities. Martin argues that this function of Churches may not be exclusively religious, in that middle-class church attendance may have become a secular or social activity. For example, middle-class people may attend church in order to be seen or because they feel it is something they should do, and not because they are more religious than other social groups.

Denominations of the Church of England

Roy Wallis (1984) argues that many denominations are slightly anti-establishment or non-conformist in character because they have broken away from the established Church of England. However, he argues that denominations such as Methodism mainly attract the skilled working class and lower middle class because such organisations are generally organised and run by their congregations. These denominations also stress standards of moral behaviour that respectable workers are happy to be associated with. For example, Methodism emphasises hard work and warns against the dangers of drinking and gambling. It encourages its members to work hard, to save for their future and to give generously to those in need. There is also evidence that the poorest socioeconomic groups may be attracted to Pentecostalism because of its 'theodicy of misfortune', which offers an explanation and a solution for their economic misfortune (see Chapter 2).

Sects

Glock (1964) argues that some social groups may be attracted to sects because of their experience of various types of deprivation (see Chapter 3). The poorest social groups' experience of economic deprivation may mean that they are or were attracted to sects such as the Nation of Islam, Rastafarianism, the Branch Davidians and Jim Jones' People's Temple, because these offer or offered divine compensation for their low economic status. Such sects may provide a way for economically deprived people to cope with their disadvantages.

Andrew Holden's (2002) research on the Jehovah's Witnesses suggests that many members of this sect are drawn from the skilled working class, the self-employed and the lower middle class. Many converts work in jobs that involve little interaction with colleagues or the general public. Consequently, these workers tend to feel unfulfilled in their jobs and isolated from others. They often express disillusion with the social, political and economic system. Holden argues that the Jehovah's Witnesses compensate for this deprivation by providing a safe haven and a strong sense of identity and community. Moreover, Holden identifies a number of factors within the Jehovah's Witnesses movement that provide converts with a sense of status and purpose that counteracts their lack of status at work. First, conversion is presented as a "heroic act that requires self-sacrifice, courage and conviction". Second, their commitment to the Witnesses' theology and ethics assures them of their heavenly salvation. Third, membership of the Jehovah's Witnesses involves a compulsory evangelical role, which instils in them a strong sense of self-worth.

Wallis notes that the sects that appeared in the 1960s and 1970s such as the Children of God, the Jesus Army, the Unification Church and the International Society for Krishna Consciousness, mainly attracted middle-class, university-educated students who were experiencing psychic deprivation. This means they felt disillusioned with the values of capitalist society and their parents' culture. They consequently turned to these sects, which claimed to offer alternative spiritual fulfilment and enlightenment.

Ethical deprivation may also explain the appeal of Islamic fundamentalism to some members of the young, upwardly-mobile Muslim middle class. Bruce (2002) argues that university-educated young Muslims may feel that the Western capitalist system is too dependent on materialism and is therefore spiritually corrupt. They may be attracted to **Islamism** because this fundamentalist movement stresses a return to what they see as traditional values. It therefore represents an attempt to reclaim the past and attain a sense of certainty in an uncertain world.

UNDERSTAND THE CONCEPT

Islamism refers to militant or fundamentalist versions of Islam.

Cults and new age movements

Active participants in the courses put on by cults, such as Landmark Worldwide, or who invest in new age activities, are overwhelmingly middle-class because the cost of investing in these spiritual interests can be quite high. Bruce (1995) argues that new age movements appeal most to those whose material and financial needs are satisfied, but who feel there may be more to life than material possessions and money. In particular, Heelas (2008) argues that new age ideas and activities appeal specifically to highly educated professionals, especially females and people who work in creative fields, who have a deep interest in exploring their full potential.

Conclusions: social class and religion

Little in-depth research has been conducted in this field, which makes it difficult to generalise with any confidence about the relationship between social class and religion. Moreover, religions in the UK do not collect data about the occupational status of their congregations. However, we can broadly speculate from the limited data that has been collected that the middle classes probably dominate mainstream Anglican and Catholic congregations in the UK. Meanwhile, the skilled working class and lower middle class dominate the congregations of denominations such as Methodism and Pentecostalism, as well as older, more established sects such as Mormons and Jehovah's Witnesses. There is evidence that in the past, working-class people were more heavily involved in non-conformist religions because these symbolised their contempt of the ruling establishment. However, the evidence today suggests that the White working class rarely involves itself with religious practice. It is important to acknowledge, however, that this does not mean they subscribe to atheist ideas. Rather, the few surveys that have been carried out, that are either dated or restricted to a sample of young people, indicate that working-class people are apathetic about or uninterested in religion because it offers no meaningful contribution to their daily lives. It therefore may be the case that they 'believe without belonging'. However, in contrast, the evidence suggests that ethnic minorities, particularly working-class Muslims, African-Caribbeans and Africans tend to be more religious than their White peers.

RELIGIOSITY AND ETHNICITY

'Ethnicity' refers to the shared culture of a social group that gives its members a common identity that is different in some ways from other social groups. A minority ethnic group is a social group that shares a cultural identity that differs from that of the majority population of a society. These differences may include religious belief and practice, tradition, marriage and family customs, dress and diet. In the UK, the main minority ethnic groups are Pakistani, Bangladeshi, Indian, Irish, African–Caribbean, Black African and Chinese.

The UK in the 21st century is a multi-faith and multicultural society. Every ethnic group enjoys the right to religious freedom. A wide variety of ethnic minority religious organisations and groups are permitted to conduct their rites and ceremonies, to promote their beliefs within the limits of the law, to own property and to run schools and to conduct a range of other charitable activities.

The 2011 census (see Table 6.4.1) showed that non-Christian religions were practised by nearly 5 million people or 7.7 per cent of the population in the UK. However, as this section will show, participation in Christian religions in the UK by ethnic minorities is also high.

Religious affiliation	Number	Percentage of population
Christian	37,583,962	59.5
Buddhist	261,584	0.4
Hindu	835,394	1.3
Jewish	269,568	0.4
Muslim	2,786,635	4.4
Sikh	432,429	0.7
Other	262,774	0.4
Total for non-Christian religions	4,848,384	7.7
No religion	16,221,509	25.7
Religion not stated	4,528,323	7.2

Table 6.4.1 *People claiming religious affiliation in the UK*
Source: UK census (2011)

Davie (2015) argues that these statistics are one-dimensional because the census only asks: "What is your religion?" It does not ask questions about everyday religious practice or level of religious commitment. It also fails to distinguish between various schools of thought and belief that exist within various religions; for example, Orthodox Jews may be more religious than non-Orthodox Jews. Davie also points out that identifying as a Jew or a Sikh may symbolise an ethnic, cultural or political identity rather than religiosity.

The statistics also fail to differentiate between those who are religious as a matter of individual choice and those who identify as religious as a response to their social situation. For example, some people may have been socialised into religion as a community or family identity. Some people's affiliation, especially children's, may be claimed on their behalf by whoever fills in the census form. Finally, the categories of 'no religion' and 'religion not stated' give no clues as to whether people who responded in this way were born into a particular religion or whether they had previously had religious faith.

Trends in ethnic minority beliefs and practices

The evidence suggests that Muslims, Hindus and Black Christians see religion as more important than White Christians do. O'Beirne (2004) found that White Christians rarely saw religion as central to their identity. Social factors such as family, work, age, interests, education, nationality, gender, income and social class were deemed more important. In contrast, Asians, especially Muslims, ranked religion and family equally as markers of identity. African–Caribbeans and Black Africans ranked religion as the third most important factor in their lives.

The most recent official statistics, which date from 2008–09, show that only 32 per cent of adults aged 16 and over who reported being Christian actively practised their religion. In contrast, 80 per cent of those who reported being Muslim and two thirds or more of Hindus, Sikhs and Buddhists actively practised their religion. Jews are also more religiously observant than Christians. According to current trends, it is likely that practising Muslims will soon outnumber practising Anglicans.

According to the English Church Census of 2005, 10 per cent of churchgoers in the UK were Black, although Brierley (2006) claimed it was high as 17 per cent. Whichever figure is accepted, it is a fact that the proportion of churchgoers who are Black is at least three times higher than the proportion of Black people in the population, which the 2011 census placed at 3.3 per cent.

Observance of African forms of Christian spirituality has dramatically increased in both the mainstream Churches and in the Black-led Pentecostal and Baptist Churches over the past 25 years. This is probably because a third of all immigrants to the UK in the past 15 years have come from Africa. British African–Caribbeans are also more likely to be Pentecostal than to belong to any other Christian religion. Half of the Pentecostal churches in the UK have predominantly Black congregations. Goodhew (2012) estimates that half a million Black people in the UK are involved in Pentecostalism. This includes those who are part of a national movement (for example, affiliated to the Assemblies of God or the Elim Pentecostal Church), those who are part of a mega-church with links overseas to countries such as Nigeria and Ghana (for example, Christ Embassy), and those who belong to an independent church.

Davie (2015) suggests that London has a unique character in comparison to the rest of the UK with regard to the diversity of ethnic minority religions. She points out that London contains the largest proportion of people who self-identify as Jews, Sikhs, Muslims, Hindus and Buddhists. There has also been a growth in the number of Chinese, Croatian, Portuguese, Russian and Tamil Christian churches. Over half of all churchgoers in London are Black. Moreover, London has relatively few people who declare they have 'no religion' compared with the rest of the UK.

There is some evidence that African–Caribbeans are more likely to be involved in sects such as the Seventh-day Adventists, Jehovah's Witnesses and Rastafarianism. Rastafarianism is popular among young African–Caribbean men in inner city areas such as Brixton in London. It gives them a very distinctive group identity, which is often interpreted by the police and judicial system to be in opposition to establishment values.

Reasons why ethnic minorities have higher levels of religiosity

Functionalism

Functionalist sociologists have suggested a range of reasons why ethnic minorities in the UK are more religious than the White population. Sociologists such as Durkheim and Parsons argue that religion functions to bring about social order and solidarity. It does this by creating a sense of common identity or community and by socialising each generation into a moral code of behaviour. This can be illustrated in a number of ways with regard to ethnic minority religions in the UK.

Cultural transition

Religion can be a means of coping with the stresses of migration. It can help to ease the transition of new immigrants into a new society or culture, by providing a familiar community in an alien society. Bruce argues that religious institutions have provided a community focal point for Irish, African–Caribbean, Muslim, Hindu and Black African immigrants. For example, when Indians and Pakistanis first came to Britain in the 1950s, there was no Hindu or Muslim infrastructure in place. Building temples and mosques from scratch, often in the face of hostile opposition, reinforced their sense of solidarity

and community as well as their commitment to living in the UK. Some sociologists have stressed the role of mosques in providing Muslim women, who often have low rates of economic activity, with a focus for social life and community.

Bird points out that most minority ethnic groups in the UK today originate in societies with high levels of religiosity. When such groups migrate to a new society, religious movements and their institutions are in the vanguard of such immigration. This encourages a type of community cohesion best summarised by the saying "birds of a feather flock together". Because immigration is a relatively recent phenomenon, it is therefore unsurprising that minority ethnic groups show higher levels of religious involvement than the White population.

Bruce suggests that once a group has successfully settled into a society its commitment to its religion may weaken. For example, there is some evidence that religious commitment amongst the Irish and Asian middle class is not as strong as it is among poorer Irish and Asian people. This is because the former group has undergone assimilation and adopted some of the secular characteristics of the majority population. There is also some evidence that the children and grandchildren of immigrant groups may be less committed to religion for the same reasons.

UNDERSTAND THE CONCEPT

Assimilation refers to the process by which an immigrant group will acquire the cultural, social and psychological characteristics of a host population.

Cultural defence

Bruce (2002) argues that religion functions as a source of cultural defence. This means that it helps support and preserve identity, culture and language in an uncertain and hostile, perhaps even racist, environment. Religion may defend communities by providing emotional, social and economic supports to its members, by providing young people with opportunities to learn more about their culture and religion, and by speaking out against intolerance, discrimination and inequality.

A good illustration of cultural defence is the fact that African-Caribbeans and Black Africans were mainly Christian when they arrived in the UK, but many found that White churches in the UK did not actively welcome their presence. Beckford (2002) suggests African-Caribbeans were also put off by the conservative nature of worship in the conventional British churches, which they interpreted as lacking passion, joyousness and spirituality. They responded by either founding or joining churches led by Black people, especially those in the evangelical Baptist or Pentecostal denominations. Beckford suggests that evangelical Christianity gives Black people a sense of identity, purpose, hope, social respectability and independence.

Religious socialisation and social controls

Functionalists such as Durkheim (1912) have argued that religions provides their members with a sense of shared norms and values, symbolised through rituals that unite them as a distinct social group. Davie (1994) argues that high levels of religious belief and practice among ethnic minorities reflect conformity to religious controls that originate in societies with high levels of religiosity. She notes that ethnic-minority religions exercise strict control over many aspects of social life, such as socialisation of children, marriage, the role of women, the relationship between young people and their families, cooking, diet, dress codes and everyday codes of behaviour. These controls are often closely policed by parents, faith schools and theological leaders such as imams and priests.

In particular, Davie notes that families are extremely influential in Asian communities in disseminating religious ideas and ensuring conformity to religious social controls. For example, Kurtz (2016) describes the family as the 'body' of Islam because it is supposed to mirror the ideal Islamic society. The extended kinship networks and close-knit communities to which many Asian people in the UK belong are powerful sources of religious socialisation. This makes Asian children more likely than White children to subscribe faithfully to moral codes concerning religious belief and practice, family honour and respect for their elders. Parents expect their children to follow, in adulthood, the religion they have been brought up in. Not to do so is to betray one's upbringing or to let one's family down.

Evaluating functionalism

Critics of functionalism have suggested that the idea of ethnic-minority religions as a source of community, unity and common identity for their adherents is overstated, because it glosses over the divisions and conflicts within ethnic-minority religions. For example, the focus in Islamic culture on the worldwide Muslim community – the ummah – conveniently ignores the schism and conflict between Sunni and Shia Muslims. It also ignores the potential fragmentation in the UK between a fairly well-integrated and law-abiding Muslim majority and a very small minority of devout, disaffected

and fundamentalist Islamists who identify or sympathise with groups such as ISIS.

Contemporary Britain also subscribes to equal opportunity laws, including laws against discrimination, on the basis of sex and sexual orientation, in work and education. This means that some of values and practices associated with some Asian religions may come into conflict with the values of the majority. This can undermine value consensus and community, creating the potential for hostility and conflict.

Modood argues that ethnic minority religious communities may be undermined by generation gaps, particularly between first-generation immigrants and their third-generation grandchildren over issues such as alcohol, dress and women's education. However, Chryssides (1994) suggests that ethnic-minority religions have evolved in order to reduce the possibility of conflict between parents and children. He argues that ethnic-minority communities continue to believe and practise, but have adapted their religious beliefs and practices to fit in with modern society. For example, there is little objection to Muslim girls dressing fashionably as long as modesty prevails.

In your opinion, what generational differences may weaken commitment to a religion?

Functionalists have also been criticised for ignoring the fact that taking an exclusivist stance, for example by dismissing the majority group as non-believers or as oppressors, can separate ethnic-minority religions from wider society and create an atmosphere of suspicion and hostility. For example, Pryce argued that Rastafarianism actually undermines social solidarity and creates conflict, because it encourages young African-Caribbeans to reject the wider White social system as racist and exploitative. Such attitudes mean that Rastafarians often come into conflict with the police and judicial system.

Marxism

As seen in Chapter 2, Marxists argue that religion as an ideology uses promises of heaven and other supernatural rewards to distract the working class and the poor from the true cause of their exploitation and inequality – the capitalist system. For example, both the Nation of Islam and Rastafarianism appeal to young Black men disaffected by unemployment, poverty, discrimination and police harassment, because both religions promise the destruction of the White race. Marxists therefore argue that ethnic-minority religions, like all religions, create a sense of false consciousness. People seek comfort and compensation in religious beliefs and practices, rather than actively and practically seeking to change their social and economic situation, for example through political protest.

Marxists believe some ethnic minority religions, particularly Hinduism and Sikhism, promote the view that socio-economies are preordained by God and are therefore unchangeable. From a Marxist perspective, religious hierarchies such as the caste system divide and rule communities that should be united against powerful economic interests, in order to overcome inequalities in wealth and income.

Worshippers at a Sikh temple

Goodhew (2012) also argues that African–Caribbean worship in the UK is characterised by social stratification. Upwardly mobile African–Caribbeans and Africans tend to attend churches belonging to traditional religions such as Methodism. African–Caribbeans from poorer backgrounds are more attracted by Pentecostalism that assures them that they have been chosen by God and are promised heavenly salvation.

Evaluating Marxism
Marxism has been accused of economic reductionism and determinism. This means that it argues that ethnic-minority religions are shaped by economics, and in particular by the social class relationships generated by the capitalist economic system. However, neo-Marxists such as Gramsci and Maduro argue that religious ideas can sometimes act independently of the economic system and that ethnic-minority religions have promoted positive social change in some societies (see Chapter 3 for examples).

Supporters of Max Weber have pointed out that Pentecostalism has enabled the poor to cope with a racist and unjust society, by equipping them with the social and economic attitudes and supports they require to overcome personal hardship and poverty. Other sociologists, particularly El-Saadawi, argue that culture, particularly patriarchy, is more likely than economics to shape ethnic minority religions.

Why do you think feminists may be critical of Marxist ideas about religion?

Weberianism
Weberians have demonstrated that minority ethnic groups in the UK tend to be economically deprived and consequently socially disadvantaged compared with the majority population. For example, children from Black African and Black Caribbean backgrounds are more likely to be in poverty than White British children, according to the 2012 Poverty and Social Exclusion (PSE) survey. Weberians point out that there seems to be a strong correlation between poverty and high religiosity.

Weber (1920) suggested that some denominations and sects may be attractive to poorer people, because they provide an explanation and justification for misfortune and poverty. The existential security theory of Norris and Inglehart provides a modern version of this theory. They argue that there is low demand for religion among members of ethnic minorities in the UK, who feel economically or socially secure. This means that they enjoy a high standard of living and there is consequently little risk to their loved ones. In contrast, poorer people may face life-threatening risks such as poverty, stress and ill health on a daily basis. They are more likely to turn to religion because it provides security, comfort and compensation for that negative daily experience. Norris and Inglehart argue that the existential security offered by religion explains why poorer sections of ethnic minorities in Western societies are more religious than their middle-class peers.

This Weberian perspective is also supported by Ken Pryce's (1979) study of the African-Caribbean community in Bristol. Pryce concludes that Pentecostalism, which he describes as a highly adaptive "religion of the oppressed", was very attractve to newly arrived African-Caribbean immigrants to the UK in the 1950s because it provided them with guidance on how to adapt to British culture, whilst defending the traditional Caribbean way of life. Pentecostal theology highlighted the Caribbean concepts of family and community supports but also provided African-Caribbeans with a religious culture that stressed the need for a strong work ethic, self-reliance, thrift, prudent money management and economic and personal morality. Pentecostalism therefore compensated for the poverty and racism experienced by African-Caribbean immigrants, by providing communal support, but also provided them with practical ways in which they might over-come poverty and integrate into British society.

Critique of Weberianism

Weber believed that certain religions, notably Protestant religions such as Pentecostalism, were more suited to bringing about economic or material change while other religions, especially Eastern religions, were unlikely to promote such change, because they were more focused on spiritual fulfilment. However, this view does not explain why Hindus and Sikhs, whose religions focus on meditation, have been very economically successful in the UK.

Why might affluence increase commitment to a religion?

Conclusions: ethnicity and religion

The evidence overwhelmingly suggests that minority ethnic groups that have lived in the UK since the 1950s and recent immigrants such as Africans and Poles are generally more religious than the White majority. Religion performs many important and positive functions for such groups; in particular, it helps unite communities and preserve cultural identity. Immigrants to the UK also often come from highly religious countries. However, there is some evidence that levels of religious belief eventually decline, as ethnic minority groups experience upward social mobility and better standards of living. For example, there is some evidence that suggests middle-class Muslims may not worship as assiduously as their poorer Muslim peers.

RELIGIOSITY AND GENDER

Trends in gendered beliefs and practices

Evidence suggests that women are more religious than men, irrespective of age. In 2005, 57 per cent of regular churchgoers were female, compared with 43 per cent who were male. Field (2010) argues that "men gravitate towards the least demanding of the various levels of religious allegiance and commitment, with women seeking the maximum degree of involvement".

Trzebiatowska and Bruce (2012) report that women 'routinely' describe themselves as 'religious' and consequently demonstrate a stronger personal religious commitment than men. In a review of British Social Attitude surveys conducted between 1983 and 2008, Voas (2008) found that two-thirds of female respondents expressed unqualified faith in God. This seems to be a global phenomenon, as surveys across

Europe and the USA have uncovered similar levels of religious belief among females. Females are also more likely than males to believe in sin, a soul, heaven, life after death, the devil and hell. Women also tend to believe in a god of love, comfort and forgiveness, whereas men are more likely to believe in a god of power, planning and control.

In the Kendal Project investigation into holistic spirituality, Heelas and Woodhead (2005) found that women were more active in new age religions than men. They found that 80 per cent of active participants were female and that 78 per cent of new age groups in Kendal were led or facilitated by females. For example, there was a 23 percentage point difference in the likelihood that men and women would try practices such as yoga and meditation. However, many consider these activities to be a means of improving wellbeing rather than religious practices. This may therefore constitute a gender imbalance for reasons other than religiosity.

Surveys show that women are more likely than men to believe in aspects of the supernatural such as premonition, fate, ghosts and angels. Over a third of women, compared with only 11 per cent of men, have sought advice from fortune tellers, palmists and Tarot card readers.

Use the previous chapters to think about why, although women are more religious than men, some men may be attracted to religion, especially fundamentalist religions.

Sociological explanations for why women are more religious than men

The influence of the biological and social aspects of the feminine role

Grace Davie argues that women feel closer to God because they are involved in the creation of life through pregnancy and giving birth. Callister and Khalaf (2009) found that mothers claimed 'contact with God' intensified during childbirth. Trzebiatowska and Bruce note that being pregnant and giving birth give women opportunities for religious reflection, in addition to those available to men.

Women's traditional role in nurturing children may also raise their awareness of and interest in religion. Many religions, particularly Islam, stress women's roles in instructing children in religious mores. Even women who have lost interest in the supernatural may still feel that religious instruction is a useful tool to teach morality and good citizenship.

Trzebiatowska and Bruce suggest that there may be a religious aspect to women's role as carers of the sick, the disabled and the elderly, because they are often expected to take responsibility for providing comfort and emotional support. Women are also more involved in the management of death and often perform a crucial function in helping the bereaved cope with their emotional upheaval. This role may mean that women think more than men about God, the function of human existence and what happens after death.

Thompson (1991) argues that those who possess the ideal characteristics of femininity, based on the Bem Sex Role Inventory, are more likely to be religious. These characteristics include being emotional, intuitive, submissive, compassionate, passive, affectionate, nurturing and caring.

In criticism of these ideas, Davie admits that the evidence linking religion to biology or women's 'natural' roles is impressionistic. In other words, there is no convincing evidence that anything in the biological make-up of men and women explains gender differences in religiosity. Moreover, many feminist sociologists attribute the more religious nature of women to gender role socialisation in a male-dominated society, rather than to biology or 'natural' female roles. In other words, female religiosity is socially constructed by male culture, in order socially to control women's behaviour, particularly their sexuality. Feminists such as de Beauvoir suggest, therefore, that religious women may be the victims of a patriarchal false consciousness (see Chapter 2).

Examining holy texts suggests that aggression, violence and vengeance – traits associated with masculinity – may be regarded as religious, just as much as 'feminine' traits such as compassion. Feminists therefore argue that the supposedly feminine characteristics of religiosity may simply reflect patriarchal bias. The overrepresentation of women may also have more to do with age than gender. A substantial number of churchgoers are elderly women; there are more elderly women than men because women enjoy longer life expectancy. With regard to women's involvement in new age religions, social class may be more influential than gender, as new age activities incur costs that many working-class women cannot afford.

In your opinion, are females naturally more religious than males?

Functionalism

Parsons (1965) suggests, in his discussion of the social functions of the nuclear family, that mothers may be likely to experience double alienation because they lack an occupational identity and may also feel dissatisfied with their role as wife, mother and nurturer. Miller and Hoffman (1995) argue that women take a greater role in religious worship, because they are less likely than men to be breadwinners and more likely to be housewives, work part time and bring up children. Miller and Hoffman argue that this gives women not only more time for church-related activities, but also a greater need for religion as a source of personal identity and commitment.

Woodhead (2007), although not a functionalist, argues that this double alienation may be a reason why females are more likely to embark on spiritual quests of self-exploration via new age movements. She argues these may provide women with a sense of self-identity and self-worth. However, Trzebiatowska and Bruce criticise this rationale for four reasons. First, they point out that very few people, even women, show any interest in new age spirituality. Such religions have never been as important as conventional religions. Second, many so-called new age practices do not address the problems that Woodhead claims explain their appeal to women. For example, the Kendal Project found that women practised yoga and meditation for health and fitness reasons, and not because they were looking for 'spiritual growth' or experiencing a 'life crisis'. Third, the logic of this social role argument implies that unskilled women and married women with children should be the main groups pursuing spiritual goals. The reality is that the main consumers of new age practices are affluent, professional, middle-class women, who have fewer than average children and are less likely to be married. Fourth, supporters of the idea that new age religions are important tend to exaggerate the cohesion of the new age milieu and to define its activities too broadly. For example, is meditating at a spiritual centre comparable with attending a yoga class once a week or reading a daily horoscope?

Risk theory

Sherkat (2002) argues that men are more willing to take risks than women, and are less religious, because they are more willing to gamble that God and the afterlife do not exist. Miller and Hoffman's (1995) research shows that both men and women who are risk averse have high levels of religious belief and practice. Collett and Lizardo (2009) suggest risk preference is the product of family background – girls brought up in patriarchal families are more likely to be risk adverse, while those brought up in egalitarian families in which parents share roles are more likely to be willing to take risks. A criticism of this perspective is that people who do not believe in God or the afterlife will not be anxious about divine punishment after death. They are therefore unlikely to consider their lack of religious belief to be risky.

Do you consider your faith or lack of faith to be a form of gambling?

Postmodernism

Postmodernists have mainly focused on the decline of conventional religion in women's lives and their adoption of new age spirituality. Evidence suggests that women have begun to leave the conventional Christian churches at a much faster rate than men. According to Brierley (2006), between 1989 and 1998, more than 65,000 women left churches each year (57% of all those leaving religion). From 1998 to 2005, the figure was slightly lower (51,000 per year) but throughout this time, women were leaving churches at about twice the rate of men.

Why do you think existing male congregations are less likely than women to leave the conventional Christian churches?

Aune *et al.* (2008) cite a number of reasons for the decline in female church attendance.

› *Fertility levels* – women are having fewer children. Consequently, the older female generation lost from conventional religions is not being replaced by equal numbers of female children or younger women.

› *Feminist values*, which began to influence women in the 1960s and 1970s, have challenged the patriarchal assumptions underlying traditional Christian views about women's roles. This has led to disillusion with the religion's stance on contraception, abortion and sexuality. For example, the Church's ambivalence towards sexuality may be driving women to leave because they feel that the Church requires them to deny or be silent about sexual desire and activity. Aune *et al.* also argue that young women nowadays are likely to subscribe to egalitarian values and dislike the patriarchal traditions and hierarchies they can see are central to Church life.

› *Paid employment* – at the beginning of the 20th century, a third of women were in paid work; now,

a century later, two thirds are in the labour market. Juggling employment with childcare and housework may simply mean that women no longer have time to commit actively to religion and churchgoing.

› *Family diversity* – compared to wider society, churches include fewer non-traditional families. The last thirty years have seen an increase in non-traditional households such as single-person households, one-parent families and lesbian families. These are not well provided for and are even discouraged by mainstream religions.

Some postmodernists believe that young women are more attracted by new age religions because these are highly individualised as well as privatised. Middle-class women based in the 'private' arena of the home can easily access fashionable and flexible new age beliefs and practices such as hypnotherapy and yoga via television, DVDs and the internet. Moreover, many new age practices promote the idea of personal 'improvement', in which, Bruce argues, women are more interested, than men. Women may also be attracted to the new age because some emphasise the importance of being 'authentic' rather than merely acting out restrictive gender roles. Many spiritual movements focus on subjective experience rather than external authority and this may appeal to some women's wish for autonomy. Many new age religions emphasise the 'natural', such as herbal and homeopathic remedies, aromatherapy and massage. These may appeal more to females because femininity is traditionally interpreted as closer to nature than masculinity.

As stated earlier, it is important not to exaggerate the importance of new age religions. They are very much a minority interest. The evidence suggests that, in 2016, most women, like most men, are less likely than previous generations to take an active interest in any religion, conventional or new age. Trzebiatowska and Bruce argue that there is no real difference between genders when men and women are asked whether they are 'spiritual', 'religious' or 'neither'. However, when men and women engage with new age spirituality, men are more likely to drop out because most of the spiritual milieu is designed by women, who aim primarily to recruit other women. Trzebiatowska and Bruce argue that the main reason for women's involvement in new age religions is 'familiarity and extension'. Men are less likely to be attracted to new age religions because of their emphasis on interests perceived as feminine, such as singing, dancing and bodywork. For example, Trzebiatowska and Bruce argue that males are "less likely to be attracted to forms of massage and healing therapy such as 'Reiki' that are presented as extensions of the perfumery, beauty parlour and health spa" (2012).

Woodhead (2005) attempts to explain modern women's diverse responses towards religion by dividing contemporary women into three groups.

› Home-centred women prioritise their home and family, even when they have part-time work. They are more likely to be traditionally religious because religion affirms their priorities. There is some evidence that home-centred women may be attracted to fundamentalist Christian and Muslim beliefs and practices. Kaufman (1991) argues that some women consciously seek stricter guidelines and rules for how to live their lives because they find the individualism and freedom of choice available in liberal secular societies constraining rather than liberating. Haleem (2003) suggests that the most common reason for women in the UK to convert to Islam (about 3,700 a year) is their dissatisfaction with the social expectations that British society places on women. He argues that such women feel society unrealistically expects them to be 'superwomen' – ambitious career women, but also perfect wives and mothers. Religions that stress traditional roles for men and women, particularly Pentecostalism and Islam, may attract some women because these religions hold motherhood and femininity in high regard. Such religions may provide women with a clear sense of self, as well as control over their bodies. Trzebiatowska and Bruce argue that, in a secular society where infidelity and divorce have become the norm, fundamentalist religions are more likely to provide long-lasting marriages, because the husband and wife clearly know and accept what is expected of them.

› Jugglers are women who combine home and work. Middle class professional women in this group are most likely to invest in new age religions. These alternative belief systems help women make the most of family life as well as encouraging female empowerment and a search for fulfilment outside the home.

› Work-centred women are more likely to follow male patterns of religiosity, abandoning religion because it does not fit with their demanding work schedules.

Feminism

Chapter 2 focuses on the reasons why feminists in general view religion as exploitative, oppressive and patriarchal. As Aune et al. argue, modern career women are less likely to want to subscribe to religions that discriminate against females and that may be partly responsible for the unequal position women occupy in modern and traditional societies. Some feminists have argued that women are less likely to involve themselves in world rejecting religions such as sects, because these demand that their members serve the religion full time and defer or abandon their careers or plans for marriage and motherhood. Young women who aim to make the most of the educational and career opportunities available to them today are unlikely to follow a religion. They can also see that such religions often have an exploitative attitude towards women.

Feminists have attempted to explain why some women are attracted to fundamentalist sects and denominations. There is some evidence that women who are attracted to such religions may have suffered from childhood abuse, broken homes and domestic violence. Jacobs (1991) argues that these women are happy to sacrifice freedom for stability. However, some women hope to be emotionally rescued by the religion's leader, although this might lead to sexual exploitation and abuse.

FOCUS ON SKILLS: WOMEN AND ORTHODOX JUDAISM

Despite feminist criticisms of the prescriptive roles ascribed to women by many religions, significant numbers of women continue to be attracted to such religions. Davidman (1991) explored the reasons why middle-class American Christian women were converting to Orthodox Judaism. Davidman concludes that it is precisely because such religion maintains a clear distinction between the sexes that it becomes attractive to women who value domesticity and their future role as wives and mothers.

In contrast to the feminist goals of sexual liberation, careers and variation in family patterns, Orthodox Judaism offered clear gender norms, assistance in finding partners and explicit guidelines for family life. It legitimised their desire for the traditional identity of wife and mother in a nuclear family. Women are also seen as central in the Jewish religious world and are given a special status. In contrast to the liberal feminist goal of equality, such women seek the alternative of equity – the idea of equal but separate roles.

Questions

1. **Understand**. Identify three prescriptive roles that Christian religions ascribe to women.

2. **Understand**. What is the difference between the feminist goal of equality and the emphasis in Orthodox Judaism on equity?

3. **Analyse** the reasons why some women are converting to Orthodox Judaism.

4. **Evaluate**. Using information from this source and elsewhere, identify three ways feminists might criticise the attitude towards family and gender roles in Orthodox Judaism.

Conclusions: gender and religion

It is generally true that women in the UK have previously tended to be more religious than men, both in terms of belief and practice. The evidence suggests that women, especially young, career-oriented White females, may now be abandoning religious belief. However, belief among women in minority ethnic groups in the UK seems to be fairly strong.

PARTICIPATION IN RELIGION BY AGE

Religious belief

According to Voas (2008), people born before 1945 are more likely than people born since 1975 to state that they have no doubt that God exists, or that they believe in God despite having doubts. Those in the group born after 1975 were twice as likely as the older group to state they did not believe in God. A YouGov poll of young people in 2013 found that only 25 per cent said they believed in God, while 38 per cent said they did not. Meanwhile, 41 per cent thought that religion was the cause of more harm than good in the world. Only 14 per cent thought that religion was, on balance, a good thing.

Despite their apparent religious indifference in surveys, belief in spirituality does appear to exist among some young people. Research by Williams and Lindsey (2005) suggests that young people are interested in spiritual matters, especially those in deprived settings. However, they regard spirituality differently from the middle classes, who tend to connect it with personal growth, or the older generation, who equate it with God.

Vincent and Olson's (2012) research, in a deprived neighbourhood in East Manchester, notes that deprivation intersects with age to bring about a very privatised form of 'crisis religiosity'. This means that deprived young

people invoke the spiritual only when faced with problems and crises such as death, loss and illness. The result of these negative experiences is that young working-class people are generally indifferent to institutionalised religion and to questions about the nature of God, the afterlife, guardian angels, ghosts and spirits. However, Vincent and Olsen found that young people who were most at risk or in poverty often saw religion and religious people as middle-class, and claimed that God was not to be found in their neighbourhoods. They saw churches as exclusionary and unwelcoming to people like themselves.

How are the findings of Vincent and Olson similar to the findings of Ahern and Davie, discussed earlier in this chapter?

Attendance at Christian churches

Brierley (2014), using data from the English Churches Census, shows that about 6.3 per cent of children under the age of 15 were regularly involved with church activities in 2010, but this drops to 4 per cent for those aged 15 to 19 and falls again to 3 per cent after the age of 20. This means that half the children in church drop out of organised religion by the time they reach early adulthood. Levitt's (2001) case study of religious practices in a Cornish town found that attendance at church declines with each generation. Fahmy (2006) found that just 4 per cent of young people aged 16–24 in deprived areas regularly attended church. The only exceptions to this rule seem to be the Pentecostal and Baptist denominations. These continue to attract younger members, usually from ethnic-minority backgrounds, because of the improvisational and spiritual character of their religious services.

In 2012, about 30% of churchgoers were aged over 65, even though members of this age group are more likely to be ill or disabled. Brierley has pointed out that the congregations of denominations such as Methodism are rapidly ageing, although this does not apply to the Pentecostal churches. These religions are failing to attract the young. Brierley argues that denominations such as Methodism may consequently die out altogether in the next 30 to 40 years.

In a major longitudinal survey of retired people conducted over 20 years, Coleman (2000) suggests that even the elderly are losing faith in God. A number of the participants attributed their declining faith to disappointment with churches and the clergy. They cited insensitive handling of bereavement, the 'self-importance' of some clergy members and a lack of interest in the elderly.

Ethnicity and age

Religion has a profound influence in shaping the ethnic identity of young Asians. Although it seems to have less influence in shaping African–Caribbean culture and identity, young African and African–Caribbean people are more likely than young White people to be practising Christians, especially born-again Christians. They are especially likely to be involved in sects and cults such as Rastafarianism and the Seventh-day Adventist Church.

Modood et al. (1997) asked two generations of Asian, African–Caribbean and White people about the statement 'Religion is very important to how I live my life.' They found that Pakistani and Bangladeshi respondents were most positive towards religion. Eighty-two per cent of the sample aged above 50 and 67 per cent of the 16–34 age group valued the importance of Islam in their lives. About one third of young Indians saw their religion as important. The lowest figure was for young White people – only 5 per cent saw religion as important, compared with 18 per cent of young African–Caribbean respondents. In all ethnic groups, the older generation saw religion as more important than the younger generation did, although the age gap was smallest among the Muslim sample.

Using the section on ethnicity earlier in this chapter, can you explain why young members of minority ethnic groups are more religious than White people?

Research into new religious movements (NRMs) suggests some differences in membership and involvement between different age groups. Research by both Wallis and Barker suggests that members of world rejecting sects in the 1970s and 1980s were relatively young – that is, aged between 18 and 30 years – for two reasons. Firstly, young adults had more freedom from social and economic ties than older people. They were usually unmarried, did not have children, and had no economic responsibilities or emotional dependents. This left them free to join sects that withdrew from the world, such as the Unification Church. Secondly, young adults, especially if educated, were more likely to experience some misgivings about mainstream values. Young sect members in the 1970s and 1980s had experienced a crisis of meaning or alienation, and were consequently disillusioned with modern society. Sects such as the Unification Church and the Children of God offered young people alternative means of moral guidance and a sense of community in a fragmented world.

New age cults are especially appealing to middle-aged people who are materially advantaged but spiritually poor because they are more likely to have the spare funds to invest in the often costly services that world affirming NRMs have to offer. Ruickbie (2004) found that Wicca, a witchcraft-based cult based on Pagan beliefs, is mainly practised by women in their thirties and forties, who use their religious activities for healing and personal development.

Sociological explanations for greater religiosity among the older generation

The ageing effect

This is the view that people turn to religion as they become older. As people approach death, they 'naturally' become more concerned about spiritual matters such as the afterlife and the need to repent past misdeeds. As a result, they are more likely to go to church and to pray.

Disengagement

This is the view that people become detached from the integrating mechanisms of society such as work as they get older. For example, retirement and the death of friends and relatives often result in social isolation and loneliness. Participation in a religion may compensate for this, because religious organisations offer a community network as well social and emotional supports.

The generational effect

This is the view that each new generation is less religious than the one before, as society becomes more secular. Gill (1998) notes that most children, with the exception of Asian children, are no longer receiving a religious socialisation. Those brought up without religious beliefs are less likely to become churchgoers later in life.

The postmodernist Hervieu-Léger makes a similar argument: she suggests that modern societies have experienced a collective loss of religious memory, which she calls **cultural amnesia**. She notes that for centuries, children were taught religion in the extended family, at school and at Sunday school in the local parish church. Religion was handed down from generation to generation. However, in postmodern societies, parents often let children decide on their own religious beliefs. Hervieu-Léger also notes the decline of Sunday schools and observes that religion no longer has the status it once commanded in the education system. As a result, young people today have little religious knowledge and are less likely to inherit a fixed religious identity.

UNDERSTAND THE CONCEPT

Cultural amnesia refers to the idea that cultures or societies can forget their historical traditions, because older generations do not hand them down to younger generations via socialisation.

This view suggests that church congregations include more old people than young people today, not because people become more attracted to religion as they get older, but because older people grew up at a time when religion was more popular. A greater emphasis was probably placed on religion and traditional forms of morality during their education and family socialisation. When they were young, it was the norm to attend church. Their greater church attendance, therefore, merely reflects old habits.

Have you received much religious education? How much of it has come from your parents?

Voas (2005) argues that people in each generation are half as religious as their parents. He agrees that parental beliefs have an impact on children's religious beliefs. However, he points out that a child with two religious parents only has a 50 per cent chance of following the same beliefs, and if the child only has one religious parent, the chance of the child being religious is reduced to 25 per cent. Voas argues that these trends do not only affect attendance at a place of worship, but also faith and belief, because religious belief is declining at a faster rate than church attendance. However, Voas has been criticised on

the grounds that people may come to religion as a result of influences other than their parents.

Apart from parental socialisation, what might lead people to religion?

Explanations of young people's apparent lack of religious belief

The declining attraction of religion

Brierley (2002) found that 87 per cent of 10 to 14-year-olds thought church was boring, repetitive, uncool, old-fashioned and full of old people who were out of touch with the styles and attitudes of young people. He also found that young people today have a greater range of demands on their time compared with members of previous generations. Consequently, they simply have more interesting, stimulating and pleasurable ways to spend their waking hours.

Individualisation

Collins-Mayo (2010) argues that young people in the past felt compelled to follow religious rules, but British culture has become increasingly individualistic and now emphasises the self over social rules and constraints. The decline of religious socialisation in the family and educational system has aided this change. Most primary and secondary schools now engage in a generalised secular or moral education, from which young people are encouraged to choose aspects that suit their lifestyle.

This postmodernist idea suggests that, in 2016, religion is increasingly perceived as a private personal choice rather than as an imposition from outside. Collins-Mayo argues that religious beliefs and practices rarely come up for discussion in young people's conversations. Teens and young adults are likely to reject religious teaching or thinking that they believe conflicts with their own individual morality. Young people are generally not hostile towards religion, but they do not particularly engage with it. Collins-Mayo argues that this is because personal relationships, rather than religion, are their main source of meaning. She believes that religion only comes into play when those relationships are threatened by illness or death.

As a young person, how true is it, in your experience, that religious beliefs rarely come up in discussion with your peers?

The decline of metanarratives

Postmodernist sociologists argue that young people are more likely than most other social groups to feel disenchanted with the world because of their exposure to further and higher education. They may believe that religion has lost the power to explain the world to them because they have easy access to alternative accounts of how the world works, especially scientific explanations.

Do you agree that the exposure of your generation to alternative accounts of reality may have undermined the power of religion to influence you?

Increased spiritual choice

Religion has to compete with other belief systems and activities that claim to provide spiritual satisfaction. Lynch (2008) claims that young people today are exposed to a wider diversity of ideas and practices than previous generations. These include philosophical ideas such as atheism, humanism, existentialism, logic and rationalism. In addition to conventional mainstream religion, alternative spiritual beliefs and activities such as Wicca, are available that may be more attractive to the individualism of the young. Moreover, young people may derive spiritual satisfaction from following a football team, listening to music or taking drugs. Even 'Beliebers' – ardent Justin Bieber fans – may be following a spiritual path!

Young people and Islam

The evidence suggests that young Muslims have strong sense of their Islamic identity. In a PEW poll in 2006, 72 per cent of Muslims of all ages in the UK said they believed that Muslims have a very strong sense of Islamic identity (28 per cent) or a fairly strong sense of Islamic identity (44 per cent). Seventy-seven per cent felt that this sense of identity was increasing. Consequently, some sociologists argue that 'Muslim' has become a new ethnicity. According to Samad (2004), "as South Asian linguistic skills are lost, identification with Pakistan and Bangladesh – countries that young people may only briefly visit – becomes less significant and being Muslim as an identity becomes more important."

Young Muslim women

The evidence suggests that young Muslim women have adapted well to the challenge of maintaining their cultural and religious identity, while also becoming effective, well-integrated members of mainstream British society. Research by Samad (2006) suggests that many young South Asian Muslim women draw a distinction between 'religion' and 'culture'. This contrasts with their parents who, in their view, mistakenly confuse the two. Consequently, they are able to use their Muslim identity to resist their parents' opinions about how they should dress and behave. For example, Woodhead (2007) argues that many young Muslim women have developed "a careful and often lavish attention to style, mixed with a very deliberate nod to faith", which she terms "Muslim chic". This creatively asserts the young women's Muslim identity, while simultaneously making a commitment to a British national identity. This has often resulted in their parents permitting them greater freedoms to go out, progress to higher education and be fully involved in choosing their marriage partner.

Conclusions: age and religion

There seems little doubt that religious belief and practice among White youth have fallen to their lowest level in recorded history. Some people fear that this lack of religious culture among the youngest generation of White people may lead to intolerance and hostility, in the future, between the White majority and religious ethnic minorities, because the former may fail to understand the importance of religion for the identity of the latter. However, it may be that the youngest generation gradually acquires a religious or spiritual identity as it ages and begins to search for answers about human existence and life after death.

FOCUS ON SKILLS: YOUNG PEOPLE AND ISLAM

A number of newspapers and politicians have expressed concern about the so-called radicalisation of Muslim youth in the UK. Although this trend has been exaggerated by the mass media, some sociologists have attempted to identify why some Muslim youth might be attracted to extremist groups. Choudhury (2007) suggests it is the result of a lack of religious literacy and education. The most vulnerable are those who have been prompted by recent world events to explore their faith for the first time, yet are not in a position to evaluate objectively whether a radical group represents an accurate understanding of Islam. Akhtar (2005) believes that British military intervention in Iraq and Afghanistan, as well as foreign policy towards Palestine, alienated young Muslims from British society. She argues that radical Islamic groups are able to exploit the idea that there is a simple dichotomy between oppressors and oppressed – the West versus Islam. This places the blame for all of the problems faced by Muslims under the same banner.

According to Hopkins and Kahani-Hopkins (2004), those who are academically inclined are those who have been most susceptible to radicalisation. Extremist groups have targeted young university students who suffer from a sense of blocked social mobility. Hopkins and Kahani-Hopkins argue that university-educated young Muslims often believe that they have a stigmatised identity because they are victims of Islamophobia from employers, the police, the state and the mainstream mass media. They believe this prevents them from realising their full potential. However, according to Choudhury (2007), there are also signs that a progressive 'British Muslim' identity is forming, which is receptive to Western influences and demonstrates a desire to take a full part in British society. Choudhury sees this partly as a reaction to violent radicalism.

Questions

1. **Understand**. Describe the forms that 'radicalisation' might take in the context of young British Muslims.

2. **Understand**. What forms does Islamophobia take?

3. **Understand**. Why might academically gifted young Muslims feel a sense of blocked social mobility?

4. **Analyse** the reasons why some young Muslims might be attracted to radical or fundamentalist forms of Islam.

5. **Evaluate**. Using information from this source and elsewhere, identify three criticisms of the idea that people with an Islamic identity cannot peacefully exist alongside people with a British or Christian identity.

CHECK YOUR UNDERSTANDING

1. Explain what is meant by the term 'disengagement' with regard to age and religiosity.

2. Explain what is meant by 'cultural defence' in the context of ethnicity and religion.

3. Explain what is meant by 'risk theory' in the context of gender and religiosity.

4. Explain what is meant by 'cultural amnesia' in the context of age and religiosity.

5. Identify and briefly outline two reasons why older people are more religious than younger people.

6. Identify and briefly explain some of the reasons working-class people tend to oppose religions associated with the establishment.

7. Analyse three sociological explanations for women's greater involvement in religion.

8. Analyse two differences in the way that the very poor and the very rich use religion.

9. Assess the postmodern explanations for women being more involved than men in new-age spirituality.

10. Evaluate the sociological theories discussed above, that explain why ethnic minorities are generally more religious than the White majority.

TAKE IT FURTHER

Using an equal sample of males and females from among your acquaintances, try to assess the extent of gender, ethnic and age differences in religiosity. Focus on formal religious practice such as church attendance, belief and non-belief in God, perceptions of the nature of God as compassionate or powerful, and alternative beliefs such as spirituality.

Visit the British Religion in Numbers website at www.brin.ac.uk. This site monitors religiosity in the UK. It often includes analysis of official statistics and research studies that focus on social class, ethnicity, gender and age.

6.5 SECULARISATION, GLOBALISATION AND FUNDAMENTALISM

LEARNING OBJECTIVES

> Demonstrate knowledge and understanding of the secularisation debate (AO1).

> Demonstrate knowledge and understanding of religiosity and secularisation in the global context of religion (AO1).

> Apply this knowledge to contemporary society (AO2).

> Analyse the role of globalisation in the spread of religions (AO3)

> Analyse the reasons for the growth of fundamentalist religions (AO3).

> Evaluate sociological explanations in order to make judgements and draw conclusions about the secularisation debate (AO3).

INTRODUCING THE DEBATE

One of the major disputes in the sociology of religion concerns whether religion is still an important influence in society in the modern industrial age. Some sociologists, notably Bryan Wilson (1982) and Steve Bruce (2002), argue that society is experiencing 'secularisation'. They describe this as a decline in the social significance of religious beliefs, practices and institutions. This chapter outlines some of the problems sociologists face in assessing this process. It looks critically at the statistical evidence and examines other aspects of secularisation such as disengagement, rationalisation, religious pluralism and fundamentalism from a British and a global perspective.

DEFINING RELIGIOSITY

In order to judge whether secularisation is or is not taking place, sociologists need to define and measure key concepts such as religiosity, as well as secularisation itself. This is by no means straightforward.

Religiosity, in its broadest sense, is a comprehensive sociological term used to refer to the numerous aspects of religious activity, including:

> regular attendance at a place of worship, such as a church, mosque, temple, or synagogue

> identification with a particular theological outlook or membership of a particular movement, such as Christianity, Islam or Judaism

> practices such as prayer, religious rites of passage such as baptism, and commitment to codes of behaviour, especially those constructed around morality, which affect how everyday life is lived and experienced

> faith or dedication; that is, a strong belief in religious doctrine based on spiritual conviction rather than proof or evidence.

Clements (2015) sums up these characteristics of religiosity very succinctly when he suggests that "scholars of religion often analyse how faith influences individuals' experiences, attitudes and values by looking at the three Bs: belonging (identification and membership), behaving (attendance) and believing (in God)."

Thus, sociologists have identified the core components of religiosity. However, the **operationalisation** of the concept, particularly for measurement purposes, still remains complex and therefore problematic. For example, the concepts of 'faith' and 'commitment' are notoriously difficult to operationalise, and therefore quantify, because they are subjective. People often claim that religion is very important to them personally, but it is often unclear how. Moreover, faith is highly individualised and consequently, it is difficult to make sociological generalisations about its causes or levels.

UNDERSTAND THE CONCEPT

Operationalisation refers to the process of breaking down a sociological hypothesis or concept into measurable and observable components or questions.

The operationalisation of religiosity is also shaped by whether the sociologist adopts a substantive or inclusive approach to religiosity. Wilson (1982) argues that those who define religiosity in substantive terms, for instance as an expression of belief in the supernatural (see Chapter 1), are more likely to suggest that religiosity is in decline, because people are now more likely to accept more rational views of the world. However, sociologists who adopt inclusive approaches (see Chapter 1) would probably reject this view, because they see religiosity as essential to the smooth and ordered running of society. From this perspective, religiosity may be less visible but still has an influence, albeit in a changed and more subtle way.

DEFINING AND MEASURING SECULARISATION

Wilson (1966) provides the following 'classic' definition of secularisation: "the process whereby religious thinking, practices and institutions lose social significance". This seems like a general, catch-all statement, and it is one that has been widely adopted. However, problems occur straight away in terms of operationalisation and consequently measurement. What exactly is 'religious thinking'? What is meant by 'social significance'? What is the benchmark in terms of 'losing' significance? For example, must this have occurred since medieval times or over the last 100 or 50 years? Should the sociologist focus exclusively on mainstream Christianity, or should the beliefs and practices of other religions be included too, such as the world religions of the UK's ethnic minorities and new religious movements, such as sects, cults and new-age movements?

Bruce (2002) attempts to be more detailed. He defines secularisation as a "social condition manifest in (a) the declining importance of religion for the operation of non-religious roles and institutions such as those of the state and the economy; (b) a decline In the social standing of religious roles and institutions; and (c) a decline in the extent to which people engage in religious practices, display beliefs of a religious kind, and conduct other aspects of their lives in a manner informed by such beliefs."

EVIDENCE IN FAVOUR OF SECULARISATION IN THE UK

The statistical evidence
The first set of evidence that this chapter will examine supports the view that secularisation is occurring in the UK and revolves around a range of quantitative data relating

to what Clements called "belonging, behaving and believing", which Wilson and Bruce refer to as "religious thinking or beliefs and visible religious practices."

Belonging

Clements compiled data showing levels of Christian identification across the period from 1963 to 2012, using the British Election Surveys (BES) dated 1963–2010 and the British Social Attitudes (BSA) surveys dated 1983–2012. He identifies two trends that seem to support the secularisation thesis. First, the proportion of people who identify themselves as Anglican is in major decline: two-thirds of the survey samples (64.5 per cent) claimed to be Church of England in 1963 compared with only a fifth (20.7 per cent) in 2012. Bruce (2013) argues that this is a fall from 10 per cent to 2 per cent of the population of the UK. Second, there has been a significant increase (1400 per cent) over the past 48 years in the number of people who claim 'no religion', which has risen from 3.2 per cent in 1963 to 48.1 per cent in 2010. Although the exact percentage fluctuates, this figure is thought to be rising.

Why might using combined data from these two surveys be problematic?

However, Clements also uncovered three more patterns that give pause to the secularisation argument. First, the number of those who belong to non-Christian faiths such as Islam has increased steadily from 0.6 per cent in 1963 to 6 per cent in 2012. This represents a 900 per cent increase, although, as Davie (2015) argues, this group is still relatively small as it makes up less than 10 per cent of the UK population. Second, the proportion of Christians who do not identify with the major Churches and denominations has increased threefold in the past 40 years to 10.5 per cent. Third, the proportion of people who identify as Catholic in the UK has remained fairly stable over the past 50 years, despite a moderate decline between 1983 and 2012.

A comparison of the 2001 and 2011 census statistics supports the secularisation thesis because it clearly demonstrates a decline in religious affiliation. In 2001, 72 per cent of the population self-identified as Christian, but this dropped to 59 per cent in 2011. The proportion of those claiming to have no religious affiliation rose from 15 per cent in 2001 to 25 per cent in 2011. However, the 2011 census also showed that the number of people who claimed to have no religion was significantly higher

in Wales (32 per cent) and Scotland (36.7 per cent) than in other parts of the UK. Only 10 per cent of people in Northern Ireland claimed that they had no religion. Northern Ireland is probably the most religious place in the UK: over 80 per cent of the population claimed a Christian affiliation in 2011.

The work of Brierley (2014) on church membership also supports the secularisation argument. His analysis of membership statistics suggests that in 1930 almost 30 per cent of the UK adult population regarded themselves as members of specific denominations, but this had fallen to 10 per cent by 2013. More specifically, the Methodist denomination lost a third of its membership between 2005 and 2015, while membership of the United Reformed Church dropped by 13 per cent to 62,000 between 2008 and 2013. The Roman Catholic Church has lost about 30 per cent of its members since 1998. Note that this conflicts with Clements' earlier observation.

Evidence from Scotland, Wales and Ireland also bodes poorly for the future of mainstream Christianity. Between 2004 and 2014, the Church of Scotland lost nearly 156,000 members – a 29 per cent fall.

According to Davie, Brierley's picture of declining membership needs to be qualified in three ways. Firstly, it is partly shaped by age. Religious affiliation is closely linked with year of birth. Among people aged 50 and above, one in two self-identified as Anglicans, while among those aged 30 that figure is only one in 20. Secondly, Davie notes that membership fell steeply for men during the course of the 20th century, but women have begun to leave the mainstream churches and denominations at a much faster rate than men since 1989. Thirdly, there are geographical variations. For example, membership of Christian religions has actually increased in London, which could be due in part to immigration.

Why do you think Northern Ireland has a higher proportion of Christians than anywhere else in the UK?

Behaving

Attendance statistics largely support the secularisation theory. Using statistics gathered by Brierley, McAndrew (2011) observes that total church attendance in England fell dramatically between 1980 and 2005 (see Table 6.5.1).

Religion	1980	2005
Anglican	1.37 million	870,000
Methodist	606,000	289,000
Roman Catholic	2.06 million	893,000
United Reformed Church	188,000	70,000
Baptist	287,000	255,000
Pentecostal	221,000	287,000
Other new Churches	75,000	184,000

Table 6.5.1 *Church attendance in England*
Based on McAndrew (2011)

Clements' data also reveal interesting attendance patterns across time. Anglicans have always had much lower levels of regular church attendance than Catholics and other Christians. Only a fifth of Anglicans claim to be frequent attenders. Clements also observes that although 70 per cent of Catholics attended church in the 1960s, which was significantly higher than the 42 per cent claimed by Anglicans, this has now declined to about 42 per cent in 2012, compared with 36 per cent for Anglicans.

Declining attendance is also apparent in other areas of the British Isles. In 2013, only 8 per cent of the Scottish population attended church once a week, compared with 14 per cent in 1999. Less than a third had been to church within the past year, except for special ceremonies such as weddings and christenings, while a further third reported they 'never or practically never' go.

Davie argues that other aspects of religious behaviour also seem to be in decline, especially the 'core' business of the religious rites of passage known as 'hatching, matching and despatching'. In 1950, the Anglican Church conducted 672 baptisms per thousand births, but by 2011 this had fallen to 120 per thousand. Baptisms conducted by the Church of Scotland declined by a third between 2004 and 2014. According to Bruce (2013), over two-thirds of English weddings were carried out by the Church of England in 1900, but this had fallen to one quarter by 2011. Even the number of funerals conducted in churches is in decline; about 30,000 funerals a year are now non-religious.

Believing

Davie argues that 'belief' is a tricky term because it is unclear what this vague and flexible category should and should not include. She argues that the evidence suggests

between half and two-thirds of the UK population continue to believe in some sort of God or supernatural force. However, she says there is a continuing shift away from belief in a personal God to an enormously diverse set of less orthodox spiritual beliefs including "healing, the paranormal, fortune telling, fate and destiny, life after death, ghosts, spiritual experiences, prayer and meditation, luck and superstition" (2015).

Perfect (2011) observes that belief in God as measured by BSA surveys has generally declined since 1991. The category 'believe and always have' decreased from 45.8 per cent in 1991 to 36.7 per cent in 2009. In contrast, the categories 'not believe, did before' and 'not believe, never have' increased from 23.7 per cent in 1991 to 35.1 per cent in 2008. However, the category 'can't choose' has remained fairly stable at about one-fifth of the population.

What reasons might account for people who previously believed in God abandoning their faith?

Clements, too, found that between 1991 and 2008 there was a steady decline in the number of people who claimed a very firm belief in God. However, this differed depending on denomination. Less than a fifth of Anglicans were very certain that God exists, compared with a third of Catholics and other Christians. However, Woodhead (2013) suggests that Catholics, who have traditionally demonstrated higher levels of belonging, behaving and believing than members of other Christian denominations, are increasingly turning away from God and their church because they disagree with the Catholic Church's stand on social morality issues.

What social morality issues may cause Catholics to question their religion?

Criticising the statistical evidence

On the face of it, the statistical evidence with regard to belonging, behaving and believing seems to support the view that religiosity is in decline and the UK is becoming a secular society. However, several criticisms of this evidence can be made, which suggests that the quantitative data may not be sufficiently robust to 'prove' secularisation. These criticisms include the following.

The statistics for membership and attendance may be unreliable because they are collected by specific religious organisations, using criteria that are unique to them. Religions do not all share a standardised way of enumerating membership or attendance, so sociological analysis of such data does not compare like with like. For example, the Catholic Church does not use the concept of formal membership – statistics emanating from the Catholic Church usually comprise either an estimate of the Catholic population in the UK or how many people attended mass on a particular Sunday. In contrast, the Anglican Church uses a formal electoral roll of membership, as well as instructing the 16,000 Anglican churches to report on attendance over the course of October of each year, as well as Easter and Christmas. Interestingly the membership roll tends to be higher than the attendance figures. The former probably includes the elderly who might not be able to attend on a regular basis, as well as those who are baptised or married within the Church.

Why has the Church of England chosen the month of October to count attendance? Why might Easter or Christmas counting be problematical?

Membership statistics are particularly difficult for sociologists to interpret, because there is often a huge gap in commitment between those who inherit membership of a religion through birth or baptism and those who have been converted and/or actively and regularly practise that religion. These two sets of statistics, which are often used together to demonstrate secularisation, do not measure the same thing.

Clements qualifies his use of the BES and BSA surveys by observing that people may exaggerate their religious belonging, behaving and believing for social rather than religious reasons. This may undermine such research, as some people appear to be more religious than they actually are.

Day (2011) identifies three social reasons that may explain why some people end up exaggerating their Christian credentials.

> The fact that some people are born and baptised into a particular religion is part of the socialisation process – it is ingrained into them at a very early stage. They therefore identify with a religion automatically, despite not actively engaging with it.

> Identifying oneself as Christian may be a proxy for being English, Scottish, Welsh and Irish. It may be a public marker of identity that differentiates some

people from social trends that they fear could overwhelm British culture, such as immigration, multiculturalism or the increase in the number of Muslims in UK society. It distinguishes people from what they see as alien 'others'. This may particularly be the case in Northern Ireland, which has been racked by sectarian violence between Protestants and Catholics. Identifying with either of these religions may indicate political rather than religious beliefs: most Protestants want to maintain the union with the UK, while most Catholics want to see a United Ireland.

> Some people may simply see their Christian identity as a marker of respectability, decency and morality. They are sending out the message that they are 'good' people. This is a type of **social desirability bias**.

UNDERSTAND THE CONCEPT

Social desirability bias is a methodological problem that undermines the validity of the collected data. When filling in questionnaires or responding to interview questions, some respondents will be concerned about how the sociologists see and judge them. They may therefore give the answers the respondent thinks the researchers want to hear, either because they want to please them or because they want to create a positive and respectable impression.

Day suggests that there is probably a big gap between agreeing in a survey that you hold a particular belief, and actually having strong convictions or engaging in religious behaviour on a daily basis. Hamilton (1998) argues that what surveys show "is not that people are still religious but that they have a propensity to say yes to this sort of question." This is because in a situation where there is uncertainty or doubt about the existence of God, most people are inclined to agree that he exists rather than disagree. Hamilton also points out that people may pray to God for help in times of great stress and anxiety, but it does not necessarily follow that they believe such help will come or that they believe God exists.

Some sociologists have suggested that the statistics may be distorted by **belonging without believing**. This means that elderly and middle-class people may claim religiosity despite their motives for religious affiliation and attendance actually being social. For example, elderly people may attend church because they desire company. Middle-class people may do so in order to reinforce feelings of social respectability or to ensure their children have access to high-achieving church schools. The upper-class elite may do so because it is expected of them.

Hamilton (2001) argues that in order to demonstrate secularisation, sociologists have to be able to show how important religion was in the past. However, he argues that the implied idea that the Middle Ages were an "age of faith" in which most people attended church regularly and uncritically subscribed to religious doctrine is an illusion. Stark (1999) agrees and argues that the historical records suggest there was widespread indifference to religion among the general population and ordinary people were contemptuous of clerics. Stark therefore concludes it is wrong to claim that religiosity is in long-term decline, because most people, whether in the Middle Ages or even in the Victorian era, were never that religious in the first place. In criticism of Stark, Bruce (2001) points out that both the Anglican and Catholic Churches could not have become so rich and powerful, or have built such massive cathedrals, if vast numbers of the population had been indifferent about religion.

Davie argues that the statistics say very little about the social meaning of religion; that is, what religious belief or churchgoing means to particular individuals. She suggests that greater levels of personal freedom and individualism have resulted in a general decline in membership of collective organisations, such as political parties, trade unions and Churches. People may now be more committed to spending their spare time with their family or on other personal priorities. Individualisation may also have led to people feeling that their religious beliefs are private. Consequently, they may not feel the need to make them public by worshipping alongside others in a church. Davie calls this **believing without belonging** and suggests that it means the true extent of religious belief may always be unknown to sociologists. It also challenges the secularisation thesis.

UNDERSTAND THE CONCEPT

Belonging without believing refers to the idea that people attend church for non-religious reasons; for example, to show how respectable they are. **Believing without belonging** refers to the idea that people no longer feel the need to make their religious beliefs public by attending church with others.

The idea of 'believing without belonging' has been criticised by Voas (2013), who points out that surveys consistently show religious belief is declining at a much faster rate than attendance. Woodhead (2013) counters this argument with the observation that the number of atheists has never risen above 20 per cent of the population. However, measuring atheism in a society may be just as problematic as measuring religiosity and secularisation. Many people may be reluctant to call themselves atheists despite the fact that they do not believe in God, because they choose not to be associated with a label that attracts hostile and negative reactions from others. In the past, atheism was regarded as a cultural sin. As Ricker (2007) observes, in some societies today atheists are "shunned, imprisoned and sometimes executed for their lack of piety. Being an atheist has always been difficult, at least for those willing to admit to it." People may use more neutral labels instead, such as **agnostic** or 'humanist'. It may therefore be that the proportion of atheists has risen significantly higher than Woodhead's figure of 20 per cent, which would support Voas' observation.

UNDERSTAND THE CONCEPT

An **agnostic** is a person who is not sure whether God exists or not.

Woodhead also supports the 'believing without belonging' argument, by claiming that large numbers of people still subscribe to unorthodox beliefs such as belief in the supernatural and spirituality. However, Voas criticises the notion of using people's belief in "everything from angels to zombies" to support the argument. He argues that such beliefs are "casual in the extreme: cultivated by popular culture and its delight in magic and Gothic romanticism, held in the most tentative and experimental way, with no connection to any meaningful spirituality."

Davie (2015) has attempted to reinforce the idea of 'believing without belonging' by developing the concept of 'vicarious religion'. She suggests that religion is not practised overtly or regularly by the majority in Europe, but that most people engage with religion 'vicariously' through others. In other words, a minority of people are religious on behalf of a silent majority. She argues that "Churches and church leaders perform (religious) ritual on behalf of others; church leaders and churchgoers believe on behalf of others; church leaders and churchgoers embody moral codes on behalf of others." She also observes that churches can at times offer space for debate about controversial issues such as same-sex relationships, and for the community to come together occasionally to mourn in times of national tragedy. In this sense, religions and churches do not exclusively belong to those who use them regularly. Rather, churches are public utilities that the majority of the population only use at critical moments in their lives, such as birth, marriage and death, and in times of national tragedy.

According to Davie, religion therefore involves rituals performed by an active minority on behalf of a much larger number of others. At least implicitly, this majority not only understands, but also clearly approves of what the minority is doing. Davie suggests that vicarious religion is particularly visible when there are radical "interruptions in the normality of societies", such as those caused by disasters or the death of a national icon. For example, the ferry *MS Estonia* sank in 1994, with the loss of almost 900 lives, many of them Swedish. Large numbers of Swedish people went to their churches, some to light candles and to mourn privately, but often also to hear the sentiments of the Swedish population and the meaning of the tragedy for the country, articulated on their behalf. Similarly, the death of Princess Diana in Paris, in a car crash in 1997, drew large numbers of British people to church as a similar gesture. More recently, following the 2015 attacks on Paris, churches put on special services which were observed around the world.

Davie argues that the concept of vicarious religion suggests that religion is far from unimportant. However, the concept has been criticised. Bruce (1996) argues that vicarious religion and 'believing without belonging' are at best evidence of a weakening and nostalgic commitment to Christianity. Davie acknowledges this by noting that vicarious religion will probably die out in the next 30 years, because members of the younger generation are less likely to inherit a religious identity. They are less likely than previous generations to regard religious utilities and rituals as necessary. Survey evidence also suggests there is little evidence of a silent majority of European believers in 2016. Furthermore, people may attend church in times of disaster because it provides a community focal point where people can come together and express grief, rather than because they hold religious beliefs.

Some sociologists argue that those who support the secularisation thesis have analysed the statistics in a very selective manner. They point to three factors that they claim suggest religion is still fairly healthy in the UK. First, the significant growth in non-Christian religions in the UK such as Islam, Hinduism and Sikhism, which tend to demand a greater degree of commitment than mainstream Christianity. Pentecostalism has also claimed more new followers than mainstream Christianity,

especially among Black worshippers; for example, a third of all Christian worshippers in London are Pentecostals while only 12 per cent are Anglican. Second, memberships of sects such as the Jehovah's Witnesses (135,000) and Mormons (190,000) remain healthy. Third, Heelas and Woodhead argue, there has been an upsurge in interest in new-age spirituality. However, in criticism of these arguments, ethnic minority groups only make up 12 per cent of the British population and there is little sign of religious commitment among the other 88 per cent of the British population who are White. Voas also argues that the interest in new-age religiosity and spirituality is insignificant compared with the millions of worshippers lost from mainstream Christianity since the 1960s.

In conclusion, the statistical evidence sociologists have used to support the secularisation thesis lacks both reliability and validity and may be a little one-dimensional. Other sociologists therefore argue that, in order to demonstrate secularisation, analysis needs to go beyond belonging, behaving and believing, and examine the role that religion plays in political and social life.

THEORIES OF SECULARISATION

Societalisation and disengagement

Bruce claims that capitalism is responsible for secularisation because it has brought about a process called **societalisation**. This has three components.

1. *Urbanisation* – compared with tight-knit rural communities, the clergy are less able to exercise social control over the large number of people living in towns and cities.

2. *Structural or social differentiation* – state-sponsored specialised agencies and secular charities have taken over many concerns previously dominated by religion. This is particularly true in the non-religious spheres of education, health and povertyy.

3. *Impersonal bureaucratic rules* mean that people expect to be rewarded here and now on the basis of merit and hard work, rather than because God has chosen them.

UNDERSTAND THE CONCEPT

Societalisation refers to the process by which aspects of life increasingly become the responsibility of the state and are decreasingly matters for religion and local communities.

Bruce (2002) therefore argues that the disengagement, or separation, of the Church from wider society is an important effect of societalisation. Bruce claims that the Church was once very influential in politics, local communities and family life but this is no longer the case today. In 2015, the Commission on Religion and Belief in British Public Life (CRBBPL) called for public life in Britain to be systematically de-Christianised. Wilson argues that the mass media have replaced religion and the family as the main source of moral values, especially for the young. Bruce observes that the number and status of the Christian clergy have severely declined.

Bruce argues that societalisation also increased individualism and secularisation, because it resulted in people taking responsibility for their own interests and becoming less concerned with how the clergy and churches saw and judged them. The postmodernist sociologist Hervieu-Leger argues that fewer and fewer Catholic parents in France feel a duty to socialise their children into the Catholic faith, because they believe they should bring up their children to make up their own minds. She argues that it is no longer the case in France that religious faith is an inherited culture. She concludes that secularisation in France is caused by "cultural amnesia". This means that each generation tends to know less and less about religion and the collective religious memory is composed of only 'bits and pieces'. Consequently, secularisation is a growing feature of French society as the young engage less with Catholicism.

Hamilton (2001) suggests that the Churches themselves have compromised their beliefs because of these social changes. For example, he argues that the Church of England has attempted to rationalise ideas such as the Virgin Birth and the physical resurrection of Christ by suggesting they are allegorical stories that aim to convey a spiritual or moral message, rather than events that actually happened.

Critique of disengagement

The disengagement argument has, however, been criticised. Some sociologists, notably Parsons (1965), have argued that disengagement actually allows Churches to focus more effectively on their central role of providing moral goals for society to achieve. The liberation of religion from the functions of education, law, politics and economic production means that religions can now concentrate on the core questions of human existence, particularly those posed by death, evil and suffering. Parsons argues that the success of religion in answering these questions has resulted in the continuing commitment of citizens to value consensus and therefore social order. He observes that religion produces a "moral economy" that keeps its citizens motivated, despite the existence of evil, suffering and so on.

Woodhead (2008) observes that religion still has a significant influence over the establishment in the UK. She argues that religious communities still enjoy great privileges: they benefit from 7,000 state-funded faith schools, charitable status and an influence in the House of Lords that is disproportionate to the actual size of their congregations. She notes that Churches still play a major role during national celebrations and mourning rituals, such as the funerals of Diana, Princess of Wales and the Queen Mother. She observes that the British legal system is still underpinned by religion, for example, through the swearing of oaths on the Bible. She notes that Christianity still shapes how British people experience time, through holidays such as Easter and Christmas. She points out that large numbers of people still use church services for rites of passage such as baptisms, weddings and funerals. In December 2015, the Education Secretary, Nicky Morgan, announced that schools must teach that the UK is a Christian country and that they have no obligation to teach atheism.

Woodhead argues that religion still plays a significant role in education

In addition, the media continue to show a great interest in religious issues. In January 2016, for example, the Anglican Church's attitude to the LGBT community, the scheduling of Easter, and David Cameron's focus on the segregation of Muslim women in the UK were presented as big news stories, which challenges the idea that the general population is no longer engaged by religious issues.

The Enlightenment and rationalisation

The Enlightenment was a European intellectual movement of the late 17th and 18th centuries which resulted in the decline in the dominance of traditional authority and in particular, superstitious thinking. This period was characterised by a growth in rational forms of thought and particularly the emergence of the scientific and technological innovations that underpinned the Industrial Revolution in Britain and other European countries.

Rationalisation refers to the idea that the sacred and religious has little or no place in contemporary Western society and that the world is no longer under the control of irrational religious forces, based on emotion, superstition and faith. Rational scientific thought based on empirical evidence now has a higher status. Bruce (2002) argues that people now have a greater sense of control over the natural world than in previous times. This has contributed to secularisation, especially of the mind; or **secularisation of consciousness**. This is because people have less need to resort to religious explanations and solutions to shape how they live their daily lives.

UNDERSTAND THE CONCEPT

The **secularisation of consciousness** is an idea developed by Peter Berger (1969), who argues that modern life means people no longer think about how they can serve God's will – they are now more concerned with serving themselves.

The rationalisation argument is particularly associated with Weber (1976), who saw rationalisation as responsible for desacrilisation – the idea that the sacred has become less influential. Science now explains natural events that were once given primarily religious or supernatural explanations; for example, how the universe was created, how the human race developed and the reasons for phenomena such as earthquakes and the weather. Developments in biotechnology and medical science also suggest that humans can achieve feats comparable with God in terms of producing new life and healing. Bruce (2002) argues that this has led to 'disenchantment' with God among the mass of the population. However, Bruce argues that secularisation has not been caused by a war between science and religion. Christianity has not been fatally wounded by science. Bruce describes the conflicts between science and religion over, for example, evolution in the USA, as 'local skirmishes' and points out that many scientists are attracted to conservative religions, because they find in them the same concepts of certainty and objectivity found in the natural sciences. Bruce argues that disenchantment is caused by a consequence of science – specifically its "general encouragement to a rationalistic

orientation of the world…to the embodiment of that rationalistic outlook in bureaucracy as the dominant form of social organisation and the role of technology in increasing our sense of mastery over our own fate."

Berger argues that, ironically, the Protestant religion has contributed to secularisation in three ways. First, it encouraged its followers to engage in free enquiry; that is, to think for themselves. This inevitably led to people questioning and turning away from religious ideas. Second, it focused the attention of its followers on work and the pursuit of profit and prosperity. Third, it created a concept of God so distant that he was no longer seen as having any relevance in a modern capitalist world that was producing tangible benefits, such as improved life expectancy and living standards. In this sense, Berger describes Christianity as its own gravedigger.

Critique of rationalisation

However, the idea that society has become more rational is difficult to measure and evaluate. Ironically, it is based on anecdotal evidence rather than on hard scientific evidence. Thompson (1986) suggests that the rationalisation argument exaggerates the rationality of modern societies. He argues it is doubtful that rational thought underpins actions such as people's choice of consumer goods, partners and voting behaviour. On the other hand, popular culture reflects a very strong public interest in the irrational: this includes the popularity of the horror genre in books and films, which often focus uncritically on supernatural beings such as wizards, werewolves and zombies, the popularity of horoscopes, which are based on the irrational idea that people's futures depend on the position of the stars at the moment of their birth, and the popularity of new-age spiritual activities. These may often be forms of entertainment rather than reflections of belief, but their continuing appearance reinforces the importance of the irrational in modern societies.

Stark and Bainbridge (1996) argue that choosing to believe in God, or to belong to a religious organisation, is actually the product of rational choice. They suggest that people seek rewards but these are often scarce or unavailable. A rational response to this is that some people may be willing to accept a substitute as compensation. Religion offers such a substitute because it often offers the promise of a future reward if a person is willing to postpone rewards in the short term. Stark and Bainbridge argue that everybody desires the rewards that only a religion can offer. For example, nobody wants to die, but this reward is unobtainable. Everybody therefore has a strong motive for being religious, because the idea of an after-life is a rational answer to the fact that we cannot physically live forever. Belief in God, from Stark and Bainbridge's perspective, is a sensible and rational bet. If God exists, believers profit. If God does not exist, they have lost very little. Unbelievers have more to lose so to be an atheist is more of a gamble.

What problems can you see in the idea that belief in God is a rational gamble?

Existential security theory

Norris and Inglehart (2011) suggest that the cause of secularisation in European societies is the increase in existential security. If people feel insecure about their future existence or that of their children, they may turn to religion for comfort and compensation. They place themselves in God's hands. However, if they feel secure because they and their families enjoy a high standard of living, there is less need for religious comfort. They can take their survival for granted.

Norris and Inglehart argue it is unsurprising that secularisation is on the increase, given that Europe enjoys an excellent standard of living compared with many other parts of the world. They argue that virtually all high-income countries have been moving towards more secular orientations during the past 50 years but, in contrast, a growing proportion of the developing world's population holds traditional religious values, because people in these countries are more likely to feel vulnerability, due to physical, societal and personal risks. People who live in low-income countries are most susceptible to death from malnutrition, disease or natural disasters. They are on the margins of survival and lack defences against threats such as war, crime, poverty and so on. Religion is attractive to people living in these situations because it provides a sense of reassurance that one's fate is in the hands of a "benevolent higher power even when it is uncertain that one's family will have enough to eat". Although people in rich societies also face external threats, these do not tend to be life-threatening, because rich societies often have welfare systems that provide their citizens with assistance.

Critique of existential security theory

Critics of this thesis argue that it does not explain why religious institutions continue to exert influence in rich societies such as the UK. The Church of England, for example, still has a fairly close relationship with the Establishment, as does the Catholic Church with the political elite of several European societies. Also, it

has been suggested that education, rather than the alleviation of poverty or the growing wealth of a society, may be more responsible for secularisation, because it encourages individualisation, relativism, rational modes of thought and so on. Some critics argue that the concept of existential security is vague and needs more precise operationalisation so that it can measured more accurately across diverse conditions and contexts.

Industrialisation and religious pluralism

Bruce (1996) suggests that industrialisation has fragmented society into a marketplace or plurality of religions and other community organisations. Aldridge (2013) notes that this argument presents religions as peddling their products to consumers who are fastidious and fickle and consequently, the pluralism argument suggests, religion has degenerated into a consumer product.

Bruce (2002) argues that plurality has partly been brought by relativism – all beliefs have come to be seen as plausible in modern societies. However, this acceptance of religious diversity may be destructive in two ways. First it may result in the suspicion that if there are so many religions, some may be man-made and therefore false. Second, Wilson (1966) argues that religion may no longer act as a unifying force in society. As a result, people may no longer feel controlled by the religion into which they are born, because alternative ways of thinking and behaving exist. Wilson points to the **ecumenical movement** as an attempt by institutionalised religion to reverse secularisation. He argues that such unification only occurs when religious influence is weak.

UNDERSTAND THE CONCEPT

The **ecumenical movement** generally refers to a movement that promotes unity among Christian churches and denominations by finding common theological ground. In practical terms, it may mean that different denominations come together because of declining congregations and the rising costs of keeping churches open when attendance is lower.

In particular, the growth in the number of sects, cults and NRMs has also been seen by Wilson as evidence of secularisation. He argues that sects are "the last outpost of religion in a secular society" and that sect members are often attracted less by religious belief than by an exotic lifestyle, the charismatic leader of these religious 'novelties', or a desire to escape a life crisis. Berger, too, sees sects as the "last refuge of the supernatural in a secular society". In other words, they mark the final desperate stand of religion – Berger claims that that they are merely "islands in a secular sea". Bruce (2002) also interprets the growth of sects as evidence of secularisation, as they further undermine the authority of the established Church on central issues of moral concern, because they all claim to have the 'right' answer. Moreover, the existence of a religious marketplace means that customer loyalty can no longer be taken for granted.

Critique of religious pluralism

Not all sociologists accept that religious pluralism is a sign that the influence of religion is declining. Heelas *et al.* claim that a spiritual revolution is taking place in the 21st century. They argue that current trends suggest the new-age movement – belief systems with a spiritual element, such as alternative therapies and techniques aimed at self-improvement – may become more popular than all conventional religions put together by around 2020. However, Bruce argues that new-age beliefs are weak, largely personal and have little or no influence on wider society. Moreover, the religious element of these beliefs is often not clearly visible.

Greeley (1972) and Nelson (1986) argue that the growth in the number of evangelical churches, especially those associated with the Pentecostal and charismatic movements, suggests that UK society is undergoing a religious revival. Nelson argues that institutional religion lost contact with the spiritual needs of society in the 1980s, because it had become too ritualised and predictable. In this sense, Nelson agrees with Wilson that established religion is undergoing secularisation. The young, in particular, find such religion unappealing. However, Nelson argues that a religious revival is underway and is being helped by the success of evangelical churches. These churches offer a more spontaneous religion, which is less reliant on ritual and consequently more attractive to the young. However, Brierley (2014) estimates that the growth of the evangelical churches amounts to about only one-sixth of the number of followers lost from the established Churches.

Postmodernity and Disneyfication

Postmodernists suggest that religion is in a state of change rather than decline. They argue that there is a demand for spirituality motivated by increasing **individuation** that cannot be catered for by any one religion. They observe that many people have embarked on 'spiritual journeys' in search of themselves, as an alternative to uncritically accepting institutionalised

religion. Therefore, the importance of religion has not declined, but its form of expression may have changed.

UNDERSTAND THE CONCEPT

Individuation refers to an individual's search for meaning and identity.

One such postmodernist is Lyon (2000), who argues that the centrality of global computer and information technologies and consumerism in postmodern life means that the nature of religious worship has changed. For example, people no longer feel obliged to follow local religions as, because of the internet, satellite television and cheap travel, they now have greater access to virtually every religious or spiritual belief and practice that exists across the world. Furthermore, the growing importance of consumerism means that people increasingly feel able to choose how they should live, rather than passively accepting traditional and externally imposed forms of religious and moral authority. However, he argues that this does not mean the decline of religion, but rather the transformation of it, as religion is re-located to what he calls the "sphere of consumption". In other words, he argues that religion has become a commodity to be marketed and used selectively by consumers, like any other product.

In particular, Lyon argues that religion is undergoing a process of Disneyfication. He observes that in the postmodern age, Disneyfication – a process of mass marketing that uses a range of global media including films, television, music, websites, social networking sites and theme parks – to sell its products, has become paradigmatic or the norm for the way most cultural institutions now present themselves to potential customers or consumers. Lyon observes that the process of Disneyfication involves activities such as shopping and consumption becoming de-differentiated from other activities in the postmodern world. This means that all forms of activity now involve shopping and consumption – they are no longer separate economic activities. People in postmodern societies shop around for the 'best' political party to vote for, the 'best' schools to send their children to, the 'best' health care and the 'best' religions from which to select personal beliefs. Lyon suggests that there is now a 'religious marketplace' competing for spiritual shoppers in which they are offered a fantastic range of religious and spiritual ideas and practices.

Lyon argues that Disneyfication goes beyond the marketing of manufactured goods and ideas. It is also about representation – events and spectacles are presented as symbolic of culture, history, nostalgia, entertainment, fantasy and so on. However, this presentation often blurs the line between reality and symbolic image. For example, Lyon observes that at the Disneyland theme park, people often seek the autograph of Mickey Mouse and other Disney characters (who in reality are only park workers in costume). Lyon argues that religions are increasingly adapting to and interacting with postmodern settings. In his book *Jesus in Disneyland*, Lyon cites the example of a Harvest Day Crusade held at Disneyland California, attended by 10,000 Christians, in which several Christian artists and a preacher performed across several stages. Normally these two worlds – the fantasy world of Disney and the world of evangelical Christianity – would clash, because the latter have been very critical of the magical worldview and practices found in many Disney films. However, Lyon observes that this evangelical Christian movement deliberately chose strategically to place itself within Disneyland, which suggests that some Christians are aware of the need to market themselves within a popular culture, to appeal to as many consumers as possible. Lyon concludes that the boundaries between religion, shopping and popular culture are now not so clear-cut. Religion in postmodern societies is increasingly found in a range of settings and contexts that would be rejected as blasphemous in traditional societies; for example, in Texas, a tattooed Jesus has been used as part of a Christian advertising campaign, whilst Jesus action figures are available via the internet. Lyon therefore argues that people in the postmodern world are seeking credible contemporary ways of expressing faith outside conventional Churches and the context of popular culture is no longer out of bounds as a means of expressing religious beliefs.

RELIGIOSITY OR SECULARISATION: THE GLOBAL PERSPECTIVE

Many writers have pointed out that secularisation has tended to be seen in terms of the decline of organised established Churches in Northern Europe. However, according to surveys, some European societies continue to experience reasonably high levels of church attendance, especially the mainly Catholic countries of Ireland, Malta, Poland, Slovakia and Italy, whereas the Pew Center (2014) has reported that between 1991 and 2008 the share of Russian adults identifying as Orthodox Christian rose from 31 per cent to 72 per cent. Moreover, an examination of societies outside Europe

also suggests that religion is still an extremely influential force. Hamilton (1998) observes that the role of religion in some developed and industrialised non-Western countries is central to cultural life. For example, Japan is highly developed but more than 180,000 groups were registered as religious corporations in 2011 and visits to religious shrines are a deep-rooted part of Japanese holidays. Prayers are left at shrines on the eve of important exams and interviews, and in the quest for a suitable husband or wife.

The USA

One society that seems to contradict the secularisation thesis is the USA, in which 40 per cent of the adult population regularly attend church and in which 20 million watch religious 'televangelist' programmes every week. About 90 per cent of Americans claim to believe in God. Only 2 per cent of American adults claim to be atheists, although some critics have pointed out that it is probably more difficult to be an atheist in the USA than in the UK. The Secular Student Alliance reported in 2014 that many Americans worried about being ostracised by parents, friends, employers and the community if they revealed they did not believe in God. Some were even scared of violence. The Pew Research Center found that American Christians regarded atheists as less trustworthy than rapists. Consequently, there is huge pressure to conform to a religious identity. This undermines the validity of statistics for religiosity and atheism.

However, Scharf (1970) suggests American Churches have developed in a secular way. He argues that they subordinate religious belief to the American way of life and stress the values of democracy, freedom, attainment and material success. Warner (1993) argues that religion is popular in the USA because it has both equality of faith and a separation of Church and state. This has encouraged different religious traditions to compete with each other for members, on an equal basis. Religion has therefore become a commodity and, consequently, religions in the USA tailor their product to meet market demand. Many advertise their unique characteristics in much the same way as schools in the UK market themselves. The result of competition in the USA is a pluralistic religious economy composed of over 320,000 religious denominations, which are happy to be flexible in their beliefs. This marketplace works hard to attract new customers, rather than relying on the loyalty of a fixed number of participants. These observations have led sociologists to conclude that religion in the USA is a form of civil religion (see Chapter 2).

Bruce (1996) argues that religion in the USA has mainly developed as a means of handling cultural transition.

It eases the process of integration and adaptation in a mainly immigrant society. Americans have also turned to religion as a form of **cultural defence** against the rapid social changes that the USA has experienced in terms of demography, ethnic and racial composition, technology and conditions of life. Putnam and Campbell (2010) argue that this concept may also explain why particular ethnic groups in the USA, such as the Hispanic and African-American population, have higher levels of religious attendance and commitment than the American population in general, as immigrants cling to familiar institutions in a strange land.

UNDERSTAND THE CONCEPT

The concept of **cultural defence** refers to the idea that where a religious culture, identity and sense of worth are challenged by an alien religion or secular ideas, religion provides resources for its defence, for example, by maintaining its own educational system.

The ideas of Scharf, Warner and Bruce suggest that USA churches are more secular than religious. However, the dominance of fundamentalist Protestant religions in the southern Bible Belt suggests that religious belief and devotion cannot be dismissed so easily: these faiths tend to commit strongly to a literal interpretation of the Bible and to strict moral codes based on the 'word of God'. There is also evidence that Christian fundamentalism has had a disproportionate conservative influence on American political life, particularly in opposing the teaching of evolution in schools, abortion rights and gay rights.

A 'pro-life' campaign, protesting against abortion

Casanova (1994) argues that a great deal of the war and conflict that has occurred in the past 50 years across the world has been based on religious differences either between the world's major religions or between sects within the same world religion, for example, the Sunni and Shia Muslim sects. (For a more detailed analysis and critique of these ideas, see pages 454–456 of Chapter 6.2). There is evidence too that Islam played a major role in the Arab Spring movement, which resulted in civil uprisings in Bahrain and Syria and major protests in Algeria, Iraq, Jordan, Kuwait, Morocco, and Sudan against high levels of unemployment, persistent poverty, corruption, nepotism, the one-party state and police brutality. Micklethwait and Wooldridge (2010) argue that in some societies, such as Saudi Arabia and Iran, Islam permeates all aspects of cultural and political life whilst Pentecostal Christianity is sweeping across South America (most notably Brazil, Chile and Peru), Africa, China and South Korea. India too has seen the rise of a nationalistic movement, powered by Hinduism, known as 'hindutva'. This religious Ideology, which is extremely anti-Muslim and which seeks to establish the dominance of the Hindu way of life, was adopted by the Bharatiya Janata party (BJP) which became the government of India in 2014.

FUNDAMENTALISM

A key feature of global postmodern society has been the emergence of fundamentalist religious factions within all the major world religions. Fundamentalist wings can be seen in Catholic and Protestant Christianity, Judaism, Hinduism and Islam.

The late 20th century and early 21st century in particular have seen a rise in religious fundamentalism among Zionists in Israel, Muslims in Saudi Arabia, Iran, Iraq and Afghanistan and Christian groups in the USA. The number of people who can be described as fundamentalists is probably only a small fraction of religious people across the world. However, it is important to examine fundamentalists because of the disproportionate effect they have had both locally and globally.

What effects have fundamentalists had on UK and world affairs?

Bruce (2008) differentiates between two different sorts of fundamentalism which he terms "the communal" and "the individual". He suggests that communal fundamentalism is the type associated with Islamism, Zionism and Hinduism because it is mainly concerned with defending communities from what are perceived to be 'modern' threats such as Western materialism, democracy, human rights, multiculturalism and so on. In contrast, individual fundamentalism is mainly found in modern societies, particularly the USA. It is particularly associated with conservative and evangelical Protestants who are "competing to define the culture of a stable nation-state". Despite their differing religious roots, fundamentalist movements often share key characteristics.

> They usually subscribe to a literal interpretation of their religious texts, which they see as infallible. They use scripture selectively to support their moral codes, which are usually inflexible and which they wish to impose on others. Fundamentalists also tend to look nostalgically to a golden past age of their religion when it was supposedly at its purest. They use this to judge the spiritual state of the society in which they operate.

> Fundamentalists regard all areas of social life as sacred, and consequently closely police people's behaviour. In Iran in 2014, six young people who appeared in a viral video on YouTube dancing to Pharrell Williams' song 'Happy' were given suspended prison sentences. They had broken religious laws that prohibit dancing with the opposite sex and prohibit women from appearing without a headscarf.

> Fundamentalists often do not tolerate other religions. In Syria and Iraq, ISIS insists that followers of other religions either convert to their form of Islamism or die.

> They also tend to subscribe to conservative beliefs and generally oppose the liberalisation of society, (such as equal rights for women or LGBT people). Malala Yousafzai, for example, was shot by the Taliban for campaigning in favour of girls' education.

Finally, some fundamentalist groups see mainstream society as a threat to their value system. They may adopt 'defensive aggressive' strategies in reaction to this perceived 'threat' to their existence. For example, the terrorist attacks by IS in Paris in 2015 and the bombing of abortion clinics in the USA by Christians are examples of fundamentalist defensive-aggression.

The causes of fundamentalism

Giddens (1999) sees communal fundamentalism as a response to the globalisation of Western culture and lifestyles. Some members of traditional societies view this as a threat to traditional authority in three respects. First, Western culture generally encourages liberal ideas that advocate equality for females and minority groups such as gay people, as well as free speech and democracy, which challenge traditional forms of authority, such as patriarchal religion. Second, Western material lifestyles are interpreted as spiritually empty, corrupt and a potential threat to the faith of the young. Third, globalisation causes uncertainty because its modernity challenges established ideals and behaviour that have been in place for hundreds of years. For example, modernity encourages rationalism and relativism, which challenges monolithic religion, whilst the modern values of education for all, meritocracy, democracy and bureaucracy challenge autocratic religious power. Fundamentalism may therefore appeal to some people, particularly those concerned by religious pluralism and the growing popularity of secular thinking, because it promises certainty, submission to a higher spiritual authority and a retreat from modernity. As Ruthven (2007) argues, fundamentalism can provide a source of authority in a global environment in which actual power is diffused and impersonal and provide psychological reassurance in a world characterised by doubt and risk.

A similar analysis by Bauman (1992) sees fundamentalism as a response to life in a postmodern world. This brings with it a greater variety of choices and relativist ideas, as well as uncertainties and greater risks. For example, there is some evidence that a very small minority of women reject the postmodern world's emphasis on women 'having it all' by juggling several identities such as career women, wife, mother and so on. Instead, these women may turn to fundamentalist sects, because they offer absolute truth and certainty in the traditional female roles of wife and mother. Fundamentalists may therefore feel threatened by postmodern society. They may seek comfort in a traditional religious community of like-minded individuals, who wish for a return to more traditional and conservative values that promote certainty and absolute truth.

Norris and Inglehart's (2011) existential security theory argues that people in developing societies may face life-threatening risks such as famine, poverty, disease and environmental disasters on a daily basis. They may be more anxious than people living in Western societies about their future or that of their children. This may lead them to turn to fundamentalist religions that provide comfort, compensation, certainty and emotional security in the context of their experience of everyday hardship.

Norris and Inglehart observe that people's need for the **existential security** provided by religion is lessened when these hardships are removed.

UNDERSTAND THE CONCEPT

Existential security refers to the idea that people are more likely to turn to religion for comfort and to secure their future or their children's future in the afterlife, if they feel their existence is regularly threatened by dangers such as poverty, famine, war or natural disasters.

Finally, Bruce observes that fundamentalist movements may share particular characteristics but the causes of their popularity are often different. For example, Bruce argues that Christian fundamentalism is caused by internal social change in Western society. Such changes include secularisation, equal opportunity laws that permit homosexuality, abortion and women's rights, and the rise of science, especially the theory of evolution. In contrast, Bruce argues that fundamentalism in the developing world is caused by external social change that is thrust upon traditional societies, such as economic development, the Americanisation of global culture and the impact of Western foreign policies, particularly the invasions of Afghanistan and Iraq.

CONCLUSIONS

It is impossible to say with any degree of certainty that secularisation is occurring. The global evidence is clear. Outside Europe, the levels of religiosity are high and have probably increased in recent years. Fundamentalists continue to have a disproportionate effect on people's sense of risk wherever they might live in the world.

It is probably true that the UK is a more secular society today than in the past because of social influences such as disengagement, the decline of religious socialisation, rationalisation, the rise of religious pluralism, individuation and existential security. However, there is little sign that a more secular society produces more atheism: secular society is not necessarily anti-religious. Woodhead (2008) describes the modern UK as a 'post-Christian' society in which most people are happy to identify with some core Christian values such as love, kindness, fairness and compassion, but reject others such as dogmatism and anti-liberalism. She notes that the UK "is no longer a Christian country in the way that it was in the 19th century, or even in the 1950s. It is much more plural in cultural and religious terms than ever before, and its conscience is now shaped by a whole range of sources – both secular and religious" (2008). At most, then, sociologists can only conclude that religion is changing in the UK. It is doubtful that religion will ever disappear altogether because it meets a very basic human need, that science and other non-religious belief systems have difficulty in providing: emotional comfort in times of need, crisis and tragedy.

FOCUS ON SKILLS: ARISE, SECULAR BRETHREN, GOD'S FANATICS ARE BACK

The return of God to international affairs is one of the most astonishing developments of the past decades. In Europe we decided to put restrictions on God in the 17th century. The wars of religion proved to be so bloody, killing perhaps 10% of the European population, that the continent's leaders devised rules to keep faith out of politics. What followed was the secularisation of European life. A succession of thinkers said religion was dying. Marx dismissed it as a tool of class oppression. Max Weber, one of the fathers of sociology, announced the "disenchantment of the world". Freud dismissed religion as a collective neurosis. People followed these advanced thinkers with unseemly haste. The masses abandoned the churches for the music hall and the cinema. The churches abandoned fire and brimstone for social work. Politicians gave up on God.

However, 13 years of living in the United States and making numerous visits to the Middle East, Latin America and Africa have convinced me the European secular mindset is hopelessly parochial. Religion is on display across the non-European world – in the overflowing mega-churches of American suburbs, in the millions who perform the hajj every year, in daily headlines in every newspaper. Modernity has had an astonishing effect – astonishing, that is, if you regard secular Europe as the measure of all things – of stimulating religion rather than smothering it. People regard religion not as a constraint on their freedom but as a storm shelter in a hostile world.

There is every reason to believe the trend is gathering pace. The armies of God have fortified their territories. Hamas and its Hasidic opposite numbers have succeeded in turning the Israeli-Palestinian conflict from a secular battle over land into a religious battle over God's kingdom. The Pentecostal churches have put down deep roots across Latin America and Africa. Look closely at the most unstable regions of the world and you can see hot religions competing for people's souls. By 2050 the People's Republic of China will be the world's largest Christian country and the largest Muslim country.

We need to avoid a number of errors when dealing with fundamentalist religions. The first is the idea that the religious revival is an illusion, that religious anger is a distorted expression of something deeper or just a passing madness. Secular-minded people like to look for the "real" causes of religious riots in lack of opportunities or injustice. But "reality" lies in the eye of the believer. Many religious fanatics come from the most privileged, educated strata of society. Another error is the reducing of religion to a caricature. American conservatives reduce Muslims to a bunch of weird-beard fanatics. European liberals reduce American Christians to warmongering, homophobic anthropoids. It is not only bigoted to think of believers in terms of stereotypes. It is also counter-productive. The best way to defeat militant Islam is to recognise that it represents a tiny minority — most Muslims regard the protests as embarrassing and repulsive. The best way to strengthen militancy is to tar all Muslims with the same brush.

Based on Wooldridge, A. 'Arise, secular brethren, God's fanatics are back' *The Times*, 16 September 2012

Questions

1. **Understand**. Give three reasons Wooldridge identifies for secularisation in Europe.

2. **Understand**. What is the future of China with regard to religion?

3. **Analyse** the errors that Wooldridge argues should be avoided when dealing with fundamentalism in its various forms.

4. **Evaluate**. Using information from this source and elsewhere, evaluate the view that modernity has had the "astonishing effect [...] of stimulating [fundamentalist] religion rather than smothering it".

CHECK YOUR UNDERSTANDING

1. Explain what is meant by the term 'secularisation'.

2. Explain what is meant by 'believing without belonging'.

3. Explain what is meant by the 'ecumenical movement'.

4. Explain what is meant by 'vicarious religion'.

5. Define what is meant by 'desacrilisation'.

6. Identify and briefly outline two examples of how religion may have disengaged from society.

7. Identify and briefly explain three ways in which statistics can be used to support the secularisation thesis.

8. Analyse two reasons why religious pluralism is seen as evidence of secularisation.

9. Analyse how postmodern theories have contributed to the secularisation debate.

10. Analyse two ways in which the UK differs from the rest of the world in terms of religiosity.

11. Evaluate the view that people turn to religion because they are experiencing existential insecurity.

12. Evaluate the view that the UK is now a post-Christian society.

TAKE IT FURTHER

1. Interview 12 young people and 12 people aged 50 or above. Ask the young people whether they attend church, whether they 'believe without belonging' and whether they are interested in religious, supernatural and spiritual ideas. Ask the older sample the same questions, but also ask whether they have noticed a change or decline in religious beliefs and practices as they have grown older. Ask them how they feel about this.

2. Visit the 'FutureFirst' page at www.brierleyconsultancy.com, run by Peter Brierley, and the 'Figures' page at www.brin.ac.uk, which is partly run by David Voas. These two excellent websites monitor religiosity and secularisation. They are well worth visiting for up-to-date statistics and research studies.

APPLY YOUR LEARNING

1. Outline and explain **two** ways in which science differs from religion. [10 marks]

2. Read **Item A** below and answer the question that follows.

ITEM A

Religious affiliation in the USA
According to Tom Shakespeare, one in three Americans now define themselves as spiritual but not religious. Putnam and Campbell have highlighted the number of 'Nones' in the USA. These are people who belong to no religion but still believe in God. Grace Davie has used the terms 'believing without belonging' and 'vicarious religion' to explain why affiliation with particular churches and religions is in decline.

Applying material from **Item A** and your knowledge, analyse **two** reasons why 'affiliation with particular churches and religions is in decline'. [10 marks]

3. Read **Item B** below and answer the question that follows.

ITEM B

Religion and social change
Functionalists believe that religion performs a number of positive but conservative functions for society that help preserve consensus and community, and therefore social order. Marx also believed that religion was a conservative force because he saw it as an ideology aimed at preserving class inequality. However, the neo-Marxists Gramsci and Maduro both agreed that religion was sometimes capable of bringing about revolutionary change and improving the lives of the poor. Weber saw most religions as conservative ideologies but claimed that Protestantism brought about massive economic change in the 17th and 18th centuries.

Applying material from **Item B** and your knowledge, evaluate the relationship between religion and social change. [20 marks]

You can find example answers and accompanying teachers' comments for this topic at www.collins.co.uk/AQAAlevelSociology. Please note that these example answers and teacher's comments have not been approved by AQA.

LOOKING AHEAD

You are reading this section of the book because you are about to begin the second year of the AQA A-level specification for Sociology. You may have already sat the AS examination or you may just be sitting the A-level exam. In either case, this section of the textbook explains what is in the specification, and what skills and knowledge you will develop through your course.

Year 1 specification content
The first year of study is divided into two units that lay out what you will learn.

> Unit 3.1 will involve the study of two compulsory topics: *Education* and *Methods in Context*. This involves the study of the educational system and how sociological research methods have been employed to study aspects of it.

> Unit 3.2 also involves a compulsory *Research Methods* section and the study of a minimum of one optional sociological topic from a choice of *Culture and Identity*, *Families and Households*, *Health*, and *Work, Welfare and Poverty*.

Year 2 specification content
The second year of study is divided into two units that lay out what you will learn.

> Unit 4.2 will involve the study of a minimum of one sociological topic from a choice of *Beliefs in Society*, *Global Development*, *The Media* and *Stratification and Differentiation*.

> Unit 4.3 involves the study of a compulsory topic *Crime and Deviance* with *Theory and Methods*. This involves the study of crime and deviance, sociological research methods and sociological theories of society.

Year 2 assessment
You will sit three examinations in this subject, even if you have already achieved the AS qualification. You should take a look at the table on the next page, which shows the structure of the A-level examination.

What skills are you expected to acquire during your course of study?
The skills you will acquire and develop during this course are split into three main strands or assessment objectives. As you work through the course you will be expected to demonstrate these skills in your work and in the exams you take at the end of the course.

1: Knowledge and understanding
To meet this objective successfully, you have to show your knowledge and understanding of the chosen topic on which you are answering a question. This knowledge and understanding covers the full range of relevant sociological material, including concepts, theories, perspectives, the findings of sociological studies, relevant facts (from official sources, for example) and sociological methods.

You will also develop and be assessed on the quality of your written communication. In other words, you need to be able to express yourself clearly in writing. This is a really important skill for sociologists.

2: Application
To meet this objective successfully, you will have to apply sociological theories, concepts, evidence and research methods to the question that you have been asked. This means that while it is probably obvious that you need to know some sociological material, you need to be able to use and discuss it in ways that actually address and answer the question.

For example, you need to be able to *interpret* or work out what the question is asking and respond by selecting relevant material (theories, studies, sociological observations and so on) from what you know. Some questions will specifically ask you to use material from an attached item of information as well. You should then aim to *apply* all of this knowledge to the question in an appropriate way.

3: Analysis and evaluation
To meet this objective successfully, you will have to *analyse* and *evaluate* sociological theories, concepts, evidence and research methods in order to:

> present arguments

> make judgements

> draw conclusions.

Analysis refers to the ability to show how arguments and ideas logically fit together. Good analysis is shown by presenting an informed, detailed and accurate discussion of a particular theory, perspective, study or event, and also by the ability to present your arguments in a clear and logical manner.

Evaluation involves being able to recognise and weigh up strengths and weaknesses; advantages and disadvantages; evidence and arguments of a sociological theory, perspective, study, argument or research method to reach an appropriate conclusion.

A-level units of study and assessment

Unit	Topics covered	Forms of assessment
1 80 marks 33.3% of A-level	› *Education* › *Methods in Context* › *Theory and Methods*	PAPER 1: EDUCATION with THEORY and METHODS Written examination of two hours. All questions are compulsory. Two short questions focused on *Education* worth 4 & 6 marks respectively; one question worth 10 marks based on a data response item and an essay question worth 30 marks partly based on a data response item. A 20 mark *Methods in Context* question focused on a data response item that describes an aspect of education and a research method. A 10 mark question focused on an aspect of *Theory and Methods*.
2 80 marks 33.3% of A-level	SECTION A › *Culture and Identity* › *Families and Households* › *Health* › *Work, Welfare and Poverty* SECTION B › *Beliefs in Society* › *Global development* › *The Media* › *Stratification and Differentiation*	PAPER 2: TOPICS in SOCIOLOGY Written examination of two hours. All questions need to be answered from *one* topic from Section A and *one* topic from Section B. Both sections will contain three questions per topic: one question worth 10 marks; one question worth 10 marks partly based on a data response item and one question worth 20 marks partly based on a data response item.
3 80 marks 33.3% of A-level	› *Crime and Deviance* › *Theory and Methods*	PAPER 3: TOPICS in SOCIOLOGY: CRIME and DEVIANCE with THEORY and METHODS Written examination of two hours. All questions are compulsory. Two short questions focused on *Crime and Deviance* worth 4 & 6 marks respectively; one question worth 10 marks partly based on a data response item and an essay question worth 30 marks partly based on a data response item. Two questions focused on *Theory and Methods*: one is worth 10 marks and the other that is partly based on a data response item, is worth 20 marks.

Please refer to the AQA website for the full A-level Sociology specification and other resources.

Understanding questions and instructions

It is really important that you become familiar with the meaning of the 'command words' that you will use during your course. Command words tell you how to go about a task or how to approach an answer to a question. The following command words are used throughout this book:

> *Analyse* – separate sociological information into components or sections and identify their characteristics.

> *Define* – Specify the meaning of a concept.

> *Identify* – Name whatever you have been asked for, such as a concept or theory. It is often a good idea to include an example to illustrate your understanding.

> *Explain* – Set out the reasons or distinguishing features of a theory, sociological study, and so on and say why they are important.

> *Outline* – Set out the main features or characteristics of something.

> *Outline and explain* – Set out the main features of something such as a sociological theory and explain the reasons why these features are important.

> *Using one example, briefly explain* – Give a brief account of something.

> *Examine* – Look at the advantages and disadvantages of a theory, or look at evidence for and against a sociological view contained in an essay title.

> *Evaluate* – Judge the strengths and weaknesses of something from the evidence available and/or by looking at all sides and come to an informed conclusion.

> *Assess* – Look at all sides, or all theories that relate to the sociological debate in question and come to an informed conclusion.

> *Applying material from Item A* – Draw on material from the data or information in the item that accompanies the question. Remember: there may be more than one useful point in the item. Also, bear in mind that this is an *instruction*, not a suggestion, so make sure you use the information that you have been given to its full potential.

The command word descriptions above may not match the definitions in the AQA specification. A full list of AQA command words and definitions can be found on the AQA website.

Communication tips

> Read the whole question or instruction very carefully before you begin your answer. Reading the question thoroughly will help you to recognise which aspects of the topic are covered. Identify any command words and decide what type of answer is required.

> Read the item(s) provided. They are there to help you and contain essential information. Think of them like a map that gives you clues to the direction in which to take your answer. To make the most of the items, read them through several times, picking out or underlining key points and letting your mind digest them. Then, try to link them up with your own knowledge.

> When you have read the question and items, make a brief plan for any longer questions before you begin writing. As you write your other answers, you may well remember things that you wish to slot into these answers. Stick to your plan and refer back to it when writing.

> Plan your time carefully. Make sure you have time to answer all of the questions to the best of your ability.

> If you are giving multiple reasons or suggesting several examples to make your point, you may wish to use bullet points. This will help you set out and deliver your argument clearly.

> Start each point on a separate line or begin a new paragraph. By doing so, the structure of your writing will be much easier to follow.

> When writing longer, more involved arguments, you should refer to appropriate theories, perspectives, studies and evidence to support and inform your point. Where possible, bring in examples of recent or current events, policies and so on, to illustrate the points you are making.

> Finally, make sure that you answer the question that is being asked, rather than the one that you wished had been set! It is very easy to want to write down everything you know about a topic, particularly if you have studied hard, but this does not show that you have understood the topic as well as a carefully-constructed response.

REFERENCES

Abbott, P. and Wallace, C. (1997) *An Introduction to Sociology: Feminist Perspectives* (3rd edn). London: Routledge

Adamson, P. (1986) 'The rich, the poor, the pregnant', *New Internationalist*, 270

Addison, T. et al. (2013) 'Aid to Africa: The Changing Context', Available at: http://ssrn.com/abstract=2499357

Adonis, A. and Pollard, S. (1998) *A Class Act: The Myth of Britain's Classless Society*, Harmondsworth: Penguin

Adorno, T.W. (1991) *The Culture Industry: Selected Essays on Mass Culture*, London: Routledge

Age Concern (2005) How Ageist is Britain? London: Age Concern

Ahern, G. (1987) ' "I do Believe in Christmas": White Working Class People and Anglican Clergy in Inner City London', in *Inner City God: The Nature of Belief in the Inner City*. Ed. by G, Ahern and G Davie, London: Hodder

Aherne, G and Davie, G (1987) *Inner City God: The Nature of Belief in the Inner City*, London: Hodder and Stoughton

Akhtar, P (2005) '(Re)turn to Religion and Radical Islam', in *Muslim Britain: Communities Under Pressure*. Ed. by ABBAS, T. London: Zed Books

Aldridge, A. (2013) *Religion in the Contemporary World: A Sociological Introduction* (3rd edn), Cambridge: Polity

Althusser, L. (1969) *For Marx*, Harmondsworth: Penguin

Ameli, S et al. (2007) *The British Media and Muslim Representation: The Ideology of Demonisation*, London: Islamic Human Rights Commission

Andsager, J. (2000) 'How Interest Groups Attempt to Shape Public Opinion with Competing News Frames' *Journalism and Mass Communication Quarterly*, 77(3), pp. 577-592

Archer, M.S. (1982) Morphogenesis versus structure and action. *British Journal of Sociology*, 33 (4)

Arweck, E. (2002) *Theorizing Faith: The Insider//Outsider Problem in the Study of Ritual*. Birmingham: University of Birmingham Press

Ashley, L et al. (2015) 'A Qualitative Evaluation of Non-Educational Barriers to the Elite Professions', Social Mobility and Child Poverty Commission

Ashworth, J. H. and Farthing, I. (2007) *Churchgoing in the UK: A research report on church attendance in the UK*, Middlesex: Tearfund

Atkinson, J.M. (1971) 'Social reactions to suicide: the role of coroners' definitions', in S. Cohen (ed.) *Images of Deviance*, Harmondsworth: Penguin

Atkinson, W. (2010) 'Class, Individualisation and Perceived (Dis)advantages: Not Either/Or but Both/And?', *Sociological Research Online*, 15(4)

Aune, K & Redfern, C. (2010) *Reclaiming the F Word*. London: Zed Books

Aune, K., Sharma, S. and Vincett, G. (eds) (2008) *Women and Religion in the West: Challenging Secularization*, Aldershot: Ashgate

Back, L. (2002) 'Youth, "race" and violent disorder', *Sociology Review*, 11(4)

Baechler, J. (1979) *Suicides* Oxford: Blackwell

Bagdikian, B. (2004) *The New Media Monopoly*, Boston: Beacon Press

Bailey, G. (2012) 'Precarious or Precariat?', *International Socialist Review*, 85(September)

Bakan, J. (2004) *Corporation: The Pathological Pursuit of Profit and Power*, London: Constable and Robinson

Bandura, A. et al. (1963) 'The imitation of film mediated aggressive models', *Journal of Abnormal and Social Psychology*, 66(1), pp. 3–11

Bandyopadhyay, S and Vermann, E. (2013) 'Donor Motives for Foreign Aid' *Federal Reserve Bank of St Louis Review* 95(4), pp. 327-36

Banyard, K. (2010) *The Equality Illusion: The Truth about Women and Men Today*, London: Faber and Faber

Barber, B.R. (2003) *Jihad Vs McWorld: Terrorism's Challenge to Democracy* (2nd edn). London: Corgi

Barber, B.R. and Schulz, A. (1995) *Jihad vs McWorld*, New York: Ballantyne Books

Barder, O. (2011) 'Should We Pay Less for Vaccines?' Available at: www.cgdev.org

Barnes, C. (1992) *Disabling Imagery and the Media: an exploration of the principles for media representations of disabled people*, Halifax: British Council of Organisations of Disabled People and Ryburn Publishing

Barnett, S and Seymour, E (1999) *A Shrinking Iceberg Slowly Travelling South: Changing Trends in British Television*, London: Campaign for Quality Television

Barrett, D. (2001) *World Christian Encyclopaedia*. Oxford: Oxford University Press

Barrett, D. (2008) *A Brief History of Secret Societies*. London: Robinson

Barron, R. D. and Norris, G.M. (1976) 'Sexual Divisions and the Dual Labour Market', in D. Barker and S. Allen (eds) *Dependence and Exploitation in Work and Marriage*, Conference Proceedings, London: Prentice Hall Press

Barsamian and Roy. (2004) *The Checkbook and the Cruise Missile: Conversations with Arundhati Roy*, Boston: South End Press

Batchelor et al. (2004) 'Representing young people's sexuality in the 'youth' media', *Health Education Research*, 19(6), pp. 669–76

Bateman, M. (2012) 'The rise and fall of microcredit in post-apartheid South Africa', Available at: mondediplo.comt

Bates, L. (2014) *Everyday Sexism*. London: Simon & Schuster

Baudrillard, J. (1980) *For a Critique of the Political Economy of the Sign*, New York: Telos Press

Baudrillard, J. (1994) *The Illusion of the End*, Cambridge: Polity Press

Baudrillard, J. (1998) *Selected Writings* (M. Poster ed.), Cambridge: Polity Press

Bauer, P.T. (1981) *Equality, the Third World, and Economic Delusion*, London: Methuen

Bauman, Z. (1988) *Freedom*, Milton Keynes: Open University Press

Bauman, Z. (1992) *Intimations of Postmodernity*, London: Routledge

Bauman, Z. (2007) *Consuming Life*, Cambridge: Polity Press

BBC (2010) *Portrayal of Lesbian, Gay and Bisexual People on the BBC*. Available at: www.bbc.co.uk

Beck, U (2002) 'A life of one's own in a runaway world: individualisation, globalisation and politics', in U. Beck and E. Beck-Gernsheim, *Individualisation*, London: Sage

Beck, U. (1992) *Risk Society: Towards a New Modernity*, London: Sage

Beck, U. (1999) *World Risk Society*, Cambridge: Polity

Beck, U. (2009) *World at Risk*, Cambridge: Polity

Becker, H. (1963) *The Outsiders: Studies in the Sociology of Deviance*, New York: Free Press

Becker, H. (1970) 'Whose side are we on?', in H. Becker, *Sociological Work*, New Brunswick: Transaction Books

Beckford, J (2003) *Social Theory and Religion*. Cambridge: Cambridge University Press

Beckford, J. (1975) *Trumpet of Prophecy: Sociological Study of Jehovah's Witnesses*. New York: Wiley-Blackwell

Beckford, J. (2010) 'The Uses of Religion in Public Institutions: the Case of Prisons'. In A, Molendijk (ed.) *Exploring the Postsecular* University of Groningen

Beckford, R. (2002) *Jesus Dub: Theology, Music and Social Change*. Abington: Taylor & Francis

Bell, E. (2015) 'Can Twitter reinvent itself with packaged news before it gets sold?' *Observer*, 18 October

Bello (2015) Industrialisation in Africa: More a Marathon than a Sprint. Available at: www.economist.com

Belson, W. (1978) *Television Violence and the Adolescent Boy*, Farnborough: Teakfield

Bennett, A. et al. (2006) *Media Culture: The Social Organisation of Media Practices in Contemporary Britain: A Report for The British Film Institute*, London: British Film Institute

Bennett, T. et al (2009) *Class, Culture, Distinction*, London: Routledge

Benson, R. (2010) 'Futures of the news: international considerations and further reflection' in N. Fenton (ed) *New Media, Old News*, London: Sage

Benston, M. (1972) 'The political economy of women's liberation', in N. Glazer-Mahlbin and H.Y. Wahrer (eds) *Women in a Man-made World*, Chicago: Rand MacNally

Berger, P (2003) 'Religions and Globalisation.' *European Judaism: A Journal for the New Europe*. 36(1): 4 -10

Berger, P. (1969) *A Rumour of Angels: Modern Society and the Rediscovery of the Supernatural*. Boston: Doubleday

Berger, P. (1971) *A Rumour of Angels*, Harmondsworth: Penguin

Bergesen (1990) 'Turning world-system theory on its head', in M. Featherstone (ed.) *Global Culture: Rationalism, Globalisation and Modernity*, London: Sage

Berry, C. (1986) 'Message misunderstood', *The Listener*, 27 Nov

Best, S. (2005) *Understanding Social Divisions*, London: Sage

Best, S. and Kellner, D. (1999) 'Rap, Black rage, and racial difference', *Enculturation*, 2(2), Spring

Bingham, J. (2014) 'Multiculturalism in reverse as teenagers buck the trend towards integration', *The Telegraph*, 29 June

Bird, J. (1999) *Investigating Religion*, London: HarperCollins

Black (2002) *The No-Nonsense Guide to International Development*, London: Verso

Blaikie, A. (1999) *Ageing and Popular Culture*, Cambridge: Cambridge University Press

Blanden, J., Gregg, P. and Machin, S. (2005) *Intergenerational Mobility in Europe and North America*, London, Centre for Economic Performance, LSE

Blanden, J., Gregg, P. and Macmillan, L. (2013) 'Intergenerational persistence in income and social class', *Journal of the Royal Statistical Society* Series A, 176(2)

Bloor, D. (1976) *Knowledge and Social Imagery*, London: Routledge

Blumer, H. (1962) 'Society as symbolic interaction', in N. Rose (ed.) *Symbolic Interactionism*, Englewood Hills, NJ: Prentice-Hall

Blumer, H. (1969) *Symbolic Interactionism: Perspective and Method*. Englewood Cliffs: Prentice Hall

Blumler, J.G. and McQuail, D. (1968) *Television in Politics: Its Uses and Influence*, London: Faber & Faber

Bottero, W. (2005) *Stratification: Social Division and Inequality*, London: Routledge

Bourdieu, P. (1984) *Distinction: A Social Critique of the Judgement of Taste*, London: Routledge and Kegan Paul

Boyle, R. (2005) 'Press the red button now: television and technology', *Sociology Review*, Nov

Boyle, R. (2007) 'The "now" media generation', *Sociology Review*, Sept

Bradley, H. (1996) *Fractured Identities: Changing Patterns of Inequality*, Cambridge: Polity

Brandt Report (1981), authored by the Independent Commission. Available at: www.sharing.org

Brasher, B. (1998) *Godly Women: Fundamentalism and Female Power*. New Brunswick: Rutgers University Press

Breman, J. (2013) 'A bogus concept?', *New Left Review*, No 84

Brewer, J.D. (2014) 'The Public Value of Peace Processes' Innovation and Engagement Public Lecture Series, Cardiff University

Brierley, P. (2002) *Reaching and Keeping Tweenagers*, London: Christian Research

Brierley, P. (2006) *Pulling Out of the Nose Dive: A Contemporary Picture of Churchgoing; What the 2005 English Church Census Reveals*, London: Christian Research

Brierley, P. (ed.) (1999) *Christian Research Association, UK Christian Handbook, Religious Trend*, London: HarperCollins

Brighton, P. and Foy, D. (2007) *News Values*, London: Sage

Britain Thinks (2011) *What about the workers?* June, www.britainthinks.com

British Academy (2015) 'The Race Relations Act at 50', Available at: Home Office

Brookings Institute (2015) "Why Wait 100 Years? Bridging the Gap in Global Education" June 2015

Bruce, S. (1995) *Religion in Modern Britain*, Oxford: Oxford University Press

Bruce, S. (1996) *Religion in the Modern World: From Cathedrals to Cults*, Oxford: Oxford University Press

Bruce, S. (2001) 'The social process of secularisation' in R.K. Fenn (2004) *The Blackwell Companion to the Sociology of Religion*, Oxford: Blackwell

Bruce, S. (2002) *God is Dead: Secularization in the West*, Oxford: Blackwell

Bruce, S. (2008) *Fundamentalism*. Cambridge: Polity

Bruce, S. (2013) 'Secularisation and Church Growth in the UK' *Journal of Religion in Europe*. 6(3), pp. 273-296

Bryman, A. (2004) *The Disneyization of Society*, London: Sage

Brynin, M. and Longhi, S. (2015) *The effect of occupation on poverty among ethnic minority groups*, JRF

Burchill, J. (2001) 'Some People Will Believe Anything'. *Guardian*, Sat 18 Aug

Burkey, S. (1993) *People First*, London: Zed Books

Burnley, J. (2010) *21st Century Aid: Recognizing Success and Tackling Failure*. Oxfam Briefing Paper (137). Available at: policy-practice.oxfam.org.uk

Bushman, B., & Anderson, C. (2009) 'Comfortably numb: Desensitizing effects of violent media on helping others', *Psychological Science*, 20, pp. 273– 277

Butler, J. (1990) *Gender Trouble: Feminism and the Subversion of Identity*, Abingdon: Routledge

Butler, R. (1969) 'Ageism: another form of bigotry', *The Gerontologist*, 9(4), pp. 243-246

Calderisi ,R. (2006) *The Trouble with Africa*, New Haven: Yale University Press

Callinicos, A. (2006) *The Resources of Critique*, Cambridge: Polity

Callister, L and Khalaf, I (2009) Culturally Diverse Women Giving Birth: Their Stories. *Science Across Cultures*. 5, pp. 33-39

Campbell, B. (1985) *Wigan Pier Revisited*, London: Virago

Campbell, B. (1993) *Goliath: Britain's Dangerous Places*, London: Methuen

Carmen, R. (1996) *Autonomous Development: Humanising the Landscape*, London: Zed Books

Carnell, B. (2000) 'Paul Ehrlich', 17 May 2000. Available at: www.overpopulation.com

Carrigan, M. and Szmigin, I. (2000) 'The ethical advertising covenant: regulating ageism in UK advertising', *International Journal of Advertising*, 19(4), pp. 509-528

Carspecken, P, F. (1996)*Critical Ethnography in Education Research: A Theoretical and Practical Guide*. London: Routledge

Casanova, J (1994) *Public Religions in the Modern World*. Chicago: University of Chicago Press

Castells, M. (2010) *End of Millennium* (2nd edn), Chichester: Blackwell

Castles, S. and Kosack, G.C. (1973) *Immigrant Workers and Class Structure in Western Europe*, Oxford: Oxford University Press

Catley-Carlson, M. (1994) 'Population policies and reproductive rights – always

in conflict?', in B. Hartmann (ed.) *Reproductive Rights and Wrongs: the Global Politics of Population Control*, Boston MA: South End Press

Centre for the Analysis of Social Exclusion (CASE) (2013) *Wealth distribution, accumulation and policy*. Casebrief 33, May, 2013

Cerezo, A. (2013) 'CCTV and crime displacement: A quasi-experimental evaluation' *European Journal of Criminology*, 10(2), pp. 222-236

Chakravarty, S et al. (2012) *Global Perspectives on Sustainable Forest Management*, InTech

Chambliss, W.J. 'The Saints and the Roughnecks' *Society*, Volume 11

Chang H. J. (2007) *The Myth of Free trade and the Secret History of Capitalism*. London: Bloomsbury

Chang, H. J. (2007) *The East Asian Development Experience: The Miracle, the Crisis and the Future*. Cambridge: Zed Books

Chang, P. L. (2009) 'The Evolution and Utilization of the GATT/WTO Dispute Settlement Mechanism' in *Trade Disputes and Dispute Settlement Understanding of the WTO: An Interdisciplinary Assessment*. Available at: ink.library.smu.edu.

Chapman, S. (2008) 'Is social class still important?', *Sociology Review*, 18(2), pp. 28-32

Charlton, T et al. (2000) *Broadcast Television Effects in a Remote Community*, Hillsdale, NJ: Lawrence Erlbaum

Chestnut, A (2014) 'Why has Pentecostalism grown so dramatically in Latin America' (interviewer: David Masci). Available at: www.pewresearch.org

Chidgey, R. (2008) 'Labours left unfinished', *the f word*, 10 March

Children Now (1999) *Boys to Men: Entertainment Media Messages about Masculinity*, Oakland, CA: Children Now

Choudhury, T. (2007) *The Role of Muslim Identity Politics in Radicalization (a study in progress)*, London: Department for Communities and Local Government

Choudury, T (2007) 'The Role of Muslim Identity Politics in Radicalisation (a study in progress)' Department for Communities and Local Government: London

Chowdhry, G. (1995). "Engendering Development?: Women in Development (WID) in International Development Regimes" in Marchand, M.H. and Parpart, J.L. (eds). Feminism/Postmodernism/Development. London and New York: Routledge, pp. 26-39

Christiano, K and Swatos, W (2015) *Sociology of Religion: Contemporary Developments* (3rd edn). Lanham: Rowman & Littlefield

Chryssides, George D. (1994) 'Britain's Changing Faiths: Adaptation in a New Environment', in G. Parsons (ed.), *The Growth of Religious Diversity – Volume Two: Issues*, London: Routledge

Cixous, Helene (1993) "The Laugh of the Medusa"

Clark, K. and Drinkwater, S. (2007) *Ethnic Minorities in the Labour Market: dynamics and diversity*, JRF

Clark, T.N. and Hoffman-Martinot, V. (eds) (1998) *The New Political Culture*, Boulder: Westview

Clements, B (2015) *Religion and Public Opinion in Britain: Continuity and Change.* Basingstoke: Palgrave Macmillan

Cochrane, A and Pain, K. (2000) 'A globalising society' in D. Held (ed.) *A Globalising World: Culture, Economics and Politics*, London: Routledge

Cochrane, K. (2011) 'Why is British public life dominated by men?', *Guardian*, 4 December

Cockburn, C. (2013) *"Beyond the Fragments": I'm a socialist feminist. Can I be a radical feminist too?* opendemocracy.net (17 May)

CODE (Centre on Dynamics of Ethnicity) (2013) 'Addressing Ethnic Inequalities in Social Mobility'. Available at: www.ethnicity.ac.uk

Cohen, Lawrence E. and Felson, M. (1979). "Social Change and Crime Rate Trends: A Routine Activity Approach." American Sociological Review. 44: 588-605

Cohen, N. (2005) 'Capital Punishment', *The Observer*, 6 Nov

Cohen, N. (2009) *Waiting for the Etonians: Reports from the Sickbed of Liberal England*, London: Fourth Estate

Cohen, R. and Kennedy, P. (2000) *Global Sociology*, Basingstoke: Macmillan

Cohen, S. (1972), *Folk Devils and Moral Panics.* London: MacGibbon and Kee

Cohen, S. (1985) *Visions of Social Control*, Cambridge: Polity

Cohen, S. (2001) *States of Denial: Knowing about atrocities and suffering*, Cambridge: Polity

Cohen, S. and Young, J. (1981) *The Manufacture of News: Deviance, Social Problems and the Mass Media* (2nd edn), London: Constable

Coleman, P. (2000) Aging and the Satisfaction of Psychological Needs. *Psychological Inquiry.* 11, pp. 291-293

Collett, J and Lizardo, O. (2009) A Power-Control Theory of Gender and Religiosity. *Journal for the Scientific Study of Religion.* 48(2), pp. 213-231

Collier, P. (2007) *The Bottom Billion: Why the Poorest Countries are Failing and What Can Be Done About It*, Oxford: Oxford University Press

Collins-Mayo, S. (2010) *The Faith of Generation Y.* London: Church House Publishing

Columbia Journalism Review (2000) 'Self-censorship', *Columbia Journalism Review*, May/Jun

Commission for Africa (2005) *Our Common Interest*, London: Penguin

Connell, R.W. (1995) *Masculinities*, Cambridge: Polity Press

Coontz, S and Henerson, P. (1986) *Women's Work, Men's Property: The Origins of Gender and Class.* London: Verso

Corak, M. (2013) 'Income inequality, equality of opportunity and intergenerational mobility', *The Journal of Economic Perspectives*, 27(3)

Corby, H. (1982) 'White women listen!' in *C.C.C.S. The Empire Strikes Back*, London: Hutchison

Cornford, J and Robins, K. (1999) 'New media', in J. Stokes and A. Reading (eds) *The Media in Britain: Current debates and developments*, London: MacMillan

Couldry, N. (2010) 'New online news sources and writer-gatherers', in N. Fenton (ed) *New Media, Old News*, London: Sage

Coussins, J. (1976) *The Equality Report*, London, NCCL Rights for Women Unit

Cowen, T (2007), 'Some Countries Remain Resistant to American Cultural Exports', *New York Times*, 22 February

Craig, I. (1992) *Men, Masculinity and the Media*, Newbury Park, CA: Sage

Crawford, A. & Evans, K. (2013) 'Crime prevention and Community Safety' in Maguire, M., Morgan, R. & Reiner, R. (eds) (2012) *The Oxford Handbook of Criminology* (5th edn), Oxford: Oxford University Press

Critcher, C. (2009) 'Widening the Focus: Moral Panics as Moral regulation', *British Journal of Criminology*, 49, pp. 17-34

Croall, H. (2011) *Crime and Society in Britain* (2nd edn), London: Longman

Crook, S., Pakulski, J. and Waters, M. (1992) *Postmodernisation: Change in Advanced Society*, London: Sage

Cross, M. (1979) *Urbanisation and Urban Growth in the Caribbean*, Cambridge: Cambridge University Press, cited in M. O'Donnell (1983) *New Introductory Reader in Sociology*, London: Nelson Harrap

Crothers, L. (2012) G*lobalization and American Popular* Culture (3rd Edn). Lanham: Rowman & Littlefield Publishers

Cumberbatch, G. (2004) *Video Violence: Villain or Victim?* Report for the Video Standards Council

Cummings, E. and Henry, W. (1961) *Growing Old: The Process of Disengagement*, New York: Basic Books

Curran (2003) 'Press history', in J. Curran and J. Seaton (2003) *Power without Responsibility: the press, broadcasting, and new media in Britain* (6th edn), London: Routledge

Curran, J and Seaton, J. (2003) *Power without Responsibility: the press, broadcasting, and new media in Britain* (6th edn), London: Routledge

Cushion, S, Moore, K. and Jewell, J. (2011) 'Media representations of black young men and boys', Report of the REACH media monitoring project, REACH/University of Cardiff/DCLG

Dale, A., Gilbert, G. & Arber, S., (1985) 'Integrating Women into Class Theory', *Sociology*, 19(3), pp. 384-408

Daly, M. (1973) *Beyond God the Father*, Boston, MA: Beacon Press

Daly, M. (1978) *Gyn/Ecology: The Meta-ethics of Radical Feminism*, Boston, MA: Beacon

Daniels, J. (2009) 'Rethinking Cyberfeminism(s): Race, Gender, and Embodiment', in *WSQ: Women's Studies Quarterly*, 37 (1 & 2), pp. 101-124

Dar, A. and Mirza-Davies, J. (2015) Unemployment by ethnic background, www.researchonline.org.uk

Darnton, A and Kirk, M. (2011) 'Finding Frames: New ways to engage the UK public in global poverty'. Available at: http://findingframes.org/index.htm

Davidman, L. (1991) *Religion in a Rootless World: Women turn to Orthodox Judaism*, Berkeley: University of California Press

Davidson, K. (2006) 'Gender and an ageing population', *Sociology Review*, 15(4)

Davie, G (2013) *The Sociology of Religion: A Critical Agenda.* London: Sage

Davie, G. (1994) *Religion in Britain 1945–1990, Believing Without Belonging*, Oxford: Blackwell

Davie, G. (2015) *Religion in Britain: a Persistent Paradox* (2nd edn) New York: Wiley-Blackwell

Davies, P., Francis, P., *et al.* (2007) *Victims, Crime and Society.* London: Sage

Davies, T. (1994) 'Disabled by Society?', *Sociology Review*, 3(4)

Davis, K. and Moore, W.E. (1945) 'Some Principles of Stratification', *American Sociological Review*, 10(2). pp. 242-249

Dawkins, R. (2006) *The God Delusion.* New York: Bantam

de Beauvoir, S. (1953) *The Second Sex*, London: Jonathan Cape

Deaton, A. (2013) *The Great Escape: Health, Wealth, and the Origins of Inequality.* Princeton: Princeton University Press

Digby , B. et al (2001) *Global Challenges*, Oxford: Heinnemann

Dixon, T. (2013) *Science and Religion: A Very Short Introduction.* Oxford: Oxford University Press

Dodani, S and LaPorte, R. (2005) 'Brain Drain from Developing Countries: how can Brain Drain be Converted in Wisdom Gain?' *J R Soc Medi*, 98(11) pp. 487-491

Dorais, M (2004) *Dead Boys Can't Dance: Sexual Orientation, Masculinity and Suicide* Montreal: McGill Queen's University Press

Dorling, D. (2013) 'If you are young in Britain today, you are being taken for a ride', *New Statesman*, 07 November

Douglas, J.D. (1967) *The Social Meaning of Suicide*, Princeton, N.J: Princeton University Press

Doyle, G. (2002) *Media Ownership*, London: Sage

Drudge. M., quoted in Chris Cizilla (2013), 'Matt Drudge was right', The Washington Post, 6 June. Available at: www.washingtonpost.com

Duffield, M. (1998) 'Post-modern conflict: warlords, post-adjustment states and private protection', *Civil Wars*, Spring 1(1), pp.65–102

Duffield, M. (2001) *Global Governance and the New Wars*, London: Zed Books

Duffield, M. (2007) *Development Security and Unending War; Governing the World of Peoples*, Cambridge: Polity

Duncan, M. C. and Messner , M.A. (2005) *Gender in Televised Sports: News and Highlights Shows, 1989–2004*, Los Angeles: Amateur Athletic Foundation of Los Angeles

Duncan, R (2015) 'China: The New Face of Development' in McGann, G and McCloskey, S (eds.) *From the Local to the Global: Key Issues in Development Studies*, London: Pluto Press

Durkheim, E. (1897/1952 reissue) *Suicide: A Study in Sociology*, London: Routledge

Durkheim, E. (1912/1915/1961 reissue) *The Elementary Forms of Religious Life*, London: Allen & Unwin

Durkheim, E. (1933, 1st edn, 1893) *The Division of Labour in Society*, Glencoe: Free Press

Durrant, S. (2009) 'The Chore Wars', *The Guardian*, 11 February

Dutton, B. (1997) *The Media*, London: Longman

Dyer, R. (2002) *The Matter of Images: Essays on Representation*, London: Routledge

Eagleton, T. (2011), 'In Praise of Marx', *The Chronicle of Higher Education*, 10 April

Eaves, End Violence Against Women Coalition, Equality Now and OBJECT 'Just the Women' (2012) www.equalitynow.org

Edwards, C. (1992) 'Industrialisation in South Korea', in T. Hewitt, H. Johnson and D. Wield (eds) *Industrialisation* and Development, Oxford: Oxford University Press

Edwards, D and Cromwell, E. (2006) Guardians of Power: The myth of the liberal media, London: Pluto Press

Ehrlich, P. (1968) The Population Bomb, New York: Ballantyne

Elias, N. (1978) The Civilizing Process: The History of Manners, Oxford: Blackwell Publishing

Elkington, J. (1999) Cannibals With Forks: The Triple Bottom Line of 21st Century Businesses, Oxford Capestone

Elliot, A. (2002) 'Beck's sociology of risk: a critical assessment', Sociology, 36(2), pp.293–315

Elliott, D and Harvey, J (2000) 'Underdevelopment in Jamaica: An Institutonalist perspective', Journal of Economic Issues, 34(2), pp. 393-401

Ellison, N.B., Steinfield, C., & Lampe, C. (2007) 'The benefits of Facebook "friends:" Social capital and college students' use of online social network sites', Journal of Computer-mediated Communication, 12

Ellwood, W. (2010) The No Nonsense Guide to Globalization. 2nd edn. London: New Internationalist Press

Ellwood. W. (2004) 'The World Trading System is Corrupt and Unjust'. New Internationalist. December 2004 Issue

Elson, D. and Pearson, R. (1981) 'The subordination of women and the internationalisation of factory production', in K. Young et al. (eds) Of Marriage and the Market: Women's Subordination in International Perspective, London: CSE Books

Engels, F. (1884/1902) The Origin of the Family, Private Property and the State. Chicago: Charles H. Kerr and Co

EOC (2006) 'Facts about women and men in Great Britain 2006', Manchester: Equal Opportunities Commission

Erixon, F. (2005) 'Why Aid Does Not Work', www.news.bbc.co.uk

Escobar, A. (2008) Territories of Difference: Place, Movements, Life, Redes, Durham, NC: Duke University Press

Esteva, G (1992) 'Development' in W. Sachs (ed.) The Development Dictionary: A Guide for Knowledge and Power, London: Zed Books

Esteva, G and Austin, J.E. (1987) Food Policy in Mexico: the Search for Self-Sufficiency, Ithaca: Cornell University Press

European Commission (2009) 'Gender segregation in the labour market: root causes, implications and policy responses in the EU'. Luxembourg: Publications Office of the European Union

Evans, J. and Chandler, J. (2006) 'To buy or not to buy: family dynamics and children's consumption', Sociological Research Online, 11(2) www.socresonline.org.uk

Evans, P. (1979) Dependent Development: The Alliance of Multinational, State and Local Capital in Brazil, Princeton: Princeton University Press

Fahmy, E. (2006) 'Youth, Poverty and Social Exclusion', in Poverty and Social Exclusion. Ed. by Gordon, D et al. Bristol: Policy Press

Farrington, D. (2007) 'Childhood Risk Factors and Risk-Focussed Prevention' in Maguire, M, Morgan, R. & Reiner, R. The Oxford Handbook of Criminology (4th edn), Oxford: Oxford University Press

Farrington, J and Bebbington, A.J. (1993) Reluctant Partners: Non-Governmental Organizations, the State and Sustainable Agricultural Development. London: Routledge

Featherstone, M. and Hepworth, M. (1991) 'The Mask of Ageing and the postmodern life-course', in M. Featherstone, M. Hepworth and B.S.Turner (eds) The Body: Social Process and Cultural Theory, London: Sage

Felson, M. & Clarke, R.V. (1998) Opportunity Makes the Thief, London: Home Office

Felson, M. (1998) Crime and Everyday Life (2nd edn), Thousand Oaks: Pine Forge Press

Felson, M. (2002) Crime and Everyday Life (3rd edn), London: Sage

Ferguson, C. (2015) 'Are Video Games Really that Bad?' Horizon, BBC

Ferguson, N. (2011) Civilisation: the West and the Rest, London: Penguin

Fesbach, S. and Sanger, J.L. (1971) Television and Aggression, San Francisco: Jessey-Bass

Festinger, L. A. (1957) A Theory of Dissonance, Stanford, CA: Stanford University Press

Feuerbach, L. (1854) The Essence of Christianity. London: John Chapman

Feyerabend, P. (1975) Against Method, London: New Left Review Editions

Field, C. (2010) 'Zion's People: Profile of English Nonconformity', Available at: www.brin.ac.uk

Fields, G. S. (2014) Self-Employment and Poverty in Developing Countries, IZA World of Labor

Firestone, S. (1970) The Dialectic of Sex: The Case for Feminist Revolution, New York: Bantam Books

Fisher, W, F. (1997) 'DOING GOOD? The Politics and Antipolitics of NGO Practices', Annual Review of Anthropology. 26. pp. 439-464

Fiske, J (1987) Television Culture, London: Methuen

Fitzpatrick, T. (2011) Welfare Theory: An Introduction to the Theoretical Debates, Basingstoke: Palgrave Macmillan

Flew, T. (2007) Understanding Global Media, Basingstoke: Palgrave

Foster, P. (2004) 'Globalising Greenwash', New Internationalist, March

Foster-Carter, A. (1993) 'Development', in Haralambos, M. (ed.) Developments in Sociology, Vol 9, Ormskirk: Causeway Press

Foucault, M. (1977) Discipline and Punish: The Birth of the Prison, London: Allen Lane

Frank, A. (1967) Capitalism and Underdevelopment in Latin America: Historical Studies of Chile and Brazil. New York: Monthly Review Press

Frank, A.G. (1971) The Sociology of Development and the Underdevelopment of Sociology, London: Pluto Press

Franklin, B. (1997) Newszak and the News Media. London: Arnold

Freedland, J. (2015) 'Religion is like sex – it can be absurd, but it works' The Guardian, 26 September 2015

Freedman, D. (2010) 'The political economy of the 'new' news environment', in N. Fenton (ed) New Media, Old News. London: Sage

Freire, P. (1972) Pedagogy of the Oppressed. Harmondsworth: Penguin

Freston, P. (2008) 'Researching the Heartland of Pentecostalism: Latin Americans at Home and Abroad' Fieldwork in Religion 3(2)

Friedan, B. (1963) The Feminine Mystique, New York: Norton & Co

Friedman, L. M. (1999) The Horizontal Society, New Haven: Yale University Press

Friedman, S. and Laurison, D. (2014) 'Introducing the "Class" Ceiling', Available at: www.lse.ac.uk/sociology/

Friedman, T. (2000) The Lexus and the Olive Tree, London: Collins

Frobel et al. (1979) The New International Division of Labour, Cambridge: Cambridge University Press

Frobel et al. (1980) The New International Division of Labour: Structural Unemployment in Industrialised Countries and industrialisation in Developing Countries. Cambridge: Cambridge University Press

Frobel, F. et al. (1980) The New International Division of Labour, Cambridge: Cambridge University Press

Fuchs, C. (2014) Social Media: a critical introduction, London: Sage

Fulcher, J. and Scott, J. (1999) Sociology, Oxford: Oxford University Press

Furlong, A., Cartmel, F., Biggart, A., Sweeting, H. and West, P. (2006) "Social class in an 'individualised' society", Sociology Review, 15(4)

Gaffney, D. and Baumberg, B. (2014) Dismantling the Barriers to Social Mobility, London: Touchstone Extra, TUC

Galeano, E (1992) Open Veins of Latin America, New York: Monthly Press Review

Galtung, J and Ruge, M, H. (1970) 'The structure of foreign news', in J. Tunstall (ed.) Media Sociology: A Reader, London: Constable

Garrod, J. (2011) 'In the news: social mobility', Sociology Review, 20(4)

Gauntlett, D. (2008) Media, Gender and Identity: An Introduction (2nd edn), London: Routledge

Gerbner, G et al. (1986) Television's Mean World: Violence profile No. 14–15, Philadelphia: Annandale School of Communications, University of Pennsylvania

Gereffi, G. (1994) 'Rethinking development theory: insights from East Asia and Latin America', in A. Douglas-Kincaid and A. Portes (eds) Comparative National Development: Society and Economy in the New Global Order, North Carolina: University of North Carolina Press

Gerth, H.H and Mills, C.W. (1948) From Max Weber: Essays in Sociology, London: Routledge and Kegan Paul

Giddens, A. (1973) The Class Structure of the Advanced Societies, London: Hutchinson

Giddens, A. (1979) 'Positivism and its Critics' in Bottomore, T. & Nisbet, R. (eds) A History of Sociological Analysis, London: Heinemann (in the text this is referenced as 1 1978 text)

Giddens, A. (1984) The Constitution of Society Cambridge: Polity

Giddens, A. (1990) The Consequences of Modernity, Cambridge: Polity

Giddens, A. (1999) A Runaway World? The BBC Reith Lectures, London: BBC Radio 4, BBC Education

Giddens, A. (1999) The Third Way - The Renewal of Social Democracy. Cambridge: Polity

Giddens, A. (2002) *Runaway World* (2nd edn), London: Profile Books

Giddens, A. (2013) *Sociology* (7ᵗʰ edn) Cambridge: Polity

Giddens, A. and Diamond, P. (2005) *The New Egalitarianism*, Cambridge: Polity

Gill, B. (2009) 'New Ethnic Identities', *Sociology Review*, 19(1).

Gill, R. (1998) Is Religious Belief Declining in Britain? *Journal for the Scientific Study of Religion* 37(3) pp. 507-516

Gillat-Ray, S. (2010) *Muslims in Britain: An Introduction*. Cambridge: Cambridge University Press

Gilleard, C.J. and Higgs, P. (2000) *Cultures of Ageing: Self, Citizen and the Body*, Harlow: Prentice Hall

Gillmor, D. (2006) *We the Media: Grassroots Journalism By the People, For the People*. Sebastapol: O'Reilly Media

Glaad (2015) 'Glaad Studio Responsibility Index 2015', Available at: www.glaad.org/sri/2015

Glasgow University Media Group (GUMG) (1981) *Bad News*, London: Routledge

Glock, C and Stark, R. (1965) *Religion and Society in Tension*. Chicago: Rand McNally

Glock, C, Y. (1964) 'The Role of Deprivation in the Origin and Evolution of Religious Groups' in *Religion and Social Conflict* ed. Lee, R and Marty, M. Oxford: Oxford University Press

Glover, C. (2010) *Crime and Inequality*. Collumpton: Willan Press

Goffman A. (2014) *On the Run: Fugitive Life In an American City*, Chicago: University of Chicago Press

Goffman, E (1961) *Asylums*, London: Anchor Books

Goffman, E. (1968) *Asylums*, Harmondsworth: Penguin

Goldthorpe, J. E. (1975) *The Sociology of the Third World: Disparity and Involvement* Cambridge: Cambridge University Press

Goldthorpe, J.H. (1980) *Social Mobility and Class Structure in Modern Britain*, Oxford: Clarendon Press

Goldthorpe, J.H. (2012) Understanding – and Misunderstanding – Social Mobility in Britain. Barnett Papers in Social Research, 2/2012, Oxford: University of Oxford

Goldthorpe, J.H. and Mills, C. (2008) 'Trends in intergenerational class mobility in modern Britain: evidence from national surveys, 1972-2005', *National Institute Economic Review*, 205

Gomm, R. (1982) *Handbook for Sociology Teachers*. London: Heinemann

Goodhew, D. (2012) *Church Growth in Britain: 1980 to the Present*. London: Routledge

Gorard, S. (2008) Researching social mobility, *Sociology Review*, 18(1) pp. 26-29

Gordon, D. (1976) 'Class and the economics of crime' in Chambliss, W.J. & Mankoff, M. (eds.) *Whose Law? What Order? A Conflict Approach to Criminology*, New York: Wiley

Gordon, O. (2015) 'He's not a list of characteristics. He's my son', *The Guardian* 17th October

Gouldner, A (1970) *The Coming Crisis of Western Sociology*. New York: Basic Books

Gouldner, A, W. (1973) *For Sociology: Renewal and Critique in Sociology Today*. Harmondsworth: Penguin

Gouldner, A.W. (1968) 'The sociologist as partisan: sociology and the welfare state', *The American Sociologist*, May

Gouldner, A.W. (1968) *The Coming of Western Sociology*. New York: Basic Books

Gramsci, A. (1971) *Selections from the Prison Notebooks*, London: Lawrence and Wishart

Greeley, A. (1972) *Unsecular Man*, New York: Schocken Books, Inc

Green, E. and Singleton, C. (2013) 'Gendering the Digital: The Impact of Gender and Technology Perspectives on the Sociological Imagination', in *Digital Sociology*, ed by Orton-Johnson, K & Prior, N. Basingstoke: Palgrave

Green, P. & Ward, T. (2012) 'State Crime: A Dialectical View' in Maguire, M., Morgan, R. & Reiner, R. (eds) (2012) *The Oxford Handbook of Criminology* (5ᵗʰ edn) Oxford: Oxford University Press

Green, P. (2010) 'The state, terrorism and crimes against humanity' in Muncie, J., Talbot, D. & Walters, R. (eds) *Crime: Local and Global*, Cullompton, Willan Publishing

Greenfield, G. "Free Market Freefall: Declining Agricultural Commodity Prices and the 'Market Access' Myth", Focus on Trade, No 100, June 2004, pp.20-28

Greengross, S. (2004) 'Why ageism must be eradicated', BBC News, 07 December

Greenslade, R. (2005) *Seeking Scapegoats: The coverage of asylum in the UK press*, Information Centre about Asylums and Refugees (ICAR)

Greer, C. & Reiner, R. (2012) 'Mediated mayhem: media, crime criminal justice' in in Maguire, M., Morgan, R. & Reiner, R. (eds) (2012) *The Oxford Handbook of Criminology*(5ᵗʰ edn), Oxford: Oxford University Press

Greer, G. (2000) *The Whole Woman*. London: Anchor Books

Grint, K. and Nixon, D. (2015) *The Sociology of Work*, Cambridge: Polity

GSMA (2014) The Mobile Economy: Sub-Saharan Africa 2014, Available at: www.gsmamobileeconomyafrica.com

Hader L. T. (2011) 'Start the Twitter revolution without me', Cato Institute Blog, vol.2011. Available at: www.cato.org

Hakim, C. (1979) *Occupational Segregation*, Department of Employment Research Paper No 9, London: HMSO

Hakim, C. (2000) *Work: Lifestyle Choices in the 21ˢᵗ Century*, Oxford: Oxford University Press

Haleem, H, A. (2003) 'Experiences, Needs and Potentials of New Muslim Women in Britain.' In *Muslim Women in the United Kingdom and Beyond*. Ed. by Benn, T and Jawad, H. Leiden: Brill

Hales, J. Nevill, C., Pudney S. and Tipping, S. (2009) *Longitudinal analysis of the Offending, Crime and Justice Survey 2003–06* London: Home Office

Halevy, E. (1927) *A History of the English People in 1815*, London: Unwin

Hall, C.M. (2007). Pro-poor tourism: Do 'tourism exchanges benefit primarily the countries of the south'? Current Issues in Tourism, 10(2-3), 111-118

Hall, S. (1973) *Encoding and Decoding in the Television Discourse*, Birmingham: University of Birmingham, Centre for Contemporary Cultural Studies

Hall, S. (1978) *Policing the Crisis*, London: Macmillan

Hall, S. *et al.* (1978) *Policing the Crisis: Mugging, the State and Law and Order*, London: Palgrave Macmillan

Hall, S., Winlow, S. & Ancrum, C. (2008) *Criminal Identities and Consumer Culture*, Cullompton: Willan Press

Hamilton, M. (1998) *Sociology and the World's Religions*. Basingstoke: MacMillan

Hamilton, M. (2001) *The Sociology of Religion* (2nd edn) London: Routledge

Hamilton, M. (2012) *The Sociology of Religion: Theoretical and Comparative Perspectives*. London: Routledge

Hammersley, M. (1992) 'By what criteria should ethnographic research be judged?', in M. Hammersley, *What's Wrong with Ethnography?*, London: Routledge

Hammersley, M. (2015) 'Methodology: The Essence of Sociology?' in Holborn. M. (ed) *Contemporary Sociology*, Cambridge: Polity

Hancock, G. (1989) *Lords of Poverty*, New York: Atlantic Monthly Press

Hannerz, U. (1992) *Cultural Complexity: Studies in the Social Organisation of Meaning*, New York: Columbia University Press

Haralambos, M. & Holborn, M. (2013) *Sociology Themes and Perspectives* (8th edn) London: Collins

Harcup, T. and O'Neill, D. (2001) 'What is News? Galtung and Ruge Revisited', *Journalism Studies*, 2 (2): 261-280

Harding, S. (1986) *The Science Question in Feminism*, Ithaca & London: Cornell University Press

Haridakis, P., & Hanson, G. (2009) 'Social interaction and co-viewing with YouTube: Blendingmass communication receptions and social connection', *Journal of Broadcasting & Electronic Media*, 53

Harris, G (1989) *The Sociology of Development*, London: Longman

Harrison, D. (2008). Pro-poor tourism: A critique. *Third World Quarterly*, 29(5)

Harrison, J. (2006) *News*, Abingdon: Routledge

Harrison, P. (1990) *Inside the Third World: The Anatomy of Poverty* (2nd edn), Harmondsworth: Penguin

Hartmann, T. & Klimmt, C., 2006. Gender and Computer Games: Exploring Females' Dislikes. *Journal of Computer-Mediated Communication*, 11(4), pp. 910–931

Hartnett, O. (1990) *The Sex-Role System* in P. Mayes (ed) Gender, London: Longman

Harvey, D. *The Condition of Postmodernity: An Enquiry into the Origins of Cultural Change*. Oxford: Wiley Blackwell

Harvey, L. (1990) *Critical Social Research*, London: Unwin Hyman

Harvey, S. (2008) *Maintaining and Strengthening Public Service Broadcasting: The Limits of Competition. A response to Ofcom's Second Review of Public Service Broadcasting, Phase Two: Preparing for the Digital Future*, London: AHRB Centre for British Film and Television Studies

Haslam, P. *et al.* (2012) *Introduction to International Development: Approaches, Actors and Issues* (2nd edn). Oxford: Oxford University Press

Hayek, F. A. (1944/1986) *The Road to Serfdom*, London: Routledge

Hayter. T. (1981) *The Creation of World Poverty* (2nd edn), London: Pluto Press

Hayward, K.J, and Yar, M. (2006) 'The "Chav" phenomenon: consumption, media and the construction of a new underclass', *Crime, Media, Culture*, 2(1), pp.9–28

Hedderman, C. (2010) 'Government policy on women offenders: Labour's legacy and the Coalition's Challenge' *Punishment and Society* 12(4)

Hedderman, C. (2015) 'Gender and Criminal Justice' *Sociology Review* Feb. 2015, 24(3)

Heelas, P. (1996) *The New Age Movement: Religion, Culture, and Society in the Age of Postmodernity*. Hoboken: Wiley-Blackwell

Heelas, P. (2004) *The Spiritual Revolution: Why Religion Is Giving Way to Spirituality*. Oxford: Blackwell

Heelas, P. (2008) *Spiritualities of Life: New Age Romanticism and Consumptive Capitalism*. Oxford: Blackwell

Heelas, P. and Woodhead, L. (2005) *The Spiritual Revolution: Why Religion is Giving Way to Spirituality*. New York: Wiley-Blackwell

Heidensohn, F. (1985) *Women and Crime*, London: Macmillan

Heidensohn, F., & Silvestri, M. (2012) 'Gender and Crime' in Maguire, M., Morgan, R. & Reiner, R. (eds) (2012) *The Oxford Handbook of Criminology* (5th edn), Oxford: Oxford University Press

Heintz-Knowles (2002) *The Reflection on the Screen: Television's Image of Children*, Oakland, CA: Children Now

Held, D *et al.* (2003) *The Global Transformations Reader: an introduction to the Globalization Debate*. Cambridge: Polity

Helpser, E. (2011) - The Emergence of a Digital Underclass: Digital Policies in the UK and Evidence for Inclusion. Available at: www.scribd.com

Henderson (2015) 'Serious issues for George Osborne on China's role in the UK's nuclear future'. Available at: theconversation.com

Herman, E and Chomsky, N. (1988) *Manufacturing Consent*, New York: Pantheon Books

Hervieu-Léger, D. (2000) *Religion as a Chain of Memory*. Cambridge: Polity

Hilary, J. (2013) *The Poverty of Capitalism: Economic Meltdown and the Struggle for What Comes Next*. London: Pluto Press

Hill, K. A and Hughes, J. E. (1997) 'Computer-mediated political communication: The Usenet and political communities', *Political Communication*, 14, pp.3-14

Hobbs, D. & Dunningham, C. (1998) 'Glocal organized crime: context and pretext' in Ruggiero, V., South, N. and Taylor, I. (eds) *The New European Criminology* London: Routledge

Holborn, M (2015) *Contemporary Sociology*. Cambridge: Polity

Holborn, M. (2005) 'Towards a Sociology of Homicide' in Holborn, M. (ed) *Developments in Sociology: San Annual Review Volume 21* Ormskirk: Causeway Press

Holden, A. (2002) *Jehovah's Witnesses: Portrait of a Contemporary Religious Movement*, London/New York: Routledge

Holmes, C. and Mayhew, K. (2012) *The Changing Shape of the UK Job Market*. London: Resolution Foundation

Hood, R. (1992) *Race and sentencing*, Oxford: Clarendon Press

Hoogvelt, A. (2001) *Globalisation and the Post Colonial World* (2nd edn), Basingstoke: Palgrave

hooks, bell (1981) *Ain't I a Woman: Black Women and Feminism*. New York: South End Press

Hopkins, N and Kahani-Hopkins, V (2004) Identity Construction and British Muslims' Political Activity: Beyond Rational Actor Theory. *British Journal of Social Psychology*. 43(3) pp. 339-356

Horkheimer, M. (1974) *Eclipse of Reason*, Oxford: Oxford University Press

Hoselitz, B. (1960) *Sociological Aspects of Economic Growth*, Chicago: Chicago Free Press

Houchin, R. (2005) Social Exclusion and Imprisonment in Scotland: A Report, Glasgow, Glasgow Caledonian University [online]. Available at: www.scotpho.org.uk

HSE (2015) 'Health and Safety Statistics 2013/14' [online] Available at: www.hse.gov.uk/statistics

Huesmann, L.R. *et al.* (2003) 'Longtitudinal Relations Betweem Children's Exposure to TV Violence and Their Aggressive and Violent Behavior in Yioung Adulthood: 1977-1992. *Developmental Psychology*, 39(2), pp. 201-221

Hulme, D and Edwards, M. (1997) *NGOs, States and Donors: Too Close for Comfort*. London: St Martin's Press

Human Rights Watch (2015)*World Report 2015 Saudi Arabia* [online] Available at: www.hrw.org/world-report

Hunt, J. (2004) 'Gender and development', in D. Kingsbury, J. Remenyi, J. McKay and J. Hunt (eds) *Key Issues in Development*, Basingstoke: Palgrave

Huntington, S. (1993) 'The Clash of Civilisations', *Foreign Affairs*, 72

Hutton, W. (2010), 'Of course class still matters', *The Observer*, 10 January

Hyde, M. (2001) 'Disabled people in Britain today: discrimination, social disadvantage and empowerment', *Sociology Review*, 10(4) pp 8-11

Inequality Briefing (2015) Available at: http://inequalitybriefing.org/

Inglehart, R and Baker, W (2000) 'Modernization, Cultural Change, and the Persistence of Traditional Values', *American Sociological Review* 65(1), pp.20-51

Inkeles, A and Smith, D. (1974) *Becoming Modern: Individual Changes in Six Developing Countries*, Cambridge MA: Harvard University Press

Itzoe, M. A. (1995) *A Regulatory Scheme for Cyberporn*, University of Indiana

Iyengar, S and Simon, A. (1993) 'News Coverage of the Gulf Crisis and Public Opnion: A Study of Agenda-Setting, Priming and Framing', *Communication Research*, 20(3), pp. 365-383

Jacobs, J. (1991) 'Gender and Power in New Religious Movements: A Feminist Discourse on the Social Scientific Study of Religion' *Religion* 21: 345-56

Jacobs, S. (2008) 'Out of Africa' The Guardian, 24/4/2008

Jenkins, H. (2008) *Convergence Culture: Where Old and New Media Collide*. New York: New York University Press

Jenkins, H., Ford, S., and Green, J. (2013) *Spreadable media: Creating value and meaning in a networked culture*, New York: New York University Press

Jewkes, Y. (2015) *Media and Crime: Third edition* London: Sage

Jivraj, S. (2012) How has ethnic diversity grown: 1991-2001-2011? ESRC Centre on Dynamics of Ethnicity, www.ethnicity.ac.uk

Johnson, J *et al.* (2002) 'Television Viewing and Aggressive Behaviour During Adolescence and Adulthood' *Science*, 295 (5564), pp. 2468-2471

Jones, O. (2011) *Chavs: The Demonisation of the Working Class*, London: Verso

Jones, O. (2014) *The Establishment: And How they Get Away With It*, London: Penguin Random House

Jones, S. (2009) *Criminology* (4th edn) London: Butterworths

Jones, T., Maclean, B. and Young, J. (1986) *The Islington Crime Survey*. Aldershot: Gower

Joyce, P. (2006) *Criminal Justice: An Introduction to Crime and the Criminal Justice System*, Cullompton: Willan Publishing

JRF. (2014) 'Monitoring Poverty and Social Exclusion', November

Kaldor, M. (2006) *New and Old Wars: Organized Violence in a Global Era* (2nd edn), Cambridge: Polity Press

Kaplan, A. (1964) *The Conduct of Inquiry: Methodology for Behavioural Science*. San Francisco: Chandler Publishing Company

Karat, P. (1988) *Foreign Funding and the Philosophy of Volunatry Organizations: A Factor in Imperialist Strategy*. New Delhi: National Book Centre

Kassim, S. (2012) 'Twitter Revolution: How the Arab Spring Was Helped By Social Media', Available at: www.mic.com/articles

Katz, E and Lazarsfeld, P. (1965) *Personal Influence*, New York: Free Press

Kaufman, D. (1991) *Rachel's Daughters: Newly Orthodox Jewish Women*. New Brunswick, NJ: Rutgers University Press

Kaur-Singh, K. (1994) 'Sikhism', in J. Holm and J. Bowker (eds) *Women in Religion*, London: Pinter

Kautsky, K. (1953) *Foundations of Christianity*, New York: Russell

Keeble, R.L. and Mair, J. (eds) (2012) *The Phone Hacking Scandal: Journalism on Trial*, Abramis, Bury St. Edmunds

Keen (1995) 'When war itself is privatised', *Times Literary Supplement*, Dec

Keen, A (2008) *The Cult of the Amateur: How Blogs, MySpace, YouTube and the rest of Today's User-Generated Media Are Killing Our Culture and Economy*, London: Nicholas Brealey

Kellner, D. (1999) in B. Smart (ed.) *Resisting McDonaldisation*, London: Sage

Kennedy (2014) 'Don't get caught by the man in the middle', *The Sunday Times*, 2 February

Kersley, H. and Shaheen, F. (2014) Addressing Economic Inequality at Root, London, New Economic Foundation

Kilbourne (1995) 'Beauty and the beast of advertising', in G. Dines and M. Humez (eds) *Gender, Race and Class in Media*, Thousand Oaks: Sage Publications

Kilby, P. (2001) quoted in D. Kingsbury, J. Remenyi, J. McKay and J. Hunt (eds) *Key Issues in Development*, Basingstoke: Palgrave

Kingsbury *et al.* (2004) *Key Issues in Development*, Basingstoke: Palgrave

Klapper, J. T. (1960) *The Effects of Mass Communication*, New York: Free Press

Klein, N. (2001) *No Logo*. London: Flamingo

Korten, D. (1995) 'Steps towards people-centered development: vision and strategies', in N. Heyzer, J.V. Ricker and A.B. Quizon (eds) *Government–NGO Relations in Asia: Prospects and Challenges for People-centred Development*, Basingstoke: Palgrave

Korten, D. (1990) *Getting to the 21st: Voluntary Action and the Global Agenda.* West Hartford: Kumarian Press

Kuhn, T.S. (1962/1970) *The Structure of Scientific Revolutions* (2nd edn), Chicago: University of Chicago Press

Kurtz, W. and Kurtz, M. (2016) *Women, War and Violence: Topography, Resistance and Hope.* Westport: Praeger

Kynaston, D. (2008) 'The road to meritocracy is blocked by private schools', *The Guardian*, 22 February

Lakatos, I. (1970) 'Falsification and the methodology of scientific research programmes', in I. Lakatos and A. Musgrave (eds) *Criticism and the Growth of Knowledge*, Cambridge: Cambridge University Press

Landes (2008) (1998?) *The Wealth and Poverty of Nations*, London: Little Brown and Company

Lansley, S. (2011) *Making a Contribution: Social Security for the Future*, London: TUC

Latour, B. & Woolgar, S. (1979) *Laboratory Life: The Social Construction of Scientific Facts*, London, Sage

Lauzen, M. (2015) 'Boxed In: Portrayals of Female Characters and Employment of Behind-the-Scenes Women in 2014-15 Prime-time Television', Avialable at: http://womenintvfilm.sdsu.edu

Law, I. (2002) *Race in the News*, Basingstoke: Palgrave

Lawes, C. (2009) *Faith and Darwin: Harmony, conflict or confusion?* London: Theos

Lawler, S. (2005) 'Introduction: class, culture, identity', *Sociology* 2005, 39(5)

Lea, J. and Young, J. (1984) *What is to be Done About Law and Order?* (2nd edn) London: Pluto Press

Leach, E. (1982) *Social Anthropology*. Oxford: Oxford University Press

Leach, E. (1988) *Culture and Communication*, Cambridge: Cambridge University Press

Lee et al. (2007) 'Representation of older adults in television adverts', *Journal of Ageing Studies*, 21, pp.23–30

Legrain, P. (2002) *Open World: the Truth about Globalisation*. London: Abacus

Leonard Cheshire Disability (2014) *Disability facts and figures*, Available at: www.leonardcheshire.org

Leonard, M. (1992) 'Women and Development', *Sociology Review*, Sept

Levene, T. (2007) 'HSBC faced down on Facebook', *Guardian* 1st September

Levitt, P (2001) *The Transnational Villagers*. Berkeley: University of California Press

LGBT.co.uk, *LGBT Character Portrayal in Media*, Avialble at www.lgbt.co.uk/leisure

Li, N. and Kirkup, G. (2007) 'Gender and cultural differences in Internet use: a study of China and the UK', *Computers and Education*, 48(2), Feb

Li, Y. and Devine, F. (2011) 'Is social mobility really declining?', *Sociological Research Online*, 16(3)

Liebling, A & Crewe, B. (2012) 'Prison life, penal power and prison effects' in Maguire, M., Morgan, R. & Reiner, R. (eds) (2012) *The Oxford Handbook of Criminology* (5th edn), Oxford: Oxford University Press

Ligali (2006) www.ligali.org/

Livingstone, S. (2009) *Children and the Internet: Great Expectations, Challenging Realities*, Cambridge: Polity Press

Lizardo, O. (2008) 'Globalization and culture: A sociological perspective', Centre for the Critical Study of Global Power and Politics, Working Paper CSGP 07/8 Trent University, Peterborough, Ontario, Canada www.trentu.ca/globalpolitics

Llosa, M. V. (2000) 'The culture of liberty', *Foreign Policy*, 5, pp.66–72

Lockwood, D. (1966) 'Sources of variation in working class images of society', *Sociological Review*, 14(3), pp. 249-267

London School of Economics/The Guardian (2012) *Reading the Riots: Investigating England's Summer of Disorder.* Available at: http://eprints.lse.ac.uk

Lorber, J. (2010) *Gender Inequality: Feminist Theories and Politics*, Oxford: Oxford University Press

Lugg, C (2000) *For God and Country: Conservatism and American School Policy.* Bern: Switzerland

Lull, J. (1995) *Media, Communication, Culture: A global approach*, New York: Columbia University Press

Lynch, G. (2008) 'Religious Experience and Popular Culture: Developing a Critical Framework of Enquiry' in *At the Crossroads of Art and Religion*. Ed. by Zock, T. Leuvan: Peeters

Lyon, D. (2000) *Jesus in Disneyland: Religion in Postmodern Times*, Cambridge: Polity Press

Lyotard, J. F. (1984) *The Post-Modern Condition: A Report on Knowledge*, Manchester: University of Manchester Press

M. Hammersley, *What's Wrong with Ethnography?*, London: Routledge

Maduro, O. (1982) *Religion and Social Conflicts*, New York: Orbis Books

Malešević. S. (2015) 'Violence, Coercion and Human Rights: Understanding Organized Brutality in Holborn, M. (ed) *Contemporary Sociology*, Cambridge: Polity Press

Manning, P. (2001) *News and News Sources: A Critical Introduction*, London: Sage

Marcuse, H. (1964) *One-Dimensional Man*, Beacon Press. London: Routledge

Marmot, M. (2010) *Fair Society, Healthy Lives*, www.ucl.ac.uk/marmotreview

Marren, P. (2015) 'Overseas Development Aid: Is it Working? Patrick Marren in From the Local to the Global: Key Issues in Development Studies (3rd Edn) by G. McCann & S. McCloskey, London: Pluto Press

Marsh, I and Keating, M (2006) *Sociology: Making Sense of Society* (3rd edn), New Jersey: Prentice Hall

Marshall, G. (1982) *In Search of the Spirit of Capitalism: Max Weber and the Protestant Ethic Thesis*, London: Hutchison

Martin, D. (1990) *Tongues of Fire: The Explosion of Protestantism in Latin America*. Oxford: Blackwell

Martin, D. (2005) *On Secularization: Towards a Revised General Theory*. Aldershot: Ashgate

Martin, W. (2005) *With God on Our Side: The Rise of the Religious Right in America*. New York: Broadway Books

Martinez-Alier, J. (2013) 'What is de-growth? From an Activist Slogan to a Social Movement' *Environmental Values*, 22, pp. 191-215

Martinson, J., Cochrane, K., Ryan, S., Corrigan, T. and Bawdon, F. (2012) 'Seen But Not Heard: How Women Make Front Page News, Women in Journalism,' Available at: womeninjournalism.co.uk

Marx, K. (1844) *Selected Writings* (2000 edn), Oxford: Oxford University Press

Marx, K. (1845) 'The German Ideology', extract in T. Bottomore and M. Rubel (eds, 1963 edn) *Karl Marx: Selected Writings in Sociology and Social Philosophy*, Harmondsworth: Penguin

Marx, K. (1867/1973) *Capital: A Critique of Political Economy*, Harmondsworth: Penguin

Matthews, R. (1992) 'Replacing 'Broken Windows': crime, incivilities and urban change' in Matthews, R. and Young, J. (eds) *Issues in Realist criminology*, London: Sage

Matthews, R. (1993) 'Squaring up to crime' *Sociology Review*, 2(3)

McAndrew, S. (2011) Church Attendance in England 1980-2005. Available at: www.brin.ac.uk

McCabe and Martin (2005) *School Violence, the Media, and Criminal Justice Responses*, York: Peter Lang Publishing

McChesney, R (2002) *Our Media, Not Theirs: the Democratic Struggle Against Corporate Media.* New York: Seven Stories Press

McChesney, R. (2000) *Rich Media, Poor Democracy: Communication Politics in Dubious Times.* New York: The New Press

McChesney, R. (2002) in K. Borjesson (ed.) *Into the Buzzsaw: Leading Journalists Expose the Myth of a Free Press*, Amherst, NY: Prometheus

McCloskey, S. (2015) *Development Education in Policy and Practice.* London: Palgrave Macmillan

McKay, H. (2000) 'The globalisation of culture', in D.Held (2000) *A Globalising World? Culture, Economics, Politics*, London: Routledge

McKay, J. (2004) 'Reassessing development theory: "modernization" and beyond', in D. Kingsbury, J. Remenyi, J. McKay and J. Hunt (eds) *Key Issues in Development*, Basingstoke: Palgrave

McKendrick, J.H. *et al.* (2008) *The Media, Poverty and Public Opinion in the UK*, York: Joseph Rowntree Foundation

McKnight, A. (2015) 'Downward mobility and opportunity hoarding', Available at: www.gov.uk

McLaughlin, E. (2001) 'State Crime' in McLaughlin, E. & Muncie, J. (eds) *The Sage Dictionary of Criminology*, London: Sage

McMahon (2015) 'Have you got FOBO? – What obsessive-compulsive phone checking is doing to your brain', *The Times*, July 18

McMichael, P. (2011) *Development and Social Change: A Global Perspective.* New York: SAGE

McNamara, J.R. (2006) *Media and Male Identity: The Making and Remaking of Men*, Basingstoke: Palgrave

McQuail, D. (1992) *Mass Communication Theory* (5th edn), London: Sage

McRobbie, A. & Thorton, S. (1995) Rethinking 'Moral Panic' for multi-mediated social worlds, *British Journal of Sociology*, 46(4)

Mead, G.H. (1934) *Mind, Self and Society* (ed. C. Morris) Chicago: University of Chicago Press

Merton, R. (1957) *Social Theory and Social Structure*. New York: Free Press

Messner, M. and DiStaso, M.W. (2008) 'The Source Cycle', *Journalism Studies*, 9(3), pp. 447-463

Meyer, B. (1999) *Globalisation and Identity: Dialectics of Flow and Closure*. Oxford: Blackwell

Micklethwait, J and Wooldridge, A (2010) *God is Back: How the Global Rise of Faith is Changing the World*. London: Penguin

Miles, R. (1989) *Racism*, London: Routledge

Miliband, R. (1973) *Parliamentary Socialism* (2nd ed), London: Merlin

Miller W. B. (1958) 'Lower-class culture as a generating milieu of gang delinquency' *Journal of Social Issues* 14(3)

Miller, A.S. and Hoffman, J.P. (1995) 'Risk and Religion: an Explanation of Gender Differences in Religiosity', *Journal for the Scientific Study of Religion*, 34, pp.63–75

Millett, K. (1970) *Sexual Politics*, New York: Doubleday

Mills, E. (2014) 'Why do the best jobs go to men?', *British Journalism Review*, 25(3), pp. 17-23

Millwood Hargrave. (2003) 'How Children Interpret Screen Violence', BBC, Available at: bbc.co.uk

Ministry of Justice. (2014) *Statistics on Women and the Criminal Justice System 2013*, London: Ministry of Justice

Ministry of Justice. (2015) Prison Population Figures [online] available at: www.gov.uk

Mirza (2007) quoted in 'Revealed: Racism in Schools', *Channel 4 News*, 24 May

Mirza, H. (ed) (1997) *Black British Feminism: A Reader*, London: Routledge

Modelski, G. (2003) *World Cities: 3000 to 2000*, Faros: 2000

Modood, T. (1992) *Not Easy Being British: Colour, Culture and Citizenship*, Runnymede Trust and Trentham Books

Modood, T. (1997) *Ethnic Minorities in Britain: Diversity and Disadvantage. The Fourth National Survey of Ethnic Minorities*. London: Policy Studies Institute

Mohanty, C. (1997) 'Under western eyes: feminist scholarship and colonial discourse', in, N. Visuanathan, L. Duggan, L. Nisonoff and N.Wiergersma (eds), *The Women, Gender and Development Reader*, London: Zed Books

Molyneux, M. (1981) 'Women in socialist societies: problems of theory and practice', in K.Young et al. (eds) *Of Marriage and the Market: Women's Subordination in International Perspective*, London: CSE Books

Moore, K., Mason, P., and Lewis, J. (2008) 'Images of Islam in the UK: The Representation of British Muslims in the National Print News Media 2000-2008', Cardiff School of Journalism, Media and Cultural Studies, and Channel 4 Dispatches

Moosa, E (2010) Civil Religion and Beyond. Available at: http://blogs.ssrc.org/tif/2010/01/22/civil-religion-and-beyond/

Mordaunt, S., Rake, K., Wanless, H. and Mitchell, R. (2003) *One in Four*, Age Concern

Morgan, R, & Liebling, A. (2007) 'Imprisonment: An Expanding Scene' in

Maguire, M., Morgan, R & Reiner, R. (eds) *The Oxford Handbook of Criminology* (4th edn), Oxford : Oxford University Press

Morley, D. (1980) *The Nationwide Audience*, London: BFI

Morris, J. (1992) *Disabled Lives: Many Voices, One Message*, BBC Education

Morrison, D.E. (1999) *Defining Violence: The Search for Understanding*, Luton: University of Luton Press

Moyo, D. (2009) *Dead Aid: Why aid is not working and how there is another way for Africa*. London: Penguin

Mulvey, L. (1975) 'Visual pleasures and narrative cinema', *Screen*, 16(3)

Murdock, G, P. (1949) *Social Structure*. New York: The Free Press

Murray, C. (1984) *Losing Ground: American Social Policy 1950-1980*. New York: Basic Books

Murthi, M, et al. (1995) 'Mortality, Fertility and Gender Bias in India: A District-Level Analysis', *Population and Development Review*, 21, pp. 745-82

Murthy, D. (2013) *Twitter: Digital Media and Society Series*. Cambridge: Polity Press

Myrdal, G (1968) *Asian Drama: An Enquiry into the Poverty of Nations*, New York: The Twentieth Century Fund

Nahdi, F. (2003) 'Doublespeak: Islam and the media', *Open Democracy*, 3 Apr

Nairn, T. (1988) *The Enchanted Glass: Britain and its Monarchy*, London: Radius

Nanda, M (2008) 'Rush Hour of the Gods' Available at: newhumanist.org.uk

Narlikar, A. (2005) *The World Trade Organisation: A Very Short Introduction*. Oxford: Oxford University Press

Nelson, G. (1987) *Cults, New Religions and Religious Creativity*. London: Routledge

Nelson, G.K. (1986) 'Religion', in M. Haralambos (ed.) *Developments in Sociology* (Vol. 2), Ormskirk: Causeway Press

Nelson, J. (2014) *Building the future: women in construction*, The Smith Institute

Newburn, T. & Reiner, R. (2012) 'Policing and the Police' in Maguire, M., Morgan, R., and Reiner, R. (2012) *The Oxford Handbook of Criminology* (5th edn) Oxford: Oxford University Press

Newburn, T. (2013) *Criminology* (2nd edn) London: Routledge

Newman, D. (2006) *The Architecture of Stratification: Social Class and Inequality*, London: Sage

Newson, E. (1994) *Video Violence and the Protection of Children*, Report of the Home Affairs Committee, London: HMSO

Ni Chasaide, N (2015) 'Debt Injustice in the Global North and South' in McGann, G and McCloskey, S (eds.) From the Local to the Global: Key Issues in Development Studies, London: Pluto Press

Ní Chasaide, Nessa (2014) speaking at Joint Oireachtas Committee on Foreign Affairs and Trade on 1 April 2014

Niebuhr, R. (1957) *Love and Justice: Selections from the Shorter Writings of Reinhold Niebuhri*. Westminster: John Knox Press

Nomis (2015) 'Labour Market Profile – Great Britain' Available at: www.nomisweb.co.uk

Norris, P and Inglehart, R (2011) *Sacred and Secular: Religion and Politics Worldwide*. Cambridge: Cambridge University Press

O'Beirne, M (2004) *Religion in England and Wales: Findings from the 2001 Home*

Office Citizenship Survey. London: Home Office

O'Connell Davidson, J. and Layder, D. (1994) *Methods, Sex and Madness*, London: Routledge

Oakley, A. (1972) *Sex, Gender and Society* London, Temple Smith

Oakley, A. (1972) *Sex, Gender and Society*, London: Maurice Temple Smith

Oakley, A. (1981) 'Interviewing women: a contradiction in terms', in H. Roberts (ed.) *Doing Feminist Research*, London: Routledge

ODI, (2014) 'Disability Facts and Figures' January

OECD (2015), Income inequality (indicator). doi: 10.1787/459aa7f1-en

Ofcom (2014) 'Adults' Media Use and Attitudes Report'

Ofcom (2015) 'Social Uses and Attitudes Survey'

Oliver, M. (1990) *The Politics of Disablement*, Basingstoke: Macmillan

Olsen, W. and Walby, S. (2004) *Modelling Gender Pay Gaps*, Manchester: Equal Opportunities Commission

Olson, C. K., Kutner, L. A., & Warner, D. E. (2008). The role of violent video game content in adolescent development: Boys' perspectives. *Journal of Adolescent Research*, 23, 55–75

Omolade, S. (2014) *The needs and characteristics of older prisoners: Results from the Surveying Prisoner Crime Reduction* (SPCR) survey. London: Ministry of Justice

ONS (2014) Crime in England and Wales, Year Ending September 2014: Statistical Bulletin. Available at: www.ons.gov.uk

Oppenheim, C. and Harker, L. (1996) *Poverty: The Facts*, London: CPAG

Orbach, S. (1991) *Fat is a Feminist Issue*, London: Hamlyn

Outhwaite, W. (2015) 'Sociological Theory: Formal and Informal' in Holborn, M. (ed) *Contemporary Sociology*, Cambridge: Polity

Packer, C. et al. (2015) 'No lasting legacy: no change in reporting of women's sports in the British print media with the London 2012 Olympics and Paralympics', *Journal of Public Health*, 37(1). pp. 50-56

Pakko, M and Pollard, P (2003) 'Burgernomics: A Big Mac Guide to Purchasing Power Parity', *Review*, pp. 9-28

Pakulski, J. (2001) 'Anti-Class Analysis: social inequality and post-modern trends', in E. O. Wright (ed) *Alternative Foundations of Class Analysis* (pdf online)

Pakulski, J. and Waters, M. (1996) *The Death of Class*, London: Sage

Park, N., Kee, K., & Valenzuela, S. (2009) 'Being immersed in social networking environment: Facebook groups, uses and gratifications, and social outcomes', *CyberPsychology & Behavior*, 12

Parliamentary Office of Science and Technology (2007) 'Ethnicity and Health' Postnote 276, January

Parsons, T (1951) *The Social System*. London: Routledge

Parsons, T (1964a) 'Evolutionary universals in society', *American Sociological Review*, 29 June

Parsons, T. (1949) 'Social Classes and Class Conflict in the Light of Recent Sociological Theory', *American Sociological Review*, 39 (3) pp. 16-26

Parsons, T. (1965) 'Religious perspectives in sociology and social psychology', in W.A. Lessa and E.Z. Vogt (eds) *Reader in Comparative Religion: An Anthropological Approach* (2nd edn), New York: Harper & Row

Paterson, L. and Iannelli, C. (2007) 'Patterns of Absolute and Relative Social Mobility: a Comparative Study of England, Wales and Scotland', *Sociological Research Online*, 12(6)

Patterson, S. (1965) *Dark Strangers*, Harmondsworth: Penguin

Pawson, R. (1992) 'Feminist Methodology' in Haralambos, M. (ed) *Developments in Sociology* Vol. 8. Ormskirk: Causeway Press

Peace, M. (2005) quoted on www.sociologystuff.com

Pearson, R (2001) 'Rethinking gender matters in development' in T. Allen and A. Thomas (2001) *Poverty and Development in the 21st Century*, Oxford: Oxford University Press

Peelo, M., Francis, B., Soothill, K., Pearson, J. & Ackerley, E. (2004) 'Newspaper Reporting and the Public Reporting of Homicide' *British Journal of Criminology* 44(2) pp. 256-75

Peet, R. (2007) Geography of Power: The Making of Global Economic Policy, London: Zed Press

Peet, R., and Hartwick, E. (2015) , *Theories of Development: Contentions, Arguments, Alternatives* (3rd edition) New York: Guilford Press

Perfect, D (2011) 'Religion or Belief', *Equality and Human Rights Commission*, Manchester

Peter, J and Valkenburg, P (2008) 'Adolescents Exposure to Sexually Explicit Internet Material, Sexual Uncertainty, and Attitudes Toward Uncommitted Sexula Exploration—Is There a Link?' , *Communication Research*, 35(5), pp. 579-601

Pew Research Center (2014) 'Cell Phones in Africa: Communication Lifeline', Available at: www.pewglobal.org

Pew Research Centre (2014) Russians Return to Religion, But Not to Church. Available at: www.pewforum.org

Phillips, A. (2010) 'Old Sources: New Bottles' in N. Fenton (ed) *New Media, Old News*, London: Sage

Phillipson, C. (1998) *Reconstructing Old Age*, London: Sage

Philo (2002) 'Circuits of communication and power; recent developments in media sociology', in Holborn, M. (ed) *Developments in Sociology*, Vol. 21, Causeway Press

Philo, G and Miller, D (2005) 'The Sociology of Mass Media: circuits of communication and structures of power' in Holborn, M (ed.) *Contemporary Sociology*. Cambridge: Polity

Philo, G and Miller, D. (2000) *Market Killings: What the free market does and what social scientists can do about it*. London: Routledge

Piacentini, L. and Walters, R. (2006) 'The politicization of youth crime in Scotland and the rise of the "Burberry Court"', *Youth Justice*, 6, pp.43-59

Picketty, T (2014) *Capital in the Twenty-First Century*. Cambridge: Belknap Press

Pierskalla, J and Hollenbach, F (2013) 'Technology and Collective Action: The Effect of Cell Phone Coverage on Political Violence in Africa', *American Political Science Review*, 107(2), pp. 207-224

Pike, S. (2004) *New Age and Neopagan Religions in America*. New York: Colombia University Press

Pilkington, A. (2015) 'Race, Ethnicity and Nationality: The Future of Multiculturalism in a Global Age', in M. Holborn (ed) *Contemporary Sociology*, Cambridge: Polity

Plant, S. (1997) *Zeros and Ones: Digital Women and the New Technoculture*, London: Fourth Estate

Platt, L. (2005) 'The intergenerational social mobility of minority ethnic groups', *BSA Publications*, 39(3)

Platt, L. (2007) *Poverty and Ethnicity in the UK*, JRF

Plummer, K. (2000) *Documents of Life*, Thousand Oaks, CA: Sage

Policy Exchange (2014) 'Moving public services could isolate the elderly'

Policy Exchange (2014) 'Technology Manifesto'

Pollert, A. (1996) "Gender and Class Revisited; Or, The Poverty of 'Patriarchy'", *Sociology* 30(4): 639-659

Poole, E. (2000) 'Media representation and British Muslims', *Dialogue Magazine*, Apr

Popper, K. (1959) *The Logic of Scientific Discovery*, London: Hutchinson

Porritt, J. (1985) *Seeing Green: The Politics of Ecology*, Oxford: Blackwell

Postman, N. (1986) *Amusing Ourselves to Death*, London: Methuen

Power, M. and Stacey, T. (2014). Unfair and unclear: The effects and perception of the UK tax system. London: The Equality Trust

Prison Reform Working Group (2002) *Locked Up Potential A strategy for reforming prisons and rehabilitating prisoners* London: Prison Reform Working Group

Pryce, K. (1979) *Endless Pressure: A Study of West Indian Lifestyles in Bristol.* Harmonsworth: Penguin

Putnam, R and Campbell, E (2010) *American Grace: How Religion Divides and Unites Us*. New York: Schuster & Schuster

Putnam, R. (1995) 'Bowling alone: America's declining social capital', *Journal of Democracy*, (6)1, Jan pp. 65-78

Raacke, J., & Bonds-Raacke, J. (2008) 'MySpace and Facebook: Applying the uses and gratifications theory to exploring friend-networking sites', *CyberPsychology & Behavior*, 11

Radelet, S. (2004) Aid effectiveness and the Millenium Development Goals. *Centre for Global Development*. 39

Rahnema, M. (1997) *The Post Development Reader*, London: Zed Books

Ramos, Raul A., Ferguson, Christopher J., Frailing, Kelly, and Romero-Ramirez, Maria (2013) 'Comfortably Numb or Just Yet Another Movie? Media Violence Exposure Does Not Reduce Viewer Empathy for Victims of Real Violence Among Primarily Hispanic Viewers', *Psychology of Popular Media Culture*, 2(1), pp. 2–10

Rampton, M. (2014) *The Three Waves of Feminism*, Oregon, Pacific University, 23-10-2014

Ray, S., Sharp, E. and Abrams, D. (2006) *Ageism*, London, Age Concern

Raynor, P. (2012) 'Community Penalties, Probation and Offender Management'in Maguire, M., Morgan, R. & Reiner, R. (eds) (2012) *The Oxford Handbook of Criminology* (5th edn), Oxford: Oxford University Press

Redding, G. (1990) *The Spirit of Chinese Capitalism*. Berlin: De Guyter

Rees (1996) quoted in M. Wackernagel and W. Rees, *Our Ecological Footprint: Reducing Human Impact On Human Health*, Gabriola Island, BC: New Society Publishers

Reese, S and Lewis, S (2009) 'Framing the War on Terror: The Internalization of Policy in the US Press' *Journalism*, 10(6), pp. 777-797

Reid-Henry, S. (2012) 'Neoliberalism's "trade not aid" approach to development ignored past lessons'. Available at: www.theguardian.com

Reiman, J. (2009) The Rich Get Richer and the Poor Get Prison: Ideology, Class and Criminal Justice, Boston: Allyn and Bacon

Reiner, R. (2007) 'Political Economy, Crime and Criminal Justice' in Maguire, M., Morgan, R & Reiner, R. (eds) *The Oxford Handbook of Criminology* (4th edn), Oxford: Oxford University Press

Reiner, R. (2007) *Law and Order*, Cambridge: Polity

Reiner, R. (2012) 'Casino Capital's Crimes' in Maguire, M., Morgan, R. & Reiner, R. (eds) (2012) *The Oxford Handbook of Criminology* (5th edn), Oxford: Oxford University Press

Reiner, R. (2015) 'Crime: Concepts, Causes, Control' in Holborn, M. (ed) *Contemporary Sociology*, Cambridge: Polity Press

Rescare (2012) 'History of Legislation on Disability', Available at: *www.rescare.org.uk*

Rex, J. and Tomlinson, S. (1979) *Colonial Immigrants in a British City*, London: RKP

Ricker, G (2007) *Mere Atheism*. Lincoln: IUniverse

Riddell, R.C. (2007) *Does Foreign Aid Really Work?*, Oxford: Oxford University Press

Riddell, R.C. (2014) 'Does Foreign Aid Really Work', Keynote address to the Australasian and International Development Workshop, Canberra

Rist, G (2010). 'Development as a buzzword', *Development in Practice* 17(4-5) pp. 485-491

Ritzer, G. (1993) *The McDonaldisation of Society*, Thousand Oaks, California: Pine Forge Press

Roberts, K. (1995) *Youth Unemployment in Modern Britain*, Oxford: Oxford University Press

Roberts, K. (2001) *Class in Modern Britain*, Basingstoke: Palgrave

Roberts, K., Cook, F.G., Clark, S.C. and Semeonoff, E. (1977) *The Fragmentary Class Structure*, London: Heinemann

Robertson, R. (1992) *Globalisation: Social Theory and Global Culture*, London: Sage

Robinson, T., Gustafson, B. and Popovich, M. (2008) 'Perceptions of negative stereotypes of older people in magazine adverts: comparing the perceptions of older adults and college students', *Ageing and Society*, 28, pp.233–51

Robinson, W. I. (2004) *A Theory of Global Capitalism: Production, Class and State in a Transnational World*, Baltimore: John Hopkins University Press

Roe, S. and Ashe, (2008) *Young people and crime: findings from the 2006 Offending, Crime and Justice Survey*, London: Home Office

Roper, L. (2003) 'Disability in Media', *The Media Education Journal*

Rorty, R. (1980) *Philosophy and the Mirror of Nature*, Oxford: Blackwell

Rose, D. and Harrison, E. (2013) Letter in *The Guardian*, 05-04-2013

Rose, D. and Pevalin, D. (with K. O'Reilly) (2001) *The National Statistics Socio-economic Classification: Genesis and Overview*, London: ONS

Rosenau, J, N. (1990) *Turbulence in World Politics: A Theory of Change and Continuity*, Princeton: Princeton University Press

Rosenthal, R. and Jacobson, L. (1968) *Pygmalion in the Classroom*, New York: Holt, Rinehart & Winston

Ross (1996) 'Disability and the media: a suitable case for treatment?', Available at: archive.waccglobal.org

Ross, G.W. (2014) 'The European Union' in Kesselamn, M (ed) *International and Comparative Politics*. Boston: Cengage

Ross, T. (2014) David Cameron: Tories will keep pension 'triple lock' guarantee. *Daily Telegraph* June 4th, 2014

Rostow, W.W. (1971) *The Stages of Economic Growth*, Cambridge: Cambridge University Press

Rothon, C. and Heath, A. (2003) 'Trends in Racial Prejudice', in A. Park, J. Curtice, K. Thompon, L. Jarvis and C. Bromley (eds) *British Social Attitudes: The 20th Report*, London: Sage

Rowbotham, S., Segal, L. and Wainwright, H. (2012, orig. 1979) *Beyond the Fragments: Feminism and the making of Socialism*, Pontypool, Merlin Press

Royse, P., Joon, L., Undrahbuyan, B., Hopson, M. and Consalvo, M. (2007) Women and games: technologies of the gendered self, *New Media and Society*, 9(4), 555-576

Ruggiero, V. & Khan, K. (2007) 'The Organisation of Drug Supply: South Asian Criminal Enterprise in the UK' Asian Journal of Criminology 2(2)

Ruggiero, V. (1996) *Organised and Corporate Crime in Europe*, Aldershot: Dartmouth

Ruickbie, L. *Witchcraft out of the Shadows*. London: Robert Hale

Runciman, G. (1990) 'How many classes are there in contemporary British society?', *Sociology*, 24(3) pp. 377-396

Runnymede Trust (2012) 'Briefing on Ethnicity and Educational Attainment', June

Ruthven, M (2007) *Fundamentalism: A Very Short Introduction*. Oxford: Oxford University Press

Ruthwen, M. (2007) *Fundamentalism: A Very Short Introduction*. Oxford: Oxford University Press

Saadawi, N, L. (1980) *The Hidden Face of Eve: Women in the Arab World*. London: ZED Press

Sachs, J. (2005) *Why Aid Does Work*, www.news.bbc.co.uk

Sachs, W. (1992) 'Where all the world's a stooge', *Guardian*, 29 May

Sahlins, M. (1997) 'The original affluent society' in M. Rahnema and V. Bawtree (eds) (1997) *The Post Development Reader*, London: Zed Books

Said, E. W. (2003) *Orientalism: Western Conceptions of the Orient*, Harmondsworth: Penguin

Salinas, E. (2015) 'Challenging media and film stereotypes on gender sexuality and women's rights', Commission on the Status of Women Panel Discussion paper

Samad, Y. (2004) 'Muslim Youth Britain: Ethnic to Religious Identity' (Paper presented at International Conference Muslim Youth in Europe, *Eduardo Agnelli Centre for Comparative Religious Studies*, Turin, 11th June)

Samad, Y. (2006) 'Muslims in Britain today', *Sociology Review*, 15(4)

Sankara, T. (1988) *Thomas Sankara Speaks: The Burkina Faso Revolution 1983–1987*, New York: Pathfinder Press

Sarnaik, R. (2001) What is Civil Society? BBC World Service

Saunders, P. (1990) *Social Class and Stratification*, London: Routledge

Saunders, P. (1996) *Unequal but Fair?* London: IEA

Saunders, P. (2010) *Social Mobility Myths*, London: Civitas

Savage, M. (2000) *Class Analysis and Social Transformation*, Buckingham: Open University Press

Savage, M. (2013) 'Concerned about the BBC's Class Calculator? Let me explain', *The Guardian*, 10 April

Savage, M., Bagnall, G. and Longhurst, B. (2001) 'Ordinary, ambivalent and defensive class identities in the North West of England', *Sociology*, 35(4), pp. 875-892

Savage, M., Barlow, J., Dickens, P. and Fielding, I. (1992) *Prosperity, Bureaucracy and Culture: Middle-Class Formation in Contemporary Britain*, London: Routledge

Savage, M., Devine, F., Cunningham, N., Taylor, M., Li, Y., Hjellbrekke, J., Le Roux, B., Friedman, S. and Miles, A. (2013) 'A New Model of Social Class?', Sociology, 47(2), pp. 219-250

Sayer, A. (1992) *Method in Social Science: A Realist Approach* (2nd edn), London: Routledge

Sayer, A. (2011) *Why Things Matter to People*, Cambridge: Cambridge University Press

Sayer, A. (2015) *Why We Can't Afford the Rich* Bristol: Policy Press

Scharf, E.R. (1970) *The Sociological Study of Religion*, London: Hutchinson University Library

Schlesinger, P. (1990) 'Rethinking the sociology of journalism: source strategies and the limits of media-centrism', in M. Ferguson (ed.) *Public Communication: the new imperatives*, London: Sage

Scott, J. (1982) *The Upper Classes: Poverty and Privilege in Britain*, London: Macmillan

Scott, J. and Marshall, G. (2009) *A Dictionary of Sociology*. Oxford: Oxford University Press

Scott, J., Dex, S. and Joshi, H. (2008) *Women and Employment: Changing Lives and New Challenges*, Cheltenham: Edward Elgar Publishing

Scott, R. (1995) *Institutions and Organizations*. London: Sage

Scourfield, J., Fincham, B., Langer, S. and Shiner, M. (2012) 'Sociological autopsy: an integrated approach to the study of suicide in men', *Social Science and Medicine*, 74(4)

Scwendinger, H, & Shwendinger, J. (1975) 'Defenders of order or guardians of human rights' in Taylor, I., Walton, P. & Young, J. (eds) *Critical Criminology*, London, RKP

Seabrook, J. (2005) 'Globalization: a War on Local Cultures', *Sociology Review*, 15(2), Nov

Seager, J. (2003) *The Penguin Atlas of Women in the World: Completely Revised and Updated*, New York: Penguin Books

Seaton, J. (2003) 'Broadcasting futures', in J. Curran and J. Seaton (2003) *Power without Responsibility: the press, broadcasting, and new media in Britain* (6th edn), London: Routledge

Sen, A. (1987) *Hunger and Entitlements*, Helsinki: World Institute for Development Economics Research

Sen, A. (1999) *Beyond the Crisis: The Development Strategies in Asia*. Singapore: Institute of South East Asian Studies

Sen, A. (2002) 'Does globalization equal Westernisation?', *The Globalist*, 25 March

Shah, S. (2008) 'Too many black and Asian faces on TV', *Guardian*, 26 Jun

Shakespeare, T. (1998) 'Down's but not out', *The Guardian*, 5 November

Shakespeare, T. (1999) 'Art and lies? Representations of disability on film' in M. Corker and S.French (eds) *Disability Discourse*, Buckingham: Open University Press

Shakespeare, T. and Watson, N. (2002) 'The Social Model of Disability: an outdated ideology?', *Research in Social Science and Disability*, Vol 2

Sharpe, S. (1994) *Just like a Girl: How Girls Learn to be Women*, Harmondsworth: Penguin

Sharples, N. (2015) *Brain Drain: migrants are the Lifeblood of the NHS, it's time the UK paid for them*. Available at: www.theguardian.com

Sharrock, W. et al (2003) *Understanding Modern Sociology*. London: Sage

Shaw, M. (2000) 'War and globality: the role and character of war in the global transition', in Ho-Won Jeong (ed.) *Peace and Conflict: A New Agenda*, Aldershot: Ashgate

Shaxson, N. (2011) *Treasure Islands: Tax Havens and the Men who Stole the World*, London: Vintage

Shearer, A. (1981) *Disability: Whose Handicap?* Oxford: Blackwell

Sherkat, D. (2002) 'Sexuality and Religious Commitment in the United States: An Empirical Examination' *Journal for the Scientific Study of Religion*. 41, pp. 313-23

Shildrick, T. and MacDonald, R. (2007) 'Class, consumption and prejudice: contemporary representations of "the social scum"', ESRC research seminar series on identities and consumption, University of Teesside

Shirky, C. (2011) 'The political power of social media', *Foreign Affairs* 90(1): 28-41

Short, C. (1999) House of Commons Hansard Written Answers, 23 Nov

Skeggs, B. (1997) *Formations of Class and Gender*, London: Sage

Skeggs, B. (2015) 'The Idea of class: A Measure of Value' in Holborn, M. (ed.) *Contemporary Sociology*, Cambridge: Polity

Sklair, L. (2000) 'The transnational capitalist class and the discourse of globalisation', *Cambridge Review of International Affairs*, 14(1), pp. 67-85

Smith, M. J. (2008) *Environment and Citizenship: Integrating Justice, Responsibility and Civic Engagement*, London: Zed Publications

Snider, L. (1993) 'The Politics of Corporate Crime Control' in Pearce, F. & Woodiwiss *Global Crime Connections*, Basingstoke: Macmillan

So, A and Chiu, S. (1995) *East Asia and the World Economy*. New York: SAGE

Soothill, K, & Wlaby S. (1991) *Sex Crimes in the News* London: Routledge

South, N. (1998) 'A green field for criminology?' *Theoretical Criminology* 2(2)

Southerton, D. (2009) *Communities of Consumption*, Saarbrucken, VDM Verlag Dr. Muller

Spencer-Thomas, O. (2008) What is Newsworthy? Available at: www. owenspencer-thomas.com

Spender, D. (1985) *Man Made Language*, London: Routledge

Standing, G. (2009) *Work after Globalisation*, Cheltenham: Edward Elgar

Standing, G. (2011) *The Precariat: The New Dangerous Class*, London: Bloomsbury

Standing, G. (2013) Letter in *The Guardian*, 05-04-2013

Standing, G. (2014) 'The Precariat and Class Struggle', *Revista Critica de Ciencias Sociais*, Issue 103, May

Stanko, B. (2000) *The Day to Count: A Snapshot of the Impact of Domestic Abuse in the UK*, London: Royal Holloway

Stanley, L. and Wise, S. (1993) *Breaking out Again, Feminist Epistemology and Ontology*, London: Routledge

Stark, R (1999) Secularisation RIP. *Sociology of Religion*. 60(3)

Stark, R and Bainbridge, W (1996) *A Theory of Religion*. New Brunswick: Rutgers University Press

Stark, R and Bainbridge, W. (1985) *The Future of Religions: Secularization, Revival and Cult Formation*. Berkeley: University of California Press

Steger, M.B. (2005) *Globalism: Market Ideology Meets Terrorism*, (2nd edn), Lanham: Rowman & Littlefield

Steinem, G. (1995) 'Words and Change', *Ms Magazine*, Sept/Oct

Steinem, G. (2015) *My Life on the Road*. New York: Random House

Steven, P. (2004) *The No-Nonsense Guide to Global Media*, London: Verso

Steward, K. (2006) 'Gender considerations in remand decision-making' in Heidensohn, F. (ed.) *Gender and Justivce: New Concepts and Approaches*, Cullompton: Willan

Stewart, H. (2015) 'Borders are closing and banks are in retreat. Is globalisation dead'. Available at: www.theguardian.com

Stiglitz, J.(2001) 'Failure of the Fund: Rethinking the IMF Response', *Harvard International Review*, 23(2) pp. 14-18

Stoller, R. (1968)*Sex and Gender: On the Development of Masculinity and Femininity* New York: Science House

Stonewall (2011) 'Unseen on Screen: Research into the representation of lesbian, gay and bisexual people on youth television'. Avaialable at: www.stonewall.org.uk

Strinati, D. (1995) *An Introduction to Theories of Popular Culture*, London: Routledge

Stromquist, N.P, (1998) NGOs in a New Paradigm of Civil Society, *Current Issues in Comparative Education* 1

Sutton Trust. (2007) *The Educational Background of the UK's 500 Leading People*, London

Sutton, P. (2015) 'The environment: sociology at its [natural] limits' in Holborn, M. (ed) *Contemporary Sociology*, Cambridge: Polity

Sveinsson, K. P. l. (2008) *A Tale of Two Englands: "Race" and Violent Crime in the Press*, London: Runnymede

Swain, J., French, S. and Cameron, C. (eds) (2003) *Controversial Issues In a Disabling Society*, Maidenhead: Open University Press

Swale, J. (2004) 'Education: A World Perspective', *Sociology Review*, 14(1), Sept

Talbot, D. & Walters, R. (eds)(2010) *Crime: Local and Global* The Open University, Milton Keynes

Taylor, J., Walton, P. and Young, J. (1973) *The New Criminology*, London: Routledge

Taylor-Gooby, P. (with Vic George) (1996) *Welfare Policy: Squaring the Welfare Circle*, Basingstoke: Macmillan

Terry, G (2014) Feminism, Gender and Women's Experiences: Research Approaches to Postnatal Depression. *International Journal of Innovative Interdisciplinary Research* 2(3)

The Commission on Older Women, (2013) Interim Report, September 2013. Available at: www.yourbritain.org.uk

The Fawcett Society (2015) *The Gender Pay Gap*, London

Thompson, E, H. (1991) Beneath the Status Characteristic: Gender Variations in Religiousness. *Journal for the Scientific Study of Religion*. 30(4), pp. 381-394

Thompson, I. (1986) *Sociology in Focus: Religion*, Harlow: Longman

Thompson, J.B. (1995) *The Media and Modernity: A Social Theory of the Media*, Cambridge: Polity

Thompson, N. (1993) *Antidiscriminatory Practice*, Basingstoke: Macmillan

Timmons Roberts, J. and Hite, A (2000) *From Modernisation to Globalization*, Oxford: Blackwell

Tombs, S. and Whyte, D. (2010) 'Crime, harm and corporate power' in Muncie, J., Talbot, D. & Walters, R. (eds) *Crime: Local and Global* Cullompton, Willan Press

Tong, R. (1998) *Feminist Thought: A More Comprehensive Introduction*. Boulder: Westview Press

Toor, S. (2009) 'British Asian Girls, Crime and Youth Justice' *Youth Justice* 9(3)

Travis, A. (2015) 'Crime rate in England and Wales soars as cybercrime is included for first time' *The Guardian*, October 15th 2015

Troeltsch, E. (1931/1976) *The Social Teachings of the Christian Churches*, Chicago: University of Chicago Press

Trowler, P. (2008) 'Mass Media and Communications' in Haralambos, M, and Holborn, M. (eds.) *Sociology: Themes and Perspectives* (7th Edn) London: Collins Education

Trzebiatowska, M and Bruce, S (2014) *Why are Women More Religious than Men?* Oxford: Oxford University Press

Tuchman, G *et al.* (1978) *Hearth and Home: Images of Women in the Mass Media*, New York: Oxford University Press

Tunstall, J and Palmer, M. (1991) *Media Moguls*, London: Routledge

Tunstall, J. (2000) *The Media in Britain*, London: Constable

Turkle, S. (2011) *Alone Together: Why we expect more from technology and less from each other*, Basic Books: NY

Turner, B.S. (1994) 'From regulation to risk', in B.S. Turner (ed.) *Orientalism, Postmodernism and Globalism*, London: Routledge

Turner, J. (2015) The Tome, May 2 2015

Tyler, S.A. (1997/1986) 'Post-modern ethnography' in K. Gelder and S. Thornton (eds) *The Subcultures Reader*, London: Routledge

Tylor, E.B. (1903, originally 1871) *Primitive Culture*, London: Murray

UK Government (2013) Conviction Tables. [online]

United Nations (1987), *The Brundtland Report*, October

United Nations (1995) *Beijing Declaration and Platform for Action*, in Report of the Fourth World Conference on Women

United Nations (2015) *Women globally live longer, healthier lives with better education, reveals new UN report*. Available at: http://www.un.org

Urry, J. (1990). The Tourist Gaze: Leisure and Travel in Contemporary Societies

Urry, J. (2014) The Rich Class and Offshore Worlds, www.discoversociety.org

Van der Gaag, N. (2004) *The No-Nonsense Guide to Women's Rights*, London: Verso

Van Dijk, T. (1991) *Racism and the Press*, London: Routledge

Voas, D. (2008) 'The Continuing Secular Tradition' in *The Role of Religion in Modern Societies* ed. by Pollack, D. London: Routledge

Voas, D. (2013) Modernization and the Gender Gap in Religiosity: Evidence from Cross National European Surveys. *Koln Z Soziol*, 65, pp. 259-283

Voas, D. and Crockett, A. (2005) 'Religion in Britain: neither Believing nor Belonging', *Sociology*, 39(1), pp.11–28

Walby, S (2011) *Globalisation and Inequalities: Complexity and Contested Modernities*. London: Sage

Walby, S. (1990) *Theorising Patriarchy*, Oxford: Blackwell

Walby, S. (1992) "Post-post modernism? Theorizing social complexity", in M, Barrett and A, Phillips (eds) *Destabilising Theory: Contemporary Feminist Debates*. Oxford: Polity

Walby, S. (2011) *The Future of Feminism*, Cambridge: Polity Press

Walker, A. (2014) *A New Vision of Later Life*, presentation at the British Academy, Available at: www.britac.ac.uk

Walker, A. and Foster, L. (2006) 'Ageing and social class: an enduring relationship', in J.A.Vincent, C.R.Phillipson and M. Downs (eds) *The Futures of Old Age*, London: Sage

Walklate, S. (2004) *Gender, Crime and Criminal Justice* (2nd edn) Cullompton: Willan Publishing

Wallerstein, I. (1979) '*The Rise and Future Demise of the World Capitalist System: Concepts for Comparative Analysis from the Capitalist World-economy*, Cambridge: Cambridge University Press

Wallis, R. (1984) *The Elementary Forms of New Religious Life*, London: Routledge

Walter, N. (1998) *The New Feminism*. London: Virago

Walter, N. (2010) *Living Dolls: The Return of Sexism*. London: Virago

Walters, R. & Hope, T (2008) 'Critical Thinking about the Uses of Research' Centre for Justice and Crime Studies (31 March 2008)

Walters, R. (2010) 'Eco-crime' in Muncie, J., Talbot, D. & Walters, R. (eds) *Crime: Local and Global*, Cullompton: Willan Publishing

Warner, R.S. (1993) 'Work in progress toward a new paradigm for the sociological study of religion in the United States', *American Journal of Sociology*, 98(5), pp.1044–93

Watson, H. (1994) 'Women and the veil: personal responses to global process', in A. Ahmed and H. Donnan (eds) *Islam, Globalisation and Postmodernity*, London: Routledge

Watson, J. (2008) *Media Communication: An Introduction to the Theory and Process* (3rd edn), Basingstoke: Palgrave

Watson, N., Philo, G., and Briant, E. (2011) 'Bad News for Disabled People: How the newspapers are reporting disability', Strathclyde Centre for Disability Research and Glasgow Media Unit

Watson, S. (2008) 'Security in the City' in Carter, S., Jordan, T. & Watson, S. (eds) (2008) *Security: Sociology and Social Worlds*, Manchester: Manchester University Press

Watt, N. & Treanor, J (2012) 'Osborne accuses Labour over rate-fixing scandal' *Guardian*, 5 July

Watts (2010) 'China warns of problems facing Three Gorges dam' [online] Available at: www.theguardian.com

Watts, R. Bessant, & Hill, R., (2008) *International Criminology: A Critical Introduction* London, Routledge

Wayne, M. *et al.* (2007) 'The media and young people – hyping up the new folk devils', *Socialist Worker*, 2069, 22 Sep

Weber, M. (1905/1958) *The Protestant Ethic and the Spirit of Capitalism*, London: Unwin

Weber, M. (1920/1963) *The Sociology of Religion*, Boston, Mass: Beacon Press

Weber, M. (1976) *Peasants Into Frenchmen: The Modernization of Modern France 1870-1914*. Palo Alto: Stanford University Press

Weber, M. (Translated 1947) *The Theory of Social and Economic Organisation*, New York: Free Press

WEF (2014) *Global Information Technology Report 2014*. Available at: reports. weforum.org

West, C. and Zimmerman, D.H. (1991) 'Doing Gender', in J. Larber and S.A.Farrell (eds) *The Social Construction of Gender*, London: Sage

Whale, J. (1977) *The Politics of the Media*, London: Fontana

Whitaker, B. (2002) 'David Beckham, identity and masculinity', *Sociology Review*, 11, pp.2–4

WHO (2002) 'Towards a Common Language for Functioning', *Disability and Health: Beginner's Guide*

Wilkinson, H. (1994) *No Turning Back: Generations and the Genderquake*, London: Demos

Wilkinson, R. and Picket, K. (2010) *The Spirit Level: Why Equality is Better for Everyone*, London: Penguin

Williams, K. (2010) *Get Me A Murder A Day! A History of Media and Communication in Britain* (2nd edn), London: Bloomsbury

Williams, N and Lindsey, E (2005) 'Spirituality and Religion in the Lives of Runaway and Homeless Youth: Coping with Adversity', *Journal of Religion and Spirituality in Social Work*, 24(4). pp. 19-38

Williams, P. & Dickinson, J. (1993) 'Fear of Crime: Read All About It', *British Journal of Criminology*, 33(1), pp. 33-56

Williams-Findlay, R. (2009) 'Is there evidence to support the view that the language and subject matter selected by the Times and the Guardian in relation to disabled people has changed over the last twenty years?', The School of Sociology and Social Policy, The University of Leeds, http://disability-studies.leeds.ac.uk/library/titles/l/

Willis, P. (1977) *Learning to Labour: How Working-class Kids get Working-class Jobs*, Farnborough: Saxon House

Wilson, B. (1961) *Sects and Society*. Berkeley: University of California Press

Wilson, B. (1982) *Religion in Sociological Perspective*, Oxford: Oxford University Press

Wilson, B.R. (1966) *Religion in a Secular Society*, London: B.A. Watts

Wilson, J. Q and Kelling, G. (1982) 'Crime and Broken Windows' *Atlantic Monthly* March, pp. 29-38

Wilson, J. Q. (1975) *Thinking About Crime*, New York: Basic Books

Wolf, N. (1990) *The Beauty Myth*, London: Vintage

Women and Work Commission (2005) *Shaping a Fairer Future*

Women's Business Council (2012) Second evidence paper, Chapter 5. London: Home Office

Wood, J. (1993) 'Repeatable pleasures: notes on young people's use of video', in D. Buckingham (ed.) *Reading Audiences: Young People and the Media*, Manchester: Manchester University Press

Wood, L. (2012) 'A critical analysis of Media representation of disabled people', Available at: www.disabilityplanet.co.uk

Woodhead, L (2002) *Religions in the Modern World: Traditions and Transformations*. London: Routledge

Woodhead, L (2008) Gendering Secularization Theory. *Social Compass*, 55(2), pp. 187-193

Woodhead, L (2013) 'Neither Religious Nor Secular: The British Situation and its Implications for Religion-State Relations' in Berg-Sorensen, A. Farnham: Ashgate (ed.) *Contesting Secularism*. London: Routledge

Woodhead, L. (2007) cited in R. Pigott 'Lifting the veil on religion and identity', *The Edge*, Spring 2007, pp.16–20

Woodhead, L. (2012) Liberal Religion and Illiberal Secularism. In Berg-Sorensen, A. (ed.) *Contesting Secularism*. Franham: Ashgate

Wood-Wallace, D. (2009) 'Globalisation, Homogeneity and Cultural Diversity'. Available at: www.academia.edu

World Bank (2012) 'Mobile Phone Access Reaches Three Quarters of Planet's Population.' Available at: www. worldbank.org

World Bank (2015). World Development Report: Mind, Society and Behavior (2015) Washington D.C. Available at: openknowledge.worldbank.org

World Trade Organization (2007) *International Trade Statistics* [online]

Worsley, P. (1977/1964) *The Third World*. Chicago: The University of Chicago Press

Wright, E. O.(1995) *Classes*, London: Verso

Wright, E.O. (2000) *Class Counts* (Student Edition), Cambridge: Cambridge University Press

Yinger, M. (1970) *The Scientific Study of Religion*, London: Routledge

Yong, A. (2012) *Pentecostalism and Prosperity: The Socio-Economics of the Global Charismatic Movement*. London: Palgrave Macmillan

Young, J. (1997) 'Left realist criminology: radical in its analysis, realist in its policy' in Maguire, M. et a. (eds.) *The Oxford Handbook of Criminology* (2nd edn) Oxford: Oxford University Press

Young, J. (1999) *The Exclusive Society* London: Sage

Young, M. (1958) *The Rise of the Meritocracy 1870-2033*, London: Transaction Publishers

INDEX

Page numbers in bold refer to definitions/explanations of key terms.

A

active audience models
  Marxist 'cultural effects'
    model 336–7
  postmodernist model 337–8
  reception analysis model 335–6
  selective filter model 333
  two-step flow model 333
  uses and gratifications model 334
advanced industrial societies **345,**
  359
ageism **326,** 395–6
agnostic **504**
aid 222
  for and against perspectives 223–6
  debt and 226
  future of 226
  reason to give 222–3
  types and sources of 222
Althusser 116
American Dream **449**
animism 435–6
anomie 5–6
anthropology **447**
anti-social behaviour orders
  (ASBOs) 35, 96
anti-trust legislation (law against
  monopolies) 22
appeal to higher loyalties 82
arrests of ethnic groups 51
assault 27
assimilation **486**
asylum seekers 14
Atkinson, Maxwell 120

B

Bauman, Zygmunt 355
Beck, Ulrick 77–8, 135–7, 355–6
believing without belonging **504**
belonging without believing **504**
biopiracy 78
Black feminism 130–1, 354
boundary maintenance 323
Bourgeoisie **359**
bread and circuses approach **277**
bribery 23
broken windows theory 34, 36

C

Calvinism 457–8
capitalism 23, 25–7, 30, 53–4, 75–6,
  78, 111, 114–15, 127–8, 141, 148,
  155, 166, 187, 189–91, 194,
  216–17, 219, 242, 255, 288–9, 298,
  300, 302, 343, 345–50, 352–4,
  391–2, 397, 407, 411–12, 417, 442,
  451, 457–9, 505
caste system 343

Catholic Church 475
censorship 330
chavs 14
chivalry thesis **58**
Christocentric **432**
churnalism 296–7
citizen journalism 297
civil society **81, 217**
class bias in law enforcement 22–3
clientism **83**
collective conscience 4, **5**
colonialism 192–3
committed sociology 165–8
condemnation of the condemners 82
conflict 9
conflict theories 397–8
conflict theorists 346–52
conformity 7
conglomeration **269**
consensus **112**
consensus theories in sociology 344
conservative force **446**
conspicuous consumption **399**
consumerism **69**
consumer society **139**
corporate crimes **22,** 67
  environmental harm 78
  punishment and 24
Corporate Manslaughter and
  Corporate Homicide Act 2007 24
corruption 23, 74
cosmopolitanism 356
crime films 91
crime prevention
  environmental 95–6
  situational 94–5
  social and community 96–7
crimes
  against the environment 76–7
  employment, role in boosting 5
  explanation of 31–2
  government and law
    enforcement agencies, role in
    controlling 43
  influence on functioning of
    society 4–6
  Marxist theory of 20–6
  negative side of 4–6
  neo-Marxist approaches 26–7
  of obedience 82
  positive side of 4–5
  as a safety valve 5
  seductions of 10
crime statistics 39–45
  official statistics of crimes 43,
    47–8
  perspectives on 45
  police-recorded statistics 39–43
  self-report studies 40, 43–5, 48–9

victimisation studies 49
victim surveys 39, 43
Crime Survey for England and Wales
  (CSEW) 40, 42, 49, 57
criminal careers 9
criminalisation **48**
criminal justice 27
criminal justice system 99–101
  bias or racism in 50–2
  double standards in 59
  statistics 47–8
critical criminology 27–8
critical social science 175–6
critical sociology 147–8
critical victimology 105
crowd-labour **416**
cultural defence **511**
culture
  high 285
  popular 285–8
culture of control 100–1

D

dark figure of crime 42
decadence **257**
delinquents 17
demographic time-bomb 396
denial, culture of 81–2
dependency theory 192–4, 228, 230,
  246–8, 252
desensitisation 329–30
designing out crime **95**
deterrence 98
development 182–5, 187–8
  demographic change and 249
  employment as a result of 241–5
  relationship between environment
    and 234–8
  role of education in 245–7
  significance of gender in
    relation 253–7
deviance 12–14
  influence on functioning of
    society 4–6
  neo-Marxist approaches to 26
  phenomenological approaches 17
  primary 13–14
  responding to and enforcing rules
    against 13
  secondary 14
deviance amplification spiral 14
deviancy amplification **90**
deviant careers 15
deviant values 10
dialectic 82, **83**
digital divide 265–6

disability
  composition of the disabled
    population   402
  demographics of   402
  disadvantaged position of   406–9
  government anti-austerity policy
    and   404
  life chances and   402–3
  myths and misunderstandings   402
  as a social phenomenon,
    models   404–9
disappearances   81
discourse   **101**
disengagement   505–6
disestablishment   **469**
disinhibition   **329**
disintegrative shaming   18
doctrine of identification   24
dramaturgy   **119**
drug users
  cannabis   16
  marijuana smoking   15
dual consciousness   **454**
dual labour-market theory   376–7, 389
Durkheim, Émile   4, 25, 98–9, 111,
  144–5, 153, 344–5, 446–7, 487
  concept of anomie   6
  evaluation of sociological thinking
    on crime   7
  positive aspects of crime   5
dysfunctional   **448**
dysfunctional society   **7**

E

eco-crime   76–7
economic reductionism   **456**
ecumenical movement   **508**
edgework   10
egoism   5–6
elderly   394–5
elite class   413
empathy   **330**
empiricism   **154**
employment   241–5
  race and ethnicity   384–5
Enlightenment thinking   134–5, 506–8
environmental crime prevention   95–6
epistemology   **149**
Equal Pay Act (EPA), 1970   374
ethnic groups
  arrests of   51
  crime statistics   47–9
  cultural factors and crime rate   54
  frequently stopping and
    searching of   51
  religiosity and   484–9
  sentencing and imprisonment   52
  victimisation of   49–52
ethnocentrism   387
European Union (EU)   213
Exclusive Brethren   431
excommunication   **475**
existential security   **513**
existential security theory   508

F

Fair Trade movement   229
false class consciousness   **451**
false consciousness   **288**
female conformity and criminality
  biological explanations   59
  liberationist perspective   60
  sex-role theory   59–60
feminism   176, 352–6, 460–3, 492
  Black   130–1, 354
  contribution to sociology   132–3
  feminist interviewing   148–9
  liberal   128–9, 352–3
  Marxist and socialist   127–8
  postmodern   131–2, 354
  radical   125–6, 353
  science and   443
  socialism   353–4
  social science methodology
    and   148–9
  sociology and   124–5
  theories of gender
    stratification   377–8
  waves of   123–4
feminist perspectives on women and
  crime   60–2
feminist research   166
fertility rate   **253**
feudal estate system   343
Firestone, Shulamith   126
focal concerns   **68**
football violence   26
Foucault, Michel   99–101
Frankfurt School of Marxists   116–17,
  349
functionalism   25, 111–12, 144–5, 173,
  344–6, 397, 446–50, 486–7, 490
  criticisms   113
  neo-functionalism   113
functional rebels   5
fundamentalism   **465,** 511–13
fundamentalists   **317**

G

gangs   10–11
Garland, David   100–1
gender
  education and   380
  health and   380
  inequality and   374–80
  pay gap   374–5
  religiosity and   489–93
  stratification in employment   375–8
  work and   374
gender differences
  in criminal justice and chivalry
    thesis   57–9
  feminist perspectives on women
    and crime   60–2
  in offending rates   56–7
  offending rates of men   62–4
  victimisation   57
gendered   **59**
genocide   81
Giddens, Anthony   121, 359, 434

glass ceiling   **375,** 424
global criminal networks   74–5
globalisation   137
  as Americanisation   288–91
  causes of   200
  cultural   200–1
  defined   200, 284
  economic   203
  impacts of   411
  media and   284–5
  political   201
  of popular culture   285–8
  theories of   204–8
globalisation of crime   74–5
  capitalism and   75–6
  development of networks   74–5
  effects of   75
global risks   203–4
Gramsci, Antonio   115–16
gratification   **334**
Great British Class Survey
  (GBCS)   363–4, 413
The Great Gatsby Curve   426
green crime   76–8
grey pound   **326**
Group of Eight (G8)   213–14

H

hate crimes   385, **386,** 404
health and illness in developing
  countries   247–9
hegemony   **279**
Heidensohn, Frances   56, 59–60
  radical feminism and social
    control   61
hidden female offenders   57–8
high modernity   135–7
high-profile crimes   70, 89
holistic approach to health   **249**
homicides   85–6
homogenisation of culture   **286**
homophobia   **312**
Hope-Goldthorpe scale   361–2
human capital   **375**
human rights, violation of   80–1
Husserl, Edmund   120
hybrid identities   **391**
hybridity   **137**
hyper-globalism   204

I

ideology   **276,** 441–2
illegal trafficking in weapons   74
illegitimate opportunity structure   8–9
illicit drugs, dealing in   74
impairment   **313**
imperialism   **186, 284**
imprisonment of ethnic groups   52
incapacitation   98
individualisation   136
individuation   **509**
induction   **154**
industrialisation, theories of   229–31

inequality
  age and   394–5, 397
  class-based structure of   367–8
  distribution of income and
    wealth   368–9
  economic inequality in the
    UK   369–70
  gender and   374–80
innovation   7–8
institutional racism   50, **51**, 387
integration   **144**
interactionism   25, 27
interactivity   **294**
International Monetary Fund
  (IMF)   214–16
Islamism   **484**
Islamophobia   **317**

J

journalistic ethics   299

K

kleptocracy   **194**
knife crime   14
Kuhn, Thomas   158–9

L

labelling theory   12–**13**, 14–17, 53,
  398
  criticism of   13–15, 17–18
  evaluation of   13–14
  process of labelling   16
  values and policy implications   17–
    18
late modernity   135–7
late modern society   77, **78**
least economically developed societies
  (LLEDCs)   183
left realism   30–3, 52
  evaluation of   33
  policies and   32–3
left-wing   **367**
left-wing views   **30**
less economically developed societies
  (LEDCs)   183
liberal feminism   128–9, 352–3
lifelong atheists   **482**
lifelong theism   **482**
locally based criminal activities   76

M

macro   110–**11**
malestream   **254**
Malinowski, Bronislaw   447–8
Mandela, Nelson   5
manslaughter   24
marginalisation   **32**
marijuana smoking   15
marriage institution   5
Marx, Karl   114, 346–8, 350
  committed sociology   166
  criticisms of   115
  five periods or epochs of
    history   114
  means of production   114

model to capitalism   114–15
  modes of production   114
Marxism   114–17, 175–6, 191–2, 225,
  276–80, 299–300, 320, 450–6,
  487–8
  neo-Marxist perspectives   115–17
  religion and   442–3
  theories of globalisation   206–7
Marxist feminism   127–8
Marxist perspectives
  on capitalist societies   420
  on ethnic minorities   390–1
  on the law and punishment   99
Marxist theory of crime   20–6
  basis of the criminal law   21
  causes of offending   23
  comparison with
    interactionism   25
  evaluation of   25
  law and ruling class ideology   21
  law enforcement and harm   22–3
  law-making process   22
  strengths   25
  weaknesses   25
masculinity and crime   62–4
mass political killings   81
Mead, George Herbert   118
media   387
  active audience approaches   333–8
  effects, hypodermic syringe model
    of   329–33
  news, construction of   294–301
  ownership and control   273–82
  scapegoating   332–3
media, representations of
  based on age   323–7
  disability   312–14
  ethnicity and minority
    people   316–20
  femininity and masculinity   305–7
  lesbians, gays, bisexuals and
    transsexuals (LGBT)   310–12
  poverty   322–3
  sexuality   309–10
  social classes   321–3
  theoretical perspectives   307–9
media on crime
  construction of crime coverage   87
  coverage of crime   85
  effects of   87–92
  media as a direct cause of
    crime   88–9
  offenders in the media   86
  selection of news content   86–7
meritocracy   **344**, 420
Merton, Robert   6–8, 67–8, 113
  evaluation of work   7–8
  idea of the innovator   9
  middle-class values and
    aspirations   9
metanarrative   **138**
methodological pluralism   151
methodology   146
metrosexual male   **307**
micro   **111**
middle class   414–15

Millennium Development Goals
  (MDGs)   185–6
Millet, Kate   126
mixed economy   **174**
modernisation theory   187–91, 229–30
modernity   134–5, 157
money-laundering   75
moral crusade   16
moral panics   14–15, 27, 89–90, 301–2
more economically developed
  countries (MEDCs)   183
moving equilibrium   112
muggers   14
muggings   27
multiculturalism   **386**

N

narrative   **165**
National Statistics Socio-Economic
  Classification (NS-SEC) scale   362–
  3, 413
Nazism   431
negotiation   17
neo-colonialism   193
neo-functionalism   449–50
neoliberalism   173–4, 191–4, 226–7,
  229–30, **346**
neoliberal structural adjustment
  programmes   **411**
neo-Malthusian modernisation
  theory   249–52
neo-Marxism   **26**, 348–51, 453–4
  to crime   26–7, 53–4
  subcultural theory   26
neo-modernisation theory   189
neo-tribes   10
networks   **74**
new-age   **441**
'new age movements' (NAMs)   474–5,
  479, 484
  impact of social change   476–7
The New Criminology (Stuart
  Hall)   27–8, 53
New International Division of Labour
  (NIDL)   230–1
newly industrialised countries
  (NICs)   183
new media
  characteristics of   263–4
  debates about   266–71
  users of   264–6
'new religious movement'
  (NRM)   469–74, 479
New Right   173–4
newsworthy   **294**
non-government organisations
  (NGOs)   216–19
norms   **285**

O

objectivity   **162**
offending   47–9
  causes of   23
  patterns of   45
official statistics of crimes   43, 47–8
operationalisation   **500**

organised criminal groups   11
overpolicing   31

P

paedophiles   14
Pakulski, Jan   355
paradigm   **158**
Parsons, Talcott   111–12, 144, 345, 376, 447
pattern variables   112–13
peer groups or 'crews'   10
Pentecostalism   459
pessimistic globalism   204–6
pester power   **324**
phenomenology   120, 146–7
pink economy   **311**
pink pound   **311**
plea-bargaining   43
pluralism   86
pluralists   **86**
pluralist societies   **464**
police-recorded statistics   39–43
    recording of crime   40
policing   50–1
polygyny   **457**
polysemic   **281**
Popper, Karl   154–6
positivism   150, 153–4, 173
positivist victimology   103–5
post-development theory   194–6
postmodern feminism   131–2, 354
postmodernity/postmodernism   135, 137–42, 157, 164, 281–2, 355–6, 391–2, 463–5, 491–2, 509–10
    age-determined inequality   398
    theories of globalisation   207–8
postmodern methodology   150
precariat   416–17
preference theory   378
primary definers   **300**
primary deviance   13–14
prisons   101–2
proletarianisation   114
Protestant ethic   457–9
Protestantism   **469**
punishments   33–4, 47
    functionalist and Marxist perspectives on   98–101

Q

quasi-religious   **433**

R

race   **383**
race and ethnicity   383
    disadvantages   386–92
    education   385
    employment and unemployment   384–5
    health   385
    media representations of   316–20
    misunderstandings and misconceptions   383
    poverty and deprivation   385

self-report studies of offending   48–9
    sentencing of ethnic groups   52
racial discrimination   387
racial prejudice   386
racism   386
radical feminism   125–6, 353
radical victimology   105
rationalisation   506–8
realism   159–60
rebellion   8, 10
reflexive modernisation   136
reflexive modernisation theory   **200**
reflexivity   **136**
Registrar General's scale   361
regulation   **144**
rehabilitation   98
reintegrative shaming   18
relative deprivation   **31, 477**
religion
    by age   493–6
    as ideology   450–1
    ideology and   441–2
    issues in defining   432–5
    Marxism and   442–3
    relationship between science   436–41
    social change and   454–5, 457
    types of   435–6
religiosity
    defined   500
    ethnicity and   484–9
    gender and   489–93
    social class and   482–3
religious organisation   483–4
    Churches   468
    denominations   468–9, 483–4
religious pluralism   469, 509
research
    link between theory and methods   150
    theory and choices in   143–4
reserve army of labour   **127,** 377–8
retreatism   8
retreatist   9
retribution   98
right realism   33–6
    evaluation of   35–6
    influence of   35
right-wing   **367**
right-wing views   **30**
risk society   75, 77–8, 135–6
risk theory   490–1
ritualism   8
robbery   23, 27
Roman Catholicism   431, 458
Roughnecks   69
routine activities theory   34–5
rule enforcement   13
    consequences of   14–15
rules and laws, creation of   15–16
ruling class ideology   **21**

S

Saints   69
Saunders, Peter   346, 423–4

scapegoating   332–3, 390–1
Scientology   431
secondary deviance   14
secularisation   500–6, 510–11
    theories of   505–10
secularisation of consciousness   **507**
self-fulfilling prophecy   14–15
self-report studies   40, 43–5, 52, 57
    of ethnicity and offending   48–9
    patterns of offending and   45
    social class and crime rate   67
    weaknesses   43–4
semiology   26
sentencing of ethnic groups   52
service class   **361**
sex-role socialisation   60
sex-role theory   59–60
shaming   18
Sharia law   **317**
shoplifting   56, 58, 64
simulacrum   **139**
situational crime prevention   94–5
skinheads   26
slavery   192–3
social and community crime prevention   96–7
social class   357–9
    class-based structure of inequality   367–8
    class structure, competing views about   359–60
    distribution of income and wealth   368–9
    divisions   368
    education and   370
    growing economic inequality in the UK   369–70
    health and   370
    problems of measuring   360–4
    religiosity and   482–3
    religious organisations and   483–4
    scales of   361–4
    subjective measurements of   364–5
social class and crime rate
    cultural explanations   68–9
    higher-status offenders   70
    lower-class backgrounds   66–7
    process of criminalisation and class bias   69–70
    working-class criminality   67–8
social closure   **351**
social cohesion   5
social construct   **434**
social control   61, 99–101
social desirability bias   **503**
social determinism   **378**
social evolution and differentiation   112–13
social exclusion   367–8
social fact   **146**
socialist feminism   127–8
socialist feminism and crime   61–2
social learning   **88**
social mobility   420–3
    education, economic inequality and   426

myths related to 424
social policy **169,** 170–1, 173–6
social solidarity **345**
social stigmatisation 323
social stratification 344–6
    'dysfunctions' of 346
    forms of 342–3
    social class in 343–4
societalisation **505**
sociological problems and social
    problems 170
sociology as science 154–61
square of crime 32
state crime
    culture of denial and 81–2
    defined 80
    dialectical approach to 82–3
    explanations of 82–3
    of Gaddafi regime 83
    human rights and 80–1
    integrated theory of 82
    nature and extent of 79–80
    obedience approach to 82
status frustration 8–9
strain theory 7–8
structural differentiation 113
structuration theory 121
subcultural theory 26, 32–3
subcultures **8,** 9–11, 14, 31–2
    criticism of the Marxist
        approach 26–7
    neo-Marxist 26
    skinhead 26
    in terms of fluidity 10
subterranean values 10
suicide 151
    study of 145–6
    types of 145
Surrey Occupational Class
    Schema 362
sustainable development 185, 235–6,
    236
symbolic interactionism 12–**13,**
    118–20, 145–6
symmetry **157**
synergy 274

T

target hardening 35
tax avoidance 21
tax evasion 70

terrorism 14, 81
theistic religions 436
theodicy **456**
theories of society
    difference between structural
        theories and social action
        theory 118
    social action and interpretivist
        theories 111, 118–20
    structural theory 110–17
Third Way **175**
tokenism **318**
torture 81
Total Fertility Rate (TFR) **253**
total institutions **408**
totemism 436
tourism 231–2
trade, theories on 226–9
trafficking of children and
    women 74–5
Transcendental Meditation (TM) 430
transformationalists 207–8
transgender **311**
transnational capitalist class
    (TCC) 411–12
transnational corporations (TNCs) 211
    theoretical perspectives 212–13
triangulation 150
trolling **270**

U

underclass 35, 68, 417
underdevelopment 182, 187–8
underpolicing 31
United Kingdom
    British newspaper and
        broadcasting media 273
    economic inequality in 369–70
    issue of meritocracy in 423–4
    as a multi-ethnic society 383–4
    secularisation in 500–5
    UK class structure 412
United Nations 213
urbanisation 232–4

V

value-free sociology 162–3
value judgements **181**
value-laden sociology 163–4
values **285**

vandalism 9
victimisation
    of ethnic groups 49–52
    gender differences 57
    of personal crime 57
    of sexual abuse 57
    studies 49
victim precipitation 104
victim proneness 104
victims of crime 103–5
victim surveys 39, 43
    local 43
    victimisation research 43
    weaknesses of 43
violent crimes 74

W

war crimes 74
wars of the developing world 237–8
    armed conflicts 238
Waters, Malcolm 355
Weber, Max 351–2, 389, 456–9
    denominations and sects 488–9
'what works' approach **97**
white-collar crimes **22**–3
    gender and 63
White-dominated police culture 51
working class 416
working-class criminality 67–8, 75
    cultural explanations 68
working-class culture 10, 26
World Bank 214–16
World Trade Organisation (WTO) 214
Wright, Erik Olin 348–9

Y

young 396–7
young male prostitutes 15
youth cultures of 1960s 14

Z

zemiology 28, **77**
zero tolerance policies **34**

William Collins' dream of knowledge for all began with the publication of his first book in 1819.

A self-educated mill worker, he not only enriched millions of lives, but also founded a flourishing publishing house. Today, staying true to this spirit, Collins books are packed with inspiration, innovation and practical expertise. They place you at the centre of a world of possibility and give you exactly what you need to explore it.

Collins. Freedom to teach

HarperCollins*Publishers*

The News Building, 1 London Bridge Street, London, SE1 9GF

Browse the complete Collins catalogue at www.collins.co.uk

© HarperCollins*Publishers* 2016

10 9 8 7 6 5 4 3 2

ISBN 978-0-00-759749-9

A catalogue record for this book is available from the British Library

Contributing author: Tim Davies

Commissioned by Alexandra Riley and Tom Guy

Project managed by Elektra Media

Development edited by Kim Vernon

Copyedited by Sarah Patey

Proofread by Joan Miller

Illustrations by Elektra Media and Oxford Designers & Illustrators

Typeset by Jouve India Private Limited

Design and cover design by We Are Laura

Indexed by Jouve India Private Limited

Production by Rachel Weaver

Printed and bound by Grafica Veneta S.p.A

The publishers gratefully acknowledge the permissions granted to reproduce copyright material in this book. Every effort has been made to contact the holders of copyright material, but if any have been inadvertently overlooked, the publisher will be pleased to make the necessary arrangements at the first opportunity.

The Department for Education do not accept responsibility for any inferences or conclusions derived from the NPD Data by third parties.

Approval Message from AQA

This textbook has been approved by AQA for use with our qualification. This means that we have checked that it broadly covers the specification and we are satisfied with the overall quality. Full details for our approval process can be found on our website.

We approve textbooks because we know how important it is for teachers and students to have the right resources to support their teaching and learning. However, the publisher is ultimately responsible for the editorial control and quality of this book.

Please note that when teaching the AS and A-level Sociology course, you must refer to AQA's specification as your definitive source of information. While this book has been written to match the specification, it cannot provide complete coverage of every aspect of the course.

A wide range of other useful resources can be found on the relevant subject pages of our website: www.aqa.org.uk

Photo credits: p6 © Michael Kemp/Alamy, p18 POOL/Getty Images, p20 © wronaphoto.com/Alamy, p24 © Frances Roberts/Alamy, p30 Pacific Press/Getty, p47 © Janine Wiedel Photolibrary/Alamy, p50 AFP/Getty Images, p51 © Janine Wiedel Photolibrary/Alamy, p63 Graeme Robertson/Getty Images, p66 © ZUMA Press, Inc./Alamy, p70l © WENN Ltd / Alamy, p70r Sandy Young/Alamy, p81 Richard Jones/REX/Shutterstock, p91 Michael Ochs Archives/Getty Images, p93 © Matthew Chattle/Alamy, p100 Daniel Berehulak/Getty Images, p102 Christopher Furlong/Getty images, p123 Chris Ratcliffe/Getty Images, p129 Anadolu Agency/Getty Images, p131 The Washington Post/Getty Images, p140 David M. Benett/Getty Images, p162 Eye Ubiquitous/Getty Images, p166 Anadolu Agency/Getty Images, p167 © christopher Pillitz/Alamy, p169 Tristan Fewings/Getty Images, p172 © Martin Parker/Alamy, p175 Jeff J Mitchell/Getty Images, p180 Macduff Everton/Getty Images, p181 ranplett/iStock.com, p197 Dmitry Chulov/iStock.com, p205 Raquel Maria Carbonell Pagola/Getty Images, p215 AFP/Getty Images, p236 AFP/Getty Images, p239 Chris Hondros/Getty Images, p251 Peter Charlesworth/Getty Images, p256 Pacific Press/Getty Images, p272 Bloomberg/Getty, p280 Lintao Zhang/Getty Images, p287 Thierry Falise/Getty Images, p293 George Clerk/iStock, p297 PHILIPPE LOPEZ/Getty Images, p304 LEON NEAL/Getty Images, p309 Yoeml/iStock.com, p311 © Stacy Walsh Rosenstock/Alamy, p319 ©Universal/Courtesy Everett/Col/REX/Shutterstock, p328 chrisjohnsson/iStock.com, p331t © Moviestore collection Ltd/Alamy, p331b © AF archive/Alamy, p335 Fertnig/iStock.com, p340 Leonardo Patrizi/iStock.com, p352 Bob Aylott/Getty Images, p357 © dov makabaw/Alamy, p371 George Clerk / iStock.com, p405 DavidCallan/iStock.com, p425 © Percy Ryall/Alamy, p445 WPA Pool/Getty Images, p452 Chris Ratcliffe/Getty Images, p459 Godong/Getty Images, p472 AFP/Getty Images, p483 Max Mumby/Indigo/Getty Images, p506 © Piero Cruciatti/Alamy